SEX MATTERS

THE SEXUALITY AND SOCIETY READER

FIFTH EDITION

MINDY STOMBLER

DAWN M. BAUNACH

ELISABETH O. BURGESS

WENDY SIMONDS

ELROI J. WINDSOR

W. W. NORTON & COMPANY

New York · London

W. W. Norton & Company has been independent since its founding in 1923, when William Warder Norton and Mary D. Herter Norton first published lectures delivered at the People's Institute, the adult education division of New York City's Cooper Union. The firm soon expanded its program beyond the Institute, publishing books by celebrated academics from America and abroad. By midcentury, the two major pillars of Norton's publishing program—trade books and college texts—were firmly established. In the 1950s, the Norton family transferred control of the company to its employees, and today—with a staff of four hundred and a comparable number of trade, college, and professional titles published each year—W. W. Norton & Company stands as the largest and oldest publishing house owned wholly by its employees.

Editor: Sasha Levitt
Project Editors: Sujin Hong, Diane Cipollone, Laura Dragonette
Editorial Assistant: Erika Nakagawa
Managing Editor, College: Marian Johnson
Managing Editor, College Digital Media: Kim Yi
Production Manager: Stephen Sajdak
Media Editor: Eileen Connell
Associate Media Editor: Ariel Eaton
Media Project Editor: Danielle Belfiore

Media Editorial Assistant: Samuel Tang
Ebook Production Manager: Michael Hicks
Marketing Manager, Sociology: Julia Hall
Design Director: Rubina Yeh
Director of College Permissions: Megan Schindel
College Permissions Associate: Elizabeth Trammell
Photo Editor: Travis Carr
Composition: Six Red Marbles
Manufacturing: LSC Crawfordsville

Photo credits: p. 1, Courtesy of Fe Delos-Santos; p. 65, Courtesy of Barnard College; p. 111, Courtesy of Ericka McConnell; p. 169, Courtesy of Jen Gilbert; p. 253, Courtesy of Leonore Tiefer; p. 327, Courtesy, Indiana University School of Public Health-Bloomington; p. 419, Courtesy of Steven Epstein; p. 487, Photo courtesy of David Mejias; p. 585, Courtesy of Ashlyn Swartout; p. 653, Courtesy of Kari Lerum.

Library of Congress Cataloging-in-Publication Data

Names: Stombler, Mindy.
Title: Sex matters : the sexuality and society reader / [edited by] Mindy
  Stombler [and four others].
Description: Fifth edition. | New York : W.W. Norton & Company, [2019] |
  Includes bibliographical references and index.
Identifiers: LCCN 2018044515 | **ISBN 9780393623581** (pbk.)
Subjects: LCSH: Sex—Social aspects. | Sex—Social aspects—United States. |
  Sex in popular culture—United States. | Sex customs—United States.
Classification: LCC HQ16 .S46 2019 | DDC 306.70973—dc23 LC record available at
  https://lccn.loc.gov/2018044515

W. W. Norton & Company, Inc., 500 Fifth Avenue, New York, NY 10110
wwnorton.com

W. W. Norton & Company Ltd., 15 Carlisle Street, London W1D 3BS

2 3 4 5 6 7 8 9 0

In honor of those resisting attacks on sex education, the rights of sexual minorities, evidence-based research on sexuality, procreative justice, and access to medical services, who strive for a sex-positive environment for us all.

CONTENTS

CHAPTER 7 Sexual Health 419

CHAPTER 8 Social Control 487

PREFACE

We live in a sex-saturated society. We hear of sex drive, sex toys, sex machines, sex slaves, sex scandals, sex gods, sex crimes, and sexaholics. Sex permeates every aspect of our lives from advertising to politics to our relationships with others. Yet we rarely consider the historical, legal, and sociocultural contexts of sexuality. Many people take the current state of sexual attitudes and practices in our society for granted, as if they are natural and thus unchangeable. Understanding contemporary sexual matters requires considering how sexuality varies across time and place and how it is modeled, molded, and even manipulated by those around us. Consider, for instance, the influence of social contexts as you read the following scenarios:

- Imagine that you've chosen to have sex for the first time. How would you know what to do? How would you plan on pleasing your partner? Yourself? Would you turn for guidance to books or magazines, pornography, websites on the internet, or the wall of the public bathroom? What makes you excited? Nervous? Would you practice safe sex?

- Imagine that you and your partner do things together that you've never heard about before but that make you feel transported, ecstatic, or orgasmic. Or imagine you feel nothing much during your encounters, or that you feel disgusted, or that you're not even sure if you have "had sex." Imagine that you want to stop but your partner won't. What would you do? Whom would you tell?

- Imagine that you and your partner are the same sex. Would you feel comfortable showing affection in public? Can you imagine a cultural context in which you wouldn't have to worry about others' reactions? Can you imagine how dating someone of the same sex might be beneficial to you?

- Imagine that an evening of partying ends in an unplanned "one-night stand." You or your partner becomes pregnant. Would you see the pregnancy as something to celebrate? To ignore? To hide? To terminate? Would your family and friends share your feelings? Would their reaction be the same if you were 15 or you were 45? What if your partner were much older or younger than you? Or of a different race, ethnicity, or religion?

- Imagine that you've made a careful decision to refrain from sexual activity. Which circumstances might compel such a decision? Would it be hard to maintain your resolve? Or imagine, by contrast, that you've sought out as much sexual activity as you can find. Either way, who would support your decision to be celibate or sexually adventurous? Who might challenge it? How would these responses be different, depending on your age, gender, or social status?

SEXUALITY AND SOCIETY

If you vary the time, place, or cultural setting of the scenarios, you'll find that your feelings, the decisions you would make, and the reactions of those around you will probably change. These variations occur because the social norms governing sexual behavior are continually in flux. Other social factors, such as your religious beliefs, level of education, economic status, ethnicity, gender, and age, influence sexual activity and its meaning. All of the following are influenced by society: what counts as a sex act, how often we have sex, what is considered erotic, where we have sex, the age when we begin having sex, with whom we have sex, what we do when we are having sex, how often we desire sex, our reasons for having or avoiding sex, whether we pay others or get paid for sex, and how we define consensual sex. Although often characterized as a purely biological and often uncontrollable phenomenon, sex is, in fact, social. The readings we have selected portray sex as a social issue influenced by culture, politics, economics, media, education, medicine, law, family, and friends.

SEX MATTERS

Our title reflects the content of the book in two ways. First, we have included research articles and essays on a variety of sexual matters. Second, the title supports our assertion that sex, and the study of sexuality, matters. There is much to learn about sexuality. Despite the prevalence of sexual matters in public life and the media, as well as their private significance, scholars researching sexuality often have difficulty getting institutional and financial support. Many funding agencies, politicians, and even academics do not take sexuality seriously.

Yet the study of sexuality is burgeoning, as evidenced by the proliferation of courses on sexuality in colleges and universities throughout the United States. This book applies social theory and methods to the study of sexuality. The Spotlight on Research feature, which profiles the work of sex researchers, enhances the empirical focus in each chapter. Each of these interviews echoes the fact that sex really does matter.

THEMES OF THIS BOOK

This book is designed to promote sex-positivity and to provide an opportunity for students to reflect on the ways that contexts affect sexual meanings. We believe that consensual sex, in all its forms, regardless of actors, can be beneficial. We have selected pieces that historicize and thus challenge the cultural stigmatization and marginalization of some sexualities and the valorization of others. To us, part of sex-positivity means, for example, promoting the pursuit of sexual pleasure and not centering sex education around danger and disease. To be sex-positive is to recognize that sex can be enriching and to affirm that sex matters.

Each of our chapters highlights the dual themes of social construction and social control. In other words, society—composed of social institutions and the individuals within them—constructs our understanding of sexuality and influences our behaviors, attitudes, and sexual identities. The readings illustrate that some social institutions and some members of society have more power to control and define a society's sexual agenda than others. At the same time, social control is usually met with social resistance, and we offer readings that feature examples of successful individual and cultural resistance to societal expectations and oppression.

Chapter 1, "Categorizing Sex," explores how society constructs and socially controls sexual categories. We challenge readers to question what should count as having sex, a topic with wide-ranging legal and health implications. Readings on intersex and transgender sexualities encourage us to consider the viability of our current categories of "male" and "female," and "man" and "woman," and how these constructions affect sexual behaviors and sexual identities. Other readings question current methods of categorizing sexual orientation and sexual identity. What does it mean to be straight, gay, lesbian, queer, or bisexual? Is sexual identity a matter of behavior, erotic attraction, or self-definition, and do these categories always align with one another? What role does community or politics play in the construction of our sexual identities? In what ways are sex and sexuality more fluid, and is this fluidity consistent across gender and other social categories? Although existing categories can be helpful for understanding commonalities, they also collapse a wide variety of experiences and feelings into inflexible and essentialized divisions. As the readings show, sexual categories vary across societies, cultures, and time.

Chapter 2, "Investigating Sexuality," presents historical and contemporary sex research and considers ethical, political, and methodological issues involved in conducting sex research. The readings introduce the unique challenges and rewards of conducting sex research. The association of sex with privacy creates a level of anxiety and reluctance among would-be research participants that is unmatched in other areas of research. For example, the cultural unwillingness to see adolescents as sexual beings discourages parents from allowing minors to participate in sex research, yet adolescents report benefiting from participating in sex research. Chapter 2 also illustrates the effect of researcher bias and how, for example, racist ideologies guiding research have resulted, historically, in serious harm to minority populations. Differing religious teachings on sexuality add to the controversial nature of sex research. The protest efforts of fundamentalist religious groups have successfully limited governmental support of art, health, and research programs that involve sexuality.

Chapter 3, "Representing Sex," presents a variety of interpretations of the ways that U.S. culture depicts sexualities and sexual activities. For example, media (books, songs, magazines, videos, internet imagery, etc.) both reflect and create ideas about sexuality. Cultural representations of sexuality affect viewers or readers in a variety of ways by telling powerful stories about appropriate sexual activity and what happens to individuals who deviate from cultural expectations. Cultural representations tell us about who we are, where we've been, and where we're going. Cultural texts document how racism, misogyny, and homophobia circulate in public discourses on sexuality. The critical perspectives presented in the readings demonstrate the varieties of possible interpretations of various representations.

Chapter 4, "Learning about Sex," examines the messages about sexuality people receive and how they engage with the meanings of these messages. Youth (ranging from young children to older teenagers) confront a variety of sex information—and misinformation—that informs their sexual attitudes and behaviors. The readings in this chapter explore the different messages youth encounter in media, school, and family contexts. Across cultures, race groups, and genders, youth are taught rather differently about sex, based on assumptions about their capacities to act as autonomous sexual beings. Across the board, sex education in the United States, as reported by educators, parents, and students, has room for much improvement, lacking sex-positive messaging, failing to be inclusive of LGBTQ and disabled sexual needs and experiences. As active consumers of messages, youth make sense of sexuality meanings in ways that vary across gender, race, class, and sexual identity. And as lifelong learners, adults continue to learn from formal sex education and less formal contexts across the life course.

Chapter 5, "Sexual Bodies," addresses how we eroticize bodies, body parts, and bodily functions and explores how notions of the erotic can affect the way we feel about our bodies. Societal discourse both celebrates and stigmatizes the body and its functions. What is sexy about a person's body? Most people can come up with distinct body types or features that are appealing or unappealing to them. Yet ideas about what is sexy and what is not are culturally constructed. For example, some people groom their genitals to craft "sexier" bodies using methods that are just recently becoming popular. Others have surgeries to change their bodies, challenging norms about bodily function and sexuality. Cultural constructions of the sexual body also function as a form of social control—shaping how we feel about our own bodies, framing our interactions with others, and even forcing us to manipulate our bodies to meet cultural expectations. The articles in this chapter explore many traditional ideas about sexuality that emphasize the gendered nature of sexual bodies.

Chapter 6, "Sexual Practices," examines how people behave sexually. As you read the articles in this section, think about how social norms, laws, religion, media, families, friends, and partners influence our sexuality and shape our behavior. From the absence of sexual desire to the interest in kink play, human sexuality is tremendously diverse. Although how we enact our sexuality varies immensely, these readings demonstrate what can happen when we vary from expected and accepted ways of acting sexually. Finally, these articles also remind us that the ways we enact sexual behaviors profoundly impact social relationships across the life course.

Chapter 7, "Sexual Health," illustrates how society treats sexual health and sexually transmitted infections (STIs, also commonly called sexually transmitted diseases, or STDs) quite differently from other forms of health and disease. STIs are the only major group of diseases categorized by their method of transmission, rather than by their symptoms or the parts of the body they affect. People infected with STIs are stigmatized, creating a shield of secrecy in which some people deny to themselves that they have an STI, fail to tell their partners, and avoid seeking treatment. The stigma and perceptions of risk surrounding STIs affect the resources that the government and medical agencies opt to dedicate to public sexual health. For example, when AIDS was first discovered, it was seen as a "gay" or "African"

disease and received little attention. In spite of intense efforts by queer activists, AIDS was considered a national emergency in the United States only when it began infecting white, middle-class, heterosexual Americans. Regardless of the manageability of sexually transmitted infections (as with the vaccine against many strains of HPV or the prophylactic use of PrEP to avoid HIV infection), fears associated with them continue to be a powerful tool in the control of sexuality.

Chapter 8, "Social Control," illustrates how sexuality is managed and directed by forces both internal and external to individuals. Whereas much research on sexuality emphasizes individual responsibility, in this section we explore the structural factors that influence sexual attitudes and behaviors. Social institutions such as family, law, and medicine control sexual behavior through systems of rewards and punishments. Interpersonal interactions further constrain sexual choices through means such as harassment and labeling. This chapter explores how the mechanisms of social control are often turned against certain groups and how the social control of sexuality is a powerful weapon of oppression. Some selections highlight how social control is a two-way street, with the forces of control and resistance in constant conflict.

Although people like to think of sex as an intimate—and ideally pleasant—activity, it can be used as a weapon of violence and control to humiliate, degrade, and hurt. The readings in Chapter 9, "Sexual Violence," illustrate the complexities of defining rape and rape victimization. They deal with various types of sexual assault, rape of sex workers, date or acquaintance rape, the rape of men, rape on campus, rape during war, and nuances of giving consent to sexual activities. The articles presented in this section also illustrate the diversity of sexual violence and the sociocultural contexts that support this violence. Although women are the primary targets of sexual violence, no group is exempt. Sexual violence cuts across all social categories. This chapter also questions assumptions about what counts as sexual violence when consent is not clearly defined. The articles presented here contain graphic and sometimes upsetting or shocking information; it is our hope that readers will not simply be overwhelmed, but will learn how sexual violence is prevalent in our culture as a form of social control and how it is "structured" into our society in a myriad of ways. With knowledge, we can work more effectively for change.

Chapter 10, "Commercial Sex," explores the commodification of sexuality. Despite numerous laws regulating the sale of sexual services, commercial sex continues to be both a profitable business and a source of abuse. We address the tensions between the freedom to express sexuality through commercial avenues and the exploitation and control of sexuality through its sale. The readings examine who profits financially from the sex industry, who works in the sex industry and their working conditions, who consumes its products, and attempts to stem that consumption.

ACKNOWLEDGMENTS

Revising this book for the fifth edition was a challenging yet rewarding experience. We would like to thank our editor, Sasha Levitt, for her patience and unparalleled flexibility, as well as project editors Sujin Hong and Diane Cipollone and assistant editor Erika Nakagawa. Other wonderful Norton team members included Elizabeth Trammell, permissions manager; Stephen Sajdak, production manager; Rubina Yeh, design director; Julia Hall, marketing manager; Eileen Connell, media editor; Ariel Eaton, associate media editor; Travis Carr, photo editor; Harry Haskell, copyeditor; Carol Sawyer, proofreader; and Heather Dubnick, indexer. The W. W. Norton staff has worked incredibly hard to publish this edition in record time with white-glove service. We love a publisher that works hard and plays hard (and we enjoy being included in both)!

We are grateful to the researchers and scholars who took time out of their busy schedules to be interviewed for the Spotlight on Research features. Their dedication to the field of sex research, their humor in the face of monetary and political challenges, and their willingness to share personal experiences make us optimistic about the future of sex research. We want to thank the authors who wrote original pieces for the fifth edition. Their contributions make the book bigger and better (not that size matters . . .).

We received crucial assistance from Leanna Greenwood, Samantha Howat, and Sierra Nicely at Georgia State University, and Jayme Mendez at Salem College. Special thanks to librarians extraordinaire Mandy Swygart-Hobaugh, who assisted with our obscure search requests, and Laura Carscaddon, who held books hostage on our behalf.

Thanks to our families and friends for their encouragement and support. In particular, Mindy would like to thank her son, Moey Rojas, for his independence, allowing her to focus on book work; her parents, Lynne and Milton Stombler, for their seemingly unending support; and her partner, Nate Steiner, for being a mensch in every way. Dawn thanks Jeff Mullis and their four cats. Wendy thanks Jake Simonds-Malamud, Ben Simonds-Malamud, Gregg Rice, Hinky Simonds (RIP), and Puff Simonds for their sweetness. Elroi thanks Aly, Avie, and Izzy Windsor for being a fantastic family. Elisabeth appreciates the support of Leila Burgess-Kattoula, Ehsan Kattoula, and the rest of her family and friends.

This book would not have been possible without our dedicated and discerning undergraduate and graduate students. We appreciate them for letting us know their favorite readings, for fearlessly voicing their opinions, and for asking tough questions.

This project is truly an example of collaborative feminist work. With Mindy Stombler as the team's "dominatrix," and the constant mutual support among all team members, creating this book often felt more like fun than work. We hope you have as much fun reading this book as we had putting it together.

ABOUT THE CONTRIBUTORS

THE EDITORS

Mindy Stombler is a principal senior lecturer of sociology at Georgia State University. Her past research has focused on the production of sexual collective identities. For example, she explored how men in gay fraternities negotiated their dual identities of being gay and being Greek and how they reproduced hegemonic masculinity. Her current research focuses on power relations and oral sex as well as a variety of pedagogical issues. She is also co-editor with Amanda M. Jungels of *Focus on Social Problems: A Contemporary Reader* (Oxford University Press).

Dawn M. Baunach is the chair of the Department of Sociology and Criminal Justice and a professor of sociology at Kennesaw State University. Her research interests include sexuality and gender inequalities, statistics and methodologies, social demography, and the sociology of food. She is currently studying various sexual attitudes and behaviors, including same-sex marriage, sexual prejudices, sexual disclosure, and bullying.

Elisabeth O. Burgess is the director of the Gerontology Institute and a professor of gerontology and sociology at Georgia State University. Her research interests focus on changes in intimate relations over the life course, including involuntary celibacy, sexuality and aging, and intergenerational relationships. In addition, she writes on theories of aging and attitudes toward older adults.

Wendy Simonds is a professor of sociology and gerontology at Georgia State University. She is the author of *Hospital Land USA: Sociological Adventures in Medicalization; Abor-*
tion at Work: Ideology and Practice in a Feminist Clinic; Women and Self-Help Culture: Reading between the Lines; and co-author of *Centuries of Solace: Expressions of Maternal Grief in Popular Literature* and *Laboring On: Birth in Transition in the U.S.* She is currently doing research on affirmative action policies and programs on U.S. college and university campuses.

Elroi J. Windsor is an associate professor and chair of the Department of Sociology at the University of West Georgia. Windsor's teaching and research interests include gender, sexuality, and embodiment. Windsor's past research focused on the disparate regulation of transgender and cisgender consumers of surgical body modification. Currently, Windsor is writing a book about health care providers who work with body parts and dead bodies and co-editing *Male Femininities* with Dana Berkowitz and C. Winter Han (New York University Press).

CONTRIBUTORS

Katie Acosta is an associate professor of sociology at Georgia State University.

Brandon Ambrosino is a PhD student in theology and ethics at Villanova University.

Orit Avishai is an associate professor of sociology and the co-director of Women, Gender, and Sexuality Studies at Fordham University.

Christina Barmon is an assistant professor of sociology at Central Connecticut State University.

Jonathon J. Beckmeyer is an assistant professor in the School of Public Health at Indiana University.

Alexis A. Bender is an assistant professor of medicine in the Division of General Medicine and Geriatrics in the Emory University School of Medicine.

Allan M. Brandt is the Amalie Moses Kass Professor of the History of Medicine and a professor of the history of science at Harvard University.

Virginia Braun is a professor of psychology at the University of Auckland.

Eliza Brown is a doctoral student at New York University.

Jamie Budnick is a doctoral candidate at the University of Michigan.

Vern L. Bullough was, before his death, a distinguished scholar and professor emeritus in the History Department at California State University, Northridge.

Kelsy Burke is an assistant professor of sociology at the University of Nebraska, Lincoln.

Caroline Catlin is a storyteller and mental health worker in Seattle, Washington.

Elizabeth Cavalier is an associate professor of sociology at Georgia Gwinnett College.

Wendy Chapkis is a professor of women and gender studies and sociology at the University of Southern Maine.

Greta Christina is an author, editor, and public speaker in San Francisco.

Georgiann Davis is an assistant professor of sociology at the University of Nevada, Las Vegas.

Saskia de Melker is a Peabody award–winning broadcast and multimedia producer who works extensively for the public television program *PBS NewsHour Weekend*.

Brian D. Earp is associate director of the Yale-Hastings Program in Ethics and Health Policy at Yale University and the Hastings Center, as well as a research fellow in the Uehiro Centre for Practical Ethics at the University of Oxford.

Paula England is a professor of sociology at New York University.

Loree Erickson is a community organizer and porn star academic in Toronto, Ontario.

Breanne Fahs is a professor of women and gender studies at Arizona State University.

Lauren Fannin is a doctoral student in sociology at Georgia State University.

Elizabeth Fee is a professor of health policy and management at the Johns Hopkins University Bloomberg School of Public Health.

Katherine Frank is a faculty associate in anthropology at the College of the Atlantic and affiliate research faculty at the University of Nevada, Las Vegas.

Nicola Gavey is a professor of psychology at the University of Auckland, New Zealand.

Desmond F. Goss is a lecturer of sociology at Georgia State University.

Mary L. Gray is a senior researcher at Microsoft Research, associate professor in the School of Informatics, Computing, and Engineering at Indiana University, and fellow at Harvard University's Berkman Klein Center for Internet and Society.

Lea Grover is a blogger and public speaker.

Matthew Hall is a research associate at Ulster University.

Corie J. Hammers is an associate professor of women's, gender, and sexuality studies at Macalester College.

C. Winter Han is an associate professor of sociology at Middlebury College.

Stacy Gorman Harmon is a research scientist at the Centers for Disease Control (CDC) Foundation.

Kimberly Kay Hoang is an assistant professor of sociology at the University of Chicago.

Jocelyn A. Hollander is a professor of sociology at the University of Oregon.

Brooke Jarvis is a contributing writer to the *New York Times Magazine* and the *California Sunday Magazine* and a winner of the Livingston Award for National Reporting.

Robin E. Jensen is a professor of communication at the University of Utah.

Maggie Jones is a contributing writer for the *New York Times Magazine* and a visiting assistant professor of English at the University of Pittsburgh.

Amanda M. Jungels is an assistant director of Faculty Programs and Services in the Center for Teaching and Learning, Columbia University.

Jillian Keenan is a freelance writer in Dakar, Senegal.

Alyson Krueger is a freelance journalist writing for the *New York Times*, the *Washington Post*, *Elle*, and *Forbes,* among other publications.

Roger N. Lancaster is a professor of anthropology and cultural studies at George Mason University.

Jill Lepore is the David Woods Kemper '41 Professor of American History at Harvard University.

Kathryn Graff Low is the interim vice president for academic affairs and dean of the faculty at Bates College.

Zakiya Luna is an assistant professor of sociology at the University of California, Santa Barbara and faculty affiliate of the Center on Reproductive Rights and Justice at Berkeley Law.

Mona Malacane is an assistant instructor at the Media School at Indiana University.

Patricia Yancey Martin is a professor emeritus of sociology at Florida State University.

PJ McGann is a lecturer of sociology at the University of Michigan, Ann Arbor.

Glenn J. Meaney is a lecturer of psychology and sexuality, marriage, and family studies at St. Jerome's University at the University of Waterloo in Ontario, Canada.

Chet Meeks was, before his death, an assistant professor of sociology at Georgia State University.

Ilan H. Meyer is a Williams Distinguished Senior Scholar of Public Policy at the Williams Institute for Sexual Orientation Law and Public Policy at the UCLA School of Law.

Sarah A. Miller is a doctoral candidate in sociology at the University of Massachusetts, Amherst.

Lisa Jean Moore is a medical sociologist and professor of sociology and gender studies at Purchase College, State University of New York.

Adina Nack is a professor of sociology at California Lutheran University.

Joane Nagel is chair of the Anthropology Department and University Distinguished Professor of Sociology at the University of Kansas.

Jake New is a reporter for *Inside Higher Ed.*

Jessica A. Nodulman is an assistant professor of communication studies at Augustana College.

Amy Palder is the assistant dean of students and chief conduct officer at Oglethorpe University.

Cat Pausé is a senior lecturer at Massey University in New Zealand.

Anna N. Query is a practicing child and family clinician in the field of early education.

Katie Rodgers is an assistant professor of sociology at Coe College.

Jennifer Rosen is an assistant professor of sociology at Ashford University.

Maura Ryan is a senior lecturer of sociology at Georgia State University.

B. J. Rye is an associate professor of psychology and sexuality, marriage, and family studies at St. Jerome's University.

Teela Sanders is a professor of criminology at the University of Leicester.

Amy T. Schalet is an associate professor of sociology at the University of Massachusetts, Amherst.

Kelsey K. Sewell is a postdoctoral fellow in behavioral medicine/psycho-oncology at the University of Kansas Medical Center.

Elisabeth Sheff is an expert witness, researcher, educator, and speaker.

Tobin Siebers was, before his death, co-chair of the university's Initiative on Disability Studies, V. L. Parrington Collegiate Professor, and professor of English language and literature, and art and design at the University of Michigan.

Tony Silva is a doctoral candidate in sociology at the University of Oregon.

Adam Sonfield is a senior policy manager at the Guttmacher Institute's Washington, DC, office.

Lara Stemple is the assistant dean for graduate studies and international student programs and the director of the Health and Human Rights Law Project at the UCLA School of Law.

Evelina Sterling is an assistant professor of sociology at Kennesaw State University.

Bethany Stevens is a doctoral student in sociology at Georgia State University.

Donald S. Strassberg is a professor of clinical psychology at the University of Utah.

Jasmine Suryawan is a doctoral student in sociology at the University of Colorado, Boulder.

Eric Swank is an associate professor of practice at Arizona State University (Social and Cultural Analysis at ASU West).

Megan M. Tesene is a doctoral candidate in sociology and adaptive learning program manager at the Center for Excellence in Teaching and Learning at Georgia State University.

Griff Tester is an assistant professor of sociology at Central Washington University.

Harper Jean Tobin is director of policy at the National Center for Transgender Equality.

Tycho Vandenburg is a doctoral candidate at the University of Auckland, New Zealand.

Chris M. Vidmar is a doctoral student in sociology at Georgia State University.

Linda Villarosa is a contributing writer to the *New York Times Magazine*. She is also the director of the journalism program at the City College of New York in Harlem and an assistant professor of media and communication arts.

Zhana Vrangalova is an adjunct professor of psychology and sexuality at New York University.

Lisa Wade is an associate professor of sociology at Occidental College.

Kevin Walby is an associate professor and Chancellor's Research Chair in the Department of Criminal Justice at the University of Winnipeg.

Margot Weiss is an associate professor of American studies and chair of the Anthropology Department at Wesleyan University.

Elizabeth A. Williams is an associate professor of organizational communication at Colorado State University.

Marik Xavier-Brier is a civil rights analyst at the U.S. Commission on Civil Rights.

Nicolette Zangari is a doctoral student of clinical psychology at the University of Kansas.

1

CATEGORIZING SEX

AN INTERVIEW WITH

MARYSOL ASENCIO

Marysol Asencio, MPH, DrPH, is a full professor at the University of Connecticut with a joint appointment in sociology and El Instituto: The Institute of Latina/o, Caribbean, and Latin American Studies. Dr. Asencio focuses on the intersections of Latina/o sexualities and sexual health with gender, race/racialization, socioeconomic status, and migration. Dr. Asencio has authored, edited, and coedited a number of books and special issues of journals on Latinas/os and their sexualities, in addition to peer-reviewed articles, chapters, and other publications. Her research and projects have been supported by both internal and external grants, such as the Ford Foundation. Her edited volume, Latina/o Sexualities: Probing Powers, Passions, Practices, and Policies *(Rutgers University Press, 2010), helped coalesce Latina/o sexualities research and scholarship as a field of study. She is currently working on a research project on Latina lesbian-queer visibility, which was funded through the UConn Collaborative to Advance Equity through Research on Women and Girls of Color.*

What led you to begin studying sexuality?

I entered graduate school with a research interest in women's reproductive health issues, which at the time ironically rarely dealt with issues of sexuality. It was mostly focused on family planning, contraceptive use, and maternal-child issues. However, this was also shortly after the medical community had identified AIDS when it was briefly referred to as GRID (Gay-Related Immune-Deficiency). It was a time when the lack of understanding of sexuality, as well as the biases about sexuality and certain racial/ethnic and sexual minorities, was exposed in a dramatic and deadly manner. The quickly advancing epidemic affected me personally as well, with the loss of several friends and colleagues. It was a frightening and frustrating time. It not only influenced me to enter sex research but it also awakened me to the need for community-based research and social justice advocacy for marginalized populations in order to promote evidence-based health and social policy.

How do people react when you tell them you study sexuality?

Over the course of my career, I have gotten the impression that for some colleagues who do not do this type of research, sex research is not viewed as serious or important. This is a big concern in terms of having an academic career in sexuality research. Will you be hired because the work is seen as being in the margins of a particular discipline or in academia as a whole? When you tell the average person that you teach human sexuality, there is usually some laughter and a perception that it is a course that provides sexual entertainment rather than a forum for serious, rigorous, and challenging research and scholarship.

What ethical dilemmas have you faced as you've studied sexuality? Could you tell us about a particularly thorny dilemma and how you solved it?

I was working on a research project on gay men and prostate health with a couple of colleagues. Given that at the time there were no published studies on gay men with prostate cancer, we decided to conduct focus groups with diverse populations of gay men (racial/ethnic and socioeconomic) to see what concerns they had around prostate screening, diagnosis, treatment and its after-effects (many of them being sexual in nature). We used standard procedures that were established for recruiting men into the study, including a $40 stipend for participation. Toward the end of the study, we were trying to move away from middle-class participants and reach out to poorer, marginalized, and in some cases homeless, gay men. What resulted was that our outreach efforts yielded potential participants who seemed as if they were claiming to be "gay" or "transgendered women" in order to receive the stipend. It was difficult to determine if someone was "gay" or "transgender" since we depend on reported self-identity.[1] If we accepted their assertions that they were gay men or transgendered women when there were signs that they may not be, we would bias our results. Also, given that they said they "matched" the criteria, there was very little rationale for turning them away other than none of the researchers believing this was the case based on other arguably unreliable cues. There was no way to know for sure.

We addressed this ethical dilemma[2] by providing every participant with the stipend and then reiterating the fact that although they consented to participate, they could leave at any time without having to give back the stipend. We hoped that those who were questionable in terms of meeting the study criteria would not feel they needed to participate. We went from around 22 people who showed up for the focus group to seven who remained. All the participants we had serious questions about left. It cost us some funds, but we had few options given our approved human subjects protocol and the volatility of the situation. This incident allowed us to consider ways to minimize this problem in future studies. However, it also demonstrates that the use and/or amount of stipends for research participation as well as the self-identification of sexual orientation and gender can in some cases become problematic depending on the particular research population and research needs.

What do you think is most challenging about studying sexuality?

While I think the field as a whole has become more accepted, the research is still "suspect." It is assumed to be potentially harmful until proven not harmful, in particular when dealing with the sexuality of those under the age of 18. There are significant barriers to getting detailed sexual histories of participants; discussing sexual acts; and attending locations that are designated as sexual such as strip clubs, brothels, etc. Sex research often depends on non-sex researchers (institutional review boards [IRBs], funders, and communities) who may view this type of research as different from other forms of research or who believe that we ought not to ask about sex or that it is a voyeuristic enterprise.

Why is sex research important?

Sexuality is central to understanding a great deal about humanity and society. As someone who researches Latinas/os and sexuality, I was once asked why I "waste" my time as a researcher on sexuality when I could be studying more important issues for the Latina/o community, such as poverty and racism. First of all, studying sexuality involves understanding all its intersections and connections with issues such as poverty and racism. Second, if you look at political debates in this country, sexuality plays a major role (e.g., contraception, abortion, same-sex marriage, teen pregnancy, etc.). Moreover, the outcomes of those debates many times affect racial/ethnic and sexual minorities and low-income individuals and families in ways that disadvantage or minimize their experiences. Therefore, sex research furthers our understanding of power, marginalization, and other social issues.

Of the projects you've done over the course of your academic career, which was most interesting and why?

My first large independent qualitative research on adolescent sexuality was most interesting because I was still learning about sexuality research. It was eye-opening. I remember when I asked one of my female respondents about the first time she had sexual intercourse, she went on to explain how she was raped as a child by an uncle and she wanted to make it clear to me that she saw herself as a "virgin" and would like me to characterize her as such. She had still not had, at the age of 18, "consensual" first sexual intercourse. It was very important to her sense of dignity and control of her sexuality to be seen as a virgin. She also told me that what she did not like about questionnaires that asked her "if she had ever had sexual intercourse" was that they did not reflect her experience or her wish "not" to be characterized as a "sexually active" teen or not a "virgin." I learned a great deal about the meanings attached to sexuality from those adolescents and I am very grateful that they shared their lives with me.

If you could teach people one thing about sexuality, what would it be?

I would say that sexuality is not just about identity and behaviors; it is a portal to understand society and issues of power.

Is there anything else you'd like to add?

One thing that I would like to add is that I hope as the field continues to grow it will attract researchers from many different backgrounds and experiences. I believe, as with any subject matter, that the more diverse the researchers are, in terms of demographic backgrounds and life experiences, the more opportunity there is for various perspectives and insights to be brought into our understanding of sex and sexuality.

NOTES

1. It is important to note that many transgender women do maintain their prostate even if they have had hormonal and surgical alterations to their bodies.

2. For a full account, see Descartes, Lara, Marysol Asencio, and Thomas O. Blank. 2011. "Paying Project Participants: Dilemmas in Research with Poor, Marginalized Populations." *Advances in Social Work* 12, no. 2: 218–25.

ARE WE HAVING SEX NOW OR WHAT?

GRETA CHRISTINA

When I first started having sex with other people, I used to like to count them. I wanted to keep track of how many there had been. It was a source of some kind of pride, or identity anyway, to know how many people I'd had sex with in my lifetime. So, in my mind, Len was number one, Chris was number two, that slimy awful little heavy metal barbiturate addict whose name I can't remember was number three, Alan was number four, and so on. It got to the point where, when I'd start having sex with a new person for the first time, when he first entered my body (I was only having sex with men at the time), what would flash through my head wouldn't be "Oh, baby, baby you feel so good inside me," or "What the hell am I doing with this creep," or "This is boring, I wonder what's on TV." What flashed through my head was "Seven!"

Doing this had some interesting results. I'd look for patterns in the numbers. I had a theory for a while that every fourth lover turned out to be really great in bed, and would ponder what the cosmic significance of the phenomenon might be. Sometimes I'd try to determine what kind of person I was by how many people I'd had sex with. At eighteen, I'd had sex with ten different people. Did that make me normal, repressed, a total slut, a free-spirited bohemian, or what? Not that I compared my numbers with anyone else's—I didn't. It was my own exclusive structure, a game I played in the privacy of my own head.

Then the numbers started getting a little larger, as numbers tend to do, and keeping track became more difficult. I'd remember that the last one was *seventeen* and so this one must be *eighteen*, but then I'd start having doubts about whether I'd been keeping score accurately or not. I'd lie awake at night thinking to myself, well, there was Brad, and there was that guy on my birthday, and there was David and . . . no, wait, I forgot that guy I got drunk with at the social my first week at college . . . so that's seven, eight, nine . . . and by two in the morning I'd finally have it figured out. But there was always a nagging suspicion that maybe I'd missed someone, some dreadful tacky little scumball that I was trying to forget about having invited inside my body. And as much as I maybe wanted to forget about the sleazy little scumball, I wanted more to get that number right.

It kept getting harder, though. I began to question what counted as sex and what didn't. There was that time with Gene, for instance. I was pissed off at my boyfriend, David, for cheating on me. It was a major crisis, and Gene and I were friends and he'd been trying to get at me for weeks and I hadn't exactly been discouraging him. I went to see him that night to gripe about David. He was very sympathetic of course, and he gave me a backrub, and we talked and touched and confided and hugged, and then we started kissing, and then we snuggled up a little closer, and then we started fondling each other, you know, and then all heck broke loose, and we rolled around on the bed groping and rubbing and grabbing and smooching and pushing and pressing and squeezing. He never did actually get it in. He wanted to, and I wanted to too, but I had this thing about being faithful to my boyfriend, so I kept saying, "No, you can't do that, Yes, that feels so good, No, wait that's too much. Yes, yes, don't stop. No, stop that's enough." We never even got our clothes off. Jesus Christ, though, it was some night. One of the best, really. But for a long time I didn't count it as one of the times I'd had sex. He never got inside, so it didn't count.

Later, months and years later, when I lay awake putting my list together, I'd start to wonder: Why doesn't Gene count? Does he not count because he never got inside? Or does he not count because I had to preserve my moral edge over David, my status as the patient, ever-faithful, cheated-on, martyred girlfriend, and if what I did with Gene counts then I don't get to feel wounded and superior?

Years later, I did end up fucking Gene and I felt a profound relief because, at last, he definitely had a number, and I knew for sure that he did in fact count.

Then I started having sex with women, and, boy, howdy, did *that* ever shoot holes in the system. I'd always made my list of sex partners by defining sex as penile-vaginal intercourse—you know, screwing. It's a pretty simple distinction, a straightforward binary system. Did it go in or didn't it? Yes or no? One or zero? On or off? Granted, it's a pretty arbitrary definition, but it's the customary one, with an ancient and respected tradition behind it, and when I was just screwing men, there was no compelling reason to question it.

But with women, well, first of all there's [generally] no penis, so right from the start the tracking system is defective. And then, there are so many ways women can have sex with each other, touching and licking and grinding and fingering and fisting—with dildoes or vibrators or vegetables or whatever happens to be lying around the house, or with nothing at

all except human bodies. Of course, that's true for sex between women and men as well. But between women, no one method has a centuries-old tradition of being the one that counts. Even when [cisgender women] do fuck each other, there's no dick, so you don't get that feeling of This Is What's Important, We Are Now Having Sex, objectively speaking, and all that other stuff is just foreplay or afterplay. So when I started having sex with women, the binary system had to go, in favor of a more inclusive definition.

Which meant, of course, that my list of how many people I'd had sex with was completely trashed. In order to maintain it I would have had to go back and reconstruct the whole thing and include all those people I'd necked with and gone down on and dry-humped and played touchy-feely games with. Even the question of who filled the all-important Number One slot, something I'd never had any doubts about before, would have to be re-evaluated.

By this time I'd kind of lost interest in the list anyway. Reconstructing it would be more trouble than it was worth. But the crucial question remained: What counts as having sex with someone?

It was important for me to know. You have to know what qualifies as sex because when you have sex with someone your relationship changes. Right? *Right?* It's not that sex itself has to change things all that much. But knowing you've had sex, being conscious of a sexual connection, standing around making polite conversation with someone while thinking to yourself, "I've had sex with this person," that's what changes things. Or so I believed. And if having sex with a friend can confuse or change the friendship, think how bizarre things can get when you're not sure whether you've had sex with them or not.

The problem was, as I kept doing more kinds of sexual things, the line between *sex* and *not-sex* kept getting more hazy and indistinct. As I brought more into my sexual experience, things were showing up on the dividing line demanding my attention. It wasn't just that the territory I labeled *sex* was expanding. The line itself had swollen, dilated, been transformed into a vast gray region. It had become less like a border and more like a demilitarized zone.

Which is a strange place to live. Not a bad place, just strange. It's like juggling, or watch-making, or playing the piano—anything that demands complete concentrated awareness and attention. It feels like cognitive dissonance, only pleasant. It feels like waking up from a compelling and realistic bad dream. It feels like the way you feel when you realize that everything you know is wrong, and a bloody good thing too, because it was painful and stupid and it really screwed you up.

But, for me, living in a question naturally leads to searching for an answer. I can't simply shrug, throw up my hands, and say, "Damned if I know." I have to explore the unknown frontiers, even if I don't bring back any secret treasure. So even if it's incomplete or provisional, I do want to find some sort of definition of what is and isn't sex.

I know when I'm *feeling* sexual. I'm feeling sexual if my pussy's wet, my nipples are hard, my palms are clammy, my brain is fogged, my skin is tingly and super-sensitive, my butt muscles clench, my heartbeat speeds up, I have an orgasm (that's the real giveaway), and so on. But feeling sexual with someone isn't the same as having sex with them. Good Lord, if I called it sex every time I was attracted to someone who returned the favor I'd be even more bewildered than I am now. Even *being* sexual with someone isn't the same as *having* sex with them. I've danced and flirted with too many people, given and received too many sexy, would-be-seductive backrubs, to believe otherwise.

I have friends who say, if you thought of it as sex when you were doing it, then it was. That's an interesting idea. It's certainly helped me construct a coherent sexual history without being a revisionist swine: redefining my past according to current definitions. But it really just begs the question. It's fine to say that sex is whatever I think it is; but then what do I think it *is*? What if, when I was doing it, I was *wondering* whether it counted?

Perhaps having sex with someone is the conscious, consenting, mutually acknowledged pursuit of shared sexual pleasure. Not a bad definition. If you are turning each other on and you say so and you keep doing it, then it's sex. It's broad enough to encompass a lot of sexual behavior beyond genital contact/orgasm; it's distinct enough *not* to include every instance of sexual awareness or arousal; and it contains the elements I feel are vital—acknowledgment, consent, reciprocity, and the pursuit of pleasure. But what about the situation where one person consents to sex without really enjoying it? Lots of people (myself included) have had sexual interactions that we didn't find satisfying or didn't really want and, unless they were actually forced on us against our will, I think most of us would still classify them as sex.

Maybe if *both* of you (or all of you) think of it as sex, then it's sex whether you're having fun or not. That clears up the problem of sex that's consented to but not wished-for or enjoyed. Unfortunately, it begs the question again, only worse: now you have to mesh different people's vague and inarticulate notions of what is and isn't sex and find the place where they overlap. Too messy.

How about sex as the conscious, consenting, mutually acknowledged pursuit of sexual pleasure of *at least one* of the people involved. That's better. It has all the key components, and it includes the situation where one person is doing it for a reason other than sexual pleasure—status, reassurance, money, the satisfaction and pleasure of someone they love, etc. But what if *neither* of you is enjoying it, if you're both doing it because you think the other one wants to? Ugh.

I'm having trouble here. Even the conventional standby—sex equals intercourse—has a serious flaw: it includes rape, which is something I emphatically refuse to accept. As far as I'm concerned, if there's no consent, it ain't sex. But I feel that's about the only place in this whole quagmire where I have a grip. The longer I think about the subject, the more questions I come up with. At what point in an encounter does it *become* sexual? If an interaction that begins nonsexually turns into sex, was it sex all along? What about sex with someone who's asleep? Can you have a situation where one person is having sex and the other isn't? It seems that no matter what definition I come up with, I can think of some real-life experience that calls it into question.

For instance, a couple of years ago I attended (well, hosted) an all-girl sex party. Out of the twelve other women there, there were only a few with whom I got seriously physically nasty. The rest I kissed or hugged or talked dirty with or just smiled at, or watched while they did seriously physically nasty things with each other. If we'd been alone, I'd probably say that what I'd done with most of the women there didn't count as having sex. But the experience, which was hot and sweet and silly and very, very special, had been created by all of us, and although I only really got down with a few, I felt that I'd been sexual with all of the women there. Now, when I meet one of the women from that party, I always ask myself: Have we had sex?

For instance, when I was first experimenting with sadomasochism, I got together with a really hot woman. We were negotiat-ing about what we were going to do, what would and wouldn't be okay, and she said she wasn't sure she wanted to have sex. Now we'd been explicitly planning all kinds of fun and games—spanking, bondage, obedience—which I strongly identified as sexual activity. In her mind, though, *sex* meant direct genital contact, and she didn't necessarily want to do that with me. Playing with her turned out to be a tremendously erotic experience, arousing and stimulating and almost unbearably satisfying. But we spent the whole evening without even touching each other's genitals. And the fact that our definitions were so different made me wonder: Was it sex?

For instance, I worked for a few months as a nude dancer at a peep show. In case you've never been to a peep show, it works like this: the customer goes into a tiny, dingy black box, kind of like a phone booth, puts in quarters, and a metal plate goes up; the customer looks through a window at a little room/stage where naked women are dancing. One time, a guy came into one of the booths and started watching me and masturbating. I came over and squatted in front of him and started masturbating too, and we grinned at each other and watched each other and masturbated, and we both had a fabulous time. (I couldn't believe I was being paid to masturbate—tough job, but somebody has to do it . . . .) After he left I thought to myself: Did we just have sex? I mean, if it had been someone I knew, and if there had been no glass and no quarters, there'd be no question in my mind. Sitting two feet apart from someone, watching each other masturbate? Yup, I'd call that sex all right. But this was different, because it was a stranger, and because of the glass and the quarters. Was it sex?

I still don't have an answer.

How Do Heterosexual Undergraduate Students Define Having Sex?

Kelsey K. Sewell and Donald S. Strassberg

A number of studies have examined which physically intimate behaviors individuals consider to be "having sex" (e.g., Sanders & Reinisch, 1999). . . . Though there has been some disagreement among these studies regarding how often some behaviors were considered sex (e.g., for oral stimulation, 24% to 40% across studies), the list of behaviors from most to least likely to be considered sex has proven to be very consistent, being replicated both within (Gute, Eshbaugh, & Wiersma, 2008) and outside (e.g., Pitts & Rahman, 2001) the United States, as well as across time (Sanders & Reinisch, 1999; Horowitz & Spicer, 2013). Nearly all of these studies have been limited (or nearly so) to exclusively heterosexual participants, the sole exception being a study on gay men in the United States and United Kingdom (Hill et al., 2010). . . .

Several recent studies have explored the idea that definitions of sex may be flexible or ambiguous. Peterson and Muehlenhard (2007) suggested that underlying many studies is the implicit assumption that individuals have clear definitions of what behaviors do and do not constitute having sex. In contrast to this assumption, however, they found that almost everyone they surveyed could describe previously experiencing an ambiguous sexual situation (e.g., "not quite sex" or "unsure"). Further, they found that participants' definitions of sex sometimes seemed to be motivated. That is, their decisions about whether to label an ambiguous sexual encounter as "having sex" seemed to be influenced by their perception of the consequences of labeling it as such (e.g., negative self-evaluation). These authors called those circumstances in which participants considered the possible consequences of the label when choosing their definition "motivated definitions" (Peterson & Muehlenhard, 2007, p. 257). They suggested these motivated definitions may serve to protect an individual's self-image but could also have the negative consequence of justifying sexually risky behaviors. . . .

THE PRESENT STUDY

. . . Utilizing a mixed-method design, participants rated their degree of confidence that each of a variety of behaviors constituted "having sex," assuming (a) they and (b) their significant other (with someone else) were engaging in the behavior, with the order in which these judgments were made (i.e., for self or significant other first) systematically manipulated so that possible order effects could be evaluated. . . . [T]he final sample consisted of 594 individuals, 267 men and 327 women. Participants ranged in age from 18 to 62 (M = 23.3, SD = 6.55). . . . None of the demographic variables (e.g., age, race, religious importance) was significantly related to the variables of interest.

Quantitative Findings

Descriptive Information for Intimate Behavior Rankings

INTIMATE BEHAVIORS	DEFINITELY NOT SEX (%)	PROBABLY NOT SEX (%)	PROBABLY SEX (%)	DEFINITELY SEX (%)
Deep kissing	92.3	4.7	1.9	0.8
SO stimulates your nipples	73.2	16.8	6.1	3.5
You stimulate SO's nipples	69.7	19.9	7.1	3.4
Self-stimulation on computer	64.6	21.5	9.8	3.9
Self-stimulation on phone	63.1	22.6	10.1	3.7
Mutual self-stimulation	59.3	23.4	10.8	6.2
SO manually stimulates you	49.3	26.1	15.0	9.4
You manually stimulate SO	47.6	28.3	15.2	8.9
SO manually stimulates you, org	41.2	25.9	18.5	14.1
You manually stimulate SO, org	40.7	26.8	18.2	14.0
SO orally stimulates you	28.8	23.1	23.4	24.6
You orally stimulate SO	27.4	25.1	22.9	24.6
SO orally stimulates you, org	23.1	23.6	22.2	31.0
You orally stimulate SO, org	21.7	24.2	22.9	31.0
69 position (mutual oral stimulation)	20.0	20.7	25.6	33.2
Anal intercourse, NO	3.5	4.5	21.5	70.0
Anal intercourse, org	3.7	3.7	18.4	74.1
Penile-vaginal intercourse, NO	2.0	0.5	8.4	88.9
Penile-vaginal intercourse, MO	0.8	0.2	3.5	95.3
Penile-vaginal intercourse, FO	0.7	0.2	3.7	94.9
Penile-vaginal intercourse, BO	0.7	0.2	0.3	98.7

Note: SO = significant other; org = orgasm; NO = nobody orgasms; MO = male orgasms; FO = female orgasms; BO = both orgasm.

SUPPORT AND IMPLICATIONS FOR UNCERTAINTY

In contrast to almost every published study in this area, our use of a four-point (rather than a Yes/No) scale allowed participants to express either absolute certainty (i.e., *Definitely not sex* or *Definitely sex*) or a degree of uncertainty (i.e., *Probably not sex* or *Probably sex*) in their judgments. The value in doing so is evident by the fact that our intermediate answer choices were frequently used, especially for those behaviors found in previous studies for which there was the least participant agreement regarding whether the behavior counted as sex. In fact, some behaviors we included received almost evenly distributed responses across choices. For example, while Sanders and Reinisch (1999) found that 40% of those they surveyed checked *Yes* (and 60% checked *No*) when rating oral-genital stimulation, nearly half of our participants expressed some uncertainty by selecting an intermediate answer choice (25.1% picked *Probably not sex* and 22.9% chose *Probably sex*). Providing participants only a Yes/No option would have failed to capture this uncertainty. . . .

Uncertainty about which behaviors are and are not sex may increase the likelihood of risky behavior. For example, someone's experience of uncertainty about the extent to which anal intercourse is "sex" could discourage the use of proper protection (e.g., condoms) when engaging in this behavior, increasing the risk of spreading or contracting sexually transmitted infections (STIs; e.g., "Why practice 'safe sex' if I don't think the behavior is definitely having sex?"). Though this study was able to measure uncertainty, it could not link uncertainty with behavioral outcomes. Future work should consider the potential relationship between certainty levels in categorizing a behavior as "sex" and the perceived health risks involved in engaging in this behavior.

QUALITATIVE FINDINGS

Qualitative follow-up encouraged participants to explain their answers, providing the opportunity to begin to understand why people do and do not consider various behaviors as sex. It was clear from the responses that a number of factors can influence one's definition of sex and that people differ in which of these factors play a role in their decisions.

The most popular themes mentioned were physical reasons, such as whether physical contact with the other person occurred (mentioned by 50% of our sample), whether penetration occurred (46.3%), and whether the genitals were involved, with 28.7% saying that at least one person's genitals must be touched and 17.1% specifying that a person's genitals must be touching the other person's genitals to count as sex. Consistent with this, lack of physical contact was used most often to describe why a behavior did not count as sex (e.g., for phone/computer sex: "no physical contact, no sex"). Using physical reasons to distinguish when a behavior counts as sex may represent a way

individuals try to use clear rules when navigating their physically intimate experiences and negotiating acceptable boundaries with a new partner. For example, if an individual considers penile penetration to be a requisite for "having sex," oral-genital stimulation may be a way to be intimate with a partner without having sex.

Some of our participants wrote that considering the potential outcome of engaging in the behavior influenced their certainty regarding whether a particular behavior should be considered as sex. Many such explanations referred to physical outcomes (e.g., 18.5% mentioned sexual arousal; 29.2% mentioned orgasm). Others wrote about situational outcomes, such as the potential for the act to result in pregnancy, STIs, and virginity loss. Outcome-based definitions can easily impact the sexual choices people make. For example, if a person believes only behaviors that can result in pregnancy constitute having sex, they might feel quite comfortable (e.g., nonguilty) engaging in oral sex or anal intercourse, perhaps leaving them at risk for negative outcomes, such as STIs. This supports Peterson and Muehlenhard's (2007) suggestion that some individuals use "motivated definitions" in their definitions of sex.

Our results suggest that there exists a very strong social norm that PVI [penile-vaginal intercourse] counts as "having sex." Quantitative results in our study and every other previous study in this area have indicated that almost 100% of people consider PVI (at least when orgasm occurs) to be sex. Further, our qualitative results found that almost half of the comments offered nothing more than "this is sex" in explanation for PVI, suggesting many people considered PVI to be so obviously and widely considered sex that they struggled to explain or felt an explanation was unnecessary. This idea of PVI as the "gold standard" of sexual encounters is not new. Research has suggested that many people tend to think about having sex within a strictly heterosexual, patriarchal model of insertive sex (Maines, 1999), where a sex act does not fully occur unless PVI happens and is not over until the man orgasms (Jackson & Scott, 2001).

. . . Among participants in our study, no consistent sex differences were found: Men and women were equally certain about whether the presented behaviors constituted sex. In contrast, we did find gender differences in the qualitative findings. Specifically, when compared to men, women (1) offered significantly more reasons and (2) were significantly more likely to mention specific reasons for defining a behavior as sex (e.g., "virginity loss," "foreplay," "only penis in vagina is sex"), while men were significantly more likely to offer no reason or to compare a behavior to one previously rated (e.g., "nipple stimulation is closer to sex than kissing"). It is possible that women were simply more thoughtful and complete in their explanations than were men in this study. However, this finding might also suggest that though men and women may not differ in which behaviors they consider as "having sex," they may differ in why behaviors fit (or do not fit) their definitions of sex.

CONCLUSION

Our findings suggest that, at least within a research setting, the context in which physically intimate behaviors are presented can significantly affect judgments regarding whether they constitute having sex (Gute, Eshbaugh, & Wiersma, 2008). This appears to include (but is certainly not limited to) (1) whether one is rating one's own behavior or that of another, (2) whether the ratings for one's own or another's behavior are made before or after the other, and (3) various aspects of the intimate behavior (i.e., the presence or absence of an orgasm). However, there appear to be some

limits to these effects. Specifically, though context can influence the degree of certainty that a given behavior is considered sex, it does not appear to change the overall hierarchical order of behaviors. That is, in all of these contextual conditions, the overall rank orderings of the certainty ratings did not change. For example, while oral-genital stimulation was rated higher (i.e., greater certainty it was sex) when an orgasm did versus did not occur, it still received lower certainty ratings than anal intercourse and greater certainty ratings than manual-genital stimulation under both orgasm conditions. This supports the idea of a robust hierarchical structure of behaviors defined as sex (Horowitz & Spicer, 2013). In summary, though this study supported the idea of a widely agreed upon hierarchy of behaviors, it was clear that many individuals experienced varying degrees of uncertainty for some behaviors, especially when the context is varied. . . .

REFERENCES

Gute, G., Eshbaugh, E., & Wiersma, J. (2008). Sex for you, but not for me: Discontinuity in undergraduate emerging adults' definitions of "having sex." *Journal of Sex Research*, 45(4), 329–37.

Hall, J. H., & Fincham, F. D. (2006). Relationship dissolution following infidelity: The roles of attributions and forgiveness. *Journal of Social and Clinical Psychology*, 25(5), 508–22.

Hill, B. J., Rahman, Q., Bright, D. A., & Sanders, S. A. (2010). The semantics of sexual behavior and their implications for HIV/AIDS research and sexual health: U.S. and U.K. gay men's definitions of having "had sex." *AIDS Care*, 22(10), 1245–51.

Horowitz, A., & Spicer, L. (2013). "Having sex" as a graded and hierarchical construct: A comparison of sexual definitions among heterosexual and lesbian emerging adults in the U.K. *Journal of Sex Research*, 50(2), 139–50.

Jackson, S., & Scott, S. (2001). Embodying orgasm: Gendered power relations and sexual pleasure. *Women and Therapy*, 24, 99–110.

Maines, R. P. (1999). The technology of orgasm: "Hysteria," the vibrator, and women's sexual satisfaction. Baltimore, MD: Johns Hopkins University Press.

Peterson, Z., & Muehlenhard, C. (2007). What is sex and why does it matter? A motivational approach to exploring individuals' definitions of sex. *Journal of Sex Research*, 44, 256–68.

Pitts, M., & Rahman, Q. (2001). Which behaviors constitute "having sex" among university students in the U.K.? *Archives of Sexual Behavior*, 30, 169–76.

Randall, H., & Byers, E. S. (2003). What is sex? Students' definitions of having sex, sexual partners, and unfaithful sexual behavior. *Canadian Journal of Human Sexuality*, 12, 87–96.

Sanders, S. A., & Reinisch, J. M. (1999). Would you say you "had sex" if . . .? *Journal of the American Medical Association*, 281, 275–77.

Source: "How Do Heterosexual Undergraduate Students Define Having Sex? A New Approach to an Old Question," *The Journal of Sex Research* Vol. 52, No. 5, pp. 507–16. Copyright © the Society for the Scientific Study of Sexuality (SSSS), http://www.sexscience.org/, reprinted by permission of Taylor & Francis Ltd, http://www.tandfonline.com on behalf of the Society for the Scientific Study of Sexuality (SSSS).

"BRINGING INTERSEXY BACK"?
INTERSEXUALS AND SEXUAL SATISFACTION

GEORGIANN DAVIS

From as early as a prenatal ultrasound image, genitalia are classified into a sex binary—males have penises and females have vaginas. However, for decades now, scholars have argued that this troubling two-sex model is socially constructed through processes that begin in the medical profession (e.g., Dreger, 1998a; Fausto-Sterling, 1993; Karkazis, 2008; Kessler, 1990; Preves, 2003). One of the very best examples of both the problem with the two-sex model and evidence that it is socially constructed is intersexuality,[1] conditions where one is born with "ambiguous genitalia, sexual organs, or sex chromosomes" that deviate from the "norm" (Preves, 2003: 2). According to the Intersex Society of North America, over twenty different intersex conditions have been identified by the medical profession (Consortium, 2006).

One example of intersexed bodies occurs among people with androgen insensitivity syndrome (AIS). Individuals with AIS have XY sex chromosomes yet are unable to, during gestation and beyond, partially (PAIS) or completely (CAIS) metabolize androgens, an umbrella term for male sex hormones, most notably testosterone. Individuals with PAIS are usually diagnosed at birth because it results in ambiguous external genitalia (usually a larger clitoris that resembles a small penis) with either internal or external testes. Individuals with CAIS also have XY sex chromosomes, but unlike those with PAIS, they do not have ambiguous external genitalia. Instead, they commonly have what appears to be a "normal"-looking vagina and internal undescended testes. Since the genital ambiguity of CAIS lies internally rather than externally, it is generally not diagnosed until adolescence, when females are expected to begin menstruation. Rather than accept intersexuality as a naturally occurring disruption of the two-sex model,[2] the medical profession surgically removes or modifies intersex genitalia to fit into the sex binary, providing evidence that sex is a socially constructed phenomenon (Fausto-Sterling, 1993: 24; see also Dreger, 1998a, b; Fausto-Sterling, 2000a, b; Karkazis, 2008; Kessler, 1998, 1990; Preves, 2003, 2000).

Background

Intersexuality makes the two-sex model that organizes our bodies visible, and it also challenges any form of sex categorization. Although some scholars have argued that we should organize bodies into multiple sex categories, going beyond the two we currently recognize (e.g., Fausto-Sterling, 1993), plural sex categorization is neither truly possible nor entirely logical (Kessler, 1998). To categorize bodies by sex, regardless of the number of sex categories made available, is a difficult task because "few, if any, physical characteristics are exclusive to one sex" (Karkazis, 2008: 22–23). For example, testosterone is not found exclusively in male bodies; nor is estrogen. Instead of attempting to sex-categorize intersex bodies by biological markers, medical professionals need to shift their focus to "sexual variability," embracing the diverse appearance of genitals without requiring categorization (Kessler, 1998).

A BRIEF HISTORY OF INTERSEX GENITAL SURGERY

Rather than accept intersexuality as a challenge to the sex binary and evidence of naturally occurring sexual variability, the medical profession has historically approached it as an abnormality that can be surgically corrected. In the twentieth century, technological advancements provided the medical profession at large with the tools to surgically "shoehorn" individuals who deviated from the sex binary system to fit into a male or female body (Fausto-Sterling, 1993: 24; see also Dreger, 1998a, b; Fausto-Sterling, 2000a, b; Karkazis, 2008; Kessler, 1998, 1990; Preves, 2003, 2000). Doctors assumed that surgery would reduce the stigma and shame associated with not comfortably fitting into the narrow sex, gender, and sexuality categorization system (Dreger, 1998a; Fausto-Sterling, 2000a, 1996; Kessler, 1998, 1990; Preves, 2003, 2002). However, in many cases, intersex genital surgery isn't medically necessary. For example, although intersexuals were often told that they were at a high risk for developing gonadal cancer (e.g., Preves, 2003), there is minimal evidence to support this claim. The presumed strong correlation between intersexuality and cancerous germ cell tumors is not consistently predicted (see Cools et al., 2006).

The surgical modification of genitalia impacts all aspects of intersexuals' lives, especially sexual pleasure, by disrupting genital sensation (Karkazis, 2008; Preves, 2003). Genital surgeries leave many intersexuals feeling mutilated, unable to achieve sexual satisfaction, and in some instances, incontinent (Preves, 2003). A recent study documented that almost half of all intersexuals who underwent genital surgery were dissatisfied with surgical outcomes (Köhler et al., 2012). While such evidence raises awareness of intersexuals' sexual dissatisfaction, it also situates the problem narrowly onto scalpels and the medical providers who

use them. Some medical professionals who are experts on intersexuality have themselves advocated for the end of intersex genital surgeries (Köhler et al., 2011; Lee et al., 2006).

Given that intersexuality is usually diagnosed when one is a minor, it is up to the individual's parent(s) to grant surgical consent. It might seem unusual for any parent to authorize a medical provider to perform a surgery that in many cases is cosmetic, medically unnecessary, or purely preventative (see Cools et al., 2006). However, parents of intersexual children, like many in our society, are uninformed about sexual variability and consequently follow medical recommendations without hesitation. For this reason, the validity of parental consent has been questioned (Dreger, 1998b).

Feminist critiques of intersex genital surgery (e.g., Dreger, 1998b; Fausto-Sterling, 1993; Kessler, 1998) helped adult intersexuals organize collectively together in the 1990s (Karkazis, 2008; Preves, 2003). The goal of the intersex rights movement was simple: to end the surgical modification of intersex genitalia (see e.g., Karkazis, 2008; Preves, 2003). Since the surgeries are usually performed on minor children who do not have a legal voice of their own, intersex activists accused medical professionals of performing nonconsensual female genital cutting, which is an illegal practice in the United States among non-intersexed females (Chase, 2002).

FROM "INTERSEX" TO "DISORDERS OF SEX DEVELOPMENT"

By the year 2000, after a decade of protests by adult intersex activists, the American Academy of Pediatrics issued a consensus statement on the medical management of intersex conditions. The document had a number of recommendations including that intersex infants should be referred to as "your baby" or "your child"—not "it," "he," or "she" (Committee, 2000: 138). However, surgery was still an option. The guidelines advised doctors to inform parents that their baby's "abnormal appearance can be corrected and the child raised as a boy or a girl as appropriate" (Committee, 2000: 138). The guidelines also stated that a number of factors should be considered when determining which "gender assignment" should be recommended for a given intersex child. Most notably, these factors included "fertility potential" and "capacity for normal sexual function" (Committee, 2000: 141).

Many medical professionals hold cissexist and heteronormative ideologies, which are especially problematic in the case of the medical management of intersexuality, because these ideologies are relied on during gender assignment and imposed on intersexuals and their bodies. Cissexism is the belief that gender is authentic only when it is neatly aligned with sex (Serano, 2007), and heteronormativity is "the suite of cultural, legal, and institutional practices that maintain normative assumptions that there are two and only two genders, that gender reflects biological sex, and that only sexual attraction between these 'opposite' genders is natural or acceptable" (Schilt and Westbrook, 2009: 441; see also Kitzinger, 2005). For example, an intersexual's gender assignment is recommended based on capacity for "normal [hetero]sexual function" and "fertility potential" (Committee, 2000: 141). Only women can become pregnant in the eyes of most medical professionals, and thus, many seem to think that all bodies capable of pregnancy must then be "female." The guidelines suggested that "[a]ll female infants virilized because of [congenital adrenal hyperplasia, or CAH] or maternal androgens are potentially fertile and should therefore be raised as girls" (Committee, 2000: 141). And assessments of prospects for "normal" sexual function presume heterosexual partnering, which exemplifies a heteronormative ideology. Because those born with CAH, a type of intersexuality, are capable of pregnancy despite having

a large clitoris that resembles a small penis, medical professionals will only define them as female.[3] They ignore the possibility that this person might desire to penetrate using their phallus, so to them, surgery is only logical. In other words, medical professionals fail to see any possibilities beyond gender- and sexual-normative bodies when they make their gender and medical intervention recommendations.

In 2006, the American Academy of Pediatrics revised their policy regarding the treatment of intersexual infants due to "progress in diagnosis, surgical techniques, understanding psychosocial issues, and recognizing and accepting the place of patient advocacy" (Lee et al., 2006: 488). They offered new recommendations in this policy revision, including avoiding unnecessary surgical intervention. The consensus statement notes:

Because orgasmic function and erectile sensation may be disturbed by clitoral surgery, the surgical procedure should be anatomically based to preserve erectile function and the innervation of the clitoris. Emphasis is on functional outcome rather than a strictly cosmetic appearance. It is generally felt that surgery that is performed for cosmetic reasons in the first year of life relieves parental distress and improves attachment between the child and the parents; the systematic evidence for this belief is lacking. (Lee et al., 2006: 491)

The guidelines also recommend a nomenclature shift away from "intersex" and "sex reversal" terminology in favor of new "disorders of sex development (DSD)" language (Lee, 2006: 488).

Only five years after the consensus statement was published, current evidence suggests that intersexuality has become an outdated term in the medical profession (Davis, 2011). Medical terminology is a concern because history has shown us that there are implications to naming and defining conditions as disorders (e.g., Brown, 2007, 1995, 1990; Conrad, 2007; Cooksey and Brown, 1998). Consider, for example, attention deficit hyperactivity disorder

(ADHD). In the 1990s, Conrad (2007) argues, ADHD diagnosis expanded to include adults who weren't previously diagnosed in ways that had lasting implications on how individuals, after diagnosis, understood and explained their behaviors.

Given what is known about the medicalization process, is it possible that the sexual struggles intersexuals experience are not only due to genital surgery? If surgery were the only cause of sexual dissatisfaction, there would be significant differences in sexual satisfaction between those who were surgically modified and those who were not. Yet, empirical studies do not support such expectations (Köhler et al., 2012; van der Zwan et al., 2012). In a study of intersexuals that included those who had genital surgeries and those who had not, sexual dissatisfaction was still alarmingly high. Regardless of surgical history, 37.5 percent of intersexuals reported dissatisfaction with their sex life and 44.2 percent reported sexual anxieties. The majority of intersexuals (68.2%) reported that their sexual dissatisfaction was the result of their "abnormality" (Köhler et al., 2012). In a different study, similar results were obtained, with 41 percent of intersex women reporting sexual distress, irrespective of surgical status (van der Zwan et al., 2012). Would ending genital surgeries solve the dissatisfaction experienced by intersexuals? Is it possible that the sexual dissatisfaction reported by intersexuals is situated in a larger medicalization process and not just in the operating room? What can we learn from intersexuals who report more positive sexual experiences?

Methods

Relying on extensive qualitative data including over 300 hours of informal observations in the public meeting spaces of intersex organizational meetings and 65 in-depth interviews with intersexuals, intersex activists, parents of intersex children, and medical professionals who are experts on such conditions, I studied how intersexuality is understood, contested, and experienced by those in the community. Most data were collected from October 2008 to August 2010. A few additional interviews took place in April 2011. As a feminist with an intersex condition, I collected the data from an informed standpoint.

Informants were initially recruited from four organizations: the Intersex Society of North America (ISNA), Accord Alliance, the Androgen Insensitivity Syndrome Support Group-USA[4] (AISSG-USA), and Organisation Intersex International (OII). Participants were targeted from these four organizations because, based on my initial assessment of their websites, each organization appeared to be involved in the intersex rights movement in a different way. For instance, ISNA and OII are activist organizations, while AISSG-USA is a support group, and Accord Alliance is an organization that seeks to distribute educational resources to medical professionals. I also employed snowball sampling by asking initial informants to name others who might share different views from their own (Biernacki and Waldorf, 1981).

Findings

Regardless of surgical history, all of the intersexuals I interviewed reported experiencing sexual struggles at some point in their lives. Everyone was also critical of surgical interventions when conducted on minor children who weren't capable of refusing or legally allowed to refuse consent for medical treatment. The intersex rights movement was formed in the 1990s, united by this critique (e.g., Chase, 2002; Preves, 2003). However, intersexuality remains medicalized, most recently with the disorder of sex development (DSD) terminology (Davis, 2011). Support for the new DSD terminology was mixed[5] among the 37[6] individuals with intersex/DSD conditions whom

I interviewed. While it is outside the scope of this reading to adequately explain *why* individuals with such conditions embraced the DSD nomenclature while others rejected it, the decision can briefly be explained as resulting from DSD proponents desiring to work alongside medical professionals in a medical context with medical terms to promote social change. Here, I focus specifically on *how* the terminology—which is situated in a larger medicalization process—is connected to sexual dis/satisfaction rather than focus on *why* individuals chose the terminology that they did.

I begin my analysis by establishing that intersexuals who were surgically modified commonly reported emotional and physical struggles because of their genital surgery. I next highlight the differences between those who embrace the new DSD terminology that upholds the two-sex model and those who reject it. I then describe the sexual struggles that surfaced, regardless of sexual history, for many intersexuals who sought sexual pleasure. I end by reporting three different responses to sexual struggles that involved avoiding intimacy, seeking heterosexual encounters, or rejecting medicalization and the *disorder* of sex development terminology that pathologizes bodies.

THE CONSEQUENCES OF INTERSEX GENITAL SURGERY

Consistent with previous research (e.g., Karkazis, 2008; Preves, 2003), of the 37 intersexuals I interviewed, 33 underwent genital surgery as children, leaving them emotionally and physically scarred (89%). The emotional consequences of surgery resulted from individuals being lied to by their parents and doctors who attempted to keep their diagnoses a secret (see also Karkazis, 2008; Preves, 2003). For example, Ana shared:

When I was 12 . . . I was told [by my parents and doctors] that my ovaries had not formed correctly

and that there was a risk of cancer and that they needed to be removed. And I had lots of examinations including of my genitals, but I was never made aware [prior to surgery] that anything was going to be taken away [from down] there. So it was a big shock to me [when I woke up after surgery]. And I really had some work to do when I was eventually ready to do it . . . from the trauma that I had from waking up from my surgery to realize that what was between my legs was gone.

Prior to the 2000 medical consensus statement that advised against such deception, intersexuals like Ana were often lied to about their diagnosis because doctors were concerned that the intersex diagnosis might disrupt a child's gender identity formation. While this deception is far less common today, possibly reducing the emotional consequences of surgery, intersex genital surgeries continue (see Davis, 2011).

Intersex genital surgeries are also problematic because they can result in physical consequences. Pidgeon[7] shared, "My clitoris is gone. . . . My vagina looks really fucked up. . . . There's some scar tissue there and . . . penetration hurts." Only four of the 37 intersexuals interviewed were not surgically modified (11%). Given the physical consequences of surgery, it wasn't a surprise that only one of the four unaltered intersexuals interviewed desired surgical modification. Although Pidgeon indicated she would ultimately support any intersexual adult who chose to have genital surgery, she still would passionately advise against it:

[N]ever let them touch you in terms of surgery. That's number one. If they ask about surgery or ask your opinion, don't do that. Don't do surgery, no matter what they say. . . . You'll love your body somehow, some way, and you don't need surgery to love your body and love yourself. . . . If you fuck with your body, you can never change that. But if you don't fuck with your body, you can change your acceptance of your body.

Given that intersex genital surgeries result in a loss of sexual pleasure, the question that arises is, why do they continue? Many medical professionals claim intersex genital surgeries promote health by minimizing cancer risks, despite minimal evidence for such claims (see Cools et al., 2006). Another, more plausible explanation for why intersex genital surgeries continue has to do with the two-sex binary model that medical professionals, like many throughout society, believe should neatly map onto gender and sexual binaries (Davis, 2011). For instance, Donna was told by her doctor, "you can go to college . . . have sex with any boy you want to." She also shared that "he pushed [her] to be feminine, he pushed [her] to be heterosexual, [and] he pushed [her] to give in to boys." Pidgeon had a similar experience. When she was 10 or 11 in the 1990s, a doctor asked her:

Wouldn't you like to have normal sex with your husband when you're older? We can just fix [your vagina], we can make it a little bit bigger for you. It's just a little snip incision, and [your vagina] will just be a little bit bigger. And then you can feel like normal women and have normal sex.

Intersexuals like Donna and Pidgeon were pressured by medical professionals to undergo surgery in order to fit into the sex binary. Doctors assumed Donna and Pidgeon, surgically constructed as females, would adopt a feminine identity and partner with men. However, as I show in the sections that follow, the sex binary model isn't enforced exclusively through surgery. Even those who were able to avoid surgical intervention reported emotional and physical insecurities at some point in their lives, which suggests that the sex binary is connected to a much broader medicalization process beyond surgery.

SEXUAL IDENTITIES AND MEDICAL TERMINOLOGY

Medical professionals frame intersex normalcy (especially after genital surgery) as something one can achieve by romantically partnering with someone of the "opposite" gender. This might, in part, explain why many of the intersexuals I interviewed identified as "straight" or "heterosexual" (32%). However, almost as many intersexuals identified as lesbian, gay, or homosexual (30%). Fewer intersexuals identified themselves as bisexual (11%), queer (11%), or asexual (8%), and several others (8%) either refused to identify themselves, reported that their sexuality was "complicated," or noted that they were "unsure."

DSD is medical terminology that upholds the two-sex system, while intersex language is an identity characteristic that challenges its existence. Given that medical professionals favor DSD terminology because it maintains ideologies that sex, gender, and sexuality are all neatly biologically correlated (Davis, 2011), it makes sense that those who preferred the DSD nomenclature were also more likely to claim a "straight" or "heterosexual" sexuality and actively sought, or maintained, a romantic relationship with an individual of the "opposite" gender. More specifically, among the 32 percent of individuals with an intersex/DSD condition who identified as straight or heterosexual, 75 percent preferred the DSD nomenclature over intersex terminology. When I asked Vanessa what terminology she preferred, she shared, "disorder of sex development . . . I'm pretty comfortable with that. . . . Intersex [terminology] rubs me the wrong way." Although Hannah wasn't as critical of intersex terminology as Vanessa, she still preferred DSD language: "I like 'DSD' . . . because if you say 'DSD' [sex is] kind of camouflaged. When you say 'intersex,' it has the word 'sex' right in it and it's like, 'what?' It's kind of a red flag for people."

On the other hand, those who preferred intersex terminology over the DSD nomenclature more often than not identified as lesbian, gay, bisexual, asexual, or queer. To be exact, just over 86 percent of those who identified as LGBA or Q preferred intersex terminology while the others either welcomed DSD language (9%) or reported being indifferent about the terminology (5%). They were usually not concerned with fitting into a sex binary that medical professionals believed could neatly be mapped onto gender and sexuality binaries; instead, they typically rejected it. Kimberly shared, "I love the term 'intersex.' For me, it really truly describes me. I am somewhere in between. I believe there's a continuum; it's not a dichotomy." While most who favorably viewed intersex terminology were in same-gender relationships, not all were. Several were, in fact, living in one gender, usually as women, while partnered with a person of the "opposite" gender, usually men. For example, Leigh, a woman who identified as queer, was in a long-term committed relationship with a man. Jeanne, a woman who identified as bisexual, was also involved with a man. Similarly, Chris, a man who identified as asexual, was also partnered with an individual of the "opposite" gender before her untimely death. By rejecting the DSD nomenclature, some intersexuals are able to avoid the medical profession's attempt to force their bodies into sex, gender, and sexuality categories assumed to be neatly biologically correlated.

IN SEARCH OF SEXUAL SATISFACTION

Regardless of surgical history and position on DSD terminology, all of the intersexuals I interviewed indicated some form of sexual anxiety about their "abnormal" bodies. Aimee, who has had surgery, expressed that even the very thought of a romantic relationship resulted in a "crippling effect of fear." Mariela, who also has had surgery, commented, "I'm worried about falling in love and when to disclose. . . . What if . . . he decides he doesn't want to be with me anymore?" Stevie, who had surgery as a young child, explained how the

silencing of her experience affected her ability to relate to others:

So not only was I wounded physically through surgery . . . which I still am dealing with and may surgically revise at some point . . . I was wounded by the mantling of my very existence being something that should not be discussed . . . the whole notion of connecting with other people especially in intimate relationships.

The few individuals who were not surgically modified offer evidence that the sexual struggles common to intersexuality are not exclusively due to surgery. Kimberly, who has not had surgery, shared, "In relationships I have had, it's always really bothered me that I feel I have to disclose that I'm intersex before I get physically intimate with anybody because it's not like I could fake being normal. . . . I've always resented that." Caitlyn, who also has not had surgery, echoed this sentiment: "Being in sexual relationships with people, that was really hard. I didn't have a positive relationship with my sexuality when I wasn't being honest with the people I was sleeping with." As I describe in the following section, these sexual struggles are dealt with in different ways.

RESPONDING TO SEXUAL STRUGGLES

Intersexuals in this study often employed one of three strategies to handle their sexual struggles: 1) avoid sexual intimacy; 2) seek out heterosexual encounters; or 3) reject medicalization. Intersexuals were not confined to a particular strategy, although most chose one and never shifted from it.

The first strategy involved avoiding sexual intimacy, and is perhaps the most disheartening. Emily explained, "I don't do intimacy very well. . . . Somewhere around 30 [years old] or so I decided to screw it. I might just not even bother anymore. . . . I'll just be single. . . . That's worked out better." Marilyn, a 50-year-old woman, expressed something similar: "I still haven't had sex. . . . I haven't had a date in the last 20 years. Not a single date." Aimee also avoided intimacy, which even her therapist could not help her overcome. Aimee reported her therapist would say, "I don't really know how to help you with this, other than to tell you: you need to just get out there and get some experience and get over it." Avoiding sexual intimacy was a reliable response to sexual struggles because it offered intersexuals the ability to escape their fears of abnormality. However, this strategy was limited because it left the sexual struggles avoided rather than confronted.

The second strategy of dealing with the sexual struggles associated with intersexuality centered on heterosexual encounters that served to validate one's assigned sex (presumed to be neatly biologically correlated with gender and sexuality). This strategy was encouraged by medical professionals who (as described earlier) urge intersexuals to romantically partner with individuals of the "opposite" gender. In the eyes of medical professionals, heterosexuality is the desired outcome of medical intervention. Individuals with intersex conditions often worry that they are "freaks" or "abnormal" because of their atypical sex anatomies. One way to overcome these feelings was to engage in sexual encounters with the "opposite" gender. Tara said, "I slept with a decent amount of guys that I . . . don't think I should have, but I think it was the whole fact that I wanted to feel like a . . . a woman." Leigh had a similar experience: "When I was a young adult . . . like 16 through . . . 20, I went through this period where I was trying to prove to myself that I was feminine and I just engaged in some risky sexual behaviors [with men]. I think that really interfered with my life, and left some lasting marks." Jenna also

looked to heterosexual encounters to normalize her body and feel appropriately gendered. She shared:

I still have issues with the fact that I have AIS. . . . It's not a debilitating sort of thing . . . but . . . I think about it frequently. . . . I don't feel like I'm less of a woman or anything . . . but one thing I have noticed about me like sexually is that . . . I have something to prove. . . . I'm like . . . I'm a woman, damn it! . . . And I'm going to take care of business and . . . you're gonna be like: . . . "That's the best I ever had!" . . . . It's like on some sort of subconscious level . . . I want to prove that I'm a woman and I can take care of this man's needs.

When I asked Jenna to elaborate, she provided an example:

Let's say that your orgasm is a 100 on a scale of 0 to 100. . . . For me, having my partner reach climax, which obviously with a dude it's ridiculously easy . . . but having my partner climax is 95 out of 100. . . . It doesn't make me . . . but the satisfaction I get from that . . . is almost as much as me orgasming . . . 'cause I'm like: FUCK YEAH! I DID THAT!!! THIS XY!! BA BAM! I'm not joking that's how I am! . . . I'm like THAT'S WHAT I'M TALKING ABOUT!

Tara, Leigh, and Jenna all sought out heterosexual activity in order to normalize their intersex conditions. By engaging in heterosexual activity, they were able to feel, in Leigh's words, "feminine."

The third strategy involved rejecting medicalization by holding onto intersex as an identity characteristic in the face of the new DSD nomenclature. Caitlin described what the term "intersex" meant to her: "I feel very emotionally connected to that word because it really did change my life for the better. So kind of moving away from that word does definitely bring up some emotional response of like no! [Intersex] really empowered me." Those who chose to employ this third strategy reached liberation without relying on others, something they wished everyone with intersex conditions could experience. Consequently, they were critical of those who supported DSD terminology. Millarca explained:

These girls [who favor DSD] are in relationships because they're trying to be normal. They don't want to be different, but they are different and they can't accept that. We're different. You're different, and I'm different. That's where the turmoil lies . . . in trying to be something you're not. If you can accept who you are, like I have, like other people have, what other people say don't mean shit. You're not trying to switch into some other box where you know damn well you can't fit into.

The first step in this strategy's process of overcoming sexual struggles involved embracing intersexuality while rejecting the search for normalcy.

Although Millarca was critical of those "trying to be normal," she was also sympathetic. She hoped they would eventually come around. Many of those who hold onto intersex terminology spoke of sexual satisfaction as a process that began with information about the condition. Irene shared, "I grew up being heterosexual, and . . . I think I evolved as I found out my condition. I felt more in touch with both sides of how I feel and so I feel I'm somewhere in between." Leigh, who earlier in her life had used the strategy of seeking out heterosexual encounters to minimize feelings of abnormality (the second strategy), decided in her twenties to embrace her intersexuality and reject the two-sex model. Although she remained interested in men, she now identifies as queer. This strategy reduced the sexual struggles she experienced as a teenager. Similarly, as a teenager, Ana adopted the first strategy of avoiding intimacy by burying "any hint of sexuality at all." Now, as a partnered woman in her late thirties, she embraces her sexuality, and a more fluid one at that. She revealed, "I probably could have gone either way. But I probably decided at one point that women are for me and I'll put my energy there and I won't

think about it anymore." Kimberly had a similar experience:

Growing up, and dealing with being intersexed and ashamed and the secrecy, I was very asexual. I simply didn't allow myself to have an orientation. I didn't allow myself to be attracted to anybody. Now I can be, and I'm really enjoying it. I think [my female partner's right], I never wore dresses before because I never felt I could pull them off. Now I feel like I can. I've got enough ego to really enjoy the body [*laughing*].

Rejecting the medicalization of intersexuality by rejecting the language of "disorder" resulted in a very real form of liberation that was often enforced by supportive friendship networks. Leigh expressed: "My friends have been incredibly supportive and really love me for this. One of my friends actually made me a T-shirt for my birthday one year that said, 'She's bringing intersexy back.'"

CONCLUSION

The sexual struggles associated with intersexuality need to be understood as part of a broader medicalization process and not just in relation to surgical history. The danger of focusing exclusively on surgery is that it reduces the medicalization process to the operating room. Intersex genital surgery poses real problems for intersexuals, but it is not the only piece in the medicalization puzzle. While sexual struggles are common to people's experience of intersexuality, some intersexuals minimized them by enacting one or more of three strategies: avoiding intimacy; seeking out heterosexual encounters; or rejecting medicalization by "bringing intersexy back." If we accept that sex is something that everyone should be able to experience if they so desire, the first strategy seems to fall short. Many intersexuals who adopt this strategy do not voluntarily *choose* it. Instead, they feel it is the only option, given their sexual insecurities. The second strategy is also inadequate in that it involves engaging in heterosexual encounters not for one's own sexual pleasure, but for validation that one is appropriately gendered. Rather than eliminate insecurities, this strategy tended to create new ones. The third strategy seems to be the most liberatory. By rejecting the medicalization of intersexuality, and the pathologizing *disorder* of sex development terminology that goes along with it, intersexuals can begin to overcome their sexual anxieties in the search for sexual pleasure. Kimberly says it best:

There is a lot of freedom in living outside the rules. If you can make that switch into seeing the freedom, it's really fabulous. . . . You get to really, truly, have an authentic experience that's all your own, and you start seeing how being "normal" is so limiting.

NOTES

1. I use the language of "intersex" and "intersexuality" throughout this paper as opposed to "disorders of sex development" for three reasons. First, due to the greater visibility such words have had in academic publications over the newer terminology "disorders of sex development," I felt it was necessary to continue to reach a broader audience. Second, recent publications in the medical sciences have, for the most part, abandoned "intersex" language despite the fact that not all individuals with such conditions prefer "disorders of sex development" terminology. Third, and the main reason for my choice in terminology, as an individual with an intersex condition, I prefer intersex language over DSD nomenclature.

2. Although we don't have any reliable estimates that capture the frequency of intersexuality in the population, attempts at estimating the intersexed population have been made. Blackless et al. (2000), for example, have estimated that intersexuality appears in 1 in 100 births. However, Fausto-Sterling (2000a) offers a different estimate that ranges from 1 in 1,000 to 1 in 2,000. These different estimates warrant skepticism of any attempts to estimate the prevalence of intersexuality.

3. It should be noted that infertile heterosexuals are still understood as appropriately gendered.

4. Androgen Insensitivity Syndrome Support Group-USA was recently renamed AIS-DSD Support Group for Women and Families.

5. Since the numbers of individuals who supported DSD terminology and those who were against it were similar, I find it misleading to use majority and minority terminology in this context.

6. One intersexed individual out of the 37 noted here is a medical professional with an intersex condition.

7. Participant has indicated preference for this spelling of the chosen pseudonym. In an earlier publication, the pseudonym was spelled "Pigeon" (see Davis, 2011).

REFERENCES

Biernacki, Patrick, and Dan Waldorf. 1981. "Snowball Sampling: Problems and Techniques of Chain Referral Sampling." *Sociological Methodology* 10:141–63.

Blackless, Melanie, Anthony Charuvastra, Amanda Derryck, Anne Fausto-Sterling, Karl Lauzanne, and Ellen Lee. 2000. "How Sexually Dimorphic Are We? Review and Synthesis." *American Journal of Human Biology* 12:151–66.

Brown, Phil. 2007. *Toxic Exposures: Contested Illnesses and the Environmental Health Movement.* New York: Columbia University Press.

———. 1995. "Naming and Framing: The Social Construction of Diagnosis and Illness." *Journal of Health and Social Behavior*, 35: 34–52.

———. 1990. "The Name Game: Towards a Sociology of Diagnosis." *The Journal of Mind and Behavior* 11(3/4): 385–406.

Chase, Cheryl. 2002. "'Cultural Practice' or 'Reconstructive Surgery'? U.S. Genital Cutting, the Intersex Movement, and Medical Double Standards." In Stanlie M. James and Claire C. Robertson, eds., *Genital Cutting and Transnational Sisterhood: Disputing U.S. Polemics.* Chicago: University of Illinois Press. 126–51.

Committee on Genetics: Section on Endocrinology and Section on Urology. 2000. "Evaluation of the Newborn with Developmental Anomalies of the External Genitalia." *Pediatrics* 106:138–42.

Conrad, Peter. 2007. *The Medicalization of Society: On the Transformation of Society.* Baltimore, MD: Johns Hopkins University Press.

Consortium on the Management of Disorders of Sex Development. 2006. "Clinical Guidelines for the Management of Disorders of Sex Development in Childhood." Retrieved January 13, 2012 from www.accordalliance.org/dsd-guidelines.html.

Cooksey, Elizabeth C., and Phil Brown. 1998. "Spinning on Its Axes: DSM and the Social Construction of Psychiatric Diagnosis." *International Journal of Health Services* 28(3):525–54.

Cools, Martine, Stenvert L. S. Drop, Katja P. Wolffenbuttel, J. Wolter Oosterhuis, and Leendert H. J. Looijenga. 2006. "Germ Cell Tumors in the Intersex Gonad: Old Paths, New Directions, Moving Frontiers." *Endocrine Reviews* 27(5):468–84.

Davis, Georgiann. 2011. "'DSD Is a Perfectly Fine Term': Reasserting Medical Authority through a Shift in Intersex Terminology." In P. J. McGann and D. J. Hutson, eds., *Sociology of Diagnosis*. United Kingdom: Emerald. 155–82.

Dreger, Alice Domurat. 1998a. *Hermaphrodites and the Medical Intervention of Sex*. Cambridge, MA: Harvard University Press.

———. 1998b. "Ambiguous Sex—or Ambivalent Medicine? Ethical Issues in the Treatment of Intersexuality." *Hastings Center Report* 28(3):24–35.

Fausto-Sterling, Anne. 2000a. *Sexing the Body: Gender Politics and the Construction of Sexuality*. New York, NY: Basic Books.

———. 2000b. "The Five Sexes, Revisited." *The Sciences* 40(4):18–23.

———. 1996. "How to Build a Man." In *Science and Homosexualities*, ed. Vernon A. Rosario. New York: Routledge. 219–25.

———. 1993. "The Five Sexes: Why Male and Female Are Not Enough." *The Sciences* 33(2):20–25.

Karkazis, Katrina. 2008. *Fixing Sex: Intersex, Medical Authority, and Lived Experience*. Durham, NC: Duke University Press.

Kessler, Suzanne J. 1998. *Lessons from the Intersexed*. New Brunswick, NJ: Rutgers University Press.

———. 1990. "The Medical Construction of Gender: Case Management of Intersexed Infants." *Signs* 16(1):3–26.

Kitzinger, Celia. 2005. "Heteronormativity in Action: Reproducing the Heterosexual Nuclear Family in After-hours Medical Calls." *Social Problems* 52(4): 477–98.

Köhler, Birgit, Eva Kleinemeier, Anke Lux, Olaf Hiort, Annette Gruters, Ute Thyen, and the DSD Network Working Group. 2012. "Satisfaction with Genital Surgery and Sexual Life of Adults with XY Disorders of Sex Development: Results from the German Clinical Evaluation Study." *Journal of Clinical Endocrinology & Metabolism* 97(2): 577–88.

Lee, Peter A., Christopher P. Houk, S. Faisal Ahmed, and Ieuan A. Hughes. 2006. "Consensus Statement on Management of Intersex Disorders." *Pediatrics* 118(2):488–500.

Preves, Sharon E. 2003. *Intersex and Identity: The Contested Self*. New Brunswick, NJ: Rutgers University Press.

———. 2002. "Sexing the Intersexed: An Analysis of Sociocultural Responses to Intersexuality." *Signs* 27(2):523–56.

———. 2000. "Negotiating the Constraints of Gender Binarism: Intersexuals Challenge Gender Categorization." *Current Sociology* 48(3):27–50.

Schilt, Kristen, and Laurel Westbrook. 2009. "Doing Gender, Doing Heteronormativity: 'Gender Normals,' Transgender People, and the Social Maintenance of Heterosexuality." *Gender & Society* 23(4):440–64.

Serano, Julia. 2007. *Whipping Girl: A Transsexual Woman on Sexism and the Scapegoating of Femininity*. Emeryville, CA: Seal Press.

van der Zwan, Yvonne G., Nina Callens, Stenvert Drop, Martine Cools, Catharina Beerendonk, Katja P. Wolffenbuttel, and Arianne Dessens 2012. Retrieved from www.ncbi.nlm.nih.gov/pmc/articles/PMC3313564/. "Do Surgical Interventions Influence Psychosexual and Cosmetic Outcomes in Women with Disorders of Sex Development?" *ISRN Endocrinology*.

THE PERILS AND PLEASURES OF SEX FOR TRANS PEOPLE

HARPER JEAN TOBIN

In the popular imagination, people who cross gender boundaries are rarely seen as happy, healthy people in satisfying sexual relationships. We are typically slotted into stereotypes such as asexual confidante, freaky fetish object, lonely tragic hero(ine), or conniving deceiver. Think of films like *The Crying Game, Boys Don't Cry, All About My Mother, Transamerica,* or even *Hedwig and the Angry Inch*. In reality, transgender people are as sexually diverse as anyone else, just as we are diverse in race, class, gender, age, and geography. In recent surveys, one-quarter to one-third of trans people identified themselves as gay or lesbian (transgender men who love men and transgender women who love women), and another one-quarter to one-third identified as heterosexual. A similar number of transgender people identified as bisexual, and the rest identified as "queer" or something else.[1] Fifty percent of transgender people are partnered or married, according to a recent national survey,[2] and many others are single and happily sexually active. Transgender people practice monogamy, polyamory, abstinence, recreational sex, kinky sex, and conventional sex. We have the same range of desires for intimacy, power, vulnerability, security, intense sensations, orgasms, creativity, playfulness, and more. And we face the same sexual challenges: inhibition, difficulty communicating effectively, difficulty getting aroused or reaching orgasm, sexual trauma, and anxieties about our performance and our bodies. This essay explores how these desires and challenges are impacted by having an identity, a life experience, and in many cases a body that does not conform to cultural expectations about gender.

WHO ARE TRANS PEOPLE?

Every person has a *gender identity*—an internal sense of self that we are aware of from a young age, which usually corresponds to the gender we are assigned at birth. You've probably most often encountered the word *transgender* in reference to people who are assigned one gender at birth but who strongly identify and eventually go through a *gender transition* to live their daily lives as members of the "opposite" gender. Such a person may be a transgender woman (such as myself) who was assigned male at birth but lives and identifies as a woman, or a transgender man, who was assigned female at birth but lives and identifies as a man. When used in this way, the term *transgender* is roughly synonymous with the older term *transsexual*.

But "transgender" can also refer to a wide variety of people whose identities and self-expressions vary from gender norms. *Transgender* (used interchangeably in this essay with the abbreviated *trans*) can encompass identities that don't fit the narrative of male-to-female or female-to-male transition. Many people identify as *genderqueer*, meaning that they identify and express themselves in ways that mix or defy categories of male and female, but which feel simply authentic to them. Genderqueer individuals "describe their gender identity as being a combination of female and male; as neither female nor male but as a different gender altogether; or as somewhere 'in between' female and male."[3] Some genderqueer folks prefer to use gender-neutral pronouns such as *ze* and *hir*.

Whether we identify as male, female, genderqueer, or something else, trans people often reshape our bodies to better reflect our internal sense of self. This can involve daily steps such as binding one's chest to present a flatter appearance, as well as more permanent steps such as hormone therapy or surgery. A common misconception is that gender transition equals genital reconstruction surgery. While genital reconstruction is essential for some people, genitals are not the end-all and be-all of gender. Some of us have arrived at this truth because we accept that the bodily changes we might want are out of reach, for financial or medical reasons. Some of us, taking into account the limitations of current surgical techniques and the stress, pain, and risk of complications that accompany any major surgery, have simply not felt the need to take every possible medical step. According to national survey data, only about 20 percent of transsexual women have had some sort of genital surgery, and only about 5 percent of transsexual men have. While "top" surgery to achieve a flatter chest is the most common gender surgery for trans men, not all of them have that either.[4]

That means that most (though not all) trans people have bodies that, to varying degrees, differ from the norm. A trans woman like myself may have breasts that are curvy or completely flat. She may still have the genitals she was born with, their size and function perhaps altered by estrogen and testosterone blockers. She may call that part of her body her *clit*, her *cock*, her *ladystick*, her *girldick*, her *strapless* (as opposed to strap-on), or any other term, or she may prefer not to refer to it explicitly. These variations in language reflect the basic fact that every person's genitals develop from the same fetal anatomical structures; the penis and clitoris, labia and scrotum, are basically the same body parts to begin with. A trans man may have a surgically flattened chest or a fleshier one that has not been surgically altered, which he may or may not bind, may

or may not refer to as *breasts*, and may or may not like to have touched. He may have a hormonally and perhaps also surgically enhanced phallus, smaller than most *cisgender* (i.e., non-transgender) men's phalluses, but much larger than a cisgender woman's clitoris. And he may have an orifice he refers to as a *pussy*, a *front hole*, a *manhole*, or any other terms, or he may prefer not to talk about that body part in such explicit ways.

Being trans can present some dating challenges. If you are genderqueer, it can be uncomfortable to explain to a potential date that you aren't the girl or boy they think you look like. If you've transitioned to living as a gender different from the one you were assigned at birth, there is no perfect moment on a date to tell someone that certain things about your body or your history aren't what they might expect. Coming out as trans to a potential partner carries risks: encountering reactions of shock and disdain; being rejected by way of mockery and humiliation; being reduced to a freaky fetish object; and possibly even experiencing a violent reaction. Dating or hooking up with a trans or genderqueer person can inspire insecurities for some people about their own identities. Jakob Hero, a gay trans man, relates the dilemma this can present when one is the catalyst for such anxieties: "From my first interactions with gay men I have had to hold, comfort, and reassure them while they go through total crises about my body. For the first few years after transition I was very open to them and to their struggles [regarding my body and gender history], but eventually it took its toll."[5] I've heard a lot of stories like that—about lovers, dates, tricks, gay and straight, men and women, freaking out that they're attracted to someone with an unexpected identity or body part. But as the statistics previously cited would suggest, many trans folks of all sexualities are happy and successful in their romantic partnerships and dating adventures, such as Bryn Kelly, a trans woman who wrote in an essay about her boyfriend:

I love how I can drag his ass to trans [events] and he is totally nonplussed. I love how he can be the only non-trans person in a room and not think there's anything all that unusual. . . . I know that some people who know about my trans history might have a few questions about his sexuality but one thing I love about him is how he really has no problems with it. When I ask him, "Are you ever worried that people might think you're gay?" He says, "Nah. Besides, there's nothing wrong with being gay."[6]

NAVIGATING BODIES AND IDENTITIES

Once trans people connect with a sexual partner—for a night or a lifetime—we have to figure out what to do together, and that is my main subject here. Many of us, trans and cisgender, struggle with cultural ideals about male and female bodies and beauty that our own bodies and gender expressions may not match—worrying whether your body is thin enough, pretty enough, hairless enough, normal enough, ad nauseam, can be a real obstacle to intimacy. Many of us have sometimes felt that, as S. Bear Bergman writes, "There's no part of me able to trust that this complicated body with all its speed bumps and dead ends will remain a viable route once someone is seriously considering setting off on it, when all the limitations are so visible."[7]

Trans people frequently experience a gap between our innate sense of identity and the meanings inscribed on specific parts of our bodies. Our culture assigns gendered names and meanings to body parts. *This body part*, says our culture, *is a penis—it is a male part, and it makes you a man. And this*, it says, *is a vulva—it is a female part, and it makes you a woman.*[8] The disconnect many people feel between their gender identity and these cultural definitions assigned to body parts has been crudely described as

being *trapped in the wrong body*. For some trans people, this disconnect manifests as discomfort or ambivalence about certain parts of our bodies. The prospect of letting other people see and touch certain parts of our bodies, and receiving and giving pleasure through them, can be frightening. Sometimes we fear that particular sexual activities would contradict our deepest sense of self, or even invalidate it.

For some of us, our anxiety is not so much about our own relationship with our bodies, as about whether another person will see, understand, and accept our bodies, our identities, and our desires. Sometimes we fear that seeing and interacting with our bodies will cause our lovers, our health care providers, or others in our lives to doubt or reject our identities—and, perhaps, to either reject us or reduce us to a sexual fetish. Or, we fear that others will desire us, or will truly see us as we see ourselves, only so long as our own desires don't include sexual activities that they might deem inconsistent with our identities. We might have been told in the past that our identities or desires are not valid, and we may have struggled not to internalize those messages. We may struggle to find a language to communicate to our partners how we see our bodies and our desires in a way that honors who we are.

We all have the right to sexual pleasure, regardless of our gender identity, our anatomy, or the steps we have or have not taken to outwardly affirm that identity. Even if we expect to make (further) changes to our bodies to make them better reflect our identity at some point in the future, we shouldn't have to wait that long to have a sexual relationship, or just a sexual fling. We deserve to have intimacy and pleasure with the bodies we have, right here, right now. To do that, we have to ask ourselves questions that anyone might ask, such as: *What is it that I value or need sexually? Physical closeness? Emotional intimacy? The opportunity to be vulnerable, or to experience my partner's vulnerability? The opportunity to take or to surrender control? To have or to give a partner orgasms? To feel affirmed as a man, a woman, masculine, feminine, beautiful, strong, dominant, submissive, boy, girl, or something else?*

To those questions trans people must add an understanding of what stands between us and our desires. *What is it about sex, or the prospect of sex, that is uncomfortable for me in the body I have?* It may be engaging in particular acts that we tend to think of as male or female, masculine or feminine. It may be being unable to engage in particular physical acts we long for. For some, it is having a partner see, touch, talk about, or think about certain parts of their body. Or, it may be seeing, touching, talking, or thinking about certain parts of one's own body, certain ways of being touched that feel better or worse, more discordant or "just right." The answers are different for every trans person. Together with our partners, we figure out how to move away from the feelings and associations that make good sex difficult, and toward being our truest and most satisfied sexual selves. That means not only identifying sexual acts that do and don't work for us, but also finding ways to approach and contextualize specific acts so that they feel right for us.

Some trans people prefer to focus their sexual energy on their partner's body instead of their own. Driving one's partner wild can, for many, be the most exciting and satisfying part of sex. Butch queer activist Koja Adeyoha—who prefers to mix gendered pronouns—spoke at a recent sexuality conference about identifying as a *stone butch*, which s/he explained means that "I limit access to myself sexually and emotionally . . . and I express my desire through other people." Bastien said that s/he used to struggle with this and experience it as "a really pathologized identity for me," feeling that somehow s/he ought to want and be comfortable with his body being the center of sexual attention. But, s/he reflected, s/he and her partner ultimately realized that "this can

just be a hot thing that we embrace." Wanting to control or limit how we are sexually viewed or touched doesn't have to be viewed as a hang-up to get over. On the contrary, embracing the kinds of sex that work for you, and clearly identifying and letting go of the kinds that don't, can be incredibly freeing.

For some of us, it's not so much about whether or not our bodies are touched and stimulated, but *how*. Certain kinds of touch can feel affirming and others discordant. A man may like to have his chest stroked and his nipples played with, but dislike having his chest cupped or squeezed like a woman's breasts. A trans woman may not like to have her genitals directly touched by a partner, but may get off from grinding against a lover's body, wearing a strap-on dildo, or stimulating herself while being anally penetrated. A genderqueer person might enjoy receiving oral sex, but dislike having hir genitals licked in a way ze associates with going down on a woman. Instead, ze may want hir partner to wrap her lips around hir *dicklet* (hir term for the body part that cisgender women call the clitoris) and suck it, more in the manner we associate with a blow job.

Talking about the acts we're sharing with our partners in a way that reflects our own conception of our bodies and identities can also be essential to feeling connected to our identities. A friend of mine, a gay trans man, relates struggling in one of his past relationships to navigate sex acts he physically enjoyed in a way that allowed him to feel affirmed in his male identity. Notice the ways he reimagines and renames his sexual body in this struggle:

[O]ne of the many reasons why it didn't work was totally different assumptions we came to sex with. I rarely [fucked my partner], because there wasn't room for the communication and logistics required for me to strap-on without completely derailing the sex for him. . . . After I got naked with him (which was after we'd had what I consider sex many times), we almost exclusively had coitus. Coitus is easy, [but challenged my ability to feel seen as a gay man because] gay men didn't have coitus. But all the same, I love [coitus], and I love it best when my partner tells me how good it feels to have my cock in his vagina, even though the physical reality is the opposite [i.e., that my partner is penetrating me]. That kind of mental play and flexibility requires imagination and talking dirty to show everyone else how you're imagining things[.][9]

The "mental play and flexibility" and dirty talk my friend describes can make all the difference in bridging the apparent gap between body and identity—and between ambivalent sex and good sex. It can allow him to collaborate with his partner to feel confident and sexy putting on a strap-on cock, rather than to feel that his lack of typical male genitals was highlighted by the need to pause to put on a harness. Similarly, it can allow him to feel seen and affirmed in his maleness while enjoying being penetrated in a body part associated with femaleness.

For some trans folks, less common sexual practices such as BDSM (short for bondage/discipline, dominance/submission, and sadomasochism) can provide spaces of erotic empowerment—a space in which top and bottom, dominant and submissive, or other erotic roles can be much more salient than gender. In BDSM communities, explicit and detailed sexual negotiation, including discussing specific language in an encounter, is also more normalized, which can make hooking up with someone new a less intimidating prospect. Moreover, BDSM practices can involve intense erotic experiences that aren't focused on genital sex, such as flogging, spanking, or temporary piercing—providing intense physical excitement and release without genitals or orgasms even being involved.

A trans woman in a BDSM relationship with another woman shared the following:

My girlfriend is also my submissive. I love making her suck my cock—and that is the way we talk about it. I'm embarrassed by my body in so many ways.

I usually don't like being seen naked or talking about my genitals explicitly—but when we are playing, it's different. When I am in control of her, whatever I desire is okay and she is eager to give it to me. Penetrating her with my body, any part of my body, makes sense.[10]

Erotic role-play can also provide, for some, a space to enact scenarios that allow us to explore or affirm our identities. Genderqueer and mixed-race writer A. P. Andre, for example, writes about experimenting with gender roles during sex as a key part of

trying to figure out what genders I am or might be and also figure out my personal relationship to black masculinity. That's been, at times, a scary process for me. So, when we're having sex and I'm able to use the space to play with the male parts of my identity and to play with being a boy, it feels very safe for me. I really appreciate that, because I feel like it's not a very safe world for the expression of black masculinity in any body. But in bed, in a sexual context [with partners I trust], I can go there with myself and see what it means to be masculine—well, I'm not a very masculine boy!—but see what it means to be a very femme-y boy, and have it celebrated and eroticized.[11]

We all have the right to define our identities, and to choose and define the meanings of our sexual practices, rather than having them assigned based on any cultural script. Queer communities have effectively modeled and affirmed myriad combinations of masculinity/femininity, male/female, active/passive, and penetrating/receiving. Plenty of cisgender women enjoy penetrating their partners, and plenty of cisgender men love being penetrated. This is demonstrated by many heterosexual couples who enjoy strap-on "pegging" (i.e., a woman penetrating her male partner with a strap-on dildo). From these increasingly commonplace insights, it also follows that if (for example) you identify, as a man, no one can tell you that any part of your body, or anything you choose to do with it, is not male. In this way, trans and genderqueer people strive to claim ownership of our bodies, resisting dominant cultural scripts, and refusing to acknowledge any incongruity or reason for shame in our bodies or our desires—a fine aspiration for anyone and everyone.

HOW TO HAVE SEX WITH A (TRANS) PERSON

In hir essay "Made Real," Sassafras Lowrey observes that for trans and genderqueer people, sex can be a minefield, riddled with dangers—the danger of feeling divorced from our bodies, of being misperceived, and of being unable to realize our true desires. "Our minds," Lowrey writes, are "so indoctrinated by narrow definitions of sex, we come to think it's an act which can never include us." At the same time, ze observes, sex can affirm who we are, make us feel whole and at home in ourselves. To be seen and to connect with someone as just who you truly are—a sweet boy, a strong woman, a beautiful gender-fluid person—can heal and strengthen. "Sex," Lowrey writes, "gave me my body back."[12]

As previously noted, sex can be complicated for everyone, and trans and genderqueer people are not so different from cisgender people in that regard. We all would benefit from more and better communication with our partners about the kinds of sex we want to have. For that reason, this essay concludes with some specific suggestions for sexual communication that may be particularly salient if one's partner is trans, but which are applicable to—and would probably make for better sex with—anyone.

First, *avoid relying on assumptions about your partner.* Try not to assume what a person's identity is, what their body is like, what words they like to use for it, or what they like to do with it. These assumptions can limit your ability to truly see and connect with each other. Second, *ask where and how your partner wants to be touched.* This is more effective—and more fun—than trial and error. They may be able to tell you exactly what works and doesn't for them—or they may be in the process of figuring that out, in which case your asking helps give them permission to be unsure and to explore and figure it out with you. Third, *ask what words they use for their body parts.* The right words can be huge turn-ons and the wrong ones huge turn-offs, and which is which is different for everyone. Just ask, "What do you call this part of you?"—then you can talk dirty with confidence. Again, your partner may still be figuring out what works for them, and you can help them do that by being flexible and open to trying different terms and seeing how each one feels for them. Fourth, *communicate your own desires.* It takes (at least) two to connect, and while what you have in mind may not be the same, you won't know if you don't express it. Fifth, *respect your partner's boundaries.* This is the basic obligation we owe all our sexual partners. We all have different boundaries, and they may fluctuate. Respecting them makes hot, connected sex possible. Finally, and critically, *make space for creativity.* The ways people can connect sexually are virtually unlimited, and they aren't—or don't need to be—determined or limited by our identities. It may take negotiation and practice to discover the places where your partner's desires and boundaries can match up with your own. Although our sexual needs and desires are infinitely varied, the fundamentals of good sex are similar for everyone. For trans people—and indeed for everyone—sex can and should be a safe place where we can connect with, explore, and affirm ourselves and one another.

NOTES

1. J. M. Grant, L. A. Mottet, J. Tanis et al. 2011. *Injustice at Every Turn: A Report of the National Transgender Discrimination Survey*, 29. Washington, DC: National Center for Transgender Equality and National Gay and Lesbian Task Force; Genny Beemyn and Susan Rankin. 2011. *The Lives of Transgender People.* New York, NY: Columbia University Press. 33–34.

2. Grant et al., *Injustice at Every Turn.*

3. Genny Beemyn and Susan Rankin. 2011. *The Lives of Transgender People*, 147. New York, NY: Columbia University Press.

4. J. M. Grant, L. A. Mottet, J. Tanis et al. 2011. *Injustice at Every Turn: A Report of the National Transgender Discrimination Survey*, 79. Washington, DC: National Center for Transgender Equality and National Gay and Lesbian Task Force.

5. Jakob Hero, "Out of the Darkness." 2011. In Morty Diamond, ed. *Trans/love: Radical Sex, Love & Relationships Beyond the Gender Binary*, 26, 27–28. San Francisco: Manic D. Press.

6. Brynn Kelly, "Fifty Reasons I Love My Man." 2011. In Morty Diamond, ed. *Trans/love: Radical Sex, Love & Relationships Beyond the Gender Binary*, 60, 62–63. San Francisco: Manic D. Press.

7. S. Bear Bergman, "Gay Men, Queer Men, and Me." 2009. In *The Nearest Exit May Be Behind You: Essays*. Vancouver: Arsenal Pulp Press. 164, 168.

8. On the social construction of gendered bodies, see generally Suzanne J. Kessler and Wendy McKenna. 1978. *Gender: An Ethnomethodological Approach*. University of Chicago Press; Anne Fausto-Sterling, *Sexing the Body: Gender Politics and the Construction of Sexuality*. 2000. New York, NY: Basic Books. The Australian Family Court succinctly summarized the issue when it concluded, after a review of current medical science, that "[a]ttributing some kind of primacy to [a particular] aspect of the person [in determining a person's gender] is not a medical conclusion. It is a social or legal one." *Kevin v. Att'y Gen.* (Re Kevin), (2001) 165 Fam. L.R. 404, 463 (Austl.).

9. Personal communication, October 2009.

10. Personal communication, October 2009.

11. A. P. Andre and Luis Gutierrez-Mock, "In Our Skin." 2010. In Kate Bornstein and S. Bear Bergman (eds.). *Gender Outlaws: The Next Generation*. Berkeley, CA: Seal Press. 157, 159.

12. Sassafras Lowrey, "Made Real." 2011. In Morty Diamond, ed., *Trans/love: Radical Sex, Love & Relationships Beyond the Gender Binary*. San Francisco: Manic D. Press. 96–97.

I AM GAY—BUT I WASN'T BORN THIS WAY

BRANDON AMBROSINO

"You can't be gay."
She was on top of me.

It wasn't a command—it was a challenge. *You so obviously cannot be gay*, was her implication, *because this is good sex.*

It was 2006, a full five years before Lady Gaga would set the Born This Way argument atop its unassailable cultural perch, but even then, the popular understanding of [sexual] orientation was that it was something you were born with, something you couldn't change. If you happened to engage in activity that ran counter to your sexual identity, then you had two options: you were lying to yourself and everyone else, or you were just experimenting. The sexual categories were rigid. Fixed. They weren't subject to human imagination or experimentation—to the frustration of many sociologists, and kids, like myself, who found themselves inexplicably in bed with a player from the other team.

My sexual journey through college was anything but run-of-the-mill. I came out at a conservative Christian college in the U.S. and was in a gay relationship for around two years with a basketball player who ended up marrying a woman. During that time, we both pal'd around with girls on the side. I even went so far as to fall in love with one. To this day, she and I joke about how she was the only girl I was ever in love with, and how I would've been quite happy marrying her. As a writer, this kind of complicated story is incredibly interesting to me—mostly because it shows that my own personal history resists the kind of easy classifications that have come to dominate discussions of sexuality. *Well, you must have been gay the whole time*, some might think, *and because of some religious shame, you decided to lie to yourself and experiment with a girl. But that was nothing more than a blip in the road. After all, most kids experiment with heterosexuality in college, don't they?* If so, that "blip in the road" has always been a thorn in my flesh. How do I explain that I was honestly in love with a woman? Some people might argue that I am innately bisexual, with the capacity to love both women and men. But that doesn't feel like an accurate description of my sexual history, either. I'm only speaking for myself here. But what feels most accurate to say is that I'm gay—but I wasn't born this way.

In 1977, just over 10% of Americans thought gayness was something you were born with, according to Gallup. That number has steadily risen over time and is currently somewhere between 42% and 50%, depending on the poll. Throughout the same period, the number of Americans who believe homosexuality is "due to someone's upbringing/environment" fell from just under 60% to 37%. These ideas reached critical mass in pop culture, first with Lady Gaga's 2011 *Born This Way* and one year later with Macklemore's *Same Love*, the chorus of which has a gay person singing, "I can't change even if I tried, even if I wanted to." Videos started circulating on the internet featuring gay people asking straight people "when they chose to be straight." Around the same time, the Human Rights Campaign

From "I am Gay—But I Wasn't Born this Way," BBC Future, 28 June 2016. Reprinted by permission.

declared unequivocally that "being gay is not a choice," and to claim that it is "gives unwarranted credence to roundly disproven practices such as conversion or reparative therapy."

As Jane Ward notes in *Not Gay: Sex Between Straight White Men*, what's interesting about many of these claims is how transparent their speakers are with their political motivations. "Such statements," she writes, "infuse biological accounts with an obligatory and nearly coercive force, suggesting that anyone who describes homosexual desire as a choice or social construction is playing into the hands of the enemy." People who challenge the Born This Way narrative are often cast as homophobic, and their thinking is considered backward—even if they are themselves gay. Take, for example, Cynthia Nixon of *Sex and the City* fame. In a 2012 interview with *New York Times Magazine,* the actress casually mentioned that homosexuality was, for her, a choice. "I understand that for many people it's not, but for me it's a choice, and you don't get to define my gayness for me." The blogger John Aravosis was one of many critics who pounced on Nixon. "Every religious right hatemonger is now going to quote this woman every single time they want to deny us our civil rights." Aravosis leveled the same accusations against me in 2014 when I wrote a piece for *The New Republic* discussing my own complicated sexual history. Calling me "idiotic" and "patently absurd," Aravosis wrote, "The gay haters at the religious right couldn't have written it any better." For Aravosis, and many gay activists like him, the public will only accept and affirm gay people if they think they were born gay. And yet the available research does not support this view. Patrick Grzanka, assistant professor of psychology at the University of Tennessee, for instance, has shown that some people who believe that homosexuality is innate still hold negative views of gays. In fact, the homophobic and non-homophobic respondents he studied shared similar levels of belief in a Born This Way ideology.

As Samantha Allen notes at *The Daily Beast*, the growing public support for gays and lesbians has grown out of proportion with the rise in the number of people who believe homosexuality is fixed at birth; it would be unlikely that this small change in opinion could explain the spike in support for gay marriage, for instance. Instead, she suggests it hinges on the fact that far more people are now personally acquainted with someone who is gay. In 1985, only 24% of American respondents said they had a gay friend, relative or co-worker—in 2013, that number was at 75%. "It doesn't seem to matter as much whether or not people believe that gay people are born that way as it does that they simply know someone who is currently gay," Allen concludes. In spite of these studies, those who push against Born This Way narratives have been heavily criticized by gay activists. "They tell me my own homo-negativity is being manifested in my work," says Grzanka. Similarly, Ward has received her own hate mail for pushing against the ruling LGB narratives. . . . And when I published my essay on choosing to be gay, an irate American lesbian activist wrote me that it had "just been confirmed" to her that my writing was "directly responsible for four gay deaths in Russia."

While I can understand why some contemporary activists (and the journalists who seem beholden to their agendas) might chalk up recent gains in LGB acceptance to Born This Way's cultural infiltration, activism must be founded upon facts and truths, or the whole program will eventually turn out to be a sham. Drowning out every voice that dares to question dominant cultural narratives is not the same thing as invalidating the arguments those voices are making. As Ward says, "Just because an argument is politically expedient doesn't make it true." So what does the science say about Born This Way?

Let's first be clear that whatever the origins of our sexual orientation, there is a unanimous opinion that gay "conversion therapy" should be rejected. These efforts are potentially harmful, according to the APA, "because they present the view that the sexual orientation of lesbian, gay and bisexual youth is a mental illness or disorder, and they often frame the inability to change one's sexual orientation as a personal and moral failure." Little wonder these therapies have been shown to provoke anxiety, depression and even suicide. In other words, the question of the efficacy of conversion therapies is a non-issue. We condemn these efforts not just because we don't think they work—perhaps anyone could be tortured into liking or disliking anything?—but because they're immoral. The question of what leads to homosexuality in the first place, however, is obscure, even to the experts. The APA, for example, while noting that most people *experience* little to no choice over their orientations, says this of homosexuality's origins: "Although much research has examined the possible genetic, hormonal, developmental, social and cultural influences on sexual orientation, no findings have emerged that permit scientists to conclude that sexual orientation is determined by any particular factor or factors." Similarly, the American Psychiatric Association writes in a 2013 statement that while the causes of heterosexuality and homosexuality are currently unknown, they are likely "multifactorial including biological and behavioral roots which may vary between different individuals and may even vary over time."

True, various eye-grabbing headlines over the years have claimed that some scientists have found something like The Gay Gene. In 1991, for example, neuroscientist Simon LeVay published findings that he claimed suggest that "sexual orientation has a biological substrate." According to LeVay's research, a specific part of the brain, the third interstitial nucleus of the anterior hypothalamus (INAH-3), is smaller in homosexual men than it is in heterosexual men. You can spot the problem with this study a mile away: were the gay brains LeVay studied born that way, or did they become that way? LeVay himself pointed this out to *Discover* magazine in 1994: "Since I looked at adult brains, we don't know if the differences I found were there at birth or if they appeared later." Further, the brains LeVay studied belonged to AIDS victims, so he couldn't even be sure if what he was seeing had something to do with the disease.

Another landmark paper on the origins of homosexuality was published in 1993 by a geneticist named Dean Hamer, who was interested to learn whether homosexuality could be inherited. Beginning from his observation that there are more gay relatives on a mother's side than a father's, Hamer turned his attention to the X chromosome (which is passed on by the mother). He then recruited 40 pairs of gay brothers and got to work. What he found was that 33 of those brothers shared matching DNA in the Xq28, a region in the X chromosome. Hamer's conclusion? He believes there's about "99.5% certainty that there is a gene (or genes) in this area of the X chromosome that predisposes a male to become a heterosexual." A 2015 study sought to confirm Hamer's findings, this time with a much larger sample: 409 pairs of gay brothers. Researchers were pleased with their findings, which they claimed "support the existence of genes on . . . Xq28 influencing development of male sexual orientation." But not everyone finds the results convincing, according to *Science*. For one thing, the study relied on a technique called genetic linkage, which has been widely replaced by genome-wide association studies. It's also noteworthy that Sanders himself urged his study to be viewed with a certain caution. "We don't think genetics is the whole story," he said. "It's not." And as Allen points out, there have also been studies that found no "X-linked gene underlying male homosexuality." Perhaps predictably, these studies haven't received as much media coverage. Besides the individual critiques leveled against each new study announcing some gay gene discovery, there are major methodological criticisms to make about the entire enterprise in general, as Grzanka points out: "If we look at the ravenous pursuit, particularly among American scientists, to find a gay gene, what we see is that the conclusion has already been arrived at. All science is doing is waiting to find the proof."

The other problem with Born This Way science is summed up nicely by Simon Copland: "Scientists are asking whether homosexuality is natural when we can't even agree exactly what homosexuality is." Grzanka agrees. "If you know anything about social constructionism, then you know these sexual categories are very recent. How then could they be rooted in our genome?" Our desires may express themselves in many different ways that do not all conform to existing notions of "gay," "straight" or "bisexual." This is one of the best takeaways of Ward's *Not Gay*, a penetrating analysis of sex between straight white men. Gay men make up only a fraction of the U.S. population—yet Ward says that there are many men not included in that number who engage in homosexual behavior. Why, then, do some men who have sex with men identify as gay, and others identify as heterosexual? This question interests her far more than "how were they born?" Ward stresses that not all straight-identifying men who have sex with men are bisexual or closeted, and we do a disservice if we force those words on them. That's because terms like "heterosexual" and "straight" and "bisexual" and "gay" come with all sorts of cultural baggage attached. Crucially, she argues, "whether or not this baggage is appealing is a separate matter altogether from the appeal of homosexual or heterosexual sex." Even if you accept that sexual desire may exist on a kind of spectrum, the predominant idea is still that these desires are innate and immutable—but this runs counter to what we know about human taste, says Ward. "Our desires are oriented and re-oriented based on our experiences throughout our lives." In fact, the straight-identified men Ward studied for her book sometimes found themselves in situations that sparked the desire for homosexual sex: fraternities, deployments, public restrooms, etc. But Ward doesn't conclude these are somehow repressed or latent gay men. Rather, she argues that they—like all of us—have come to desire bodies and genitals within specific social contexts pregnant with "significant cultural and erotically charged meanings." In other words, what they want isn't the "raw fact" of a man's body, but what it represents in a certain context. Why might we be uncomfortable asking whether and how much control we each possess over our "full range of erotic possibilities," as Ward calls it? "What would it mean to think about people's capacity to cultivate their own sexual desires, in the same way we might cultivate a taste for food?" she asks. Ward thinks this question is the next frontier of queer thought.

When I first said I chose to be gay, a queer American journalist challenged me to name the time and date of my choice. But this is an absurd way to look at desire. You might as well ask someone to name the exact moment they began liking Chaucer or disliking Hemingway. When did I begin to prefer lilies to roses? What time did the clock read at the exact moment I fell in love with my partner? All of our desires are continually being shaped throughout our lives, in the very specific contexts in which we discover and rehearse them.

Thinking back to my college romances with women and men, I can begin to understand how my own experiences might have helped me to cultivate my desire for homosexuality. I want to be very clear: I'm not claiming I simply began to "grow into" my homosexuality, or that as I became more comfortable with being gay, I allowed myself the freedom to express what had always been latent within me. I'm claiming that at some point during college, my sexual and romantic desires became reoriented toward men. These desires suggested to me a queer identity, which I at first reluctantly accepted and then passionately embraced. This new identity in turn helped reinforce and grow new gay desires within me. Granted, none of this means that there were no genetic or prenatal factors that went into the construction of my or any other sexual orientation. It just means that even if those factors exist, many more factors do too. So why not encourage conversations about those other things?

Humans aren't who and what we are because of one gene. We're who and what we are for a variety of reasons, and some of it might have something to do with how our genes randomly interact with our environments. But that's not the whole story, and to engage in discourse that pretends it is—regardless of the nobility of the intentions—could have "profound and very negative consequences" for the LGBT community, says Grzanka. "Limiting our understanding of any complex human experience is always going to be worse than allowing it to be complicated," he says.

So what are we to do with the Born This Way rhetoric? I would suggest that it's time to build a more nuanced argument—regardless of how good a pop song the current one makes. There are several reasons for this. Firstly, and most importantly, it's just not the truth, as we currently understand it. The evidence to date offers no consensus that the Born This Way argument is the beginning and end of the story. We should stop pretending that it does.

Secondly, the entire search for a gay gene is predicated upon the assumption that homosexuality is not the natural or "default" state of a developing human. "Something had to happen to make that man gay!" But why cede such enormous ground to those who believe something has "gone wrong" inside gay bodies and brains? For that matter, why play their game and pretend the only forms of difference that deserve justice are those we were born with? "That's a very narrow understanding of what justice looks like," says Ward. What about the concern that homophobes will want to "encourage" gay people to be straight if there's no biological basis for sexuality? Let's turn it around. Is it not equally true that "finding a gay gene" might inspire the same homophobes to "find a cure" for homosexuals? It doesn't take too much creativity to imagine a scenario in which homophobic parents, upon being informed their fetus has "the gay gene," choose what to them may seem the lesser of two evils: abortion.

Finally, I would argue that the Born This Way narrative can actively damage our perceptions of ourselves. In my sophomore year of college, I attended a Gay Student Alliance event at a nearby campus. It was the last meeting before Thanksgiving break, and the theme was coming out to your families. The idea was that the students would rehearse the coming-out speech that they'd deliver while they were home. Student after student, while sobbing hysterically, said something like this: "Mom, you see how much pain this is causing me! Of course I'd want to be straight if it were up to me. This is just who I am! You have to accept that because I can't change that." I wanted to grab each of them and say, "Being gay is not a handicap. It's OK to be queer even if you choose to be queer—and you should want to be queer! Because we are beautiful and fabulous." Ward sees this as a self-hating narrative. "Could you imagine if the dominant narrative of people of color was, 'Well, of course I'd want to be white if I could. Wouldn't everyone want to be white?' That's so racist! We'd never accept that story."

Perhaps it is time to look to the beginning of the gay rights movement. "Queer Nation and earlier movements in the U.S. were not fundamentally organized around Born This Way explanations," says Grzanka. "They were organized around sexual liberation, and the radical notion of challenging heteronormativity." Gay and lesbian activists, says Ward, used to draw on religion parallels to argue for inclusion. "People aren't born with their religions. They're born into religious cultures, and they can convert if they'd like. But there are still legal protections for them." Eventually activists decided that argument wasn't working fast enough, particularly in the shadow of the AIDS epidemic. "Then there was a shift, and the leaders of the movement chose to jump on board with a less nuanced argument that people already understood: just like race, people are born with their homosexuality."

Fortunately, we have now made enormous strides in understanding and affirming our queer sexualities. Some experts have even started using categories like "mostly straight" and "mostly gay" to try and expand our limited ways of viewing human sexuality. A recent UK poll from J. Walter Thompson Innovation group found that only 48% of Generation Z (ages 18–24) identify as "100% heterosexual." Respondents were asked to rate themselves on a scale from zero (which signified "completely straight") to six ("completely homosexual"). More than a third chose a number between one and five. . . . [T]he Generation Z findings don't signal some evolutionary shift over the last 15 years. Rather, they show that the times—the "nurture" part of the nature/nurture dichotomy—are changing. Homosexuality isn't considered taboo. Heterosexuality isn't (always) considered the compulsory norm. And importantly, each isn't always constructed in opposition to the other.

I'm thankful for a new generation that is capable of imagining sexuality in a way that transcends the gay/straight binary, that couldn't care less about what happened to their bodies and minds to make them who they are today. I'm hopeful that for this generation, sexual histories like mine and Cynthia Nixon's aren't seen as threatening, but liberating. I don't think I was born gay. I don't think I was born straight. I was born the way all of us are born: as a human being with a seemingly infinite capacity to announce myself, to re-announce myself, to try on new identities like spring raincoats, to play with limiting categories, to challenge them and topple them, to cultivate my tastes and preferences, and, most importantly, to love and to receive love.

Queer: Identity and Praxis

Maura Ryan

You're probably familiar with the word *queer* being used as a catchall term for all gender and sexual minorities (GSMs), and it *is* often used for brevity in place of listing various LGBT identities. Certainly, some of its appeal is that it can be used as an umbrella term that simply identifies an individual as not heterosexual rather than tying them to a particular identity. But in addition to being an umbrella term, *queer* also has its own specific social history, its own unique meaning, and a particular political stance.

The word *queer* was once only a slur the dominant society used to mock nonnormative sexualities and genders, which is why some LGBT people are still offended by the term. However, for a segment of this community, it became formally reclaimed and redefined following the onset of the AIDS epidemic in the late 1980s. The government was hostile toward the marginalized communities affected, perceived at first to be only gay men, IV drug users, and sex workers. President Ronald Reagan eschewed discussion of HIV/AIDS while in office and his successor, President George H. W. Bush, remarked that the government had no business helping people who are in their predicament because of their immoral behaviors (Gould, 2009). Politicians, media pundits, and religious figures were either completely silent on the matter or celebratory about the deaths of social "misfits." In short, "AIDS offered the wish fulfillment of a homicidal culture that knows fags have always been, and must always be, already dead" (Stanley, 2012: 159). Rather than allowing the government to rationalize its negligence with the narrative that gay promiscuity caused the outbreak of the illness, a radical direct-action organization called ACT UP (AIDS Coalition to Unleash Power) reasoned that it was homophobia itself that was responsible for what they called a genocide of gay people, and that the proper way to fight their inaction was to flaunt their nonconformity unapologetically. They wanted a word that was gender neutral—that could be used to describe gay men or lesbians— and that made it clear they were no longer playing nice. By 1990, this word that had been used against them—*queer*—now meant "to be righteously angry about homophobia and the AIDS crisis, politically militant, free of shame about nonnormative sexualities, and unconcerned about social acceptance" (Gould, 2009: 191). In fact, in 1990 the first specifically queer organization formed: Queer Nation. In their manifesto, "Queers Read This," they defined *queer* this way:

Being queer is not about a right to privacy; it is about the freedom to be public, to just be who we are. It means every day fighting oppression: homophobia, racism, misogyny, the bigotry of religious hypocrites, and our own self-hatred. (We have been carefully taught to hate ourselves.) And now, of course, it means fighting a virus as well, and all those homo-haters who are using AIDS to wipe us off the face of the earth. Being queer means leading a different sort of life. It's not about the mainstream, profit-margins, patriotism, patriarchy or being assimilated. It's not about executive directors, privilege and elitism. It's about being on the margins, defining ourselves; it's about gender-fuck and secrets, what's beneath the belt and deep inside the heart; it's about the night. (Anonymous Queers, 1990: 2)

According to Berlant and Freeman (1993), Queer Nation "always refuse[d] closeting strategies of assimilation and [went] for the broadest and most explicit assertion of presence." Their demand to be acknowledged as part of the culture is expressed in their most recognizable protest chant, "We're here! We're Queer! Get used to it!" They reject a "politics of respectability" that would be a faster avenue to legislative change; actually, they often reject legislative change altogether. As opposed to the liberal "add and stir" approach of asking for entry into institutions that have previously excluded them (e.g., marriage, military service), they follow a radical approach that problematizes those very institutions. While gay and lesbian activists would call for same-sex couples to be included in the institution of marriage, a queer politics would assert that marriage is a patriarchal institution by which the state regulates sexuality, relationships, and families. Queer activists would call for the rights associated with marriage to flow through other channels, working on national health care and immigration reform rather than marriage equality.

These different perspectives on social change, one for equality and one for liberation, flow from different perspectives on identity. The mainstream liberal agenda for civil rights is influenced by an identity politics: Gay and lesbian identities are neatly and objectively defined, homophobia is the problem, and gay people deserve the same access as heterosexuals to society's institutions.

The queer radical agenda for cultural transformation is influenced by a deconstructivist politics: gender and sexuality are fluid and believed to be socially constructed labels; heteronormativity (the structuring of social life around heterosexuality and its mores, such as monogamy and gender conformity) is the problem, and all people deserve the right to sexual freedom (Gamson, 1995). According to Shepard (2001), this division between those who believe it's best to assimilate to the dominant culture (the group he calls "the suits") and those who believe full sexual liberation is the only objective (the group he calls "the sluts") has always been present in modern LGBT communities, which in the United States is traceable back to the 1940s, but it was the rise of queer identity and queer politics that cemented this divide.

The queer politics has a "deconstructivist" aim; queer activists want to deconstruct what they believe is a meaningless social construct— the divide between heterosexual and homosexual and between man and woman. Queer offers a new way to conceive of desire that does not conform to the binary of straight and gay; it offers ways of being a person, dressing, and acting that cannot be boxed within the limited framework of man and woman. In fact, queer activists believe that these either/or binaries were only created to control people.

The discourses which particularly oppress all of us, lesbians, women, and homosexual men, are those discourses which take for granted that what founds society, any society, is heterosexuality. . . . These discourses of heterosexuality oppress us in the sense that they prevent us from speaking unless we speak in their terms. . . . These discourses deny us every possibility of creating our own categories. (Wittig, 1990: 53)

In this view, *homosexual* is a label created by the dominant group to mark a subordinate group. The very language people are given to describe themselves is a social control mechanism that warps their ability to be true to themselves; queer discourse seeks to disrupt the false consciousness that human sexuality or gender can be understood within a binary.

But not all oppressive structures were equally critiqued in the formation of queer identity and politics. Cohen (1997) has argued that the early manifestation of queer politics lacked an intersectional analysis. White queer people created an us/them logic that saw all queers as oppressed and all heterosexuals as oppressing, with no context for how white supremacy, class status, or male privilege may insulate someone from queer oppression. It is an astounding testament to the power of privilege that white queer people did not see the problem with their righteous anger over heteronormativity and their silence around how whiteness advantaged them. This is perhaps why some lesbian, gay, and bi people of color still associate queer identity with whiteness and a flawed idealistic radicalism. However, it is also important to note that some people of color see queerness as an ideal conceptual space for POC sexual and gender minorities.

In Ferguson's (2003) call for a "queer of color critique," he argues that queer people of color are ideally positioned to dissolve the oppressive pillars of white supremacy, capitalism, heterosexism, and patriarchy because their lived experiences give them special insight into how power operates. Muñoz (1999) also argues this through his concept of *disidentifications*, that queers of color exist as racial and sexual outsiders who are especially positioned to go against the currents of our oppressive culture. Although it may not have been true for everyone who subscribed to queer identity in the early years of its usage, it is now an obvious and unarguable tenet of queerness that if sexual liberation and bodily autonomy are going to be realized, white supremacy and patriarchy have to fall, too.

Queer stands as the underbelly of everything enforced as a norm; it understands that sexual liberation requires a cultural overhaul of every shame-inducing tenet of idealized social behavior. In their zine *Toward the Queerest Insurrection*, the Mary Nardini Gang writes, "Queer is the cohesion of everything in conflict with the heterosexual capitalist world. Queer is a total rejection of the regime of the Normal" (2014: 3). Perhaps most straightforwardly, it could be said that queerness is about reverence for difference. As Dean Spade has said:

We have long critiqued powerful shame-inducing norms about sexual practices, family structures, appearance, and behavior. We have celebrated sexual desires, gender expressions, and relationships that are marked as abnormal, criminal, or pathological by our cultures. We have done this despite disapproval from our families, vulnerability, and significant loss of security. We have felt the excitement of entering a queer space where we can see ways of life that are hidden or despised played up and celebrated, where we can exist for a moment in an alternative world, in which the most beautiful people are those reaching most daringly away from norms, even mocking them. (Spade, 2010: Para. 8)

It is in this revolutionary valuing of difference that queerness creates an alternative universe, one that encompasses new ways of loving and creating social networks. As Malachi (2017) said:

Queer is asking permission of our lovers, and not asking forgiveness for the ways we don't fit in. Queerness is thinking about the space we occupy and how we move through it because we have had so little space in our own lives and refuse to contribute to minimizing the space of others. Queerness is assuming our friends and lovers have been hurt, because we have been hurt, and know what it feels like when people assume we haven't. Queerness is wanting to know the wounds before we reach them, instead of apologizing after for reopening them. (Para. 4)

For many, queer identity has become synonymous with a radical political agenda. It is not just exploring the potential of sexual and gender diversity; it's ending white supremacy and capitalist exploitation. Queerness is about finding value in what is not valued and working to undo the harm of social oppression. It is about the possibility of a completely different way of life. The real value of queerness is its openness, that it is not supposed to be defined. Because it is nothing in particular, it is everything. Because it is not one central identity, it can be anything an individual wants it to be.

REFERENCES

Anonymous Queers 1990. "Queers Read This." Leaflet. Retrieved from http://www.qrd.org/qrd/misc/text/queers.read.this.

Berlant, L., and E. Freeman. 1993. Queer Nationality. In M. Warner, ed., *Fear of a Queer Planet: Queer Politics and Social Theory*. Minneapolis: University of Minnesota Press. 213–46.

Cohen, C. J. 1997. "Punks, Bulldaggers, and Welfare Queens: The Radical Potential of Queer Politics?" *GLQ: A Journal of Lesbian and Gay Studies*, 3(4): 437–65.

Ferguson, R. 2003. *Aberrations in Black: Toward a Queer of Color Critique*. Minneapolis: University of Minnesota Press.

Gamson, J. 1995. "Must Identity Movements Self-destruct?: A Queer Dilemma." *Social Problems*, 42(3): 390–407.

Gould, D. B. 2009. *Moving Politics: Emotion and ACT UP's Fight against AIDS*. Chicago: University of Chicago Press.

Malachi. 2017. "Don't Tell Me You're Queer." Retrieved from https://monomaniacism.com/2017/04/16/dont-tell-me-youre-queer/.

Mary Nardini Gang. 2014. *Toward the Queerest Insurrection*. Zine. Retrieved from https://theanarchistlibrary.org/library/mary-nardini-gang-toward-the-queerest-insurrection.

Muñoz, J. E. 1999. *Disidentifications: Queers of Color and the Performance of Politics*. Vol. 2. Minneapolis: University of Minnesota Press.

Shepard, B. H. 2001. "The Queer/Gay Assimilationist Split: The Suits vs. the Sluts." *Monthly Review*, 53(1): 49–62.

Spade, D. 2010. "It's So Queer to Give Away Money." *Tikkun*, 25(4): 63–74.

Stanley, E.A. 2012. "Slow Boil." In M. B. Sycamore, ed., *Why Are Faggots So Afraid of Faggots?: Flaming Challenges to Masculinity, Objectification, and the Desire to Conform*. Oakland, CA: AK Press. 157–61.

Wittig, M. 1990. "Homo sum." *Gender Issues*, 10(1): 3–11.

BUD-SEX: CONSTRUCTING NORMATIVE MASCULINITY AMONG RURAL STRAIGHT MEN THAT HAVE SEX WITH MEN

TONY SILVA

Mainstream understandings of hetero-sexuality emphasize that straight men's attractions, behaviors, and desires should be oriented exclusively toward women, and yet research indicates that some straight-identified men have sex with other men. There are multiple reasons why some men who have sex with men (MSM) identify as straight, incl-uding internalized heterosexism, participation in other-sex marriage and child rearing, and enjoyment of straight privilege and culture (Ward 2015). Few interview-based studies of straight MSM exist, and previous studies focus on urban, military, or prison contexts. . . . Addi-tionally, there is a widespread urban focus in sexualities and gender literatures (Halberstam 2005), which obscures the role of geography in the construction, maintenance, perception, and experience of gender and sexuality. . . . [T]his study is one of the first to examine how straight MSM themselves understand their own gen-ders and sexualities, and how rurality affects these perceptions.

How do rural, white, straight MSM unde-rstand their gender? Through complex inter-pretive processes, participants reworked non-normative sexual practices usually anti-thetical to rural masculinities to actually con-struct normative masculinity. Participants selected male sexual partners on the basis of masculinity, race, and sexual identity. Most chose other masculine, white, and straight or secretly bisexual men for secretive sex with-out romantic involvement. By choosing these partners and having this type of sex, the par-ticipants normalized and authenticated their

sexual encounters as straight and normatively masculine. The married men framed sex with men as less threatening to their marriages than extramarital sex with women, helping to pre-serve a part of their lives that most described as central to their straightness.

Rather than referring to participants as MSM, a public health term, I describe them as guys who engage in *bud-sex*. I use "bud-sex" when referring to the participants' sexual activi-ties and "MSM" when referring to broader pop-ulations of straight men that have sex with men.[1] Similar sexual practices carry different mean-ings across populations and contexts, including among different groups of MSM. Ward (2015) examines *dude-sex*, a type of male–male sex that white, masculine, straight men in urban or military contexts frame as a way to bond and build masculinity with other, similar "bros." Carrillo and Hoffman (2016) refer to their pri-marily urban participants as *heteroflexible*, given that they were exclusively or primarily attracted to women. While the participants in this study share overlap with those groups, they also frame their same-sex sex in subtly different ways: not as an opportunity to bond with urban "bros," and only sometimes—but not always—as a novel sexual pursuit, given that they had sexual attractions all across the spectrum. Instead, as Silva (forthcoming) explores, the participants reinforced their straightness through unconven-tional interpretations of same-sex sex: as "helpin'

From "Bud-Sex: Constructing Normative Masculinity among Rural Straight Men That Have Sex with Men," *Gender & Society* 31(1), pp. 51–73. Copyright © 2017 by the Author. Reprinted by permission of SAGE Publications, Ltd.

a buddy out," relieving "urges," acting on sexual desires for men without sexual attractions to them, relieving general sexual needs, and/or a way to act on sexual attractions. "Bud-sex" captures these interpretations, as well as how the participants had sex and with whom they partnered. The specific type of sex the participants had with other men—bud-sex—cemented their rural masculinity and heterosexuality, and distinguishes them from other MSM. . . .

THE SOCIAL CONSTRUCTION OF SEXUALITY

How individuals understand and experience sexuality is profoundly social: scripts (Simon and Gagnon 1986), discourses (Foucault 1978), and interactions between individuals (Plummer 1996) and among structures, agency, and practice (Stein 1989) all inform perceptions of sexuality and the forms sexualities take. Cultural norms about what sexual practices are acceptable, their significance, their relation to identity, and even what practices are considered sexual are all socially constructed (Foucault 1978). Identification based on sexual behavior emerged only in the late nineteenth century (Chauncey 1994; Foucault 1978). As Sedgwick (1990) explains, defining individuals in this way is only one of many ways sexual identities could potentially operate. Sexual identities are socially constructed and differ by culture and time period (Katz 1995), and often these identities cannot fully describe complex combinations of sexual practices, attractions, and desires. Relatedly, the relationship between sexual identity and gender practices differs between cultures and time periods. . . . Within the United States, individuals with similar sexual attractions may adopt different sexual identities because of a differing emphasis placed on sexual attractions and current sexual behaviors (Rust 1992) or the presence—or lack thereof—of emotional attrac-

tions (Adam 2000). In addition, stereotypical views of sexual identities (e.g., lesbian women are butch) may affect the one that individuals adopt (Kitzinger and Wilkinson 1995). Sexual identities reflect culture, time period, social structures, and personal interpretations.

Despite increasing acceptance of same-sex sexuality, hegemonic masculinity remains distinctly heterosexual (Connell 1987). Homophobia is often a key aspect of normative masculinity (Kimmel 1994), and from a young age: Pascoe (2011) explores how boys utilize a "fag discourse" to regulate the masculinity and heterosexuality of peers. Similarly, many measures of normative masculinity—such as support for all-male institutions—are related to homophobia (Britton 1990). The relationship between heterosexuality and normative masculinity remains, even as overt homophobia has lessened in many contexts (Anderson 2008; Bridges 2014; Connell 2005; Dean 2014; McCormack 2013). . . . "[N]ormative masculinity" in this [reading] refers to gender practices that eschew femininity and reinforce white, straight, male, and masculine (i.e., nonfeminine) dominance. Because rural spaces in different regions (e.g., rural Alabama vs. rural Québec) are distinct and will consequently develop unique masculinities in those spaces, this [reading] specifically examines normative masculinity in U.S.-based rural regions in the Midwest and Pacific Northwest—areas that share social conservatism and demographic white majorities (Bump 2014; United States Census Bureau 2016).

INTERSECTIONS OF RURAL MASCULINITIES AND SEXUALITIES

. . . "Rural masculinity" refers to masculinity as it is "constructed within what rural social scientists would recognize as rural spaces and sites" (Campbell and Bell 2000, 540). Rural masculinities differ based on local context as well as intersections of social identities, and central to many of them are physical labor and toughness (Morris 2008; Kazyak 2012). The strong link between heterosexuality and masculinity is especially evident in rural areas, which are often more conservative than urban locales (Bump 2014). Rural men are likelier than urban men to engage in unsafe behaviors, and intersections with non-normative sexualities can exacerbate these dangers (Courtenay 2006). For rural men with marginalized sexualities, normative rural masculinity is particularly important because it provides them a degree of social acceptance (Boulden 2001; Fellows 2001). Many rural gay men even distance themselves from feminine gay men and point out their similarities with (purportedly masculine) straight men (Annes and Redlin 2012). Relatedly, in her interview study of rural Midwestern gays and lesbians, Kazyak (2012) found that gay men had little flexibility in gender practices; they either performed conventional rural masculinities or were rejected by their community. Research on rural queer youth (Gray 2009) and rural trans men (Abelson 2014) indicates that challenging gender norms often leads to fear of physical harm, encouraging gender normativity. . . .

METHODS

I posted advertisements in several men-for-men casual encounters sections of Craigslist, which is organized regionally. Unlike most other apps/websites, Craigslist is widely used, anonymous, free, and frequented by individuals with a variety of sexual identities. I also included project information on Grindr, an app catering to gay and bisexual men, which recruited two participants. Of the approximately 100 men who inquired about participation, 19 agreed to participate: 15 over the phone and four in person. This study utilizes phone/in-person semistructured interviews. During each interview,

I used an interview guide. Inquiries included the following: Describe yourself in terms of masculinity and femininity. How has [growing up/living in] a rural area affected how you see yourself in terms of [masculinity/femininity]? Describe the kind of guy you prefer to meet up with. Do you view sex with men outside of your [marriage/partnership] as cheating, and why or why not? Walk me through the last time you met up with another guy for action. In what ways was this encounter typical or not typical of other encounters you've had? I reordered and rephrased questions to make the interview less formal, which allowed me to follow up on leads. Interviews lasted approximately one-and-a-half hours. . . .

All the participants live in Missouri, Illinois, Oregon, Washington, or Idaho; these rural spaces share similarities by virtue of their social conservatism and predominant white populations (Bump 2014; United States Census Bureau 2016). All but two participants currently live in, or were raised in, a rural area. Thirteen currently live in a rural area, and 15 were raised in rural areas. By rural, I refer to an area with fewer than 25,000 residents. The only two exceptions were participants who were raised in urban areas but currently live in what I term *semirural areas*: cities with 25,000–60,000 residents in isolated areas of the Pacific Northwest. All the participants are white, challenging the perception of straight MSM as urban blacks on the "down low" (Ward 2015). They are skewed toward older ages with the majority over 50: 20s (1), 30s (3), 40s (1), 50s (6), 60s (6), and 70s (2). The participants have a variety of educational and occupational backgrounds, but most are middle class. One reported a doctorate as his highest degree, five a master's, three a bachelor's, five an associate's, two some college, and three high school. . . . [T]he sample has considerable diversity in sexual attraction. Further, although all tell others they identify as straight, 17 actually identify as straight or some variation thereof, one as gay, and one as bisexual. Thus, while all are secretive about their same-sex sex, only two are "closeted" in terms of sexual identity, as only two identify as gay or bisexual but tell others they identify as straight.

CONSTRUCTING BUD-SEX

"Strictly Masculine": Average, Rural, Masculine Guys

. . . The men's gender self-descriptions largely conform to conventional understandings of masculinity. Brad (48) is a "T-shirt and Levi kind of guy" who is "straight-acting [and] masculine." Jon (39) is "pretty much masculine" because "I'm a . . . straight guy that likes to hunt, fish, camp, and I raise cattle for a living." Jack (52) shared similar sentiments: "The things I do, interests, all masculine. I like to shoot, I like to hunt. . . ." Cain (50) explained, "My demeanor may be more gentleman-like than . . . the rugged cowboy type," but described himself as having "a type A personality" with the potential to "be kind of aggressive." Similarly, David (74) is an "alpha male" who enjoys shooting and fishing. Richard (75) described himself "as masculine as John Wayne; I'm definitely not feminine in any way, shape, or form." Kevin (69) noted, "I've always done blue-collar type work, I live in a rural area, I'm a farmer." Will (52) leans "a lot toward masculine," because "I can clean a deer . . . I can catch some fish . . . and I'm a very good handyman," while Billy (59) enjoys "trudgin' in the wilderness, cuttin' firewood and throwin' logs.". . .

The participants' rural locations played a large role in their self-descriptions as masculine. Eleven described themselves using elements of rurality, such as hobbies (hunting, fishing, shooting, cutting firewood), occupations (farming, ranching), ways of dressing (camo, T-shirts, and Levi's jeans), or images of rugged rurality (John Wayne). Another used

rural tropes (rugged cowboys) as a comparison to his own masculinity. Central to the men's self-understanding is their rural background; they perform a rural masculinity, which they seek to reaffirm through their same-sex sexual encounters. . . .

"Guys Like Me": Partnering with Other Masculine, White, Non-Gay Men

The participants overwhelmingly preferred to have sex with men like themselves: masculine, white, and not gay—straight or secretly bisexual. This is a key element of bud-sex. Partnering with other men similarly privileged on several intersecting axes—gender, race, and sexual identity—allowed the participants to normalize and authenticate their sexual experiences as normatively masculine, as Ward (2015) also describes. . . .

Seventeen participants—all of those who identify as straight—stated that they prefer masculine male sexual partners, and each explained that the majority of their male sexual partners are masculine. Masculinity in sexual partners helped construct and validate their own normative masculinity. The straight participants often equated masculinity with non-gayness (heterosexuality or secretive bisexuality) or normality. As Cain said, "I'm really not drawn to what I would consider really effeminate faggot type[s]," but he does "like the masculine looking guy who maybe is more bi." Similarly, Matt (60) explained, "If they're too flamboyant they just turn me off," and Jack noted, "Femininity in a man is a turn off." Ryan (60) explained, "I'm not comfortable around femme" and "masculinity is what attracts me," while David shared that "femme guys don't do anything for me at all, in fact actually I don't care for 'em." Jon shared, "I don't really like flamin' queers." Mike (50) similarly said, "I don't want the effeminate ones. I want the manly guys. . . . If I wanted someone that acts girlish, I got a wife at home.". . .

The four participants who reported exclusive sexual attractions to women also stated a preference for normatively masculine male sexual partners, revealing the social origins of their attractions. . . . Like Jeff, Marcus finds normative straight, masculine men like himself better sex partners than feminine and/or gay men. Echoing Mike, Richard stated, "Given a choice I prefer masculine; I don't want a substitute woman," and Joe (63) shared, "Feminine guys don't interest me at all." Preferences for masculine men both validate the participants' own normative masculinity and reveal the socially constructed nature of sexual desires.

Similarly, the vast majority of the past and present male sexual partners of 16 participants—all except Reuben, Tom (59), and Mark—are white. Unlike many urban straight MSM who fetishize interracial sex, as Robinson and Vidal-Ortiz (2013) found with the largest proportion of their sample and Ward (2015) found with a sizable minority, the participants in this study fetishized whiteness. For most of the straight participants, racial sameness was a strategy to align themselves with normativity and, in so doing, to construct normative masculinity. Thus, whiteness is central to bud-sex, which reinforces the participants' straightness and normative rural masculinity. Twelve participants stated that they prefer white male sexual partners, and four others explained their mostly white sexual history as happenstance. When explaining why he prefers white men, Kevin noted, "I guess because I'm white and, I guess you'd say more normal for me to be with white guys.". . .

Of the 17 straight participants, nine reported preferences for straight or bisexual men and 13 noted that a majority of their sexual partners are straight, bisexual, and/or married to a woman. Their partners' not-gay sexual identities—straight or secretly bisexual—are an important component of the men's normative masculinity. . . . Many of the straight participants who noted preferences for straight or bisexual men did so because of perceived greater compatibility and greater confidence in discreetness. As Jeff stated, he is "basically seeking the same" kind of guy as himself. . . . Marcus feels more comfortable with straight or bisexual men because he dislikes a "gay vibe," reinforcing how social factors such as culture affect sexual desires. Similarly, Tom noted choosing a bisexual man as his ideal male sexual partner because he would "kinda be closer in tune to what I am." Joe would also choose a bisexual man "because he would be of the same mind that I am. He would understand what I'm feeling, and would respond probably similarly. So we could engage with common knowledge." Jack noted, "He would be in the same boat as me. He would be straight, preferably married or definitely partnered up with a female, with one thing on his mind, getting his rocks off with me. . . . They're not gonna out me.". . .

That a majority of 13 straight participants' male sexual partners are straight or secretly bisexual, despite bountiful opportunities for sex with gay and openly bisexual men on Craigslist, indicates that partnering with non-gay men is a strategy to reaffirm their own normatively masculine sense of self. It also reflects that the sexual meanings attributed to encounters are socially produced; while many gay men are also masculine and enjoy romance-free sex, most of the participants view straight or secretly bisexual partners as more desirable because of the link between normativity and non-gayness. Given the centrality of heterosexuality to normative rural masculinity, the participants were able to align themselves closer to both by selecting straight and secretly bisexual male sexual partners. While most expressed frustration about the difficulty of finding sexual partners in rural areas, they nonetheless mostly chose men who are masculine, white, and straight or secretly bisexual, underscoring the importance of these characteristics for their normative masculinity and bud-sex.

Secretive and Nonromantic: Ingredients for Bud-Sex

. . . [T]he participants preferred secretive, nonromantic same-sex sex, key ingredients of bud-sex. They did not necessarily prefer one-time meet-ups, however; their histories with "regular" male sexual partners indicate they appreciate the benefits of a sexual friendship. Departing from content analyses, data indicate that relationships with sexual partners are not necessarily *emotionless*, but are rather *nonromantic*. Further, like Robinson and Vidal-Ortiz's (2013) findings, the participants had a wide range of sexual preferences—all had either oral or anal sex (or both). Few, however, tied specific sex acts with masculinity or straightness. For these men, what was paramount to their masculinity was not *what* they did sexually, but *how* they did it. All 19 participants described the need for sexual encounters to be secretive, and this secrecy was tied to rurality. Rurality had both its advantages and drawbacks. On one hand, vast expanses of unpopulated land meant participants could easily find places to have secretive sex. On the other, community interconnectedness necessitated increased caution. As Pat said, "[I]n a small town everyone knows more about your business than you do. . . . I suppose in the city you don't have to be discreet. But here in [a] small rural area, yes, you've gotta be discreet." . . . The absence of romance reframed encounters as normatively masculine and compatible with straightness. Even while avoiding romantic attachments, 13 participants currently have regulars, three others had regulars in the past, and two others would like one or are open to it. While most are open to one-time hookups, most also prefer regulars. By doing so, they reinforce their masculinity by seeking consistent partners on the same page about what sex between straight guys should constitute. This is especially important in rural areas, given

that each attempt to find a new sexual partner opens the participants to potential discovery in a small pool of acquaintances.

While relationships with regulars were free of romance and deep emotional ties, they were not necessarily devoid of feeling; participants enjoyed regulars for multiple reasons: convenience, comfort, sexual compatibility, or even friendship. Pat described a typical meetup with his regular: "We talk for an hour or so, over coffee . . . then we'll go get a blow job and then, part our ways." Similarly, Richard noted, "Sex is a very small part of our relationship. It's more friends, we discuss politics . . . all sorts of shit." Likewise, with several of his regulars, Billy noted, "I go on road trips, drink beer, go down to the city [to] look at chicks, go out and eat, shoot pool, I got one friend I hike with. It normally leads to sex, but we go out and do activities other than we meet and suck." While Kevin noted that his regular relationship "has no emotional connection at all," it also has a friendship-like quality, as evidenced by occasional visits and sleepovers despite almost 100 miles of distance. . . .

No Big Deal: Extramarital Same-Sex Sex

For the 17 straight participants, a key aspect of their straightness was marriage and/or child rearing. Each currently married man indicated a desire to stay married. As they explained, sex with men either does not constitute cheating or is less threatening to their marriage than extramarital sex with women, because it is devoid of deep emotional ties. Sex with women is far more threatening to marriage, as this breaks vows and/or has the potential to involve emotional attachment. As Tom explained, "Being romantic and emotional is more cheating than just havin' sex." Similarly, Cain shared, "I'm not cheating on my wife. I don't have the intention of leaving her." Kevin echoed this: "Meetin' up with women would be cheating on my wife. And when I meet up with guys, I justify it by sayin' 'well it's only fun between me and the other guy, it's not like I have another woman. . . . ' I'm sure she or other people would argue [with] that, but that's just the way I feel."

For the currently married straight men, their perceptions of their extramarital same-sex sex bolster their normative masculinity: sex with men is simply a way for them to fulfill sexual desires without affecting any other part of their lives. Four framed sex with men as not cheating in part because they no longer had sex with their wives. . . . [B]y framing same-sex extramarital sex as insignificant, the men interpret their sexual practices in ways that make them compatible with the marriages that are central to their heterosexuality and normative rural masculinity.

Aging: Not Ready to Give Up Sex

Age affected the participants' interpretations of their sexuality and gender, both because of generational dynamics and aging itself. Fourteen participants are 50 or older and internalized heteronormativity and strict masculine norms during some of the most difficult decades to express sexual or gender non-normativity (Seidman 2002). This, combined with the lack of visibility of non-normative sexualities and gender expressions in most rural areas in the 1950s–1980s, shaped the participants' relationship with masculinity and straightness. As Kevin shared, "I grew up in an area where that [being gay/bisexual] wasn't an option, in a time and area both," and Jack noted, "Back in the day when I was growing up, it was absolutely not accepted."

Additionally, sex with men helped nine participants bolster their masculinity, despite the fact that they or their wives were experiencing age-related bodily changes that made sex more difficult. Seven explained that sex became uncomfortable or undesirable for their wives, and sex with men helped relieve sexual desires. As Ryan shared, "As physically there's been changes to our bodies and it's even pain-

ful for my wife to have sex, I have no problem taking care of myself with another guy." Similarly, David explained, "I'm not getting sex at home, and I want sex," and "older men are a lot more receptive to sex; they're more enthusiastic," because "senior women have kinda lost their desire to do much of anything." Two others began having sex with men because of erectile dysfunction, which limited their ability to penetrate. As Tom described, "I'm a straight guy that has ED and doesn't want to give up havin' sex." Turning to sex with men or increasing the relative frequency of sex with men was a way for each to maintain their sex lives and masculinity despite bodily changes related to aging. . . .

CONCLUSION

The results demonstrate that some rural straight men who have same-sex sex construct normative masculinity through their choice of sexual partners on the axes of masculinity, race, and sexual identity, as well as through the type of sex they prefer. By having sex mostly with other privileged men—conventionally masculine, white, and not gay—and by enjoying secretive and romance-free same-sex sex, the participants framed their encounters as straight and normatively masculine. Through complex interpretive processes, they reframed same-sex sex, usually antithetical to rural masculinities, such that it actually helped them construct normative rural masculinity. The type of same-sex sex they have is distinguishable from that of other groups of MSM: *bud-sex* captures their unique sexual interpretations (Silva, forthcoming), as well as their partnering preferences and the type of sex they have, and it helps construct their normative masculinity and straightness. The concept of bud-sex helps clarify that similar sex practices have different meanings across contexts and populations. Non-normative sexual practices—same-sex sex—can actually be used to reinforce normative masculinity and straightness. The results also demonstrate the flexibility of male heterosexuality over the life course, and the importance of heterosexuality to rural masculinity. Given the centrality of heterosexuality to normative masculinity in rural areas, the participants' identification with straightness— bolstered by their interpretations of their sexual practices—reinforced their normative rural masculinity. Because normative masculinity is critical for social acceptance in rural areas, identification with heterosexuality to bolster normative masculinity was especially important. . . .

The social implications of straight masculinities open to same-sex sex are complex. On one hand, diversity within expressions of heterosexuality and masculinities demonstrates that normativity can be unintentionally challenged from within dominant identities. On the other, the participants' masculinity reinforces inequality. All 19 participants in this study maintain straight privilege by publicly identifying as straight and keeping secret their same-sex encounters. All of the straight men avoid effeminate men, and several disparaged male effeminacy, contributing to the widespread devaluation of femininities. Moreover, 13 were married and had extramarital sex without their wives' knowledge, underscoring their male entitlement and unwillingness to consider ethical nonmonogamy.[2] The participants enjoy marginalized sexual practices, but they are unwilling to challenge heterosexism or other forms of domination, maintaining numerous systems of inequality.

NOTES

1. The participants did not use any particular phrasing to describe their sex, necessitating a new term. I use "MSM" to refer to broader populations of men that have sex with men, given that there are few other terms that can describe them.

2. Only Joe was in an open relationship with his wife; as he said, "I like big dicks; she likes big tits."

REFERENCES

Abelson, Miriam J. 2014. *Men in context: Transmasculinities and transgender experiences in three US regions.* Ph.D. diss., University of Oregon, Eugene, OR.

Adam, Barry. 2000. Love and sex in constructing identity among men who have sex with men. *International Journal of Sexuality and Gender Studies* 5 (4): 325–39.

Anderson, Eric. 2008. "Being masculine is not about who you sleep with . . . ": Heterosexual athletes contesting masculinity and the one-time rule of homosexuality. *Sex Roles* 58 (1–2): 104–15.

Annes, Alexis, and Meredith Redlin. 2012. The careful balance of gender and sexuality: Rural gay men, the heterosexual matrix, and "effeminophobia." *Journal of Homosexuality* 59 (2): 256–88.

Boulden, Walter. 2001. Gay men living in a rural environment. *Journal of Gay and Lesbian Social Services* 12 (3/4): 63–75.

Bridges, Tristan. 2014. A very "gay" straight? Hybrid masculinities, sexual aesthetics, and the changing relationship between masculinity and homophobia. *Gender & Society* 28 (1): 58–82.

Britton, Dana. 1990. Homophobia and homosociality: An analysis of boundary maintenance. *Sociological Quarterly* 31 (3): 423–39.

Bump, Philip. 2014. There really are two Americas. An urban one and a rural one. *The Washington Post*, 21 April.

Campbell, Hugh, and Michael Bell. 2000. The question of rural masculinities. *Rural Sociology* 65 (4): 532–46.

Carrillo, Héctor, and Amanda Hoffman. 2016. From MSM to heteroflexibilities: Non-exclusive straight male identities and their implications for HIV prevention and health promotion. *Global Public Health* 11 (7–8): 923–36.

Chauncey, George. 1994. *Gay New York: Gender, urban culture, and the making of the gay male world 1890–1940.* New York: Basic Books.

Connell, R. W. 1987. *Gender and power: Society, the person, and sexual politics.* Palo Alto, CA: Stanford University Press.

Connell, R. W. 2005. *Masculinities*, 2nd ed. Berkeley: University of California Press.

Courtenay, Will. 2006. Rural men's health: Situating risk in the negotiation of masculinity. In *Country boys: Masculinity and rural life*, edited by Hugh Campbell, Michael M. Bell, and Margaret Finney. University Park, PA: Pennsylvania State University Press.

Dean, James. 2014. *Straights: Heterosexuality in post-closeted culture.* New York: New York University Press.

Fellows, Will. 2001. *Farm boys: Lives of gay men from the rural Midwest.* Madison: University of Wisconsin Press.

Foucault, Michel. 1978. *The history of sexuality: An introduction*, volume 1. New York: Vintage Books.

Gray, Mary. 2009. *Out in the country: Youth, media, and queer visibility in rural America.* New York: New York University Press.

Halberstam, Judith. 2005. *In a queer time and place: Transgender bodies, subcultural lives.* New York: New York University Press.

Katz, Jonathan. 1995. *The invention of heterosexuality.* New York: Dutton.

Kazyak, Emily. 2012. Midwest or lesbian? Gender, rurality, and sexuality. *Gender & Society* 26 (6): 825–48.

Kimmel, Michael. 1994. Masculinity as homophobia. In *Theorizing masculinities*, edited by Harry Brod and Michael Kaufman. Thousand Oaks, CA: Sage.

Kitzinger, Celia, and Sue Wilkinson. 1995. Transitions from heterosexuality to lesbianism: The discursive production of lesbian identities. *Developmental Psychology* 31 (1): 95–104.

McCormack, Mark. 2013. *The declining significance of homophobia*. Oxford: Oxford University Press.

Morris, Edward. 2008. "Rednecks," "rutters," and 'rithmetic: Social class, masculinity, and schooling in a rural context. *Gender & Society* 22 (6): 728–51.

Pascoe, C. J. 2011. *Dude, you're a fag: Masculinity and sexuality in high school*, 2nd ed. Berkeley: University of California Press.

Plummer, Ken. 1996. Symbolic interactionism and the forms of homosexuality. In *Queer theory/sociology*, edited by Steven Seidman. Cambridge, MA: Blackwell.

Robinson, Brandon, and Salvador Vidal-Ortiz. 2013. Displacing the dominant "down low" discourse: Deviance, same-sex desire, and Craigslist.org. *Deviant Behavior* 34 (3): 224–41.

Rust, Paula. 1992. The politics of sexual identity: Sexual attraction and behavior among lesbian and bisexual women. *Social Problems* 39 (4): 366–86.

Sedgwick, Eve. 1990. *Epistemology of the closet*. Berkeley: University of California Press.

Seidman, Steven. 2002. *Beyond the closet: The transformation of gay and lesbian life*. London: Routledge.

Silva, Tony. Forthcoming. "Helpin' a buddy out": Perceptions of identity and behavior among rural straight men that have sex with each other. *Sexualities*.

Simon, William, and John Gagnon. 1986. Sexual scripts: Permanence and change. *Archives of Sexual Behavior* 15 (2): 97–120.

Stein, Arlene. 1989. Three models of sexuality: Drives, identities, and practices. *Sociological Theory* 7 (1): 1–13.

United States Census Bureau. 2016. Annual estimates of the resident population by sex, age, race alone or in combination, and Hispanic origin for the United States and states: April 1, 2010, to July 1, 2015. Washington, DC: United States Census Bureau, Population Division. http://factfinder.census.gov/faces/tableservices/jsf/pages/productview.xhtml?src=bkmk#.

Ward, Jane. 2015. *Not gay: Sex between straight white men*. New York: New York University Press.

Bisexuality and Bi Identity

P J McGann

"Sexuality" conceals significant complexity. Even when limited to basic components, sexuality is an amalgamation of what we do, what we wish we could do, what we think about doing, how we see ourselves, and how others see us.[1] Which of these components is (or should be) most important when defining "sexuality" is socially and individually variable. Social groups also "package" the basic components of sexuality—behavior, desire, and identity—in different ways. Thus, different cultures, different historical moments, even subcultures within a larger society sometimes have different "sexualities." Contemporary forms of desire are defined by the sexual anatomy of the partners; hence,

homo, hetero, and bi. As recently as the 1930s, though, sexualities were defined by gender expression. Thus, traditionally masculine men who had sex with effeminate males were considered "normal" men, but their "fairy" partners were seen as "third-sexers" (Chauncey, 1994). Although the categories of sexuality are social creations, we don't usually experience them that way. Sexualities seem natural. We take for granted that there are sexual "types" of people, and presume that sexual behavior, desire, and identity "line up"—that what we *do* and what we *think* "match" who we *are*, and that who we are corresponds to our society's sexual categories.

Identity, though, is a complex thing. *Individual* identity is who we are to ourselves; *social* identity is who we are to others. These facets of identity don't always align; sometimes this is intentional (as when someone is "in the closet"), sometimes not (as when we think somebody's sexuality is one thing, but it is something else). Either way, sexual identity is built on a culture's sexual categories and is dependent on others for recognition. Identity, then, isn't just something individuals "have." It is instead a process that emerges from dynamic interplay with the social world. Consider how we "know" someone's sexual identity. Even if they don't tell us directly, individuals "announce" identity through appearance, gestures, and acts. For such announcements to work, others must know how to interpret the signs (a wedding ring, for instance), know which sexuality they point to, and accept the signs as legitimate indicators of the person's sexuality. However, the prevalence, persistence, and visibility of the hetero–homo binary underpin a belief that most people are "really" straight or gay/lesbian. Such "monosexism" fuels anti-bisexual stereotypes and skepticism of the reality of bisexuality, leaving bi identity in a precarious position (James, 1996; Rust, 1993, 2002).[2]

Contemporary bisexual *identity*—a sense of self based on attraction to more than one gender—is linked to the emergence of bisexual politics in the early to mid-1970s. Bisexual behavior existed before then, of course, as did bisexuality as a category of sexuality, but people didn't necessarily think of themselves as bi (Savin-Williams, 2005; Weinberg et al., 1994). Even when they did, bi often wasn't an identity recognized by others (Rust, 2000, 2002; Storr, 1999; Udis-Kessler, 1996). This changed when a newly visible bisexuality[3] converged with countercultural ideals of sexual and gender experimentation, leading to the creation of local bisexual groups. The first were mostly male, and by 1978 there were only four such groups in the United States. Things changed significantly in the 1980s, as women—many of whom had previously identified as lesbian—founded bi networks in cities such as Minneapolis, Chicago, New York, and Boston. By the mid-1980s explicitly political organizations had formed, ultimately leading to regional, national, and international conferences. By the early 1990s there were college courses and several books on bisexuality, as well as a national bisexual organization. After initial resistance, in 1993 lesbian and gay organizations formally recognized bisexuality (Hutchins, 1996; Rust, 2000, 2002; Udis-Kessler, 1996). As bisexuality became socially visible and more positively defined, it became possible not only to act bisexually, but to *be* a bisexual.

Visibility and recognition created a base for bi identity, but even today, bisexuality is still not necessarily valued. Stereotypes of bisexuals as immature, deceitful, and promiscuous persist. The gendered nature of the images means female and male bisexuals face different attitudes. For example, both gays and lesbians have criticized bisexuals for a presumed unwillingness to "fully" come out. But gay men have historically been more tolerant of bisexual behavior than have lesbians, a discrepancy rooted in critique of male control of female sexuality and the politicization of lesbianism (Echols, 1989; Rust, 1995; Stein, 1992; Udis-Kessler, 1996).

In contrast to the suspicion and, at times, hostility female bisexuals have faced from some lesbians, straight society sometimes celebrates female bi behavior. Indeed, some forms are deeply eroticized. But even ostensibly positive "hot bi babe" stereotypes—more liberated, more daring, with a large if not insatiable sexual appetite—constrain, given how easily such images facilitate objectification (Sheff, 2005). What's more, in a context of gender inequality, female bisexuality is consumed for male pleasure, yet dismissed as not "really" sex. This situation may provide cover for "hetero-flexible" sexual exploration but the hyper-visibility may undermine bi identity (however unintentionally). In contrast, male bi behavior is less visible but more roundly denounced in the dominant culture. Concerns about the "Down Low" phenomenon demonize African American and Latino men as dishonest and scorn them as sources of contaminating disease, attitudes which reflect racial inequality and historic fear of Black male sexuality (see "No Brokeback for Black Men" in Chapter 8). There may be less overt hostility directed at the private sex of white "str8 dudes," but the clandestine nature of it and Down Low sexuality alike suggest homophobia and underscore the threat male same-sex activity may pose to heterosexuality and masculinity.

The depiction of male bisexual activity as the deceitful selfishness of closeted gays and the "embrace" of female bisexuality are two sides of the same monosexist coin. Despite bisexual activism, many insist that everyone is "really" either gay or straight. The rigidity of the hetero–homo binary leaves little room for the both/and of bisexuality. Confusion and disagreement as to what bisexuality is—attraction to *both* genders? attraction *regardless* of gender?—compound the instability, yet underscore the social nature of identity. The "in betweenness" of bisexuality provokes debate. As discussion proceeds, new categories emerge—queer, fluid, pan- and omni-sexual—giving individuals new ways to make sense of their sexual experience in terms (potentially) intelligible to others.

NOTES

1. A more complete consideration of sexuality would include things such as emotional connection, capacity, preference, lifestyle, group membership, community involvement, political commitment, and so on.

2. The complexity of heterosexual identity is often overlooked—not because heterosexuality is inherently more stable or natural, but because it is the default, taken-for-granted form of sexuality woven into (and thus supported by) nearly every other social institution.

3. The visibility was linked to the high-profile coming-out of pop icons such as David Bowie, Elton John, and Kate

Millet; films such as *Cabaret* (1972) and *The Rocky Horror Picture Show* (1975); and stories about "bisexual chic" in *Time* and *Newsweek* (1974).

REFERENCES

Armstrong, Elizabeth. 1995. "Traitors to the Cause? Understanding the Lesbian/Gay 'Bisexuality Debates.'" In Naomi Tucker, ed., *Bisexual Politics: Theories, Queries, and Visions*. Binghamton, NY: Haworth.

Chauncey, George. 1994. *Gay New York: Gender, Urban Culture, and the Gay Male World, 1890–1940*. New York: Basic Books.

Echols, Alice. 1989. *Daring to Be Bad: Radical Feminism in America, 1967–1975*. Minneapolis: University of Minnesota Press.

Hutchins, Loraine. 1996. "Bisexuality: Politics and Community." In Beth A. Firestein, ed., *Bisexuality: The Psychology and Politics of an Invisible Minority*. Thousand Oaks, CA: Sage.

James, Christopher. 1996. "Denying Complexity: The Dismissal and Appropriation of Bisexuality in Queer, Lesbian, and Gay Theory." In Brett Beemyn and Mickey Eliason (eds.) *Queer Studies: A Lesbian, Gay, Bisexual, and Transgender Anthology*. New York: NYU Press.

Rust, Paula C. Rodriguez. 1993. "'Coming Out' in the Age of Social Constructionism: Sexual Identity Formation Among Lesbian and Bisexual Women." *Gender & Society*, 71: 50–77.

———. 1995. *Bisexuality and the Challenge to Lesbian Politics*. New York: NYU Press.

———. 2000. "Popular Images and the Growth of Bisexual Community and Visibility." In *Bisexuality in the United States: A Social Science Reader*. New York: Columbia University Press.

———. 2002. "Bisexuality: The State of the Union." *Annual Review of Sex Research*, 13: 31–68.

Savin-Williams, Ritch C. 2005. *The New Gay Teenager*. Cambridge, MA: Harvard University Press.

Sheff, Elisabeth. 2005. "Polyamorous Women, Sexual Subjectivity, and Power." *Journal of Contemporary Ethnography*, 34, 3: 251–83.

Stein, Arlene. 1992. "Sisters and Queers: The Decentering of Lesbian Feminism." *Socialist Review*, 22, 1: 33–55.

Storr, Merl. 1999. "Editor's Introduction." In *Bisexuality: A Critical Reader*. London: Routledge.

Udis-Kessler, Amanda. 1996. "Identity/Politics: Historical Sources of the Bisexual Movement." In Brett Beemyn and Mickey Eliason (eds.) *Queer Studies: A Lesbian, Gay, Bisexual, and Transgender Anthology*. New York: NYU Press.

Weinberg, Martin S., Colin J. Williams, and Douglas W. Pryor. 1994. *Dual Attraction: Understanding Bisexuality*. New York, NY: Oxford University Press.

"STRAIGHT GIRLS KISSING"? UNDERSTANDING SAME-GENDER SEXUALITY BEYOND THE ELITE COLLEGE CAMPUS

JAMIE BUDNICK

Contrary to stereotypes of college as a "hive of same-sex experimentation" (Lewin 2011), women with the *lowest* levels of educational attainment report the *highest* lifetime prevalence of same-gender sex (Chandra et al. 2011).[1] Straight-identified young women commonly have same-gender sexual or romantic experiences, but existing research cannot adequately explain this behavior among young mothers or women who never attended college. Research on sexual fluidity (Diamond 2008), hooking up (Armstrong, England, and Fogarty 2012; England, Shafer, and Fogarty 2007; Hamilton and Armstrong 2009; Rupp et al. 2014), and "straight girls kissing" (Hamilton 2007; Rupp and Taylor 2010) has largely focused on white women living on the progressive campuses of selective universities. In the same age group, less privileged women report higher rates of same-gender sex but have earlier paths toward family formation (Edin and Kefalas 2005; Finer and Zolna 2011) and access to different sexual discourses. This leaves sociologists of sexuality with a puzzle: how does context shape the experience, consequence, and meaning of same-gender sexuality[2] for women beyond the elite college campus? . . .

DEMOGRAPHY, LIFE COURSE TRAJECTORIES, AND SEXUAL IDENTITY

...The National Survey of Family Growth (NSFG) has asked questions about sexual behavior, attraction, and identity over the last 15 years. Several consistent patterns have emerged. Same-gender sex is common—the lifetime prevalence among women ages 18–44 was 17 percent (triple that of men)—and "bisexual" identification is more common than "lesbian" or "gay." Sexual behavior, attraction, and identity do not necessarily correlate: 85 percent of women who said they were "mostly [but not exclusively] attracted to the opposite sex" identified as straight, and 13 percent of straight-identified women reported same-gender sex (Copen, Chandra, and Fabo-Vezquez 2016). These patterns have been replicated across different national surveys (Baumle 2013; Savin-Williams and Vrangalova 2013).

HOW COLLEGE CAMPUSES SHAPE YOUNG WOMEN'S SEXUALITY

Qualitative research on young women's sexualities has relied disproportionately on convenience samples drawn from student populations. This scholarship routinely recognizes this sampling strategy as a limitation, calling for greater race and class diversity (Allison and Risman 2014; Armstrong, England, and Fogarty 2012; Diamond 2008; Manning, Giordano, and Longmore 2006; Rupp et al. 2014); nonetheless, it has provided rich insight into how college campuses shape young women's sexuality. Once functioning as an "extended adolescence" for an elite minority of women "in the transition to adulthood," higher education's "new majority" includes students who are older, people of

From "'Straight Girls Kissing'? Understanding Same-Gender Sexuality beyond the Elite College Campus," *Gender & Society* 30(5), pp. 745–68. Copyright © 2016 by the Author. Reprinted by permission of SAGE Publications, Ltd.

color, and [students] balancing work and family responsibilities (Armstrong and Hamilton 2013). "College" has expanded beyond selective, residential, nonvocational four-year institutions (Armstrong and Hamilton 2013), but sexualities research is disproportionately conducted at schools meeting this elite definition (Allison and Risman 2014). Even within selective universities, there is considerable diversity of student experiences: "pathways" through college vary significantly by race and socioeconomic status, contributing to the reproduction of social class and stratification (Armstrong and Hamilton 2013). . . .

[R]esearch on sexuality at college has identified "straight girls kissing" as an increasingly common phenomenon—the latest iteration of stereotypes about experimental college women (such as the older trope of "lesbian until graduation") (Lewin 2011). Sociological research characterized this behavior as attention-seeking performances for men, now part of the heteronormative sexual scripts of college party culture (Hamilton 2007; Rupp and Taylor 2010). More recently, this behavior also has been recognized as a way for queer college women to explore and legitimate their sexualities (Rupp et al. 2014) without adopting stigmatized and isolating lesbian identities (Stone and Gorga 2014). "Straight girls kissing" has largely been framed as a white and middle-class phenomenon, and we know little about the experience and meaning of similar behavior outside the college hookup scene. . . .

THEORIZING YOUNG WOMEN'S SEXUALITIES

Sexual fluidity has become the paradigmatic way of understanding young women's same-gender experiences, especially in the context of inconsistent or changing sexual identification. This influential model, proposed by developmental psychologist Lisa Diamond to improve understandings of female bisexuality, argues that in addition to their stable underlying sexual orientation, women have a varying capacity for fluidity, defined as a "sensitivity to situations and relationships that might facilitate erotic feelings" (2008, 84). Diamond's influence looms large in the study of women's sexuality, but her work, like that of most sexualities scholars, draws disproportionately on the experiences of white and middle-class women. Given that sexuality can be fluid, who gets to act on fluidity and how does context shape how it is expressed and understood? . . .

METHODS

. . . Data come from 35 in-depth semistructured interviews with participants systematically recruited from the Relationship Dynamics and Social Life (RDSL) study. RDSL is a federally funded longitudinal survey (2008–2012) primarily interested in exploring the context and consequences of unintended pregnancy. RDSL followed a representative sample of 1,003 young women living in a socioeconomically diverse Michigan county (aged 18–19 when enrolled in RDSL, and 22–23 when interviewed in Fall 2013).[3] . . .

The weekly RDSL survey asked a standard question about (presumably heterosexual) romantic and sexual experiences, which I rephrased to specify same-gender *behavior*: "Have you ever had physical or emotional contact, such as kissing, dating, spending time together, sex, or other activities with a woman?" The response options were "Yes" and "No." Twenty-nine percent of respondents answered "Yes." The *attraction* question read, "When I think about who I am romantically and sexually attracted to, it is:." The response options were "Always women," "Usually women, but sometimes men," "A person's gender isn't really important when it comes to who I'm attracted to," "Usually men, but sometimes women," and

"Always men." Twenty-three percent of respondents chose answers other than "Always men." The *identity* question read, "Please choose the description that best fits how you think about yourself." The response options were "Lesbian, gay, or queer," "Bisexual," "Straight," and "I don't label myself in this way." Sixteen percent of respondents selected a response other than "Straight." In total, 37 percent of all survey respondents (213 women) gave at least one non-heterosexual response (that is, they reported same-gender sexual or romantic experiences, attraction to women, and/or an identity other than "straight"). I invited all 213 women to participate in a one-time interview, continuing contact attempts until I had recruited a similar number of Black and white women with the most common combinations of survey responses.

Among interviewees, approximately one-third reported same-gender *behavior only*; one-third reported *consistent* non-heterosexual behavior, attraction, and identity; and one-third reported some *other* combination. During interviews, I asked participants about their current sexual identity and to reflect on changes from their original survey responses. Nearly everyone wanted to revise or explain their original answers. Specifically, many who chose "straight" on the survey complicated the definition and described themselves with considerably more flexibility. Probing uncovered a variety of same-gender romantic and sexual experiences that interviewees were comfortable discussing but were unsure "mattered," including adolescent experiences, intimate friendships with ambiguous boundaries, or hooking up with women while maintaining a straight identity. . . .

Among the 35 interview participants . . . , 19 were white and 16 were women of color (14 of whom identified as Black; the absence of many non-Black women of color in my sample is a limitation reflecting the region where they live).

Interviewees varied in their class backgrounds and educational experiences. About a quarter grew up in poverty or on public assistance, about a third grew up with a single parent, and more than half had neither a mother nor a father with a bachelor's degree. Nearly half of interviewees were living at home (typically with parents in the residence where they grew up). Fewer than half of participants attended any four-year college. With one exception, the colleges attended were not selective universities but regional commuter colleges, low- to midrange state schools, or satellite campuses of the state flagship university. The colleges represented here were located in rural Midwest towns or in economically depressed urban centers, were largely nonresidential, and offered night and online courses for commuting and working students. The sexual possibilities enabled by these locations differed from the progressive campuses of selective universities reflected in much of the sexualities literature. The personal lives of my interviewees presented a contrast to elite college students: about a quarter of the white women and about half of the women of color were already mothers. An additional quarter of white women and 13 percent of women of color were preparing to become mothers, meaning they had gone off birth control to try to conceive or were actively planning to do so in the near future. Many were married, engaged, or cohabiting (63 percent of white women and 56 percent of women of color; almost all of whom were in relationships with men).

SAME-GENDER SEXUALITY BEYOND THE ELITE COLLEGE CAMPUS

How are young women's experiences and understandings of same-gender sexuality shaped by their context? To answer this question, I leverage comparisons to women attending the elite colleges disproportionately reflected in sexualities scholarship. In what follows, I discuss three findings that emerged from my interviews: the first looks at life course considerations in identification, the second at strategies for and meanings of same-gender sex, and the third at discourses of identification.

Foreclosed Possibilities Following Early Motherhood

Both on and off campus, women of lower socioeconomic status have earlier trajectories toward family formation (Edin and Kefalas 2005; Kost and Henshaw 2012) and are less comfortable hooking up (Allison and Risman 2014; Armstrong and Hamilton 2013). At the same time, bisexual and unlabeled women report declines in same-gender sex over time (Diamond 2008). These patterns intersect earlier in the lives of my interviewees. These classed timelines foreclose possibilities for same-gender sexual identification in two ways: young moms prioritize their identity as good and self-sacrificing parents over LGBTQ identification, and women in committed relationships with their child's father or other men felt their same-gender sexualities were rendered irrelevant.

My interviewees described reconsidering sexual identities, relationships, and values after becoming mothers. Jayla, a Black woman with a recent bachelor's degree from a regional state university, became pregnant after her on-again/off-again boyfriend pressured her to stop using condoms. Cradling her sleeping daughter, she described how "humbled" she was since moving back in with her parents. Jayla isolated herself from her best friend (a gay man) and refused to reciprocate a godmother relationship with her lesbian-identified friend. . . . Jayla described emotionally walling herself off from the attraction and love she felt for her lesbian-identified friend, feelings overshadowed by the hope of meeting a man who could be a father figure to her child and a partner in parenting. Summer, a Black woman with a high school diploma, similarly reconsidered her progressive sexual values and the place of same-gender attraction in her life after becoming a mom in her late teens. She struggles to answer her four-year-old daughter's questions about her cousin, who has two moms. Summer calls herself "protective," explaining, "I know my nephew got teased a lot for having two moms. . . . I don't want her to have to go through that." Jayla and Summer are confronting observations about what it is like for their gay friends and lesbian cousins to be "out" in their communities.

The mothers I interviewed describe the waning salience of their same-gender attraction and romantic or sexual experiences, instead drawing on raced, classed, and heteronormative discourses of "good motherhood" (Bell 2014), foregrounding self-sacrifice and "settling down." If their child's father was in the picture, this could mean going to great lengths to work things out—these expectations differed by current relationship status, which is itself raced and classed. White women were more likely to be married, describing their non-heterosexuality as "moot," while Black women were more likely to be single, dating, or cohabiting and experiencing social and family pressures to marry. Marriage may have a waning salience for many Americans' definition of family (Powell et al. 2012), and it remains to be seen how options and expectations might broaden following federal recognition of marriage equality. But for my interviewees, the idea of settling down with a woman is an unintelligible option for themselves and in conflict with the discursive imperatives of "good motherhood."

Monogamy similarly forecloses possibilities for LGBTQ identification. Noel, a white woman working on her GED, had her son shortly after dropping out of high school and leaving her impoverished family to marry her husband. Before this tumultuous period, she strongly identified as bisexual, but feels her monogamous relationship renders her attraction to women moot: "I'm with my husband, and I don't intend on being with anybody else for my future. That's where I'm at now." For Noel, same-gender attraction and identity labels became irrelevant when she married her husband. Rachel, a white woman with a high school diploma, embraces and even acts on her same-gender attraction, but her marriage similarly forecloses identification. She had a threesome with her husband and a close woman friend to whom she had long been attracted, but does not want to label herself: "I'm pretty *open*. I don't know that it's because I'm *married*—because I know that I'm with [my husband] and I always plan on being with [him]—that I would be straight. But I don't know. . . . Maybe just no label is easier to think about."

Having or planning threesomes was one possible way to act on same-gender attraction without threatening my interviewees' primary identity as a mother or their committed relationships. Although it was not a topic included in my initial interview guide, many women brought up threesomes: they reacted to stereotypes that bisexual women want threesomes (many were offended), recalled stories of friends who had threesomes, or discussed the role threesomes had in their own sex lives. For women in this latter category, threesomes were a low-stakes way to raise the issue of same-gender attraction within a relationship without making any threatening claims about identity, thus involving their partner in their sexuality without challenging their relationship. Threesomes functioned as a site of possibility for some of my interviewees to offload attraction and longing. . . .

Sexual Friendships and Safety Strategies

Certain circumstances more prevalent among women of lower socioeconomic status (such as earlier paths toward family formation) may foreclose possibilities to develop and express same-gender sexual identities. Conversely, those same circumstances may facilitate possibilities for acting on same-gender desire. At elite colleges, women are confronted with sexual discourses that pressure them to name their experiences and label themselves (Armstrong and Hamilton 2013; Rupp et al. 2014). Women outside this environment draw on different discourses when describing their identity, and may have more leeway to act on same-gender desire. My interviewees' descriptions of sexual friendships present a contrast to same-gender relationships among privileged white college students. However, their narratives of strategically choosing same-gender hookups based on perceptions of safety looked remarkably similar.

Some interviewees described exploring same-gender desire within sexual friendships. Chantelle, a Black woman with a high school diploma, lives with her parents so that she can make ends meet raising her two-year-old son. She says she is too busy parenting and too frustrated with her child's father to date, but described reconnecting with a woman she knew in high school. . . . She laughs about the situation, and describes preferring the openness of a sexual friendship to expectation-laden relationships: "It's funny, because it actually brought us a lot closer. . . . She didn't know if she was ready for a girlfriend. I didn't either. . . . That could have ruined our friendship, because relationships have a different degree and different standards. But with a friendship it's kind of like everything is an open book." Chantelle's sexual friendship exists in a space unconstrained by identity or relationship labels that presents a contrast to both heterosexual "friends with benefits" hookups and the intimate female friendships of comparatively privileged women engaging LGBTQ discourses. . . .

With less pressure to label sexual identities and experiences, the boundary between intimate and sexual friendships is difficult to discern. Jayla (introduced above) describes her relationship with one particular close friend as intimate but not sexual. . . . Their friendship is serious (Jayla was chosen to be godmother to her friend's daughter), but also playful. Their playfulness is expressed both physically and in how they characterize their relationship. . . . Lost in her recollection, Jayla suddenly stops and remembers that her friend once had a "forbidden relationship" with another woman, exclaiming, "To this day, my friend will tell you that the best relationship that she's ever been in has been with a woman. *I can't believe I forgot about that.*" This recollection surprises her, and as she struggles to make sense of their friendship, her sleeping daughter begins to stir and Jayla asks to end our interview. . . .

Some interviewees described choosing hookups with women based on perceptions of safety—physical safety and safety for their reputation. Tara, a white woman with a bachelor's degree from a regional public university, explicitly said she thought same-gender hookups would decrease her risk of being sexually assaulted and simultaneously safeguard her reputation. She lives with her grandma and has a boyfriend, but in college she shared an off-campus apartment with a lesbian couple and frequently made out with women when they all went to parties together. She describes always feeling open and comfortable expressing her sexuality, but says she experienced less negativity at parties when hooking up with women than men. . . . In her experience, making out at parties with women not only has fewer repercussions for her reputation, it's physically safer as well: "It's *safer* too, because you never know if you're making out with a guy, what might happen in that situation. Like if I want to make out with you, it doesn't mean I want to have sex with you. But in a lot of guys in party scenes, that's their mentality." . . .

These narratives of sexual friendships and safety strategies shed light on how young mothers and poor and working-class women meaningfully explore same-gender sexuality. Something that young mothers seem to be getting out of their sexual friendships is *friendship* with a woman who deeply understands and shares their experience as struggling, often isolated, single parents navigating frustrating relationships with unsupportive men. Public lesbian relationships are described as "impossible" or "unimaginable," and conversations acknowledging a sexual friendship might be something more are dismissed as "joking" or "playing around." . . . While college-attending women describe a preference to socialize and hook up with women based on perceptions of physical and reputational safety (Hamilton 2007; Rupp et al. 2014), these strategies enacted by women from lower socioeconomic positions are embedded in their increased risk of sexual assault (Barber, Kusunoki, and Budnick 2015) and better awareness of crime (Jones 2009; Levine 2013).

Labels Outside the Women's Studies Classroom

Rejecting sexual identity labels is increasingly common across different populations (Diamond 2008; Savin-Williams and Vrangalova 2013), but working-class and non–college attending women draw on different discourses when doing so. My interviewees embrace "bisexual" and reject "queer" in the exact opposite pattern observed among women sampled from women's studies courses and LGBTQ student spaces at selective universities. The latter characterize "bisexual" as an outdated term rife with negative connotations circulating in straight society and lesbian subcultures (Rust 1992), and they say that it incorrectly suggests "equal, continuous, or simultaneous attraction to both men and women" (Tabatabai 2015, 26). For my interviewees, "bisexual" is a relatively untainted and utterly intelligible term, and "queer" is an alienating slur rather than an anti-label panacea.

My interviewees who rejected labels did not draw on queer discourses challenging sexual classification, but rather discourses about individualism and openness (in addition to discourses about self-sacrifice and good motherhood, as described earlier). . . . "Bisexual" was viewed as an acceptable and intelligible label among my interviewees. Nikki, a Black woman and part-time commuting student working on a bachelor's degree at a regional public university, succinctly concludes, "I always thought 'bisexual' was a pretty good term for it." Krystina, a white woman with a bachelor's degree from a regional public university, explains, "I feel like that's much more acceptable in today's society."

"Queer" was overwhelmingly viewed as a derogatory slur among my interviewees. . . . Taylor, a white woman and full-time commuting student working on a bachelor's degree at a regional public university, has identified as lesbian and bisexual, but about queer says, "I personally feel it's a slur word. I would never use queer to identify my own sexual identity. In my opinion, 'queer,' regardless of a gay connotation, just means weird. I don't think my sexuality is weird. So I wouldn't feel comfortable identifying with queer." . . .

CONCLUSIONS

. . . I find that early motherhood forecloses possibilities to develop or claim LGBTQ identities as women prioritize seemingly incompatible discourses of self-sacrifice and good motherhood. At the same time, sexual friendships provide opportunities to explore same-gender sex and desire. These findings demonstrate how sexual fluidity is enacted among women outside spaces permeated with LGBTQ discourses (Diamond 2008), and present meanings of same-gender sex for "straight girls kissing" located outside the college hookup scene (Hamilton 2007; Rupp and Taylor 2010). For women in lower socioeconomic positions, choosing same-gender hookups is a strategy embedded in their increased risk of sexual assault and better awareness of crime (Barber, Kusunoki, and Budnick 2015; Jones 2009; Levine 2013). My interviewees reject "queer" and embrace "bisexual" in the opposite pattern observed among their more privileged peers. . . .

Processes of sexual identification and the enactment of desire are intersectional. Too often, this fundamental observation of feminist sexualities research remains at the level of theory alone and is undermined by the entrenched focus on samples of educated middle-class white women. My study contributes to the growing body of scholarship on same-gender sexuality among working-class women and women of color (Acosta 2013; García 2012; Kazyak et al. 2014; Moore 2011; Rust 1992; Trautner 2005), underscoring how our knowledge about sexual fluidity is critically situated—driven by research with women residing on elite college campuses. I offer an intersectional analysis of the everyday expectations and structural constraints encountered by working-class women and women of color navigating their sexuality *beyond* the elite campus. I describe the specific strategies and negotiations these women use to enact sexual desire, foster intimate connections with other women, and cultivate sexual identities that are intelligible to themselves and their communities.

NOTES

1. The National Survey of Family Growth has continuously collected data since 1973. The patterns described here draw on national data available at the time of my study (Chandra et al. 2011). The latest report presents a slightly different picture: women reporting same-gender sex increased (from 13 to 17 percent), but no statistically significant pattern by education was found. However, prevalence among women with the lowest educational attainment remains high and under-examined (Copen, Chandra, and Fabo-Vezquez 2016).

2. In this [reading], I use "same-gender sexuality" (except when directly citing others) because I am referring to intimacies between *women,* and we—as gender scholars—need to take seriously the distinction between terms used to describe sex and gender. "Same-gender sexuality" is one specific language choice available to us that has been used in fundamental sexualities scholarship, including *Social Organization of Sexuality* (Laumann et al. 1994). For a recent *Gender & Society* article theorizing the relationship between scientists' use of sex and gender language and the construction sex/gender knowledge in social life, see Westbrook and Saperstein (2015).

3. For more information on the Relationship Dynamics and Social Life (RDSL) study, see Barber, Kusunoki, and Gatny (2011).

REFERENCES

Acosta, Katie. 2013. *Amigas y amantes: Sexually nonconforming Latinas negotiate family.* New Brunswick, NJ: Rutgers University Press.

Allison, Rachel, and Barbara J. Risman. 2014. "It goes hand in hand with the parties": Race, class, and residence in college student negotiations of hooking up. *Sociological Perspectives* 57 (1): 102–23.

Armstrong, Elizabeth A., Paula England, and Alison Fogarty. 2012. Accounting for women's orgasm and sexual enjoyment in college hookups and relationships. *American Sociological Review* 77 (3): 435–62.

Armstrong, Elizabeth A., and Laura Hamilton. 2013. *Paying for the party: How college maintains inequality.* Cambridge, MA: Harvard University Press.

Barber, Jennifer S., Yasamin Kusunoki, and Jamie Budnick. 2015. Women not enrolled in four-year universities and colleges have higher risk of sexual assault. Council on Contemporary Families. https://contemporaryfamilies .org/not-enrolled-brief-report/.

Barber, Jennifer S., Yasamin Kusunoki, and Heather Gatny. 2011. Design and implementation of an online weekly journal to study unintended pregnancies.

Baumle, Amanda K. 2013. Introduction: The demography of sexuality. In *International handbook on the demography of sexuality,* edited by Amanda K. Baumle. Dordrecht, the Netherlands: Springer.

Bell, Ann. 2014. "I'm good at the job": How women achieve "good" motherhood. Chapter 2 in *Misconception: Social class and infertility in America.* New Brunswick, NJ: Rutgers University Press.

Chandra, Anjani, William Mosher, Casey Copen, and Catlainn Sionean. 2011. Sexual behavior, sexual attraction, and sexual identity in the United States: Data from the 2006–2008 National Survey of Family Growth. *National Health Statistics Reports* 36.

Copen, Casey, Anjani Chandra, and Isaedmarie Fabo-Vezquez. 2016. Sexual behavior, sexual attraction, and sexual orientation among adults aged 18–44 in the United States: Data from the 2011–2013 National Survey of Family Growth. *National Health Statistics Reports* 88.

Diamond, Lisa. 2008. *Sexual fluidity: Understanding women's love and desire.* Cambridge, MA: Harvard University Press.

Edin, Kathryn, and Maria Kefalas. 2005. *Promises I can keep: Why poor women put motherhood before marriage.* Berkeley: University of California Press.

England, Paula, Emily Fitzgibbons Shafer, and Alison Fogarty. 2007. Hooking up and forming romantic relationships on today's college campuses. In *The Gendered Society Reader,* edited by Michael Kimmel and Amy Aronson. New York: Oxford University Press.

Finer, Lawrence, and Mia Zolna. 2011. Unintended pregnancy in the United States: Incidence and disparities, 2006. *Contraception* 84 (5): 478–85.

García, Lorena. 2012. *Respect yourself, protect yourself: Latina girls and sexual identity.* New York: New York University Press.

Hamilton, Laura. 2007. Trading on heterosexuality: College women's gender strategies and homophobia. *Gender & Society* 21 (2): 145–72.

Hamilton, Laura, and Elizabeth A. Armstrong. 2009. Gendered sexuality in young adulthood: Double binds and flawed options. *Gender & Society* 23 (5): 589–616.

Jones, Nikki. 2009. *Between good and ghetto: African American girls and inner-city violence.* New Brunswick, NJ: Rutgers University Press.

Kazyak, Emily, Nicholas Park, Julia McQuillan, and Arthur Greil. 2014. Attitudes toward motherhood among sexual minority women in the United States. *Journal of Family Issues* October: 1–26.

Kost, Kathryn, and Stanley Henshaw. 2012. *U.S. teenage pregnancies, births and abortions, 2008: National trends by age, race and ethnicity.* Guttmacher Institute. http://www .guttmacher.org/pubs/USTPtrends08.pdf (accessed July 31, 2015).

Laumann, Edward, John Gagnon, Robert Michael, and Stuart Michaels. 1994. *The social organization of sexuality: Sexual practices in the United States.* Chicago: University of Chicago Press.

Levine, Judith. 2013. *Ain't no trust: How bosses, boyfriends, and bureaucrats fail low-income mothers and why it matters.* Berkeley: University of California Press.

Lewin, Tamar. 2011. Study undercuts view of college as a place of same-sex experimentation. *The New York Times,* 17 March.

Manning, Wendy, Peggy Giordano, and Monica Longmore. 2006. Hooking up: The relationship contexts of "nonrelationship" sex. *Journal of Adolescent Research* 21 (5): 459–83.

Moore, Mignon. 2011. *Invisible families: Gay identities, relationships, and motherhood among Black women.* Berkeley: University of California Press.

Powell, Brian, Catherine Bolzendahl, Claudia Geist, and Lala Carr Steelman. 2012. *Counted out: Same-sex relations and Americans' definitions of family.* New York: Russell Sage.

Rupp, Leila J., and Verta Taylor. 2010. Straight girls kissing. *Contexts* 9 (3): 28–32.

Rupp, Leila J., Verta Taylor, Shiri Regev-Messalem, Alison Fogarty, and Paula England. 2014. Queer women in the hookup scene: Beyond the closet? *Gender & Society* 28 (2): 212–35.

Rust, Paula C. 1992. The politics of sexual identity: Sexual attraction and behavior among lesbian and bisexual women. *Social Problems* 39 (4): 366–86.

Savin-Williams, Ritch, and Zhana Vrangalova. 2013. Mostly heterosexual as a distinct sexual orientation group: A systematic review of the empirical evidence. *Developmental Review* 33 (1): 58–88.

Stone, Amy L., and Allison Gorga. 2014. Containing pariah femininities: Lesbians in the sorority rush process. *Sexualities* 17 (3): 348–64.

Tabatabai, Ahoo. 2015. *Lesbian, queer, and bisexual women in heterosexual relationships: Narratives of sexual identity.* Lanham, MD: Lexington Books.

Trautner, Mary Nell. 2005. Doing gender, doing class: The performance of sexuality in exotic dance clubs. *Gender & Society* 19 (6): 771–88.

Westbrook, Laurel, and Aliya Saperstein. 2015. New categories are not enough: Rethinking the measurement of sex and gender in social surveys. *Gender & Society* 29 (4): 534–60.

Sexual Orientation versus Behavior—Different for Men and Women?

Eliza Brown and Paula England

If you know which sexual orientation people identify with, how much does that tell you about whether they have sex with women, men, or both? How similar or different are the links between identity and behavior for women and men? . . .

We're using data from the 2002, 2006–2010, and 2011–2013 National Survey of Family Growth for men and women 15 to 44 years of age. . . . Here we focus on a few specific questions:

HOW COMMON IS IT FOR HETEROSEXUAL MEN AND WOMEN TO HAVE SEX WITH SAME-SEX SEXUAL PARTNERS?

Unsurprisingly, almost none of the men identifying as heterosexual have had only male sexual partners and only 2% say they have had even one male sexual partner. For women, like men, almost none of those who identify as heterosexual have had only female partners, but 10% say they have had at least one same-sex partner, five times the rate reported by men. . . . In sum, it is more common for heterosexual women than men to have had sex with members of their same sex.

We can get a little closer to assessing how common inconsistency between identity and behavior is by comparing men and women's current identity with whether they've had same-sex sexual partners *in the last year.* Here we get a much smaller figure—only 0.4% of men and 2% of women who called themselves heterosexual on the survey report that they had sex with a same-sex partner in the last year. . . . Thus, behavior usually aligns with identity in any short (one year) time range. But here, too, the percent of heterosexuals having same-sex partners is larger for women than men.

How should we interpret the finding that some men and women who identify as heterosexual have had sex with same-sex partners? It may mean that they had sex that doesn't match their stated sexual orientation at the time, perhaps because of the stigma associated with same-sex partnerships in some quarters. Another possibility is that, although they see themselves as straight now, they identified as gay/lesbian or bisexual at the time they had same-sex partners, so there was no inconsistency between identity and behavior. This is especially plausible regarding with whom one has had sex "ever." If that is the explanation, then women's higher rate may mean that they are more likely than men to change the sexual orientation they identify with. But we are speculating; we would need panel data following the same people over time and repeatedly asking about orientation and recent behavior to distinguish (a) changing sexual orientation where behavior and identity are almost always consistent from (b) inconsistency between current identity and current behavior. It is also possible that the ways people see their own orientations don't fit neatly into the three categories provided in the survey in most years, so some respondents choose the best fit of not-well-fitting categories.

HOW COMMON IS IT FOR GAY MEN AND LESBIANS TO HAVE SEX WITH OTHER-SEX SEXUAL PARTNERS?

. . . Thirty-nine percent (37% + 2%) of gay men have had a female sexual partner sometime in their lives, whereas a much higher 59% (5% + 54%) of lesbians have had a male sexual partner sometime. The proportion of either gay men or lesbians who have ever had sex with other-sex sexual partners is much larger than the proportion of heterosexual men and women who have had sex with same-sex sexual partners. And it is much larger than the proportion of gay men/lesbians who have had sex with an other-sex partner in the last year, 5% (3% + 2%) for men and 18% (5% + 13%) for women.

As for how things differ by gender, it is clear that lesbians are more likely than gay men to have ever had sex with an other-sex sexual partner, whether in the last year (5% for men and 18% for women) or ever (39% for men and 59% for women). The larger share of lesbians than gay men who had other-sex partners in the past year comes both from lesbians being more likely than gay men to have partners of both sexes (13% of lesbians), as well as being more likely to have had sex with only other-sex partners (5% of lesbians).

Why would this be, that lesbians have sex with men more than gay men have sex with women? One explanation is that women's sexual attractions don't fit the three categories allowed by the survey as well, or that women are more likely than men to change the sexual orientation with which they identify. Either can be seen as more fluidity in women's sexuality than men's, a topic taken up by Lisa Diamond and Leila Rupp and her coauthors.[1] Another possibility is that either evolution or cultural conditioning make . . . [men] the initiators in sex. So it is probably a less likely scenario that a young man who thinks that he may be gay is approached by a woman for sex and acquiesces despite not wanting it, compared to an analogous scenario in which a young queer woman has sex with a man she doesn't want. Indeed, both lesbians and gay men are likely to have men as their first sexual partners, according to research conducted by Karin Martin and Ritch C. Savin-Williams. In some cases, these early partners may have raped them, as indicated by research on the prevalence of sexual assault among gay, lesbian, and bisexual individuals by Emily Rothman and her coauthors. We suspect, however, that greater sexual fluidity among women and the frequency of male initiation contribute more to the gender differences in partnership patterns than sexual assault.

HOW DOES THE BEHAVIOR OF BISEXUAL MEN AND WOMEN DIFFER FROM THAT OF GAY AND HETEROSEXUAL MEN AND WOMEN?

Given that the commonsense meaning of the term "bisexual" is an interest in having sex and romantic relationships with men and women, we would expect more bisexual than heterosexual or lesbian/gay individuals to have had sex with both men and women. Indeed, we find that 62% of bisexual men and 73% of bisexual women have (ever) had sex with both sexes, higher than the analogous figures for gay men and lesbians, and drastically higher than the figures for heterosexual men and heterosexual women.

Who have bisexual men and women had sex with *in the last year*? . . . [T]he percent that have had sex with both women and men in the last year is 33% for bisexual men, 27% for bisexual women; 2% for gay men, 13% for lesbians; and 0.4% for heterosexual men, and 2% for heterosexual women. Thus, as we would expect, bisexuals are much more likely than either gays/lesbians or straight men or women to have had sex with both sexes. They are also more likely to have had sex only with other-sex partners in the last year than are gay men or lesbians, but are less likely to have done so than are heterosexuals.

. . . What about gender differences between bisexual men and bisexual women? The two groups have a similarly low percent who have ever had sex only with the other sex (14% for

men and 12% for women), but it is much more likely for bisexual women than men to have had sex only with the other sex in the last year— 34% for men but 53% for women. . . .

CONCLUSION

We have shown that identity—the sexual orientation one identifies with—is strongly, but by no means perfectly, associated with whether men and women have had sex with women, men, or both. Heterosexual men and women are the most likely to have had sex only with other-sex partners, bisexual men and women are the most likely to have had sex with both women and men, and gay men and lesbians are the most likely to have had sex only with same-sex partners. In this sense, behavior is roughly consistent with sexual orientation. Unsurprisingly, this consistency between current identity and behavior is much stronger when the behavior being asked about is in the last year rather than over the whole lifetime.

However, the patterns differ between men and women. Women, both lesbian and straight, are more flexible with either their identities or behavior than men. Thus, they are more likely than men to have what could be seen as mismatches between identity and behavior. As an example of this, looking at behavior in the last year, heterosexual women are more likely than heterosexual men to have had sex with women, and lesbians are more likely than gay men to have had sex with an other-sex partner.

As part of women's "flexibility," women are more likely to have partners of both sexes than men are. Taking people of all sexual orientations combined, 14% of women but only 4% of men have ever had both male and female sexual partners. . . . Similarly, in the past year, 3% of all women had both male and female sexual partners, compared with less than 1% of men. This is partly because more women than men identify as bisexual, but is also influenced by the higher proportion of women than men among those who identify as either heterosexual or gay having had *both* male and female sexual partners. . . .

NOTE

1. *Editor's note:* In her book *Sexual Fluidity: Understanding Women's Love and Desire*, Lisa Diamond defined sexual fluidity as "situation-dependent flexibility in women's sexual responsiveness." Diamond studied 100 women with a same-sex sexual or romantic orientation for a decade. She found that most women showed signs of this capacity to change, shifting either their sexual identity, behavior, or general attraction during the study. While timing wasn't fixed, she found increased fluidity as women aged. Single powerful relationships could shift a person's identity, in the short or long term. While Diamond's book focused on women's sexuality, she has also called attention to sexual fluidity among men. Men's sexuality can also be fluid, although the patterns of this fluidity may differ across genders.

Source: "Sexual Orientation versus Behavior: Different for Men and Women?" *Contexts Blog*, February 29, 2016. Reprinted by permission of the authors.

2

INVESTIGATING SEXUALITY

AN INTERVIEW WITH

MIGNON R. MOORE

Mignon R. Moore, PhD, is an associate professor of sociology at Barnard College, Columbia University. Professor Moore received a Faculty Career Award from the Woodrow Wilson Foundation and a national award from the Human Rights Campaign for her professional work and outreach with LGBT communities of color. She was also selected as a Russell Sage Foundation Visiting Scholar. She holds a grant from the National Institutes of Health for her study examining the social histories, current health outcomes, and sources of social support for older African American sexual minorities. Her 2011 book, Invisible Families: Gay Identities, Relationships, and Motherhood among Black Women *(University of California Press), examines how lesbian women of color form and raise families and experience their gay identities while retaining connections to their racial/ethnic communities. Her current research includes a new book project on the social histories of LGBT seniors in New York and Los Angeles, the negotiation of religious and community life for lesbians and gay men of faith, and the promotion of healthy aging for racial and ethnic minority elders.*

What led you to begin studying sexuality?

I became interested in studying various aspects of sexuality, particularly as they relate to African American women, in part because of the existing negative stereotypes in society and in the literature regarding Black women and their processes of family formation. Much of the research on this population lacks an in-depth analysis of the choices Black women and girls make around their bodies, their relationships, and more generally their lives. My dissertation examined the predictors of early sexual debut and pregnancy among African American adolescents in high-poverty neighborhoods. Rather than compare them to their White, middle-class peers as other work had done, I looked at the risk and protective factors within these social contexts that were associated with more positive outcomes for these young women.

I began studying lesbian, gay, and bisexual women in 2003. After meeting and getting to know a working-class Black lesbian couple, I realized that the literature in LGBT studies, family studies, and even African American studies provided almost no information about the family experiences of Black gay women. I wrote *Invisible Families: Gay Identities, Relationships and Motherhood among Black Women* as a corrective to these literatures, and as a way to increase the visibility of working-class and middle-class gay women of color.

How do people react when you tell them you study sexuality?

These days, people usually show great interest in the type of work I do and the methods I use for uncovering and studying LGBT populations. However, when I first started my book project, the country was not talking as openly about gay sexuality. This was before many of the political debates on legalizing same-sex marriage had really begun to permeate the discourse of regular, everyday people. At earlier stages in my career I was hesitant to let people know that the focus of my research was Black gay women. I feared I would be marginalized in the scholarly community, or that my work would be ignored and seen as insignificant. However, I knew that there were important sociological understandings that would come from this work, and that it was necessary to be brave and to take the lead in helping several areas of study move forward.

What ethical dilemmas have you faced as you've studied sexuality? Could you tell us about a particularly thorny dilemma and how you solved it?

When writing my book *Invisible Families*, I had to decide how much to reveal about my own sexuality. I knew that readers would want to know whether I am gay and how that might have influenced my research, both in the data collection and in the way I portray the families in the study. I knew that once it was written in the book that I am a gay woman, it would stand forever and anyone who read the book would know. I grew up in a conservative Christian denomination and knew that some of the parishioners in my family's church might read the book. I worried that my parents would be uncomfortable with their friends knowing about my sexuality.

Nevertheless I decided to be upfront about my sexuality in the book because I did not want fear of knowledge to be present in the work or in my own personal life. Thus far, my parents have only had positive things to say about my work. They are proud of my accomplishments.

What do you think is most challenging about studying sexuality?

One of the most challenging things about studying sexuality is that it elicits such strong feelings from so many groups! Sexuality is something that is difficult for people to talk about, particularly those who deem themselves "respectable." Several studies have shown, for example, that even many physicians are uncomfortable talking about sexuality with their patients. It is an area of scholarship that has not always received serious consideration in the field of sociology, so as a sociologist studying lesbian families I have had to show connections between sexuality and other areas of the discipline that are more easily accepted, such as family and gender.

Why is sex research important?

The study of sexuality in society is important because it gives us a window into an important aspect of human behavior. Studying the sexuality of different groups adds to our understandings of how social groups operate. I focus on the ways context influences how individuals in groups understand their own sexuality.

Of the projects you've done over the course of your academic career, which was most interesting and why?

Completing my book *Invisible Families* was one of the most challenging and rewarding feats of my career because it required me to forge new ground in several fields of study. In the book I challenge several assumptions in the feminist literature, I show a new applicability to the intersectionality paradigm, and I make visible the multifaceted lives of a stigmatized population. Ultimately I want people to know that social contexts—including race, ethnicity, gender, region, social class, and religiosity—all influence how individuals enact a sexuality.

ALFRED KINSEY AND THE KINSEY REPORT

VERN L. BULLOUGH

The more I study the development of modern sexuality, the more I believe in the importance and significance of Alfred Kinsey. Although his research was on Americans, it came to be a worldwide source of information about human sexuality and set standards for sex research everywhere. In America and much of the world, his work was a decisive factor in changing attitudes toward sex. Within the field of sexuality, he reoriented the field, moving it away from the medical model and medical dominance, to one encompassing a variety of disciplines and approaches. In short, his work has proved revolutionary.

To understand what Kinsey wrought, one must look at the field of sexuality when Kinsey began his studies. One must also look briefly at Kinsey as an individual to understand his accomplishments.

SEX RESEARCH, 1890–1940

The modern study of sexuality began in the nineteenth century, and these early studies were dominated by physicians. It was assumed that since physicians were the experts on body functions, they should be the experts regarding sexual activities. In a sense, this was a divergence from the past, when sexuality had been regarded almost entirely as a moral issue. And although there were still moral issues involved, physicians were also judged as qualified to speak on these issues as well. Although few physicians had any specialized knowledge on most sexual topics, except perhaps for sexually transmitted diseases, this did not prevent them from speaking with authority on most aspects of human sexuality.

Havelock Ellis, one of the dominant figures in promoting sexual knowledge in the first third of the twentieth century, said that he sought a medical degree primarily because it was the only profession in which he could safely study sex. Inevitably, most of the so-called experts were physicians. Equal in influence to Ellis was Magnus Hirschfeld, another physician. Both Ellis and Hirschfeld compiled what could be called sexual histories, as Kinsey later compiled. Ellis, however, acquired almost all of his histories from correspondence of volunteers and, as far as I know, never interviewed anyone. Hirschfeld, later in his career, compiled many case histories based on interviews, but early on he depended mainly on historical data and personal knowledge. Unfortunately, Hirschfeld used only a small portion of his data in his published books, and before he could complete a comprehensive study of sexuality, his files were destroyed by the Nazis (Bullough, 1994).

Although some of the data physicians reported about sex [were] gathered from their own practices, these [data] were usually interpreted in terms of traditional views and were supplemented by historical materials or reports of anthropologists [in order] to increase their authenticity. Simply put, most physicians writing about sex were influenced more by the zeitgeist of the time rather than by any specialized base of knowledge. A few early physician investigators, such as the American obstetrician

From "Alfred Kinsey and the Kinsey Report: Historical Overview and Lasting Contributions," *Journal of Sex Research*, Vol. 35, Issue 2, 1998, pp. 127–31. Copyright © 1998 Routledge, reprinted by permission of the publisher (Taylor & Francis Ltd, http://www.tandfonline.com).

Robert Latou Dickinson (Dickinson and Beam, 1931, 1934), had over 1,000 case studies, but most had only a handful. As the twentieth century progressed, the ordinary physician probably was regarded as the most easily available authority on sex, but most of the medical writings on sexual topics came from psychiatrists, particularly those who were psychoanalytically trained (Bullough, 1997). Unfortunately, even the most comprehensive sex studies undertaken by psychiatrists, such as that of George Henry, were flawed by the assumptions of the investigators interpreting data. For example, they assumed that homosexuals were ill. Moreover, whether the answers to their questions were valid for determining differences with heterosexuals is uncertain, as there was a lack of any comparative study of heterosexuals (Henry, 1941).

Still, assumptions about medical expertise remained. When the Committee for Research in the Problems in Sex (CRPS), the Rockefeller-funded grant-giving body operating under the umbrella of the National Research Council, began to explore the possibilities of carrying out surveys of sexual behavior, they first sought out physicians. For example, Adolf Meyer of Johns Hopkins University was commissioned to complete a study of attitudes of medical students, but failed to complete his work. The only social scientists funded in the first 20 years of the CRPS were psychologists, although anthropological consultants and members of other fields provided occasional input. Lewis Terman, for example, was given funds to carry out studies on attitudes toward sex and marriage. Though his and similar studies were valuable, they depended on questionnaires rather than interviews to gather their data (Terman, Buttenweiser, Ferguson, Johnson, and Wilson, 1938), and the sexual part of their studies was secondary to other interests. Even though one of the major reasons the CRPS had been created

in 1921 was to complete such general studies, the committee members were either unwilling or unable to find a person to carry out this kind of study. I suspect that the first factor was more important than the second: There is considerable evidence to indicate that the committee members were uncomfortable with studies on actual sexual behavior and much preferred to fund what might be called bench (i.e., laboratory-based) scientists to social scientists. I should add that this attitude was not shared by the Rockefeller Foundation or John D. Rockefeller, Jr.: both funded other survey projects dealing with sex, including that of Katherine Bement Davis (1929).

Funding for research projects when Kinsey began his work operated much more according to an old-boy network than it does today. There was little advertisement of fund availability and individuals were invited to apply, had to be nominated to apply, or had to have a connection. Certain universities and individuals dominated the disbursement of the money available. To an observer [today] examining most of the research grants given for sex research, the relationships look almost incestuous.

Unfortunately for the committee, sex activity could not be studied exclusively in the laboratory or even in the field by observing animals or gathering historical data. There had been nongrant-supported popular studies of sex, but their samples were not representative and the questionnaires were poorly designed. Moreover, in keeping with its reliance on academia, the committee seemed reluctant to give its imprimatur to individuals conducting such studies. What was needed was a person willing to blaze new trails, dispassionately examining sex without the preconceived notions of most of the physicians then involved in writing about sex. The qualified individual or individuals needed an academic connection, preferably one with an established reputation for scientific studies.

KINSEY COMES ON THE SCENE

It was in this setting that Kinsey entered the scene. He was the right person at the right time; that is, a significant amount of money was available for sex research and there was an interest within the CRPS for some general kind of survey of American sex behavior. Who was Kinsey?

In terms of overall qualification, Kinsey's best asset was that he was a bench scientist, a biologist with a Ph.D. from Harvard, and an internationally known expert on gall wasps. But he was also a broad-based scientist. Unlike most research scientists today, who often are part of a team, researchers in the 1930s in the United States were self-dedicated and carried a major teaching load. Kinsey, for example, simultaneously taught general biology, published two editions of a popular introductory general biology text, two editions of a workbook, and a general text on methods in biology, and carried out major research. His entry into sex seems to have been serendipitous, taking place after he had completed his studies on gall wasps. Professors at the University of Indiana had discussed the possibility of an introductory cross-discipline course on marriage, then a topic beginning to receive some attention in academic circles. Kinsey was not only involved in such discussions but took the lead. In 1938, he was invited to coordinate and direct the new course on marriage and family. As a sign of the time, the course was taught by an all-male faculty from a variety of disciplines, including law, economics, sociology, philosophy, medicine, and biology.

Before the appearance of courses on marriage and family, the academic discussion of human sexuality had been confined to lectures in the hygiene-type courses that had been established on many campuses in the second decade of the twentieth century, largely through the efforts of the American Social Hygiene Association. The approach to sex of these hygiene classes was quite different from that of the marriage and family courses, as they generally emphasized the dangers of sexually transmitted diseases and masturbation. In a sense, these hygiene-type courses were conceived to preserve sexual purity, whereas the sexual portions of marriage and family courses provided information, following the outlines of the better sex manuals of the time.

Kinsey went even further in his discussion of sexuality than the sex-positive marriage manuals, and soon clashed with Thurman Rice, a bacteriology professor who had written extensively on sex, primarily from the point of view of eugenics. For many years, Rice had delivered the sex lectures in the required hygiene course, where the males were separated from the females when he gave his lectures. Kinsey deliberately had not included Rice in his recruited faculty, which probably furthered Rice's antagonism. Rice was typical of an earlier generation of sex educators in that he considered moral education an essential part of sex education. He believed and taught that masturbation was harmful, condemned premarital intercourse, and was fearful that Kinsey's course on marriage was a perversion of academic standards. For example, he charged Kinsey with asking some of the women students about the length of their clitorises. To show that his accusations were based on more than gossip, Rice demanded the names of students in Kinsey's class so that he could verify such classroom voyeurism. Rice opposed Kinsey's questioning of students because he believed that sexual behavior could not and should not be analyzed by scientific methods because it was a moral topic, not a scientific one. Rice's perspective thus was perhaps typical of the hygiene approach to sex.

Kinsey had probably been doing at least some of the things that Rice mentioned because he had approached sex as a taxonomist—as one interested in classifying and describing—as a dispassionate scientist and not as a reformer or politician. In a sense, he was a political innocent. He believed that science could speak for itself, and he criticized his faculty colleagues who took any kind of political stand. He refused to join organizations that he felt had any kind of political agenda, including the Society for the Scientific Study of Sexuality (SSSS) in its early years.

There is, however, much more to Kinsey's interest in sex than the dispassionate scientist. In his personal life, he was not inhibited about body functions. Even before starting his course on marriage, he had sought information about the sex life of his students. His openness about sex (see Jones, 1997; 1997a) was what Rice objected to.

It might well be that when Kinsey began teaching the sex course, he was undergoing a kind of midlife crisis, feeling that he had come to know all he wanted to know about gall wasps and needing to explore new fields. Sex to him represented an unexplored new field where comparatively little was known, and where there was much information to be gleaned. He began his study as he had that of gall wasps: finding out what was known and, in the process, building up a personal library of serious books on sex (hardly any of these had found their way into university libraries) and reading extensively. He also sought first-hand information by questioning his students about topics such as their age at first premarital intercourse, frequency of sexual activity, and number of partners.

All this gave fodder to Rice and his allies, including a number of parents who, perhaps at Rice's urging, complained about the specific sexual data given in the course and particularly about questions that Kinsey asked of his students. The president of the university, Herman Wells, a personal friend of Kinsey who had appointed him coordinator of the course, counseled him and gave him two options: to continue to teach the course and give up some

of his probing of student lives, or to devote more time to his sex research and not teach the course. Because Kinsey had already begun to extend his interviews off campus, the answer was perhaps inevitable. Although Kinsey continued to teach courses in biology, his load was reduced, and much of his life came to be devoted to sex research.

Because Kinsey was already well connected to the scientific establishment, his initial efforts to study sex received encouragement from the CRPS. He received an exploratory grant from them in 1941, during which time he would be evaluated as to suitability for a larger grant. George W. Corner, a physician member and later the chair of the CRPS, visited Kinsey as one of the grant investigators to determine whether Kinsey deserved further funding. He was tremendously impressed and reported that Kinsey was the most intense scientist he had ever met. He added that Kinsey could talk about little besides his research. According to Corner (1981), Kinsey was an ideal person for a grant to study sex:

He was a full professor, married with adolescent children. While carrying on his teaching duties in the zoology department he worked every available hour, day and night, traveling anywhere that people would give him interviews. He was training a couple of young men in his method of interviewing. Dr. Yerkes and I submitted separately to his technique. I was astonished at his skill in eliciting the most intimate details of the subject's sexual history. Introducing his queries gradually, he managed to convey an assurance of complete confidentiality by recording the answers on special sheets printed with a grid on which he set down the information gained, by unintelligible signs, explaining that the code had never been written down and only his two colleagues could read it. His questions included subtle tricks to detect deliberate misinformation. (p. 268)

Important to the continuation of the grant was the support of the university administration and its president, which Kinsey received despite sniping by some fellow faculty members such as Rice and others who regarded Kinsey's interest in sex with suspicion. As Corner's reference to Kinsey's family indicates, the committee wanted to make certain that the researcher had no special agenda except, perhaps, to establish some guides to better marriages. Kinsey satisfied them on this account and was well aware that any indication otherwise might endanger his grant. Thus, his own sex life remained a closed book, only to be opened by later generations of scholars (Jones, 1997). The CRPS came to be so committed to Kinsey that by the 1946–1947 academic year, he was receiving half of the committee's total budget.

Before the interviews stopped with Kinsey's death, about 18,000 individuals had been interviewed, 8,000 by Kinsey himself. Kinsey strongly believed that people would not always tell the truth when questioned about their sexual activities and that the only way to deal with this was through personal interviews in which the contradictions could be explored. He did not believe that self-administered questionnaires produced accurate responses: He regarded them as encouraging dishonest answers. He also recognized that respondents might lie even in a personal interview, but he provided a variety of checks to detect this and believed his checks were successful. Subjects were usually told that there were some contradictions in their answers and were asked to explain them. If they refused to do so, the interview was terminated and the information not used. Kinsey was also aware of potential bias of the interviewer. He sought to overcome this bias by occasionally having two people conduct the interviews at different times and by relying mainly on four interviewers, including himself, to conduct the study. If there was a bias, it came to be a shared one. The questions, however, were so wide-ranging that this too would limit much of the potential for slanting the data in any one direction. Following taxonomic principles, he wanted to gather data from as many

subjects as possible, and he hoped initially to conduct 20,000 interviews and later to conduct 80,000 more. He did not live to achieve this. Before he died, the funding sources had dried up for such research, and other methods based on statistical sampling grew more popular.

WHAT KINSEY DID

Kinsey's major accomplishment was to challenge most of the assumptions about sexual activity in the United States. In so doing, he aroused great antagonism among many who opposed making sexual issues a matter of public discussion and debate. One reason for the antagonism is that he brought to public notice many sexual practices that previously had not been publicly discussed. Although Kinsey prided himself as an objective scientist, it was his very attempt to establish a taxonomy of sexual behaviors—treating all activities as more or less within the range of human behavior— that got him into trouble. Karl Menninger, for example, said that "Kinsey's compulsion to force human sexual behavior into a zoological frame of reference leads him to repudiate or neglect human psychology, and to see normality as that which is natural in the sense that it is what is practiced by animals" (quoted in Pomeroy, 1972, p. 367).

Most sex researchers today accept the fact that total objectivity in our field is probably impossible. Some of Kinsey's difficulty resulted from his belief that he could be totally objective. He did not realize that the way he organized his data sometimes could challenge his objectivity, even though the organization seemed logical. For example, Kinsey developed a seven-point bipolar scale, which was one of the standard methods of organizing data in social science research at that time. He did not trust people's self-classification as homosexual or heterosexual. Therefore, he decided that regardless of how they might have classified themselves, the only objective indicator that he could use was to define sex in terms of outlet—namely, what activity resulted in orgasms.

In most seven-point scales, the extremes are represented by 0 and 6 (or by 1 and 7, depending upon the number with which the scale starts). Most people tend to respond using the middle of the scale. When one rates heterosexual orgasm as 0 and homosexual orgasm 6, a logical decision in terms of taxonomy, he in effect weights the scale by seeming to imply that exclusive heterosexuality is one extreme and exclusive homosexuality the other. Although his data demonstrated that far more people were identified as exclusively heterosexual than as any other category, his scale also implied that homosexuality was just another form of sexual activity, something that I think Kinsey believed was true. For his time and place this was revolutionary. His discussion of homosexuality and its prevalence resulted in the most serious attacks upon him and his data (Kinsey, Pomeroy, and Martin, 1948).

Kinsey was a trailblazer, openly and willingly challenging many basic societal beliefs. It was not only his dispassionate discussion of homosexuality that roused controversy, but also his tendency to raise questions that society at that time preferred to ignore. In his book on males, for example, he questioned the assumption that extramarital intercourse always undermined the stability of marriage and held that the full story was more complex than the most highly publicized cases led one to assume. He seemed to feel that the most appropriate extramarital affair, from the standpoint of preserving a marriage, was an alliance in which neither party became overly involved emotionally. Concerned over the reaction to this, however, he became somewhat more cautious in the book on females. He conceded that extramarital affairs probably contributed to divorces in more ways and to a "greater extent than the subjects themselves realized" (Kinsey, Pomeroy, Martin, and Gebhard, 1953, p. 31).

Kinsey was interested in many different sexual behaviors, including that between generations (i.e., adults with children or minors). One of his more criticized sections in recent years is the table based on data he gathered from pedophiles. He is accused of not turning these people over to authorities, although one of the major informants was already serving time in jail for his sexual activities when interviewed. Kinsey gathered his data wherever he could find it, but he also reported on the source of his data. His own retrospective data tended to show that many individuals who experienced intergenerational sex as children were not seriously harmed by it, another statement that got him into trouble.

Kinsey is also criticized for his statistical sampling. Although his critics (even before his studies were published) attempted to get him to validate his data with a random sample of individuals, he refused on the grounds that not all of those included in the random sample would answer the questions put to them and that, therefore, the random sample would be biased. It is quite clear that Kinsey's sample is not random and that it overrepresents some segments of the population, including students and residents of Indiana. Part of the criticism, however, is also due to the use and misuse of the Kinsey data without his qualifications. This is particularly true of his data on same-sex relationships, which are broken down by age and other variables and therefore allowed others to choose the number or percentage of the sample they wanted to use in their own reports.

Another assumption of American society that Kinsey also challenged was the asexuality of women. This proved the issue of greatest controversy in his book on females. A total of 40% of the females he studied had experienced orgasm within the first months of marriage, 67% by the first six months, and 75% by the end of the first year. Twenty-five percent of his sample had experienced orgasm by age of 15, more than 50% by the age of 20, and 64% before marriage. On the other hand, he also reported cases in which women failed to reach orgasm after 20 years of marriage. In spite of the controversies over his data on orgasms, it helped move the issue of female sexuality on to the agenda of the growing women's movement of the late 1960s and the 1970s, and to encourage further studies of female sexuality.

In light of the challenges against him, Kinsey ignored in his writings what might be called sexual adventurers, paying almost no attention to swinging, group sex, and alternate lifestyles such as sadism, masochism, transvestism, voyeurism, and exhibitionism. He justified this neglect by arguing that such practices were statistically insignificant. It is more likely that Kinsey was either not interested in them or not interested in exploring them. He was also not particularly interested in pregnancy or sexually transmitted diseases. However, he demystified discussion of sex insofar as that was possible. Sex, to him, was just another aspect of human behavior, albeit an important part. He made Americans and the world at large aware of just how big a part human sexuality played in the life cycle of the individual and how widespread many kinds of sexual activities were.

Kinsey was determined to make the study of sex a science, a subject that could be studied in colleges much the same way that animal reproduction was, with succeeding generations of researchers adding to the knowledge base. He succeeded, at least in the long run. He had a vision of the kind of studies that still needed to be done, some of which were later done by his successors at Indiana and elsewhere, but he himself died before he could do them and the funds dried up.

Another of his significant contributions was to establish a library and to gather sources about sexuality from all over the world. He blazed a trail for future sex researchers: The library he established at Indiana University served as an example that helped many of us to persuade other university libraries to collect works from this field. Although there are now several impressive collections of this kind in the country, Kinsey's collection is still tremendously important.

In sum, Kinsey was the major factor in changing attitudes about sex in the twentieth century. His limitations and his personal foibles are appropriately overshadowed by his courage to go where others had not gone before. In spite of the vicious attacks upon him during his last few years of life, and the continuing attacks today, his data continue to be cited and used (and misused). He changed the nature of sexual studies, forced a reexamination of public attitudes toward sex, challenged the medical and psychiatric establishment to reassess its own views, influenced both the feminist movement and the gay and lesbian movement, and built a library and an institution devoted to sex research. His reputation continues to grow, and he has become one of the legends of the twentieth century. . . .

REFERENCES

Bullough, V. L. 1994. *Science in the bedroom: A history of sex research.* New York: Basic Books.

Bullough, V. L. 1997. American physicians and sex research. *Journal of the History of Medicine,* 57, 236–53.

Corner, G. W. 1981. *The seven ages of a medical scientist.* Philadelphia: University of Pennsylvania Press.

Davis, K. B. 1929. *Factors in the sex life of twenty-two hundred women.* New York: Harper.

Dickinson, R. L., and Beam, L. 1931. *A thousand marriages.* Baltimore: Williams and Wilkins.

Dickinson, R. L., and Beam, L. 1934. *The single woman.* Baltimore: Williams and Wilkins.

Henry, G. 1941. *Sex variants: a study of homosexual patterns* (2 vols.). New York: Hoeber.

Jones, J. H. 1997, August 25 and September 1. Annals of sexology: Dr. Yes. *New Yorker,* pp. 99–113.

Jones, J. H. 1997a. *Kinsey: A Public/Private Life.* New York: Norton.

Kinsey, A., Pomeroy, W., and Martin, C. 1948. *Sexual behavior in the human male.* Philadelphia: Saunders.

Kinsey, A., Pomeroy, W., Martin, C., and Gebhard, P. 1953. *Sexual behavior in the human female.* Philadelphia: Saunders.

Pomeroy, W. B. 1972. *Dr. Kinsey and the Institute for Sex Research.* New York: Harper and Row.

Terman, L., Buttenweiser, P., Ferguson. L., Johnson, W. B., and Wilson, D. P. 1938. *Psychological factors in marital happiness.* New York: McGraw-Hill.

LARGE-SCALE SEX: METHODS, CHALLENGES, AND FINDINGS OF NATIONALLY REPRESENTATIVE SEX RESEARCH

AMANDA M. JUNGELS AND STACY GORMAN HARMON

We know gossip about the sex lives of famous people. . . . What we don't know—and what is of immensely greater importance—is what the rest of us ordinary folks have been doing between the sheets.

—Erickson and Steffen, 1999: 207

Have you ever wondered how old the average American is when they lose their virginity? Or how many sexual partners they have in a lifetime? Since Alfred Kinsey completed his revolutionary sex research in the 1950s, sex researchers have been struggling to answer these questions (and many more) about Americans' sexual practices. While Kinsey's research was large-scale (collecting the sexual histories of more than 11,000 Americans), his sample was not representative of the general population. At the time, Kinsey did not believe that it was possible to collect data on sexual practices successfully from a random sample of Americans (Kinsey Institute, 2011; Michael et al., 1994). Since the 1950s, few researchers have taken on the challenge of conducting large-scale representative studies on the sexual practices of Americans, "perhaps because it was considered too dull, trivial, and self-evident to deserve attention" (Laumann et al., 1994a: 37).

More recently, sexuality researchers have reported feeling marginalized or stigmatized because of their research, as well as being subjected to undue oversight or interference by institutional review boards (committees intended to ensure research is conducted ethically and with minimal harm to participants) (Irvine, 2012, 2015). The absence of reliable research did not allay Americans' curiosity about sex and sexuality; instead, they turned to less-than-reliable data gathered by mainstream publications like *Cosmopolitan*, *Redbook*, and *Playboy* (Laumann et al., 1994a; Michael et al., 1994). Unfortunately, magazine surveys are fraught with problems; a major one is that their samples are usually drawn from a small portion of the magazine's own readers. Thus, their samples are not representative of the general American population (i.e., *Redbook* readers are mostly affluent married white women). In addition, those who volunteer to participate in such surveys may be very different from those who do not (Michael et al., 1994). So, when we want to learn about Americans' sexual behavior—to answer these questions about the "average American," or Americans in general—a nationally representative sample is necessary.

Nationally representative research is useful in a number of ways, but foremost is the fact that it is the only kind of research that allows us to generalize to the overall population. Representative samples use probability sampling techniques, which means that everyone in the population has an equal and known chance of being selected to participate. But how does one randomly select a set of Americans in a way that ensures that everyone has an equal chance of participating? There is no "list" of Americans that one could randomly select from; even a semicomplete list (from each state's Department of Motor Vehicles, for example) would exclude some people, like those who cannot afford to own a car, cannot drive, or use public transportation.

There are a variety of ways to do it, but many researchers use multistage area probability sampling. Two of the studies reviewed in this reading used this form of sampling—the National Health and Social Life Survey (NHSLS), conducted in the early 1990s, and the National Survey of Family Growth (NSFG), which has been conducted every few years since the 1970s. Both of these studies began their sampling by using primary sampling units (PSUs), which are large geographic areas (including major metropolitan areas or several counties grouped together). The researchers randomly selected a set of PSUs; within these larger areas, smaller areas that are analogous to neighborhoods (called "segments") were selected. After segments were randomly selected, all addresses in that segment were listed. Not every address in a given neighborhood is a residential address—there are vacant lots, empty houses, and businesses. To address this issue, researchers would often dispatch an assistant who traveled the neighborhood and confirmed which addresses were residences. After this information had been confirmed, the researchers randomly selected addresses to include, and then randomly selected someone from the household to participate.

While nationally representative surveys are an important part of understanding the lives of the general population, there are many challenges to conducting such large-scale research. The greatest of these challenges—whether the research is about sexual behavior or not—is ensuring that the sample reflects the demographic characteristics of the population and that no groups are left out of the sample. For example, while researchers acknowledge that sampling "households" is an acceptable method of drawing a national sample, around 3 percent of the population in this country do not live in households and will be excluded, such as those in institutional settings like college dorm residents, incarcerated individuals, seniors in assisted living facilities, and homeless people (Laumann et al., 1994a). A related challenge is that members of racial and ethnic minority groups are often underrepresented in national samples. To combat this pattern, most nationally representative surveys "oversample" minority groups to ensure that they are represented in final samples in high enough numbers for analysis. Sexual minorities (particularly salient to sex researchers) such as gay men and lesbians are not as "easily identifiable" as members of racial and ethnic minority groups, making it challenging to oversample for them (Michael et al., 1994: 29). A final challenge of large-scale research is that it describes "general" experiences and patterns; these patterns do not always coincide with an individual's specific experience. Large-scale representative studies offer us a snapshot of the American population at the time the research is conducted (Michael et al., 1994).

But selecting a representative sample is not the only challenge that researchers have to face. In addition to practical design challenges, researchers also must contend with the cost of implementing such large surveys. Outside of government agencies, there are few organizations with the resources to fund large projects, and receiving government funding is fraught with complications and problems [see "Funding Sex Research" in Reading 10]. Two of the studies reviewed in this reading had major funding challenges—the NHSLS lost its government funding in the 1990s, and the National Survey of Sexual Health and Behavior (NSSHB) used exclusively private funding because of the lack of available government funding (Reece et al., 2010a). The government funds the NSFG, but it does not focus exclusively on sexual practices or attitudes.

We present findings in the next section for all three of these nationally representative surveys, as well as discuss their strengths, their limitations, and the challenges the researchers faced. Ideally, comparisons would be made across studies to look for changes across time in the sexual behaviors of the participants.

However, this is difficult because of major differences across the studies themselves. The methods used and questions asked are not the same across all three studies, and there are even differences in the specific focuses and goals of the researchers. For these reasons, we highlight what we consider to be major findings that might be new or different in comparison to other studies, or that challenge mainstream perceptions of the "average American's" sexual experiences.

NATIONAL HEALTH AND SOCIAL LIFE SURVEY (1994)

The National Health and Social Life Survey began in 1987 as a government-funded effort to better understand Americans' sexual practices, largely in response to the developing HIV/AIDS crisis (Laumann, Michael, and Gagnon, 1994b). Besides Kinsey's results, scholars had very little information about Americans' sexual behaviors. What was missing was how sexual behaviors had changed in the intervening years and how sexual behaviors and attitudes would impact sexually transmitted infection rates (Laumann et al., 1994a).

Designing and implementing the study was complicated by the fact that the researchers from the University of Chicago and the government officials who were spearheading the project seemed to have different goals (Michael et al., 1994). The researchers wanted to include broad questions about sexual behavior, but government officials wanted a strict focus on sexually transmitted infections (STIs) and HIV/AIDS. The researchers wanted to focus on a wide variety of issues connected to sexuality, arguing that so little was known about Americans' sexual practices that they would not assume to know what factors were relevant; government officials argued that some topics (including masturbation) had nothing to do with the transmission of STIs and thus should

be excluded from the research (Michael et al., 1994). Given that government approval (and funding) was necessary to conduct the research, the research team relented and narrowed their field of study to specific sexual health and HIV/AIDS-related questions (Michael et al., 1994).

After the research team had refined the survey and research design, they awaited approval from several government agencies that were involved with the funding of the project. During this review process, the magazine *Science* ran a story about the project, illustrated with a picture from *Bob and Carol and Ted and Alice*—a film about two couples that partner-swap (Laumann, Michael, and Gagnon, 1994b). Several conservative members of Congress honed in on the article and photo and began attacking the research. Representative William Dannemeyer argued that the research was "a plot by homosexuals to legitimate the normality of gay and lesbian lifestyles . . . and the project staff had an anti-family agenda" (Laumann, Michael, and Gagnon, 1994b: 35). Dannemeyer also deliberately sensationalized the content of the study by reading questions from the survey out of context on the floor of Congress and to the press (Laumann, Michael, and Gagon, 1994b). Defending the scientific merits of the study was left to the few in Congress and government who supported the project because the research team was under a government gag order (Laumann, Michael, and Gagnon, 1994b). In 1991, after several years of debate and deadlock, the House of Representatives removed all funding for the project (Laumann, Michael, and Gagnon, 1994b). The research team eventually received private funding from several organizations (although the amount was significantly reduced) and, "freed of political constraints," was able to conduct much broader research. Unfortunately, the reduction in funding meant dramatically reducing the scale of the project, from 20,000 to fewer than 4,000 individuals (Michael et al., 1994: 28).

During these delays and funding negotiations, the research team conducted a number of pilot studies, which heavily informed their research methods and survey questions. For example, researchers learned that many Americans at the time did not understand terms like vaginal or heterosexual, requiring the researchers to think carefully about question wording and ordering to avoid terminology that participants might consider confusing, offensive, provocative, or "sexy." After deciding to conduct interviews rather than distributing self-administered surveys, the researchers held focus groups to determine how to select interviewers who would be able to gain the trust of the participants and with whom participants would be comfortable discussing their sexual histories. Almost everyone who participated in the focus groups, including men, and Hispanic and African-American men and women, said they would prefer to be interviewed by middle-aged white women (Michael et al., 1994). In the end, 220 highly trained interviewers conducted 3,432 face-to-face interviews across the United States, each of which lasted about 90 minutes (Michael et al., 1994). Nearly 80 percent of those who were selected for participation completed their interview, a rate that challenged the widely held belief that Americans would simply not participate in a study about sex (Michael et al., 1994).

Findings of the National Health and Social Life Survey[1]

The researchers behind the NHSLS approached their task from a distinctly sociological perspective, acknowledging that "an individual's social environment affects sexual behavior" (Laumann et al., 1994a: 4). Any number of social factors, including age, race, socioeconomic status, and gender, affect an individual's sexual behavior, the meanings they associate with sex, and even what they believe "counts" as sex. The NHSLS attempted to describe the relationships among an individual's social position, sexual practices, and attitudes by looking at patterns that developed between them.

Sexual Behaviors and Number of Sexual Partners

Popular media often tell us that the average American has a varied and exciting sex life, including high numbers of sex partners and very frequent sex; the NHSLS suggests that these representations are inaccurate. According to the NHSLS, the vast majority of Americans tended to be monogamous, had either zero or one partner per year, and had sex with fewer than four partners after age 18. In terms of gender differences, men had sex earlier in life and reported more sexual partners over their lifetimes than did women.

Sexual Orientation

One of the most innovative parts of the NHSLS was how the researchers measured sexual orientation. Many Americans believe that same-sex sexual behavior, identity, and desire are intrinsically linked. Guided by a sociological perspective, the researchers measured these concepts separately. While there was, of course, some overlap between desire, behavior, and identity (for example, most individuals who self-identified as gay or lesbian also reported same-sex desire and behaviors), there were significant numbers of participants who reported either same-sex desire without corresponding behavior or same-sex behavior without corresponding self-identification. Further reinforcing the idea that desire, behavior, and self-identity are conceptually different is the fact that 10 percent of men reported either same-sex attraction, desire, or identity but less than 3 percent of men indicated all three; similarly, 8 percent of women reported some form of same-sex sexuality (either desire, behavior, or self-identity) but less than 2 percent of women reported all three (Erickson and Steffen, 1999).

Forced Sex

One of the results that Laumann and his colleagues found most shocking were the rates of forced and coerced sex among the respondents. The researchers found that almost 22 percent of women reported that they had been forced by a man to do something sexual that they did not want to do; almost all (over 95 percent) reported that they knew the person that forced them. Interestingly, less than 3 percent of men reported that they had forced a woman to do something sexual they did not want to do. One of the explanations that Laumann and his colleagues offered for this gap was a difference in sexual scripts: Men, they argued, are encouraged to "negotiate" for sex with women, and women are encouraged through traditional gender roles to resist sex. The resultant conflict creates "not a gender gap, but a gender chasm" between men and women's understanding of forced sex (Michael et al., 1994: 221).

Limitations of the National Health and Social Life Survey

Because it used an area probability sample, the NHSLS excluded those individuals who do not live in a household. The limited availability of funding forced the researchers to limit the sample size, which resulted in some minority groups (gays and lesbians, for example, and some racial/ethnic groups) being inadequately represented. In addition, the sample age range had to be limited to those between 18 and 59 (Michael et al., 1994).

Despite the care with which the interview questions were created, the wording of some of the questions has been criticized. For example, one of the major findings of the NHSLS was that women had less sexual experience than men and reported being less interested in every type of sexual activity compared to men (Erickson and Steffen, 1999; Michael et al., 1994). To understand what kinds of activities

people found appealing, respondents were asked to rate a wide variety of sexual activities, ranging from oral sex and anal stimulation to group sex and sex with a stranger. Some critics have argued that what was excluded from this list are "activities that women's sexual scripts define as pleasurable, such as kissing and mutual masturbation. . . . The authors, like many male researchers before them, described a world in which men owned desire and initiated sexual activity and women chose whether to respond" (Erickson and Steffen, 1999: 215).

CONTINUOUS NATIONAL SURVEY OF FAMILY GROWTH (2006–2010)

The National Survey of Family Growth (NSFG) was created in 1971 by the Centers for Disease Control and Prevention. Over time, the NSFG has changed dramatically, but the goal of the study—to interview a nationally representative sample of Americans about pregnancy, marriage, and contraceptive use through in-person interviews—has remained the same (Groves et al., 2009). Since 1973, data have been gathered every few years using the area probability technique. All the interviews are conducted by women interviewers. Each time a cycle was completed, major changes were made. When the survey was first conducted in 1973, for example, only women who had been or were married were included because it was deemed "too sensitive" to ask women who had never been married about pregnancy and marriage (Martinez, Copen, and Abma, 2011). Over the years, many modifications have been made: young people, never-married women, and adult men were added to the sample, and changes in technology have allowed researchers to use laptops and interviewing software to encourage participants to give honest answers to questions about sensitive topics (Groves et al., 2009; Martinez, Copen, and Abma, 2011).

By the time the sixth cycle of the NSFG was completed in 2002, American society had changed dramatically. It was becoming prohibitively expensive to continue using the same data-collection methods (including recruiting and interviewing participants) because Americans were less willing to participate in large-scale research (Groves et al., 2009). To address these changes, the NSFG underwent a major methodological and design change in 2006. Rather than doing data collection in one 12-month cycle, the researchers decided to collect data continuously throughout the year by using a rotating sample of PSUs (Groves et al., 2009). Collecting data continuously saved the researchers money by allowing them to employ a smaller number of highly skilled interviewers. It also meant researchers could release results more often. More than three-quarters of those contacted participated in the 2006–2010 cycles of the NSFG. Interviewers conducted 22,682 face-to-face interviews with men and women between the ages of 15 and 44 over that four-year period (Martinez, Copen, and Abma, 2011). Interviewing has continued in the years since. From 2011 to 2015, 20,621 interviews were conducted with men and women around the country (U.S. Department of Health and Human Services, 2016). In September 2015, the NSFG expanded the age range for participants by five years to include men and women up to age 49 (U.S. Department of Health and Human Services, 2016).

Findings of the 2006–2008 National Survey of Family Growth[2]

Sexual Behaviors and Number of Sexual Partners

Many of the findings across the most recent cycles of the NSFG have remained remarkably consistent. The median number of lifetime sexual partners has remained essentially the same since 2002, about 4 for women and 6.5 for men aged 25–44 (U.S. Department of Health and Human Services, 2015). Some behaviors are quite common among adults; for example, almost all adult women (94 percent) and adult men (92 percent) have engaged in vaginal intercourse. Oral sex is also quite common among adults. The vast majority of those aged 18–24 have engaged in heterosexual oral sex (78 percent of men and 77 percent of women). There are, however, differences in this behavior by education level among women and men (see table below). For men and women, there is a greater likelihood of having engaged in oral sex as education level increases. This effect of education, though, seems to be greater for women than for men.

Percent of Men and Women Who Have Engaged in Oral Sex with Opposite-Sex Partner by Education Level

	WOMEN	MEN
No high school	72.6%	80.2%
High school/GED	87.3%	90.9%
Some college	92.2%	92.7%
Bachelor's or higher	91.5%	91.7%

Women and men with no high school education are less likely to report having engaged in oral sex (72.6 percent for women, 80.2 percent for men) than those with more education. When we compare those with the highest level of education, we find that a similar proportion of men (91.7 percent) and women (91.5 percent) have engaged in oral sex and in greater percentages than those with either no or only a high school education.

Sexual Identity

Like the National Health and Social Life Survey from the 1990s, the NSFG assessed sexual orientation in a variety of ways and found differing levels of same-sex activities depending on how they were measured; the survey also found large gender differences in the reporting of same-sex sexual experiences. For example, in the 2011–2013 NSFG, approximately 1 percent of women and 2 percent of men self-identified as "homosexual, gay, or lesbian," and approximately 5 percent of women and 2 percent of men self-identified as bisexual. Those numbers are significantly lower than the percentage of women (17.4) and men (6.2) who reported having "any same-sex sexual experiences." The ability to compare findings across time is one of the major strengths of the NSFG, especially since there is "considerable fluidity in the development and expression of sexual behavior and orientation over time" (Gartrell, Bos, and Goldberg, 2011: 3). For example, comparing the data for adolescent girls across the cycles shows that since 2002, the percentage of girls who had sex with boys dropped significantly, while the percentage of girls reporting same-sex contact doubled (from 5 to 10 percent) (Gartrell, Bos, and Goldberg, 2011). The adolescent girls in the most recent cycles were also older the first time they had sexual contact with boys compared with girls in the earlier cycles, and were less likely than the earlier cohorts to have experienced a pregnancy (Gartrell, Gos, and Goldberg, 2011).

Condom and Contraceptive Use

In addition to sexual practices and identity, the NSFG also collects information about reproductive health, including condom and contraceptive use (U.S. Department of Health and Human Services, 2015). Overall, condom use has increased in the last 15 years. In 2002, 42 percent of women and 48 percent of men reported having used a condom the first time they had sexual intercourse. When this was measured again from 2011–2013, 56 percent of women and 66 percent of men reported using a condom at first sex. Condom use has increased for teenagers as well. In 2002, 66 percent of girls and 71 percent of boys aged 15–19 used condoms the first time they had sex; by

2013–2015, these numbers had increased to 72 percent of girls and 78 percent of boys. The NSFG also assesses the consistency with which people use condoms by asking unmarried men and women who had ever used a condom and who had sex within the four weeks prior to the interview whether they used condoms "none of the time," "some of the time," or "every time" they had sex. For men in this age range, condom use became more consistent over time. The percentage of men answering "none of the time" fell from 71 percent in 2002 to 64 percent in 2013, and the percentage reporting they used condoms "some of the time" and "every time" increased by 4 percent and 2 percent, respectively. Women's consistency in condom use has fluctuated a small amount over time. Approximately 74 percent of women reported using condoms none of the time in the four weeks prior to their interview, about 7 percent reported using condoms some of the time, and between 19 percent and 21 percent reported using condoms every time they had sex. Though their condom use may be slightly less consistent than men's, women's use of contraceptives over the lifetime and at last sex have remained relatively consistent over time (98 percent and 62 percent, respectively). While condoms and long-acting reversible contraceptives (e.g., Depo-Provera, intrauterine devices), emergency contraceptives, and contraceptive patches have increased in popularity over time, other methods (such as the hormonal birth control pill) have decreased slightly in popularity.

Limitations of the National Survey of Family Growth

Like the National Health and Social Life Survey, the NSFG excludes those who do not live in a household. In addition, because the original focus of the NSFG was fertility and marriage, it only includes people who are in their reproductive years. While it would certainly be beneficial to include teens in the study, it is especially important because the baby boomer generation is rapidly aging out of their reproductive years—excluding a large portion of the population from participating in the NSFG.

Another concern with the NSFG is how the survey measures same-sex sexual behaviors. Although the most recent cycle of the NSFG measures same-sex sex between men based on giving or receiving oral sex and anal sex, it asks women about less specific practices (giving or receiving oral sex with another woman and vague "sexual experiences"). This could lead to larger numbers of women being classified as having same-sex sexual behavior. The difference in wording might also reflect heteronormative understandings of gender and sexuality; namely, that sexual acts can be quantified as events that prioritize penile penetration.

NATIONAL SURVEY OF SEXUAL HEALTH AND BEHAVIOR (2010)

By the early 2000s, sexual norms and attitudes in the United States had shifted again. Doctors were frequently prescribing Viagra and other medications to help with sexual dysfunction, allowing older adults to engage in sexual practices later in the life course. Attitudes about same-sex practices were liberalizing, sex education in schools continued on an abstinence-only path, and access to the internet and social networking sites became widespread (Reece et al., 2010a). Clearly, more research was needed to understand how these changes in American society were affecting our sexual lives, especially with regard to adults who were past middle age. In 2007, researchers at the Center for Sexual Health Promotion at Indiana University partnered with Church & Dwight Co. Inc. (the makers of Trojan condoms) to conduct a nationally representative study on sexual behavior (Herbenick et al., 2010a).

The National Survey of Sexual Health and Behavior (NSSHB) was designed with the intention of assessing how individuals "make health-related decisions once they decide to become sexually active" (Reece et al., 2010a: 245). Unlike the earlier large-scale studies that used face-to-face interviews, the NSSHB relied on an internet-based survey—the first of its kind. The researchers partnered with a private company to create a representative sample that was then used to conduct research online (Herbenick et al., 2010a). The probability sample they created used both phone numbers and addresses, allowing those individuals who only used cell phones to be included. Respondents were initially contacted through mailings and phone calls. When they agreed to participate, they either accessed the internet on their own to complete the survey or were provided a computer and internet access by the research company (Herbenick et al., 2010a). In total, there were 5,865 participants in the NSSHB (Herbenick et al., 2010a). The researchers continued to collect data annually from 2012 to 2015, using a diverse set of questions (Dodge et al., 2016).

Findings from the National Survey of Sexual Health and Behavior[3]

Sexual Behaviors over the Life Course

One of the major strengths of the NSSHB is the broad age range of the respondents, which allowed the researchers to better understand the "developmental trajectory of sexual expression" (Herbenick et al., 2010a: 261). The NSSHB demonstrated how the behaviors individuals engaged in changed over the life course. For example, masturbation was more common than partnered sexual activities for men under age 24 and over age 50. Vaginal intercourse, too, was quite common—it was the most common sexual activity for men and women between the ages of 25 and 49, but became less frequent among women beginning at age 30. Oral sex and anal sex "appear to be well established aspects of a contemporary sexual repertoire" (Herbenick et al., 2010a: 259). Forty percent of respondents had engaged in anal sex during their lifetime (an increase since the NHSLS in 1994). Despite cultural fears of rampant sexual activity among young people, teen sex was episodic and "safer" than anticipated. Less than one-third of teens had partnered sex in the past year, and during sex, "condom use appears to have become a normative behavior for many adolescents" (Fortenberry et al., 2010: 314).

Sexual Behaviors at Last Sexual Encounter

Some of the most interesting findings from the NSSHB concerned what types of behaviors people engaged in when they last had sex. The researchers investigated where individuals had sex, with whom they had sex (i.e., a relationship partner, a friend/acquaintance, etc.), any sexual difficulties that occurred, whether they had an orgasm, and how pleasurable they rated the encounter (Herbenick et al., 2010c). While vaginal intercourse was most common, participants reported more than 41 combinations of sexual activities (including giving and receiving oral sex, anal sex, and partnered masturbation) (Herbenick et al., 2010c). Men and women reported that they were more likely to have an orgasm if they engaged in a variety of behaviors. Women in particular reported higher rates of orgasm if vaginal intercourse was paired with other behaviors (Herbenick et al., 2010c). Despite everyone reporting high rates of pleasure at their last encounter, men tended to overestimate how often their female partner had an orgasm. The vast majority of men (85 percent) reported their partner had an orgasm, compared to the 64 percent of women who said they did. This gap is too large to be explained by same-sex couples included in the study. While there may be a variety of explanations

for this, more research is needed to explore the inconsistency (Herbenick et al., 2010c).

With whom individuals had sex also appeared to affect both their evaluations of their last encounter and the rates that they orgasmed, but the effects were different for men and women. Men reported that they experienced greater arousal, greater pleasure, and fewer problems when their last encounter was with a relationship partner than when it was with someone with whom they were not in a relationship. The researchers concluded that this difference might occur because as men age and experience sexual difficulty, being comfortable with and receiving patience from a partner is important (Herbenick et al., 2010c). Women, on the other hand, reported more sexual difficulties when their last encounter was with a relationship partner than not. This finding challenges the common notion that for women, love and emotional connection are necessary in order to be sexually satisfied. Though the majority of those who participated in the NSSHB were in a relationship, a significant proportion of men (30 percent) and women (18 percent) of all ages reported that their last sexual encounter was with a "friend" or "new acquaintance," indicating that the "friends with benefits" phenomenon is not limited to young adults (Herbenick et al., 2010c).

Limitations of the National Survey of Sexual Health and Behavior

Like the other nationally representative studies already described, the NSSHB relied on household-level data, which excludes institutionalized individuals. And although the NSSHB features a broader age range than any other large-scale sex survey, it is not representative of older adults, who may be more likely than adults of younger ages to be in an institutional setting (i.e., hospitalized or in an assisted-living facility). Older adults might also be less comfortable using computers and the internet. Like the other studies reviewed in this reading, the NSSHB did not oversample some minority groups (in particular, those with same-sex behaviors) (Herbenick et al., 2010a). Because the NSSHB focused more on public health and the life course than the previous studies, the questions were structured differently. This makes it difficult to compare results across time (to, for example, the NHSLS). The use of the internet was both a strength and a weakness. While the internet might create the feeling of increased confidentiality when reporting stigmatized behaviors, it was unclear whether this held true for all ages. Also, it was unclear whether individuals who could not read or were not comfortable using a computer would have been as likely to participate (Reece et al., 2010a).

Although the NSSHB collected detailed information about sexuality across age groups, what it lacks is contextual data. One of the benefits of in-person interviewing is that it allows the researcher to build rapport with the participant, promoting disclosure and offering insight into the individual's sexual experiences. Previous studies allowed for analysis of sexual experiences based on individuals' life experiences and social demographics (like age, race, and class), something that the NSSHB cannot offer (Reece et al., 2010a). The NSSHB is less sociological than the National Health and Social Life Survey; while health information is certainly valuable, it is equally important to understand the sociological context of sexual behaviors, including how social groups and culture shape our understanding of sex and our sexual practices.

CONCLUSION

Using probability sampling methods and conducting representative research is an important way for us to understand the sexual behaviors of large portions of Americans. Though these methods are complex and come with a host of challenges (including inadequate funding, limited government support, and the shortcomings of the methods themselves), the studies outlined in this article show the value of large-scale research on sexual behaviors. Research conducted by mainstream publications, such as *Cosmopolitan* and *Playboy*, is inadequate and often misleading, giving a false impression of what is "normal" under the guise of "research." Readers must be critical of these studies, analyzing the research design and sampling methodology to fully understand how the research was conducted and whether it is valid. In addition to large-scale sexual surveys, many qualitative and in-depth studies have been done on small populations. Although these studies are not generalizable to the larger population, they do contribute a nuanced understanding of sexual practices, attitudes, and identities that is often lost in large-scale representative research. If we want to continue to answer questions about "average Americans" and what their sexual lives are like, the government and the general public must support both quantitative and qualitative research projects.

NOTES

1. All results from Laumann et al., 1994a (unless otherwise noted).

2. All data from Copen, Chandra, and Febo-Vazquez, 2016 (unless otherwise noted).

3. All data from Herbenick et al., 2010a (unless otherwise noted).

REFERENCES

Chandra, Anjani, William D. Mosher, Casey Copen and Catlainn Sionean. 2011. "Sexual Behavior, Sexual Attraction and Sexual Identity in the United States: Data from the 2006–2008 National Survey of Family Growth." National Center for Health Statistics, *National Health Statistics Reports* 36.

Copen, Casey E., Anjani Chandra, and Isaedmarie Febo-Vazquez. 2016. "Sexual Behavior, Sexual Attraction, and Sexual Orientation among Adults Aged 18–44 in the United States: Data from the 2011–2013 National Survey of Family Growth." National Center for Health Statistics, *National Health Statistics Reports* 88.

Dodge, Brian, Debby Herbenick, M. Reuel Friedman, Vanessa Schick, Tsung-Chieh (Jane) Fu, Wendy

Bostwick, Elizabeth Bartelt, Miguel Muñoz-Laboy, David Pletta, Michael Reece, and Theo G. M. Sandfort. 2016. "Attitudes towards Bisexual Men and Women among a Nationally Representative Probability Sample of Adults in the United States." *PLoS One*, 11(10): 1–18.

Erickson, Julia A., with Sally A. Steffen. 1999. *Kiss and Tell: Surveying Sex in the Twentieth Century*. Cambridge, MA: Harvard University Press.

Fortenberry, J. Dennis, Vanessa Schick, Debby Herbenick, Stephanie Sanders, Brian Dodge, and Michael Reece. 2010. "Sexual Behaviors and Condom Use at Last Vaginal Intercourse: A National Sample of Adolescents Ages 14 to 17 Years." *Journal of Sexual Medicine*, 7(5): 305–14.

Gartrell, Nanette K., Henny M. W. Bos, and Naomi G. Goldberg. 2011. "New Trends in Same-Sex Sexual Contact for American Adolescents?" *Archives of Sexual Behavior*, 40(6): 1–3.

Groves, Robert M., William D. Mosher, James M. Lepkowski, Nicole G. Kirgis. 2009. "Planning and Development of the Continuous National Survey of Family Growth." National Center for Health Statistics, *Vital Health Statistics*, 1: 48.

Herbenick, Debby, Michael Reece, Vanessa Schick, Stephanie Sanders, Brian Dodge and J. Dennis Fortenberry. 2010a. "Sexual Behavior in the United States: Results from a National Probability Sample of Men and Women Ages 14–94." *Journal of Sexual Medicine*, 7(5): 255–65.

———. 2010b. "Sexual Behaviors, Relationships, and Perceived Status among Adult Women in the United States: Results from a Probability Sample." *Journal of Sexual Medicine,* 7(5): 277–90.

———. 2010c. "Event-Level Analysis of the Sexual Characteristics and Composition Among Adults Ages 18–59: Results from a National Probability Sample." *Journal of Sexual Medicine*, 7(5): 346–61.

Irvine, Janice M. 2012. "Can't Ask, Can't Tell." *Contexts*, 11(2): 28–33.

———. 2015. "The Other Sex Work: Stigma in Sexuality Research." *Social Currents* 2(2): 116–25.

Kinsey Institute. "Alfred Kinsey's 1948 and 1953 Studies." Retrieved December 8, 2011 from http://www .kinseyinstitute.org/research/ak-data.html.

Laumann, Edward O., John H. Gagnon, Robert T. Michael and Stuart Michaels. 1994a. *The Social Organization of Sexuality: Sexual Practices in the United States*. Chicago: University of Chicago Press.

Laumann, Edward O., Robert T. Michael, and John H. Gagnon. 1994b. "A Political History of the National Sex Survey of Adults." *Family Planning Perspectives*, 26(1): 34–38.

Martinez, Gladys, Casey E. Copen, and Joyce C. Abma. 2011. "Teenagers in the United States: Sexual Activity, Contraceptive Use and Childbearing, 2006–2010." National Survey of Family Growth, National Center for Health Statistics. *Vital Health Statistics*, 23: 31.

Michael, Robert T., John H. Gagnon, Edward O. Laumann and Gina Kolata. 1994. *Sex in America: A Definitive Survey*. Boston: Little Brown.

Reece, Michael, Debby Herbenick, Vanessa Schick, Stephanie Sanders, Brian Dodge and J. Dennis Fortenberry. 2010a. "Guest Editorial: Background and Considerations on the National Survey of Sexual Health and Behavior (NSSHB) from the Investigators." *Journal of Sexual Medicine*, 7(5): 243–45.

——— 2010b. "Sexual Behaviors, Relationships, and Perceived Health Status among Adult Women in the United States: Results from a Probability Sample." *Journal of Sexual Medicine*, 7(5): 291–304.

U.S. Department of Health and Human Services, Centers for Disease Control and Prevention. 2015. "Key Statistics from the National Survey of Family Growth." Retrieved from https://www.cdc.gov/nchs/nsfg /key_statistics.htm.

———. 2016. "User's Guide: Public Use Data File Documentation, 2013–2015." National Survey of Family Growth, National Center for Health Statistics.

Doing It Differently: Women's and Men's Estimates of Their Number of Lifetime Sexual Partners

Mindy Stombler and Dawn M. Baunach

A national survey of sexual practices found that men report having more sexual partners than women over the course of their lifetimes (Smith et al., 2011). Theoretically, heterosexual men's and women's estimates should be the same, because for each new female partner a man adds to his "lifetime account," a woman adds a new male partner to her "lifetime account." The discrepancy between women's and men's estimates remains even when researchers define *sexual partners* very specifically and account for possible sampling problems (such as undersampling female sex workers). What explains the gender gap in claims people make about numbers of sexual partners?

One possibility is that women and men misrepresent their number of lifetime sexual partners to others. Our society tends to hold a double standard regarding the sexual behavior of women and men. Men who have a great deal of sexual experience generally are not subject to shame (and in some circles their behavior is lauded), whereas women with "too many" lifetime partners are stigmatized. Attempts to give interviewers the socially approved response (called *social desirability bias*) may lead women to intentionally underreport their numbers or men to inflate theirs.

Another possibility is that people misrepresent their behaviors to themselves. If women discount partners for whom they feel little affection, such partners could slip from memory, thereby erroneously lowering their reported lifetime account. Women and men also rely on different estimation strategies. Women tend to enumerate (actually count), whereas men tend to give rough estimates (Brown and Sinclair, 1999; Weiderman, 1997). Weiderman notes a clear tendency for men reporting larger numbers of lifetime sexual partners to choose numbers that end in 0 or 5. Men prefer "round" numbers rather than exact counts.

The number of sexual partners that women and men report does become more similar when researchers shorten the time frame for estimation to the past year or the past five years (see table below), indicating that both men and women estimate more accurately over a shorter period of time. In addition, the cultural meaning that we attach to our accumulated lifetime number of sexual partners carries more weight than, say, the number of partners we might have in a year. Taking the double standard into account, it might be in women's best interest to carefully consider their number of lifetime sexual partners and in men's best interest to round up.

Mean Number of Sexual Partners

	WOMEN	MEN	DIFFERENCE (MEN–WOMEN)
Last five years	1.59 ($n = 942$)	2.08 ($n = 803$)	0.49
Last year	1.01 ($n = 953$)	1.26 ($n = 804$)	0.25

Note: Weighted sample sizes used.
Source: General Social Survey, 2016.

REFERENCES

Brown, Norman R., and Robert C. Sinclair. 1999. "Estimating Number of Lifetime Sexual Partners: Men and Women Do It Differently." *Journal of Sex Research,* 36(3): 292–97.

Smith, Tom W., Peter Marsden, Michael Hout, and Jibum Kim. 2011. *General Social Surveys, 1972–2010* [machine-readable data file]. Principal Investigator, Tom W. Smith; Co-Principal Investigator, Peter V. Marsden; Co-Principal Investigator, Michael Hout; Sponsored by National Science Foundation. Chicago, IL: National Opinion Research Center [producers]; Storrs, CT: Roper Center for Public Opinion Research, University of Connecticut [distributor].

Weiderman, Michael. 1997. "The Truth Must Be in Here Somewhere: Examining the Gender Discrepancy in Self-Reported Lifetime Number of Partners." *Journal of Sex Research,* 34(4): 375–86.

RACISM AND RESEARCH: THE CASE OF THE TUSKEGEE SYPHILIS STUDY

ALLAN M. BRANDT

In 1932 the U.S. Public Health Service (USPHS) initiated an experiment in Macon County, Alabama, to determine the natural course of untreated, latent syphilis in black males. The test comprised 400 syphilitic men, as well as 200 uninfected men who served as controls. The first published report of the study appeared in 1936 with subsequent papers issued every four to six years, through the 1960s. When penicillin became widely available by the early 1950s as the preferred treatment for syphilis, the men did not receive therapy. In fact, on several occasions, the USPHS actually sought to prevent treatment. Moreover, a committee at the federally operated Centers for Disease Control (CDC) decided in 1969 that the study should be continued. Only in 1972, when accounts of the study first appeared in the national press, did the Department of Health, Education, and Welfare (HEW) halt the experiment. At that time seventy-four of the test subjects were still alive; at least twenty-eight, but perhaps more than 100, had died directly from advanced syphilitic lesions.[1] In August 1972, HEW appointed an investigatory panel which issued a report the following year. The panel found the study to have been "ethically unjustified," and argued that penicillin should have been provided to the men.[2]

This [reading] attempts to place the Tuskegee Study in a historical context and to assess its ethical implications. Despite the media attention which the study received, the HEW *Final Report,* and the criticism expressed by several professional organizations, the experiment has been largely misunderstood. The most basic questions of *how* the study was undertaken in the first place and *why* it continued for forty years were never addressed by the HEW investigation. Moreover, the panel misconstrued the nature of the experiment, failing to consult important documents available at the National Archives which bear significantly on its ethical assessment. Only by examining the specific ways in which values are engaged in scientific research can the study be understood.

RACISM AND MEDICAL OPINION

A brief review of the prevailing scientific thought regarding race and heredity in the early twentieth century is fundamental for an understanding of the Tuskegee Study. By the turn of the century, Darwinism had provided a new rationale for American racism.[3] Essentially primitive peoples, it was argued, could not be assimilated into a complex, white civilization. Scientists speculated that in the struggle for survival the Negro in America was doomed. Particularly prone to disease, vice, and crime, black Americans could not be helped by education or philanthropy. Social [Darwinists] analyzed census data to predict the virtual extinction of the Negro in the twentieth century, for they believed the Negro race in America was in the throes of a degenerative evolutionary process.[4]

From "Racism and Research: The Case of the Tuskegee Syphilis Study," *Hastings Center Report*, Vol. 8, No. 6, 1978, pp. 21–29. © 1978 The Hastings Center. Reprinted by permission of John Wiley & Sons, Inc.

The medical profession supported these findings of late nineteenth- and early twentieth-century anthropologists, ethnologists, and biologists. Physicians studying the effects of emancipation on health concluded almost universally that freedom had caused the mental, moral, and physical deterioration of the black population.[5] They substantiated this argument by citing examples in the comparative anatomy of the black and white races. As Dr. W. T. English wrote: "A careful inspection reveals the body of the negro a mass of minor defects and imperfections from the crown of the head to the soles of the feet. . . ."[6] Cranial structures, wide nasal apertures, receding chins, projecting jaws, all typed the Negro as the lowest species in the Darwinian hierarchy.[7]

Interest in racial differences centered on the sexual nature of blacks. The Negro, doctors explained, possessed an excessive sexual desire, which threatened the very foundations of white society. As one physician noted in the *Journal of the American Medical Association*, "The negro springs from a southern race, and as such his sexual appetite is strong; all of his environments stimulate this appetite, and as a general rule his emotional type of religion certainly does not decrease it."[8] Doctors reported a complete lack of morality on the part of blacks:

Virtue in the negro race is like angels' visits—few and far between. In a practice of sixteen years I have never examined a virgin negro over fourteen years of age.[9]

A particularly ominous feature of this overzealous sexuality, doctors argued, was the black males' desire for white women. "A perversion from which most races are exempt," wrote Dr. English, "prompts the negro's inclination towards white women, whereas other races incline towards females of their own."[10] Though English estimated the "gray matter of the negro brain" to be at least a thousand years behind that of the white races, his genital organs were overdeveloped. As Dr. William Lee Howard noted:

The attacks on defenseless white women are evidences of racial instincts that are about as amenable to ethical culture as is the inherent odor of the race. . . . When education will reduce the size of the negro's penis as well as bring about the sensitiveness of the terminal fibers which exist in the Caucasian, then will it also be able to prevent the African's birth-right to sexual madness and excess.[11]

One southern medical journal proposed "Castration Instead of Lynching" as retribution for black sexual crimes. "An impressive trial by a ghost-like kuklux klan [sic] and a 'ghost' physician or surgeon to perform the operation would make it an event the 'patient' would never forget," noted the editorial.[12]

According to these physicians, lust and immorality, unstable families, and reversion to barbaric tendencies made blacks especially prone to venereal diseases. One doctor estimated that over 50 percent of all Negroes over the age of twenty-five were syphilitic.[13] Virtually free of disease as slaves, they were now overwhelmed by it, according to informed medical opinion. Moreover, doctors believed that treatment for venereal disease among blacks was impossible, particularly because in its latent stage the symptoms of syphilis become quiescent. As Dr. Thomas W. Murrell wrote:

They come for treatment at the beginning and at the end. When there are visible manifestations or when harried by pain, they readily come, for as a race they are not averse to physic; but tell them not, though they look well and feel well, that they are still diseased. Here ignorance rates science a fool. . . .[14]

Even the best educated black, according to Murrell, could not be convinced to seek treatment for syphilis.[15] Venereal disease, according to some doctors, threatened the future of the race. The medical profession attributed the low birth rate among blacks to the high prevalence of venereal disease which caused stillbirths and miscarriages. Moreover, the high rates of syphilis were thought to lead to increased insanity and crime. One doctor writing at the turn of the century estimated that the number of insane Negroes had increased thirteen-fold since the end of the Civil War.[16] Dr. Murrell's conclusion echoed the most informed anthropological and ethnological data:

So the scourge sweeps among them. Those that are treated are only half cured, and the effort to assimilate a complex civilization [is] driving their diseased minds until the results are criminal records. Perhaps here, in conjunction with tuberculosis, will be the end of the negro problem. Disease will accomplish what man cannot do.[17]

This particular configuration of ideas formed the core of medical opinion concerning blacks, sex, and disease in the early twentieth century. Doctors generally discounted socioeconomic explanations of the state of black health, arguing that better medical care could not alter the evolutionary scheme.[18] These assumptions provide the backdrop for examining the Tuskegee Syphilis Study.

THE ORIGINS OF THE EXPERIMENT

In 1929, under a grant from the Julius Rosenwald Fund, the USPHS conducted studies in the rural South to determine the prevalence of syphilis among blacks and explore possibilities for mass treatment. The USPHS found Macon County, Alabama, in which the town of Tuskegee is located, to have the highest syphilis rate of the six counties surveyed. The Rosenwald Study concluded that mass treatment could be successfully implemented among rural blacks.[19] Although it is doubtful that the necessary funds would have been allocated even in the best economic conditions, after the economy collapsed in 1929, the findings were ignored. It is, however, ironic that the Tuskegee Study came to be based on findings of the Rosenwald Study that demonstrated the possibilities of mass treatment.

Three years later, in 1932, Dr. Taliaferro Clark, chief of the USPHS Venereal Disease Division and author of the Rosenwald Study report, decided that conditions in Macon County merited renewed attention. Clark believed the high prevalence of syphilis offered an "unusual opportunity" for observation. From its inception, the USPHS regarded the Tuskegee Study as a classic "study in nature,"* rather than an experiment.[20] As long as syphilis was so prevalent in Macon and most of the blacks went untreated throughout life, it seemed only natural to Clark that it would be valuable to observe the consequences. He described it as a "ready-made situation."[21] Surgeon General H. S. Cumming wrote to R. R. Moton, director of the Tuskegee Institute:

The recent syphilis control demonstration carried out in Macon County, with the financial assistance of the Julius Rosenwald Fund, revealed the presence of an unusually high rate in this county and, what is more remarkable, the fact that 99 per cent of this group was entirely without previous treatment. This combination, together with the expected cooperation of your hospital, offers an unparalleled opportunity for carrying on this piece of scientific research which probably cannot be duplicated anywhere else in the world.[22]

Although no formal protocol appears to have been written, several letters of Clark and Cumming suggest what the USPHS hoped to find. Clark indicated that it would be important to see how disease affected the daily lives of the men:

The results of these studies of case records suggest the desirability of making a further study of the effect of untreated syphilis on the human economy among people now living and engaged in their daily pursuits.[23]

It also seems that the USPHS believed the experiment might demonstrate that antisyphilitic treatment was unnecessary. As Cumming noted: "It is expected the results of this study may have a marked bearing on the treatment, or conversely the non-necessity of treatment, of cases of latent syphilis."[24] . . .

SELECTING THE SUBJECTS

Clark sent Dr. Raymond Vonderlehr to Tuskegee in September 1932 to assemble a sample of men with latent syphilis for the experiment. The basic design of the study called for the selection of syphilitic black males between the ages of twenty-five and sixty, a thorough physical examination including x-rays, and finally, a spinal tap to determine the incidence of neurosyphilis.[25] They had no intention of providing any treatment for the infected men.[26] The USPHS originally scheduled the whole experiment to last six months; it seemed to be both a simple and inexpensive project.

The task of collecting the sample, however, proved to be more difficult than the USPHS had supposed. Vonderlehr canvassed the largely illiterate, poverty-stricken population of sharecroppers and tenant farmers in search of test subjects. If his circulars requested only men over twenty-five to attend his clinics, none would appear, suspecting he was conducting draft physicals. Therefore, he was forced to test large numbers of women and men who did not fit the experiment's specifications. This involved considerable expense since the USPHS had promised the Macon County Board of Health that it would treat those who were infected but not included in the study.[27] Clark wrote to Vonderlehr about the situation: "It never once occurred to me that we would be called upon to treat a large part of the county as return for the privilege of making this study. . . . I am anxious to keep the expenditures for treatment down to the lowest possible point because it is the one item of expenditure in connection with the study most difficult to defend despite our knowledge of the need therefor."[28] Vonderlehr responded: "If we could find from 100 to 200 cases . . . we would not have to do another Wassermann on useless individuals. . . ."[29]

Significantly, the attempt to develop the sample contradicted the prediction the USPHS had made initially regarding the prevalence of the disease in Macon County. Overall rates of syphilis fell well below expectations; as opposed to the USPHS projection of 35 percent, 20 percent of those tested were actually diseased.[30] Moreover, those who had sought and received previous treatment far exceeded the expectations of the USPHS. Clark noted in a letter to Vonderlehr:

I find your report of March 6th quite interesting but regret the necessity for Wassermanning [sic] . . . such a large number of individuals in order to uncover this relatively limited number of untreated cases.[31]

Further difficulties arose in enlisting the subjects to participate in the experiment, to be "Wassermanned," and to return for a subsequent series of examinations. Vonderlehr found that only the offer of treatment elicited the cooperation of the men. They were told they were ill and were promised free care. Offered therapy, they became willing subjects.[32] The USPHS did not tell the men that they were participants in an experiment; on the contrary, the subjects believed they were being treated for "bad blood"—the rural South's colloquialism for syphilis. They thought they were participating in a public health demonstration similar to the one that had been conducted by the Julius Rosenwald Fund in Tuskegee several years earlier. In the end, the men were so eager for medical care that the number of defaulters in the experiment proved to be insignificant.[33]

To preserve the subjects' interest, Vonderlehr gave most of the men mercurial ointment, a noneffective drug, while some of the younger men apparently received inadequate dosages of neoarsphenamine.[34] This required Vonderlehr to write frequently to Clark requesting supplies. He feared the experiment would fail if the men were not offered treatment. . . .

The readiness of the test subjects to participate of course contradicted the notion that blacks would not seek or continue therapy.

The final procedure of the experiment was to be a spinal tap to test for evidence of neurosyphilis. The USPHS presented this purely diagnostic exam, which often entails considerable pain and complications, to the men as a "special treatment." Clark explained to Moore:

We have not yet commenced the spinal punctures. This operation will be deferred to the last in order not to unduly disturb our field work by any adverse reports by the patients subjected to spinal puncture because of some disagreeable sensations following this procedure. These negroes are very ignorant and easily influenced by things that would be of minor significance in a more intelligent group.[35]

The letter to the subjects announcing the spinal tap read:

Some time ago you were given a thorough examination and since that time we hope you have gotten a great deal of treatment for bad blood. You will now be given your last chance to get a second examination. This examination is a very special one and after it is finished you will be given a special treatment if it is believed you are in a condition to stand it. . . .
REMEMBER THIS IS YOUR LAST CHANCE FOR SPECIAL FREE TREATMENT. BE SURE TO MEET THE NURSE.[36]

The HEW investigation did not uncover this crucial fact: the men participated in the study under the guise of treatment.

Despite the fact that their assumption regarding prevalence and black attitudes toward treatment had proved wrong, the USPHS decided in the summer of 1933 to continue the study. Once again, it seemed only "natural" to pursue the research since the sample already existed, and with a depressed economy, the cost of treatment appeared prohibitive—although there is no indication it was ever considered. Vonderlehr first suggested extending the study in letters to Clark and Wenger:

At the end of this project we shall have a considerable number of cases presenting various complications of syphilis, who have received only mercury and may still be considered untreated in the modern sense of therapy. Should these cases be followed over a period of from five to ten years many interesting facts could be learned regarding the course and complications of untreated syphilis.[37]

"As I see it," responded Wenger, "we have no further interest in these patients *until they die.*"[38] Apparently, the physicians engaged in the experiment believed that only autopsies could scientifically confirm the findings of the study. . . .

Bringing the men to autopsy required the USPHS to devise a further series of deceptions and inducements. Wenger warned Vonderlehr that the men must not realize that they would be autopsied:

There is one danger in the latter plan and that is if the colored population become aware that accepting free hospital care means a post-mortem, every darkey will leave Macon County and it will hurt [Dr. Eugene] Dibble's hospital.[39]

The USPHS offered several inducements to maintain contact and to procure the continued cooperation of the men. Eunice Rivers, a black nurse, was hired to follow their health and to secure approval for autopsies. She gave the men non-effective medicines—"spring tonic" and aspirin—as well as transportation and hot meals on the days of their examinations.[40] More important, Nurse Rivers provided continuity to the project over the entire forty-year period. By supplying "medicinals," the USPHS was able to continue to deceive the participants, who believed that they were receiving therapy from the government doctors. Deceit was integral to the study. When the test subjects complained about spinal taps, one doctor wrote:

They simply do not like spinal punctures. A few of those who were tapped are enthusiastic over the results but to most, the suggestion causes violent shaking of the head; others claim they were robbed of their procreative powers (regardless of the fact that I claim it stimulates them).[41]

Letters to the subjects announcing an impending USPHS visit to Tuskegee explained: "[The doctor] wants to make a special examination to find out how you have been feeling and whether the treatment has improved your health."[42] In fact, after the first six months of the study, the USPHS had furnished no treatment whatsoever.

Finally, because it proved difficult to persuade the men to come to the hospital when they became severely ill, the USPHS promised to cover their burial expenses. The Milbank Memorial Fund provided approximately $50 per man for this purpose beginning in 1935. This was a particularly strong inducement as funeral rites constituted an important component of the cultural life of rural blacks.[43] One report of the study concluded, "Without this suasion it would, we believe, have been impossible to secure the cooperation of the group and their families."[44]

Reports of the study's findings, which appeared regularly in the medical press beginning in 1936, consistently cited the ravages of untreated syphilis. The first paper, read at the 1936 American Medical Association annual meeting, found "that syphilis in this period [latency] tends to greatly increase the frequency of manifestations of cardiovascular disease."[45] Only 16 percent of the subjects gave no sign of morbidity as opposed to 61 percent of the controls. Ten years later, a report noted coldly, "The fact that nearly twice as large a proportion of the syphilitic individuals as of the control group has died is a very striking one." Life expectancy, concluded the doctors, is reduced by about 20 percent.[46]

A 1955 article found that slightly more than 30 percent of the test group autopsied had died *directly* from advanced syphilitic lesions of either the cardiovascular or the central nervous system.[47] Another published account stated, "Review of those still living reveals that an appreciable number have late complications of syphilis which probably will result, for some at least, in contributing materially to the ultimate cause of death."[48] In 1950, Dr. Wenger had concluded, "We now know, where we could only surmise before, that we have contributed to their ailments and shortened their lives."[49] As black physician Vernal Cave, a member of the HEW panel, later wrote, "They proved a point, then proved a point, then proved a point."[50]

During the forty years of the experiment the USPHS had sought on several occasions to ensure that the subjects did not receive treatment from other sources. To this end, Vonderlehr met with groups of local black doctors in 1934, to ask their cooperation in not treating the men. Lists of subjects were distributed to Macon County physicians along with letters requesting them to refer these men back to the USPHS if they sought care.[51] The USPHS warned the Alabama Health Department not to treat the test subjects when they took a mobile VD unit into Tuskegee in the early 1940s.[52] In 1941, the Army drafted several subjects and told them to begin antisyphilitic treatment immediately. The USPHS supplied the draft board with a list of 256 names they desired to have excluded from treatment, and the board complied.[53]

In spite of these efforts, by the early 1950s many of the men had secured some treatment on their own. By 1952, almost 30 percent of the test subjects had received some penicillin, although only 7.5 percent had received what could be considered adequate doses.[54] Vonderlehr wrote to one of the participating physicians, "I hope that the availability of antibiotics has not interfered too much with this project."[55] A report published in 1955 considered whether the treatment that some of the men had obtained had "defeated" the study. The article attempted to explain the relatively low exposure to penicillin in an age of antibiotics, suggesting as a reason: "the stoicism of these men as a group; they still regard hospitals and medicines with suspicion and prefer an occasional dose of time-honored herbs or tonics to modern drugs."[56] The authors failed to note that the men believed they already were under the care of the government doctors and thus saw no need to seek treatment elsewhere. Any treatment which the men might have received, concluded the report, had been insufficient to compromise the experiment.

When the USPHS evaluated the status of the study in the 1960s, they continued to rationalize the racial aspects of the experiment. For example, the minutes of a 1965 meeting at the CDC recorded:

Racial issue was mentioned briefly. Will not affect the study. Any questions can be handled by saying these people were at the point that therapy would no longer help them. They are getting better medical care than they would under any other circumstances.[57]

A group of physicians met again at the CDC in 1969 to decide whether or not to terminate the study. Although one doctor argued that the study should be stopped and the men treated, the consensus was to continue. Dr. J. Lawton Smith remarked, "You will never have another study like this; take advantage of it."[58] A memo prepared by Dr. James B. Lucas, assistant chief of the Venereal Disease Branch, stated: "Nothing learned will prevent, find, or cure a single case of infectious syphilis or bring us closer to our basic mission of controlling venereal disease in the United States."[59] He concluded, however, that the study should be continued "along its present lines." When the first accounts of the experiment appeared in the national press in July 1972, data were still being collected and autopsies performed.[60]

THE HEW FINAL REPORT

HEW finally formed the Tuskegee Syphilis Study Ad Hoc Advisory Panel on August 28, 1972, in response to criticism that the press descriptions of the experiment had triggered. The panel, composed of nine members, five

of them black, concentrated on two issues. First, was the study justified in 1932 and had the men given their informed consent? Second, should penicillin have been provided when it became available in the early 1950s? The panel was also charged with determining if the study should be terminated and assessing current policies regarding experimentation with human subjects.[61] The group issued their report in June 1973.

By focusing on the issues of penicillin therapy and informed consent, the *Final Report* and the investigation betrayed a basic misunderstanding of the experiment's purposes and design. The HEW report implied that the failure to provide penicillin constituted the study's major ethical misjudgment; implicit was the assumption that no adequate therapy existed prior to penicillin. Nonetheless medical authorities firmly believed in the efficacy of arsenotherapy for treating syphilis at the time of the experiment's inception in 1932. The panel further failed to recognize that the entire study had been predicated on nontreatment. Provision of effective medication would have violated the rationale of the experiment—to study the natural course of the disease until death. On several occasions, in fact, the USPHS had prevented the men from receiving proper treatment. Indeed, there is no evidence that the USPHS ever considered providing penicillin.

The other focus of the *Final Report*—informed consent—also served to obscure the historical facts of the experiment. In light of the deceptions and exploitations which the experiment perpetrated, it is an understatement to declare, as the *Report* did, that the experiment was "ethically unjustified" because it failed to obtain informed consent from the subjects. The *Final Report*'s statement, "Submitting voluntarily is not informed consent," indicated that the panel believed that the men had volunteered *for the experiment*.[62] The records in the National Archives make clear that the men did not submit voluntarily to an experiment; they were told and they believed that they were getting free treatment from expert government doctors for a serious disease. The failure of the HEW *Final Report* to expose this critical fact—that the USPHS lied to the subjects—calls into question the thoroughness and credibility of their investigation.

Failure to place the study in a historical context also made it impossible for the investigation to deal with the essentially racist nature of the experiment. The panel treated the study as an aberration, well-intentioned but misguided.[63] Moreover, concern that the *Final Report* might be viewed as a critique of human experimentation in general seems to have severely limited the scope of the inquiry. The *Final Report* is quick to remind the reader on two occasions: "The position of the Panel must not be construed to be a general repudiation of scientific research with human subjects."[64] The *Report* assures us that a better designed experiment could have been justified:

It is possible that a scientific study in 1932 of untreated syphilis, properly conceived with a clear protocol and conducted with suitable subjects who fully understood the implications of their involvement, might have been justified in the pre-penicillin era. This is especially true when one considers the uncertain nature of the results of treatment of late latent syphilis and the highly toxic nature of therapeutic agents then available.[65]

This statement is questionable in view of the proven dangers of untreated syphilis known in 1932.

Since the publication of the HEW *Final Report,* a defense of the Tuskegee Study has emerged. These arguments, most clearly articulated by Dr. R. H. Kampmeier in the *Southern Medical Journal,* center on the limited knowledge of effective therapy for latent syphilis when the experiment began. Kampmeier argues that by 1950, penicillin would have been of no value for these men.[66] Others have suggested that the

men were fortunate to have been spared the highly toxic treatments of the earlier period.[67] Moreover, even these contemporary defenses assume that the men never would have been treated anyway. As Dr. Charles Barnett of Stanford University wrote in 1974, "The lack of treatment was not contrived by the USPHS but was an established fact of which they proposed to take advantage."[68] Several doctors who participated in the study continued to justify the experiment. Dr. J. R. Heller, who on one occasion had referred to the test subjects as the "Ethiopian population," told reporters in 1972:

I don't see why they should be shocked or horrified. There was no racial side to this. It just happened to be in a black community. I feel this was a perfectly straightforward study, perfectly ethical, with controls. Part of our mission as physicians is to find out what happens to individuals with disease and without disease.[69]

These apologies, as well as the HEW *Final Report,* ignore many of the essential ethical issues which the study poses. The Tuskegee Study reveals the persistence of beliefs within the medical profession about the nature of blacks, sex, and disease—beliefs that had tragic repercussions long after their alleged "scientific" bases were known to be incorrect. Most strikingly, the entire health of a community was jeopardized by leaving a communicable disease untreated.[70] There can be little doubt that the Tuskegee researchers regarded their subjects as less than human.[71] As a result, the ethical canons of experimenting on human subjects were completely disregarded.

The study also raises significant questions about professional self-regulation and scientific bureaucracy. Once the USPHS decided to extend the experiment in the summer of 1933, it was unlikely that the test would be halted short of the men's deaths. The experiment was widely reported for forty years without evoking any significant protest within the medical community. Nor did any bureaucratic mechanism exist within the government for the periodic reassessment of the Tuskegee experiment's ethics and scientific value. The USPHS sent physicians to Tuskegee every several years to check on the study's progress, but never subjected the morality or usefulness of the experiment to serious scrutiny. Only the press accounts of 1972 finally punctured the continued rationalizations of the USPHS and brought the study to an end. Even the HEW investigation was compromised by fear that it would be considered a threat to future human experimentation.

In retrospect the Tuskegee Study revealed more about the pathology of racism than it did about the pathology of syphilis; more about the nature of scientific inquiry than the nature of the disease process. The injustice committed by the experiment went well beyond the facts outlined in the press and the HEW *Final Report*. The degree of deception and damages have been seriously underestimated. As this history of the study suggests, the notion that science is a value-free discipline must be rejected. The need for greater vigilance in assessing the specific ways in which social values and attitudes affect professional behavior is clearly indicated.

EDITOR'S NOTE

On May 16, 1997, President Bill Clinton apologized to the participants in the Tuskegee Study. He acknowledged that the U.S. government had done "something that was wrong—deeply, profoundly, and morally wrong."

NOTES

* In 1865, Claude Bernard, the famous French physiologist, outlined the distinction between a "study in nature" and experimentation. A study in nature required simple observation, an essentially passive act, while experimentation demanded intervention which altered the original condition. The Tuskegee Study was thus clearly not a study in nature. The very act of diagnosis altered the original conditions. "It is on this very possibility of acting or not acting on a body," wrote Bernard, "that the distinction will exclusively rest between sciences called sciences of observation and sciences called experimental."

1. The best general accounts of the study are "The 40-Year Death Watch," *Medical World News* (August 18, 1972), pp. 15–17; and Dolores Katz, "Why 430 Blacks with Syphilis Went Uncured for 40 Years," Detroit *Free Press* (November 5, 1972). The mortality figure is based on a published report of the study which appeared in 1955. See Jesse J. Peters, James H. Peers, Sidney Olansky, John C. Cutler, and Geraldine Gleeson, "Untreated Syphilis in the Male Negro: Pathologic Findings in Syphilitic and Nonsyphilitic Patients," *Journal of Chronic Diseases* 1 (February 1955), 127–48. The article estimated that 30.4 percent of the untreated men would die from syphilitic lesions.

2. *Final Report* of the Tuskegee Syphilis Study Ad Hoc Advisory Panel, Department of Health, Education, and Welfare (Washington, D.C.: GPO, 1973). (Hereafter, HEW *Final Report*.)

3. See George M. Frederickson, *The Black Image in the White Mind* (New York: Harper and Row, 1971), pp. 228–55. Also, John H. Haller, *Outcasts From Evolution* (Urbana, Ill.: University of Illinois Press, 1971), pp. 40–68.

4. Frederickson, pp. 247–49.

5. "Deterioration of the American Negro," *Atlanta Journal-Record of Medicine* 5 (July 1903), 287–88. See also, J. A. Rodgers, "The Effect of Freedom upon the Psychological Development of the Negro," *Proceedings* of the American Medico-Psychological Association 7 (1900), 88–99. "From the most healthy race in the country forty years ago," concluded Dr. Henry McHatton, "he is today the most diseased." "The Sexual Status of the Negro—Past and Present," *American Journal of Dermatology and Genito-Urinary Diseases* 10 (January 1906), 7–9.

6. W. T. English, "The Negro Problem from the Physician's Point of View," *Atlanta Journal-Record of Medicine* 5 (October 1903), 461. See also, "Racial Anatomical Peculiarities," *New York Medical Journal* 63 (April 1896), 500–01.

7. "Racial Anatomical Peculiarities," p. 501. Also, Charles S. Bacon, "The Race Problem," *Medicine* (Detroit) 9 (May 1903), 338–43.

8. H. H. Hazen, "Syphilis in the American Negro," *Journal of the American Medical Association* 63 (August 8, 1914), 463. For deeper background into the historical relationship of racism and sexuality see Winthrop D. Jordan, *White Over Black* (Chapel Hill: University of North Carolina Press, 1968: Pelican Books, 1969), pp. 32–40.

9. Daniel David Quillian, "Racial Peculiarities: A Cause of the Prevalence of Syphilis in Negroes," *American Journal of Dermatology and Genito-Urinary Diseases* 10 (July 1906), p. 277.

10. English, p. 463.

11. William Lee Howard, "The Negro as a Distinct Ethnic Factor in Civilization," *Medicine* (Detroit) 9 (June 1903), 424. See also, Thomas W. Murrell, "Syphilis

in the American Negro," *Journal of the American Medical Association* 54 (March 12, 1910), 848.

12. "Castration Instead of Lynching," *Atlanta Journal-Record of Medicine* 8 (October 1906), 457. The editorial added: "The badge of disgrace and emasculation might be branded upon the face or forehead, as a warning, in the form of an 'R,' emblematic of the crime for which this punishment was and will be inflicted."

13. Searle Harris, "The Future of the Negro from the Standpoint of the Southern Physician," *Alabama Medical Journal* 14 (January 1902), 62. Other articles on the prevalence of venereal disease among blacks are: H. L. McNeil, "Syphilis in the Southern Negro," *Journal of the American Medical Association* 67 (September 1916), 1001–04; Ernest Philip Boas, "The Relative Prevalence of Syphilis Among Negroes and Whites," *Social Hygiene* 1 (September 1915), 610–16. Doctors went to considerable trouble to distinguish the morbidity and mortality of various diseases among blacks and whites. See, for example, Marion M. Torchia, "Tuberculosis Among American Negroes: Medical Research on a Racial Disease, 1830–1950," *Journal of the History of Medicine and Allied Sciences* 32 (July 1977), 252–79.

14. Thomas W. Murrell, "Syphilis in the Negro: Its Bearing on the Race Problem," *American Journal of Dermatology and Genito-Urinary Diseases* 10 (August 1906), 307.

15. "Even among the educated, only a very few will carry out the most elementary instructions as to personal hygiene. One thing you cannot do, and that is to convince the negro that he has a disease that he cannot see or feel. This is due to lack of concentration rather than lack of faith; even if he does believe, he does not care; a child of fancy, the sensations of the passing hour are his only guides to the future." Murrell, "Syphilis in the American Negro," p. 847.

16. "Deterioration of the American Negro," *Atlanta Journal-Record of Medicine* 5 (July 1903), 288.

17. Murrell, "Syphilis in the Negro: Its Bearing on the Race Problem," p. 307.

18. "The anatomical and physiological conditions of the African must be understood, his place in the anthropological scale realized, and his biological basis accepted as being unchangeable by man, before we shall be able to govern his natural uncontrollable sexual passions." See, "As Ye Sow That Shall Ye Also Reap," *Atlanta Journal-Record of Medicine* 1 (June 1899), 266.

19. Taliaferro Clark, *The Control of Syphilis in Southern Rural Areas* (Chicago: Julius Rosenwald Fund, 1932), 53–58. Approximately 35 percent of the inhabitants of Macon County who were examined were found to be syphilitic.

20. See Claude Bernard, *An Introduction to the Study of Experimental Medicine* (New York: Dover, 1865, 1957), pp. 5–26.

21. Taliaferro Clark to M. M. Davis, October 29, 1932. Records of the USPHS Venereal Disease Division, Record Group 90, Box 239, National Archives, Washington National Records Center, Suitland, Maryland. (Hereafter, NA-WNRC.) Materials in this collection which relate to the early history of the study were apparently never consulted by the HEW investigation. Included are letters, reports, and memoranda written by the physicians engaged in the study.

22. H. S. Cumming to R. R. Moton, September 20, 1932, NA-WNRC.

23. Clark to Davis, October 29, 1932, NA-WNRC.

24. Cumming to Moton, September 20, 1932, NA-WNRC.

25. Clark Memorandum, September 26, 1932, NA-WNRC. See also, Clark to Davis, October 29, 1932, NA-WNRC.

26. As Clark wrote: "You will observe that our plan has nothing to do with treatment. It is purely a diagnostic procedure carried out to determine what has happened to the syphilitic Negro who has had no treatment." Clark to Paul A. O'Leary, September 27, 1932, NA-WNRC.

27. D. G. Gill to O. C. Wenger, October 10, 1932, NA-WNRC.

28. Clark to Vonderlehr, January 25, 1933, NA-WNRC.

29. Vonderlehr to Clark, February 28, 1933, NA-WNRC.

30. Vonderlehr to Clark, November 2, 1932, NA-WNRC. Also, Vonderlehr to Clark, February 6, 1933, NA-WNRC.

31. Clark to Vonderlehr, March 9, 1933, NA-WNRC.

32. Vonderlehr later explained: "The reason treatment was given to many of these men was twofold: First, when the study was started in the fall of 1932, no plans had been made for its continuation and a few of the patients were treated before we fully realized the need for continuing the project on a permanent basis. Second it was difficult to hold the interest of the group of Negroes in Macon County unless some treatment was given. Vonderlehr to Austin V. Diebert, December 5, 1938. Tuskegee Syphilis Study Ad Hoc Advisory Panel Papers, Box 1, National Library of Medicine, Bethesda, Maryland. (Hereafter, TSS-NLM.) This collection contains the materials assembled by the HEW investigation in 1972.

33. Vonderlehr to Clark, February 6, 1933, NA-WNRC.

34. H. S. Cumming to J. N. Baker, August 5, 1933, NA-WNRC.

35. Clark to Moore, March 25, 1933, NA-WNRC.

36. Macon County Health Department, "Letter to Subjects," n.d., NA-WNRC.

37. Vonderlehr to Clark, April 8, 1933, NA-WNRC. See also, Vonderlehr to Wenger, July 18, 1933, NA-WNRC.

38. Wenger to Vonderlehr, July 21, 1933, NA-WNRC. The emphasis is Wenger's.

39. Wenger to Vonderlehr, July 21, 1933, NA-WNRC.

40. Eunice Rivers, Stanely Schuman, Lloyd Simpson, Sidney Olansky, "Twenty-Years of Followup Experience in a Long-Range Medical Study," *Public Health Reports* 68 (April 1953), 391–95. In this article Nurse Rivers explains her role in the

experiment. She wrote: "Because of the low educational status of the majority of the patients, it was impossible to appeal to them from a purely scientific approach. Therefore, various methods were used to maintain their interest. Free medicines, burial assistance of insurance (the project being referred to as 'Miss Rivers' Lodge'), free hot meals on the days of examination, transportation to and from the hospital, and an opportunity to stop in town on the return trip to shop or visit with their friends on the streets all helped. In spite of these attractions, there were some who refused their examinations because they were not sick and did not see that they were being benefited" (p. 393).

41. Austin V. Diebert to Raymond Vonderlehr, March 20, 1939, TSS-NLM, Box 1.

42. Murray Smith to Subjects, (1938), TSS-NLM, Box 1. See also, Sidney Olansky to John C. Cutler, November 6, 1951, TSS-NLM, Box 2.

43. The USPHS originally requested that the Julius Rosenwald Fund meet this expense. See Cumming to Davis, October 4, 1934, NA-WNRC. This money was usually divided between the undertaker, pathologist, and hospital. Lloyd Isaacs to Raymond Vonderlehr, April 23, 1940, TSS-NLM, Box 1.

44. Stanley H. Schuman, Sidney Olansky, Eunice Rivers, C. A. Smith, Dorothy S. Rambo, "Untreated Syphilis in the Male Negro: Background and Current Status of Patients in the Tuskegee Study," *Journal of Chronic Diseases* 2 (November 1955), 555.

45. R. A. Vonderlehr and Taliaferro Clark, "Untreated Syphilis in the Male Negro," *Venereal Disease Information* 17 (September 1936), 262.

46. J. R. Heller and P. T. Bruyere, "Untreated Syphilis in the Male Negro: II. Mortality During 12 Years of Observation," *Venereal Disease Information* 27 (February 1946), 34–38.

47. Jesse J. Peters, James H. Peers, Sidney Olansky, John C. Cutler, and Geraldine Gleeson, "Untreated Syphilis in the Male Negro: Pathologic Findings in Syphilitic and Non-Syphilitic Patients," *Journal of Chronic Diseases* 1 (February 1955), 127–48.

48. Sidney Olansky, Standley H. Schuman, Jesse J. Peters, C. A. Smith, and Dorothy S. Rambo, "Untreated Syphilis in the Male Negro, X. Twenty Years of Clinical Observation of Untreated Syphilitic and Presumably Nonsyphilitic Groups," *Journal of Chronic Diseases* 4 (August 1956), 184.

49. O. C. Wenger, "Untreated Syphilis in Male Negro," unpublished typescript, 1950, p. 3. Tuskegee Files, Centers for Disease Control, Atlanta, Georgia. (Hereafter TF-CDC.)

50. Vernal G. Cave, "Proper Uses and Abuses of the Health Care Delivery System for Minorities with Special Reference to the Tuskegee Syphilis Study," *Journal of the National Medical Association* 67 (January 1975), 83.

51. See, for example, Vonderlehr to B. W. Booth, April 18, 1934; Vonderlehr to E. R. Lett, November 20, 1933, NA-WNRC.

52. "Transcript of Proceedings—Tuskegee Syphilis Ad Hoc Advisory Panel," February 23, 1973, unpublished typescript, TSS-NLM, Box 1.

53. Raymond Vonderlehr to Murray Smith, April 30, 1942; and Smith to Vonderlehr, June 8, 1942, TSS-NLM, Box 1.

54. Stanley H. Schuman, Sidney Olansky, Eunice Rivers, C. A. Smith, and Dorothy S. Rambo, "Untreated Syphilis in the Male Negro: Background and Current Status of Patients in the Tuskegee Study," *Journal of Chronic Diseases* 2 (November 1955), 550–53.

55. Raymond Vonderlehr to Stanley H. Schuman, February 5, 1952, TSS-NLM, Box 2.

56. Schuman et al., p. 550.

57. "Minutes, April 5, 1965," unpublished typescript, TSS-NLM, Box 1.

58. "Tuskegee Ad Hoc Committee Meeting—Minutes, February 6, 1969," TF-CDC.

59. James B. Lucas to William J. Brown, September 10, 1970, TF-CDC.

60. Elizabeth M. Kennebrew to Arnold C. Schroeter, February 24, 1971, TSS-NLM, Box 1.

61. See *Medical Tribune* (September 13, 1972), pp. 1, 20; and "Report on HEW's Tuskegee Report," *Medical World News* (September 14, 1973), pp. 57–58.

62. HEW *Final Report*, p. 7.

63. The notable exception is Jay Katz's eloquent "Reservations About the Panel Report on Charge 1," HEW *Final Report*, pp. 14–15.

64. HEW *Final Report*, pp. 8, 12.

65. Hew *Final Report*, pp. 8, 12.

66. See R. H. Kampmeier, "The Tuskegee Study of Untreated Syphilis," *Southern Medical Journal* 65 (October 1972), 1247–51; and "Final Report on the Tuskegee Syphilis Study,'" *Southern Medical Journal* 67 (November 1974), 1349–53.

67. Leonard J. Goldwater, "The Tuskegee Study in Historical Perspective," unpublished typescript, TSS-NLM; see also, "Treponemes and Tuskegee," *Lancet* (June 23, 1973), p. 1438; and Louis Lasagna, *The VD Epidemic* (Philadelphia: Temple University Press, 1975), pp. 64–66.

68. Quoted in "Debate Revives on the PHS Study," *Medical World News* (April 19, 1974), p. 37.

69. Heller to Vonderlehr, November 28, 1933, NA-WNRC; quoted in *Medical Tribune* (August 23, 1972), p. 14.

70. Although it is now known that syphilis is rarely infectious after its early phase, at the time of the study's inception latent syphilis was thought to be communicable.

The fact that members of the control group were placed in the test group when they became syphilitic proves that at least some infectious men were denied treatment.

71. When the subjects are drawn from minority groups, especially those with which the researcher cannot identify, basic human rights may be compromised. Hans Jonas has clearly explicated the problem in his "Philosophical Reflections on Experimentation," *Daedalus* 98 (Spring 1969), 234–37. As Jonas writes: "If the properties we adduced as the particular qualifications of the members of the scientific fraternity itself are taken as general criteria of selection, then one should look for additional subjects where a maximum of identification, understanding, and spontaneity can be expected—that is, among the most highly motivated, the most highly educated, and the least 'captive' members of the community."

SEXING UP THE SUBJECT: METHODOLOGICAL NUANCES IN RESEARCHING THE FEMALE SEX INDUSTRY

TEELA SANDERS

Despite the interdisciplinary accounts of the sex industry, apart from some reflective revelations (for instance by Hart, 1998; Hubbard, 1999a; Maher, 2000; Melrose, 2002; O'Connell Davidson, 1998; O'Neill, 1996; Sharpe, 2000; Shaver, 2005), researchers have been reluctant to report on the methodological demands of this topic. These pieces of work highlight the importance of reflexivity in the researcher process—a research account that is aware that the researcher is of the world being studied and therefore should be included in the process of analysis. . . . This article explores the methodological challenges that question existing procedural boundaries and push the parameters of the qualitative method as the subject becomes increasingly sexual. Drawing on my own ethnography in the indoor prostitution markets (see Sanders, 2005a), this article reflects mostly on research into female adult consensual prostitution but will refer to other aspects of the non-contact sexual services such as pornography and erotic dancing.

STUMBLING AT THE FIRST HURDLE: ETHICS COMMITTEES

Much of what has been written about the ethics of fieldwork and the sex industry focuses on what happens in the field. Yet increasingly, one of the first stumbling blocks for the researcher (especially students) is gaining approval for the project from the internal institution's ethics committee. With these regulatory bodies becoming an increasing part of funding applications and university bureaucracies, having a vague plan and heading into the field is becoming less of an option. Anecdotally it can be said that ethics committees have treated the sex industry as a problematic area of inquiry, which can sometimes result in projects failing at this initial stage. An example from Mattely (1997) demonstrates how funding research into prostitution continues to be stifled by stigma and excluded by research councils. This section teases out three familiar areas of suspicion that are charged at those wanting to research sex work: the methods employed, the setting of the fieldwork and concerns for the reputation of the institution.

Methodological concerns are often raised at ethics committees when the method of inquiry is based on an ethnographic style that places informality at the heart of the data collection. Invariably this method requires lengthy periods of observation, interviews that can take the form of informal conversations and other methods that are unorthodox in the minds of positivist thinkers. As a result, committees can query the validity of the methods, whether enough information will be collected and the quality of the data. For instance, in situations where interviews cannot be taped, data collection relies on fieldnotes and memory, which raises questions about how information can be accurately recorded. In addition, as Shaver (2005) documents, researchers in

From "Sexing Up the Subject: Methodological Nuances in Researching the Female Sex Industry," *Sexualities* 9(4), pp. 449–68. Copyright © 2006 by the Author. Reprinted by permission of SAGE Publications, Ltd.

the sex industry are constantly struggling with the unknown size and boundaries of the population, leading to queries of sample representation. Covert methods have also been adopted in sex work research, highlighting the difficulties of informing all parties that are being observed, often for the sake of access and at the request of sex workers and managers. Ethics committees are usually hostile to covert methods, as they can appear unethical and potentially dangerous for the researcher. Stereotypes and misunderstandings about the research setting exacerbate these generic concerns about the methods often employed when studying the sex work field.

The setting, whether it is a "red light district," crack house or illegal brothel, is often the focus of concern raised by ethics committees. Is this the correct environment for research to be conducted, or for a student to be initiated into the research culture? Questions of danger always arise because of stereotypes that link prostitution to criminality, especially drug-related crimes. Associations between HIV, drug-injecting sex workers, vicious and violent male pimps and the sex work setting all surface with the prospects of researching the sex industry. Fuelled by assumptions about the type of people who organize and work in the sex industry, as well as the men who buy sex, the researcher is expected to take extra precautions when assessing participants and field sites. In addition, the routines that the researcher will be expected to engage in usually entail long hours in fairly unknown or secluded locations, often late at night, and sometimes alone.

The danger that the researcher is exposed to is a central concern of officials, but this can sometimes be a disguise for more pressing anxieties about the reputation of the institution. As a postgraduate student, my own research (which was originally based on an internet survey of the sex work community) was scrutinized by the senior officials in the university before it was vetoed as an unacceptable area of inquiry and methodological design (see Sanders, 2005b). Behind this decision was apprehension related to preserving the reputation of the university and concerns about media headlines that linked students to the seedy underworld environment in the name of completing a doctorate. . . .

However, there are solutions to these ethical trials. The plethora of successful work in this field, using both ethnographic and more mainstream methods, is a testament to the appropriateness of the sex industry as a field site. The general literature that explains the limitations of informed consent in all circumstances and the acceptability of covert inquiry within an ethical framework that prioritizes the anonymity of those being studied, can be used to demonstrate the feasibility of the design. There are few horror stories reported (this does not mean that researchers have not experienced some difficult and vulnerable situations), and good quality accounts of ethnography explain the basic rules of engagement, such as finding a gatekeeper who acts as a protector (Hart, 1998: 55; O'Connell Davidson and Layder, 1994). Therefore, it can be demonstrated that despite common conceptions, there are regulators (health workers, sauna owners, police, key informants) in the sex industry who researchers can align themselves with in order to stay out of trouble and learn the local scene.

In addition, researchers in this field can rely on the professional codes of practice promoted by the subject discipline that set out procedures, obligations and expectations of the research process (for example, the British Sociological Association produces guidelines for its members). Often, universities have their own codes of etiquette, which can include safety procedures when researchers are working alone or at night, for instance. Basic safety checks such as never meeting people alone in private, always in a public place, letting a third party know of your whereabouts and checking in after the session has ended, are assurances that go a long way to maintaining safety (see Shaver, 2005: 302 for a thorough account of safety procedures for sex work researchers). The potential dangers and strong stereotypes associated with the sex industry are issues that researchers have to confront before the project gets off the ground. Although this means that research designs are perhaps over-scrutinized and charged with queries that expect more insight from the novice researcher, this encourages the researcher to be reflective even at this initial stage. Thinking ahead to foreseeable problems, having a set of plan B's if the initial methods fail, and taking time out of the fieldwork to reassess are good practice in an intense and volatile environment.

ACCESS AND ACCEPTANCE INTO THE SEX INDUSTRY

For the researcher, the legal status of prostitution and the actual environment are the key considerations when planning the access route.

Prostitution is often located outside a legitimate legal framework and even where the sex industry is legitimate, there are always issues of stigma and deviancy to consider. The different environments that facilitate street and off-street prostitution offer some peculiarities (for a lengthy discussion, see Shaver, 2005). On the street, the environment is vulnerable, as women mainly work at night, in deserted and unlit industrial areas, in an economy that can be linked to other forms of acquisitive crime. Indoors, although not usually characterized by the violence and vulnerabilities of the street scene, the premises of illegal brothels may be well known but getting a foot in the door is a difficult prospect—especially if the researcher

is a woman. Owners, managers and workers are suspicious of unknown inquirers, and women who enter the building are normally looking for work (i.e., competition) or are spying for the opposition. Rarely has it been reported that a researcher has introduced herself or himself to sex workers without a third party mediating the initial introductions.

To sidestep these closed environments, researchers use various gatekeepers to overcome initial hostilities. Some access routes have been outside the sex work environment. For example, the criminal justice system (prisons, bail hostels, courts, probation service and so on) or sexual health and welfare services have traditionally been a successful introduction route to women and men involved in prostitution. Specific sex work outreach projects (see Cooper et al., 2001) have been the most prolific gatekeepers, as their established and trusted ties with street workers and indoor establishments provide researchers with the opportunity to prove their credibility. Hubbard (1999b: 233) explains four principles that must be demonstrated to outreach projects and sex workers to achieve success in the negotiation phase. First, the investigator must establish how the research will produce knowledge to help reduce stigma surrounding prostitution; second, that the researcher has an insight into the reality of prostitution and the circumstances in which sex is sold; third, a recognition that prostitution is a legitimate form of work; and fourth, a belief that health and safety risks should be minimized for sex workers. However, as Melrose (2002: 340) documents, securing access through sexual health projects is not straightforward. This route can be met with refusal because of concerns that the research will demand too much time from the project, disagreement with the premise of the research or the worry that their clients are "over-researched" or exploited. . . .

ACCESSING PRIVATE AND THE PUBLIC LIVES

Once access to sex establishments or sex workers has been achieved, researchers then negotiate whether the research will be conducted in either the working environment or in the private lives and spaces of the sex workers. Despite the difficulties of the prostitution environment, research is often conducted in the working spaces of the commercial sex exchange. By striking "research bargains" and "exchanges" that involve giving out condoms, sterile needle equipment and hot drinks on the street, researchers have been able to observe successfully how the street markets operate. . . . A combination of methods (usually a mixed approach that includes observations and interviews) appears to be a successful recipe for data collection. . . .

Entering the private worlds of women who are involved in activities that are largely disapproved of presented additional ethical issues. On the few occasions I was permitted into the private worlds of participants, I would often be asked to collude with the secrecy stories that sex workers had constructed to hide their money-making activities. I would have to pretend I was a colleague from the office or an acquaintance whilst I chatted to a participant's husband or was invited to stay for tea with the children. An example of the role-playing that I describe in the next section shows how it is an essential tool in the field.

MAKING SENSE OF THE SEXUAL FIELD

When actually doing research in the sex industry where the exchange of sexual services, bodily functions and flesh-to-flesh contact is the everyday trade, the reality of research cannot avoid these characteristics. Although there are similarities with other illicit economies, the setting of the sex industry is unique because the combination of studying sex and money in an illegal arena affects how the research is executed, the dilemmas for the researcher and the immediacy of making decisions in the "sexual" field. For those who are unaware, a typical sauna or brothel can be characterized by televisions showing hard-core pornography, pornographic magazines, sex toys, domination equipment, a menu of sexual services on offer, an explicit photographic gallery of the women who are available and other sex paraphernalia. This environment can be distasteful at best but is often violently shocking and disturbing.

The sexual subtext of the environment is impossible to escape as participants are in their work clothes (which usually consist of very little), buying into the fantasies that tempt customers to part with their cash (see Sanders, 2005c). The physical sexual environment is not the only sexualized element to the fieldwork setting. Men are constantly wandering into the premises and engaging in a set of negotiations with the receptionist (maid) and then (often in private) with the sex worker. Men linger in the communal lounge while they wait for a worker to finish her current client, idling the time away by flicking through a pornographic magazine or watching graphic images on the screen, before they are called to the shower room and finally the specifically chosen bedroom, until, 30 minutes later they come out the other side, £60 lighter. This routinization of the sexual negotiation is a process with which the observer becomes familiar (and perhaps desensitized) and after several sessions of data collection, the process of negotiating sexual services becomes part of the momentum of the fieldwork. . . .

My own experiences of being in the sexual field of the sauna and brothel involved two other methodological nuances that at the time became routinized yet had an intrinsic effect on the way in which information was collected, my role in this foreign arena, and establishing rapport with participants. First, as my role in the sauna was overt to the sex workers but, at the request of the managers, the clients were unaware of my researcher status, I was often propositioned by interested customers. Men would assume I was another worker or a new member of the team and would make propositions and innuendo that had to be managed. Initially flustered, embarrassed and uncomfortable, I soon adopted strategies to deflect their requests: I would either pretend I was "fully booked," a friend of a worker or a sexual health professional, switching between these roles depending on how confident I felt at the time and the amount of backup I had from those around me. Ultimately, role-playing became a necessity in the field, especially where a delicate "research bargain" existed that required keeping my researcher status anonymous to one party while others were aware of the investigation.

Second, the majority of the fieldwork in the indoor sex work venues was conducted amongst women who were semi-naked for most of the time. For instance, my interviews with Beryl, a 39-year-old mother of four who had worked in a range of sex markets for 20 years, took place in the 30-minute slot she allocated each day as her "preparation time" before she welcomed her first customer. In this time, Beryl was showering, shaving, applying makeup, styling her hair, putting on lingerie and at the same time answering my questions. It became natural to see women naked as they changed from one outfit to another, were flitting between bathroom and bedroom or needed a hand squeezing into a particular costume. These situations were non-sexualized and non-erotic, as the women conducted their behaviour in a professional matter-of-fact manner, relegating luxurious lingerie or kinky outfits to the function of a work uniform. Participants approached their work and ultimately the display of their bodies in an entirely pragmatic, de-sexualized and business-like manner with no sense of shame, embarrassment or vulnerability. Explaining their trade as a combination of physical, sexual and emotional labour, the role of the body and their sexuality was afforded different meanings in the context of a money-making economic exchange.

WHAT IS PARTICIPANT OBSERVATION IN THE SEX INDUSTRY?

The ethnographic method in the sex work arena brings into question what participation means, and whilst there are those who maintain "going native" jeopardizes the professional status of the researcher (Hart, 1998: 55), others have used complete participation as the key to the insider status. For example, Wahab (2003: 629) describes how she not only conducted observations in strip clubs but decided to engage in the sex work venue. Encouraged by her participants, who insisted that to really understand the job it had to be lived, Wahab took part in a peep show as a dancer, immersing herself in the context of the culture. . . .

Like the familiar debates in qualitative social science inquiry (see Labaree, 2002), the insider–outsider dilemma is a point of negotiation, confusion and reflection for the researcher in the sex work setting. Rarely are researchers' identities clearly defined as only "information gatherers." In the spirit of transparency, researchers interested in sex work qualify their intentions and character, which often means blurring the roles and boundaries that other types of research and methods have the luxury of maintaining. . . .

PLEASURES AND DANGERS OF THE RESEARCH PROCESS

One account of my fieldwork experience in the sex work setting could read as a list of uncomfortable moments, scary confrontations, mistakes that led to insults, embarrassments, treading on toes and appearing unprofessional and out of my depth. Another positive account could reflect the strong bonds and lasting friend-ships I built with key informants, idling time away putting the world to rights, and sharing our histories, hopes and expectations. This section will reflect on some of the contrasting experi-ences of dangers and pleasures when conducting research in the sex work environment, highlight-ing the complexity of the method and the neces-sity of investing oneself in the process.

The practical challenges of doing research in the field have been discussed in relation to dan-gerous fieldwork settings or sensitive topics of inquiry (Ferrell and Hamm, 1998; Lee, 1995; Sharpe, 2000). . . . In the sexual field, despite the advantages of collecting different types of live data when immersed in the working environ-ment, there are inherent dangers for research-ers who operate in illegal environments that are isolated. Several researchers describe how they have met with opposition from potential par-ticipants, other hustlers on the street and ter-ritorial pimps who take issue with a researcher on their patch (see O'Neill, 1996). . . . Some-times obvious risks are expected when working with populations at the margins of society, but, as I describe later, the emotional risks of such work are often unknown when the research is designed. Other hazards in the field make sex work a tricky subject for the well-intended researcher. Researchers have been mistaken for plainclothes police (see Barnard, 1992: 145; Sharpe, 2000: 366), journalists (Sanders, 2005b), or accused of spying for rival competi-tors (Lever and Dolnick, 2000)—all of which add extra hurdles to achieving safety, credibility and, of course, a sample! . . .

THE EMOTIONAL TOIL OF DATA GATHERING

The emotional effort needed to research sex work is stark in both the pragmatics of the field-work and the efforts needed to dissect, reflect and understand the researcher's own position in a complex social activity. What Melrose (2002) calls the "labour pains" of researching sensitive areas like prostitution are often given little attention, as the researcher is expected to apply emotional labour to manage the feel-ings of others as well as their own responses. Although not always the case, informal conver-sations and taped interviews with women who work in prostitution can involve the disclosure of disturbing and unpleasant data consisting of tales of exploitation, abuse, violence, despera-tion, drug use and hopelessness.

Melrose, like others (Miller, 1997; O'Connell Davidson and Layder, 1994: 216–7; Sharpe, 2000: 365), documents how stories provoke feelings of anger, rage and despair both in the data-collection phase and again in the analysis stage. In a current project with men who buy sex from female sex workers, such feelings of anger and contempt have been a consequence of listening to the other side of the story. In a minority of cases, as interviewees have left my office, I have felt pure rage at their misogynist attitudes and belief that if they buy the services of a sex worker, then they can do as they please. It is difficult to understand or accept these experiences as research but maintaining a pro-fessional attitude and response to people who incite such negative feelings is the only reason why the project has not been shelved.

The dangers of the sexual field are not only related to the physical safety of the researcher, as the emotional investment in the endeavour is significant and needs to be reflected upon and managed. At times the field relations with participants can prove to be very intense. To bridge the scepticism and doubts held by potential participants, the researcher know-ingly or unknowingly enters into a degree of self-disclosure. . . . Participants always wanted to know why I was interested in sex work and whether I could be tempted or indeed had the guts to sell sexual services for money. Such curi-osity could not be ignored and a natural process of self-disclosure and identification became an integral part of how field relations were secured. I recall this process as natural rather than manipulative because it was not a chore to engage in in-depth conversation with the participants as I shared many experiences with them. Yet, although disclosure brought me closer to the women, this self-investment also opened up vulnerabilities and concerns about keeping my private life protected from the demands of the fieldwork setting and the public academic eye. At the same time, having to do some personal soul searching also made me confront my stereotypes and prejudices about sexuality and lifestyles. Not something that is generally written into the research design.

The intensity of the research does not necessarily decrease as time lapses between the fieldwork and the safety of the academic corridors. In processes of self-reflection, what was experienced cannot be fully understood until the "after" phase of the data collection, writing up and dissemination (see Roberts and Sanders, 2005). It is in the after phases that the journey can be considered as a whole, the mistakes highlighted and good practice recognized as worthy of repeating or sharing with peers. It is also in the "after" phase that there are dilemmas about whether we make our academic careers off the backs of the people who have supplied the material. Making a successful academic career through permanent positions, book contracts and promotions from the experiences of those in the sex industry brings added suspicions of exploitation. The information used to make that career is based on experiences of individuals involved in what some consider an immoral or inhumane exchange of sex for money, or an institution that exists as a prop for patriarchy and wider unequal power structures that subjugate women. . . . Collaborative research partnerships that work alongside informants, offering directorship and control to those who are normally subjected to

the research process, is a step toward reducing the exploitative nature of social science research. . . .

CONCLUDING COMMENTS

Despite its criticisms and dwindling application, here I have argued that there is great value in small-scale ethnographic research, especially collaborative in nature, into the sex industry that is concentrated both in time and space. Yet, at every stage, there are hurdles and challenges, often from within the institution, as questions are posed by ethics committees of the appropriateness and feasibility of the sex industry as a worthy topic of study.

Sex work research diverges from institutional patterns and accepted paths of information gathering, transgressing expectations of the types of group that are worthy of research or will produce useful knowledge (Pyett, 1998). In addition, the nature of the sex work environment and the political issues surrounding prostitution demand that the researcher make personal investment (such as self-disclosure) into the research process. The demands of emotional labour on the researcher are complex and intense. Researchers have to confront hostile and volatile environments that need to be managed with care, making skills in negotiation, conflict management, role-playing and keeping quiet an essential part of the fieldwork tool kit.

The challenges do not stop as the researcher leaves the field. The writing-up process demands considerable reflection on all aspects of the fieldwork and decisions have to be made about what to reveal and what to confine to the fieldwork diary. Continually promoting research into sex work, tirelessly applying (and re-applying) for funding, and pushing to disseminate findings amongst the decision-makers are also part of the methodological challenges that face those committed to this important social issue. Pragmatics aside, to advance the theoretical arguments and knowledge regarding the nature and place of prostitution in contemporary life, research needs to be directed at wider issues relating to the politics of gender and social issues. O'Neill (2001: 187) suggests some of these wider social issues, such as the feminization of poverty, violence and abuse in the home, and routes into sex work such as homelessness and leaving care are intrinsically linked to finding out more about prostitution. Researchers have the responsibility not to produce more of the same but to address the questions and areas that are often pushed to one side, constantly rejected by funding bodies, and appear to be in discord with national political objectives. As Shaver (2005: 307) comments, challenges to stereotypes and the victimization of sex workers need to be implicit in the methods that are employed to produce knowledge about these groups. If there is to be any advancement in the sociology of sex work, separate aspects of the industry should not be studied in isolation, and female sex workers should not remain the only focus of investigation.

REFERENCES

Barnard, M. 1992. "Working in the Dark: Researching Female Prostitution," in H. Roberts (ed.). *Women's Health Matters*, pp. 141–56. London: Routledge.

Cooper, K., Kilvington, J., Day, S., Ziersch, A., and Ward, H. 2001. "HIV Prevention and Sexual Health Services for Sex Workers in the UK," *Health Education Journal* 60(1): 26–34.

Ferrell, J., and Hamm, M. S. 1998. *Ethnography at the Edge: Crime, Deviance and Field Research*. Boston. MA: Northeastern University Press.

Hart, A. 1998. *Buying and Selling Power: Anthropological Reflections on Prostitution in Spain*. Oxford: Westview Press.

Hubbard, P. 1999a. *Sex and the City. Geographies of Prostitution in the Urban West*. Aldershot: Ashgate.

Hubbard, P. 1999b. "Researching Female Sex Work: Reflections on Geographical Exclusion, Critical Methodologies and 'Useful' Knowledge," *Area* 31(3): 229–37.

Labaree, R. 2002. "The Risk of 'Going Observationalist': Negotiating the Hidden Dilemmas of Being an Insider Participant Observer," *Qualitative Research* 2(1): 97–122.

Lee, R. 1995. *Dangerous Fieldwork*. London: Sage.

Lever, J., and Dolnick, D. 2000. "Clients and Call Girls: Seeking Sex and Intimacy," in R. Weitzer (ed.). *Sex for Sale*, pp. 85–100. London: Routledge.

Maher, L. 2000. *Sexed Work: Gender, Race and Resistance in a Brooklyn Drug Market*. Oxford: Oxford University Press.

Mattley, C. 1997. "Field Research with Phone Sex Workers," in M. Schwartz (ed.). *Researching Violence Against Women*, pp. 146–58. London: Sage.

Melrose, M. 2002. "Labour Pains: Some Considerations on the Difficulties of Researching Juvenile Prostitution," *International Journal of Social Research Methodology* 5(4): 333–51.

Miller, J. 1997. "Researching Violence Against Street Prostitutes," in M. Schwartz (ed.). *Researching Sexual Violence Against Women*, pp. 144–56. London: Sage.

O'Connell Davidson, J. 1998. *Prostitution, Power and Freedom*. London: Polity.

O'Connell Davidson, J., and Layder, D. 1994. *Methods, Sex and Madness*. London: Routledge.

O'Neill, M. 1996. "Researching Prostitution and Violence: Towards a Feminist Praxis," in M. Hester, L. Kelly and J. Radford (eds.). *Women, Violence and Male Power*, pp. 130–47. London: Open University Press.

O'Neill, M. 2001. *Prostitution and Feminism*. London: Polity Press.

Pyett, P. 1998. "Doing It Together: Sex Workers and Researchers," *Research for Sex Work*, 1. URL (accessed June 2006): http://hcc.med.vu.nl/artikelen/pyett.htm.

Roberts, J. M., and Sanders, T. 2005. "'Before, During and After': Ethnography, Reflexivity and Pragmatic Realism," *Sociological Review* 53(2): 294–313.

Sanders, T. 2005a. *Sex Work. A Risky Business*. Cullompton, UK: Willan.

Sanders, T. 2005b. "Researching the Online Sex Work Community," in C. Hine (ed.). *Virtual Methods in Social Research on the Internet*, pp. 66–79. Oxford: Berg.

Sanders, T. 2005c. "It's Just Acting: Sex Workers' Strategies for Capitalising on Sexuality," *Gender, Work and Organization* 12(4): 319–42.

Sharpe, K. 2000. "Sad, Bad and (Sometimes) Dangerous to Know: Street Corner Research with Prostitutes, Punters and the Police," in R. King and E. Wincup (eds.). *Doing Research on Crime and Justice*, pp. 362–72. Oxford: Oxford University Press.

Shaver, F. 2005. "Sex Work Research: Methodological and Ethical Challenges," *Journal of Interpersonal Violence* 20(3): 296–319.

Wahab, S. 2003. "Creating Knowledge Collaboratively with Female Sex Workers: Insights from a Qualitative Feminist and Participatory Study," *Qualitative Inquiry* 9(4): 625–42.

Funding Sex Research

Mindy Stombler and Amanda M. Jungels

Getting funding for sex research has always been challenging. In the 1950s, Alfred Kinsey and his colleagues lost funding from the Rockefeller Foundation following publication of their controversial report on women's sexuality. The National Health and Social Life Survey (1994)—the closest we've come to a national sexual "census"—lost federal funding following Republican opposition led by Representative William Dannemeyer and Senator Jesse Helms.[1] The researchers were subsequently forced to dramatically reduce the scope of their project. Other grant-seekers report that they find themselves in a very defensive position. According to James Wagoner, president of Advocates for Youth, "For 20 years it was about health and science, and now we have a political ideological approach. . . . Never have we experienced a climate of intimidation and censorship as we have today [2004]."[2]

In 2003, there was a strong congressional effort to block the funding of four National Institutes of Health (NIH) grants. These grants had already been judged as outstanding by peer scientists in an independent review process. The grants called for research on sexual risk taking and its link to sexual arousal, the sexual habits of older men, Asian sex workers, and sexual and gender identity among American Indians. Conservative politicians argued that the government had no business funding research on such inappropriate topics. Efforts to block the funding were narrowly defeated by two votes in the House.[3]

The economic climate caused by the Great Recession has made funding sex research even more tenuous. As local, state, and federal governments wrestle with reduced budgets and increasing debts, funding for many types of research has been threatened—but sexuality research is often singled out as "wasteful" and "bizarre." In 2011, the Traditional Values Coalition (TVC) called for a moratorium on grants awarded by the NIH and a federal investigation of the NIH's granting process because of "bizarre projects" that amounted to "institutional waste."[4] One study that was heavily criticized was characterized by the TVC as a ten-year, $10 million study to determine the average penis size of gay men; in reality, this study was conducted to understand the relationship among penis size, condom slippage/breakage, and sexually transmitted infection (STI) rates—and it was not federally funded.[5] In 2017, the Trump administration canceled more than $213 million in awarded grants for already-in-progress research intended to evaluate evidence-based interventions to reduce teen pregnancy, leaving researchers scrambling to find funds to complete their projects.[6] Canceling funding in the middle of multiyear grants, as happened in these cases, is quite unusual because it means researchers are unable to analyze the data they have already collected or make modifications to social problems based on the results. Thus, the money spent and work completed prior to cancellation are often wasted.[7]

Although some scientists will continue to apply for large government grants, others are becoming increasingly discouraged and are turning to alternative sources. The National

Survey of Sexual Health and Behavior, discussed in Reading 8, turned to the makers of Trojan condoms to fund the project.[8] Aside from the federal government and select corporations, sources for funding sex research tend to include a handful of private institutions and universities. Convincing private foundations to fund sex research can be challenging, as Dr. Miro Gudelsky, a sex therapist, explains: "Few individuals are willing to put up their money, or their family's money, behind sex-related research. 'Grandpa worked really hard so that we can find out the most sensitive part of the penis' generally isn't the sort of story family foundations want to tell."[9] Even when researchers can find nongovernmental funding, these resource pools are often more limited.[10] This lack of available funding reduces the scope of the sex-related research projects that do get carried out. For example, an extensive sex survey conducted by the Centers for Disease Control and Prevention (CDC) (see Reading 8) initially had to cap its sample at age 44, ignoring the sexual behaviors of the older generation that brought us the sexual liberation movement.[11] The economic stimulus package of 2009 (formally known as the American Recovery and Reinvestment Act) included additional funding for scientific research, but those projects that would not "reap economic rewards in the foreseeable future" (including social science and public health research) were criticized by John McCain of Arizona and other Republican senators as being wasteful.[12]

As conservative politicians fight to reduce funding available for sex research, researchers feel pressured to focus on topics for which funding is available, such as pharmaceutical research. This trend necessarily narrows the breadth of researchable topics to those connected to potential profit making. This trajectory was advanced in 2011 when Senator Tom Coburn (a Republican from Oklahoma) singled out the National Science Foundation and suggested

the elimination of all funding for research that did not have "practical uses outside of academic circles and clear benefits to mankind and the world."[13] Psychologist Geoffrey Miller claims that his research on kissing (why couples kiss less the longer they remain involved) is valuable for society but not necessarily fundable: "Kissing could help couples rejuvenate a marriage and reduce divorce rates . . . but it's less threatening and more profitable to study orgasms."[14] In fact, Mark Schwartz, former director of the Masters and Johnson Institute, claims that the survival of the study of sexual behavior is a result of the HIV/AIDS epidemic and the development of Viagra "because the pharmaceutical companies suddenly became very interested in the fact that they can make huge amounts of money off the genitals."[15] Leonore Tiefer, a sex researcher interviewed in Chapter 5, cautions sex researchers about their overreliance on pharmaceutical money, insisting it contributes to a medical model of sexuality where all sexual problems can be fixed with a pill.[16] In her research on the stigmatization of sexuality research, Janice Irvine notes that sexuality researchers whose research critically examines pharmaceutical companies' "promise of better sex" will likely not receive funding from this industry.[17]

Following the AIDS crisis and the public's concern with teen pregnancy rates, researchers who studied sexually transmitted infections (STIs) and reproductive health had a decent chance of being funded. But today, even these researchers have their share of challenges. Recently, scientists who study HIV/AIDS and other STIs claim they have been warned by government officials to avoid the use of certain key words in their grant applications. Grants that include terms like *sex workers*, *men who sleep with men*, *anal sex*, *needle exchange*, *prostitute*, *gay*, *homosexual*, and *transgender* are rumored to face additional scrutiny in an already fiercely competitive arena.[18] In her study of sexuality researchers, Irvine found that 18 percent reported a funding organization seeking modification of researchers' grant proposals "in a way that downplayed its focus on sexuality." This included removing words the funder saw as "dirty." Funders labeled sex research as less serious and more controversial than other research.[19] In one case, a researcher seeking a grant was told that "we do not wish to support research that will land [the university] on the front page of the newspaper."[20] Ironically, this self-censorship of controversial terms and topics has made it harder to assess whether funding has declined for sex research, as it is difficult to determine what researchers are actually studying when they submit disguised or reframed research proposals.[21] Even research that is clearly related to public health concerns (such as why young men do not use condoms correctly or the effect alcohol has on college students' casual sex habits) can come under fire as being inappropriate uses of federal funding.[22] Other researchers have found that this stigma about sex research exists beyond funding agencies, noting that "some people who were not directly involved in our research field, either as a participant, peer, or colleague, viewed our topic and our jobs as researchers as a 'joke' and 'unworthy' of academic research."[23] These researchers frequently had to carefully manage whether to disclose information about their research, and if so, how much.

In addition to reframing how they present their research proposals to funding sources, researchers must tackle the issue of how to present their research results to the media: Issues of inaccurate, politicized, sensationalized, or misused findings are common concerns for sex researchers.[24] Presenting sensitive or controversial findings to the public is viewed as a "fundamental skill" by many researchers, especially those who fear that their results may be "misused or misinterpreted."[25] While controversy generates publicity for the researchers

and the media outlets, it can also "threaten funding, result in restrictive policies, and lead to negative consequences for the individual or the field."[26] This fear of reprisal has led some researchers to avoid appearing in the media at all to report findings; in today's global media culture, local media coverage of a research controversy can quickly turn into "unwelcome" national attention.[27]

Frustrated by the increasing interference of politicians, researchers—and even federal agency directors—have been fighting back. For example, scientists from a range of disciplines have formed the Coalition to Protect Research, an organization "committed to promoting public health through research [and promoting the idea that] sexual health and behavior research is essential to providing a scientific foundation for sound public health prevention and intervention programs."[28] Organizations like the Coalition to Protect Research and the Society for the Scientific Study of Sexuality call for politicians to respect the scientific peer-review process and to actively fund sex research. Some researchers, particularly those targeted by the congressional effort to block NIH funding in 2003, have been reinvigorated by the controversy brought on by their research, wearing it as a "badge of honor" and insisting that they will continue to do sex research, even if they must engage in self-censorship to do so.[29]

NOTES

1. Senator Helms and Representative Dannemeyer were also leaders in the successful effort to de-fund the American Teenage Study, a project designed to study "patterns of adolescent sexual and contraceptive behavior and the cause of these patterns" (106). In Udry, J. Richard. 1993. "The Politics of Sex Research." *Journal of Sex Research*, 30(2): 103–10.

2. Navarro, Mireya. 2004. "Experts in Sex Field Say Conservatives Interfere with Health and Research." *New York Times*, July 11.

3. McCain, Robert Stacy. 2003. "Sex and Child Health: Critics Wonder Why NICHD Funds Studies." *Washington Times*, September 19, A2.

4. Traditional Values Coalition (TVC). 2011. "NIH Wastes Millions on Bizarre 'Research.'" Retrieved September 28, 2011 from http://www.traditionalvalues.org/content /Press%20Releases/31645/NIH%20Wastes%20Millions.

5. Moisse, Katie, and Mikaela Conley. 2011. "Study of Gay Men's Sexual Health Called Waste of Taxpayer Money; Study Not Government-Funded." Retrieved September 28, 2011 from http://abcnews.go.com/Health/MensHealth /study-gay-mens-sexual-health-called-waste-taxpayer /story?id=14125898.

6. Molteni, Megan. 2017. "Teen Pregnancy Researchers Regroup after Trump's HHS Pulls Funding." *Wired*, July 19. Retrieved July 27, 2017 from https://www.wired.com/story /teen-pregnancy-researchers-regroup-after-trumps-hhs -pulls-funding/.

7. Kay, Jane. 2017. "Trump Administration Suddenly Pulls Plug on Teen Pregnancy Programs." *Reveal from the Center for Investigative Reporting*, July 14. Retrieved July 27, 2017 from https://www.revealnews.org/article/trump -administration-suddenly-pulls-plug-on-teen-pregnancy -programs/.

8. Herbenick, Debby, Michael Reece, Vanessa Schick, Stephanie Sanders, Brian Dodge and J. Dennis Fortenberry. 2010a. "Sexual Behavior in the United States: Results from a National Probability Sample of Men and Women Ages 14–94." *Journal of Sexual Medicine* 7(s5): 255–65.

9. Alptraum, Lux. 2015. "Masters of Sex and the Ongoing Stigma of Sex Research." *The Verge*, July 15. Retrieved July 26, 2017 from https://www.theverge .com/2015/7/14/8958097/masters-of-sex-science-research -sexuality.

10. *American Experience: Kinsey*, Online Forum, Day 2. February 15, 2005. Retrieved December 12, 2005 from www.pbs.org/wgbh/amex/kinsey/sfeature/sf_forum_0215 .html.

11. Hunter, Jennifer. 2005. "Sex Study Spurns Generation of Love." *Chicago Sun-Times*, October 5: 63.

12. Radnofsky, Louise. 2010. "Science Stimulus Funds Called Wasteful." *Wall Street Journal*, August 12. Retrieved September 28, 2011 from http://online.wsj.com/article /SB10001424052748704268004575417541178463762.html.

13. Coburn, Tom A. 2011. "The National Science Foundation: Under the Microscope." Retrieved September 28, 2011 from http://coburn.senate.gov/public /index.cfm?a=Files.Serve&File_id=2dccf06d-65fe-4087 -b58d-b43ff68987fa.

14. Clark, Justin. 2005. "Sex: The Big Turnoff." *Psychology Today,* January/February.

15. Clay, Rebecca. 2003. "Sex Research Faces New Obstacles." *APA Online.* Retrieved December 12, 2005 from www.apa.org/monitor/apr03/obstacles.html.

16. Tiefer, Leonore. 1995. *Sex Is Not a Natural Act and Other Essays.* Boulder, CO: Westview Press.

17. Irvine, Janice. 2014. "Is Sexuality Research 'Dirty Work'?: Institutionalized Stigma in the Production of Knowledge." *Sexualities,* 17(5–6): 632–56.

18. Goode, Erica. 2003. "Certain Words Can Trip Up AIDS Grants, Scientists Say." *New York Times,* April 18, A10.

19. Irvine, 2014.

20. Irvine, 2014: 648.

21. Kempner, Joanna. 2008. "The Chilling Effect: How Do Researchers React to Controversy?" *PLoS Medicine,* 5(11): 1–8.

22. Radnofsky, Louise. 2010. "Science Stimulus Funds Called Wasteful." *Wall Street Journal*, August 12. Retrieved September 28, 2011 from http://online.wsj.com/article /SB10001424052748704268004575417541178463762.html.

23. Hammond, Natalie, and Sarah Kingston. 2014. "Experiencing Stigma as Sex Work Researchers in Professional and Personal Lives." *Sexualities,* 17(3): 329–47.

24. McBride, Kimberly R., Stephanie A. Sanders, Erick Janssen, Maria Elizabeth Grabe, Jennifer Bass, Johnny V. Sparks, Trevor R. Brown, Julia R. Heiman. 2007. "Turning Sexual Science into News: Sex Research and the Media." *Journal of Sex Research*, 44(4): 347–58.

25. Kempner, Joanna, Jon F. Merz, and Charles L. Bosk. 2011. "Forbidden Knowledge: Public Controversy and the Production of Nonknowledge." *Sociological Forum,* 26 (3): 475–500.

26. McBride et al., 2007.

27. Kempner et al., 2011.

28. Coalition to Protect Research (CPR). Retrieved December 16, 2005 from www.cossa.org/CPR/cpr.html.

29. Kempner, 2008.

3

REPRESENTING SEX

AN INTERVIEW WITH

JOSHUA GAMSON

Joshua Gamson, PhD, is a professor of sociology and assistant dean at the University of San Francisco. His research and teaching focus on the sociology of culture, with an emphasis on contemporary Western commercial culture and mass media; social movements, especially on cultural aspects of contemporary movements; participant-observation methodology and techniques, particularly as applied in urban settings; and the history, theory, and sociology of sexuality. He is the author of Claims to Fame: Celebrity in Contemporary America *(University of California Press, 1994);* Freaks Talk Back: Tabloid Talk Shows and Sexual Nonconformity *(University of Chicago Press, 1998);* The Fabulous Sylvester: The Legend, the Music, the Seventies in San Francisco *(Henry Holt, 2005), and* Modern Families: Stories of Extraordinary Journeys to Kinship *(New York University Press, 2015).*

What led you to begin studying sexuality?

I didn't know it at the time, but studying sexuality began for me as part of what some scholars have called "identity work." I was a 23-year-old graduate student at UC Berkeley, and I'd decided it was time to figure myself out a bit better, and a big part of that seemed to be figuring out my sexuality a bit better. I knew that the Bay Area was a great place to do that, given the history of sexual subcultures—gay ones, especially—but somehow I didn't want to just take myself out exploring. So I decided to study it, come at my personal life from the outside in, as it were. When I had a statistics paper to do, I made it about public opinion about homosexuality, for instance. When I took a graduate seminar in participant-observation research, I eventually decided on a field site that would get me into San Francisco, among gay and lesbian people: the AIDS activist group ACT UP. That turned into a very rewarding research experience, and to do it I had to teach myself some of the literature on sexuality-based social movements, so it fed my head. But it also fed my identity. That work moved me into a part of the gay community that I liked, felt comfortable in, and identified with; it helped me see myself as gay, and to actually experience gayness without shame or apology. It was a case of personal identity leading to intellectual pursuit and then back to personal identity. That back and forth continues to this day.

How do people react when you tell them you study sexuality?

It depends on which people are doing the reacting, I suppose. Back when I started, my more senior colleagues would generally seem mystified, as if they couldn't quite figure out what there was to study about sexuality. Some, I'm certain, didn't and still don't think it's a legitimate area of study, but I think a lot of people just didn't know how to have a conversation about studying sexuality. That's rarely the case anymore, partly because over the last decade the field has become much more established and much less marginalized in sociology—and partly because sexuality has been such a significant political and public policy focal point. Younger people seem to think it's kind of cool that I study sexuality, or cool that there is such a field of study. Then there are always those who want to joke about how much fun the "research process" must be.

Which of your projects have you found most interesting? Why?

The book on TV talk shows, *Freaks Talk Back*, was interesting to me for a whole slew of reasons. I found it really interesting to investigate how the everyday production routines—the kinds of things talk show producers think about, talk about, worry about, and do all the time to get a show made—affected LGBT topics. Usually, when scholars and activists talk about "cultural visibility," they have only a vague sense of what kinds of institutional and organizational processes shape that visibility, and I felt like I was pushing past that vagueness. I was also really interested in the experiences of guests, and learned a lot about sexuality politics from that—in particular, the internal struggle over who best represents "gayness," which is very much a class-based divide. I became very interested in how complicated media visibility was for sexually stigmatized and gender-nonconforming populations: how gay and lesbian respectability was shored up on the shows by demeaning or stereo-typing transgender and bisexual guests; how the exposure of class and race diversity among LGBT populations only really came about through the extraordinarily exploitative, confess–accuse–pull hair kind of shows, like [Jerry] Springer. Media visibility has really changed since then, but that project tuned me in to dynamics of gay visibility I still see all around me.

My book *The Fabulous Sylvester* was interesting in a whole other kind of way. It's a sort of combination biography (of the 1970s openly gay, sometimes crossdressing, African American disco star Sylvester) and cultural history (of San Francisco's gay subcultures, in which Sylvester lived and through which he rose to fame; and of AIDS, from which Sylvester died). So it was interesting partly because it was a different sort of project, more narrative and less analytical scholarly. It was interesting to me because it put me into contact with Sylvester's life and friends, and his story is just beautiful, and beautiful largely because his sexuality was such an integrated part of who he was—he was never closeted, and he suffered quite a bit for that, but he eventually became an international disco star by putting gay "fabulousness" to music, while refusing to be reduced to, or by, sexuality, and by never apologizing for being gay and sexual. I also loved delving into 1970s gay liberation cultures, which were so creative and novel and important, and which have been largely lost to AIDS, assimilation, and fear.

What ethical dilemmas have you faced as you've studied sexuality?

I haven't really experienced ethical dilemmas, frankly. I'm not studying sexual behavior, and I've never studied covert sexual populations, so I've never had concerns about revealing things that might hurt the subjects. I always tell people I'm a researcher, and give them the option of not participating, or of participating without having their name used, and sometimes people take me up on that. When I'm interviewing, they always have the option of having me turn off the tape recorder. The closest I've come to an ethical dilemma is in dealing with the question of how what I write might be used by others, such as journalists or policymakers who have an anti-gay agenda—which is, of course, totally out of my control. I don't think I've ever made a decision to censor myself for fear that the wrong people would use it in a way that damages those to whom I'm loyal and allied, but I certainly am careful how I frame and phrase things.

What do you think is most challenging about studying sexuality?

The most challenging thing for me is that it's a constantly moving target. Again, I don't study sexual behaviors, but instead sexual identities, movements, politics, cultures, and cultural representations. One can easily be at the end of a project and find the phenomenon entering some radically different new phase, so one has to be ready to always rethink and revise. (Maybe that's one of the reasons I enjoyed doing the Sylvester book, since it was more historical.) Media visibility is a good example: When I finished the talk show book, the issue was still that LGBT people were mainly invisible on television or restricted to narrow stereotypes; the issues now, after *Ellen, Will and Grace, Queer as Folk, The L Word, Queer Eye*, and so on, are quite different. The talk show study, over the course of just a few years, went from being a statement about the limits and paradoxes of LGBT media visibility to being an account of a historical moment. That's not an insurmountable challenge, and I'd rather study something that is active and volatile than something inert. But sexual cultures and politics don't stand still for their snapshot.

Why is it important to do sex research?

Most basically, because sex is an important part of human existence, and it's been so smothered by shame and negativity that there's still plenty that's not well understood. Although it hasn't always been the case, and I suspect won't be forever, sexuality has also become a significant basis for people's identities and self-understandings, and it affects their life chances and life paths in various ways—where they wind up living, what kinds of jobs they can and can't get. And sexuality is one of several significant bases of social inequality, and therefore is a very significant arena of politics. These are things that need to be understood, both just because more knowledge is better than less, and because sexualities research can help us figure out what needs to be changed and how to change it—the research can inform the pursuit of social justice.

If you could teach people one thing about sexuality, what would it be?

That it's both more significant and less significant than it's been made out to be: Sexuality is not just a phenomenon of nature, and not just "personal," but a phenomenon of society, and political; at the same time, at the root of all of this politics is just sex, just the fun and sometimes funny things people do with their bodies, together and alone.

SEXY LIKE A GIRL AND HORNY LIKE A BOY: CONTEMPORARY GAY "WESTERN" NARRATIVES ABOUT GAY "ASIAN" MEN

C. WINTER HAN

In the recent HBO documentary *Middle Sexes: Redefining He and She*, narrator Gore Vidal introduces us to Qui, a Thai katoey, or ladyboy, who posted her picture online looking for a partner. The ad, placed when Qui was still a teenager, was answered by Mark, a 40-something white man who "left wife, family, and job behind to follow an obsession." Describing the first time he met Qui, Mark explains:

First time I'd ever been to Asia in my life. First country in Asia I've ever been to. And she met me at the airport, so she was the very first person I ever met, about 8 o'clock at night, looking, she's 19, I think, just turned 19 years old, just looking cute as a button.

About their first night together, Mark continues:

Took me to a hotel, you know, our first, I still remember our first kiss. Of course, I never kissed a boy before so that was interesting. I still remember how it feels like. The smell of her and every single thing.

As for Qui, she explains:

I never planned on having a foreign lover. I just wanted someone who wouldn't exploit me, someone to give me opportunities. To be born a katoey in a poor family is difficult.

One might wonder why a seemingly heterosexual man would leave behind a wife, his family, and his career for such an "obsession." When such a question is posed to Mark, that is, when he is asked what he finds so attractive about a katoey, particularly Qui, he answers simply:

She's very feminine. She's sexy like a girl is sexy, but she's also horny like a boy is horny. You couldn't really ask for more than that in a person.

Later Mark explains that he would prefer that Qui not undergo surgery to remove his male sex organs. . . . Mark explains:

Yeah, I mean I enjoy it. I find it a big turn-on. I find very feminine Asian ladyboys who can perform the same as I can, who can't, definitely can't, fake an orgasm, I find that a huge turn-on. I mean, when I first met Qui, when we were first getting together and doing interesting things in private, I was shooting bullets into the headboard. It was really just the best sex I've ever had.

This exchange is more than just a narrative from a television special. While a self-described straight white man and a Thai katoey are hardly representative of the gay community, the preceding narrative is representative of how western media presents gay Asian men. Long vilified in popular western press, images of Asian men in the popular media, by the mid-1980s, "[were] at their best, effeminate closet queens like Charlie Chan and, at their worst, [were] homosexual menaces like Fu Manchu."[1] The feminization of Asian men in popular western media can be traced to the growing yellow peril of the early twentieth century, the Cold War years of the mid- and late twentieth century, and the continuing xenophobia surrounding global labor and capital that has had the chilling consequence of equating Asian Americans with Asians, thereby making them perpetually foreign, and desexualizing Asian men in a society that values masculinity over femininity.[2] By neutralizing Asian male sexuality with feminine undertones, western masculinity was able to maintain its sense of superiority, particularly over those it was dominating.[3]

In more recent decades, the rise of media activism among Asian Americans, along with texts and images created by them, has begun to challenge these stereotypes. Gay men and women of color have also begun to challenge old assumptions regarding what it means to be gay, posing a threat to older notions of gay identity.[4] When previously marginalized groups begin to challenge dominant narratives and images used to marginalize them, they also challenge the taken-for-granted beliefs that help to maintain group hierarchies. When the hierarchies that maintain domination over marginalized groups become weaker, social representations about "others" may emerge more strongly because the dominant group's identity is also threatened.[5] In this [reading], I analyze *The Advocate* and *OUT* magazines from 2005 to 2010 in order to examine how images of gay Asian men are constructed and maintained within larger western gay narratives. . . .

A MATTER OF REPRESENTATION

. . . [S]ocial representations don't exist outside of the individual, inherent in the object they describe, but lie within individual and group experiences.[6] Therefore, representations are embedded in historical, cultural, and social conditions confronted by those who create these representations at the time that they are created. . . .

According to [Edward] Said, representations are never neutral but reflect the power dynamics inherent in stratified social systems.[7] In such systems, representations are deployed for the purpose of creating and maintaining ideological definitions of "difference." Once created, representations have the power to define

racial and cultural boundaries while outlining who does and does not "belong" to a nation or a people. . . .

Perhaps in no other arena of social life is the act of identity construction and contestation more evident than in media productions. As Stuart Hall reminds us, cultural identities are born and maintained "within, not outside, representations."[8] It is these representations that shape how we come to see ourselves and others. . . . Intimately tied to this notion is that representations reflect power differentials within the larger society. Representations of "oppressed groups were, and by and large still are, a relentless parade of insults."[9] . . . [N]egative representations of oppressed groups have the consequence of representing the dominant group in a positive light along the dichotomy of *difference*. It's a simple logic—if *we* are different from *them*, and *they* are bad, *we* must be good. For those who control the images, it is in their best interest to either (a) portray other groups negatively or, in the event that such negative portrayals will have unacceptable consequences, (b) erase them altogether when attempting to patrol the borders of inclusion. . . .

To maintain racial borders, media productions rely on stereotypes to patrol the margins, and gay media is no exception. Within the gay press, stereotypes are deployed to delineate between those who belong in the gay community and those who do not. . . . Stereotypes reflect the values and beliefs of those who create them and work to maintain the privilege of those who deploy them for use.[10] When thought about in this way, stereotypes tell us more about those who manufacture them than those who are actually stereotyped. More important, the ability to deploy stereotypes implies a power relationship where the group with power is able not only to deploy stereotypes but to actually have those stereotypes taken as reality.[11] . . .

Given "journalism's centrality in politics and culture, as well as its vested economic and occupational interests, questions regarding its boundaries, uses and contingencies [are] more than idle concern."[12] Rather, it becomes critical to examine the role that journalism plays in maintaining and promoting social inequality by exposing journalistic practices that add to further marginalization of subaltern groups.

WHERE ARE ALL THE GAY ASIAN MEN?

Looking at gay media, it is clear that the strategy deployed by gay publications to maintain white male privilege is one of exclusion. Asian men, and other men of color, rarely appear as subjects of a story and are rarely represented as contributors to the debates. Because of this, gay print media often speaks only to white men. . . . The invisibility of Asian men in gay media is most evident in the pages of *The Advocate* and *OUT* magazines, the largest gay and lesbian news magazines in the United States.

Gay Asian men (and other gay men of color) are virtually nonexistent within the pages of *The Advocate* and *OUT* magazines. For example, during the year 2010, gay Asian men appeared in *OUT* only four times. . . . In fact, during the entire period covering 2005 through 2010, gay Asian men were the subjects of only four feature stories, two stories each in *The Advocate* and *OUT* magazines. Ironically enough, the first of these was about the invisibility of gay Asian American men in the larger gay community, which appeared in *The Advocate* in 2005. . . . To be fair, Asian men appear in the magazines much more frequently than four times. However, they often appear as a wink and nod toward diversity, rather than as the subjects of stories. For example, they are most likely to be included as a respondent in *The Advocate*'s recurring feature "Out on the Streets," where random gay and lesbian people are asked questions while they are out and about. Yet in this recurring feature, Asian

homophobia is subtly implied repeatedly, marking Asians as somehow not really a part of the gay community. For example, while questions asked in western localities such as Las Vegas are usually mundane and neutral, such as, "Is Las Vegas a gay Mecca?" the question asked on the streets of Shanghai was, "How openly can gays and lesbians live in China?" The question, when asked this way, is rather loaded as it assumes that the answer is that they can't live openly in China but are celebrated in the gay Mecca of Las Vegas.

While feature stories about gay Asian men were rare, Asian men were often included in profile stories. However, when Asian men were the subject of a profile story in *The Advocate* or *OUT*, either alone or as a part of a group of people being featured, their race was only an issue when discussing homophobia in the Asian American community but not racism in the gay community. The subtle message, of course, is that homophobia is a problem to be addressed in the magazine, but racism is not.

Likewise, while gay Asian men were included in a small number of covers for *The Advocate* that consisted of a composite of people . . . there were no issues of the magazine that featured a gay Asian man as the primary focus of the cover during the entire period, with the exception of the July 19, 2005, issue that featured voiceover actor James Sie.

. . . [I]n 2005[, *The Advocate* ran a] review of an article that [first] appeared in the magazine on June 25, 1985, called "Gays in China." The review is reproduced verbatim:

While we look at the struggles faced by gay Asian-Americans in the current issue of *The Advocate*, 20 years ago we were examining the difficult lives of gay men in China. Author "Jay Michael" used a pseudonym so that he would be able to later return to the People's Republic.

While there he met a Shanghai local known as "Chang Fulai," another pseudonym. Homosexuality was illegal, and gays were often thrown in jail, so Fulai had to be careful not to get caught with other men. Because the government assigned housing, Fulai had not lived with any of his boyfriends. When he did occasionally bring them home, he had to sneak them into his room.

Fulai saw himself as "very modern" because he had sex with Western foreigners, dressed in elegant Western-style clothes, and identified himself as "gay." And he was cautiously hopeful that Chinese leader Deng Xiaoping's push for increased personal wealth and openness to Western trade might improve the lives of gays.

. . . [I]ncluding this short narrative . . . accomplishes two goals. First, it conveniently places gay Asian American men outside of the gay mainstream. The "From *The Advocate* Archives" column is solely intended to draw a connection between the main feature and a *similar* issue from the past and showcase the continuity of the issues covered by the magazine. . . . Using a story on gay men in China to reflect on the situations encountered by gay Asian American men in the United States, the editors of *The Advocate* equate Asian Americans with Asia and conflate gay Asian Americans with gay men in Asia, marking them as foreigners. Also, the vivid descriptions of how difficult it is to be gay in China are reminiscent of the racist defense that Asian Americans, who by popular imagination are foreign, should not complain about any mistreatment they receive by "Americans" because it is inevitably better than how "Americans" would be treated in . . . Asian nations. By marking gay Asian American men as foreigners, it takes away from the validity of their complaints about racist treatment. . . . [N]o article about gay life in Europe is used to harken back to a feature story about gay whites.

The narrative images created by the "From *The Advocate* Archives" column are more striking when compared to the main Asian-themed feature titled "Invisible No More." In this piece, the author sets the narrative stage by beginning

with the story of Andy Wong, who, despite having gotten over his "mistake" of joining the Mormon Church in high school, nonetheless "still struggles with being gay in his traditional Chinese immigrant family." Ironically, little is said about his Mormon background, which one might suspect had a lot to do with his remaining closeted as a gay man. Instead, numerous references are made throughout the article about gay Asian American men and women who are hesitant to come out of the closet because of traditional Asian values and pressure from Asian families. While his struggle with homophobia by Asian Americans is highlighted, there is virtually no mention of racism that is routinely experienced by gay Asian American men in the gay community or the homophobia inherent in the Mormon Church. In fact, when racism is mentioned at all, it seems to be in order to minimize the effects of racism on gay Asian American men. For example, [the author] quotes Pauline Park, a transgender Asian American activist, as stating: "There's racism in the gay community. But there's a bigger problem of homophobia in the Asian Pacific Islander community."

This quote, along with the tone of the article, is problematic given that existing academic studies do not support this conclusion. While homophobia may prevent some gay Asian American men from coming out of the closet, several scholars have noted that racism from the gay community plays an equal, if not greater, role in the lives of gay Asian American men.[13] So while *The Advocate* presents the issue of homophobia as the "big problem" among gay Asian Americans and nearly ignores the racism that they experience from gay white men, evidence suggests otherwise. . . . [The author] does address issues of racism within the gay community, but at the same time, the larger gay community is portrayed as actively working to address this issue as allies of gay Asian Americans. . . . [T]he struggle for recognition in the Asian American community is portrayed as being a lonely battle waged by gay Asian Americans, without straight allies, to win acceptance in a largely homophobic community. . . .

. . . [In the] June 21, [2005,] issue, . . . *The Advocate* ran a brief sidebar article called "Ending Hong Kong's Homophobia." Much like the retrospective piece "Gays in China" discussed earlier, this short piece also discussed the rigid homophobia in Chinese societies and described how protesters were encouraged to wear masks to show that gays and lesbians in Hong Kong "lived in the shadow of homophobia.". . .

. . . [T]he July 19, 2005, issue of *The Advocate* featured a gay Asian man on the cover, making him the only Asian person, man or woman, to appear on the cover of *The Advocate* in 2005 and the only Asian man to be featured prominently on the cover of either magazine for the entire six-year period. Voiceover actor James Sie, [pictured] with his partner, musician Douglas Wood, was featured as a part of the magazine's coverage of gay parenting and adoption. In both the photos, one on the cover and the photo accompanying the story, Wood is shown holding their adopted son while Sie is in the background. . . . [P]resenting Wood as the active parent and Sie as the passive parent blatantly gives Wood primacy in the article while relegating Sie to the background. In addition, . . . Wood's occupation, and by extension his role as family provider, is given primacy, while Sie's work is merely a footnote. . . .

While depicting Chinese officials as being overly homophobic and Asian American women as unwilling to "give up" their children, the article makes no mention of laws in the United States that forbid gay men and women from adopting any children, or the scarcity of white babies available for adoption. In fact, the trials endured by Wood and Sie in having to seek a child outside of the United States are blamed on Asian American women's unwillingness to "give up" their children and the Chinese government's homophobic attitudes. As compared to this homophobia in Asian cultures, whites, whether in the United States or elsewhere, are given a pass. . . .

Although there are a number of profiles of gay Asian men between 2005 and 2010, . . . gay Asian men do not appear as the subject of a full-length feature story in *The Advocate* again until September 2010, . . . in an article about author Michael Lowenthal's trip to Nanjing, China. The tagline to the story, which reads, "Author Michael Lowenthal travels across 12 time zones to find a gay experience as foreign as the culinary delicacies his hosts won't stop serving," preestablishes the inherent and essentialistic "difference" between gay Asian men and Lowenthal, a gay white man. Sadly, the article is full of stereotypes that are already well-established in the western imagination about Asian men. For example, Lowenthal notes: "Homosexuality was classified as a mental disorder in China until less than a decade ago, and it was only in December that the first government-backed gay bar in the country opened."

True as that statement might be, the passage is meant to highlight the homophobia among the Chinese, an extension of the "Asians are homophobic" trope encountered in many of the articles about people in Asia and Asian Americans in both *The Advocate* and *OUT*. What Lowenthal doesn't mention, or even allude to, is that homosexuality was also classified as a mental disorder in the United States during his own lifetime, making the classification of homosexuality as a mental disorder a recent part of America's past as well, rather than an ancient homophobic legacy that is well in our historical past. So, while China's recent labeling of homosexuality as a mental disorder is condemned, America's similar practices are ignored. Rather than being an isolated incident, Lowenthal's discussion about the way homosexuality is criminalized and marginalized simply echoed an earlier article in *The Advocate* titled "Gay China Comes Out Online" about China-based gay websites, written by Morgan Kroll, that noted, "The show reflects slowly changing attitudes in China. Sodomy was decriminalized in 1997, though homosexuality was still considered a mental illness by the government until 2001." Again, while portraying Chinese people and the Chinese government as homophobic, no mention was made that sodomy laws remained on the books in 14 states in the United States until 2013. . . .

Lowenthal's description of the gay Chinese men that he meets is also emblematic of the western view of Asian men, both gay and straight. In describing the first person he encounters at a Nanjing gay bar, Lowenthal had this to say:

A femmy man—or a butch woman: again my gaydar failed me—emerged from a shadow toward some stairs. When I approached, the person, in a panic, waved me off. "Please," I said. I smiled and showed my map. The nervous nelly (even this close, I couldn't tell the gender) made a rueful book-shutting gesture and scuttled up the stairs.

. . . Through . . . Lowenthal's western eyes, it is difficult to ascertain if the Asian person in front of [him] is a man or a woman, quite simply because all Asian men are, by nature, feminine.

Lowenthal's attempt to subtly exotify and foreignize gay life in Asia through descriptions of dark alleys and confusing signs seems even more problematic given his own admission that the gay life he finds in China is neither exotic nor foreign to him. In his own words:

The queen on stage, peddling her cartoonish sexuality, her stringy wig, the cheesy disco lighting: The club resembled ones I've seen from Kansas to Cape Cod, from Copenhagen to Lisbon to Havana. It called to mind the set of *RuPaul's Drag Race*. But I had crossed 12 time zones to a vast, exotic land, had braved its maze of mystifications, *for this?*

Rather than the exotic difference that the title and tagline suggest, what he finds in the dingily lit bar is no different than what gay men would find from Kansas to Copenhagen. One would be hard-pressed to find a well-lit gay bar anywhere in the world, east or west. Given these similarities, what exactly is this "gay experience as foreign as the culinary delicacies his hosts won't stop serving"? The foreign experience that Lowenthal encounters is not one of exotic and essentialistically different men with exotic and essentialistically different lives, but an intimate encounter with a drag queen in the bathroom of a rather mundane and typical gay bar. As the author writes: "Next I knew, Miss Ming smashed her lipsticked mouth on mine. I started to resist: *Sorry—not into drag queens.* But how would I know? When had I ever tried one? I had journeyed all this way, and finally, here I was."

The "foreign experience" that the article's tagline refers to is not one of exotic lands or exotic people but one of an exotic sexual experience, with a drag queen, which the author engages in for the first time, one that he could have easily and readily experienced in the United States. . . . The irony is that the author finds nothing that is exotic, including the "culinary delicacies" alluded to in the title. . . . What is exotic is his sexual encounter with a drag queen, an Asian drag queen no less. In this way, the gay Asian man, drag queen or not, is clearly a sexual other, outside of the author's normative definition of sexually desirable and, thus, a "foreign" and "exotic" experience only to be indulged 12 time zones away.

ASIANS ARE HOMOPHOBIC BUT GAYS ARE NOT RACIST

. . . The trope of Asian homophobia is presented in both subtle and blatant ways. For example, the March 14, 2006, issue of *The Advocate* included a sidebar article as part of their "World Focus" series that discusses gay issues from around the globe. In this particular issue, the column discussed the "Gay in Japan" cover story that appeared in the Japanese edition of *Newsweek* magazine. The sidebar begins with the sentence, "Coming out is still very difficult in Japan's traditional culture" and continues to discuss the difficulty of being gay in Japan. The very next issue, March 28, 2006, includes another "World Focus" sidebar article on the South Korean military's policy of discharging gay men from military service. The tone of the article, which is clearly meant to highlight homophobia in the South Korean military, ignores the homophobia in the U.S. military while denouncing the alleged homophobia in the South Korean military. Ironic given the policy of "don't ask, don't tell" that the U.S. military was practicing at the time of the article's printing, a policy that also discharged gay men from military service in the United States. In another sidebar article, which appeared in the April 25, 2006, issue on a gay Hmong support group in Minneapolis and St. Paul, author Bao Ong writes: "When Phia Xiong came out to his family at a young age, he was disowned, accused of recruiting straight people, and told there was no such thing as gay—there's not even a word for gay in Hmong."

The fact that there is no word for "gay" in the Hmong language is immediately associated with homophobia rather than a cultural tradition that did not mark and stigmatize homosexual behaviors or think of sexuality as a central core of a person's identity. Because the judgment is made entirely from a western perspective, with no regard to Hmong cultural history, the Hmong community is condemned for what the magazine deems homophobic behavior. The formation of the [support] group, and its continued growth, is attributed entirely to homophobia among Hmong community members rather than to any potential or actual

racism that the members of this group might experience from the gay community. While Phia Xiong's personal experiences with his family may have led to the formation of the group, his experiences with his family are presented as a universal Asian American experience by tying his racial background to a specific familial experience. More important, while the formation of a gay Asian American group in the twin cities is covered by the magazine, other gay Asian American groups, such as Queer and Asian in Seattle, GAPIMNY in New York City, and Gay Asian Pacific Alliance in San Francisco, that have a much larger membership and a much longer history, as well as a history of confronting racism in the gay community, are not mentioned at all. . . .

The problem is that the "Asians are homophobic" trope is often used by gay white men to justify gay racism toward gay Asian American men. For example, in a rare online discussion about racism in the gay community hosted by mainstream gay website Queerty. com, the first comment to the editorial titled "Is the Gay Community Racist?" was: "Is the black, Asian, and Latino community homophobic?" As this example demonstrates, for many gay white men, it isn't important if members of the gay community are racist. Nor does it matter how they treat other members of the gay community. What is important is how people who *look* like *those* gay men might allegedly treat them. The realization that if there is homophobia in communities of color, *those* particular gay men would also be victims of that homophobia is entirely lost on some of the gay white men who continue to conflate all people of color. In addition, any accusation of racism on the part of gay white men can be easily dismissed with references to the "homophobic" communities of color. This alleged homophobia in the Asian American community, and other communities of color, is used to excuse gay racism and provide cover for gay white men's racist behaviors, making these behaviors almost justified in their eyes. These justifications erase the existence of gay men and women of color, marking the boundaries of group membership along either race or sexuality, but not both.

Racism toward gay Asian American men by gay white men is not only ignored but actively dismissed as trivial. Perhaps the most direct discussion about gay racism is in the "Minute Rice Queens" column by writer Q. Allan Brocka that appeared in the November 6, 2007, issue of *The Advocate*. In this column, Brocka addresses the well-noted phenomenon of racial "preference" among gay white men and the racist tone that underlines these supposed "preferences." As noted by several gay commentators of color and discussed on websites such as sexualracismsux.com and sexual racismonmanhunt.blogspot.com, white men's defense of "racial preference" is deeply rooted in racist beliefs about the social worth of men of color.[14] . . . [G]ay white men often resort to a biological rationale when confronted with sexual racism, largely ignoring the racialized language that they use to describe their racial preferences of sexual partners or the racialized hierarchy that defines who is and is not desirable. For example, one online poster on the public forum hosted by Queerty.com noted, "Not liking women doesn't make me sexist, so not liking Asians doesn't make me racist." Rather than confront this absurd assumption, Brocka justifies it by stating, "I suppose if we could choose whom we are physically attracted to, there might be no gay community." The idea, of course, is that if we can indeed "choose" whom we are physically attracted to, we would all choose women, therefore leaving no gay men. Even putting aside the ridiculous idea that one's sexuality is "chosen" the way one prefers blond hair or blue eyes, the absurdity of his own defense of gay white men's racial preferences in sexual

partners as being biologically determined is contradicted by his own observation that "tastes even change sometimes. I've had friends whose lack of sexual interest in black or Asian men was reversed after a trip to Africa or Asia." It is fairly safe to assume that Brocka has no gay male friends whose sexual orientation changed. So, while sexual orientations don't change, a preference for certain attributes certainly does. Clearly, racial preferences, much like preferences for blue eyes or blond hair, are socially determined, not biologically determined, and do therefore "change sometimes." And while Brocka notes that "any number of things could shape what we look for in a partner," he further states, "all that matters to me is that people aren't jerks about their tastes." One wonders why the racist beliefs surrounding alleged racial preferences do not matter to the author.

The photo accompanying the column is doubly problematic. An image of a gay Asian man wearing a shirt imprinted with the line "Imported from Asia" marks all Asian men as foreign and part of an immigrant wave rather than as native to American soil. The idea that Asian men are all immigrants is further promoted by the author's closing remark, "Maybe you can't control whom you're attracted to, but you can control how you respond to finding an IMPORTED FROM ASIA label on your date." Why is there an expectation that Asian American men would have an "imported from Asia" label on them, while white men would never have an "imported from Europe" label? The stereotype that all Asian American men are immigrants, therefore foreign, is not only left unchallenged but is promoted. Furthermore, with this closing comment, Brocka transforms a structural problem of racism in the gay community into a personal matter that could be addressed by encouraging gay white men to simply be more polite as they are engaging in racist behavior.

ADDING INSULT TO INJURY

While the treatment of gay Asian men by *The Advocate* may be lacking, at least it is not outright degrading. In fact, given the relatively small number of gay Asian American men in the United States compared to gay white men, a few articles that represent the needs of a small portion of their potential readers might be expected. However, articles in *OUT* magazine seem to actively degrade gay Asian men for entertainment value while relegating gay Asian American men to the margins of the gay community or placing them outside of the gay community altogether. For example, the February 2005 issue of *OUT* magazine ran a column titled "How to Gab in Gaysian." A pitiful and unfortunate attempt at comic relief, *OUT* magazine introduced the column in this way:

Sometimes members of a group pepper their conversations with sexual euphemisms, saucy slang terms, and just flat-out un-PC parlance. Since there isn't an official English-Gaysian dictionary, OUT offers you a small menu of words you might want to know in order to verbal-vogue it like a queer Asian.

Included in the list of words to be translated into English were *FOBulous*, an adjective meaning "fresh off the boat and fabulous," and *dogeater*, a noun to describe a "gaysian who unapologetically uses men for all their emotional, sexual, and financial worth because they feel men are dogs by nature."

First, the column works to highlight the foreignness of gay Asian American men compared to gay white men. . . . In implying that readers of *OUT* magazine would need an "English-Gaysian dictionary," the column presupposes that such readers are white, or at least not Asian. It is the implied gay white reader who is provided with a lesson on how to decipher the "foreign" language of gay Asian American men, and it is the implied gay white reader who is to receive a "lesson" about a "foreign" group.

In addition, the column plays upon old stereotypes of Asian Americans; for one, it suggests that Asian men are perpetually foreign, and as such are outside of the gay mainstream. While an adjective to describe a recent immigrant is provided, there is no attempt to define slang terms that describe American-born Asians. Not surprising is the inclusion of the term *dogeater*, meant to conjure up stereotypical images of Asians and perceived dietary patterns. . . .

The same issue of *OUT* magazine also included an article titled "A Whole New Playing Field," about the supposed emerging gay culture and politics in Thailand. . . .

Despite the purported focus of the article being about the increase in gay visibility in Thailand, the alleged new gay movement in Thailand is largely attributed to western influences. As [Chandler] Burr argues: "Two forces are moving gay rights: the Internet—Thai gay people are connecting with U.S. and European gay people, thus learning about Western identity politics—and HIV/AIDS. Just as it did in the West, HIV/AIDS is relentlessly forcing the growth of gay political power."

While Burr states that two forces are moving gay rights in Thailand, western gays are given credit in both. It is the western gays who are providing Thai men with a lesson about gay identities, and it is the "western" model that Thai men are following in responding to HIV/AIDS. Here, gay white men are seen as coming to the aid of gay Thai men who, before the onset of western influence, had "no vocabulary" for being gay and thus, "use the English word 'gay' for men whose sexual orientations are homosexual." Much like *The Advocate* article on the formation of the gay Hmong support group, the author takes it as a given that having no word for "gay" is equated with being homophobic. Rather than examine cultural patterns that may have excluded labels for exclusively "gay" men and the westernized notions of equating sexual behavior with sexual identity, the author implies that the lack of such labels is an indication of a society that has not yet come to terms with having homosexual members. Yet any reading of Thai sexual history would show that Thailand has a long history of accepting men who have sex with men.[15]

Western gay men are also given credit for the rising "gay consciousness" found in Thailand. . . .

Gay white men are also portrayed as helping Thai men who are inept at simple rational activities such as planning. Burr explains that after [gay activist] Pakorn [Pimton] organized the first Bangkok Gay Festival in 1999, Bangkok Pride "almost died several times" because of what Burr characterizes as a lack of planning and coordination. . . .

Despite Burr's own contention that HIV/AIDS is central to political organizing among gay Thai men, little is said about the role that sex tourism by white men contributed to the rising epidemic. Instead, Burr attempts to remove blame from western tourists on what he presents as largely a Thai problem. . . .

. . . [D]escriptions of white male celebrities, gay and straight, as being "hot" or sexually desirable are routine in OUT magazine. Yet, despite the fact that a number of Asian celebrities . . . are profiled or discussed in the magazine, none of them is described as being sexually desirable in any way. In fact, allusions to their attractiveness are strikingly absent. Even when a man is described as "handsome," as is nightclub host Xiao Gang in Dan Levin's article "Comrades and Boundaries," in the October 2008 issue, about gay nightlife in China, the description is torturously desexualized by describing him as "a slim, handsome man of 31 with an impish face and great hair." So, while an Asian man may be considered "handsome," it is in a child-like "impish" way, devoid of sexual connotations. . . .

To be fair, two Asian men do appear on the "hot list" in 2005. However, one is Buddhist monk Dzongsar Khyentse Rinpoche, who the magazine features as the "hottest Lama" for being "open about his gay 'tendency'" rather than for being sexually desirable, and an Asian stripper who is used to feature Remington's in Toronto, which the magazine notes is the "hottest male strip club." The use of a nameless Asian stripper, whose most prominent asset in the photo is his ass, to represent a strip club where bodies on display are specifically meant for consumption, is an interesting contrast to the named white men who are included as the hottest alt-rock record executive, hottest DJ, hottest reality personality, hottest straight guy we wish was gay, hottest crooner, hottest returning gay rock icon, hottest up-and-coming filmmaker, hottest has-been, hottest author, hottest photographer, hottest gay romance-writing couple, hottest contractor, hottest porn star, and hottest designers. . . .

The only other images of Asian men to appear in OUT magazine before the yearend issue in 2005 are in a September review of the nude photography book The Asian Male. Although the brief review states that the photos in the book "clearly challenge the stereotype of Asian men as passive geeks," it nonetheless quotes the photographer as stating that the thing that makes Asian men sexy is their "delicious skin; really nice butts; sensuous, alluring eyes." It's good to know that the author of the review is aware of the geek stereotype thrust upon all Asian men; however, it's obvious that they believe it is the stereotypical beliefs about Asian male femininity that make Asian men attractive to white audiences. . . .

Gay Asian men don't make it onto the "hot list" again until 2009, when three gay Asian men are featured. The first is designer Jason Wu, who is quoted as stating, "I played with dolls. I made little clothes for them." . . . Wu . . . also [states] that it would have been "traumatic" if his family did not immigrate to Vancouver from Taipei when he was a young child, given his own description of Taiwan as an "extremely conventional society." The allusion, of course, is that a young boy dressing dolls would have been persecuted in Taiwan but was somehow fully accepted in Vancouver, an allusion that is laughable at best. Yet, characterizing Asian countries as conventional, and thus homophobic, and western nations as progressive on issues of gender and sexuality allows *OUT* magazine to continue to promote the trope of Asian homophobia and western acceptance. . . .

NO SHORTAGE OF ASIAN MEN HERE

While virtually invisible in feature stories, gay Asian men are amply present in advertisements placed in gay periodicals. Full-page ads for pornographic films with all-Asian casts are scattered generously throughout the pages of gay publications, although Asian men are excluded from the features. While advertisements in gay periodicals seem to advertise to gay white men, they advertise gay Asian men as a commodity for consumption. Perhaps this is nowhere more evident than in the pages of *Oriental Guys Magazine*. Originally published in Sydney, the recently defunct *Oriental Guys Magazine* was essentially a nine-year advertisement of gay Asian men for white men. The Asian men who grace the pages of *Oriental Guys Magazine* and other such "rice queen magazines," named in reference to *rice queens*—gay white men who prefer Asian sex partners—are meant for white male consumption, and sexual narratives regarding the men pictured are almost always written by white men.[16] Further highlighting this

argument, gay Asian American film director Quentin Lee writes:

I often get slightly depressed when I wander through queer stores, whether it's in San Francisco, Montreal or Hawaii. It's the same everywhere, in every part of North America. There are so few porno products about us Asian queers, and these few are not created by us, they are exotified for the pleasure of the white man.[17]

To illustrate his point, Lee discusses a story in *Beau Magazine* titled "Thai'ed up for the evening," about a sailor, presumed to be white, and his sexual encounter with two Thai "boys." Lee quotes from the story as follows:

Their childlike, scrawny bodies didn't do much for me, I dream of the Jeff Stryker type, and these kids weren't it. Even when I had been a boy I never lusted after boys, only strong adult men. These were going to take some getting used to. Let's face it: A scrawny five-foot kid isn't going to have the size of Godzilla. They told me they were 20 and 23. When I asked them their names and got some Thai back in return, I told the one with the big dick that his name was "Butch" and the other that his was "Sundance." I doubt they saw the humor, but did I give a fuck?[18]

Although not common in gay pornographic magazines, these are the only such stories that feature Asian characters. Asian characters are never the narrators, rather they are the narrated. As Lee notes, in these stories, the subject is the assumed white male, while Asian men are simply the objects present for sexual gratification. . . . By making the sharp contrast with Stryker, a famous porn actor notorious for being the muscular, masculine, and active "top" in gay porn films, the narrator constructs the Thai boys as feminine, passive, and submissive. . . .

Richard Fung also notes that gay Asian actors in gay porn exist only for the pleasure of white men.[19] In . . . "Looking for My Penis," Fung finds that gay Asian porn actors always, with the exception of one instance, take the bottom role of passive recipient of anal sex. Even in the one exception where the Asian porn actor plays the active sexual partner, the narrative of the plot has him performing the role of the white man's domestic servant. In this way, even the normally aggressive and active sexual role of the top is couched in the Asian man's "service" of the white man. . . .

DISMANTLING HEGEMONIC MASCULINITY

It's not surprising that the feminine image of all Asian men has been easily superimposed onto gay media. Contrasting the "feminine" gay Asian man to the "masculine" gay white man places gay white men in the dominant position in a society and culture that value masculinity over femininity, active over passive, and virile over submissive. In doing so, gay publications create a hierarchy of those who belong in the gay community and those who are simply marginal members. . . .

The real goal needs to be an attempt at changing the dominant view of masculinity within the gay community rather than buying into the existing model provided by the gay mainstream. Doing so, however, is hardly an easy task. Rather than focusing on reproducing the dominant gay images of masculinity with Asian faces, I believe, as Jachinson Chan suggests, that "an ambivalent or ambiguous model of masculinity is a more effective way to counter a hegemonic model of masculinity."[20] However, doing so is a daunting task. But what other options are there if the ultimate goal is to dismantle the very system of gendered expectations that continually places gay men of color in the subordinate position to gay white men? . . .

NOTES

1. Jeffrey Chan et al., *The Big Aiiieeee! An Anthology of Chinese American and Japanese American Literature* (New York: Meridian, 1991), xiii.

2. David Eng, *Racial Castration: Managing Masculinity in Asian America* (Durham: Duke University Press, 2001). See also, Darrell Hamamoto, *Monitored Peril: Asian Americans and the Politics of TV Representation* (Minneapolis: University of Minnesota Press, 1994) and Robert Lee, *Orientals: Asian Americans in Popular Culture* (Philadelphia: Temple University Press, 1999).

3. Lisa Lowe, *Immigrant Acts: On Asian American Cultural Politics* (Durham: Duke University Press, 1996).

4. Roderick Ferguson, *Aberrations in Black: Toward a Queer of Color Critique* (Minneapolis: University of Minnesota Press, 2003). . . .

5. Serge Moscovici, "Introduction," in *Health and Illness: A Social Psychological Analysis*, ed. Claudine Herzlich (London: Academic Press, 1973).

6. Ibid., xi.

7. Edward Said, *Culture and Imperialism* (New York: Alfred A. Knopf, 1993), 314.

8. Stuart Hall, "Cultural Identity and Cinematic Representation," *Framework*, 36 (1989): 69.

9. Richard Dyer, *The Matter of Images: Essays on Representation* (London: Routledge, 2002), 1.

10. Walter Lippman, *Public Opinion* (New York: Harcourt, Brace and Company, 1922), 96.

11. Peter Berger and Thomas Luckman, *The Social Construction of Reality* (London: Allen Lane, 1967).

12. Peter Dahlgren, "Introduction," in *Journalism and Popular Culture*, ed. Peter Dahlgren and Colin Spark (London: Sage, 1992), 18. See also, John Storey, *Cultural Studies and the Study of Popular Culture* (Athens: University of Georgia Press, 1996).

13. Stephen Murray. "Representations of Desire in Some Recent Gay Asian-American Writing," *Journal of Homosexuality*, 45 (2003). See also, Maurice Poon, "The Discourse of Oppression in Contemporary Gay Asian Diasporal Literature: Liberation or Limitation?" *Sexuality and Culture*, 10 (2006).

14. Alex Blaze, "John Mayer and Sexual Racism: *The Bilerico Project*," February 11, 2010, http://www.bilerico.com/2010/02/john_mayer_and_sexual_racism.php. Daniel W. K. Lee, "Don't Ask, Just Tell: Sexual Racism Is at the Core of What Many Gay Men Believe to Be 'Preferences,'" *Metro Weekly*, September 23, 2010, http://metroweekly.com/news/opinion/?ak=5613. Andy Quan, "I Don't Have a Racist Bone in My Body," *Crank Magazine*, 2 (2002). Alex Rowlson. "Not Just a Preference," *FAB Magazine*, October 12, 2011, http://www.fabmagazine.com/story/not-just-a-preference.

15. Peter A. Jackson and Gerard Sullivan, eds., *Lady Boys, Tom Boys, Rent Boys: Male and Female Homosexualities in Contemporary Thailand* (Binghamton, NY: Haworth Press, 1999).

16. Paul Hagland, "'Undressing the Oriental Boy': The Gay Asian in the Social Imagination of the Gay White Male," in *Looking Queer: Body Image and Identity in Lesbian, Bisexual, Gay and Transgender Communities*, ed. Dawn Atkin (New York: Harrington Park Press, 1998).

17. Quentin Lee, "The Sailor and the Thai Boys," *Lavender Godzilla*, 8 (1999): 12.

18. Ibid, 11.

19. Richard Fung, "Looking for My Penis," in *How Do I Look? Queer Film and Video*, ed. Bad Object Choices (Seattle: Bay Press, 1991).

20. Jachinson W. Chan, "Bruce Lee's Fictional Model of Masculinity," *Men and Masculinities*, 2 (2000): 385.

WHAT TEENAGERS ARE LEARNING FROM ONLINE PORN

MAGGIE JONES

Drew was 8 years old when he was flipping through TV channels at home and landed on "Girls Gone Wild." A few years later, he came across HBO's late-night soft-core pornography. Then in ninth grade, he found online porn sites on his phone. The videos were good for getting off, he said, but also sources for ideas for future sex positions with future girlfriends. From porn, he learned that guys need to be buff and dominant in bed, doing things like flipping girls over on their stomach during sex. Girls moan a lot and are turned on by pretty much everything a confident guy does. One particular porn scene stuck with him: A woman was bored by a man who approached sex gently but became ecstatic with a far more aggressive guy.

But around 10th grade, it began bothering Drew, an honor-roll student who loves baseball and writing rap lyrics and still confides in his mom, that porn influenced how he thought about girls at school. Were their breasts, he wondered, like the ones in porn? Would girls look at him the way women do in porn when they had sex? Would they give him blow jobs and do the other stuff he saw?

Drew, who asked me to use one of his nicknames, was a junior when I first met him in late 2016, and he told me some of this one Thursday afternoon, as we sat in a small conference room with several other high school boys, eating chips and drinking soda and waiting for an after-school program to begin. Next to Drew was Q., who asked me to identify him by the first initial of his nickname. He was 15, a good student and a baseball fan, too, and pretty perplexed about how porn translated into real life. Q. hadn't had sex—he liked older, out-of-reach

girls, and the last time he had a girlfriend was in sixth grade, and they just fooled around a bit. So he wasn't exactly in a good position to ask girls directly what they liked. But as he told me over several conversations, it wasn't just porn but rough images on Snapchat, Facebook and other social media that confused him. Like the GIF he saw of a man pushing a woman against a wall with a girl commenting: "I want a guy like this." And the one Drew mentioned of the "pain room" in "Fifty Shades of Grey" with a caption by a girl: "This is awesome!"

Watching porn also heightened Q.'s performance anxiety. "You are looking at an adult," he told me. "The guys are built and dominant and have a big penis, and they last a long time." And if you don't do it like the guys in porn, Drew added, "you fear she's not going to like you."

Leaning back in his chair, Drew said some girls acted as if they wanted some thug rather than a smart, sensitive guy. But was it true desire? Was it posturing? Was it what girls thought they were supposed to want? Neither Q. nor Drew knew. A couple of seats away, a sophomore who had been quiet until then added that maybe the girls didn't know either. "I think social media makes girls think they want something," he said, noting he hadn't seen porn more than a handful of times and disliked it. "But I think some of the girls are afraid."

"It gets in your head," Q. said. "If this girl wants it, then maybe the majority of girls want it." He'd heard about the importance of consent in sex, but it felt pretty abstract, and it didn't seem as if it would always be realistic in the heat of the moment. Out of nowhere was he supposed to say: Can I pull your hair? Or could he try something and see how a girl responded? He knew that there were certain things—"big things, like sex toys or anal"—that he would not try without asking.

"I would just do it," said another boy, in jeans and a sweatshirt. When I asked what he meant, he said anal sex. He assumed that girls like it, because the women in porn do.

"I would never do something that looked uncomfortable," Drew said, jumping back into the conversation. "I might say, 'I've seen this in porn—do you want to try it?'"

It was almost 4 p.m., and the boys started to gather their backpacks to head to a class known as Porn Literacy. The course, with the official title The Truth About Pornography: A Pornography-Literacy Curriculum for High School Students Designed to Reduce Sexual and Dating Violence, is a recent addition to Start Strong, a peer-leadership program for teenagers headquartered in Boston's South End and funded by the city's public-health agency. About two dozen selected high school students attend every year, most of them black or Latino, along with a few Asian students, from Boston public high schools, including the city's competitive exam schools, and a couple of parochial schools. During most of the year, the teenagers learn about healthy relationships, dating violence and L.G.B.T. issues, often through group discussions, role-playing and other exercises.

But for around two hours each week, for five weeks, the students—sophomores, juniors and seniors—take part in Porn Literacy, which aims to make them savvier, more critical consumers of porn by examining how gender, sexuality, aggression, consent, race, queer sex, relationships and body images are portrayed (or, in the case of consent, not portrayed) in porn.

On average, boys are around 13, and girls are around 14, when they first see pornography, says Bryant Paul, an associate professor at Indiana University's Media School and the author of studies on porn content and adolescent and adult viewing habits. In a 2008 University of New Hampshire survey, 93 percent of male college students and 62 percent of female students said they saw online porn before they were 18. Many females, in particular, weren't seeking it out. Thirty-five percent of males said they had watched it 10 or more times during adolescence.

Porn Literacy, which began in 2016 and is the focus of a pilot study, was created in part by Emily Rothman, an associate professor at Boston University's School of Public Health who has conducted several studies on dating violence, as well as on porn use by adolescents. She told me that the curriculum isn't designed to scare kids into believing porn is addictive, or that it will ruin their lives and relationships and warp their libidos. Instead it is grounded in the reality that most adolescents do see porn and takes the approach that teaching them to analyze its messages is far more effective than simply wishing our children could live in a porn-free world.

Imagine that you are a 14-year-old today. A friend might show you a short porn clip on his phone during the bus ride to school or after soccer practice. A pornographic GIF appears on Snapchat. Or you mistype the word "fishing" and end up with a bunch of links to "fisting" videos. Like most 14-year-olds, you haven't had sex, but you're curious, so maybe you start searching and land on one of the many porn sites that work much like YouTube—XVideos.com, Xnxx.com, BongaCams.com, all of them among the 100 most-frequented websites in the world, according to Alexa Top Sites. Or you find Pornhub, the most popular of the group, with 80 million visitors a day and more traffic than Pinterest, Tumblr or PayPal. The mainstream websites aren't verifying your age, and your phone allows you to watch porn away from the scrutinizing eyes of adults. If you still have parental-control filters, you probably have ways around them.

Besides, there's a decent chance your parents don't think you are watching porn. Preliminary analysis of data from a 2016 Indiana University survey of more than 600 pairs of children and their parents reveals a parental naïveté gap: Half as many parents thought their 14- and 18-year-olds had seen porn as had in fact watched it. And depending on the sex act, parents underestimated what their kids saw by as much as 10 times.

What teenagers see on Pornhub depends partly on algorithms and the clips they've clicked on in the past. Along with stacks of videos on the opening page, there are several dozen categories ("teen," "anal," "blonde," "girl on girl," "ebony," "milf") that can take them to more than six million videos. The clips tend to be short, low on production value, free and, though Pornhub tries to prevent it, sometimes pirated from paid sites. Many of the heterosexual videos are shot from the male point of view, as if the man were holding the camera while he has sex with a woman whose main job, via oral sex, intercourse or anal sex, is to make him orgasm. Plot lines are thin to nonexistent as the camera zooms in for up-close shots of genitals and penetration that are repetitive, pounding and—though perhaps not through the eyes of a 14-year-old—banal. (There are alternative narratives in L.G.B.T. and feminist porn, and studies show that for gay and bisexual youth, porn can provide affirmation that they are not alone in their sexual desires.)

We don't have many specifics on what kids actually view, in large part because it's extremely difficult to get federal funding for research on children and pornography. A few years ago, frustrated by the dearth of large, recent United States studies, Rashida Jones,

Jill Bauer and Ronna Gradus, creators of the 2017 Netflix documentary series "Hot Girls Wanted: Turned On," about technology and porn, paired with several foundations and philanthropists to fund a national survey about porn viewing, sexual attitudes and behaviors. As part of the survey, led by Debby Herbenick, a professor at the Indiana University School of Public Health and director of the university's Center for Sexual Health Promotion, along with her colleague Bryant Paul, 614 teenagers ages 14 to 18 reported what their experiences were with porn. In preliminary data analysis from the study (Herbenick is submitting an academic paper for publication [in 2018]), of the roughly 300 who did watch porn, one-quarter of the girls and 36 percent of the boys said they had seen videos of men ejaculating on women's faces (known as "facials"), Paul says. Almost one-third of both sexes saw B.D.S.M. (bondage, domination, sadism, masochism), and 26 percent of males and 20 percent of females watched videos with double penetration, described in the study as one or more penises or objects in a woman's anus and/or in her vagina. Also, 31 percent of boys said they had seen "gang bangs," or group sex, and "rough oral sex" (a man aggressively thrusting his penis in and out of a mouth); less than half as many girls had.

It's hard to know if, and how, this translates into behavior. While some studies show that a small number of teenagers who watch higher rates of porn engage in earlier sex, as well as in gender stereotyping and in sexual relationships that are less affectionate than their peers', these findings only indicate correlations, not cause and effect. But surveys do suggest that the kinds of sex some teenagers have may be shifting. The percentage of 18- to 24-year-old women who reported trying anal sex rose to 40 percent in 2009 from 16 percent in 1992, according to the largest survey on American sexual behavior in decades, co-authored by

Herbenick and published in the Journal of Sexual Medicine. In data from that same survey, 20 percent of 18- to 19-year-old females had tried anal sex; about 6 percent of 14- to 17-year-old females had. And in a 2016 Swedish study of nearly 400 16-year-old girls, the percentage of girls who had tried anal sex doubled if they watched pornography. Like other studies about sex and porn, it only showed a correlation, and girls who are more sexually curious may also be drawn to porn. In addition, some girls may view anal sex as a "safer" alternative to vaginal sex, as there's little risk of pregnancy.

The Indiana University national survey of teenagers asked about other sex behaviors as well. Though the data have not been fully analyzed, preliminary findings suggest that of the teenagers who had had sex, around one-sixth of boys said they had ejaculated on someone's face or choked a sex partner. The survey didn't define choking, but the high school and college-age students I spoke to referred to it as anything from placing a hand gently on a partner's neck to squeezing it.

We don't have longitudinal data on the frequency of ejaculating on a girl's face or choking among American teenagers to know whether either practice is more common now. And, as David Finkelhor, director of the Crimes Against Children Research Center at the University of New Hampshire, told me, fewer teenagers have early sex than in the past (in a recent study, 24 percent of American ninth graders had sex; in 1995 about 37 percent had), and arrests of teenagers for sexual assault are also down. But you don't have to believe that porn leads to sexual assault or that it's creating a generation of brutal men to wonder how it helps shape how teenagers talk and think about sex and, by extension, their ideas about masculinity, femininity, intimacy and power.

Over the year in which I spoke to dozens of older teenagers at Start Strong and around the country, many said that both porn and mainstream media—everything from the TV show "Family Guy" (which references choking and anal sex) to Nicki Minaj's song "Truffle Butter" (with an apparent allusion to anal sex followed by vaginal sex) to the lyrics in Rihanna's "S&M" ("Sticks and stones may break my bones, but chains and whips excite me")—made anal and rough sex seem almost commonplace. Drew told me he got the sense that girls wanted to be dominated not only from reading a few pages of "Fifty Shades of Grey" but also from watching the movie "Mr. & Mrs. Smith," with Brad Pitt and Angelina Jolie. "She's on the table, and she's getting pounded by him. That's all I've seen growing up."

These images confound many teenagers about the kinds of sex they want or think they should have. In part, that's because they aren't always sure what is fake and what is real in porn. Though some told me that porn was fantasy or exaggerated, others said that porn wasn't real only insofar as it wasn't typically two lovers having sex on film. Some of those same teenagers assumed the portrayal of how sex and pleasure worked was largely accurate. That seems to be in keeping with a 2016 survey of 1,001 11- to 16-year-olds in Britain. Of the roughly half who had seen pornography, 53 percent of boys and 39 percent of girls said it was "realistic." And in the recent Indiana University national survey, only one in six boys and one in four girls believed that women in online porn were not actually experiencing pleasure: As one suburban high school senior boy told me recently, "I've never seen a girl in porn who doesn't look like she's having a good time."

It's not surprising, then, that some adolescents use porn as a how-to guide. In a study that Rothman carried out in 2016 of 72 high schoolers ages 16 and 17, teenagers reported that porn was their primary source for information about sex—more than friends, siblings, schools or parents.

"There's nowhere else to learn about sex," the suburban boy told me. "And porn stars know what they are doing." His words reflect a paradox about sex and pornography in this country. Even as smartphones have made it easier for teenagers to watch porn, sex education in the United States—where abstinence-based sex education remains the norm—is meager. Massachusetts is among 26 states that do not mandate sex ed. And a mere 13 require that the material be medically and scientifically accurate. After some gains by the Obama administration to promote more comprehensive sex ed, which includes pregnancy prevention, discussions of anatomy, birth control, disease prevention, abstinence and healthy relationships, the Trump administration did not include the program in its proposed 2018 budget; it also has requested increased funding for abstinence education. Easy-to-access online porn fills the vacuum, making porn the de facto sex educator for American youth.

One Thursday afternoon, about a dozen teenagers sat in a semicircle of North Face zip-ups, Jordans, combat boots, big hoop earrings and the slumped shoulders of late afternoon. It was the third week of Porn Literacy, and everyone already knew the rules: You don't have to have watched porn to attend; no yucking someone else's yum—no disparaging a student's sexual tastes or sexuality. And avoid sharing personal stories about sex in class. Nicole Daley and Jess Alder, who wrote the curriculum with Emily Rothman and led most of the exercises and discussion, are in their 30s, warm and easygoing. Daley, who until last month was the director of Start Strong, played the slightly more serious favorite-aunt role, while Alder, who runs Start Strong's classes for teenagers, was the goofier, ask-me-anything big sister. Rothman also attended most of the classes, offering information about pornography studies and explaining to them, for example, that there is no scientific evidence that porn is addictive, but that people can become compulsive about it.

In the first class, Daley led an exercise in which the group defined porn terms (B.D.S.M., kink, soft-core, hard-core), so that, as she put it, "everyone is on the same page" and "you can avoid clicking on things you don't want to see." The students also "values voted"— agreeing or disagreeing about whether the legal viewing age of 18 for porn is too high, if working in the porn industry is a good way to make money and if pornography should be illegal. Later, Daley held up images of a 1940s pinup girl, a Japanese geisha and Kim Kardashian, to talk about how cultural values about beauty and bodies change over time. In future classes, they would talk about types of intimacy not depicted in porn and nonsexist pickup lines. Finally, Daley would offer a lesson about sexting and sexting laws and the risks of so-called revenge porn (in which, say, a teenager circulates a naked selfie of an ex without consent). And to the teenagers' surprise, they learned that receiving or sending consensual naked photos, even to your boyfriend or girlfriend, can be against the law if the person in the photo is a minor.

Now, in the third week of class, Daley's goal was to undercut porn's allure for teenagers by exposing the underbelly of the business. "When you understand it's not just two people on the screen but an industry," she told me, "it's not as sexy."

To that end, Daley started class by detailing a midlevel female performer's salary (taken from the 2008 documentary "The Price of Pleasure"): "Blow job: $300," Daley read from a list. "Anal: $1,000. Double penetration: $1,200. Gang bang: $1,300 for three guys. $100 for each additional guy."

"Wow," Drew muttered. "That makes it nasty now."

"That's nothing for being penetrated on camera," another boy said.

Then, as if they had been given a green light to ask about a world that grown-ups rarely acknowledge, they began peppering Daley, Rothman and Alder with questions.

"How much do men get paid?" one girl asked. It is one of the few professions in which men are paid less, Rothman explained, but they also typically have longer careers. How long do women stay in their jobs? On average, six to 18 months. How do guys get erections if they aren't turned on? Often Viagra, Rothman offered, and sometimes a "fluffer," as an off-screen human stimulator is known.

Daley then asked the teenagers to pretend they were contestants on a reality-TV show, in which they had to decide if they were willing to participate in certain challenges (your parents might be watching) and for how much money. In one scenario, she said, you would kneel on the ground while someone poured a goopy substance over your face. In another, you'd lick a spoon that had touched fecal matter. The kids debated the fecal-matter challenge—most wouldn't do it for less than $2 million. One wanted know if the goop smelled. "Can we find out what it is?" asked another.

Then Daley explained that each was in fact a simulation of a porn act. The goopy substance was what's called a "baker's dozen," in which 13 men ejaculate on a woman's face, breasts and mouth.

"What?" a girl named Tiffany protested.

The second scenario—licking the spoon with fecal matter—was from a porn act known as A.T.M., in which a man puts his penis in a woman's anus and then immediately follows by sticking it in her mouth.

"No way," a 15-year-old boy said. "Can't you wash in between?"

Nope, Daley said.

"We don't question it when we see it in porn, right?" Daley went on. "There's no judgment here, but some of you guys are squeamish about it."

"I never knew any of this," Drew said, sounding a bit glum.

Daley went on to detail a 2010 study that coded incidents of aggression in best-selling 2004 and 2005 porn videos. She noted that 88 percent of scenes showed verbal or physical aggression, mostly spanking, slapping and gagging. (A more recent content analysis of more than 6,000 mainstream online heterosexual porn scenes by Bryant Paul and his colleagues defined aggression specifically as any purposeful action appearing to cause physical or psychological harm to another person and found that 33 percent of scenes met that criterion. In each study, women were on the receiving end of the aggression more than 90 percent of the time.)

"Do you think," Daley said, standing in front of the students, "watching porn leads to violence against women? There's no right or wrong here. It's a debate."

Kyrah, a 10th-grade feminist with an athlete's compact body and a tendency to speak her opinions, didn't hesitate. "In porn they glamorize calling women a slut or a whore, and younger kids think this is how it is. Or when they have those weird porn scenes and the woman is saying, 'Stop touching me,' and then she ends up enjoying it!"

Tiffany, her best friend, snapped her fingers in approval.

"Yes and no," one guy interjected. "When a man is choking a woman in porn, people know it is not real, and they aren't supposed to do it, because it's violence." He was the same teenager who told me he would just "do" anal sex without asking a girl, because the women in porn like it.

Pornography didn't create the narrative that male pleasure should be first and foremost. But that idea is certainly reinforced by "a male-dominated porn industry shot through a male lens," as Cindy Gallop puts it. Gallop is the creator of an online platform called

MakeLoveNotPorn, where users can submit videos of their sexual encounters—which she describes as "real world," consensual sex with "good values"—and pay to watch videos of others.

For years, Gallop has been a one-woman laboratory witnessing how easy-to-access mainstream porn influences sex. Now in her 50s, she has spent more than a decade dating 20-something men. She finds them through "cougar" dating sites—where older women connect with younger men—and her main criterion is that they are "nice." Even so, she told me, during sex with these significantly younger nice men, she repeatedly encounters porn memes: facials, "jackhammering" intercourse, more frequent requests for anal sex and men who seem less focused on female orgasms than men were when she was younger. Gallop takes it upon herself to "re-educate," as she half-jokingly puts it, men raised on porn. Some people, of course, do enjoy these acts. But speaking of teenagers in particular, she told me she worries that hard-core porn leads many girls to think, for example, that "all boys love coming on girls' faces, and all girls love having their faces come on. And therefore, girls feel they must let boys come on their face and pretend to like it."

Though none of the boys I spoke to at Start Strong told me they had ejaculated on a girl's face, Gallop's words reminded me of conversations I had with some older high schoolers in various cities. One senior said that ejaculating on a woman's face was in a majority of porn scenes he had watched, and that he had done it with a girlfriend. "I brought it up, or she would say, 'Come on my face.' It was an aspect I liked—and she did, too."

Another noted that the act is "talked about a lot" among guys, but said that "a girl's got to be down with it" before he'd ever consider doing it. "There is something that's appealing for guys. The dominance and intimacy and that whole opportunity for eye contact. Guys are obsessed with their come displayed on a girl."

Many girls at Start Strong were decidedly less enthusiastic. One senior told me a boyfriend asked to ejaculate on her face; she said no. And during a conversation I had with three girls, one senior wondered aloud: "What if you don't want a facial? What are you supposed to do? Friends say a boy cleans it with a napkin. A lot of girls my age like facials." But a few moments later, she reversed course. "I actually don't think they like it. They do it because their partner likes it." Next to her, a sophomore added that when older girls talk among themselves, many say it's gross. "But they say you gotta do what you gotta do." And if you don't, the first girl added, "then someone else will."

These are not new power dynamics between girls and boys. In a 2014 British study about anal sex and teenagers, girls expressed a similar lack of sexual agency and experienced physical pain. In the survey, of 130 heterosexual teenagers ages 16 to 18, teenagers often said they believed porn was a motivating factor for why males wanted anal sex. And among the guys who reported trying it, many said friends encouraged them, or they felt competitive with other guys to do it. At the same time, a majority of girls who had tried anal sex said they didn't actually want to; their partners persuaded or coerced them. Some males took a "try it and see" approach, as researchers called it, attempting to put their finger or penis in a girl's anus and hoping she didn't stop them. Sometimes, one teenager reported, you "just keep going till they just get fed up and let you do it anyway." Both boys and girls blamed the girls for pain they felt during anal sex and some told researchers the girls needed to "relax" more or "get used to it." Only one girl said she enjoyed it, and only a few boys did. Teenagers may not know that even while porn makes it seem commonplace, in the 2009 national survey of American sex habits, most men and women who tried anal sex didn't make it a regular part of their sex lives. And in another study, by Indiana University's Debby Herbenick and others in 2015, about 70 percent of women who had anal sex said they experienced pain.

Drew had firsthand experience with what he had seen in porn not translating into actual pleasure. The first time he had sex, he thought he was supposed to exert some physical control over his girlfriend. But the whole thing felt awkward, too rough and not all that fun. And things that looked easy in porn, like sex while taking a shower or mutual oral sex, didn't go so well.

At one point during sex, Drew's girlfriend at the time, who was a year older and more experienced, asked him to put his hand around her neck during sex. He did it, without squeezing, and though it didn't exactly bother him, it felt uncomfortable. Drew never asked if she got the idea from porn, but it made him wonder. Had she also picked up other ways of acting? "Like, how do you really know a girl has had a good time?" he said one afternoon, musing aloud while sitting with some friends before Porn Literacy class. "My girlfriend said she had a good time," he went on. "She was moaning. But that's the thing: Is it fake moaning?"

Even if you know porn isn't realistic, it still sets up expectations, one senior told me. In porn, he said, "the clothes are off, and the girl goes down on the guy, he gets hard and he starts having sex with her. It's all very simple and well lit." Before he had sex, porn had supplied his images of oral sex, including scenes in which a woman is on her knees as a man stands over her. At one point, he thought that's how it might go one day when he had sex. But when he talked with his girlfriend, they realized they didn't want to re-enact that power dynamic.

I spent a couple of hours on a Wednesday afternoon at Start Strong with a senior girl who took the first Porn Literacy class in the summer of 2016. Looking back over the last several years of middle and high school, A., who

asked me to identify her by the first initial of her middle name, said she wished she had had someplace—home, school, a community sex-ed program—to learn about sex. Instead, she learned about it from porn. She saw it for the first time by accident, after a group of sixth-grade boys cajoled her to look at tube8.com, which she didn't know was a porn site. She was fascinated. She had never seen a penis before, "not a drawing of one, nothing." A few years later, she searched online for porn again, after listening to girls in the high school locker room talk about masturbation. A.'s parents, whom she describes as conservative about sex, hadn't talked to her about female anatomy or sex, and her school didn't offer any sex education before ninth grade; even then, it focused mostly on the dangers—sexually transmitted infections and diseases and pregnancy.

Aside from some private schools and innovative community programs, relatively few sex-ed classes in middle and high school delve in detail into anatomy (female, especially), intimacy, healthy relationships, sexual diversity. Even more rare are discussions of female desire and pleasure. Porn taught A. the basics of masturbation. And porn served as her study guide when she was 16 and was the first among her friends to have sex. She clicked through videos to watch women giving oral sex. She focused on how they moved during sex and listened to how they moaned. She began shaving her vulva ("I've never seen anyone in porn have sex with hair on it").

Porn is "not all bad," said A., who was frank and funny, with a slew of Advanced Placement classes on her transcript and a self-assured manner that impresses adults. "I got my sexual ways from porn, and I like the way I am." But what she learned from porn had downsides too. Because she assumed women's pleasure in porn was real, when she first had intercourse and didn't have an orgasm, she figured that was just how it went.

For A., it wasn't enough to know that porn was fake sex. She wanted to understand how real sex worked. Rothman and her team did consult a sex educator while they were writing the Porn Literacy curriculum but decided to include only some basic information about safe sex. It came in the form of a "Porn Jeopardy" game during one class. The teenagers, clustered in teams, chose from four categories: S.T.D./S.T.I.s, Birth Control, Teen Violence/Sexual Assault and Porn on the Brain.

"S.T.I.s/S.T.D.s for $300," one student called out.

"Why is lubrication important for sex?" Alder asked.

"What's lubrication?" Drew asked.

"It's lube," another teenager said, in an attempt to explain.

"Is lubrication only the little tube-y things?" a girl with long black hair asked. "Or can it be natural?"

"I never learned this before," Drew announced to the class after it was mentioned that lubrication decreased friction, increased pleasure and could reduce the risk of tearing and therefore of S.T.I.s and S.T.D.s. Drew's only sliver of sex ed was in sixth grade with the school gym teacher, who sweated as he talked about sex, "and it was all about it being bad and we shouldn't do it."

As if to rectify that, Alder offered a quick anatomy lesson, drawing a vulva on the whiteboard and pointing out the clitoris, the vagina, the urethra. "This is called a vulva," she said. Alder repeated the word slowly and loudly, as if instructing the students in a foreign language. It was both for humor and to normalize a word that some of them may have been hearing for the first time. "This is the clitoris," Alder went on. "This is where women get most pleasure. Most women do not have a G spot. If you want to know how to give a woman pleasure, it's the clitoris."

"Let's move on," Rothman said quietly. Alder had just inched across a line in which anatomy rested on one side and female desire and pleasure on the other. It was a reminder that as controversial as it is to teach kids about pornography, it can be more taboo to teach them how their bodies work sexually. "The class is about critically analyzing sexually explicit media," Rothman told me later, "not how to have sex. We want to stay in our narrow lane and not be seen as promoting anything parents are uncomfortable with." Daley added: "I wish it were different, but we have to be aware of the limitations of where we are as a society."

Porn education is such new territory that no one knows the best practices, what material should be included and where to teach it. (Few people are optimistic that it will be taught anytime soon in public schools.) Several years ago, L. Kris Gowen, a sexuality educator and author of the 2017 book "Sexual Decisions: The Ultimate Teen Guide," wrote extensive guidelines for teaching teenagers to critique "sexually explicit media" (she avoided the more provocative term "porn literacy"). Even though Oregon, where Gowen lives, has one of the most comprehensive sex ed programs in the country, Gowen said that teachers felt unequipped to talk about porn. And though the guidelines have been circulated at education conferences and made publicly available, Gowen doesn't know of a single educator who has implemented them. In part, she says, people may be waiting for a better sense of what's effective. But also, many schools and teachers are nervous about anything that risks them being "accused of promoting porn." The most recent sex education guidelines from the World Health Organization's European office note that educators should include discussions about the influence of pornography on sexuality starting with late elementary school and through high school. The guidelines don't, however, provide specific ideas on how to have those conversations.

In Britain, nonprofit organizations and a teachers' union, along with members of Parliament, have recommended that schools include discussions about the influence of porn on how children view sex and relationships. Magdalena Mattebo, a researcher at Uppsala University in Sweden who studies pornography and adolescents, would like porn literacy mandated in her country. "We are a little lost in how to handle this," Mattebo told me.

More than 300 schools, youth and community groups and government agencies in Australia and New Zealand use components of a porn-education resource called "In the Picture" that includes statistics, studies and exercises primarily for teenagers. It was created by Maree Crabbe, an expert on sexual violence and pornography education, who lives near Melbourne, Australia. As she put it during a United States training program for educators and social workers that I attended in 2016: "We want to be positive about sex, positive about masturbation and critical of pornography." One key component of the program is often neglected in porn literacy: providing training to help parents understand and talk about these issues.

Last year, a feminist porn producer, Erika Lust, in consultation with sex educators, created a porn-education website for parents. The Porn Conversation links to research and articles and provides practical tips for parents, including talking to kids about the ways mainstream porn doesn't represent typical bodies or mutually satisfying sex and avoiding accusatory questions about why your kid is watching porn and who showed it to them. "We can't just say, 'I don't like mainstream porn because it's chauvinistic,'" says Lust, whose films feature female-centered pleasure. "We have given our children technology, so we need to teach them how to handle it." But she takes it a step further by suggesting that parents of middle- and high schoolers talk to their teenagers about "healthy porn," which she says includes showing female desire and pleasure and being made under fair working conditions. I asked Lust if she would steer her daughters in that direction when they are older (they are 7 and 10). "I would recommend good sites to my daughters at age 15, when I think they are mature enough. We are so curious to find out about sex. People have doubts and insecurities about themselves sexually. 'Is it O.K. that I like that, or this?' I think porn can be a good thing to have as an outlet. I'm not scared by explicit sex per se. I'm afraid of the bad values."

Tristan Taormino, another feminist porn filmmaker and author, speaks frequently on college campuses and produces explicit sex ed videos for adults. "The party line is we don't want teenagers watching our videos," she says, noting they are rated XXX. "But do I wish teenagers had access to some of the elements of it?" In addition to seeing consent, she said, "they would see people talking to each other, and they'd see a lot of warm-up. We show lube, we show sex toys."

That may be more than most parents, even of older teenagers, can bear. But even if parents decided to help their teenagers find these sites, not only is it illegal to show any kind of porn—good or bad—to anyone under 18, but, really, do teenagers want their parents to do so? And which ones would parents recommend for teenagers? "Unlike organic food, there's no coding system for ethical or feminist porn," Crabbe notes. "They might use condoms and dental dams and still convey the same gender and aggression dynamics." Also, "good porn" isn't typically free or nearly as accessible as the millions of videos streaming on mainstream sites.

Al Vernacchio, a nationally known sexuality educator who teaches progressive sex ed at a private Quaker school outside Philadelphia, believes the better solution is to make porn literacy part of the larger umbrella of comprehensive sex education. Vernacchio, who is the author of the 2014 book "For Goodness Sex:

Changing the Way We Talk to Teens About Sexuality, Values, and Health," is one of those rare teenage-sex educators who talks directly to his high school students about sexual pleasure and mutuality, along with the ingredients for healthy relationships. The problem with porn "is not just that it often shows misogynistic, unhealthy representations of relationships," Vernacchio says. "You can't learn relationship skills from porn, and if you are looking for pleasure and connection, porn can't teach you how to have those."

Crabbe notes one effective way to get young men to take fewer lessons from porn: "Tell them if you want to be a lazy, selfish lover, look at porn. If you want to be a lover where your partner says, 'That was great,' you won't learn it from porn." And parents should want their teenagers to be generous lovers, Cindy Gallop argues. "Our parents bring us up to have good manners, a work ethic. But nobody brings us up to behave well in bed."

To prepare his students to be comfortable and respectful in sexual situations, Vernacchio shows photos, not just drawings, of genitalia to his high schoolers. "Most people are having sex with real people, not porn stars, and real bodies are highly variable. I would much rather my students have that moment of asking questions or confusion or even laughter in my classroom, rather than when they see their partner's naked body for the first time." He, along with Herbenick, who is also the author of the 2012 book "Sex Made Easy: Your Awkward Questions Answered for Better, Smarter, Amazing Sex," advocates that adolescents should understand that most females don't have orgasms by penetration alone, and that clitoral stimulation often requires oral sex, fingers and sex toys, as she notes: "It's part of human life, and you teach it in smart, sensitive ways."

As the students from the first Porn Literacy classes moved through their lives in the year after their courses ended, some things from the discussions stayed with them. In surveys from the first three sets of classes, one-third of the students still said they would agree to do things from porn if their partner asked them to. Several also wanted to try things they saw in porn. They were, after all, normal, sexually curious, experimenting teenagers. But only a tiny number of students agreed in the post-class survey that "most people like to be slapped, spanked or have their hair pulled during sex," compared with 27 percent at the start of class. And while at the beginning, 45 percent said that porn was a good way for young people to learn about sex, now only 18 percent agreed. By the end of the class, no one said pornography was realistic; just over one quarter had believed that at the outset. The survey didn't reveal the catalyst for the changes. Was it the curriculum itself? Was it something about Daley and Alder's teaching style? It's possible the students created the changes themselves, teaching one another through their in-class debates and discussions.

A., the young woman who said she had never seen an image of a penis until she watched porn, resisted the idea that porn was uniformly bad for teenagers. "At least kids are watching porn and not going out and getting pregnant," she said. But recently, she told me that she'd given up watching it altogether. She disliked looking at women's expressions now, believing that they probably weren't experiencing pleasure and might be in pain. When Drew watched porn, he found himself wondering if women were having sex against their will. As another student said with a sigh: "Nicole and Jess ruined porn for us."

In the months after the class, A. had created a new mission for herself: She was going to always have orgasms during sex. "And I did it!" she told me. It helped that she had been in a relationship with a guy who was open and asked what she liked. But even if Porn Literacy didn't go into as many details about sex as she would have liked, "in this indirect way, the class shows what you deserve and don't deserve," she said. "In porn, the guy cares only about himself. I used to think more about 'Am I doing something right or wrong?'" Porn may neglect women's orgasms, but A. wasn't going to anymore.

Drew, who had once used porn as his main sex educator, was now thinking about sex differently. "Some things need to come to us naturally, not by watching it and seeing what turns you on," he told me. The discussions about anatomy and fake displays of pleasure made him realize that girls didn't always respond as they did in porn and that they didn't all want the same things. And guys didn't, either. Maybe that porn clip in which the nice, tender guy didn't excite the girl was wrong. What Drew needed was a girl who was open and honest, as he was, and with whom he could start to figure out how to have good sex. It would take some time and most likely involve some fumbling. But Drew was O.K. with that. He was just starting out.

Virtual Reality Gets Naughty

Alyson Krueger

In early 2014 Ela Darling, 31, a pornographic actress, recorded her first virtual reality sex scene. She was in a college dorm room at the University of Maryland dressed in an R2-D2 swimsuit and high athletic socks. She sat on a twin bed, next to a wooden desk, and spoke to the camera as if it were a real person. There was no story line and no other actors.

"It was a solo masturbation scene," she said. "I was coy and flirty and then a little bit dirty. I felt sexy as hell."

Ms. Darling had been filming pornography since she was 22 and took her job seriously. It was her responsibility to convince audiences to connect with her physically and emotionally. She tried everything, including acting out bondage fetishes, performing erotic electrostimulation ("electrosex") on another woman, and dressing as a real-estate agent. Yet no matter what she did to entice and engage, the results had always been voyeuristic, since there was always a screen separating her and her fans.

This time, though, was different. Virtual reality uses many camera lenses to record the same scene from hundreds of angles. When the takes are stitched together, the viewer gets a 180—or 240—degree view of the room and the feeling that he or she is there, participating. As soon as Ms. Darling viewed the scene she recorded, she knew virtual reality would be a sea change to her job and the adult entertainment industry.

"You can pretend like you are in the bedroom with me, and it is someone you have a crush on," she said. "You are in the experience."

While virtual reality pornography may feel like something out of a science fiction movie, it already has a formidable, if underground, presence. According to the website Pornhub, views of VR porn are up 275 percent since it debuted in the summer of 2016. . . .

By 2025 pornography will be the third-largest VR sector, according to estimates prepared by Piper Jaffray, an investment and management firm. Only video games and N.F.L.-related content will be larger, it predicted, and the market will be worth $1 billion.

"We're getting more and more of it every day," said Mark Kernes, a senior editor at AVN Media Network, which covers the industry. "We are leading the technology in this area. Sex sells, and where there is money to be made, there will be entrepreneurs who want to adopt it and make money from it," some by offering it for free to increase clicks.

Pornography is what rushed along the first printing press, and spurred developments in the internet, online payment systems, and other technology. Now it's time for virtual reality, Mr. Kernes said: "I'm pretty sure there is more porn VR out there than regular VR."

. . . Ms. Darling first experienced regular old VR at E3, a conference for the video-game industry. Excited by the pornography possibilities, she found a college student on Reddit who knew the technology but lacked a star. Before long, Ms. Darling started streaming weekly VR segments live from her bedroom in Los Angeles. . . .

She then started a company named VRTube .xxx to make the technology, now licensed to Cam4.com, which employs over 40 performers.

Though the pornography industry as a whole is challenging to regulate, considering the potential for abuse, disease, and exploitation, the virtual kind comes with extra moral and maybe legal issues. For example, can you use someone's likeness to have sex with them in virtual reality?

"Virtual reality is like the Wild Wild West," said Bryony Cole, the host of *Future of Sex*, a podcast that explores technology and sexuality.

At . . . [the 2017] AVN Adult Entertainment Expo, a convention and trade show held each January in Las Vegas, the latest advancements in virtual reality pornography were on display.

CamSoda, a website that specializes in live sex videos, had an exhibit featuring pornography stars dressed in plunging bathing suits and waving visitors into the booth. They were showing off OhRama, a small canister that attaches to virtual reality headsets and releases scent during the action. . . .

There are also companies that are adding taste and touch to the experience.

Another big player is CamasutraVR, a start-up using 142 cameras that all look at one person, or one body part. "They are creating images from that, which they are hoping will be indistinguishable from an actual person," Mr. Kernes said. . . .

Still other virtual reality companies were showing off their partnerships with sex toy companies to create vibrators or penis pumps that link to VR material. "As the action ramps up so does the vibrations of the vibrator," he said.

One of the most buzzed-about inventions has been the sex robot. The first one, Harmony, was introduced in May [2017] by a company named Realbotix. In seductive videos posted on YouTube, Harmony shows off her long legs, her firm breasts, her full lips, her lifelike hand gestures, even her intellect.

"How do you feel about sex?" an unknown presenter asks her in one video.

"Sex is one of the most fascinating things in the world," she responds in a raspy voice. "I don't see anything wrong with it." Harmony can connect with virtual reality so the user can interact with her in that space; she can perform all the acts the viewer is watching.

"It's a little bit of a video game combined with sci-fi," said Matt McMullen, the C.E.O. and creative director of Realbotix. The company has been making dolls for 20 years that were linked to artificial intelligence but not virtual reality. "Based on our experiences with thousands of clients," Mr. McMullen said, "people do use them for sex, but there is something more that exists. We focus on companionship."

Virtual reality has been nicknamed the empathy machine because it allows people to feel like they are truly connected to the action. "It's neurological," said Holly Richmond, a somatic psychologist based in Los Angeles and Portland, OR. "You aren't just watching and thinking about it. You are feeling it, and it's not just your genitals. There is literally a mind-body connection."

When Ms. Darling does live X-rated performances, users can leave comments and chat to one another on the side of the screen. "The people who are in virtual reality tell the other people watching me in 2-D to stop being jerks and knock it off," she said. "They feel like they know me and are in the bedroom with me."

Many sex therapists and educators are interested in the new technology. . . . Ms. Richmond worked with BaDoinkVR, a virtual reality company in Rochester, N.Y., to create *Virtual Sexology*, a series of free videos that help men and women overcome common sex problems. . . .

The first video, aimed at men, was the most downloaded video on BaDoinkVR.com in 2016—an impressive feat considering it was competing with noneducational pornography.

Ms. Cole, the podcast host, is most excited about how virtual reality can be used in sex education.

"What if we had young people watch videos where they practice consent or practice identifying at-risk behaviors?" she said. "Or they can be in a room with someone who said, 'I contacted herpes and this is my experience.' That is way more informative than a gonorrhea slide."

Indeed.

Barbara Rothbaum, a professor in the department of psychiatry and behavioral sciences at Emory University School of Medicine and the director of Emory's Veterans Program, is studying how virtual reality can help treat people suffering from post-traumatic stress disorder caused by military sexual trauma.

The program is building scenes that take victims to barracks, tents, private living quarters, latrines, offices, or remote buildings and vehicles where the trauma may have taken place. The idea is that going back to these places virtually will help victims confront their memories so they can move forward with more internal peace.

But for virtual reality to work, the scenes have to be so lifelike that users get lost in them and take them for reality. They have to feel like they are participants, not just observers. "We can create 3-D bodies in virtual reality and do whatever we want with them," Ms. Cole said. As the technology becomes good enough to make that happen, issues are bound to arise.

Mr. McMullen said an issue his company has is clients commissioning dolls that look exactly like people they know in real life, maybe an ex-girlfriend they never got over or someone about whom they fantasize. His company requires written consent from the model for his or her likeness to be used.

Ms. Cole said VR companies are going to have to address this same problem as they get better at customizing avatars to look exactly like what their customers desire. "What are the lines between reality and fantasy and what can we do in this space?" she said. "What does consent mean in virtual reality? Can you do something to your girlfriend in virtual reality that you wouldn't do in real life? If you are using someone's likeness in virtual reality, do you require their permission? And what about revenge porn? That will be even harsher in virtual reality."

She is worried about the technology assimilating into the culture as easily as dating apps, drawing people away from flesh-and-blood encounters.

Certainly partners will also have to negotiate whether virtual reality sex constitutes cheating. It is, after all, much more lifelike than traditional pornography.

But Mr. McMullen said a lot of people accuse his sex robot of doing that, but he believes he is helping alleviate a bad situation, not causing

it. "There are people who are already lonely, and people who live their lives being alone. They work all day and come home to an empty house," he said. "This is just offering an alternative to those types of people. They don't have anyone else."

RACE AND MASCULINITY IN GAY PORN

DESMOND F. GOSS

Academic researchers and cultural critics have primarily focused on gender relations in porn created for heterosexual men and manufactured by corporate producers. Overall, these discussions illuminate the racist and sexist sexual discourses that pervade such pornography (Collins, 1993). However, the sociocultural phenomena that create and maintain the "age of the selfie" suggest that we extend these explorations. For instance, the widespread availability of porn on the internet has likely encouraged the proliferation of pornography intended for nonheterosexual communities, particularly gay men. In addition, user-created social media have opened new avenues for individuals to consume and create self-produced erotica. Other than policies of the host sites—which tend to function more as suggestions than mandates—users produce pornography with very little, if any, corporate (or other) oversight. My goal here is to unpack attitudes and behaviors at the intersection of gender and race in gay men's pornography. I do so by comparing discussions of race in an "ebony" category versus categories that do not specifically advertise black men's participation. I contrast themes in content produced by users versus corporate enterprises. To do so, I investigate how gay men's sexual culture represents and understands black men, as well as how black participants reaffirm or resist sexual stereotypes of black masculinity.

THE SEPARATION OF BLACK AND QUEER

In so many contexts, society portrays and understands blackness and queerness as incompatible (Ferguson, 2004). Consequently, mainstream black cultures disenfranchise black queer and trans folks, while mainstream queer cultures disenfranchise people of color. These cultural representations are associated with white and black men occupying racially segregated spaces. And the infrequent inclusion of gay black men in the mainstream gay community is often predicated on white sexual fantasy, where encounters with black men mean little more than sexual conquest. Thus, the only places in which some white and black gay men meaningfully interact are hookup sites like Grindr.

For black men, maintaining a healthy sense of self in such an environment can be difficult. Few have the social resources necessary to overcome the cultural barriers that prevent their queerness and blackness from interlocking into a single cohesive sense of self. To cope, black men who have sex with men (or MSM) often privilege one identity over the other, seeing themselves as "black then gay," while others separate their private identity as gay men from their public identity as black men (Hunter, 2010). Social institutions, too, present extraordinary barriers to queer men of color—and negotiating them with intersecting minority identities "produces a new set of structured choices and survival strategies" (Green, 2007: 758). As such, spaces generally deemed safe for black communities or LGBT communities may not be safe for queer black folks. In black churches and families or LGBT-oriented establishments, black gay men must often reshape themselves in ways that minimize sexual or racial identification.

PORNOGRAPHIC REPRESENTATIONS

Pornography has probably existed in some form for as long as there has been human record; however, its context and contents evolve with changing social environments. Throughout its history, porn has been extensively critiqued by agents of both liberal and conservative political orientations. On the right, local, state, and federal governments have attempted to regulate and even ban pornography (Lehman, 2012). On the left, some radical feminists deride porn as a catalyst for the sexual objectification and victimization of women—for them, "pornography is the theory, and rape the practice" (Morgan, 1980: 128). And in the 1990s, feminists of color began critiquing and protesting the portrayal of women of color in pornography, noting the uniqueness of such representations at the intersection of womanhood and black identity (Bernardi, 2007).

In 2007, an art exhibit titled *Seduced: Art and Sex from Antiquity to Now* opened in London, celebrating artistic representation of sexuality through history. Folding under pressure from the surrounding community, the Barbican Gallery prohibited visitors under 18 from viewing the show (Chittenden, 2009). Of particular concern were several photographs by New York photographer Robert Mapplethorpe, which presented nude and erotic images of black men. Nearly two decades earlier, a Mapplethorpe exhibition at the Contemporary Arts Center in Cincinnati, Ohio, led to large antipornography protests, an executive resignation, and an obscenity trial (Dobush, 2015). Although other photographic art in the Barbican exhibition featured homoerotic and sadomasochistic portrayals of nude subjects, the racial character of Mapplethorpe's series of photographs seemed to add insult to the already sexually explicit, and thus problematic, presentation (Chittenden, 2009). In a way, the inclusion of

nonwhite bodies pushed Mapplethorpe's photos out of the sunnier realm of nude art and into the darker underworld of pornography. Moreover, Mapplethorpe (a gay white man) has been extensively critiqued for fetishizing black masculinity in this series (Chittenden, 2009). Such situations illustrate the malleability of definitions of pornography, as they are undoubtedly delineated with intersecting social parameters like age and race.

Few studies have examined the presentation of nonnormative (that is, nonwhite, less fit, or older) bodies in gay porn. In these studies, researchers typically find a contradictory relationship between fetishism and empowerment in corporatized pornography. In other words, though such representations create space for marginalized communities, they also reinforce stereotypical beliefs and exclusionary sexual practices. For example, "Daddy porn" and "bear porn" present older men and fat men as sexually desirable, in contrast to the emphasis on youth and muscularity that dominates mainstream gay men's sexual culture (Highberg, 2011). However, participants in such pornography are often typecast to restrictive niches; it is uncommon, for instance, to see "Daddies" penetrated by younger men. Moreover, neither "Daddy" nor "bear" porn typically features men of color.

METHODS

I collected most of the data for this study from Xtube.com, a website where viewers can access pornography for free produced by both individual users and companies. I used Xtube as a source of data because, unlike other similar sites, it archives videos, allows users' comments, centers on gay men's pornography, and fosters a unique sense of community among consumers. I sampled the 20 most-viewed user-generated, noncorporate gay men's videos categorized as "ebony"; the 20 most-viewed corporate gay videos categorized as "ebony"; and the 20 most-viewed gay videos (without the "ebony" classification). I did not split most-viewed videos like the other categories because my interest in the relationship between corporatization and agency concerns only black performers, who are rare in this category. Since these lists change, I collected all videos in one sitting. I recorded descriptive information about the videos (including tags, number of views, run time, etc.), summaries of the videos, and any viewer comments that alluded to race. The race of commenters or producers was either inferred from profile pictures or explicitly stated in profiles or usernames. I also sampled related content by searching material linked to each case, such as advertisements, user profiles, and images from other websites, to supplement the primary data. With the assistance of NVivo analytic software, I reviewed explicit content and interpreted deeper latent meanings from the data. I also relied on the "constant comparison" grounded theory method: I grouped emergent themes into broader categories, and then connected these categories theoretically through the themes that emerged (Seale, 2004). Ultimately, three significant categories emerged: *dark phalluses, missing links,* and *separate spaces.*

DARK PHALLUSES: PREOCCUPATION AND DISMEMBERMENT

The first category of findings concerned the symbolic transformation of black men's penises into *dark phalluses*—that is, from mundane anatomy to a powerful symbol of black masculine sexuality. This is accomplished in gay men's pornography through two rhetorical mechanisms. The first is *preoccupation*: Almost every video featuring black participants made some reference to a "BBC" (big black cock).

Overall, ebony videos were considerably more focused on penises than non-ebony videos. In fact, videos featuring black participants gave more camera time to penises than faces, while the opposite was true in videos with only white participants. Size was of particular interest to both white and black producers and consumers of ebony porn, and there were twice as many references to penis size in video descriptions and viewer comments in ebony than in non-ebony videos.

Transforming ordinary anatomy into dark phalluses involves a process I call *dismemberment*. In gay porn, this process of detachment transmuted black men's penises into cultural matter that fits into one or more of just three categories. When black men's penises became *dissociated organs*, consumers conceptualized and discussed them in ways that render the persona and often the rest of its "owner" invisible, even useless. For example, users often used relative rather than possessive pronouns (referring to "that" penis instead of "his" penis), or they simply referred to black men's penises as "meat." Producers and consumers also more often characterized black men's penises as *wielded tools*, often referring to specific objects of utility like "poles," "towers," "pipes," and "machines." Not only did such references sever black men's genitalia and bodies from the rest of their humanity, they also recalled the history of white America's exploitation of black productivity through systems such as chattel slavery, indentured servitude, cheapened labor, and prison labor. Moreover, a few "tool" references are also infused with undertones of violence, such as one commenter's praise of a "weapon of mass destruction." The final archetype—the *sentient monster*—was more than twice as prevalent as the dissociated organs and wielded tools archetypes combined. In contrast to the lifelessness of dissociated organs and wielded tools, sentient monsters are directly or indirectly endowed with personality and animus. For instance, site users frequently made reference to black men's penises as humanoid creatures, especially gods ("that is God") and monsters ("you have a monster out there!"), as a metaphor for the intimidating posture of large creatures.

MISSING LINKS: PRIMITIVENESS AND PRIMALITY

The second category of findings concerned the portrayal of black men as *missing links* in the context of *primitiveness* and *primality*. In gay men's pornography, consumers and producers construed black men as less human (that is, more primitive) than their counterparts, and this image then served as a source of erotic attraction. Typically, this process involves relegating black men to one or more of three *subordinating* associations: *natural rawness, rancidity,* and *animality*. For instance, in gay men's pornography, black men demonstrated the definition of "real" masculinity. In a video titled *Chino in the Raw*, three young black men engaged in various sexual activities, as a superimposed text reads, "Aight, yo, the thugs are back with some serious gangtsa lovin. . . . No bullshit—just straight up gangstas doing it raw." Here, rawness redefined gay sex as both natural phenomena and perilous adventure, based in a conceptualization of black masculinity as less defined by femininity and thus more realized by naturality: "No bitches allowed . . . this da real shit nigga." A rhetorical association with the concepts of *raw* and *natural* epitomized the "realness" of black men in gay porn, who are apparently unaltered by the supposedly feminizing forces of civilized humanity. Paradoxically, however, these same forces produce socially valued qualities such as intelligence, emotional aptitude, and others that account for the human capacity for self-control. As one user (whose favorited videos included *Latin Jerkoff 2* and *huge black dick cuming loads*) summarized,

"A bitch instinctively surrenders to a real Man, who exercises His natural right to relentlessly fuck the cunt or cunts of His choice. . . . When the power of His loins can no longer be contained, He triumphantly spurts His sacred essence in or on the reamed bitch, and His victory is complete." This comment typified white commenters' view of black masculine "realness" as a coercive, phallocentric, barbaric, competitive sexual authoritarianism that is in opposition to femininity.

Another aspect of the subordination of black men in gay porn entailed an association with *rancidity*. In gay men's pornography, noxious odors ("amazing piece of black meat, i would hope it smells bad too"), noncircumcision, hairiness, and bare-backing (condomless anal sex) all contributed to the fetishized primitiveness of black masculine sexuality. Each is deployed to link black masculinity with the lack of hygiene implied by primitiveness, and this link is especially eroticized by white consumers and producers (e.g., "Thank goodness your bush is not shaved, you're still a real man!").

The project of primitivizing black men also included portraying black men as less human (more *animalistic*) than white men. Here, producers and consumers characterized black men as aliens ("The black guy must be from another world") and associated them with imagined ancestral African communities ("gorgeous face with a mandingo cock"), as well as with nonhuman animal behavior, especially "feeding" ("THERES ENOUGH HUNGRY FAGS IN THE WORLD TO FEED WITH THAT"). In addition to *subordination*, black men are primitivized in gay men's porn through *diminution*. So, despite the bombastic allocation of power and prowess to black masculinity, gay men's pornography simultaneously diminished black masculinity to juvenility. Typically, this process entails referring to black men as "boys" ("YEAAAHHHHHHHHHHHHH Dadddy feed his cute Black Boyyy mouth"), as well as the concerted infantilization of black participants in corporate "bait" films, where straight men are coerced into performing in gay pornography. In these films, "straight" white participants are generally portrayed as participating only for pay, while "straight" black participants, too simple to know better, are more often portrayed as having been tricked into participating.

On the one hand, *primitivity* entailed an ideology that positions black masculinity as a prehistoric state of identity located within modern surroundings. On the other hand, *primality* emphasized primeval savagery. This is the difference between an ape in a cage at the zoo and an ape on the loose in your neighborhood. Both are spectacle, for sure, but the latter stimulates a tension not present in the former. And it is this sexual tension, this implication of danger, that drove the erotic allure of presumed black masculine primality in gay men's pornography. For black men in gay porn, the portrayal of primality entailed presenting black masculinity as violent and powerful, intended to arouse the viewer by offering an image of black masculinity as "sensuous but dangerous." For instance, the ebony category was saturated with references to "monsters"—eight times as many references compared to non-ebony videos. There is even a website where viewers can "see monsters fuck innocent humans." Most of the animated men on the site were slim and white, in stark contrast to the animated monsters that are much larger and darker. All the monsters are menacing, and since our cultural notion of "monster" is inherently violent, the presentation of consent in these fantasies is inherently problematic. But this was part of the allure—to be taken by the big, dark monster, to lose the power of consent, and to revel in that loss, *is* the fantasy. And the symbolism of such a tagline ("see monsters fuck innocent humans") was significant given the network of racialized sexual ideologies that inform gay

men's culture. Here, black men are to "monsters" as white men are to "innocent humans." Thus, it is no surprise that several of the profiles of white users I reviewed named violence as a desired quality in sexual encounters with black men ("Turn Ons: Being used like a slut by black men"). Racist portrayals of black men in gay porn were normalized through the association of monstrosity and violence with power, which commands fascination and admiration from black and white users alike ("it is clear that as white people we have no choice but to surrender to the superiority of blacks").

SEPARATE SPACE: BIFURCATED PERFORMANCES AND ESSENTIALIZED IDENTITIES

The final category of findings concerns how racial ideology in gay men's pornography emphasized separation through *bifurcated performances* (performances divided into two parts) and *essentialized identities* (identities assumed to be innate or inherent). The performances of black and white men in gay porn diverged starkly by race, particularly in terms of sexual desirability. These divergences dichotomized black and white gay identities by emphasizing or deemphasizing racial visibility. For instance, a non-ebony video featured a white man performing oral sex on several different men in succession. In the comments, many viewers were enamored with the performer's eye color ("so blue!"). In this case, regardless of intention, there was an unspoken but clear relation between the celebration of blue eye color and the celebration of whiteness, especially when considering the lack of similar comments about physical features (other than penises) in ebony videos. However, the most obvious way gay men's pornography bifurcated black and white masculinity was by making black men's genitals hypervisible. Here, penis sizes did not simply vary across communities but were instead an essential trait of every man's racial identity. For example, a viewer expressing his disappointment in a black performer's endowment sarcastically suggested that "he is definitely half black and half Chinese." Through such discourses, gay pornography works to solidify a perspective of irreconcilable difference between black and white men. Moreover, this dichotomization essentialized blackness and whiteness by linking race with longstanding gender archetypes regarding sexual behavior. In essence, black men were almost always penetrating partners ("tops") while white men tended to be penetrated partners ("bottoms"), a set-up that mimics the gendered assumptions of agency in heterosexual relationships, where "man fucks woman; subject verb object" (MacKinnon, 1982: 124).

Furthermore, pornographic performances, and evaluations of these performances, had racially distinct *focuses*. Producers and consumers of gay porn were much more attentive to technique, occupation, hairiness, and age in non-ebony versus ebony videos. In this way, it seemed that whiteness allowed for more variation in pornographic norms. For example, sexual scripts about hair and age in "Daddy" and "bear" porn provided discourses through which gay white men could simultaneously pray at the altar of youth, revere the wisdom and confidence that accompany aging, and play with the normative dynamics of heteropatriarchal family ("The hard determined face of Dad as he pile drives his [son] and the final ejaculation of both [son] and Dad"). In ebony porn, however, the significance of youth was implicit in its overemphasis on black virility. And without the platform provided by "bear" culture, older black men were generally denied a space in the zeitgeist of gay men's sexuality. Moreover, given the history of misrepresenting and dismantling black families in North America, the sort of "Daddy–son" play where many older

men find a place in gay porn may be off-limits to black performers, as well as less palatable to black viewers.

In *Queering the Color Line*, Somerville (2000) illustrates how dichotomization aids essentialism (that is, an interpretation of human attitudes and behaviors as created and maintained by biology or divinity rather than social practices) by positioning social variables as oppositional. By defining one in contrast to the other, social psychologies are transformed into embodied identities. In gay men's sexual culture, "white or black," "man or woman," and "gay or straight" continue to define and concretize one another through the deployment of gendered and racialized archetypes of sexuality. For example, the type of sex acts performed and appreciated in gay men's pornography was highly dependent upon the race of the participants. In ebony porn, there was much less discussion and portrayal of rimming, masturbation, and any activity that was not anal sex. And whatever the activity, white commenters assigned blanket sexual characteristics to participants of color based on preexisting ideas about the sexual behaviors supposedly endemic to their racial communities ("Blatinos so rico suave"). Nowhere was the essentializing force of gay men's sexual culture more apparent than in discourses surrounding topping and bottoming. Who tops and who bottoms, who's "femme" and who's "masc," as well as how these roles were successfully fulfilled or disrupted, demonstrated the impact of rooted and racialized sex and gender scripts. And there was very little deviation from the norm of black tops and white bottoms.

While viewers consistently praised white bottoms for their masculine physique and virility (best demonstrated by how well they "take it"), almost all evaluations of black bottoms were critical, with most expressing disappointment in performers' feminine qualities. Though femininity was frowned upon in non-ebony porn, it was expressly condemned in sex between black men, as it disrupted the continual attempt to de-gay sex between black men, in preservation of the "dark phallus" and "missing link" fantasies. For instance, there were high premiums for "straightness" and "virginity" in gay men's pornography, and both concepts were heavily advertised and policed, yet they were barely mentioned in the ebony category. Blackness, therefore, implied heterosexuality and hypersexuality, and whiteness homosexuality and virginity. The use of concepts and language borrowed from heterosexual culture also aided the co-constitution of racial, gendered, and sexual identities in gay men's pornography. This process involved the rhetorical and conceptual reconfiguring of men's mouths and anuses into "pussies," "cunts," and even "wombs," and suggests that bodies cannot be both penetrated and masculine. Race was an important delineator of such references, and there were two times as many in ebony versus non-ebony pornography. This language gendered gay sex acts by borrowing discursive concepts from heterosexual culture. In this way, gay pornography operated as a tool of racialized homonormativity, denying black men any characterization other than heterosexual hypermasculinity.

THE PORNOGRAPHIC IS POLITICAL

On the whole, by helping solidify a sociocultural image of black men as "missing links," by reducing black masculinity to a "dark phallus," and by aggravating the segregation of black and white men, gay men's pornography reifies existing stereotypes about black masculinity and extends them into queer contexts. In doing so, gay men's porn participates in the ongoing exclusion of black men from equal and just queer citizenship. In theory, user-submitted pornography offers black participants more agency to perform sexuality without explicit

intrusion from capitalist marketing, which may more readily bend to pressures of racist, sexist, and femme-antagonistic public demand. Indeed, some aspects of user-submitted videos in this sample are somewhat more inclusive than corporate producers. For example, corporate producers are more than twice as likely to reproduce gendered archetypes about gay men's sexuality, with a focus on straightness and youth. Corporatized pornography more frequently borrows language from heterosexual romantic culture to characterize same-sex sex acts between men. Black men in user-submitted porn are also more likely to engage in masturbation and oral sex, while corporate ebony videos are more likely to depict anal penetration and focus on penis size. However, comparing indicators reveals far more similarities than differences between corporate and noncorporate pornography. Many of the discrepancies are small, and problematic rhetoric remains steady across categories. Thus, though user-submission clearly offers black performers the agency to deconstruct and challenge racist sexual imagery, it does not automatically translate into such resistance. Moreover, black participants cannot control the interpretation of their performances by white consumers. Thus, the power of porn self-produced by black men to transform gay men's sexual culture may be limited by white men's continuing fetishization of black masculinity.

In any regard, a thorough analysis of gay men's pornography illustrates the political significance of sexual desire, despite cultural attitudes that position gay sex as "color-blind." If academics and activists interested in the intersection of race, gender, and queerness are to ever deconstruct such politics of desire, we must begin with this premise: Sexual preference is not, in any circumstance, an apolitical phenomenon. Of course, this may mean reintroducing uncomfortable conversations about the origins of sexual attraction in sex studies—

conversations that have historically been used to pathologize queerness and marginalize queer people. But, for too long, queers and academics alike have unproblematized the "my preference, my business" explanation of sexual desirability (Robinson, 2015). Such an individualized and neoliberal discourse only upholds the "right" of gay white men to proclaim "no fats, no femmes, no blacks, no Asians" without recourse. Moreover, this sort of exclusion can have negative implications for the physical and mental health of gay black men, as well as the well-being of queer black communities. Public health research, for example, has already linked racism and risk taking among people of color, such as lack of condom use among black and Latino MSM (Smith, 2012).

CONCLUSION

Despite the display of cultural messages to the contrary, sex is a social interaction steeped in identity politics. Though there is plenty of existing research critiquing pornography as an institutional and cultural transmitter of white supremacist heteropatriarchal messaging, much of it lacks a queer-intersectional perspective. As such, many of the current ideological conclusions on the topic frame masculinity as singularly white and heterosexual. However, as the perspectives of Johnson (2001), Du Bois (2008), and Anzaldúa (1999) suggest, the masculinities of queer men of color are experienced and understood in a different political, social, and cultural context, as they are situated at the intersection of more than one marginalized identity. Uniting relevant queer, critical race, and black feminist perspectives is useful for deconstructing racialized expressions and interpretations of masculinity and sexuality in gay pornography. Du Bois reasoned that black Americans move through American culture and institutions with two separate consciousnesses: one for all U.S. citizens and

another reserved for members of black communities (Du Bois, 2008). Similarly, Anzaldúa—a queer, Chicana, indigenous woman—describes life at the border of multiple identities as being a member of many different communities but never fully accepted into any one as "borderlands" (Anzaldúa, 1999). In the development of "quare theory," Johnson retools the perspectives of Du Bois and Anzaldúa to match the particular common experiences of black MSM (Johnson, 2001). Here, Johnson provides a "queer of color critique" by attending to the connection between these experiences and black cultures—a connection historically ignored, diminished, or denigrated by white-centered queer theory. Moreover, because sexuality is crucial to the practice of masculinity, we cannot separate sexual performance from masculine identity. Therefore, since normative expression of masculinity is limited to cis, heterosexual, middle-class white men, the masculinity of queer men of color is socially marginalized and subordinated.

Collins's concept of "controlling images" delineates how these performances legitimize the structural oppression of black Americans (Collins, 2005). Controlling images, Collins argues, construct racial difference by providing stereotypical images of black people to which Americans constantly compare to the white ideal. For example, the racist notion of black "welfare queens" who produce offspring to game "the system" symbolically contrasts with the idealized stereotypical nurturing, responsible, suburban white mother. Images of black men in gay pornography may contribute to a similar process of constant evaluation, where the standardization of white bodies is contrasted to the fetishization of black bodies. Controlling images of black masculinity buttress the eroticism of gay men's pornography (Collins, 2005). By supporting a sociocultural image of black men as "missing links," by reducing black masculinity to a "dark phallus," and by aggravating the segregation of black and white men, gay men's pornography participates in the ongoing exclusion of black men from community.

Future research should attempt to address the following methodological limitations of this study. First, the data used here are not representative and should therefore not be generalized to make causal explanations of social attitudes and behaviors. Although procuring a representative sample of internet pornography is unrealistic, future projects may collect a more varied representation of content. Second, despite all attempts to avoid doing so, this study likely reproduces cultural ideology that conceptualizes gay men as a community without internal differences. It is especially important to acknowledge this limitation as it applies to gay black men, as the experiences of oppressed communities are too often singularized. However, for ease of analysis and discussion, it was most efficient at times to discuss gay men in these terms. Third, Xtube's declining popularity should prompt future research projects to analyze websites at the forefront of user-submitted pornography to give a timelier account of how race works in gay men's porn presently. Fourth, I did not include in-depth analyses of nonwhite and nonblack ethno-racial categories because of time and resource constraints, but further research into the representations of these identities is certainly warranted.

Problematizing white masculinity in gay pornography also has serious and interesting implications for social organizing concerned with the experiences of queer people of color. Sex is a social interaction steeped in the politics of racial and gender identities. As such, we must appreciate that racism in gay men's pornography is a symbolically violent phenomenon in which "all of [our] culture's racist myths become just another turn-on" (Leidholdt, 1981: 20). Therefore, the discussions presented are framed by the broader culture of sexual

oppression experienced by trans folks, people of color, people with disabilities, fat people, and femmes in gay communities. Though seemingly unrelated, all such experiences are linked by white supremacist heteropatriarchy, and each is a manifestation of its impact on the social psychologies of LGBT communities. Nevertheless, marginalized queer and trans people are already making space for themselves. However, macro-level changes in cultures and institutions are difficult to accomplish without cis, able-bodied, "masc" white men acknowledging and deconstructing their participation, either passive or active, in systemic oppression.

REFERENCES

Anzaldúa, Gloria. 1999. *Borderlands La Frontera: The New Mestiza*. San Francisco: Aunt Lute Books.

Bernardi, Daniel. 2007. "Racism and Pornography: Evidence, Paradigms, and Publishing." *Cinema Journal*, 46(4): 116–21.

Chittenden, Tara. 2009. "Sexing Up the Secondary Art Curriculum: A Strategy for Discussing Robert Mapplethorpe's Photographs of S&M and the Black Male Nude in Art Classrooms." *International Journal of Education through Art*, 5(2): 157–67.

Collins, Patricia Hill. 1993. "Pornography and Black Women's Bodies." In D. Russell, ed. *Making Violence Sexy*. 97–104. New York: Teacher's College Press.

———. 2005. *Black Sexual Politics: African Americans, Gender and the New Racism*. New York: Routledge.

Dobush, Grace. 2015. "25 Years Later: Cincinnati and the Obscenity Trial Over Mapplethorpe Art." *The Washington Post*, October 24. Retrieved October 7, 2016 from https://www.washingtonpost.com/entertainment /museums/25-years-later-cincinnati-and-the-obscenity -trial-over-mapplethorpe-art/2015/10/22/07c6aba2-6dcb -11e5-9bfe-e59f5e244f92_story.html.

Du Bois, W. E. B. 2008 [1903]. *The Souls of Black Folk*. Oxford: Oxford University Press.

Ferguson, Roderick. 2004. *Aberrations in Black: Toward a Queer of Color Critique*. Minneapolis: University of Minnesota Press.

Foucault, Michel. 1978. *The History of Sexuality*. Vol 1: *An Introduction*. Trans. Robert Hurley. New York: Pantheon Books.

Green, Adam Isaiah. 2007. "On the Horns of a Dilemma: Institutional Dimensions of the Sexual Career in a Sample of Middle-Class, Urban, Black, Gay Men." *Journal of Black Studies*, 37(5): 753–74.

Highberg, Nels. 2011. "More Than a Comic Sidekick: Fat Men in Gay Porn." *Performing Ethos*, 2(2): 109–20.

Hunter, Marcus Anthony. 2010. "All the Gays Are White and All the Blacks Are Straight: Black Gay Men, Identity, and Community." *Sexuality Research and Social Policy*, 7(2): 81–92.

Johnson, E. Patrick. 2001. "'Quare' Studies or (Almost) Everything I Know About Queer Studies I Learned from My Grandmother." *Text and Performance Quarterly*, 21(1): 1–25.

Lehman, Peter. 2012. "Bad, Worse, Worst: 8MM and Hollywood's Bad Boys of Porn." In M. Pomerance, ed. *Bad: Infamy, Darkness, Evil, and Slime on Screen*. 79–92. Albany, NY: SUNY Press.

Leidholdt, Dorchen. 1981. "Where Pornography Meets Fascism." *Women's International Newsletter*, March: 18–22.

MacKinnon, Catherine. 1982. "Feminism, Marxism, Method and the State: An Agenda for Theory." *Signs: Journal of Women in Culture and Society*, 7: 515–33.

Morgan, Robin. 1980. "Theory and Practice: Pornography and Rape." In L. Lederer, ed., *Take Back the Night: Women on Pornography*. 134–40. New York: HarperCollins.

Robinson, Brandon Andrew. 2015. "'Personal Preference' as the New Racism." *Sociology of Race and Ethnicity*, 1(2): 317–30.

Seale, Clive. 2004. "Generating Grounded Theory." In C. Seale, ed., *Researching Society and Culture*. 240–47. London: Sage Publications.

Smith, William Pastor. 2012. "Exploring Dimensions of Racism, Homophobia, and Social Network as Concomitant Predictors of Condom Use in a Sample of Black MSM." *Journal of Gay & Lesbian Social Services*, 24(4): 417–45.

Somerville, Siobhan. 2000. *Queering the Color Line*. Durham, NC: Duke University Press.

OUT OF LINE: THE SEXY FEMMEGIMP POLITICS OF FLAUNTING IT!

LOREE ERICKSON

I'd like to tell you a story, which as it turns out, is in fact at least three related stories.

STORY ONE: A DAY LIKE ANY OTHER DAY

One day, which really could be any day, I left my house in a rather good mood. I had found a lovely patch of sunshine to sit in while I waited for the bus. Soon I was joined by another bus rider who stood about four or five feet away from me. In a minute or two another person passed by with no real difficulty but found it necessary to grumble at me while passing that I should have "parked [my] car" (more appropriately called a wheelchair) elsewhere, as I was blocking the sidewalk. I wasn't blocking anything. The person who was waiting with me was shocked that this other person had made such a rude, ableist comment. I was not surprised. Nor was I surprised by the message behind his words, which was: *You are in the way. You and "your car" are taking up too much space.* I just let it go and waited. I was relieved when the bus that arrived moments later was accessible, and was a bit surprised when the other person waiting stepped to the side to allow me on, rather than rushing/pushing past me—as many people tend to do, making the bus more difficult to navigate.

As I waited for the driver to ready the bus, the person who had been waiting with me looked at the step of the bus and then to my power wheelchair and asked if I needed help. I simply replied that the bus has a ramp. Behind this sort of well-intentioned query is the ever-present assumption that I am in need of help. I get this also when I am sitting somewhere waiting to meet a friend. People just come up to me and ask if I am okay.

As the bus pulled away, I was thinking about how back-to-back these moments were when I heard a loud shrill voice from the back of the bus, "you're *amazing!*" I froze. "The way you just whipped that little cart of yours right in that spot." I ignored it, too tired after three ableist encounters in ten minutes to offer any witty comebacks in response, and too angry to feel like educating anyone.

These three encounters are not isolated or individual experiences. Sadly, they are common and systemic. These three moments only tell us some of what disability means, how it appears, and how it is done. Disabilities, and many associated experiences, are often reduced to essentialized biomedical[1] limitations or malfunctions of certain bodies. Disability can more accurately be described as a process enacted through social relations. While the term *disability* appears to describe bodies and how they act/move/inhabit/sense/think/exist/communicate, the label carries the weight of how these bodies are deemed inferior to other bodies through illusory, arbitrary, and compulsory social and economic standards designed to enable certain ways of being over

From "Out of Line: The Sexy Femmegimp Politics of Flaunting It!" by Loree Erickson, http://www.femmegimp.org/femmegimp%20files/outofline.pdf. Reprinted by permission of the author.

others. Disability is a complex, intersectional, cultural, and fluid constellation of experiences and constructs.

While this is my story of systemic ableism, it is not—and could not be—every story of systemic ableism. My story is reliant on my particular embodiment and cultural context, which includes, but is not limited to, physical disability, whiteness, with a high level of education. As a thirty-something-year-old queer femmegimp who lives below the poverty line, I am marked by a unique interplay of identities. Disability never appears in isolation; it is always interrelated with a matrix of other marginalities and privileges. Systemic ableism manifests based on other marginalities (race, other experiences of disability, class, gender, and beyond).

The encounters in the story above tell something about how people make sense of my body: both the anxieties they project onto it and the simultaneous erasures they enact. These are moments among many where the relations of power reveal themselves. For example, the idea that people take up "too much space" underscores the notion that some people are worthy of occupying space and others are not—and is reminiscent of other sociohistorical practices of isolation and segregation. In *Reading and Writing Disability Differently*, Tanya Titchkosky writes, "The meaning of disability is composed of conflicts of inclusion and exclusion as this intersects with our ordinary ways of recognizing people . . . or not." (2007: 6)

STORY TWO: WHY I BECAME A PORN STAR

Disabled people are often imagined as being in the way, unimportant, in need of help, or called "inspirational" for doing ordinary things. Disabled people are imagined as less capable than or not as good as "normal" people (a problematic term as well). All of these attitudes simultaneously bolster and create policies and practices that propagate the association of disability with undesirability. We see this in state-sponsored practices of funding and mandating institutionalization via incarceration in prisons, psychiatric wards/hospitals, group homes, and nursing homes over community-based support; immigration policies using racist, capitalist, and ableist definitions of who counts as a desirable citizen; in historic and contemporary eugenic ideals (affecting marginalized bodies and minds of all varieties), "lives not worth living" rhetoric and consequent denial of medical treatment to those deemed unworthy; as well as welfare and disability income programs that keep us impoverished and hungry.

The same structures that impact other areas of our lives, creating an overwhelming climate of devaluation, also regulate our sexual lives.[2] From forced and coerced sterilization to institutional surveillance that limits privacy, there are multiple systems that pathologize, control, and punish the sexual explorations and expression of disabled people. Common paternalistic assumptions hypersexualize and/or portray disabled people as hypervulnerable. This damaging ideology is used to justify segregation. Disabled people—all people—need affirming resources, sex-positive information, and ways to realize their sexual potentials. Anti-sex laws in many U.S. states criminalize certain sexual activities that may be preferred ways for some disabled people to experience pleasure and express desire.

Disabled people are also often subjected to medical and psychological gawking that objectifies, stigmatizes, and pathologizes our experiences of our bodies, including our minds (Blumberg, 1994). Many children who are born with or acquire their disabilities early on are told directly and indirectly to not expect to have a family or anyone ever romantically love them (*Willing and Able: Sex, Love and Disability*, 2003). Disabled people experience the cumulative effects of this extensive system of desexualization every day.

People have begun organizing around this site of oppression as honestly and effectively as we have for other issues of access and justice. There are many particular barriers associated with this type of organizing and it is often deprioritized. In part, this is because there has been a disconnection between sexuality and other needs. It can be argued that one should focus more on needs such as housing, adequate attendant care, employment, transportation, and the like. However, this omission of sexuality ignores how profoundly interconnected all of these aspects of our lives are. Another part of the struggle to include sexuality as an organizing goal requires us to challenge the way sex operates in Western society. We learn to associate shame with sex. We are surrounded by images that convey a very narrow definition of sex and of desirable bodies. We learn we are not supposed to talk about sex. This framing of normative desire is larger than life and does not make room for a whole range of enjoyable experiences and possibilities. When sex is thought of as a bountiful playground for the relatively few who can approximate the illusory ideals of the desirable body (skinny, white, able-bodied, rich, etc.), then sex, desire, and pleasure for the rest of us remain relatively invisible. Sex and sexual expression are also often dismissed as frivolous "wants" rather than fundamental aspects of humanity. This is especially true for people with disabilities.

Felt as a personal and private emotion, shame is spun to internalize, naturalize, and individualize many of the oppressions mentioned above as well as others. As Abby Wilkerson argues, "Shame is not so much a psychological state of individuals as such (even though it may shape individual subjectivity), but rather a socially based harm which oppressed groups are subject to in particular ways. . . . Shame is deployed as a 'political resourc[e] that some people use to

silence or isolate others'" (Wilkerson, 2002: 45). I would like to expand this idea to include how shame is used not only as a tool of social control to isolate us from each other, but to keep us from accessing those very parts of ourselves, our bodies, our desires, and our experiences (usually wrapped up in our differences from that illusory ideal mentioned earlier) that hold the most potential for change by offering us a different way of being in the world.

Rather than hide away, deny, and ignore those very sites of the deepest shame, we must not only embrace them and learn from them, we need to *flaunt* them.

What better way to flaunt conventions of sexuality than by making porn? Pornography is surrounded by shame. We feel shame for watching it, enjoying it, making it, and buying it. The content of porn also often instills shame in us. We can feel badly for not living up to certain standards (both in terms of not fitting the mold of which bodies are seen as beautiful and in terms of not measuring up in regards to sexual prowess and skills). There is porn that demeans our identities and experiences and replicates oppressive power dynamics. Porn is complex, multifaceted—and yes—powerful. Rather than attempt to regulate and control it, which only drives it more underground and into the hands of those with privilege, we need to follow in the work of sex-positive feminists and explore the many benefits that pornography made from such alternative perspectives has to offer (Erickson, 2007).

This all may seem an unlikely beginning to porn stardom. By making queercrip porn, I moved out of line and took the "queer" and "wonky" path to place new stories within reach. I took this path to open up new possibilities and imaginings.

My journey began in a progressive sex shop in San Francisco in 2000; I was looking at an issue of *On Our Backs*, a lesbian porn magazine, featuring an article on sex and disability.

I was so excited—until I opened to the article. There was *one* picture of someone in a wheelchair with someone sitting on their lap kissing them. This one picture—the only image combining sex and disability I had found up to that point in my life—was inverted, so the image was obscured and barely recognizable. I wanted to see bodies that looked and moved and felt like mine represented in the exciting, but clearly still problematic, queer sexual culture. I wanted to see something that reflected my desires! I wanted to know that desiring people like me was possible. I resolved then and there to become a porn star.

I began with a series of photos and in the summer of 2006, I made a short film called *want*. *Want* weaves together sexually explicit images with everyday moments and scenes of the ableist world. It works to get people hot *and* poses an insightful, complex, honest, and sexy image of disability and gender-transgressive bodies. *Want* was clearly wanted. It won several awards, and continues to screen internationally at numerous film festivals, conferences, and workshops.

I wouldn't be making porn right now if I weren't so pissed off. I would not be making porn if I hadn't struggled for most of my life to be recognized as a sexy and sexual being, or if the world wasn't so fucked up. But making porn is one of the best things I've ever done. On a political level it allowed me to make a movie that would offer not only a moment of recognition of how sexy queercrips could be, but also a way to tell others how I wanted to be seen. Making this video allowed me to take up space and reconceptualize what is sexy.

Personally, it was an amazing experience—and not just because of all the really great sex. The three of us (my co-star, the video artist, and I) created a space of comfort, beauty, respect, and desire. To be able to share that with others is truly remarkable. That day was one of the first times in my life that I truly felt

wanted for exactly who I am. The first time was with my first lover. Unfortunately, experiences like these are rare for many people. Despite the sheer joy of the day—I must have been smiling for days afterward—it took me a while to work up the nerve to watch the video footage. I was afraid that what I might see would allow all those stories I was trying to erase to reemerge and pollute my experience of that day. While there were some bits that were hard to watch, it turned out to be not so bad—and kind of hot. I could see that I was sexy. I still feel that pull of doubt, but I am building up a whole host of stories, salacious stories, to counter the other ones.

STORY THREE: BEING A PORN STAR IS HARD WORK

Before this turns into a simple story of overcoming adversity, I would like to complicate things a bit. "Flaunting it" is not without its difficulties, but it does help to loosen up the knots a bit and free up more space for imagining. Our bodies, identities, desires, and experiences have multiple meanings, and thus, we need multiple stories. We need stories of love, lust, and other stuff. We need the success stories and the stories of pain and frustration. We also need stories about the work that stories being told about us, *without* us, do. These stories still inform our stories. We also need to look at the work that our stories do. Here are some stories that attempt to do that work.

Mainstream porn uses a series of conventions to shape the discourse of what is considered sexy. As I mentioned earlier, we can feel shame for not measuring up to these standards. Despite my politics, while editing, I found myself tempted to recreate those standards. I wanted to edit out the messy stuff, the very things that made this particular porn different. Wouldn't leaving in these sites of shame make it so that we wouldn't have to feel bad when we don't fall seamlessly into bed with our hair splayed out perfectly on the pillow? I've seen other porns that do this; they show pauses for gloves and lube, the negotiation process: "try moving my leg here," or "I like this," or "touch me here." How powerful would it be to show that when we fell back or slipped, it didn't ruin anything? We just kept going. Then I realized that, within the constellation of power relations, I had somewhat contradictory aims. How far could I go toward a new vision of sexy and still be recognized as sexy? How far could I go away from that standard referent and not be discounted as too different or have my film written off as a fetish film? If, as Foucault contends, we can never get outside of power, then how do we create something new without reinforcing oppressive ideologies? In the end I compromised; I showed bits of both.

Despite all the recognition, there are also times of misrecognition. I find these particular moments quite revealing. They are useful not just in highlighting how difficult it can be to unlearn conceiving of only certain bodies as desirable, but also what possibilities there are for bodies to take. A perfect example of this is how people assume that my co-star and I are lesbians. I only have space to offer partial explanations here. Some of this assumption is explained by normative readings of gender, which argue that a certain tone of voice implies a corresponding gender or that a dildo is a dildo, when sometimes what may appear to some as a dildo is someone's cock. Another explanation is that representations of genderqueer boy/femmegimp love are still rare, leaving many to not even realize that these experiences and identities are imaginable. I am also interested in thinking through what work it does to read the film and thus the identities and bodies portrayed in the film as lesbian. I am often either seen as straight or a lesbian—this is more complicated and interesting than I can really take up here—but both readings (straight or lesbian)

erase the desiring of gender-transgressive bodies (both his and mine). This assumption also presumes that desire occurs along heteronormative binary axes of gender and sex and sexuality. In addition, the way that disabled people are often denied agency contributes to a lack of recognition of subversively performed gender expression. Hot boy/femme lovin' action must be made unintelligible, yet again, to keep certain bodies and desires in line.

The first time I screened *want* at a festival, during the Q and A section, one of the other directors commented that "eventually your chair just faded away and you were just a hot girl getting fucked." For this viewer, this was meant as praise: the all-too-familiar "I was so hot he forgot I was in a wheelchair" compliment. I was not fulfilling the asexual poster-child stereotype that he views as being what disability *is*; and thus, disability and hot sexiness could not exist simultaneously. So in his viewing, he made what he considered to be the less desirable bit disappear. But my wheelchair will not just fade away; when I am hot, I am still disabled. I feel it is important to mention here that I had to win an obnoxious email argument about why my screening had to be held in an accessible theatre to make the exchange even possible. And sorry, no, you can't keep your little bubble of queer sex-positivity or the locations of said activities exactly the same and include me. The alignment of the inaccessible location of the event and his ableist views of hotness are not accidental.

Films like mine are unsettling as well as productive. What is made possible in the moments where we recognize being out of line, being crooked, being variant, as red smoking hot? This is especially true when being *in* line means hiding the parts that *don't* fall in line so that we never feel fully recognized. As already discussed, shame is a panoptical device used to urge bodies toward assimilation and normalcy. In my life, the many ways of not having the privilege of hiding certain sites of shame has been complicated and in some ways hard, but it has also opened up new possibilities and ways of being in the world. In *want* I show myself as a body that is explicitly sexual and also needs intimate daily personal care. Bodies that cannot or do not hide their interdependence, needs, and leakiness as well as others do, have faced a long history of violence, discrimination, and desexualization. Being regarded as a dependent body is certainly one of the major ways that disabled bodies have been cast as undesirables. I wanted to bring these two supposedly disparate parts of me together because I am certain that disability will never be fully desirable until notions of dependency and care are reworked. I also wanted to show how adopting a nontraditional model of meeting my care needs through a collective of people has not only enabled my sexual expression, but opened up a space for so much more. The mutuality of these caring relationships contributes to new ways of being-in-the-world-with-others.

In the article "Loving You Loving Me: Tranny/Crip/Queer Love and Overcoming Shame in Relationships," Samuel Lurie states, "being desired, trusting that, reciprocating that cracks us open" (2002: n.p.). Remaining open and vulnerable is scary because of shame, past hurts (both systemic and interpersonal), and the very real chance of harm, but it is also hard because it means we have to tell new stories. We have to tell stories that contradict the omnipresent chorus that tells us that we are not good enough to be wanted. These stories can be hard to tell because they can sometimes be hard to believe, but they need to be told because in their telling, they make change possible. As Eli Clare argues:

Never are we seen, heard, believed to be the creators of our own desires, our own passions, our own sexual selves. Inside this maze, the lives of queer crips truly disappear. And I say it's time for us to reappear. Time for us to talk sex, be sex, wear sex, relish our sex, both the sex we do have and the sex we want to be having. I say it's time for some queer disability erotica, time for an anthology of crip smut, queer style. Time for us to write, film, perform, read, talk porn. I'm serious. It's time (Clare, 2002: n.p.)

I screened *want* at a queer conference in Massachusetts; afterward, a young woman with a disability thanked me for my video and told me she had never had a romantic relationship. She said before that moment she had never even thought it was a possibility for her. So while my story tells many stories, there is most definitely a love story or two in there that are also stories of resistance and systemic change.

NOTES

1. The term *biomedical* here is used to encompass biological, psychological, intellectual, and medical practices and praxis not acting as interrelated systems.

2. This is true of many experiences of marginalization. An easy comparison is made when looking at laws regarding marriage in the prohibition of interracial marriages, same-sex marriages, and so on.

REFERENCES

Blumberg, L. 1994. Public Stripping. In B. Shaw (ed.). *The Ragged Edge: the Disability Experience from the Pages of the First Fifteen Years of The Disability Rag.* Lousiville, KY: Advocado Press. 77–81.

Clare, E. 2002. *Sex, Celebration, and Justice: A Keynote for QD2002.* Paper presented at the Queer Disability Conference, San Francisco, CA.

Erickson, Loree. 2007. Revealing Femmegimp: Sites of Shame as Sites of Resistance for People with Disabilities. *Atlantis: A Journal of Women's Studies* 32: 1.

Lurie, S. 2002. *Loving You Loving Me: Tranny/Crip/Queer Love and Overcoming Shame in Relationships.* Retrieved July 15, 2004, from www.bentvoices.org.

Titchkosky, Tanya. 2007. *Reading and Writing Disability Differently: The Textured Life of Embodiment.* Toronto: University of Toronto Press.

Wilkerson, A. 2002. Disability, Sex Radicalism, and Political Agency. *NWSA Journal,* 14(3): 33–57.

Willing and Able: Sex, Love and Disability, SexTV Documentary, 2003.

CONSTRUCTING VICTIMS: THE ERASURE OF WOMEN'S RESISTANCE TO SEXUAL ASSAULT

JOCELYN A. HOLLANDER AND KATIE RODGERS

On April 25, 2008, Melissa Bruen, then a senior at the University of Connecticut, was sexually assaulted as she walked home from a party during the campus's Spring Weekend Celebration. The Hartford *Courant* reported that "a young man pinned her to a tree, thrust himself against her and began moaning as a crowd gathered" (Merritt 2008). Then, another young man pulled down her tube top and grabbed her bare breasts as the drunken crowd cheered. The *Courant* painted this episode as an assault on a vulnerable female victim. For example, it described the aftermath of the assault in the following way: "Bruen's friend Kevin Meacham found Bruen after the incident. She had collapsed on the ground and was frantically calling his name. 'She was hysterical,' he said. 'She was almost hyperventilating.'" The article also mentions the warnings Bruen had received that women should not walk alone at night, as well as her boyfriend's sense of guilt that he wasn't with her to protect her. In other words, the *Courant*'s description of this assault fits well with our societal ideas about how assaults happen to women: they are attacked, generally by male strangers, in public places. They are vulnerable and helpless, and even if they do manage to escape rape or other serious assault, they are hysterical, weeping, and calling for male support.

But does this report portray what really happened? At the time of the assault, Bruen was the editor of the University of Connecticut's *Daily Campus*. In one of her final contributions to the paper, she published her first-person account of her experience. Here, in part, is how she describes what unfolded as she walked along a path nicknamed the "Rape Trail":

When he came toward me, I grabbed him by the shoulders and pushed him down to the ground. I held onto his shoulders and climbed on top to straddle him. He started thrashing side to side, but I was able to hit him with a closed fist, full force, in the face. A small crowd had gathered, mostly men. Now they seemed shocked. I was supposed to have been a victim, and I was breaking out of the mold. I hit him in the stomach, while clenching my legs around him to prevent another man from pushing me off. In all, it took three men to pull me off my assailant. . . . Another man, around 6'1", approached me and said, "You think that was assault?" and he pulled down my tube top, and grabbed my breasts. More men started to cheer. . . . I punched him in the face, and someone shoved me into a throng of others. I was surrounded, but I kept swinging and hitting until I was able to break free. (Bruen 2008)

This is a very different description than the one offered by the *Courant*. In her full account, Bruen does blame herself for walking alone at night. She focuses not on her escape but on what might have happened if she hadn't fought back. But regardless, she used her fists and determination to break free not just from one man, but from many. She sustained only bruises, not rape.

From "Constructing Victims: The Erasure of Women's Resistance to Sexual Assault," *Sociological Forum*, Vol. 29, No. 2, 2014, pp. 342–64. © 2014 Eastern Sociological Society. Reprinted by permission of John Wiley & Sons, Inc.

Bruen's case offers an unusual opportunity to compare two accounts of a single assault: a first-person narrative by the target of the assault and the news media's reporting of the same event. In this case, it seems clear that the *Courant*'s writer reframed Bruen's experience. In her own account, she is brave and powerful and ultimately successful—even if she was also, understandably, scared and shocked. In the *Courant*'s description, she is only vulnerable and weak, with very little attention to her resourcefulness and strength in resisting a crowd of drunken and abusive men.

Most of the time, however, we do not have access to the intended victim's version of what happened, but are exposed only to the news media's account of an assault. As we discuss below, large-scale survey research over the past two decades has found that, as in Melissa Bruen's case, women resist sexual assault—and do so successfully—in the majority of attempted attacks. Of course, we do not expect the details of newspaper reports to perfectly mirror the findings of social science research. Media accounts of sexual assault are influenced by both patterns of police reporting and the perceived "newsworthiness" of a particular incident. Nonetheless, the news media are an influential source of information for the public on crime and other events outside their own experience. The question we ask in this [reading] is what information about women's responses to sexual assault is available to newspaper readers. Are readers exposed to information about women's resistance and successful self-defense? Or do news reports tend to emphasize a conventional story line of vulnerability, as they did in the Bruen case, ignoring women's strength and highlighting their weakness? If so, these stories may reinforce the belief that women cannot defend themselves from men's violence, distorting readers' understanding of sexual assault.

LITERATURE REVIEW

Rape Resistance

There is now an abundance of evidence that on average, actively resisting sexual assault reduces the risk of completed rape (see Ullman 1997, 2007 for a comprehensive review of this literature). In particular, forceful physical resistance (e.g., kicking or hitting), nonforceful physical resistance (e.g., blocking an assailant's blows or fleeing), and forceful verbal resistance (e.g., yelling) are all associated with avoiding rape. Nonforceful verbal resistance (e.g., pleading or reasoning), on the other hand, does not seem to reduce the likelihood of rape. Moreover, it is now clear that women's physical or forceful verbal resistance does not, on average, increase their risk of serious injury beyond the sexual assault itself. Rather, while there is an association between victim resistance and injury, research that examines the sequence of assault finds that it is the injury that typically occurs first (Tark and Kleck 2004; Ullman 1998). In the most comprehensive study of this issue, Tark and Kleck (2004) concluded that in all types of crimes, including sexual assaults, victim resistance is nearly always the most effective course of action.[1]

National surveys find that women take self-protective action in the majority of assaults.[2] According to the National Crime Victimization Survey (NCVS), 66% of U.S. women who reported being sexually assaulted also reported taking some sort of self-protective action (Bureau of Justice Statistics 2007). . . .

In addition to increasing women's likelihood of escape, resisting assault also confers other benefits. For example, women who resist assault report fewer post-assault symptoms, both physical and psychological (Koss, Woodruff, and Koss 1991). They also report more rapid psychological healing (Bart and O'Brien 1985) and less self-blame (Rozee and

Koss 2001). Finally, fighting back can result in more compelling physical evidence for any later criminal justice process (Rozee 2005).

Media and the Social Construction of Reality

These findings about women's resistance to violence stand in contrast to societal beliefs about women's ability to resist sexual assault. For example, women are believed to be naturally weaker than men and thus inevitably vulnerable to violence, especially sexual assault (Hollander 2001; McCaughey 1997). Men, in contrast, are believed to be both inherently dangerous and, paradoxically, the source of women's protection. These beliefs make the idea of women's resistance to violence literally unthinkable (Hollander 2009). . . .

How the media portray social problems can have real consequences. The news media provide information about events that we have not personally experienced and frame that information for us, suggesting particular interpretations and meanings (Heath, Gordon, and LeBailly 1981). Media framings of social issues influence public opinion and perception (Berns 2004; Gilliam and Iyengar 2000; Holbert, Shah, and Kwak 2004; Leverentz 2012; Lowney and Holstein 2001; Repogle 2011; Wozniak and McCloskey 2010). . . . For women in particular, media depictions of sexual assault and other forms of violence have been argued to disempower them (Reid and Finchilescu 1995), induce fear (Chiricos, Eschholz, and Gertz 1997), teach them the "victim role" (Gerbner and Gross 1976), and serve as a form of social control, instructing women on the boundaries of virtuous behavior as well as "safe" and "unsafe" environments (Meyers 1997). Through its influence on public perception, news coverage of violence against women can also affect public policy (Berns 2004; Carll 2003) and facilitate continued violence against women (Meyers 1997: ix). . . .

METHODS

Data

We used the Lexis-Nexis Academic online database of U.S. newspapers as the source of data for our analysis. . . . To capture a diverse group of newspapers, we stratified the sample by region (Northeast, Midwest, Southeast, Southwest, and West) and circulation (over 1 million, 400,000 to 1 million, 100,000 to 400,000, and below 100,000). We included two newspapers with over 1 million circulation, *USA Today* and the *New York Times*, because they command a national audience. We then used a random number generator to choose one newspaper from each of the remaining geographic area/circulation size groups.[3] The final sample included 16 newspapers from communities of various sizes around the United States. . . .

We then returned to the Lexis-Nexis database to search for articles in these newspapers that focused on the sexual assault of women. We used three search terms: *sexual assault*, *sex offenses*, and *rape*. Because there may be seasonal differences in rates of sexual assault, we searched for all articles on these topics over a full calendar year, January 1–December 31, 2007. We scanned each article and selected for inclusion those articles that involved male assailants and female targets, focused on a particular incident, and included some description of the sequence of the assault (thus providing an opportunity for writers to include details about women's resistance to attacks). . . .

The final sample included 922 articles that described 1,084 incidents of assault. . . .

Coding and Analysis

We developed a coding scheme to capture descriptions of women's resistance, as well as representations of the assault, the perpetrator, and the target. We distinguished between two types of resistance based on previous discussions of women's self-defense in the research literature. *Active resistance* includes what other scholars have described as forceful physical and verbal resistance, and is characterized by targets using their own physical or verbal resources to assertively attempt to prevent an attack in progress. This may mean striking an assailant, yelling, or simply running away. *Passive resistance* includes nonforceful reactions that convey that the sexual interaction is unwanted but do not assertively refuse victimization, instead relying on the perpetrator or outside intervention to stop the assault. Examples include crying, pleading, or going limp. We also coded other characteristics of the article and assault; most relevant for this analysis are the type of article, the relationship between target and perpetrator, and the outcome of the resistance (successful or unsuccessful at ending the assault). . . .

We focused our analysis on two questions. First, did the article mention women's resistance to assault? And second, if it did so, what was the outcome of this resistance and how was it described? . . . Because past research has found that media reports of violence against women tend to mirror societal beliefs about gender, we hypothesized that newspapers would neglect to include information on women's resistance to violence, especially when it is successful at stopping an assault.

RESULTS

Do Newspapers Report Women's Resistance?

Of the 1,084 incidents in our sample, 689, or 63.6%, included no information about resistance by the target of the assault . . . , leaving readers to draw their own conclusions—and perhaps, given societal narratives of women's vulnerability and weakness, to assume that she did not resist or that her resistance was unsuccessful. In 34 incidents (3.1%), the writer noted explicitly that the target chose not to resist. Of those articles that did mention resistance, 73 cases, or 6.7% of all incidents, mentioned only passive resistance; as noted above, passive resistance has been found to be associated with completed rape. Of these mentions of passive resistance, approximately three-quarters were verbal (e.g., crying or begging) and one-quarter were physical (e.g., going limp). In only 26.6% (288 cases) of all incidents did the newspaper article mention women's active resistance. These cases were fairly evenly divided between physical resistance (12% of all incidents), verbal resistance (14%), and escape (10%).[4]

In only about one-third of the total sample of incidents, then, did the newspaper report mention any kind of resistance on the part of the target of the assault. . . .

Resistance Outcomes

When women resist a sexual assault, what happens? Survey research has found that active resistance reduces women's risk of rape. According to Clay-Warner's (2002) analysis of NCVS data, for example, there is an 87% reduction in the probability of completed rape when women use any form of self-protective action. In newspaper accounts, however, resistance is not strongly associated with avoiding completed rape. Of the 361 incidents for which some form of resistance was reported, that resistance was successful in stopping the assault in only 42% of the cases. . . . In the other 58% of incidents, the woman's resistance was described as unsuccessful (38%), the assault outcome was unclear (14%), or the assault was ended by outside intervention (6%). Women's active physical and verbal resistance was more frequently reported as successful (48.2% of 311 incidents) than unsuccessful (35.4% of incidents). In contrast, passive resistance (nonforceful physical and verbal resistance) was reported as unsuccessful (64.6% of 73 incidents) more frequently than as successful (12.3% of incidents). These results mirror the findings of social science research, which also find active resistance to be more effective than passive resistance (e.g., Clay-Warner 2002; Ullman 2007).

When articles did report women's resistance, the power of those actions was frequently diluted by the way they were described. For example, reporters often wrote that resistance or escape was something women "managed" to do, implying that it was not easy and that women were lucky, rather than skillful, if they achieved it. In other cases, a strong action such as escape was modified by descriptions of weak emotions, such as a description of a target who "ran into the house crying" (Anon. 2007). Only rarely was women's forceful resistance described with unmodified verbs such as "fought," "hit," or "resisted.". . .

Relationship between Perpetrator and Target

In about one-third of all incidents (31.9%), the newspaper report did not specify the relationship between the perpetrator and the target. Of the remainder, slightly more than half (51.7%) involved perpetrators who were described as strangers to the target, 41.0% involved acquaintances and other known assailants, and 7.3% involved intimate partners or family members. . . .

Interestingly, there were few differences in the reporting of women's resistance across different types of perpetrators. . . . This finding is surprising given that most research has found that women are much more likely to resist attacks by strangers than by known assailants (see Ullman 1997, 2002).

However, *successful* resistance was much more frequently reported in incidents involving strangers: 60% of these incidents, compared with 24% of incidents involving acquaintances

and 16.7% involving family members, described women's successful resistance to violence. . . . Although there is little research on the efficacy of resistance to strangers versus known perpetrators, the few studies that do measure this find forceful resistance to be equally effective in both situations (Ullman and Siegel 1993).

It is impossible to be certain *why* newspapers overrepresent stranger rapes but underreport resistance to them, or why they underreport the effectiveness of resistance to assaults by acquaintances and intimates. One possibility is the fact that newspapers often obtain information about sexual assaults from police reports, and women are more likely to report assaults by strangers than acquaintances or intimates. Another possibility is that reports of assaults by strangers are seen as more "newsworthy," either because they fit with widespread stereotypes about rape or because they are more sensational. Whatever the reason, these patterns distort the information available to readers and thus may perpetuate myths about sexual assault.

Variation by Type of Article and Type of Newspaper

Although the patterns described above held true for virtually all articles in the sample, we found some variation by article type. The articles fell into four categories based on length, level of detail, and focus. *Crime reports* (18% of the 922 articles) are brief, formulaic descriptions of reports made to the police, and average 48 words per article. . . . *Short reports* (31%), which average 163 words per article, are concise descriptions of a specific, very recent event. *Long reports* (46%) also focus on a single crime or series of related crimes but tend to be longer (averaging 547 words per article) and more detailed, often following up on a short report and providing context or interview quotes. *Feature stories* (6%), in contrast, tend to be much longer (1,576 words per article, on average) and focus not on a single event but rather on a larger story or issue (e.g., sexual assault in the military), embedding accounts of specific assaults within this larger context. . . .

[The crime and short reports provide] a simple reporting of the facts, rather than a detailed narrative about why she chose not to fight back. Of course, longer articles inevitably provide more details than short crime reports. What we found notable, however, was that only some types of information were elaborated in longer reports. There were virtually no lengthy or detailed descriptions of women's resistance, for example, even though resistance was reported much more frequently than submission. Descriptions in different article types, then, differ in both quantity and quality: Longer articles not only more frequently report women's submission; they also include additional detail that focuses on women's vulnerability and fear.

The four types of articles also varied in the way they reported the outcomes of women's resistance. About one-third of all types of articles noted a resistance outcome. Overall, longer articles were less likely to report successful resistance. . . .

Longer articles also tended to emphasize the ways in which outsiders helped facilitate a woman's escape or resistance, downplaying her own efforts at self-protection. One article, for example, reported that a woman fought off an attacker in an elevator but concluded by noting that "Workers chased him down and held him until police arrived" (Cooper 2007). . . . Instead, feature stories and long reports tended to describe passive resistance such as begging, ignoring, or going limp. . . .

At the other end of the spectrum, shorter articles were not only more likely to report successful resistance, but also tended to frame this resistance in more empowering ways. For example, some short articles describe women as "fighting," rather than "struggling," and some even provide details about the resistance. . . .

Depictions of unsuccessful resistance, unsurprisingly, follow the opposite pattern: longer articles provide more detail about unsuccessful resistance, while shorter articles provide less. A notable pattern here was that in longer articles, women were portrayed as being overwhelmed by men's strength and speed. . . .

Crime reports, however, describe the opposite pattern: although women's initial attempts at resistance may be unsuccessful, they keep trying and often get away or escape greater harm. . . .

Overall, the longer the article, the closer the story adhered to conventional narratives of female vulnerability and weakness. In the brief, "just-the-facts" articles, women's resistance was more evident, though still less frequent than victimization surveys report. This pattern is particularly striking because one might expect longer stories to describe more, not less, female resistance. Longer stories present the writer with the greatest opportunity to elaborate the details of the assault, and might be expected to describe the actions women took to protect themselves. Instead, however, writers appear to use this extra space to sketch a conventional picture of sexual assault, emphasizing women's weakness and minimizing or ignoring their agency. It is notable that resistance is virtually invisible in this type of reporting. Our data cannot tell us, of course, whether the focus on women's vulnerability in these articles reflects the types of incidents that feature stories choose to focus on or the writers' interpretations of these incidents. In either case, however, these stories serve to make conventional narratives of women's vulnerability more available to readers. . . .

CONCLUSIONS

What information do newspapers present about women's resistance to sexual assault? According to our analysis of a representative sample of 16 newspapers across 1 full year, newspaper reports of sexual assault reinforce a conventional narrative that assumes women's vulnerability to assault and their inability to respond to it effectively. About two-thirds of the newspaper descriptions contain no mention of women's resistance. When newspapers do report women's self-defensive behavior, they often do so only to note its failure; this was especially true when the assailant was known to the victim. The variation by article length multiplies this effect. . . . And in the relatively few cases when successful resistance is described, the fact that the woman defended herself is frequently undermined by the language used to describe it. In only a very small minority of cases are women described as strong, competent social actors who possess the ability to protect themselves from men's violence. . . .

Newspaper descriptions of victims of sexual assault, as we have described, nearly always conform to interpretations of women as weak, vulnerable, and dependent on others for their safety. This is true even for women who resist violence: although these situations present writers with the opportunity to deviate from the typical gender script, they virtually never do so. Newspapers "victimize" the targets of sexual assault even when they fight back, constructing them as victims (and particular kinds of *feminized* victims) rather than resisters. . . .

If women are presented with a barrage of information confirming their vulnerability, why would they believe themselves capable of fighting off a male attacker?[5] These patterns may also affect women's everyday behavior outside of assault situations. For example, if women believe self-defense to be impossible, they are left only with infantilizing options for preventing assault: limiting their participation in public life (though of course this may not protect them, since so much violence against women is perpetrated by acquaintances and intimates) or relying on others, particularly

men, for protection (Hollander 2009; Meyers 1997; Stanko 1995). Conversely, potential attackers may learn from newspaper reports that women are vulnerable and unlikely to resist assault; this portrait of weakness may actually encourage sexual assaults (Reid and Finchilescu 1995).

An alternate presentation of sexual assault, however, could have very different effects. Presenting full accounts of women's active resistance could challenge gender expectations, according agency to women and making resistance a more cognitively available response to assault (Cermele 2010). Melissa Bruen's firsthand account of her assault, with which we began this [reading], is a good example of how newspapers could report sexual assaults in ways that are empowering to women. Although Bruen does not discount the fear and pain she suffered, her account makes clear that she was not a passive victim. She fought back ferociously and ultimately succeeded in escaping her attackers. . . .

Although we believe that newspapers should more fully report women's resistance to violence, it is important to acknowledge the potential pitfalls. As other writers have argued, encouraging women's resistance can be used to blame victims by implying that women should resist assault or that they are at fault if they are unable to do so effectively. Moreover, focusing on women's resistance can reduce sympathy for victims or reinforce myths about "real rape" as occurring only when a woman resists and is physically overpowered. In our view (see Hollander 2009 for a more extended discussion), saying that women *can* effectively resist sexual assault does not imply that women *should* resist or that they should be blamed if they could not do so. Responsibility for sexual assault always lies squarely on the shoulders of the assailant, not the target. Moreover, as the recent revision of the definition of rape in the Uniform Crime Reports makes clear (U.S. Department of Justice 2012), women's resistance is not necessary for "real rape" to have occurred.

Despite these risks, we speculate that if depictions of women's resistance became more widespread, they could both encourage women to resist attackers and discourage men from attempting such attacks. Women, armed with the knowledge that they have both the power to defend themselves and a good chance of succeeding, would be able to participate more fully in social life. Empowering women in this way could not only prevent sexual violence but would also "challenge the status quo by encouraging women to break with traditional role expectations" in all areas of their lives (Meyers 1997:82). Reporting women's resistance to violence against women, in other words, could play an important role in deconstructing gender inequality.

NOTES

1. Of course, every assault situation is different, and in some situations resistance may not be the most effective response.

2. Most women who resist sexual assault do so without any formal self-defense training. A growing body of research suggests, however, that such training can reduce women's risk of victimization (e.g., Brecklin and Ullman 2005; Hollander 2014; Orchowski, Gidycz, and Raffle 2008; Senn, Gee, and Thake 2011; Sinclair et al. 2013), as well as increasing their self-confidence and changing gender scripts that prescribe female passivity and vulnerability (Brecklin 2008; Hollander 2004; McCaughey 1997).

3. Because there were no newspapers in the southeast region with a circulation between 400,000 and 1 million, the sample includes no paper from this geographic/circulation group.

4. Note that the number of descriptions of resistance sum to more than the number of incidents mentioning resistance because in some incidents women used more than one resistance strategy. In addition, in some incidents women initially resisted but then decided to submit to the assault; in others, the assault had multiple parts, some of which the woman resisted.

5. Of course, the large-scale survey research discussed above reports that women often *do* fight back when they are attacked. Our argument here is not that women do not resist sexual assault, but that the patterns of newspaper reporting we discuss here may reduce their belief that they can be successful in doing so.

REFERENCES

Bart, Pauline B., and Patricia H. O'Brien. 1985. *Stopping Rape: Successful Survival Strategies*. Elmsford, NY: Pergamon.

Berns, Nancy. 2004. *Framing the Victim: Domestic Violence, Media, and Social Problems*. New York: Aldine de Gruyter.

Brecklin, Leanne R. 2008. "Evaluation Outcomes of Self-Defense Training for Women: A Review." *Aggression and Violent Behavior* 13: 1: 60–76.

Brecklin, Leanne R. and Sarah E. Ullman. 2005. "Self-Defense or Assertiveness Training and Women's Responses to Sexual Attacks." *Journal of Interpersonal Violence* 20: 6: 738–62.

Bruen, Melissa. 2008. "My Spring Weekend Nightmare: A Firsthand Account of Sexual Assault on 'The Rape Trail.'" *The Daily Campus*, May 2. Retrieved May 27, 2011 from www.dailycampus.com/2.7440/my-spring-weekend-nightmare-1.1053994.

Bureau of Justice Statistics. 2007. *National Crime Victimization Survey*. Washington, DC: Bureau of Justice Statistics. Retrieved May 25, 2011 from http://bjs.ojp.usdoj.gov/index.cfm?ty=pbdetail&iid=1743.

Carll, E. K. 2003. "News Portrayal of Violence and Women: Implications for Public Policy." *American Behavioral Scientist* 46: 12: 1601–10.

Cermele, Jill. 2010. "Telling Our Stories: The Importance of Women's Narratives of Resistance." *Violence against Women* 16: 10: 1162–72.

Chiricos, Ted, Sarah Eschholz, and Marc Gertz. 1997. "Crime, News and Fear of Crime: Toward an Identification of Audience Effects." *Social Problems* 44: 3: 342–57.

Clay-Warner, Jody. 2002. "Avoiding Rape: The Effects of Protective Actions and Situational Factors on Rape Outcome." *Violence and Victims* 17: 6: 691–705.

Eschholz, Sarah, Ted Chiricos, and Marc Gertz. 2003. "Television and Fear of Crime: Program Types, Audience Traits, and the Mediating Effect of Perceived Neighborhood Racial Composition." *Social Problems* 50: 3: 395–415.

Gerbner, George, and Larry Gross. 1976. "Living with Television: The Violence Profile." *Journal of Communication* 26: 2: 172–99.

Gilliam, Franklin D., and Shanto Iyengar. 2000. "Prime Suspects: The Influence of Local Television News on the Viewing Public." *American Journal of Political Science* 44: 3: 560–73.

Heath, Linda, Margaret T. Gordon, and R. LeBailly. 1981. "What Newspapers Tell Us (and Don't Tell Us) about Rape." *Newspaper Research Journal* 2: 1: 48–55.

Holbert, R. Lance, Dhavan V. Shah, and Nojin Kwak. 2004. "Fear, Authority, and Justice: Crime-Related TV Viewing and Endorsements of Capital Punishment and

Gun Ownership." *Journalism & Mass Communication Quarterly* 81: 2: 343–63.

Hollander, Jocelyn A. 2001. "Vulnerability and Dangerousness: The Construction of Gender through Conversation about Violence." *Gender & Society* 15: 1: 83–109.

Hollander, Jocelyn A. 2004. "'I Can Take Care of Myself': The Impact of Self-Defense Training on Women's Lives." *Violence against Women* 10: 3: 205–35.

Hollander, Jocelyn A. 2009. "The Roots of Resistance to Women's Self-Defense." *Violence against Women* 15: 4: 574–94.

Hollander, Jocelyn A. 2014. "Does Self-Defense Training Prevent Sexual Violence against Women?" *Violence Against Women* 20: 3.

Koss, Mary P., W. J. Woodruff, and Paul G. Koss. 1991. "Criminal Victimization among Primary Care Medical Patients: Incidence, Prevalence, and Physician Usage." *Behavioral Sciences and the Law* 9: 1: 85–96.

Leverentz, Andrea. 2012. "Narratives of Crime and Criminals: How Places Socially Construct the Crime Problem." *Sociological Forum* 27: 2: 348–71.

Lowney, Kathleen, and James A. Holstein. 2001. "Victims, Villains, and Talk Show Selves." In Jaber F. Gubrium and Holstein, James A. (eds.), *Institutional Selves: Troubled Identities in a Postmodern World*: pp. 23–45. New York: Oxford University Press.

McCaughey, Martha. 1997. *Real Knockouts: The Physical Feminism of Women's Self-Defense*. New York: New York University Press.

Merritt, Grace E. 2008. "UConn Student Editor Describes Being Sexually Assaulted." *Hartford Courant*, May 3. Retrieved May 9, 2008 from articles.courant.com/2008 -05-03/news/uconnassault0503.art_l_three-sexual -assaults-university-and-police-path.

Meyers, Marian. 1997. *News Coverage of Violence against Women: Engendering Blame*. Thousand Oaks, CA: Sage.

Orchowski, Lindsay M., Christine A. Gidycz, and Holly Raffle. 2008. "Evaluation of a Sexual Assault Risk Reduction and Self-Defense Program: A Prospective Analysis of a Revised Protocol." *Psychology of Women Quarterly* 32: 2: 204–18.

Reid, Penny, and Gillian Finchilescu. 1995. "The Disempowering Effects of Media Violence against Women on College Women." *Psychology of Women Quarterly* 19: 3: 397–411.

Rozee, Patricia D. 2005. "Rape Resistance: Successes and Challenges." In Andrea Barnes (ed.), *The Handbook of Women, Psychology, and the Law*: pp. 265–79. San Francisco, CA: Wiley.

Rozee, Patricia D., and Mary P. Koss. 2001. "Rape: A Century of Resistance." *Psychology of Women Quarterly* 25: 4: 295–311.

Senn, Charlene Y., Stephanie S. Gee, and Jennifer Thake. 2011. "Emancipatory Sexuality Education and Sexual Assault Resistance: Does the Former Enhance the Latter?" *Psychology of Women Quarterly* 35: 1: 72–91.

Sinclair, Jake, Lee Sinclair, Evans Otieno, Munyae Mulinge, Cynthia Kapphahn, and Neville H. Golden. 2013. "A Self-Defense Program Reduces the Incidence of Sexual Assault in Kenyan Adolescent Girls." *Journal of Adolescent Health* 53: 3: 374–80.

Stanko, Elizabeth A. 1995. "Women, Crime, and Fear." *The Annals of the American Academy of Political and Social Science* 539: 46–58.

Tark, Jongyeon, and Gary Kleck. 2004. "Resisting Crime: The Effects of Victim Action on the Outcomes of Crimes." *Criminology* 42: 4: 861–910.

U.S. Department of Justice. 2012. "Attorney General Eric Holder Announces Revisions to the Uniform Crime Report's Definition of Rape." January 6. Retrieved March 27, 2012 from www.fbi.gov/news/pressrel/press-releases /attorney-general-eric-holder-announces-revisions-to-the -uniform-crime-reports-definition-of-rape.

Ullman, Sarah E. 1997. "Review and Critique of Empirical Studies of Rape Avoidance." *Criminal Justice and Behavior* 24: 4: 177–204.

Ullman, Sarah E. 1998. "Does Offender Violence Escalate When Women Fight Back?" *Journal of Interpersonal Violence* 13: 2: 179–92.

Ullman, Sarah E. 2002. "Rape Avoidance: Self-Protection Strategies for Women." In Paul A. Schewe (ed.), *Preventing Violence in Relationships: Interventions across the Lifespan*: pp. 137–62. Washington, DC: American Psychological Association.

Ullman, Sarah E. 2007. "A 10-Year Update of 'Review and Critique of Empirical Studies of Rape Avoidance.'" *Criminal Justice and Behavior* 34: 3: 1–19.

Ullman, Sarah E., and J. M. Siegel. 1993. "Victim–Offender Relationship and Sexual Assault." *Violence and Victims* 8: 2: 121–34.

Wozniak, Jessica A., and Kathy A. McCloskey. 2010. "Fact or Fiction? Gender Issues Related to Newspaper Reports of Intimate Partner Homicide." *Violence against Women* 16: 8: 934–52.

APPENDIX A: NEWSPAPER ARTICLES QUOTED IN TEXT

Anon. 2007. "Man Accused of Assault on a Woman in Orem." *Deseret Morning News*, July 24.

Cooper, Todd. 2007. "Reversal of DNA Ruling Pleases Victims; A Judge Says a Convicted Rapist Can't Seek Evidence That Wasn't Originally Part of the Case against Him." *Omaha World-Herald*, August 8, 01A.

4

LEARNING ABOUT SEX

AN INTERVIEW WITH

JESSICA FIELDS

Jessica Fields is a professor of sociology and sexuality studies at San Francisco State University and the author of Risky Lessons: Sex Education and Social Inequality *(Rutgers University Press, 2008), which received the Distinguished Contribution to Scholarship Book Award from the American Sociological Association's Race, Class, and Gender Section. Her second book,* Problems We Pose: Feeling Differently about Qualitative Research *(University of Minnesota Press) explores emotion as an opportunity to reimagine power and knowledge production.*

What led you to begin studying sexuality?

My research focus is teaching and learning about sexuality in a variety of settings, including middle school sexuality education classrooms; sexuality education debates and policy; lessons schools offer about lesbian, gay, bisexual, transgender, and queer (LGBTQ) gender and sexuality; and participatory sexuality education for incarcerated women. I'm especially interested in intersections among sexuality, gender, and race, and I'm interested in teaching and learning as opportunities to reimagine sexual possibilities.

While I was a graduate student in North Carolina, the state passed legislation requiring public schools to teach abstinence until marriage. School boards and teachers had to decide what the legislation would mean for local practice. I recognized that those debates would be a chance to observe communities debating the relationship between schooling and sexuality and articulating a vision of what sort of sexual lives they would value and what sort of learning they would promote.

How do people react when you tell them you study sexuality?

To state the obvious: People think that if I study sexuality, I am interested in sexuality. And, of course, I am interested in what I study. But this interest can confuse people. For some, my interest in sexuality becomes permission to speak freely and comfortably about a topic that is often taboo. Sometimes people imagine I am a confessor—someone with whom they can share secrets: an identity they haven't disclosed to many people or a troubling experience in their past. Other times, they think I have the knowledge and authority of a trained sexuality educator and can help them answer a question they have about their own or a loved one's sexual health. I try to receive those disclosures respectfully, answer as best I can, and, if necessary, direct people to those who can be more helpful: a friend, teacher, counselor, or other resource.

What ethical dilemmas have you faced as you've studied sexuality? Could you tell us about one particularly thorny dilemma and how you solved it?

University institutional review boards (IRBs) have many concerns about research with vulnerable populations, and my work with young people in schools and with women of color in jails raises lots of ethical questions with IRBs. I have spent a lot of time designing studies that ensure I've protected participants from exploitation, given them adequate opportunity to offer and refuse consent to participate, and protected their privacy.

Ironically, responding to IRB requirements sometimes raises an even thornier dilemma. In order to work inside schools and jails, I have to comply with institutional regulations that I otherwise critique. Our research team has to reassure the jail warden and staff that our study will not undo the logic of the jail—an institution we consider oppressive. Similarly, we have to promise school principals that we will respect the rules and culture of their schools, even though we know that those rules and cultures routinely work against the interests of queer youth, youth of color, and other disenfranchised groups. In order to conduct research that interrogates inequalities, I first have to bear witness to those inequalities and that has meant being, at least momentarily, complicit.

What do you think is most challenging about studying sexuality? Could you share any particular challenges you've faced conducting sex research?

I am lucky to be a sociology professor at San Francisco State University, where sexuality studies has been integral to the university's teaching and research mission for decades. In general, across disciplines, departments, and generations, my colleagues respect my work and share my interests. On many campuses and in academia more broadly, this isn't the case. Sexuality is often considered a peripheral and even suspect subfield in sociology—a topic less prestigious and less fundamental to social life than more established subfields. Janice Irvine has demonstrated that this thinking has all sorts of material consequences for sociologists: IRBs are more forbidding, funding is more difficult to obtain, and journals are harder to break into. These consequences make it harder to secure and retain professional positions, support students, disseminate research, and launch ambitious studies. Even for someone like me—employed in a supportive department—these conditions limit the possibilities for sexuality research. Overall, my colleagues and I do our work with fewer resources than our colleagues in other fields, and that limits the reach and impact of our work.

Can you describe some of the findings from your recent research?

My latest project began with a worry: In focusing so much attention and so many resources on preventing anti-gay bullying, were schools muting other experiences of LGBTQ sexuality and gender? With funding from the Ford Foundation, my colleagues (Jen Gilbert, Nancy Lesko, Laura Mamo) and I conducted the Beyond Bullying Project, a school-based study of LGBTQ gender and sexualities in high schools. We set up storytelling booths inside three high schools and invited students and educators to step inside to tell their stories of LGBTQ sexuality and gender. Our aim was to identify and explore stories of LGBTQ sexuality and gender beyond the bullying framework that dominates schools' approach. We also wanted to know what might be required of schools who want to think "beyond bullying" in their teaching and learning about LGBTQ sexuality and lives.

In the hundreds of stories we collected in three U.S. schools, we heard accounts of friendship, family, love, activism, and—sometimes—vulnerability and bullying. One of the most important findings is that students' friendships are a crucial site for learning about and trying on LGBTQ sexual identities and affiliations. Some students told stories about losing friends after coming out; other students talked about struggling to be good friends to those who had recently come out as LGBTQ. Many students learned about the challenges of coming out by witnessing their friends' struggles, and still others talked about how a friend's coming-out put their own sexuality into question—could they survive the stigma that often comes with being friends with a member of the LGBTQ community? In story after story, students called out for ideas and support that would help them sustain friendships in the wake of anti-gay sentiment. The stories suggest that schools, adults, and teachers would do well to explore friendship in sexuality education.

Why is sex research important? How does your research relate to everyday life?

Sexuality research helps us understand, among other things, how everyday concerns like intimacy, desire, and health are implicated in broader social identities, differences, hierarchies, and injustices. Too often, these concerns feel simply natural—we are hardwired for certain sorts of relationships and not others, we like who and what we like, or policies and norms are just well-intentioned efforts to promote and protect the health of community members. Sexuality research illuminates the many ways those seemingly organic sensations and inclinations emerge from, sustain, or challenge existing conditions. With that insight in mind, sexuality education becomes an opportunity for educators and students to do more than prevent disease, infection, and unwanted pregnancies. Sexuality education becomes an opportunity to reimagine social and sexual realities.

Of the projects you've completed over the course of your career thus far, which is the most interesting and why?

The insight that most interests me spans multiple research projects. In studies of middle school students, African American girls and young women, LGBTQ teachers and students, and incarcerated adult women of color, I've realized these disparate groups share an important experience: youth, queers, and women in jail are all assumed to have poor judgment and not to know how to take care of themselves and others. Education becomes a necessary correction to their bad inclinations and habits—not an opportunity to think critically and creatively about their sexual lives. Not everyone has access to my experience of education as sexually liberatory; access is tied to racial, socioeconomic, and other social privileges. Efforts to transform sexuality education must confront social stratification in order to ensure all students have access to teaching and learning built on a sense of possibility.

If you could teach people one thing about sexuality, what would it be?

I want people to ask more of sexuality education, to hold on to a utopian vision of what we could pursue in the classrooms, hallways, assemblies, and informal spaces of schooling. In the face of limited funding, shrinking budgets, contentious debate, and vulnerable youth, our hopes for sexuality education easily become modest. I encourage people to resist the urge simply to be practical. Sure, compromise may be necessary, but let's always remember that we've compromised and hold out for more next time.

THE DEATH OF THE STORK: SEX EDUCATION RESOURCES FOR CHILDREN AND PARENTS

WENDY SIMONDS AND AMANDA M. JUNGELS

WHY NOT THE STORK?

You may say, "Isn't it easier and less embarrassing to tell them about the stork?" There are several reasons. . . . Even if he doesn't suspect anything at 3, he is surely going to find out the truth or the half-truth when he's 5 or 7 or 9. It's better not to start him off wrong and have him later decide that you're something of a liar. And if he finds out that you didn't dare tell him the truth, it puts a barrier between you, makes him uneasy. He's less likely to ask you other questions later, no matter how troubled he is. (Spock and Rothenberg, 1992: 511)

"Does it feel good when a mommy and daddy make a baby?" he asked.

Joey's father answered, "It feels very nice, especially since you're able to be so close to someone you love."

"Hey," Joey said in an excited voice, "maybe sometime you two can show me how you do it."

Joey's parents smiled and laughed, but Joey knew it was a nice laugh and they weren't making fun of him.

"Joey, when a mommy and daddy make love, it's private, just something for the two of them," said Joey's father.

"Well, when can I do it? When can I make a baby?"

"When you get older, Joey," said Joey's mother. (Brooks and Perl, 1983)

This hokey conversation excerpted from *So That's How I Was Born!*, a sex education book aimed at preschoolers, exemplifies the sort of sexual honesty Spock and Rothenberg prescribe in advising against the stork story in the first extract. And certainly everyone believes that honesty is the best policy. But there's more than one way to be honest, and there are multiple truths about sexuality. We educate kids based on our perceptions of social reality, often without questioning norms to which we've grown accustomed. We also educate kids without knowing we're doing it—with offhand remarks or behaviors that we're not aware they notice. When we do intend to teach, we can now select from a variety of texts designed to help us. Parents may choose sex education books (or other resources) because doing so gets them off the hook altogether from discussing sex with their kids, or they may use them as supplementary material. Many of these books have introductory notes to parents instructing them about instructing their kids. Sex education resources for children both represent and shape cultural ideologies about children, sexuality, and procreation.

In the United States, teaching sex to children in any form seems to induce cultural anxiety and controversy. An early sex ed pamphlet addressed to teens by Mary Ware Dennett, *The Sex Side of Life: An Explanation for Young People* (1919), was deemed obscene under the Comstock Law in 1922, which banned sending any materials related to sexuality, contraception, or abortion through the U.S. mail (see Moore, 2007, and Solinger, 2005, for more complete historical discussions). This decision was overturned on appeal in 1930; the ruling stated: "an accurate exposition of the relevant facts of the sex side of life in decent language and in manifestly serious and disinterested spirit cannot ordinarily be regarded as obscene" (cited in Solinger: 106). Sex ed books gained legal respectability on shaky grounds. What, after all, constitutes "accuracy"? Who decides what the "facts" are and which of them are "relevant" to children? Authors, since this time, have continually asserted their credibility by presenting themselves as *scientific* authorities on what morally constitutes "accurate facts about sex."

In this reading, we discuss sex ed media for children from the 1970s to the 2010s. In our research, we found no books about sex targeted to young children published before the late 1960s. Publishers apparently began to perceive young children as a market for this sort of didactic material in the late 1960s and early 1970s as a result of a particular combination of cultural forces that promoted resistance to authority and more openness about sexual matters: the student movement, the feminist movement, the gay rights movement (all of which are indebted to the civil rights movement); hippie subculture; the so-called sexual revolution; and the human potential movement (promoting psychological growth techniques and practices). Advice books on sexuality for adults also flourished during this time (see, e.g., Ehrenreich and English, 1986; Simonds, 1992), and sex education programs proliferated in U.S. public schools (Moran, 2000). The notion that children should be educated about sex before adolescence developed as cultural views of adolescents *as* sexual became accepted by educators and doctors. Thus, adolescents were in need of sexual education—especially regarding management and control. Moran describes the development of these ideas, beginning at the turn of the twentieth century (2000). Patton (1996) writes that the way in which we now conceive of adolescence is "as a time of turmoil between a period of innocence (childhood) and one of accomplished identity and safety (adulthood)" (75). So how do we present sexuality to innocents to prepare them for impending turmoil?

We analyze a range of androgynous (not addressed specifically to one gender), nonreligious picture books about sex geared toward young children, sex ed books for older kids, and advice books for parents regarding talking with children about sex that were available through Amazon. com. (The books we surveyed are arranged by category in the references.) In earlier versions of this reading, we limited ourselves to what we felt were "professional" publishers, but, as in the past, used Amazon "popularity" as our source. Now there are so many online and self-publishing outlets that it can be difficult to define or tell what's "professional." This time, we did not limit our investigation to books produced by established publishing companies. Additionally, we include a chart that lists current websites offering secular advice about sex to older children and parents (though we do not discuss these resources here).

These sources, taken together, address a loose set of problems parents face in their presumed desire to present a variety of complex, baggage-laden topics to children in an understandable way without feeling deeply uncomfortable in the process. Talking about sexuality and childbearing with children creates a multifaceted dilemma. Parents are, in essence, attempting to create openness about a range of topics they may feel unable to be truly open about. First there is the issue of deterrence: How can parents present sex without making it seem too appealing? Second, how should adults avoid frightening children with all the ways that sexual encounters and their outcomes can be painful, even horrible? Third, how can parents balance a desire not to frighten with the goal of offering kids information that might protect them from sexual dangers and unintended consequences (sexual predators, rape, sexually transmitted diseases, teen pregnancy, abortion, not to mention heartbreak)? Fourth, how can parents deal with, acknowledge, respond to evidence of, and instruct children about their own sexuality? And fifth, how do adults teach children appropriate contexts for expressions of sexuality?

What are appropriate contexts, after all? In the rest of this reading, we look at how authors of sex ed books for children and advice books for parents contextualize sexuality. Authors tend to reify (and occasionally resist) heteronormative, gendered, and medicalized sociosexual conventions through an examination of five general topics: procreative/sexual anatomy; procreative sex; childbirth; managing childhood sexuality; and alternatives to procreative sex. Our primary focus is on the books for young children; we supplement the discussion of these books with interpretations of the books for older children and for parents.

CHANGING BODIES

In sex ed books for young and older kids, authors foreground the primary discussion of procreative sex with brief anatomy lessons. Until recently, they have almost universally equated biological sex with gender, telling this general narrative: There are people with penises and people with vaginas, and this is what makes them boys or girls. Eventually, boys and girls grow up into men and women and make babies together utilizing these parts. Brown and Brown (1997) preface their presentation of genital difference with a litany of ways in which boys and girls *may* be different (clothes, hairstyles, playing styles, emotions). After each example, they write that the difference is "sometimes, but not always" evident. Harris (2006) has a similar discussion (including that "girls play with dolls and teddy bears! And so do boys!" and "boys have very big and strong muscles. So do girls!"), and concludes that boys and girls are "not all that different" (12–13).

Despite claims of similarity, divergent anatomy is central in these discussions of difference: "Actually the only sure way to tell boys and girls apart is by their bodies. If you're a boy, you have a penis, scrotum, and testicles. If you're a girl, you have a vulva, clitoris, and vagina" (11–12). This text appears alongside illustrations of a naked boy and girl, with labeled body parts. The cartoon girl proclaims, "Look! Our bodies are more alike than different!" Harris and Emberley (1999) include a similar picture, with the text "Most parts of our bodies . . . are the same and look quite the same whether we are female or male. . . . The parts that are different are the parts that make each of us a female or a male" (10). Occasionally, authors omit the clitoris from their depictions of girls' bodies, as in Saltz's (2005) book *Amazing You,* or describe girls' sex organs as if they are somehow based on boys' sex organs. For example, in a description of sexual arousal in girls, Foster (2005) describes the elongation of the clitoris as an example of how, "in some ways, a female's clitoris is like a male penis" (29). In the book *Boys, Girls and Body Science,* Hickling (2002) frames her discussion of sexual development with the device of a teacher interacting with elementary-aged students; these students present their ideas about sexual development and the teacher redirects them along the "correct" path. For instance, a student asks whether "girls have balls," and the teacher responds that "girls have two ovaries inside their abdomen and they are sort of like balls" (n.p.). Early fetal development begins with undifferentiated female internal sex organs, not male parts. So, in actuality, "balls" are like ovaries, not vice versa. Yet authors' language tends to centralize boys' bodies and make girls' bodies secondary and/or deviant.

Authors typically do not mention the possibility of not being able to tell bodies apart easily, or of gender identity that doesn't "match" genitalia, nor question the bifurcated social constructs of girl and boy, man and woman. As Joey's mother says in *So That's How I Was Born!* (Brooks and Perl, 1983), "a boy's body isn't better than a girl's body and a girl's body isn't better than a boy's. They're just different from the time they're born and each is special in their own way." In this way, most authors proclaim gender difference as essential (rooted in dimorphic biological sex), while also contradictorily claiming the difference doesn't matter. Perhaps they think that introducing sex and gender ambiguity and fluidity would confuse kids. The majority of babies *are* born genetically dimorphous, after all, and most people appear to grow up relatively comfortable with socially constructed gender divisions. Yet in many other instances, it is not the frequency of a phenomenon that determines whether authors present it; many books include discussions of occurrences at least as infrequent as intersexuality or gender-bending identities (e.g., multiple births, home births, adoption), apparently without worrying about the confusion these mentions might cause. Authors seek to demystify some social practices but leave others untouched and, in so doing, appear to take most cultural norms for granted.

A recent exception is Silberberg and Smyth's *Sex Is a Funny Word: A Book about Bodies, Feelings, and You* (2015), where diversity and difference recur throughout in the text. Silverberg clearly describes gender as a social construction: "When we are born, a doctor or midwife calls us boy or girl because of what we look like on the outside." They also say that these assignments could be wrong, and that they are "based on who *they* think we are. What about our whole body, inside and out? What about who we think we are?" (81).

Authors of books for older kids tend to discuss the social construction of gender and sexual identity explicitly. In *Sex: A Book for Teens: An Uncensored Guide to Your Body, Sex, and Safety* (2010), Nicole Hasler explains:

While most biological boys feel more or less like boys and most biological girls feel more or less like girls (regardless of being gay or straight), some people really feel they do not identify with the gender they are given at birth. Some people also identify with more than one gender or do not identify with any gender at all. (34)

Hasler goes on to discuss people who "change genders," though most trans people see becoming trans as a full realization of their gender, not a "change." Hasler, like many authors, conflates gender and sex in her discussion of trans kids: "Some people hide their desire to be the opposite sex. . . . It sucks because you can't live your life the way you feel most comfortable (dressing and living as someone of the opposite gender) out of fear of people judging you or being jerks about it" (2010: 35).

Authors try to be accepting of diversity, even when their discussions are short and reify binary rather than fluid notions of sexual and gender identity. In *100 Questions You'd Never Ask Your Parents* (2013), in response to the question, "I'm unsure about my sexual orientation. What do I do?" the authors recommend: "Give yourself some more time to figure it out. With time, you will begin to notice yourself becoming attracted to people, and your orientation will show itself to you. . . . Some guys and girls are sure about their orientation early on; for others it takes time, doubt, and exploration. Discover your feelings and you'll discover your orientation" (77). The authors don't address gender identity specifically, but here they suggest that there are two categories ("guys" and "girls"), and four categories for sexual identity ("guys" and "girls" who like "guys," and "guys" and "girls" who like "girls").

The vast majority of illustrations and photographs of children and their families in these books only show racially alike families. Though the majority of those pictured are white, illustrators and photographers include children and adults interacting with each other across racial boundaries. Over time, illustrations have become more diverse. In the original version of this reading, written in 2001, we cited only one clear depiction of an interracial family

(Smith and Wheatley, 1997: 14), and Harris and Emberley (1999) had a few illustrations that might have been interracial family groups. Harris's books typically depict and discuss families in a multitude of other ways, including multiracial, foster, adoptive, blended, queer, and intergenerational families (2004, 2006, 2013). While other authors do discuss different family forms (adoptive, foster, and intergenerational), and also present and promote multicultural interactions among people, depictions of interracial intimacy within families still occur relatively infrequently.

MAKING LOVE AND MAKING BABIES

Children do indeed ask their parents, "Where did I come from?" or "How are babies made?" Thus, many parents find themselves working backward from baby (or pregnancy) to heterosexual sexuality. We suspect that if children initiate conversations about sexuality apart from procreation, many parents don't know what to do or say, so they may end up in the procreation story because it's easier for them to deal with than sexuality on its own.

Sexual information conveyed in the books for young children tends to be vague, to reinforce heteronormativity, and to represent penile–vaginal intercourse as the only example of sexual activity in which men and women engage. Sometimes authors omit the act altogether, as in Joanna Cole's *How You Were Born* (1993) and Cory Silverberg's *What Makes a Baby* (2012).

In a woman's body are egg cells. The egg cell is round. It does not have a shell like a chicken's egg. In a man's body are sperm cells. The sperm cells have long tails and can swim. When a sperm and an egg join together, they form a special cell that can grow into a baby. (Cole, 1993: 19)

When grown ups want to make a baby they need to get an egg from one body and sperm from another body. . . . When an egg and sperm meet, they swirl together in a special kind of dance. As they dance, they talk to each other. . . . When their dance is done they are not two things anymore. They danced around and shared so much that they became one brand new thing. (Silverberg, 2012: n.p.)

Fewer than half of the books for young children depict sexual acts. When they do, men are either on top of women, or the man and woman are side by side. In almost all cases, the copulators are under the covers. When authors do discuss penile–vaginal intercourse, they describe it as pleasurable and functional for both men and women, and portray it taking place within the context of loving relationships. For instance, Harris and Emberley warn explicitly that, however enticing it may seem, "kids" should not have "sexual intercourse":

Sexual intercourse may seem gross or nice, scary or funny, weird or cool—or even unbelievable to you. But when two people care for each other, sexual intercourse is very loving. Kids are much too young to have sexual intercourse. (Harris and Emberley, 1999: 29)

None of the authors writing for young children describes orgasm, though clearly they present the emission of sperm as momentous. Eggs and sperm are personified in gendered ways: Lisa Jean Moore writes, "There is a preponderance of narratives describing the exceptionalness of the one sperm that gets to fertilize the egg. Other than primping and batting eyes to be attractive to the sperm, eggs typically are passive" (2007: 62). Authors depict sex cells as engaged in analogous romances to those of their producers.

The reason for sex in these books is parenthood. Brooks and Perl (1983) label the lovers "mommy" and "daddy" before the fact, thus presenting sex as predicated on this goal of future parenthood:

One of the ways a mommy and daddy show they love one another is by hugging each other very close.

In bed, they can get really close when a daddy puts his **penis** inside the special opening between a mommy's legs which is called a **vagina**. The sperm comes out of the daddy's penis and goes into the mommy's vagina, and then the sperm meets the egg and a baby starts. (Brooks and Perl, 1983: 9)

Andry, Schepp, and Hampton's *How Babies Are Made* (1979) and Baker's *The Birds and the Bees* (1990) are more lackluster than the others in their descriptions of procreative sex:

The sperm, which come from the father's testicles, are sent into the mother through his penis. To do this, the father and mother lie down facing each other and the father places his penis in the mother's vagina. Unlike plants and animals, when human mothers and fathers create a new baby they are sharing a very personal and special relationship. (Andry, Schepp, and Hampton, 1979: n.p.)

When men and women mate, the penis becomes stiff and is inserted into the vagina, which has become larger and moist, ready to receive it. (Baker, 1990: n.p.)

Many books present humans' procreative method after first laboriously introducing habits of other plant and animal species. This approach makes sex seem natural and scientific. "By relying on science, these children's books bolster their contents as being objective and truthful" (Moore, 2007: 51). Andry, Schepp, and Hampton (1979) interestingly sever this naturalistic connection with other living things, separating humans out by insisting on our emotional superiority ("unlike plants and animals . . ."). They want to show that sex is more than just the casual rubbing together of stamens and pistils. The experts writing for parents endorse grounding sex in satisfying long-term connections between adults. For instance, Spock and Rothenberg (1992) advise, "Parents shouldn't ever let the anatomical and physiological explanation of sex stand alone but always connect it with the idealistic, spiritual aspects" (509).

One of our favorites among the books for young children is Babette Cole's *Mommy Laid an Egg OR Where Do Babies Come From?* (1993). Cole uses humor throughout the book, both in the prose and in her illustrations, which mix a cartoon family together with raucous, childlike stick-figure drawings. The book begins with the cartoon parents misinforming their children that "some babies are delivered by dinosaurs," "you can make them out of gingerbread," and "sometimes you just find them under stones." The children respond with laughter, and say, "What a bunch of nonsense!" They proceed to instruct their parents about procreative sex, all the while pointing to their crude, comical illustrations.

Girl: "Mommies do have eggs. They are inside their bodies."
Boy: "And daddies have seeds in seed pods outside their bodies. Daddies also have a tube. The seeds come out of the pods and through the tube."
Girl: "The tube goes into the mommy's body through a hole. Then the seeds swim inside using their tails." (Cole, 1993)

On the page where the boy proclaims, "here are some ways . . . mommies and daddies fit together," Cole illustrates his words with childlike drawings of the mommy and daddy cavorting in a variety of imaginative positions while linked at the crotch, including holding balloons, bouncing on a big ball (labeled "space hopper"), and lying on a skateboard. These are raunchy yet clean, because they are children's drawings (and do not depict genitalia, only breasts). The language is crude in a childish way, yet the botanical allegories don't seem embarrassingly goofy, just goofy in a fun way. Sex seems fun for once—not just a pleasant sperm-delivery arrangement. Why else would the participants wear party hats? Yet, at the same time, this language of "fitting together" and identifying the participants as "mommies and daddies," which recurs in several books, reinforces the notion that heteronormative, procreative sex is natural and right.

HAVING BABIES

The next step after procreative sex in all these books is pregnancy and birth. After a brief discussion of the growth of the fetus and changes in the mother's body, authors explain how babies are born. Many authors tell the story of birth from the point of view of the baby, which is apparently the perspective with which they imagine child readers will identify. Authors typically do not discuss pain in childbirth, although Silverberg (2012) does, stating that "sometimes it takes a long time, sometimes it is quick, sometimes it hurts a little, and sometimes it hurts A LOT." Authors portray labor as a biological (muscular) activity, as hard work that a woman does, or both. They depict childbearing as wonderful, a job to be done together by a mommy and a daddy (who cheers her on).

Typically, birthing women are depicted in the lithotomy positions (on their backs, with feet in stirrups), surrounded by masked and gowned people (Brown and Brown, 1997; Harris and Emberley, 1999; Cole, 2001; Harris, 2013). Frequently, the daddy is also decked out in medical garb, though in some illustrations he doesn't wear a mask. Laura Krasny Brown (1997) writes, "When a baby is ready to be born, muscles in the mother's womb begin to tighten and relax, tighten and relax, helping her push out the baby. In most births, the baby comes out the vagina, which stretches to let it pass through" (28). Similarly, the text accompanying Emberley's drawing reads:

When a baby is about to be born, the muscles in the mother's uterus begin to squeeze tight. This is called "labor." "Labor" is another word for "work." A mother's muscles work very hard to push and squeeze the baby out of the uterus and into the vagina. Then the mother's muscles push and squeeze the baby's body through the vagina. The vagina stretches wide as the baby's soft, wet, and slippery body travels through it. (Harris and Emberley, 1999: 56–57)

Even though these authors' descriptions of labor and birth sound like they might have been written by midwives, they tend to depict the medical management of the process as normal. Few authors mention alternatives to hospital birth, and even fewer depict it. Joanna Cole (1993) writes: "Your mother and father went to the hospital or childbirth center where you were to be born. If you were born at home, then the doctor or midwife came to your house" (31). The photographs accompanying this text show couples in more casual hospital or birth center settings than the settings depicted in the other books, but none are at home. Sol and Judith Gordon write: "Some babies are born at home. But most women like to go to the hospital for the birth of their baby" (1992). This text is accompanied by a drawing of a woman lying in the lithotomy position in a hospital, a masked woman birth attendant standing between her legs holding a screaming baby up for her (and us) to see. We are positioned behind and above the woman's head, watching the baby come out from her vantage point, but we can also see her face, and she looks happy. We rarely see a vaginal view of birth: in Cole's (1993) child drawing, we see a baby sticking out of a round-blob mother and saying, "Hello Mommy!"; and in Harris's (2004) illustration, we see both a vaginal view of birth and a woman in the lithotomy position in the same set of illustrations (63). In *What Makes a Baby* (Silverberg, 2012), we see one illustration of a cesarean section, *and* the only illustration of a nonmedical birth in the collection of books we reviewed: from the same "above and behind" vantage point, we see a woman being attended by a person not in medical garb, on what appears to be a blanket on a hardwood floor (possibly at home). All other illustrations show babies attended by medical personnel in medical settings both during and after birth.

As mentioned, authors writing for young children often seek to present labor and birth from the baby's perspective—these authors tend to present the birthing process as both fun and exciting. In *Boys, Girls and Body Science* (Hickling, 2005), Nurse Meg describes to a class of elementary students how the birthing process happens. This dialogue is accompanied by a picture of a woman in the lithotomy position who appears serene and peaceful—if not unconscious:

"But what would happen if you kept squeezing on a balloon?" asked Meg.

"It would pop," said Nicholas.

"That is exactly what happens," said Meg. "After a few hours, the water bag breaks and the water comes pouring out of the mum's vagina and makes it all wet and slippery, just like a water slide. So, the first water slide that you ever had was the day you were born when you came slip-sliding down your mum's vagina."

All the children loved the water slide story and made swooshy noises as they waved their arms around.

Harris (2006) uses the same "balloon" analogy in a much more effective way, explaining that a pregnant woman's uterus does *not* pop because her uterus and skin are stretchy—"like a balloon." This response is an excellent example of how an analogy can be used to explain a phenomenon to a young child in a way that is correct yet still understandable.

TEACHING ABOUT TOUCHING

Over time, books for young children have increasingly come to address children's sexuality within the context of danger; the number of books dedicated solely to this issue has also increased. The primary goals of authors who address the theme of "good touch/bad touch" or sexual abuse are to teach kids to recognize dangerous abusive touch, and to encourage them to seek help if they feel something bad has happened or could happen to them. Brown and Brown (1997) and Harris and Emberley (1999) attempt to differentiate between touching that is "okay" and "not okay"—that is, between

masturbation and sexual abuse. Brown and Brown (1997) write:

Touching and rubbing your genitals to feel good is called masturbation. Some of us try this; some of us don't. However, it's best to do this private kind of touching off by yourself.

Touching others is just as important. . . . If someone doesn't want to be touched, then respect his or her wishes—don't do it! . . . Everyone needs good touches to feel loved and happy. . . . But no one has the right to touch you in a way that feels wrong or uncomfortable.

If you don't like the way someone touches you, speak up and tell him or her to stop. If that doesn't work, tell your mom or dad or another grownup. Your body belongs to you, and you should say who touches it! (16–19)

Harris (1999) goes into more detail about both masturbation and abuse, and as in Brown and Brown, the discussion of masturbation leads into the issue of abuse. The Browns differentiate between self-touches that feel good, touches from others that *are* good, and those that feel wrong or are somehow dislikable. Harris (1999) makes the same points, and goes into more detail about contentious views on masturbation: "Every family has its own thoughts and feelings about masturbation. . . . Some people and some religions think it's wrong to masturbate. But most doctors agree that masturbation is perfectly healthy and perfectly normal, and cannot hurt you or your body" (69). Apparently, doctors are the authority on the subject and have the last word. This is ironic, given that well into the twentieth century, sex educators backed up denouncements of masturbation as pathological with medical authority. (See Conrad and Schneider, 1992: 180–81, on nineteenth-century conceptualizations of masturbation as disease; and Moran, 2000: 57, on lasting sex educational prohibitions.)

In Kleven's book *The Right Touch* (1997), a mother tells her son the story of the attempted sexual abuse of a young girl by a neighbor. The text is accompanied by Bergsma's illustrations of "whimsical, elfin-like people" (n.p.) that seem too cute to us for this topic. Kleven portrays child abuse as potentially everywhere: "grown-ups, babysitters, and bigger kids" can be abusers. Child readers are urged to be self-protective at all times. The mother in the story says, "No one has the right to touch private parts of your body without a good reason, not even Dad or me" (Kleven, 1997). How a child determines what constitutes a "good reason" is not clear. Kleven asserts that many children in bad-touch-situations-in-the-making have "warning feelings" when "things are not safe." This position suggests that knowing how to recognize a sexual predator is innate and universal, so if one fails to escape danger, one may be somehow to blame.

These books have a lot of explanations to offer about how confusing bodies, emotions, and relationships can be. Authors work hard to provide clear warnings that can make adults *and* other kids sound pretty scary. Telling the difference between safety and danger is complicated, so authors recommend kids consider whom they can trust among their adult significant others. Sanders and Hancock offer "5 BODY SAFETY RULES" for young kids (2016):

1. MY BODY IS MY BODY . . . and it belongs to me. I can say "NO!" if I don't want to kiss or hug someone. . . .

2. SAFETY NETWORK . . . These are 3 to 5 adults who I trust. I can tell these people anything and they will believe me. . . .

3. EARLY WARNING SIGNS. If I feel frightened or unsafe, I might feel sick in the tummy or my heart might beat really fast. . . . If I feel this way about anything, I must tell an adult on my Safety Network straightaway.

4. PRIVATE PARTS. I always call my private parts by their correct names. No one can touch my private parts. No one can ask me to touch their private parts,

and no one should show me pictures of private parts. If any of these things happen, I must tell a trusted adult on my Safety Network. . . .

5. NO SECRETS. I don't keep secrets, only happy surprises that will be told. If someone asks me to keep a secret, I tell them I don't keep secrets. If someone asks me to keep a secret that makes me feel unsafe or uncomfortable, I must tell an adult on my Safety Network straightaway. (7)

A mother-son team pair up in *I Said No! A Kid-to-Kid Guide to Keeping Private Parts Private* (King and King, 2017 [2010]) to explain "special rules" about "private parts" (4–6), and warning signs of inappropriate "red flag" touching or coercion toward abuse (8–20). The book culminates in a story about Zack going to his "first ever sleepover party with [his] best friend" (22), and being confronted with a "red flag" situation. The "best friend" tells him, "Did you know that all cool kids touch each other's privates?" and "If you don't touch mine, I'll never be your friend again." Zack knew that the first question was a "big lie," and that the second statement was a "threat." He thought, "DANGER RED FLAG! Private parts are not for sharing with friends! I SAID NO! NO WAY! I was loud and clear!" There is absolutely no space for consensual touching between friends here, nor any discussion of masturbation; the only examples of "green flag" touching the Kings discuss are "grownups that take care of you have to wipe your private parts to keep them healthy and clean" and a doctor (depicted as a man) who "wants to make sure that all of the parts of your body are healthy" (3–4). There is minimal discussion about how trusted adults may abuse their positions of authority in order to abuse children using just this type of language.

In *Sex Is a Funny Word*, Silberberg and Smyth (2015) offer a slightly less alarmist approach to discerning what's dangerous and what's safe. They also refuse the language of "private" parts, referring instead to "middle parts." They discuss "secret touching," so called because the person doing it "make[s] you keep it a secret" (110). They describe the confusion that could be involved ("they might try to scare you so you won't tell. They might be nice to you so you won't tell" [110]). They acknowledge (as do the Kings) that the person *could* be "someone you thought you could trust," and endorse the idea that "you should never feel like you have to keep a secret when it's about touching" (119). Their description of "secret touching" follows their discussion of "touching yourself," as is common in books for young children. The common proximity of these topics—masturbation and sexual abuse—in books for small children is logical on the one hand (they are both types of touch, after all), yet we are troubled by their repeated linkage.

Authors writing for teenagers typically discuss masturbation and sexual abuse in terms similar to those utilized by those writing for young children (but they are less likely to segue from one to the other). Authors writing for teens describe masturbation as normal and healthy (but occasionally pathological); they describe sexual abuse/violence as always wrong (even as they occasionally blame the victims).

In *Changing Bodies, Changing Lives* (1998), Bell writes that "having masturbated helps you enjoy lovemaking more," and gives descriptions of how boys and girls masturbate (1998: 83). In addition, Bell provides advice for what to do "if you don't have orgasms and want to," and addresses the pressure that many teenagers, especially girls, feel about orgasms, as a result of a lack of sex education and "the double standard." Bell discusses the "sexual script" that occurs because the "man is 'supposed' to be dominant, to be sexually powerful and demanding. The woman, on the other hand, is 'supposed' to be coy and shy and passive, to lead men on but not let them get 'too far'" (1998: 128). She argues that girls have to learn to "give straightforward messages. Boys have to learn to believe what girls are saying. It is important to say yes *only* when you mean yes; and to really mean no when you say no" (1998: 129).

Basso discusses date rape and stranger rape in a way that infantilizes women and reinforces heteronormative sexual scripts, victim-blaming, and male dominance. His definition of rape seems only to include those cases that include physical harm, verbal threats, or limited capacity due to drugs or alcohol (2003: 233). Even though Basso argues that "it doesn't matter what a female wears, says, or does, there is never any excuse for rape" (234), and that "ladies, you are free to wear anything you want any way you want, and you can act any way you want" (237), he contradicts these statements, advising young women to be careful about what they wear; to know their dancing might be interpreted as sexually provocative; and to avoid casual touches to avoid sending the wrong message to their dates. He advises boys that "when a female says no, she means no. Although the female may have led you on, she has every right to change her mind, and you must honor her decision" (234). Basso continues with a bizarre analogy, in which he compares committing rape to getting ticketed for speeding:

It's like driving a shiny red Corvette with a racing stripe down the side. Suddenly a police officer pulls up behind you, flashes his/her lights and gives you a speeding ticket. Is it fair to get a speeding ticket just because you're driving a shiny red Corvette? Just because a female dresses a certain way doesn't mean she should be treated a certain way based on YOUR assumptions. Of course, comparing rape to a speeding ticket is like comparing a nuclear explosion to a firecracker—rape is a devastating crime. (234)

Well, the good news is that boys "can avoid the embarrassment of being arrested as a rapist" if they just drive their dates home and behave like a "gentleman" (Basso, 2003: 240). Basso clearly identifies with male readers. Beyond the offensive analogy, we are troubled by the message that what a boy should seek to avoid is the "embarrassment of being arrested as a rapist," rather than *being* a rapist.

In these books, sexual touching and sexual activity during childhood are almost *never* okay, no matter who does it, and no matter the context. In adolescence, the messages become mixed: unwanted sexual touching and sexual activity is usually not all right, unless you confused your partner—then, can you blame them? It's not always clear-cut, according to authors. Didactic presentations of boundaries can become mired in a discourse of thwarted or dangerous desires for boys and provocative yet (rightfully) reluctant girls, as in Basso's presentation, in which he ultimately places the responsibility for control of sexual limits on young women, and implicitly blames girls when boys feel "led on." It is not possible that a girl might pressure a boy to have sex or attempt to rape him. Same-gender situations are notably absent in most of these discussions of coercive sexual requests or acts.

In contrast to the warnings authors offer about abusive sex, when they do discuss "sex play" between children, they describe it as generally harmless. In books for parents where masturbation and/or sex-play are discussed, the goal seems to be allaying parents' fears of impending gayness or sexual excessiveness (non-normativity). Most authors endorse masturbation as normal and healthy for young children. But a few warn against too much of this good thing (Eyre and Eyre, 1998; Maxwell, 2008; Spock and Rothenberg, 1992). Spock and Rothenberg discuss what they call "excessive masturbation," never specifying how often is too much. Even as they introduce this behavior as abnormal, Spock and Rothenberg (1992) reassure parents that sexual exploration is natural:

I think that whatever your personal beliefs or feelings, you should avoid threatening or punishing your children when they reveal their natural sexuality. . . . It's important to try to say something about how normal and universal the activity is. It's good for children to feel they can ask their parents about sex. (506)

This seemingly conflicting advice could be confusing to parents, especially those who have themselves been brought up by parents who disapproved of masturbation.

The Eyres (1998) propose telling children who ask about masturbation: "Everyone at least experiments with it. But it can be a problem if it becomes a habit or happens too often" (105). Maxwell (2008) warns that "obsessive masturbation to only one kind of stimulation" can lead to "difficulty reaching orgasm within a relationship" (58). She claims to have seen this in her practice as a clinical psychologist, but admits that "there is no current research to support that this is the case with most men" (58). Thus, she urges parents to talk to their children (read: boys) about porn. She proclaims, "Demeaning pictures or pictures that promote dominance of one person over another, can, over time, train a person to respond only to that form of stimulation" (58–59). All authors who write about sexual urges in children emphasize that urges are natural or normal, even as they coach parents about how to best protect, contain, constrain, and train their children's desires in socially desirable ways.

WORDS YOU MAY HAVE HEARD

Authors of sex books for young children tend to limit discussion of sexual issues to procreative sex and occasional mentions of masturbation and child abuse. Authors of sex books for adolescents typically cover masturbation and sexual abuse, but beyond this they tend to discuss sexual diversity (anything other than penile–vaginal intercourse) in a very limited way. For instance, Westheimer offhandedly mentions anal and oral sex in her section on AIDS: "some people think they can avoid AIDS by practicing anal intercourse (putting the penis in the anus) or oral sex (putting it in the mouth). They are dead wrong" (Westheimer and deGroat, 1998:74).

Throughout books for teens, authors depict loving sexual relationships between men and women as normative. When they do discuss alternatives, gayness, lesbianism, and bisexuality predominate. Only a few authors discuss trans or intersex people. Authors treat all these topics with a liberal touch, yet cordon them off into short sections of their own, which connotes otherness. These authors advocate acceptance but are careful to avoid endorsing or advocating nonheterosexual activities. The following are examples of discussions of "homosexuality" from two books for teens:

Some people prefer to have sexual experiences with persons of their own sex. They are called homosexuals. Most boys and girls have homosexual thoughts occasionally. Some even have homosexual experiences. This doesn't mean that they are homosexual. The people properly called homosexual are those who, as adults, have sexual contacts only with persons of their own sex. . . . Some people enjoy sexual relations with both sexes throughout their adult life. They are called bisexuals. Modern psychologists no longer see homosexual or bisexual behavior between consenting adults as a disorder. (Gordon and Cohen, 1992: 28)

Why Are Some People Straight and Others Gay?
Psychologists do not really know what causes a person's sexual preferences. Some believe that whether a person is straight or gay depends on experiences in early childhood. Others think homosexuality might be an inherited, or built-in preference. . . .

Is Homosexuality a Sickness?
No. People used to believe that homosexuality was a form of mental illness, but now psychiatrists say that it is not. Homosexuality is just one way people can express sexual love.

Can Homosexuals Choose Not to Be Gay?
Homosexuals can choose not to practice homosexuality. . . . But for most gay people, it is probably not possible to choose how they feel inside and which sex they are attracted to. (Cole and Tiegreen, 1988: 75)

Even as they attempt to advocate open-mindedness, authors frame sexual nonconformity as deviant by using the clinical term *homosexual*, by discussing lesbian/bisexual/gay sexuality via questions that are pointedly negative, and by emphasizing that it was once officially pathological. By consistently presenting medicine as the arbiter of the current nonpathology of "homosexuality," authors do not question medical authority or effectively critique its past or enduring homophobia.

The Eyres (1998) are the only authors among our sample who are *overtly* homophobic. They discuss "homosexuality" in one paragraph (which precedes a paragraph on AIDS), saying, "we shouldn't judge a person who is gay, but it can be a sad situation because it doesn't allow for the birth of children or for the kind of family that a heterosexual couple can have" (97). In contrast, many authors do actually denounce homophobia, usually by explaining that gayness is "not a choice" (Levkoff, 2007: 89), and then proclaiming that, anyway, discrimination is morally wrong:

There has never been a reason to treat people with disrespect. Homophobia is as bad as any other type of hatred—including racism and religious persecution. People should be judged according to their character, not who they sleep with. (Levkoff, 2007: 90)

Some people disapprove of gay men and lesbians. Some even hate homosexuals only because they are homosexuals. Usually these people know little or nothing about homosexuals, and their views are based on fears or misinformation, not facts. People are often afraid of things that they know little or nothing about. (Harris, 2004: 18)

Even advocates of respect for sexual diversity tread with a great deal of caution, and in so doing, undercut their affirmation of gayness in children.

Many of the authors writing for older kids and adults seek to reassure readers that nonheterosexual urges and experiences might well be transitory. Though the categories they introduce have the same essentialist ring to them as gender does in the books for young kids, authors recognize some flux on the road to a permanent sexual identity. But because authors explain that eventually sexual identity (straight, gay, lesbian, bisexual) is permanent, this changeability often comes across as an experimentation phase before settling into a heterosexual identity.

Are you homosexual? It's difficult to know. Some people don't figure out if they're gay or straight until their late teens or their twenties. Having a crush on, or even kissing or touching, someone of your own sex does not necessarily mean that you're gay. (Westheimer, 1993: 54)

Because there are so many negative ideas in our society about being gay, young people may panic if they have any feelings or daydreams about people of their own sex. Yet most of them will not end up being gay. Naturally, a small percentage will—about five to ten percent. . . . But most will not. They are simply going through a stage of growing up. (Cole, 1988: 76)

An exception to many of the implicitly negative approaches to LGBT topics and to this "cordoned off" approach occurs in Corinna's (2007) book S.E.X.: The All-You-Need-to-Know Progressive Sexuality Guide to Get You through High School and College. Corrina's book explicitly addresses "The Gay Chapter" that is present in many books for teenagers, while also addressing the notion that teens should "wait a while longer" before deciding their sexual orientation:

This isn't The Gay Chapter: you know, the one that says it's okay to be gay and it really will all be okay, but maybe we should wait a while longer before we decide we're not heterosexual. Any of us who are queer and who needed that chapter have already read it in most sex books before, and already know that people tell us it's okay. Heterosexuality is a sexual orientation. Bisexuality is a sexual orientation. "I'm attracted to whom I'm attracted to, and I don't know or care why," is also a sexual orientation. Everyone has one, and none of them is a default. And in case you haven't read The Gay Chapter before? It's all okay. (82)

Corinna explicitly states that sexual orientation occurs on a spectrum, that no sexual orientation is "normal" or the default, and reassures teen readers that sexual development is a process for all teens, not just those who are "deciding" to be LGBT (2007).

Most of the books addressed to parents offer advice about what parents should do if they think their kids aren't straight. Ratner and Chamlin (1985) pose the hypothetical question, "Will my son's love of 'dressing up' lead to homosexuality?" And they respond, "No. Many parents discourage boys from playing 'dress-up' and 'house,' but at certain ages, certainly preschool, it's appropriate. Preschoolers actively assume many different roles" (35). They imply that at a certain age, gender-bending will—and should—straighten out. Spock and Rothenberg (1992) imply this as well, saying, "When parents think that their little boy is effeminate or their little girl too masculine, they may worry that the child will grow up to be a homosexual or lesbian. In fact, the majority of such children will grow up to be heterosexual" (52). However, they then recommend therapy for a boy who wants to play with girls and dolls and who wants to wear dresses ("I would assume that something had gotten mixed up in his identification"), as well as for a girl who plays "only with boys" and is "always unhappy about being a girl" (52). A girl who prefers to play with boys and who "occasionally" wishes she were a boy, "but also [enjoys] playing with girls" does not concern them (52).

Increasingly, authors addressing parents are discussing the social construction of gender and of sexual identity. For instance, Levkoff endorses parental acceptance of all forms of self-expression among kids, yet she simultaneously presents parental emotional responses to a child's coming out as gay as almost entirely unpleasant: "It can be an emotionally challenging time. . . . Most people speak of grief and mourning, as if they have lost a loved one. . . . It is natural and it will pass. What we hope is that these turbulent and complex feelings will bring you, in the end, to acceptance. But it isn't an easy road" (2007: 99). Similarly, Heffner (2004: 187) describes parents as having mostly unpleasant feelings, even if they find their feelings surprising: "you may be scared, confused, worried, or upset. Even the most liberal heterosexual parents I know have told me their initial response to their child's coming out to them was surprising. One woman confided in me that she was surprised by her reaction: 'We have gay friends, we march in pride parades, so why am I feeling so disappointed?'"

Harris and Emberley (1999) were the first authors of books for young children to explore alternatives to heterosexuality, and they, along with Levkoff, are among the few authors who explain that love and sexual behavior can be multifaceted without invoking the past pathologizing or current acceptance of medical experts: "There are lots of kinds of love—like love between a parent and child, love between friends, love between kids, love between teenagers, and love between grownups. There can be love between a female and a male, or a male and a male, or a female and a female" (Harris and Emberley, 1999: 31). They go on to explain the terms *homosexual, heterosexual, gay, lesbian, bisexual,* and *straight,* and proclaim, "A person's daily life—having friends, having fun, going to work, being a mom or dad, loving another person—is mostly the same whether a person is straight or gay." This text appears with an illustration of a possibly interracial gay male couple and their two kids eating dinner (32). Similarly, Silverberg (2015) notes that heteronormativity is common (without using the term *heteronormativity*), and that some terminology and concepts may be new to kids and to their adult readers:

You may have noticed that people often talk about relationships between men and women as if those are the only kinds of relationships that can have a crush, love, or sexy feelings. But they aren't. Have you heard people use the words gay or lesbian? How about asexual or queer? Those are words people use to describe themselves, the kinds of relationships they have, and who they have them with. Every community has its own words. . . . Some of these words may be new to you. (They may be new to a grown-up you're reading this with too!) (151)

Authors seek to promote harmony across difference by positing that difference is overshadowed by commonalities among people, regardless of sexual identity.

SO WHAT SHOULD WE TELL THE KIDS?

First, let us sum up what we *do* tell the kids in the discourse of these didactic books: that the central focus of sexuality is procreative penile–vaginal intercourse; that this form of sexuality is "natural" and good; that participants should be monogamous adults; and that proper sexual expression is based in love and enacted in private. Many authors writing for older kids and adults do acknowledge other sorts of sexual behavior, but these discussions are limited and not integrated into presentations of what is clearly the main event. Nonheterosexual activities are marginalized. The books can be seen as precursors to school-based sex education programs, which increase the focus on dangers, often advocate abstinence, and are notoriously heterosexist and devoid of discussions of gendered or sexual power dynamics (see, e.g., Irvine, 2004; Luker, 2007; Raymond, 1994; Watney, 1991). Over time, there has been an increase in feminist approaches to gender and sexuality in these resources that offer kids some views of unconventional sexual practices. Despite the centrality of heterosexuality in these resources, some authors do depict sexuality and gender as fluid and advocate acceptance of unconventional identities, but these resources are not the norm.

When do we tell children that some sex is amazing, some is lovely, some is dull, some becomes repugnant in retrospect, and some is horrible while it's happening? When do we tell them about its potential variety and variability? When do we expose children to a peerlike level of sexual honesty in which we speak to them of the intensity of desire, the fickleness of lust, the pain of rejection? Or do we simply not venture this far into the murky depths of sexuality? Do we just let them find out whatever they'll find out by themselves from people we can only hope will not hurt them or mess up their lives? All the while, we must bear in mind that something we say to them today could be the impetus for therapy later. What truths, warnings, and recommendations do we dare to communicate? In short, our task is absurd and impossible the more we ponder it, yet most of us would agree that to say nothing would be worse than to make some kind of attempt.

So we're back where we started, with Spock and Rothenberg's (1992) admonition against the stork, in favor of the truth. There is no absolute truth about sexuality, so we have to decide what and how we want to discuss sexuality with our children. Sex education books for children and parents are generally a step in the right direction, and are certainly better than nothing, in our view. But they are not as comprehensive or critical or political as they could be.

Imagine if most sex education books presented gender and genitals as socially constructed, as Silverberg's work best exemplifies; sexuality could then more easily be conceived by young readers as taking place on a continuum rather than as written in stone. Imagine books that present sex as not only the cause of procreation but also as recreational, as indeed it is for most people engaged in it most of the time. Imagine books that present sexual activities other than penile–vaginal intercourse as satisfying and good for body and soul (or even just for body!). Imagine sex education books that acknowledge and contest power dynamics based on gender and sexual categories, as Corrina's book does—books that would urge children to interrogate, rather than reify, these categories—and affirm for children that their experiences and desires are valid and worthy of respect. Imagine the sex lives that might develop out of such an anti-foundational foundation. Would you buy these books for your children?

REFERENCES

Sex Books for Young Children

Andry, Andrew, Steven Schepp, and Blake Hampton (Ill.). 1979 (1968). *How Babies Are Made.* Boston: Little, Brown.

Baker, Sue. 1990. *The Birds and the Bees.* Swindon, Bologna, New York: M. Twinn.

Brooks, Robert, and Susan Perl (Ill.). 1983. *So That's How I Was Born!* New York: Aladdin.

Brown, Laura Krasny, and Marc Brown. 1997. *What's the Big Secret?: Talking about Sex with Girls and Boys.* Boston: Little, Brown.

Cole, Babette. 1993. *Mommy Laid an Egg OR Where Do Babies Come From?* New York: Chronicle Books.

Cole, Joanna, and Margaret Miller (Photo.). 1993 (1984). *How You Were Born.* New York: Mulberry.

Davis, Jennifer, and Laura Cornell (Ill.). 1997. *Before You Were Born: A Lift-the-Flap Book.* New York: Workman.

Gordon, Sol, Judith Gordon, and Vivien Cohen (Ill.). 1992 (1974). *Did the Sun Shine before You Were Born?: A Sex Education Primer.* Amherst, NY: Prometheus Books.

Harris, Robie H., and Michael Emberley (Ill.). 2006. *It's Not the Stork! A Book about Boys, Girls, Babies, Bodies, Families and Friends.* Cambridge, MA: Candlewick Press.

———. 2014 (1999). *It's So Amazing!: A Book about Eggs, Sperm, Birth, Babies, and Families.* Cambridge, MA: Candlewick Press.

Harris, Robie H., and Nadine Bernard Wescott. 2013. *What's in There? All about Before You Were Born.* Cambridge, MA: Candlewick Press.

Hickling, Meg, and Kim La Fave (Ill.) 2002. *Boys, Girls and Body Science.* Maderia Park, British Columbia, Canada: Harbour Publishing.

King, Zack, Kimberly King, and Sue Rama (Ill.). 2017 [2010]. *I Said No!: A Kid-to-Kid Guide to Keeping Private Parts Private.* Weaverville, CA: Boulden Publishing.

Kleven, Sandy, and Jody Bergsma (Ill.). 1997. *The Right Touch: A Read Aloud Story to Help Prevent Child Abuse.* Bellevue, WA: Illumination Arts.

Saltz, Dr. Gail, and Lynne Cravath (Ill.). 2005. *Amazing You! Getting Smart about Your Private Parts.* New York: Penguin Group USA.

Sanders, Jayneed, and Anna Hancock. 2016. *My Body! What I Say Goes!: A Book to Empower and Teach Children about Personal Body Safety, Feelings, Safe and Unsafe Touch, Private Parts, Secrets and Surprises, Consent and Respectful Relationships.* Educate2Empower Publishing (online).

Silverberg, Cory, and Fiona Smyth (Ill.). 2012. *What Makes a Baby.* New York: Seven Stories Press.

———. 2015. *Sex Is a Funny Word: A Book about Bodies, Feelings, and You.* New York: Seven Stories Press.

Smith, Alastair, and Maria Wheatley (Ill.). 1997. *How Are Babies Made?* London: Usborne Publishing.

Sex Books for Older Children

Basso, Michael J. 2003 (1998). *The Underground Guide to Teenage Sexuality.* 2nd ed. Minneapolis: Fairview Press.

Bell, Ruth. 1987. *Changing Bodies, Changing Lives.* New York: Random House.

Cole, Joanna, and Alan Tiegreen (Ill.). 1988. *Asking about Sex and Growing Up: A Question-and-Answer Book for Boys and Girls.* New York: Beech Tree.

Corrina, Heather. 2007. *S.E.X.: The All-You-Need-to-Know Progressive Sexuality Guide to Get You through High School and College.* Philadelphia: Perseus Books.

Foster, Lorri. 2005. *Let's Talk about S-E-X.* 2nd ed. Minnetonka, MN: Book Peddlers.

Gordon, Sol, and Vivien Cohen (Ill.). 1992 (1977). *Facts about Sex for Today's Youth.* Amherst, NY: Prometheus Books.

Harris, Robie H., and Michael Emberley (Ill.) 2004. *It's Perfectly Normal: Changing Bodies, Growing Up, Sex and Sexual Health.* Cambridge, MA: Candlewick Press.

Hasler, Nikol. 2010. *Sex: A Book for Teens: An Uncensored Guide to Your Body, Sex and Safety.* San Francisco: Zest Books.

———. 2015. *Sex: An Uncensored Introduction.* Revised and expanded edition. San Francisco: Zest Books.

Henderson, Elizabeth, and Nancy Armstrong. 2013. *100 Questions You'd Never Ask Your Parents: Straight Answers to Teens' Questions about Sex, Sexuality, and Health.* New York: Roaring Brook Press.

Pardes, Bronwen. 2013 (2007). *Doing It Right: Making Smart, Safe, and Satisfying Choices about Sex.* New York: Simon Pulse.

Westheimer, Ruth, and Diane deGroat (Ill.). 1998 (1993). *Dr. Ruth Talks to Kids: Where You Came From, How Your Body Changes, and What Sex Is All About.* New York: Aladdin.

Sex Books for Parents

Berkenkamp, Lauri, and Steven C. Atkins. 2002. *Talking to Your Kids about Sex from Toddlers to Preteens: A Go Parents! Guide.* Chicago: Nomad Press.

Calderone, Mary S., and James W. Ramey. 1982. *Talking with Your Child about Sex: Questions and Answers for Children from Birth to Puberty.* New York: Random House.

Eyre, Linda, and Richard Eyre. 1998. *How to Talk to Your Child about Sex.* New York: Saint Martin's Griffin.

Haffner, Debra W. 2004. *From Diapers to Dating: A Parent's Guide to Raising Sexually Healthy Children.* New York: Newmarket Press.

Levkoff, Logan. 2007. *Third Base Ain't What It Used to Be: What Your Kids are Learning about Sex Today—and How to Teach Them to Become Sexually Healthy Adults.* New York: New American Library.

Maxwell, Sharon. 2008. *The Talk: What Your Kids Need to Hear from YOU about Sex.* New York: Avery.

Morris, Lois B. 1984. *Talking Sex with Your Kids.* New York: Simon and Schuster.

Ratner, Marilyn, and Susan Chamlin. 1985. *Straight Talk: Sexuality Education for Parents and Kids 4–7.* New York: Viking.

Richardson, Justin, and Mark A. Schuster. 2003. *Everything You Never Wanted Your Kids to Know about Sex (But Were Afraid They'd Ask).* New York: Three Rivers Press.

Roffman, Deborah M. 2002. *How'd I Get in There in the First Place?: Talking to Your Young Child about Sex.* New York: Perseus Publishing.

Schwartz, Pepper, and Dominic Cappello. 2000. *Ten Talks Parents Must Have with Their Children about Sex and Character.* New York: Hyperion.

Spock, Benjamin, and Michael B. Rothenberg. 1992 (1945). *Dr. Spock's Baby and Child Care.* New York: Pocket Books.

Online Resources (compiled by Samantha Howat)

| sex, etc. | https://sexetc.org | • "By teens, for teens"
 • Run by Rutgers University |
| Planned Parenthood "For Teens" | https://www.plannedparenthood.org /learn/teens | • Includes chat feature
 • Includes "Find Birth Control" feature |

teensource.org "SEX + HEALTH + YOU"	http://www.teensource.org	• Run by Essential Access Health • Focus on California resources (e.g., includes "FIND A CLINIC" feature for CA only)
SCaRLeTeeN "sex ed for the real world"	http://www.scarleteen.com	• "Most popular and most widely used site" • Includes "Sex and Disability/Disabled Sex Yes!" feature (others do not)
Teen Health Source	http://teenhealthsource.com	• Located in Toronto; peer educators available by phone and chat • Includes "queering sexual education" videos
STAYTEEN	http://stayteen.org	• Run by National Campaign to Prevent Teen and Unplanned Pregnancy • Includes "Ask Us Anything" feature
I Wanna Know: Sexual Health for Teens and Young Adults	http://www.iwannaknow.org	• Run by American Sexual Health Association
Advocates for Youth "Rights. Respect. Responsibility"	http://www.advocatesforyouth.org	• Geared more toward advocacy and policy, but provides some info for teens and parents
KidsHealth	http://kidshealth.org	• Run by Nemours Children's Health System (pediatricians) • Covers overall health • Sections for parents, kids, teens, and educators
SexInfo Online	http://www.soc.ucsb.edu/sexinfo	• Run by UC-Santa Barbara • Sex ed for people in general, but also has a section for teens
Go Ask Alice!	http://www.goaskalice.columbia.edu	• Run by Columbia University • Overall health (sexuality a part of it)
It's Your (Sex) Life	http://www.itsyoursexlife.com	• Run by MTV • Focus on pregnancy prevention and STDs

Other Sources

Conrad, Peter, and Joseph W. Schneider. 1992. *Deviance and Medicalization: From Badness to Sickness.* Philadelphia: Temple University Press.

Ehrenreich, Barbara, and Deirdre English. 1986. *ReMaking Love: The Feminization of Sex.* Garden City, NY: Anchor Press/Doubleday.

Irvine, Janice. 2004. *Talk about Sex: The Battles over Sex Education in the United States.* Berkeley: University of California Press.

Luker, Kristin. 2007. *When Sex Goes to School: Warring Views on Sex and Sex Education since the Sixties.* New York: W. W. Norton.

Moran, Jeffrey P. 2000. *Teaching Sex: The Shaping of Adolescence in the 20th Century.* Cambridge, MA: Harvard University Press.

Moore, Lisa Jean. 2007. *Sperm Counts: Overcome by Man's Most Precious Fluid.* New York: NYU Press.

Patton, Cindy. 1996. *Fatal Advice: How Safe-Sex Education Went Wrong.* Durham, NC: Duke University Press.

Raymond, Diane. 1994. "Homophobia, Identity, and the Meanings of Desire: Reflections on the Cultural Construction of Gay and Lesbian Adolescent Sexuality." In Janice M. Irvine, ed., *Sexual Cultures and the Construction of Adolescent Identities*. Philadelphia: Temple University Press. 115–50.

Simonds, Wendy. 1992. *Women and Self-Help Culture: Reading between the Lines*. New Brunswick, NJ: Rutgers University Press.

Solinger, Rickie. 2005. *Pregnancy and Power: A Short History of Reproductive Politics in America*. New York: NYU Press.

Watney, Simon. 1991. "School's Out." In Diana Fuss, ed., *Inside/Out: Lesbian Theories, Gay Theories*. New York: Routledge. 387–401.

Sex-Positive Parenting, or We Don't Touch Our Vulvas at the Table

Lea Grover

It happened yet again. As I was sitting at the table for dinner with my children, I noticed my daughter's hand fishing around under her skirt.

"We don't play with our vulvas at the table. Go wash your hands and finish your food," I scolded. She nodded, ran off to wash her hands, and resumed picking at her dinner instead.

Small children, they touch themselves. A lot. It's fascinating to them. And when you're a small child, you have no sense of shame or disgust or fear of your body. Your body is what it is. It does what it does. And everything that it does is kind of amazing, because you're not old enough for lower back pain. It's not sexual, it's just . . . fact. The first time I caught one of my kids playing with their genitals, I said absolutely nothing. I was momentarily paralyzed with indecision. One thing I knew for a fact I did *not* want to do was to shout, "No!" or "Stop!" What good could that possibly do? Sure, I would be spared the awkwardness of catching my child playing with her genitals on the living room floor, but what kind of lesson is that? To fear or ignore your own vagina? I thought about it almost constantly for two days, and of course she gave me a second chance to react.

"Sweetie, we don't play with our vulvas in the living room," I said. Which sounded ridiculous and strange, but nonetheless true. *Why is everything with little kids "we" statements?* "It's okay to touch your vulva, but people are private, and it's a private thing. The only places where you should touch your vulva are in the bathroom or in your bedroom. If you want to play with your vulva, please go to the bedroom." And she smiled and did, without question, because compartmentalizing where you do certain activities makes sense to little kids.

"We don't eat in the bathroom, and we don't touch our vulvas in the living room," became the new mantra. And yes, eventually it became, "We don't touch our vulvas at the table."

I'm what some people call "sex positive." That doesn't mean I talk with my four-year-olds about how great sex is and how good it feels. It means I don't pretend it's something other than it is. As parents, we lie all the time. About the Easter Bunny or Santa or the Tooth Fairy, about how long ten minutes is, about whether or not we remembered they wanted to have grilled cheese for dinner *again*, we lie a lot. But one thing I never lie about is sex. I don't want them to grow up ashamed of their bodies or confused about what they do. I don't tell them about Cabbage Patches or storks; I make an effort, always, to be honest about human reproduction. Every aspect of it.

I've had talks with lots of other moms about having "the talk." I don't think my kids and I will ever have that particular talk, because they already know. And we talk about it often—kids are obsessive creatures. We read *Where Did I Come From?* and *What Makes a Baby*, which together cover every aspect of the subject. We can talk about IVF and C-sections, because both of those are part of the story of their births, and we can talk about the fact that yes, mommy and daddy still have sex regardless. And when they're older, we'll start talking about contraception. Because lying to your kids about sex helps nobody. Telling them that sex is "only between mommies and daddies" is a lie that leads to confused, hormone-charged teenagers. Telling them that sex is "only something that happens when two people love each other very much" is a lie that causes hormone-charged teenagers to confuse "love" with "lust," or "obsession." It leads to leaps of logic like, "If I have sex with them, we must be in love." Or worse—"If I love them, I have to have sex with them." And how many teenage tragedies are based on that misconception?

The truth is that human beings, almost universally, like sex. It feels good. And it's *supposed* to feel good. If it didn't, the human race would die out. The truth is that sex isn't special and magical just because it's sex. The truth is that you *can* have spectacular sex with strangers whose names you don't even know. The truth is that just because you *can*, that doesn't necessarily mean you *should*. And that's what sex-positive parenting really is. Not telling my kids lies about sex to keep them from behaviors I don't think are healthy. It's telling them the truth, the whole truth, and letting it sink in so they can make their own good choices.

It's telling them that sex is good, but that it's dangerous if you're not careful. It's teaching them to require their partners to use condoms, to buy their own condoms if they're planning on having sex. It's teaching them that while sex feels good, they can feel good on their own too. (Just not at the table.) That while sex combined with love is often the best sex—transcendent sex—that grows the bond of love and builds a closeness that is almost impossible to find otherwise, sex isn't always like that—even with people you love. That sex can lead to pregnancy, even with protection, so engaging in it is a commitment to deal with any consequences. It's telling them they're not wrong, or sinful, or bad, if they have sexual feelings. Or even if they have sex. It's teaching them that sex happens, whether people always make good choices or not. And it's giving them the tools to ensure that when they're ready, they're smart and cautious and conscientious.

There's a lot of black and white comparisons when it comes to sex education. Some people think that once kids hit puberty, if they don't have a strong fear of sex they'll have as much as they can, as often as they can. There's a lot of abstinence-only sex education based on telling kids, "SEX IS SCARY! DON'T DO IT!" and it's about the least successful program anyone has ever invented. In states with abstinence-only sex ed, teen pregnancy rates only go up and up and up. Telling children the truth about sex isn't giving permission for them to have it—and this is the most important part—because nobody has the right to deny them permission for sex but themselves. And that's the thing I try to keep in mind when I say things like, "We don't touch our vulvas at the table." Sex is something that ONLY happens when both people WANT it to happen. And that means that the only people in the entire world with any kind of say over whether or not my daughters have sex is *them*. I don't get to tell my daughters they have to have sex, but I also don't get to tell them they can't.

They're in charge. Your body, your decision. I never want to be responsible for setting the precedent that another person gets to tell them what to do with their bodies, and especially with their sexuality. I don't want to be the gateway for a manipulative, potentially abusive boyfriend. So I teach boundaries. Appropriate places. Hygiene. I teach my children that nobody is allowed to touch their bodies without permission. When we get in tickle fights and they say, "Stop!" I stop. And when we talk about pregnant friends, we talk about uteruses and sperm and eggs. And most of the time, it's not uncomfortable. Most of the time, I'm verifying information and the conversation lasts fifteen seconds.

And someday the conversation is going to be a lot uglier. Someday, we'll have to actually talk about rape, and explicit and enthusiastic consent, and contraception. Someday we'll have to talk about healthy masturbation and pornography and realistic expectations of sex and sex partners and body image and a lack of shame for their bodies. And those conversations are not going to be as brief or straightforward. But I'm ready. Whenever that day comes, I'm prepared. Because the groundwork is there.

"We don't touch our vulvas at the table." It's absurd, but it's got all the important pieces. It's a micro-lesson in safety and consent and social propriety. I don't think I'll be able to say, "We don't lose our virginity in the back seat of a car after a prom party" with a straight face, but I will be able to say, "We don't have sex without thinking long and hard about it first, and we certainly don't do it without being careful, and being safe, and being totally confident in the maturity of our partner and our ability to handle the repercussions if we get a disease or get pregnant."

Because it's true. We don't.

But I like that when that time comes, I'm part of the "we." Because if I can tell my girls "we" have to be careful, they'll know that no matter what happens, I'm still in their corner. I've still got their backs. Even if "we" make bad choices, I'll still be there to help make things right again.

Source: "Sex Positive Parenting, or 'We Don't Touch Our Vulvas at the Table,'" Becomingsupermommy.blogspot .com, June 19, 2014. Reprinted by permission of the author.

TALKING TO TEENS ABOUT SEX: PARENT–ADOLESCENT COMMUNICATION ABOUT SEX AND SEXUALITY

MONA MALACANE AND JONATHON J. BECKMEYER

Interest and curiosity regarding sexual behavior and sexuality are normal and healthy for adolescents (Tolman & McClelland, 2011); however, sexual activity can carry significant costs (e.g., unintended pregnancy, sexually transmitted infections [STIs], and depressive symptoms) for adolescents' well-being (Deptula, Henry, & Schoeny, 2010; Zimmer-Gembeck & Helfand, 2008). Often what distinguishes healthy from unhealthy sexual development is the degree to which adolescents are knowledgeable about sexual health practices, possess self-efficacy over their sexual decision making, and consistently use safer sex practices (Beckmeyer & Jamison, 2015; Hoff, Greene, & Davis, 2003; Martino, Collins, Kanouse, Elliott, & Berry, 2005). Parents play a key role in promoting healthy sexual development for adolescents by initiating and discussing sexuality with their children. Unfortunately, it is rare for parents and/or caregivers to be adolescents' primary or even secondary source of sexual health information (Bleakley, Hennessy, Fishbein, Coles, & Jordan, 2009; Epstein & Ward, 2007). To help sex and family educators promote greater parent–adolescent sexual health communication, we conducted a literature review to identify common reasons why parents do or do not engage in sexual health conversations with their children. The goal of this review was to identify barriers that could be influenced by sex and family educators. After summarizing the prior literature, we formulated strategies that sex and family educators can follow to promote parent-initiated sexual health conversations.[1] . . .

PARENT–ADOLESCENT COMMUNICATION ABOUT SEX

Although adolescents and parents do report discussing sexuality (see Jerman & Constantine, 2010; Stidman-Hall, Moreau, & Trussell, 2012), estimates of discussion frequency can be misleading since they are typically derived from global measures of parent–adolescent sexual communication (e.g., have you ever talked to your parent about birth control?), which do not convey the consistency, frequency, or duration of these discussions. Open and frequent sexual health conversations are associated with indicators of adolescent sexual development, including delayed sexual initiation (DiIorio, Kelley, & Hockenberry-Eaton, 1999; Martinez, Abma, & Copen, 2010), increased use of condoms (DiIorio, McCarty, Resnicow, Lehr, & Denzmore, 2007), fewer sexual partners (Secor-Turner, Sieving, Eisenberg, & Skay, 2011), lower risk of STIs (Deptula et al., 2010), and discussing sexual issues with romantic partners (Widman, Coukas-Bradley, Helms, Golin, & Prinstein, 2013). Those results are consistent with a broader literature noting that higher-quality parent–adolescent relationships, parental knowledge of adolescents' daily lives, and

From "A Review of Parent-Based Barriers to Parent–Adolescent Communication about Sex and Sexuality: Implications for Sex and Family Educators," *American Journal of Sexuality Education*, Vol. 11, Issue 1, 2016, pp. 27–40. Copyright © 2016 Taylor & Francis Group, LLC, reprinted by permission of the publisher (Taylor & Francis Ltd, http://www.tandfonline.com).

positive parenting behaviors are associated with better sexual health among adolescents.[2] . . .

BARRIERS TO PARENT–ADOLESCENT COMMUNICATION ABOUT SEX

Adolescents want to learn about sex from their parents (Somers & Surmann, 2004). However, researchers have consistently found that peers and the media are more common sources of sexual health information for adolescents than are parents (Epstein & Ward, 2007; Secor-Turner et al., 2011; Whitfield, Jomeen, Hayter, & Gardiner, 2013). Additionally, researchers have found that when parents do discuss sex with their adolescents, they tend to shy away from "tougher" topics (e.g., how to say no and where to access birth control; Hyde et al., 2013; Planned Parenthood, 2014). Parents do have the ability to promote adolescents' healthy sexual development, but research illustrating that they rarely serve as adolescents' primary source of sexual health information would suggest that they may be reluctant to directly engage their adolescents in conversations about sex and sexuality. In order to better understand why this is the case, we searched article databases (e.g., Psych-INFO and Academic Search/EBSCO) to identify empirical literature pertaining to parent–adolescent sexual health communication. After reviewing this literature, we identified four broad categories of barriers to parent–adolescent sexual health communication: limited sexual health knowledge, perceptions of adolescents' readiness for sex, parental comfort discussing sex, and demographic factors.

Limited Sexual Health Knowledge

Parents with a real or perceived lack of knowledge about sexuality and sexual behavior are unlikely to engage in conversations about sex with their children (Guilamo-Ramos, Jaccard, Dittus, & Bouris, 2006; Jaccard et al., 2000; Jaccard, Dodge, & Dittus, 2002). For example, in a study of inner-city youth, Jaccard et al. (2000) found that the second most reported reservation to discussing sex with their child was fear that the child would ask a question to which the parent did not know the answer. When parents perceive that they are unknowledgeable about sexual health, the conversations they do have with their children tend to be brief, vague, and indirect (Hyde et al., 2013). When parents are educated about sexual health, have confidence in their knowledge of sexual health topics, and believe they have the skills to effectively communicate this information, they are more likely to self-initiate communication with their child (Byers, Sears, & Weaver, 2008; Villarruel, Loveland-Cherry, & Ronis, 2010). Similarly, when adolescents perceive their parents to be knowledgeable, they are less likely to avoid sexual discussions with them and are also less anxious about the discussions (Afifi, Joseph, & Aldeis, 2008). Moreover, when adolescents report that their parents have a moderate amount of general expertise (i.e., general competence), they feel they can trust their parents more and subsequently are more open to having discussions about sex (Guilamo-Ramos et al., 2006). Based on prior research, it is clear that parental knowledge of sexual health plays a key role in promoting open parent–adolescent communication about sexuality and sexual behavior (Miller et al., 2009).

Perceptions of Adolescents' Readiness for Sex

Parents also avoid discussions about sex when they perceive their children are not ready to have these conversations. Parents' perceptions of readiness for sexual health conversations may be based on age (e.g., thinking that their child is too young) (Pluhar, DiIorio, & Mccarty, 2008; Wilson, Dalberth, Koo, & Gard, 2010) and [a belief] that children are not involved in romantic relationships and/or are not yet sexually active (Eisenberg, Sieving, Bearinger, Swain, & Resnick, 2006; Swain, Ackerman, & Ackerman, 2006). Such apprehensions are, to a degree, understandable, as parents have reported being concerned that these discussions could expose their children to topics that are inappropriate for their age or tacitly encourage sexual behavior (Hyde et al., 2013; Wilson et al., 2010). Therefore, parents may believe they are acting in their children's best interest by delaying conversations about sex until they are older or exhibit signs of becoming sexually active. However, by avoiding conversations about sex because they perceive their children are "not ready," parents are missing crucial opportunities to convey their expectations for adolescents' sexual behavior and to help adolescents make healthy sexual choices. Finally, adolescents commonly conceal information about dating and romantic relationships from their parents (e.g., Daddis & Randolph, 2010); therefore, parents may not truly know when their child has begun dating, again missing opportunities to promote sexual health.

Parental Comfort with Discussing Sex

Parents have reported they feel embarrassed when discussing sex, making it difficult to know what to say to adolescents (Eisenberg et al., 2006; Lefkowitz, 2002; Wilson et al., 2010). Relatedly, parents have also reported feeling that they lack the communication skills or tact necessary to facilitate conversations about sex (Pluhar et al., 2008; Wilson et al., 2010). Some parents also believe that adolescents will feel uncomfortable talking about sex and avoid conversations based on this assumption (Afifi et al., 2008; Guilamo-Ramos, Jaccard, Dittus, & Collins, 2008; Mazur & Ebesu Hubbard, 2004). However, in a recent study, Goldfarb, Lieberman, Kwiatkowski, and Santos (2015) interviewed college students about their experiences discussing

sex with their parents when they were teenagers and found that when parents avoided discussing sex, adolescents felt closed off from an important and reliable source of information. Therefore, by avoiding discussions with adolescents, parents are potentially creating an environment in which adolescents will be reluctant to seek them out for sexual health information.

Demographic Factors

Researchers have noted that cultural, political, and demographic factors are associated with parent–adolescent sexual communication. . . . Among non-Caucasian racial and ethnic groups, African American parents report significantly more sexual communication and talks about birth control with their children than Asian American or Hispanic parents (Widman et al., 2013). Asian American parents report the least frequent and fewest number of sexual topics discussed with their children (Kim & Ward, 2007; Martino, Elliott, Corona, Kanouse, & Schuster, 2008). Mothers communicate with adolescents about sex more than fathers do (DiIorio et al., 1999; Rosenthal & Feldman, 1999; Swain et al., 2006), and mothers are more likely to have had conversations with daughters than sons (Kim & Ward, 2007; Martin & Luke, 2010; Miller et al., 2009; Pluhar et al., 2008). Differences in the frequency of mothers' and fathers' communication about sex with their adolescents may reflect gender norms pertaining to parenting roles. Researchers have also found that girls report talking about more sex-related topics with their parents than do boys (Jerman & Constantine, 2010; Widman et al., 2013). Lastly, parents' political and religious beliefs can influence the decision to discuss sexuality. A recent study found that politically conservative and religious parents—those who report attending a religious service more than once per week—discuss the negative consequences of sex with their children more often than liberal and less religious counterparts (Swain et al., 2006). The same study found conservative parents are also less likely to believe that birth control and condoms are safe and effective; subsequently, they are less likely to discuss where to obtain birth control with their children.

FACILITATING PARENT–ADOLESCENT SEXUAL HEALTH DISCUSSIONS

The second aim of this review was to identify specific practical approaches for sexual health and family educators and medical professionals (e.g., family doctors and nurses) to assist parents in overcoming barriers to sexual health communication with their adolescents. Our focus is on parents' behavioral decision to engage in sexual health conversations with their adolescents. Therefore, we used the Theory of Planned Behavior (TPB) to guide and organize our suggestions. In the TPB model individual behaviors are the result of behavioral intentions (i.e., the motivation to engage in specific behaviors), which are determined by three constructs: behavioral beliefs, normative beliefs, and perceived behavioral control (Azjen, 1991, 2002). In order to increase the frequency of parent–adolescent communication about sex and sexuality, we must first increase parents' intentions to have those conversations, which are derived from parents' attitudes toward talking to adolescents about sex and sexuality (i.e., behavioral beliefs), their beliefs regarding whether their children and other individuals (e.g., other parents, teachers, doctors) think such communication is important and/or also engage in the behavior (i.e., normative beliefs), and how much control they perceive having over such communication with adolescents (i.e., perceived behavioral control). We believe that the barriers we identified in the literature can be organized using the

constructs of the TPB, supporting its use as a framework to illustrate how sexual health and family educators can increase parent–adolescent communication about sex and sexuality. . . . Additionally, sex and family educators may find that presenting the TPB model to parents (e.g., in a workshop or a print or web-based resource) could help them recognize reasons for why they are or are not choosing to engage in sexual communication with their children so they are able to identify the most personally useful resources and information.

Strategies to Improve Behavioral Beliefs

In the TPB, behavioral beliefs are the positive and negative attitudes individuals hold about the outcome of a behavior as well as how they feel about the behavior (i.e., if it is valuable, helpful, or appropriate). These beliefs are shaped by past experiences and consequences of the same or similar behaviors (Azjen, 1991, 2002). Therefore, communication with adolescents about sex and sexuality should be more likely when parents are comfortable with such conversations, when they believe they will benefit adolescents, and when they have had positive experiences with prior conversations. We believe existing workshops and classes for parents would be appropriate venues to help parents gain confidence using sexual health terms, initiating conversations, and even handling negative responses from their children. For example, parents could be taught techniques regarding how to use the media that adolescents are already consuming (e.g., TV shows and movies) to initiate sexual health conversations. Although researchers have not typically viewed sexually laden media content as a positive influence on adolescent sexual socialization (e.g., Collins et al., 2004), it can be used to facilitate conversations with adolescents about sex and sexuality. Instances of sexual innuendos and precursory sexual behaviors can help parents segue into conversations with adolescents about sex. Parents and adolescents may find discussing the hypothetical sexuality of fictional characters more comfortable than speaking directly about adolescents' own experiences. Even when discussing hypothetical or fictional sexual experiences parents are able to communicate their values and expectations to their children. Doing so is critically important, as communicating values and expectations have been shown to decrease adolescent sexual risk behavior (Dancy et al., 2009; Jaccard et al., 2002).

Additionally, there are existing online evidence-based resources that sex and family educators can direct parents to about the benefits of these conversations. For instance, Advocates for Youth . . . has a parent-specific section of its website with articles explaining the importance and protective factors of parent–child communication, as well as advice from parenting experts and conversation starters and activities. The Centers for Disease Control and Prevention (CDC) Division of Adolescent and School Health . . . also contains a wealth of free and accessible resources, including podcasts, webinars, brochures, and fact sheets. Educators can use this site to learn about successful evidence-based programs as well as strategies to engage parents and families in supporting adolescent healthy behaviors.

Parents are also concerned that they will hasten sexual activity, leading to a belief that discussing sex and sexuality may be harmful for adolescents. This is related to parents' expectations regarding the outcomes of sexual health conversations with adolescents. However, the existing literature illustrates parent–adolescent sexual health conversations are more likely to do the opposite (Beckett et al., 2010; Deptula et al., 2010; Eisenberg et al., 2006; Martino et al., 2008). Therefore, the role of sex and family educators, family doctors, and nurses is to inform parents of the benefits

of early and frequent conversations about sex and that these early conversations may actually promote the health of their adolescent children. Educators can encourage parents to focus on age-appropriate discussion topics such as . . . the names of different body parts, characteristics of healthy and unhealthy relationships, being responsible for your actions, privacy, and respecting other people's bodies as well as your own (Levine, 2011; Richardson, 2004). Preparing to discuss specific topics may help parents feel more comfortable approaching these discussions, but they should also be encouraged to be open to topics adolescents are curious about.

Strategies to Improve Normative Beliefs

Normative beliefs reflect individuals' perceptions of what important others (e.g., other parents, family doctors, and sex and family educators) think about the behavior, if these important others have engaged in the behavior themselves, and if they are motivated to comply with those expectations (Azjen, 1991, 2002). A potential approach to impact normative beliefs is through mass media campaigns aimed at parents of adolescents. These campaigns typically involve promoting factual information to specific groups in order to overcome misperceptions regarding health behaviors (Davis, Evans, & Kamyab, 2012; DuRant, Wolfson, LaFrance, Balkrishnan, & Altman, 2006). Applied to parent–adolescent communication about sex, campaigns could focus on the importance of sexual health discussions, how frequently most parents talk about sex with their adolescents, adolescents' own interest in having conversations with their parents, and what are other, less reliable, sources of adolescents' sexual health information. Sex and family educators can be involved in these campaigns by working with interventionists to ensure that the content is appropriate and reflects current knowledge and best practices on this topic. They can also implement smaller-scale, more targeted programs within their communities. An example of an effective mass media campaign is Parents Speak Up, which seeks to promote sexual communication "early and often" with children (Evans, Davis, Ashley, & Khan, 2012). The campaign used television, radio, and print advertisements as well as an accompanying website to target parent self-efficacy to have conversations about sex, explain the long-term benefits of talking to your children, and [share] norms surrounding adolescent sexual activity (Davis, Blitstein, Evans, & Kamyab, 2010). Research on parents exposed to the campaign messages reported more frequent sexual communication and discussions about abstinence with their children (Davis et al., 2012; Evans et al., 2012).

Strategies to Increase Perceived Behavioral Control

The final area of the TPB model is perceived behavioral control, reflecting one's belief in their ability to perform a behavior (Ajzen, 1991, 2002). Based on the literature we reviewed, parents' perceived behavioral control appears to be related to their sexual health knowledge and self-efficacy in initiating conversations with adolescents. Sex and family educators can play a significant role in helping parents learn (or relearn) information about sexual behavior, safer sex practices, and STIs. Sex and family educators can help parents identify appropriate sources of sexual health information such as the Advocates for Youth website noted above. Further, many sexual health websites for teens contain accurate information from qualified professionals (Buhi et al., 2010; Noar, Clark, Cole, & Lustria, 2006), and Guilamo-Ramos and colleagues (2014) found that parents perceived a number of benefits to using resources on the Internet with their children, such as the immediacy and convenience to access information and the scope of topics available. The CDC and the Sexuality Information and Education Council of the United States (SIECUS) provide research-supported information on their websites for parents and caregivers to become informed and also learn about adolescent sexual development (CDC, 2014; SIECUS, n.d.). Sex and family educators can also increase parents' sexual health knowledge through parent-focused interventions . . . , which have found positive associations between knowledge and increased self-efficacy (DiIorio et al., 2007) and comfort (Kirby & Miller, 2002; Pluhar et al., 2008) in having sexual talks with children.

There are no "perfect" times or methods guaranteed to make parents' discussion with adolescents about sexuality comfortable. However, an easy and flexible way to broach the subject is to use everyday experiences to initiate conversations (Wilson et al., 2010), for example, talking during a commercial break about a romantic moment in a television show, listening to song lyrics and discussing what they mean while driving in the car, seeing a group of co-ed teenagers at the mall, or simply asking what their peers do in co-ed groups. Educators can also assist parents by modeling and teaching active communication techniques. During the discussions, parents should keep the tone informal and temper their emotional reactions to questions asked by their children (Afifi et al., 2008). By moderating their emotional responses, parents can foster a judgment-free environment where their children feel more comfortable and open to discuss sensitive topics with them. By working . . . sex-related topics into day-to-day life, parents can gradually become more comfortable with discussing these topics and subsequently change their behavioral norms toward them. The more frequent these conversations are, the easier and more comfortable it becomes to talk about sex topics in general, thereby reducing the embarrassment felt by both parent and child (Guzman et al., 2003).

Although this review was primarily focused on parents as sexual health educators due to the well-documented associations between parent–adolescent communication and adolescent sexual health outcomes (Wight & Fullerton, 2013), other family members such as siblings and cousins can be sources of sexual health information. For example, adolescents have reported talking to siblings about sex more frequently than to parents (Bleakley et al., 2009; Secor-Turner et al., 2011; Wood, Senn, Desmarais, Park, & Verberg, 2002). Older siblings in particular may be viewed as more approachable than parents as sources of sex information given that they generally grow up together, share similar experiences, and their relationships have a mix of peer and familial qualities (Grusec, Chapparro, Johnston, & Sherman, 2012; Haurin & Mott, 1990; Smetana, Campione-Barr, & Metzger, 2006). Future studies could investigate the effectiveness and outcomes associated with sibling communication about sex. Another avenue of research could investigate [whether and] why parents choose to take advantage of the wealth of resources designed specifically for this audience and this topic. We believe the resources discussed in the sections above contain reputable, evidence-based information; however, given that parents still report feeling unprepared, uncomfortable, and unsure about sexual health discussions, it is likely that resources designed to address these concerns among parents are not being widely used despite their availability. Future research should investigate the barriers to access and knowledge of resources for parents seeking this information. Finally, the research reviewed above has primarily been conducted with American or European samples and the recommendations would likely be different for other countries and cultural, religious, and social contexts. It was beyond the scope of this review to do a cross-cultural review or comparison and we direct readers elsewhere for this type of research (e.g., Asampong, Osafo, Bingenheimer, & Ahiadeke, 2013).

CONCLUSION

It is unfortunate that the media, friends, and peers, which typically provide adolescents with inaccurate information about sex and sexuality, are more common sources of sexual health information than parents (Whitfield et al., 2013). Unmediated, sex information from the media can lead to misinformation among adolescents. For example, content analyses of TV shows popular among adolescents have found that although shows are skilled at showing and talking about sex (Kunkel et al., 2003; Kunkel, Eyal, Finnerty, Biely, & Donnerstein, 2005), they generally lack messages about sexual risk and responsibility and do not show teens using safer sex practices (Kunkel et al., 2005; Wright, 2009) and frequently couch sexual health topics in jokes or portray sexual development as embarrassing and uncomfortable (Hust, Brown, & L'Engle, 2008). Similarly, relying on friends and peers for sexual health information can lead to misperceptions about the prevalence and consequences of sexual behavior during adolescence (Bleakley et al., 2009; L'Engle & Jackson, 2008). Sex and family educators can promote parent–adolescent communication about sex and sexuality by actively targeting parents' sexual health knowledge, perceptions of adolescents' readiness for conversations about sex, and how comfortable they are discussing sex with adolescents. Regardless of why parents avoid or do not discuss sex and sexuality with their adolescents, it is important for them to remember, and be reminded, that their adolescents will be confronted with sex-related issues whether they have private conversations with them or not. Therefore, having control over the accuracy of this information, and making oneself available as a resource in spite of the initial discomfort that comes along with the talks, is healthier for adolescents in the long run (Guzman et al., 2003).

NOTES

1. We note that this review did not focus on the consequences or effectiveness of parent–adolescent sexual health communication because there are recent, high-quality summaries of those topics (e.g., Akers, Holland, & Bost, 2011; Santa Maria, Markham, Bluethmann, & Mullen, 2015); rather we concentrated on what can prevent such communication in order to develop practical recommendations to overcome those barriers.

2. . . . [F]or reviews, see Jaccard, Dittus, & Gordon, 2000; Zimmer-Gembeck & Helfand, 2008).

REFERENCES

Afifi, T., Joseph, A., & Aldeis, D. (2008). Why can't we just talk about it? An observational study of parents' and adolescents' conversations about sex. *Journal of Adolescent Research*, 23: 689–721. doi:10.1177/0743558408323841.

Ajzen, I. (1991). The Theory of Planned Behavior. Organizational Behavior and Human Decision Processes, 50, 179–211. doi:10.1016/0749-5978(91)90020-T.

Ajzen, I. (2002). Perceived behavioral control, self-efficacy, locus of control, and the Theory of Planned Behavior. *Journal of Applied Social Psychology*, 32(4): 665–83. doi:10.1111/J.1559-1816.2002.Tb00236.X.

Akers, A. Y., Holland, C. L., & Bost, J. (2011). Interventions to improve parental communication about sex: A systematic review. *Pediatrics*, 127: 494–510. doi:10.1542/peds.2010-2194.

Asampong, E., Osafo, J., Bingenheimer, J., & Ahiadeke, C. (2013). Adolescents' and parents' perceptions of best time for sex and sexual communications from two communities in the Eastern and Volta Regions of Ghana: Implications for HIV and AIDS education. *BMC International Health and Human Rights*, 13: 40–51. doi:10.1186/1472-698X-13-40.

Beckett, M. K., Elliott, M. N., Martino, S., Kanouse, D. E., Corona, R., Klein, D. J., & Schuster, M. A. (2010). Timing of parent and child communication about sexuality relative to children's sexual behaviors. *Pediatrics*, 125: 34–42. doi:10.1542/peds.2009-0806.

Beckmeyer, J. J., & Jamison, T. B. (2015). Identifying demographic and attitudinal correlates of young adults' safer-sex self-efficacy. *International Journal of Sexual Health*, 27: 36–42. doi:10.1080/19317611.2014.933151.

Bleakley, A., Hennessy, M., Fishbein, M., Coles, H. C., & Jordan, A. (2009). How sources of sexual information relate to adolescents' beliefs about sex. *American Journal of Health Behavior*, 33: 37–48. doi:10.5993/AJHB.33.1.4.

Buhi, E. R., Daley, E. M., Oberne, A., Smith, S. A., Schneider, T., & Fuhrmann, H. J. (2010). Quality and accuracy of sexual health information web sites visited by young people. *The Journal of Adolescent Health*, 47: 206–08. doi:10.1016/j.jadohealth.2010.01.002.

Byers, E. S., Sears, H. A., & Weaver, A. D. (2008). Parents' reports of sexual communication with children in kindergarten to grade 8. *Journal of Marriage and Family*, 70: 86–96. doi:10.1111/j.1741-3737.2007.00463.x.

Centers for Disease Control and Prevention (CDC) (2014, June). Parent and guardian resources. Retrieved from http://www.cdc.gov/teenpregnancy/parent-guardian-resources/index.htm.

Collins, R. L., Elliott, M. N., Berry, S. H., Kanouse, D. E., Kunkel, D., Hunter, S. B., & Miu, A. (2004). Watching sex on television predicts adolescent initiation of sexual behavior. *Pediatrics*, 114: 280–89.

Daddis, C., & Randolph, D. (2010). Dating and disclosure: Adolescent management of information regarding romantic involvement. *Journal of Adolescence*, 33: 309–20. doi:10.1016/j.adolescence.2009.05.002.

Dancy, B. L., Hsieh, Y. L., Crittenden, K. S., Kennedy, A., Spencer, B., & Ashford, D. (2009). African American adolescent females: Mother-involved HIV risk-reduction intervention. *Journal of HIV/AIDS & Social Services*, 8; 292–307. doi:10.1016/j.biotechadv.2011.08.021. Secreted.

Davis, K. C., Blitstein, J. L., Evans, W. D., & Kamyab, K. (2010). Impact of a parent–child sexual communication campaign: Results from a controlled efficacy trial of parents. *Reproductive Health*, 7; 1–12. doi:10.1186/1742-4755-7-17.

Davis, K. C., Evans, W. D., & Kamyab, K. (2012). Effectiveness of a national media campaign to promote parent–child communication about sex. *Health Education & Behavior*, 40: 97–106. doi:10.1177/1090198112440009.

Deptula, D. P., Henry, D. B., & Schoeny, M. E. (2010). How can parents make a difference? Longitudinal associations with adolescent sexual behavior. *Journal of Family Psychology*, 24: 731–39. doi:10.1037/a0021760.

DiIorio, C., Kelley, M., & Hockenberry-Eaton, M. (1999). Communication about sexual issues: Mothers, fathers, and friends. *The Journal of Adolescent Health*, 24: 181–89.

DiIorio, C., McCarty, F., Resnicow, K., Lehr, S., & Denzmore, P. (2007). REAL men: A group randomized trial of an HIV prevention intervention for adolescent boys. *American Journal of Public Health*, 97: 1084–89. doi:10.2105/AJPH.2005.073411.

DuRant, R. H., Wolfson, M., LaFrance, B., Balkrishnan, R., & Altman, D. (2006). An evaluation of a mass media campaign to encourage parents of adolescents to talk to their children about sex. *The Journal of Adolescent Health*, 38: 298. doi:10.1016/j.jadohealth.2004.11.133.

Eisenberg, M. E., Sieving, R. E., Bearinger, L. H., Swain, C., & Resnick, M. D. (2006). Parents' communication with adolescents about sexual behavior: A missed opportunity for prevention? *Journal of Youth and Adolescence*, 35: 893–902. doi:10.1007/s10964-0069093-y.

Epstein, M., & Ward, L. M. (2007). "Always use protection": Communication boys receive about sex from parents, peers, and the media. *Journal of Youth and Adolescence*, 37: 113–26. doi:10.1007/s10964-007-9187-1.

Evans, W. D., Davis, K. C., Ashley, O. S., & Khan, M. (2012). Effects of media messages on parent–child sexual communication. *Journal of Health Communication*, 17: 498–514. doi:10.1080/10810730.2011.635772.

Goldfarb, E., Lieberman, L., Kwiatkowski, S., & Santos, P. (2015). Silence and censure: A qualitative analysis of young adults' reflections on communication with parents prior to first sex. *Journal of Family Issues*. Advance online publication. doi:10.1177/0192513Å~15593576.

Grusec, J. E., Chapparro, M. P., Johnston, M., & Sherman, A. (2012). Social development and social relationships in middle childhood. In I. B. Weiner, R. M. Lerner, A. M. Easterbrooks, & J. Mistry, eds., *Handbook of Psychology*, vol. 6: *Developmental psychology* (2nd ed., pp. 243–64). Somerset, NJ: Wiley & Sons.

Guilamo-Ramos, V., Jaccard, J., Dittus, P., & Bouris, A. M. (2006). Parental expertise, trustworthiness, and accessibility: Parent–adolescent communication and risk behavior. *Journal of Marriage and Family*, 68: 1229–46.

Guilamo-Ramos, V., Jaccard, J., Dittus, P., & Collins, S. (2008). Parent–adolescent communication about sexual intercourse: An analysis of maternal reluctance to communicate. *Health Psychology*, 27: 760–69. doi:10.1037/a0013833.

Guilamo-Ramos, V., Lee, J. J., Kantor, L. M., Levine, D. S., Baum, S., & Johnsen, J. (2014). Potential for using online and mobile education with parents and adolescents to impact sexual and reproductive health. *Prevention Science*, 16: 53–60. doi:10.1007/s11121-014-0469-z.

Guzmán, B. L., Schlehofer-Sutton, M. M., Villanueva, C. M., Dello Stritto, M. E., Casad, B. J., & Feria, A. (2003). Let's talk about sex: How comfortable discussions about sex impact teen sexual behavior. *Journal of Health Communication*, 8: 583–98. doi:10.1080/716100416.

Haurin, R. J., & Mott, F. L. (1990). Adolescent sexual activity in the family context: The impact of older siblings. *Demography*, 27: 537–57. doi:10.2307/2061569.

Hoff, T., Greene, L., & Davis, J. (2003). National survey of adolescents and young adults: Sexual health knowledge, attitudes, and experiences. Menlo Park, CA: Kaiser Family Foundation. Retrieved from http://kff.org /hivaids/report/national-survey-of-adolescentsand -young-adults/.

Hust, S. J. T., Brown, J. D., & L'Engle, K. L. (2008). Boys will be boys and girls better be prepared: An analysis of the rare sexual health messages in young adolescents' media. *Mass Communication and Society*, 11: 3–23. doi:10.1080/15205430701668139.

Hyde, A., Drennan, J., Butler, M., Howlett, E., Carney, M., & Lohan, M. (2013). Parents' constructions of communication with their children about safer sex. *Journal of Clinical Nursing*, 22: 3438–46. doi:10.1111/jocn.12367.

Jaccard, J., Dittus, P. J., & Gordon, V. V. (2000). Parent–teen communication about premarital sex: Factors associated with the extent of communication. *Journal of Adolescent Research*, 15: 187–208. doi:10.1177/0743558400152001.

Jaccard, J., Dodge, T., & Dittus, P. (2002). Parent–adolescent communication about sex and birth control: A conceptual framework. *New Directions for Child and Adolescent Development*, 97: 9–41. doi:10.1002/cd.48.

Jerman, P., & Constantine, N. A. (2010). Demographic and psychological predictors of parent–adolescent communication about sex: A representative statewide analysis. *Journal of Youth and Adolescence*, 39: 1164–74. doi:10.1007/s10964-010-9546-1.

Kim, J. L., & Ward, L. M. (2007). Silence speaks volumes: Parental sexual communication among Asian American emerging adults. *Journal of Adolescent Research*, 22: 3–31. doi:10.1177/0743558406294916.

Kirby, D., & Miller, B. C. (2002). Interventions designed to promote parent–teen communication about sexuality. *New Directions for Child and Adolescent Development*, 97: 93–110. doi:10.1002/cd.52.

Kunkel, D., Biely, E., Eyal, K., Cope-Farrar, K. M., Donnerstein, E., & Fandrich, R. (2003). Sex on TV 3: A biennial report to the Kaiser Family Foundation. Menlo Park, CA: Kaiser Family Foundation.

Kunkel, D., Eyal, K., Finnerty, K., Biely, E., & Donnerstein, D. (2005). Sex on TV 4: A biennial report to the Kaiser Family Foundation. Menlo Park, CA: Kaiser Family Foundation.

Lefkowitz, E. S. (2002). Beyond the yes-no question: Measuring parent–adolescent communication about sex. *New Directions for Child and Adolescent Development*, 97: 43–56. doi:10.1002/cd.49.

L'Engle, K. L., & Jackson, C. (2008). Socialization influences on early adolescents' cognitive susceptibility and transition to sexual intercourse. *Journal of Research on Adolescence*, 18: 353–78. doi:10.1111/j.1532-7795.2008.00563.x.

Levine, S. B. (2011). Facilitating parent–child adolescent communication about sexuality. *Pediatrics in Review*, 32: 129–30. doi:10.1057/pt.2010.28.

Martin, K. A., & Luke, K. (2010). Gender differences in the ABC's of the birds and the bees: What mothers teach young children about sexuality and reproduction. *Sex Roles*, 62: 278–91. doi:10.1007/s11199-009-9731-4.

Martinez, G., Abma, J., & Copen, C. (2010). Educating teenagers about sex in the United States (NCHS data brief no. 44). Hyattsville, MD: National Center for Health Statistics.

Martino, S. C., Collins, R. L., Kanouse, D. E., Elliott, M., & Berry, S. H. (2005). Social cognitive processes mediating the relationship between exposure to television's sexual content and adolescents' sexual behavior. *Journal of Personality and Social Psychology*, 89: 914–24. doi:10.1037/0022-3514.89.6.914.

Martino, S. C., Elliott, M. N., Corona, R., Kanouse, D. E., & Schuster, M. A. (2008). Beyond the "big talk": The roles of breadth and repetition in parent–adolescent communication about sexual topics. *Pediatrics*, 121: 612–18. doi:10.1542/peds.2007-2156.

Mazur, M. A., & Ebesu Hubbard, A. S. (2004). "Is there something I should know?": Topic avoidant responses in parent–adolescent communication. *Communication Reports*, 17: 27–37. doi:10.1080/08934210409389371.

Miller, K. S., Fasula, A. M., Dittus, P., Wiegand, R. E., Wyckoff, S. C., & McNair, L. (2009). Barriers and facilitators to maternal communication with preadolescents about age relevant sexual topics. *AIDS and Behavior*, 13: 365–74. doi:10.1007/s10461-007-9324-6.

Noar, S. M., Clark, A., Cole, C., & Lustria, M. L. (2006). Review of interactive safer sex web sites: Practice and potential. *Health Communication*, 20: 233–41. doi:10.1207/s15327027hc2003_3.

Planned Parenthood. (2014, July). Parents and teens talk about sexuality: A national survey. Planned Parenthood Federation of America. Retrieved from http://www.plannedparenthood.org/files/2914/1322/5667/NationalPoll_09-14_V2_1.pdf.

Pluhar, E. I., DiIorio, C. K., & McCarty, F. (2008). Correlates of sexuality communication among mothers and 6–12-year-old children. *Child: Care, Health and Development*, 34: 283–90. doi:10.1111/j.1365-2214.2007.00807.x.

Richardson, R. A. (2004). Early adolescence talking points: Questions that middle school students want to ask their parents. *Family Relations*, 53(1): 87–94.

Rosenthal, D. A., & Feldman, S. (1999). The importance of importance: Adolescents' perceptions of parental communication about sexuality. *Journal of Adolescence*, 22: 835–51. doi:10.1006/jado.1999.0279.

Santa Maria, D., Markham, C., Bluethmann, S., & Mullen, P. D. (2015). Parent-based adolescent sexual health interventions and effect on communication outcomes: A systematic review and meta-analyses. *Perspectives on Sexual and Reproductive Health*, 47: 37–50. doi:10.1363/47e2415.

Secor-Turner, M., Sieving, R. E., Eisenberg, M. E., & Skay, C. (2011). Associations between sexually experienced adolescents' sources of information about sex and sexual risk outcomes. *Sex Education*, 11: 489–500. doi:10.1080/14681811.2011.601137.

Sexuality Information and Education Council of the United States (SIECUS). (n.d.). Resources from SIECUS for parents. Retrieved from http://www.cdc.gov/teenpregnancy/parentguardian-resources/index.htm.

Smetana, J. G., Campione-Barr, N., & Metzger, A. (2006). Adolescent development in interpersonal and societal contexts. *Annual Review of Psychology*, 57: 255–84. doi:10.1146/annurev.psych.57.102904.190124.

Somers, C. L., & Surmann, A. T. (2004). Adolescents' preferences for source of sex education. *Child Study Journal*, 34: 47–59.

Stidham-Hall, K., Moreau, C., & Trussell, J. (2012). Patterns and correlates of parental and formal sexual and reproductive health communication for adolescent women in the United States, 2002–2008. *Journal of Adolescent Health*, 50: 410–13. doi:10.1016/j.jadohealth.2011.06.007.

Swain, C. R., Ackerman, L. K., & Ackerman, M. A. (2006). The influence of individual characteristics and contraceptive beliefs on parent–teen sexual communications: A structural model. *Journal of Adolescent Health*, 38(6): 753.e9–e18. doi:10.1016/j.jadohealth.2005.08.015.

Tolman, D. L., & McClelland, S. I. (2011). Normative sexuality development in adolescence: A decade in review, 2000–2009. *Journal of Research on Adolescence*, 21: 242–55. doi:10.1111/j.1532-7795.2010.00726.x.

Villarruel, A. M., Loveland-Cherry, C. J., & Ronis, D. L. (2010). Testing the efficacy of a computer based parent–adolescent sexual communication intervention for Latino parents. *Family Relations*, 59(5): 533–43. doi:10.1111/j.1741-3729.2010.00621.x.

Whitfield, C., Jomeen, J., Hayter, M., & Gardiner, E. (2013). Sexual health information seeking: A survey of adolescent practices. *Journal of Clinical Nursing*, 22: 3259–69. doi:10.1111/jocn.12192.

Widman, L., Choukas-Bradley, S., Helms, S. W., Golin, C. E., & Prinstein, M. J. (2013). Sexual communication between early adolescents and their dating partners, parents, and best friends. *The Journal of Sex Research*, 51: 731–41. doi:10.1080/00224499.2013.843148.

Wight, D., & Fullerton, D. (2013). A review of interventions with parents to promote the sexual health of their children. *Journal of Adolescent Health*, 52(1): 4–27. doi:10.1016/j.jadohealth.2012.04.014.

Wilson, E. K., Dalberth, B. T., Koo, H. P., & Gard, J. C. (2010). Parents' perspectives on talking to preteenage children about sex. *Perspectives on Sexual and Reproductive Health*, 42: 56–63. doi:10.1363/4205610.

Wood, E., Senn, C. Y., Desmarais, S., Park, L., & Verberg, N. (2002). Sources of information about dating and their perceived influence on adolescents. *Journal of Adolescent Research*, 17: 401–17. doi:10.1177/07458402017004005.

Wright, P. J. (2009). Sexual socialization messages in mainstream entertainment mass media: A review and synthesis. *Sexuality & Culture*, 13: 181–200.

Zimmer-Gembeck, M. J., & Helfand, M. (2008). Ten years of longitudinal research on U.S. adolescent sexual behavior: Developmental correlates of sexual intercourse, and the importance of age, gender and ethnic background. *Developmental Review*, 28: 153–224. doi:10.1016/j.dr.2007.06.001.

Let's Talk about Sex: How Parents of Color Communicate with Teens

Lauren Fannin

Sex talks. They may make many parents anxious, but talking to teens about sex is an essential part of parenting. Thanks to research on sexual communication between parents and teens, we know that teens who talk to their parents about sex have sex later in life and are more likely to use condoms when they do (Whitaker and Miller, 2000; Widman et al., 2016). Traditionally, sexual communication research centered the experiences and perspectives of white families, using them as the standard. In more recent years, however, researchers have shifted focus to explore how parents of color communicate with their teens about sex.

Much of the literature on young people of color, particularly African American and Latino teenagers, focuses on sexual risk behaviors and the prevention of the social problems commonly associated with these groups, such as unplanned pregnancy and sexually transmitted infections (STIs). Researchers have paid less attention to the ways in which parent sexual communication contributes to the sexual health and emotional well-being of their teens, or the specific types of messages teens of color receive from their parents about sex. I discuss some of the common themes found in the literature.

Like white teens, teens of color report having more frequent conversations with their mothers than their fathers (Raffaelli and Green, 2003; Hutchinson and Cederbaum, 2011; Sneed et al., 2013), which essentially makes parent sexual communication a gendered activity. In fact, mother–daughter communication is associated with reduced sexual activity and increased condom use for African American and Latina teens (Hutchinson et al., 2003; Hutchinson and Montgomery, 2007). But how do parents of color talk about sex with their teens? Awkwardly, as it turns out.

African American, Latina, and Asian American mothers report feeling less comfortable communicating with their teens about sex than do white mothers (Meneses et al., 2006), and this discomfort is often detected by their children (Dennis and Wood, 2012). Despite their discomfort, African American parents have been found to have more frequent talks with their teens than parents of other groups (Hutchinson & Cooney, 1998; Hutchinson, 2002). Yet more frequent discussions about sex do not necessarily translate to open communication; compared to white, Asian American, and Latina mothers, African American mothers are least likely to know how much sexual experience their teens actually have (Meneses et al., 2006).

For black parents, firmly rooted ideas and stereotypes about sexuality and respectability inform the way they talk to their children about sex; the gendered messages African American teens receive from their parents are a reflection of those ideas. One study of mother–teen pairs revealed an underlying theme of "clean versus dirty" girls in discussions about sex. The moms admonished their sons to avoid being infected by "dirty" girls by using condoms, while teaching their daughters to avoid being labeled "dirty." Many of the mothers attempted to control their daughters by forbidding them to date and discouraging them from obtaining birth control (which they felt was for promiscuous girls). Most of the moms reported providing their sons with condoms, but only one mom provided them to her daughter (Fasula, Miller, and Wiener, 2007). Subsequent research uncovered similar themes: black girls are more likely than black boys to be taught about waiting until marriage, protecting their reputation (being a good girl), and not allowing boys to use them for sex, while black boys are more likely to be taught to use condoms and prevent pregnancy (Santa Maria et al., 2014; Fletcher et al., 2015). A study of African American father–daughter dyads revealed similar patterns in sexual communication: girls were encouraged by their fathers to be "good," protect their reputations, and be wary of boys, who the fathers believed have bad intentions (Brown et al., 2014).

Throughout the literature, there is a consistent lack of discussion about sexual assertiveness or sex-positivity, particularly for girls (Kapungu et al., 2010). In fact, some African American young women perceived sexual conversations with their mothers to be fraught with negativity about and criticism of the act itself, framing sex as dangerous or harmful (Dennis and Wood, 2012). Mothers' negative attitudes toward sex may be related to black women's centuries-long experiences with racist stereotypes about their sexuality. Since their arrival in the Americas, black women's bodies and sexuality have been subject to surveillance,

control, and legalized exploitation. Controlling images like the "Jezebel"—a sexually promiscuous black woman—were used to justify the abuse black women endured while simultaneously blaming and shaming black women (Collins, 2004). In light of this history, the emphasis on being a good girl may be a protective measure.

For Latino families, deeply held beliefs about gender and tradition influence the messages parents communicate to their teens. Like African American mothers, Latina mothers' discussions with their daughters tend to be protective in nature, focusing on preventing pregnancy and STIs, and many also encourage abstinence or delaying sex until adulthood (Romo et al., 2010; Stauss et al., 2011). There are diverse themes in the messages Mexican American mothers send to their daughters about sex. While some mothers view sex as strictly a male domain and encourage their daughters to remain chaste until marriage, others acknowledge that their daughters have sexual feelings (Reyes, 2016). That Latino male teens do not receive the same messages may be attributed in part to the traditional gender values, notions of female purity (Caal et al., 2013), and the concepts of *machismo* and *marianismo*[1] present in many Hispanic cultures (Guilamo-Ramos et al., 2006; Guilamo-Ramos et al., 2007).

For Asian American families, taboos about sex talk and cultural conservatism impede open sexual communication, but the dearth of parent–teen sexual communication does not affect Asian American youth the way it affects other groups. Asian American parents are least likely of all groups to engage in sexual communication with their teens. Asian American teenagers report that their parents talk more about dating norms and general standards of behavior with romantic partners than they do about sex, likely because explicit sexual discourse is considered taboo due to cultural norms (Kim and Ward, 2007). A survey of Chinese, Korean,

Filipina, and Vietnamese students found that among school, peers, medical professionals, and parents, the students learned the *least* about sex education from their parents (Lee et al., 2013). When sexual communication did occur, Asian American parents were much more likely to talk about abstinence than birth control (Lee et al., 2013). In the absence of direct messages about sex, Asian American teens rely on indirect messages from their parents through observation; listening to what their parents say about other members of their community and watching how their own parents behave yield important information regarding sexual norms and expectations (Kim, 2009). Despite minimal parent–teen sexual communication, Asian American youth begin having sex later and take fewer sexual risks than other groups, a paradox that deserves further study (Trinh et al., 2014).

The methods, themes, frequency, and impact of sexual communication between parents and teens vary across racial and ethnic groups. It is imperative that researchers do not overlook these differences when conducting research on teens and young adults. Additionally, we must move past descriptive data to understand *why* these differences occur, as each group's unique cultural history informs the sexual socialization that occurs in their families. We have a responsibility to understand the diversity of the human experience, especially when it comes to sex, one of the most natural human experiences there is.

NOTE

1. *Machismo* and *marianismo* are gender constructions. *Machismo* stresses the man's dominant role as the head of household. *Marianismo*, inspired by the Virgin Mary, emphasizes the woman's role as mother and nurturer (Cauce and Domenech-Rodriguez, 2002).

REFERENCES

Aspy, Cheryl B., Sara K. Vesely, Roy F. Oman, Sharon Rodine, LaDonna Marshall, and Ken McLeroy. 2007. "Parental Communication and Youth Sexual Behaviour." *Journal of Adolescence*, 30(3): 449–66.

Brown, Danice L., Christopher B. Rosnick, Traice Webb-Bradley, and Jonathan Kirner. 2014. "Does Daddy Know Best? Exploring the Relationship between Paternal Sexual Communication and Safe Sex Practices among African-American Women." *Sex Education*, 14(3): 241–56.

Caal, Selma, Lina Guzman, Amanda Berger, Manica Ramos, and Elisabeth Golub. 2013. "Because You're on Birth Control, It Automatically Makes You Promiscuous or Something": Latina Women's Perceptions of Parental Approval to Use Reproductive Health Care." *Journal of Adolescent Health*, 53(5): 617–22.

Cauce, Ana Mari, and Melanie Domenech-Rodriguez. 2002. "Latino Families: Myths and Realities." In *Latino Children and Families in the United States: Current Research and Future Directions*. 3–25.

Collins, Patricia Hill. 2004. *Black Sexual Politics: African Americans, Gender, and the New Racism*. New York: Routledge.

Dennis, Alexis C., and Julia T. Wood. 2012. "We're Not Going to Have This Conversation, But You Get It": Black Mother–Daughter Communication about Sexual Relations." *Women's Studies in Communication*, 35(2): 204–23.

Fasula, Amy M., Kim S. Miller, and Jeffrey Wiener. 2007. "The Sexual Double Standard in African American Adolescent Women's Sexual Risk Reduction Socialization." *Women & Health*, 46(2–3): 3–21.

Fletcher, Kyla Day, L. Monique Ward, Khia Thomas, Monica Foust, Dana Levin, and Sarah Trinh. 2012. "Will It Help? Identifying Socialization Discourses That Promote Sexual Risk and Sexual Health among African American Youth." *The Journal of Sex Research*, 52(2): 199–212.

Guilamo-Ramos, Vincent, Patricia Dittus, James Jaccard, Vincent Goldberg, Eileen Casillas, and Alida Bouris. 2006. "The Content and Process of Mother–Adolescent Communication about Sex in Latino Families." *Social Work Research*, 30(3): 169–81.

Guilamo-Ramos, Vincent, Patricia Dittus, James Jaccard, Margaret Johansson, Alida Bouris, and Neifi Acosta. 2007. "Parenting Practices among Dominican and Puerto Rican Mothers." *Social Work*, 52(1): 17–30.

Hutchinson, M. Katherine. 2002. "The Influence of Sexual Risk Communication between Parents and Daughters on Sexual Risk Behaviors." *Family Relations*, 51(3): 238–47.

Hutchinson, M. Katherine, and Julie A. Cederbaum. 2011. "Talking to Daddy's Little Girl about Sex: Daughters' Reports of Sexual Communication and Support from Fathers." *Journal of Family Issues*, 32(4): 550–72.

Hutchinson, M. Katherine, and Teresa M. Cooney. 1998. "Patterns of Parent–Teen Sexual Risk Communication: Implications for Intervention." *Family Relations*, 185–94.

Hutchinson, M. Katherine, John B. Jemmott, Loretta Sweet Jemmott, Paula Braverman, and Geoffrey T. Fong. 2003. "The Role of Mother–Daughter Sexual Risk Communication in Reducing Sexual Risk Behaviors among Urban Adolescent Females: A Prospective Study." *Journal of Adolescent Health,* 33(2): 98–107.

Hutchinson, M. Katherine, and Arlene J. Montgomery. 2007. "Parent Communication and Sexual Risk Among African Americans." *Western Journal of Nursing Research*, 29(6): 691–707.

Kapungu, Chisina Tsvakayi, Donna Baptiste, Grayson Holmbeck, Cami McBride, Melissa Robinson-Brown, Allyse Sturdivant, Laurel Crown, and Roberta Paikoff. 2010. "Beyond the 'Birds and the Bees': Gender Differences in Sex-Related Communication among Urban African-American Adolescents." *Family Process*, 49(2): 251–64.

Kim, Janna L. 2009. "Asian American Women's Retrospective Reports of Their Sexual Socialization." *Psychology of Women Quarterly*, 33(3), 334–50.

Kim, Janna L., and L. Monique Ward. 2007. "Silence Speaks Volumes: Parental Sexual Communication among Asian American Emerging Adults." *Journal of Adolescent Research*, 22(1): 3–31.

Lee, Christine, Denise Yen Tran, Deanna Thoi, Melissa Chang, Lisa Wu, and Sang Leng Trieu. 2013. "Sex Education among Asian American College Females: Who Is Teaching Them and What Is Being Taught." *Journal of Immigrant and Minority Health*, 15(2): 350–56.

Meneses, Lisa M., Joan K. Orrell-Valente, Sylvia R. Guendelman, Doug Oman, and Charles E. Irwin. 2006. "Racial/Ethnic Differences in Mother-Daughter Communication about Sex." *Journal of Adolescent Health*, 39(1): 128–31.

Raffaelli, Marcela, and Stephanie Green. 2003. "Parent–Adolescent Communication about Sex: Retrospective Reports by Latino College Students." *Journal of Marriage and Family*, 65(2): 474–81.

Regnerus, Mark D. 2005. "Talking about Sex: Religion and Patterns of Parent–Child Communication about Sex and Contraception." *The Sociological Quarterly*, 46(1): 79–105.

Reyes, Daisy Verduzco. 2016. "Conundrums of Desire: Sexual Discourses of Mexican-Origin Mothers." *Sexuality & Culture*, 20(4): 1020–41.

Romo, Laura F., Magali Bravo, Maria Elena Cruz, Rebeca M. Rios, and Claudia Kouyoumdjian. 2010. "'El Sexo no es Malo': Maternal Values Accompanying Contraceptive Use Advice to Young Latina Adolescent Daughters." *Sexuality Research and Social Policy*, 7(2): 118–27.

Santa Maria, D., C. Markham, J. Engebretson, E. Baumler, and S. McCurdy. 2014. "Parent–Child Communication about Sex in African American Mother–Son Dyads." *Family Medicine & Medical Science Research*, 3(3): 134.

Sneed, Carl D., Christian G. Somoza, Taurean Jones, and Sandra Alfaro. 2013. "Topics Discussed with Mothers and Fathers for Parent–Child Sex Communication among African-American Adolescents." *Sex Education*, 13(4): 450–58.

Stauss, Kimberly, Yvette Murphy-Erby, Javier Boyas, and Van Bivens. 2011. "Parent–Child Communication Related to Sexual Health: The Contextual Experiences of Rural Latino Parents and Youth." *Advances in Social Work*, 12(2): 181–200.

Trinh, Sarah L., L. Monique Ward, Kyla Day, Khia Thomas, and Dana Levin. 2014. "Contributions of Divergent Peer and Parent Sexual Messages to Asian American College Students' Sexual Behaviors." *The Journal of Sex Research*, 51(2): 208–20.

Whitaker, Daniel J., and Kim S. Miller. 2000. "Parent–Adolescent Discussions about Sex and Condoms: Impact on Peer Influences of Sexual Risk Behavior." *Journal of Adolescent Research*, 15(2): 251–73.

Widman, Laura, Sophia Choukas-Bradley, Seth M. Noar, Jacqueline Nesi, and Kyla Garrett. 2016. "Parent–Adolescent Sexual Communication and Adolescent Safer Sex Behavior: A Meta-Analysis." *JAMA Pediatrics*, 170(1): 52–61.

CONFLICTED IDENTIFICATION IN THE SEX EDUCATION CLASSROOM

ELIZABETH A. WILLIAMS AND ROBIN E. JENSEN

All U.S. states require public schools to teach sex education in some form (National Conference on State Legislatures, 2012), and well over 200 million federal dollars are earmarked for sex education each year (Boonstra, 2010). Decisions about what is included in sex education curricula in public schools occur at the state level and at the discretion of the local school boards, who may expand upon, but not violate, state mandates (Sexuality Information and Education Council of the United States, 2015). The enactment of these regulations on sex education curricula falls to sex educators. As sex education curricula are legislated, these educators are bound, by law, to teach according to approved mandates or risk losing their jobs. In this study, sex educators are defined as individuals who teach human sexuality curricula. However, as participants in this study made clear, this is often just a small part of their teaching load, and the level of training they receive varies, with some receiving little to no formal training in sex education instruction.

Although numerous studies have evaluated the effectiveness of various types of programs (e.g., Byers et al., 2003; Caron & Free, 2008; Spriggs & Halpern, 2008), few have taken into account the experiences of the individuals who are responsible for implementing sex education programs within the confines of organizational structures. Existing research that does account for health educator experiences has explored educators' enactive mastery experiences, as well as their curricular decision-making processes (Carrion & Jensen, 2014; Jensen, 2012).

These studies demonstrate how sex educators' experiences and choices play a role in the quality of sex education programs and, by extension, in students' sexual-health outcomes. What remains unexplored, however, is how educators negotiate conflicting ideological viewpoints concerning that which they are required to teach by their employing organization and that which they believe is professionally appropriate and/or effective.

In the present study, we address this gap in the literature by drawing from semi-structured interviews with 50 sex educators employed at public secondary schools throughout a Midwestern U.S. state, 22 of whom expressed a degree of conflicted identification within the context of their employment. Conflicted identification refers to a state in which an individual alternates between (and/or otherwise negotiates) feelings of connection with and disconnection from a social collective (e.g., their profession or organization; Pratt, 2000; Williams & Connaughton, 2012). We begin our study by reviewing extant literature on identification in general and conflicted identification in particular. Next, we provide an overview of our data collection methods before analyzing how interview participants described their experiences with conflicted identification in the sex education classroom. Finally, we delineate the implications of our findings.

From "Conflicted Identification in the Sex Education Classroom: Balancing Professional Values with Organizational Mandates," *Qualitative Health Research* 26(11), pp. 1574–86. Copyright © the Authors, 2015. Reprinted by permission of SAGE Publications, Ltd.

THEORIES OF ORGANIZATIONAL IDENTIFICATION

Identification has been conceptualized as the psychological attachment that an individual feels to a social collective (i.e., an organization, a team, a professional community). Many identification studies trace their theoretical roots to Burke (1969) and his theory of consubstantiality, or what Sass and Canary (1991) have interpreted as "the extent to which one shares one's substance with another idea, value, person, organization, etcetera" (p. 280). Likewise, Larson and Pepper (2003) have defined identification as "the communicative process through which individuals either align themselves with or distance themselves from . . . targets/sources of identity" (p. 530). In this respect, identification is the process by which individuals form their identity through their relationship with various social collectives, including organizations, teams, and professions (Lammers, Atouba, & Carlson, 2013).

Indeed, research suggests individuals' sense of identity creates a series of premises upon which they are likely to rely as they make choices and develop an understanding of the world around them (Tompkins & Cheney, 1985). For instance, individuals who become ingrained within a social collective's value structure rely on those values as they interact with others and make decisions both within and outside the confines of the social collective. Using this framework, one would assume educators' decisions about what, how, and why to teach their students are influenced by the school or school district through which they are employed.

To date, a growing body of research is dedicated to examining diverse categories of alternative identifications (i.e., neutral, deidentification, disidentification), including conflicted identification (Kreiner & Ashforth, 2004; Pratt,

2000). Pratt (2000) explained that conflicted identification emerges when individuals "alternatively move toward, away, or against the organization" (p. 480).[1] For instance, individuals may develop a sense of conflicted identification when they identify strongly with some aspects of the organization's (or other social collective's) ideological positioning at the same time they actively (although not necessarily openly) disagree with other key elements of the organization's values or endorsements. Kreiner and Ashforth (2004) offered several more specific examples of this including "critical theorists in business schools (who embrace the general ideologies of scholarship and learning, but are at odds with the predominant positivist paradigm)," or "gays in conservative institutions (who could feel strong identification with most of the values of the organization, but perceive that their lifestyle is not accepted)" (p. 4). These authors have argued that conflicted identification and other similar states "may predict a host of cognitive, affective, and behavioral outcomes, ranging from satisfaction to intentions to quit, and from organizational citizenship behaviors to whistle-blowing" (Kreiner & Ashforth, 2004, p. 22). Correspondingly, Scott (2007) noted the continued need to study the experience and expression of various forms of attachment, as little is known about their communicative indicators and the potential implications of their discursive manifestations. The present study joins diverse attempts to answer this call within the context of U.S. public sex education and poses the following research questions:

Research Question 1: What identification-oriented conflicts do sex educators describe encountering in the context of their employment?

Research Question 2: What strategies do sex educators identify as mechanisms they use for alleviating identification-oriented conflict in the context of their employment?

METHOD

Participants

Fifty sex educators employed at public schools throughout a Midwestern, U.S. state participated in this study. Participants were employed at junior high schools (n = 27), high schools (n = 22), or at a joint junior/senior high school (n = 1). Their self-reported ages ranged from 23 to 65 years (M = 40.68, SD = 12.38), with 13 identifying as male and 37 as female, and all participants reporting their race/ethnicity to be either White or Caucasian. Correspondingly, 95% of public school teachers identified as White in the state in which the study took place and during the school year in which this study took place (K. Lane, personal communication, April 28, 2009). Sixty percent (n = 30) of the participants had gone beyond the required bachelor's degree and obtained a master's degree. Participants' tenure in their position ranged from 1 to 40 years (M = 17, SD = 13.18). Of these 50 sex educators, 22 (44% of the sample as a whole) expressed in their interviews a sense of conflicted identification (see the subsequent Analysis section for discussion of construct operationalization). Their demographics largely aligned with the demographics of the sample as a whole. They were employed at junior high schools (n = 11), high schools (n = 10), or at a joint junior/senior high school (n = 1). Their self-reported ages ranged from 23 to 65 years (M = 41.5, SD = 12.25), with 5 identifying as male and 17 as female. Sixty-three percent (n = 14) of the participants had gone beyond the required bachelor's degree and obtained a master's degree. Participants' tenure in their position ranged from 2 to 40 years (M = 20.86, SD = 12.33).

Procedures

Following the attainment of institutional review board approval, sex educators were recruited to participate in this study. The sampling frame came from the list of public school teachers designated to teach health on the state's Department of Education website. Depending on available contact information, individuals were recruited by either email or formal letter. Four hundred teachers were contacted with a final sample size of 50 sex educators. Recruitment ended when the authors felt they had achieved a maximum variation sample representing a wide range of participant demographics and experiences (Lindlof & Taylor, 2002).

A semi-structured interview protocol was used to conduct telephone interviews with participants. The semi-structured format not only allowed for consistency across interviews but also provided flexibility to inquire about participants' unique experiences (Corbin & Strauss, 2008). Telephone interviews allowed individuals to participate when it was convenient for them and alleviated some of the limitations inherent to a statewide study.

Dr. Jensen conducted all of the interviews. During the interviews, she first explained informed consent to each of the participants and, upon receiving verbal consent to audio-record the interview, a short battery of demographic questions was given. This was followed by a series of open-ended questions about participants' experiences derived, in part, from existing research on the communication of sex information targeting young people (Allen, 2009; Buston, Wight, Hart, & Scott, 2002). These questions focused on (a) their training and job history, (b) how they obtained information about what to include in their curriculum, (c) their description of the curriculum, (d) their perceived self-efficacy in the classroom, and (e) specific strategies they used to teach sex education. Taped interviews ranged from 20 to 60 minutes in length with an average length of 40.94 minutes (SD = 10.14). Interviews were transcribed verbatim. All participants were given a U.S. $20 gift certificate following the interview.

Analysis

The authors did not go into the analysis expecting to find conflicted identification, but, rather, conflicted identification emerged through the analysis, which was guided by constant-comparative techniques (Charmez, 2006). Each transcript was read in its entirety before coding commenced. As the authors began to see themes emerge, memos were generated exploring those themes. Open coding (Strauss & Corbin, 1998) then occurred, during which the authors began a list of theoretical categories and continuously compared the readings of the interview transcripts with the theoretical categories and revised as necessary. Themes were collapsed and refined throughout the process of coding and after discussion between the authors (Strauss & Corbin, 1998). During this process, it became clear that a number of participants were experiencing identification conflicts related to the curricular mandates of their employing organization. Thus, the authors decided to focus their analysis on the conflicted identification participants were describing and the ways in which educators reported managing these conflicts.

After creating coding criteria for conflicted identification, the authors divided the remaining 40 transcripts and coded them individually to ascertain how many participants expressed conflicted identification, as well as to collect examples of its expression and explore communicative responses to these conflicts. The examples provided throughout this [reading] are drawn from the 22 cases in which conflicted identification was recognized. Pseudonyms are used in place of interviewees' names.

RESULTS

Our analysis suggests that a number of participants (n = 22) reported an ideological perspective on sex education (i.e., beliefs about how and what to teach) at odds with the perspective mandated by the school/district of their employment. For the majority of these educators, this discrepancy was experienced as a significant ideological difference. But, for a number of reasons (e.g., job security, normative pressure from parents), they nonetheless tended to follow the dominant ideology and adhere to the goals/objectives of their organization (i.e., their school/school district). We argue that the identification experiences described by these individuals mirror what scholars have termed conflicted identification. The remainder of this section delineates the ideological struggles facing participants, why many participants reported following the dominant ideology despite personal concerns, and how these dominant ideologies are discursively negotiated and even subverted.

Sources of Conflicted Identification

Our participants described a range of diverse identification-oriented conflicts they encountered while teaching sex education. Although participants were not explicitly asked to speak about their identification(s), interviewees used language suggesting they felt connections with the various social collectives of which they were a part. Specifically, participants expressed degrees of both implicit and explicit identification with their profession. This identification was evidenced in statements from participants that noted (a) a calling to the profession (e.g., "I had a gift, so I was gonna pursue that. . . . I've been told, I've always been told I was a born teacher."—Nathan, a 30-year-old junior high school teacher), (b) significant work to maintain professional standards (e.g., conference participation, continuing education), (c) their position as one they personally selected and perceived as valuable (e.g., "I started teaching because I wanted to teach."—Julie, a 55-year-old junior/senior high school teacher), and/or (d) their role as significant as it involved educating youth for the betterment of the community (i.e., several educators noted they taught in schools/communities in which they had grown up and, thus, had vested interests in teaching students how to contribute to those communities). Although participants seemed strongly entrenched within their professions, they also explained how these identification-oriented connections become stressed at times, particularly in the context of teaching sex education in mandated ways. Their interviews revealed conflicts of identification, which manifested in terms of feelings of inauthenticity, fear for job security, and concerns about angering community stakeholders. Many participants expressed having more than one of these feelings concurrently.

Feelings of Inauthenticity

For some interviewees, the conflict they experienced seemed to originate from a sense of potential inauthenticity in carrying out their job. Nathan, a 30-year-old junior high school teacher, explained the moments he struggled with these feelings:

When I have to say what abstinence is, I don't feel, I don't feel successful because I hate it. I hate saying that. I hate, only because I feel like I'm Bible-pushing. I feel like religion is getting into the schools and it's supposed to be that church and state are separated and I don't feel like that's what it is. Again, I don't have a religious affiliation and that may be a component of that. But people should have a choice. I guess it's my American-ism talking but I hate it because, kids, we're trying to teach them to be decision makers and now we are telling them, "No, you can't do that." And I was the type of kid that if you were to tell me "No," I'm going to find a way to do it. So that's personal. I don't, I just have a hard time saying abstinence.

Earlier in the interview, Nathan had expressed a strong degree of identification with his profession and the mission of his school. But, in this case, he also noted he closely identified

with an ideology of "American-ism" involving the separation of church and state. Nathan suggested the organizational mandate to teach abstinence-only curricula was so closely aligned with religious messages that he "hated it" when he had to follow this dictate in the context of public schools.

Other participants expressed a similar sense of inauthenticity emerging when their beliefs about the goals of their profession (i.e., teaching children to be decision makers, providing accurate information) were at odds with what they had to teach as educators in organizations endorsing abstinence-only programs. These feelings stemmed from a belief that the curriculum was ineffective because some students were already engaging in sexual practices. For instance, John, a 26-year-old high school teacher, shared,

I am not a proponent of abstinence-only sexual education. It doesn't work. . . . I feel that I'm doing the students kind of an injustice because it's kind of like teaching with textbooks from the 1800s. You know, the information they need is not there.

Similarly, Paige, a 56-year-old junior high school teacher, explained that she had been able to teach what she wished until the HIV/AIDS epidemic forced the district to revise their sex education curricula, which resulted in what she saw as an inappropriate and ineffective mandate:

Paige: And when this committee began I was told that these are the things I could not address in my classroom: masturbation, homosexuality, birth control.
Interviewer: Wow, birth control entirely.
Paige: Yeah. And I'm thinking that's it. So I said, "I've taught too long to know that that wasn't gonna work! How do you do any AIDS instruction without any of those kinds of issues or even sexuality education?"

Julie, a 55-year-old junior/senior high school teacher, expressed a similar degree of frustration about a curriculum she deemed unrealistic and a student body she felt was due information about contraception and abortion. She explained, "The only [guideline] was, supposedly, I wasn't supposed to talk about birth-control options, abortion. I think those were the main two. And I just argued and said, 'That's unrealistic.' . . . And I just, truthfully, ignored it." For both Paige and Julie, rather than take on a role they found at odds with their sense of professional ethics, they decided to teach a curriculum that was not endorsed by their employers. This choice did not necessarily alleviate feelings of conflicted identification, but it nonetheless seemed to alleviate feelings of inauthenticity.

Concern for Job Security

For other participants, the biggest source of their sense of conflicted identification was their concern for job security. These participants disagreed with their employing organization's sex education policy but emphasized the fact that, if they were not to adhere to the policy, it would put them in danger of losing their jobs. As Eloise, a 60-year-old junior high school teacher, shared, "No matter how much you enjoy the students or you know the students, it's just not safe, as a teacher, to explain those kinds of things." Safety was not something Eloise could be assured if she overstepped the bounds of her school mandate.

Heidi, a 27-year-old high school teacher, admitted she had discussed things in the classroom that could have led to her dismissal:

Yeah there's kind of like a black hole there . . . and when I look back on it, if somebody really wanted to cite me on it, I guess I technically could have lost my job if someone, and I guess I'm still in that same situation, I mean I hope to god that somebody doesn't want to take it that far.

Heidi described the tension of having to choose whether or not to jump in the black hole and risk one's own job security. This was a struggle echoed by Samantha, a 35-year-old high school teacher, who indicated she felt an ongoing sense

of conflict that sometimes led her to thwart the rules, thus putting her job on the line, because key decision makers in her organization were unwilling to address the problems at hand:

Well, the problem, I think, is that [the school board] is not comfortable with [discussing birth control]. You know they knew that there is a problem with teen pregnancy, however it's not something they're willing to budge on, so in lieu of job security you kinda have to [discuss birth control in class despite the abstinence-only mandate] sometimes, unfortunately.

Samantha's use of the word "unfortunately" at the end of her comment highlights the dissonance and even disappointment she felt at the prospect of having to risk her job for the sake of the children she was appointed to educate. For many participants, their experiences teaching sex education repeatedly put them in a precarious position where they were forced to balance or choose between their organization's policies, perceived student needs, and their own job security.

Fear of Angering Organizational Stakeholders

For still other participants, the key source of identification-oriented conflict they encountered in teaching sex education came from their perception/fear of angering organizational stakeholders such as parents or community members. Belinda, a 27-year-old junior high school teacher, highlighted the seemingly unresolvable tension she experienced in the face of this concern:

Some parents want me to teach their child how to put on a condom, other parents would prefer that their child stay naïve and innocent. Parents who don't care about their child, they're not involved in their child's life, they don't care one way or the other, but parents who are involved with their child, they're usually either, "No, I don't want you to talk about it," or "Yes, please talk about it, BUT don't talk about this." There are a lot of "buts.". . . So, you know, it's just a trial by fire.

From this perspective, sex educators feeling conflicted about diverse parental goals will likely always face dissent. However, without an employer sharing ideological perspectives about curricula, educators may feel especially ungrounded in their professional choices.

In a number of these cases, participants' sense of conflicted identification was revealed in light of their concerns about potentially negative parental responses. Nathan, the 30-year-old junior high teacher who expressed anger at being forced to teach an abstinence-only curriculum, indicated that he *only* teaches out of the textbook "because I don't want parents calling me" and because "I'm scared of getting sued. I'm so scared of getting sued. You get sued left and right and it's all based on that." Nathan, an individual adamant about what should be taught, still followed the organization's mandate because of the potential for stakeholder objections. Similarly, Joy, a 65-year-old junior high school teacher, explained, "Parents—they can be pretty scary." Concerns about "scary" organizational stakeholders and getting sued were compounded by concerns about job security, as well as acceptance within the larger community. Jake, a 52-year-old junior high teacher, explained,

And it's like anything else, it only takes one person to write a letter to the editor, to call a school board member, and if those people don't want to deal with it, it comes from the top down. Watch what you do, watch what you say, don't be controversial. And like I said, you have to pick your battles and most of the time it's not worth the hassle.

Jake argued that a single disgruntled stakeholder had the power to set off a chain reaction in which an employee would be framed as, at best, problematic and, at worst, unfit for their job. Given that parents may become upset regardless of course content or teaching methods, sex educators in this sample seemed to feel an almost constant tension related to the choices they made in their job and their sense of identification with employing organizations

they felt would not support them in the face of stakeholder objections.

Discursive Strategies for Managing Conflicted Identification

In spite of the sense of futility individuals such as Jake seemed to associate with their experiences of conflicted identification in the sex education classroom, a number of participants nonetheless delineated distinct communicative strategies allowing them to subvert the dominant ideology and lessen their feelings of conflict and futility. These strategies included finding ways to be student-focused, relying on sources external to the organization, and choosing silence or evasion.

Student-Centered Communication Strategies

Throughout the interviews, participants repeatedly indicated that they sought out ways to be student-centered in the classroom and thereby limit their sense that they were doing either their students or their employing organizations a disservice. In other organizational contexts, this strategy may be best translated as a client-focused orientation. In this sample, participants reasoned, given that the schools' objective is to educate and thereby meet the needs of students, the choices teachers made to respond to students' experiences and inquiries would always align with schools' objectives in some respect, even if they technically defied schools' abstinence-only mandates. As Keri, a 52-year-old high school teacher, explained, being student-centered and thereby serving the needs of the employing organization in an overarching sense involved accounting for the specific subjectivities and experiences of the populations served:

Well, in the inner city I answer [questions that fall outside of the scope of the abstinence-only curriculum]. If I know it. Otherwise, if I tell them I don't know it, I'll go find out. Because you can't, with inner-city kids, I mean you have to answer the questions or they'll get, I'm telling you, they just won't believe in the curriculum. They won't think you're authentic.

It takes a long time to get their trust anyway. Once you've got their trust, then you can help educate them. But these kids are not trusting people. But their lives are not trusting; these kids have hard lives. They come to school; we have a 99% attendance rate. So they come to school because they live in unsafe neighborhoods. They don't have stable home lives. A lot of time, they're switching places to live every 2 months. I mean, it's just not, and they need someone they can trust that can give them the right information. My kids have really hard lives.

In accounting for the lived experiences of her students, Keri came to the conclusion that student questions must guide her curriculum because anything other than a student-led discussion would result in students' lack of faith in her and her ability to teach.

Other participants explained how they created the space in which to answer the difficult questions students might ask and thereby extend the mandated curriculum. Several participants indicated they utilized question boxes for students to submit inquiries, or they opened the floor for discussion. These participants operated under the philosophy that if the student asked the question, they, as educators, were at liberty to answer said question. Heidi, a 27-year-old high school teacher, explained her approach, stating:

I kind of have an environment where the kids can feel open to ask questions and I like that because kind of where our school stands on how you go about teaching it is abstinence-only. That's all that they really want us to tell our students but I feel that if they ask the question, I feel that I have the obligation to tell them, at least give them the knowledge or where they can go to find the correct answer.

Emily, a 47-year-old high school teacher, echoed that she had also found success with this approach:

In the [state] that's all we're supposed to teach [abstinence], but the little leeway is that if somebody asks then I can teach it. So I usually do a lead-in and get them to ask a question about, well, "If you don't want to have a kid but you want to have sex, then

what do we do?" And that's all I have to do, and then I can teach it.

This strategy offers the added benefit of giving teachers additional control over when, where, how, and whether specific questions were answered, as Jennie, a 47-year-old high school teacher, made clear:

Yeah, and I've had, you know, just very few times over the course of 25 years where a kid has taken me some place where, uncharted waters or what not, and if I know that there's no malice on their part, I can respectfully say just within the normal classroom management, I can say, "Let's you and I chat about that at a different time," not trying to be demeaning to them, but yeah, I'll deal with it at some point, maybe not in front of 32 of them, but I'll deal with it.

Beyond speaking with specific students one-on-one, other teachers drew from student-submitted questions and rephrased them in ways they deemed more appropriate for class discussion. That these discussions ultimately seemed to be generated from students, rather than from the teacher, offered teachers a degree of justification for extending the curriculum and alleviated their sense of conflicted identification.

Employing Sources External to the Organization

Another strategy participants used for providing students with information outside of the mandated curriculum, without explicitly defying the mandate itself, involved directing students to external resources. Evan, a 49-year-old junior high school teacher, explained he would provide students with abbreviated answers to their questions and then refer them to a nurse for further information. Other participants, such as Carolyn, a 43-year-old junior high school teacher, relied on resources outside of the school for student referrals:

I said there were [questions about things like abortion or pregnancy], I will give them that lady's number [an external organization], because she's been ok'd by the school and then she can get into it further and she can keep it quiet if she wants or whatever she wants to do.

Similarly, Eloise, a 60-year-old junior high teacher, relied extensively on external resources. One of the external presenters who visited her classes ultimately became a long-term resource for students as he

gives a telephone number, where they [the students] can call if they need help with anything or if they have any more questions. He has a website that he really encourages them to use, to keep in touch with him, let him know [what] they're doing, if they're having any questions or feelings that they're having some trouble with.

Furthermore, Eloise explained that she actively fostered a persona that encourages students to go to others with their questions: "Students don't generally talk to me. I'm not one that they come talk to. I'm pretty strict."

This practice of encouraging students to ask other individuals about their questions seemed to help teachers feel they were staying within the bounds of their employing organization's directives without denying students the information they felt was needed. In some cases, this strategy involved directly answering some beyond-the-pale questions first and then referring students elsewhere. For instance, Keri, the 52-year-old inner-city high school teacher quoted above, explained to her students "come and talk to me about STDs and I refer them to the County health department and get the social worker involved." But in other cases, such as that of Carolyn and Eloise, this strategy involved no more than a referral and thereby offered a relatively conservative approach to stretching the limits of organizational mandates and alleviating the tensions of conflicted identification.

Evasion

A final strategy several participants delineated for alleviating their sense of conflicted identification was silence or evasion. That is, they indicated that they simply did not share their curriculum or teaching strategies with others. The following interview exchange with Justine, a 29-year-old high school teacher, highlights this strategy:

Justine: I guess I go by the "don't ask, don't tell" philosophy but I've never had anybody question as far as . . .

Interviewer: And so if they do start asking, it sounds like people start getting concerned about what's going on.

Justine: Right, right.

By keeping to herself, Justine suggested she evaded the extra attention and corresponding concern that might be generated from discussions about her teaching. Later in the same interview, Justine explained she makes information from Planned Parenthood available to students, but she has to be strategic in how she does so:

Interviewer: Do you think that your school board would find [giving students information about Planned Parenthood] problematic, or do you think that would be okay . . . ?

Justine: It's hard to say. I'm thinking that, again, they would be, if they found out it was going on, I think they would have a problem with it. So I would be hesitant just to . . .

Interviewer: Right. Just to have the [Planned Parenthood] cards [handed out to all students].

Justine: Yeah, but I might put a number on a bulletin board so it's there.

In this case, Justine, like Carolyn, Eloise, and Keri, used the strategy of referring students to sources external to the organization.

Another example of evasion strategies at work involved situations wherein educators felt compelled to expand on the information provided by external sources. For example, Katie, a 31-year-old junior high teacher, noted her district contracts with a religious-based organization to teach an abstinence-only curriculum. In their presentations, this contracted organization takes the stance "no birth control is 100% effective except for self-control. . . . They say condoms do not work effectively 100% of the time." Katie explained that explanation results in "a lot of kids they walk away with the attitude 'Well, if condoms don't work, why bother?'" In response, she gives what she calls the "seat belt speech" once the organization has finished their presentation:

So I address it as, well, you can say that seat belts don't always save your life in a crash, but you could say why bother, but if you are going to do something that's risky, it's probably a better idea to try to protect yourself in some way, than not protect yourself at all. "Would it be safer to never get into a car?" Yeah, probably. But you have to protect yourself somehow.

Katie, it seems, took liberty to expand on the mandated curriculum, and she did so without making that information known to others in her organization.

What set this strategy apart from some of the examples discussed earlier is that the teachers were fairly certain that their employing organization would not approve of the external source (in Justine's case) or the message provided (for Katie). In this way, this strategy may actually function to heighten, rather than alleviate, the sense of conflicted identification employees experience as they are forced to carry out their job from within a context fraught with evasion and potential exposure.

DISCUSSION

The results of this study suggest that many of the sex educators who participated (n = 22) experienced an ideological conflict between what they were required to teach by an employing organization and what they personally and professionally believed needed to be taught. This conflict left them in a precarious organizational position as they constructed lesson plans and navigated classroom interaction.

Pragmatic Implications

In the context of teaching sex education specifically, participants who expressed a sense of conflicted identification cited specific sources of conflict (i.e., feelings of inauthenticity, concerns about job security, concerns about organizational stakeholder disapproval), all of which may actually be grounded in overarching structural issues related to the organization as a whole. For instance, some participants pointed to a lack of formal training or guidance about what should/could be covered in their sex education courses. They were familiar with the overarching ideology of the program but were not given formal training about how their teaching should mirror this ideology. Therefore, these individuals were left in a quandary, deciding what is and what is not appropriate as they balanced their desire to follow organizational rules with their personal beliefs concerning what students needed to be taught. Furthermore, many participants also noted they received no training on teaching techniques specifically useful for teaching sex education. They indicated their particular teaching techniques came from trial and error. This suggests a more formalized training program for sex educators, either as part of college curricula or district/state-wide initiatives, may help ameliorate the organizational conflicts sex educators face and provide them with useful educational tools for communicating pertinent information. This suggestion is in line with Petrieglieri's (2011) model proposing social support as a moderator between identity threats and individuals' responses to said threats.

In an applied sense, regardless of whether participants' sense of professional conflict was the result of a lack of guidance/training or of something else, participants in these interviews provided many comments suggesting their own sense of conflicted identification affected their ability to do their job and students' ability to learn. Students, they argued, could tell when they were being inauthentic and feeling conflicted about their degree of honesty and forthrightness in the classroom. Participants implied students probably picked up on this feeling and were less forthcoming with questions and less aggressive about seeking out sexual-health information than if they had encountered a more centered, open, and supportive instructor. These comments not only support research highlighting negative professional and organizational outcomes of conflicted identification among employees (Kreiner & Ashforth, 2004) but also provide one possible reason why sex education in this country is, and long has been, failing. Future research needs to further explore the relationship between conflicted identification among sex educators and students' learning and health outcomes.

Limitations

The present study is limited in that participants were all employed in the same state and, thus, do not represent the experiences of sex educators employed in other parts of the United States, particularly those states with different educational mandates. In addition, the study was not able to include information about individual teacher rankings and reviews and, therefore, cannot speak objectively about the potential relationship between, for instance, professional success and the experience and negotiation of conflicted identification. What the study does provide insight into, however, is the possibility that conflicted identification is often central to the experience of teaching sex education, and this subjectivity, and its implications may be managed via more-or-less subtle discursive mechanisms.

DECLARATION OF CONFLICTING INTERESTS

The authors declared no potential conflicts of interest with respect to the research, authorship, and/or publication of this [reading].

FUNDING

The authors disclosed receipt of the following financial support for the research, authorship, and/or publication of this [reading]: This research was supported by a research incentive grant from Purdue University's College of Liberal Arts.

NOTE

1. Conflicted identification has also been termed ambivalent or schizo-identification (see Elsbach, 1999).

REFERENCES

Allen, L. (2009). "It's not who they are it's what they are like": Re-conceptualising sexuality education's "best educator" debate. *Sex Education, 9,* 33–49. doi:10.1080/14681810802639814.

Boonstra, H. (2010). Sex education: Another big step forward—and a step back. *The Guttmacher Policy Review, 13,* 27–28. Retrieved from http://www.guttmacher.org/pubs/gpr/13/2/gpr130227.pdf.

Burke, K. (1969). *A rhetoric of motives.* Berkeley: University of California Press.

Buston, K., Wight, D., Hart, G., & Scott, S. (2002). Implementation of a teacher-delivered sex education programme: Obstacles and facilitating factors. *Health Education Research, 17,* 59–72. doi:10.1093/her/17.1.59.

Byers, E. S., Sears, H. A., Weaver, A. D., Cohen, J. N., Voyer, S. D., & Thurlow, J. L. (2003). An adolescent perspective on sexual health education at school and at home. *The Canadian Journal of Human Sexuality, 12,* 1–17. Retrieved from http://www.utpjournals.com/Canadian-Journal-of-Human-Sexuality.

Caron, K. R., & Free, C. (2008). Recent evaluations of the peer-led approach in adolescent sexual health education: A systematic review. *Perspectives on Sexual and Reproductive Health, 40,* 144–51. doi:10.1363/4014408.

Carrion, M. L., & Jensen, R. E. (2014). Curricular decision-making among public sex educators. *Sex Education, 14,* 623–34. doi:10.1080/14681811.2014.919444.

Charmez, K. (2006). *Constructing grounded theory.* Thousand Oaks, CA: Sage.

Corbin, J., & Strauss, A. (2008). *Basics of qualitative research* (3rd ed.). Thousand Oaks, CA: Sage.

Elsbach, K. D. (1999). An expanded model of organizational identification. *Research in Organizational Behavior, 21,* 163–200. Retrieved from http://www.journals.elsevier.com/research-in-organizational-behavior/.

Jensen, R. E. (2012). Sex educators and self-efficacy: Toward a taxonomy of enactive mastery experiences. *Health Education & Behavior, 39,* 259–67. doi:10.1177/1090198111399756.

Kirby, D. K. (2006). Comprehensive sex education: Strong public support and persuasive evidence of impact, but little funding. *Archives of Pediatrics & Adolescent Medicine, 160,* 1182–84. doi:10.1001/archpedi.160.11.1182.

Kreiner, G. E., & Ashforth, B. E. (2004). Evidence toward an expanded model of organizational identification. *Journal of Organizational Behavior, 25,* 1–27. doi:10.1002/job.234.

Lammers, J. C., Atouba, Y. L., & Carlson, E. J. (2013). Which identities matter? A mixed-method study of group, organizational, and professional identities and their relationship to burnout. *Management Communication Quarterly, 27,* 503–36. doi:10.1177/0893318913498824.

Lammers, J. C., & Garcia, M. A. (2009). Exploring the concept of "profession" for organizational communication research: Institutional influences in a veterinary organization. *Management Communication Quarterly, 22,* 357–84. doi:10.1177/0893318908327007.

Larson, G. S., & Pepper, G. L. (2003). Strategies for managing multiple organizational identifications: A case of competing identities. *Management Communication Quarterly, 16,* 528–57. doi:10.1177/0893318903251626.

Lindlof, T. R., & Taylor, B. C. (2002). *Qualitative communication research methods.* Thousand Oaks, CA: Sage.

National Conference on State Legislatures. (2012, March). *State policies on sex education in schools.* Retrieved from http://www.ncsl.org/issues-research/health/state-policies -on-sex-education-in-schools.aspx.

Petriglieri, J. L. (2011). Under threat: Responses to and the consequences of threats to individuals' identities. *Academy of Management Review, 36,* 641–62. doi:10.5465/amr.2009.0087.

Pratt, M. G. (2000). The good, the bad, and the ambivalent: Managing identification among Amway distributors. *Administrative Science Quarterly, 45,* 456–93. doi:10.2307/2667106.

Santelli, J., Ott, M. A., Lyon, M., Rogers, J., Summers, D., & Schleifer, R. (2006). Abstinence and abstinence -only education: A review of U.S. policies and programs. *Journal of Adolescent Health, 38,* 72–81. doi:10.1016/j.jado-health.2005.10.006.

Sass, J. S., & Canary, D. J. (1991). Organizational commitment and identification: An examination of conceptual and operational convergence. *Western Journal of Communication, 55,* 275–93. doi:10.1080/10570319109374385.

Scott, C. R. (2007). Communication and social identity theory: Existing and potential connections in organizational identification research. *Communication Studies, 58,* 123–38. doi:10.1080/10510970701341063.

Scott, C. R., Connaughton, S. L., Diaz-Saenz, H. R., Maguire, K., Ramirez, R., Richardson, B., . . . Morgan, D. (1999). The impacts of communication and multiple identifications on intent to leave. *Management Communication Quarterly, 12,* 400–35. doi:10.1177/0893318999123002.

Sexuality Information and Education Council of the United States. (2015). *Sexuality education Q&A.* Retrieved from http://www.siecus.org/index.cfm? fuseaction=page.viewpage&;pageid=521&grandparent ID=477&parentID=514.

Spriggs, A. L., & Halpern, C. T. (2008). Timing of sexual debut and initiation of postsecondary education by early adulthood. *Perspectives on Sexual and Reproductive Health, 40,* 152–61. doi:10.1363/4015208.

Strauss, A., & Corbin, J. (1998). *Basics of qualitative research: Techniques and procedures for developing grounded theory.* Thousand Oaks, CA: Sage.

Tompkins, P. K., & Cheney, G. (1985). Communication and unobtrusive control in contemporary organizations. In R. D. McPhee & P. K. Tompkins, eds., *Organizational communication: Traditional themes and new directions* (pp.179–210). Newbury Park, CA: Sage.

Williams, E. A., & Connaughton, S. L. (2012). Expressions of identifications: The nature of talk and identity tensions among organizational members in a struggling organization. *Communication Studies, 63,* 457–81.

The Case for Starting Sex Education in Kindergarten

Saskia de Melker

"Who here has been in love?" Anniek Pheifer asks a crowd of Dutch elementary school students. It's a spring morning in Utrecht, and the St. Jan de Doper elementary school gym is decked in heart-shaped balloons and streamers. Pheifer and Pepijn Gunneweg are hosts of a kids' television program in the Netherlands, and they're performing a song about having a crush. Kids giggle at the question. Hands— little and bigger—shoot up. Welcome to "Spring Fever" week in primary schools across the Netherlands, the week of focused sex ed classes . . . for four-year-olds. Of course, it's not just for four-year-olds. Eight-year-olds learn about self-image and gender stereotypes. Eleven-year-olds discuss sexual orientation and contraceptive options. But in the Netherlands, the approach, known as "comprehensive sex education,"[1] starts as early as age four.

You'll never hear an explicit reference to sex in a kindergarten class. In fact, the term for what's being taught here is sexuality education rather than sex education. That's because the goal is bigger than that, says Ineke van der Vlugt, an expert on youth sexual development for Rutgers WPF, the Dutch sexuality research institute behind the curriculum. It's about having open, honest conversations about love and relationships. By law, all primary school students in the Netherlands must receive some form of sexuality education. The system allows for flexibility in how it's taught. But it must address certain core principles—among them, sexual diversity and sexual assertiveness. That means encouraging respect for all sexual preferences and helping students develop skills to protect against sexual coercion, intimidation and abuse. The underlying principle is straightforward: Sexual development is a normal process that all young people experience, and they have the right to frank, trustworthy information on the subject. "There were societal concerns that sexualization in the media could be having a negative impact on kids," van der Vlugt said. "We wanted to show that sexuality also has to do with respect, intimacy, and safety."

BEYOND RISK PREVENTION

The Dutch approach to sex ed has garnered international attention, largely because the Netherlands boasts some of the best outcomes when it comes to teen sexual health. On average, teens in the Netherlands do not have sex at an earlier age than those in other European countries[2] or in the United States.[3] Researchers found that among 12- to 25-year-olds in the Netherlands, most say they had "wanted and

fun" first sexual experiences. By comparison, 66 percent of sexually active American teens surveyed said they wished that they had waited longer to have sex for the first time.[4] When they do have sex, a Rutgers WPF study found that 9 out of 10 Dutch adolescents used contraceptives the first time,[5] and World Health Organization data shows that Dutch teens are among the top users of the birth control pill.[6] According to the World Bank, the teen pregnancy rate in the Netherlands is one of the lowest in the world, rates of HIV infection are five times lower than in the United States, and sexually transmitted diseases are also low.[7]

There are multiple factors that likely contribute to these numbers. Easy access to contraception is one. Condoms, for example, are available in vending machines, and the birth control pill is free for anyone under age 21. But there's also a growing body of research that specifically credits comprehensive sexuality education. A recent study from Georgetown University shows that starting sex ed in primary school helps avoid unintended pregnancies, maternal deaths, unsafe abortions and STDs.[8] Proponents of the Dutch model argue that their approach extends beyond those risks. Their brand of sex ed reflects a broader emphasis on young people's rights, responsibility and respect that many public health experts say is the foundation of sexual health. A 2008 United Nations report found that comprehensive sex ed, when taught effectively, allows young people to "explore their attitudes and values, and to practice the decision-making and other life skills they will need to be able to make informed choices about their sexual lives."[9] Students who had completed comprehensive sex education in the Netherlands were also found to be more assertive and better communicators, according to an independent health research agency that conducted a study of the Dutch programs.[10] "We have to help young people navigate all the choices they face and stand up for themselves in all situations, sexual and otherwise," said Robert van der Gaag, a health promotion official at Central Holland's regional public health center.

"LITTLE BUTTERFLIES IN MY STOMACH"

At the St. Jan de Doper school, a group of kindergartners sit in a circle as their teacher, Marian Jochems, flips through a picture book. The pages contain animals like bears and alligators hugging. "Why are they hugging?" she asks the class. "Because they like each other," one girl answers. Jochems asks them to think about who they like the most. Several kids say their mom or dad. One girl names her little sister. A few name other children at school. "How does it feel when that person hugs you?" Jochems asks. "I feel warm from the inside," one boy replies. "It's like there are little butterflies in my stomach." Lessons like this are designed to get kids thinking and talking about the kind of intimacy that feels good and the kind that doesn't. Other early lessons focus on body awareness. For example, students draw boys' and girls' bodies, tell stories about friends taking a bath together, and discuss who likes doing that and who doesn't. By age seven, students are expected to be able to properly name body parts including genitals. They also learn about different types of families, what it means to be a good friend, and that a baby grows in a mother's womb. "People often think we are starting right away to talk about sexual intercourse [with kindergartners]," van der Vlugt says. "Sexuality is so much more than that. It's also about self-image, developing your own identity, gender roles, and it's about learning to express yourself, your wishes and your boundaries."

That means the kindergartners are also learning how to communicate when they don't want to be touched. The goal is that by age 11, students are comfortable enough to navigate pointed discussions about reproduction, safe sex, and sexual abuse.

LET'S NOT TALK ABOUT SEX

In the United States, sexual education varies widely from state to state. Fewer than half of U.S. states require schools to teach sex ed, according to the Guttmacher Institute, a global nonprofit that researches sexual and reproductive health.[11] Just last month Congress extended the Personal Responsibility Education Program (PREP), which funds comprehensive adolescent sexual health initiatives across the country.[12] At the same time they increased funding for programs that promote sexual abstinence until marriage to $75 million a year. And Deb Hauser, president of Advocates for Youth, a nonprofit dedicated to sexuality education, says that sex ed in the U.S. still overwhelmingly focuses on minimizing the risk of pregnancy and STDs from heterosexual intercourse.[13] And nearly 4 in 10 millennials report that the sex education they received was not helpful, according to a survey by the Public Religion Research Institute.[14] "We have failed to see that sexual health is far more than simply the prevention of disease or unplanned pregnancy," says Hauser. That narrow focus, she says, leaves young people with few skills to cope with their feelings and make decisions in sexual encounters.

Not everyone agrees. In fact, comprehensive sex ed has yet to take hold in most parts of the country. Utah, for example, requires that abstinence be the dominant message given to students. It bans discussing details of sexual intercourse and advocating for homosexuality, the use of contraceptives or sexual activity outside of marriage. Utah state representative Bill Wright has further tried to restrict sex ed. In 2012, he proposed a bill requiring that abstinence-only be taught and that it be an optional subject. It passed but was vetoed by the governor. Sex ed is "not an important part of our curriculum," Wright said.[15] "It is just basically something out there that takes away from the character in our schools and takes away from the character of our students."

Utah is far from alone. Half of U.S. states require that abstinence be stressed.[16] "We have created generations of people who are not comfortable with their own sexuality," says Dr. David Satcher, the former U.S. surgeon general. That extends to parents and teachers, he says. In other places, the tide is shifting toward an approach closer to that of the Dutch. Two of the largest school districts in the country—Chicago Public Schools and Florida's Broward County—have recently mandated sex education for elementary school students. Chicago Public Schools requires at least 300 minutes a year of sex education for kindergarten through fourth-grade students and twice as much time for fifth through twelfth graders.[17] In 2014, schools in Broward County began teaching sex education at least once a year in every grade,[18] and the curriculum includes information about topics like body image, sexting and social media.

In the Netherlands, schools aim to educate parents too. Parents' nights are held to give parents tools to talk to their kids about sex. Public health experts recommend that parents take cues from their kids and make it an ongoing conversation, rather than one awkward, all-encompassing "birds and the bees" talk. For example, they advise, if you walk in on your child masturbating, don't react shocked; don't punish or scold them. Have a talk about where it is appropriate for such behavior to occur. "We talk about [sex] over dinner," said one father at a Spring Fever Parents' Night. Another said he recently answered questions about homosexuality posed by his twin six-year-olds during bath time.

LESSONS IN LOVE

Sabine Hasselaar teaches 11-year-olds. In a recent class, Hasselaar posed a series of hypothetical situations to her students: *you're kissing someone and they start using their tongue, which you don't want. A girl starts dancing close to a guy at a party, causing him to get an erection. Your friend is showing off pornographic photos that make you feel uncomfortable.*

The class discusses each scenario. "Everyone has the right to set their own limits and no one should ever cross those limits," Hasselaar says. There is an anonymous "Question Box" in her class during "Spring Fever" week. Students submit questions that teachers later address in class. "Nothing is taboo," Hasselaar says. One of her students, for example, wrote: "I think I am lesbian. What should I do?" Hasselaar addressed the issue in class: "It's not strange for some girls to like other girls more than boys. It's a feeling that you can't change, just like being in love. The only difference is that it's with someone that is the same sex as you." And in fact, most of the questions from her students aren't about sex at all. "Mostly they are curious about love. I get a lot of questions like, 'What do I do if I like someone?' or 'How do I ask someone to go out with me?'" Questions like these are taken just as seriously as the ones about sex. "Of course, we want kids to be safe and to understand the risks involved with sex, but we also want them to know about the positive and fun side of caring for someone and being in a healthy relationship," van der Vlugt says. That's why you'll find teachers discussing the difference between liking someone (as a friend) and liking someone. There's even a lesson on dating during which a teacher talked about how to break up with someone in a decent way: "Please do not do it via text message," the teacher said.

After elementary school, these students will likely go on to receive lessons from a widely used curriculum called Long Live Love.[19] "In the U.S., adults tend to view young people as these bundles of exploding hormones. In the Netherlands, there's a strong belief that young people can be in love and in relationships," says Amy Schalet, an American sociologist who was raised in the Netherlands and now studies cultural attitudes toward adolescent sexuality, with a focus on these two countries.[20] "If you see love and relationships as the anchor for sex, then it's much easier to talk about it with a child," Schalet says. "Even a young one."

NOTES

1. http://www.unfpa.org/comprehensive-sexuality-education.

2. http://www.euro.who.int/__data/assets/pdf_file/0003/163857/Social-determinants-of-health-and-well-being-among-young-people.pdf.

3. https://www.cdc.gov/nchs/data/series/sr_23/sr23_031.pdf.

4. http://www.whijournal.com/article/S1049-3867%2811%2900008-9/abstract.

5. https://www.rutgers.nl/sites/rutgersnl/files/PDF-Onderzoek/Factsheet_Seksonderje25ste_ENG.pdf.

6. http://www.euro.who.int/en/health-topics/Life-stages/child-and-adolescent-health/child-and-adolescent-health2/youth-friendly-services/health-behaviour-in-school-aged-children-hbsc2.-who-collaborative-cross-national-study-of-children-aged-1115.

7. https://data.worldbank.org/indicator/SP.ADO.TFRT.

8. http://irh.org/wp-content/uploads/2014/05/Investing_in_VYAs_SRH_2014.pdf.

9. http://unesdoc.unesco.org/images/0018/001832/183281e.pdf.

10. http://www.rescon.nl/.

11. https://www.guttmacher.org/state-policy/explore/sex-and-hiv-education. [*Editors' note*: While all U.S. states and the District of Columbia provide some level of sexuality education (see Reading 20), only 24 states and the District of Columbia mandate sex education. Other states may allow school districts or individual schools to opt out of sex education or provide limited content such as HIV education.]

12. https://www.acf.hhs.gov/opre/research/project/personal-responsibility-education-program-prep-multi-component.

13. http://www.advocatesforyouth.org/.

14. https://www.prri.org/wp-content/uploads/2015/03/PRRI-Millennials-Web-FINAL.pdf.

15. https://www.ksl.com/?sid=19180217.

16. https://www.guttmacher.org/state-policy/explore/sex-and-hiv-education.

17. http://www.siecus.org/index.cfm?fuseaction=Feature.showFeature&featureID=2297.

18. http://miami.cbslocal.com/2014/05/06/broward-school-board-to-vote-on-new-sex-ed-policy/.

19. https://www.langlevedeliefde.nl/docenten.

20. http://www.amyschalet.com/not-under-my-roof-parents-teens-and-the-culture-of-sex/.

Source: "The Case for Starting Sex Education in Kindergarten," PBS NewsHour, May 27, 2015. Reprinted by permission of Creative News Group.

LGBTQ YOUTH NEED INCLUSIVE SEX EDUCATION

HUMAN RIGHTS CAMPAIGN, IN COLLABORATION WITH
ADVOCATES FOR YOUTH, ANSWER, GLSEN, PLANNED
PARENTHOOD FEDERATION OF AMERICA, AND THE SEXUALITY
INFORMATION AND EDUCATION COUNCIL OF THE U.S. (SIECUS)

Lesbian, gay, bisexual, transgender, queer and questioning (LGBTQ) youth need and deserve to learn in settings that are inclusive of their experiences and that give them the education necessary to stay safe and healthy. Far too many LGBTQ youth are sitting in classrooms where their teachers and textbooks fail to appropriately address their identities, behaviors, and experiences. Nowhere is this absence more clear, and potentially more damaging, than in sex education.

Sex education can be one of the few sources of reliable information on sexuality and sexual health for youth. Hundreds of studies have shown that well-designed and well-implemented sex education can reduce risk behavior and support positive sexual health outcomes among teens, such as reducing teen pregnancy and sexually transmitted infection (STI) rates.[1]

For LGBTQ youth to experience comparable health benefits to their non-LGBTQ peers, sex education programs must be LGBTQ-inclusive. Inclusive programs are those that help youth understand gender identity and sexual orientation with age-appropriate and medically accurate information; incorporate positive examples of LGBTQ individuals, romantic relationships, and families; emphasize the need for protection during sex for people of all identities; and dispel common myths and stereotypes about behavior and identity.

Whether legally barred or simply ignored, LGBTQ-inclusive sex education is not available for most youth. The GLSEN 2013 National School Climate Survey found that fewer than 5 percent of LGBT students had health classes that included positive representations of LGBT-related topics.[2] Among Millennials surveyed in 2015, only 12 percent said their sex education classes covered same-sex relationships.[3]

To right these inequities, Advocates for Youth, Answer, GLSEN, the Human Rights Campaign, Planned Parenthood Federation of America, and the Sexuality Information and Education Council of the U.S. (SIECUS) are calling on parents, youth, educators, and policymakers to help by:

1. Becoming advocates for LGBTQ-inclusive sex education
2. Ensuring that school is a safe and accepting space for LGBTQ students
3. Implementing LGBTQ-inclusive sex education in schools, community settings, and online
4. Talking to their own children and teens about sex and sexuality
5. Working to remove state-level legal and policy barriers to LGBTQ-inclusive sex education in schools and to require inclusive programs

THE PROBLEM

Background and Funding

The provision of sex education in public schools has a long and complicated history in the United States that is fraught with controversy stemming from disagreements over what youth should be taught about sex. Abstinence-only-until-marriage education, which began receiving major federal funding in the early 1980s during the Reagan administration, promotes abstaining from sex outside of marriage, emphasizes the failure rates of condoms and other methods of birth control, and generally overlooks or stigmatizes LGBTQ people.[4]

Despite evidence of its ineffectiveness,[5] it then went on to receive significant funding increases during the George W. Bush administration. Since 1996, abstinence-only-until-marriage education has received more than $1.8 billion in federal taxpayer funding.

The Legal Landscape

State laws regarding sex education vary widely across the country. Sex education is legally mandated in [24] states and the District of Columbia.[6] When sex education is provided in schools, only 13 states require that the instruction be medically accurate; 26 states and the District of Columbia require that the information be appropriate for the students' age; and 18 states and the District of Columbia require that information on birth control be provided.[7]

There are also laws and policies that explicitly or in effect prohibit inclusion of LGBTQ content in sex education. There are eight states that explicitly restrict the teaching of LGBTQ-related content in schools: Alabama, Arizona, Louisiana, Mississippi, Oklahoma, South Carolina, Texas and Utah. While some states, like Arizona, prohibit instruction that "promotes a homosexual lifestyle," others like Alabama, require teachers to "emphasize [. . .] that homosexuality is not a lifestyle acceptable to the general public and

that homosexual conduct is a criminal offense under the laws of the state."[8] In addition to this list, states such as Florida and North Carolina mandate that sex education focus on "monogamous heterosexual marriage."[9]

While there are many other states that do not have such prohibitions against discussing homosexuality, few states require education about sexual orientation or programs that are inclusive of LGBTQ youth. According to HRC's 2014 State Equality Index, only four states—California, Colorado, Iowa, and Washington—and the District of Columbia have state laws or regulatory guidance requiring sex education provided to students to be specifically inclusive of LGBTQ youth.[10] Only 12 states require that sexual orientation be discussed in sex education at all. The lack of such requirements leaves states without clear guidance.[11] The specific content of sex education is typically decided on a local level by school boards, advisory committees, or even individual teachers—the result too often being the exclusion of LGBTQ youth.

Exclusionary and Hostile School Environments for LGBTQ Youth

Only 12 percent of Millennials said their sex education class covered same-sex relationships.[12] Across the United States, less than 5 percent of middle and high school students reported having positive discussions of LGBT-related topics in their health classes.[13] According to the CDC, in states that allow LGBTQ-inclusive content, the percentage of secondary schools that actually provided sex education curricula or supplementary materials that were LGBTQ-inclusive ranged from 8 to 44 percent.[14] In other words, even in the states where educators are allowed to include LGBTQ-specific information, the vast majority of them do not.

In areas that implement abstinence-only curricula, students may hear messages that:[15]

- **Promote fear of same-sex attraction:** "Young persons may sense affection and even infatuation for a member of the same sex. This is not the same thing as 'being' homosexual. Any same-sex 'sexual experimentation' can be confusing to young persons and should be strongly discouraged."[16]

- **Reinforce gender stereotypes and heterosexual relationships:** "What do guys talk about in the locker room? (Girls) What do girls talk about at sleepover parties? (Guys)"[17]
- **Mandate heterosexual marriage:** "The only safe sex is in a marriage relationship where a man and a woman are faithful to each other for life."[18]
- **Disparage nontraditional families:** "Single women are trying to be both mother and father. The absentee dad has become a norm in many communities. It is interesting that domestic violence, child abuse, and poverty have also increased in proportion to the decline in the sanctity of marriage."[19]

Sex education programs that stigmatize LGBTQ people help cultivate hostile school environments by ignoring LGBTQ identities and experiences, or worse, actively promoting LGBTQ stigma. LGBT students who reported receiving an abstinence-only sex education curriculum were less likely to feel safe at school, more likely to miss school because they felt unsafe or uncomfortable, less likely to feel comfortable talking about LGBT issues with school personnel, and less likely to be able to identify educators who were supportive of LGBT students.[20] In the eight states that prohibit the positive discussion of homosexuality in schools, students were more likely to hear homophobic remarks from school staff, less likely to report feeling supported by school staff, less likely to receive an effective response to harassment from school staff, and less likely to have LGBTQ resources in schools such as comprehensive anti-harassment/assault policies and Gay-Straight Alliances.[21] Furthermore, LGBT

students who reported high levels of victimization and discrimination at school because of their sexual orientation or gender expression were more than three times as likely as their peers to have missed school in the past month, have lower GPAs, lower self-esteem, and higher levels of depression compared to their less frequently victimized peers.[22]

THE SOLUTION

LGBTQ-Inclusive Sex Education

Quality sex education provides students with opportunities for learning sexual health information, exploring attitudes and values about sexuality and relationships, and developing critical interpersonal skills. Sex education encourages students to talk with their parents about sex and teaches students communication, negotiation, and refusal skills they can use to form healthy relationships. Hundreds of studies have shown that well-designed and well-implemented sex education programs can reduce sexual risk and support positive sexual health outcomes among teens:[23]

- delaying the age of first sexual intercourse
- reducing the overall number of sexual partners
- reducing unprotected sex and increasing use of condoms and contraception
- reducing unintended teen pregnancy
- reducing rates of teen HIV and other STIs

LGBTQ youth deserve to receive the same benefits from sex education as their non-LGBTQ peers. Overcoming the current health disparities experienced by LGBTQ youth requires supportive learning environments and sex education programs that are inclusive of their identities, needs, and experiences.

Sex education that is LGBTQ-inclusive should, at a minimum:

- Include information for all students about sexual orientation and gender identity that is medically accurate and age-appropriate.

- Be designed with the needs of LGBTQ students in mind and be implemented with awareness that all classes are likely to have some LGBTQ students.
- Include depictions of LGBTQ people and same-sex relationships in a positive light in stories and role-plays.
- Use gender-neutral terms such as "they/them" and "partner" whenever possible.
- Ensure that prevention messages related to condom and birth control use are not relayed in a way that suggests only heterosexual youth or cisgender male/female couples need to be concerned about unintended pregnancy and STI prevention.
- Avoid making assumptions about students' sexual orientation or gender identity.

Comprehensive sex education delivered in schools from kindergarten through 12th grade is the best way to provide truly LGBTQ-inclusive sex education and ensure positive sexual health outcomes for all youth. These programs provide medically accurate and age-appropriate information on human development, relationships, personal skills, sexual behavior, including abstinence, sexual health, and society and culture.[24] Most importantly for LGBTQ youth, comprehensive sex education provides factual, non-stigmatizing information on sexual orientation and gender identity as a part of human development and teaches youth to respect LGBTQ people with messages like "Making fun of people for not acting the way society expects them to based on their biological sex [sic] is disrespectful and hurtful" and "People deserve respect regardless of who they are attracted to."[25]

Though comprehensive sex education is far from common in U.S. schools, sex education of any kind is a logical venue to help young people learn about identity and encourage acceptance for LGBTQ people and families. Even smaller-scope programs delivered in schools, community settings, or online that are designed or adapted to be LGBTQ-inclusive can make a difference for LGBTQ youth—particularly if they are evidence-based.

A study of the impact of LGB-inclusive HIV education found that LGB students receiving inclusive education reported fewer sexual partners, less recent sex, and less substance use before having sex than LGB youth in other schools.[26] In a survey of more than 1,200 middle and high school students across California, students whose health and sexuality classes expressed support for LGBTQ people were less likely to report bullying based on sexual orientation and gender expression.[27] These students were also more likely to feel safe at school. Inclusive content in other subjects made a difference, but sexuality and health education classes mattered most across various measures of school climate.

Public Support for LGBTQ-Inclusive Sex Education

Parents and leading health organizations alike support providing more LGBTQ-inclusive sex education. Ninety-six percent of parents support providing sex education in high school and 94 percent support it in middle school. Further, 85 percent of parents specifically support discussion of sexual orientation as part of sex education in high school and 78 percent support it in middle school.[28]

Many health organizations have issued statements and position papers expressing their support for LGBTQ-inclusive education:

- **The Society for Adolescent Medicine:** "Health educators and clinicians caring for adolescents should promote social and cultural sensitivity to sexually active youth and gay, lesbian, bisexual, transgendered [sic], and questioning youth. Health education curricula should also reflect such sensitivity."[29]

- **The American Public Health Association:** "Urges all states to require and adequately fund local school districts and schools to plan and implement comprehensive sexuality education as an integral part of comprehensive K-12 school health education. This education must be . . . consistent with community standards and efforts to foster safe and welcoming schools [and] be implemented in a nonjudgmental manner that does not impose specific religious viewpoints on students. . . . Districts should use multiple sources of data regarding students' needs, knowledge, and behaviors so that they can plan programs that meet the prevention needs of all students, with due attention to those who might be at greater risk for HIV, other STIs, and pregnancy, such as young men who have sex with men and members of populations with high prevalence rates."[30]
- **The American Medical Association:** "The American Medical Association (AMA) urges schools to implement comprehensive, developmentally appropriate sexuality education programs that . . . utilize classroom teachers and other professionals who have shown an aptitude for working with young people and who have received special training that includes addressing the needs of gay, lesbian, and bisexual youth."[31]

A CALL TO ACTION FOR YOUTH, PARENTS, COMMUNITY MEMBERS, EDUCATORS, AND POLICYMAKERS

Youth

Become an advocate for inclusive sex education. LGBTQ youth and allies can speak to school health advisory committees (SHACs), school boards, school administrators, and teachers about the need for sex education programs that meet their needs. Some SHACs include student members, so consider joining to advocate for inclusive curricula. School clubs, such as Gay-Straight Alliances, can also play a role in educating peers and advocating with educators at school for inclusive sex education. When possible, organize other people to advocate with you. Consult Youth Activist's Toolkit from Advocates for Youth for more ideas. GLSEN and the Gay-Straight Alliance Network also have many resources to help build or strengthen Gay-Straight Alliances.

Parents and Community Members

Find out what is being taught in your local schools. Many people have no idea whether their schools are providing abstinence-only-until-marriage education, sex education programs that are non-inclusive, or truly inclusive programs.

Become an advocate. The way that decisions about sex education curricula are structured varies by school district but there is generally a school health advisory committee that helps oversee curriculum choice. Parents and other community members can speak to school health advisory committees (SHACs), school boards, school administrators, and teachers about the need for LGBTQ-inclusive sex education programs. When possible, join the health advisory committee to help positively influence curriculum decisions.

Talk about sex with your own children. Learn about parent–child communication techniques and talk to your own children about the range of gender identities and expressions, as well as healthy sexuality and relationships. Advocates for Youth has a comprehensive guide to help parents through difficult conversations and Planned Parenthood has a section on its website with tools for parents.

Educators

Develop and implement LGBTQ-inclusive sex education curricula. Educators should incorporate best practices for LGBTQ inclusion in sex education curricula delivered in schools, community settings, and online. Resources for developing inclusive programs include your local Planned Parenthood affiliate, Answer's professional development workshop, LGBTQ Issues in Schools, and "Responsive Classroom Curriculum for Lesbian, Gay, Bisexual, Transgender, and Questioning Students" in *Creating Safe and Supportive Learning Environments: A Guide for Working with Lesbian, Gay, Bisexual, and Questioning Youth and Families.*[32]

Promote inclusivity throughout the school experience. The more that LGBTQ topics are discussed in the classroom and visible on campus, the better it is for LGBTQ youth. It is safe to assume that you have LGBTQ students in your class, whether you know it or not. Support or help students start affirming student organizations like Gay-Straight Alliances. Ensure an early and integrated approach to all LGBTQ issues by talking about LGBTQ people in history, using examples of same-sex couples in math word problems, and using terminology that acknowledges different family structures and gender identities. For more ideas on creating inclusive classrooms, consult GLSEN's LGBTQ-Inclusive Curriculum Guide for Educators and lesson plans on bullying, bias, and diversity.

Policymakers

Remove legal barriers. Policymakers are in a unique position to create change and clear legal roadblocks to LGBTQ-inclusive sex education. Federal, state, and local policymakers should work to address gaps and remove restrictions in the policy landscape, requiring sex education that goes beyond disease or pregnancy and is truly LGBTQ-inclusive. Policymakers can also support funding for effective sex education and resources for teacher training, program evaluation, and research.

NOTES

1. Advocates for Youth. (2008). *Science and Success: Sex Education and Other Programs that Work to Prevent Teen Pregnancy, HIV & Sexually Transmitted Infections.* Washington, D.C.: Alford, S. et al.; Kohler, P. K., Manhart, L. E., & Lafferty, W. E. (2008). Abstinence-only and comprehensive sex education and the initiation of sexual activity and teen pregnancy. *Journal of Adolescent Health,* 42(4), 344–51; Kirby, D. B., Laris, B. A., & Rolleri, L. A. (2007). Sex and HIV education programs: their impact on sexual behaviors of young people throughout the world. *Journal of Adolescent Health,* 40(3), 206–17.

2. GLSEN. (2014). *The 2013 National School Climate Survey: The experiences of lesbian, gay, bisexual and transgender youth in our nation's schools.* New York: Kosciw, J. G., Greytak, E. A., Palmer, N. A., & Boesen, M. J. (2014).

3. Public Religion Research Institute. *How Race and Religion Shape Millennial Attitudes on Sexuality and Reproductive Health: Findings from the 2015 Millennials, Sexuality, and Reproductive Health Survey.* Washington, D.C.: Jones, R. P., & Cox, D.

4. Sexuality Information and Education Council of the United States. *A History of Federal Funding for Abstinence-Only-Until-Marriage Programs.* Retrieved from http://www.siecus.org/index.cfm?fuseaction=page.viewpage&pageid=1340&nodeid=1.

5. Kantor, L. M., Santelli, J. S., Teitler, J., & Balmer, R. (2008). Abstinence-only policies and programs: An overview. *Sexuality Research & Social Policy,* 5(3), 6–17.

6. Guttmacher Institute. (2018, July 1). *State Laws and Policies: Sex and HIV Education.* Retrieved from https://www.guttmacher.org/state-policy/explore/sex-and-hiv-education.

7. Ibid.

8. GLSEN. *"No Promo Homo" Laws.* Retrieved from http://www.glsen.org/learn/policy/issues/nopromohomo.

9. National Coalition to Support Sexuality Education. *State Mandates and Coalitions.* Retrieved from http://www.ncsse.com/index.cfm?pageid=939.

10. Human Rights Campaign Foundation. (2015). *2014 State Equality Index.* Washington, D.C.: Gill, A.M.

11. Guttmacher Institute. (2018, July. 1). *State Laws and Policies: Sex and HIV Education.* Retrieved from https://www.guttmacher.org/state-policy/explore/sex-and-hiv-education.

12. Public Religion Research Institute. *How Race and Religion Shape Millennial Attitudes on Sexuality and Reproductive Health: Findings from the 2015 Millennials, Sexuality, and Reproductive Health Survey.* Washington DC: Jones, R. P., & Cox, D.

13. Kosciw, J. G., Greytak, E. A., Palmer, N. A., & Boesen, M. J. (2014). *The 2013 National School Climate Survey: The experiences of lesbian, gay, bisexual and transgender youth in our nation's schools*. New York: GLSEN.

14. Demissie, Z., Brener, N. D., McManus, T., Shanklin, S. L., Hawkins, J., & Kann, L. (2013). *School Health Profiles 2012: Characteristics of Health Programs among Secondary Schools*. Atlanta: Centers for Disease Control and Prevention.

15. Sexuality Information and Education Council of the United States. (2008). *Pride or Prejudice: How Fear-Based Abstinence-Only-Until-Marriage Curricula Present Sexual Orientation*. Retrieved from http://www.communityactionkit.org/index.cfm?fuseaction=page.viewPage&pageID=1095&nodeID=3&stopRedirect=1.

16. Fuller, R., McLaughlin, J., & Asato, A. (2000). *FACTS —Family Accountability Communicating Teen Sexuality, Middle School and Senior High School Editions*. Portland, OR: Northwest Family Services.

17. Cook, B. (2000 & 2003). *Choosing the Best LIFE*. Atlanta, GA: Choosing the Best, Inc.

18. Phelps, S., & Gray, L. *A. C. Green's Game Plan*. Glenview, IL: Project Reality, undated.

19. Frainie, K. (2002). *Why kNOw*. Chattanooga, TN: Abstinence Education Inc.

20. Kosciw, J. G., Diaz, E. M., and Greytak, E. A. (2008). *2007 National School Climate Survey: The experiences of lesbian, gay, bisexual and transgender youth in our nation's schools*. New York: GLSEN.

21. Kosciw, J. G., Greytak, E. A., Diaz, E. M., and Bartkiewicz, M. J. (2010). *The 2009 National School Climate Survey: The experiences of lesbian, gay, bisexual and transgender youth in our nation's schools*. New York: GLSEN.

22. Kosciw, J. G., Greytak, E. A., Palmer, N. A., & Boesen, M. J. (2014). *The 2013 National School Climate Survey: The experiences of lesbian, gay, bisexual and transgender youth in our nation's schools*. New York: GLSEN.

23. Advocates for Youth. (2008). *Science and Success: Sex Education and Other Programs that Work to Prevent Teen Pregnancy, HIV & Sexually Transmitted Infections*. Washington, D.C.: Alford, S., et al.; Kohler, P. K., Manhart, L. E., & Lafferty, W. E. (2008). Abstinence-only and comprehensive sex education and the initiation of sexual activity and teen pregnancy. *Journal of Adolescent Health*, 42(4), 344–51; Kirby, D. B., Laris, B. A., & Rolleri, L. A. (2007). Sex and HIV education programs: Their impact on sexual behaviors of young people throughout the world. *Journal of Adolescent Health*, 40(3), 206–17.

24. Sexuality Information and Education Council of the United States. *The Guidelines for Comprehensive Sexuality Education; Kindergarten–12th Grade*, 3rd Ed. Retrieved from http://www.siecus.org/_data/global/images/guidelines.pdf.

25. Ibid.

26. Blake, S. M., Ledsky, R., Lehman, T., Goodenow, C., Sawyer, R., & Hack, T. (2001). Preventing sexual risk behaviors among gay, lesbian, and bisexual adolescents: The benefits of gay-sensitive HIV instruction in schools. *American Journal of Public Health*, 91(6), 940–46.

27. Snapp, S. D., McGuire, J. K., Sinclair, K. O., Gabrion, K., & Russell, S. T. (2015). LGBTQ-inclusive curricula: Why supportive curricula matter. *Sex Education*, (ahead-of-print), 1–17.DOI: 10.1080/14681811.2015.1042573.

28. Let's Talk Poll. (2015). New York: Planned Parenthood Federation of America and Center for Latino Adolescent and Family Health.

29. Santelli, J., Ott, M. A., Lyon, M., Rogers, J., Summers, D., & Schleifer, R. (2006). Abstinence and abstinence-only education: A review of U.S. policies and programs. *Journal of Adolescent Health*, 38(1), 72–81.

30. American Public Health Association. *Policy Statement: Sexuality Education as Part of a Comprehensive Health Education Program in K to 12 Schools*. Retrieved from http://www.apha.org/policies-and-advocacy/public-health-policy-statements/policy-database/2015/01/23/09/37/sexuality-education-as-part-of-a-comprehensive-health-education-program-in-k-to-12-schools.

31. Council on Scientific Affairs. *Report of the Council on Scientific Affairs*. [Action of the AMA House of Delegates 1999 Interim Meeting, CSA Report 7-I-99]. Chicago, IL: American Medical Association, 1999.

32. Greytak, E. G., & Kosciw, J. G. (2013). Responsive classroom curriculum for lesbian, gay, bisexual, transgender, and questioning students. In E. Fisher & K. Komosa-Hawkins, eds., *Creating Safe and Supportive Learning Environments: A Guide for Working with Lesbian, Gay, Bisexual, and Questioning Youth and Families*. New York: Routledge. 157–75.

Disability and Sexuality Myth-Busting: Non-normative Sex Liberates Us All

Bethany Stevens[1]

For the past decade, as a disabled sex educator, I have traveled the nation speaking at conferences, taught classes at the university level, and engaged in community-based sexual education. I have worked with other disabled people, their parents, and academics. Along the way I have run up against some commonly held myths about disability and sexuality. In this process, I have found "flipping the script" useful. Instead of merely ranting about social barriers to robust sexual lives for disabled people, I offer lessons that all people can learn from by dismantling tired disability and sexuality myths! Most of these myths are so widespread and ingrained in our psyches that few people are prepared to challenge these fallacies.

The most prominent disability and sexuality myth is that disabled people are either desexual or hypersexual. I intentionally use the term *desexual* rather than *asexual*. Desexualization is a social process in which people perceive others as not having sexual interest or activities (Silverberg, Odette, & Kaufman, 2003), whereas asexuality is a sexual orientation, usually referring to an absence of sexual attraction to others. In contrast, the term *hypersexual*, often associated with a clinical diagnosis, suggests an unnatural obsession with sex (Shakespeare, Gillespie-Sells, & Davies, 1996). People with mental health or intellectual disabilities often are viewed as hypersexual, while those with mobility or sensory disabilities are thought to be desexual. The lack of positive media representation about the nuances of life with a disability reinforces these misconceptions, like too many oppressive cultural tropes. Too often we are flattened into characters that reflect lives that are fundamentally different from nondisabled lives; we are either inspirational or depressed and angry about our disabilities (Barnes, 1992). We are only our disabilities. Many portrayals of disability and actual encounters in society are loaded with patronizing tones and assumptions of our childlike nature, leading to a desexualizing conclusion (Silverberg, Odette, & Kaufman, 2003). Disability is a unique marginalized identity because anyone can join at any moment due to accident or illness, and it cuts across all identity markers (e.g., political leaning, sexual orientation, race, class). It is then only logical that there are many sexual permutations among disabled people. Most of us are having sex or working on it. Some of us have clinical issues with hypersexuality. Some of us are asexual. We are just as diverse sexually as members of nondisabled communities, despite contending with barriers erected socially. Ask yourself: If you had an injury or acquired a disability, would it cancel your desire? Would it increase your libido?

The second disability and sexuality myth is that disabled people are undesirable. Close your eyes and visualize what you consider to be a beautiful person. Reflecting on characteristics of beauty, my students often rely on societal norms that represent interlocking systems of oppression (or how racism, homophobia, classism, fatphobia, transphobia, and ableism connect) (Collins, 2004). This means that when they think about beauty, they tend to talk about young, thin, often white (though that depends on the crowd), gender-typical people. When asked about whether disability was part of their conception of beauty, most students admit it was not. It is sometimes assumed that if a non-disabled person is dating a disabled person the nondisabled person must have a perverted fetish; it is "unnatural" to find disabled people unattractive. The media reinforces what beauty entails, disenfranchising not just those with disabilities but anyone who does not meet the media's unachievable standards.

Pornography and mainstream media also teach us that we should be orgasming simultaneously and that our hair and makeup should look perfect in the process (Paul, 2006). People expect bodies to conform to a certain grammar of movement, in which people walk, move, talk, and even have sex in typical ways (Garland-Thomson, 1997). Although so-called beautiful imagery often defines sexual activity, the reality for all is much more diverse and messy. The cinematic climax is vastly different than intimate climax. For example, it's absolutely normal not to climax at the same time as your partner(s), and most people don't look like perfectly coiffed models while doing it. The website Beautiful Agony (beautifulagony.com) offers a great myth-busting series of videos of the faces of people orgasming. Most seem to be consumed in the moment and not concerned at all that their faces are contorted in odd, lovely ways. Disability provides space to expand what beauty and sexuality can look, move, and feel like. How do we identify beauty beyond socially sanctioned Eurocentric youthful nondisabled imagery?

The third myth is that disabled people are pathetic partners who lack an adventurous spirit. Undoubtedly, this is tied to the widely held belief that disabled people are pitiable or frail. This notion is reinforced by telethons and organized races to raise money to cure us of our disabilities and chronic conditions. At times, it is assumed our lives are not worth living, something one can see in movies such as *Million Dollar Baby* (Eastwood, 2004) and *Me Before You* (Sharrock, 2016). The nondisabled people who opt to date, marry, and/or love us are assumed to be sacrificing good sex and therefore are often viewed as valiant. While modifications may be necessary when approaching sex and modes of living, these adjustments often enhance intimacy and strengthen relationships by requiring people to think outside the box of traditional sexual tropes.

The mainstream media and pornography tend to view passionate sex as spontaneous in nature. Women are expected to be slammed against a wall and penetrated without communication about desires or safe-sex practices; the process cannot slow down because that would break the passionate thrust of the moment and the need to attend to men's erections with immediacy. Yet, slowing down and having open and honest communication about needs and abilities, as well as formal negotiation of triggers and possible positions, can actually serve to reinforce sexual pleasure for all. While that may not be viewed as "hot" by some, planned sex can be just as hot or hotter than spontaneous sex because you know your body will be protected (one of the best ways to show you love yourself), and fun activities such as role-playing can be added with just a bit of pre-sex conversation! How often do you have these conversations with your partners? How would it change your sexual script?

The fourth disability and sexuality myth is that disabled people do not have "real sex." Some types of disabilities entail the inability to engage in penile–vaginal intercourse (PVI); others are more limited. While PVI can be pleasurable or exciting for many people, it reinforces heteronormative sexual norms and simply should not be exalted as the ideal or the only appropriate sexual activity. Along with assuming PVI sex is the best sex, many also assume it's the one way to orgasm. Thank goodness there are multiple ways to orgasm, so people can have their choice of g-spot, breast or nipple, anal, mental, clitoral, or prostrate orgasms (Otto, 1999). Each type of orgasm can manifest differently in different people. An exciting truth about sexual activity is that it does not necessarily need to be genital-focused or end in an orgasm; we all have the capacity to experience pleasure in different parts of our body. Being sexually goal-oriented (or viewing sex as a staircase in which one sequentially moves from kissing, to fondling, to genital touching, and then to coitus with expectations of orgasm) can be anxiety-provoking and not pleasurable to some. Instead of thinking of sexual activity in steps, it's useful to consider sexual activity as a wheel in which one can choose from a buffet of activities and enjoy the play. Sexual activity need not even include a partner. Indeed, masturbation is one of the suggested practices to learn more about your body and sexual needs. Sexual activity may not even require touch. Drs. Barry Komisaruk, Carlos Beyer-Flores, and Beverly Whipple (2006) completed fMRIs (or colorful brain scans) to demonstrate that people can even experience orgasms through fantasy alone; some people working in tantra— the art of merging meditation and sexual activity to encourage mindfulness and attention to the breath—call this "thinking off" (Carrellas, 2007). Disability helps liberate orgasms by expanding our notions of what sex looks and feels like. It helps us learn that sex can be what we want it to be, not what we have learned from the media.

A really wonderful activity one can do alone or with partner/s to learn about their pleasure points is to complete a sexual blueprint. This entails going over the entire body—head to toe—with various forms of touch and pressure. Through touching softly, scratching, or pressing with fingers, feathers, or leather floggers,

one gets the experience of figuring out pleasure points in the body. I have my students do this and write about it. They marvel at hidden sexual gems in their body, such as finding the back of their knees are sensitive to touch. Additionally, we do breathing exercises in class to help instill some tantra principles. Directed and conscious breathing can focus pleasure in an area of the body; it also has the capacity to elongate moments of pleasure peaking or orgasming. For example, Rafe Biggs explains that his training in tantra enabled him to shift his orgasmic body part away from his penis after acquiring a spinal cord injury. Through focused breath and mindfulness practices, he can achieve an orgasm through having someone suck on his thumb (http://sexability.org). The *bodymind*—a term used by mental health scholars to show the interconnectedness between the mind and body, where when the body is in pain the brain may be foggy and vice versa—is remarkable when working in tandem to facilitate sexual pleasure in ways that do not meet the norm. How could you move beyond heteronormative, PVI-focused ideas of sex?

I hope this reading challenges your perceptions of sexuality, enhancing your sexual life and helping you see disabled people as typical humans. I will end with some insight into my sexological life focus; it is largely inspired by one of the first leaders in disability and sexuality, Barbara Waxman Fiduccia, as well as my own experiences in disability and sexuality. Waxman Fiduccia brazenly encouraged the politicizing of disability and sexuality at a time when no one in the movement was discussing it. This was a time when more "important" social change was afoot with the passing of a major piece of civil rights legislation: the Americans with Disabilities Act (ADA). In 1991, Waxman Fiduccia wrote, "Our movement has never addressed sexuality as a key political issue, though many of us find sexuality to be the area of our greatest oppression. That's because we are afraid we are ultimately to blame for not getting laid" (Waxman, 1991: 25). Regardless of how life-changing and empowering the ADA continues to be in the United States, Waxman Fiduccia's thoughts about disability and sexuality remain true today.

I work to continue the legacy of Barbara Waxman Fiduccia by bringing disability to sexuality spaces, and sexuality to disability spaces. I try to spread the good word about disability and sexuality to anyone who will listen! This is an important issue in my life because it has been such a strong force in sculpting my self-esteem, interactions with others, and overall socialization. As a teenager, I was sexually eager; I was aching to throw my (socially constructed) virginity at anyone who would take it. It was not until college that I started dating and having sex, and most of it was not so wonderful sex. I went from hating myself for not having sex to not loving myself enough to believe I deserved something better than the people I had sex with. I also had the youthful problem of having not figured out how to say what I want and get it.

A love of my life committed suicide because he was so exhausted from not being able to achieve nonchemically assisted erections after acquiring a spinal cord injury. It did not matter what I said, or anyone else really; his mind was made up. When I learned of his death, I wailed from deep inside of me for what seemed like a month. I realized in that intense grieving process that I was not just grieving the death of a loved one, I was grieving all my comrades in disability communities who come close to losing or do lose their lives due to sexual stigma. As Durkheim (2007) showed, suicide is a public problem, and considering many of us think in patterns, it makes sense that myths and assumptions about manhood and disabled sexuality could destroy a person. Every day I work

on refuting the myths I have been taught about disability, sexuality, and beauty. It is important to critically engage with these issues as though your life depends on it, because for some of us, it does. Sexuality does not have to remain a silenced social problem; it can be our screamed solution to confining bonds of our sexualities. It can be a needed push against the acculturated hate of our bodyminds. It can be a space for needed moments of sexual utopia.

NOTE

1. Follow Bethany Stevens on Twitter as @disaBethany and her blog cripconfessions.com.

REFERENCES

Barnes, Colin. 1992. *Disability Imagery and the Media: An Exploration of the Principles of Media Representations of Disabled People.* Halifax: Ryburn Publishing Limited.

Carrellas, Barbara. 2007. *Urban Tantra: Sacred Sexuality for the Twenty-First Century.* New York: Ten Speed Press.

Collins, Patricia Hill. 2004. *Black Sexual Politics: African Americans, Gender, and the New Racism.* New York: Routledge.

Durkheim, Emile. 2007 (1897). *On Suicide.* Trans. Robin Buss. London: Penguin Classics.

Garland-Thomson, Rosemarie. 1997. *Extraordinary Bodies: Figuring Physical Disability in American Culture and Literature.* New York: Columbia University Press.

Kauman, Miriam, Cory Silverberg, and Fran Odette. 2007. *The Ultimate Guide to Sex and Disability: For All of Us Who Live with Disabilities, Chronic Pain, and Illness.* San Francisco, CA: Cleis Press Inc.

Komisaruk, Barry, Carlos Beyer-Flores, and Beverly Whipple. 2006. *The Science of Orgasm.* Baltimore, MD: The Johns Hopkins University Press.

Otto, Herbert Arthur. 1999. *Liberated Orgasm: The Orgasmic Revolution.* Silverado, CA: Liberating Creations, Inc.

Paul, Pamela. 2006. *Pornified: How Pornography Is Transforming Our Lives, Our Relationships, and Our Families.* New York: Times Books.

Shakespeare, Tom, Kath Gillespie-Sells, and Dominic Davies. 1996. *The Sexual Politics of Disability: Untold Desires.* London and New York: Cassell Wellington House.

Waxman, Barbara. 1991. "It's time to politicize our sexual oppression." *The Disability Rag:* 23–26.

SEX, LOVE, AND AUTONOMY IN THE TEENAGE SLEEPOVER

AMY T. SCHALET

The vast majority of American parents oppose a sleepover for high school–aged teenagers, while Dutch teenagers who have steady boyfriends or girlfriends are typically allowed to spend the night with them in their rooms. This contrast is all the more striking when we consider the trends toward a liberalization of sexual behavior and attitudes that have taken place throughout Europe and the United States since the 1960s. In similar environments, both parents and kids are experiencing adolescent sex, gender, and relationships very differently. A sociological exploration of these contrasts reveals as much about the cultural differences between these two countries as it does about views on adolescent sexuality and child rearing.

ADOLESCENT SEXUALITY IN CONTEMPORARY AMERICA

Today, most adolescents in the United States, like their peers across the industrialized world, engage in intercourse—either opposite- or same-sex—before leaving their teens (usually around seventeen). Initiating sex and exploring romantic relationships, often with several successive partners before settling into long-term cohabitation or marriage, are now normative parts of adolescence and young adulthood in the developed world. But in the United States, teenage sex has been fraught with cultural ambivalences, heated political struggles, and poor health outcomes, generating concern among the public, policy makers, scholars, and parents. American adolescent sexuality has been dramatized rather than normalized.

In some respects, the problems associated with adolescent sexuality in America are surprising. Certainly, age at first intercourse has dropped in the United States since the sexual revolution, but not as steeply as often assumed. In a recent survey of the adult American population, sociologist Edward Laumann and colleagues found that even in the 1950s and 1960s, only a quarter of men and less than half of women were virgins at age nineteen. The majority of young men had multiple sexual partners by age twenty. And while women especially were supposed to enter marriage as virgins, demographer Lawrence Finer has shown that women who came of age in the late 1950s and early 1960s almost never held to that norm. Still, a 1969 Gallup poll found that two-thirds of Americans said it was wrong for "a man and a woman to have sex relations before marriage."

But by 1985, Gallup found that a slim majority of Americans no longer believed such relations were wrong. Analyzing shifts in public opinion following the sexual revolution, sociologists Larry Petersen and Gregory Donnenwerth showed that among Americans with a religious affiliation, only conservative Protestants who attended church frequently remained unchanged. Among all other religious groups, acceptance of premarital sex actually grew, although Laumann and colleagues reported a majority of Americans continued to believe sex among *teenagers* was always wrong. Even youth agreed: six in ten fifteen- to nineteen-year-olds surveyed in

From "Sex, Love, and Autonomy in the Teenage Sleepover," *Contexts* 9(3), pp. 17–21. Copyright © 2010, American Sociological Association. Reprinted by permission of SAGE Publications, Ltd.

the 2002 National Survey of Family Growth said sixteen-year-olds with strong feelings for one another shouldn't have sex.

Part of the opposition to adolescent sexuality is its association with unintended consequences such as pregnancy and sexually transmitted diseases. In the United States, the rate of unintended pregnancies among teenagers rose during the 1970s and 1980s, dropping only in the early 1990s. However, despite almost a decade and a half of impressive decreases in pregnancy and birth rates, the teen birth rate remains many times higher in the United States than it is in most European countries. In 2007, births to American teens (aged fifteen to nineteen) were eight times as high as in the Netherlands.

One would imagine the predominant public policy approach would be to improve education about, and access to, contraception. But "abstinence-only-until-marriage" programs, initiated in the early 1980s, have received generous federal funding over the past fifteen years, and were even written into the recent U.S. health reform law (which also supports comprehensive sex education). For years, schools funded under the federal "abstinence-only" policy were prohibited from educating teens about condoms and contraception and required to teach that sex outside of heterosexual marriage was damaging. A 2004 survey by NPR, the Kaiser Family Foundation, and Harvard University found that most parents actually thought that contraception and condom education should be included, but two-thirds still agreed sex education should teach that abstinence outside of marriage is "the accepted standard for school-aged children." And for most parents, abstinence means no oral sex or intimate touching.

While American parents of the post–sexual revolution era have wanted minors to abstain, few teens have complied. Many American teenagers have had positive and enriching sexual experiences; however, researchers have also documented intense struggles. Comparing teenage boys and girls, for example, University of Michigan sociologist Karin Martin found that puberty and first sex empowered boys but decreased self-esteem among girls. Psychologist Deborah Tolman found the girls she interviewed confronted dilemmas of desire because of a double standard that denies or stigmatizes their sexual desires, making girls fear being labeled "sluts." Analyzing the National Longitudinal Study of Adolescent Health, researchers Kara Joyner and Richard Udry found that even without sex, first romance brings girls "down" because their relationship with their parents deteriorates.

Nor are American girls of the post–sexual revolution era the only ones who must navigate gender dilemmas. Sociologist Laura Carpenter found that many of the young men she interviewed in the 1990s viewed their virginity as a stigma, which they sought to cast off as rapidly as possible. And in her ethnography *Dude, You're a Fag*, C. J. Pascoe found boys are pressured by other boys to treat girls as sex objects and sometimes derided for showing affection for their girlfriends. But despite public pressures, privately boys are as emotionally invested in relationships as girls, found Peggy Giordano and her associates in a recent national study out of Toledo, Ohio. Within those relationships, however, boys are less confident.

In the 1990s, the National Longitudinal Study of Adolescent Health found that steady romantic relationships are common among American teenagers. Girls and boys typically have their first intercourse with people they are dating. But the Toledo group found that once they are sexually experienced, the majority of boys and girls also have sex in non-dating relationships, often with a friend or acquaintance. And even when they have sex in dating relationships, a quarter of American girls and almost half of boys say they are "seeing other people" (which may or may not include sexual intercourse).

TEEN SEXUALITY IN THE NETHERLANDS

In a late 1980s qualitative study with 120 parents and older teenagers, Dutch sociologist Janita Ravesloot concluded that in most families, parents accepted that sexuality "from the first kiss to the first coitus" was part of the youth phase. In middle-class families, teenagers reported that parents accepted their sexual autonomy, but didn't engage in elaborate conversations with them because of lingering feelings of shame. Working-class parents were more likely to use their authority to impose norms, including that sex belonged only in steady relationships. In a few strongly religious families—Christian or Islamic—parents categorically opposed sex before marriage: here there were "no overnights with steady boy- or girlfriends at home."[1] But such families remain a minority. A 2003 survey by *Statistics Netherlands* found that two-thirds of Dutch fifteen- to seventeen-year-olds with steady boy- or girlfriends are allowed to spend the night with them in their bedrooms, and that boys and girls are equally likely to get permission for a sleepover.

This could hardly have been predicted in the 1950s. Then, women *and* men typically initiated intercourse in their early twenties, usually in a serious relationship (if not engagement or marriage). In the late 1960s, a national survey conducted by sociologist G. A. Kooy found most respondents still rejected premarital sex when a couple was not married or planning to do so very shortly. But by the early 1980s, the same survey found that six out of ten respondents no longer objected to a girl having intercourse with a boy as long as she was in love with him. Noting the shift in attitudes since the 1950s, Kooy spoke of a "moral landslide." His colleague, sociologist Evert Ketting, even went as far as to speak of a "moral revolution."

What changed was not just a greater acceptance of sex outside of the context of heterosexual marriage. There was also serious new deliberation among the general public, health professionals, and the media about the need to adjust the moral rules governing sexual life to real behavior. As researchers for the Guttmacher Institute later noted, "One might say the entire society has experienced a course in sex education." The new moral rules cast sexuality as a part of life that should be governed by self-determination, mutual respect, frank conversation, and the prevention of unintended consequences. Notably, these new rules were applied to minors and institutionalized in Dutch health care policies that removed financial and emotional barriers to accessing contraceptives—including the requirements for a pelvic examination and parental consent.

Indeed, even as the age of first sexual intercourse was decreasing, the rate of births among Dutch teenagers dropped steeply between 1970 and 1996 to one of the lowest in the world. What distinguished the very low Dutch teenage birth rate from, for instance, that of their Swedish counterparts, was that it was accompanied by a very low teen abortion rate. Despite the AIDS crisis, by the mid-1990s, funding agencies were so confident that, in the words of demographer Joop Garssen, youth were doing "wonderfully well," they decided further study of adolescent sexual attitudes and behavior wasn't warranted.

Sex education has played a key role. Sociologists Jane Lewis and Trudie Knijn find that Dutch sex education curricula are more likely than programs elsewhere to openly discuss female sexual pleasure, masturbation, and homosexuality. The Dutch curricula also emphasize the importance of self-reliance and mutual respect in negotiating enjoyable and healthy sexual relationships during adolescence.

A 2005 survey of Dutch youth, ages twelve to twenty-five, found the majority described their first sexual experiences—broadly defined—as well-timed, within their control, and fun. About first intercourse, 86 percent of women and 93 percent of men said, "We both were equally eager to have it." This doesn't mean that gender doesn't matter. Researcher Janita Ravesloot found that more girls than boys reported that their parents expected them to only have intercourse in relationships. Girls were also aware that they might be called sluts for having sex too soon or with too many successive partners. And although most of the 2005 respondents said they were (very) satisfied with the pleasure and contact they felt with their partner during sex, men were much more likely to usually or always orgasm during sex and less likely to report having experienced pain.

It also appears that having sex outside of the context of monogamous romantic relationships isn't as common among Dutch adolescents, especially older ones, as among their American counterparts. Again in the 2005 survey, two-thirds of male youth and 81 percent of Dutch females had their last sex in a monogamous steady relationship, usually with a partner with whom they were "very much in love." Certainly, Dutch adolescents have "non-relational" sex—indeed, one in three males and one in five females had their last vaginal or anal sex outside of a monogamous romantic relationship. That said, relational sex seems to remain the norm, especially as young people age: two-thirds of fifteen- to seventeen-year-olds, and three-quarters of those eighteen to twenty, had their last intercourse in a monogamous relationship. Among the oldest group—nineteen- to twenty-four-year-olds—almost half of gay men surveyed, six in ten straight men and lesbians, and nearly three-quarters of straight women were in long-term relationships.

EXPLAINING THE DIFFERENCES

So why do parents in two countries with similar levels of development and reproductive technologies have such different attitudes toward the sexual experiences of teenagers? Two factors immediately spring to mind. The first is religion. As the Laumann team found, Americans who do not view religion as a central force in their decision-making are much less likely to categorically condemn teenage sex. And devout Christians and Muslims in the Netherlands are more likely to exhibit attitudes toward sexuality and marriage that are similar to those of their American counterparts. That Americans are far more likely to be religiously devout than the Dutch, many of whom left their houses of worship in the 1960s and 1970s, explains part of the difference between the two countries.

A second factor is economic security. Like most European countries, the Dutch government provides a range of what sociologists call "social" and what reproductive health advocates call "human" rights: the right to housing, health care, and a minimum income. Not only do such rights ensure access, if need be, to free contraceptive and abortion services, government supports make coming of age less perilous for both teenagers and parents. This might make the prospect of sex derailing a child's life less haunting. Ironically, the very lack of such rights and high rates of childhood poverty in the United States contribute to high rates of births among teenagers. Without adequate support systems or educational and job opportunities, young people are simply more likely to start parenthood early in life.

While they no doubt contribute, neither religion nor economics can solve the whole puzzle. Even Dutch and American families matched on these dimensions still have radically divergent views of teenage sexuality and the sleepover. After interviewing 130 white middle-class Dutch and American teenagers (mostly 10th graders) and parents, I became convinced that a fuller solution is to look at the different cultures of independence and control that characterize these two middle classes.

In responding to adolescent sexuality, American parents emphasize its dangerous and conflicted elements, describing it in terms of "raging hormones" that are difficult for young people to control and in terms of antagonistic relationships between the sexes (girls and boys pursue love and sex respectively, and girls are often the losers of the battle). Moreover, American parents see it as their obligation to encourage adolescents' separation from home before accepting their sexual activity. Viewing sex as part of a larger tug-of-war between separation and control, the response to the question of the sleepover, even among many otherwise socially liberal parents is, "Not under my roof!"

Dutch parents, by contrast, downplay the dangerous and difficult sides of teenage sexuality, tending to normalize it. They speak of . . . a process of becoming physically and emotionally ready for sex that they believe young people can self-regulate, provided they've been encouraged to pace themselves and prepare adequately. Rather than emphasizing gender battles, Dutch parents talk about sexuality as emerging from relationships and are strikingly silent about gender conflicts. And unlike Americans who are often skeptical about teenagers' capacities to fall in love, they assume that even those in their early teens fall in love. They permit sleepovers, even if that requires an "adjustment" period to overcome their feelings of discomfort, because they feel obliged to stay connected and accepting as sex becomes part of their children's lives.

These different approaches to adolescent sexuality are part of the different cultures of independence and control. American middle-class culture conceptualizes the self and (adult) society as inherently oppositional during adolescence. Breaking away from the family is necessary for autonomy, as is the occasional use of parental control (for instance, in the arena of sexuality), until teenagers are full adults. Dutch middle-class culture, in contrast, con-

ceptualizes the self and society as interdependent. Based upon the assumption that young people develop autonomy in the context of ongoing relationships of interdependence, Dutch parents don't see teenage sexuality in the household as a threat to their children's autonomy or to their own authority. To the contrary, allowing teenage sexuality in the home—"domesticating" it, as it were—allows Dutch parents to exert more informal social control.

WHAT IT MEANS FOR KIDS

The acceptance of adolescent sexuality in the family creates the opportunity for Dutch girls to integrate their sexual selves with their roles as family members, even if they may be subject to a greater level of surveillance. . . . By contrast, many American girls must physically and psychically bifurcate their sexual selves and their roles as daughters. . . .

American boys receive messages ranging from blanket prohibition to open encouragement. One key message is that sex is a symbol and a threat—in the event of pregnancy—to their adult autonomy. . . . By contrast, Dutch boys, . . . like their female counterparts . . . say permission comes with a social control that encourages a relational sexuality and girlfriends their parents like. . . .

These different templates for adolescent sex, gender, and autonomy also affect boys' and girls' own navigation of the dilemmas of gender. The category "slut" appears much more salient in the interviews with American girls than Dutch girls. One reason may be that the cultural assumption that teenagers can and do fall in love lends credence to Dutch girls' claims to being in love, while the cultural skepticism about whether they can sustain the feelings and form the attachments that legitimate sexual activity puts American girls on the defensive. . . .

In both countries, boys confront the belief and sometimes the reality that they are interested in sex but not relationships. But there is evidence in both countries that boys are often emotionally invested. The American boys I have interviewed tend to view themselves as unique for their romantic aspirations and describe themselves, as Jesse does, as "romantic rebels." "The most important thing to me is maintaining love between me and my girlfriend," while "most guys are pretty much in it for the sex," he says. The Dutch boys I interviewed did not perceive themselves as unusual for falling in love (or for wanting to) before having sex. Sam, for instance, believes that "everyone wants [a relationship]." He explains why: "Someone you can talk to about your feelings and such, a feeling of safety, I think that everyone, the largest percentage of people wants a relationship."

CULTURE'S COST

How sexuality, love, and autonomy are perceived and negotiated in parent-child relationships and among teenagers depends on the cultural templates people have available. Normalization and dramatization each has "costs" and "benefits." On balance, however, the dramatization of adolescent sexuality makes it more difficult for parents to communicate with teenagers about sex and relationships, and more challenging for girls and boys to integrate their sexual and relational selves. The normalization of adolescent sexuality does not eradicate the tensions between parents and teenagers or the gender constructs that confine both girls and boys. But it does provide a more favorable cultural climate in which to address them.

NOTE

1. This quote and subsequent quotes from Dutch sources are the author's translations. Names have been changed to protect anonymity.

"PUT ME IN, COACH, I'M READY TO PLAY": SEXUALITY EDUCATION FOR ADULTS AT *GOOD VIBRATIONS*

JESSICA A. NODULMAN

Copious amounts of literature have examined sexuality education for adolescents and emerging adults; however, few studies have investigated sexuality education for the general public over 18 years of age. Sexuality education that only targets adolescents mistakenly assumes that it is only young people who encounter sexual health problems and require education (Paiva 2005; The National Campaign to Prevent Teen and Unplanned Pregnancy 2008). Rates of unintended pregnancy, abortion and sexually transmitted infection (STI) among those over 18 tell us otherwise. For example, in 2013, reported cases of gonorrhea in the USA were highest among men and women aged 20–24 years, and cases of chlamydia were highest among women aged 19–20 and men aged 20–24 years (CDC 2014). Older adults are also at risk for STIs. In 2014, people aged 50 and over accounted for more than 16% of new HIV diagnoses (CDC 2015).

Although these statistics suggest that adults need sexuality education, there are few places where adults can receive this education (Schick et al. 2013; Sexuality Information and Education Council of the United States 2015). College sex education programs (Eisenberg et al. 2012) or progressive church programs such as *Our Whole Lives*, developed jointly by the Unitarian Universalist Association and the United Church of Christ, are available for segments of the population, but not the general public (Lamb, Lustig, and Graling 2013). The internet has also been examined as a setting that can provide advantages and disadvantages for adults seeking to learn about sex (Adams, Oye, and Parker 2003). However, the most commonly investigated setting remains the health care professional's office (Penna and Sheehy 2000; Brandenburg and Bitzer 2009; Golin et al. 2010; Bahouq et al. 2013; Ussher et al. 2013; Dyer and das Nair 2014).

Research reveals that adult patients and physicians often have difficulty communicating about sex for a variety of reasons, including lack of awareness about sexual concerns, embarrassment and time constraints (Brandenburg and Bitzer 2009; Jeffers and DiBartolo 2011). Lindau et al. (2007) found that although men and women aged 57–85 years reported having at least one sexual problem, only 38% of men and 22% of women discussed sex with their doctors. In a study of 1150 obstetrician-gynecologists, the majority reported not discussing sexual problems or sexual satisfaction with their patients (Sobecki et al. 2012). Furthermore, there is a gender difference with respect to mature patient–provider conversations. According to Noland (2010), physicians are more likely to discuss sex with male patients than with female patients. In contrast, Politi et al.'s research reveals that women would like their physician to initiate discussions about sexual health with them. Thomas, Hess, and Thurston's (2015) research stresses the importance of clinicians discussing sexual relationships and sexual satisfaction with women patients, as

From "Put Me in, Coach, I'm Ready to Play: Sexuality Education for Adults at *Good Vibrations*," *Sex Education* Vol. 16, No. 6, 2016, pp. 649–62. Copyright © Informa UK Limited, reprinted by permission of the publisher (Taylor & Francis Ltd, http://www.tandfonline.com).

sexual activity is common among older women. Initiatives to incorporate sexual health communication training to medical students (Ferrara et al. 2003; Jayasuriya and Dennick 2011) and other health care professionals (Macdowall et al. 2010) may help adults and practitioners discuss these issues during a medical encounter, but there still remain few other non-clinical settings where adults can learn about sex.

One less traditional setting is the adult retail industry—including in-home sex toy parties and adult sexual retail stores. Reece, Herbenick, and Sherwood-Puzzello (2004) have investigated the adult retail industry (e.g. adult bookstores, sex shops, adult video and retail outlets) as a venue of sexual health information. They argue:

Given the magnitude of the adult retail industry and the fact that a significant percentage of the US population looks to it for products related to safer sex, sexual pleasure, or alleviating sexual dysfunction, it is logical to consider whether its retail establishments might be able to serve as resources that could simultaneously promote sexual health and sexual pleasure while retaining, and perhaps expanding, a profitable consumer base. (Reece, Herbenick, and Sherwood-Puzzello 2004, 177)

In-home sex toy parties are a way in which "literally millions of women now learn about (and often purchase) sexual enhancement products" (Herbenick and Reece 2009, 191). Previous research has investigated the types of questions asked by consumers and answered by facilitators at these in-home parties and found that there are teachable moments to educate women on a host of topics, including human development, relationships, sexual behavior, health, and society and culture (McCaughey and French 2001; Storr 2003; Herbenick and Reece 2009; Fisher et al. 2010). However, in-home sex toy or lingerie parties are usually marketed toward heterosexual women (McCaughey and French 2001; Storr 2003). Therefore, it is important to explore other adult

retail venues—such as adult retail stores—that cater to a more diverse population. Herbenick and Reece (2006) report that employees of adult retail stores frequently disseminated sexual health information to customers, often with a focus on maximizing pleasure. However, they also answer questions on a range of other topics, including relationships as well as health and safety. Even adult sexual retail stores that have a mission to educate the community are still profit-motivated and, as a result, adult retailers face challenges in their role as providers of adult sexuality education (McCaughey and French 2001; Herbenick and Reece 2006; Black 2012). It is clear that adult retail stores are venues of sexuality education, and it is important to investigate how these organizations actually accomplish sexuality education for adults.

In this paper, I investigate the sex-positive approach to sexuality education at *Good Vibrations* (GV), an adult sexual retail store with eight locations predominately in the San Francisco, California, area and an online presence. Sex-positive approaches focus on sex as a positive component of life, are honest about the positive and negative consequences to sex, aim to remove fear and shame, do not focus solely on reproduction, are inclusive of diverse genders and sexualities, teach competent communication skills such as gaining enthusiastic consent before engaging in sexual activities, and embrace the idea that pleasure for all people—but with special attention to women—is a crucial component to sex and sexuality (Nodulman 2014). GV embodies the philosophy of sex-positive sexuality education in its organizational mission, promotes education and career opportunities for women, promotes sexual diversity, provides sexual health resources, and participates in social activism and community building (Comella 2010). Being in business for nearly 40 years, GV is something of a trendsetter in the community and a pioneer among feminist sex stores. It is also a relevant site to study because the staff includes some of the founders and pioneers of sex-positive sexuality education, such as Carol Queen, an originator of the sex-positive movement in the USA. GV has been recognized as a leader in the adult retail field. In 2015, the company was named Boutique Adult Retailer of the Year by xBiz (an adult industry news publisher) and the Best Place to Shop for Sex Toys by *San Francisco* magazine (*San Francisco* magazine 2015; xBiz 2015).

METHODS

I evaluated the sexuality education provided at GV using observation, interview and textual analysis. I observed four GV stores . . . in one- to two-hour time blocks between June and July of 2011, spending an average of 10 hours in each store and a total of 50 hours in the field. . . . In order to understand how sexuality education was accomplished, I investigated shop design, products, floor plans, product layout, and other nonverbal elements such as color and smells. I also observed employees' and customers' verbal and nonverbal communication. In addition to observing the stores as a participant, I also observed and participated in the GV booth at the Dyke Rally in Dolores Park, the GV Pink Pleasure Party, a tour of the Mission Street store by a GV administrator, and an educational workshop entitled "Strap it to me! with Dr. Carol Queen," held at the Valencia Street store. During the observation of these events, I gathered data on the language the educators used, the materials that were used (videos, handouts, diagrams, etc.), what questions patrons were asked and information about the overall experience.

I also conducted in-depth interviews with three representatives from GV: Charlie Glickman,[1] the Education Program manager; Carol Queen, the Staff Sexologist; and a Sex Educator/Sales Associate (SESA) called Vickie.[2] During my interviews with administrators,

I focused on how they make decisions that affect the company, SESAs and the community. In the interview with an SESA, I inquired about the day-to-day operations of GV and her job as both a sex educator and sales associate. I was not allowed to discuss my role as a researcher when I was observing in the stores (a request Glickman made at the onset of my project to protect the privacy of the customers); therefore, I did not interview any patrons about their experiences at GV.

The last type of data I analyzed was 11 educational brochures about various sexuality and sex-toy topics. These free brochures were placed next to their corresponding products within the stores. Brochure topics were as follows: "Lubricants," "Vibrators," "Silicone & Glass/Cleaning Your Toys," "Prostate," "Anal Sex," "G-Spot," "Condoms," "PC muscle & Kegels/Pumps," "Harnesses/ Dildos," "Cock Rings" and "Bondage & Spanking." They provided quick, key information and were written in a conversational tone.

All research activities were reviewed and approved by the University of New Mexico's institutional review board. Interviewees gave informed consent, and all observations were conducted in public with no identifying information recorded in my field notes. . . .

FINDINGS

Based on an analysis of my observations, interviews and texts from GV, three factors emerged for understanding how sex-positive sexuality education is enacted in this context: communicational, organizational and environmental factors. To inquire more deeply into sex-positive sexuality education as practiced in this particular context, I kept analyzing the data. Categories developed during this subsequent analysis included preparation, instruction, development, encouragement, critique, ensuring and recruitment. Because of the affinity between these activities and the practice of "coaching," I thereafter used a coaching framework to specifically address how GV prepares, instructs, develops, encourages, critiques, ensures and recruits their patrons.[3]

Preparing

Coaches need to be knowledgeable about what they are coaching and have competent strategies to pass to participants. They are also responsible for providing the participant the necessary equipment and . . . [ensuring] the event meets the needs of the participant. This is true of GV as well, whose staff are experts in sexuality education: Charlie Glickman has an interdisciplinary studies doctorate with a focus in adult sexuality education and Carol Queen also has a doctorate with a focus on human sexuality. All GV's SESAs receive extensive training in sexuality education. This sex-positive training enables them to work with customers of varying needs. As SESA Vickie recalled:

At GV, when I first started, my manager would catch me saying terms that even as a gender [studies] student I should know better. Like I was showing someone a toy and I would say, "Oh, this would go into a women's vagina," and she'd be like, "You know what, you need to be careful when you say that because men can have vaginas as well." So, that really stuck out, because that was like my first week. (Vickie, Personal communication, July 2011)

In addition to education that prepares the SESAs to be competent, the variety of products GV retails supports a multitude of customer interests and needs. For example, along with selling female condoms and vegan condoms, the store also sells "snugger fit" and larger condoms. The store's approach also does not assume that all of its customers want the same things. In the brochure on Bondage & Spanking, for example, it is explained that "different desires mean different approaches to bondage" (Bondage and Spanking, n.d.). Furthermore,

GV works from a broad definition of what constitutes pleasure and is prepared for customers to find pleasure in a variety of ways. For example, some customers may find pleasure in reading about sex and sexuality, and therefore the stores carry numerous titles of erotica. Other customers may want to experience the pleasure of relaxing, and various products are available that customers can use alone or with a partner to help relax, such as luxury oils, bath balls, lotions and scented candles. To promote enjoyment and fun, the stores also sell products such as edible body paint, couples' board games, candy bras and G-strings, and even pasta in the shape of penises or breasts.

Stores are also designed to provide customers with a positive experience. City zoning laws often limit sex stores to industrial rather than residential or commercial spaces; therefore, the public often associates sex stores with being in dirty, dark and seedy sections of town (Comella 2010; Riley 2014). GV's locations are just the opposite. The stores are bright, clean and located in the midst of bustling neighborhoods that serve both tourists and locals. All of the stores ensured the privacy of patrons through the use of frosted glass or window coverings or partitions; however, the doors were always propped slightly open. . . . Across all of the stores, the floor plans were open and all of the products and display cases were in pristine condition.

Instructing

Having knowledge and preparing the environment are important to being a good coach, but coaches also need to instruct their participants on an individual and team basis. GV does this instructing in many ways. During Queen's workshop on strap-on/hands-free sex, she was extremely clear in her instruction. Since the class was for beginners interested in this type of activity, she made sure to start off with basic information—explaining what harnesses and dildos are and how they operate. When she described how something works, she made sure to demonstrate it using demo products she pulled from the shelf. When topics arose and she realized she did not have the products handy, she made sure to get relevant products to demonstrate.

Queen's teaching also included referring people to other products that could help them best understand the process. Since GV does not demonstrate live sexual acts within their store, it can be difficult to teach about specific acts without showing the learners how they are done. To remedy this, Queen listed many resources, including DVDs or books, for people to learn more about the topics discussed. Since the presentation lasted only an hour, these resources provided learners with access to trusted sources from which to receive additional instruction.

At certain stores, beneath every product is a business card size "info card." This card details the product title alongside several bullet points explaining the product. Sometimes the cards provide recommendations. For example, on one card, the information encouraged the use of condoms with non-silicone-based toys. The brief instructions are also useful because some customers may have lower literacy skills or may be apprehensive discussing these products with an SESA.

In addition, the staff at GV provides instruction for practitioners and the community, as Glickman explained:

Carol Queen and I do a lot of interviews for things or organizations. For that matter, we are also a resource for anytime or anything people have a question about something. They are welcome to email us, and we get quite a few. Everything from doctors who aren't sure how to answer a question . . . [to] therapists saying, you know, what books are there on this topic? And we do outreach. Our OFSE program, Off-Site Sex Education, that's where we send sex educators to college groups, student groups, nonprofits, a few companies here and there. Last year I think we did almost 100 of those over the course of a year, and that is in addition to the 70 or 80 workshops that happen in our stores. (Glickman, Personal communication, July 2011)

Developing

Another responsibility of a coach is to develop the skills of the individual participant. This may be done through personalized attention. GV does this individual development in many ways. SESA Vickie explained that the most important skills are to be able to listen to a customer and negotiate the customer's individual needs and wants (Personal communication, July 7, 2011). Such practices were observed repeatedly throughout the fieldwork. For example, because some customers may feel intimidated by the variety of lubricants available, when individuals were looking at the lubricants, an SESA might walk over and describe the differences between them and explain why one lubricant might serve their needs better than another.

At times, GV staff appeared to be personal shoppers for patrons, even though SESAs do not work on commission. I commonly observed SESAs working for a half hour to an hour with one customer. During these interactions, the SESA first would find out what the patron was looking for and then provide them with options. However, explaining each option can be a lengthy process. At the Berkeley store, I observed an SESA spend over an hour with one woman interested in buying a vibrator. The SESA explained in great detail what the different vibrators provided and then encouraged the woman to touch each one and get a sense for what she liked best. Once the woman had narrowed her selection down, she continued to ask the SESA more questions about vibrator use until she made her final choice.

In order to develop the individual customer's knowledge and skills, GV encourages its customers to experiment with products in the store and at home. Having a demo version or tester of most every product allows SESAs to work with customers to find the best option. In addition, GV also provides opportunities for personal experimentation. Glickman explained on a tour of the Mission Street store that GV makes a conscious decision to sell products that are inexpensive, single size or "loose" to encourage such experimentation. For example, single-use packets of lubricants, individually wrapped condoms and $10 vibrators are sold to enable customers to find a product that works best for them. Glickman said that these opportunities for experimentation are "similar to the philosophy behind a wine tasting"—a person needs to try something first to be able to determine whether it is a good match to their palate (Author's notes, July 2011).

In sum, development of a customer's knowledge and skills is not an isolated event; rather, it is seen as a mission.

I will say, one of my most favorite customers ever . . . was in her fifties and she had just gotten divorced. And for the first time in her life she was exploring what she wanted to do. She was coming to every single workshop, and for about six months she was like a kid in a candy store. And every time she would see me she would come up and tell me about this new thing that she had just done. And one of the things that I like most about working here is knowing that she is out there, and other people are out there somewhere having a happier sex life because of what we do. And if somebody is not getting that, we want to do what we can to help them find what that means. (Glickman, Personal communication, July 2011)

Encouraging

Competent coaches teach their participants skills but must also find ways to motivate and reassure them. GV uses a variety of methods of encouragement. The staff at GV encourages customers by putting them at ease. As Glickman explained:

What we do is let folks know, yeah, alright, let me give you the information that you need. And I will make whatever level of eye contact you are comfortable with, and I will share this information with you. And I will show you that I don't think there is anything wrong with it. I don't think this [way of communicating] is something you can learn from like a website or book. It is something that happens in relation to someone else, and we put a lot of energy into our relationships with our customers. (Glickman, Personal communication, July 2011)

After initially greeting a customer, an SESA usually would follow up with the person in an encouraging manner in order to break the ice. For example, at the Polk Street store, when one customer was looking at vibrators, an SESA came up to her and said, "That is a really great product. Let me know if you have any questions, okay?" (Author's notes, June 2011). The SESA broke the ice by reassuring the customer that the product she was looking at was a good choice, and also provided a nonthreatening way for the customer to follow up with her that came across as just a friendly conversation. I often observed SESAs explaining the benefits of products. On another occasion, at the Polk Street store, I observed an SESA asking a customer who was looking at cock rings if she had ever tried one. The SESA explained to her how "awesome" they were and how they can provide an amazing sensation for both men and women (Author's notes, July 2011).

In addition to verbal encouragement, a variety of nonverbal techniques are used by GV to motivate and encourage customers to feel comfortable. Each store plays upbeat pop or light rock music from artists such as Britney Spears, Lenny Kravitz, the Scissor Sisters and Ke$ha. The songs were played at a comfortable volume so as not to distract customers, but keep a lively feeling in the store. There are also store displays to encourage customers to feel at ease in the store. One of the promotions happening during my visit was "water fun." In line with this promotion, the Berkeley store had a red betta fish swimming in a fish bowl with blue gravel on a table next to blue vibrators, lubricants with blue labels and GV shot glasses with blue ribbons in them as a decoration. . . . SESAs' clothing also aims to give an uplifting impression. The SESAs generally dress in a casual style that may include unique and funky accents. . . .

Critiquing

In order for participants to improve or master certain skills, coaches must critique and evaluate the participants. GV, while being very welcoming, is not afraid to criticize stereotypes and reprimand customers who may not be upholding the spirit of the store.

Glickman, during the tour of the Mission Street store, was a harsh critic of using pornography to judge one's sexual ability or performance. He discussed how oftentimes people who have viewed pornography mistakenly believe that anal sex should be easy. However, once they try it themselves they are upset because they encounter difficulties. Glickman explained that in reality, anal sex takes a lot of time and practice in order to ease physical and emotional tension. He explained that the performers in pornography are professionals who have used lubricants and "warmed up." However, these actions are edited out of the film and/or are done offscreen (Author's notes, July 2011). Although GV sells numerous titles of pornography, Glickman went out of his way to explain that pornography is not real sex and should not be treated as such.

It is also important to critique some commonly held myths their customers have. Carol Queen explained in her workshop that anal sex is often mistakenly stereotyped as a sexual act only between gay men. In reality, research shows that heterosexual women constitute the largest percentage of people to engage in anal sex. According to Glickman, it is also common for men with women sexual partners

to be hesitant to use lubricants because men feel inadequate sexually if they cannot arouse a woman. Thus, some men believe a woman's lack of arousal is a reflection of how good of a sex partner they are or is an indictment of their masculinity. Glickman explained that GV staff tell customers that this is a myth, and that a variety of factors, including medications, cigarette or marijuana smoking, birth control, post-childbirth and menopause, can impact women's arousal.

I observed many instances where SESAs approached customers and asked them to not play inappropriately with products. In one instance, an SESA asked a young man to put his shirt back on because they try to "de-sexualize" the store (Author's notes, June 2011). A sign posted in front of the spankers and floggers in the Mission Street store read, "Spanking! We love it, but for the safety and consideration of our customers we ask that you refrain from doing it in the store" (Author's notes, July 2011). Glickman explained how SESAs work actively to maintain a positive but professional environment:

If some customers are getting a little rowdy or raucous, which does happen sometimes . . . we will go up to them and say, "Look, we are glad you are here. We are glad you are having a great time, and we need you to tone it down because it is making other people uncomfortable." (Glickman, Personal communication, July 2011)

Ensuring

Coaches help to ensure a participant's health and wellness by informing of any risks, discussing safety measures and promoting healthy behaviors. Based on my observations and fieldwork, GV appears to take this responsibility seriously. Shops ensure their customers understand the risks that can be associated with sex and inform them about how to be healthy and safe. Throughout Queen's "Strap It to Me" presentation, for example, it was repeated several times that dildos and harnesses must be cleaned. She also encouraged learners to put dildos in the dishwasher as a way to keep them clean[4] and stressed that harness activity should not hurt unless that is something more advanced users are aiming for. Similarly, every brochure discusses some aspect of health and safety. For example, in the Vibrators brochure, there is a section entitled "Care & Cleaning." Along with cleaning reminders, it also tells the reader to "never insert any object into the anus if it doesn't have a base. It may slip all the way inside, requiring a trip to the emergency room" (Vibrators, n.d.).

Ensuring the health and wellness of patrons was also witnessed in the products sold. In addition to selling dozens of different types of male condoms, stores also sell female condoms. GV also sells less mainstream safer sex materials such as finger cots, dental dams and gloves. Along with safer sex materials, the stores also sell numerous books that promote health, wellness and safety. Some of the titles of the books I observed included *Our Bodies, Ourselves* by the Boston Women's Health Collective, *Talking to Your Kids about Sex* by Laura Berman, *Anal Pleasure and Health* by Jack Morin and *The Ultimate Guide to Sex and Disability* by Miriam Kaufman, Cory Silverberg and Fran Odette.

Recruiting

In a sports context, participants often search out a program that fits their interests, but many times coaches need to recruit participants. Coaches often use a variety of methods to advertise and build their brand with potential participants. Similarly, although many customers seek out GV, they also utilize recruitment strategies. One way in which GV recruits potential customers is by hosting events that incorporate or appeal to the community. The Dyke March during Pride Week passes along Valencia Street, right in front of the Valencia Street GV store. The shop celebrates this fact by hosting a

party within their store for marchers and rally-goers to celebrate Pride. When I got to the party, many people were standing outside the shop laughing, dancing and taking photos. Two young women, wearing pasties (stickers that cover the nipples), lingerie, high heels and stylish hair and make-up, took turns dancing in the store's one display window with a sign that read "Photos for Tips." People were stopping in front to take photos with them, without always tipping, or dancing alongside them. Some people would go into the store and place dollar bills into the dancers' garters (Author's notes, June 2011). The laughter, loudness of the music and overall party atmosphere could be heard outside of the store and helped to welcome and encourage other people to come inside. As I exited the store, night had fallen. However, the streets were still crowded with people milling about and partying, and GV remained crowded as well (Author's notes, June 2011).

GV also recruits new customers by serving as a resource for local organizations. During my visit, the back room of the Polk Street store was being used as a gallery for an art exhibit of work by the noted erotic photographer Phyllis Christopher. According to Glickman:

We also host events for other [non–*Good Vibrations*] groups. There was one organization, an organization that teaches people about bicycle safety. And so we let them use our room. 'Cause we weren't using it, so come on in and bring your folks in, and no problem. (Glickman, Personal communication, July 2011)

GV also recruits through their large online presence. Much time is spent maintaining and updating the company's Facebook and Twitter accounts. Through these social media accounts, GV advertises special promotions, provides links to articles about sex and sexuality from a variety of sources, including nonprofit and government agencies, and distributes information about community and cultural events. The store's social media presence serves to remind existing customers about the store and entice them to visit. It also serves to promote the store to potential new customers. Through the use of social media, people can see when their Facebook friends "Like" a GV post or re-tweet a GV message.

In addition to a social media presence that serves to brand the store and promote it to potential customers, GV also sells branded merchandise. Participants on sports teams often wear "gear" from their team or collect memorabilia. GV also provides customers with that option. Merchandise includes shot glasses, coffee mugs, stickers and sweatshirts that have the GV logo on them and read, "Creating a Buzz since 1977" (Author's notes, July 2011).

DISCUSSION AND CONCLUSIONS

Previous research and commentary (Reece, Herbenick, and Sherwood-Puzzello 2004; Herbenick and Reece 2006; Black 2012) indicate that adult sexual retail stores are a place for adults to receive much-needed sexuality education. However, to date, besides Comella's (2010) ethnographic analysis of the environment of feminist sex stores, no other research using qualitative ethnographic methods has examined how adult sexual retail stores educate adults about sex. In this paper, I describe how GV—a pioneer in the field of sex-positive sexuality education—uses a coaching framework to transmit sex-positive sexuality education in the retail environment.

The coaching framework used by GV starts with an educated staff who instructs customers and develops their skills, encourages and critiques customers when necessary, ensures customer safety by discussing health and wellness and recruits new participants. This framework carries useful implications for those interested in sexuality education. First, a coaching framework implies a shared responsibility in the process of sexuality education. Coaches have responsibilities to their participants. GV does

many things to make itself an inviting place for customers to learn about sex and purchase products. However, in a coaching framework, an individual's achievement is ultimately left up to the participant. GV can instruct and develop a customer's knowledge about sex, but it is up to the customer to choose to act upon this knowledge. This shared responsibility between coach and participant balances a tension in sexuality education—that people want to know more about sex (Hilton 2007; Fields 2008), but that they are also agentic individuals who can make decisions about sex for themselves (Fine and McClelland 2006; Tolman 2012; Niccolini 2013).

A coaching framework implies that sexuality education should be inclusive and accessible. Coaches work with participants of varying skill levels, and they help all participants, from novice to advanced, succeed. GV seeks to be inclusive and accessible by withholding assumptions and letting customers lead the conversation. Furthermore, coaches realize that participants will have different goals. While one participant may just hope to learn specific techniques to better her skill for participation in a sport for hobby, others may be hoping to specialize in something specific. Using a coaching framework, GV does not privilege particular experiences, acts or sexualities and thus lets everyone become a player.

A coaching framework also stresses the importance of communication. The importance of good communication skills as part of high-quality sexuality education cannot be underestimated (Fisher et al. 2010; Noland 2010; Thomas, Hess, and Thurston 2015). The coaching functions that GV performs, such as encouraging or critiquing their customers, cannot be accomplished without competent communication skills.

Finally, a coaching framework implies that people participate in activities in order to gain positive and exciting experiences whereby they can better themselves and receive pleasure from participation.[5] GV plays upbeat music to their customers to feel good in the stores and sells tester-size products so customers can experiment with what product feels the best to them.

In the past, much sexuality education has downplayed the importance of pleasure. More recently, pleasure has been conflated with risk, excess or danger (Fine and McClelland 2006; Lamb, Lustig, and Graling 2013). As Hirst (2013) discusses, pleasure and positivity within sexuality education are crucial to "improving sexual health, rights, and equality" (432). A coaching framework can provide an opportunity for individuals to experience satisfaction and pleasure through sexuality education.

In sum, a coaching framework provides a way to fill the gaps in teaching sexuality education. It promotes shared responsibility between learner and teacher; enacts sexuality education that is inclusive, accessible and tailored; highlights communication skills; and honors the importance of pleasure and positivity. The coaching framework described here contributes to the evidence concerning how adult sexual retail stores can disseminate sex-positive sexuality education. The principles involved are something that other sex educators can emulate as well. . . .

NOTES

1. Glickman left GV in 2013.

2. Vickie requested that I use her real name.

3. This coaching framework should not be confused with sex coaching, which is performed in private and includes touching and homework. That said, sex coaching is a client-centered sex-positive approach to educating people of all genders and sexual identities and therefore does share some of the same characteristics of the work done at GV (Britton and Bright 2014).

4. Recent research (Anderson et al. 2014) suggests STIs may still be transmitted via sex toys even after standard cleaning procedures. As my data were collected in 2011, I am not aware of whether GV has updated the information provided to patrons.

5. Certainly, there are instances when people are coerced into, or are not interested in participating in, a particular activity. Just as there is no excuse for sexual coercion, I base my coaching framework on the assumption that parties fully and enthusiastically consent to participate.

REFERENCES

Adams, M. S., J. Oye, and T. S. Parker. 2003. "Sexuality of Older Adults and the Internet: From Sex Education to Cybersex." *Sexual and Relationship Therapy* 18 (3): 405–15.

Anderson, T. A., V. Schick, D. Herbenick, B. Dodge, and J. D. Fortenberry. 2014. "A Study of Human Papillomavirus on Vaginally Inserted Sex Toys, before and after Cleaning, among Women Who Have Sex with Women and Men." *Sexually Transmitted Infections* 90 (7): 529–31.

Bahouq, H., F. Allali, H. Rkain, and N. Hajjaj-Hassouni. 2013. "Discussing Sexual Concerns with Chronic Low Back Pain Patients: Barriers and Patients' Expectations." *Clinical Rheumatology* 32 (10): 1487–92.

Black, M. 2012. "Letter to the Editor: Bridging Sex Education and Adult Retail." *American Journal of Sexuality Education* 7 (4): 480–82.

Bondage & Spanking. n.d. *Brochure*. San Francisco, CA: Good Vibrations.

Brandenburg, U., and J. Bitzer. 2009. "The Challenge of Talking about Sex: The Importance of Patient–Physician Interaction." *Maturitas* 63 (2): 124–27.

Britton, P., and S. R. Bright. 2014. "'Extraordinary' Sex Coaching: An Inside Look." *Sexual and Relationship Therapy* 29 (1): 98–108.

CDC (Centers for Disease Control and Prevention). 2014. *Sexually Transmitted Disease Surveillance 2013*. Atlanta, GA: US Department of Health and Human Services.

CDC (Centers for Disease Control and Prevention). 2015. "HIV Surveillance Report 2014." http://www.cdc.gov/hiv/library/reports/surveillance/.

Charmaz, K. 2006. *Constructing Grounded Theory: A Practical Guide through Qualitative Analysis*. London: Sage.

Comella, L. 2010. "Repackaging Sex: Class, Crass, and the Good Vibrations Model of Sexual Retail." In *New Sociologies of Sex Work*, edited by Kate Hardy, S. Kingston, and T. Sanders, 213–26. Farnham: Ashgate.

Dyer, K., and R. das Nair. 2014. "Talking about Sex after Traumatic Brain Injury: Perceptions and Experiences of Multidisciplinary Rehabilitation Professionals." *Disability and Rehabilitation* 36 (17): 1431–38.

Eisenberg, M., K. Lechner, E. Frerich, K. Lust, and C. Garcia. 2012. "Characterizing Sexual Health Resources on College Campuses." *Journal of Community Health* 37 (5): 940–48.

Ferrara, E., M. P. Pugnaire, J. A. Jonassen, K. O'Dell, M. Clay, D. Hatem, and M. Carlin. 2003. "Sexual Health

Innovations in Undergraduate Medical Education." *International Journal of Impotence Research* 15 (S5): S46–S50.

Fields, J. 2008. *Risky Lessons: Sex Education and Social Inequality*. New Brunswick, NJ: Rutgers University Press.

Fine, M., and S. McClelland. 2006. "Sexuality Education and Desire: Still missing after All These Years." *Harvard Educational Review* 76 (3): 297–338.

Fisher, C., D. Herbenick, M. Reece, B. Dodge, S. Satinsky, and D. Fischtein. 2010. "Exploring Sexuality Education Opportunities at In-home Sex-toy Parties in the United States." *Sex Education* 10 (2): 131–44.

Golin, C. E., R. A. Davis, S. M. Przybyla, B. Fowler, S. Parker, J. Earp, B. E. Quinlivan, S. C. Kalichman, S. N. Patel, and C. A. Grodensky. 2010. "SafeTalk, a Multicomponent, Motivational Interviewing-based, Safer Sex Counseling Program for People Living with HIV/AIDS: A Qualitative Assessment of Patients' Views." *AIDS Patient Care and STDs* 24 (4): 237–45.

Herbenick, D., and M. Reece. 2006. "Sex Education in Adult Retail Stores: Positioning Consumers' Questions as Teachable Moments." *American Journal of Sexuality Education* 2 (1): 57–75.

Herbenick, D., and M. Reece. 2009. "In-home Sex Toy Party Facilitators as Sex Educators: What Questions Are They Asked and What Makes Them More 'Askable'?" *American Journal of Sexuality Education* 4 (2): 178–93.

Hilton, G. L. S. 2007. "Listening to the Boys Again: An Exploration of What Boys Want to Learn in Sex Education Classes and How They Want to Be Taught." *Sex Education* 7 (2): 161–74.

Hirst, J. 2013. "'It's Got to Be about Enjoying Yourself': Young People, Sexual Pleasure, and Sex and Relationships Education." *Sex Education* 13 (4): 423–36.

Jayasuriya, A. N., and R. Dennick. 2011. "Sexual History-taking: Using Educational Interventions to Overcome Barriers to Learning." *Sex Education* 11 (1): 99–112.

Jeffers, L. A., and M. C. DiBartolo. 2011. "Raising Health Care Provider Awareness of Sexually Transmitted Disease in Patients over Age 50." *MEDSURG Nursing* 20 (6): 285–90.

Lamb, S., K. Lustig, and K. Graling. 2013. "The Use and Misuse of Pleasure in Sex Education Curricula." *Sex Education* 13 (3): 305–18.

Lindau, S. T., P. L. Schumm, E. O. Laumann, W. Levinson, C. A. O'Muircheartaigh, and L. J. Waite. 2007. "A Study of Sexuality and Health among Older Adults in the United States." *New England Journal of Medicine* 357 (8): 762–74.

Macdowall, W., R. Parker, K. Nanchahal, C. Ford, R. Lowbury, A. Robinson, J. Sherrard, H. Martins, N. Fasey, and K. Wellings. 2010. "'Talking of Sex': Developing and

Piloting a Sexual Health Communication Tool for Use in Primary Care." *Patient Education and Counseling* 81 (3): 332–37. doi:10.1016/j. pec.2010.10.027.

McCaughey, M., and C. French. 2001. "Women's Sex-toy Parties: Technology, Orgasm, and Commodification." *Sexuality and Culture* 5 (3): 77–96.

National Campaign to Prevent Teen and Unplanned Pregnancy. 2008. "Fast Facts: The Consequences of Unplanned Pregnancy." http://www.thenationalcampaign .org/resources/pdf/fast-facts-consequences-of-unplanned -pregnancy.pdf.

Niccolini, A. D. 2013. "Straight Talk and Thick Desire in Erotica Noir: Reworking the Textures of Sex Education in and out of the Classroom." *Sex Education* 13 (S1): S7–S19.

Nodulman, J. A. 2014. "Communicating Sex-positive Sexuality Education: Benefits and Strategies of an Emerging Approach." In *Applications in Health Communication: Emerging Trends*, edited by Michael Eaves, 341–59. Dubuque, IA: Kendall Hunt.

Noland, C. M. 2010. *Sex Talk: The Role of Communication in Intimate Relationships*. Santa Barbara, CA: Praeger.

Paiva, V. 2005. "Analysing Sexual Experiences through 'Scenes': A Framework for the Evaluation of Sexuality Education." *Sex Education* 5 (4): 345–58.

Penna, S., and K. Sheehy. 2000. "Sex Education and Schizophrenia: Should Occupational Therapists Offer Sex Education to People with Schizophrenia?" *Scandinavian Journal of Occupational Therapy* 7 (3): 126–31.

Reece, M., D. Herbenick, and C. Sherwood-Puzzello. 2004. "Sexual Health Promotion and Adult Retail Stores." *Journal of Sex Research* 41 (2): 173–80.

Riley, H. 2014. "Zoning Regulations Cock Block Sex Shops." *Santa Fe Reporter*. Accessed June 3. http:// www.sfreporter .com/santafe/article-8741-zoning-regulations-cock-block -sex-shops.html.

San Francisco magazine. 2015. "The Best Places to Shop in SF in 2015." *San Francisco* magazine. Accessed June 19. http://www.modernluxury.com/san-francisco/story /the-best-places-shop-sf-2015.

Schick, V., D. Herbenick, K. N. Jozkowski, S. Jawed-Wessel, and M. Reece. 2013. "The Sexual Consumer: Characteristics, Expectations, and Experiences of Women Attending In-home Sex Toy Parties." *Journal of Sex & Marital Therapy* 39 (2): 160–75.

Sexuality Information and Education Council of the United States. 2015. "Sexuality Education Q & A." http://www.siecus.org/index.cfm?fuseaction=page.viewpage &pageid=521&grandparentID=477&parentID=514.

Sobecki, J. N., F. A. Curlin, K. A. Rasinski, and S. T. Lindau. 2012. "What We Don't Talk about When We Don't Talk about Sex: Results of a National Survey of U.S.

Obstetrician/Gynecologists." *Journal of Sexual Medicine* 9 (5): 1285–94.

Storr, M. 2003. *Latex and Lingerie: Shopping for Pleasure at Ann Summers Parties*. Oxford: Berg.

Thomas, H. N., R. Hess, and R. C. Thurston. 2015. "Correlates of Sexual Activity and Satisfaction in Midlife and Older Women." *Annals of Family Medicine* 13 (4): 336–42.

Tolman, D. L. 2012. "Female Adolescents, Sexual Empowerment and Desire: A Missing Discourse of Gender Inequity." *Sex Roles* 66 (11/12): 746–57.

Ussher, J. M., J. Perz, E. Gilbert, W. K. T. Wong, C. Mason, K. Hobbs, and L. Kirsten. 2013. "Talking about Sex after Cancer: A Discourse Analytic Study of Health Care Professional Accounts of Sexual Communication with Patients." *Psychology and Health* 28 (12): 1370–90.

Vibrators. n.d. *Brochure*. San Francisco, CA: Good Vibrations.

xBiz. 2015. "Award Winners." http://xbizawards.xbiz.com /winners.php.

5

SEXUAL BODIES

AN INTERVIEW WITH

LEONORE TIEFER

Leonore Tiefer, PhD, is an independent scholar, sex researcher, therapist, author, and critic. Dr. Tiefer has become internationally known as the primary spokesperson for a movement that challenges the medicalization of women's sexual problems by the pharmaceutical industry (for more information, see www.newviewcampaign .org). Dr. Tiefer organized the 2016 Feminist Scholar Activism and the New View Campaign conference and made a video about the conference and the campaign. Dr. Tiefer gave the inaugural Masters and Johnson lecture at Washington University in St. Louis in November 2017. Both the Society for the Scientific Study of Sexuality and the Association for Women in Psychology selected her for their Distinguished Career awards in 2004.

What led you to begin studying sexuality?

I see sexuality as one of the most interesting and complex topics in all of academia. In the 1960s I majored in psychology, and in psychology grad school (UC Berkeley), I was at first attracted to the subject of learning and conditioning. But after two years of research on learning in rats I felt bored, and I became more interested in physiological psychology—the study of the biological bases of behavior. Frank Beach had a very active research group studying mating behavior in rodents and dogs, and although at that time (he changed later) he wouldn't fund women grad students to work in his lab, he allowed us to do experiments and participate in seminars. I studied hamster sexuality for my dissertation and then directed an animal lab for seven years in my first academic job. *But*, and this is a big but, I began to question the value of animal research on sexuality when the women's liberation movement (now called "second wave") hit me in the 1970s. After a sabbatical working with human sexuality issues, I decided I was really interested in sexuality, but that I wasn't suited to animal work and I doubted its ultimate significance. I re-specialized as a clinical psychologist specializing in sexuality. I also studied the new work in sexuality emerging from women's and gay and lesbian studies. Feminist politics combined with my biological and psychological background provided a well-rounded view of sexuality.

How do people react when you tell them you study sexuality?

Usually they express political opinions first (about abortion or porn or sex ed), and ask personal questions about their own sexual life second. I have learned that no matter how strong the opinions, most people feel undereducated when it comes to sexuality and appreciate the opportunity to talk with an "expert." Ironically, however, my "expert" opinion is that sexuality is complicated and my answers to their questions usually involve more variables than they had anticipated.

Which of your projects have you found most interesting? Why?

I had the opportunity to participate in a monthly New York intellectual seminar on sexuality that lasted 11 years (1982–1993). Participants were journalists, writers, political activists, and a wide range of humanities professors. I was the only "official" sex expert. Members presented papers on topics ranging from gays in World War II to Picasso's sojourn in Barcelona to histories of food to "dirty" postcards. You cover a lot of ground in 11 years! The seminar always focused on how these various cultural events arose from and affected sexuality. The seminar completely changed my idea of what kind of thing sexuality was—from a biopsychological aspect of individual experience to a socially constructed ever-changing sociocultural phenomenon. This consciousness-changing occurred slowly. Standards of evidence were completely different than in my psychological training and the topics taxed my general knowledge base (World War II? Barcelona?). But when, slowly and gradually, I finally got it that sex was constructed differently within groups, generations, genders, religions, and regions, my eyes were permanently opened in a way few conventionally trained sexologists can understand.

What ethical dilemmas have you faced studying sexuality?

I became an activist against the medicalization of sexuality after Viagra was approved in 1998. I saw corporations taking advantage of people's lack of education about sexuality to promote drugs with marginal benefits and various dangers. It made me angry to see few other sexologists resisting the financial opportunities and propaganda of the pharmaceutical industry, but I have found many allies in public health, women's health, investigative journalism, and health reform. My ethical dilemma has occurred because throughout my years of activism, I have continued my clinical private practice doing sex therapy. People come to me for help with their personal sexual problems and I have to put their concerns and perspectives first, and refrain from lecturing or moralizing about the things that are on my mind. On occasion I even recommend that someone try one of the new sex drugs because in his or her individual case they might be helpful, even though I believe that for society at large they are the very opposite. Even when I think a person's problem has been caused by all the exaggerated public relations claims about the new drugs, I don't ever say, "I told you so." That's not my role as a clinical psychologist.

What do you think is most challenging about studying sexuality?

The subject is very complicated, and many professionals and academics are unwilling to read widely outside their primary field. I think to be a good sexologist you have to be somewhat well versed in psychology, physiology, sociology, anthropology, history, law, religion, media studies, and gender studies.

Why is it important to do sex research?

It's important to do good sex research, but it's a waste of time to do foolish or trivial sex research. Good-quality research—qualitative research, especially—can help shed light on topics many areas of society want to be hidden in darkness. Ignorant people can be shamed, guilt-tripped, and manipulated, and they raise ignorant children. Our media-saturated world requires an informed public, and good sex research is part of the information base essential in modern culture. For example, many states in the United States now have grossly uninformed laws about the dangers of "sex offenders" and are punishing people far too harshly for minor offenses. Ambitious politicians manipulate an ignorant public. The same thing happens with sex education or new contraceptive methods. The public is easily scared into taking a repressive position because they are uninformed. Movies and TV (and drug ads) promote ecstatic sex, but the public lacks the knowledge to assess these images. Good sex research will narrow the gap.

If you could teach people one thing about sexuality, what would it be?

As the title of my book says, I believe that "Sex Is Not a Natural Act." At least in the twenty-first century it's not. Everything about sex is the result of cultural influences and totally saturated with cultural meaning. Madison Avenue has hyped the pleasures and right-wing values have hyped the dangers—and, oddly, both insist that sex is a "natural" result of evolution (or God)—and that learning, practice, reading, reflection, conversation, and research are unnecessary. I believe just the opposite.

Is there anything else you'd like to add?

Every college and university should have a department of sexuality studies. At the present time it is impossible to get the kind of multidisciplinary education I think every sexologist needs. You have to do it all on your own. As a consequence, few sexologists are well trained. Such departments would employ sexuality scholars who would generate interesting new theory and research. I wish I could be in such a department.

THE G-SPOT AND OTHER MYSTERIES

ELISABETH O. BURGESS AND AMY PALDER

Is there a G-spot? One common question about female sexuality is whether there is a localized place in the vagina, often referred to as the G-spot, which causes especially pleasurable sensations when stimulated. The G-spot, or Grafenburg spot, was named for Dr. Ernst Grafenburg, a German gynecologist who first described this spot in 1950. Although Grafenburg often is credited with discovering this spot, descriptions of sensitivity in a specific area of the vagina can be found across cultures and historical periods (Sevely and Bennett, 1978; Ladas, Whipple, and Perry, 1982). Yet, contemporary sexologists disagree about the significance of the G-spot and its prevalence in the female population. Those in support of the G-spot claim that it is either a bundle of nerves, possibly representing the root of the clitoris, or a gland, or series of glands, that produces lubrication. More recently, Ostrzenski and colleagues have identified a complex neurovascular structure on the anterior wall of the vaginas of cadavers. They believe that this verifies the existence of the G-spot (Ostrzenski, 2012; Ostrzenski et al., 2014). Those who believe the G-spot is a myth argue that there is no anatomical evidence that it exists (Kilchevsky, Vardi, Lowenstein, and Gruenwald, 2012; Pan, Leung, Shah and Kichevsky, 2015) and dispute Ostrzenski's research (Puppo, 2014).

Over the past few decades, the G-spot has gained widespread acceptance by the mass media. Numerous articles on sexual pleasure in the popular press, self-help literature, and on the Internet describe the G-spot and provide instructions on using it for sexual pleasure (for instance, Cass, 2007; Hicks, 2006; Miller, 2016; Paget, 2004; Solot and Miller, 2007; Sundahl, Ladas, and Sprinkle, 2003; and Winks, 1998). New media provide an infinite array of good and bad information about sexual health and often focus on locating the G-spot to enhance sexual pleasure. Ladas, Whipple, and Perry (1982) argue that the G-spot feels like a spongy mass, about the size of a quarter and the shape of a bean, and can be found about halfway up the anterior (or belly) side of the vagina. The mass becomes more rigid or identifiable when a woman is sexually aroused (Perry and Whipple, 1981; Zaviacic, Zaviacicova, Holoman and Molcan, 1988; Zaviacic and Whipple, 1993). According to self-reports, the G-spot produces "full body" orgasms and orgasms that are "more intense" than other female orgasms (Davidson, Darling, and Conway-Welch, 1989; Ladas et al., 1982; Perry and Whipple, 1981). Ladas et al. (1982) report that in a study supervised by Perry and Whipple, a medical professional was able to locate a G-spot in each of over 400 female volunteers (p. 43). Because Ladas et al. found that all women in their study had G-spots, they explain that women who have not been able to locate their G-spot are either not sufficiently aroused or not using the proper technique to locate it.

Yet, while many women believe the G-spot exists, not all women have heard about the G-spot and many women have not found their own G-spot. A survey of over 1,000 women found that although 85.3 percent of the women surveyed believed that a sensitive area existed in the vagina, only 65.9 percent reported having such an area (Davidson et al., 1989). This survey also found that angle of vaginal entry, position of vaginal intercourse, and a woman's degree of emotional involvement with her partner affected her ability to orgasm from being stimulated in this area. Because traditional sexual positions such as the "missionary position" fail to stimulate the anterior wall of the vagina, women who explore other sexual practices such as manual stimulation from a partner or vibrator may be more likely to discover a G-spot (Ladas et al., 1982).

In contrast, some researchers strongly dispute the existence of the G-spot. Alzate and colleagues (Alzate and Hoch, 1986; Alzate, 1985) argue that the walls of the vagina are sensitive to touch, but there is no specific area in the vagina that produces orgasm. These authors also argue that there is no anatomical evidence of a G-spot and critique previous research for using small clinical samples and anecdotal evidence. In recent reviews of the literature on the G-spot, Hines (2001) and Kilchevsky and colleagues (2012) call it a myth and argue that despite widespread acceptance, there is little scientific evidence to support its existence. Other prominent sex researchers, including Masters and Johnson, do not discuss the G-spot or an especially sensitive area in the vagina but instead focus on the clitoris as the locus of female orgasms (Masters and Johnson, 1966). Others suggest that the focus on a G-spot or vaginal orgasm sets women up for sexual frustration (Hines, 2001; Jannini et al., 2010; Kilchevsky et al., 2012; Puppo and Gruenwald, 2012).

Some feminist sex researchers also dispute the existence of the G-spot, but for different reasons. These scholars fear that the "discovery of the G-spot" and subsequent emphasis on vaginal orgasms support Freudian notions about the female orgasm and privilege heterosexual male-centered models of sexuality. These authors emphasize the clitoris as the primary location of the female orgasm and sexual empowerment for women (Ehrenreich, Hess,

and Jacobs, 1987; Gerhard, 2004). Other feminist researchers believe that, because of cultural preferences about (hetero) sexual behavior, many women prefer to view the vagina as an important location of orgasmic response. These scholars recognize that orgasm is not merely a physiological response but is also an emotional and psychological response to sexual stimuli and, as such, orgasms centered in the vagina should not be ignored (Hite, 1976; Schneider and Gould, 1987). However, if such a spot does exist, even supporters such as Ladas (2001) argue that it is harmful to think of the G-spot as the holy grail of female sexuality. In a critical review of the discourse of female orgasm, Tuana (2004) argues that this false dichotomy of clitoral and vaginal orgasm ignores the perspective that the majority of the clitoris is internal (see also Moore and Clarke, 1995; O'Connell, Sanjeevan, and Hutson, 2005). Moreover, Tuana finds that some models of female anatomy that do include the G-spot ignore the feminist argument for a perineal sponge which is located between the posterior wall of the vagina and the rectum and also can become engorged during sexual stimulation.

Recent medicalization of women's sexual health has led to cluster of procedures loosely referred to as female genital cosmetic surgery (FGCS). The latest procedure, G-spot amplification or G-shot, is designed to expand the size of the G-spot by injecting it with a collagen-based filler with the intent of increasing sexual pleasure. There is no scientific evidence that FGCS improves sexual function (Barbara, Facchin, Meschia, and Vercellini, 2015), and Puppo (2014) argues that the focus on proving the existence of the G-spot only promotes industries such as G-spot amplification. Puppo and Gruenwald (2012) go even further, arguing that these "procedures have been quickly and unprofessionally introduced" and "are widely performed without monitoring or control" (p. 1668).

In sum, regardless of the politics of measuring and defining female genitalia, the female body contains many potential erogenous zones. Whether individuals find stimulation of these locations pleasurable depends on the social context, the expertise of their partner, and personal preference. Women (and men) should continue to seek out reliable information to understand their sexual bodies. One interesting new development doing just that is the subscription website OMGYES (www.omgyes.com), which provides research-based information about sexual health through videos and how-to guides for individuals and couples.

Do women ejaculate? Another common debate about the sexual body is whether women ejaculate. For centuries, erotic literature and sex research have alluded to the elusive female orgasm that results in a squirt of liquid from the woman (Belzer, 1981; Korda, Goldsein, and Sommer, 2010). Contemporary researchers disagree as to where it comes from, what it is, and whether it is something that all women are capable of releasing.

Most often associated with G-spot stimulation, female ejaculation is the release of fluid through the urethra at the climax of an orgasm. One common concern about female ejaculation is whether the fluid is urine, a result of incontinence, or whether it is similar to male ejaculate. Self-reports indicate that this fluid is different from urine in smell, consistency, and color (Davidson et al., 1989; Belzer, 1981; Taormini, 2000). Chemical analyses of female ejaculate have been less conclusive. While Goldberg et al. (1983) found the expelled fluid to be chemically similar to urine, numerous other clinical studies argue that the consistency of this fluid is significantly different from urine (Addiego, Belzer, Moger, Perry, and Whipple, 1981; Belzer, Whipple, and Moger, 1984; Wimpissinger, Stifter, Grin, and Stackl, 2007; Zaviacic et al., 1988). Additionally, a recent study concluded that women who reported experiencing female ejaculation are not more likely to experience urinary problems than women who do not report ejaculation (Cartwright, Elvy, and Cardozo, 2007). One reason for the confusion is that the ejaculate may be from different sources. In a review of the literature, Pastor (2013) found that women may expel several kinds of fluids during sexual stimulation, including vaginal fluids, female ejaculate, and urine, or a combination of these fluids. Regardless of these findings, without larger samples of ejaculate, it would be difficult to reach any definitive conclusions.

A related controversy associated with female ejaculation concerns the source of the fluid. The most common theory is that the Skene's glands (also known as the female prostate), which surround the urethra, secrete fluid into the urethra that is then ejaculated upon orgasm. Researchers who support this theory argue that female ejaculate may have a different consistency, at different times, for different women. In addition, reported rates of ejaculation among women vary from 10 to over 50 percent (Ladas et al., 1983; Bullough, David, Whipple, Dixon, Allgeier, Rice, and Drury, 1984). Only a few women report ejaculating fluid with every orgasm. Although manipulation of the G-spot is not required to produce female ejaculation, women who experience pleasure or orgasms through stimulation of the G-spot are more likely to report experiencing ejaculation (Davidson et al., 1989). Either way, by focusing solely on chemical components of the fluid, researchers are ignoring the role this event plays in sexual satisfaction.

Female ejaculation also has become the subject of several self-help sexuality books and sexuality workshops. According to an article by Taormino (2000), female ejaculation was the subject of one of the workshops at the 2000 Michigan Womyn's Festival. After the workshop, several women participated in the "First Annual Ejaculation Contest," competing in categories such as "speed," "distance," "quantity," and "best single-handed job." While reports based on nonclinical trials do not receive scientific approval, the nature of this contest helps to alter negative stigma associated with female ejaculation.

There are several important implications of this research on female ejaculation. Because female ejaculation is not a widely known phenomenon, women who experience the expulsion of fluids frequently feel shame or anxiety (Davidson et al., 1989). Many women, particularly those who are uncomfortable examining the fluid, assume that any release of fluid is urine and a sign of urinary incontinence. In some cases, women may seek and receive medical treatment for urinary incontinence when this is not, in fact, the problem. If women were aware that the expulsion of fluid was a normal and healthy bodily function, they would feel free to enjoy a pleasurable event rather than perceiving themselves as deviant (Cartwright et al., 2007; Winton, 1989).

REFERENCES

Addiego, Frank, Edwin G. Belzer, Jill Comolli, William Moger, John D. Perry, and Beverly Whipple. 1981. "Female Ejaculation: A Case Study." *The Journal of Sex Research*, 17: 13–21.

Alzate, Heli. 1985. "Vaginal Eroticism: A Replication Study." *Archives of Sexual Behavior*, 14: 529–37.

Alzate, Heli, and Zwi Hoch. 1986. "The 'G-Spot' and 'Female Ejaculation': A Current Appraisal." *Journal of Sex and Marital Therapy*, 12: 211–20.

Barbara, G., F. Facchin, M. Meschia, and P. Vercellini. 2015. "'The First Cut Is the Deepest': A Psychological, Sexological and Gynecological Perspective on Female Genital Cosmetic Surgery." *Acta obstetricia et gynecologica Scandinavica*, 94(9): 915–20.

Belzer, Edwin G. 1981. "Orgasmic Expulsions of Women: A Review and Heuristic Inquiry." *Journal of Sex Research*, 17: 1–12.

Belzer, Edwin G, Beverly Whipple, and William Moger. 1984. "On Female Ejaculation." *Journal of Sex Research*, 20: 403–06.

Bullough, Bonnie, Madeline David, Beverly Whipple, Joan Dixon, Elizabeth Rice Allgeier, and Kate Cosgrove Drury. 1984. "Subjective Reports of Female Orgasmic Expulsion of Fluid." *Nurse Practitioner*, 9: 55–59.

Cartwright, Rufus, Susannah Elvy, and Linda Cardozo. 2007. "Do Women with Female Ejaculation Have Detrusor Overactivity?" *Journal of Sexual Medicine*, 4(6): 1655–58.

Cass, Vivienne. 2007. *The Elusive Orgasm: A Woman's Guide to Why She Can't and How She Can Orgasm*. New York: Marlowe and Company.

Davidson, J. Kenneth, Carol A. Darling, and Colleen Conway-Welch. 1989. "The Role of the Grafenburg Spot and Female Ejaculation in the Female Orgasmic Response: An Empirical Analysis." *Journal of Sex and Marital Therapy*, 15: 102–20.

Ehrenreich, Barbara, Elizabeth Hess, and Gloria Jacobs. 1986. *Re-Making Love: The Feminization of Sex*. New York: Anchor Books.

Gerhard, Jane. 2004. "The Politics of the Female Orgasm." In M. Stombler, D. M. Baunach, E. O. Burgess, D. Donnelly, and W. Simonds, eds., *Sex Matters: The Sexuality and Society Reader*. Boston: Allyn and Bacon. 213–24.

Goldberg, Daniel C., Beverly Whipple, Ralph E. Fishkin, Howard Waxman, Paul J. Fink, and Martin Weisberg. 1983. "The Grafenberg Spot and Female Ejaculation: A Review of Initial Hypotheses." *Journal of Sex and Marital Therapy*, 9: 27–38.

Hicks, Donald L. 2006. *Unleashing Her G-Spot Orgasm: A Step-by-Step Guide to Giving a Woman Ultimate Sexual Ecstasy*. Berkeley, CA: Amorato Press.

Hines, Terence M. 2001. "The G-Spot: A Modern Gynecological Myth." *American Journal of Obstetrics and Gynecology*, 185: 359–62.

Hite, Shere. 1976. *The Hite Report: A Nationwide Study of Female Sexuality*. New York: Dell.

Jannini, E. A., B. Whipple, S. A. Kingsberg, O. Buisson, P. Foldès, and Y. Vardi. 2010. "Who's Afraid of the G-Spot?" *Journal of Sexual Medicine*, 7(1pt1): 25–34.

Kilchevsky, A., Y. Vardi, L. Lowenstein, and I. Gruenwald. 2012. "Is the Female G-Spot Truly a Distinct Anatomic Entity?" *Journal of Sexual Medicine*, 9(3): 719–26.

Korda, J. B., S. W. Goldstein, and F. Sommer. 2010. "Sexual Medicine History: The History of Female Ejaculation." *Journal of Sexual Medicine*, 7(5): 1965–75.

Ladas, Alice. 2001. "Review of Secrets of Sensual Lovemaking and the Good Vibrations Guide." *Journal of Sex Education and Therapy*, 26: 150–51.

Ladas, Alice, Beverly Whipple, and John Perry. 1982. *The G-Spot and Other Recent Discoveries about Human Sexuality*. New York: Plenum.

Masters, W. H., and V. E. Johnson, 1966. *Human Sexual Response*. Boston: Little, Brown.

Miller, Korin. 2016. "How to Find Your G-Spot." *Cosmopolitan*. Retrieved January 15, 2018 from http://www.cosmopolitan.com/sex-love/advice/g2126/how-to-find-your-g-spot/.

Moore, Lisa Jean, and Adele E. Clarke. 1995. "Clitoral Conventions and Transgressions: Graphic

Representations in Anatomy Texts, c. 1900–1991." *Feminist Studies*, 21(2): 255–301.

O'Connell, H. E., K. V. Sanjeevan, and J. M. Hudson. 2005. "Anatomy of the Clitoris." *Journal of Urology*, 174: 1189–95.

Ostrzenski, A. 2012. "G-Spot Anatomy: A New Discovery." *The Journal of Sexual Medicine*, 9(5): 1355–59.

Ostrzenski, A., P. Krajewski, P. Ganjei-Azar, A. J. Wasiutynski, M. N. Scheinberg, S. Tarka, and M. Fudalej. 2014. "Verification of the Anatomy and Newly Discovered Histology of the G-Spot Complex." *BJOG: An International Journal of Obstetrics and Gynaecology*, 121(11): 1333–40.

Paget, Lou. 2004. *Orgasms: How to Have Them, Give Them, and Keep Them Coming*. New York: Broadway Books.

Pan, S., C. Leung, J. Shah, and A. Kilchevsky. 2015. "Clinical Anatomy of the G-Spot." *Clinical Anatomy*, 28(3): 363–67.

Pastor, Z. 2013. "Female Ejaculation Orgasm vs. Coital Incontinence: A Systematic Review." *Journal of Sexual Medicine*, 10(7): 1682–91.

Perry, John D., and Beverly Whipple. 1981. "The Varieties of Female Orgasm and Female Ejaculation. SIECUS Report.

Puppo, V. 2014. "The G-Spot Does Not Exist." *BJOG: An International Journal of Obstetrics and Gynaecology*, 121(11): 1341–41.

Puppo, V., and I. Gruenwald. 2012. "Does the G-Spot Exist? A Review of the Current Literature." *International Urogynecology Journal*, 23(12): 1665–69.

Schneider, Beth E., and Meredith Gould. 1987. "Female Sexuality Looking Back into the Future." In Beth B. Hess and Myra Marx Ferree, eds., *Analyzing Gender: A Handbook of Social Science Research*. Newbury Park, CA: Sage. 120–53.

Sevely, J. L., and J. W. Bennett. 1978. "Concerning Female Ejaculation and the Female Prostate." *Journal of Sex Research*, 14: 1–20.

Solot, Dorian, and Marshall Miller. 2007. *I Love Female Orgasm: An Extraordinary Orgasm Guide*. New York: Marlowe and Company.

Sundahl, Deborah, Alice Ladas, and Annie Sprinkle. 2003. *Female Ejaculation and the G-Spot: Not Your Mother's Orgasm Book!* Alameda, CA: Hunter House, Inc.

Taormini, Tristan. 2000. "Pucker Up." *Village Voice*, September 5, 45(35): 130.

Tuana, Nancy. 2004. "Coming to Understand: Orgasm and the Epistemology of Ignorance." *Hypatia*, 19(1): 194–232.

Wimpissinger, Florian, Karl Stifter, Wolfgang Grin, and Walter Stackl. 2007. "The Female Prostate Revisited: Perineal Ultrasound and Biochemical Studies of Female Ejaculate." *Journal of Sexual Medicine*, 4(5): 1388–93.

Winks, Cathy. 1998. *The Good Vibrations Guide: The G-Spot*. San Francisco: Down There Press.

Winton, Mark A. 1989. "Editorial: The Social Construction of the G-Spot and Female Ejaculation." *Journal of Sex Education and Therapy*, 15: 151–62.

Zaviacic, Milan, and Beverly Whipple. 1993. "Update on the Female Prostate and the Phenomenon of Female Ejaculation." *Journal of Sex Research*, 30: 148–51.

Zaviacic, Milan, Alexandra Zaviacicova, Igor Karol Holoman, and Jan Molcan, 1988. "Female Urethral Explusions Evoked by Local Digital Stimulation of the G-Spot: Differences in the Response Patterns." *Journal of Sex Research*, 24: 311–18.

FEMALE GENITAL MUTILATION AND MALE CIRCUMCISION: TOWARD AN AUTONOMY-BASED ETHICAL FRAMEWORK

BRIAN D. EARP

The cutting of healthy genital organs for non-medical reasons is at its essence a basic violation of girls' and women's right to physical integrity. This is true regardless of the degree of cutting or the extent of the complications that may or may not ensue.

—Anika Rahman and Nahid Toubia[1]

Most illogical is the use of the term "'male genital mutilation" to refer to male circumcision . . . in an attempt to equate the latter with female genital mutilation, with which it has little in common, either anatomically or health-wise.

—Brian J Morris[2]

The non-therapeutic surgical alteration of children's genitals is treated very differently in Western societies depending on the sex or gender of the child whose genitals are being altered.[3–8] Why such divergent treatment? As one prominent ethicist has noted, "these two practices, dramatically separated in the public imagination, actually have significant areas of overlap."[9] For example, both types of intervention involve the incision (and usually, though not always, the excision) of healthy, erogenous tissue.[10–12] Both concern an individual's "private parts," yet are done without the person's own consent. And neither involves the treatment of disease, nor the correction of an acknowledged deformity.[13] *Prima facie*, then, at least according to this way of thinking, a similar medical-ethical analysis—based on conventional bioethical principles—would seem to apply to both.

Yet this is not the predominant opinion expressed in Western popular discourse, nor in much of the scholarly literature. In these domains, as well as in many others, the two types of intervention are rarely discussed in the same context.[14] Moreover, when they are characterized as being potentially comparable, the reaction is often incredulous. For example, when the anthropologist Kirsten Bell put forward such a comparison in her university lectures, the response from her students was "immediate and hostile": "How dare I mention these two entirely different operations in the same breath! How dare I compare the innocuous and beneficial removal of the foreskin with the extreme mutilations enacted against females in other societies!"[15]

One recurrent claim is that FGM [female genital mutilation] is analogous to "castration" or a "total penectomy," such that any sort of comparison between it and male circumcision is entirely inappropriate.[16] This perspective alludes to a harm-based argument for the (distinctive) impermissibility of female forms of genital alteration. On this sort of view, the sheer level of harm entailed by FGM passes a threshold of intolerability that is not passed by male circumcision. FGM is also seen as lacking in any benefit (as the World Health Organization states: FGM has "no health benefits, [and] only [causes] harm"),[17] whereas potential health-based benefits are not infrequently raised in support of male circumcision.[18–19]

In the first section of this essay, I call into question the claims upon which these distinctions are typically premised. Specifically, I show

From "Female Genital Mutilation and Male Circumcision: Toward an Autonomy-based Ethical Framework," *Medicolegal and Bioethics*, 2015, Vol. 5, pp. 89–104. Published by Dove Press Ltd. Reprinted by permission.

that at least certain forms of FGM (or female genital alteration [FGA]),[9] including forms that are legally prohibited in Western societies, are demonstrably less harmful than the most prevalent forms of male circumcision. I also show that certain forms of male circumcision (or male genital alteration [MGA]), including forms that are common in parts of Africa and elsewhere, can be at least as harmful as the most extreme forms of FGA as practiced in any context. I will also question the claims that have been made on the point of health benefits, with respect to both types of genital alteration.

The harm-based argument, then, does not turn out to be sufficient to draw a strict moral distinction between male and female forms of genital cutting practices. The consequence of this conclusion can be stated as a conditional: if the degree of harm vs. benefit commonly attributed to male circumcision is seen as being compatible with its permissibility in Western societies, then forms of female genital cutting that result in a similar degree of harm vs. benefit must also be considered permissible on these grounds.[20] Yet many would resist this conclusion. Indeed, the official position of such influential bodies as the World Health Organization (WHO) and the United Nations is that *any* kind of medically unnecessary, non-consensual alteration of the female genitalia—no matter how minor the incision, no matter what type of tissue is or is not removed, no matter how slim the degree of risk, and no matter how sterile the equipment used—is by definition an impermissible "mutilation."[10]

Granting this view for now (although it is not uncontroversial),[10,9] perhaps we can find some other moral basis on which to ground a gender- or sex-based distinction. The philosopher Joseph Mazor has recently advanced an intuitive-sounding possibility:

There is an important *moral* difference [between male and female forms of genital alteration] that does not have to do with the physical effects of the operation[s]. Namely, in some . . . of the cultures in which female genital cutting is practiced, the practice reflects deeply rooted attitudes about the lower status of women. Thus, even if male and female genital cutting were perfectly identical in terms of net health benefits and effects on sexual pleasure, the relationship in some cultures between female genital cutting and a failure to respect women as moral equals would give an additional reason to object to female circumcision.[21] (emphasis added)

This line of thought, which I will refer to as the "symbolic meanings" argument, will be the focus of the second section of my paper. In this section, I argue that Mazor's proposed distinction, while potentially appealing on a first-pass assessment, is ultimately untenable. First, as Mazor himself concedes, male and female forms of genital alteration are carried out for different reasons, and reflect different norms and attitudes, in different cultural contexts. In some cases, the "symbolic meanings" of these respective alterations are in fact quite similar. Indeed, contrary to common wisdom, non-therapeutic FGA is not always associated with, nor a reflection of, sexist and patriarchal norms; nor are the norms associated with male genital cutting always as morally innocent as is typically assumed.

Accordingly, even if one were to grant that the moral permissibility of each type of genital cutting—stipulated to be equally (physically) harmful for the sake of this analysis—hinged on the attitudes or norms that they "reflected," it would still be necessary to distinguish between such attitudes and norms on a context-specific basis, and possibly even case-by-case. Apart from the practical difficulties that would be incurred by such a task, there are a number of epistemological difficulties as well.

As I conclude, therefore, the Western habit of drawing a stark moral distinction between male and female forms of non-therapeutic, non-consensual genital alteration may be impossible to maintain on principled grounds—or if not impossible, certainly much more difficult than is commonly assumed. In the final section of this paper, I provide a very brief sketch of an ethical framework that could be used to evaluate such alterations in a more consistent and principled way. Instead of being based on considerations of sex or gender, my proposed framework will be based on considerations of bodily autonomy and informed consent.

MALE AND FEMALE FORMS OF GENITAL ALTERATION: THE QUESTION OF HARM

That FGA is harmful to women and girls—and certainly much more harmful than MGA—is a truism in Western societies. This is the harm-based argument to which I alluded earlier, and I have already suggested that it cannot succeed. To see why this is the case, it is necessary to begin with a widely accepted definition of FGM . . . so that we can understand what is at stake in such a procedure, followed by an analysis of male circumcision. The WHO gives us the following typology:[22]

FGM Type 1—This refers to the partial or total removal of the clitoral glans (the part of the clitoris that is visible to the naked eye) and/or the clitoral prepuce ("hood"). This is sometimes called a "clitoridectomy,"[17] although such a designation is misleading: the external clitoral glans is not always removed in this type of FGM, and in some versions of the procedure—such as with so-called "hoodectomies"—it is deliberately left untouched.[23] There are two major sub-types. *Type 1(a)* is the partial or total removal of just the clitoral prepuce (i.e., the fold of skin that covers the clitoral glans, much as the penile prepuce covers the penile glans in boys; in fact, the two structures are embryonically homologous).[24–25] *Type 1(b)* is the same as *Type 1(a)*, but includes the partial or total removal of the external clitoral glans. Note that two-thirds or more of the entire clitoris (including most of its erectile tissue) is internal to the body envelope,[26] and is therefore not removed by this type, or any type, of FGM.

FGM Type 2—This refers to the partial or total removal of the external clitoral glans and/or the clitoral hood (in the senses described above), and/or the labia minora, with or without removal of the labia majora. This form of FGM is sometimes termed "excision." *Type 2(a)* is the "trimming" or removal of the labia minora only; this is also known as labiaplasty when it is performed in a Western context by a professional surgeon (in which case it is usually intended as a form of cosmetic "enhancement").[23] In this context, such an intervention is not typically regarded as being a form of "mutilation," even though it formally fits the WHO definition. Moreover, even though such "enhancement" is most often carried out on consenting adult women in this cultural context, it is also sometimes performed on minors, apparently with the permission of their parents.[10,27] There are two further subtypes of *FGM Type 2*, involving combinations of the above interventions.

FGM Type 3—This refers to a narrowing of the vaginal orifice with the creation of a seal by cutting and repositioning the labia minora and/or the labia majora, with or without excision of the external clitoris. This is the most extreme type of FGM, although it is also one of the rarest, occurring in approximately 10% of cases.[10,28] When the "seal" is left in place, there is only a very small hole to allow for the passage of urine and menstrual blood, and sexual intercourse is rendered essentially impossible. This type of FGM is commonly called "infibulation" or "pharaonic circumcision" and has two additional subtypes.

FGM Type 4—This refers to "all other harmful procedures to the female genitalia for non-medical purposes" and includes such interventions as pricking, nicking, piercing, stretching, scraping, and cauterization.[22] Counterintuitively for this final category—which one might expect to be even "worse" than the ones before it—several of the interventions just mentioned are among the least severe forms of FGM. Piercing, for example, is another instance of a procedure—along with labiaplasty (*FGM Type 2*) and "clitoral unhooding"[23] (*FGM Type 1*)—that is popular in Western countries for "non-medical purposes," and can be performed hygienically under appropriate conditions.[10,29–31]

The Harms of FGM/A

Several points can now be emphasized. First, "FGM" is not just one thing. Instead, there are many ways to nick, scratch, or cut off parts of a girl's vulva, ranging from (at the lowest end of the harm spectrum) an anaesthetized prick on the clitoral hood, as is common in Malaysia and in some other Muslim communities,[10,32] to (at the highest end of the spectrum) the excision of the outer clitoris with a shard of glass, and the suturing of the labia with thorns.[33] It should be clear that these different forms of intervention are likely to result in different degrees of harm, with different effects on sexual function and satisfaction, different chances of developing an infection, and so on, among the other possible adverse consequences that may be associated with these procedures.[34] But as Carla Obermeyer has observed:

It is rarely pointed out that the frequency and severity of complications are a function of the extent and circumstances of the operation, and it is not usually recognized that much of [our] information comes from studies of the Sudan, where most women [in contrast to the majority of other contexts] are infibulated. The ill-health and death that these practices are thought to cause are difficult to reconcile with the reality of their persistence in so many societies, and raises the question of a possible discrepancy between our "knowledge" of their harmful effects and the behavior of millions of women and their families.[35]

A further point to consider is that many of the risks and harms that are associated with FGM—such as pain, infection, and hemorrhage—could be substantially reduced, if not eliminated, by transitioning toward the less invasive forms of the procedure, coupled with an increased focus on "medicalization."[36–37] In light of this recognition, more minor forms of female genital alteration are indeed being performed in hospital settings in an increasing number of communities worldwide, on the model of routine male circumcision as performed in the United States.[38] This trend has not been welcomed, however, by those who oppose FGM regardless of implementation or type,[10,38–39] and it has been explicitly condemned by both the WHO and the United Nations.[10]

What about effects on sexuality?[40] While a popular assumption is that any form of FGM deprives women of all sexual feeling, "[r]esearch by gynecologists and others has demonstrated that a high percentage of women who have had genital surgery have rich sexual lives, including desire, arousal, orgasm, and satisfaction, and their frequency of sexual activity is not reduced."[41] Indeed, in one study,[42] up to 86% of women—some of whom had undergone even "extreme" forms of FGM—reported the ability to orgasm, and "the majority of the interviewed women (90.51%) reported that sex gives them pleasure." These counterintuitive findings might be explained by the fact, noted earlier, that much of the clitoris is actually underneath the skin layer and is therefore not removed by even the most invasive types of FGM. Of course, there are other parts of the vulva/vagina to consider as well, whose stimulation can likewise contribute to sexual pleasure. All told, the degree and quality of subjective sexual feeling are likely to vary considerably. . . .[43]

On the other side of the ledger, there is a great deal of evidence that FGM can be harmful to sexual function and experience, especially when one considers the more extreme forms.[44–46] Women in some studies have reported feeling "cold" during sex, deriving "no satisfaction" from intercourse, and "having pain during sex."[47]. . . FGM—of whatever degree of severity—will lead to different psychologically mediated outcomes, depending upon the beliefs, attitudes, and other internal states of the affected individual.[42–43] As I have argued elsewhere:

While many African women feel *enhanced* by having modified genitals—feeling more beautiful, "cleaner," more "smooth" and "neat"—increasing numbers of them are aware of just how controversial their local customs have become on the world stage. Many of them are learning about how other cultures and societies regard the innervation and functions of the clitoris. Some of them are dating outside of their cultural groups [and finding] out that "cut" genitals are *not* considered beautiful by the prevailing group in such contexts, and so on. Accordingly, they may feel humiliated, deprived, diminished—and yes, "mutilated." There is even [some] evidence of women seeking reconstructive surgery of their genitals to try to reclaim what was "taken from them" when they were too young to fully understand what was happening.[10]

. . . [I]t is clear that FGM, and especially its more invasive forms, poses a distinct risk of causing sexual harm, even if this harm may not be experienced in the same way, or to the same degree, by every woman who has been subjected to genital surgery. . . .

The Harms of MGA

These same considerations apply to male circumcision. As with FGM/A, circumcision is not a monolith: it isn't just one kind of thing. The original form of circumcision within Judaism, for example, until about 150 AD, was comparatively minor: it involved cutting off the overhanging tip of the foreskin—whatever stretched out over the end of the glans—thus preserving (most of) the foreskin's protective and motile functions, as well as limiting the amount of erogenous tissue removed.[48] The "modern" form adopted by the United States[49] is significantly more invasive: it typically removes between one-third to one-half of the movable skin system of the penis,[50] or about 50 square centimeters of sensitive tissue in the adult organ.[51–52] The operation also eliminates the gliding function of the prepuce (which may help to reduce chafing in the female sexual partner), as well as any and all sexual sensation in the prepuce itself;[12,52] and it exposes the head of the penis to environmental irritation.[12,50] Just as with various forms of non-therapeutic FGA, male circumcision has been associated with numerous sexual difficulties, ranging from reduced sensitivity in the exposed glans, to problems with orgasm, to pain in the receptive female partner.[53–55] Nevertheless, many, if not most, circumcised men report being able to enjoy their sexual experiences, notwithstanding the loss of erotogenic tissue. . . .[56–57]

The literature concerning the sexual effects of male circumcision is hotly contested. . . .[58–59] "Adverse self-reported outcomes associated with foreskin removal in adulthood include impaired erectile functioning, orgasm difficulties, decreased masturbatory functioning (loss in pleasure and increase in difficulty), an increase in penile pain, a loss of penile sensitivity with age, and lower subjective ratings of penile sensitivity" (internal references omitted).[57] While "other studies have found no significant differences in self-reported sexual functioning following adult circumcision," it must be remembered that (a) adult vs. infant/child circumcision may not necessarily yield equivalent outcomes,[12] and (b) that a lack of statistical significance does not entail a lack of underlying effect. . . .[60]

Just as with FGA, male genital cutting can take many different forms. In Pakistan, traditional Muslim circumcisions are done while the boy is fully conscious, usually between the ages of 3 and 7. . . . "[T]he child is held in a seated position, with both legs apart . . . [then] a probe, a cutter made of wood, and a razor are used [to excise] the prepuce," at which point "ashes of burnt wood are [applied] to establish haemostasis."[61] The operation is performed "with no anaesthesia, no sutures and with unsterilized instruments."[61] In the United States, routine (non-religious) circumcisions are performed in a hospital setting, and take place in the first few days of life. These, too, often involve inadequate (or no) pain control, and have been known to result in serious "botches," including partial amputations of the penis. While such an outcome is typically described as "rare," the true incidence of complications is unknown.[7,62–63] Metzitzah b'peh, done by some ultra-Orthodox Jews, requires the sucking of blood from the circumcision wound, and carries the risk of herpes infection and permanent brain damage.[64] Subincision, performed by some Australian aboriginal groups, involves slicing open the urethral passage on the underside of the penis from the scrotum to the glans, often affecting urination as well as sexual function.[65–66] . . . "[T]he bleeding is staunched with sand, and the edges of the wound may be cauterized . . . the resultant defect in the urethral wall is kept open [with] pieces of wood, bone, or clay."[65] Circumcision among the Xhosa in South Africa is traditionally done in the bush as a rite of passage, sometimes with the use of spearheads and dirty knives, and frequently by medically untrained practitioners. Just as with female genital altering rites performed under comparable conditions (and often by the very same groups), these kinds of operations frequently cause hemorrhage, infection, mangling, and loss of the sexual organ.[67] In fact, between 2008 and 2014, more than half a million boys were hospitalized due to botched circumcisions in South Africa alone; more than 400 lost their lives.[68–69] But even when performed in a modern clinical setting, circumcisions are not without their risks and complications. In 2011, nearly a dozen infant boys were treated for "life-threatening

hemorrhage, shock or sepsis" as a result of their non-therapeutic circumcisions at a single children's hospital in Birmingham, England.[70]

. . . [B]oth male and female forms of genital alteration fall on a wide spectrum, and . . . the harms they may entail substantially overlap.[9] That this is not commonly understood in the popular discourse is most likely due to the fact that when Westerners hear the term "FGM," they tend to think of the most extreme forms of female genital cutting, done in the least sterilized environments, with the most drastic consequences likeliest to follow (since these are the forms to which they will typically have been exposed, due to their disproportionate representation in the media and in other popular accounts).[41] When people hear the term "male circumcision," by contrast, they are much more likely to think of the *least* severe forms of male genital cutting, done in the most sterilized environments, with the least drastic consequences likeliest to follow, largely because this is the form with which they are culturally familiar. . . .[10,71]

THE OTHER SIDE OF THE COIN: THE QUESTION OF BENEFITS

So far, I have discussed the potential harms of male and female genital alterations, but I have not yet considered the question of benefits. MGA, but not FGA, is believed by some medical professionals to confer a number of possible health benefits—most notably, a small reduction in the absolute risk of female-to-male, heterosexually transmitted HIV in areas with high base rates of such infection[62,72–75]—although the likelihood and the magnitude of such benefits outside of sub-Saharan Africa are the subject of considerable dispute. If these authorities are correct, then the benefits of circumcision might conceivably offset the drawbacks and risks in a way that is not the case for FGA, thereby preserving the moral distinction between them.

An important qualification is in order. First, almost all of the controlled evidence pointing to potential health benefits for MGA has been derived from studies of adult (and hence voluntary) circumcision, rather than from infant/child (and hence involuntary) circumcision.[57] Since "the spread of disease, including sexually transmitted infections, is determined much more by socio-behavioral and situational factors than by strictly anatomical-biological factors, such as the presence or absence of a foreskin . . . the apparent findings from these studies cannot be simply mapped on [to] circumcisions performed earlier in life, i.e., before an age of sexual debut."[76] This distinction is important. From an ethical perspective, few people would argue that fully informed adult males should not be permitted to undergo elective surgeries on their own genitals. . . .

With respect to neonatal or childhood circumcision, by contrast, the primary health benefit that has been attributed to this version of the surgery is a slight reduction in the absolute risk of urinary tract infections.[77] However, the overall chance of contracting such an infection (in the first year of life) is low—approximately 1%—regardless of one's circumcision status. . . .[78] In the rare event that a child does in fact become infected, UTIs are both "easily diagnosed and treatable, with low morbidity and mortality."[79] A further point to consider is that: according to one recent estimate, about 111 circumcisions would have to be performed to prevent a single case of UTI.[80] Accordingly, "a more conservative, humane, and effective course of treatment would be to prescribe oral antibiotics—if and when an infection does occur. This is just what we do for girls, who get UTIs (after the age of 1) about 10 times more frequently than boys do, with no pre-emptive surgery recommended."[52]

But what if such surgery were recommended? . . . [W]e do not actually know whether some minor form of FGA might confer health benefits, because it is illegal—and would be unethical[12,34]—to conduct a study to find this out. Obviously, the more extreme types of FGA will not contribute to good health on balance, but neither will the spearheads-and-dirty-knives versions of MGA performed on boys. What about more mild forms of FGA? As I have noted elsewhere, "the vulva has all sorts of warm, moist places where bacteria or viruses could get trapped, such as underneath the clitoral hood, or among the folds of the labia; so who is to say that removing some of that tissue (with a sterile surgical tool) might not reduce the risk of various diseases?"[71]

As a matter of fact, defenders of FGA in some countries actually do cite such "health benefits" as "a lower risk of vaginal cancer . . . less nervous anxiety, fewer infections from microbes gathering under the hood of the clitoris, and protection against herpes and genital ulcers."[14] Moreover, at least one study by Western scientists has shown a link between "female circumcision" and reduced transmission of HIV—a result that the authors, both experienced statisticians, characterized as a "significant and perplexing inverse association between reported female circumcision and HIV seropositivity."[81–82]

. . . The thought experiment can be taken a step further. With respect to causal plausibility, it is often argued that the biological mechanism through which the foreskin in males becomes a vector for HIV transmission (although the details are somewhat contentious)[81–82] is the presence of Langerhans cells in the inner mucosa of the foreskin. What is rarely mentioned in these discussions, however, is that the external female genitalia are also richly endowed with Langerhans cells.[83] If the removal of tissue with Langerhans cells is seen as an acceptable means of reducing HIV transmission, then the excision of portions of the female genitalia (on these grounds) should logically be entertained as well.

The point here is . . . that regardless of any evidence for such a possibility, serious research into the question is unlikely ever to be considered, simply because such procedures are unacceptable to Western ethical and cultural norms.[84] Bell has highlighted the contradictory policies of international health organizations on this point, "which seek to medicalize male circumcision on the one hand, oppose the medicalization of female circumcision on the other, while simultaneously basing their opposition to female operations on grounds that could legitimately be used to condemn the male operations."[15]

IS THERE A "SYMBOLIC" DIFFERENCE?

. . . [T]here may be a "symbolic" difference to consider as well. This is the view suggested by the philosopher Joseph Mazor, as indicated in the introduction, and it is one that has been advanced by Martha Nussbaum, among many others. "Female genital mutilation is unambiguously linked to customs of male domination,"[85] Nussbaum has written; whereas male circumcision is not ordinarily seen as being linked to such customs, nor perhaps to other problematic norms.[86]

In contrast to this perspective, I suggest that male genital cutting can indeed "be understood as a gendering practice tied to [patriarchal notions of] masculinity" as well as to customs of male domination;[87] and also, following Ahmadu,[88] that female forms of genital cutting are *not* "unambiguously" tied to such customs. . . .

The Symbolic Meanings of FGA

[. . .] As is increasingly being emphasized by scholars in this area, female genital cutting is performed for different reasons in different social contexts, and is not always associated with a lower status for women and girls, nor with the aim of reducing their sexual plea-

sure.[41,88] Indeed, such cutting is nearly always carried out by women themselves, who do not typically view their rites as being an expression of patriarchal norms, but rather as conducive to good hygiene, beautifying,[28,89] empowering, and as a rite of passage with high cultural value.[28,88] As Lisa Wade has argued, "attributing [the] persistence [of female genital altering rites] to patriarchy grossly oversimplifies their social, cultural, and economic functions" in the diverse societies in which they are performed.[90]

It has sometimes been argued that women who endorse FGA are victims of "false consciousness" and are thus mistaken about the nature of their own most cherished customs— that they are so oppressed, for example, that they have become unwitting instruments to their own oppression.[91] However, this sort of argument is increasingly being seen as both simplistic and condescending.[10,28,91-94] . . . [T]he supportive voices of women who have actually undergone genital alterations are "almost entirely absent, literally silenced by [a Western] insistence that the horrendousness of the practice precludes any possible positive evaluation."[95] . . .

. . . [A]s Ahmadu has argued, there has been an "unjustified conflation" of the varied practices of FGA in the popular discourse, resulting in an overemphasis on the most symbolically problematic form, namely infibulation. . . .[88] This conflation is unjustified, she suggests, because infibulation is simultaneously the most extreme form of FGA, the rarest, and the form most closely associated with norms of male dominance and sexual control. It is also "associated with a specific region and interpretation of Muslim purdah ideology,"[88] and appears to be concentrated in northeast Africa.

In most other African contexts, by contrast, both FGA and MGA are at least superficially egalitarian: they are carried out regardless of the sex or gender of the child, and are intended as a means of conferring adult status within the group.[41,84] Among the Kono of Sierra Leone, for example, "there is no cultural obsession with feminine chastity, virginity, or women's sexual fidelity, perhaps because the role of the biological father is considered marginal and peripheral to the central 'matricentric unit.'"[108] In this context, male and female genital alterations are performed in parallel ceremonies, are not primarily intended to reduce sexual pleasure, and the operations are seen as mirror images of each other.[10,41,84]

Nancy Ehrenreich and Mark Barr provide a general lesson:

[. . .] The mainstream anti-FG[A] position is premised upon an orientalizing construction of FG[A] societies as primitive, patriarchal, and barbaric, and of female circumcision as a harmful, unnecessary cultural practice based on patriarchal gender norms and ritualistic beliefs. . . . Lambasting African societies and practices (while failing to critique similar practices in the United States [and Europe]) . . . essentially implies that North American [and European] understandings of the body are "scientific" (i.e., rational, civilized, and based on universally acknowledged expertise), while African understandings are "cultural" (i.e., superstitious, uncivilized, and based on false, socially constructed beliefs). [Yet] neither of these depictions is accurate. North American medicine is not free of cultural influence, and FG[A] practices are not bound by culture—at least not in the uniform way imagined by opponents.[96]

The Symbolic Meanings of MGA

What about the other side of things? The usual claim is that male circumcision is not associated with a lowered status for women, but in Judaism, at least, this is not obviously the case. Indeed, only the males are permitted to "seal the divine covenant" by having their foreskins removed, so the custom is sexist on its face.[9] . . . "Jews of antiquity seem not to have been bothered by this question probably because the fundamental Otherness of women was clear to them.

Jewish women were Jewish by birth, but their Jewishness was assumed to be inferior to that of Jewish men."[97–98] "A true egalitarian would think it unfair that a boy is cut while a girl is not [and would] either extend the burden [of circumcision] to girls or remove it from [the] boys."[99] The sociologist Michael Kimmel goes a step further:

Circumcision means . . . the reproduction of patriarchy. [In the Jewish tradition] Abraham cements his relationship to God by a symbolic genital mutilation of his son. It is on the body of his son that Abraham writes his own beliefs. In a religion marked by the ritual exclusion of women, such a marking not only enables Isaac to be included within the community of men . . . but he can also lay claim to all the privileges to which being a Jewish male now entitles him. . . . To circumcise [one's son, therefore, is] to accept as legitimate 4000 years [of] patriarchal domination of women.[100]

Male circumcision may be related to other problematic norms as well. One connection that has been raised in the literature is with an attempt to exercise control over boys' sexualities.[9,101] While most contemporary Western parents who choose circumcision for their sons do not (very likely) have such a motivation consciously in mind, neither, apparently, do most African parents when they choose "circumcision" for their daughters. Instead, as the renowned anti-FGA activist Hanny Lightfoot-Klein has stated: "The [main] reasons given for female circumcision in Africa and for routine male circumcision in the United States are essentially the same. Both promise cleanliness and the absence of odors as well as greater attractiveness and acceptability."[102]

Nevertheless, male genital cutting has indeed been used as a form of sexual control, and even punishment, for a very long time.[9,101] The Jewish philosopher Maimonides (b. 1135) argued that diminished sexual sensitivity was part of the point of performing circumcisions (to reduce excessive "lust" as well as "weaken . . . the organ in question");[103] circumcision was adopted into Western medicine in the Victorian period largely as a means to combat masturbation and other expressions of juvenile sexuality. . . .[104]

. . . [I]t could be argued that these apparent associations with problematic norms are superficial,[105] outdated, or only apply to a limited number of cases. But this is exactly the point. Neither male nor female forms of genital cutting can be successfully "boiled down" in terms of the attitudes that they supposedly express, and both have been plausibly associated with both (seemingly) unproblematic as well as (seemingly) extremely problematic norms. . . .

Given that both male and female forms of genital cutting express different cultural norms depending upon the context, and are performed for different reasons in different cultures, and even in different communities or individual families, how shall we assess the permissibility of either? Do we need to interview each set of parents to make sure that their proposed act of cutting is intended as an expression of acceptable norms? If they promise that it isn't about "sexual control" in their specific case, but rather about "hygiene" or "aesthetics" or something less symbolically problematic, should they be permitted to go ahead? But this is bound to fail.[71]

TOWARD AN AUTONOMY-BASED ETHICAL FRAMEWORK

At a first glance, there seem to be at least two ways of resolving this inconsistency. First, if Western societies remain convinced that the non-therapeutic alteration of boys' genitalia should be considered permissible so long as it does not cross an arbitrary threshold of "harm," then they should consider allowing similar alterations to the genitals of little girls (if requested by the parents). Some authors . . . have in fact made just such a suggestion.[9,10,106–107] It seems evident, however,

that this "solution" would create more problems than it would solve. For example, it would require that Western laws regarding physical assault on a minor be rewritten, potentially creating large-scale disturbances throughout the legal system. This is because—as others have argued—cutting into a child's genitals without a medical diagnosis, and without its informed consent, meets the formal definition of criminal assault under the legal codes of most of these societies. . . .[108]

Another problem . . . is that it would be very difficult indeed to "police" such newly approved "minimal" forms of FGA, to ensure that they were not being used as a cover for more invasive and harmful procedures. In fact, a very basic problem with the suggestion of harm-tolerance is the difficulty it presents in terms of specifying an appropriate threshold for harm that could be measured in an objective way. As Blackstone noted more than 200 years ago, "the law cannot draw [a] line between different degrees of violence. . . . The law is an important symbol and if [it] allows parents, carers and teachers to [so much as hit their] children, it is sending a message to these people and to the community generally that children are not entitled to the same right to bodily integrity as adults."[109]

The question of rights is arguably central to this issue. In Western societies, we teach our citizens (including our children) that they have a right to bodily integrity:[110] "a right to make decisions about what happens to [their] own body, [a] right to say no to unwanted touching, [a] right not to be physically or sexually assaulted."[109] This, Ludbrook argues, is "the most personal and arguably the most important of all human rights," next to the right to life itself.[109] Some authors have argued that FGA performed before an age of consent is a violation of such a right, "regardless of the degree of cutting or the extent of the complications that may or may not ensue."[1]

Undoubtedly, such a view is motivated at least in part by the fact that such cutting involves a very "private" part of the body—i.e., a part with unique psycho-sexual significance—and that it is done before a girl can understand what is at stake in such a procedure, much less offer effective resistance. Indeed, genitals are not like other parts of the body. This can be seen in the fact that sexual assault, in Western societies, is typically regarded as a more severe and more personal violation than other kinds of bodily assault. Accordingly, the outright cutting and/or alteration of a child's genitals seems much more likely to be the sort of interference that would later be experienced as a harm, compared against various other childhood bodily alterations that are sometimes raised in the literature. . . .

A New Ethical Framework

Taking all of these considerations into account, let me offer a second approach to resolving the "inconsistency" alluded to above, which has the potential to avoid the serious disadvantages that seem likely to follow from an increased tolerance for FGA. This approach would involve a decreased tolerance for MGA, and on the same grounds that have just been discussed. According to this approach, the test for moral permissibility (if not legal permissibility, as that may raise a different set of issues)[111] would rest not so much on considerations of sex or gender—according to which boys, compared to girls, are treated less favorably—but more on considerations of informed consent, reflecting an underlying concern for the "genital autonomy"[112-113] of children.

Moira Dustin has described just such an approach. She suggests that one way to resolve the apparent double standard regarding male vs. female forms of genital alteration in Western societies, "would be to argue for the application of consistent principles of choice . . . and the recognition of all non-therapeutic bodily modifications" as being "culturally" motivated.[94] "This could mean making a distinction," she continues, "between adults who can choose how to modify their bodies in irreversible ways—however much the majority might deplore their choices—and children who cannot."[94] The application of this framework would have several important implications:

It would mean saying that male circumcision of baby boys, where it has been established that it has no . . . medical benefits, is unacceptable; it would mean that it would be illegal to circumcise a girl under the age of consent; and it would mean [by contrast] that if an adult woman wants to have her genitals "tidied up" after childbirth or her labia reduced through "cosmetic" surgery, then she should be allowed to make that choice. This may not be a satisfactory position but it is a way of avoiding double standards while the real work of changing the attitudes that produce these practices takes place.[94]

I am sympathetic with this general framework. As I have argued elsewhere, "Children of whatever [sex or] gender should not have healthy parts of their most intimate sexual organs removed, before such a time as they can understand what is at stake in such a surgery and agree to it themselves."[34] Conversely, . . . adults should be free to use medical technologies to modify their own bodies and minds, in a process of self-creation, if that is what they truly want.[114-116] While I do not suggest that (non-therapeutic) MGA should be banned, necessarily,[117-119] it is clear that the current *laissez-faire* attitude toward this practice that is typical of Western societies—and in particular the United States—can no longer be maintained without facing serious objection. FGA and MGA are both highly problematic practices, with far more overlap between them . . . than is commonly understood: they should not be discussed, therefore, in hermetically sealed moral discourses.[9,84] Instead, the relevant framework is one that analyses a child's right to bodily integrity, and carefully considers how tolerant we are willing to be, in these societies, of practices which irreversibly alter a person's "private parts" in a non-trivial fashion, in the absence of medical necessity,[120] and before the person has a chance to say "no.". . .

REFERENCES

1. Rahman A, Toubia N. *Female Genital Mutilation: A Practical Guide to Worldwide Laws and Policies*. London: Zed Books. 2000.

2. Morris B. Science supports infant circumcision, so should skeptics. *The Skeptic*. 2013; Autumn: 30–33.

3. United Nations Population Fund. *Promoting Gender Equality*. 2014. Available at http://www.unfpa.org /gender/practices2.htm#12.

4. UN Women. *United Nations Bans Female Genital Mutilation*. 2012. Available at http://www.unwomen .org/en/news/stories/2012/12/united- nations-bans -female-genital-mutilation/.

5. Earp, BD. Between moral relativism and moral hypocrisy: reframing the debate on "FGM." *Kennedy Institute of Ethics Journal*. In press. Available online ahead of print at https://www.academia.edu/10197867 /Between_moral_relativism_and_moral_hypocrisy _The_case_of_FGM.

6. Van den Brink M, Tigchelaar J. Shaping genitals, shaping perceptions: a frame analysis of male and female circumcision. *Netherlands Quarterly of Human Rights*. 2012; 30:417–45.

7. Geisheker JV. The completely unregulated practice of male circumcision: human rights abuse enshrined in law? *New Male Studies*. 2013; 2(1):18–45.

8. Solomon LM, Noll RC. Male versus female genital alteration: differences in legal, medical, and socioethical responses. *Gender Medicine*. 2007; 4(2): 89–96.

9. Davis DS. Male and female genital alteration: a collision course with the law. *Health Matrix*. 2001; 11:487–687.

10. Earp, BD. Between moral relativism and moral hypocrisy: reframing the debate on "FGM." *Kennedy Institute of Ethics Journal*. In press. Available online ahead of print at https://www.academia.edu/10197867 /Between_moral_relativism_and_moral_hypocrisy _The_case_of_FGM.

11. Cold CJ, Taylor JR. The prepuce. *BJU International*. 1999; 83(S1):34–44.

12. Earp BD. Sex and circumcision. *American Journal of Bioethics*. 2015; 15(2):43–45.

13. Dekkers W, Hoffer C, Wils J-P. Bodily integrity and male and female circumcision. *Medicine, Health Care and Philosophy*. 2005; 8(2):179–91.

14. Svoboda JS, Darby R. A rose by any other name: symmetry and asymmetry in male and female genital cutting. In *Fearful Symmetries: Essays and Testimonies Around Excision and Circumcision*, ed. Zabus C. Amsterdam and New York: Rodopi. 2008; 272–86.

15. Bell K. Genital cutting and Western discourses on sexuality. *Medical Anthropology Quarterly*. 2005; 19(2):125–48.

16. Schwartz RL, Johnson D, Burke N. Multiculturalism, medicine, and the limits of autonomy: the practice of female circumcision. *Cambridge Quarterly of Healthcare Ethics*. 1994; 3(3):431–41.

17. World Health Organization. *Female Genital Mutilation*. 2014. Available at http://www.who.int/mediacentre /factsheets/fs241/en/.

18. Tobian AA, Gray RH. The medical benefits of male circumcision. *Journal of the American Medical Association*. 2011; 306(13):1479–80.

19. Blank S, Brady M, Buerk E, et al. Circumcision policy statement. *Pediatrics*. 2012; 130(3):585–86.

20. And conversely, if the degree of net harm commonly attributed to FGA is seen as being incompatible with its permissibility in Western societies, then forms of MGA that result in a similar (or greater) degree of net harm must also be considered impermissible on these grounds.

21. Mazor J. The child's interests and the case for the permissibility of male infant circumcision. *Journal of Medical Ethics*. 2013; 39(7):421–28.

22. World Health Organization. *Global Strategy to Stop Healthcare Providers from Performing Female Genital Mutilation*. 2010. Available at http://whqlibdoc.who .int/hq/2010/WHO_RHR_10.9_eng.pdf?ua=1.

23. Renganathan A, Cartwright R, Cardozo L. Gynecological cosmetic surgery. *Expert Review of Obstetrics and Gynecology*. 2009; 4(2):101–04.

24. Cold CJ, McGrath KA. Anatomy and histology of the penile and clitoral prepuce in primates. *Male and Female Circumcision*. New York: Springer. 1999; 19–29.

25. Note that, on some interpretations, FGM Type 1(a) is the strict anatomical equivalent of male circumcision, since both procedures constitute the removal of the genital prepuce. However, such comparisons are not quite exact: in the male version of the procedure, many more square centimeters of erogenous tissue are removed due to the larger size of the penile prepuce.

26. O'Connell HE, Sanjeevan KV, Hutson JM. Anatomy of the clitoris. *The Journal of Urology*. 2005; 174(4): 1189–95.

27. Liao L-M, Taghinejadi N, Creighton SM. An analysis of the content and clinical implications of online advertisements for female genital cosmetic surgery. *BMJ Open*. 2012; 2(6):e001908.

28. Shell-Duncan B, Hernlund Y. *Female "Circumcision" in Africa: Culture, Controversy, and Change*: Boulder: Lynn Reinner Publishers. 2000.

29. Rodriguez, S. *Female Circumcision and Clitoridectomy in the United States: A History of a Medical Treatment*. University of Rochester Press. 2014.

30. Kelly B, Foster C. Should female genital cosmetic surgery and genital piercing be regarded ethically and legally as female genital mutilation? *BJOG: An International Journal of Obstetrics and Gynaecology*. 2012; 119(4):389–92.

31. Sheldon S, Wilkinson S. Female genital mutilation and cosmetic surgery: regulating non-therapeutic body modification. *Bioethics*. 1998; 12(4):263–85.

32. MacReady N. AAP retracts statement on controversial procedure. *The Lancet*. 2010; 376(9734):15.

33. Brady M. Female genital mutilation: complications and risk of HIV transmission. *AIDS Patient Care and STDs*. 1999; 13(12):709–16.

34. Earp BD. Female genital mutilation (FGM) and male circumcision: Should there be a separate ethical discourse? *Practical Ethics*. University of Oxford. 2014. Available at https://www.academia.edu/8817976/Female_genital_mutilation_FGM_and_male_circumcision_Should_there_be_a_separate_ethical_discourse.

35. Obermeyer CM. Female genital surgeries: the known, the unknown, and the unknowable. *Medical Anthropology Quarterly*. 1999; 13(1):79–106.

36. Chambers C. Are breast implants better than female genital mutilation? Autonomy, gender equality and Nussbaum's political liberalism. *Critical Review of International Social and Political Philosophy*. 2004; 7(3):1–33.

37. Shell-Duncan B. The medicalization of female "circumcision": harm reduction or promotion of a dangerous practice? *Social Science and Medicine*. 2001; 52(7):1013–28.

38. Shell-Duncan B, Hernlund Y. Female circumcision in Africa: dimensions of the practice and debates. In *Female "Circumcision" in Africa: Culture, Controversy, and Change*, ed. Shell-Duncan B, Hernlund Y. Boulder: Lynne Rienner Publishers. 2000; 1–40, 48.

39. Toubia N. *Female Genital Mutilation: A Call for Global Action*. New York: Rainbow/Women Ink. 1993.

40. Obermeyer CM. Female genital surgeries: the known, the unknown, and the unknowable. *Medical Anthropology Quarterly*. 1999; 13(1):79–106.

41. Abdulcadir J, Ahmadu FS, Catania L, et al. Seven things to know about female genital surgeries in Africa. *Hastings Center Report*. 2012; 42(6):19–27.

42. Catania L, Abdulcadir O, Puppo V, Verde JB, Abdulcadir J, Abdulcadir D. Pleasure and orgasm in women with female genital mutilation/cutting (FGM/C). *The Journal of Sexual Medicine*. 2007; 4(6):1666–78.

43. Johnsdotter S. Discourses on sexual pleasure after genital modifications: the fallacy of genital determinism (a response to J Steven Svoboda). *Global Discourse*. 2013; 3(2):256–65.

44. Alsibiani SA, Rouzi AA. Sexual function in women with female genital mutilation. *Fertility and Sterility*. 2010; 93(3):722–24.

45. Berg RC, Denison E, Fretheim A. Psychological, social and sexual consequences of female genital mutilation/cutting (FGM/C): a systematic review of quantitative studies. *Report from Kunnskapssenteret*. 2010; 13:3–77.

46. Berg RC, Denison E. Does female genital mutilation/cutting (FGM/C) affect women's sexual functioning? A systematic review of the sexual consequences of FGM/C. *Sexuality Research and Social Policy*. 2012; 9(1):41–56.

47. Fahmy A, El-Mouelhy MT, Ragab AR. Female genital mutilation/cutting and issues of sexuality in Egypt. *Reproductive Health Matters*. 2010; 18(36):181–90.

48. Glick LB. *Marked in Your Flesh: Circumcision from Ancient Judea to Modern America*. Oxford: Oxford University Press. 2005.

49. Gollaher DL. From ritual to science: the medical transformation of circumcision in America. *Journal of Social History*. 1994; 28(1):5–36.

50. Taylor JR, Lockwood AP, Taylor A. The prepuce: specialized mucosa of the penis and its loss to circumcision. *BJU International*. 1996; 77(2):291–95.

51. Werker PM, Terng AS, Kon M. The prepuce free flap: dissection feasibility study and clinical application of a super-thin new flap. *Plastic and Reconstructive Surgery*. 1998; 102(4):1075–82.

52. Earp BD, Darby R. Does science support infant circumcision? *The Skeptic*. 2015; 25(3):23–30.

53. Frisch M, Lindholm M, Grønbæk M. Male circumcision and sexual function in men and women: a survey-based, cross-sectional study in Denmark. *International Journal of Epidemiology*. 2011; 40(5):1367–81.

54. Morris BJ, Waskett JH, Gray RH. Does sexual function survey in Denmark offer any support for male circumcision having an adverse effect? *International Journal of Epidemiology*. 2012; 41(1):310–26.

55. Frisch, M. Author's response to: Does sexual function survey in Denmark offer any support for male circumcision having an adverse effect? *International Journal of Epidemiology*. 2012; 41(1):312–14.

56. Morris BJ, Krieger JN. Does male circumcision affect sexual function, sensitivity, or satisfaction?—A systematic review. *The Journal of Sexual Medicine*. 2013; 10(11):2644–57.

57. Bossio JA, Pukall CF, Steele S. A review of the current state of the male circumcision literature. *The Journal of Sexual Medicine*. 2014; 11(12):2847–64.

58. Earp BD. Addressing polarization in science. *Journal of Medical Ethics*. 2015; 41:782–84.

59. Earp BD. How can journal editors fight bias in polarized scientific communities? *Journal of Medical Ethics Blog*. 2015. Available at http:// blogs.bmj.com /medical-ethics/2015/04/30/how-can-journal-editors -fight-bias-in-polarized-scientific-communities/.

60. Aberson C. Interpreting null results: Improving presentation and conclusions with confidence intervals. *Journal of Articles in Support of the Null Hypothesis*. 2002; 1(3):36–42.

61. Rizvi SA, Naqvi S, Hussain M, Hasan A. Religious circumcision: a Muslim view. *BJU International*. 1999; 83(S1):13–16.

62. AAP. Male circumcision. *Pediatrics*. 2012; 130(3): e746–e785.

63. Stang HJ, Snellman LW. Circumcision practice patterns in the United States. *Pediatrics*. 1998; 101(6):e5.

64. Davis DS. Ancient rites and new laws: how should we regulate religious circumcision of minors? *Journal of Medical Ethics*. 2013; 39(7):456–58.

65. Pounder DJ. Ritual mutilation: subincision of the penis among Australian Aborigines. *The American Journal of Forensic Medicine and Pathology*. 1983; 4(3):227–30.

66. Willis J. Heteronormativity and the deflection of male same-sex attraction among the Pitjantjatjara people of Australia's Western Desert. *Culture, Health and Sexuality*. 2003; 5(2):137–51.

67. Anike U, Govender I, Ndimande JV, Tumbo J. Complications of traditional circumcision amongst young Xhosa males seen at St Lucy's Hospital, Tsolo, Eastern Cape, South Africa: original research. *African Primary Health Care and Family Medicine*. 2013; 5(1):1–5.

68. Gonzalez L. South Africa: over half a million initiates maimed under the knife. *All Africa*. 2014. Available at http://allafrica.com/stories/201406251112.html.

69. Maseko N. When circumcision can mean death in South Africa. *BBC News Africa*. 2013. Available at http://www.bbc.co.uk/news/world-africa-23378694.

70. Checketts R. Response to freedom of information request, FOI/0742. Birmingham Children's Hospital, NHS Foundation Trust. 2012. Available at http:// www.secularism.org.uk/uploads/foi-bch-response -received-260612.pdf.

71. Earp BD. Boys and girls alike. *Aeon Magazine*. 2015. Available at http://aeon.co/magazine/philosophy/male -and-female-circumcision-are-equally-wrong/.

72. CDC. *Recommendations for Providers Counseling Male Patients and Parents Regarding Male Circumcision and the Prevention of HIV Infection, STIs, and Other Health Outcomes*. 2014. Available at http://www.regulations .gov/#!documentDetail;D=CDC-2014-0012-0003.

73. CDC. *Draft CDC Recommendations for Providers Counseling Male Patients and Parents Regarding Male Circumcision and the Prevention of HIV Infection, STIs,*

and Other Health Outcomes. 2014. Available at http:// www.cdc.gov/nchhstp/newsroom/docs/MC-factsheet -508.pdf.

74. World Health Organization. *Male Circumcision for HIV Prevention*. 2015.

75. Garenne M, Giami A, Perrey C. Male circumcision and HIV control in Africa: questioning scientific evidence and decision making process. In *Global Health in Africa: Historical Perspectives on Disease Control*, ed. Giles-Vernick T, Webb JLA Jr. Athens, Ohio: Ohio University Press. 2013:185–210.

76. Earp BD. Do the benefits of male circumcision outweigh the risks? A critique of the proposed CDC guidelines. *Frontiers in Pediatrics*. 2014; 3(18):1–6.

77. Frisch M, Aigrain Y, Barauskas V, et al. Cultural bias in the AAP's 2012 Technical Report and Policy Statement on male circumcision. *Pediatrics*. 2013; 131(4):796–800.

78. Wettergren B, Jodal U, Jonasson G. Epidemiology of bacteriuria during the first year of life. *Acta Paediatrica Scandinavica*. 1985; 74:925–33.

79. Benatar M, Benatar D. Between prophylaxis and child abuse: the ethics of neonatal male circumcision. *American Journal of Bioethics*. 2003; 3(2):35–48.

80. Singh-Grewal D, Macdessi J, Craig J. Circumcision for the prevention of urinary tract infection in boys: a systematic review of randomised trials and observational studies. *Archives of Disease in Childhood*. 2005; 90(8):853–58.

81. Van Howe RS. *A CDC-Requested, Evidence-Based Critique of the Centers for Disease Control and Prevention 2014 Draft on Male Circumcision: How Ideology and Selective Science Lead to Superficial, Culturally-Biased Recommendations by the CDC*. 2015. Available at https://www.academia.edu/10553782/A_CDC -requested_Evidence-based_Critique_of_the _Centers_for_Disease_Control_and_Prevention_2014 _Draft_on_Male_Circumcision_How_Ideology_and _Selective_Science_Lead_to_Superficial_Culturally -biased_Recommendations_by_the_CDC.

82. de Witte L, Nabatov A, Pion M, et al. Langerin is a natural barrier to HIV-1 transmission by Langerhans cells. *Nature Medicine*. 2007; 13(3):367–71.

83. Edwards JNT, Morris, HB. Langerhans cells and lymphocyte subsets in the female genital tract. *BJOG: An International Journal of Obstetrics & Gynaecology*. 1985; 92(9):974–82.

84. Caldwell JC, Orubuloye IO, Caldwell P. Male and female circumcision in Africa from a regional to a specific Nigerian examination. *Social Science and Medicine*. 1997; 44(8):1181–93.

85. Nussbaum MC. *Sex and Social Justice*. Oxford: Oxford University Press. 1999.

86. Johnson M. Male genital mutilation: beyond the tolerable? *Ethnicities*. 2010; 10(2):181–207.

87. Fox M, Thomson M. Foreskin is a feminist issue. *Australian Feminist Studies*. 2009; 24(60):195–210.

88. Ahmadu F. Rites and wrongs: an insider/outsider reflects on power and excision. In *Female "Circumcision" in Africa: Culture, Controversy, and Change*. 2000; 283–312.

89. Manderson L. Local rites and body politics: tensions between cultural diversity and human rights. *International Feminist Journal of Politics*. 2004; 6(2):285–307.

90. Wade L. Learning from "Female Genital Mutilation": lessons from 30 years of academic discourse. *Ethnicities*. 2012; 12(1):26–49.

91. James SM, Robertson CC. *Genital Cutting and Transnational Sisterhood: Disputing US Polemics*. Champaign: University of Illinois Press. 2002.

92. Kirby V. On the cutting edge: feminism and clitoridectomy. *Australian Feminist Studies*. 1987; 2(5):35–55.

93. Shaheed F. Constructing identities: culture, women's agency and the Muslim world. *International Social Science Journal*. 1999; 51(159):61–73.

94. Dustin M. Female genital mutilation/cutting in the UK: challenging the inconsistencies. *European Journal of Women's Studies*. 2010; 17(1):7–23.

95. Wax D. *Female Genital Cutting, Sexuality, and Anti-FGC Advocacy*. University of Nevada: Las Vegas. 2006. Available at https://www.academia.edu /1622829/Female_Genital_Cutting_Sexuality_and _Anti-FGC_Advocacy.

96. Ehrenreich N, Barr M. Intersex surgery, female genital cutting, and the selective condemnation of cultural practices. *Harvard Civil Rights–Civil Liberties Law Review*. 2005; 40:71–539.

97. Cohen SJ. Why aren't Jewish women circumcised? *Gender and History*. 1997; 9(3):560–78.

98. Cohen SJ. *Why Aren't Jewish Women Circumcised? Gender and Covenant in Judaism*. Berkeley: University of California Press. 2005.

99. Benatar D. Why do Jewish egalitarians not circumcise their daughters? *Jewish Affairs*. 2008; Chanukah:21–23.

100. Kimmel MS. The kindest un-cut. *Tikkun*. 2001; 16(3):43–48. Available at http://www.cirp.org/pages /cultural/kimmel1/.

101. Aggleton P. "Just a snip"?: A social history of male circumcision. *Reproductive Health Matters*. 2007; 15(29):15–21.

102. Lightfoot-Klein H. *Prisoners of Ritual: An Odyssey into Female Genital Circumcision in Africa*. Philadelphia: Haworth Press, Inc. 1989.

103. Boyle GJ, Goldman R, Svoboda JS, Fernandez E. Male circumcision: pain, trauma and psychosexual sequelae. *Journal of Health Psychology*. 2002; 7(3):329–43.

104. Darby R. *A Surgical Temptation: The Demonization of the Foreskin and the Rise of Circumcision in Britain*. Chicago: University of Chicago Press. 2005.

105. Plaskow J. Blaming Jews for inventing patriarchy. *Lilith*. 1980; 7:11–12.

106. Abdulcadir J, Margairaz C, Boulvain M, Irion O. Care of women with female genital mutilation /cutting. *Swiss Medical Weekly*. 2011; 140:w13137.

107. Coleman DL. The Seattle compromise: multicultural sensitivity and Americanization. *Duke Law Journal*. 1998:717–83.

108. Merkel R, Putzke H. After Cologne: male circumcision and the law. Parental right, religious liberty or criminal assault? *Journal of Medical Ethics*. 2013; 39(7):444–49.

109. Ludbrook R. The child's right to bodily integrity. *Current Issues in Criminal Justice*. 1995; 7(2):123–32.

110. Dekkers W. Routine (non-religious) neonatal circumcision and bodily integrity: a transatlantic dialogue. *Kennedy Institute of Ethics Journal*. 2009; 19(2):125–46.

111. Darby R. The mysterious disappearance of the object of inquiry: Jacobs and Arora's defense of circumcision. *American Journal of Bioethics*. 2015; 15(5):70–72.

112. Svoboda JS. Promoting genital autonomy by exploring commonalities between male, female, intersex, and cosmetic female genital cutting. *Global Discourse*. 2013; 3(2):237–55.

113. Darby R. The child's right to an open future: is the principle applicable to non-therapeutic circumcision? *Journal of Medical Ethics*. 2013; 39(7):463–68.

114. Mason C. Exorcising excision: medico-legal issues arising from male and female genital surgery in Australia. *Journal of Law and Medicine*. 2001; 9(1): 58–67.

115. Earp BD, Sandberg A, Savulescu J. Brave new love: The threat of high-tech "conversion" therapy and the bio-oppression of sexual minorities. *AJOB Neuroscience*. 2014; 5(1):4–12.

116. Earp BD, Wudarczyk OA, Sandberg A, Savulescu J. If I could just stop loving you: Anti-love biotechnology and the ethics of a chemical breakup. *American Journal of Bioethics*. 2013; 13(11):3–17.

117. Earp BD. The ethics of infant male circumcision. *Journal of Medical Ethics*. 2013; 39(7):418–20.

118. Earp BD. Things I have learned (so far) about how to do practical ethics. *Practical Ethics*. University of Oxford. 2014. Available at http://blog. practicalethics .ox.ac.uk/2014/03/things-ive-learned-so-far-about -how-to-do-practical-ethics/.

119. Earp BD. Prostitution, harm, and disability: Should only people with disabilities be allowed to pay for sex? *Journal of Medical Ethics*. 2015. E-letter. Available at https://www.academia.edu/13252176/Prostitution _harm_and_disability_Should_only_people_with _disabilities_be_allowed_to_pay_for_sex.

120. Hutson JM. Circumcision: a surgeon's perspective. *Journal of Medical Ethics*. 2004; 30(3):238–40.

THE POLITICS OF ACCULTURATION: FEMALE GENITAL CUTTING

LISA WADE

Modern democracies around the globe are struggling to build functional, integrated, egalitarian nations in the face of social conflicts deemed "cultural." This crisis of culture derives, in part, from the multiplicitous and paradoxical meanings of the term. Used to describe time-honored traditions, unconscious habits, group identities (racial, ethnic, and other), the character of nation-states, religious practices, and both "high" and "folk" art, culture is both condemned as a primary obstacle to the spread of human rights and celebrated as a human right in itself (Benhabib, 2002; Cowan, Dembour, and Wilson, 2001; Merry, 2006). Indeed, the term seems to have lost any coherent meaning even as it has become increasingly politicized (Eriksen, 2001; Fraser, 1995; Turner, 1993).

As illustrated by Susan Okin's (1997) famous question, "Is multiculturalism bad for women?" the challenge of managing (so-called) cultural difference is crystallized in conflicts over women's rights. Practices like dowry murders, honor crimes, sex-selective abortion, forced or arranged marriage, and female genital cutting (FGC) are all framed as cultural problems that test the limits of cross-cultural tolerance. Culture itself is often held accountable for the perpetuation of these practices, alongside or instead of individuals, such that the well-being of girls and women seems to be incompatible with cultural preservation (Narayan, 1997). The apparent incommensurability between feminism and multiculturalism has spurred a voluminous literature in which culture has been both defended and derided. . . .

More recently, however, scholars have been interrogating the assumptions behind this discussion of Okin's question. These scholars have argued that the object driving the multiculturalism/feminism debates is not "culture," but our model of culture. While most anthropologists and sociologists of culture adopt various dynamic models (e.g., Bourdieu, 1977; Sewell, 1992; Swidler, 2001), public debates often assume a reified model, selectively applied, in which culture is characterized by timelessness, internal coherence, clear boundaries, and determinism (Benhabib, 2002; Merry, 2006; Narayan, 2000). It is this reified model that makes the answer to Okin's question appear to be "yes" by presupposing that some groups, but not others, are rigidly bound to an un-reformable (patriarchal) culture.

I contribute to this emerging literature in two ways. First, instead of looking at cultural practices and cultural groups, I focus on cultural change. I show that the reified model of culture also shapes our perception of acculturation, with serious consequences for our ability to manage the compromise and accommodation essential to multicultural democracies. Second, I interrogate how the dynamic model of culture is discursively mobilized. I show that the dynamic model, just like the reified model,

From "The Politics of Acculturation: Female Genital Cutting," *Social Problems*, Vol. 58, Issue 4, 2011, pp. 518–37. Copyright © 2011, The Society for the Study of Social Problems Inc. By permission of Oxford University Press.

can be used by actors to shape perceptions of social change in troubling ways. The adoption of a dynamic model, then, does not necessarily mean that contests will be more civil, inclusive, or productive.

I make these arguments with an examination of the role that culture played in a debate over a proposal by U.S. physicians to offer a modified female genital cutting procedure to immigrants. Somali patients at Seattle, Washington's Harborview Medical Center were requesting that physicians perform genital cutting on their daughters. In Somalia, 98 percent of women undergo infibulation, a practice that involves the removal of labial tissue, trimming of the clitoris, and fusing of the anterior vulva (WHO, 2008). Wanting to attend to their patients' "cultural needs," and desiring to reduce the chance that girls would be subjected to infibulation, a group of physicians proposed to offer a procedure in the clinic: a one-centimeter incision in the clitoral foreskin. Before they could implement the plan, however, opponents to the procedure began calling and writing the hospital. Those targeted reported that the objectors were angry and sometimes threatening. Cowed by the level of controversy and the intensity of the opposition, the medical center revoked its support for the proposal . . .

Drawing on interviews, original documents, and newspaper coverage, I analyze how advocates and critics of the proposal used culture to defend and attack the procedure. I show that the conflict rested on whether the move from infibulation to an incision was framed as cultural change or persistence. Opponents of the proposal (hereafter: "opponents") argued that Somali interest in the incision was proof of their *in*ability to throw off the ancient patriarchal practices to which they were obedient. They critiqued Somalis for being *in*flexible and physicians for being *grossly* flexible. From the physicians' perspective, however, this was a stunning mischaracterization. They saw the procedure as essentially symbolic; it was, literally, the *least* they could do. From their perspective, then, adoption of the alternative procedure would be a testament to Somali cultural flexibility and their own respect for cultural differences.

I argue that these dramatically different interpretations of the physicians' proposal are explained by differences in the implicit models of culture used by opponents and physicians. Physicians assumed a dynamic model of culture that attributed to Somalis an ability to adapt to (a presumably egalitarian) U.S. culture. Opponents, in contrast, applied a reified model of culture that made anything but abandonment appear to be cultural persistence. I argue, further, that both models, as mobilized by these actors, failed to capture the complexity of this difficult compromise. Because opponents used the reified model of culture, they reinforced negative stereotypes and fomented cross-cultural intolerance. They failed to recognize Somali women's autonomy, privileged Western over Somali ideas about the symbolic meaning of genital cutting, and trivialized the abandonment of infibulation. Physicians using the dynamic model of culture did not make these mistakes, granting Somali women autonomy from culture, independence from the men in their lives, and the ability to reflect thoughtfully. Physicians, however, used the dynamic model against opponents. Romanticizing acculturation to the United States, and their own ability to rather effortlessly chaperone the abandonment of infibulation and its patriarchal meanings, they felt comfortable excluding socially relevant constituencies such as feminists and anthropologists from their deliberations and, when their proposal brought opposition, they dismissed opponents' concerns as irrelevant, even ridiculous.

This incident occured in 1996, but the intervening years have brought little clarity. In 2010, the American Academy of Pediatrics published a position statement endorsing a "ritual nick." Their logic, and that of those who emerged to oppose them—which I discuss in more detail below—was essentially the same as in 1996. And, just as they did 15 years [earlier], the physicians responded to the opposition by revoking their recommendation. This case study, then, remains timely and illuminates a still active debate. . . .

REVIEW OF THE LITERATURE

The Politics of Culture

Many sociologists of culture, even when they otherwise disagree, understand culture to be a complex collective repertoire of practices and ideas (e.g., Bourdicu, 1977; Sewell, 1992; Swidler, 2001). Because its logics and imperatives are often contradictory, people's values and behaviors are not determined; instead, culture serves as a resource with which people strategically and pragmatically make sense of the world. Culture inevitably evolves as actors accept and challenge meanings, borrow from other cultures, negotiate with other individuals, and react to economic, political, and technological change. Among sociologists, Ann Swidler's (1986) "toolkit" is the most well-known metaphor for what I will call a "dynamic model of culture."

One of the tools in this cultural toolkit is "culture" itself (hereafter sans quotations) and politics is one arena in which the idea is mobilized (Fraser, 2000). Indeed, it is now common to use culture as a basis for rights claims and resource allocation at both national and transnational levels (Cowan et al., 2001; Eriksen, 2001; Fraser, 1995; Turner, 1993). In some cases we see strategic essentialism (Spivak, 1985). Indigenous groups "orientalize" themselves (Said, 1978) to appeal to both national and international audiences and national leaders defend against "Westernization" by claiming

that it amounts to cultural imperialism (Jackson, 1995:19; see also Chanock, 2002; Cowan, 2001; Merry, 2001; Narayan, 1997; Sieder and Witchell, 2001). Western countries have made similar moves: French lawmakers, for example, resisted passing anti-sexual harassment laws with the argument that doing so required seeing France through an American cultural lens (Saguy, 2003). Individuals can also use respect for cultural difference to claim special rights based on cultural membership, such as the right of Sikhs to refrain from wearing motorcycle helmets and hardhats and the right to turn to faith-based conflict resolution instead of secular law (Cowan et al., 2001; Razack, 2007). Groups not previously identified as cultural are also tapping into pro-multiculturalism discourses. For example, some religious groups are fighting the separation of church and state by claiming that the inclusion of their beliefs in public education is consistent with multiculturalism (Davies, 1999).

Culture, however, can also be used to negatively portray group members and justify the withdrawal of rights and resources. Economically and politically powerful nation-states penalize less powerful nation-states who do not work to eradicate "harmful traditional practices" (Boyle, 2002; Merry, 2006), wars and other aggressive interventions are justified with references to backward, barbaric, and evil cultures (Abu-Lughod, 2002; Cooke, 2002; Stabile and Kumar, 2005), and cultural practices, like veiling, are banned on the premise that they are incompatible with a "neutral" public sphere (Bloul, 1994; Dustin and Phillips, 2008; Mushaben, 2005). Individuals can also demonize their own culture for individual gain. They can, for example, obtain asylum by claiming that they are persecuted members of an oppressive culture (Piot, 2007; Razack, 1995) and gain leniency in sentencing on the supposition that "their culture made them do it" (Fournier, 2002; Phillips, 2003; Volpp, 1994).

The Power of Culture: Reified and Dynamic Models

The power of culture in these arguments comes from its reification. To reify culture is to (1) presume that cultural groups have nonambiguous boundaries and nonoverlapping memberships (Benhabib, 2002; Gupta and Ferguson, 1992; Narayan, 1997, 2000); (2) essentialize cultural content as unchanging, internally coherent, and universally embraced (Abu-Lughod, 1991; Anthias, 2002; Parekh, 1995; Rudy, 2000); and (3) attribute causal power to culture such that it is "superautonomous" relative to the autonomy of its members (Calmore, 1992:2185; see also Appadurai, 1988; Benhabib, 2002; Phillips, 2007). Widely criticized by academics, this view of culture is also called a "package picture" (Narayan, 1998, 2000), a "billiard ball conception" (Tully, 1995), an "essentialist model" (Cowan et al., 2001; Merry, 2006), and a "reductionist sociology of culture" (Benhabib, 2002). Following Nancy Fraser (2000), I call it a "reified model of culture."

A reified model is strategically useful because only a culture that is presumed to persist independent of historical change and interpenetration with other cultural groups can be argued to deserve perfect preservation or require total destruction. When the culture or cultural practice in question is celebrated, a reified model allows insiders to insist on protectionism and isolationism; only if we imagine cultures to be unchanging is change threatening to cultural survival. When a culture or cultural practice is condemned, the same model calls for intervention to force cultural group members to abandon their culture; only if we imagine culture to be totalizing is forced abandonment the route to the enhancement of human rights. In contrast, a dynamic model takes for granted that cultures change and, thus, are never perfectly authentic or entirely unredeemable. To frame a practice as cultural in this context does not mean, then, that the practice must be preserved exactly as is, nor eradicated completely for the sake of human rights.

Importantly, powerful groups often characterize themselves as culture-less or only lightly cultural (the dynamic model) at the same time that they frame others as culture-bound (the reified model). . . . Members of non-Western societies, then, are often portrayed as hopelessly backward, incapable of change and, ultimately, "imperfectible" (Lazreg, 1988:87; see also Pournier, 2002; Merry, 2006; Mohanty, 1988; Volpp, 1994, 2000).

These divergent relationships to culture attributed to Western and non-Western societies influence not just portrayals of cultural groups, but portrayals of their cultural practices, and even what practices are understood to be cultural at all. In many instances, social problems in societies deemed culture-bound are described by members of other societies as *cultural* practices related to the beliefs, values, and traditions of the entire group. In contrast, social problems in Western societies are often individualized, understood to be caused by bad people, not bad societies. Uma Narayan (1997), for example, has shown that the rationale behind "dowry murders" in India is framed in U.S. discourse as cultural and characterized as a normative national characteristic with deep historical roots. Domestic murders in the United States, however, which occur at a similar frequency, are seen as the unfortunate result of a few unusually bad men and not reflective of American culture. . . . Meanwhile, Pascale Fournier (2002), examining the use of the "cultural defense" to moderate sentencing in sexual assault cases, has found that lawyers sometimes argue that immigrants are prone to violence by virtue of their membership in a "primitive" culture; lesser sentences are justified by pointing to culture as a co-perpetrator. Drawing on Narayan's observation that dowry murders are often framed as "death by culture"

(p. 103), Fournier calls the cultural defense "rape by culture" (p. 81).

In each of these cases, culture is identified as the cause of social problems, a tendency that functions primarily to condemn the culture in question, at the expense of providing an explanation for why a problematic practice persists. Foreign men rape, murder, and mutilate women, the culture frame implies, because that is "how they are." At best, to say "they do it because they do it" is tautological and, at worst, it *mis*represents cultural beliefs and practices as independent from the economic, technological, and political forces that influence their persistence, emergence, and disappearance (Narayan, 1997; Turner, 1993). . . .

Models of Culture and the Compatibility of Multicultural and Feminism

Just as the reified model gives cultural arguments their power, it is this model, especially as it is applied asymmetrically, that makes it seem as if feminism and multiculturalism are incompatible. A dynamic model of culture assumes that women in different cultural contexts can use their own cultural tools to empower themselves. This is the premise behind the insistence on the existence of feminisms. Pluralizing the term acknowledges that women's liberation may look differently for different women (e.g., Abu-Lughod, 2002; Collins, 1991; Narayan, 1997). . . .

If we believe that the culture to be integrated is *immutably* patriarchal, however, embracing [it] is equivalent to embracing patriarchy, logically leading to a denial of the agency of some women. [They] must reject [their] culture, we imagine, or embrace patriarchy. When women contest the idea that their choices are manifestations of their complicity with patriarchy, they can be dismissed as falsely conscious. Since they are believed to be incapable of liberating themselves, it is concluded that they must be liberated by members of societies to which we ascribe gender egalitarianism and dynamism. Lightly cultural people, then, must step in to help the culture-bound. The phenomenon is succinctly described by Gayatri Spivak's (1988) phrase "white men [and women] are saving brown women from brown men" (p. 296). . . .

[This logic is] used to invalidate the opinions of women who support female genital cutting. Wairimu Ngaruiya Njambi (2004) argues that the "decision to avoid as well as to opt for female circumcision is both within the realm of cultural possibility" (p. 283; see also Ahmadu 2001). Yet, U.S. discourse about FGCs all too often portrays women who support genital cutting as patriarchal pawns, contrasting them with a supposedly liberated American woman (Wade, 2009). . . .

Okin's question as to whether multiculturalism is bad for women, then, depends very much on how the idea of culture is mobilized. Insofar as a reified model of culture is driving our national and transnational politics—and there is good evidence to suggest it is (Benhabib, 2002; Fraser, 1995; Merry, 2006; Narayan, 1997)—then societies can either be multicultural or egalitarian, but not both. Driven by this logic, states take the counterintuitive step of restricting women's rights in the interest of their own liberation. . . .

Cultural change, like practices and peoples, is subject to social construction. The perception that a culture has changed, or not, is the product of ideological and discursive projects, as well as practical and material realities. Whether something counts as cultural preservation or disruption, then, is the outcome of contests between social agents who select and fetishize certain aspects of cultural practice and specific time periods as "traditional." Describing research by Olayinka Koso-Thomas (1987), Narayan (1998) offers the example of changes in genital cutting rituals in Sierra Leone. Some Sierra Leonean proponents of the cutting insisted that continuing the practice was crucial to the survival of local culture. Koso-Thomas observed that almost all of the related ceremonial and educational practices had disappeared in response to other economic and social changes. The cutting itself, however, was fetishized as the critical link between the present and the past, while the fact that the practice of genital cutting was very different today was dismissed as unimportant. . . .

METHODS

Data used to investigate the controversy at Harborview Medical Center (hereafter: "Harborview") included newspaper coverage, material from the University of Washington archives, and interviews. . . .

The first set of interviewees was culled from . . . newspaper accounts. Using a snowball method of sampling, I identified additional individuals to interview, ultimately completing nine interviews with physicians, other hospital staff, and individuals involved with the media.[1] . . . I attempted to determine the trajectory of events, the important participants, and perceptions of various actors and their motivations. . . . When I include quotations from these interviews, I indicate the interviewee with an "Int" for "interview" and a number ranging from one to nine (e.g., Int9). Because of the small number of high-profile individuals involved in this controversy, I offer no additional details as to their identities in order to protect confidentiality. . . . I reconstituted a timeline and the facts of the controversy with the newspaper accounts, archived documents, and interviews. . . .

FINDINGS

Overview of the Controversy

Harborview Medical Center's mission is to provide culturally responsive health care. To achieve this goal, the hospital disseminates knowledge about different healing traditions through a website, EthnoMed (ethnomed.org). Aimed at the wider medical community, the site is a repository of "cultural information" about ethnic groups and their health beliefs. Harborview also modifies standards of care in ways that satisfy "cultural" as well as "medical" needs. . . .

Blending Western with non-Western medicine placed significant demands on the hospital and its employees, but they prided themselves on trying to live up to their mission. Accordingly, when a resident obstetrician/gynecologist, Leslie Miller, asked her colleagues if they could devise a productive way to respond to Somali mothers' requests for female "circumcision," the response was positive. My informant, describing their reaction, continued: "it didn't seem to be an odd and unusual thing . . . that's what we do, is we try to make sure that everybody is really comfortable . . . that's what we were so proud of doing at Harborview . . . meeting people's cultural needs" (Int6). Finding a way to fold genital cutting into Harborview's practice, then, fit nicely with the mission of the institution, which both ascribed cultural motivations to its patients and counted upon their ability to adapt to a modified Western medical approach.

On this rationale, the medical director approved a plan to hold focus groups with Somali mothers. The initiating physician, Miller, facilitated three discussions with a total of 36 women. Notes from the focus groups indicate that the mothers were amenable to a modified version of genital cutting. Because they had all undergone infibulation as girls, they were intimately familiar with the short- and long-term suffering that often accompanied the practice and they did not want their daughters to be infibulated. But neither did they want to abandon the practice entirely. An informant reported: "[T]hey were not interested in their daughters having *that* [infibulation] done to them. But at the same time they weren't interested in the daughters not having *anything* done" (Int8). The mothers explained that they desired to preserve some form of the practice as a nod to their religion and tradition, but also because they believed that it bonded their daughters to their community and marked the transition from girl to woman. Aesthetics, "purity," and the prevention of premarital sex, they claimed, were not considerations.

The notes revealed that the mothers asked that clinics offer a procedure in which a small piece of tissue would be removed as painlessly as possible. Miller explained that they would not remove tissue, but could possibly offer a small incision in the prepuce (or foreskin) of the clitoris that would draw blood. The mothers, with one exception, agreed that this would be sufficient. Similar compromises had been made in East Africa and elsewhere, so some of the mothers may have been familiar with this kind of alternative (though Somalia has been particularly isolated in this regard) (Gruenbaum, 1991; see also Abed et al., 1995; Isa, Shuib, and Othman, 1999).

The following June a committee convened to discuss whether Miller's proposal satisfied principles of medical ethics and, if so, to work out the details of its delivery. The eight-member committee included only physicians: a urologist, a plastic surgeon, and five pediatricians, one of whom was a specialist in bioethics. Defending the idea of an impermeable professional boundary, physicians saw the issue as firmly within their "scope of practice" and subject to the same privacy laws that guarantee the right to abortion in the United States. When asked if nonphysicians had been consulted, one informant insisted: "this is a matter of privacy between a patient and a family. . . . [It's not any] outsiders' business if there is consent with discussion with a patient and family. So, no . . ." (Int3). In line with this thinking, the physicians did not consult with other experts or interest groups, such as anthropologists or anti-FGC activists.

Subsequent to deliberation, the committee wrote a proposal recommending that the medical staff at the Children's Clinic offer a one-centimeter incision in the prepuce (foreskin of the clitoris) under a topically applied local anesthetic. Described as a "prepotomy" ("prep" referring to the prepuce and "otomy" meaning incision), there would be no tissue removal, no need for sutures, and little or no scarring. The procedure would be performed on girls 11 and older who signed a consent form after being interviewed separately from their parents to ascertain their understanding of and desire for the procedure. It would then be performed by physicians under "direct supervision and assistance of Somali midwives," with a follow-up three days later. The clinic and the midwife would split a $40 fee. The medical director sent the recommendation to the state attorney general for review in light of the (then-pending, but soon to be passed) federal law against "female genital mutilation."

The effort to stop implementation of the proposal was led by Patricia Schroeder, Meserak Ramsey, and Mariama Barrie-Diamond. Schroeder was a U.S. Representative (D–Colorado) and the sponsor of the anti-FGM law. Ramsey and Barrie-Diamond grew up in Ethiopia and Sierra Leone, respectively, and later moved to the United States; both underwent infibulation as children. Barrie-Diamond had written about her genital cutting experience for *Essence* magazine. Ramsey had founded the U.S. arm of an organization dedicated to the eradication of FGCs, the Foundation for Women's Health Research and Development. In addition to contacting the hospital personally, all three publicized the proposal through the media, activist networks, and conferences. As a result, the hospital began receiving letters and phone calls from individuals opposed to the proposal.

My informants interpreted the outcry to be the machinations of "rabid feminists" (Int5), "zealots" (Int3), and "radicals" (Int2). Nevertheless, the opponents were ultimately successful in halting the implementation of the physicians' proposal. The attorney general concluded that the procedure would not violate the law, but told the medical director to abandon the proposal nonetheless. Still frustrated many years later, one informant behind the proposal remarked that they had made a "spectacular misjudgment of the political climate" (Int6). Reflecting the weariness of the proposal's advocates, *The Seattle Times* (1996) story about the decision to abandon the proposal was four sentences long and quoted a hospital spokesperson saying only: "we're not going to do it." How did the physicians and their opponents come to have such diametrically opposed evaluations of the proposed procedure?

The Physicians' Logic

The minutes from the committee meeting, my interviews, and the quotations from physicians included in newspaper accounts reveal physicians' rationale for endorsing the proposal. Prepotomy, they argued, was a significant departure from infibulation and, therefore, a meaningful cultural change enacted thoughtfully by a self-conscious community. Though they were proposing to cut girls' genitals, physicians and hospital staff insisted that the prepotomy was different: "No one was out to practice female genital mutilation," said one informant (Int6); while another explained, "It's not *that* you are doing a procedure down there, it's *what* you're doing down there" (Int1). When pushed in the news coverage, the hospital staff insisted that they were not proposing to perform "female genital mutilation" or "female circumcision." The medical director, for example, explained: "No one is contemplating doing those rituals most people associate

with female circumcision. . . . Medical and ethical standards would prohibit any procedures that mutilate or unnecessarily remove tissue from a female's genitals" (Paulson, 1996). Similarly, the obstetrician-gynecologist who initiated the deliberations was quoted saying that the mothers were "asking for a small incision, a bloodletting. . . . It's very different than what happened to them" (Paulson, 1996). And a public relations officer explained: "We are not now doing female circumcisions at Harborview, nor are we considering doing female circumcisions" (Brune, 1996). From their perspective, prepotomy was not "mutilation"; the move to prepotomy, then, marked a significant and positive cultural change.

Reflecting the medical center's commitment to cultural compromise, physicians expressed mixed ideas about Somali culture. Ultimately, though, they applied a dynamic model of culture, believing that the Somalis were capable of choosing to adapt to U.S. culture without entirely abandoning their traditions. On the one hand, physicians saw culture as a powerful force in the lives of their patients. They expressed this with the language of "cultural need," a phrase that was used by four of my informants and appeared in two news articles and four of the archived correspondences. That they took cultural influence seriously is evident in their concerns that the mothers of their Somali patients would have their daughters infibulated in the absence of an alternative. Physicians remarked that the mothers threatened to take their daughters to Somalia if Harborview did not offer a procedure; others mentioned that there was a traditional practitioner in Vancouver who was known to do infibulations, and they discussed one focus group participant who said that, if the physicians did not offer a procedure, she would do it herself. Physicians believed, then, that immigrants held "traditional" or "historical" health-related beliefs that they could not be expected to abandon wholesale upon arrival in the United States.

On the other hand, physicians did not see Somalis as culture-bound. In fact, they envisioned that prepotomy would be a "bridg[e]" between infibulation and abandonment of genital cutting altogether. One informant explained:

We were dealing with a group that's not yet fully acculturated into the United States. . . . You are probably more likely to make progress by working with them in a way that didn't harm their children, and then sort of allowing them to . . . recognize that this past practice was not such a good idea. . . . The odds were that their daughters who would become acculturated to the United States would probably not be coming back in 20 years seeking the same sort of thing for their daughters. And so this was seen as sort of a bridging procedure (Int1).

Instead of a blind following of tradition, physicians argued that the Somalis' desire for genital cutting was "analogous" to that of Jewish families in the U.S. who practice male circumcision (Int5):

So the male circumcision . . . is very important and everybody recognizes it as a legitimate cultural need. Female circumcision, you know, has not had that same recognition. But it certainly has the same long tradition. It's been done for thousands of years. It's been done over many different religious groups. It continues to be done, even though it's been made illegal in many countries. And so I think you have to ask, well, why are people doing it? Are they doing it just because they are uneducated and, you know, don't understand this is a barbaric procedure? Or is it really meeting some need within the society (Int5)?

Comparing FGCs and male circumcision, physicians resisted the idea that Americans were culture-less and Somalis culture-bound. Instead, they drew connections between Somali and American culture. From their perspective, Somalis were not incomprehensibly "traditional"; they were like Jewish Americans who also followed a tradition of medically unnecessary genital cutting because of its symbolic meaning.

Physicians and hospital staff also believed that the ritual could be modified symbolically as well as physically. One informant suggested that

there was a possibility to transform this particular procedure into really a coming-of-age procedure that involved a lot of intergenerational communication, really history, health training, and education; that you could transform this into something that could be very positive for families and for their own communities (Int6).

They believed, then, that something quite good could come out of prepotomy. This sense was facilitated by their dismissal of the concern that genital cutting was a way to symbolically indoctrinate Somali girls into a gendered subservience. They saw Somali women as powerful members of their community. One informant said:

The stereotype of, you know, the submissive woman being forced to have this procedure by sort of a patriarchal society doesn't really hold up, you know, in my own personal experience with this culture. These [Somali women] are very strong, capable women who run their families with a usually pretty clear control (Int6).

Drawing on familiar feminist ideas, committee members agreed that, if anything, it would be *inequitable* to deny girls the procedure, especially given that the procedure they had in mind involved less physical alteration and risk than male circumcision. Prepotomy, committee members felt, was simply a matter of "medical equity" or equal treatment for different kinds of patients (Int9). They had already modified the standard of care for Somali boys: they were circumcising them at puberty instead of infancy, per Somali tradition. Offering a procedure to girls, too, seemed only fair.

In sum, committee members believed that the Somali community "needed" an alternative to infibulation. They felt strongly that, if they failed to offer a procedure, girls would undergo a procedure that was more extensive, painful, and dangerous than the one they could offer. In that sense, they ascribed power to culture to shape Somali choices. However, they rejected the idea that Somalis could not change and the notion that Somali women were subject to a superautonomous culture. Instead, Somali culture included traditions that were followed for complex reasons that Somalis could be reflective about, just like Americans. With the support and encouragement of physicians, they believed, Somalis would choose prepotomy and later abandon cutting altogether. Even as they saw culture as an influential force, then, their model of culture allowed for cultural evolution. This was a dynamic model. . . .

The Opponents' Logic

One of the physicians named in the newspaper coverage received phone calls and letters from opponents of the proposal. He kept and archived 25 letters and 17 postcards from an elementary school class (which I count as one "letter"); all but one objected to the proposal. These letters reveal that the resistance to the physicians' proposal centered around disagreement as to whether the move from infibulation to prepotomy was, truly, change.

The opponents' contrasting evaluation of the Somali interest in abandoning infibulation in favor of a prepotomy reflected a belief that they were essentially culture-bound. Opponents' arguments against the proposal involved a contrast between a "traditional" Somali culture and a culture-less or lightly cultural America characterized primarily by its commitment to protecting the supposedly universal rights of its citizens. For many opponents, the United States was an exemplar of social progress,

whereas Somalis were "traditional" and genital cutting was the embodiment of their cultural backwardness. Representative Schroeder's letter is illustrative of this approach, contrasting "mainstream" Western medicine with "barbari[sm]." She writes: "Quite frankly this apparent push for such a barbaric procedure by a respected, mainstream medical establishment both baffles and horrifies me." Another opponent insists, simply, "This horrible violence has no place in a civilized and democratic society . . ." (Manitoba, Canada).

Echoing Okin, some opponents explicitly placed the idea that Somalis have a right to culture in opposition to human rights. One, for example, argued: "even if the parents of children are authorising this operation, the rights of little girls should be considered above the so-called 'cultural rights' of ignorant parents" (West Sussex, UK). Other speakers also freely described the difference between "them" and "us" in terms of a linear notion of progress. One, who used the term "slice" (instead of the physicians' preferred "incision"), wrote:

We, as a civilized society must be vigilant in protecting the rights of all children, especially in this country. . . . The little girl's [sic] whose parents come from Somalia or wherever, are growing up American, which means equality and protection is their right (New York, NY).

This opponent contrasted America, a civilized country that protects children's rights, to Somalia, a country that does not. Similarly, Ramsey, one of the activists who spearheaded the opposition, was quoted in *The Seattle Times* (Ostrom, 1996) arguing that girls "*in this country . . . have a right to protect their bodies*" (emphasis added). Another opponent echoed her: "this is taking away their rights." Opponents' arguments against the proposal, then, characterized Somalis as irrational and ignorant carriers of old traditions. In contrast, the United States was culturally superior or, perhaps, culture-less, having evolved into a rational society organized around universal truths.

Believing the Somalis to be culture-bound, opponents evaluated the move to prepotomy as a continuation instead of an interruption of their cultural practices. While the extent of cutting and tissue removal was significant to physicians, it failed to impress opponents. They asserted that all forms of genital cutting were unacceptable, prepotomy no less than infibulation. They noted, correctly, that the prepotomy involved cutting genitals and was, thus, genital cutting. One informant explained that opponents argued that the practice was "a bad thing *in any form* and we can't do it" (Int8). Another, recalling a conversation with a particular opponent, explained that she objected to "*anybody* having *anything* to do with anything about sexual parts of a woman's body . . ." (Int5).

The letters, too, suggested that opponents felt that both infibulation and prepotomy were fairly and accurately described by the phrase "female genital mutilation." One opponent, who described the prepotomy as a "limited form of female genital mutilation," explicitly objected to any genital cutting, no matter how minimal; she headlined her letter: "STOP ANY TYPE OF FEMALE GENITAL MUTILATION" (Seattle, WAa; capitalization in the original). For this opponent, that the procedure was "limited" did not mean it was not "mutilation." Likewise, Representative Schroeder warned physicians that she entirely intended for a "ritual bloodletting" to be equivalent to infibulation under the law. She wrote: "The clear intent of the legislation the President signed was to criminalize *any* medically unnecessary procedure involving female genitalia. What Harborview appears to be considering would violate that clear intent."

In addition to objecting to the prepotomy, some opponents were concerned that offering one version of genital cutting would open the door to others. Physicians might perform increasingly extensive procedures once

becoming comfortable with the idea of cutting female genitals and facing an "escalation" of "demands and pressures" from immigrants (Seattle, WAb). This concern is certainly not baseless. Given that physicians perform male circumcisions and intersex and cosmetic female genital surgeries, it seems reasonable to worry that they might do to Somali teenagers what they are already doing to adult women and children of both sexes.

For opponents, prepotomy also represented the persistence of Somali cultural practice because they believed that the ritual, however minor, would allow the *symbolic* meaning of cutting to survive. Less optimistic than physicians about the possibility that the move to prepotomy would be accompanied by change in the practice's meaning, opponents argued that genital cutting was designed to teach girls their subordinate place in Somali society and, therefore, infibulation and prepotomy were symbolically identical. They explained: it "is the manifestation of society's fear of women's sexuality" (Manitoba, Canada) and is done "solely to make men feel as though they are in control of the womyn [sic] in their lives" (Ontario, Canada). The reporter for *The Seattle Times* (Ostrom, 1996) articulated this objection when, after describing the proposed procedure and discussing the medical rationale, she noted that: "None of that has placated those who say that even talking about cutting female genitals legitimizes a barbaric practice, one that disempowers women and serves to keep them out of the American mainstream." The reporter explains that opponents are uncomfortable entertaining the idea of an alternative cutting procedure on the assumption that doing so threatens to prop up foreign patriarchy in the United States. So, when physicians argued that the prepotomy was only "symbolic," opponents explained that this was *precisely* the problem. In truth, how exactly prepotomy would have been made meaningful is difficult to know.

The extent of the cutting and potential for harm was significant for physicians, then, but not for opponents who felt that the prepotomy was physically and symbolically equivalent. For them, a move to prepotomy represented a continuance of the Somali's genital cutting practice, not its end. Therefore, it was not cultural change, it was cultural persistence.

Based on the beliefs that compromise was impossible (because Somali culture was deeply traditional and resistant to change) and that adoption of the prepotomy represented continuance and not adaptation, opponents concluded that the physicians were capitulating to, instead of compromising with, Somali culture. Criticizing physicians for being *excessively* flexible, one opponent wrote: "Are we bending over backwards to meet demands from an immigrant cultural group that we envision as not having much power in the United States?" (Seattle, WA). For opponents, then, offering a genital cutting procedure did not help Somalis adapt to American culture through compromise; rather, it was adopting (backward) Somali values wholesale. The physicians' flexibility was equivalent to becoming "barbaric" and "uncivilized."

Indeed, if prepotomy was "savage," "evil," and "an act of barbarism," then so were the physicians and their procedure (East Sussex, UK; also Hempstead, NY; New York, NY; San Jose, CAa; Washington, DC; Westhung, NY; West Sussex, UK). One opponent wrote: "Whatever your reasoning concerning cutting young girls, it is clearly wrong. Even if a child asks for this ritual, she is only speaking the words of her parents. Barbaric, uncivilized words. Just like yours" (New York, NY). For the opponents, offering a prepotomy was a misguided attempt at political correctness and a ceding of American values to an immigrant group who was "insist[ing]" upon cultural accommodation (Napa, CA; San Jose, CA).

These arguments are consistent with a reified model of culture that wraps some cultures but not others in nonpermeable packages with straightforward memberships and discrete boundaries. Their description of Somali culture as "traditional" and the unfavorable comparison with a modern, progressive United States, placed Somalis among those people [who] are assumed to bring an ancient culture unchanged through time. Attributing a profound resilience to Somali culture, they foreclosed the possibility of (true) cultural adaptation. Even if the material practice changed, they argued, the symbolic meaning of genital cutting would persist. From the opponents' point of view, then, Somalis were not compromising, they were demanding that the United States adapt to them. Likewise, physicians were not multicultural heroes modeling cross-cultural tolerance, they were culturally relativist villains who were sacrificing sacred American values by capitulating to the backward beliefs of an immigrant group.

Despite their strong language and use of a reified model, however, opponents raised important questions. We do not know how prepotomy would have been made meaningful by the Somalis. Nor could we ensure that social pressure would not make adolescent consent meaningless. And physicians do, indeed, perform more extensive procedures on infants and adult women; it is not unreasonable to be concerned that we might add adolescent girls to the list of individuals who can legally undergo genital cutting practices.

SUMMARY OF FINDINGS AND ONGOING RELEVANCE

. . . The physicians' argument that the adoption of prepotomy signified meaningful cultural change was driven by a commitment to a dynamic model of culture. They rejected the idea that Somalis were irrationally committed to uniquely barbaric practices as well as the idea that Americans were entirely autonomous from culture. Comparing FGCs to male circumcision and emphasizing Somali women's autonomy from both men and their culture, physicians described a group of women who were negotiating issues familiar to Americans: imperfect traditions and sensitive family and community relationships. . . .

In contrast, opponents subscribed to a reified model of culture that led them to interpret the request for the modified procedure as the persistence of a genital cutting tradition. Opponents characterized Somali culture as obstinately tied to an ancient patriarchy. They observed that the change was only a move from one form of genital cutting to another and they imbued the practice with a stable, discernable, coherent meaning that would persist even in the face of changing contexts (from Somalia to Seattle) and practices (from infibulation to prepotomy). . . .

This debate is far from resolved. In 2010, the American Academy of Pediatrics (2010b) released an official statement in support of a similar procedure in clinics: a "pricking or incising the clitoral skin . . . no more of an alteration than ear piercing" (p. 1092). They supported such a procedure with the same logic articulated by the physicians in 1996. "The ritual nick," they argued:

is not physically harmful and is much less extensive than routine newborn male genital cutting . . . [and it] may build trust between hospitals and immigrant communities, save some girls from undergoing disfiguring and life-threatening procedures in their native countries, and play a role in the eventual eradication of FGC (p. 1092).

Using a now-familiar logic, Equality Now (2010) mobilized an opposition movement in response. In their "Urgent Alert," they argued that "pricking, piercing and incising of girls' genitalia are forms of female genital mutilation . . ." designed to oppress women and they recommended a letter writing campaign to pressure the AAP to retract its recommendation (p. 1).

The World Health Organization, United Nations Population Fund, United Nations Children's Fund, and United Nations Development Fund for Women also issued a joint press release condemning the AAP recommendation (WHO et al., 2010). Joining Equality Now in using the term "mutilation" instead of the physicians' "cutting," they described a nick as a violation of human rights, contesting the claim that "some forms of FGM are not harmful," and they argued that offering a "nick" may "give way to more invasive procedures" (pp. 1-2).

One month after the statement, the AAP revoked their recommendation (AAP 2010a).

CONCLUSIONS

The lessons learned from the controversy at Harborview Medical Center are consistent with the literature on debates about veiling in Western societies . . . and other practices like voluntary sex segregation, the desire to enter polygamous relationships, and arranged marriages (Ahmed, 1982; Arndt, 2000; Deveaux, 2007; Dustin and Phillips, 2008). This research has shown that a reified model of culture can harden cross-cultural antagonism, in part by making cultural tolerance seem incompatible with feminist principles, thereby justifying controlling and penalizing policies. In my case study, opponents of the prepotomy, informed by this model, reinforced negative stereotypes of Africa and rejected the possibility that the Somalis could transform genital cutting into something materially and symbolically consistent with gender equality. They also trivialized

---

Editor's note: In November 2012, the United Nations Member States approved a groundbreaking resolution calling for an end to "female genital mutilation" worldwide (United Nations, 2012).

the abandonment of infibulation, castigating physicians for pursuing a harm reduction strategy designed to protect girls from the worst kind of genital cutting. Instead, they endorsed zero tolerance, a position echoed in the federal U.S. law against "female genital mutilation" that would pass that year. Meanwhile, American culture remained uninterrogated on the assumption that it was superior, based on rational truths, or both. For the opponents, feminism was indeed incompatible with multiculturalism.

In addition to confirming the existing literature on cultural groups and practices, this case shows that a reified model can also shape perceptions of cultural *change* by disallowing the possibility of meaningful cultural adaptation altogether. If opponents could perceive the move from infibulation to prepotomy as no change at all—if they objected to both the potential symbolic meaning of the practice as well as the material outcome—then it is likely that there is nothing the Somalis could have done, short of an overt rejection of Somali culture in favor of mainstream American values, that would have been satisfying to the opponents.

This is a suggestive finding. It suggests that, for some, perceptions of a lack of autonomy from culture are not dependent on the choices a presumably culture-bound person makes. Instead, insofar as the reified model of culture drives perceptions, the fact that people are believed to be culture-bound may shape the evaluation of *all* of their choices. As a hypothetical, imagine that a Somali girl who immigrated with her parents as a child, and who was spared genital cutting, elects to undergo labiaplasty as an adult. Imagine she approaches the plastic surgeon with the same concerns that nonimmigrant American women bring: a concern that her labia are too large, too long, or asymmetrical. If the same dynamics are at play in the interpretation of her motivations

as were at play in the opponents' framing of prepotomy, it is likely that some will say that she is seeking "female genital mutilation." No matter how similar "their" practices become to "ours," then, Somalis and other members of groups deemed culture-bound may face scrutiny that others do not. The same choices that nonimmigrant American women make—the choice to undergo cosmetic genital surgery, but perhaps also the choice to marry young, be a stay-at-home mother, eschew higher education, dress modestly, or attend a fundamentalist or orthodox church—may be more likely to be interpreted as a sign of internalized oppression when Somali women make them. In other words, all choices made by someone who is presumably culture-bound can be interpreted as manifestations of her lack of autonomy, and can be used to condemn her culture as well.

It remains to be seen if using this lens to analyze similar debates will reveal similar phenomenon. If a young Somali girl did not submit to any kind of genital cutting, but still chose to protect her "honor" until marriage, is she interpreted as principled or traditional? If a Muslim woman chooses not to cover her hair, but wears, instead, a cloth-covered barrette as a reference to the hijāb, is she oppressed or innovative? Likewise, if an Indian woman refuses to allow her parents to arrange her marriage, but promises not to marry unless she has their approval, is this compromise or submission? Understanding how models of culture shape perceptions of cultural change may shed great light on these debates. . . .

The dynamic model of culture . . . may be used to mischaracterize cultural change in two ways. First, it may undersell cultural resilience, offering those who mobilize it an opportunity to trivialize social justice concerns and dismiss activists and scholars as irrelevant. This is the concern that Okin (1997) was articulating when she posed her question: "is multiculturalism bad for women?" Okin is taking seriously whether we are able to *ensure* that we are protecting both marginalized communities and their most vulnerable members. While the reified model of culture suggests that we cannot do both, the dynamic model can be used to suggest that her question is not worth asking.

Second, the dynamic model of culture allows one to dismiss the possibility that acculturation into American society may reinforce or even introduce the ideology and practice of women's subordination. An immigrant group can be acculturated into *new* ways of oppressing its women (Espiritu, 2000; Hondagneu-Sotelo, 1994). The physicians believed that the prepotomy would initiate acculturation to a society in which "genital mutilation" did not happen. In fact, however, adult women increasingly undergo genital alteration in U.S. clinics and hospitals: a woman can legally have collagen injected into her "g-spot" or her hymen "reconstructed"; she can have her clitoral foreskin removed (circumcision proper) or her clitoris reduced in size; she can have her labia trimmed if she thinks they are "obtrusive" or engorged with injections of fat if she thinks they are "too thin"; and she can have [the] size of her vaginal opening reduced with stitches for a tighter fit during penile-vaginal intercourse (colloquially known as a "husband's stitch" when it is performed during an episiotomy repair). These are defined by some as "enhancing" instead of "mutilating," but in some cases the effect is not dissimilar to what we include under the label "female genital mutilation" when it occurs elsewhere (Lewis and Gunning, 1998; Sheldon and Wilkinson, 1998). In other words, while the physicians saw the prepotomy as a "bridging" procedure between infibulation and the abandonment of genital cutting, it could just as easily become a bridge between American-reviled and American-endorsed genital cutting, with an already available, legal cosmetic procedure emerging as a new coming-of-age ritual for young Somali girls.

This hypothetical suggests that people drawing on the dynamic model of culture may take for granted that acculturation will conform to a set of progressive values that they believe permeate their own culture. This may lead to overly simple evaluations of the ease with which cultural change can be chaperoned and the easy dismissal of the need to engage with other constituencies. An analysis informed by the dynamic model, in other words, can be facile if it suggests that life-affirming cultural change is easy and inevitable, erasing the vision and vigilance required to establish truly functional, integrated, egalitarian nations.

NOTE

1. My university's institutional review board (IRB) did not grant me permission to interview Somali community members because of concerns that they might self-incriminate.

REFERENCES

Abed, Asali, Naif Khamaysi, Yunis Aburabia, Simha Letzer, Buteina Halihal, Mōshe Sadovsky, Benjamin Maoz, and R. Belmaker. 1995. "Ritual Female Genital Surgery among Bedouin in Israel." *Archives of Sexual Behavior* 24(5): 573–77.

Abu-Lughod, Lila. 1991. "Writing Against Culture." Pp. 137–62 in *Recapturing Anthropology: Working in the Present*, edited by R. G. Fox. Santa Fe, NM: School of American Research Press.

———. 2002, "Do Muslim Women Really Need Saving? Anthropological Reflections on Cultural Relativism and Its Others." *American Anthropologist* 104(3): 783–90.

Ahmadu, Fuambai. 2001. "Rites and Wrongs: An Insider/Outsider Reflects on Power and Excision." Pp. 283–312 in *Female 'Circumcision' in Africa: Culture, Controversy, and Change,* edited by Bettina Shell-Duncan and Ylva Hernlund. Boulder, CO: Lynne Rienner Publishers.

Ahmed, Leila. 1982. "Western Ethnocentrism and Perceptions of the Harem." *Feminist Studies* 8(3): 521–34.

American Academy of Pediatrics (AAP) Committee on Bioethics. 2010a. "American Academy of Pediatrics withdraws Policy Statement on Female Genital Cutting." *AAP News Room,* May 27. Retrieved June 14, 2010 (www.aap.org/advocacy/releases/fgc-may27-2010 .htm).

———. 2010b. "Policy Statement on Ritual Genital Cutting of Female Minors." *Pediatrics* 125(5): 1088–93.

Anthias, Floya. 2002. "Beyond Feminism and Multi-culturalism: Locating Difference and the Politics of Location." *Women's Studies International Forum* 25(3): 275–86.

Appadurai, Arjun, 1988. "Putting Hierarchy in Its Place." *Cultural Anthropology* 3(1): 36–49.

Arndt, Susan. 2000. "African Gender Trouble and African Womanism: An Interview with Chikwenye Ogunyemi and Wanjira Muthoni." *Signs* 25(3): 709–26.

Benhabib, Seyla. 2002. *The Claims of Culture: Equality and Diversity in the Global Era.* Princeton, NJ and Oxford, UK: Princeton University Press.

Bloul, Rachel. 1994. "Victims or Offenders? 'Other' Women in French Sexual Politics." *The European Journal of Women's Studies* 3(3): 251–68.

Bourdieu, Pierre. 1977. *Outline of a Theory of Practice.* Cambridge, UK: Cambridge University Press.

Boyle, Elizabeth Heger. 2002. *Female Genital Cutting: Cultural Conflict in the Global Community.* Baltimore, MD: Johns Hopkins University Press.

Brune, Tom. 1996. "Refugees' Beliefs Don't Travel Well: Compromise Plan on Circumcision of Girls Gets Little Support." *Chicago Tribune*, October 28. Retrieved December 11, 2004 (http://articles.chicagotribune.com/1996-10-28/news/9610280094_1_somali-community-circumcision-refugees).

Calmore, John, 1992. "Critical Race Theory, Archie Shepp, and Fire Music: Securing an Authentic Intellectual Life in a Multicultural World." *Southern California Law Review,* 65: 2129–230.

Chanock, Martin. 2002. "Human Rights and Cultural Branding: Who Speaks and How." Pp. 38–67 in *Cultural Transformation and Human Rights in Africa,* edited by Abdullahi An-Na'im. London, UK and New York; Zed Books.

Collins, Patricia Hill. 1991. *Black Feminist Thought: Knowledge, Consciousness, and the Politics of Empowerment.* New York: Routledge.

Cooke, Miriam. 2002. "Saving Brown Women." *Signs* 28(1): 468–70.

Cowan, Jane, 2001. "Ambiguities of an Emancipatory Discourse: The Making of a Macedonian Minority in Greece." Pp. 152–76 in *Culture and Rights: Anthropological Perspectives,* edited by Jane Cowan, Marie-Bénédicte Dembour, and Richard Wilson. Cambridge, UK: Cambridge University Press.

Cowan, Jane, Marie-Bénédicte Dembour, and Richard Wilson, 2001. "Introduction," Pp. 1–26 in *Culture and Rights: Anthropological Perspectives,* edited by Jane Cowan, Marie-Bénédicte Dembour, and Richard Wilson. Cambridge, UK; Cambridge University Press.

Davies, Scott. 1999. "From Moral Duty to Cultural Rights: A Case Study of Political Framing in Education." *Sociology of Education* 72(1):1–21.

Deveaux, Monique. 2007. "Personal Autonomy and Cultural Tradition." Pp. 139–66 in *Sexual Justice/Cultural Justice: Critical Perspectives in Political Theory and Practice,* edited by Barbara Arneil, Monique Deveaux, Rhita Dhamoon, and Avigail Eisenberg. London, UK and New York: Routledge.

Dustin, Moira and Anne Phillips. 2008. "Whose Agenda Is It? Abuses of Women and Abuses of 'Culture' in Britain." *Ethnicities* 8(3): 405–24.

Equality Now. 2010. "Urgent Alert (April 29): Equality Now Calls on the American Academy of Pediatrics to Retract a Portion of their Policy Statement Endorsing Type (IV) Female Genital Mutilation of Female Minors." Retrieved May 9, 2010 (www.equalitynow.org/node/584).

Eriksen, Thomas. 2001. "Between Universalism and Relativism: A Critique of the UNESCO Concept of Culture." Pp. 127–48 in *Culture and Rights: Anthropological Perspectives,* edited by Jane Cowan, Marie-Bénédicte Dembour, and Richard Wilson. Cambridge, UK: Cambridge University Press.

Espiritu, Yen Le. 2000. *Asian American Women and Men: Labor, Laws, and Love.* Walnut Creek, CA: Alta Mira Press.

Fournier, Pascale. 2002. "The Ghettoisation of Difference in Canada: 'Rape by Culture' and the Danger of a 'Cultural Defence' in Criminal Law Trials." *Manitoba Law Journal* 29: 81–119.

Fraser, Nancy, 1995. "From Redistribution to Recognition? Dilemmas of Justice in a 'Post-Socialist' Age." *New Left Review* I/212 (July/August): 67–93.

———. 2000. "Rethinking Recognition." *New Left Review* 3 (May-June): 107–20.

Gruenbaum, Ellen. 1991. "The Islamic Movement, Development and Health Education: Recent Changes in the Health of Rural Women in Central Sudan." *Social Science and Medicine* 33 (6):637–45.

Gupta, Akhil and James Ferguson. 1992. "Space, Identity, and the Politics of Difference." *Cultural Anthropology* 7(1): 6–23.

Hondagneu-Sotelo, Pierrette. 1994. *Gendered Transition: Mexican Experiences in Immigration.* Berkeley: University of California Press.

Isa, Ab. Rahman, Rashidah Shuib, and M. Shukri Othman. 1999. "The Practice of Female Circumcision among Muslims in Kelantan, Malaysia." *Reproductive Health Matters* 7(13): 137–44.

Jackson, Jean. 1995. "Culture, Genuine, and Spurious: The Politics of Indianness in the Vaupés, Colombia." *American Ethnologist* 22(1): 3–27.

Koso-Thomas, Olayinka. 1987. *The Circumcision of Women: A Strategy for Eradication.* London, UK: Zed Books.

Lazreg, Marnia. 1988. "Feminism and Difference: The Perils of Writing as a Woman on Women in Algeria." *Feminist Studies* 14(1): 81–107.

Lewis, Hope and Isabelle Gunning. 1998. "Cleaning Our Own House: 'Exotic' and Familial Human Rights Violations." *Buffalo Human Rights Law Review* 4:123–40.

Merry, Sally Engle. 2001. "Changing Rights, Changing Culture." Pp. 31–55 in *Culture and Rights: Anthropological Perspectives,* edited by Jane Cowan, Marie-Bénédicte Dembour, and Richard Wilson, Cambridge, UK: Cambridge University Press.

———. 2006. *Human Rights and Gender Violence: Translating International Law into Local Justice.* Chicago and London, UK: The University of Chicago Press.

Mohanty, Chandra. 1988. "Under Western Eyes: Feminist Scholarship and Colonial Discourses." Pp. 51–80 in *Third World Women and the Politics of Feminism*, edited by Chandra Mohanty, Ann Russo, and Lourdes Torres. Indianapolis: Indiana University Press.

Mushaben, Joyce. 2005. "More Than Just a Bad Hair Day." Pp. 182–223 In *Crossing Over: Comparing Recent Migration in the United States and Europe*, edited by Holger Henke. Lanham, MD: Lexington Books.

Narayan, Uma. 1997. *Dislocating Cultures: Identities, Traditions, and Third World Feminism.* New York: Routledge.

———. 1998. "Essence of Culture and a Sense of History: A Feminist Critique of Cultural Essentialism." *Hypatia* 13(2): 86–106.

———. 2000. "Undoing the 'Package Picture' of Cultures." *Signs* 25(4): 1083–86.

Njambi, Wairimu Ngaruiya. 2004. "Dualisms and Female Bodies in Representations of African Female Circumcision: A Feminist Critique." *Feminist Theory* 5(3): 281–303.

Okin, Susan. 1997. "Is Multiculturalism Bad for Women?" *Boston Review* 22(5): 25–28.

Ostrom, Carol. 1996. "Harborview Debates Issue of Circumcision of Muslim Girls." *The Seattle Times*, September 6, Retrieved December 11, 2004 (http://community.seattletimes.nwsource.com/archive/?date=19960913&slug=2348974).

Parekh, Bhikhu. 1995. "Cultural Pluralism and the Limits of Diversity." *Alternatives* 20(4): 431–57.

Paulson, Tom. 1996. "Harborview, Somalis Try to Compromise on Female Circumcision." *Seattle Post-Intelligencer*, September 13. Retrieved December 11, 2004 (www.highbeam.com/doc/1G1-64677311.html).

Phillips, Anne. 2003. "When Culture Means Gender: Issues of Cultural Defence in the English Courts." *Modern Law Review* 66(4): 510–31.

———. 2007. "What is 'Culture'?" Pp. 15–29 in *Sexual Justice/Cultural Justice: Critical Perspectives in Political Theory and Practice,* edited by Barbara Ameil, Monique Deveaux, Rita Dhamoon, and Avigail Eisenberg, London, UK and New York: Routledge.

Piot, Charles. 2007. "Representing Africa and the Kasinga Asylum Case." Pp. 157–66 in *Transcultural Bodies:*

Female Genital Cutting in Global Context, edited by Ylva Hernlund and Bettina Shell-Duncan. New Brunswick, NJ and London, UK: Rutgers University Press.

Razack, Sherene, 1995. "Domestic Violence as Gender Persecution: Policing the Borders of Nation, Race and Gender." *Canadian Journal of Women and the Law* 8(1): 45–88.

———. 2007. "The 'Sharla Law Debate' in Ontario: The Modernity/Premodernity Distinction in Legal Efforts to Protect Women from Culture." *Feminist Legal Studies* 15(1): 3–32.

Rudy, Kathy. 2000. "Difference and Indifference: A U.S. Feminist Response to Global Politics." *Signs* 25(4): 1051–53.

Saguy, Abigail C. 2003. *What is Sexual Harassment?: From Capitol Hill to the Sorbonne.* Berkeley: University of California Press.

Said, Edward. 1978. *Orientalism.* New York: Vintage.

Seattle Times, The. 1996. "Hospital Won't Circumcise Girls." *The Seattle Times,* December 5. Retrieved December 11, 2004 (http://community.seattletimes.nwsource.com/archive/?date=19961205&slug=2363272).

Sewell, William. 1992. "A Theory of Structure: Duality, Agency, and Transformation." *American Journal of Sociology* 98(1): 1–29.

Sheldon, Sally and Stephen Wilkinson. 1998. "Female Genital Mutilation and Cosmetic Surgery: Regulating Non-Therapeutic Body Modification." *Bioethics* 12(4): 263–85.

Sieder, Rachel and Jessica Witchell. 2001. "Advancing Indigenous Claims through the Law: Reflections on the Guatemalan Peace Process." Pp. 201–25 in *Culture and Rights: Anthropological Perspectives*, edited by Jane Cowan, Marie-Bénédicte Dembour, and Richard Wilson. Cambridge, UK: Cambridge University Press.

Spivak, Gayatri Chakravorty. 1985. "Subaltern Studies: Deconstructing Historiography." Pp. 337–38 in *Subaltern Studies IV*, edited by Ranajlt Guha. Delhi, India: Oxford University Press.

———. 1988. "Can the Subaltern Speak?" Pp. 271–313 in *Marxism and the Interpretation of Culture*, edited by C. Nelson and L. Grossberg, Chicago: University of Illinois Press.

Stabile, Carol and Deepa Kumar. 2005. "Unveiling Imperialism: Media, Gender, and the War on Afghanistan." *Media, Culture, and Society* 27(5): 765–82.

Swidler, Ann. 1986. "Culture in Action: Symbols and Strategies." *American Sociological Review* 51:273–86.

———. 2001. *Talk of Love: How Culture Matters.* Chicago: University of Chicago Press.

Tully, James. 1995. *Strange Multiplicity: Constitutionalism in an Age of Diversity.* Cambridge, UK: Cambridge University Press.

Turner, Terence. 1993. "Anthropology and Multiculturalism: What is Anthropology that Multiculturalists Should be Mindful of It?" *Cultural Anthropology* 8(4): 411–29.

United Nations. 2012. "UN Committee Approves First-ever Text Calling for End to Female Genital Mutilation." Retrieved December 19, 2012 (http://www.un.org/apps/news/story.asp?NewsID=43625&Cr=violence+against+women&Crl=#.UNIaKKzheSo).

Volpp, Leti. 1994. "(Mis)Identifying Culture: Asian Women and the 'Cultural Defense'." *Harvard Women's Law Journal* 17: 57–80.

———. 2000. "Blaming Culture for Bad Behavior." *Yale Journal of Law and the Humanities* 12: 89–117.

Wade, Lisa. 2009. "Defining Gendered Oppression in U.S. Newspapers: The Strategic Value of 'Female Genital Mutilation.'" *Gender and Society* 23(3): 293–314.

World Health Organization (WHO). 2008. *Eliminating Female Genital Mutilation: An Interagency Statement.* Geneva, Switzerland: World Health Organization.

WHO, UNFPA, UNICEF, and UNJFEM. 2010. "Regarding the 'Policy Statement-Ritual Genital Cutting of Female Minors' from the AAP." Retrieved June 14, 2010 (www.who.int/reproductivehealth/topics/fgm/fgm_app_statement.pdf).

"WHEN THERE'S NO UNDERBRUSH THE TREE LOOKS TALLER": A DISCOURSE ANALYSIS OF MEN'S ONLINE GROIN SHAVING TALK

MATTHEW HALL

Appearance for men (and women) is becoming an increasingly important feature of modern consumerist and individualistic societies and a key resource for identity construction (Featherstone, 1991; Giddens, 1991). Where once a man's identity was largely drawn from work, sport and family discourses, the exponential growth in consumerism and the media has provided men with a multitude of alternative identity discourses— ones which they are tasked with, and accountable for, designing and maintaining (Giddens, 1991). The payoff for such identity and body work is social and psychological well-being, that is, as many marketers promote, "look good, feel good" (Featherstone, 1991; D'Alessandro and Chitty, 2011). Whilst more traditional discourses clearly remain available and influential, men are increasingly held accountable if they fail to invest time and resources in their appearance (see Hall et al., 2012a, 2012b). As Grogan (2010) points out, these modern pressures often lead to men and boys (and women and girls) developing anxieties around body image—size, shape, colour, muscularity, thinness and tone for the body as a whole and its individual body parts.

Men's genital size and shape appear to be no exception (Tiggemann et al., 2008; Veale et al., 2013; Wylie and Eardley, 2007). Indeed, the *Online Slang Dictionary* (http://onlineslangdictionary.com/) boasts 165 English slang terms for the penis. Many of these refer to size and specifically the penis as long and thick. For example: babies arm, bratwurst, chopper, dong, one-eyed-monster, one-eyed-trouser-snake, pocket rocket, pork sword, trouser meat, whanger and so on. This isn't surprising given that penis size has traditionally been a symbol of masculinity, particularly when erect. Wylie and Eardley (2007: 1449) point out that "in many cultures it has come to symbolise attributes such as largeness, strength, endurance, ability, courage, intelligence, knowledge, dominance over men, possession of women; a symbol of loving and being loved," and also fertility. Given this symbolism, it's understandable that some men may feel inadequate if they don't meet perceived cultural norms. Indeed, two-thirds of men in a recent UK study (Veale et al., 2013) reported some dissatisfaction with their genital size and shape. Tiggemann et al.'s (2008) research reported penis size as the third biggest concern for men (behind body weight and muscularity).

Much of this is arguably perpetuated by perceptions of the penis in the media. For example, the UK newspaper *The Daily Mail* (Gayle and Jones, 2012) ran an article titled "Sorry boys, size DOES matter: Scientific journal confirms men's worst bedroom fear." Apparently, researchers found that women who reported regular vaginal orgasms (as opposed to clitoral) said size is a key factor. Similarly, *Time* magazine (Szalavitz, 2013) ran an article titled "Size does matter: Study shows women

From "'When There's No Underbrush the Tree Looks Taller': A Discourse Analysis of Men's Online Groin Shaving Talk," *Sexualities* 18(8), pp. 997–1017. Copyright © the Author, 2015. Reprinted by permission of SAGE Publications, Ltd.

judge male attractiveness by penis size." Yet men might be consoled in other media articles such as "Does size matter to women?" (Burton, 2013), reporting that "women simply don't care about size. There will be the odd ones who say it is very important, but they are usually the ones who love aggressive sex." With such mixed messages it's not surprising then that some men are sensitive about their genitals. For some, an inordinate fascination with size leads to the development of "small penis syndrome" and associated psychological issues (Wylie and Eardley, 2007; see below).

Penis size is not the only concern for men. Besides the traditional importance of symbolism and function, men are increasingly interested in its aesthetics. Flowers et al.'s (2013) paper elegantly presents an overview of recent trends in which long-standing penis anxieties have been reframed within the context of health and aesthetics. New penis enhancement possibilities for size and aesthetics, not previously available, mean that men are increasingly confronted with ideas that they should change their penis. Marketers now capitalize upon and promote penis-related products, helping to increase mediated penis anxieties. Size and aesthetic concerns are reported to produce a multitude of psychological problems such as body dysmorphophobia.[1] Phillips and Castle (2001) argue that about 15% of men have presented to physicians in the UK with this more severe body image disturbance condition which manifests itself as a preoccupation with an imagined or slight defect in the appearance of their penis, which has caused clinically significant distress or impairment in its function. Indeed, conditions such as erectile dysfunction, obsessive-compulsive disorder, social phobia, relationship and emotional problems, along with anxiety and depression, were also reported in Lever et al.'s (2006; see also Levine, 2000, for a more detailed examination) internet survey of 52,031 heterosexual men and women. Kilmartin (2000: 215–16) points out that psychological-based issues with the penis manifest because "Real men are . . . described as having huge penises." Wylie and Eardley (2007) report "these concerns, when severe, can lead a man to go to extreme lengths to try to change the size of his penis."

Many marketers now offer remedies and procedures for those interested in altering their penis. One only has to look in one's "junk mail" box or conduct a simple Google search to see the vast array of quick fix solutions such as non-surgical remedies to extend and reshape the penis. These range from weights . . . to electrical devices . . . and pumps . . . , herbal . . . and pharmaceutical interventions . . . , self-administrable such as clamping . . . and Jelqing (massaging blood flow). On a more extreme level penile-augmentation surgery procedures such as penoplasty or phalloplasty[2] are available. The numbers of men opting for these types of cosmetic procedures are steadily increasing according to the American Society for Aesthetic Plastic Surgery and the British Association of Aesthetic Plastic Surgeons (see Aitkenhead, 2005).

The plethora of penis enhancement products, along with men's psychological presentation to physicians (Lever et al., 2006; Levine, 2000; Kilmartin, 2000; Phillips and Castle, 2001; Wylie and Eardley, 2007), are markers of men's penis size disturbances. Marketers such as Gillette—the global men's grooming giant (Forbes, 2012)—have been quick to furnish and contribute to such insecurities by expanding the use of their product range from facial hair to include non-head body hair removal. For example, in a recent animated tutorial video, doubling as an advert, Gillette instruct men on how to shave their groin. Apparently shaving the groin area makes the penis look bigger and better, marketed with the amusing and catchy slogan "when there's no underbrush the tree looks taller." "How to Shave Down There" [was] the most popular viral video on groin shaving out of the seven specifically targeted at men, with over 6,074,474 views and 5129 comments (as of 6 June 2014). . . .

There are two potential problems for men who openly ascribe to undertaking groin shaving. Firstly, to do so might imply one is concerned with their penis size and, secondly, genital grooming, like many modes of grooming for men, has traditionally been associated with women and femininity (Edwards, 2003). Indeed, Edwards (2003: 141–42) argues that men and image-enhancement practices are still considered "antithetical if not an outright oxymoron." Other image-conscious research on the metrosexual (Hall et al., 2012a, 2012b), men's health and lifestyle practices (Watson, 2000), obesity (Gough et al., 2013), illness (Robertson et al., 2010) and body hair removal (Immergut, 2010) support this view, showing that men must simultaneously disavow any "inappropriate" interest in their own appearance in order to maintain "manliness" or risk being cast as vain, weak, effeminate or gay. In other words, they can't appear to be feminine but neither can they get away with being a slob (Gill et al., 2005). Building on this work, I examine how men account for pubic hair grooming.

Focusing on men's electronic responses to the Gillette groin shaving advert also offers several important points of entry into the study of men and masculinities. Firstly, examining men's talk offers an example of how some men construct and negotiate masculinity in relation to a traditionally non-typical gender activity. Secondly, the focus on men's groin shaving offers an important example of a wider trend in men's image-conscious practices (Hall et al., 2012a, 2012b) and what that means for our understanding of men's embodiment (Grogan, 2007, 2010). Lastly, examining the deployment of masculinities in situ helps us evaluate the application of existing theoretical concepts on masculinities and men's body image to men's everyday practices and signal whether all, or aspects of these, might need to be reworked or rethought in light of modern developments. These would include concepts such as "hegemonic masculinity," which is understood to be the variety of masculine identities amassed around expectations of what masculinity is presumed to be; even though most men do not enact them, all men are required to position themselves in relation to them (Connell, 1995: 77). Such masculinities are often portrayed in films by characters played by Vin Diesel—tough, emotionally stoic and muscular. Yet many men seem to reject some aspects of the dominant attitudes or traits in various contexts and are more willing to embrace traditional feminized ones instead (e.g., childcare and grooming). Bridges (2014) argues such practices indicate that masculinities are becoming more "hybrid." Yet other scholars, such as MacInnes (2001), argue that because of feminist equality pressures, some men have found it difficult to orientate to traditional gender-distinct identities or embrace aspects of femininity (e.g., work in traditionally feminine jobs) and, as such, this has resulted in masculinities being in "crisis." In the realm of body image, too, men's increasing attention to the body to enhance image suggests that theoretical notions of gender-discrete practices (e.g., cosmetics use, body hair removal) and body structure (e.g., muscularity, thinness, curvature) might be in the process of being challenged and reworked (Grogan, 2007, 2010). . . .

DATA AND METHOD

The dataset is drawn from the premier internet video publisher YouTube (Nielsen, 2009). Founded in February 2005, YouTube allows people to easily upload and share video clips on a range of topics, including "how to" demonstrations and adverts. As with other online sites, YouTube provides viewers with the ability to engage with the material they encounter through computer-mediated communication channels—text and video comments. These allow viewers to write comments on, and rate responses to, their favourite videos. . . .

Having downloaded all 5129 comments from the Gillette video "How to Shave Down There," I coded the talk by response type. Admittedly, some responses could have fitted into two or more response types. For these I added an additional code to avoid overlooking their potential importance. Since my interest was in why men shave their pubic hair, I further clustered responses drawing out the main themes. . . .

The analysis I present is a selection of the accounts that emphasized eloquently the specific reasons for their groin shaving. I present the extracts in full as they appear on YouTube, including spelling mistakes, colloquial language and emoticons.

Before analysing the electronic data it's important to discuss the goals of discourse analysis in general. A general aim is to explore how "versions of world, of society, events and inner psychological worlds are produced in discourse," and so discourse analysis has "a concern with participants' constructions and how they are accomplished and undermined" (Potter, 1996: 146). In other words, there is a multiplicity of versions of the world that can be worked up at any given time and on a moment-to-moment basis during conversational interaction. . . .

In order to see how such things come into play within a stretch of talk I follow a step-by-step procedure identifying how each extract fits together and what the respondent was achieving at each and every stage (Edwards and Potter, 1992). Each segment of text is analysed for its individual, sequential, relational and contextual relevance following these three steps: locate the central themes that are named and/or implied in the talk; focus on

the discursive activities with each text; look at how respondents construct accounts, produce descriptions, manage stake, frame specific activities and make connections for the implied social actions. . . .

ANALYSIS

One would expect most respondents to be male given the focus of the video. However, research suggests that some online users present unrealistic or deceptive images of themselves (Epstein, 2007; Gibbs et al., 2006; Schmitt, 2002; Toma et al., 2008; Wiszniewski and Coyne, 2002), creating a "mask." Individuals and groups are able to do this because they are in a position to control the flow of information that others receive (Hollingshead, 2001). Since the "true" identity of the respondents is almost impossible to ascertain without direct contact, the gender of the respondent can be presumed through their gender indexing. Indexing can be explicit with traditional names for men (now anonymized), male positioning in relation to females (girls, women, their, us), male action references . . . and invoking typical masculine markers. . . . These are treatable as "male" even without this identity being "named out aloud" (Antaki and Widdicombe, 1998: 4). In the following analytical section I examine the response types; size, health and hygiene, heterosexual pay-off, equality, self-respect and individuality. For ease of understanding and reading I have loosely presented them within the analytical sections: "(Dis)engaging with Size," "A Female and Heterosexual Imperative," "Gender Distinction or Equality?," and "Individuality and Minimization."

As expected, size was evident in many responses. The following two extracts show interesting ways in which men both engaged or disengaged with size concerns. The respondent in the next extract is orientating to Gillette's claim that 'the tree looks taller':

(Dis)engaging with Size

Extract 1: *Jimbob*

Nope, it reveals nothing. Because no matter how big dick is, it still is good when it looks even bigger . . .

Jimbob's opening line "Nope, it reveals nothing" contains a definitive "Nope" and an extreme-case formulation "nothing" (Pomerantz, 1986). As Edwards (2000: 348) points out, these serve as discursive devices in "defending positions against refutation, making complaints, and justifying factual claims." Therefore Jimbob's initial sentence is readable as a refutation. In refuting people tend to, or are required by others to, provide an account for this discursive action (Potter, 1996). Jimbob's account centres on the presumption that any practice that makes . . . one's "dick" "look even bigger" is "good" regardless of "how big dick is." In doing so he is refuting Gillette's implied claim that this practice is for those with a smaller penis. What this also does, however, is imply that penis size is important for many men (see Kilmartin, 2000: 215–16; i.e., and Eardley, 2007: 1449), and so any practice that increases size potentially also increases one's masculinity (Wylie and Eardley, 2007). In contrast to this response, the poster's comment in the next extract discounts size concerns.

Extract 2: *Ontherodney*

They put a negative spin on it with a corrupt motive—to "make the tree look taller." Bad idea. Don't fall for that crap. Most of us aren't trying to fool anyone. [It's] just getting it cleaner and free of unwanted hair. I don't see why they have to repeat that juvenile deceptive crap. It sends a bad message about insecurity and trickery. Gillette hits a sour note for no reason. It's about hygiene and natural beauty of the skin, nothing else.

The overall context of Ontherodney's response is a critique of the advert for containing a "negative spin," "a corrupt motive," "juvenile deceptive crap" regarding penis size. Indeed, penis size "insecurities" are presented as predominantly adolescent ("juvenile"). Like Jimbob, Ontherodney's critique requires an account, which centres on the presented "fact" that "Most of us" (men) aren't concerned with trying to make our penis look longer; genital grooming is about "hygiene and natural beauty." In other words, cleanliness and aesthetics. The implication is that this pubic hair shaving is a common practice for men and a modern aspect of masculinity. What's also notable is that "Most" is a "softener" or "non-extreme-case formulation" (Edwards, 2000: 352). The use of softeners indicates the possibility of some readers undermining his claims (Edwards and Potter, 1992). That is, if a respondent anticipates others questioning their claims an account may be worked up beforehand, especially if, like pubic hair shaving, it is a "delicate" topic or non-typical gender activity (Silverman and Perakyla, 2008). So, although Ontherodney positions pubic hair grooming as common for men, it also references it as a non-traditional practice for some men—a point made more explicit in other responses, as we will see.

The non-normativity of genital grooming for some men combined with his pragmatic justification ("It's just getting it cleaner and free of unwanted hair") summons discourses of choice, individuality and self-respect. . . . Ontherodney is therefore reframing this masculine activity with recourse to conventional masculine markers. In doing so, he masculinizes this activity but also inoculates it from charges of penis size and feminine interests. . . . Since body hair removal has traditionally been seen as an activity of women and femininity (Edwards, 2003), and since nearly two-thirds of men have genital dissatisfaction (Veale et al., 2013), it is hardly surprising that this topic is "delicate," requiring careful management to avoid unwarranted charges.

In the following extracts Diamondgeezer, Sammyboy and Justintime reframe pubic hair grooming as a requirement of female preference and heterosexual endeavour, albeit in differing ways.

A Female and Heterosexual Imperative

Extract 3: *Diamondgeezer*

Ffs i shaved down there before I watched this video and now its itchy as fuck. Btw if you have no pubes girls will give head easier and won't be disgusted by your pubes

Diamondgeezer's opener "Ffs" (Acronym for, for fuck's sake; Urban Dictionary, 2014) acts as an exclamation for the activity "i shaved down there" which "now its itchy as fuck." What's also evident is that the marker of time "before" works to position himself as a novice who should have watched the advert before trying this activity. Yet we get a sense of the "delicacy" in the account which he provides (Silverman and Perakyla, 2008). Diamondgeezer manages his "stake" (Edwards and Potter, 1992) in this practice by stating as "fact" that "girls will give head easier" (fellatio), which centres on pubic hair as unpalatable "disgusted by your pubes." This achieves several things. It places some accountability for shaving pubic hair with women's preferences but ultimately with men's own pleasure. The implied pleasure payoff "girls will give head easier" draws on a classic marker of masculine status—frequent heterosexual activity. . . . The final point to note is that by undertaking this reframing action, Diamondgeezer deflects attention from charges that he is doing this to enhance his penis. Similarly, this framing of genital grooming as sexual pleasure and female preference is evident in the next extract, albeit differently:

Extract 4: *Sammyboy*

I really didn't want to do that but my girl said I had to or else I don't get any :(

Sammyboy begins by personalizing his account "I," which is immediately followed by an extreme-case formulation (Pomerantz, 1986) "really." The deployment of this maximizes the properties of his claim "I . . . didn't want to," reducing the basis for others to search for . . . additional accounts—possibly penis size or aesthetic interests. Yet like other posters, Sammyboy still manages his stake in this non-typical masculine practice by offering an account which centres on framing it as his girlfriend's demand . . . (like Diamondgeezer the payoff is heterosexual activity).

Extract 5: *Justintime*

Most of the (str8) young males that I know say they shave-off their bush. It is b/c females want the guys to shave their bush so it doesn't scratch their sensitive shaved pubic area during sexual intercourse. Twenty years ago it was unheard of, or weird, for a guy shave-off his bush

It would be easy to simply gloss this response as another "(str8) young male" justifying pubic hair shaving as a female requirement for intercourse. Yet that would miss many other important features of the text. For example, although "most" is a softener (Edwards, 2000), it also acts as an orientation device for him as a member of the collective category ["(str8) young male"] but in referencing "their." His membership of this category of men is affirmed by his access to other members ("young males that I know") and members' knowledge ("they shave-off their bush"). In doing so, Justintime sets up a contrasting pair of identity categories—those who do/ don't shave pubic hair (Smith, 1978). By invoking the commonality of "Most," it positions those who don't shave pubic hair as in the minority and therefore accountable for their non-activity. Like the previous two extracts, this is accounted for by recourse to heterosexuality . . . and what women want. . . . Also like Diamondgeezer, Justintime provides this as a "factual" description "so it doesn't scratch their sensitive pubic area," which works to strengthen his position. However, Justintime does still recognize that some might not agree with his participation in this activity and so further positions this act as modern . . . and in doing so is able to hold those who don't participate in this action as outmoded.

Implicating women for men's actions was a common feature of the dataset even when men (and teenage boys) did state that they "shave their junk becuz it can get pretty sweaty and stuff down there" or "i like the feel of no hair down there" for personal reasons. Yet what was also evident from all the comments that did reframe pubic hair shaving in this way was that none of them said that women wanted it removed so that their penis size would be enhanced (sexual activity and pleasure were instead foregrounded).

In the following sequence the debate centres on gender equity and whether this practice should be suitable for either sex as a practice for cleanliness.

Gender Distinction or Equality?

Extract 6: *Silversimon*

Why should women be expected to keep it clean down there but not guys? Its respect. I don't like hair, and I'm sure women don't either. They appreciate a clean shaven man and I'm happy to give it to them. Welcome to the 21st century.

Dannyboy

Women shouldn't be shaving "down there" either. You can be clean without removing every piece of hair on your body. Certain aspects of shaving (men's faces and backs, women's legs and underarms) I will admit make a person look neat and contribute to a nice appearance. Woman with matted leg hair under stockings or men with messy long

beards and shaggy hair look gross. But this is an extreme.

Silversimon

I disagree. For one, I have a tongue ring, hair wrappes around that easily. Plus, it don't matter how short you trim it, you have the prickly feeling on your tongue, and for some people, its like a jungle down there. Disgusting. I don't shave/remove hair all over my body, there are many places I like hair to be, but thats just a place I think is so 70's and its just gross looking. Skin against skin will ALWAYS feel better then skin against hair.

Silversimon links pubic hair shaving as an activity for keeping genitalia clean. . . . His questioning of gender inequity based on "Its respect" identifies this as a typical activity for women and femininity, supported also by Silversimon's personalized perspective . . . which suggests others may not agree. Like previous accounts, Silversimon presents this firstly as a desire of women . . . which is then upgraded to a fact-based assessment. . . . This upgrading of his knowledge from "presumed" to "known" supports his discursive strategy of inoculation from charges of doing this for reasons other than equality. What's also interesting is that, like Justintime, this activity is seen as a modern aspect of masculinity . . . one that draws on contemporary notions of the equality of the sexes and a rejection of some aspects of conventional masculinities. . . . In doing so, those who don't participate in this activity can be held accountable for being sexist.

Similarly, Dannyboy invokes a reverse style of equality ("Women shouldn't be shaving 'down there' either"), presenting it as a critique ("You can be clean without removing every piece of hair on your body"). But risking advocating no body hair removal at all he genders aspects of body hair removal ("men's faces and backs, womens legs and underarms"), accounting for non-participation as "gross." What is evident from Dannyboy's post is that whilst he critiques modern body hair practices as "extreme," he is simultaneously advocating the status quo, that is, gender-specific grooming to "look neat and contribute to a nice appearance.". . .

Silversimon's initial rebuttal centres on Dannyboy's account as being outdated, since keeping pubic hair "wrappes around" a tongue ring—aspects of some modern identities (Carroll and Anderson, 2002). Yet "I dont shave/remove hair all over my body, there are many places I like hair to be" suggests he doesn't want to risk appearing too "extreme" and distances himself from Dannyboy's more normative gender position. Interestingly, the second way he manages stake is in recycling his earlier comment of this being a modern aspect of masculine identity. . . . Combined with supporting gender equality, Silversimon's account can be read as both an "inclusive" masculinity (Bridges, 2014) but also a "gender rebel" (Wetherell and Edley, 1999).

Positioning oneself as "gender rebel" was a similar tact by Cityboy in the following extract. However, unlike Silversimon, he doesn't draw on more modern "inclusive" aspects of masculinity, but rather draws on more conventional "individuality" (Gill et al., 2005).

Individuality and Minimization

Extract 7: *Cityboy*
I have been shaving down there for a long time and I like and prefer it that way. To each his own and everyone should respect that. I'm sure people have searched much more weird and bizarre things than that! Groin shaving is tame compared to things I've seen here.

Cityboy's initial sentence . . . marks him as seasoned and perhaps a fair bit older than some of the other posters. What this does is lend authority to the account he is about to deliver. But rather than a simple account of personal preference . . . and tolerance and respect . . . , Cityboy draws on experience to counter potential critiques. . . . Indeed, in positioning himself as a "man-of-the-world" and inviting others to recall their own experiences . . . he is able to trivialize this activity and anybody who wishes to challenge him.

This style of countering and reframing of groin shaving as seasoned masculinity, individuality and rebelliousness was also deployed by Davetherave. But what is interesting and novel about this response is the way the respondent is able to discount conventional gender-discrete activities.

Extract 8: *Davetherave*
I have pretty much always lived my life in an unorthodox fashion. I never really TRIED to be different for the sake of being different . . . just interested in new and unusual things and experimentation. You only live once so I want to do more than everyday mundane things to make life a bit more exciting. And I do mean more exciting than groin shaving . . . HaHah!!

As with other posters, Davetherave personalizes his account. . . . But whereas Sammyboy's deployment of "I" positioned himself as like many other men . . . , Davetherave positions himself outside gender norms. . . . In doing so he draws on the masculine markers of individuality . . . , rebelliousness . . . , and a man-of-the-world . . . (Bridges, 2014; Donaldson, 1993; Gill et al., 2005; Wetherell and Edley, 1999). What also supports his masculinized account of groin shaving is that it is presented as authoritative, marked by experience and time . . . , and additionally supported by the deployment of several extreme-case formulations. . . . What's also notable is the way he manages his "stake" as non-accountable and an inherent aspect of his identity. . . . In other words, his "effort-lessness" repertoire allows him to orient to potential critiques regarding vanity and sensation-seeking.

DISCUSSION

Clearly, in-depth discourse analysis of men and teenage boys' accounts of groin shaving can cast light on the manifold ways interest in penis size and aesthetic practices are accounted for in masculine ways. For example, in contemporary terms groin shaving was practised for cleanliness ("hygiene and natural beauty") and gender equality ("It is b/c females want the guys to shave their bush"). Whereas, in more conventional terms, individuality was signalled ("You only live once") along with rebelliousness ("unorthodox") and being worldly ("Groin shaving is tame compared to things I've seen here"). Indeed, having a "dick" that "looks even bigger" was also presented as advantageous. Reframing groin shaving in masculine ways isn't surprising given that a concern with the body (other than perhaps muscularity, thinness and function; Gill et al., 2005; Grogan, 2007, 2010) and hair-removal (Toerien and Wilkinson, 2003) have traditionally been seen as in the realm of women and femininity.

What was also noticeable was that only two respondents engaged with size issues (Extracts 1 and 2). Jimbob implied he already had a "big dick" . . . , whereas Ontherodney vehemently dismissed size concerns. . . . The absence of posts stating that they wanted to "make the tree appear taller" is also not surprising since to suggest that is one's objective signals to other readers and respondents that one has penis-size anxieties. Whilst it would be foolish to speculate on whether the respondents suffered more extreme psychological issues (e.g., dysmorphophobia; Wylie and Eardley; 2007: 1449), we do get a sense of the changing dynamics of heterosexual relationships and emotional interactions when respondents report shaving for women. . . . But what is evident from an increasing number of men and teenage boys willing to engage with this non-typical gender activity, whether by action or response (more than six million hits and over 5000 comments), is that it supports Veale et al.'s (2013) findings that men and boys are both fascinated by and dissatisfied with their genitals. Men's interest in and concern with their penises is not a new phenomenon, but what this paper suggests is that men and boys may be developing a new fascination and anxiety with the aesthetics of their penis. Fascination with the aesthetics of the penis also fits with other studies which report men increasingly "window dressing" their bodies (e.g., cosmetic use, tattoos, hair removal etc.; see Hall et al., 2012a, 2012b and Grogan, 2007, 2010) to the demands of an image-conscious society in which the body and identity are becoming more fluid.

Although some men talked about wanting to enhance the size and look of their penis, there was no evidence to suggest these respondents had anxieties about penis size ("small penis syndrome"; Wylie and Eardley, 2007). One might speculate that men may not openly admit to shaving the groin for this reason since it would potentially invite ridicule. Perhaps an open, widely available public forum is not the best place to examine these issues. Yet what this study does show is that penis size is not the only concern for men. Men seem to be increasingly interested in penis aesthetics (see Flowers et al., 2013). New penis-enhancement possibilities mean that men are increasingly confronted with ideas that they should change their penis. As we saw, marketers have been quick to capitalize upon and promote penis-related products. However, for men to invest in these, they risk being cast as insecure or vain (Edwards, 2003). Therefore, men must simultaneously negotiate (dis)interest in their penis.

The analysis demonstrated the complex ways in which men achieved this and how many men swept charges of insecurity and vanity under the carpet in favour of heterosexual pleasure, cleanliness, self-respect and individuality.

Framing groin shaving with more traditional masculine markers . . . indicates that the concept of "hegemonic masculinity" still has some analytical mileage (Connell, 1995). That is, non-typical practices are reframed in traditional ways in order to avoid having one's masculine credentials questioned (see Hall et al.'s [2012a, 2012b] studies of metrosexuality). However, whilst men must position their masculinities in relation to more dominant notions, these notions are subject to change in different eras in light of current trends and demands. The invocation of modern masculine scripts such as caring ("It is b/c females want the guys to shave their bush so it doesn't scratch their sensitive shaved pubic area"; Justintime, Extract 5) and equality . . . may challenge such dominant notions of masculinities. These, combined with men's willingness to engage the traditional feminized practice of body-hair removal, suggest that many men now display more hybrid masculinities (Bridges, 2014). Whilst modern demands (e.g., to be well-presented) mean many men's masculinities are more hybrid, they must also simultaneously reframe their nontraditional gender practices in more conventional terms. Although there is an inherent tension here, I would caution the reader in thinking this means masculinities are in "crisis" (MacInnes, 2001). What this does suggest is that masculinities are being reworked in light of contemporary demands in an image-conscious society.

Clearly more work needs to be undertaken if we are to gain a clearer understanding of men's relationship with their penis, but also how masculinities are being reworked for contemporary requirements such as presenting the body as healthy and aesthetically pleasing.

Other research might focus on other aspects of men's body work such as "back, sack and crack," "manscaping" or changing masculinity pre-, peri-, post-penis-augmentation surgery. Such insight may help practitioners deal with men in vulnerable contexts, e.g., during prostate screening or when managing sexually transmitted disease. Investing time in examining men's penis concerns and activities offers the potential to identify valuable insights in which to help men (and boys) deal with the demands of modern society.

NOTES

1. Dysmorphophobia or body dysmorphic disorder (BDD) is a psychiatric condition in which the individual has a fixation on a perceived imagined flaw, leading to an inordinate amount of anguish.

2. Penoplasty refers to the enlargement of the penis by surgery. Although phalloplasty is often used interchangeably with penoplasty, phalloplasty more specifically refers to the surgical (re-)construction or artificial modification of the penis for cosmetic purposes.

REFERENCES

Aitkenhead D (2005) Most British woman now expect to have cosmetic surgery in their lifetime: How did the ultimate feminist taboo become just another lifestyle choice? *The Guardian*, 14 September, p. 13.

Antaki C and Widdicombe S (eds) (1998) *Identities in Talk*. London: SAGE.

Bridges T (2014) A very "gay" straight? Hybrid masculinities, sexual aesthetics, and the changing relationship between masculinity and homophobia. *Gender & Society* 28(1): 58–82.

Burton V (2013) Does size matter to women? Askmen.com. Available at: http://uk.askmen.com/dating/vanessa/vanessa4.html (accessed 13 November 2013).

Carroll L and Anderson R (2002) Body piercing, tattooing, self-esteem, and body investment in adolescent girls. *Adolescence* 37(147): 627–37.

Connell RW (1995) *Masculinities*. Cambridge: Polity.

D'Alessandro S and Chitty B (2011) Real or relevant beauty? Body shape and endorser effects on brand attitude and body image. *Psychology & Marketing* 28: 843–78.

Donaldson M (1993) What is hegemonic masculinity? *Theory and Society* 22: 643–57.

Edwards D (2000) Extreme case formulations: Softeners, investment, and doing nonliteral. *Research on Language and Social Interaction* 33(4): 347–73.

Edwards D and Potter J (1992) *Discursive Psychology: Inquiries in Social Construction*. London: SAGE.

Edwards T (2003) Sex, booze and fags: masculinity, style and men's magazines. In: Benwell B, ed., *Masculinity and Men's Lifestyle Magazines*. Oxford: Blackwell Publishing/ Sociological Review, pp. 132–46.

Epstein R (2007) The truth about online dating. *Scientific American Mind*. Available at: http://drrobertepstein .com/pdf/Epstein-TheTruthAboutOnlineDating-2-07.pdf (accessed 19 June 2010).

Featherstone M (1991) The body in consumer culture. In: Featherstone M, Hepworth M and Turner BS, eds., *The Body: Social Process and Cultural Theory*. London: SAGE, pp. 170–96.

Flowers P, Langdridge D, Gough B and Holliday R (2013) On the biomedicalisation of the penis: The commodification of function and aesthetics. *International Journal of Men's Health* 12(2): 121–37.

Forbes (2012) The world's most powerful brands. October. Available at: http://www.for bes.com/powerful-brands /list/ (accessed 31 October 2013).

Gayle D and Jones T (2012) Sorry boys, size DOES matter: Scientific journal confirms men's worst bedroom fear. *The Daily Mail*, 20 June. Available at: http://www .dailymail.co.uk/femail/article-2231751/Sorry-boys-size -DOES-matter-Scientific-journal-confirms-mens-worst -bedroom-fear.html (accessed 28 July 2005).

Gibbs JL, Ellison NB and Heino RD (2006) Self-presentation in online personals: The role of anticipated future interaction, self-disclosure, and perceived success in internet dating. *Communication Research* 33: 152–76.

Giddens A (1991) *Modernity and Self-Identity: Self and Society in the Late Modern Age*. Cambridge: Polity Press.

Gill R, Henwood K and McLean C (2005) Body projects and the regulation of normative masculinity. *Body & Society* 11(1): 39–62.

Gillette (2009). How to shave down there. Available at: http://www.youtube.com/watch?v¼1TiJNewpCnY (accessed 22 November 2012).

Gough B, Seymour-Smith S, Matthews C, Rutherford Z and Wilcox J (2013) How do male clients evaluate, and benefit from [i] a new male-targeted weight management service, [ii] an established service, and how can we engage more men to access and adhere to weight loss programmes within Nottingham City? Project Report to NHS Nottingham City, September.

Grogan S (2007) *Body Image: Understanding Body Dissatisfaction in Men, Women and Children*. London: Routledge.

Grogan S (2010) Gender and body image: Implications for promoting body satisfaction. *Sex Roles* 63: 757–65.

Hall M, Gough B, Seymour-Smith S and Hansen S (2012a) On-line constructions of metro-sexuality and masculinities: A membership categorisation analysis. *Gender & Language* 6(2): 379–403.

Hall M, Gough B and Seymour-Smith S (2012b) "I'm METRO, NOT gay!": A discursive analysis of men's accounts of makeup use on YouTube. *Journal of Men's Studies* 20(3): 209–26.

Hollingshead AB (2001) Communication technologies, the internet and group research. In: Hogg MA and Tindale RS (eds) *Blackwell Handbook of Social Psychology: Group Processes*. London: SAGE, pp. 221–35.

Immergut M (2010) Manscaping: The tangle of nature, culture and male body hair. In: Moore L and Kosut ME, eds., *The Body Reader: Essential Social and Cultural Readings*. New York: New York University Press, pp. 287–304.

Kilmartin CT (2000) *The Masculine Self*, (2nd edn). Boston: McGraw-Hill.

Lever J, Frederick DA and Peplau LA (2006) Does size matter? Men's and women's views on penis size across the lifespan. *Psychology of Men & Masculinity* 7(3): 129–43.

Levine LA (2000) Diagnosis and treatment of erectile dysfunction. *The American Journal of Medicine* 109(9): Suppl. 1, 3–12.

MacInnes J (2001) The crisis of masculinity and the politics of identity. In: Whitehead SM and Barrett FJ, eds., *The Masculinities Reader*. Cambridge: Polity Press.

Nielsen (2009) Time spent viewing video online up 25% per viewer. Available at: http://blog.nielsen.com /nielsenwire/online_mobile/time-spent-viewing-video -online-up-25-per-viewer/ (accessed 24 October 2013).

Online Slang Dictionary (2013) Penis. Available at: http:// onlineslangdictionary.com/thesaurus/words+meaning+ penis.html (accessed 28 October 2013).

Phillips KA and Castle DJ (2001) Body dysmorphic disorder in men. *British Medical Journal* 323: 1015–16.

Pomerantz A (1986) Extreme case formulations: A way of legitimizing claims. *Human Studies* 9: 219–29.

Potter J (1996) *Representing Reality: Discourse, Rhetoric and Social Construction*. London: SAGE.

Robertson S, Sheik K and Moore A (2010) Embodied masculinities in the context of cardiac rehabilitation. *Sociology of Health & Illness* 32(5): 695–710.

Schmitt DP (2002) A meta-analysis of sex differences in romantic attraction: Do rating contexts moderate tactic effectiveness judgments? *British Journal of Social Psychology* 41: 387–402.

Silverman D and Perakyla A (2008) AIDS counselling: The interactional organisation of talk about "delicate" issues. *Sociology of Health & Illness* 12(3): 293–318.

Smith D (1978) K is mentally ill: The anatomy of a factual account. *Sociology* 12: 23–53.

Szalavitz M (2013). Size does matter: Study shows women judge male attractiveness by penis size. *Time*, 9 April. Available at: http://healthland.time.com/2013/04/09 /size-does-matter-study-shows-women-judge-male -attractiveness-by-penis-size/ (accessed 13 November 2013).

Tiggemann M, Martins Y and Churchett L (2008) Beyond muscles: Unexplored parts of men's body image. *Journal of Health Psychology* 13: 1163–72.

Toerien M and Wilkinson S (2003) Gender and body hair: Constructing the feminine woman. *Women's Studies International Forum* 26(4): 333–44.

Toma CL, Hancock JT and Ellison NB (2008) Separating fact from fiction: An examination of deceptive self-presentation in online dating profiles. *Personality & Social Psychology* Bulletin 34: 1023–36.

Urban Dictionary (2012) Ffs. Available at: http://www.urbandictionary.com/define.php?term¼ffs) (accessed 5 April 2014).

Veale D, Eshkevari E, Read J, Miles S, Troglia A, Phillips R, Echeverria LMC, Fiorito C, Wylie K and Muir G (2013) Beliefs about penis size: Validation of a scale for men ashamed about their penis size. *Journal of Sexual Medicine* 10(9). DOI: 10.1111/ jsm.12294.

Watson J (2000) *Male Bodies: Health Culture and Identity*. Buckingham: Open University Press.

Wetherell M and Edley N (1999) Negotiating hegemonic masculinity: Imaginary positions and psycho-discursive practices. *Feminism & Psychology* 9(3): 335–56.

Wiszniewski D and Coyne R (2002) Mask and identity: The hermeneutics of self-construction in the information age. In: Renninger KA and Shumar W, eds., *Building Virtual Communities*. New York: Cambridge University Press, pp. 191–214.

Wylie RR and Eardley I (2007) Penile size and the "small penis syndrome." *BJU International* 99(6): 1449–55.

"BASICALLY, IT'S SORCERY FOR YOUR VAGINA": UNPACKING WESTERN REPRESENTATIONS OF VAGINAL STEAMING

TYCHO VANDENBURG AND VIRGINIA BRAUN

You sit on what is essentially a mini-throne, and a combination of infrared and mugwort steam cleanses your uterus, et al. It is an energetic release—not just a steam douche—that balances female hormone levels.

—Goop, 2015

A practice called vaginal steaming (aka "v-steam" "yoni steam," "chai-yok") has been offered by "holistic health spa clinics" in Australia, New Zealand, the UK and the USA for some time (Heifetz 2010). Widespread public attention and media coverage only occurred after celebrity and self-professed health and lifestyle guru Gwyneth Paltrow blogged enthusiastically about it on her popular site *Goop.com* in early 2015. In this practice, the vulva is exposed to heated steam, typically infused with herbs such as mugwort and wormwood (Burd 2015). Various "medicinal" benefits, often evidenced by client testimonials, are claimed; responses to vaginal steaming have ranged from adoration to scepticism, rejection and concern, with some, often medical professionals, critiquing the practice as potentially hazardous (e.g., Gunter 2015).

We can conceptualise vaginal steaming as the newest addition to an existing arsenal of practices available to Western women to "improve" their (troublesome) genitalia, including douching, pubic hair removal (Braun, Tricklebank, and Clarke 2013; Herbenick et al. 2013) and even cosmetic surgery (Braun 2005, 2010). Vaginal douching, the existing Western practice most akin to steaming, involves "cleansing" the vagina through an injected liquid solution, such as vinegar and water (Martino,

Youngpairoj, and Vermund 2004). Douching has a long history (Nicoletti 2006), but now is usually practised after menstruation or sexual intercourse, for perceived hygiene, cleanliness, the elimination of odour, relief of vaginal irritations and to tighten the vagina (Anderson et al. 2008; Cottrell, 2010; Martino, Youngpairoj, and Vermund 2004). It is a practice most common in the USA (Farage and Lennon 2006)—one quarter of US women aged 15–44 are believed to douche regularly (Office of Women's Health 2015). Public health professionals dismiss douching as at best unnecessary and at worst unhealthy, linked with various adverse gynaecological outcomes (see Luong et al. 2010; Martino and Vermund 2002; Zhang, Thomas, and Leybovich 1997). Regular douching can damage the mucosal lining of the vagina and increase women's vulnerability to infection (Fashemi et al. 2013; Luong et al. 2010; Martino and Vermund 2002).

Vaginal steaming also bears similarities to practices associated with "dry sex" in various African, South American and Southeast Asian countries (van Andel et al. 2008; Hilber et al. 2010; Hull et al. 2011), which aim to dry the vagina and/or alter or eliminate "unpleasant" odours and discharge (Hilber et al. 2010; Hull et al. 2011). Performed most commonly postpartum, to purify the body and "make it attractive again" for male partners (van Andel et al.

From "'Basically, It's Sorcery for Your Vagina': Unpacking Western Representations of Vaginal Steaming," *Culture, Health & Sexuality* Vol. 19, No. 4, 2016, pp. 470–85. Copyright © 2016 Informa UK Limited, reprinted by permission of the publisher (Taylor & Francis Ltd, http://www.tandfonline.com).

2008, 86; Hull et al. 2011), these practices are also potentially risky—heated steam may disrupt healthy vaginal flora, leading to infection, or result in scalding of sensitive vulvar tissues; women report experiencing vaginal irritation, pain, bleeding and sores; "dry sex" has been linked to increased risk of infection (Hull et al. 2011; Smit et al. 2011).

Vaginal steaming is worth examining as part of a broader pattern of imperatives to work on and improve the female body, and for how it potentially re-inscribes ideas of the female body as (always, potentially) defective or even disgusting, to be feared and managed (Fahs 2015). Women's genitalia have long been a source of both fear and fascination, positioned as abhorrent, uncontrollable, dangerous and to be feared (Braun and Wilkinson 2001; Ussher 2006). Contemporary Western sociocultural representations of women's genitalia tend to be more nuanced than in the past, but still in subtle ways position them as unhygienic, disgusting and/or shameful (Braun and Wilkinson 2001; Fahs 2014). Our aim is to examine online media coverage of Western vaginal steaming to explore the constructions and rationalities the practice relies on, and reinforces, including ideas about women, women's bodies and women's engagement with such modificatory practices, and to interrogate their implications for women's well-being.

Our analysis is situated within constructionist theoretical frameworks (Burr 2015) and an understanding of the meanings and practices of the female body as socially produced rather than inherent or natural (Braun and Wilkinson 2001). . . . The concept of neoliberalism (Brown 2006; Rose 1996) has also proved fruitful for analyses of the body (Phipps 2014) and genital modification practices (e.g., Braun 2009). Neoliberalism's ideology of "privatisation, personal responsibility, agentic individualism, autonomy, and personal freedom" (Weiss 2008, 89) has quite radically shaped the ways Westerners now think about their selves, their bodies, their sexuality and their well-being, as well as the practices they engage in (Brown 2006). Neoliberalism asserts "an almost hyper-responsible self," who understands themself as "free from the influence of cultural norms and expectations" (Braun 2009, 236) in how they choose to act and what they desire (Brown 2006; Gill 2008a; Phipps 2014), an "enterprising" self, invested in "self-help" and transformation (Rose 1996) towards perfection. The ideology dubbed "healthism" situates the pursuit of not just health, but health optimisation, as a moral obligation (Cairns and Johnston 2015; Crawford 1980, 2006) and vital to contemporary (neoliberal) selfhood. . . .

The ideology of neoliberalism folds into and congeals with postfeminism (Gill 2007; McRobbie 2004), where the female subject is positioned as "liberated," free to choose and enact any femininity, how and when they see fit. Postfeminist rhetoric of "choice" and "empowerment" has become central to how body modification practices are marketed to women (Braun 2009; Gill 2003, 2008a, 2008b; Lazar 2006; McRobbie 2004). The self-as-project, "improved" through "proper" consumption, produces a culture of self-scrutiny (Gill 2007) in which women engage in constant self-monitoring and body-disciplining practices, such as "routine surveillance and maintenance" (Fahs 2014, 214) of their genitalia. The possession of "perfect" genitalia becomes vital to empowered (authentic and sexy) womanhood. This context produces accountability and culpability: women who do not engage in bodily (and psychological) "improvement" options become responsible for a less-than-desirable self/body, knowable as somehow defective or deficient (Lazar 2006; Phipps 2014). Women who use vaginal douches report perceiving those that do not as dirty and irresponsible, as not taking care of themselves (Lichtenstein and Nansel 2001); unmodified or visible pubic hair is similarly read as dirty or disgusting (Braun et al. 2013; Tiggemann and Hodgson

2008). Despite "free choice" rhetoric, choice has a strong moral dimension—certain choices are "right" (genital "improvement"); others are "wrong" (no genital modifications). The individual woman is expected—even obliged—to make the right choice (Braun 2009); non-compliance is seldom feasible (Bordo 2003).

METHODS

The data-set comprised a stratified sample of 90 online items related to vaginal steaming, from a number of predetermined site types (news/magazines [30]; health/lifestyle [20]; blogs [20]; spa/provider sites [20]). Data were collected through web searches (April–June 2015) using Google regional search engines (Australia, Canada, New Zealand, the UK, the USA). Search terms used were "vaginal steaming" and "v steam"; as search results were initially saturated with news and magazine articles pertaining to Paltrow's recent blog post, search terms were delimited to include sites specific to "health and lifestyle" ("lifestyle"), spas and service providers ("spa") and personal blogs ("blog"). Our sampling criteria excluded certain other site types (YouTube; online marketplace/classified advertisements; discussion forums; non-English websites). The 90 items in the sample represent the top-ranked hits from each search, after removal of duplication, as we were interested in accessing the types of text-based pages laypersons are likely to encounter if they turn to the Internet for information about vaginal steaming. After review, we decided to exclude user comments, as we were interested in the initial construction of vaginal steaming.

We followed Hookway's (2008) ethical "fair game–public domain" (105) approach when determining what content was suitable to collect and analyse: the content of webpages that were open access. Information that could potentially identify the individual respondent was disguised or excluded from data extracts presented (Convery and Cox 2012; Hookway 2008). Data were analysed using a social constructionist version of thematic analysis (Braun and Clarke 2006, 2012). . . . Data extracts are numbered sequentially (e1, e2, etc.) and identified by type of data item and a number (N = news/magazine; L = health/lifestyle; S = spa/ providers; B = personal blogs). Spelling errors/typos have been corrected to facilitate readability.

ANALYSIS: A SELF-IMPROVING WOMAN WHO STEAMS

E1: Often, I think some take the care of their vaginal/perianal area a little too lightly. It is the core of who and what we are as women; it brings forth life, love, pleasure, etc. We must learn to take care, treat and respect our vagina and womb. (B5)

A woman[1] who engages in various "self-improvement" strategies for both body and mind was the imagined subject who dominated the data-set. A perfect child of neoliberalism, this imagined subject operates within the ideology of "healthism" (Crawford 1980, 2006), where the pursuit of not just health, but health optimisation, becomes a moral obligation and vital to contemporary selfhood. We discuss four themes that evoke the self-improving woman in distinct ways. The first two—(1) the naturally deteriorating, dirty female body and (2) contemporary life is harmful—construct vaginal steaming as effectively a solution for a (health) problem. The others—(3) physical optimisation and the enhancement of health and (4) vaginal steaming for life optimisation—construct vaginal steaming as enhancement for already healthy women.

The Naturally Deteriorating, Dirty Female Body

The first way this self-improving woman was evidenced was in constructions of an inherently "faulty" female reproductive body, which reinforced and justified a need for self-surveillance and action:

E2: The combination of steam and essential oils from the plants penetrates deeply into the cervix and uterus to dislodge indurated menstrual fluids and pathological accumulations that have not properly sloughed off with each monthly cycle. (S12)

E3: After the steam you may notice some slight cramping or vaginal discharge. This is normal and ok. The cramping is a way for the uterus to rid itself of toxins and any blood that is stagnant and old. (P4)

The female reproductive body here is inevitably "unclean" and "toxic." Concern about toxicity reflects and reinforces the entrenched cultural narrative around women's genitalia as a dirty contaminating "liability" that require ongoing maintenance and purification (Braun and Wilkinson 2001, 2003; Fahs 2014), part of a broader discourse of women's bodies as polluting (Douglas 2002). In these extracts, a specific defectiveness is applied to menstruation, a metaphoric construction of menstruation as a "machine in disrepair" (Martin 1987, 45) which permeated the data-set. Here, women suffer through their defective bodies, with defectiveness evident in both mechanical and structural aspects. The uterus, an organ with an amazingly long history of blame related to women's health (Meyer 1997), was itself singled out as faulty:

E4: My uterus sits pretty far back and is slightly tilted and as a result old blood gets stuck up in there relatively easily. Unfortunately this means that with each new period, my uterus has to contract something fierce to get all this hardened and thickened old blood out, hence the painful cramping. What a job our uteruses have, huh?! (B8)

E5: A lot of discomfort to do with menstruation et al. can actually be caused by having a misaligned uterus. I never knew that the uterus could become misaligned, but I guess it makes sense. I mean, the uterus does a lot of work. (B20)

These extracts link design faults (location, orientation, alignment) with problematic menstrual experiences. However, reflecting the contradictory social meanings ascribed to women's genitalia (e.g., Braun and Wilkinson 2001, 2003; Fahs 2014), negative constructions coexisted with a more positive account of a "hardworking" organ. At the same time, this ultimately relies on an imagined problematic female body—a body that requires hard work. Building on the idea of defective-by-design, women's reproductive bodies were also described as reaching a point of "stagnation":

E6: Many infertility problems are related to coldness and stagnation. . . . The chai-yok treatment is effective for coldness or poor circulation in the lower part of the body because it increases the blood circulation, and blood supplies nutrition, so the more blood supply, the faster the healing process. (L2)

E7: Stagnation is not a good thing when it comes to any organ system, but when it comes to the uterus it can cause a myriad of issues with menstruation and fertility. (L3)

. . . The female body was regularly positioned as inevitably deteriorating from an optimal to a sub-optimal state, a process depicted as both natural and inherently problematic, and to be battled against. Vaginal steaming was, for instance, framed as a "detox":

E8: Vaginal steam baths are basically a detoxing facial for your lady parts. They cleanse, tone, and nourish your cervix, uterus, and vaginal tissues. (B4)

E9: I was drawn to it as a way to detoxify a part of my body that is not easily accessible yet important to keep clean. (L14)

A claim to "detox" evokes a needed cleansing process, and a starting state of pathology that is removed. Through a factually oriented claim around "importance" (E9), a responsible and self-policing neoliberal subject (Neasbitt and Rodriguez 2011) is evoked, a woman who recognises a problem and seeks to resolve it.

Within the data, the female body was situated within this biologically determinist narrative of inevitable decline (Twigg 2004), but decay was positioned as something that could and should be resisted. . . . [V]aginal steaming is positioned as a (new) technique women can now use to disrupt decline and dirtiness, the "solution" that rational, responsible women should utilise to maintain their declining "unruly" bodies and bodily processes.

This was particularly evident in relation to fertility enhancement, a key desired outcome of vaginal steaming processes. Fertility was constructed as inherently fraught; always at risk, always potentially sub-optimal or declining—that ticking "biological clock" (Friese, Becker, and Nachtigall 2006). Given that gendered identity for women and childbearing are almost inextricably linked in pronatalist Western societies (Greil, Slauson-Blevin, and McQuillan 2011), women were unsurprisingly often depicted in states from eagerness to improve fertility to desperation to (re)gain fertility:

E10: That brings me to the story of my one experiment with vaginal steaming, when I was a desperate woman about to try IVF [in vitro fertilization] for the second and last time and was willing to give anything a shot. . . . When you're dealing with infertility, you end up reading about anything and everything that has ever helped a woman get pregnant. (L16)

Stories of "the miracle pregnancy" following vaginal steaming were not uncommon:

E11: In fact, Niki Han Schwarz, owner of Tikkun Spa (where Gwyneth gets steamed), told the LA Times that after battling three years of infertility, she was able to get pregnant at age 45 after only five V-Steam treatments. (L15)

Decay (infertility) is here conquered through vaginal steaming. Infertility was often described using warfare metaphors, such as "battling" (E30), explicitly as well as implicitly framing the female body as an enemy, something to be "battled" against and beaten. So although decline was positioned as inherent in womanhood, it was to be resisted by the self-improving woman who steams.

"Modern Women Are Really Suffering": Contemporary Life Is Harmful

E12: What's really ruining our health is all the toxic sh*t we keep putting into our bodies, not a traditional practice that's been used by women for a very long time. (B8)

The female body wasn't only positioned as naturally defective and deteriorating. The deterioration of women's bodies and health was frequently positioned as a result of contemporary Western cultural contexts and meanings, with vaginal steaming situated as a practice that women should use to liberate themselves from these forms of sociocultural oppression. The female body was situated often as effectively under assault:

E13: With all the torture we inflict on our vaginas these days—waxing, lasering, chemical-laden douches, synthetic tampons and pads, antibiotics, hormonal birth control, vaginal rejuvenation surgery, bleaching, spermicides. I could go on and on—I'm frankly shocked at the recent backlash in the media about vaginal steaming. (B8)

E14: We live in a culture that likes to [traumatize] its vaginas. We wax it, shave it, give it a buzz cut and pluck it within an inch of its life. We pierce it. We vajazzle it. We "cleanse" it even though it cleans itself just fine. And we are constantly bombarded with perfumed products to douse it with because some people are afraid of what a real woman smells like. But this steamy vagina business sounds like something I could get on board with. (L19)

In such accounts, genital modification and "maintenance" become normalised, the "we" positioning *all* women as participating, as complicit. Here, the damage or risk to women's bodies effectively comes from the practices women (choose to) engage in. While some women referred to contemporary life in a generalised way ("toxic sh*t"; E10), others singled out specific practices as a point of comparison:

E15: I question why people are up in arms about hot water near a vulva when people are still putting toxic cotton tampons IN their vaginas . . . talk about changing the vaginal flora! (L11)

Setting up a contrast between contemporary "damaging" practice and vaginal steaming achieves two things: it legitimates vaginal steaming as normative within a range of modificatory practices *and* it situates it as inherently different to those. . . . [V]aginal steaming is explicitly positioned as a "safe" alternative that contrasts with toxic and damaging yet normative practices. . . . This constructs a sort of imperative that "responsible" women would take up vaginal steaming in an effort to preserve their health, as conscientious consumers in postfeminist neoliberal times (Evans and Riley 2013; Gill 2007; Lazar 2011).

The theme of a female body damaged by Western culture was also evident in accounts of a medicalised and pathologised female (reproductive) body:

E16: You may snicker at the idea of steaming your vagina, but in a culture that pathologises our bodies and medicalises our reproductive ailments, bringing back this time-tested technique could serve a lot of women well. (N4)

Western biomedicine was often positioned negatively in data items that promoted vaginal steaming:

E17: Maybe you'd like to turn this into a protective rite, to ensure that various institutional ignoramuses keep their grubby paws off of your vagina . . . and stop treating your body as the property of their dubious enterprises. (S16)

Here, the entire medical establishment is suspect, a "dubious" mode of control of women's bodies. The caution in extract E17 extends a long (feminist) critique of both the institution of medicine and the processes around the medicalisation of women's "normal" bodies and bodily changes, particularly related to women's genitalia, sexuality and fertility (e.g., Braun and Tiefer 2009; Cacchioni 2015; Moynihan and Cassels 2005). Medicalisation relies on,

and reproduces, very particular and normative ideas of what is ideal for women's "reproductive" body and sexuality, and indeed what is normal. Through evocation of this critique, vaginal steaming is positioned as a holistic modality that women can use as both alternative, and resistance, to Western medicine, as potentially empowering (Barrett et al. 2003; Madden 2012) and authentic. However, the language of Western medicine remains in the texts, through reference to "symptoms," "conditions" and "ailments," which vaginal steaming is claimed to resolve. Despite a critique of medicalisation, the terms of reference blend and blur, used to legitimate vaginal steaming as a "cure" for real problems.

"Isn't Your Health Worth That?" Physical Optimisation and the Enhancement of Health

E18: The periodic use of the yoni steam technique can enhance overall reproductive health for women. (S17)

Women's health was situated as something to endlessly be "improved," "enhanced" and "optimised." Vaginal steaming was routinely portrayed as a means to optimise the body and maintain general health:

E19: The V-Steam can be used to maintain health and wellness in addition to treating more complex issues. (B19)

E20: The vaginal steam bath is used for just about everything, it is used to promote . . . healing and rejuvenation for just about any woman's reproductive health ailment. (S3)

Vaginal steaming is constructed here as an almost all-in-one solution to whatever ails a woman—both specific "ailments" as well as more ephemeral well-being. Reflecting healthism, the only acceptable body becomes situated as the ultimately health-optimised body (Cairns and Johnston 2015). In some cases, a state of perfection was positioned as something women had had, and could return to, evoking the narrative of decline evidenced in the previous theme:

E21: The 30-minute service—which costs $75 for one session, or $750 for 12—uses healing herbs to irrigate the vaginal passage to restore optimum health. (N16)

E22: Vaginal steaming to help maintain internal health as well as keep your skin looking young and healthy. (S1)

Although sometimes situated as "maintenance" (E19, E22), others evoked restoration, and a return to an optimal past. "Youth" and "health" were conflated—implicitly positioning change as bad, and resonating with broader discourse not only of healthism, but a related "successful aging" discourse (Meletiou and Meylahn 2015). Fertility and sexual pleasure were particularly targeted for optimisation. . . . Women were encouraged to use vaginal steaming as a preventive measure, a way of optimising something not (yet) "broken":

E23: Vagi-steam is best done every two weeks when used for treating a fertility issue. For general fertile vitality (preventative maintenance), Vagi-steam baths are best done twice a year. (L3)

E24: Renew Fertility V-Steam: For women who are trying to get pregnant or are interested in preserving their fertility. (S13)

Vaginal steaming here becomes a practice for every woman who cares about her fertility—something to be attended to, worked on and optimised. . . . Within the neoliberalist discourse evident in the data, women are encouraged to adopt a "self-policing gaze" (Gill 2003) to work to ameliorate the risks to fertility; fertility optimisation via vaginal steaming becomes positioned as a key marker of "productive and conscientious citizenship" (Lavrence and Lozanski 2014, 85).

Vaginal steaming was regularly depicted as a tool to improve women's sexual experiences:

E25: For women looking to boost their sexual energy. An energetic steam that aids in increasing blood flow and circulation enhancing chi thereby improving sexual response and sexual vigour. (S13)

This appears to offer an "empowered" narrative: with women the primary beneficiaries of "increase[d] sexual gratification" (S11), they are situated as entitled to sexual pleasure (Braun 2005). Such sexual pleasure was, however, often situated within very heteronormative framings: sexual pleasure was framed as occurring typically only within heterosexual couplings, and even often specifically heterosexual marriage:

E26: We have some clients who say that after they've had the V-steam their husbands can't stay away from them. (N16)

The claim that vaginal steaming would "improve the marital relationship" (S11) was sometimes explicit. The (often) unspoken risk of not having a vaginal steam becomes marriage decline, through her inattention to body or sexual response. Like the domain of female genital cosmetic surgery (Braun 2005), vaginal steaming becomes a legitimate, potentially even obligatory, practice for women in pursuit of an optimal body and (through that) hetero-relationship.

The texts frequently utilised "feminist" language evoking an empowered woman, to frame this as an activity women undertook for themselves. Concepts such as being "in contro'" (N4) or having (self)confidence appeared regularly:

E27: It can be used to enhance sexual arousal and self-confidence. (S11)

E28: And why should you do this before Valentine's Day?? Nicole specifically told me that after the treatment, many of her clients feel confident, refreshed and ready to hurry home to their man!! (L17)

A claim to self-confidence and/or increased sexual control affords a "moral justification" (Braun 2005) for vaginal steaming, through evoking an empowered, confident woman whose sexuality is her own—even if it was depicted, as in extract E25, as revolving around a man. This discourse echoes contemporary "sex advice" texts where women are coached on how to become sexually "self-assured" (Gill 2009). Such claims situate vaginal steaming within the cluster of practices marketed to women under "because you're worth it" rhetoric (see Gill 2008b), where physical actions are psychological actions, with broader and widespread ramifications. In a medicalised context where a "sex for health" discourse is prevalent, and sex positioned as crucial to diverse facets of well-being (see Gupta and Cacchioni 2013; Marshall 2012), vaginal steaming for better sex becomes steaming for better health and well-being.

Overall, vaginal steaming was depicted as a tool already-well women should utilise to optimise their body, and in particular, their reproductive capacity and sexuality. Despite the neoliberal tone, the rhetoric employed echoes longstanding Western-cultural definitions of the vagina (Braun and Wilkinson 2001, 2005) as the "centre of a woman's being" (S14); the sexual and reproductive enhancement focus mirrors the two modes through which Western societies have traditionally valued women: sexual availability for men (within marriage) and childbearing.

"Go for It—Pamper Yourself!" Vaginal Steaming for Life-Optimisation

E29: I have a great vagina. Really, I do. I've never had a problem with yeast infections, never had a Pap smear come back abnormal, never had to deal with menstrual cramps. I have the kind of vagina that deserves to be pampered, so when I heard about "vaginal steaming," I thought to myself: *Vagina, you deserve a spa day.* (N15)

Finally, vaginal steaming was situated as a way for women to "pamper" themselves:

E30: It is called a Vagina Steam and yes, my Vagina really loves it! It feels really cleansing and is perfect to do just after your monthly or if you just feel like giving your little friend a little special treat! (B17)

E31: Think of this luxurious modality as a facial for your lady parts. (S13)

Comparison to the "facial" and evocations of "TLC" (tender loving care) situates vaginal steaming within the domain of luxury, and for the perfectly fine body rather than a body in deficit that needs some improvement. Again echoing "because you're worth it," this situates certain (sometimes painful) female body practices as "pampering" (Gill 2007). The spa visit has been positioned as an important part of women's regular health-and-well-being routines (Little 2013) and steaming is here linked with practices presented to women as entitlement, the "earned" right to be "pampered" (Lazar 2009). Positioned thus within neoliberal framing, vaginal steaming becomes a treat women should do for themselves, if they really value themselves. This final theme reveals an inherent paradox in many of these texts: vaginal steaming is depicted as both a necessity for health, and a "treat" that a woman does "for herself." This sets up an ontological state for women's genitalia as never there, as always available for (more) intervention, whether "faulty" or fine.

Frequent references were also made to the notion that women will be able to "reconnect" with their bodies or selves as a result of vaginal steaming:

E32: Yoni steaming is about more than uterine health. . . . The practice brings a reconnection to the female body and to the wisdom of plant medicine. It is an opportunity for women to celebrate and cherish our bodies, and learning to enjoy our wombs as the beautiful, sacred center from which we radiate our capacity to change the world. (S7)

E33: It was a beautiful experience! Every woman should do this because it does feel good. It sensually awakens the senses of my yoni. It feels different afterwards, like, I am in touch with myself as a woman. It feels very intimate and sexy. (B14)

Some made reference to the idea of "reawakening" (L12) an "inner goddess":

E34: To awaken your inner goddess, please call us at . . . (S4)

E35: For women who want to connect to "their inner goddess." A pampering, nurturing and relaxing steam for your "down there area." (S13)

Located within new-age "inner self" discourse, this argument appears the opposite of neoliberal "pampering" discourse, yet both rely on the logic of improvement of an essentially OK (reproductive) body—and through that, self. And, albeit in a different way to the idea of a facial, the notion that vaginal steaming can unlock an "inner power" (S20) constructs it as a transformative practice. . . . The outcome of vaginal steaming is more than a "toned" reproductive system or even "comfort and relaxation" (S15); it offers an opportunity to become the "sensual" and "divine" goddess the woman already has the *potential* to be. Metaphors of interiority—references to "reconnecting with" or "reawakening" something "inside" (see also Donaghue, Kurz, and Whitehead 2011)—evoke an unknown entity blocking a woman from accessing her "true" self. Vaginal steaming, resembling a search and rescue device tailored to discover/recover formerly neglected, repressed or forgotten qualities, liberates. It is presented as a way for women to experience the self-exploration and self-realisation that are a crucial element of both the neoliberal "project of the self" (Rose 1996) and new-age discourse. . . .

DISCUSSION

. . . Accounts of vaginal steaming are sites of meaning-making and meaning-contestation. Cutting across the themes discussed, three notable and distinct epistemological frameworks were utilised to make and refute truth claims: *Eastern mysticism, Western biomedicine* and/ or *Experience.* Each oriented to a quite different truth-base to validate their promotion or debunking (sometimes both!) of vaginal steaming. *Eastern mysticism,* which appeared most commonly in data items that sought to promote vaginal steaming (e.g., spa sites, personal blogs), rationalised the practice by chronicling a tradition of vaginal steaming and attributing its origin to one or more non-Western cultures, typically within Asia. Vaginal steaming tended to be described as a long-standing practice that has "stood the test of time" (L1), evoking effectiveness and credibility. Exhibiting orientalist (Said 1978) discourse, "the East" was exoticised and implicitly positioned as more authentic and "uncontaminated" than Western nations. Vaginal steaming, constructed as a "holistic" practice that "incorporates body, mind and spirit wellness" (S8), was often contrasted with Western medicine, which was positioned as too heavily focused on the body, or extensively critiqued (as noted in theme 2). Vaginal steaming was, in contrast, often depicted as completely natural and non-invasive, and positioned as therefore a safe alternative to many "conventional" medicines. Indeed, claims based within Eastern mysticism often portrayed vaginal steaming as a form of resistance to Western medicine and, sometimes, Western culture more broadly.

In contrast, *Western biomedicine* privileged scientific evidence and rationality, and was typically deployed to dispute beneficial claims about the practice, and the practice itself, not least through highlighting the lack of "credible evidence" (L20). Claims used to justify the practice were often positioned as "dubious" (N7) and pseudo-scientific, both anatomically and physiologically. Texts drawing on Western biomedicine often positioned the female body as basically naturally physiologically competent—with vaginal steaming positioned as a threat to that. Risks were emphasised—"Worst case scenario? Death" (N21)—and claimed-healthy alternatives (e.g., diet, exercise, medication) were encouraged for anyone experiencing the conditions vaginal steaming was claimed to cure. This epistemological framing situated Western biomedicine as the authority on women's bodies; women who promote and engage in vaginal steaming were positioned as "dupes."

The *Experience* epistemological frame—used to argue both for and against the practice by women who have tried it—based claims in the author's personal, embodied experiences of vaginal steaming—evoking a hard-to-dispute "experiential authority" (Kitzinger 1994). Personal testimony–based framing was used to dispute the validity of "any randomised controlled double-blinded clinical trial" (L2) as the basis for deciding whether the practice had merit, situating it as more important or valid than Western biomedical "evidence" standards. Vaginal steaming was commonly promoted on the merit that it felt good—"I *felt* great: clean, relaxed, at ease" (N15, emphasis in original)—even if it did not deliver the claimed or desired effects.

. . . The way vaginal steaming is promoted online simultaneously reflects and reinforces traditional derogatory understandings of the vagina and women's reproductive bodies as dirty and defective (e.g., Braun and Wilkinson 2001) and, despite the rhetoric of liberation and empowerment, appears to operate as a conservative regulatory practice (Ussher 2006). It appears to promote very particular forms of feminine embodiment, and particular modes of selfhood practice for women, which fit with neoliberalism, healthism, postfeminism and the production of self-hood through consumption.

We examined a range of easily accessible online texts. Examination of online texts offers a way to understand and unpack sociocultural assumptions and logics, but it does not tell us how women make sense of these texts. The ways everyday women make sense of these practices is another important step for understanding their implications for women's health and well-being. . . . This study contributes to the wider literature on genital modification practices and sociocultural constructions of women's bodies and genitalia, and to the question of what selves, subjectivities and practices are offered to women in neoliberal times. Our analysis suggests the meanings associated with vaginal steaming are still highly contested, and not (yet) socioculturally solidified, but the practice, and the way it is discussed and described, remains familiar and resonant. Whether it poses the same risks as vaginal douching remains to be seen.

NOTE

1. An essentialised notion of womanhood, whereby (1) a woman has a vagina and (2) a vagina is regarded as central to being a woman (Braun and Wilkinson 2005), as well as an orientation to the female body as reproductive, permeated the data-set. Although such cis- and heteronormative assumptions trouble us, we use the terms "woman," "women" and "female" in a way consistent with the data—to reference cissexual/cisgender women (women whose sex and gender identities match those assigned at birth). In noting these assumptions, we attempt to avoid simply reproducing societal heterosexism and cisgenderism in and through research (see Ansara and Hegarty 2014).

REFERENCES

van Andel, T., S. de Korte, D. Koopmans, J. Behari-ramdas, and S. Ruysschaert. 2008. "Dry Sex in Suriname." *Journal of Ethnopharmacology* 116 (1): 84–88.

Anderson, M. R., D. Mckee, J. Yukes, A. Alvarez, and A. Karasz. 2008. "An Investigation of Douching Practices in the Botanicas of the Bronx." *Culture, Health & Sexuality* 10 (1): 1–11.

Ansara, Y. G., and P. Hegarty. 2014. "Methodologies of Misgendering: Recommendations for Reducing Cisgenderism in Psychological Research." *Feminism & Psychology* 24 (2): 259–70.

Barrett, B., L. Marchand, J. Scheder, M. B. Plane, R. Maberry, D. Appelbaum, D. Rakel, and D. Rabago. 2003. "Themes of Holism, Empowerment, Access, and Legitimacy Define Complementary, Alternative, and Integrative Medicine in Relation to Conventional Biomedicine." *The Journal of Alternative and Complementary Medicine* 9 (6): 937–47.

Bordo, S. 2003. *Unbearable Weight: Feminism, Western Culture and the Body.* Berkeley: University of California Press.

Braun, V. 2005. "In Search of (Better) Sexual Pleasure: Female Genital 'Cosmetic' Surgery." *Sexualities* 8 (4): 407–24.

Braun, V. 2009. "'The Women Are Doing It for Themselves': The Rhetoric of Choice and Agency around Female Genital Cosmetic Surgery." *Australian Feminist Studies* 24 (60): 233–49.

Braun, V. 2010. "Female Genital Cosmetic Surgery: A Critical Review of Current Knowledge and Contemporary Debates." *Journal of Women's Health* 19 (7): 1393–407.

Braun, V., and V. Clarke. 2006. "Using Thematic Analysis in Psychology." *Qualitative Research in Psychology* 3: 77–101.

Braun, V., and V. Clarke. 2012. "Thematic Analysis." In *APA Handbook of Research Methods in Psychology*, edited by H. Cooper, 57–71. Washington, DC: APA Books.

Braun, V. and L. Tiefer. 2009. "The 'Designer Vagina' and the Pathologisation of Female Genital Diversity: Interventions for Change." *Radical Psychology* 8 (1): 1–21.

Braun, V., and S. Wilkinson. 2001. "Socio-Cultural Representations of the Vagina." *Journal of Reproductive and Infant Psychology* 19 (1): 17–32.

Braun, V., and S. Wilkinson. 2003. "Liability or Asset? Women Talk about the Vagina." *Psychology of Women Section Review* 5 (2): 28–42.

Braun, V., and S. Wilkinson. 2005. "Vagina Equals Woman? On Genitals and Gendered Identity." *Women's Studies International Forum* 28 (6): 509–22.

Braun, V., G. Tricklebank, and V. Clarke. 2013. "'It Shouldn't Stick Out from Your Bikini at the Beach': Meaning, Gender, and the Hairy/Hairless Body." *Psychology of Women Quarterly* 37 (4): 478–93.

Brown, W. 2006. "American Nightmare Neoliberalism, Neoconservatism, and De-Democratization." *Political Theory* 34 (6): 690–714.

Burd, J. 2015. "The Mysterious Origins of Vaginal Steaming." https://skeptoid.com/blog/2015/01/18/the-mysterious-origins-of-vaginal-steaming/.

Burr, V. 2015. *Social Constructionism*. 3rd ed. New York: Routledge.

Cacchioni, T. 2015. "The Medicalization of Sexual Deviance, Reproduction, and Functioning." In *Handbook of the Sociology of Sexualities*, edited by J. DeLamater, and R. F. Plante, 435–52. Cham: Springer.

Cairns, K., and J. Johnston. 2015. "Choosing Health: Embodied Neoliberalism, Postfeminism, and the 'Do-diet.'" *Theory and Society* 44 (2): 153–75.

Convery, I., and D. Cox. 2012. "A Review of Research Ethics in Internet-based Research." *Practitioner Research in Higher Education* 6 (1): 50–57.

Cottrell, B. H. 2010. "An Updated Review of Evidence to Discourage Douching." *MCN: The American Journal of Maternal/Child Nursing* 35 (2): 102–07.

Crawford, R. 1980. "Healthism and the Medicalization of Everyday Life." *International Journal of Health Services* 10: 365–88.

Crawford, R. 2006. "Health as a Meaningful Social Practice." *Health* 10 (4): 401–20.

Donaghue, N., T. Kurz, and K. Whitehead. 2011. "Spinning the Pole: A Discursive Analysis of the Websites of Recreational Pole Dancing Studios." *Feminism & Psychology* 21 (4): 443–57.

Douglas, M. 2002. *Purity and Danger: An Analysis of Concepts of Pollution and Taboo*. New York: Routledge.

Evans, A., and S. Riley. 2013. "Immaculate Consumption: Negotiating the Sex Symbol in Postfeminist Celebrity Culture." *Journal of Gender Studies* 22 (3): 268–81.

Fahs, B. 2014. "Genital Panics: Constructing the Vagina in Women's Qualitative Narratives about Pubic Hair, Menstrual Sex, and Vaginal Self-Image." *Body Image* 11 (3): 210–18.

Fahs, B. 2015. "The Dreaded Body: Disgust and the Production of 'Appropriate' Femininity." *Journal of Gender Studies* 1–13.

Farage, M. A. and L. Lennon. 2006. "Products for Vulva Hygiene." *In the Vulva: Anatomy, Physiology and Pathology*, edited by M. A. Farage and H. I. Maibach, 217–33. New York: CRC Press.

Fashemi, B., M. L. Delaney, A. B. Onderdonk, and R. N. Fichorova. 2013. "Effects of Feminine Hygiene Products on the Vaginal Mucosal Biome." *Microbial Ecology in Health and Disease* 24: 1–6.

Friese, C., G. Becker, and R. D. Nachtigall. 2006. "Rethinking the Biological Clock: Eleventh-Hour Moms, Miracle Moms and Meanings of Age-related Infertility." *Social Science and Medicine* 63 (6): 1550–60.

Gill, R. 2003. "From Sexual Objectification to Sexual Subjectification: The Resexualisation of Women's Bodies in the Media." *Feminist Media Studies* 3 (1): 100–06.

Gill, R. 2007. "Critical Respect: The Difficulties and Dilemmas of Agency and 'Choice' for Feminism." *European Journal of Women's Studies* 14 (1): 69–80.

Gill, R. 2008a. "Culture and Subjectivity in Neoliberal and Postfeminist Times." *Subjectivity* 25 (1): 432–45.

Gill, R. 2008b. "Empowerment/Sexism: Figuring Female Sexual Agency in Contemporary Advertising." *Feminism & Psychology* 18 (1): 35–60.

Gill, R. 2009. "Mediated Intimacy and Postfeminism: A Discourse Analytic Examination of Sex and Relationships Advice in a Women's Magazine." *Discourse and Communication* 3 (4): 345–69.

Goop. 2015. "Infrared Saunas, Detox Spas, and the Best Spots for Colonics." http://goop.com/city-guide/infrared-saunas-detox-spas-and-the-best-spots-for-colonics/los-angeles/.

Greil, A. L., K. Slauson-Blevin, and J. McQuillan. 2011. "The Experience of Infertility: A Review of the Recent Literature." *Sociology of Health & Illness* 32 (1): 140–62.

Gunter, J. 2015. "Gwyneth Paltrow Says Steam Your Vagina, an OB/GYN Says Don't." https://drjengunter.wordpress.com/2015/01/27/gwyneth-paltrow-says-steam-your-vagina-an-obgyn-says-dont/.

Gupta, K., and T. Cacchioni. 2013. "Sexual Improvement as If Your Health Depends on It: An Analysis of Contemporary Sex Manuals." *Feminism & Psychology* 23 (4): 442–58.

Heifetz, S. 2010. "Vaginal Steam Bath Finds a Place among Southern California Spa Options." http://articles.latimes.com/2010/dec/20/health/la-he-v-steam-20101220.

Herbenick, D., V. Schick, M. Reece, S. A. Sanders, and J. D. Fortenberry. 2013. "Pubic Hair Removal and Sexual Behavior: Findings from a Prospective Daily Diary Study of Sexually Active Women in the United States." *The Journal of Sexual Medicine* 10 (3): 678–85.

Hilber, A. M., T. H. Hull, E. Preston-Whyte, B. Bagnol, J. Smit, C. Wacharasin, and N. Widyantoro for the World Health Organisation Gender, Sexuality, and Vaginal Practices Study Group. 2010. "A Cross Cultural Study of Vaginal Practices and Sexuality: Implications for Sexual Health." *Social Science & Medicine* 70 (3): 392–400.

Hookway, N. 2008. "'Entering the Blogosphere': Some Strategies for Using Blogs in Social Research." *Qualitative Research* 8 (1): 91–113.

Hull, T., A. M. Hilber, M. F. Chersich, B. Bagnol, A. Prohmmo, J. A. Smit, N. Widyantoro, et al. 2011. "Prevalence, Motivations, and Adverse Effects of Vaginal Practices in Africa and Asia: Findings from a Multicountry Household Survey." *Journal of Women's Health* 20 (7): 1097–109.

Kitzinger, C. 1994. "Experiential Authority and Heterosexuality." In *Changing Our Lives: Doing Women's Studies*, edited by G. Griffin, 135–44. London: Pluto Press.

Lavrence, C., and K. Lozanski. 2014. "'This Is Not Your Practice Life': Lululemon and the Neoliberal Governance of Self." *Canadian Review of Sociology* 51 (1): 76–94.

Lazar, M. M. 2006. "'Discover the Power of Femininity!' Analyzing Global 'Power Femininity' in Local Advertising." *Feminist Media Studies* 6 (4): 505–17.

Lazar, M. M. 2009. "Entitled to Consume: Postfeminist Femininity and a Culture of Post-critique." *Discourse & Communication* 3 (4): 371–400.

Lazar, M. M. 2011. "The Right to Be Beautiful: Postfeminist Identity and Consumer Beauty Advertising." In *New Femininities: Postfeminism, Neoliberalism and Subjectivity*, edited by R. Gill and C. Scharff, 37–52. New York: Palgrave Macmillan.

Lichtenstein, B., and T. R. Nansel. 2001. "Women's Douching Practices and Related Attitudes: Findings from Four Focus Groups." *Women & Health* 31 (2–3): 117–31.

Little, J. 2013. "Pampering, Well-being and Women's Bodies in the Therapeutic Spaces of the Spa." *Social & Cultural Geography* 14 (1): 41–58.

Luong, M. L., M. Libman, M. Dahhou, M. F. Chen, S. R. Kahn, L. Goulet, J. Lydon, H. McNamara, R. W. Platt, and M. S. Kramer. 2010. "Vaginal Douching, Bacterial Vaginosis, and Spontaneous Preterm Birth." *Journal of Obstetrics and Gynaecology Canada* 32 (4): 313–20.

Madden, H. 2012. "Integrative Medicine: A Contested Practice." Doctoral Thesis, Massey University.

Marshall, B. L. 2012. "Medicalization and the Refashioning of Age-related Limits on Sexuality." *Journal of Sex Research* 49 (4): 337–43.

Martin, E. 1987. *The Woman in the Body: A Cultural Analysis of Reproduction*. Boston, MA: Beacon Press.

Martino, J. L., and S. H. Vermund. 2002. "Vaginal Douching: Evidence for Risks or Benefits to Women's Health." *Epidemiologic Reviews* 24 (2): 109–24.

Martino, J. L., S. Youngpairoj, and S. H. Vermund. 2004. "Vaginal Douching: Personal Practices and Public Policies." *Journal of Women's Health* 13 (9): 1048–65.

McRobbie, A. 2004. "Post-feminism and Popular Culture." *Feminist Media Studies* 4 (3): 255–64.

Meletiou, C., and J. A. Meylahn. 2015. "Deconstructing the Cultural Confinement of the Western Menopausal Women towards a Spirituality of Liberation." *VERBUM et Ecclesia* 36 (1): 1–6.

Meyer, C. L. 1997. *The Wandering Uterus: Politics and the Reproductive Rights of Women*. New York: New York University Press.

Moynihan, R., and A. Cassels. 2005. *Selling Sickness: How the World's Biggest Pharmaceutical Companies Are Turning Us All into Patients*. New York: Nation Books.

Neasbitt, J. Y., and J. M. Rodriguez. 2011. "Lip Service(s): Discourses on Designer Vaginas." *Penn Bioethics Journal* 7 (1): 17–22.

Nicoletti, A. 2006. "To Douche or Not to Douche." *Journal of Pediatric and Adolescent Gynecology* 19 (5): 353–54.

Office of Women's Health. 2015. Douching Fact Sheet. United States Department of Health and Human Services. http://www.womenshealth.gov/publications/our-publications/fact-sheet/douching.pdf.

Phipps, A. 2014. *The Politics of the Body: Gender in a Neoliberal and Neoconservative Age*. Malden, MA: Polity Press.

Rose, N. 1996. *Inventing Our Selves: Psychology, Power, and Personhood*. New York: Cambridge University Press.

Said, E. W. 1978. *Orientalism*. London: Routledge.

Smit, J., M. F. Chersich, M. Beksinska, B. Kunene, N. Manzini, A. M. Hilber, and F. Scorgie. 2011. "Prevalence and Self-reported Health Consequences of Vaginal Practices in KwaZulu-Natal, South Africa: Findings from a Household Survey." *Tropical Medicine & International Health* 16 (2): 245–56.

Tiggemann, M., and S. Hodgson. 2008. "The Hairlessness Norm Extended: Reasons for and Predictors of Women's Body Hair Removal at Different Body Sites." *Sex Roles* 59 (11–12): 889–97.

Twigg, J. 2004. "The Body, Gender, and Age: Feminist Insights in Social Gerontology." *Journal of Aging Studies* 18 (1): 59–73.

Ussher, J. M. 2006. *Managing the Monstrous Feminine: Regulating the Reproductive Body*. London: Routledge.

Weiss, M. D. 2008. "Gay Shame and BDSM Pride: Neoliberalism, Privacy, and Sexual Politics." *Radical History Review* 2008 (100): 87–101.

Zhang, J., A. G. Thomas, and E. Leybovich. 1997. "Vaginal Douching and Adverse Health Effects: A Meta-Analysis." *American Journal of Public Health* 87 (7): 1207–11.

HUMAN NATURE: ON FAT SEXUAL IDENTITY AND AGENCY

CAT PAUSÉ

I think I'd be grossed out if I had to watch two characters with rolls and rolls of fat kissing each other . . . because I'd be grossed out if I had to watch them doing anything. To be brutally honest, even in real life, I find it aesthetically displeasing to watch a very, very fat person simply walk across a room.

In an article about the television sitcom *Mike & Molly*, Maura Kelly (2010) expressed her disgust at the idea of having to watch the fat characters engage in displays of affection. The comments on the piece demonstrated that she is not the only one to find acts of sexual expression among fat people to be gross. But agreement was not the only response Kelly's piece received. A range of responses, from the online fat community, the online feminist community, and even mainstream presses, cried out over the fat-shaming and hatred contained in the article. Emily Exton (2010) at *Entertainment Weekly* suggested in her piece that not only do viewers need to get over any objection to seeing fat people be amorous on screen, but that producers of on-screen material need to get over their reliance on fat jokes to tell a fat story.

Examining more recent mainstream media coverage around fat sexuality reinforces the negative perception that many, like Kelly, may have. In the *Sydney Morning Herald*, Matty Silver (2014) argues that a better sex life can be found through weight loss. Focusing in on issues of erectile dysfunction and sterility in heterosexual men, Silver suggests that fat men often find sex difficult because of their lack of stamina or lower levels of testosterone. She also highlights the low self-esteem that may plague fat men, noting that "fat in the abdominal area can make the penis look smaller than it really is,

which doesn't help self esteem." An article from CNN (2014) promotes a new book, *XL Love: How the Obesity Crisis Is Complicating America's Love Life*. The author of the book, Sarah Varney, suggests that fatness has a "chilling effect on sexual relationships, from physical barriers to intimacy to attitudinal shifts with weight gain and even loss." The article frames the discussion around concerns of the "obesity epidemic" and the impact it may have on the lives of fat people.

The mainstream media's representations and discussions around sex make it clear that fat people are not considered sexually attractive, or as individuals with sexual agency. As noted by LeBesco (2004), mainstream discourses on what is sexy and how sexy is embodied usually exclude fatness and fat bodies. Murray (2004) argues this is due to heteronormative systems that construct the values and meanings surrounding sex and sexual identification. Systems such as capitalism and neoliberalism place value on discipline, conformity, and fulfilling the fantasies of the dominant subject (heterosexual men in power). Fatness, according to these systems, is not desirable or valued. The rejection of fatness as acceptable has led to fat identity being classified as a spoiled identity; one in which the bearer of the stigma (fatness) is held responsible for the stigma (Pausé, 2012). All identities are constructed, maintained, and revised through an interaction of individuals' beliefs about themselves and the messages one receives from the environment. A spoiled

From "Human Nature: On Fat Sexual Identity and Agency," in Helen Hester, Caroline Walters, eds., *Fat Sex: New Directions in Theory and Activism*. © Helen Hester and Caroline Walters, 2015, reproduced by permission of Taylor & Francis Books UK.

identity, like fatness, is further complicated by the individuals' beliefs about themselves being shaped by the internalized oppression that many in marginalized populations hold. For example, fat individuals are just as likely as non-fat individuals to hold anti-fat attitudes (Schwartz, Vattanian, Nosek, and Brownell, 2006; Wang, Brownell, and Wadden, 2004). Harding (2008) illuminates this internalized oppression and how it reflects back on fat sexual identities and behaviours, "When you're a fat woman in this culture, everyone—from journalists you'll never meet to your own mother, sister, and best friend—works together to constantly reinforce the message that you are not good enough to be fucked" (p. 74). The negative messages integrated into a fat person's sexual identity are then unchallenged, as fat people are rarely included in displays and discourses related to sex; or reinforced as the discourses and displays that do exist in mainstream sex discourses do not look favourably upon fat sex.

If fat individuals are excluded from mainstream discourses around sex, what does this mean for a fat individual who is forming and performing an identity as a sexual being? As Murray points out,

One only has to reflect on the ways in which we speak about fatness in this historical moment in Western societies. . . . We talk about fatness as a major health crisis, an epidemic, a drain on resources, a symbol of the failed body, and as an aesthetic affront. We do not talk about fat and sex. (2004, p. 239).

Perhaps Murray is correct; we do not talk about fat sex as a normative part of our discourse. It is, as LeBesco (2004) suggests, excluded from constructions of normal sexuality. So how then is fat sexual activity presented? And how are fat individuals to construct positive sexual identities in a fat-hating world? This piece does not intend to propose the ways in which fat individuals construct their understanding of sexuality, or themselves as sexual beings. It does, however, attempt to consider some of the narratives presented to people around what fat sexuality means and how it is embodied and performed.

Given the prevalent anti-fat attitudes in heteronormative Western cultures, it is not surprising that most of the empirical scholarship around body size and sexuality have concluded that fat individuals, especially fat women, are significantly disadvantaged in the areas of heterosexual dating and sexual activity (Regen, 1996; Tiggemann and Rothblum, 1988; Widerman and Hurst, 2008). Focus has more recently turned to examining the impact of fatness on sexual activity and behavior.

Obesity research on sexuality can be grouped into three categories based on the sample being studied: population studies, clinical studies, and weight loss studies. In population studies, where participants are pulled from a general population, no significant relationship between weight and sexual functioning and satisfaction are found with the exception of the relationship between BMI and sexual dysfunction in men. For example, Adolfsson and others (2004) sampled 4,781 men and women, aged 18–74, and determined there to be no relationship between BIW and sexual satisfaction. In clinical studies, studies where the sample has been drawn from a specific group of individuals (such as those with an existing condition), BMI was found significant in sexual functioning and satisfaction for some clinical populations (Chung, Sohn, and Park, 1999; Esposito et al., 2007), but not all (Kadioglu et al., 2010; Paranhos et al., 2009). In weight loss studies, however, the findings are consistent. Research drawn from samples of individuals engaged in weight loss find that weight loss improves both functioning and satisfaction (Hammoud, Gibson, Hunt, Adams, Carrell, Kolotkin, and Meikle, 2009; Kolotkin, Zunker, and Østbye, 2012; Larsen, Wagner, and Heitmann, 2007). This could suggest that individuals who are unhappy with their sex lives pursue weight loss as a possible remedy; more likely it suggests that individuals who are pursuing weight loss are unhappy with their current weight and perceive improvements in all areas of life if weight loss occurs.

As noted by a review of the literature by Kolotkin, Zunker, and Østbye (2012), most of the empirical studies around fatness and sexuality in obesity research draw from samples of individuals engaged in weight loss. And the majority of the available research in this area has focused on sexual dysfunction (often measured as erectile dysfunction in men). In their conclusion, Kolotkin, Zunker, and Østbye (2012) call for a wider understanding of sexual functioning and satisfaction in the literature.

Not surprisingly, the tenor of work in obesity research is negative, assuming from the start that being fat is negative and thus impacts negatively on sexuality. For example, several studies (Kolotkin et al., 2006; Kolotkin et al., 2008) in this area assess sexual functioning and satisfaction using the Impact of Weight on Quality of Life (IWQOL) questionnaire. This questionnaire is grounded in a deficit view, with six questions around sexuality that inquire as to the impact of an individual's weight on: "not feeling sexually attractive," "not enjoying sexual activity," "avoidance of sexual encounters," "difficulty with sexual performance," and "not wanting to be seen undressed" (Kolotkin, Binks, Crosby, Østbye, Nfitchell, and Hartley, 2008). Measures such as the IWQOL work from the position that being fat must negatively affect an individual's sex life, fitting in with the standard assumption that grounds all of obesity research: fat is bad. Slightly more positive in tone is the work surrounding heterosexual men who prefer fat sexual partners. These men are labelled Fat Admirers (FAs). FAs are likely to identify fat bodies as more attractive than non-fat bodies and regularly choose fat women as sexual partners (Swami and Tovée, 2009). The research surrounding FAs often explores this sexual choice with a hint of disgusted curiosity while labelling it as "deviant." Prohaska and Gailey (2009) present a piece on hogging in the *Fat Studies Reader*. Hogging is the act of straight men pursuing fat women as sexual partners, often at the bidding of friends, and for the result of satiating sexual desire in an easy manner. They argue that hogging, to the men who participate in the activity, is based on the assumption that "fat women are sexually easy and can help men out of a losing streak" (p. 158). So we have on the one hand, men who pursue fat women as sexual partners out of deviant desire, and on the other, men who pursue fat women as sexual partners to reinforce their virility.

Most of the scholarship on sexuality has focused on men's sexual activities, behaviors, and desires. Both within and outside academic scholarship, women have often been denied sexual agency, especially those that fall outside of heteronormative culture (Richardson, 2000). Those women routinely excluded from normative representations of sexuality (fat women, lesbian women, trans women, women of colour, etc.) are presented with the dilemma as to whether to construct their own ideas of sexuality, independent from heteronormative narratives, or to deconstruct the existing narratives and position their sexual identities as contrasting.

Sitting outside of academic scholarship are books that are written by fat people about fat sex. Two such tomes are Rebecca Jane Weinstein's *Fat Sex: The Naked Truth* (2012) and Virgie Tovar's *Hot and Heavy: Fierce Fat Girls on Life, Love and Fashion* (2012). While both books are presentations on fat sex from fat individuals, the messages of the books are strikingly different.

Fat Sex: The Naked Truth presents itself as a book about fat sex. Weinstein's book has been crafted around narratives about sex from fat people, and people who enjoy having sex with fat people. Framing the narratives is commentary about society's perspective on fat sexuality and factoids about information relevant to understanding fat sex within our culture. Weinstein's book, unfortunately, often promotes tired ideas around fatness (suggesting that fat is the new gay, asserting that fat is the last acceptable form of prejudice, etc.) while also reinforcing many of the negative stereotypes held about fat people. Overall, readers of *Fat Sex* may find themselves wishing that more of the personal stories had been included in the manuscript; the individual voices of fat individuals talking about their sex lives are often muted.

A very different telling of fat sexual lives may be found in Virgie Tovar's (2012) edited collection, *Hot and Heavy: Fierce Fat Girls on Life, Love and Fashion*. In this collection, 31 fat women share their personal stories of rejecting cultural constructions of fat shame and hatred and embracing their inner fierceness. All of the narratives in Tovar's text are stories of redemption. The writers share stories of embracing sexuality, encouraging others to embrace their own sexual pleasure in their fat bodies, and finding pride in oneself through sexual identity and agency. These narratives, while more positive than those presented in *Fat Sex,* are still often problematic. Many of the stories presented rely on patriarchal assertions that a woman's worth is based in her ability to be desirable to others (specifically, heterosexual men). The focus for heterosexual fat women in mainstream media images is usually on validating their sexual desirability (Kyrölä, 2014). In contrast, representations of heterosexual fat men in media (think *Shallow Hal* or *The Nutty Professor*) focus on validating their sexual desires.

Alongside the scholarship from obesity research, and collections published by fat individuals, are the writings of fat women who embrace their bodies and enjoy the pleasure they may take from them. Much of this work is presented in a self-help fashion, written both to express the individual's own pleasure in sexuality, but also as a means of assisting others in experiencing a more satisfying sex life.

One of the best known self-help books for fat people is *Big Love* by Hanne Blank (2000, 2011). The book is a practical, instructional, and, dare it be said, inspirational guide on relationships and sexual activity for fat individuals and their partner(s). The revised text is heavily influenced by the growing fat activism movement, the emergence of fat studies within academia, and the advancement of sexual politics in the decade since the original release. Also included in the 2011 edition is information drawn from the Big Big Love Survey, collected by Blank in 2010 from over 700 participants. Blank weaves the information shared by participants into the revised edition, often using survey material to illustrate her arguments.

Blank's sex-positive tome covers a range of sexual topics, including physical accommodations with bellies for better sex, and gentle advice on how to negotiate through the internalized fat hatred that often rears to the surface when nakedness and pleasure are involved. Blank also presents discussions of ethics in fat sex, taking a considered approach to addressing Fat Admirers in the segment "How Not to Be an Asshole."

In her piece, "How to Have Sex While Fat: A Short Guide to Sexy Fun for Fatties and People Who F#&@ Them," Marianne Kirby (2013) suggests that being fat-sex positive is not advocating that all people must have sex with fat people. She suggests that the taboo that surrounds fat sex (and turns it into a fetish) often makes it difficult for fat people to develop sexual identity and enjoy sexual activity. She suggests some simple guidelines for navigating through the taboo, the internalization of fat hatred, and the myth that fat people are not sexual beings. Asserting that fat people are often denied sexual agency, Kitty Stryker takes to her blog to present tips and tricks for hot fat sex. The inclusion of tools and techniques is common in pieces about fat sex, and suggests a market for such items. Perhaps this is one way that fat sex will become more mainstream, as capitalistic systems will embrace the opportunity to provide desirable goods to individuals looking to facilitate fat sex.

In "Fat Sex: What Everyone Wants to Know but Is Afraid to Ask,"[1] msvaginascience introduces herself as a fat woman who has enjoyable sex with partners who are usually smaller than she is. Her biggest piece of advice is that fat women need to "overcome the idea that your partner doesn't know how fat you are." For a marked difference though, msvaginascience spends most of the piece exploring different sexual positions and how they can work for fat bodies. These pieces are accompanied by illustrations of her (clothed) fat body demonstrating.

This is in no way an exhaustive accounting of the materials about fat sex that have been written by fat individuals, merely a selection of the better-known offerings available. The introduction of the World Web Wide, and Web 2.0, has opened up a never-ending supply of spaces for individuals of all sizes to share information (Pausé, 2014a). It has especially been taken up by individuals in marginalized groups, whose sexuality is often denied (or, at least, ignored) by mainstream media and culture.

Participation in fat communities, both online and off, may be one way for fat people to develop positive sexual identities. "In a culture that rarely associates fat bodies with sexuality, publicly claiming sexual agency, desire, and desirability allows fat women to take pleasure in their bodies" (p. 300), writes Asbill (2009). In her qualitative work, Asbill explores the experience of fat women participating in burlesque, and considers how this activity shapes their fat identity. Engaging in explicitly sexual performance for others allowed the women

involved to "[redefine] the fat body as an object of sexual desire" (p. 300). Performance is an important part of identity, as demonstrated by the women in Asbill's work. These women were given/took permission to publicly perform as fat sexual beings, allowing themselves to develop or reinforce positive fat sexual identities. Doing so in a group allowed these women to support each other through the process. Fat-positive communities provide safe spaces for individuals to construct positive fat identities; for some, they may be the only spaces in which fat-positive identities may be constructed, maintained, and performed.

Gailey (2012) interviewed over 30 fat women from size/fat acceptance organizations about their romantic and sexual lives. The women in her study reported having poor body image and unsatisfactory romantic and sexual histories, illustrating that body image dissatisfaction often detracts from sexual agency in women. This changed for most, however, when these women became involved in size acceptance, and began to take pride in their fat bodies. "Women who accept their bodies, or are beginning to, not only experience freedom from the pressure to diet or change their bodies, but also a freedom to be sexual," argues Gailey (p. 124). Without body image satisfaction, it is difficult to construct positive sex identities, as Gailey found in her work. Engaging in fat-positive communities allowed these women to construct fat-positive sexual identities.

Is it surprising that women produce much of the fat-positive sex information? Perhaps this stems from the (re)production of dominant social phenomena that position women and their experiences as "inferior, deviant, or significant only in the ways they serve male interests" (Anderson, 2012). This may be seen as reinforced by the focus in obesity research on sexuality on sexual dysfunction, specifically erectile dysfunction. In contrast, fat-positive sex resources suggest that fat sex is enjoyable and normative. And they argue that fat people are sexual beings with sexual agency who are engaging in satisfying sex lives, a stark juxtaposition to the themes in the literature of obesity research.

As individuals increasingly produce large amounts of knowledge in the Web 2.0 age, marginalized communities are able to present their truths and suggest representations of themselves that contrast with the dominant discourses (Pausé, 2014b). If, as Gailey (2012) suggests, involvement in size acceptance leads to decreased body image dissatisfaction and greater sexual agency for fat women, then perhaps turning to fat activist communities for information about sex, and drawing on sexuality scholarship from the field of Fat Studies (a field that rejects the negative assumptions associated with fatness and the fat body) will allow more fat women to construct positive fat sexual identities and exercise their sexual agency.

NOTE

1. Find the "Fat Sex Week Table of Contents" on The Queer Fat Femme Guide to Life at http://queerfatfemme.com/tag/fat-sex-week/.

REFERENCES

Adolfsson, B., Elofsson, S., Rössner, S., and Undén, A. L. 2004. Are sexual dissatisfaction and sexual abuse associated with obesity? *Obesity Research*, 12, 1702–09.

Anderson, E. 2013. Feminist epistemology and philosophy of science. In E. N. Zalta, ed., *The Stanford encyclopedia of philosophy*. Retrieved from http://plato.stanford.edu/entries/feminist-social-epistemology (1 August 2014).

Asbill, L. 2009. "I'm allowed to be a sexual being": The distinctive social conditions of the fat burlesque stage. In E. Rothblum and S. Solovay, eds., *The fat studies reader* (pp. 299–304), New York: New York University Press.

Blank, H. 2011. *Big big love, revised: A sex and relationships guide for people of size (and those who love them)*. Berkeley: Celestial Arts.

Chung, W. S., Sohn, J. H., and Park, Y. Y. 1999. Is obesity an underlying factor in erectile dysfunction? *European Urology*, 36(1), 68–70.

Esposito, K., Ciotola, M., Giugliano, E., Bisogni, C., Schisano, B., Autorino, R., Cobellis, L., De Sio, M., Colacurci, N., and Giugliano, D. 2007. Association of body weight with sexual function in women. *International Journal of Impotence Research*, 19(4), 353–57.

Exton, E. 2010. Should "fatties" get a room? No. But it is time for TV to move beyond fat jokes. *Entertainment Weekly* [online]. Retrieved from http://popwatch.ew.com/2010/10/28/marie-claite-fatties-mike-and-molly/ (30 April 2014).

Gailey, J. A. 2012. Fat shame to fat pride: Fat women's sexual and dating experiences. *Fat Studies: An Interdisciplinary Journal of Body Weight and Society*, 1(1), 114–27.

Hammoud, A., Gibson, M., Hunt, S. C., Adams, T. D., Cattell, D. T., Kolotkin, R. L., and Meikle, A. W. 2009. Effect of Roux-en-Y gastric bypass surgery on the sex steroids and quality of life in obese men. *The Journal of Clinical Endocrinology & Metabolism*, 94(4), 1329–32.

Harding, K. 2008. How do you fuck a fat woman? In J. Friedman and J. Valenti, *Yes means yes! Visions of female sexual power & a world without rape* (pp. 67–76). Berkeley: Seal Press.

Kadioglu, P., Yetkin, D. O., Yahn, A. S., Onem, K., and Kadioglu, A. 2010. Obesity might not be a factor for female sexual dysfunction. *BJU International*, 106(9), 1357–61.

Kaukua, J., Pekkarinen, T., Sane, T., and Mustajoki, P. 2012. Sex hormones and sexual function in obese men losing weight. *Obesity Research*, 11 (6), 689–94.

Kelly, M. 2010. Should fatties get a room? (Even on TV)? *Claire* [online]. Retrieved from http://www.matieclairecom/sex-love/dating-blog/overweightcouples-on-television (29 April 2014).

Kirby, M. 2013. How to have sex while fat: A short guide to sexy fun for fatties and people who f#&@ them. *xoJane* [online]. Retrieved from http://www.xojane.com/sex/sex-with-a-fat-person (21 March 2013).

Kolotkin, R. L., Binks, M., Crosby, R. D., Østbye, T., Gress, R. E., and Adams, T. D. 2006. Obesity and sexual quality of life. *Obesity*, 14(3), 472–79.

Kolotkin, R. L., Binks, M., Crosby, R. D., Østbye, T., Mitchell, J. E., and Hartley, G. 2008. Improvements in sexual quality of life after moderate weight loss. *International Journal of Impotence Research*, 20(5), 487–92.

Kolotkin, R. L., Zunker, C., and Østbye, T. 2012. Sexual functioning and obesity: A review. *Obesity*, 20(12), 2325–33.

Kyrölä, K. 2014. *The weight of images: Affect, body image and fat in the media*. Farnham: Ashgate.

Larsen, S. H., Wagner, G., and Heitmann, B. L. 2007. Sexual function and obesity. *International Journal of Obesity*, 31, 1189–98.

LeBesco, K. 2004. *Revolting bodies? The struggle to redefine fat identity*. Amherst: University of Massachusetts Press.

LeTrent, S. 2014. "XL love": How fat is affecting our sex lives. *CNN* [online]. Retrieved from http://edition.cnn

.com/2014/07/22/living/obesity-sex-xllove-relate/ (10 August 2014).

msvaginascience. 2012. Fat sex: What everyone wants to know but is afraid to ask. *Persephone Magazine*. Retrieved from http://persephonemagazine.com/2012/03 /fat-sex-what-everyone-wants-to-know-but-is-afraid-to-ask/ (1 July 2013).

Murray, S. 2004. Locating aesthetics: Sexing the fat woman. *Social Semiotics*, 14, 237–47.

Paranhos, M., Antunes, A., Andrade, E., Freire, G., and Srougi, M. 2009. The prevalence of erectile dysfunction among Brazilian men screened for prostate cancer. *BJU International*, 104(8), 1130–33.

Pausé, C. J. 2012. Live to tell: Coming out as fat. *Somatechnics*, 2(1), 42–56.

Pausé, C. J. 2014a. Express yourself: Fat activism. In R. Chastain, ed., *The politics of size: Perspectives from the fat-acceptance movement* (pp. 1–8). Santa Barbara: Praeger Publishing.

Pausé, C. J. 2014b. Causing a commotion: Queering fatness in cyberspace. In C. Pausé, J. Wykes, and S. Murray, eds., *Queering fat embodiment* (pp. 75–88). London: Ashgate.

Prohaska, A., and Gailey, J. 2009. Fat women as "easy targets": Achieving masculinity through hogging. In E. Rothblum and S. Solovay, eds., *The fat studies reader* (pp. 158–66). New York: New York University Press.

Ratliff, J. 2013. Drawing on burlesque: Excessive display and fat desire in the work of Cristina Vela. *Fat Studies: An Interdisciplinary Journal of Body Weight and Society*, 2(2), 118–31.

Regan, P. C. 1996. Sexual outcasts: The perceived impact of body weight and gender on sexuality. *Journal of Applied Social Psychology*, 26, 1803–15.

Richardson, D. 2000. Claiming citizenship? Sexuality, citizenship and lesbian/feminist theory. *Sexualities*, 3(2), 255–72.

Schwartz, M. B., Vartanian, L. R., Nosek, B. A., and Brownell, K. D. 2006. The influence of one's own body weight on implicit and explicit anti-fat bias. *Obesity*, 14(3), 440–47.

Silver, M. 2014. Lose weight for better sex. *The Sydney Morning Herald* [online]. Retrieved from http://www .smh.com.au/lifestyle/diet-and-fitness/lose-weight-for -better-sex-20140721-zv6vv.html (5 August 2014).

Stryker. K. 2011. Fuck me, I'm fat: A hot guide to fat sex. Kitty Stryker: PurrVersatility [Weblog]. Retrieved from http://kittystryker.com/2011/06/fuck-me-im-fat-a-hot -guide-to-fat-sex/ (1 July 2013).

Swami, V. I., and Tovée, M. J. 2009. Big beautiful women: The body size preferences of male fat admirers. *Journal of Sex Research*, 46, 89–96.

Tiggemann, M., and Rothblum, E. 1988. Gender differences in social consequences of perceived overweight in the United States and Australia. *Sex Roles*, 18, 75–86.

Tovar, V. (ed.). 2012. *Hot and heavy: Fierce fat girls on life, love and fashion.* Berkeley: Seal Press.

Wang, S. S., Brownell, K. D., and Wadden, T. A. 2004. The influence of the stigma of obesity on overweight individuals. *International Journal of Obesity*, 28, 1333–37.

Weinstein, R. J. 2012. *Fat sex: The naked truth.* Self-published: CreateSpace Independent Publishing Platform.

Widerman, M., and Hurst, S. R. 2008. Body size, physical attractiveness, and body image among young adult women: Relationships to sexual experience and sexual esteem. *Journal of Sex Research*, 35, 272–81.

6

SEXUAL PRACTICES

AN INTERVIEW WITH

MICHAEL REECE

Michael Reece, PhD, MPH, is a professor of applied health science in the School of Public Health at Indiana University. Dr. Reece's research is focused on sexual health in both domestic and international settings and is conducted under the auspices of his research team, the Center for Sexual Health Promotion. The center conducts research designed to advance conceptual and methodological approaches to studying sexual health and trains the next generation of sexuality and sexual health scholars. The center's work is focused on four key areas, including (1) conducting nationally representative assessments of sexual and sexual health behaviors that provide an empirical foundation for those who need population-based data to support their work in public health and medicine, (2) advancing the methods used to study sexual behavior through innovative designs like technology-based daily diaries, (3) developing measures for sexuality-related research that are not only valid and reliable but that are attentive to unique cultural norms and changes in the human sexual repertoire, and (4) exploring the manner in which humans acquire and use products that promote sexual health and that improve sexual function and pleasure, such as vibrators, condoms, and lubricants.

What led you to begin studying sexuality?

When I was an undergraduate student, I volunteered as a peer sexuality educator at the University of Georgia. I used to conduct workshops for fraternities and sororities, mostly on the topic of sexual assault and acquaintance rape. Later, after earning my MPH degree, I led the office of HIV prevention for a state health department in the southwestern United States. In that work, I started to believe that our public health interventions were off-base; we were focused only on things like condom use, but we didn't understand that condom use doesn't occur in a vacuum, it occurs within the context of a sexual event. I became convinced that the only way to prevent public health problems like HIV, STIs, and unintended pregnancy was to better understand the nature of sexual behavior itself. I felt that we needed to understand sexual behavior at its core and that by only looking at sexuality for its potential contributions to disease we were missing something. That led me to pursue a doctoral degree and ultimately led me to Indiana University, which has always been known as a leading university for studying sexuality.

How do you tell people you study sexuality and how do they react?

It depends. I don't tell everyone. . . . However, when I do tell people, what I find is that they think that it is much more mystical than it actually is. People seem to think that it must be so exciting to know lots of things about people's sexual lives. I've never had a negative reaction actually. I think . . . that people are genuinely curious about sexuality; most have never had a chance to discuss it and they are intrigued by the fact that there is research that helps them to compare their sexual lives to those of others.

What ethical dilemmas have you faced studying sexuality?

My team is incredibly attentive to assuring people that they can trust us when they disclose information about their sexual lives. We go to extremes to inform people about what we are going to ask, why we are asking it, and what we will be doing with it. So one important ethical issue is that you have to be sincere about keeping people's data confidential and about assuring them that there is a really valid scientific purpose.

In an early study at Indiana University, my team studied the behaviors of men who were having sex with other men in campus bathrooms, locker rooms, and other locations. This was called "cruising" and it was incredibly taboo. One of the most popular places for men to "cruise" was in a bathroom that was right down the hall from my office. This study was conducted over ten years ago, but on a regular basis I still run into men who participated in that study when I am on campus or out in the community. We told these men at the beginning of the study that if we were to encounter them in a public place after the study that we would pretend that we did not know them. And I do that. When I see these men I don't make any gestures toward them at all. I think they are surprised that I still do this after ten years, but we had made a commitment that we would not acknowledge them unless they spoke first. So it is not just the notion of maintaining data confidentially in traditional ways like not using identifiers in data sets. Maintaining high ethical standards also requires a long-term pledge to being absolutely sincere in your commitments to participants.

Why is sex research important?

From an everyday perspective, sexuality research is very important because people are incredibly curious about who does what with whom and about how the behavior of others compares to their own. Particularly in the United States, we are rarely provided with the opportunity to have open discussions about sexuality, creating incredible challenges in people's romantic and sexual lives. So, sexuality research is vital to helping people have access to information that enables them to better understand their own sexuality.

From an academic perspective, sexuality research is also essential. Sexual behavior is perhaps the most common behavior of humans. . . . So, in terms of an academic commitment to understanding societies and behaviors, we must remain committed to sexuality research. Academic institutions should be willing to support sexuality research because it is among the most common of all denominators of our existence.

From a sexual health or public health perspective, we must understand sexual behaviors if we are going to change them. We can't understand condom use without understanding the relational, situational, and other factors that influence the decision-making process of two or more individuals during a sexual event. We just can't change behaviors that we don't understand.

Can you describe some of the findings from your recent research?

The National Survey of Sexual Health and Behavior (NSSHB) was the first nationally representative study of the sexual lives of Americans in close to two decades. It provided important data about the current nature of the sexual repertoires of both adolescents and adults, indicating that our sexual lives are incredibly diverse. The results also illustrated that "sex" is more than intercourse. While intercourse remains the most common behavior, there are many sexual events that don't involve intercourse, and when it does occur, it is typically accompanied by other behaviors. This study also provided data that suggested that adolescents are among the most responsible when it comes to sexuality—with those aged 14–17 having the highest rates of condom use in the country, a trend that public health has been documenting for the past decade. We followed this study with one that was very similar but was focused on gay and bisexual men. In that study, we surveyed over 25,000 men and found that gay and bisexual men also have extremely varied sexual lives. Among the least reported behaviors was anal intercourse—which is completely contrary to what most people think constitutes gay sex. The most common behavior reported by gay and bisexual men was kissing their partner. People always ask me if I'm surprised that kissing was the most frequent behavior; I usually say that I'm not surprised by the finding but instead I'm shocked that most researchers have never collected data on kissing and that when we only ask about gay sexuality in the context of HIV (and thus mostly having asked only about condom use and anal intercourse), we get very warped understandings of their lives.

Of the projects you've done over the course of your academic career, which did you find most interesting and why?

I would say that I think our early study of men's cruising on college campuses was one of the most interesting studies that I've ever done. Cruising is incredibly taboo; at its foundation, it is reliant upon anonymity and secrecy. So I learned an incredible amount about how to do sexuality research on such topics. The men's willingness to participate in extensive interviews about this behavior still fascinates me. Also, most people who had considered this issue before had never considered the positive aspects of cruising; what do men get out of it other than sex? Participants in that study were incredibly articulate about how such behaviors helped them to better understand their own sexuality and about how it often resulted in many positive outcomes—that is just something that had never been documented.

If you could teach people one thing about sexuality what would it be?

There is no "normal" when it comes to sexual behaviors. All of us have very diverse desires and needs when it comes to sexuality and communicating with your partners about those desires and needs is critical.

THE PURSUIT OF SEXUAL PLEASURE

B. J. RYE AND GLENN J. MEANEY

Sex and sexuality are surprisingly difficult terms to define. In one sense, sex can be seen as a collection of behaviors related directly or indirectly to stimulation of the genitals; our bodies then respond to this stimulation with a reflex that is pleasurable and tension-releasing (i.e., orgasm). This . . . definition does not, however, provide much insight into the role that sexuality plays in our lives. Rather, sexuality can be thought of as an institution defined by shared social meaning that is constructed around the simple stimulation of genitals; sex, in this sense, is what we make it (e.g., DeLamater and Hyde, 1998; Foucault, 1976/1978). At the individual level, human sexuality is subjective and represents how we experience and express ourselves as sexual beings. At a cultural level, sexuality can be constructed to serve a variety of needs: sex is a means of procreation, an intimate bonding ritual, even a form of social control (Foucault, 1976/1978; Hawkes, 1996; Weeks, 1981). For some, sex is work (e.g., prostitution, "spousely duty"). For others, sex is play. . . . [T]his reading will focus on the "playful" aspect of sex. In particular, we will discuss the more physical gymnastics involved in the pursuit and attainment of *sexual pleasure*—"sex for fun." We hope to show how pleasure is a primary motivator for sexual activity and how social constructions of sexuality are built around this fundamental desire for sexual pleasure. . . .

Our perspective on sexual pleasure is constructed from a review of mainly Canadian and U.S. literature concerning sexual activity and sexual behavior. We supplement this review from our own ongoing survey of Canadian university students. . . . We . . . focus our discussion on a very North American version of the pursuit of sexual pleasure.

THE PURSUIT OF SEXUAL PLEASURE

What Is Sexual Pleasure?

Broadly defined, sexual pleasure involves the positive feelings that arise from sexual stimuli (Abramson and Pinkerton, 1995). Sexual pleasure may result from a variety of activities that involve sexual arousal, genital stimulation, and/ or orgasm. . . . While it may seem self-evident, people are more likely to engage in sexual behaviors they consider pleasurable than sexual behaviors that they find less pleasurable (Browning et al., 2000; Pinkerton et al., 2003).

It is seldom overtly stated, but sexual pleasure is very important in our society. Achieving sexual arousal and orgasm is significant enough to people that manuals of sexual technique have been compiled—such as the venerable *Kama Sutra* (trans., 1994), *The Joy of Sex* (Comfort, 1972), and *Sex for Dummies* (Westheimer, 1995). There are university courses, television shows (e.g., *The Sex Files,* Colby, 2006), websites (e.g., www.sexualityandu.ca), sex stores, and shows (e.g., *The Stag Shop,* see www.stagshop.com; *The Everything to Do with Sex Show,* see www.everythingtodowithsex.com) devoted to human sexuality and the attainment of the highest level of sexual satisfaction

From "The Pursuit of Sexual Pleasure," *Sexuality & Culture*, Volume 11, Issue 1, December 2007, pp. 28–51. Copyright © 2007, Springer. Reprinted by permission of the authors.

possible. Clearly, people have a great interest in sexual pleasure. This pleasure can be pursued in many forms—and can occur in solitary and/ or partnered contexts. Perhaps the simplest sexual activities are those in which an individual can engage alone, such as masturbation and sexual fantasy.

Solitary Sex

Fantasy

Sexual fantasy has the appeal of being the safest form of sexual enjoyment: One can fantasize any time, one can have total control, and there are no (direct) consequences (Doskoch, 1995). Sexual fantasy is difficult to research, especially because it is difficult to define exactly what constitutes fantasy (see Byrne and Osland, 2000). Leitenberg and Henning (1995: 470) define sexual fantasy as "almost any mental imagery that is sexually arousing or erotic to the individual." Byers and colleagues (Byers, Purdon, and Clark, 1998; Little and Byers, 2000; Renaud and Byers, 1999) prefer the term *sexual cognitions,* which may have positive or negative connotations. Sexual thoughts can take many forms, some of which may not be pleasurable to the individual. . . .

The great majority of men and women engage in sexual fantasy, either as an activity by itself (i.e., daydreaming), or in conjunction with other sexual activities, including masturbation and partnered sex. For example, when asked "how often do you think about sex?", 97 percent of men and 86 percent of women responded with a few times a month or more (Laumann et al., 1994). In terms of content, men seem more likely to have explicitly sexual fantasies (Ellis and Symons, 1990), to imagine themselves in positions of dominance (Byers, Purdon, and Clark, 1998; Hsu et al., 1994), to see themselves as the "doer" (Byers, Purdon, and Clark, 1998; Knafo and Jaffe, 1984) and to fantasize about multiple partners (Ellis and

Symons, 1990). Women tend to have more emotional and romantic fantasies and to see themselves in positions of submission (Hsu et al., 1994; McCauley and Swann, 1978). Lesbians and gay men tend to have fantasies similar to heterosexual women and men, respectively, except that they typically imagine same-sex partners (Hurlbert and Apt, 1993; Keating and Over, 1990; Masters and Johnson, 1979; Robinson and Parks, 2003). In general, people report a wide variety of content in sexual fantasy. People who have more sexual fantasies tend to have fewer sexual problems and report more sexual satisfaction than people who have fewer fantasies (Byrne and Osland, 2000; Leitenberg and Henning, 1995).

. . . Renaud and Byers (1999) found that all of their New Brunswick university student sample reported having had sexual thoughts at some time. Both men and women reported more positive than negative thoughts, with men reporting more of both positive and negative thoughts. Participants reported a wide variety of content in sexual thoughts. . . . Little and Byers (2000) [found that] . . . [p]eople often enjoyed having sexual fantasies while in public places, and people in committed relationships were not more likely to evaluate sexual thoughts as negative. Our survey of Ontario students enrolled in an introductory sexuality course (1999–2006) indicated that 63 percent of women and 78 percent of men—who have had sex—fantasize while engaging in sexual activity with a partner. Our students fantasize in greater numbers (98 percent of men; 93 percent of women) during masturbation—sexual self-stimulation.

Masturbation

Historically, masturbation has been stigmatized and associated with immorality and pathology, but it is quickly gaining respect as a common and healthy sexual activity (Coleman, 2002). A [2002] survey of American university students (Pinkerton et al., 2002) found that about two-thirds of the women and almost all of the men reported masturbating at least once. Both genders reported frequent masturbation in the past three months. People masturbated more if they perceived social norms in support of this behavior (Pinkerton et al., 2002). More sexually active people masturbated more often, indicating that masturbation is not a substitute for other sexual activity (also see Davis et al., 1996).

Men tend to masturbate fairly uniformly whereas women tend to have more varied masturbation techniques from woman to woman (see Masters and Johnson, 1966). There were no gender differences in reasons for masturbating: the majority of men and women stated that they masturbated to relieve sexual tension and the second most commonly cited reason was for physical pleasure (Laumann et al., 1994). . . . Of all sexual behaviors, masturbation seems most clearly motivated by pleasure, or at least, release of tension. . . .

Partnered Sexual Activity

A common North American sexual script suggests that we have a shared idea about the sequence of partnered sexual behaviors that proceeds from kissing and touching ("petting" above the waist) to more intensive touching ("petting" below the waist or manual stimulation of the genitals) to oral sex to genital-to-genital contact to vaginal or anal intercourse (Gagnon and Simon, 1987; Laumann et al., 1994; McKay, 2004). Of course, there are a multitude of variations on this script and many behaviors have been omitted from this generic description. In almost all cases, kissing is a starting point.

Kissing

Kissing is a very common behavior, with same-sex and other-sex couples reporting that they usually kiss when they have sex (Blumstein and Schwartz, 1983). In a U.S. study of university students, most (96%) had "dry" kissed someone and a large majority (89%) reported having "French-kissed" (i.e., kissed with open mouths). Ninety-one percent of men and 95 percent of women who participated in our human sexuality student survey indicated that they were experienced French-kissers as well. A representative study of Canadian youth found that about a third to half of seventh-grade students, approximately two-thirds of ninth-grade students, and about eight out of ten eleventh-grade students reported engaging in "deep, open-mouth" kissing (Boyce et al., 2003). It should be noted that, while kissing is generally considered an erotic activity in North American society, it is not considered erotic in all cultures (Harvey, 2005). When kissing is considered erotic, however, it is often a precursor to petting (kissing, of course, may accompany petting).

Touching

Petting is a rather odd term for sexually touching another person—usually interpreted as meaning in the genital region. This is also known as mutual masturbation or being masturbated by a partner. This is a common behavior amongst university students . . . (Browning et al., 2000; Pinkerton et al., 2003). . . . Over a third of seventh-grade students, about two-thirds of ninth-grade students, and eight out of ten eleventh-grade students indicated that they had engaged in "touching above the waist at least once." The incidence of hand-genital contact was less common—with about a quarter to a third of seventh-grade students, slightly over half of ninth-grade students, and about three-quarters of eleventh-grade students responding yes to "touching below the waist at least once" (Boyce et al., 2003). Mutual masturbation is a common sexual behavior and being masturbated by one's partner tends to be ranked as highly pleasurable relative to some other sexual behaviors (Pinkerton et al., 2003). Another form of touching is oral sex: sexual stimulation of the genitals by mouth.

Oral Sex

People frequently engage in oral sex. Recent national surveys in the United State indicated that a large majority of adult men (79–85%) have had oral sex performed on them (called fellatio) while many women (73–83%) have received oral sex (called cunnilingus) (Laumann et al., 1994; Mosher, Chandra, and Jones, 2005). About 90 percent of adults have had oral sex (Mosher et al., 2005). This has changed somewhat since the Kinsey surveys (1949, 1953), which indicated that about 60 percent of men and women had engaged in oral sex. Our survey of sexuality students indicated that between 80 percent and 85 percent of women and men had performed and received oral sex. Not surprisingly, oral sex is becoming more common among Canadian adolescents as well (Boyce et al., 2003; McKay, 2004).

There is an emerging literature where researchers and lay people alike discuss adolescent oral sex as an activity on the rise as a "substitute" for intercourse—as this helps prevent pregnancy, reduce STIs risk, and maintain "virginity" (Barrett, 2004; McKay, 2004). Mosher and others (2005) found that just over 10 percent of teenagers (15–19 years old) have had oral sex without intercourse, with about 55 percent of all teens having had oral sex.

. . . [E]ducators and researchers consider this to be a natural increase as oral sex rates have increased for adults as well (Burnett, 2004; McKay, 2004). One of the major reasons why youth engage in oral sex is that it is fun and pleasurable (Barrett, 2004). Similarly, university students ranked receiving oral sex as the second most pleasant activity after vaginal intercourse (Pinkerton et al., 2003).

Penis-in-Vagina Intercourse

Pinkerton and others (2003) found that penis-in-vagina intercourse was rated as the most pleasurable sexual activity (as did Laumann et al., 1994). This is a behavior in which almost all adults have engaged at least once (Laumann et al., 1994; Mosher et al., 2005; Wellings et al., 1994). In terms of U.S. university students, around 80 percent have had vaginal intercourse (Browning et al., 2000; Pinkerton et al., 2003). Our sample of Canadian sexuality students had slightly fewer men indicating that they have had vaginal intercourse (75%) compared to women (79%). Most of these students (40–45%) had their first intercourse between the ages of 16–18 years; this is congruent with the representative survey of Canadian youth finding that between 40–46% of eleventh-grade students have had intercourse at least once (Boyce et al., 2003).

While there are *many* different positions for intercourse, there are four "basic" positions: man on top ("missionary"), woman on top, side by side, and rear entry ("doggie style"). Each position has certain "advantages." For example, the woman-on-top position is good when a man has poorer ejaculatory control, allows the woman to control sexual positioning and rhythm, and allows greater accessibility to the clitoris (a key organ to female sexual pleasure). Man on top is the recommended position when a couple is trying to become pregnant. Rear entry is good when a woman is pregnant or when particularly deep penile insertion is desired. . . . While vaginal intercourse is considered pleasurable by most people, a substantial minority of people also report enjoying anal sex.

Anal Sex

Anal sex can take different forms. There is penis-in-anus intercourse whereby a man inserts his penis into the rectum of his partner.

As the anus has no natural lubrication, a sterile lubricant gel is recommended (e.g., Astroglide, K-Y Jelly) so as to reduce the likelihood of trauma to the anus (e.g., tearing tissue, damaging sphincters). It is recommended that the inserter wear a condom. Because anal intercourse typically involves some tearing of the tissue, there is a direct route for pathogens into the bloodstream, making this a very efficient route for HIV transmission and other STIs. It is important that the penis be washed after anal intercourse and prior to any further genital contact. For example, if a man removes his penis from the anus and inserts it into the vagina, various bacteria can be transferred to the vagina.

Anilingus or "rimming" is oral stimulation of the anus. Again, because of the presence of bacteria and possibly other STI pathogens (e.g., gonorrhea, hepatitis), it is prudent to use a barrier (e.g., cut a condom up the side or use a dental dam). Some people enjoy digital stimulation of the anus by having fingers or the hand inserted in the anus during sexual arousal.

Anal intercourse is not as commonly performed as the other sexual activities discussed thus far. A representative U.S. sample found that roughly a third of adults have had anal sex (Mosher et al., 2005). . . . About one-fifth to a quarter of university students in two U.S. samples reported ever having experienced anal intercourse (Browning et al., 2000; Pinkerton et al., 2003). In our sexuality student survey, about one-fifth reported having had anal intercourse. Laumann and others asked their participants if they had experienced anal sex *in the past year* and approximately 5–10% had experienced anal sex that recently. Finally, Laumann and others posed an interesting set of questions to their participants about how "appealing" a variety of sexual behaviors were. When asked about various forms of anal sex, between 1% and 5% of people rated anal contact as "very appealing" (including stimulating a partner's anus, having anus stimulated by a partner's finger, and anal intercourse).

Techniques of Same-Sex Couples

A substantial minority of people are lesbian, gay, or bisexual (LGB; Laumann et al., 1994). A [2005] representative U.S. survey found that around 8–10 percent of adults identified as LGB (Mosher et al., 2005). About 9 percent of men and 6 percent of women in our human sexuality class self-identified as LGB. One does not need to be LGB to engage in same-sex behavior; 6 percent of men and 11 percent of women indicated that they have had a same-sex sexual partner in their lifetime (Mosher et al., 2005). Laumann and others (1994) found that about 3 percent of men and women rated having a same-gendered sexual partner as "very appealing."

Same-sex couples tend to engage in similar sexual behaviors as other-sex couples, including kissing, hugging, mutual masturbation, oral stimulation, and penetrative sex (Blumstein and Schwartz, 1983; Masters and Johnson, 1979). Male couples sometimes engage in interfemoral intercourse; this is where one man thrusts his penis between the thighs of the other man. Female couples may engage in tribadism whereby "two women rub their vulvae together to stimulate each other's clitoris to orgasm" (Wikimedia Foundation, 2006; also see Caster, 1993) or there may be mons-to-thigh stimulation. Other-sex couples also engage in this non-penetrative genital-to-genital stimulation (Kinsey et al. [1953] call this apposition; "dry humping" is a more common, but less sophisticated, description).

Masters and Johnson (1979) observed and compared the sexual behaviors of same-sex couples to other-sex couples and found differences in arousal *techniques* rather than sexual behaviors. In general, the same-sex couples tended to "take their time" in comparison to opposite-sex couples. That is, Masters and Johnson characterized heterosexual couples as more "performance oriented"—oriented toward the penis-in-vagina act—in contrast to the same-sex couples, who engaged more in pleasure-seeking throughout the sexual encounter. There were no differences between heterosexual and homosexual people of the same gender in terms of masturbation techniques.

Spicy Sex

Thus far, we have discussed relatively common sexual activities. There are practices that are not necessarily common or usual but that are pleasurable for many people. . . . [I]t is important to remember that uncommon does not equal pathological. Most sexual behaviors can be placed on a continuum from healthy (e.g., having a mild or strong preference) to pathological (e.g., when the behavior/object becomes a necessity or a substitute for a human relationship; see Hyde, DeLamater, and Byers, 2006). Spicier activities may be an indication of the importance of sexual pleasure. While many of the "vanilla" techniques are quite pleasurable, they are often socially scripted, and are cheap and easy in which to engage. More "spicy" techniques may require creative thought, monetary expense, or even travel plans. The trouble that people are willing to go through for the "spicier" activities might indicate that these are primarily pleasure-seeking activities.

Sex Toys

Sex toys are devices that people use to enhance their sexual pleasure (e.g., vibrators, dildos). While sex toys have been around for years (in the late 1800s, early 1900s as "medical devices"; see Maines, 1999), people have become more open about discussing sex toys perhaps because of popular media portrayals (e.g., *Sex and the City,* King, Chupack, Melfi, Bicks, Raab, et al., 2006; *The L Word,* Chaiken,

Golin, and Kennar, 2006) and books and stores devoted to sex toys (e.g., Venning and Cavanah, 2003). . . . In our survey of human sexuality students, about a third of women had experience with a "mechanical aid" compared to 8 percent of men. This is quite different from the representative survey of American adults, which found less than 1 in 20 (< 5%) of men and women rated vibrator/dildo use as appealing (Laumann et al., 1994). Laumann and others found that the more educated women in their sample found vibrator/dildo use the most appealing—education may impact attitudes toward sex toy use.

Davis et al. (1996) conducted a study of women who use vibrators. . . . The results suggested that many of the women . . . found that clitoral-vibrator stimulation usually triggers an orgasm; they used their vibrators on a variety of sexual sites (clitoral, vaginal, and anal), and in a variety of ways (circular motion, up/down, or back/forth). Most (80%) of the sample used the vibrator during partnered sex—sometimes with the partner watching the woman use the vibrator while sometimes the partner held the vibrator for the woman. Women, who were lesbians and were more likely to, reported being younger when they first used a vibrator and were slightly more likely to use a vibrator with a partner than were bisexual or heterosexual women.

Sexually Explicit Material

Use of erotica—sexually explicit depictions—is also a relatively common aid in autosexual or partnered sexual activity. Erotic materials are broad-ranging and may include books, magazines, videos/DVDs, live shows (e.g., exotic dancers), telephone sex, and cybersexuality (e.g., sex in chat rooms, webcam sex). Laumann and others (1994) found that as many as one out of five men used some form of erotic material when fantasizing/masturbating, while fewer women did (as many as one out of ten). These researchers asked about the appeal of "watching other people do sexual things" (which might be interpreted as erotica or, alternatively, voyeurism) and found that 5 percent of men and 1 percent of women found this activity sexually appealing. In the human sexuality student survey, a majority of men and women had favorable attitudes toward erotic materials, although there was a gender difference such that men were more favorable than women were.

Online sexual activities have increased in recent years. . . . A study of people who use the Internet indicated that 80 percent of participants used the web for sexual purposes. Of those people, about a third had engaged in "cybersex." Cybersex was defined as "when two or more people are engaging in sexual talk while online for the purposes of sexual pleasure and may or may not include masturbation" (Daneback, Cooper, and Månsson, 2005: 321). This cybersex most commonly took the form of a sexual encounter in a "chat room" with the second most popular medium being instant messenger–type programs.

Sexual Internet activities are probably on the rise because of the fact that these materials are affordable, readily available, and can be accessed anonymously (Cooper, McLoughlin, and Campbell, 2000). The Internet allows people with uncommon sexual proclivities to both find and support others with similar interests. As well, the Internet offers users the opportunity to experiment with new behaviors in a relatively safe setting, satisfy curiosity, and seek out new information. While there has been a substantial discussion of "Internet sex addiction," sexually compulsive Internet users typically already have a history of unconventional sexual practices (i.e., diagnosable paraphilias, risky sexual activity). Many people who are recreational users of online sexual material spend less than an hour per week, on average, visiting sexual websites (Cooper et al., 1999).

Sadomasochism

Sadomasochism (S&M) is a term that collectively describes a variety of sexual behaviors which may involve the administration of pain (e.g., use of clothespins/clamps, hot wax, spanking), deliberate humiliation (e.g., use of a gag, face slapping), physical restriction (e.g., handcuffs, chains), and hypermasculine activities (e.g., cockbinding, watersports, rimming) that are experienced as pleasurable by both partners (Alison, Santtila, Sandnabba, and Nordling, 2001; Sandnabba, Santtila, and Nordling, 1999). The S&M scene typically involves fetishistic elements such as leather clothing and whips, and ritualistic activity such as bondage. S&M has been characterized as fantasy-oriented and role-playing scripted behavior.

. . . [T]here is a distinct subculture of psychologically well-adjusted individuals who engage in S&M activities—many of whom belong to S&M "clubs" (Alison et al., 2001; Sandnabba et al., 1999). Partners in S&M activities described here refer to consenting S&M participants. People who have participated in research studies about the S&M subculture have been found to be well-integrated into society in general as they tend to be highly educated and earn high incomes (Alison et al., 2001; Mosher and Levitt, 1987; Sandnabba et al., 1999). Most of these people report engaging in S&M activities occasionally and in non-S&M sexual activities frequently—which indicates that the S&M activities were not part of a "diagnosable paraphilia" (Sandnabba et al., 1999). Most of the information known about S&M involves men; it is sometimes difficult to obtain adequate samples of women within the S&M subculture (Mosher and Levitt, 1987; Sandnabba et al., 1999). In a study of men, Sandnabba and colleagues (1999) found the most common S&M behaviors to include (in order): oral sex, bondage, wearing leather outfits, flagellation (e.g., whipping), anal intercourse, rimming, handcuffs, and the use of chains, dildos, and verbal humiliation; at least 70 percent of the men interviewed participated in each of these behaviors. The most popular role-play for heterosexual men was master/slave (for Mosher and Levitt's, 1987, sample, too) while, for gay men, the most common role-play was a "uniform scene" (e.g., police officer and arrestee).

Although we do not know how many people practice S&M, we do know that people fantasize about and/or have a sexual response to S&M activities. . . . While S&M fantasies appear to be fairly common, we do not know how many people act upon these fantasies.

Sex on Vacation

There is a phenomenon that has recently begun to be documented whereby people travel for the purpose of obtaining sex outside of their community. Much of this literature has focused on heterosexual men who travel to areas such as the Caribbean or Southeast Asia for sexual gratification. While most of these men do not view themselves as engaging prostitution services, the transactions are clearly a form of commercialized sex. Researchers and theorists in this area actually find that sex tourists of this sort tend to be racist, sexist, and believe in their own Western cultural superiority over the people in these Third World locales (O'Connell Davidson and Sánchez Taylor, 1999).

Heterosexual women are also sex tourists who "purchase" the sexual services of local men (e.g., Cabezas, 2004; Herold, Garcia, and DeMoya, 2001). In Sánchez Taylor's (2001) study of single women vacationing at resorts in the Dominican Republic and Jamaica, approximately a third had engaged in sexual relations with local men; this was significantly more new sexual contacts compared to single women vacationing in Europe. Over half of the women with "vacation" sex partners had remunerated the sex partner in some way (e.g., cash, gifts).

These women did not view themselves as being consumers of prostitution services despite the economic element to their relationship; rather, they tended to characterize these sexual behaviors as "holiday romances." However, the men tend to be in lower socioeconomic positions (e.g., "beach boys," hotel workers), often live in poverty, and earn a living through various forms of "hustling." Interviews with the men indicated that they do not conceptualize themselves as prostitutes or sex trade workers but they acknowledge that they reap financial and material benefits from entering into a series of fleeting sexual relationships with female tourists. These men even have strategies to assess which women are likely to be the most "generous" (Sánchez Taylor, 2001).

A different type of sex tourism is popular with university students who are on vacation. This involves having casual sex with a relative stranger while on spring break. By *relative stranger*, researchers mean that the individual has met the sexual partner while on vacation and typically known the sex partner for 24 hours or less. . . . Matika-Tyndale and colleagues . . . 1997; 1998) found . . . approximately 16 percent of students vacationing in Daytona Beach had engaged in sexual intercourse with a new casual partner (this excludes those traveling with their boyfriend/girlfriend). Almost half (46%) reported "fooling around in a sexual way" with a new partner; this involved sexual activity excluding intercourse. In the spring break subculture, sexual norms are more permissive than what is expected "back home" . . . (Mewhinney, Herold, and Maticka-Tyndale, 1995). Having a partner "back home" did not seem to deter vacationers from having casual sex; one-fifth to one-quarter of people who were currently in a relationship had intercourse with a casual partner while they were on vacation.

It seems that being on vacation—away from the social constraints of "home"—creates a subculture of sexual permissiveness whereby one can have sex for solely the purpose of having sex (e.g., for fun, to "let loose"). As one student characterized casual sex during spring break vacation: "It is generally expected . . . to have a great time and that includes having sex" (Mewhinney et al., 1995: 278). There are similar destinations that are known for tourist-tourist casual sex such as Ibiza and Côte d'Azur that cater to non-student populations (O'Connell Davidson and Sánchez Taylor, 1999). The fact that some will go through so much trouble for the purpose of having sex lends credence to the unspoken value we place on sexual pleasure. The pursuit of sexual pleasure can be seen clearly, not only in sex tourism, but in the multi-faceted behaviors we have chosen to call "spicy" sex.

Spicy sex encompasses a diversity of behaviors, many of which we have *not* discussed (e.g., group sex and swinging, other commercialized sex, cross-dressing, etc.). What is interesting about these diverse behaviors is that, while not popular with everyone, people who engage in these behaviors tend to find social groups that are supportive of the activities (e.g., fantasia parties for those who have an interest in sex toys, S&M clubs, online chat groups devoted to various sexual acts). It is possible that when there is a supportive social network for the "spicy" sexual behavior, people will be more comfortable with their "less common" sexual behavior (see Kutchinsky, 1976; Sandnabba et al., 1999). . . .

What Can We Conclude about Sexual Pleasure?

What is sexually pleasurable is in the eye of the beholder. "Sex" and "sexual pleasure" are very much "social constructions" in that certain attitudes, behaviors, and activities are considered taboo. Societal norms exert a great deal of social control over what is "acceptable" sexuality. In Western society dominated by Christian

values, there is a tendency to view the pursuit of sex for pleasure's sake as hedonistic; for example, a person who has casual sex tends to be viewed negatively (Parrinder, 1996). The pleasure of sex for a particular person depends not entirely on attaining orgasm but on the context and psychological state of the individuals involved (Mah and Binik, 2005). How a person has internalized the cultural messages about various aspects of sexuality will have a profound impact on the person's experience of sexual pleasure. For example, if sex is seen solely as a means of procreation—a strongly Christian perspective (Parrinder, 1996)—there may be great guilt associated with feeling pleasure if one engages in sexual behavior solely for pleasure purposes. Similarly, when sex is fundamental to the maintenance of a long-term relationship, it can become an obligatory duty (see Hawkes, 1996, . . . for a discussion). In both cases, sex can become a matter of performance pressure and anxiety.

In the eighteenth and nineteenth centuries, sex was officially defined in terms of the social and interpersonal functions it fulfilled; there was little mention of sex as a pleasurable experience (or, if so, it was pleasurable only for men). When attention was drawn to the sexual pleasure of women (somewhat ironically, by the work of Freud), social forces constrained that pleasure to marriage. People seeking sexual pleasure outside of marriage were labeled as "deviant" (Hawkes, 1996). Our current societal views on sexual pleasure have their roots in our Victorian history of sex negativity and the subsequent need to "quell" or control a dangerous instinct (Foucault, 1976/1978; Weeks, 1981, 1986).

Current North American attitudes toward sexual pleasure run the gamut from "only for procreation" to "okay when in love or when dating" to "anything goes." While there is no consensus, sex with love or in the context of a committed relationship tends to be deemed as more acceptable and changes in attitudes toward sex tend to relate to concurrent changes in sexual behavior (Barrett et al., 2004). Views about sexuality and sexual pleasure are constantly changing (DeLamater and Hyde, 2003). Enhanced discussions about sexual pleasure will occur as our society incorporates an increasingly positive perspective on sexual pleasure into the existing sexual scripts (Gagnon and Simon, 1987). This positive view of sexual pleasure will need to be incorporated into scripts at all levels: the intrapersonal (i.e., self-acceptance of sex for personal pleasure), the interpersonal (i.e., acceptance of one's partner[s], friends, family, etc., as enjoying sex for pleasure reasons), and finally, the overarching cultural scripts (i.e., schemas for the sexuality of men, schemas for the sexuality of women, environments that reinforce rather than punish the concept of sexual pleasure for pleasure's sake).

While the social discourse surrounding sexuality will continue to evolve and to complicate the meanings attached to sexuality, the avoidance and guilt associated with sexual pleasure seem to be lessening. In fact, a new discourse appears to be arising that specifically and explicitly emphasizes the often-lost pursuit of sexual pleasure (McKay, 2004; Abramson and Pinkerton, 1995). This pursuit, in itself, can become a source of enlightenment spurred by the realization of simple, physical pleasures associated with human sexuality. The dark side of sexuality will continue to exert its influence, of course, in the specters of sexual harassment, sexual coercion, stalking, paraphilias, and related phenomena. . . . But, an acceptance of sexual pleasure would open avenues for personal satisfaction that will, hopefully, serve as a safeguard against such negative outcomes.

REFERENCES

Abramson, P. R., and Pinkerton, S. D. 1995. *With pleasure: Thoughts on the nature of human sexuality*. New York: Oxford University Press.

Alison, L., Santtila, P., Sandnabba, N. K., and Nordling, N. 2001. Sadomasochistically oriented behavior: Diversity in practice and meaning. *Archives of Sexual Behavior,* 30(1): 1–12.

Barrett, A. 2004. Oral sex and teenagers: A sexual health educator's perspective. *Canadian Journal of Human Sexuality,* 13(3/4): 197–200.

Barrett, M., King, A., Lévy, J., Maticka-Tyndale, E., McKay, A., and Fraser, J. 2004. Canada. In R. T. Francoeur and R. J. Noonan, eds., *The Continuum complete international encyclopedia of sexuality* (pp. 126–81). New York: Continuum.

Blumstein, P., and Schwartz, P. 1983. *American couples*. New York: Morrow.

Boyce, W., Doherty, M., Fortin, C., and MacKinnon, D. 2003. *Canadian youth, sexual health and HIV/AIDS study*. Toronto, ON: Council of Ministers of Education.

Browning, J. R., Hatfield, E., Kessler, D., and Levine, T. 2000. Sexual motives, gender and sexual behavior. *Archives of Sexual Behavior,* 29(2): 135–53.

Byers, S., Purdon, C., and Clark, D. A. 1998. Sexual intrusive thoughts of college students. *Journal of Sex Research,* 35(4): 359–69.

Byrne, D., and Osland, J. A. 2000. Sexual fantasy and erotica/pornography: Internal and external imagery. In L. T. Szuchman and F. Muscarella, eds., *Psychological perspectives on human sexuality* (pp. 283–305). Toronto, ON: Wiley.

Cabezas, A. L. 2004. Between love and money: Sex, tourism, and citizenship in Cuba and the Dominican Republic. *Signs: Journal of Women in Culture and Society,* 29(4): 987–1015.

Caster, W. 1993. *The lesbian sex book*. Boston, MA: Alyson.

Chaiken, I., Golin, S., and Kennar, L. (Producers). 2006. *The L word* [Television series]. Showtime.

Colby, C. (Producer). 2006. *The sex files* [Television series]. Discovery Channel.

Coleman, E. 2002. Masturbation as a means of achieving sexual health. *Journal of Psychology and Human Sexuality,* 14(2/3): 5–16.

Comfort, A. 1972. *The joy of sex: A gourmet guide to love making*. New York: Simon & Schuster.

The complete kama sutra: The first unabridged translation of the classic Indian text (A. Danielou, Trans.). (1994). Rochester, VT: Rock Street Press.

Cooper, A., McLoughlin, I. P., and Campbell, K. M. 2000. Sexuality in cyberspace: Update for the 21st century. *CyberPsychology & Behavior,* 3(4): 521–36.

Cooper, A., Putnam, D. E., Planchon, L. A., and Boies, S. C. 1999. Online sexual compulsivity: Getting tangled in the net. *Sexual Addiction & Compulsivity: The Journal of Treatment and Prevention,* 6(2): 79–104.

Cooper, A., Sherer, C., Boies, S. C., and Gordon, B. 1999. Sexuality on the Internet: From sexual exploration to pathological expression. *Professional Psychology: Research and Practice,* 30(2): 154–64.

Daneback, K., Cooper, A., and Mansson, S.-A. 2005. An Internet study of cybersex participants. *Archives of Sexual Behavior,* 34(3): 321–28.

The dark side of sexuality (n.d.). Retrieved April 22, 2006 from http://www.sju.ca/courses/course.php?course=408&id=29&ad=10&dir=sexuality.

Davis, C. M., Blank, J., Lin, H.-Y., and Bonillas, C. 1996. Characteristics of vibrator use among women. *Journal of Sex Research,* 33(4): 313–20.

DeLamater, J. D., and Hyde, J. S. 1998. Essentialism vs. social constructionism in the study of human sexuality. *Journal of Sex Research,* 35(1): 10–18.

DeLamater, J. D., and Hyde, J. S. 2003. Sexuality. In J. J. Ponzetti, Jr., ed., *International encyclopedia of marriage and family, Volume 3.* (2nd ed.) (pp. 1456–62). New York: Macmillan/Thomson Gale.

Doskoch, P. 1995, September/October. The safest sex. *Psychology Today,* 28: 46–49.

Ellis, B. J., and Symons, D. 1990. Sex differences in sexual fantasy: An evolutionary psychology approach. *Journal of Sex Research,* 27(4): 527–55.

Foucault, M. 1978. *The history of sexuality: Vol. 1. An introduction* (R. Hurley, Trans.). New York: Pantheon (Original work published 1976).

Gagnon, J. H., and Simon, W. 1987. The sexual scripting of oral genital contacts. *Archives of Sexual Behavior,* 16(1): 1–25.

Harvey, K. 2005. *The kiss in history.* Manchester: Manchester University Press.

Hawkes, G. 1996. *A sociology of sex and sexuality.* Philadelphia, PA: Open University Press.

Herold, E., Garcia, R., and DeMoya, T. 2001. Female tourists and beach boys: Romance or sex tourism? *Annals of Tourism Research,* 28(4): 978–97.

Hsu, B., Kling, A., Kessler, C., Knapke, K., Diefenbach, P., and Elias, J. E. 1994. Gender differences in sexual fantasy and behavior in a college population: A ten-year replication. *Journal of Sex and Marital Therapy,* 20(2): 103–18.

Hurlbert, D. F., and Apt, C. 1993. Female sexuality: A comparative study between women in homosexual and heterosexual relationships. *Journal of Sex and Marital Therapy,* 19(4): 315–27.

Hyde, J. S., DeLamater, J. D., and Byers, E. S. 2006. *Understanding human sexuality* (3rd ed., Canadian). Toronto, ON: McGraw-Hill Ryerson.

Keating, B. A., and Over, R. 1990. Sexual fantasies of heterosexual and homosexual men. *Archives of Sexual Behavior,* 19(5): 461–75.

King, M. P., Chupack, C., Melfi, J., Bicks, J., Raab, J., et al. (Producers). 2006. *Sex and the city* [Television series]. New York: HBO.

Kinsey, A. C., Pomeroy, W. B., and Martin, C. E. 1949. *Sexual behavior in the human male.* Philadelphia, PA: Saunders.

Kinsey, A. C., Pomeroy, W. B., Martin, C. E., and Gebhard, P. H. 1953. *Sexual behavior in the human female.* Philadelphia, PA: Saunders.

Knafo, D., and Jaffe, Y. 1984. Sexual fantasizing in males and females. *Journal of Research in Personality,* 18(4): 451–62.

Kutchinsky, B. 1976. Deviance and criminality: The case of voyeur in a peepers' paradise. *Diseases of the Nervous System,* 37(3): 145–51.

Laumann, E. O., Gagnon, J. H., Michael, R. T., and Michaels, S. 1994. *The social organization of sexuality: Sexual practices in the United States.* Chicago, IL: University of Chicago Press.

Leitenberg, H., and Henning, K. 1995. Sexual fantasy. *Psychological Bulletin,* 117(3): 469–96.

Little, C. A., and Byers, E. S. 2000. Differences between positive and negative sexual cognitions. *Canadian Journal of Human Sexuality,* 9(3): 167–79.

Mah, K., and Binik, Y. M. 2005. Are orgasms in the mind or the body? Psychosocial versus physiological correlates of orgasmic pleasure and satisfaction. *Journal of Sex and Marital Therapy,* 31(3): 187–200.

Maines, R. P. 1999. *The technology of orgasm: "Hysteria," the vibrator, and women's sexual satisfaction.* Baltimore, MD: Johns Hopkins University Press.

Masters, W. H., and Johnson, V. E. 1966. *Human sexual response.* Boston, MA: Little, Brown.

Masters, W. H., and Johnson, V. E. 1979. *Homosexuality in perspective.* Boston, MA: Little, Brown.

Maticka-Tyndale, E., and Herold, E. S. 1997. The scripting of sexual behaviour: Canadian university students on spring break in Florida. *Canadian Journal of Human Sexuality,* 6(4): 317–28.

Maticka-Tyndale, E., Herold, E. S., and Mewhinney, D. 1998. Casual sex on spring break: Intentions and behaviors of Canadian students. *Journal of Sex Research,* 35(3): 254–64.

McCauley, C., and Swann, C. P. 1978. Male-female differences in sexual fantasy. *Journal of Research in Personality,* 12(1): 76–86.

McKay, A. 2004. Oral sex among teenagers: Research, discourse, and education. *Canadian Journal of Human Sexuality,* 13(3/4): 201–03.

Mewhinney, D. M., Herold, E. S., and Maticka-Tyndale, E. 1995. Sexual scripts and risk-taking of Canadian university students on spring break in Daytona Beach, Florida. *Canadian Journal of Human Sexuality,* 4(4): 273–88.

Mosher, C., and Levitt, E. E. 1987. An exploratory-descriptive study of a sadomasochistically oriented sample. *Journal of Sex Research,* 23(3): 322–37.

Mosher, W. D., Chandra, A., and Jones, J. 2005. Sexual behavior and selected health measures: Men and women 15–44 years of age, United States, 2002. *Advance data from vital and health statistics, no. 362*. Hyattsville, MD: National Center for Health Statistics.

O'Connell Davidson, J., and Sánchez Taylor, J. 1999. Fantasy islands: Exploring the demand for sex tourism. In K. Kempadoo, ed., *Sun, sex, and gold: Tourism and sex work in the Caribbean* (pp. 37–54). Oxford: Rowman and Littlefield.

Parrinder, G. 1996. *Sexual morality in the world religions*. Oxford: Oneworld.

Pinkerton, S. D., Bogart, L. M., Cecil, H., and Abramson, P. R. 2002. Factors associated with masturbation in a collegiate sample. *Journal of Psychology and Human Sexuality*, 14(2/3): 103–21.

Pinkerton, S. D., Cecil, H., Bogart, L. M., and Abramson, P. R. 2003. The pleasures of sex: An empirical investigation. *Cognition and Emotion*, 17(2): 341–53.

Renaud, C. A., and Byers, E. S. 1999. Exploring the frequency, diversity, and content of university students' positive and negative sexual cognitions. *Canadian Journal of Human Sexuality*, 8(1): 17–30.

Robinson, J. D., and Parks, C. W. 2003. Lesbian and bisexual women's sexual fantasies, psychological adjustment, and close relationship functioning. *Journal of Psychology and Human Sexuality*, 15(4): 185–203.

Sánchez Taylor, J. 2001. Dollars are a girl's best friend? Female tourists' sexual behaviour in the Carribean. *Sociology*, 35(3): 749–64.

Sandnabba, N. K., Santtila, P., and Nordling, N. 1999. Sexual behavior and social adaptation among sadomasochistically-oriented males. *Journal of Sex Research*, 36(3): 273–82.

Venning, R., and Cavanah, C. 2003. *Sex toys 101: A playfully uninhibited guide*. New York: Fireside.

Warren, W. K., and King, A. J. 1994. *Development and evaluation of an AIDS/STD/Sexuality program for Grade 9 students*. Kingston, ON: Social Program Evaluation Group, Queens University.

Weeks, J. 1981. *Sex, politics, and society*. New York: Longman.

Weeks, J. 1986. *Key ideas: Sexuality* (P. Hamilton, Series Ed.). London: Tavistock.

Wellings, K., Field, J., Johnson, A. M., and Wadsworth, J. 1994. *Sexual behavior in Britain: The national survey of sexual attitudes and lifestyles*. London: Penguin.

Westheimer, R. K. 1995. *Sex for dummies*. Chicago: IDG Books Worldwide.

Wikimedia Foundation 2006. Tribadism. Retrieved February 26, 2006 from http://en.wikipedia.org/wiki/Tribadism.

Teen Sex in the United States

Chris M. Vidmar

Moral panic about teen sex is nothing new. Most recently, parental concerns have been focused on the availability of sexually explicit content on the Internet (Bilton, 2015), the prevalence of sexting among teens (Lohmann, n.d.), and the possibility that vaccinations for sexually transmitted infections (STIs) might encourage risky behavior (Fox News, 2011). However, recent studies tell a different story about U.S. teens and sex. According to a 2017 report from the National Center for Health Statistics (NCHS), the number of teens who have ever had sex has been dropping since 1988, more teens are using contraception, and teen pregnancy has hit a historic low (Abama and Martinez, 2017). Dr. Brooke Bokor of the Children's National Health System, in comments made to the *Washington Post*, attributed these shifts to the availability of information online (Paquette and Cai, 2015). Despite parents' concerns about the Internet, the ability to privately locate reliable sexual health information has helped teens navigate sexual risk. While little empirical research on teen sexting has been completed, the current approach of criminalization under child pornography statutes has been shown to be an ineffective and arguably unconstitutional response (Lampe, 2013). As for the fear that STI vaccines might encourage casual sex, the American Academy of Pediatrics reported that HPV vaccination in girls was not associated with increased markers of sexual activity (AAP, 2012; Bednarczyk et al., 2012).

While the moral panic over teen sex may be misinformed, there is ample reason to continue researching teen sexuality. Even though teen pregnancy and birth rates in the United States have dropped to a rate of 22.3 per 1,000 females ages 15–19, the United States continues to have higher rates than other developed countries— double the rates in Canada and four times the rates in France and Germany (Abama and Martinez, 2017). Furthermore, adolescents in the United States continue to be at higher risk for STIs than adults, with an estimated one in four sexually active adolescent women having an STI (Abama and Martinez, 2017). Clearly, a lot more work needs to be done, but to help young people make healthy decisions we need evidence-based public policy, not conjecture and moral panic.

Some of the best sources for understanding teen sexuality are the reports produced by the Centers for Disease Control and Prevention (CDC). An example of these is the aforementioned 2017 NCHS report *Sexual Activity and Contraceptive Use among Teenagers in the United States, 2011–2015*, which utilizes data from the National Survey of Family Growth (NSFG) and the Youth Risk Behavior Surveillance System (YRBSS) (Abama and Martinez, 2017). Both these survey efforts produce large, nationally representative data sets. And because they are administered repeatedly, they can be used to show changes over time. The most recent NSFG data (collected from 2011 to 2015) produced a sample of 4,134 interviews with teenagers (2,047 females and 2,087 males), and the YRBSS has administered 3.8 million paper surveys to high school students since 1991.

Below are some details from the most recent CDC reports (from Abama and Martinez, 2017, unless otherwise specified).

Overall, the number of teens who have had sex has declined significantly over the last 20 years, but there are important differences based on gender, race, and family structure. The number of never-married females age 15–19 who have ever had sex has gone down from 51% in 1988 to 42.2% in the 2011–2015 data. For males, that number has decreased even more drastically: from 60.4% to 44.2%, only 2% higher than females. However, males still tend to become sexually active earlier than females, with 16% of males reporting sexual intercourse by age 15 compared to 11% of females.

Historically there were race and ethnic differences in sexual onset among female teens, but in the 2006–2010 data the rate of sexual experience for non-Hispanic black females declined significantly. Since then, among never-married females ages 15–19 there has been no significant difference in sexual onset between non-Hispanic blacks, Hispanics, or non-Hispanic whites. For males, there remains a difference, with 58.6% of non-Hispanic black males reporting they have had sex, compared to 45.7% of Hispanic males and 42.8% of non-Hispanic white males. Finally, family structure may influence when teens first have sex. In the 2011–2015 data, teens who lived with both parents at the age of 14 had lower rates of sexual onset (36.8% females; 39.4% males) compared to those living in any other family arrangement (50.8% females; 51.9% males).

Contraceptive use among sexually active teens is a major focus of the reports, with data on what kinds of contraceptives respondents have ever used, the method they used the first time they had intercourse (if any), and the method used the last time they had sex. In all data collected from 2002 on, nearly all female teens who have had intercourse have used some form of contraceptive (99.4% in the 2011–2015 data). The most common types ever used were the condom (97.4%), withdrawal (59.7), and the pill (55.5%). The number of female teens who have ever used emergency contraception increased notably from 8.1% in 2002 to 22.9% in 2011–2015. The most recent research found 81% of female teens used a contraceptive during first intercourse, with condoms as the most common method at 74.6%—an increase from 68% in the 2006–2010 data. Race and Hispanic origin are related to contraceptive use at first intercourse, with non-Hispanic black teen females having the lowest rate (62.2%) compared to Hispanics (78.8%) and non-Hispanic whites (87.2%).

According to the CDC, "data on the circumstances of first intercourse aid in understanding what underlies current differentials and potential future changes in sexual activity" (Abama and Martinez, 2017: 5). A prime example of this is the relationship between contraceptive use at first intercourse and teen pregnancy. By the age of 19, women were more than twice as likely to have had a teen birth if they didn't use contraception when they first had sex (Martinez and Abama, 2015). Whether a teen uses contraception during their first sexual encounter is also related to their age at the time. Teens who were 14 or younger when they first had sex were less likely to use a contraceptive method (70.1% females; 71.3% males) compared to teens who first had sex when they were 17–19 (84.2% females; 94.7% males).

Contraception use among teens the first time they have sex is related to relationship structure with the chosen partner. If they were going steady with a partner the first time they had sex, male teens were more likely to use contraception (88.4%) than if they were just friends or had just met (76.4%). In the 2011–2015 data, most teenagers' first sexual experience was with a steady partner, but this was more true for females (74.1%) than for males (51.1%).

Since the number of teens having sex continues to drop, one of the most important questions might be why more teens are choosing to wait. According to the newest CDC reports, 57.6% of females and 55.8% of males ages 15–19 have not yet had intercourse, and "data on their reasons for not having had sex aids in understanding the context of teen decision making about sexual activity" (Abama and Martinez, 2017: 6). According to the 2011–2015 data, ideas about morality, religion, and relationships dominated teens' reasons for not having sex. Among teens who had not had sex, 35.3% of females and 27.9% of males said their main reason was that having sex was against their religion or morals. Relationship ideas about who to have sex with and when to do it were also important: 21.9% of females and 28.5% of males reported that they had not yet found the right person, and 6.2% of females and 6.6% of males said they were in a relationship but waiting for the right time. Wanting to avoid pregnancy was reported by 19.3% of females and 21.2% of males, and only 7.1% of females and 4.7% of males said their main reason for abstinence was because they didn't want to get a sexually transmitted disease.

While these reports show that U.S. teens overall are waiting longer to have sex and being safer about it when they do, there is still room for improvement. Lower rates of safe-sex practices among blacks and Hispanics, for instance, suggest that community-outreach programs and continued research should focus on these populations. In addition, reduced rates of safe-sex practices among younger teens call for improved sexual education and availability of contraceptives earlier in life. Most important, we must approach these challenges empirically and resist reactionary policies that are based on moral panic.

REFERENCES

AAP. 2012. "HPV Vaccination Does Not Lead to Increased Sexual Activity." Retrieved November 25, 2017 from https://www.aap.org/en-us/about-the-aap/aap-press-room/pages/HPV-Vaccination-Does-Not-Lead-to-Increased-Sexual-Activity.aspx.

Abama, Joyce, and Gladys Martinez. 2017. "Sexual Activity and Contraceptive Use Among Teenagers in the United States, 2011–2015." Retrieved November 25, 2017 from https://www.cdc.gov/nchs/data/nhsr/nhsr104.pdf.

Bednarczyk, Robert A., Robert Davis, Kevin Ault, Walter Orenstein, and Saad B. Omer. 2012. "Sexual Activity–Related Outcomes After Human Papillomavirus Vaccination of 11- to 12-Year-Olds." Pediatrics (October 2012): 798–805.

Bilton, Nick. 2015. "Parenting in the Age of Online Pornography." The New York Times, January 7. Retrieved November 27, 2017 from https://www.nytimes.com/2015/01/08/style/parenting-in-the-age-of-online-porn.html.

Fox News. 2011. "The Truth about Teens, Sex and Vaccines." LiveScience. Retrieved November 27, 2017 from http://www.foxnews.com/health/2011/09/16/truth-about-teens-sex-and-vaccines.html.

Lampe, Joanna R. 2013. "A Victimless Sex Crime: The Case for Decriminalizing Consensual Teen Sexting." University of Michigan Journal of Law Reform, 46: 703.

Lohmann, Raychelle. n.d. "When Your Teen Won't Stop Sexting." Retrieved November 27, 2017 from https://health.usnews.com/wellness/for-parents/articles/2017-06-21/when-your-teen-wont-stop-sexting.

Martinez, Gladys, and Joyce Abama. 2015. "Sexual Activity, Contraceptive Use, and Childbearing of Teenagers Aged 15–19 in the United States." Retrieved November 27, 2017 from https://www.cdc.gov/nchs/data/databriefs/db209.pdf.

Paquette, Danielle, and Weiyi Cai. 2015. "Why American Teenagers Are Having Much Less Sex." Washington Post, July 22. Retrieved November 27, 2017 from https://www.washingtonpost.com/news/wonk/wp/2015/07/22/why-american-teenagers-are-having-much-less-sex/.

GOD'S CASE FOR SEX

ORIT AVISHAI AND KELSY BURKE

The church conference in a small Midwestern town was called "Intimacy in Marriage," so Kelsy expected speakers and participants to talk about sex. A graduate student just beginning research on evangelicals and sexuality, she was *not* expecting the prayers for couples to experience "the deepest sexual pleasure in the name of Jesus Christ" or a raffle for a vibrating massager that sat on a table in the sanctuary. Her field notes were punctuated with exclamation points, like after the phrase, "There is a vibrator in a church!"

On the other side of the globe, in Israel, an Orthodox Jewish bridal counselor discussed with Orit the sexual education component of a twelve-session marriage preparation course. A stern-looking woman in her fifties, she served as an example for brides-to-be of Jewish modesty codes—hair covered, she was dressed in a long skirt and shirt with long sleeves and high neckline. Yet she spoke enthusiastically and directly to the sexually uninitiated young women enrolled in the course, telling them to "Get the mood right. Tell him what you want."

Were it not for the obvious markers of religion, these scenes might not be surprising in the 21st century. At least within Western popular culture, "good sex" has seemingly won out over sexual shame and become a prerogative of modern adult life. From advice books like *The Joy of Sex* to TV shows like *Sex and the City* and popular podcasts like *Savage Love*, a fulfilling sex life is promoted as integral to happiness and personal fulfillment. But religious traditions are notorious for sexual rules and norms that seem to fly in the face of modern secular culture, with its emphasis on sexual expression, experimentation, and satisfaction. In fact, many observers associate the expansion of progressive sexual norms and practices with the decline of organized religion.

It is in this context that we examine how some religious followers live and love amid secular and religious messages about sex and sexuality. Kelsy observed, surveyed, and interviewed American evangelical Christians who used websites or attended workshops to discuss sexual pleasure in Christian marriages. Orit interviewed Orthodox Jewish women in Israel about the sexual education that is part of an elaborate marriage preparation. The believers, educators, and experts we interviewed and observed contradicted the stereotype that religiosity is incompatible with sexual pleasure. They self-identified as "traditional," "conservative," and "devout," yet insisted that their religious traditions encouraged sexual pleasure and could even improve how they experienced sexuality. Our respondents learned to navigate the religiously prescribed boundaries surrounding sexuality and embrace "good," religiously sanctioned sex.

LEARNING TO EXPERIENCE PLEASURE

How believers develop a *religious* prerogative for sexual pleasure hinges on three related tasks: learning to embrace sexual pleasure, contextualizing sex as part of a larger religious narrative, and establishing religious rules for permissible sex.

From "God's Case for Sex," *Contexts* 15(4), pp. 30–35. Copyright © 2016 American Sociological Association. Reprinted by permission of SAGE Publications, Ltd.

Historically, the list of perceived sexual sins has been much longer than that of religiously permitted sexual desires and practices. Religious rules range from the familiar—prohibitions against extramarital, premarital, and homosexual sex common to many religious traditions—to the foreign. In Orthodox Judaism, marital sex is forbidden for roughly two weeks of every menstrual cycle. Catholic teaching forbids sex acts unless they lead to procreative, penile–vaginal intercourse within marriage, and Latter-day Saints prohibit mutual masturbation within marriage. Such religious proscriptions can serve as obstacles for followers who want to learn about and experience sex in a meaningful way. Orthodox Jewish women Orit talked to drew on a range of euphemisms for sex, referencing "the first night," "physical relations," and a husband and wife "meeting" or "coming together." One evangelical woman told Kelsy that, until her marriage, she had "no idea" how her body worked "down there." Religious regulations and conversational unease among believers may seem to imply that religion is bad for one's sex life—but that's not what we found when we talked to evangelical Christians and Orthodox Jews who purport to live and love by God's rules.

For these believers, God's case for sex involves explicit sex education along with a sexual re-education that affirms the pleasures of sex. Secular sex education and advice—found in *Cosmopolitan* magazine and the like—are largely off-limits to, or are at least treated with skepticism by, religious conservatives. Followers of conservative religions must instead filter out the secular messages about sex that they believe disregard God's messages, while also filtering out religious messages that emphasize sexual sins. We call this an *inhibition paradox*—growing up, evangelicals and Orthodox Jews receive numerous negative messages about sex but are expected to embrace and enjoy sex once married. Orthodox Jewish

respondents said they struggled with making a "180-degree switch" on their wedding night. One evangelical woman described her church as "schizophrenic": "sex is bad, bad, bad, and then suddenly good, good, good."

The evangelical Christians and Orthodox Jews we spoke with emphasized that God encourages sexual pleasure, if one knows where to look. They look to sex therapists, workshops, premarital preparation classes, Internet conversations, and Christian and Jewish sex advice books, with titles that make abundantly clear that God approves of good sex: *A Celebration of Sex; The Gift of Sex; Holy Sex; Kosher Sex, Kosher Lust.* They also seek sex-positive messages in scripture while rejecting secular sexual ethics, deemed as hedonistic, and the dominant view of Christian sexual ethics, perceived to be sex negative. Indeed, religious studies scholar Jennifer Wright Knust points out that although the Bible is a political and sexual battleground in contemporary debates about sexuality, it is not a systematic or conclusive sexual code. Rather, biblical teachings on desire, sexual practices, marriage, and the body are inconsistent and open to interpretation. As such, religious adherents collectively construct interpretations claiming that sexuality is not "forbidden," "shameful," or "disgusting"—as was once their impression. Instead, sex is holy, normal, and good.

But theologically redeeming sexuality is insufficient—followers still need concrete advice on how to have good sex. In Orthodox Jewish circles, much of this education occurs during premarital preparation. One bridal counselor, a high school teacher in her fifties, told Orit how she harnesses Jewish laws of menstrual purity to help brides prepare for sex. These laws entail that women check for remnants of blood for seven days after menstruation ceases, and this counselor encourages young women to use the opportunity to explore themselves "there" as preparation for the marital relationship, especially the dreaded "first night." Her affirmation of self-exploration serves as "a way to connect with the body so it doesn't seem alien, so the place is not foreign" and flies in the face of years of teaching that masturbation is immoral and sinful, but she assures brides that "it's not negative. It's positive, permissible, essential, important for you to get to know your body. . . . It's good to arouse yourself; you have to incite yourself."

Christian sexuality websites and advice books also offer couples tools to help achieve physical pleasure: step-by-step instructions for arousal, anatomical drawings identifying "mysterious" body parts like the clitoris, advice on lubricants, suggestions about what time of day to have sex, lists of romantic gestures, and descriptions of sexual positioning. Evangelicals prioritize mutuality and consent and sex acts that benefit a heterosexual marital relationship. This gives both spouses a clear voice within a marriage, even among those Christians who support men's headship and women's submission. Authors Ed and Gaye Wheat insist that women are entitled to experience sexual pleasure: "If you [directed toward women] desire to have an orgasm, [it is] *because* you know it is your right, your provision from God. . . . Your goal, now, is satisfaction given by a loving husband, and achieving the fulfillment of orgasm." Evangelicals like the Wheats contextualize pleasure as good for the spiritual and marital lives of believers. In contrast to much secular sex advice, God's case for sex constructs sex as a means, not an end.

A GREATER GOOD

Orthodox Jews and evangelical Christians face a dilemma: how to affirm sexual desires without descending into the vulgarities associated with secular culture? Their solution is to normalize pleasure but insist that sex is fundamentally a spiritual pursuit.

Despite the "anything goes" in marriage attitude that seems to dominate Christian sex advice, the rationale for pursuing and optimizing sexual pleasure is a theological one. As historian of religion Amy DeRogatis has also argued, evangelicals believe that following God's rules makes possible a unique and exceptional sexual experience that contributes to a larger story about being born again. At the "Intimacy in Marriage" conference, David, a pastor, explained that the stakes of marital sex are high: "There's a party being thrown in heaven when married Christians have sex. Just by having sex, you are winning a battle in the war against Satan." By having sex in the way that God designed (in heterosexual, monogamous marriage), couples can help defeat the devil. David outlined specific steps that spouses could take to "use weapons to fight to keep your marriage out of Satan's hands": praying before, during, and after sex and having sex frequently. David explained, "Sex should be spiritually comforting, spiritually connecting, and spiritually productive for the two most important relationships in your life: God and your spouse." Good sex aligns with living a Christian life.

Jewish scriptures contain seemingly conflicting messages about sex. On the one hand, sexual desire is known as *yezerhara*, or the evil desire. But marital sex is also a *mitzvah*, a religiously prescribed obligation. To resolve this apparent conflict, some Orthodox Jews infuse an otherwise carnal act with spirituality and morality. As one Orthodox bridal counselor described, authentic Jewish "marital relations" can be "happy, wonderful, sanctified, as long as it's in the right place, at the right time, and with the right intention." Marriage sanctifies the sexual act: the self-exploration and arousal discussed above were sanctioned because they prepared the bride for her husband. This approach to sex posits that sex is good because it facilitates the creation of "one flesh." By connecting couples, sex strengthens the marital relationship, the building block of Jewish communities. Spiritual "marital relations" hinge on having sex with the "right intention": rather than pursue satisfaction of carnal desires, couples sanctify sex by bringing "the Almighty to it." Accordingly, one bridal counselor does not instruct brides about desire, pleasure, or the mechanics of sex, but teaches them to recite prayers about holiness and redemption before and after "relations." Another counselor instructs brides to "think pure thoughts and recite psalms before coming together."

But not everyone buys this spiritual model of sex. Increasingly, Orthodox Jews are seeking to articulate an alternative sexual ethics that would let Orthodox Jewish women "just have fun." Recent years have seen the emergence of Facebook groups (for women only) and the expansion of body-focused study groups and pools of therapists and instructors well-versed in Jewish teachings as well as the latest sexological research. Nevertheless, even in these more forgiving spaces it is clear that religious rules about marriage, bodies, and good sex still need to be followed.

PLAYING BY THE RULES

For religious authorities within Orthodox Judaism and evangelical Christianity, God's embrace of sex does not mean that anything goes. Sex requires regulation, though opinions vary about what practices are allowed. Some authorities restrict sex to acts associated with penile–vaginal intercourse, but scriptural ambiguity leaves room for some competing interpretations.

Most evangelical authorities permit heterosexual married couples to explore almost any sexual act imaginable so long as there is monogamy and mutual consent. Evangelicals who believe that the Bible is the literal word of God must read between the lines to determine God's stance on a wide range of marital sex acts that the Bible does not discuss. Author Shannon Ethridge summarizes the prevailing attitude that sex is permitted by God "as long as no harm is done and all is kept solely between consenting spouses." Similarly, a popular blogger explains: "There are far more things that you *can* enjoy together than those you cannot." Kelsy surveyed almost 800 users of Christian sexuality websites about their attitudes toward a range of sexual activities. Over 90% of respondents agreed that, within marriage, oral sex and using a vibrator are "not wrong at all." About anal sex and masturbation within marriage, only 20 and 10%, respectively, reported that the acts are "always wrong." One message board user explained her attitude about anal sex: "I am undecided. . . . It's not something DH [dear husband] and I are interested in. . . . If DH were really interested in it, I'd be willing to look into it from a Biblical and health standpoint and hope we could reach some common ground on it." Respondents who reported those acts are "sometimes" or "usually" wrong explained in follow-up interviews that they did not feel comfortable making judgments about these acts without knowing the relational context in which they occur.

Likewise, for many Jewish couples, "kosher sex" is murky terrain. Orthodox Jews draw sexual directives from the Bible, its elaborators and interpreters, and contemporary rabbis with whom they consult on all matters pertaining to Jewish law and practice. Orthodox Jewish authorities are quick to point out that Jewish sex is not about procreation. Referring to the Jewish mitzvah (religious deed) of Onah—Jewish law that regards a wife's sexual pleasure as a marital obligation—one bridal counselor explained to Orit that, "unlike Christians, in Judaism coming together is first and foremost about pleasure." Yet, this religiously prescribed pleasure is highly regulated. Expectedly, intimate and sexual acts are restricted to marriage and require mutual consent. In addition, Jewish law prescribes periods of impermissible sexual activity depending on the woman's menstrual status and prohibits "wasting of seed." This term refers to the prohibition against sexual acts in which the male's sperm is consciously wasted, and it is traditionally cited in prohibitions against male homosexual acts and masturbation, though some authorities also use it to restrict marital sex to penile–vaginal intercourse. A thirty-something woman who had been married for almost fifteen years told Orit about how she struggled early in her marriage: "the fun was lost amidst concerns about non-vaginal ejaculation!" She later took a bridal counseling course and began working with young women herself. Only then did she become comfortable speaking in such direct terms—and with alternatives to intercourse.

The people we talked to and spaces we studied suggest that conservative religions articulate a sexual ethic that blends limits on who is allowed to have sex with expansive possibilities for sexual pleasure within those limits. This is how evangelical Christians declare there is "tremendous freedom" within the (heterosexual) "marriage bed," but remain vehemently opposed to same-sex relationships and other non-heterosexual or non-monogamous sexual expressions. The co-creator of one evangelical message board that hosts supportive conversations about a wide range of sexual interests writes to the site's members: "The basic tenets of the Christian faith are not debatable issues" and later explains that "any defense of the practice of homosexuality, so called 'gay marriage,' or the like" will not be tolerated. In Orthodox Jewish marriage preparation courses, the message is clear: women prepare to wed men. In both of these faith traditions, heterosexuality is as sacrosanct as marriage itself.

SEXUAL AMBIVALENCE

Religious sexual debates operate on multiple levels: interpretations of scripture and foundational religious documents; talk about sexuality by religious leaders, teachers, and experts; and laypeople's sexual practices and ideas about sexuality. But at each level, conservative religious traditions simultaneously encourage sexual expression—albeit in specifically prescribed circumstances—while admonishing sexual sins. We have identified two reasons why this "sexual ambivalence" persists in religious communities.

First, narratives that sex is wrong remain salient in the lives of religious believers (regardless of what the Bible "really" says). Traditionally, Jewish and Christian leaders have spent far more time discussing sexual sins than sexual enjoyment, and people's minds are hard to de- and re-program. One woman told Orit about an episode that occurred three years into her marriage, when she was pregnant with her second child: "Once I woke up in the middle of the night, thinking *THERE IS A MAN IN MY BED! WHAT IS A MAN DOING IN MY BED?. . .'* I told myself, 'It's ok, this is your husband.' It's entrenched in us, the sense that this whole thing is forbidden." Evangelicals' stories about using Christian sexuality websites suggest similar unresolved anxieties about the possibility of Christian sexual pleasure. Many users turned to "Googling" their questions about sex because they felt they could not discuss them with anyone in real life. One user explained to Kelsy, "I never felt like it would be okay for me to date or have sex ever. I mean, intellectually I knew that my parents would be happy if I got married, but it didn't seem to make sense in my head."

Second, even though conservative religious communities are hardly unique bastions of sexual hang-ups, sex functions as a boundary-making mechanism that sets religious believers apart from the secular world. Discussions of sex, vibrators, and sexual pleasure are sites of ideological battles. Religious communities regulate sex not simply to suppress "worldly" pleasures but to negotiate conflicting worldviews and ethical systems about life's purpose. In the Orthodox Jewish case, yoking sex to marriage draws a bright line between a religious and secular sexual ethic. For evangelicals, embracing sexual pleasure within the criteria of heterosexual, monogamous matrimony means that they can experience the pleasures encouraged by the secular world but remain committed to their religious foundation.

For sexual pleasure to function as a religious ethic, it needs to be regulated—hence enduring sexual rules. Political debates about abortion, contraception, pornography, sexual education, and marriage equality typically present religious attitudes as constraining sexual expressions, rejecting sexual diversity, and squashing sexual pleasure. There's some truth to this. Numerous injuries have been inflicted in the name of religious morality through legislation and public debates that portray heterosexuality and modesty as normative and universal. In the coming-out stories of gays and lesbians, religion is often a hurdle on the path to self-love and acceptance.

Yet, if sexual regulations are more about communal efforts to define sexual morality than they are about unequivocal and timeless biblical sexual codes, religious groups' notions of sexual morality can incorporate a wide range of beliefs and practices—accounting for the presence of a vibrator in church and exhortations for brides-to-be to explore "down there." These religious traditions, then, are not unequivocally sexually repressive, nor are they uniformly sexually liberating. To appreciate their complexity, we need to understand religious traditions' approaches to sexuality from within their own logics and sensibilities. From there, we find that religious boundaries are not simple or fixed, and they can and do change with the broader social world in which believers practice their faith.

RECOMMENDED RESOURCES

Avishai, Orit. 2012. "What to do with the Problem of the Flesh? Negotiating Jewish sexual anxieties," *Fieldwork in Religion* 7:148–62.

Burke, Kelsy. 2016. *Christians under Covers: Evangelicals and Sexual Pleasure on the Internet.* Berkeley, CA: University of California Press.

DeRogatis, Amy. 2015. *Saving Sex: Sexuality and Salvation in American Evangelicalism.* New York: Oxford University Press.

Gardner, Christine J. 2011. *Making Chastity Sexy: The Rhetoric of Evangelical Abstinence Campaigns.* Berkeley, CA: University of California Press.

Knust, Jennifer Wright. 2011. *Unprotected Texts: The Bible's Surprising Contradictions about Sex and Desire.* New York: Harper-One.

A QUALITATIVE EXPLORATION OF THE "COMING OUT" PROCESS FOR ASEXUAL INDIVIDUALS

NICOLETTE ZANGARI, KATHRYN GRAFF LOW, AND ANNA N. QUERY

An asexual individual is commonly defined as one who does not experience sexual attraction (Bogaert, 2004; Jay, 2008a). Based on this definition, prevalence of asexuality is estimated at 1% (Bogaert, 2004; Poston & Baumle, 2010). However, the heterogeneity of the asexual community is well-documented (Bogaert, 2015; Carrigan, 2011; Chasin, 2011) and there is considerable disagreement among asexual individuals and researchers regarding the degree to which this definition truly captures asexual identity (Jay, 2003; Prause & Graham, 2007; Scherrer, 2008; Westphal, 2004).

Alternate definitions of asexuality have included a lack of sexual behavior (Rothblum & Brehony, 1993) and a lack of sexual desire (Prause & Graham, 2007). Yet, endorsing an asexual identity does not necessitate lack of affection or romantic interest toward others (Bogaert, 2006). Many see "asexual" as an umbrella term that encompasses myriad variations. For example, it might include those who seek romantic relationships devoid of sex, those who experience sexual attraction but have no desire to act on it, those who are repelled by sex, those who are disinterested in having sex, and many other attitudes and behaviors (Bogaert, 2012; Carrigan, 2011; Chasin, 2011). For the purposes of the current study, asexual individuals are self-identified.

Brotto, Knudson, Inskip, Rhodes, and Erskine (2010) identified the distinction between romantic and aromantic relationships as an important aspect of asexual identity. Aromantic asexuals are not interested in romantic relationships, sexual or otherwise. Some aromantic asexuals describe their ideal relationship as resembling a typical friendship and lacking any physical intimate activity (Scherrer, 2008). Conversely, romantic asexuality refers to those asexuals who seek closeness, companionship, and the intellectual and emotional intimacy of a romantic relationship, without a sexual component (Brotto et al., 2010). Among romantic asexuals, there are those who desire physical intimacy, excluding sex, and those who do not (Brotto et al., 2010). Endorsing a romantic asexual identity does not necessarily involve complete abstinence from sex. The data from Brotto et al. suggest that some romantic asexuals have negotiated consensual sexual relationships with non-asexual partners.

The implications of asexuality as a sexual orientation are far-reaching. Science has traditionally understood human nature to be essentially sexual, yet the presence of the asexual community challenges this assumption. Skeptics have conjectured that asexuality may be the result of some past sexual trauma, a deficiency in hormones, or a "rest stop" on the way to another sexual orientation. In fact, recent research provides support for an underlying physiological etiology for this lack of sexual attraction. Yule, Brotto, and Gorzalka (2013a) found a number of biological correlates of asexuality, including increased rates of non-right-handedness in both male and female asexuals, and a greater likelihood for asexual men to have more older brothers and fewer older sisters compared to other groups. The authors speculate that older male siblings may affect the prenatal environment, perhaps influencing the development of sexual attraction in the asexual male (Yule et al., 2013a). These results indicate that there may be certain biological pathways implicated in the development of asexuality. Furthermore, laboratory studies have shown that asexual women are physiologically similar to other sexual orientation groups in their response to sexual stimuli, despite varying subjective reports of arousal. This suggests that their lack of sexual desire cannot be explained by an organic inability or hormone deficiency (Brotto & Yule, 2011). Moreover, in Bogaert's (2006) study on conceptualizing asexuality, it was pointed out that a sizable minority of individuals across several studies chooses to identify with the term "asexual" and we must amend our clinical discourse to accommodate this designation. Although researchers do encourage further exploration of the genetic, hormonal, environmental, and social influences on the development of asexuality, there is conceptual and theoretical evidence to support asexuality as being its own unique sexual orientation (Bogaert, 2006, 2008).

Research is just beginning to explore the process of identity development for asexual individuals. Within other sexual minority communities, coming out appears to be an important aspect of identity development and has psychological as well as practical benefits. For example, research suggests that coming out may increase access to romantic or sexual partners, allow membership to a community, and increase commitment to advocacy (Vaughan & Waehler, 2010). It is unknown how generalizable these findings are to the asexual community or whether asexual individuals relate to the coming-out experience at all. . . .

In a recent study, researchers found increased mental health problems and suicidality among asexual individuals compared to their heterosexual and non-heterosexual counterparts (Yule, Brotto, & Gorzalka, 2013b). Further clarification is needed on whether or not psychological stress is associated with being asexual and how the coming-out period may play a role in such distress. Coming out as asexual may be especially difficult in a society that puts great emphasis on sex and sexuality. Prause and Graham (2007) reported that asexual participants struggled with negative public perceptions of asexuality and pressure to conform to the universal assumption that humans are sexual beings. A recent study by MacInnis and Hodson (2012) found that asexuals were more likely to be dehumanized and seen as "animalistic" and "machinelike" than other sexual minorities. Research has not explored how these challenges may influence the decision to come out, and there is a critical need to better understand this process for asexuals (Prause & Graham, 2007; Yule et al., 2013b).

Past asexuality research has employed qualitative methods to enhance general understanding of the asexual experience (Brotto et al., 2010; Carrigan, 2011; Prause & Graham, 2007). Using open-ended prompts, Scherrer (2008) found that many asexual respondents reported endorsement of an asexual identity to be affirming. Yet, many also reported challenges related to describing asexuality. AVEN, a website dedicated to education about asexuality, has been instrumental in creating both a venue and a lexicon for asexual individuals to communicate about the experience (Chasin, 2011; Scherrer, 2008). Although AVEN has facilitated discussion among asexuals in its online forums, the extent to which asexuals share their identities outside online platforms remains unknown (Jay, 2003; Westphal, 2004). Coming out may be uniquely challenging for asexual individuals because many have not yet determined how to articulate their asexual identity off-line (Jay, 2003; Scherrer, 2008). It is also possible that since asexuality is not always necessarily associated with any overt behaviors, disclosing such an identity to others may be unnecessary. Coming out as asexual may not be critical to acceptance of the identity, which may be particularly true in the case of aromantic asexuals who do not seek any type of partnership, thus eliminating the utility of coming out to others.

. . . Despite being a psychologically stressful experience, the coming-out process may lead to personal growth and improved self-esteem among sexual minority individuals (Vaughan & Waehler, 2010). . . . Research has not yet touched upon the potential benefits and outcomes of coming out as asexual, or how coming out may influence the process of forming an integrated asexual identity.

Toward that end, the current study aims to obtain a deeper understanding of how asexual individuals view their identity and the role that coming out plays in identity formation, if any. . . .

METHOD

Participants

Participants were recruited for a separate study that included 225 participants from three online communities dedicated to asexuality (AVEN, Apositive.org, Asexuality LiveJournal). Among these participants, 169 individuals provided "coming out" narratives. Of the total sample, 69% were female, 16% were male, and the remaining 15% identified as "other" or "undifferentiated."

Most participants (71%) were between 18 and 25 years of age, 20% were 26–32 years of age, and the remaining 8% were above 33 years of age. The sample was well-educated, with 48% having some college education, 28% holding a university degree, and 9.2% having

a graduate degree. Among the entire sample, 13% reported currently being in a romantic asexual relationship, 7% reported currently being in a sexual relationship, 48% identified as single seeking a non-sexual relationship, and 26% are single not seeking a relationship. In terms of masturbation frequency, 36% reported never masturbating, while 17% reported masturbating about once a month, and 7% reported masturbating once a day. According to the narratives, 84% of the sample had revealed their asexual identity to at least one person, while 16% had not disclosed their asexuality to anyone. Of note, 86% of the total sample reported no history of childhood sexual abuse, while the remaining 14% reported a possible or probable history of childhood sexual abuse. Data on the sample's racial composition were not collected.

Procedure

The narratives were collected as part of a larger project on the assessment of asexuality. . . . Participants were required to be over 18 and fluent in English. After completing a 96-item survey assessing asexuality, sexual aversion, sexual desire, and demographic information, participants were asked to respond to an open-ended prompt about the development of their asexual identity and the disclosure of that identity to others. The specific phrase "coming out" was never used in the prompt so as to facilitate an open description about the experience of disclosing asexual identity to others.

Analyses

A phenomenological approach was utilized to explore the narratives in order to facilitate open examination of lived experiences in the absence of a specific hypothesis (Shinebourne, 2011). This approach was used to identify and analyze themes related to coming out as an asexual and is supported by past qualitative research on asexuality (Brotto et al., 2010; Carrigan, 2011). . . .

RESULTS

Similar to past research, the current study found that a majority (69%) of the asexual sample identified as female (Bogaert, 2004; Brotto et al., 2010; Prause & Graham, 2007; Scherrer, 2008). As studies on asexuality have consistently shown significant gender differences within samples, researchers have speculated that these findings may be the result of a population disparity rather than a sampling flaw (Brotto et al., 2010). Bogaert (2004) suggested that women may be more likely to identify as asexual due to the societal expectation that males are more sexual than females. He also suggests that women may not report experiencing sexual attraction as frequently as men because they may not be as aware of their own sexual arousal.

Theme 1: Motives for Coming Out as Asexual

The majority of participants (84%) had come out as asexual to at least one other person. Review of the narratives revealed that participants conceptualized this process of disclosure as "coming out" as asexual. . . . Three motives emerged for those who chose to come out: response to pressure from family and friends, salience to personal identity, and membership in the asexual community.

Response to Pressure

Many participants reported that it was not necessary to come out as asexual to family members, but felt that doing so might reduce questions about dating and seeking a partner. One female participant indicated, "I decided to tell my parents in my late teens because I was starting to get pressure from family members

and friends to start dating, get married, have kids" (Asexual, Female, age 18–25). Providing an explanation for the absence of romantic involvement alleviated pressure from family. Coming out also relieved social pressure from peers, for example, to address uncomfortable questions about sexual preferences or experiences: "I told . . . some of my close friends a few years ago in college, mostly to stop them from assuming I was sexual, asking me whether I was dating and trying to set me up with people" (Panemotional Aromantic Asexual, Female, age 18–25).

Salience to Identity

Many considered asexuality to be a defining identity characteristic and chose to come out as an act of self-expression and a step toward identity integration. These respondents felt compelled to come out in order to develop authentic and meaningful relationships.

I told my parents and siblings because I thought it was vital information to help them understand me and my life experiences. . . . I wanted the people I cared about in my life to actually know me and who I am. (Hetero-affectional Asexual, Female, age 18–25)

Another participant commented, "It wasn't a difficult decision for me to reveal my discovery about this integral part of my identity to close friends and family" (Asexual, Female, age 18–25). Narrative analysis revealed a pattern: the more central asexuality was to personal identity, the more likely participants seemed to come out as asexual.

Discovering Asexuality

Discovering online information about asexuality was described as exciting and liberating for many individuals who believed that their lack of sexual desire was pathological. "I discovered that asexuality is a true orientation when I was about 16; I was thrilled that I fit in with a group that I could agree with. I don't see a reason to keep my asexuality hidden" (Asexual, Female, age 18–25). Previously, many participants had assumed that they had low libido or suffered from a sexual disorder. Learning about asexuality allowed them to legitimize their own experience and embrace their asexual identity: "I came out almost immediately after learning what asexuality was, because I knew beyond a doubt that that's what I was" (Asexual, Female, age 18–25).

Participants felt relieved and validated to find a community of other asexuals with similar experiences: "I do plan to tell my sister and close friends because I'm so happy to finally feel normal. I'm kind of bursting to tell someone outside of AVEN [asexuality.org]" (Asexual, Female, age 18–25). Finding the appropriate designation to describe their experience and joining the asexual web community was a critical moment for many participants.

Right after I discovered the asexual community, I told my mother and three of my best friends. They all said [it] was like they knew but they didn't know there was a name for it. . . . After finding out that there are many like me and I needn't any fixing, I became much more confident in my attitude and I feel more able to express my thoughts and opinions without worry. (Aromantic Asexual, Female, age 26–32)

Theme 2: Motives for Withholding Asexual Identity from Others

Among those who chose not to come out, there were several prominent reasons identified for not doing so. Some felt that the information was private, or that their asexuality was not a salient enough part of their identity to warrant coming out, while others feared the social consequences.

Selective Disclosure

Some romantically oriented participants described asexuality as irrelevant to everyone but the individual and his or her partner. "I have only told the person I'm currently in a purely romantic relationship with that I am asexual. I don't think other people need to know this fact about me. It's simply not important" (Asexual, Female, age 18–25). Another motivation to come out exclusively to a partner was the negotiation of a sexual–asexual relationship. Some respondents felt that it was necessary to disclose their asexuality in order to help their partner understand the experience of sex for an asexual or to address sexual conflicts within the relationship.

[I came out to] the "love of my life" only. It had become a bit of an obstacle between us and when I realized what I was, 1) I needed to tell someone, 2) I wanted him to know why things had gone wrong. He was fine with it. I haven't told anyone else; I don't think there's any need to. It doesn't affect anyone else. (Asexual, Female, age 26–32)

Coming out appeared to be a step toward seeking acceptance and understanding from sexual partners. In these cases, coming out became necessary because it related to negotiation of the couples' sexual activity.

My ex said, "You just need to change your attitude towards intimacy." I told him because I was sick of fighting back tears during [sex], crying quietly to myself afterwards, it feeling like rape when it wasn't, and he deserved to be with someone who likes sex and looks forward to sex as pleasurable as opposed to dreading it. (Celibacy-oriented, Female, age 26–32)

Some participants discovered their asexuality after committing to a sexual relationship or marriage. In these cases, coming out to an intimate partner was a step toward negotiating the terms of the relationship, and in some cases, determined the couple's ultimate separation.

The only person who . . . I have told that I am asexual is my ex-husband. Our differences in sexuality were a primary component in our divorce. He was supportive and recognized that it is not something I can control. (Biromantic Asexual, Female, age 33+)

Fear of "Coming Out"

A theme present in many narratives was anxiety around describing asexuality to others for fear of being ostracized or misunderstood. Many were worried about social stigma and how their relationships might change after coming out as asexual.

I have not told anyone that I am asexual because I don't want anyone to label me as weird or crazy. I don't want people to pity me for my life situation or how I feel about things. I just don't want people to think less of me or stereotype me. (Asexual-Indifferent, Female, age 18–25)

The public's general lack of knowledge and understanding of asexuality was a major deterrent for those who had not come out. As asexuality is not widely accepted as a sexual orientation, closeted participants chose to avoid the possibility of facing rejection and alienation.

I have not come out to anyone . . . because I do not think there is very much acceptance of asexuality as a valid orientation. I am afraid that my friends would think there is something wrong with me or that they would feel uncomfortable with me. (Biromantic Asexual, Female, age 33+)

Moreover, the prospect of explaining asexuality was seen as burdensome and risky. Some were even willing to endure unwanted sexual activity to maintain relationships.

I have not discussed it because I think it would deeply affect my personal relationship. I find occasionally giving into sex is worth keeping my romantic relationship going. (Asexual, Female, age 26–32)

Non-Salience to Identity

A number of respondents reported that their asexual identity did not affect their lives in any way, and was not salient at all to their identity. Because they did not define themselves in terms of their asexuality, sharing their orientation with others was unnecessary. One respondent wrote, "My orientation is not an important enough part of my identity for me to need to share it with others" (Asexual-Questioning, Female, age 26–32). Another participant noted, "I haven't told anybody yet because I don't think that my sexual orientation has anything to do with my relationships to others or my life in general" (Asexual, Female, age 18–25). These results seem to reaffirm the previous observation that asexual individuals may be more likely to come out if they consider asexuality to be central to their identity. . . .

I have not told anyone at all about my explorations of asexuality. Sexuality/asexuality is by my choice a non-issue in my life (though sometimes it feels like the elephant in the room); it's like it's not even there. It never gets talked about. (Asexual-Questioning, Female, age 18–25)

Theme 3: Explaining Indifference about "Coming Out"

Respondents also included those who did not intentionally share or conceal their asexuality. They had not put a great deal of thought into coming out, and simply accepted their asexual status. One participant exemplified this theme: "I tell people as it becomes relevant, which isn't very often. I don't really feel much one way or the other about telling people" (Homoromantic Asexual, Undifferentiated Gender, age 18–25). For those who were neutral about coming out, many opted to do so because it was simply easier than hiding their sexual identity. Acquisition of the proper vocabulary facilitated and sometimes prompted this process.

Having a word to describe myself made conversations about my future much easier to navigate. Otherwise, it doesn't affect me much. I didn't start acting differently after I came out; I was always this. All that's changed is that now I have a name for it. (Asexual, Female, age 18–25)

Endorsing a specific sexual orientation was a useful tool to promote understanding but was not central to the identity-formation process.

People knowing or not knowing doesn't really affect my life, but it's easier to avoid awkward topics when they do know and will be sensitive about topics that bore me, such as conversations about sex or relationships. (Asexual, Female, age 21)

Theme 4: Negative Reception of Asexual Identity

Among those who did choose to publicly disclose their asexuality, some reported negative reactions from friends and family members. Typically, these negative reactions tended to affect the participants' views about coming out to others in the future.

Reactions of Disbelief

The fact that asexuality is not yet widely accepted as a legitimate sexual orientation was reflected in the negative reactions to disclosure. One participant commented, "[My friends] didn't believe me when I said I was asexual or that asexual was an actual orientation; it was rather unfortunate" (Asexual, Male, age 26–32). Another female participant reported, "My friends didn't believe me. One friend's exact response was 'you're not a tree'" (Asexual, Female, age 18–25). After discovering and accepting their own asexual identity, they were dismayed to be challenged and rejected by skeptics:

I was fifteen when I told my mother and friends that I was asexual. They didn't believe me. This was kind of shocking and hurtful to me, because it made so much sense to me. It was like learning that I had brown eyes, but when I mentioned it people just said that I really had blue eyes. I just couldn't believe that they didn't believe me and worse, that they thought they knew how I felt better than I did. (Asexual, Female, age 21)

Dismissal of Asexuality

The most common negative responses to coming out were suggestions that the asexual individual was confused, that asexuality is "just a phase," and that the individual had not yet met the right person. One participant commented: "[My parents] brushed it off, saying that I probably didn't know what asexual meant" (Asexual-Questioning, Female, age 20). Some participants reported coming out to their queer or LGBT friends, seeking empathy from peers with similar experiences. "I came out to my lesbian friend. She laughed at me and told me that I was being ridiculous. . . . My local gay switchboard told me that asexuality doesn't exist and that everyone wants to f*** someone" (Asexual, Male, age 18–25).

Respondents also reported that many were insistent that asexuality was just a stage: "[One friend] took it pretty well but still wanted to believe it wasn't 'real' or that I would 'grow out of it'" (Panromantic Asexual, Female, age 18–25). Another participant commented, "My parents were insistent that it was just a phase and I would not always feel this way" (Demisexual, Female, age 26–32). Similarly, others were convinced that when they found the right person, their libido would surface. One female participant commented:

I can't even count the number of times I've been told, 'Oh, well, you just haven't met the right guy yet. When you meet the right man everything will work out and you'll enjoy having sex.' I strongly doubt that. (Asexual, Female, age 18–25)

Pathologizing asexuality was not uncommon. "They want to fix me, to the extent that I have cut communication with several of them. I've been called unnatural, and had people attempt to fix me by taking me to psychologists and therapists without my consent" (Asexual, Female, age 18–25). One participant commented,

My family seems to think everyone is sexual. If you're not you should get hormone treatment to fix yourself. Since none of my blood tests or doctors exams have shown me to be medically lacking in an area that would relate to my zero sex drive or attraction toward people, I just keep my private life just that, and don't really tell them anything. (Aromantic Demisexual, Female, age 18–25)

Theme 5: Positive Reactions to Coming Out as Asexual

Narratives also contained reports of positive reactions to coming out as asexual. One woman stated:

Communicating my asexual identity was relatively easy because my family and friends are very supportive. They had listened to me talk a lot about feeling broken or wrong, and when I found out about asexuality, it was like a light bulb went on over my head. Everyone was very accepting and open to the idea. (Asexual, Female, age 18–25)

In some cases, family members responded with apparent excitement: "When I told my parents, my mom was ecstatic. She knew that I had little to no sexual feelings growing up, so she thought it was great that I found the term 'asexual' to legitimize myself" (Asexual, Undifferentiated Gender, age 18–25).

Surprisingly, some participants even reported that those they told were already aware of their asexuality: "When I told my friends none of them were really shocked. They had figured it out long before I did. They still accept me and love me for who I am, which is great" (Asexual, Female, age 18–25). This finding suggests that perhaps acceptance and knowledge of asexuality as a legitimate sexual orientation are increasing in the public sphere.

Theme 6: The Role of the Internet in Coming Out as Asexual

One of the most prevalent themes in the process of discovering, accepting, and sharing an asexual identity was the significant role played by the internet. AVEN (asexuality.org) helped inform asexuals about their own identity and validated their experience. Searching the internet for a way to classify their experience often led them to the AVEN homepage, where an asexual is defined as "a person who does not experience sexual attraction" (asexuality.org). The discovery of an online asexual community had a profound impact on respondents, and provided a context for their experiences. AVEN was a crucial source of answers and validation for individuals questioning their sexual identities.

Most were not even aware that asexuality existed until they found AVEN and other asexual web communities. One participant noted, "I [came out] quite late in my life because I just did not know or understand the term 'asexual' until I first read about it on the Internet" (Male, Asexual, age 33?). This website even aided the coming-out process for several individuals whose loved ones were skeptical until reviewing the online information: "One friend didn't believe me and that hurt until I could show her the AVEN site and she understood" (Asexual, Female, age 18–25). Some participants simply forwarded the link to their friends and family to help explain asexuality: "[My sister] had a few questions. . . . I told her that she could look at the FAQ on AVEN." (Asexual-Questioning, Female, age 20). AVEN also provided a unique community of like-minded peers to help answer questions and give support. In fact, some respondents were only comfortable coming out to online acquaintances because they felt that others would not understand.

I've only come out to online friends so far. I think people in real life would never understand what asexuality really means; they'd think I'm not normal and send me to therapy. But coming out to my online friends was . . . fun, to say a word. It was just very natural and logical. (Asexual, Female, age 18–25)

The asexual web community is an important platform for asexuals who have accepted their identities and want to begin the process of coming out safely and anonymously.

Other internet sources aside from AVEN assist individuals in coming out as asexual without directly telling others. For example, the use of social networking sites like Facebook has simplified the passive disclosure of personal information. By posting about asexuality on Facebook in lieu of face-to-face contact, individuals can represent their orientation while avoiding the stress and potential negative outcome of more direct communication.

I came out by Facebook status on coming-out day in 2010, at 18 when I was a freshman in college. . . . I kind of copped out of fully coming out by electronically announcing my orientation, so while my family knows I identify as asexual, I've kind of avoided talking about it much, just because it's an awkward conversation to have. (Female, Asexual, age 18–25)

In these ways, participants were able to test the waters by disclosing their asexuality without great risk. "I also revealed my asexual identity on Facebook by changing my profile picture to the asexual flag and sneaking a brief mention in the 'about me' section" (Female, Asexual, age 18–25). Those who came out in this way seemed to receive milder reactions than those who took a more direct approach to coming out. "On the Internet it is easy for me to reveal my asexual identity and so far I [am] met with indifference or interest. No negative feedback" (Gray Asexual, Undifferentiated Gender, age 18–25). Another participant wrote: "I've posted a link to AVEN on Facebook to start a conversation, no one noticed" (Aromantic Asexual, Female, age 21). This response suggests that this method of coming out may not be optimal in terms of encouraging a dialog about asexuality, but it may be appealing for those who wish to come out without inviting judgment or rejection. Privacy restrictions also allow individuals to maintain control over the process by selecting who is privy to personal information.

Theme 7: Reflections After Coming Out

Coming out as asexual resulted in a deep sense of liberation and increased personal insight for most respondents. There were no reports of regret after coming out.

I felt relief after 'coming out' as asexual because I wasn't trying to pretend to be something I wasn't any longer. I tried for a good 10 years to be sexual, up to being bordering promiscuous for a time. . . . Once I realized I didn't want sex, I was so much happier. (Biromantic Asexual, Female, age 26–32)

Most participants who came out ultimately reported feeling more comfortable with themselves. One participant noted, "Mostly, telling people now just made me feel like something was off my shoulders. Life didn't change much, since I just continued not being in relationships, but I personally felt better" (Asexual, Female, age 21). Generally, coming out facilitates identity integration: "Having my asexuality known has caused me to feel less misunderstood and alienated" (Hetero-affectional Asexual, Female, age 18–25).

DISCUSSION

The current study explored the coming-out experiences of a sample of asexual individuals recruited from three internet sources and provides insight into the process of asexual identity development. Narratives revealed preliminary patterns in the process of identity formation similar to theoretical models of identity development among homosexual and bisexual samples. . . .

Coleman (1982) suggested that the function of coming out among homosexuals is to begin the process of self-acceptance. Within the asexual community, the function of coming out may instead be an expression of identity salience and may serve as an external indicator of commitment to asexuality as a way of life (Troiden, 1988). Participants also described disclosure as a strategy for coping with sexual-normative expectations, like past models for disclosure of homosexuality (Cass, 1979). The present study suggests that the desire to share crucial identity information and educate others contributed to the decision to come out. Most asexuals found meaning in coming out and reflected positively on the experience. The reports of positive reactions to disclosure demonstrate the importance of external validation.

Earlier models emphasize the implications of positive and negative reactions to disclosure, suggesting that the individual's perception of the reaction has an effect on continuing identity development (Cass, 1979). It is unclear from the narratives how a positive or negative reaction to disclosure affected the process of identity integration in the asexual samples. It is possible that negative reactions do not have the derailing effect suggested by Cass. The current sample reported reactions of incredulity, minimizing, and complete repudiation of the construct. Negative responses reflected ignorance of the changing social understanding of sexual essentialism. It is possible that being put in the position to defend the validity of asexuality may further strengthen the commitment to this identity and facilitate identity integration rather than impede it, as suggested in homosexual identity development models (Carrion & Lock, 1997; Cass, 1979; Coleman, 1982). Further research is needed to explore this idea. . . .

Like sexuality, asexuality may be a dynamic construct, constantly in flux and always being redefined. This is supported by the existence of many variations within the asexual community, including Gray-A, aromantic, romantic, biromantic, heteroromantic, homoromantic, panromantic, demisexual, demiromantic, and more (Jay, 2008b). Asexual individuals may also continue to refine the types of intimacy they are comfortable with, if any. Rust (1993) noted that "historical changes in the conceptualization of sexuality change the meaning of existing constructs and generate new constructs" (p. 68). Asexual individuals are in a unique position to help construct the social understanding of this identity and change the conceptualization of sexuality. Future research should explore in more depth what it means to have an integrated asexual identity.

LIMITATIONS

There were several important limitations to the current study that should be addressed. A central criticism of past research has been the exclusive use of asexual samples recruited from the internet, excluding those with asexual tendencies who may not identify with or be aware of online communities. Researchers have expressed concern that the diversity within the asexual population may be an artifact of using internet sites to recruit participants (Brotto & Yule, 2009; Hinderliter, 2009). For example, those who join online communities may be looking for others with similar identities. Conversely, others have argued that the asexual population contains more diversity than is represented on AVEN, not less (Chasin, 2011). To address these issues, Hinderliter (2009) suggested drawing from multiple online sources—a method employed in the current study. Nevertheless, recruiting from multiple asexual web communities presents many of the same challenges as enlisting participants from a single website. This methodology limits the generalizability of the findings to asexual individuals who are members of online asexual communities. Furthermore, the proposed model hinges on the assumption that asexual participants build their identities using these online resources. It is unknown how one would develop an asexual identity without the use of the internet to inform the process. . . . Future research may benefit from approaching asexual identity development in a more structured manner in order to collect specific demographic and descriptive data, or from using a multi-method approach. . . .

REFERENCES

Bogaert, A. F. (2004). Asexuality: Prevalence and associated factors in a national probability sample. *Journal of Sex Research*, 41, 279–87.

Bogaert, A. F. (2006). Toward a conceptual understanding of asexuality. *Review of General Psychology*, 10, 241–50.

Bogaert, A. F. (2008). *Expert commentary B: Asexuality: Dysfunction or variation?* Hauppauge, NY: Nova Biomedical Books.

Bogaert, A. F. (2012). *Understanding asexuality*. Lanham, MD: Rowman & Littlefield Inc.

Bogaert, A. F. (2015). The Demography of Asexuality. In A. Baumle, ed., *International handbook on the demography of sexuality*. New York: Springer.

Brotto, L. A., Knudson, G., Inskip, J., Rhodes, K., & Erskine, Y. (2010). Asexuality: A mixed-methods approach. *Archives of Sexual Behavior*, 39, 599–618.

Brotto, L. A., & Yule, M. A. (2009). Reply to Hinderliter (2009) [Letter to the Editor]. *Archives of Sexual Behavior*, 38, 622–23.

Brotto, L. A., & Yule, M. A. (2011). Physiological and subjective sexual arousal in self-identified asexual women. *Archives of Sexual Behavior*, 40, 699–712.

Carrigan, M. (2011). There's more to life than sex? Difference and commonality within the asexual community. *Sexualities*, 14, 462–78.

Carrion, V. G., & Lock, J. (1997). The coming out process: Developmental stages for sexual minority youth. *Clinical Child Psychology and Psychiatry*, 2, 369–77.

Cass, V. C. (1979). Homosexual identity formation: A theoretical model. *Journal of Homosexuality*, 4, 219–35.

Chasin, C. J. D. (2011). Theoretical issues in the study of asexuality. *Archives of Sexual Behavior*, 40, 713–23.

Coleman, E. (1982). Developmental stages of the coming out process. *Journal of Homosexuality*, 7, 31–43.

Hinderliter, A. (2009). Methodological issues for studying asexuality [Letter to the Editor]. *Archives of Sexual Behavior*, 38, 619–21.

Jay, D. (2003). A look at online collective identity formation. Unpublished manuscript.

Jay, D. (2008a). Overview: Asexuality visibility and education network. Retrieved from http://www.asexuality.org/home/overview/html.

Jay, D. (2008b). AVEN Survey 2008—Results: Asexuality visibility and education network. Retrieved from http://www.asexuality.org/home/2008_stats.html.

MacInnis, C. C., & Hodson, G. (2012). Intergroup bias toward "Group X": Evidence of prejudice, dehumanization, avoidance and discrimination against asexuals. *Group Processes and Intergroup Relations*, 15, 725–43.

Poston, D. L., & Baumle, A. K. (2010). Patterns of asexuality in the United States. *Demographic Research*, 23, 509–30.

Prause, N., & Graham, C. (2007). Asexuality: Classification and characterization. *Archives of Sexual Behavior*, 36, 341–56.

Rothblum, E. D., & Brehony, K. A. (1993). Boston marriages: Romantic but asexual relationships among contemporary lesbians. Amherst: University of Massachusetts Press.

Rust, P. C. (1993). "Coming out" in the age of social constructionism: Sexual identity formation among lesbian and bisexual women. *Gender & Society*, 7, 50–77.

Scherrer, K. (2008). Coming to an asexual identity: Negotiating identity, negotiating desire. *Sexualities*, 11, 621–41.

Shinebourne, P. (2011). The theoretical underpinnings of interpretative phenomenological analysis (IPA). *Existential Analysis*, 22, 16–31.

Troiden, R. R. (1988). Homosexual identity development. *Journal of Adolescent Health Care*, 9, 105–13.

Vaughan, M., & Waehler, C. (2010). Coming out growth: Conceptualizing and measuring stress-related growth associated with coming out to others as a sexual minority. *Journal of Adult Development*, 17, 94–109.

Westphal, S. P. (2004). Glad to be asexual. *New Scientist*, 184, 40–43.

Yule, M. A., Brotto, L. A., & Gorzalka, B. B. (2013a). Biological markers of asexuality: Handedness, birth order, and finger length ratios in self-identified asexual men and women. *Archives of Sexual Behavior*, 43, 299–310.

Yule, M. A., Brotto, L. A., & Gorzalka, B. B. (2013b). Mental health and interpersonal functioning in self-identified asexual mean and women. *Psychology and Sexuality*, 4, 136–51.

ADVENTURES WITH THE "PLASTIC MAN": SEX TOYS, COMPULSORY HETEROSEXUALITY, AND THE POLITICS OF WOMEN'S SEXUAL PLEASURE

BREANNE FAHS AND ERIC SWANK

For the last several decades, women in the United States have successfully advocated for the recognition of their right to sexual pleasure, with access to sex toys representing one possible avenue to women's self-pleasure. As the call to "take pleasure into your own hands" has grown—in part due to recognizing the role of clitoral stimulation and the importance of sexual self-reliance—sex toys have entered more women's sexual lives in both private and partnered sexual experiences. Building upon this momentum, much scholarly debate has ensued about whether phallic-shaped sex toys utilized in sex play between women represent literal phalluses or symbolic subversions of patriarchal power (Findlay 1992; O'Keefe et al. 2009). While those in classical semiotics have argued that lesbians utilize sex toys as a means to compensate for the relative lack of "phallus" in sex (Bolsø 2007), most postmodern and feminist scholars have theorized that lesbians' use of phallic sex toys subverts the masculinized power of the phallus and plays with the idea that men are the sole wielders of the penetrative penis (Bolsø 2007; Hamming 2001; Minge and Zimmerman 2009; Lamos 1994; Reich 1999). Curiously, though quantitative research has shown that heterosexual, bisexual, and lesbian women all use vibrators (Herbenick et al. 2010) and women generally use them to enhance sexual responsiveness and sexual pleasure (Herbenick et al. 2009a;

Davis et al. 1996; Richters et al. 2006), qualitative sex researchers have largely ignored women's own narratives about their sex toy usage, particularly across sexual identity boundaries. In other words, the empirical literature on sex toys has mostly ignored the storylines and common interpretive schemas women use when discussing and thinking about sex toys. In particular, heterosexual women's use of (phallic) sex toys has rarely received the same conceptual interrogations and empirical analysis that has been directed toward lesbian women's dildo usage. As such, this study examines women's subjective narratives about their sex toy usage (including vibrators and dildos) across sexual identity boundaries, as heterosexual, bisexual, and lesbian women discuss their complex relationship with, and meanings ascribed to, using (or not using) sex toys and the meaning of sex toys in their sexual experiences, masturbation behaviors, and sexual partnerships. By framing women's sex toy narratives within larger frameworks of feminist theory, queer theory, and the problems of compulsory heterosexuality, this study addresses many of the contemporary blind spots present in the study of women's sexual pleasure.

LITERATURE REVIEW

A Brief History

Historical studies show that people have used dildos (from the Italian *diletto*, for "to delight") since at least third-century Greece, and that modern rubber dildos first appeared in the nineteenth century (Deka 2005). Most notably, the history of vibrators suggests notable links between sex toys and the regulation and control of women, as doctors may, in some small circles, have used vibrators in the nineteenth century to "cure" hysteria and other ailments, often with women's husbands' approval (Chazan 2009; Maines 2001). Because vibrators had a distinctly medical purpose in the nineteenth century, it took several decades—well into the 1920s—to "see" vibrators as mechanisms that induce sexual pleasure. In the 1930s, women's magazines advertised "massagers" in non-sexual terms instead of "vibrators," and vibrators did not reappear in advertisements until after the sexual revolution (Lindemann 2006). Globally, dildos and vibrators currently have a tangible presence in the developed world and have started to appear in the developing world (India, in particular) (Deka 2005).

Benefits of Using Sex Toys

While there have been only a handful of explanatory studies about how women use sex toys, or what potential benefits they offer to partnered sexual dynamics (Herbenick et al. 2009a, 2010; Richters et al. 2006), research has found masturbation (with or without sex toys) to be positive and sexually affirming, noting that masturbation can improve women's self-awareness, body image, self-esteem, and overall sexual pleasure (Coleman 2002; Herbenick et al. 2009a; Hurlbert and Whittaker 1991; McFadden 2011; Shulman and Horne 2003). In the most widespread study of women's vibrator use to date (Herbenick et al. 2009a),

researchers found that 52.5% of women used vibrators, with more women stimulating the clitoris (83.8%) than penetrating their vaginas (64%). Further, those who used them described greater likelihood of engaging in other health behaviors like getting regular gynecological exams and performing genital self-examinations during the previous month and described [few] negative side effects associated with using vibrators. Also, women's vibrator [use] positively linked with many other aspects of women's sexual lives, including increased sexual desire, arousal, lubrication, orgasm, absence of sexual pain, and overall sexual functioning (Herbenick et al. 2009a, 2011; Richters et al. 2006). Women used vibrators primarily to stimulate the clitoris and to enhance sexual pleasure (Davis et al. 1996). As nearly 2/3 of women used vibrators in partnered sexual activities and masturbation, women described vibrators as contributing to intense orgasms and high levels of sexual satisfaction whether alone or with partners (Davis et al. 1996).

Sex toys have also often enhanced women's sexual lives by serving as a mechanism for women to "spice up" their sometimes-monotonous partnered sex (Zamboni and Crawford 2002), though many women also masturbate with sex toys as a complementary practice to an active, fulfilling, partnered sex life (Das 2007). Women use sex toys as part of an active masturbatory life, whether partnered or not (Tiefer 1998). With options available like vibrators, dildos, butt plugs, cock rings, and sex dolls (among others), sex toys represent a viable option for women to take pleasure into their own hands (Herbenick et al. 2009b). Across sexual identity lines, heterosexual, bisexual (see Schick et al. 2012 and Schick et al. 2011), and queer women all report relatively frequent use of vibrators and sex toys (Herbenick et al. 2009b). They may also help women to achieve stereotypical definitions of "empowered" femininity (that is, successful, "hip," nontraditional, and career-driven) outlined in fashion-oriented magazines like *Cosmopolitan*, *Essence* (Buchanan 2010), and shows like *Sex and the City* (Comella 2003). Popular women's magazines and television shows frequently advocate that women orgasm to empower their sexualities through buying sex toys (Buchanan 2010; Comella 2003; Wright 2009), as cultural norms about sexual pleasure reveal themselves both through the toys themselves and through marketing strategies directed at women (Rye and Meaney 2007).

Sex Toys as Therapeutic?

Sex therapy literatures often advocate sex toys and other sexual enhancement devices to promote "orgasm positive interventions" (Striar and Bartlik 1999) implicitly targeting heterosexual women's orgasmic functioning as something sex toys can assist with (Billups et al. 2001). While some sex therapies have successfully deconstructed the centrality of orgasm and penetrative intercourse (Tiefer 2004), the underlying premise of these "progress through technology" interventions assumes that orgasm (via sex toys) correlates with a better overall sex life (Garland 2004; Zamboni and Crawford 2002), and that women's discovery of sex toys would allow them greater happiness and fulfillment (Billups et al. 2001). Sex toy advocates within the sex therapy community argue that sex toys can add diversity to a monogamous relationship, trigger sexual desire for patients with low libido, inspire arousal and ease performance anxiety, help couples with incompatible sexual fantasies, model new ways to communicate or achieve orgasm, and assist with older patients, those with chronic pain, or those struggling with sexual aversion disorders, sexual abuse, and poor body image (Striar and Bartlik 1999; Warkentin et al. 2006). Dildos and butt plugs may also allow *men* to experience penetration from a partner . . . and thus

provide new experiences for sexual pleasure that transcend traditional gender and heteronormative scripts (Hollows 2007; Rye and Meaney 2007). Still, feminist sex therapists caution that masturbation and partnered sex, with or without sex toys, are beholden to patriarchal cultural scripts that derive from historical, biological, and cultural influences (Tiefer 1998, 2004), including racist, heterosexist, and sexist ideologies (Fahs 2011).

Within the medical world, the medicalization of women's sexuality has led to a host of "interventions" that seek to improve women's orgasmic functioning via medical "toys." Devices like vacuum pumps for women's clitorises (Billups et al. 2001) and "clitoral therapy devices" (Schroder et al. 2005) suggest that sex therapy discourses equate physiological arousal with efficient orgasm and sexual activity for women, even though other studies have found that women's physiological arousal does not always correlate with sexual *desire* (Fahs 2011; Harris 2004; O'Connor 2004). That is, medical interventions may induce women's physiological arousal (e.g., lubrication and swelling) but women still report little desire for sex with their partners (O'Connor 2004). Nevertheless, sex therapy interventions that ignore systemic sexism often equate the use of sex toys with women's "freedom" to enjoy sexuality, and too often do not adequately account for women's fluctuations in sexual desire that occur because of everyday life responsibilities and stressors (e.g., domestic responsibilities, child care, health status, full-time careers, and inequities with division of labor in most households) (Tiefer 2004).

Revisiting the "Lesbian Dildo Debates"

While theoretical debates exist about whether phallic sex toys represent the literal, symbolic, or differently imagined participation of the "symbolic man" (O'Keefe et al. 2009; Findlay 1992), most feminist theory suggests that dildos subvert the meaning of the phallus and undermine men's ultimate power to "please" women via penetration. If women can penetrate each other, or if the phallus functions as a symbolically castrated or dismembered man, this undermines men's monopoly on patriarchal and sexual power (Findlay 1992; Hamming 2001; Lamos 1994; Minge and Zimmerman 2009; Reich 1999). The dildo in lesbian sex may serve as a technological extension that mutates lesbians into "post-gender" beings; this transformation disrupts the sense that dildos represent literal penises or lesbians' repressed desire for a male partner (Hamming 2001; Preciado 2011). Lesbian dildo play may also "resignify" the dildo, reimagine violent sexual narratives, and reshape heteronormative assumptions about the relationship between the body and penetration (Minge and Zimmerman 2009).

Nevertheless, many feminist theorists have expressed concern that the phallus's role in *delivering* pleasure to women is rarely challenged in debates about the phallus's symbolic role, as penetrative pleasure still reigns. Some theorists suggest that dildos represent, for lesbians, "phallic imperialism," as dildos keep women subjugated while ensuring the maintenance of male dominance (Mondschein 2004). Rather than using dildos at all, some wonder, why not completely bar the phallus from entering the lesbian bedroom (Findlay 1992)? Why not embrace *non*-penetration? This rhetoric of the *penetration imperative* fits well with historical trends that viewed masturbation (and all non-reproductive sexuality) as trivial, deviant, and causing mental illness (Kay 1992; Laqueur 2004). Theologians, therapists, and medical doctors have historically warned that women who practiced "excessive" masturbation were "crazy" (Laqueur 2004). This characterization translates into recent medical scholarship as well, as one study in *The Journal of Sexual Medicine* portrayed women who used vibrators for clitoral stimulation as having "anxious attachment" and as fundamentally insecure (Costa and Brody 2011), suggesting, as much of their work does, that secure and mature women should primarily rely upon penises and penetration for sexual satisfaction and should avoid all clitoral stimulation. Further, heterosexual women's sexual *satisfaction* correlated most highly with their *partners' knowledge and perceived liking of vibrator use* (Herbenick et al. 2010), suggesting that partner evaluations and relationship scripts informed women's feelings about their vibrators (just as women evaluate many aspects of their bodies and sexuality based on the evaluation of others, particularly men).

Implicitly, then, there is a sharp divide between the decades-long queer theory work around lesbians using phallic sex toys compared with the relatively recent emergence of social science work that examines heterosexual women's (and *all* men's) motives for using sex toys. When women's sex toy use appears in the social science literature, it is usually framed empirically as (healthy, body-affirming) "vibrator use" (Herbenick et al. 2009a; Davis et al. 1996; Richters et al. 2006), while . . . lesbians' sex toy use is framed more theoretically and focused on (power-heavy, deviant) "dildo use" (Findlay 1992; Hamming 2001) or vibrator use and psychological impairment (Costa and Brody 2011), perhaps suggesting a discursive split between queer women and others. With regard to gender differences, existing studies of men's sex toy usage point out that men (across sexual identities) who used vibrators more often performed testicular self-exams (Reece et al. 2009), and generally report higher satisfaction (Reece et al. 2009; Satinsky et al. 2011) and higher erectile functioning, orgasmic functioning, and sexual desire (Reece et al. 2009), though debate about the symbolic meaning of sex toys for men has not appeared nearly as often as it has for women. And, to demonstrate women's "deviance" in comparison to men, women who penetrated themselves during masturbation before age 18 were found to desire vaginal and anal penetration later on, implying that those who *did not* self-penetrate developed paraphilias or other sexual dysfunctions (O'Keefe et al. 2009). No such studies of men's early masturbation experiences and correlates with paraphilic behavior exist.

Sex Toys, Capitalism, and Social Identities

Some scholars have started to question capitalistic implications of sex toys, including the dangerous and financially exploitative conditions in which sex toys are produced. For example, equating sex toy usage with sexual liberation suggests that buying things leads to sexual freedom and that sexual agents are also *sexual consumers* (Curtis 2004; Smith 2007). The sex toy industry and its targeted audiences rarely question the equation of shopping and sexual liberation, often drawing upon discourses of pleasure, fashion, consumerism, and sexuality to market "new" female sexualities (Attwood 2005). Further still, the sex toy market may indeed *produce* sexual desires and therefore *produce* sexual subjects so that women construct their sexualities around the desires that best sell sex toys (e.g., the "double dildo") (Curtis 2004) even while promoting feminist values and consciousness (Comella 2012). Progressives have only recently begun to question the labor conditions, quality of materials (particularly plastics), and eco-friendly implications of sex toys, as demand has grown for such information (Thomas 2006). These political economy critiques from progressives offer particular complexity because they arrive in tandem with conservative attacks on the morality of the sex toy industry (Glover 2009), as many states like Alabama still outlaw the purchase of sex toys (Hayes 2009; Rawls 2007).

As another way to critique the hierarchical implications of sex toys, they often replicate racist and sexist themes, particularly the racist stereotype of the gigantic (notably dismembered) black penis as a "signifier of racial terror and desire" (Findlay 1992, p. 572), and sexist imagery about women as passive sex objects (Fisher 2010; Loe 1998). As Alavi (2004) wrote, while interracial sexual relationships create moral panics in the United States, large black dildos are "constructed to reinforce the stereotype of the 'big black cock,' which supports the idea that black men are sexually aggressive" (p. 89). Additionally, sex toys advocate heterosexist ideals, as sex toys for women are phallic shaped even though women most often employ clitoral stimulation while masturbating (Davis et al. 1996). Only in the last decade have sex toy companies released sex toys shaped like tongues or amorphous shapes (e.g., JimmyJane's tongue-shaped Form 3 . . .). Though feminist-owned and woman-focused sex toy shops often differ in packaging sex toys, the typical advertising and packaging of sex toys in male-targeted sex toy shops depict women in stereotypically objectified poses, referencing themes found in mainstream pornography; though sex toys are clearly meant to stimulate women, the packaging in traditional sex toy shops portrays men as the primary purchasers and disseminators of sex toys to "their" women. Even for feminist sex toy stores that explicitly fight against these trends, they often admit to struggling between ideological feminist beliefs and the ultimate need to generate profits (Loe 1999).

The assumption that sex toys represent an inherently feminist agenda (particularly when sold in more gender-friendly packaging) also undermines the reality that, theoretically, sex toys may teach women *not* to touch their vaginas and vulvas with their own fingers and hands. In other words, sex toys may encourage women to use devices, rather than fingers, to give themselves pleasure. Women who use sex toys may learn to masturbate only with technology as an aid, thereby forgoing the potentially more intimate experience of touching their actual genitals (Fahs and Frank 2014). Further, sex toys may serve a role in infantilizing women, as sex toys in Japan were originally developed as actual *toys* (with children's toys' designs) in order to get around the country's obscenity laws that banned penis-shaped objects. Consequently, toys like the "Rabbit" and Hello Kitty vibrators that clearly mimic children's toys came onto the market (Taormino 2009). This association between sex toys, sexual pleasure, and treating women like children has largely been ignored, even though it mimics larger trends of treating women as (passive, immature, hairless) girls (Kilbourne 2007; Toerien and Wilkinson 2003).

These theoretical and empirical findings suggest that, while sex toys have received theoretical and quantitative scholarly attention, *qualitative* work has not yet explored women's narratives about using sex toys, particularly related to the ways sexual scripts (and compulsory heterosexuality) frame women's private sexual experiences. Consequently, this study asks several questions: First, what kinds of themes emerge when women talk about their experiences with using sex toys? Second, what differences, if any, appear between lesbian, bisexual, and heterosexual women, and what do these differences suggest about the relationship between sexual identity and sex toy usage? Third, how do women's narratives about sex toys reflect broader constructions of patriarchy, power, and the potential for subversive resistance?

METHOD

This study utilized qualitative data from a sample of 20 adult women recruited in 2011 in a large metropolitan Southwestern U.S. city. Participants were recruited through local entertainment and arts listings distributed free to the community as well as the volunteers section of the local online section of Craigslist. . . . The study invited women ages 18–59 to participate in [an] interview about their sexual histories, sexual practices, and feelings and attitudes about sexuality. Participants were screened only for their gender, racial/ethnic background, sexual identity, and age. . . . A purposive sample was selected to encourage greater demographic diversity in the sample: sexual minority women and racial/ethnic minority women were intentionally oversampled and a diverse range of ages was represented. . . . The sample included 55% (11 of 20) white women and 45% (9 of 20) women of color, including three African American women, four Mexican American women, and two Asian American women. For self-reported sexual identity, the sample included 12 heterosexual women (60%), six bisexual women (30%), and two lesbian women (10%). While these labels are informative, women's reported sexual *behavior* often indicated far more same-sex eroticism than these self-categorized labels suggest. As advertised in the recruitment materials (and approved by the institutional review board), participants were compensated $20.00 for participating. . . . Participants directly reported a range of socioeconomic and educational backgrounds, employment histories, and parental and relationship statuses.

Participants were interviewed using a semi-structured interview protocol that lasted for approximately 1.5–2 [hours], where participants responded to 36 questions that included aspects of their best and worst sexual experiences, feelings about contemporary sexual culture and media, personal experiences with orgasm and other sexual events, negotiations of power with partner(s), and reflections on their bodies. Several of the prompts addressed issues relevant to this study; these questions were asked as a part of a larger study on women's sexuality. For example, women were asked, "What kind of relationship do you have with sex toys or 'props' during masturbation or during partnered sex?". . . As the questions were broad and open-ended, participants could set the terms of how they would discuss sex toys and what information they wanted to share. The original questions served as "sensitizing concepts" that allowed previous research to lay the groundwork for topics and themes to look for (Charmaz 2006).

Responses were analyzed qualitatively using thematic analysis. This type of analysis was considered the most effective and useful because it allowed for groupings of responses based on women's attitudes and feelings. . . . This method of analysis also supported an examination of the intersection between sex toy usage and other components of women's sexual lives. . . . To conduct the analysis, we familiarized ourselves with the data by reading all of the transcripts thoroughly, and we then identified patterns for common interpretations posed by participants. . . .

RESULTS

Overall, 90% (18 of 20) [of the] women described using sex toys either during masturbation or partnered sex (or both), while 10% (2 women, both heterosexual identified) said that they had never used sex toys. This number is higher than earlier studies assessing women's vibrator use. Because all women reported that they had masturbated at least once, and all had much to say about sex toys, all 20 women were included in this study. . . . [S]ix main themes were generated. . . . [S]ome participants' responses overlapped between themes in that one woman's interview often addressed more than one theme. The six themes included (1) emphasis on non-penetrative use of phallic sex toys (8 out of 20); (2) embarrassment about disclosing sex toy usage to partner(s) (6 out of 20); (3) personifying vibrators and dildos (5 out of 20); (4) coercion and lack of power (4 out of

20); (5) embracing sex toys as campy, fun, and subversive (4 out of 20); and (6) resistance to sex toys as impersonal or artificial (5 out of 20). Heterosexual women far more often described experiences that fit into the first four themes, while queer women (lesbian and bisexual women) far more often described experiences that fit into the latter two themes.

Theme 1: Emphasis on Non-penetrative Use of Phallic Sex Toys

Whether as a mode of resistance to traditional scripts about how women should derive sexual pleasure, or as an indicator of the imperfect design of sex toys, women overwhelmingly described *non-penetrative* uses for (mostly phallic) sex toys. Of the 18 women who reported sex toy use, only three women penetrated themselves with sex toys yet most used phallic-shaped sex toys. Nevertheless, women used the sex toys, to stimulate their clitorises rather than to penetrate their vaginas; several women described this behavior as deviant or shameful, as they believed "normal" masturbation meant self-penetration. Keisha, a 34-year-old African-American bisexual woman, described her lack of penetration as something she believed characterized her as "weird": "I use a vibrator and to tell you the truth I don't penetrate while masturbating. I just use it on—just go around it, and it's really actually little. I just go around the clitoris and that's it. I don't even penetrate when I use a vibrator." Her perception that non-penetration was surprising or non-normative suggests that Keisha believed most women penetrated themselves with sex toys. This assumption implies that equating penetration with sexual normality has entered women's internal masturbation scripts. Keisha's response also suggests that women do not typically discuss masturbation with each other and that socializing forces found in schools, media, and within women's networks do not relay accurate information about how women masturbate.

Similarly, Sylvia, a 23-year-old white heterosexual woman, also described her masturbation behavior as not normal because she did not insert it: "I like my vibrator. It's this little thing and I have to have that on my clit or it just will not work. I don't ever like even insert it. It doesn't do anything if I do." Describing her sex toy as abnormally small, Sylvia believed that most women use larger (and more phallic) toys. By deriving pleasure from her "small" vibrator, she subverts the "bigger is better" assumptions about penis size and what pleases women while also showing that "normal" size equals "normal" (male) penis.

A few women, however, felt less uneasiness about their disinterest in penetration and chose devices not intended to resemble (penetrative) penises. Inga, a 24-year-old white bisexual, said that she frankly preferred non-phallic toys: "Anything that's inserted I just don't like. I have a sex toy with two prongs. It looks weird, like a tooth, not like most vibrators. I absolutely love it! It's waterproof so I can take it in the shower with me if I want." Together, these responses indicate that women conceptualize differences between their own (use of) sex toys and how others use them.

Theme 2: Embarrassment about Disclosing Sex Toy Usage to Partner(s)

Although women often derived pleasure from sex toys, they generally felt uncomfortable expressing these sentiments to others. As a second theme, heterosexual women felt particularly embarrassed about their sex toy usage, often constructing sex toys as a threat to their boyfriends' or husbands' sense of sexual prowess. As such, several women did not disclose their sex toy use to others (including mothers, sisters, friends, coworkers, and partners) and often *purposefully hid* sex toys from

male partners. Tania, a 25-year-old white heterosexual woman, described her experiences with past boyfriends and their jealousy about her vibrator use: "Some of the men I've chatted with about (my vibrator) become jealous that they can't perform the same act as the vibrator does, so I try to shy away from speaking to them about it. When I can't have an orgasm during sex with them, they become, you know, kind of self-conscious because I tell them that I can with a vibrator. Now I just don't talk about it at all with them." This description of shying away from disclosure starkly contrasted with her overwhelming sense of pleasure when using her vibrator: "I didn't know what I was doing at first and I just kind of played around with it and I finally had my first orgasm with it and it was incredible! I couldn't stop from there on! So now it's definitely become a regular kind of thing. I've got the Rabbit, and I can have multiple orgasms. Once I had ten orgasms in an hour and I was very, very excited!" Tania felt she could not share with her partner the sexual joy she experienced during masturbation, suggesting that lack of disclosure may correspond with uneasiness about challenging men's sexual power (or "territory"). In other words, women worried that their partners would not automatically feel superior to a machine and that disclosure of sex toy use would undermine hegemonic masculinity notions of men's (inherent) sexual mastery.

As another example of women's fear of disclosure, some worried that others would find their sex toys or discover their own personal "deviance." Several women described hiding their sex toys in special places in their houses, buying them discreetly, and worrying about their partners hearing a buzzing vibrator from the next room. Other women worried about *other men's* (non-partners) judgments. . . . Patricia, a 28-year-old African American heterosexual woman, reported her imagined shame when telling a doctor about her (misused) sex toy: "At first I was really all for using sex toys, but once your vagina starts getting wet and your muscles start contracting, I was scared because, well, what if it sucks it up in there? And then what? I gotta go to the doctor and tell him to pull out a toy?! So, that kind of discouraged me right there." Patricia's fear that a doctor would evaluate her negatively suggests a link between sex toys and implied deviance, as "good girls" would not encounter such trouble. This narrative also reveals how, even though women did not disclose sex toy use to other *women*, they felt far more distressed imagining other *men* finding their "secret" sex toys.

Theme 3: Personifying Sex Toys

As a common theme, several women admitted that they anthropomorphized and personified their sex toys by naming them, referring to them as a "substitute" for a real person, or imagining a relationship with their (male) sex toys. This personification of sex toys challenged men's assumed dominance and sexual abilities. For example, Zhang, a 36-year-old Asian American bisexual woman, referred to her vibrator as a "him" and described interactions with "him": "I had a dildo before, Mr. Cool Guy, but I got too emotionally attached to him. I really liked him and enjoyed my plastic man but my boyfriend didn't like it. Eventually I just threw him away so he and I couldn't have our sexual rendezvous anymore." In this example, Zhang feared disclosure of using "Mr. Cool Guy" while she also constructed him as a substitute man. Her dildo assumed a gender, an identity, and, most importantly, challenged the phallic power of her boyfriend and must therefore be discarded immediately.

As a more subtle example of personifying sex toys, Jane, a 59-year-old white heterosexual woman, described playing with a sex toy with her husband, using the "he" pronoun for the toy: "Generally we do the missionary style position but sometimes I would be on top. When I would be on top—generally I don't have an orgasm during intercourse—I have to have my vibrator on hand so that *he* can do what my husband can't. . . . My partner is very accommodating. He allows me to have an orgasm and it's important for him that I have one." Jane described her husband both as unable to help her orgasm but as *allowing* her to orgasm with the (masculinized) object, as she turned to "another man" (in this case, her vibrator) for assistance. Jane's vibrator imposed the presence of a *different* man rather than serving as something else altogether (e.g., female, a toy, a genderless object, etc.). The vibrator, it seems, is gendered male in heterosexual sex.

Theme 4: Coercion and Lack of Power in Using Sex Toys

Though only a few women described negative experiences with sex toys, these negative experiences often followed a similar coercive pattern. The worst cases generally happened when women said that their male partners either forced them to use sex toys to accommodate pornographic fantasies, or that sex toys symbolized their relative lack of power during sex. As the most clearly coercive example, Sylvia, a 23-year-old white heterosexual woman, recalled that her male partner coerced her into using anal sex toys to fulfill his fantasies: "He watched a lot of porn so he wanted to try every single little thing out there that had to do with anything that he had seen. He wanted to have anal sex so he used anal toys and stuff to loosen me up. It didn't do anything for me. It hurt a lot but I went along with it anyway. As long as he was happy, then I would try whatever he wanted. He also wanted to use ropes, gags, and meet up with people on Craigslist to meet other couples." For Sylvia, using anal sex toys accommodated her partner's desires even if using them caused her physical pain. In this scenario, the toys functioned as an extension of his (misogynistic) power, as she became the physical manifestation of a pornographic scene.

As a more subtle example of sex toys enabling power imbalances, Angelica, a 32-year-old Mexican American heterosexual woman, used sex toys to please her male partner even when she did not orgasm: "I've used masturbating toys while we're having sex. He liked it quite a bit and thought it was hot. He was fine with it, 'cause I still fake it and he gets what he wants out of it anyway." For Angelica, sex toys titillated her boyfriend rather than helping her orgasm, again representing the ways women often prioritize male pleasure above their own. . . .

Theme 5: Embracing Sex Toys as Campy, Fun, and Subversive

While heterosexual women more often relayed a tone of seriousness about power imbalances with sex toys, lesbian and bisexual women far more often described sex toys as fun or campy, often with a subversive and playful twist. In these examples, women embraced sex toys without as much shame and expressed more openness about enjoying them with partners. Cris, a 22-year-old white lesbian woman, described visiting an adult store and using the toy as a fun partnered interaction: "The dildo was kind of small. We got it in a kit from the adult store, so it doesn't really *do* anything. Neither of us (I guess you would say) wants it to be replicated like a penis, but it's just something different to do. It's kind of silly. Honestly, sometimes we'll be laughing because it's so funny. It's tiny and laughable and not meant to be taken seriously." Cris considered the relationship between the fake and real phallus and used humor and fun to undercut the absurdity of sex toys. She clearly did not see the dildo as a means to assert dominance or power over her partner and instead described it as a playful diversion.

Sex toys also allow same-sex couples to rethink the presence and absence of the phallus in their sex lives (often in a humorous and subversive way). Hannah, a 57-year-old white bisexual woman, used a dildo with her female partner to consciously undermine its phallic qualities: "My partner and I love to mess around with our dildo. It's kind of floppy so sometimes I'll wear it into the bedroom and she'll laugh really hard. We have this game where she'll ask me to take off the penis so she can get to my clit. When I do that, it's really sexy." Hannah constructed the dildo here as a humorous foreplay device rather than the centerpiece of quintessentially phallic intercourse, thus stripping the dildo of its (masculinized) power to *deliver* pleasure.

Theme 6: Resistance to Sex Toys as Impersonal or Artificial

As a final theme, several women saw no positive or therapeutic aspects of sex toys and described them instead as too impersonal or artificial. Often as a conscious rebellion against technological and corporate means to women's sexual pleasure, these women typically preferred to masturbate with their fingers and have partnered sex without accessories. For example, April, a 27-year-old Mexican American lesbian woman, felt that sex toys alienated her from her body: "I don't like the ways the toys feel. I mean, it's plastic and you can tell that it's different from what a person feels like. It's not as natural. I like to feel connected more than that, not like I just went shopping for a toy." Rather than admonishing sex toys as bad or immoral, April described them as not meeting her needs for bodily and emotional connection. In doing so, she expected masturbation to meet multiple needs rather than merely delivering sensations.

As another example of sex toys not fully satisfying women, Mei, a 22-year-old Asian American heterosexual woman, described giving up on using her vibrating cock ring and vibrator when they did not fully satisfy her: "We tried to use it together because it's one of those couple vibrators, like the U-shaped one. I don't know if it's the strength or the continuous buzzing, but it eventually makes you numb. We tried it a few times and we were like, 'This doesn't really add much.' Since then, I've used it once or twice alone but I don't like it that much. I prefer my fingers." Again, Mei expected sex toys to enhance partnered sex or masturbation, and when they failed in this regard, she discarded them. This description of "failing" (or impotent?) sex toys presents a striking contrast to imagining the sex toys as having *power* or *authority* over her pleasure, or as having a persona or a masculinized identity (as previous narratives showed).

DISCUSSION

While sex toy use is relatively widespread, honest and frank discussions about the meanings women assign to sex toys remains rare. These six themes—non-penetrative use of phallic sex toys, embarrassment about disclosure, personifying sex toys, coercion and lack of power, embracing sex toys as campy and fun, and resistance to sex toys as impersonal or artificial—point to vastly different experiences in women's interactions with, thoughts about, and emotional experiences of sex toys. There are clear advantages to *asking* women about sex toys rather than assuming universally positive or uncomplicated relationships between women, sex toys, and sexual pleasure. While this study used a small qualitative sample, these narratives did reveal several important (though exploratory) trends regarding sexual identity and sex toy narratives: first, a pattern (though somewhat imperfect) emerged between lesbian/bisexual women and heterosexual women's construction of sex toys, as queer women far more often resisted

thinking about sex toys as threatening to men, representative of phallic power, or coercive. Queer women more often constructed sex toys as fun, campy, and subversive and reported less shame about not using sex toys for penetration. On the other hand, heterosexual women more often described shame and secrecy about their sex toys, and far more often personified their sex toys as *men* or imagined that they were *supposed* to penetrate themselves with their sex toys. The narratives that women *should* treat sex toys as either replacements for penises, or as imagined penises, appeared far more often in heterosexual women's narratives.

This divide suggests that queer women more often constructed sex toys as non-literal in comparison to heterosexual women, and more importantly, queer women seemed less apt to treat sex toys as *masculine* in nature. With no clear patterns of sex education or educational background found among participants that could help to explain these differences, heterosexual women, on the whole, reported a greater tendency to treat sex toys as an inherent *threat* to their partners' masculinity, sometimes discussing sex toys as actually *male* gendered. Thus, men's expectations about "proper sex" affect women's relationship to sex even when men are absent. Interestingly, even though nearly all women masturbated with clitoral stimulation rather than vaginal stimulation, heterosexual women expressed the most reluctance and shame when disclosing these patterns to male partners. Queer women described masturbating without penetration as a normal and routine part of their lives while heterosexual women described this as something weird or abnormal.

Because of the relatively small sample, we do not contend that these sexual identity findings are conclusive and warn against overgeneralizing from this study. Future research (both qualitative and quantitative) should determine whether sexual identity differences exist on a larger scale or within different intersections between women (e.g., age, race, and class). Moreover, it is possible that our recruitment technique or interview questions led to conclusions that differ from earlier research. The fact that more women used sex toys in this sample compared to national samples could reflect biases in self-selection, differences in qualitative work that involves face-to-face discussions compared to quantitative pen/paper or online surveys, or more progressive populations in urban centers with more access to sex toys than those in rural areas.

Notably, some themes found in previous research—particularly the theme of women fearing addiction to, or desensitization from, sex toys (Loe 1998)—did not appear in our study, leading to additional questions about how age, media consumption, education, and cohort may affect the themes found in qualitative work on sex toys. Nevertheless, our findings add to the literature on women's sex toy usage by suggesting that, because queer women in this sample did not typically construct sex toys as "competition" for men, they could more easily use sex toys for fun, silliness, exploration, play, and subversion of normative scripts (e.g., deconstructing the phallus as all-powerful). Many of these queer women easily upended the (hetero)scripts and thereby changed the symbolic and literal meaning of the sex toys. Just as "butch" and "femme" distinctions within lesbian communities lead to different interpretations of dildos (Wilson 2009), our study suggests that differences between queer, bisexual, and heterosexual women may be worth studying. For example, heterosexual women overwhelmingly retained the patriarchal and phallic qualities of sex toys by envisioning them as literal penises or even as full-on *men*. Their worries about hiding sex toys or justifying any "competition" to their partners indicate that they perceived tension between real and fake penises rather than imagining sex toys as altogether symbolic. The naming of sex toys

("Mr. Cool Guy") or the assertion that a sex toy used in partnered sex has the pronoun *him* both suggest this as well. Nevertheless, subversive potential exists in the literal and symbolic displacement of the phallus, as both queer and heterosexual women enacted agency by *choosing* to have sexual pleasure regardless of the normative scripts that dictate their allegiance to patriarchy. Both groups complicate the "penetrative imperative." For heterosexual women, they still masturbate (often in secret) with their sex toys and, in doing so, may subvert the literal power of their (male partners') phallus by using the "plastic man." For queer women, they play with the metaphorical dimensions of the dildo and vibrator while also, at times, assuming the role of having a "penetrative cock," thereby *taking* that power from men. Neither group lack agency, though the *expression* of that agency differs and is worthy of close consideration.

These narratives also suggest that, perhaps because of the pervasive qualities of compulsory heterosexuality, women as a whole largely do not discuss their masturbation habits with others, particularly other women, and that even between partners, masturbation remains a relatively taboo subject. This points to the importance of feminist sex toy stores and sex toy parties as sites of women's personal sexual conversations (Comella 2012; McCaughey and French 2001) and openness between partners during couples and individual psychotherapy (Tiefer 1998). At its most basic level, this study suggests that women still believe that sexual pleasure during masturbation is not something they can readily discuss. Beyond this broad reading of the data, this research highlights the ways that heterosexism may enter women's private masturbatory experiences. Perhaps women believe masturbation serves as a substitute for "real" (that is, penetrative intercourse with a male partner) sex, or it may suggest that women lack a cultural lexicon for conversing about masturbation. (Consider, for example, the number of popular slang terms for men's masturbation compared to women's masturbation.) Women may not discuss masturbation because self-pleasure represents a direct challenge to the notion that *men alone* have the power to "please" women (with their penises); as such, sex toys, or other women, both threaten the power of hegemonic masculinity and sexual machismo. Just as women feel increasing pressure to kiss and fondle other women *in front of men* (Fahs 2011), perhaps "acceptable" masturbation for women involves masturbating *in front of men* for their pleasure. The silences surrounding women's sexual pleasure—particularly masturbatory pleasure—represent a pivotal avenue for the transmission of patriarchal power and control of women.

As a more broad critique, several of these themes suggest that (heterosexual) women generally assume they should orgasm from penetrative intercourse even though they often do not find this pleasurable. By relying upon clitoral stimulation in both masturbation and partnered sex (and then feeling shame about this), women reveal the tensions that exist in the mandate they feel about penetrative intercourse. Similar to the "sexual compliance" literature that suggests that women often engage in unsatisfying sexual intercourse to get or maintain approval of their male partners (Katz and Tirone 2009; Sanchez et al. 2005), cultural prescriptions that maintain men's power and dominance over women (and keep men *present* in solitary sex) take priority over women's orgasmic pleasure. Women's overwhelming sense that they *should* find penetration pleasurable (but they secretly do not) implies that sex toys propagate discourses of heteronormativity *even during women's private experiences with masturbation*. In other words, women have internalized the message that penetrative intercourse is *superior* even while masturbating alone. The masculine presence of sex toys only further entrenches the idea that *all aspects*

of women's sexualities are subject to patriarchal control, even during supposedly empowering and private experiences (Weinberg and Williams 2010). The literal descriptions of coercion with sex toys only further cement this pattern, as women mold their desires around men's fantasies and desires even when this occurs at women's expense (Fahs 2011).

Though sex toys mostly seem to replicate gender imbalances both by reinforcing patriarchy and emphasizing stringent adherence to traditional gender roles, these findings also suggest several important resistances women could enact when using, buying, talking about, or thinking about sex toys. First, as some women expressed in this study, women do question, critique, and challenge the divide between the *natural* and the *artificial*, between *phallic* and *non-phallic*, and between *serious* and *fun*. Whether via sex education, consciousness-raising experiences, women and gender studies courses, or informal networks, women can learn, as individuals and as a collective, to inject both a critical consciousness *and* a sense of fun into sexuality, as both of these elements receive far too little attention and consideration in contemporary discourses of women's sexuality (for a great example of how to do this, see Dodson 1996). Any time women take pleasure into their own hands, they subvert cultural scripts about "normal" sexuality. This does not suggest that if women merely "have fun" with dildos, they will fully negate the power-imbalanced implications of these toys. Still, women's narratives of shame about masturbation and sex toy use could change if women more often questioned the (phallic, patriarchal) implications of sex toys. To further complicate matters, subversive potential exists in a huge range of behaviors with sex toys, as women (queer or heterosexual) using sex toys as a literal "penetrative cock" as well as those playfully deconstructing the "realness" of the phallus *both* subvert norms of gender and power.

As a second mode of resistance, women can better address some of the racist, sexist, classist, and heterosexist implications of sex toys by refusing to buy certain sex toys, demanding better quality material in their sex toys, ensuring that sex toys are produced with better working conditions, and by refusing to purchase and use sex toys that replicate tired racist and heterosexist assumptions about gender and bodies. Further still, women may want to experiment with using their fingers to masturbate rather than relying upon sex toys exclusively, as they may discover new avenues to pleasure in this way. By collectively abstaining altogether from being sexual consumers, women can use boycotts to shape the industry that (falsely?) assumes women will continue to buy and use objects that perpetuate tired stereotypes, keep women connected to phallic pleasure, and define (in *highly* simplistic terms) what should please them.

As a third and final mode of resistance, women can decouple sex toys and liberation, instead looking closely at how sex toys simultaneously benefit and fail women, how they both empower and disempower women, and how sex toys represent a microcosm of broader contradictory and insidious cultural assumptions about women, gender, and bodies. Though this study serves as an early exploratory study about women's narratives of sex toy use, future research can delve further into questions about gender, power, and sexual accessories. In doing so, the discussion surrounding sex toys could expand to include questions like: How can we reimagine women's relationship to *buying* sexual liberation (however conceived), and what might it mean to *buy* liberation in the absence of a feminist education? In what other ways do women imagine men as *present* or *in control* when they could invest this power in themselves? How do the assumptions of popular culture (or sex therapy) construct women's relationship to orgasm, sexual play, and sexual pleasure? Ultimately, sex toys can serve a dual role: they reflect both the worst and most insidious aspects of patriarchy—namely that the invisibility of power allows it to infect women's private sexual experiences—and the more subversive possibilities of sexuality—that sex can *undo*, *redo*, *remake*, and *upend* much of the oppression, control, and restraint we face both individually and collectively.

REFERENCES

Alavi, A. K. (2004). Little white lies: Race, dildos, and American culture. In M. Strombler, D. M. Baunach, E. O. Burgess, D. Donnelly, & W. Simonds, eds., *Sex matters: The sexuality and society reader* (pp. 86–90). Boston: Pearson.

Attwood, F. (2005). Fashion and passion: Marketing sex to women. *Sexualities*, 8(4), 392–406.

Billups, K. L., Berman, L., Berman, J., Metz, M. E., Glennon, M. E., & Goldstein, I. (2001). A new non-pharmacological vacuum therapy for female sexual dysfunction. *Journal of Sex and Marital Therapy*, 27(5), 435–41.

Bolsø, A. (2007). Approaches to penetration—theoretical difference in practice. *Sexualities*, 10(5), 559–81.

Buchanan, J. (2010). This year I will . . . have hotter sex. *Essence*. Retrieved from http://business.highbeam.com/136977/article-1G1-213519765/year-have-hotter-sex.

Charmaz, C. (2006). *Constructing grounded theory*. London: Sage.

Chazan, A. (2009). Good vibrations: Liberating sexual freedom from the commercial regulation of sexual devices. *Texas Journal of Women and the Law*, 18(2), 263–303.

Coleman, E. (2002). Masturbation as a means of achieving sexual health. *Journal of Psychology & Human Sexuality*, 14(2–3), 5–16.

Comella, L. (2003). (Safe) sex and the city: On vibrators, masturbation, and the myth of "real" sex. *Feminist Media Studies*, 3(1), 109–12.

Comella, L. (2012). Changing the world one orgasm at a time: Sex positive retail activism. In R. Mukherjee & S. Banet-Weiser, eds., *Commodity activism: Cultural resistance in neoliberal times* (pp. 240–53). New York: New York University Press.

Costa, R. M., & Brody, S. (2011). Anxious and avoidant attachment, vibrator use, anal sex, and impaired vaginal orgasm. *The Journal of Sexual Medicine*, 8(9), 2493–500.

Curtis, D. (2004). Commodities and sexual subjectivities: A look at capitalism and its desires. *Cultural Anthropology*, 19(1), 95–121.

Das, A. (2007). Masturbation in the United States. *Journal of Sex and Marital Therapy*, 33(4), 301–17.

Davis, C. M., Blank, J., Lin, H., & Bonillas, C. (1996). Characteristics of vibrator use among women. *Journal of Sex Research*, 33(4), 313–20.

Deka, K. (2005). Durex is fine, but is India ready for sex toys? *India Times*. Retrieved from http://articles.economictimes.indiatimes.com/2005-11-24/news/27497533_1_toys-indians-durex.

Dodson, B. (1996). *Sex for one: The joy of selfloving*. New York: Three Rivers Press.

Fahs, B. (2011). *Performing sex: The making and unmaking of women's erotic lives*. Albany, NY: State University of New York Press.

Fahs, B., & Frank, E. (2014). Notes from the back room: Gender, power, and (in)visibility in women's experiences of masturbation. *Journal of Sex Research*, 51(3), 241–52.

Findlay, H. (1992). Freud's "fetishism" and the lesbian dildo debates. *Feminist Studies*, 18(3), 563–80.

Fisher, C. (2010). Exploring sexuality education opportunities at in-home sex-toy parties in the United States. *Sex Education*, 10(2), 131–44.

Garland, E. (2004). Reinventing sex: New technologies and changing attitudes. *The Futurist*, 38(6), 41–46.

Glover, R. (2009). Can't buy a thrill: Substantive due process, equal protection, and criminalizing sex toys. *Journal of Criminal Law and Criminology*, 100(2), 555–98.

Hamming, J. E. (2001). Dildonics, dykes, and the detachable masculine. *European Journal of Women's Studies*, 8(3), 329–41.

Harris, G. (2004). Pfizer gives up testing Viagra on women. *The New York Times*. Retrieved from http://www.nytimes.com/2004/02/28/business/28viagra.html.

Hayes, W. C. (2009). "Rabbit" hunting in the Supreme Court: The constitutionality of state prohibitions of sex toy sales following Lawrence v. Texas. *Georgia Law Review*, 44(1), 245–83.

Herbenick, D. D., Reece, M., & Hollub, A. A. (2009a). Inside the ordering room: Characteristics of women's in-home sex toy parties, facilitators and sexual communication. *Sexual Health*, 6(4), 318–27.

Herbenick, D. D., Reece, M., Sanders, S. A., Dodge, B. S., Ghassemi, A., & Fortenberry, J. D. (2009b). Prevalence and characteristics of vibrator use by women in the United States: Results from a nationally representative study. *Journal of Sexual Medicine*, 6(7), 1857–67.

Herbenick, D. D., Reece, M., Sanders, S. A., Dodge, B. S., Ghassemi, A., & Fortenberry, J. D. (2010).Women's vibrator use in sexual partnerships: Results from a nationally representative survey in the United States. *Journal of Sex and Marital Therapy*, 36(1), 49–65.

Herbenick, D. D., Reece, M., Schick, V., Jozkowski, K. N., Middlestadt, S. E., Sanders, S. A., et al. (2011). Beliefs about women's vibrator use: Results from a nationally representative probability survey in the United States. *Journal of Sex and Marital Therapy*, 37(5), 329–45.

Hollows, K. (2007). Anodyspareunia: A novel sexual dysfunction? An exploration into anal sexuality. *Sexual and Relationship Therapy*, 22(4), 429–43.

Hurlbert, D. F., & Whittaker, K. E. (1991). The role of masturbation in marital and sexual satisfaction: A comparative study of female masturbators and nonmasturbators. *Journal of Sex Education & Therapy*, 17(4), 272–82.

Katz, J., & Tirone, V. (2009). Women's sexual compliance with male dating partners: Associations with investment in ideal womanhood and romantic well-being. *Sex Roles*, 60(5), 347–56.

Kay, D. S. (1992). Masturbation and mental health: Uses and abuses. *Sexual & Marital Therapy*, 7(1), 97–107.

Kilbourne, J. (2007). You talkin' to me? In M. Anderson & P. Hill-Collins (Eds.), *Race, class, and gender: An anthology* (pp. 228–33). Belmont, CA: Thomson Wadsworth.

Lamos, C. (1994). The postmodern lesbian position: On our backs. In L. L. Doan, ed., *The lesbian postmodern* (pp. 86–102). New York: Columbia University Press.

Laqueur, T. (2004). *Solitary sex: A cultural history of masturbation*. Cambridge: Zone Books.

Lindemann, D. J. (2006). Pathology full course: A history of anti-vibrator legislation in the United States. *Columbia Journal of Gender and the Law*, 15(1), 326–46.

Loe, M. (1998). Dildos in our toolboxes: The production of sexuality at a pro-sex feminist sex toy store. *Berkeley Journal of Sociology*, 43, 97–136.

Loe, M. (1999). Feminism for sale: Case study of a pro-sex feminist business. *Gender & Society*, 13(6), 705–32.

Maines, R. (2001). *Technologies of orgasm: "Hysteria," the vibrator, and women's sexual satisfaction*. Baltimore: The Johns Hopkins University Press.

McCaughey, M., & French, C. (2001). Women's sex toy parties: Technology, orgasm, and commodification. *Sexuality and Culture*, 5(3), 77–97.

McFadden, J. (2011). *Your daughter's bedroom: Insights for raising confident women*. New York: Palgrave Macmillan.

Minge, J., & Zimmerman, A. L. (2009). Power, pleasure, and play: Screwing the dildo and rescripting sexual violence. *Qualitative Inquiry*, 15(2), 329–50.

Mondschein, K. (2004). Sex toys. In M. Stein, ed., *Encyclopedia of lesbian, gay, bisexual, and transgendered history in America*. New York: Charles Scribner's Sons.

O'Connor, A. (2004). In sex, brain studies show, 'la différence' still holds. *The New York Times*. Retrieved from http://www.nytimes.com/2004/03/16/health/in-sex-brain-studies-show-la-difference-still-holds.html.

O'Keefe, S. L., Beard, K. W., Stroebel, S. S., Berhie, G., Bickham, P. J., & Robinett, S. R. (2009). Correlates of inserted object-assisted sexual behaviors in women: A model for development of paraphilic and non-paraphilic urges. *Sexual Addiction & Compulsivity*, 16(2), 101–30.

Preciado, B. (2011). The contra-sexual manifesto. *Total Art Journal*, 1(1), 1–6.

Rawls, P. (2007). Court leaves Alabama sex toy ban intact. *USA Today*. Retrieved from http://www.usatoday.com/news/nation/2007-10-01-2390404063_x.htm.

Reece, M., Herbenick, D., Sanders, S. A., Dodge, B., Ghassemi, A., & Fortenberry, J. D. (2009). Prevalence and characteristics of vibrator use by men in the United States. *The Journal of Sexual Medicine*, 6(7), 1867–74.

Reich, J. L. (1999). Genderfuck: The law of the dildo. In F. Cleto, ed., *Camp: Queer aesthetics and the performing subject: A reader* (pp. 254–65). Ann Arbor: University of Michigan Press.

Richters, J., de Visser, R., Rissel, C., & Smith, A. (2006). Sexual practices at last heterosexual encounter and occurrences of orgasm in a national survey. *Journal of Sex Research*, 43(3), 217–26.

Rye, B. J., & Meaney, G. (2007). The pursuit of sexual pleasure. *Sexuality and Culture*, 11(1), 28–51.

Sanchez, D. T., Crocker, J., & Boike, K. R. (2005). Doing gender in the bedroom: Investing in gender norms and the sexual experience. *Personality and Social Psychology Bulletin*, 31(10), 1445–55.

Satinsky, S., Rosenberger, J. G., Schick, V., Novak, D. S., & Reece, M. (2011). USA study of sex toy use by HIV-positive men who have sex with other men: Implications for sexual health. *International Journal of STD and AIDS*, 22(8), 442–48.

Schick, V., Herbenick, D., Rosenberger, J. G., & Reece, M. (2011). Prevalence and characteristics of vibrator use among women who have sex with women. *Journal of Sexual Medicine*, 8, 3306–15.

Schick, V., Herbenick, D., Rosenberger, J. G., & Reece, M. (2012). Variations in sexual repertoires of bisexually-identified women from the United States and the United Kingdom. *Journal of Bisexuality*, 12(2), 198–213.

Schroder, M., Mell, L. K., Hurteau, J. A., Collins, Y. C., Rotmensch, J., Waggoner, S. E., et al. (2005). Clitoral therapy device for treatment of sexual dysfunction in irradiated cervical cancer patients. *International Journal of Radiation Oncology Biology Physics*, 61(4), 1078–86.

Shulman, J. L., & Horne, S. G. (2003). The use of self-pleasure: Masturbation and body image among African American and European American women. *Psychology of Women Quarterly*, 27(3), 262–69.

Smith, C. (2007). Designed for pleasure: Style, indulgence, and accessorized sex. *European Journal of Cultural Studies*, 10(2), 167–84.

Striar, S., & Bartlik, B. (1999). Stimulation of the libido: The use of erotica in sex therapy. *Psychiatric Annals*, 29(1), 60–62.

Taormino, R. (2009). *The big book of sex toys: From vibrators and dildos to swings and slings*. Beverly: Quiver Books.

Thomas, P. (2006). Love: Batteries not included. *Ecologist*, 36(9), 20–21.

Tiefer, L. (1998). Masturbation: Beyond caution, complacency, and contradiction. *Journal of Sex and Marital Therapy*, 13(1), 9–14.

Tiefer, L. (2004). *Sex is not a natural act and other essays*. Boulder: Westview Press.

Toerien, M., & Wilkinson, S. (2003). Gender and body hair: Constructing the feminine woman. *Women's Studies International Forum*, 26(4), 333–44.

Warkentin, K. M., Gray, R. E., & Wassersug, R. J. (2006). Restoration of satisfying sex for a castrated cancer patient with complete impotence: A case study. *Journal of Sex and Marital Therapy*, 32(5), 389–400.

Weinberg, M. S., & Williams, C. J. (2010). Bare bodies: Nudity, gender, and the looking glass body. *Sociological Forum*, 25(1), 47–67.

Wilson, D. (2009). Black lesbian gender and sexual culture. *Culture, Health, & Sexuality*, 11(3), 297–313.

Wright, P. J. (2009). Sexual socialization messages in mainstream entertainment mass media. *Sexuality and Culture*, 13(1), 181–200.

Zamboni, B. D., & Crawford, I. (2002). Using masturbation in sex therapy: Relationships between masturbation, sexual desire, and sexual fantasy. *Journal of Psychology & Human Sexuality*, 14(2–3), 123–41.

Grandma Does *WHAT!?*: Perceptions about Older Adults and Sex

Christina Barmon, Alexis A. Bender, and Elisabeth O. Burgess

When we teach about sexuality and aging, the overarching sentiment we get from students of all ages is that they don't want to know about their parents' or grandparents' sex lives. They joke that they know they must have had sex at least as many times as they have children, but they don't want to know any details or talk to them about it. Even those of us who consider ourselves open-minded in regard to sex don't necessarily want to talk to our parents or grandparents about their fantasies or kinks. In pop culture, with the recent exception of the cougar or MILF,[1] sex is the domain of the young and conventionally attractive. Many younger people mistakenly assume that older people do not want sex and are so undesirable and unattractive that nobody would want to have sex with them; they wouldn't even want sex with each other. Contrary to these sentiments, many older adults do want and have sex. Hopefully, we can start to think about parents and grandparents in a very different way, and maybe begin to communicate more effectively about these issues.

As life expectancy increases and a larger percentage of our population is over 65 years old, we are more likely to interact with older adults in our families, workplaces, and communities. Thus, we all need to be more informed about these issues. Family members, health professionals, social workers, direct care workers, and long-term-care staff members should be aware of older adults' needs for privacy, autonomy, and access to information regarding sexual health, and the ability of older adults to make their own decisions. Furthermore, institutional policies should reflect those needs and provide training as necessary.

Although the frequency of sexual activity declines with increasing age, more so for women than for men (DeLamater and Koepsel, 2015), age alone does not explain the decline. In a large nationally representative study, Waite et al. (2010) found 84 percent of men and 62 percent of women between the ages of 57 and 64 years old reported having penile–vaginal intercourse (PVI) with a partner in the past year. For people in the 75–85-year-old age group, 38 percent of men and 17 percent of women reported engaging in PVI in the last year. While fewer older adults are sexually active, those who are having PVI tend to have it once or twice a week. This trend remained fairly constant, declining only at the oldest ages (Waite et al., 2010). Additionally, many older adults are still interested in and engage in a wide variety of sexual behaviors that may not include PVI, such as oral sex, mutual masturbation, and masturbation (Barmon, 2016).

Sexual activity, such as oral sex and masturbation, tends to remain stable over the life course (Bretschneider and McCoy, 1988; DeLamater and Koepsel, 2015; Lindau et al., 2007). Variability in sexual behavior across age groups is better understood by cohort differences than age differences (Twenge, Sherman, and Wells, 2017). Waite et al. (2010) found that more than half of older adults between the ages of 57 and 64 reported engaging in oral sex compared to only 28 percent of men and 36 percent of women between the ages of 75 and 85. The trends were similar for masturbation.

This sharp difference between those two age groups most likely represents differences between those who were teenagers in the 1940s and those who came of age during the sexual revolution. In fact, a life course perspective on sexuality suggests that people most likely have similar fantasies, interests, and desires toward the end of their lives as they did in earlier years (Burgess, 2004). In other words, if someone places a higher or lower priority on sex at a younger age, this probably remains constant with age. Similarly, if someone is kinky at a younger age, they will most likely retain their kinkiness as they get older. At all ages, opportunity structure and physical functioning influence our sexual experiences.

A lack of interest in sexual activity is much more dependent on life circumstances than on age. The largest predictors of decline in sexual activity among older adults include lack of available partners, health status, and the mental and physical health of one's partner (Gott and Hinchliff, 2003; Lindau et al., 2007). The majority of sex occurs within a monogamous relationship and the likelihood of having a sexual partner decreases with age (Karraker, DeLamater, and Schwartz, 2011). Waite et al. (2010) found 89 percent of men and 74 percent of women between the ages of 57 and 64 had a current sexual partner. But for people in the 75–85-year-old age group that number decreased to 78 percent of men and 41 percent of women. Additionally, the likelihood of having a partner with health problems increases with age. Sixty-three percent of women and 20 percent of men between the ages of 57 and 64 reported not having sex because of a partner's health problems. For those between the ages of 75 and 85, this increased to 65 percent and 23 percent, respectively. These social factors disproportionately affect women because they have a higher life expectancy and are more likely to form relationships with older men (Austad, 2006; Karraker, DeLamater, and Schwartz, 2011).

Stereotypes and misconceptions about older adults and sexuality have wide implications. Because of the stigma surrounding aging and sex, many older adults themselves have difficulty talking to health care providers about sex (Gott and Hinchliff, 2003). Conversely, health professionals are not always comfortable talking to older adults about sex (Hughes, Rostant, and Curran, 2014). This discomfort can limit health-seeking behavior regarding sexual health (Lindau, Leitsch, Lundberg, and Jerome, 2006) and can diminish older adults' comfort pursuing romantic relationships (Bender, Burgess, and Barmon, 2017). These issues are further complicated for older adults who identify as LGBTQ. They face stigma and discrimination in health care broadly, not just in discussing sex, and may have had to remain in the closet or go back in the closet as they age (Fredriksen-Goldsen, Jen, Bryan, and Goldsen, 2016; Tester and Wright, 2016).

These barriers to communication about sex also affect older adults who live in long-term-care facilities. Our research in assisted-living facilities shows that even when caregivers and family members espouse an ideology supporting sexual freedom, they still act in a variety of ways that inhibit sexual autonomy, including staff seeking permission of family, discouraging interested couples, and limiting privacy (Barmon, Burgess, Bender, and Moorhead, 2017). Perceptions of sexual autonomy are further complicated by concerns about dementia, such as the ability to consent.

Understanding sexuality and older adults requires the same straightforward approach as with any age group. Sex education, access to protection, and ability to consent must be part of the conversation. For example, due to physiological changes as we age, sexual pleasure, functioning, and desire may shift (Syme, 2014). Sex education can introduce new sexual techniques, positions, and aids to enhance sexual pleasure and accommodate physiological change. Additionally, many older adults do not think they are vulnerable to sexually transmitted infections (STIs). Scholars have found that the population of older adults with HIV/AIDS is growing (Lindau et al., 2007; Fritsch, 2005; Poynten, Grulich, and Templeton, 2013), but we know less about other STIs. Lifelong sex education would provide aging individuals with the tools to make healthy decisions about sexual activity. Finally, when some older adults face limitations due to cognitive impairment, families and caregivers should openly confront ethical issues, such as the ability to consent to sex. All these subjects require efforts to achieve comfort communicating about sex across the life course. We will, no doubt, all learn something from the conversation.

NOTE

1. "MILF" (mom I'd like to fuck) is a pop culture slang term popularized by the movie *American Pie* and primarily associated with teenage boys who are lusting after a friend's mom they think is hot (Taormino, 2007). The term "cougar" is a derogatory slang term used to describe middle-aged women who are perceived as predatory and are involved in or interested in relationships with younger men.

REFERENCES

Austad, Steven N. 2006. "Why Women Live Longer Than Men: Sex Differences in Longevity." *Gender Medicine*, 3(2): 79–92. doi: 10.1016/S1550-8579(06)80198-1.

Barmon, Christina. 2016. "Successful Sexual Aging: A Feminist Gerontological Examination of Sexual Behavior and Health." PhD dissertation, Department of Sociology, Georgia State University, Atlanta.

Barmon, Christina, Elisabeth O. Burgess, Alexis A. Bender, and James R. Moorhead Jr. 2016. "Understanding Sexual Freedom and Autonomy in Assisted Living: Discourse of Residents' Rights among Staff and Administrators." *Journals of Gerontology, Series B: Psychological Sciences and Social Sciences*, 72(3): 457–67. doi: 10.1093/geronb/gbw068.

Bender, Alexis A., Elisabeth O. Burgess, and Christina Barmon. "Negotiating the Lack of Intimacy in Assisted Living: Resident Desires, Barriers, and Strategies." *Journal of Applied Gerontology*, forthcoming. doi: 10.1177/0733464817746756.

Bretschneider, Judy, G. and Norma L. McCoy. 1988. "Sexual Interest and Behavior in Healthy 80–102

Year-Olds." *Archives of Sexual Behavior*, 17(2): 109–29. doi: 10.1007/BF01542662.

Burgess, Elisabeth, O. 2004. "Sexuality in Midlife and Later Life Couples." In *The Handbook of Sexuality in Close Relationships*. John H. Harvey, Wenzel A, Sprecher S., eds., Mahwah, NJ: Lawrence Erlbaum Associates Inc. 437–54.

DeLamater, John, and Erica E. Koepsel. 2015. "Relationships and Sexual Expression in Later Life: A Biopsychosocial Perspective." *Sexual and Relationship Therapy*, 30(1): 37–59. doi: 10.1080/14681994.2014.939506.

Fredriksen-Goldsen, K. I., S. Jen, A. E. Bryan, and J. Goldsen. 2016. "Cognitive Impairment, Alzheimer's Disease, and Other Dementias in the Lives of Lesbian, Gay, Bisexual and Transgender (LGBT) Older Adults and Their Caregivers: Needs and Competencies." *Journal of Applied Gerontology*, 1(25). doi:10.1177/0733464816672047.

Fritsch, Teresa. 2005. "HIV/AIDS and the Older Adult: An Exploratory Study of Age Related Differences in Access to Medical and Social Services." *Journal of Applied Gerontology*, 24: 35–54. doi: 10.1177/0733464804271452.

Gott, Merryn, and Sharron Hinchliff. 2003. "How Important Is Sex in Later Life? The Views of Older People." *Social Science and Medicine*, 56: 1617–28. doi: 10.1016/S0277-9536(02)00180-6.

Gott, Merryn, Sharron Hinchliff, and Elisabeth Galena. 2004. "General Practitioner Attitudes to Discussing Sexual Health Issues with Older People." *Social Science and Medicine*, 58: 2093–103. doi: 10.1016/j.socscimed.2003.08.025.

Hughes, Anne K., Ola S. Rostant and Paul G. Curran, 2014. "Improving Sexual Health Communication Between Older Women and Their Providers: How the Integrative Model of Behavioral Prediction Can Help." *Research on Aging* 36(4): 450–66. doi:10.1177/0164027513500055.

Karraker, Amelia, John DeLamater, and Christine R. Schwartz. 2011. "Sexual Frequency Decline from Midlife to Later Life." *The Journals of Gerontology, Series B: Psychological Sciences and Social Sciences*, 66B(4): 502–12. doi: 10.1093/geronb/gbr058.

Lindau, Stacy T., Sara A. Leitsch, Kristina L. Lundberg, and Jessica Jerome 2006. "Older Women's Attitudes, Behavior, and Communication about Sex and HIV: A Community-Based Study." *Journal of Women's Health*, 15: 747–53. doi: 10.1089/jwh.2006.15.747.

Lindau, Stacy T., Philip L. Schumm, Edward O. Laumann, Wendy Levinson, Colm A. O'Muircheartaigh, and Linda J. Waite. 2007. "A Study of Sexuality and Health among Older Adults in the United States." *New England Journal of Medicine*, 357: 762–74. doi: 10.1056/NEJMoa067423.

Poynten, I. Mary, Andrew E. Grulich, and David J. Templeton. 2013. "Sexually Transmitted Infections in Older Populations." *Current Opinion in Infectious Diseases*, 26(1): 80–85. doi: 10.1097/QCO.0b013e 32835c2173.

Syme, Maggie. 2014. "The Evolving Concept of Older Adult Sexual Behavior and Its Benefits." *Generations*, 38(1): 35–41.

Taormino, Tristan. 2007. "The Rise of MILFs and Mommies in Sexual-Fantasy Material." *The Village Voice*, October 30. Retrieved January 26, 2012 from http://www.villagevoice.com/2007-10-30/columns/ the-rise-of-milfs-and-mommies-in-sexual-fantasy- material/.

Tester, G., and E. R. Wright. 2017. "Older Gay Men and Their Support Convoys." *The Journals of Gerontology, Series B: Psychological Sciences and Social Sciences*, 72(3): 488–97. doi: 10.1093/geronb/gbw052.

Twenge, Jean M., Ryne A. Sherman, and Brooke E. Wells. 2017. "Declines in Sexual Frequency among American Adults, 1989–2014." *Archives of Sexual Behavior*, 1–13.

Waite, Linda J., Edward O. Laumann, Aniruddha Das, and L. Philip Schumm. 2009. "Sexuality: Measures of Partnerships, Practices, Attitudes, and Problems in the National Social Life, Health, and Aging Study." *The Journals of Gerontology, Series B: Psychological Sciences and Social Sciences*, 64: i56–66. doi: 10.1093/geronb /gbp038.

A SEXUAL CULTURE FOR DISABLED PEOPLE

TOBIN SIEBERS

Sexuality is not a right which must be earned or a posses-sion that must be purchased, but a state of being acces-sible to all individuals. Even those who sometimes have to fight for that access.

—Lucy Grealy, "In the Realm of the Senses"

The emergence in recent decades of people who define their identities based on sexual preferences and prac-tices is transforming the landscape of minor-ity politics. Sexual minorities are fighting for the rights and privileges accorded to majority populations on many legal and political fronts. The fight over gay marriage is only the most public and contentious of current struggles for full and equal rights by a sexual minority. Pro-ponents of minority sexual identity attack the neat division between the private and public spheres, the relevance of the traditional fam-ily and its institutions of marriage and child-rearing, and the moral certainty that sexuality is better controlled or repressed than set free. Claims that sexuality is a major part of a per-son's identity, that sexual liberation is a good in itself, and that sexual expression is a civil right crucial to human happiness have led to new conceptions of civic life linked to sex. . . .

Disabled people have long struggled to take control of their bodies from medical authorities and to gain access to built environments and public institutions. Like [other] sexual minori-ties, . . . disabled people experience sexual repression, possess little or no sexual autonomy, and tolerate institutional and legal restrictions on their intimate conduct. Moreover, legal and institutional forces inhibit their ability to express their sexuality freely and to develop consensual relationships with sexual partners.

It would be an exaggeration to define the oppression of disabled people exclusively in the sexual context; not many people with dis-abilities consider themselves a sexual minor-ity. Nevertheless, I want to argue that disabled people do constitute a significant sexual minor-ity and that recognizing their status as sexual citizens will advance the cause of other sexually oppressed groups. "Sexuality is often," Anne Finger explains about people with disabilities, "the source of our deepest oppression; it is also often the source of our deepest pain. It's easier for us to talk about—and formulate strategies for changing—discrimination in employment, education, and housing than to talk about our exclusion from sexuality and reproduction" (9). The facets of my argument are multiple, but most of them rely on the power of disability as a critical concept to defamiliarize how we think currently about sex. First, thinking about disabled sexuality broadens the definition of sexual behavior. Second, the sexual experi-ences of disabled people expose with great clarity both the fragile separation between the private and public spheres, as well as the role played by this separation in the history of regu-lating sex. Third, co-thinking sex and disability reveals unacknowledged assumptions about the ability to have sex and how the ideology of ability determines the value of some sexual practices and ideas over others. Finally, the sex-ual history of disabled people makes it possible to theorize patterns of sexual abuse and vic-timization faced by other sexual minorities.

My argument will hinge on what I call the "sexual culture" of people with disabilities. This phrase is meant to set in motion a process of defamiliarization directed at experiences so intimate and unspoken, so familiar and yet mysterious, that few people will discuss them. These experiences are bundled under what is colloquially called a "sex life"—a term I contrast heuristically to "sexual culture." Sexual culture refers to neither gender assignation nor sexual preference, although obviously they are components of sexual being. Sexual culture references the experience of sex itself. By sexual culture, I mean to suggest two ideas about how disabled sexuality disrupts the notion of a sex life: first, sexuality assumes a larger role in the quotidian life of people with disabilities than the usual phrase "sex life" indicates; second, the idea of a sex life is ableist. Being able-bodied assumes the capacity to partition off sexuality as if it were a sector of private life: that an individual *has* sex or a sex life implies a form of private ownership based on the assumption that sexual activity occupies a particular and limited part of life determined by the measure of ability, control, or assertiveness exercised by that individual. People with disabilities do not always have this kind of sex life. On the one hand, the stigma of disability may interfere with having sex. On the other hand, the sexual activities of disabled people do not necessarily follow normative assumptions about what a sex life is. Neither fact means that people with disabilities do not exist as sexual beings. One of the chief stereotypes oppressing disabled people is the myth that they do not experience sexual feelings or that they do not have or want to have sex—in short, that they do not have a sexual culture.

Two cautions must be remarked before I undertake an extended argument about the sexual culture of disabled people. First, the distinction between sex life and sexual culture does not turn exclusively on the issue of privacy. While disabled people sometimes lack privacy for sex,

their situation is not unique. Gay, lesbian, bisexual, queer, and transgendered people also suffer from a lack of sexual privacy, and economic resources may determine whether people have sex in private or public. Crowded housing situations, for example, are as offensive to the conception of private sexual expression as health care facilities. The distinction between sex life and sexual culture relies not on privacy but on access as defined in a disability context: sexual culture increases access for disabled people not only by breaking down the barriers restricting them from sexual locations but also by bringing sexual rights to where they live. Second, the idea of sexual culture strips away what one might call the existential connotations of a sex life. Existentialism posits that identities are constructed by ourselves for ourselves, that all values are subjective, that we are responsible for our choices, and that we are condemned to be free. The notion of sexual culture relies on different presuppositions about identity. I define sexual identities as theory-laden constructions, combining both objective and subjective values, used by individuals to make choices, to test the consequences of their actions, and to explore the possibilities and responsibilities of their sexuality. Sexual culture is designed as a concept to provide a deeper, more sustained idea of how sex and identity interconnect by resisting the partitioning and privatization characteristic of a sex life. It means to liberate sex, allowing it to overflow the boundaries of secured places and to open up greater sexual access for people with disabilities.

NO WALKS ON THE BEACH

I am looking for an intelligent, literate woman for companionship and, perhaps, sexual play. I am, as you see, completely paralyzed, so there will be no walks on the beach.
—Personal ad

Sex always happens somewhere. We go to certain places to fall in love or to have sex.

A sex life, perhaps to our disappointment, tends to occur in the same places—the bedroom, hotels, automobiles, health clubs, baths, and so on. Sex will not happen if we do not have access to such places or if we cannot return to them once we discover that they permit sexual activity. If sex is walking together on the beach, if it is running across a field of flowers to meet in an embrace, what is the nature of sex apart from the ability to walk or to run? If a person's wheelchair gets stuck in the sand or if low vision makes it uncomfortable to dash across a field, does it mean that this person will have little chance of having sex? Clearly, people who do not do these things or go to these places manage to have sex, but that is not exactly the point. The point is to ask how the ideology of ability determines how we think about sex.

The ideology of ability represents the able body as the baseline of humanness. Absence of ability or lesser ability, according to this ideology, marks a person as less than human. The preference for ability permeates nearly every value in human culture, including the ability to have sex. In fact, sex may be the privileged domain of ability. Sex is the action by which most people believe that ability is reproduced, by which humanity supposedly asserts its future, and ability remains the category by which sexual reproduction as such is evaluated. As a result, sex and human ability are both ideologically and inextricably linked. Mark O'Brien recounts a story about the belief that the inability to have sex robs the disabled person of human status:

We watched a movie about disability and sexuality. The movie consisted of four or five able-bodied men joking and laughing about how they once lugged their crippled friend up a flight of stairs to a whorehouse. . . . After the movie, a doctor talked about disability and sexuality. . . . I will always remember his closing line: "You may think you'll never have sex again, but remember . . . some people do become people again." (O'Brien and Kendall, 80)

The doctor is speaking loosely about sex and membership in the human community, but he employs a widespread prejudice used against those who have lost human status along with the ability to have sex. What is it about sex that bestows human status? Barbara Waxman-Fiduccia argues that disability assumes the characteristic of a sexual perversion because disabled people are thought unable to produce "quality offspring" (168–69). It is reproduction, then, that marks sexuality as a privileged index of human ability. In fact, the ideology of ability underlies the imperative to reproduce at many levels, establishing whether an individual supposedly represents a quality human being. First, sex appeal determines the opportunity to have sex. The greater a person's capacity to attract partners, the more opportunities to have sex. Second, a person must be able physically and mentally to have sex. Third, a person must be able to reproduce, to be either virile or fertile. To fail to be able to reproduce is somehow to fail as a human being. Finally, successful reproduction is thought to pass our essential abilities and qualities to our children. The predominant assumption is that what we are will be visited upon our children. If a person does not measure up to society's ideas about ability, that person's opportunities to have sex will be limited. People with disabilities share with gay men and lesbians the suspicion by majority populations that they cannot, will not, or should not contribute to the future of the human race. They will not reproduce, but if they do, the expectation is that the results will be tainted. Social stigma would have little impact on sexual behavior if it were not for the fact that ability represents the supreme measure of human choices, actions, thoughts, and values.

The concept of a sex life encapsulates many of the ways in which the ideology of ability distorts current attitudes about sexuality. At the most superficial level, a sex life is described almost always in the context of health. A sex life must be, first and foremost, a healthy sex life, and the more healthy a person is, the better the sex life is supposed to be. Whence the imperative in today's culture to "work on" one's sex life, to "improve" or "better" it, to do special exercises or adopt a particular diet for it, "to spice it up"—all for the purpose of discovering "the ultimate pleasure." These and other catchphrases attend the commodification of sex as healthy and satisfying, but the connection between a sex life and ability runs deeper than cliché. When disability is linked to sex, it becomes a clinical matter in which each disability betrays a particular limitation of sexual opportunity, growth, or feeling. The literature on sex and disability recites a litany of limitations for each category of impairment. The blind have trouble with sex because it centers supposedly on a visualization of the body as integral whole, and lacking sight, they cannot visualize what a body is (Hamilton, 239). The mobility impaired and paralyzed are apparently cut off from sources of information about sex from peers, and their sexual development remains stunted (Shuttleworth, 265–66). Because of language delays, deaf people are believed to be emotionally and sexually immature, living without the language tools needed to meet the high standards of communication required for sex (Job, 2004, 264, 266). Disabled women are said to tolerate sexism and objectification (Fine and Asch, 29-30). In general, people with disabilities are thought to suffer from distorted body images, considering themselves ugly, and they do not feel at home with typical gender roles.

Because a sex life depends on ability, any departure from sexual norms reads as a disability, disease, or defect. Moreover, the equation runs in the other direction as well: disability signifies sexual limitation, regardless of whether the physical and mental features of a given impairment affect the ability to have sex. . . . Many people in the disability community are still waiting, as Corbett Joan O'Toole explains, to hear a story in which a man or woman who chooses to be lovers with a disabled person is congratulated by family and friends for making a good choice (217). What sea change in current scientific, medical, political, and romantic attitudes would be necessary to represent disabled sexuality as a positive contribution to the future? To reconceive sexuality apart from ability, it would be necessary to imagine the sexual benefit of a given impairment, to claim and celebrate it as a sexual advantage.

PRIVATE PARTS IN PUBLIC PLACES

I was very shy before my accident. Dealing with lots of nurses doing extremely personal things to you—sometimes in front of other people—knocks off your shyness.
                                              —A quadriplegic

If people with disabilities are to develop a sexual culture, they will need to access safe spaces where they may develop new erotic theories and modes of being. A major obstacle to this project is the separation between the private and public spheres and the history of this separation in regulating sexuality in general and disabled sexuality in particular. Feminists identify the private/public split as a source of gender and sexual oppression because it often reifies gender differences and disempowers women. First, men have more power than women to draw the lines between private and public life. Second, men often use this power to maintain or to increase their advantage over women, forcing them into dependency, using privacy to conceal sexual violence, and stifling any attempts by them at political protest. Because the state is reluctant to enter the private sphere, women are imprisoned there, made vulnerable to abuse by domestic partners and given the status of second-class citizens.

Disability studies support the feminist argument that the private/public split is responsible for political oppression, while deepening the perception that privacy is abandoned at a terrible cost. The experience of disabled people with the medical model has been key to this perception. The medical model thrives by sustaining an essential difference between nondisabled and disabled people, defining disability not as a flourishing of biological diversity but as an individual defect that medical professionals cure or eradicate in order to restore a person to the superior state of health required by the ideology of ability. . . .

The presence of disability exposes the fragility of the traditional separation between private and public because economic factors do not obtain for disabled people in expected ways. Medicalization opens privacy to assault, and while economic privilege may make this assault less intrusive, it does not eliminate it. A private room in a hospital, no matter how expensive, is not like a hotel room, although it is leased for a certain period. No "Do Not Disturb" sign, controlled by a patient, will ever hang on the doorknob. Doctors, nurses, aides, and janitorial staff enter and exit at will. Despite the persistent fantasy that doctors, nurses, and nurse assistants provide sexual services, hospital trysts and erotic sponge baths are not part of their job descriptions. In fact, their professionalization hinges on being able to invade privacy while divorcing that invasion from its sexual associations. It may be acceptable, Dominic Davies explains, for a male patient to get an erection when having his penis washed, but "consensual, vigorous washing is seen as forbidden" (183–84). As long as medical staff *act* professionally, they do not consider themselves responsible for sexual side effects, and yet they cross erotic boundaries constantly, with little real regard for the consequences of their actions. Patients in medical institutions do not possess the same rights as non-disabled staff. It is as if sick or disabled individuals surrender the right to privacy in exchange for medical care, even though caregivers work for them. "The difference between

those of us who need attendants and those who don't," Cheryl Marie Wade claims, "is the difference between those who know privacy and those who don't" (88).

Group homes and long-term-care facilities purposefully destroy opportunities for disabled people to find sexual partners or to express their sexuality. Even though inhabitants in group homes pay rent for their rooms, the money buys no functional privacy or right to use personal space. The staff usually does not allow renters to be alone in their room with anyone of sexual interest. Renters are subjected to intense surveillance, their activities entered in the day log. In many care facilities, staff will not allow two people to sit together alone in the same room. Some facilities segregate men and women. Add to these restrictions the fact that many people with disabilities are involuntarily confined in institutions, with no hope of escape, and the enormity of their oppression becomes palpable. The intimate lives of disabled men and women, as O'Toole phrases it, are "monitored, documented and discussed by others" (220). Medical authorities make decisions about access to erotic literature, masturbation, and sexual partners.

The unequal power relations between staff and patients encourage sexual abuse. We are only beginning to gather data on the sexual abuse of people with disabilities, but initial statistics indicate that the incidence of abuse is high (Ward, 2006; 1349), perhaps two to ten times more than the experience of the nondisabled population (Kaufman et al., 2003, 8; Shakespeare, 1999, "Sexual Politics" 63). It is puzzling that paralyzed women are especially vulnerable, given that disabled women are not considered sexually attractive by mainstream society, until a closer look is given to the conditions of abuse. A woman unable to leave her bed is a woman always in bed, and conventionally a bed is a sexual site. Paralysis is also pictured easily as sexual passivity or receptiveness—an invitation to sexual predators, since the erotic imagination thrives on clichéd positions and gestures. . . .

Frequently, . . . abuse is premeditated, representing acts of discipline, payback, or sexual harassment. O'Toole reports that many disabled women experience unacceptable touching by male doctors during medical examinations; they are sometimes publicly stripped and displayed to medical students. These women recount feelings of fear, embarrassment, vulnerability, and shame; they often try to separate themselves from their bodies, pretending that nothing is happening to them.

Personal choice and autonomy are constitutive features of the private sphere, but once subjected to medicalization, individual preference and self-determination evaporate. When the right to privacy and the medical model come into conflict, a new public sphere, controlled by medical figures and supportive of their authority, appears on the horizon. This medical zone of publicness replaces for people with disabilities everything formerly considered private. It engulfs them in an invasive and discriminatory space where they are viewed exclusively as medical subjects and the most casual stranger feels empowered to touch them, to comment on their disabilities, and to offer medical advice or charity. The medical model too often makes of the world a hospital where the disabled are obliged to be perpetual patients and the non-disabled have the right to play doctor.

THE EROTICS OF DISABILITY

Because I am so sensitive to touch, so acutely aware of a breeze on my neck, a ring on my finger, the rib of a sock pressing into my ankle, when I choose to participate in sexual contact, my unusually heightened physicality works for and not against me.
                              —Amy Wilensky, "The Skin I'm In"

As a sexual minority, people with disabilities face many limitations on their intimate behavior and erotic feelings. But, aware of their oppression and defiant of its injustice, they have begun to explore an alternative sexual culture based on the artfulness of disability. The progress has been slow because the fight for access has usually targeted the public sphere. . . . Consequently, we know much more about the public dimension of disability than about its private dimension; we are at the beginning of a period of sexual investigation for disabled people, where information is scarce and ethnography and sharing of practices need to be pursued.

Nevertheless, there are signs that people with disabilities are claiming a sexual culture based on different conceptions of the erotic body, new sexual temporalities, and a variety of gender and sex ed identities. These emerging sexual identities have at least two significant characteristics. First, they represent disability not as a defect that needs to be overcome to have sex but as a complex embodiment that enhances sexual activities and pleasure. Second, they give to sexuality a political dimension that redefines people with disabilities as sexual citizens. It is crucial to understand that sexual citizenship does not translate merely into being able to express sexuality in public—a charge always levied against sexual minorities—but into the right to break free of the unequal treatment of minority sexualities and to create new modes of access for sex. In the case of disabled people, sexual citizenship has particular stakes. Some specific agenda items include access to information about sexuality; freedom of association in institutions and care facilities; demedicalization of disabled sexuality; addressing sexual needs and desires as part of health care; reprofessionalization of caregivers to recognize, not deny, sexuality; and privacy on demand.

While certain aspects of the body are not open to transformation, sexual desire and erotic sensation are remarkably flexible. For example, people with paralysis, who have lost feeling in traditional erogenous zones, have found ways to eroticize other parts of their body. They also develop new ways to please their partners by creating erotic environments adjustable to differently abled bodies. As feminists have made clear, normative sexuality requires a distinctive mapping of the body into limited erogenous zones (Irigaray, 1985). A parallel geography exists between the places on the body marked for sex and the places where bodies have sex. Although it is considered kinky to have sex in out-of-the-way places, it does not usually cross one's mind to summon sexual feelings in places on the body not already demarcated by them. Andrew Vahldieck (1999) adds a particularly vivid and thoughtful account to the literature on sex after spinal cord injury about the erotics of the disabled body:

There's a bumper sticker that proclaims, "Quads Make Better Lovers" and perhaps it's true. One positive by-product of adapting to a disability is having to learn to go with the flow of experience, both mentally and physically. After severe spinal injury, one must begin again, and this includes developing alternate sense faculties. My erotic self need not be solely localized at the tip of my cock, where I've lost much sensation; I have learned that other areas of my body can be erotically sensitive and responsive. Sensation is mobile. My passion, desire and heat can be creatively restrained or refocused on more sensitive areas: ears, lips, neck, shoulders. In doing so, I can transfer sensual feeling into areas where sensation is diminished.

Just as important has been learning to free myself from a preoccupation with my own pleasure. To give myself over to my partner. To slow down, not because I'm disabled and have to, but because I want to. This has proved crucial, paradoxically, to building up my own libidinous momentum. By relaxing into a quiet, tender space while stroking and touching my lover, I can engage vicariously in her enjoyment and stimulation so intensely as to share in her—and expand upon my own—felt pleasure. How curious that pleasing women orally has never been held as a form of manly sexual expression. Speaking as a man labeled "severely disabled," this may truly be considered a high and most subtle erotic art.

Disabled sexuality not only changes the erotics of the body, Vahldieck implies, but also transforms the temporality of lovemaking. For example, in the same way that narrative temporality has a beginning, middle, and end, normative sexuality requires beginning, middle, and end points. This is especially true of penetrative sex. Penetration has a preparatory phase, a period of sustainment, and a climax—all designed to prop up the physiognomy of the penis. One gets it up, gets it in, and keeps it up for as long as possible, until one loses it. Penetrative sex figures as a race against fatigue—a performance with a beginning, middle, and end. It also smacks of the assembly or production line, where part after part is added until the product is finished. The dependence of sex on penetration, incidentally, represents one reason why people tend to partition their sex life from everyday existence. Because the temporal phases of penetrative sex are so indelible, its narrative seems relatively autonomous, and it is easy to think of it as an activity apart from all other facets of life.

Because disabled people sometimes require advanced planning to have sex, their sexual activity tends to be embedded in thinking about the day, not partitioned as a separate event. Among disabled people, the so-called sex act does not always qualify as an action or performance possessing distinct phases such as beginning, middle, and end. Moreover, the myth that sex must be spontaneous to be authentic does not always make sense for people who live with little privacy or whose sexual opportunities depend on making arrangements with personal attendants. Rather, disabled sexuality has an ebb and flow that spreads it out among other activities, and its physiognomy does not necessarily mimic conventional responses of arousal, penetration, or orgasm. "I used to get stuck, needing orgasm, needing penetration, etc.," one woman explains. "Now, my sexuality has matured. . . . For example, one of the greatest highs I get (full-body orgasms? or spiritual-like orgasms?) is from having my neck bit" (Kaufman et al., 2003, 126). Some people without bodily sensation report experiencing mental orgasms when engaged in kissing, verbal play, or sexual fantasy. Others remark that sexual pleasure grows more intense with the advent of disability, owing either to physical changes or to a greater awareness of their body: "Since I became paralyzed in both legs I have noticed that I have varying kinds of orgasms, depending upon the situation. For example, when I play with myself and rub my clit a certain way my orgasms are much more intense. Sometimes my leg will go into spasm and my crotch feels tingly" (Kaufman et al., 2003, 52).

A crucial consideration for people with disabilities is not to judge their sexuality by comparison to normative sexuality but to think expansively and experimentally about what defines sexual experience for them. Sex may have no noticeable physical signs of arousal or may not conclude with an orgasm. When touching is involved, the places being touched may not be recognizable to other people as erogenous zones, which makes sex in public possible and a lot of fun. Sex may extend beyond the limits of endurance for penetrative sex, resembling slow dancing instead of the twist. It may seem kinky by comparison to what other people are doing. According to O'Toole, disabled sex often surprises a person's community, no matter how radical. For example, in Boston in the mid-1990s, Connie Panzarino marched in a gay pride parade with a placard reading, "Trached dykes eat pussy all night without coming up for air" (O'Toole, 2000, 212). That a woman with little movement below the neck could be the active partner in sex and use her disability to enhance her partner's pleasure stunned and shocked people. "This disabled woman," O'Toole notices, "was using her disability as an advertisement for a sexual partner. She was appealing to partners

who like extended oral pleasure. She was turning her apparent severe disability into a distinct sexual advantage" (220–21). O'Toole also mentions an account given by a lesbian amputee about enhancing the pleasure of her partners: "Can I just say that my two leg stumps make fabulous sex toys. I really think my amputated body is tailor-made for lesbian sex: I can crawl on top of my lover and grind my leg into her cunt in ways that I couldn't if I had 'real' legs. Having my little stumps gives me much more freedom of motion and I can get closer, deeper into her that way. Plus, pushing myself into her and away from her and into her again, moving my hips and legs against/on her body is the closest I have come to slow-dancing in years and I love it" (215).

Disabled people may advance a different sexual geography both for the body and for the places where bodies express their sexuality. Just as disabled persons may change places on the body not usually associated with sexual feeling into erogenous zones, they reorganize places inhabited by bodies as locations for sexual culture. . . . As one woman explains it, "if you are a sexually active disabled person, and comfortable with the sexual side of your life, it is remarkable how dull and unimaginative non-disabled people's sex lives appear" (Shakespeare, 2000, 163).

New formations of gender and sex ed identity may be the final frontier of sexual citizenship for people with disabilities. Although present currents on the Left and Right wish to abolish identity entirely, especially identities connected with sickness and perceived weakness, gender and sex ed identities make sexuality present as a mode of being not easily closeted away or partitioned into isolated temporal and spatial segments. Claiming an identity based on sexual culture thrusts one's minority status into the foreground, politicizes it, and creates the opportunity to clarify sexual needs and desires. It also resists the closeting of gender and sexuality central to Western attitudes about sex. It may be especially valuable for people with disabilities to assert sex ed identities, since Western attitudes seem married to the argument that "sex is sick," giving people perceived to be "sick" extra purchase in making counterarguments.

Apart from the urgency of political resistance, it may simply be the case that different identity formations suit people with disabilities better. They often complain that conventional notions of male and female or straight and gay do not apply to them (Shakespeare, 2000, 163), and it is fairly obvious that their sexual practices depart from many of the founding myths of normative sexuality. Disabled people do not embody gender in "natural" ways because gender stereotypes do not allow it. "It's like I don't have any maleness," one disabled man complains (Shuttleworth, 2000, 272). Certain disabilities appear to offer specific gender limitations. Men with cerebral palsy cannot touch or hug their female partners in the ways to which they are accustomed (Shuttleworth, 2000, 269). Blindness changes sexual flirtation from afar between men. But another person puts a positive spin on flexible gender identity: "Why should men be dominant? Why should sex revolve around penetration? Why should sex only involve two people? Why can't disabled people be assisted to have sex by third parties?" (Shakespeare, 2000, 163). O'Toole notes that no lesbian equivalent of the missionary position exists, and that partners are not obliged to have orgasms in the same position at the same time (213). Disabled sexuality embraces a similar flexibility. The sex ed identities of disabled people are of value to all sexually active people, Shakespeare claims, because they allow for a continuum of sexual practices and encourage a greater willingness to embrace diversity, experimentation, and alternative sexual techniques (1999, 58). If we are to liberate disabled sexuality and give to disabled people a sexual culture

of their own, their status as a sexual minority requires the protection of citizenship rights similar to those being claimed by other sexual minorities. The challenge of sexual citizenship for people with disabilities is great because they remain one of the largest unrecognized minority populations; little awareness exists about the manner of their oppression; sex is a taboo subject for everyone and for disabled people in particular; and the unquestioned embrace in most societies of ability as an ideology denies participation in the public sphere to those not deemed quality human beings. Integral to sexual citizenship for people with disabilities is the creation of a safe space with different lines of communication about disabled sexuality; they need in effect to invent a new public sphere receptive to political protest, public discussion, erotic association, and the sharing of ideas about intimate practices and taboos, erotic techniques and restrictions, sexual innovation and mythologies.

In the clash of the culture wars, some people have argued for a monoculture where we abandon all identities except nationality, while other people argue for a multiculture where we embrace many identities—racial, ethnic, gendered, national, and sex ed. The call for a disability culture in general and a sexual disability culture in particular will arouse, no doubt, the anger of the first group and garner, with luck, the support of the second. But the stakes in the emergence of a sexual culture for disabled people are greater than the dispute between these two political factions. The stakes concern questions about fundamental rights expected by all citizens in a democratic society: freedom of association and intimate companionship; authority over their own body; protection from violence, abuse, and oppression; and the right to pursue a sexual future of their own choosing. Because every citizen will become sooner or later a disabled citizen, the struggle of people with disabilities for sexual rights belongs to everyone.

REFERENCES

Davies, Dominic. 2000. "Sharing Our Stories, Empowering Our Lives: Don't Dis Me!" *Sexuality and Disability* 18.3: 179–86.

Fine, Michelle, and Adrienne Asch, eds. 1988. *Women with Disabilities: Essays in Psychology, Culture, and Politics.* Philadelphia: Temple University Press.

Finger, Anne. 1992. "Forbidden Fruit." *New Internationalist* 233: 8–10.

Grealy, Lucy. "In the Realm of the Senses." *Nerve.* 25 October 2001 (http://www.nerve.com/dispatches /Grealy/RealmOfTheSenses/).

Hamilton, Toby. "Sexuality in Deaf Blind Persons." 1979. *Sexuality and Disability* 2.3: 238–46.

Irigaray, Luce. 1985. *This Sex Which Is Not One.* Trans. Catherine Porter. Ithaca: Cornell University Press.

Job, Jennifer. 2004. "Factors Involved in the Ineffective Dissemination of Sexuality Information to Individuals Who Are Deaf or Hard of Hearing." *American Annals of the Deaf* 149.3: 264–73.

Kaufman, Miriam, Cory Silverberg, and Fran Odette. 2003. *The Ultimate Guide to Sex and Disability: For All of Us Who Live with Disabilities, Chronic Pain, and Illness.* San Francisco: Cleis.

O'Brien, Mark, with Gillian Kendall. 2003. *How I Became a Human Being: A Disabled Man's Quest for Independence.* Madison: University of Wisconsin Press.

O'Toole, Corbett Joan. 2000. "The View from Below: Developing a Knowledge Base about an Unknown Population." *Sexuality and Disability* 18.3: 207–24.

Shakespeare, Tom. 1999. "The Sexual Politics of Disabled Masculinity." *Sexuality and Disability* 17.1: 53–64.

———. 2000. "Disabled Sexuality: Toward Rights and Recognition." *Sexuality and Disability* 18.3: 159–66.

Shuttleworth, Russell P. 2000. "The Search for Sexual Intimacy for Men with Cerebral Palsy." *Sexuality and Disability* 18.4: 263–82.

Vahldieck, Andrew. "Uninhibited." *Nerve.* 19 November 1999 (http://www.nerve.com/PersonalEssays/Vahldieck /uninhibited/).

Wade, Cheryl Marie. 1994. "It Ain't Exactly Sexy." *The Ragged Edge: The Disability Experience from the Pages of the First Fifteen Years of the Disability Rag.* Ed. Barrett Shaw. Louisville: Advocado Press. 88–90.

Ward, Amy Paul. 2006. "Rape." *Encyclopedia of Disability.* Ed. Gary L. Albrecht. Thousand Oaks, CA: Sage. 1348–51.

Waxman-Fiduccia, Barbara Faye. 2000. "Current Issues in Sexuality and the Disability Movement." *Sexuality and Disability* 18.3: 167–74.

Wilensky, Amy. "The Skin I'm In." *Nerve.* 24 October 2001 (http://www.nerve.com/PersonalEssays/Wilensky/skin/).

BECOMING A PRACTITIONER: THE BIOPOLITICS OF BDSM

MARGOT WEISS

BDSM is a project, a practice of developing oneself as a skilled practitioner, of learning how to be a practitioner (see Weiss, 2006). Becoming a practitioner takes work on the self: finding the community, attending events, learning techniques and skills, and educating oneself. These practices are forged in relation to the community norms and rules, but—as Foucault emphasizes—it is not a question of complying with the rules, but of transforming oneself through one's own interpretation of the rules. As he argues, the proper use of pleasure, one's self-mastery in relation to pleasure, produces a "solid and stable state of rule of the self over the self" ([1984] 1990, 69; see also 91–92). This rule is less a strict rule of conduct and more about individualizing, moderating, and elaborating conduct, subjecting the self to his own moral mastery. Foucault's understanding of self-mastery in relation to the rules of pleasure is useful here, as SM practitioners also learn to elaborate codes of conduct, to subject themselves to a kind of self-mastery that is supplementary to, rather than in strict compliance with, social and community norms. As Foucault argues, in time, these practices of the self "evolved into procedures, practiced and taught. It thus came to constitute a social practice, giving rise to relationships between individuals, to exchanges and communications, and at times even to institutions" ([1984] 1988, 45). . . . The rules, worked on as part of the labor of becoming an SM practitioner, also produce this particular SM community and the circuits and exchanges it endorses.

Working at BDSM play is also work on the self: it produces and consolidates subjectivities and communities. It is deeply class-inflected, relying not only on the income and time to attend courses and conferences, but also on shared forms of community recognition—education, expertise, and mastery—that are most available to professional-class practitioners. This exclusivity, however, is displaced and obscured in community discourse; these forms of recognition are hegemonic precisely because they construct an ideal, class-restricted community member (the professional practitioner with sufficient means and proper education) toward which other, nonaffluent practitioners aspire. Universalizing ideologies, therefore, normalize such careful work on oneself and one's pleasures. Bailey, a white, heterosexual bottom in her mid-forties, explains that she got into the scene after joining a local SM e-mail list: "I found out about munches [group meals]. I started showing up, and from there I just networked the hell out of it. So I've been active in the public community in the Bay Area going on six years now. Two years ago I did six national events. Last year I probably did four. . . . More-educated people, more-knowledgeable people, more-affluent people tend to be at the national conventions. And I'm like, 'Well, I want to learn more. That's why I'm going.'" Thinking of the rules in this way focuses attention on self-mastery and knowledge as an active practice of modulation, testing, analysis, and self-cultivation.

This form of self-mastery . . . is articulated especially strongly around the rules, especially rules—like Safe, Sane, and Consensual—that require practitioners to forge their own practices of safety. Safe, Sane, and Consensual (SSC) is the mantra of SM in the United States today. Coined in 1983 by David Stein, as part of the statement of purpose of GMSMA (Gay Male S/M Activists), the slogan was popularized across the country and is now widely endorsed by BDSM organizations.[1] . . . Stein notes that the slogan was originally understood to distinguish "defensible" SM, practiced on "willing partners for mutual satisfaction," from "harmful, antisocial, predatory behavior," "the coercive abuse of unwilling victims." Beyond being a motto, however, Safe, Sane, and Consensual has become critical to the social organization of SM; it is the primary way practitioners distinguish between good, safe, acceptable SM and bad, unsafe, unacceptable practice. To ensure that the community of practitioners corresponds to SSC rules, several practices have become standardized; the two largest, most institutionalized are negotiation and using safewords.

Although it is likely that old guard scenes involved some sort of negotiation, today, all BDSM scenes are supposed to involve fairly formal negotiation.[2] Like the infamous Antioch College rules that required explicit and specific verbal consent for every sexual act, negotiation ensures that there will be informed consent throughout the play, and that each player's desires and fantasies will be responded to in the course of the scene.[3] Unlike the Antioch rules, negotiation is supposed to be done before the play, thus requiring anticipatory foresight. During negotiation, one should divulge any emotional, physical, or sexual information that may be important (for example, one should tell one's partner about the child abuse that may crop up and force the scene to end abruptly, or how one's carpal tunnel syndrome might

impact bondage, or that the word *slut* is acceptable, but *whore* is not). One should also explain the kinds of SM play one particularly likes. Finally, one should describe one's limits; the most common limit is "dead people, kids, and shit," although there are many other limits.

SM guidebooks explain how to negotiate with a partner in excruciating detail; Wiseman's *SM 101*, one of the most popular, has a ten-page "long form" for negotiation that lists sixteen categories with spaces so that practitioners can fill in the blanks with their own desires, limits, and protocols. The categories include people involved; place; how long the scene will last; emotional and physical limits; presence and kind of sex and safe-sex procedures; presence and kind of bondage and pain; what, if any, marks can be left; and safewords (Wiseman, 1998, 58–62). Many people rely on verbal negotiation, but many others use these highly formalized checklist negotiation forms to plan a scene.

Similarly, the use of safewords—words like *red* or *safeword* or *pineapple* that are unlikely to come up during a scene—was introduced in the 1970s and has now become a crucial part of contemporary SM. Wiseman recommends having two safewords, "one for 'lighten up' and one for 'stop completely.'" He adds, "I also strongly recommend using the 'two squeezes' technique. If the players will use a gag or a hood, they *must* agree upon nonverbal 'safe signals'" (1998, 62; italics in original).[4] Semipublic play parties almost always have a house safeword, usually *safeword* or *red*. Viewed as a last resort, safewords function as an out for when the scene has gone too far—when it has exceeded the boundaries of either player. Thus, like negotiation, safewords have become an institutionalized procedure of safety.

Many practitioners find this level of planning and negotiation ridiculous. Lady Hilary, for example, explained that "rules now are for safety." "Not that safety's not important, but . . . none of the rules enhance the dynamic. 'Oh, let's over-process how we're going to play. So you want to be spanked five times—okay, fine, but six I can't do.' And then I have to do this, so that's how some people negotiate a scene. It's now lost the tension." Pam, a white, bisexual slave in her fifties, described coming out into the scene in her twenties, when "it wasn't a bunch of negotiation." "I found who he [gesturing to Vince] was as a person and his character and everything else and that was enough to serve him." With the new players, she explained, you sit down and negotiate "an hour and a half for a twenty-minute scene." "And I'm just like . . . 'you're boring the shit out of me.'" Pam is in service to her master Vince, a white, gay man in his mid-forties; they play without safewords or negotiation because, as she explains, "he knows just where I am at every moment, and plus if something does happen that he's not aware of, I can just say it. I don't have to go 'beige' or 'yellow' or 'green' or whatever the hell they're all doing." Vince agrees: "I think that we can think about sex or we can have sex. And so my question and my process has always been 'Is this someone that I can connect with? Can I sense you? Can I feel you?'. . . If that's possible, then I don't really need to negotiate because all I really need to do is pay attention."

Here, practitioners' concern that the more mechanical exercise of negotiation destroys the heart of modern BDSM parallels the mainstream press's response to the Antioch rules. Like the excessive zeal of mandatory bicycle helmet laws, the rules were seen as political correctness gone awry. These critics of both safewords and negotiation argue that by codifying very specific ways of doing SM, the intense connection that SM can create between partners is destroyed, that excessive negotiation will diminish interpersonal intimacy. Taking sex, a practice that is supposed to be spontaneous and magical, and delineating and codifying it seems counterproductive to many. Indeed, this is one of the most common vanilla responses to SM that I hear: how can a scene that is negotiated ahead of time be hot, believable, or fun?

There are two related ways to approach this question. The first is to note the pleasure that inheres in the rules. So, for example, in a front-page news story in the *New York Times* on the Antioch rules, Jane Gross reported that students liked the policy. They thought that talking about sex was erotic, that it was more about setting up "ground rules" than a rigid checklist, and that the policy effectively addressed rape (1993). In this case, negotiation is a practice that carries with it some unintended pleasures: the pleasures of describing one's desires in detail, for example, a pleasure (bound to safety) that many people—especially women who have sex with men—emphasized when contrasting SM sex with vanilla sex. . . . The second approach, which I follow here, is to note that community pressure to be safe, sane, and consensual does not ask practitioners to blindly follow the rules, but rather to negotiate their own relationship to these rules, to define safety and risk for themselves. This work creates a relationship between individual subjects and social norms, a relationship in which one's enactment, disavowal, or disregard of the rules is a form of self-subjugation and self-mastery in accordance with professional-class standards. This provides one way to read SSC SM and the rules as technique, allowing us to see the community debates about the rules and their pleasures as themselves part of the construction of SM practitioners.

For example, many of the BDSM practitioners with whom I spoke agreed that Safe, Sane, and Consensual was a simplistic slogan, but they had varying opinions about its value. Most thought that SSC was a good policy, but that it couldn't really be followed to the letter. Many also felt that it was, as Teramis puts it, "an easy sound bite for newbies to digest . . .

a good tone to strike for the masses," or "created as outreach or propaganda, and I think it's best in that role," in Anton's words. Others liked it for its usefulness in conveying to medical professionals, psychologists, or the police the difference between BDSM and abuse, rape, torture, or violence—as well as between BDSM practitioners and psychopaths.

A few unconditionally liked the phrase. For example, Monique Alexandra—a Latina, bisexual bottom/submissive/masochist in her mid-thirties—thought that the use of negotiation and safewords in the community made her feel comfortable and, more important, safe: "I want things that are exciting, but I want to know I decided to have that done, and that at any point I can say whatever the codeword is and it will stop. . . . Safety is very important to me; I would not play with anyone who has the attitude 'I won't negotiate because it's boring.'" For some, the emphasis on safety reduced the fear that people coming in to the scene may experience, but it didn't make BDSM any less erotic. As Mustang explains: "Safe doesn't mean you're driving around in your Suburban. . . . Some of these people are pretty far out on the edge. . . . It's people doing things safely and yet still getting what they need." For him, community resources, experts on things like "rope or whipping or electricity," and medical doctors and lawyers who are "kink aware," are all aspects of community development "not available ten years ago."[5] This development means that there is "community support to say, 'here's what edge play is, here's what it means, here's the things you need to do, here's what you can't do, and here are the risks you're taking when you do it,' so there's informed consent. I think that's a wonderful thing. . . . It's what saved me."

Yet many people pointed out that there was no way to be truly safe, sane, or even consensual. For example, Chris told me that "we need some way of distinguishing this [SM] from

abuse." "[But] my opinion is also that we've picked the wrong three words. I can't think of any activity . . . that I would wholeheartedly call safe . . . [and] the definition of sanity is actually a legal issue." He continued, half joking: "Now if it were something like informed, consensual, and involving a level of risk that was comparable to, say, everything that everybody on the planet does, I'd be all for that." For this reason, many prefer RACK (risk-aware consensual kink), a term coined by Gary Switch of TES in the late 1990s.[6] Teramis argues: "You can't define for somebody what's safe for them. You can't define if what somebody's doing is sane for them. [What matters is] that I'm aware of the risks, I'm informed, I've given consent, and it's making me happy."

Practice—being "informed," learning the risks, being educated—leads here to less safe, sane, and consensual SM, but this is not surprising. Rather, it is through these community practices of education, classes, orientations, and the like that practitioners take responsibility for their own practices of safety, that they map out their own relationship to the rules. So, for example, Domina and Hayden told me that they play without limits or safewords, as do Jezzie and Anton. Jezzie explained that she initially needed SSC to feel comfortable in the scene, but then she "kind of outgrew it." "Safe, well, what if I knowledgeably want to do something risky? Sane, what the hell does that mean? I mean, I'm in the mental health profession!" For her, SSC is "like training wheels." Once one is a part of this community, having learned social norms through educational structures, one should "outgrow" or cultivate one's own rules.

This is why many, like Annalee—a white, bisexual genderqueer/pervert/voyeur in her early thirties—insisted on their own definition of the terms. Annalee explains: "I'm a fan of consensual sex, however you each consent with your partner. You can each consent like, 'okay, I consent to having you push my boundaries until I say *red*,' which might not be somebody else's definition of safe, sane, and consensual, which would be like, 'we will agree on ten acts to be performed in this order.' I'm not a fan of the 'ten acts in this order.' I just think it's too much to remember. . . . If I'm playing with friends, or partners, we know each other well enough that we can push these limits and [do] whatever the hell we feel like doing. There's a lot of safety built into it, and that's how I define safe, sane, and consensual." All of these debates point to the ways practitioners work with and customize the rules and definitions of safe, sane, consensual, and negotiated. The rules provide a social structure, a scaffolding, within which people cultivate their own ways of being practitioners with—and against—the rules.

RISK AND SOCIAL PRIVILEGE

In a speech critiquing the SSC mantra of contemporary BDSM, Alison Moore argues that "when we invent these sorts of simplistic slogans to differentiate our behavior from nonconsensual violence, what we end up with is often a set of definitions that do not reflect anyone's way of doing SM." She continues: "For me, the whole beauty of SM play is that it doesn't always make sense, that it does take us outside our 'safety zone,' that it is frightening; it taps into the purest essence of sex, which is ultimately chaotic, chthonic, exhilarating, exuberant, a dizzying abyss, an electrifying scream. . . . There is no political slogan to describe this."[7] Moore neatly summarizes the desire that many people have: to have sex that is unsafe. SM sex is already edgy sex, in that it is—to the general public, at least—forbidden, dark, and prohibited. It is also risky, although generally no more physically risky than football, rock climbing, or other sports. Maintaining this allure of the clandestine, outlaw, or dangerous is important to practitioners,

and this is one reason they remain ambivalent about the rules as well as the cultural mainstreaming of SM fashion and, to some degree, practice.

At the same time, practitioners are quick to rely on precisely the binaries established by SSC to assert that SM is not what Stein referred to as "harmful, antisocial, predatory behavior," and what many would call simple, sociopathic sadism. The rules, then, solicit a complex technology: they create a social context within which SM practice is understandable—as sexual and as desirable—and they also demand that individual practitioners chart their own relationship to that edge between safety and risk, control and the "abyss."

Here, risk must be understood as productive and desirable, not merely aversive. This is, in part, a critique of the "risk society" thesis of Anthony Giddens and Ulrich Beck, which—in the words of Merryn Ekberg—suggests that societies like the United States are characterized by a "collective consciousness of anxiety, insecurity, uncertainty and ambivalence" that produces "an ethos of risk avoidance" (2007, 346, 344). As Ekberg puts it in a review essay, these understandings posit the risk society "in contrast to primary, industrial modernity, which was characterized by the safety, security, predictability and permanence of inherited traditions, such as class location, gender roles, marriage, family, lifetime employment and secure retirement." The risk society, however, "is characterized by a dislocation, disintegration and disorientation associated with the vicissitudes of detraditionalization" (346).

Although many scholars agree that risk, anxiety, and security are key discourses in the contemporary United States, this universalizing meta-theory has come under attack [too] . . . (Zaloom, 2004; see also T. Baker and Simon, 2002; Mythen, 2007). First, as Ekberg notes, "communities have not disappeared [due to social dislocation], rather they have reformed around risk and safety. . . . Risk is now the collective bond holding communities together as imaginary risk communities" (2007, 346). Second, imagining a "collective consciousness" of risk aversion "negates the possibility of a risk-seeking culture" (362). The desirability of risk—its pleasure and benefits— is part of this ethos and combines with the community- and subject-producing aspects of risk. . . .

Building and mastering BDSM skills produce new subjects in relation to an evaluative community. The community evaluates one's education, trustworthiness, experience, and skill. So, for example, Bailey explained to me that a DM at a party once stopped her friend: "One of the things he's very good at and he teaches is Japanese rope bondage, in particular suspension bondage. And . . . the last two years in a row they stopped the scene before he [had finished the] suspension because they didn't think he was safe. And if there's anyone I would trust to do that, it would be him. He knows his stuff." Here, trust is based on knowledge and skill, in terms of one's public persona. Waldemar, a white, bisexual mostly top in his early thirties, explains that he has no problem making playdates: "I'm well known, and people trust me and they like what I do." Francesca, a white, bisexual, pain slut bottom in her late forties, explains that if she were playing with a friend, she "could probably take a lot more stressful [forms of play]." "It's a matter of trust, how much do I trust this person? And trust is based on knowledge for me."

Concepts of risk also entail "edgework," or "the personal exploration of the limits of both the context and the individual's ability to control it" (Celsi, Rose, and Leigh, 1993, 16). Here, as Richard Celsi, Randall Rose, and Thomas Leigh note, in an essay exploring the motivations of skydivers, "many high-risk performers learn to like working at the edge of their abilities, 'to push the envelope'" (16). Skydivers want "thrills," but also "high-risk performers seek controllable risk contexts where their abilities can be challenged" so that they can "attain mastery, self-efficacy, and flow" (16). Of course, the edge is not a fixed limit; it changes based on ability, knowledge, experience, and confidence level. Hence risk is not to be avoided but managed; not a static relationship but a boundary of self-improvement and skill.

In SM, edgework might be productively discussed in terms of edge play, a category of play that is physically or psychologically risky or dangerous (see also Henkin and Holiday, 1996, 66). Examples of edge play include suspension bondage, electricity, cutting, piercing, branding, enemas, water sports, scat, breath play, knife play, blood play, gun play, terror play, intense humiliation, race and cultural trauma play, singletails, and fire play— all kinds of play in which the risk of physical or emotional damage is fairly high. Patrick Califia adds to this list mind games, consensual nonconsent, abduction and kidnapping, catheters and sounds, and scarification (2002, 193–215). The management of risk is central to the classification of edge play. Some of these play forms are edge play because they risk unintentional physical harm, such as falling during suspension bondage. Some risk long-term bodily damage, death (for example, heart stoppage with electricity play and suffocation during breath play), disease, or psychological trauma. Yet these definitions are not stable; familiarity changes what counts as risky SM. For example, many participants think play piercing is no longer edge play because so many people do it, and the techniques have become standardized. Single-tail whips, too, became trendy during my fieldwork, and there were many classes on how to throw or crack them correctly; this made the use of singletails at semipublic parties much less edgy. Breath play, on the other hand, is widely prohibited, at least for now.

The desirability of managed risk, in edge play, is an opportunity to fashion oneself as a person with skills and knowledge in relation to SM as a risk community. This is why many people told me that they do breath play, but not *that kind* of breath play. Domina, for example, told me: "I don't do much in the way of breath play. I might put a gas mask on somebody and put my hand over the intake, but I don't believe in breath play because you can kill people doing it."[8] Anthony described a scene in which a woman was encased in Saran Wrap: the top wrapped it around her body, over the top of her head, and finally across her face. The top then "ripped it off [from the roll] and walked away and left her there flopping and struggling for breath, and then finally when the thing [Saran Wrap] started sucking way in [to her mouth], he pops his finger in it." Anthony has adapted this scene for himself, using a latex mask that he rips off just in time. But then, he tells me, "in reality I'm only holding her nose for maybe twenty or thirty seconds; it's not really that long at all. It's not really breath play." For Anthony, the scene had what he termed "symbolic value," but it wasn't "really all that edgy." "I do some knife play, but I don't really slice anybody up. I'll cut a couple layers of epidermis and then blood will pool up on the cut." These practitioners, by claiming that their play isn't *really* dangerous, are actively redefining their practices as manageable—SSC—risk.

Other practitioners enjoy imaginatively violating community standards. There are community jokes and T-shirts that say "unsafe, insane, nonconsensual," an homage to the outlaw quality of SM play. In our interview, Vince explained that he and Pam "play with the edges, we play with that monster." Pam clarified the point: "It's kind of like running a marathon or climbing a mountain, it's like 'Can I do it? Where are my edges? Where do I stop? Where do I start?' . . . If you always stay in your safety zone, how do you know what you can do?" SM

play, for these practitioners, *should* be unsafe, a place where boundaries and limits can be pushed outside of a personal safety zone.

Yet these practitioners also forge an ethical relationship with the self based on techniques, self-mastery, and community norms or rules. Sybil—a white, bisexual dominant/mistress in her mid-fifties—told me: "This whole thing about 'edge play' is a joke. Edge play is not heavy, it's what's heavy to you. So edge play is . . . blood and heavy whipping . . . to some people, [but] that's not all there is to edge play. If you have a phobia of needles, that's edge play. If you're freaked out because you're a woman and I don't want you to wear pink lingerie, that's edge play. Whatever makes you nervous and you don't want to go there, I want to go there 'cause that's where the exchange of power comes from." Sybil's comments show how community rules incite individual or personal responses: the self-cultivation of practice. The point here is not that breath play or edge play is strictly prohibited, thus inciting the desire to do it. Rather, self-mastery as a practitioner requires the production and subsequent personal refinement of community rules.

As Liz Day notes, all the authors in the SM essay collection *Leatherfolk* (Thompson, 1991) claim that SM is transgressive (of nature, culture, materiality, and discourse) because it is "outlaw" (Day, 1994, 243). These essayists, like the practitioners who argue that SM is (or should be, or used to be) outlaw, read the limitations imposed by community rules as a coercive form of disciplinary power, forcing practitioners to choose between replication (obeying SM community rules) or transgression (operating outside of, or in violation of, these rules). Rather, these community debates about edge play, risk, and safety produce knowledges that, in turn, encourage practitioners to position themselves in relation to these rules and thus this ethical community. In edge play, then, pleasure comes from defining and marking the boundaries and limits of what can be done; in policing and enforcing these boundaries in the community and in one's own play; and in mastering the rules—the knowledge, skills, and techniques of self-improvement—that make being a practitioner possible.

Here, risk is not aversive, nor does it stand outside of or serve as an escape from the demands or "constraints of modern social routines" imagined as boring, banal, or routinized (Zaloom, 2004, 365). Although these practitioners—like high-risk hobbyists such as rock climbers and skydivers—imagine their practice as a break from the "real world" that is simultaneously closer to their authentic selves, the management of risk is actually a way of aligning their play selves with "real life." Indeed, imagining a risk community as a break from the real world is . . . a way of bracketing off SM play as a priori "safe" and "fantasy." This bracketing works as an alibi to screen off SM as safe precisely when it is most productive—of selves, communities, and social inequalities.

In this way, rather than a general ethos or collective consciousness, risk functions to produce differentiated subjects. As Bruce Braun writes, white, middle-class people "constitute themselves as middle-class and white precisely through the externalization of as many risks as possible . . . and through barricading themselves from many others. . . . Hence, if you are white and middle-class, 'risk' is something you take on voluntarily, not something you are subject to" (2003, 199). Therefore, he argues, adventure-sport advertisements both construct the "proper" risk-taking subject and naturalize racialized and classed hierarchies (199; see also Simon, 2002). Representations of risk and ability do not passively reflect but rather justify social inequality. In SM, the ability—or desire—to take on a socially constructed risk is one way in which the community is produced as white and middle class, and, cyclically,

continues to appeal to—and produce—these same practitioners. . . .

NOTES

1. David Stein's essay "Safe, Sane, Consensual" was presented in a workshop at the Leather Leadership Conference in Washington, D.C., in April 2000 and is archived at the Leather Leadership Conference website: http://www.leatherleadership.org. An updated version was published in 2002 as "Safe, Sane, Consensual: The Making of a Shibboleth" in *VASM Scene 20* (September/October).

2. This is not to say that all people negotiate; for example, most people in 24/7 (full-time) or M/s relationships do not use safewords or negotiate with each other, although they may use safewords, limits, and negotiation when they play with others. Many people also cease using safewords and negotiation when they know their partner well. For example, Bailey, who is usually a bottom, told me that she decided to top her partner: "It was awesome because I knew him long enough that I knew he didn't want to negotiate. He just wanted it to happen. I wouldn't normally do that with people if I didn't know them really well, but that's the cool part about really knowing your partner. You can make judgment calls like that."

3. The Antioch rules were created in 1992 in response to the crisis of consent in legal and social definitions of rape, especially date rape (see Soble, 1997). Anton reminded me of this link when he said he thought that SSC "has sort of infected the community with . . . this sort of safety-first mentality that I don't agree with at all. . . . There are some people who I think take [it] too far. You have to go through a rigorous checklist before you do anything—you know, this sort of . . . what is that college, the university that put those rules for dating in place where you had to ask people before you could—'May I touch your breast?'" "Antioch?" I asked, and he replied "Antioch, yeah, these sort of Antioch rules for BDSM."

4. "Two squeezes" is a way for a top to check in on a bottom. The top squeezes the bottom's arm or leg twice; if all is well, the bottom gives two squeezes in return. A "safe signal" or "drop safe" is a non-verbal safeword, such as an object that the bottom can drop on the floor.

5. Mustang is referring to an online community service managed by Race Bannon called "Kink Aware Professionals," a list of kink-friendly doctors, therapists, and lawyers across the United States.

6. Gary Switch's essay, "Origin of RACK; RACK vs. SSC," was originally posted on the Eulenspiegel Society's (TES) e-mail list in the late 1990s. An archived version of the post can be found at http://www.leathernroses.com/generalbdsm/garyswitchrack.htm.

7. Alison Moore's speech, "Out of the Safety Zone: Codes of Conduct and Identity in SM Communities," was presented at the Bob Buckley memorial discussion for Sydney Leather Pride Week, April 25, 2002.

8. This is similar to what Califia advises in his section on breath play: "Avoid any activity that may injure or kill someone . . . on the other hand, it's very common for a top to briefly cut off the bottom's air with the palm of their hand. I think this can intensify excitement in a low-risk fashion. So please don't call the S/M police if you see this being done" (2002, 203).

REFERENCES

Baker, Tom, and Jonathan Simon, eds. 2002. *Embracing Risk: The Changing Culture of Insurance and Responsibility.* Chicago: University of Chicago Press.

Braun, Bruce. 2003. "'On the Raggedy Edge of Risk': Articulations of Race and Nature after Biology." In *Race, Nature, and the Politics of Difference,* Donald S. Moore, Anand Pandian, and Jake Kosek, eds., 175–203. Durham: Duke University Press.

Califia, Patrick. 2002. *Sensuous Magic: A Guide to S/M for Adventurous Couples.* Pittsburgh: Cleis.

Celsi, Richard L., Randall L. Rose, Thomas W. Leigh. 1993. "An Exploration of High-Risk Leisure Consumption through Skydiving." *Journal of Consumer Research* 20 (1): 1–23.

Day, Liz. 1994. "'Transgression': The 'Safe Word' in S/M Discourses." *Mattoid* 48: 241–53.

Ekberg, Merryn. 2007. "The Parameters of the Risk Society: A Review and Exploration." *Current Sociology* 55 (3): 343–66.

Foucault, Michel. (1984) 1988. *The Care of the Self.* Vol. 3. *The History of Sexuality.* Translated by Robert Hurley. New York: Vintage.

Gross, Jane. 1993. "Combating Rape on Campus in a Class on Sexual Consent." *New York Times,* September 25.

Henkin, William A., and Sybil Holiday. 1996. *Consensual Sadomasochism: How to Talk about It and How to Do It Safely.* San Francisco: Daedalus.

Mythen, Gabe. 2007. "Reappraising the Risk Society Thesis: Telescopic Sight or Myopic Vision?" *Current Sociology* 55 (6): 793–813.

Simon, Jonathan. 2002. "Taking Risks: Extreme Sports and the Embrace of Risk in Advanced Liberal Societies." In *Embracing Risk: The Changing Culture of Insurance and Responsibility,* Tom Baker and Jonathan Simon, eds., 177–208. Chicago: University of Chicago Press.

Soble, Alan. 1997. "Antioch's 'Sexual Offense Policy': A Philosophical Exploration." *Journal of Social Philosophy* 28 (1): 22–36.

Thompson, Mark, ed. 1991. *Leatherfolk: Radical Sex, People, Politics, and Practice.* Boston: Alyson.

Weiss, Margot. 2006. "Working at Play: BDSM Sexuality in the San Francisco Bay Area." *Anthropologica* 48 (2): 229–45.

Wiseman, Jay. 1998. *SM 101: A Realistic Introduction.* San Francisco: Greenery.

Zaloom, Caitlin. 2004. "The Productive Life of Risk." *Cultural Anthropology* 19 (3): 365–91.

THE PRIVILEGE OF PERVERSITIES: RACE, CLASS, AND EDUCATION AMONG POLYAMORISTS AND KINKSTERS

ELISABETH SHEFF AND CORIE J. HAMMERS

This [reading] focuses on *kinksters*—people involved in "kinky" or "perverted" sexual acts and relationships frequently involving bondage/discipline, dominance/submission and/or sadism/masochism (BDSM, also referred to as sadomasochism), and *polyamorists*—people who engage in openly conducted, multiple-partner, romantic and/or sexual relationships. Popular usage among polyamorists and kinksters indicates that people who identify themselves as kinky are more likely to accept and celebrate the pervert moniker, and polyamorists who do not identify themselves as kinky appear less likely to think of themselves as perverts. Conventional society, however, generally classifies as perverts people who have multiple and concurrent romantic and/or sexual relationships, engage in group sex and/or openly espouse non-monogamy. Polyamorists are thus defined as perverts by the popular imagination, even if they themselves do not identify as such.[1]

Being accused of being a pervert can have detrimental consequences, such as alienation from family and friends (Barker, 2005a; Califia, 2000), harassment (Wright, 2006), loss of a job or custody of a child (Dalton, 2001; Hequembourg, 2007; Klein and Moser, 2006), physical attack (Keres, 1994), public excoriation and incarceration (Attias, 2004; White, 2006). Although everyone involved in "perverted" sex risks social censure, people unprotected by social advantages are more vulnerable to the discriminatory impacts of this sexual stigma than are those shielded by racial and/or class privileges. This insulation provides greater social latitude to engage in and redefine sexual or relational "deviance" than that available to those burdened by racism, poverty, inadequate education, limited job prospects and other forms of discrimination (Collins, 1996, 2005; Sanday, 2007; Steinbugler, 2005). . . .

Scholars are increasingly emphasising the intersections of sexuality with other elements of social stratification (Collins, 1996, 2005; Schippers, 2000; Sharma and Nath, 2005). Disability, (trans)gender, sexual orientation, age—these elements and more—influence the ways in which people choose to, or are able to, express their sexual selves. In this [reading], we focus on race, education and class for three reasons. First, as white, middle-class sexuality researchers, we have attempted to address the implications of the overwhelmingly white populations who participated in our research. Second, race, education and class stand out as important constants in the field, indicating their significance for analysis. Finally, researchers have identified demographic characteristics, and especially race, as important factors impacting sexuality and specifically salient to research on polyamory and BDSM (Haritaworn, Lin, and Klesse, 2006; Langdridge and Barker, 2007). For instance, Willey (2006) and Noël (2006) examined poly discourse and highlighted the ways in which whiteness and class privilege are central to polyamory and those

From "The Privilege of Perversities: Race, Class, and Education Among Polyamorists and Kinksters," *Psychology & Sexuality*, Vol. 2, No. 3, September 2011, pp. 198–223. Copyright © 2011 Routledge, reprinted by permission of the publisher (Taylor & Francis Ltd, http://www.tandfonline.com).

claims that seek to "naturalise" the practice of polyamory. As Willey noted, many feminist poly activists justify polyamory on the grounds that monogamy is unnatural and patriarchal because it works to quell our uncontainable sexual "drives" while being deeply implicated in female subjugation. Yet, this same "liberationist" rhetoric has historically been used to marginalise and stigmatise the poor and people of color for *their* "uncontrollable" urges and *their* inability to conform to the monogamous, nuclear family (white) ideal.

. . . It is our strong belief that in studying only those who are most accessible and visible within poly and BDSM subcultures—those overwhelmingly white and middle class—we fail as researchers to understand alternative mappings of non-monogamous desire and BDSM practices. . . . Our objectives here are multi-fold, and we document the affiliation between polyamory and BDSM; demonstrate through a meta-analysis of extant literature the ways in which research on alternative sexual communities has often (unwittingly) reinforced and (re) constituted a homogenous image of these nonconformist subcultures; support and augment this analysis with our own empirical data; and provide recommendations to improve research methods. By highlighting the race and class privileges that operate throughout these processes, we aim to foster dialogue about the ways in which we as sexuality researchers can mitigate this privilege and its potential impact on our collective research. . . .

COMMUNITY CHARACTERISTICS

Although polyamorous and kinky identities are distinct, the populations practicing them share such a variety of traits and considerable overlap in membership that they warrant joint analysis (Bauer, 2010). . . .

Neither academicians nor community members have achieved consensus on precise definitions of kinkiness or polyamory. In line with other researchers (Barker, 2005a, 2005b; Haritaworn et al., 2006; Weitzman, 2006, 2007), we define polyamory as a form of association in which people openly maintain multiple romantic, sexual and/or effective relationships. Polyamorists use the term *poly* as a noun . . . an adjective . . . , and an umbrella term that includes polyfidelity or relationships based in sexual and emotional fidelity among a group larger than a dyad.

With its emphasis on long-term, emotionally intimate relationships, polyamory differs from the form of swinging based on emotional exclusivity with one partner and sexual non-monogamy with multiple partners. Polyamory is also not adultery: the poly focuses on honesty and (ideally) full disclosure differs markedly from the attempted secrecy definitional to adultery. Both men and women have access to multiple partners in polyamorous relationships, distinguishing them from those that are polygynous or polyandrous. Polyamorists routinely debate the definition of the term, the groups it includes and who is qualified to claim it as an identity.

Kinky people, relationships and communities share many characteristics with polyamorists, with a myriad of potential additional dimensions that can make kink even more complex. Kinksters are people who identify as kinky, frequently including (but not limited to) those who participate in BDSM; have multiple sexual and/or play partners; engage in role-play and/or costuming as part of their sexual behaviour; have fetishes; blend gender characteristics; and/or modify their bodies in conjunction with or to augment their sexual practices. BDSM, the primary umbrella under which many of these identities are encompassed . . . is the practice of consensual exchanges of personal power, including (but not limited to) scripted "scenes" involving some combination of corporal or psychic "punishment," intense physical stimulation (often pain), role-playing and/or fantasy and/or varied sexual interactions (Langdridge and Barker, 2007; Moser and Kleinplatz, 2006a; Weinberg and Kamel, 1995). Among kinksters, definitions of who qualifies as a sexual partner and what counts as a sex act encompass far greater variety than those considered sex acts or partners among "vanilla" (non-kinky) people. Typically, BDSM and poly communities cohere around a specific gender and sexual orientation. For instance, most public play parties are geared specifically toward gay men, lesbians or bisexual/heterosexual people. This is in part due to the origins of the BDSM subculture in the United States, which began as a gay male phenomen[on] that later diverged to include lesbian, heterosexual and bi/pansexual communities (Ridinger, 2002). These various groups tend to self-segregate by sexual orientation and gender, although the growth of virtual and physical kink community has encouraged some amalgamation as well.

Poly and kinky research respondents emphasise negotiation, honesty, consent and personal growth as important components of successful relationships (Sheff, 2005a, 2005b, 2006, 2007, 2010; Barker and Ritchie, 2007; Weitzman, 2006, 2007). Similarly, many of them maintain multiple relationships with varied levels of emotional and sexual intimacy. Kinkiness appears to be a broader base for an identity than polyamory, encompassing a greater range of relationships and types of practices/identities. Many kinky people have multiple partner relationships but do not necessarily primarily identify as polyamorous—the number of people involved in their relationships is but one component among many aspects of kink identity, sexuality and relationships. For some, mostly non-kink poly people, the multiplicity of the relationships determines their status as poly. Those polys who engage in kinky sexual activities are more likely to view sexuality more broadly and numerosity as one, not necessarily the defining, element of their sexual identities. Additionally and more importantly, for the purposes of this [reading], the poly and kinky populations who have participated in research primarily comprise white, well-educated, middle-class professionals. . . .

METHODS

The data for this [reading] come from three sources: our own original research, others' studies of kinksters and polyamorists, and communication with other researchers online. . . .

Original Research

Sheff's longitudinal study of polyamorists has thus far produced two waves of data collected through participant observation, content analysis, Internet research and in-depth interviews. The first portion of the study (*Gender, family, and sexuality: Exploring polyamorous community* 1996–2003) provided the base of 40 in-depth interviews with adults who identified as poly, and extensive participant observation data collected at a wide variety of poly events, including co-ed and women's support groups, potlucks, community meetings and two national conferences. The second wave of data collection (*Polyamorous families study* 2007–[2011]) focuses on polyamorous families with children and includes 15 previous respondents[2] and has expanded the sample to incorporate an additional 41 people, for a . . . total sample of 81 across both studies. Race is the most homogeneous demographic characteristic, with 89 percent of the sample identifying as white. Socio-economic status is high among these respondents, with 74 percent in professional jobs. Fully 88 percent report some college education, with 67 percent attaining bachelor's degrees and 21 percent completing graduate degrees.

Sheff also conducted a study of intersecting sexual identities (*Overlapping identities study* 2005) examining the overlap between polyamorists, swingers, people with fetishes and those who practice BDSM. Of the 64 respondents (31 men, 27 women and 6 others),[3] 31 were involved in BDSM, 19 in polyamory and 6 in swinging. The majority of respondents (58 or 90%) identified as white, with two African Americans, one Filipina, two people of multiracial heritage and one who identified himself simply as "other" also participating. Respondents were also highly educated, with all but three respondents (95%) having completed or currently enrolled in an undergraduate degree, and 48 (75%) of them completing at least some graduate school. All of the 26 respondents who reported fetishes were also involved in BDSM, and the two groups are so intricately involved that distinguishing between them did not provide any useful analysis. Swingers, however, stood out as socially distinct—if racially, economically and educationally similar to the other respondents. They neither identified themselves strongly with the other groups, nor were they identified as integral to a joint identity the way polys and kinksters identified each other. Although there are certainly intersections between polys and swingers (and to a lesser extent kinksters and swingers), these focus groups indicated a much stronger affiliation between polyamorists and kinksters than between either group and swingers.

In her ethnographic research on Canadian lesbian/queer bathhouses (*Bathhouse culture study* 2004), Hammers also found a largely white and well-educated population. Approximately 80 percent of the 33 interview respondents identified as white, with over half attaining either undergraduate or graduate degrees. Although highly educated, most of these women were only marginally middle class (Hammers, 2008). Hammers's current project, which explores the US lesbian/queer BDSM community (2007 to present), has found this population, like the bathhouse subculture, to be a relatively homogenous one. As with the

bathhouse study, data for this BDSM project come from in-depth interviews with lesbian/queer BDSM practitioners/attendees and participant-observation data derived from attendance at a variety of public lesbian/queer/women-only BDSM events in the United States. A total of 40 in-depth interviews with BDSM practitioners and self-identified kinksters have been conducted thus far. Of these, 36 individuals identify as white. Approximately 76 percent reported some university education, with 70 percent having attained a bachelor's degree.

Thus, a major interweaving theme that binds our studies and informs our views on race in the research setting, and the inadequate attention paid to race when it comes to alternative sexual subcultures, comes through at this juncture. We find that these alternative sex publics—which encompass such things as community meetings, national conferences, bathhouse events and public BDSM play parties—are predominantly white. It is this whiteness, we believe, that sexuality scholars must address.

Others' Studies of Kinksters and Polyamorists

To find pertinent studies, we searched in Google Scholar, as well as Sociological Abstracts and Sociological Collection in the Galileo search engine, using the search terms *BDSM*, *sadomasochism*, *kink*, *SM* and *polyamor*. To be eligible for inclusion, studies had to focus on polyamory and/or kinkiness and contain at least some demographic data relevant to the target populations. Both the communities involved in and the literature on kink and BDSM share a core identity built on sadomasochism, so we include them in a single category. Polyamory is one form of non-monogamy, but other forms of non-monogamy (polygyny, infidelity) are so diverse as to lack a similar common foundation. The intersection between swinging and polyamory is complex, ambiguous and common enough to gain its own moniker of "swolly"[4] and clearly warrants further investigation, although space constraints prohibit its inclusion in this analysis.

Communication with Researchers Online

Once we had amassed a list of polyamory and kink studies, we posted our bibliography to PolyResearchers, an online discussion group composed of academicians, journalists, researchers and clinicians dedicated to the discussion of research on polyamory.[5] We asked the membership to review the list to inform us if we had missed any studies. No members were able to identify any missing studies.

The Poly Researchers' list similarly granted us access to many of the researchers whose work we reviewed, allowing us to obtain additional data that were not included in the published pieces. If a published piece did not include demographic data but did include an email address for correspondence, we would contact the investigator(s) and request the additional data. All 12 of the researchers we contacted for more information regarding their studies responded to us with the requested data. . . .

RESULTS OF STUDIES OF KINKSTERS AND POLYAMORISTS

The composite results from these 36 studies (20 of kinksters, 14 of polys and 2 of both) indicate a largely homogeneous universe populated with highly educated, white, middle- and upper-middle-class professionals, confirming numerous researchers' conclusions (Sheff, 2005a, 2005b; Sandnabba, Santtila, Alison, and Nordling, 2002; Spengler, 1977). These studies employed a variety of methods: six used surveys or e-interviews conducted entirely online; four "offline" studies reported relying heavily on the Internet to recruit their samples and for some supplementary data collection; 12 used interviews; one combined interviews and a questionnaire; and 14 used questionnaires distributed in person or through magazines, at organisation/club meetings or at events. Twenty-one of the studies were conducted in the United States, five in Western Europe, two in Australia and one in China. There are three unpublished master's theses and four unpublished dissertations. Sample sizes range from a low of six (Matthews, 2006; Mosher, Levitt, and Manley, 2006) to a high of 6,997 (Brame, 2000) and span over time from Spengler's trailblazing 1977 study of male sadomasochists in Western Germany to Barker and Langdridge's 2010 volume that includes original research on polyamory. The percent of people of color in the sample varies from a low of zero in four studies (Barker and Ritchie, 2007; Cook, 2005; Matthews, 2006; Mosher et al., 2006) to a high of 48 in Tomassilli, Golub, Bimbi, and Parson's (2009) study of lesbians and bisexual women in New York City.

Unique Cases

Some studies contribute to multiple areas or provide qualitative data unsuitable for tables. Taormino's (2008) study of 126 people in "open relationships" includes data on polys and kinksters, with 62 percent identifying as polyamorous or polyfidelitous and 51 percent identifying as kinky. Of the entire sample of 126 people, 82 percent identified as white and 77 percent as middle class or above. As previously discussed, Sheff's *Overlapping identities study* of polyamorists, swingers, kinksters and those with fetishes yielded similar results.

In the sole randomly selected sample of which we are aware, Richters, de Visser, Rissel, Grulich and Smith (2008) surveyed a representative sample of 19,307 residents of Australia aged 16–59 years old and found that 1.8 percent of the sexually active respondents

(2.2 percent of men and 1.3 percent of women) reported being involved in BDSM in the last year. Results also indicate that people involved in BDSM are more likely to have been "non-exclusive in a regular relationship (i.e., had sex with someone else besides their regular partner)" (Richters et al., 2008, p. 1663) in the last 12 months than are people with no involvement in BDSM, confirming the association between non-monogamy and BDSM. The study measured ethnicity through country of birth and language spoken at home, and only 1.3 percent of respondents spoke anything but English in their homes. Although respondents who engaged in BDSM also had higher levels of education, Richters (personal communication, 2009) cautioned that

> my impression is that we cannot be certain whether the apparent high education levels and social class of BDSM people as anecdotally reported is an artifact of self-selection for study. It may be real, which would not be surprising given that BDSM is often highly verbal and symbolic. Nonetheless, our analysis clearly showed that demographic and psychological variables were swamped by the strong differences in sexual interest and breadth of experience/repertoire.

Although this most representative sample finds virtually the same racial, ethnic, class and educational characteristics of the other studies with less-randomly selected samples, the authors note that these select demographic characteristics are overshadowed by the sample's sexual characteristics.

REASONS FOR THESE RESULTS

Although it is quite unlikely that these samples are representative of the actual range of kink and poly people, they are certainly representative of the range of people involved in mainstream poly and kink communities. . . . One plausible rationale is that poly and kinky people hold the same kind of racist views as do others of their social ilk. Living in the United States,

Australia and/or Western Europe would make it virtually impossible for polys and kinksters to escape the pervasive racism and classism endemic in those societies and the accompanying white privilege (or lack thereof) that inflects their lives. In our experiences, poly and kink communities tend to eschew open racism and often support such liberal ideals as equality and celebration of diversity. White privilege, however, generally remains as invisible in these groups as it is in more conventional society, thus becoming the dominant racial paradigm. . . .

Internet Recruitment

Because the Internet serves as a primary tool for sexuality researchers to both engage and recruit target populations (Waskul, 2004), it is no surprise that numerous respondents in these kink and poly studies identify the Internet as a crucial element of their access to sexual non-conformist communities (Sheff, 2005a; Weber, 2002; Weitzman, 2006). The web has profoundly reshaped sexual minorities' communities, identities, networks and communications, and nine of the researchers cited in this [reading] avail themselves of this expanded opportunity by examining poly and kink populations that would have previously been extremely difficult to find, or may in fact not exist, without the Internet. Although it is reasonable to recognise the Internet as an important site of community evolution, it is not sensible to rely so heavily on a single resource that will definitionally provide a limited sample.

Although the Internet has expanded sexual opportunity (for some) and created a virtual world wherein sexual minorities can find affirmation and community (Weinrich, 1997), this technological tool also reproduces (and possibly strengthens) pre-existing inequalities. Initial research indicated that the majority of Internet users were male, overwhelmingly white, middle class and well educated (Warf and Grimes, 1997), with an average income that was twice that of the national average (Kantor and Neubarth, 1996). . . . [R]esearch identifies lingering disparities in computer ownership (Ono and Zavodny, 2003) and use (Chakraborty and Bosman, 2005), which continue to disadvantage people of color (Mossberger, Tolbert, and McNeal, 2008). Internet use and its impacts are complex, however, and measuring access alone is insufficient—researchers must also account for a variety of factors that shape the ways in which people use the Internet (Jackson, Ervin, Gardnera, & Schmitt, 2001; Roderick, 2008). Thus, depending on one's race and class location, the Internet can both enhance and hinder sexual opportunity and sense of belonging for members of unconventional sexual cultures, often reproducing predominately white and relatively affluent alternative sexual communities.

Protections Afforded by Privileges

Although they do not completely insulate people from the risks associated with deviance, race and class privileges can provide buffers to mitigate the myriad potential negative outcomes related to sexual and relational non-conformity. Like other sexual minorities, kinky and poly people have lost jobs, child custody and families' and friends' esteem. Indeed, Pallotta-Chiarolli (2006, p. 51) found that two indigenous Australian children in her study of poly families

[. . .] kept to themselves in order to discourage any intimacy with other children that could lead to discovery and a further reason to harass them, as they were already experiencing ongoing racist harassment. They had also been warned by their parents not to let white teachers know or else they'd be taken away from their family, a theme that was all too real for this family whose own childhoods had been mostly spent in mission homes after being removed from their families as part of Australia's racist and assimilationist policies.

Their family's experiences with racism sensitised them to the need to remain concealed to avoid further racialised persecution.

As groups comprised mainly white people with relatively high socio-economic statuses, mainstream polyamorists' and kinksters' privileges can buffer them from some of the negative impacts people risk when they eschew conventionally sanctioned roles. Respondents' levels of education and occupations indicate that they are generally skilled professionals with careers endowed with greater job security than low-skill, low-paying jobs, where employees are far more easily replaced and often subject to greater surveillance and less autonomy. Courts have repeatedly demonstrated their endorsement of conventional heterosexual families over those with sexual and/or gender nonconforming members (Klein and Moser, 2006; Polikoff, 1993). The intersections of these varied privileges bestow middle-class people with greater freedom to engage in behaviours and relationships that risk social approbation. Coupled with a relative lack of public awareness of polyamory and kinky relationships, these privileges allow some to pass as sexually or relationally conventional when they wish to do so, thus avoiding the consequences that can accompany detection. People in disadvantaged positions are often subject to levels of surveillance that make non-conformity riskier than it would be for others with greater resources. "Perversity" then becomes another luxury more readily available to those who are already members of dominant groups.

Deterrents to Participation

There are a number of factors that can combine to dissuade people of color and those of lower socio-economic status from participating in mainstream poly and kink communities. These include expense, discomfort with being a numerical minority, the potential for discrimination, communities of colors' negative assessments of sexual minorities and issues of identity.

Expense

Scarce funds can deter people with low incomes from participating in some kink and poly community events. Fetish wear, admission to public sex environments such as "dungeons" and "toys" such as floggers can be expensive, selecting out entire categories of people with little discretionary income. This is quite problematic, because 11 of the research samples to which we refer were drawn at least in part from those attending public "play parties" and thus reflect only a portion of the population that is readily accessible—people with Internet access and the privacy to use it, who are involved in groups or organisations and/or willing and able to afford to "play" in public. . . .

Tokenism, Potential Discrimination and Community Rejection of Sexual Minorities

In her study of polyamorists in the Western United States, Sheff's respondents of color cited a number of barriers to participation in poly community events. Yansa, a 29-year-old kink- and poly-identified African American health-care provider, reported acute discomfort when attending a poly pool party in the San Francisco Bay Area. She observed that

I was not sure if they wanted me there. Like I felt like maybe I had walked in on somebody else's thing and I wasn't invited. . . . [There were] 75, 80 naked people in this huge pool and I walked in and everybody just turned and looked . . . and I realized I am the only Black person here. I was the only person in a swimming suit so that could have been another issue, too, like maybe she's lost her way, what is she doing here?

Yansa's discomfort at being the sole Black person at the party was compounded by her unawareness of the community (un)dress code. Although the setting was "clothing optional"

in that people were neither compelled to nor barred from wearing clothing, the norm was universal nudity while in the swimming pool and various stages of undress to full clothing on the pool deck.

Though Yansa's initial discomfort eased as she socialised at that and other parties, she remained uneasy about the increased potential risks she faced for sexual non-conformity. She reported already feeling vulnerable at work because of her race and fearing that being a known polyamorist would mean termination. She described her employers as

[. . .] executives who went to Wharton and Harvard and were Republicans and assholes . . . very, very closed-minded. And I got the impression that they were already not comfortable with me being a person of color. To throw in the other stuff that I did may confirm their stereotypes about Black people or they may have just thought she's the weirdest shit on the planet, I don't trust her. . . . We don't want her on this job anymore, someone may find her out.

Yansa noted several reasons other African Americans had discussed with her for their lack of desire to attend poly or kink community events or identify as polyamorous or kinky. "I've heard from Black folk that they think it's a nasty white person thing to do. And they throw out the whole scenario of slavery[—]you know they raped us and they took our women and impregnated them . . . that any respectable educated cultured Black person in their right mind wouldn't even think about doing something so disgusting." She similarly reported that

I've had Black people in the community tell me that they don't want to feel like the token Black . . . the novelty like the fat girl or the Asian girl. I don't want to feel like people are attracted to me and wanting to play with me or date me because they're trying to figure out something. Like I'm some anthropological experiment or something.

It was not only their fear of objectification and denunciation of past abuses and negative stereotypes that deterred Yansa's compatriots of color from joining the local poly community, but their active rejection of poly or kinky subcultures as white, foreign and potentially corrupt.

Victor, a poly-identified 36-year-old African American therapist, artist and college instructor, was more optimistic. He noted that the poly community in which he socialised was "monochromatic," though he was not sure if that was because of "issues of either privilege or even cultural interest." The whiteness of the setting did not bother him, in part because he had grown up in mostly white neighbourhoods and was thus "acclimated" to white people, and in part because he felt that "people who are interested in really relating with people and good whole truth telling are going to tend to be less racist. . . . I've actually felt a lot of acceptance." Victor pointed out that his socioeconomic status gave him access to a lifestyle that others did not have the freedom to enjoy. "It's sort of privilege related. . . . If you're not worrying about certain things, then you have the privilege or the space to explore alternatives. . . . The freedom to explore polyamory sort of comes from a freedom either financially or just psychologically not having to [struggle to] survive in other ways." Even so, when thinking about mainstream African American communities' possible reactions to polyamory, he noted that "I can imagine being in a room of Black people and them going 'That sounds like crazy white folks, that's some crazy shit.'"

Identity

People of color, already labouring under stigma and racism, might be more reluctant to assume a potentially disadvantageous identity than white or ethnic majority people. Laksha, a 26-year-old African American graduate student and participant in Sheff's *Overlapping*

identities study who identifies as bisexual, poly and "mostly vanilla," asserts that

I think African Americans are much less likely to go into a BDSM setting and think, ok, these are my people, this is my family, and take on that label. It is similar to feminism, in that many African American women have feminist principles and take feminist action and even participate in what some would consider feminist activism, but do not identify with the label. White people can more readily walk into the room and identify with the people, see them as their tribe, because race does not stand out to them, so kink can become their organizing identity. But it is not that easy for African Americans; race always stands out to us in a situation like that.

The disadvantage of a stigmatised identity, coupled with the added weight of racial strain that white or ethnic majorities do not experience, as well as feelings of discomfort or lack of belonging in the setting, can contribute to people of color's reluctance to identify with kink and poly subcultures.

That many who might appear to be poly or kinky by others' definitions do not self-identify as such has important implications for the construction of identities. Although Victor asserted that mainstream African Americans would reject an organised poly identity, he hypothesised that there were ". . . communities of color where there are multipartner relationships going on. I don't know whether they would call it poly or not. Probably not. . . . I think that populations tend to self select." Undoubtedly, there are people who openly maintain non-monogamous relationships or enjoy being spanked during sex, behaviours characteristic of (respectively) poly and kinky relationships, but nonetheless do not identify with those communities.

Equally certain is the existence of people who identify as poly or kinky but do not attend meetings or join groups. Again, it could be that those who feel marginalised or different from the more "visible" members of the poly and kink community will remain outside the very organisations that purportedly represent their ilk. It is also possible that people of color involved in unconventional sexual practices are just as active but more clandestine and maintain their own, more exclusive, list-servs, events and private sexual venues. Precisely how these more underground sexual networks and private play parties might differ from the more visible sexual subcultures requires additional research.

Finally, the (almost all-white) researchers' race could deter people of color from participating in research on kink and polyamory. Hammers's (2008) attempts to interview women of color who chose to participate in lesbian/queer bathhouse culture certainly testify to this issue and the power that inheres within the researcher–interviewee relationship. This power differential is particularly salient when the focus is on sex and non-normative sexual practices. Many of the women of color Hammers approached for her bathhouse study refused to speak to her precisely because she is white. Those people of color who chose to participate in the study often linked the lack of participation by other people of color to the perceived potential predation and appropriation of participants' experiences by the researcher. Only a few women of color agreed to talk to Hammers about their experiences, several of whom expressed concern about other women of color discovering their decision to do so.

RESEARCH STRATEGIES

Past Strategies

. . . Researchers examining kinky and poly populations have dealt with issues of class and race in a variety of ways. Measuring race and class is quite complex even in a single society, and when the research is international it becomes very difficult to establish common meanings indeed. . . . Class status does not necessarily translate directly from income in a single nation, much less internationally: some have middle-class status with little disposable income, and others have money to spend but are not considered middle class. Although education and class can be strongly correlated, some poly or kinky people are highly educated but "underemployed" or work in comparatively low-paid fields of counselling and academia and thus have less disposable income than their level of education might suggest.

Alternately, Bauer (2008, p. 238) questioned the stereotype of

BDSM people being overwhelmingly highly educated and of middle to upper class . . . [because] my sample is rather diverse in this regard. However, some interviewees put forth the idea that high-quality BDSM is only for those whom they perceive to be highly educated, "intelligent" or "classy" individuals, thus endorsing potentially excluding class-based criteria for membership in the community.

Bauer's (2008, p. 238) respondents report that the majority of the play parties they attend were populated primarily by white people and that "the race thing is partly class stuff and it's partly because most of the play parties that I've been to have been organized by white people."

Like class, measuring race presents a myriad of complexities, and researchers took a variety of approaches to this task. Of the reviewed studies, eight ignored the category of race altogether, rendering it virtually irrelevant in its invisibility (e.g. Sandnabba, Santtila, and Nordling, 1999, 2002). The fact that race was left unproblematised indicates that the populations were most likely white. . . . Others (14) collected data on race but refrained from addressing racial issues in their analysis. This lack of discussion indicates that many of these researchers were oblivious to, or actively chose to ignore, the impacts race can have on the construction of sexual identities. Still other researchers have attempted to oversample people of color (e.g., Sheff, 2005a, 2005b,

2006; see also Connolly, 2006; Klesse, 2007, p. 157). Sheff endeavoured to recruit as many respondents of color as possible, interviewed all three people of color in the Midwestern poly community and travelled to the California Bay Area with the explicit intent of increasing sample diversity. Even so, she found the demographic characteristics of the numerous mainstream poly communities in the Bay Area to closely mirror the Midwestern sample. . . .

Some researchers (E. Cook, personal communication, 2007; L. Wolf, personal communication, 2008) did not collect data on race because they perceived it as unrelated to their topic of study. Others intentionally avoided collecting data on race. G. Brame (personal communication, 2007) reported that

I did not set out or want to study what role if any race plays in SM. In part that is because, for economic and socio-political reasons, minorities are under-represented in the Scene. BDSM communities cut across all socio-economic, political lines; but while I suspect just as many minorities engage in kinky sex, . . . they do not tend to join sexual communities in number, the way mainstream white people do, so the population is very heavily skewed towards white. . . .

L. Wolf (personal communication, 2008) . . . pointed out that "racial categories are not readily translatable in international research; they are just not meaningful because there is no continuity or agreed-upon definitions."

The studies we review represent six different countries, and whereas most of them were conducted in the "West," one was completed in Hong Kong (Ho, 2006). Ho's study underlines the complexity of defining race, especially at an international level. As ethnic Chinese living in Hong Kong, Ho's respondents are either 0 percent people of color or 100 percent people of color, depending on the perspective used to judge. In their own social context, they are members of the social majority, and thus would not appropriately be considered people

of color (0%) in a numerical minority sense because the point of reference is the same racial and ethnic group. They would also evade the stigma, social pressures and disadvantages attached to being a "minority" not only numerically, but with the attendant deprivation of social privileges. In the larger discussion in literature, however, Ho's respondents could be classified as 100 percent people of color, because they are all Chinese. In that construction, they are people of color in relationship to the external white measure, rather than their internal measure of majority status.

This begs the question "People of color from whose perspective?" The term *people of color* implies some neutral colorless other to which they are compared—the white perspective that underlies both mainstream poly and kink communities, as well as the research that seeks to understand them. M. Pallotta-Chiarolli (personal communication, 2008) highlighted this linguistic issue and clarified that

in Australia, the respectful term is "indigenous Australians." Indigenous Australians find the term "people of color" offensive, as it doesn't differentiate between their experiences of colonialism, genocide, etc., and the experiences of Africans and others who are migrants and refugees.

Although in the United Kingdom some scholars use Black and Minority Ethnics to describe these populations, *people of color* remains the standard language in the United States. We use it here not only because it is the standard scholarly rhetoric of our academic peers, but more importantly because it is the language our respondents use. Even so, the terminology is difficult and we acknowledge the problematic nature of the term. . . .

Recommended Strategies

There are a number of strategies that scholars can use to deal with these research issues. First and most obviously, we must attend to them. Measuring class and race/ethnicity should be a standard research practice, on par with measuring gender. . . . Sexual value systems and the meanings attached to particular sex acts and arrangements stem from Western, white heteropatriarchal standards of sex/gender normativity. Race is never not related to one's topic of study: race confounds the study of sexuality precisely because of its continued neglect.

Learning to deal with the complexities of measuring race is key to the success of inclusive research and requires a broader discussion of race, nationally and internationally. Scholars can use journals, conferences and online forums to discuss methodological issues and establish greater international communication. On an individual methodological level, researchers can ask respondents to self-identify racially and/or ethnically. When reporting their results, scholars should explain their terms and respondents' social locations to give readers the information necessary to understand respondents' racial and ethnic identities in the context of their own cultures.

Second, scholars studying this area must continue to oversample people of color. This becomes complex, as who is "of color" is difficult to define. . . . This process must be accomplished with sensitivity to avoid the mistakes of previous researchers who, in the process of getting to "know and understand" certain groups, have been guilty of fetishizing "the other" (Probyn, 1993).

Third, researchers in this area must shift their recruitment strategies to include a far broader range of options rather than relying so heavily on the Internet and homogeneous snowball samples (often coordinated through email or other Internet interactions as well). Although these sampling and recruitment methods remain useful, such complete dependence on them produces skewed and monochromatic samples. . . .

Fourth, increasing the number of researchers of color examining these groups could significantly boost participation among kinksters and polyamorists of color. Methodological literature indicates that disadvantaged groups such as people of color (Collins, 1996), lesbians (England, 1994) and women (Gilbert, 1994) may be more open to participate in research conducted by those perceived as members of their own underprivileged group. . . .

Fifth, it is important to understand the reasons why individuals do *not* identify with particular alternative sexual communities, despite participating in behaviours characteristic of those communities. Such an understanding will facilitate a broader examination of the full range of people having kinky sex or multiple partners and the ways in which people select the components of their identities. Furthermore, these studies can illuminate privileges that facilitate or hinder people's associations with particular identities, and the interlocking web of characteristics such as age, gender, race/ethnicity, ability, orientation and experience that shape individuals' sexualities in idiosyncratic ways.

Sixth, researchers should study behaviour as well as identity. Studies that include only people who identify as kinky or poly will miss these potential respondents whose behaviours may match the target population but whose self-identification precludes their participation in the study. This creates a double bind, because researchers must clearly define their sample populations to conduct a coherent analysis. On the one hand, relying on self-identification as a selection criteria has a long tradition in sexualities research (Berenson, 2002; Chung and Katayama, 1996; Golden, 1996; Rust, 2000) in part because it has proven problematic in the past when researchers assigned identities to behaviours and in part because it can be difficult to build a sample when investigating sexual minorities, and seeking people who self-identify and are willing to participate in research is one of the primary ways in which sexuality scholars have been able to conduct their research. On the other hand, relying on self-identification eliminates the category of persons who engage in the behaviour but do not classify it as an organising principle for self-identification, thus missing large sections of the population of practitioners (Savin-Williams, 2005; Vrangalova and Savin-Williams, 2010).

Most importantly, researchers must move beyond simple "bean counting" to an examination of how race impacts the ways in which people "do" sexuality. How does being Black and queer impact sexuality? Asian and gay affect sexual practices? Latina and poly shape identity formations? Native American and kinky affect participation in public organisations? To date, too many studies neglect to address these issues because they begin from a white frame, often fail to problematise race and thus assume a homogenous sample, all despite (potentially) statistically accounting for race.

CONCLUSION

Finally, we must consider that, on some level, there might not be anything to be *done* about the dearth of people of color in samples of sexual minorities. It is possible that polys and kinksters of color are less interested in being studied and potentially less desirous of engaging in public sexual interactions or becoming a member of a group founded on sexual status that might then provide contact with researchers—in effect self-selecting to abstain from community and research involvement. Clearly, attempting to recruit people of color into research samples will provide a far richer analysis of kinky and poly relationships, groups and communities. But is the virtual absence of people of color in these samples so passive—so completely based on exclusion? We think not.

In fact, to assume that the "we" (the almost exclusively white researchers who study alternative sexual communities) can control what "they" (people of color who have unconventional sex lives) do is the ultimate act of hubris. Maybe "they" *elect* not to participate.

This dynamic is obviously far more complex than simple omission or self-selection. It calls into question the meanings of alternative sexualities and those who found their identities upon them. Who is authorised to determine the particular characteristics associated with any specific identity, much less function as the arbiter of those with legitimate claims to assume that identity? How people construct their identities is, to varying degrees, up to them: identity is *inherently* self-defined. To deny that choosing to claim or refraining from claiming a specific sexual identity is a self-directed, socially constructed moment is to deny people of color sexual subjectivity. . . .

Too frequently white researchers approach their studies from a white frame of reference and thus (usually unintentionally) exclude consideration of people of color from the original research design. This initial exclusion then telescopes through the research project to shape the questions researchers ask and the populations they query. Research on poly and kinky populations remains impoverished to the degree that people of color, as well as other social and numerical minorities such as people with disabilities and the aged, are absent from the analyses. There must be more sexuality research, particularly research that is mindful of privilege and intersections of oppression. . . .

NOTES

1. The authors do not claim the right to define others' identities, but rather use the term *pervert* to describe polyamorists both because conventional society views them as such and for theoretical coherency.

2. Because the initial study was not designed to be a longitudinal research project and the institutional review board (IRB) required that [Sheff] destroy all identifying

information, [Sheff] was only able to locate those members of [her] my original sample who retained enough contact with mainstream polyamorous communities to receive the calls for participation in the follow-up study. . . . Of the 17 previous respondents [Sheff] was able to locate, 15 agreed to participate in the follow-up study. Only one of the previous respondents who consented to an interview no longer identified as polyamorous and had started seeking a monogamous relationship.

3. On the questionnaire, there was a line adjacent to the *other* category for self-identification. The responses were so varied that [Sheff] aggregated them into a single category of *other* for ease of discussion.

4. Ken Haslam coined the term "swolly" to denote the intersection between poly and swing behaviours, identities and communities.

5. PolyResearchers is an online discussion group that facilitates research into polyamory by allowing members to share resources, research findings and seek each other's advice. . . .

REFERENCES

Attias, B. 2004. Police free gay slaves: Consent, sexuality, and the law. *Left History*, 10(1): 55–83.

Barker, M. 2005a. On tops, bottoms and ethical sluts: The place of BDSM and polyamory in lesbian and gay psychology. *Lesbian & Gay Psychology Review*, 6(2): 124–29.

Barker, M. 2005b. This is my partner, and this is my . . . partner's partner: Constructing a polyamorous identity in a monogamous world. *Journal of Constructivist Psychology*, 18: 75–88.

Barker, M., and Langdridge, D., eds., 2010. *Understanding non-monogamies*. London: Routledge.

Barker, M., and Ritchie, A. 2007. Hot bi babes and feminist families: Polyamorous women speak out. *Lesbian & Gay Psychology Review*, 8(2): 141–51.

Bauer, R. 2008. Transgressive and transformative gendered sexual practices and white privilege: The case of the dyke/trans/BDSM communities. *Women's Studies Quarterly*, 36(3/4): 233–53.

Bauer, R. 2010. Non-monogamy in queer BDSM communities: Putting the sex back into alternative relationship practices and discourse. In M. Barker and D. Langdridge, eds., *Understanding non-monogamies*. London: Routledge.

Berenson, C. 2002. What's in a name? Bisexual women define their terms. *Journal of Bisexuality*, 2(2/3): 9–21.

Brame, G. 2000. *BDSM/Fetish demographic survey*. Retrieved from http://www.gloriabrame.com/therapy/bdsmsurveyresults.html.

Califia, P. 2000. *Public sex: The culture of radical sex*. San Francisco, CA: Cleis Press.

Chakraborty, J., and Bosman, M. 2005. Measuring the digital divide in the United States: Race, income, and personal computer ownership. *The Professional Geographer*, 5(3): 395–410.

Chung, Y., and Katayama, M. 1996. Assessment of sexual orientation in lesbian/gay/bisexual studies. *Journal of Homosexuality*, 30(4): 49–62.

Collins, P. 1996. *Black feminist thought*. New York, NY: Routledge.

Collins, P. 2005. *Black sexual politics: African Americans, gender, and the new racism*. New York, NY: Routledge.

Connolly, P. 2006. Psychological functioning of bondage/domination/sado-masochism (BDSM) practitioners. *Journal of Psychology & Human Sexuality*, 18(1): 79–120.

Cook, E. 2005. *Commitment in polyamorous relationships* (Unpublished Master of Arts in Liberal Studies [Psychology]). Regis University, Denver, CO. Retrieved from http://www.aphroweb.net/papers/thesis/chapter-4.htm.

Dalton, S. 2001. Protecting our parent–child relationships: Understanding the strengths and weaknesses of second-parent adoption. In M. Bernstein and R. Reimann, eds., *Queer families, queer politics: Challenging culture and the state* (pp. 201–20). New York, NY: Columbia University Press.

England, K. 1994. Getting personal: Reflexivity, positionality, and feminist research. *The Professional Geographer*, 46(1): 80–89.

Gilbert, M. 1994. The politics of location: Doing feminist research at "home." *The Professional Geographer*, 46(1): 90–96.

Golden, C. 1996. What's in a name? Sexual self-identification among women. In R. Savin-Williams and K. Cohen, eds., *The lives of lesbians, gays, and bisexuals: Children to adults* (pp. 229–49). Fort Worth, TX: Harcourt Brace.

Hammers, C. 2004. Queer exclusions and corporeal silences: The promises and limitations of queer in public sexual spaces. In S. Hines and T. Sanger, eds., *Transgender Identities: Towards a social analysis of gender diversity*. London: Routledge.

Hammers, C. 2008. Making space for an agentic sexuality? The examination of a lesbian/queer bathhouse. *Sexualities*, 11(5): 547–72.

Haritaworn, J., Lin, C., and Klesso, C. 2006. Poly/logue: A critical introduction to polyamory. *Sexualities*, 9(5): 515–29.

Hequembourg, A. 2007. *Lesbian motherhood: Stories of becoming*. New York, NY: Routledge.

Ho, P. 2006. The (charmed) circle game: Reflections on sexual hierarchy through multiple sexual relationships. *Sexualities*, 9(5): 547–64.

Jackson, L., Ervin, K., Gardnera, P., and Schmitt, N. 2001. The racial digital divide: Motivational, affective, and cognitive correlates of Internet use. *Journal of Applied Social Psychology*, 31(10): 2019–46.

Kantor, A., and Neubarth, M. 1996. Off the charts: The internet. *Internet World*, 7(12): 44–51.

Keres, J. 1994. Violence against S/M women within the Lesbian community: A nationwide survey. *Female trouble*. National Coalition for Sexual Freedom. Retrieved from http://www.ncsfreedom.org/index.php?option=com _keyword&id=214.

Klein, M., and Moser, C. 2006. SM (sadomasochistic) interests in a child custody proceeding. *Journal of Homosexuality*, 50: 233–42.

Klesse, C. 2007. *The specter of promiscuity: Gay male and bisexual non-monogamies and polyamories*. London: Ashgate Publishers.

Langridge, D., and Barker, M. 2007. Situating sadomasochism. In L. Darren and B. Meg, eds., *Safe, sane and consensual*. New York, NY: Palgrave Macmillan.

Matthews, M. 2006. *Lesbians who engage in public bondage, discipline, domination, submission, and sadomasochism (BDSM)*. Ann Arbor, MI: ProQuest Company.

Moser, C., and Kleinplatz, P. 2006a. Introduction: The state of our knowledge on SM. *Journal of Homosexuality*, 50: 2–3.

Moser, C., and Kleinplatz, P. 2006b. *Sadomasochism: Powerful pleasures*. New York, NY: Routledge.

Mosher, C., Levitt, H., and Manley, E. 2006. Layers of leather. *Journal of Homosexuality*, 51(3): 93–123.

Mossberger, K., Tolbert, J., and McNeal, R. 2008. *Digital citizenship: The Internet, society, and participation*. Cambridge, MA: MIT Press.

Noel, M. 2006. Progressive polyamory: Considering issues of diversity. *Sexualities*, 9(5): 602–20.

Ono, H., and Zavodny, M. 2003. Race, Internet usage and e-commerce. *The Review of Black Political Economy*, 30(Winter): 7–22.

Pallotta-Chiarolli, M. 2006. Polyparents having children, raising children, schooling children. *Lesbian & Gay Psychology Review*, 7(1): 48–53.

Polikoff, N. 1993. We will get what we ask for: Why legalizing gay and lesbian marriage will not dismantle the legal structure of gender in every marriage. *Virginia Law Review*, 79(7): 1535–50.

Probyn, E. 1993. *Sexing the self: Gendered positions in cultural studies*. New York, NY: Routledge.

Richters, J., de Visser, R., Rissel, C., Grulich, A., and Smith, A. 2008. Demographic and psychosocial features of participants in bondage and discipline, "sadomasochism," or dominance and submission (BDSM): Data from a national survey. *The Journal of Sexual Medicine,* 5(7): 1660–68.

Ridinger, R. 2002. Things visible and invisible: The leather archives and museum. *Journal of Homosexuality*, 43, 1–9.

Roderick, G. 2008. The stylisation of internet life? Predictors of Internet leisure patterns using digital

inequality and status group perspectives. *Sociological Research Online*, 13: 5.

Rust, P. C. 2000. Bisexuality: A contemporary paradox for women. *Journal of Social Issues*, 56: 205–21.

Sanday, P. 2007. *Fraternity gang rape: Sex, brotherhood and privilege on campus*. New York, NY: NYU Press.

Sandnabba, N., Santtila, P., Alison, L., and Nordling, N. 2002. Demographics, sexual behaviour, family background and abuse experiences of practitioners of sadomasochistic sex: A review of recent research. *Sexual and Relationship Therapy*, 17(1): 39–55.

Sandnabba, N., Santtila, P., and Nordling, N. 1999. Sexual behavior and social adaptation among sadomasochistically oriented males. *The Journal of Sex Research*, 36(3): 273.

Savin-Williams, R. 2005. *The new gay teenager*. Cambridge, MA: Harvard University Press.

Schippers, M. 2000. The social organization of sexuality and gender in alternative hard rock: An analysis of intersectionality. *Gender and Society*, 14(6): 747–64.

Sharma, J., and Nath, D. 2005. Through the prism of intersectionality: Same-sex sexualities in India. In G. Misra & R. Chandiramani, eds., *Sexuality, gender, and rights: Exploring theory and practice in South and Southeast Asia*. New Delhi: Sage.

Sheff, E. 2005a. *Gender, family, and sexuality: Exploring polyamorous community* (Ph.D. dissertation). University of Colorado at Boulder, Colorado.

Sheff, E. 2005b. Polyamorous women, sexual subjectivity, and power. *Journal of Contemporary Ethnography*, 34(3): 251–83.

Sheff, E. 2006. Poly-hegemonic masculinities. *Sexualities*, 9(5): 621–42.

Sheff, E. 2007. The reluctant polyamorist: Auto-ethnographic research in a sexualized setting. In M. Stombler, D. Baunach, E. Burgess. D. Donnelly, and W. Simonds, eds., *Sex matters: The sexuality and society reader*, 2nd ed. (pp. 111–18). New York: Pearson, Allyn, and Bacon.

Sheff, E. 2010. Strategies in polyamorous parenting. In M. Barker and D. Langdridge, eds., *Understanding non-monogamies* (pp. 169–81). London: Routledge.

Spengler, A. 1977. Manifest sadomasochism of males: Results of an empirical study. *Archives of Sexual Behavior*, 6(6): 441–56.

Steinbugler, A. 2005. Visibility as privilege and danger: Heterosexual and same-sex interracial intimacy in the 21st century. *Sexualities*, 8(4): 425–43.

Taormino, T. 2008. *Opening up: A guide to creating and sustaining open relationships*. San Francisco, CA: Cleis Press.

Tomassilli, J., Golub, S., Bimbi, D., and Parsons, J. 2009. Behind closed doors: An exploration of kinky sexual behaviors in urban lesbian and bisexual women. *The Journal of Sex Research*, 46(5): 438–45.

Vrangalova, Z., and Savin-Williams, R. 2010. Correlates of same-sex sexuality in heterosexually identified young adults. *The Journal of Sex Research*, 47(1): 92–102.

Warf, B., and Grimes, J. 1997. Counterhegemonic discourses and the Internet. *Geographical Review*, 87(2): 259–74.

Waskul, D., ed., 2004. *Net.seXXX: Readings on sex, pornography, and the Internet*. New York, NY: Peter Lang.

Weber, A. 2002. Survey results: Who are we? And other interesting impressions. *Loving More Magazine*, 30: 4.

Weinberg, T., and Kamel, G. 1995. S&M: An introduction to the study of sadomasochism. In T. Weinberg, ed., *S&M: Studies in dominance & submission*. New York, NY: Prometheus Books.

Weinrich, J. D. 1997. Strange bedfellows: Homosexuality, gay liberation and the Internet. *Journal of Sex Education and Therapy*, 22(1): 58–66.

Weitzman, G. 2006. Therapy with clients who are bisexual and polyamorous. *Journal of Bisexuality*, 6(1/2): 137–64.

Weitzman, G. 2007. Counseling bisexuals in polyamorous relationships. In B. Firestein, ed., *Becoming visible: Counseling bisexuals across the lifespan* (pp. 312–35). New York, NY: Columbia University Press.

White, C. 2006. The spanner trials and changing laws on sadomasochism in the UK. In P. Kleinplatz and C. Moser, eds., *Sadomasochism: Powerful pleasures*. New York, NY: Hayworth Press.

Willey. A. 2006. Christian nations, polygamic races, and women's rights: Toward a genealogy of non/monogamy and whiteness. *Sexualities*, 9(5): 530–46.

Wright, S. 2006. Discrimination of SM-identified individuals. *Journal of Homosexuality*, 50(2): 217–31.

7

SEXUAL HEALTH

AN INTERVIEW WITH

HÉCTOR CARRILLO

Héctor Carrillo, PhD, is a professor of sociology and gender and sexuality studies at Northwestern University, where he is also the co-director of the Sexualities Project at Northwestern (SPAN). He is a member of the governing board of the Latina and Latino Studies Program; a faculty associate in the Latin American and Caribbean Studies Program; a faculty affiliate in the Science and Human Culture Program; a faculty affiliate in the Center on Social Disparities and Health (C2S) at the Institute for Policy Research; a faculty affiliate in the Institute for Gender and Sexual Minority Health and Wellbeing; and a member of the Buffett Institute Faculty Advisory Council. He is the author of two books: Pathways of Desire: The Sexual Migration of Mexican Gay Men *(University of Chicago Press, 2017) and* The Night Is Young: Sexuality in Mexico in the Time of AIDS *(University of Chicago Press, 2002). Professor Carrillo is also the author or co-author of articles in publications such as* Sexualities, Global Public Health, Archives of Sexual Behavior, *and* Citizenship Studies. *His recent awards include Faculty Fellow, Alice Kaplan Institute for the Humanities, Northwestern University; Distinguished Teaching Award, Weinberg*

College of Arts and Sciences, Northwestern University; and the Carlos Monsiváis Award–Sexualities Section, Latin American Studies Association (LASA). His areas of interest include sexualities, race and ethnicity, migration, transnationalism, health promotion, and HIV/AIDS.

What led you to begin studying sexuality?

In the late 1980s, I became a staff member at the San Francisco AIDS Foundation, where I was put in charge of creating the Spanish AIDS Hotline for Northern California. This was one of the first services of its kind in the nation. As I began to work on this project, I realized that research on the sexual cultures of Latino/a populations was scarce. The little that was known about Latino/a sexualities often reflected a somewhat stereotypical sense of cultural difference between Latinos and non-Latinos. In the literature that existed at the time, Latinos/as were frequently portrayed as Catholic and traditional, and Latino/a sexualities were assumed to always reflect the values of machismo. I felt that to design more effective HIV prevention programs we needed a more nuanced understanding of Latino/a sexual cultures—one that took into account how Latino/a sexualities were changing and that also considered a range of experiences within Latino/a communities. I decided to obtain a doctoral degree in public health at the University of California, Berkeley, and eventually to become a sexuality researcher.

How do you tell people you study sexuality and how do they react?

My experience is that people generally feel that we need to know more about this topic. People often refer to the fact that sexuality is an issue about which they learned very little in school or while growing up, and they express the view that more sex education is needed. But, of course, there is no consensus about what shape such education should take. There are also people who, upon learning about the kind of research that I do, do not ask me any further questions. Their silence makes me wonder if the topic does not interest them, whether they find it somewhat awkward or embarrassing, whether they see sexuality as a private matter that should not be publicly discussed, or whether they feel (because of conservative values) that sexuality should not be researched.

What do you think is most challenging about studying sexuality?

People often think that sexuality, because it can be such a socially charged topic, is a difficult topic to research. However, precisely because sexuality is often a taboo subject, many people want to discuss it and are willing to share their personal stories in the context of sexuality research projects. What is perhaps more challenging is the broader politics of research and the way in which sexuality research is sometimes used within the so-called culture wars. Conservative social actors who would prefer that our society not learn more about sexuality or sexual diversity see nothing valuable in funding sexuality studies; they thus often strongly oppose any efforts to conduct sexuality research.

Why is sexuality research important? Why is it important to do research on sexual health?

Sex and sexuality occupy an important place in people's lives. They can be an essential source of intimacy and pleasure, and they are powerfully linked to our human sense of connection. However, sexual contact can also result in the transmission of sexually related diseases, and the intimacy associated with sexual interaction can imply a strong emotional component that can result in some emotional vulnerabilities. It is therefore crucial for people to learn how to maximize the positive aspects of their sexualities while minimizing the possible negative ones. That requires that we know more, based on solid research, about sex and sexuality, about our sexual cultures, about our sexual desires, and more generally about how a diversity of people live their sexual lives. More broadly, sexuality also reflects many aspects of how society is organized and vice versa, and thus I find that studying sexuality from a sociological perspective is crucial to understanding our society more generally.

Can you describe some of the findings from your recent research?

My research on Mexican sexualities has revealed that, contrary to what is commonly assumed, there is considerable social change in Mexico in relation to sexuality and sexual cultures. This became evident in my research in Guadalajara, Mexico, during the 1990s, and more recently in the research that I have conducted with Mexican immigrants in California. By focusing on migration, my current research is also showing what happens to Mexican sexualities when they are "on the move." In fact, my study of Mexican gay and bisexual male immigrants has confirmed that for some immigrants, their sexuality and their desire to migrate are tightly linked, as part of a phenomenon that I call "sexual migration"—international migration that is primarily (or at least partially) motivated by sexuality. My research has also revealed that immigrants' sexualities shift some upon arrival in the United States as a result of cross-cultural interaction and participation in new sexual contexts. In this sense, my research further confirms what social scientists have been saying now for decades: that the social context considerably influences how people interpret their sexualities, a conclusion that questions the idea that sexuality reflects purely individual desires. This has also become evident in my research with heterosexually identified men who have sex with men, which is generating new knowledge about how these men, within the social contexts of the United States, make sense of their heterosexual identities and sexual behaviors with men—that is, why they see no contradiction between the two. Instead of being in denial about their sexual desires, as is commonly assumed, these men indeed have developed elaborate logics for why their heterosexual identities accurately describe them. And those logics reflect cultural expectations about men and masculinity.

If you could teach people one thing about sexuality what would it be?
A central message in my classes is that sexuality provides an interesting and helpful window to understand society and how society works. But I also emphasize that studying sexuality from a sociological perspective is helpful for us to realize that our sexualities are socially shaped and reflect not only our individual desires but also the sexual cultures and expectations to which we have been exposed over the course of our lives.

SECONDARY PREVENTION OF SEXUALLY TRANSMITTED INFECTIONS: TREATING THE COUPLE AND COMMUNITY

ADAM SONFIELD

INFECTIONS AND THEIR CONSEQUENCES

There are more than two dozen infections that are today recognized as being transmitted largely or exclusively through sexual contact. U.S. public health authorities, by and large, focus on a limited set of these STIs, according to such factors as how common and contagious they are, how easily they are to detect and treat, and how much impact they may have on the public health.

For a variety of reasons, including because the most common STIs are often or usually asymptomatic, estimates of the incidence (new cases) and prevalence (total existing cases) of most STIs are difficult to make. . . .

Despite their ubiquity, STIs far less commonly have any major, lasting impact on individuals' health. HPV is the clearest example, with several million HPV infections among Americans each year leading to 4,000 cervical cancer deaths. Pap tests are so effective, in fact, that current federal guidelines recommend testing at three-year intervals, rather than what has been the long-time standard of testing every year.

At the other end of the STI spectrum is HIV. AIDS is, despite considerable medical advances, still considered to be ultimately fatal, but early treatment with antiretroviral drugs and other medical and lifestyle interventions (such as quitting smoking and improving diet) can greatly delay the onset of the disease. And with ongoing, high-quality care, HIV-positive Americans can live long lives with minimal symptoms. Current federal guidelines, consequently, recommend routine HIV screening for all Americans, regardless of perceived risk.

Syphilis, too, is important to catch early, because if untreated for years, the infection can ultimately cause irreversible damage to the nervous system and heart, possibly leading to blindness, insanity, paralysis, and death. Because of the severity of the disease and the then-high prevalence of the infection, the discovery that penicillin can cure syphilis completely was a major public health advance in the 1940s, and the U.S. government has since attempted to eliminate the infection in this country.

Somewhere in the middle of this spectrum are chlamydia and gonorrhea. Routine screening for chlamydia among women younger than 26 is widely recommended by the government and medical associations, and is considered a cost-effective, but underutilized, form of preventive health care by the U.S. Preventive Services Task Force because of its ability to reduce rates of pelvic inflammatory disease (PID). Estimates of how often chlamydia (or other infections, including gonorrhea) lead to PID, and of how often PID leads to infertility or other serious complications, vary widely, in large part because it would be unethical to allow an infection to progress untreated. (Indeed, today's ethical standards were developed largely

From "For some sexually transmitted infections, secondary prevention may be primary," *Guttmacher Policy Review*, 2009, 12(2):2–7. Reprinted by permission of the Guttmacher Institute.

in response to the infamous Tuskegee study, which did exactly that for black men infected with syphilis.) Roughly, it appears that 10–40 percent of untreated chlamydia cases will lead to PID and that perhaps 20 percent of women with PID will develop infertility. This progress typically occurs over a matter of years, however, and antibiotic treatment will eliminate the infection and stop the progression of PID. . . .

TREATING THE COUPLE

Screening and treating a woman or man [for STIs] also provides benefits to that patient's partner. Numerous studies have found that people who know that they have HIV or another serious STI are more likely than those without such knowledge to talk with their partners about risk and protection and are less likely to engage in high-risk behavior. And treatment of infected men and women can directly protect their partners against infection—something that is true not only for curable, bacterial infections, but also for many viral infections that can only be suppressed. Recent studies have shown that common drugs to treat and suppress herpes can reduce transmission by half. The findings are even stronger for HIV, with the risk of transmission so low among HIV-positive individuals without detectable viral loads that some experts have begun to argue that condom use may not always be necessary for discordant couples (where one partner is HIV positive and the other, HIV negative).

At the same time, screening and treatment of a patient's partner are also crucial for that original patient to break the cycle of reinfection that is seen commonly among patients with curable infections such as chlamydia and gonorrhea. The need to break this cycle has long been recognized by health care providers, and they have responded in part by making rescreening three months after treatment the standard of care. But going further, by getting the partner to come in for testing and treatment, can be difficult, particularly when the partner is asymptomatic.

Distributing home-based testing kits—at health centers, schools, workplaces, shelters, or via the Internet—is one potential tactic to address this problem, as are educational and communication skills training efforts to help patients convince their partners to come in for testing and treatment. The tactic that has generated by far the most interest in recent years is expedited partner therapy (EPT), in which the original patient's health care provider will provide a supply of or prescription for antibiotics to the partner without an actual diagnosis for the partner. This tactic works best with infections like chlamydia and gonorrhea, where effective single-dose therapies are available to minimize the chance of improper or incomplete treatment. It is not considered appropriate for syphilis, in contrast, because single-dose treatment is not available and because of the frequency of allergies to penicillin, the standard treatment for that infection.

EPT has received public endorsements over the past several years by the Centers for Disease Control and Prevention (CDC), the American Medical Association, and the American Academy of Pediatrics, following several CDC-sponsored studies that found it led to substantial reductions in recurrent infections and, at the same time, saved scarce public health resources. Several studies indicate that even before those endorsements, it was widely, if quietly, practiced by providers across the country. However, the CDC has also highlighted a long list of implementation issues, including the possible presence of other STIs, missed opportunities for counseling, difficulties in obtaining funding or insurance coverage, and legal liability concerns stemming from EPT's sometimes uncertain legal status, including whether providers may treat or write a prescription for someone they have not directly evaluated.

TREATING THE COMMUNITY

The public health response to STIs has traditionally recognized that even treating the couple is not enough. By and large, people's sexual activity typically occurs within a relatively closed network, and epidemiologists have found that the behaviors—especially, having concurrent multiple partners—of even a small fraction of the members of a network can have profound ripple effects. The real-life evidence of these network effects can be seen in the disproportionately high STI rates among men who have sex with men (MSM) and among African Americans. The incidence of HIV and syphilis, for example, is significantly concentrated among MSM, and the rates of many STIs are several times higher among black women and men than among their white counterparts. . . . In both cases, there is a range of reasons for the disparities, including lack of access to health care and persistent discrimination. But the spread of STIs within these communities is fundamentally fueled by the facts that sexual networks among MSM and among African Americans are largely closed, and that a substantial minority of both communities practice high-risk behaviors.

Part of the traditional policy response to this problem has been to promote sex education to change people's behavior regarding multiple partners and condom use, and vaccination for those infections (currently, HPV and Hepatitis B) where that option is available. These efforts have had many well-documented successes and will continue to be central to addressing STIs going forward.

Yet, STI testing and treatment have also long been a central component of public health efforts to reduce STI rates in a community. The tactic of tracing, notifying, and treating the partners of infected patients, for example, was central to the U.S. campaign against gonorrhea, which reduced the prevalence of that infection by three-quarters between the mid-1970s and the mid-1990s. . . . Today, facing limited resources to carry out such a labor-intensive activity, the CDC recommends that public health authorities focus their partner services efforts on syphilis and HIV, and limit their use for other STIs to high-risk cases. In fact, EPT for chlamydia and gonorrhea is in many ways a response to the limited resources available for comprehensive partner services, which include counseling, testing, treatment, and referral services. . . . CDC guidelines emphasize that partner services should be client-centered, confidential, voluntary, nonjudgmental, culturally appropriate, and free. These ideals, however, pose serious challenges, including the potential to spark physical or emotional abuse and legal obligations related to mandatory reporting and the duty to warn against imminent danger.

Ultimately, partner services and related community-based efforts to promote STI testing and treatment can have and have had a substantial impact on STI rates. Part of that success is by identifying and exploiting the same social and sexual networks that help spread STIs in the first place. By identifying the people who are the "hubs" of a network, these efforts can educate them about their STI status and the risks of their behavior, cure or suppress the infection itself, and efficiently identify large numbers of other at-risk members of the network. All of this can have major, positive ripple effects in curbing the spread of STIs within that network.

Moreover, by linking high-risk members of a community with other key government and non-profit services—to reduce substance abuse, prevent violence, provide job training, and improve nutrition and living conditions—treating STIs can also help to address the broader problems in a community. This approach dovetails with an increasing recognition among public health experts that to effectively address STIs in the community, we need to "treat" the community itself. In this "reproductive justice" perspective, STIs are a symptom of broader community problems, from a lack of jobs and housing to high rates of crime and imprisonment to poor health care access and infrastructure.... Many other studies have demonstrated links between high-risk sexual behavior and other high-risk behavior, such as drug use and violence, indicating that they have common root causes.

POLICY AND POLITICS

Advocates, public health experts, and policymakers have all been working to turn the promise of secondary prevention into a reality. Leading the way at the federal level is the CDC's Division of STD Prevention.... [The CDC has pursued] overarching strategic goals that emphasize preventing and reducing disparities in four potential types of STI-related harm: infertility, cancers, adverse pregnancy outcomes, and increased susceptibility to HIV transmission. (The latter two dangers may stem from a wide variety of STIs, some of which—like herpes and trichomoniasis—are otherwise notable mostly as irritants and as sources of psychological distress.)

Screening and treatment for chlamydia—which can be tied to three of those four potential harms—have been an object of particular focus for the CDC and other public health authorities, as well as nonprofit groups like the American Social Health Association (ASHA). For example, in 2008 the CDC helped launch the National Chlamydia Coalition as a way of bringing together provider and consumer groups to increase knowledge of and support for efforts to increase chlamydia screening and treatment. ASHA and other members of the coalition have also pushed to expand programs that provide free or subsidized screening and treatment at safety-net health centers, such as the CDC's antichlamydia Infertility Prevention Program. Fred Wyand, media and communications manager with ASHA, notes that "a key part in breaking the cycle of infection with chlamydia is for all partners to be treated, but this presupposes that individuals (and their health care providers) know their status to begin with. That so many chlamydia infections are asymptomatic underlines the importance of testing, and the need for adherence to screening guidelines."

On a related front, the CDC has worked ... to eliminate the legal confusion surrounding EPT for chlamydia and gonorrhea, partnering with researchers at Georgetown and Johns Hopkins universities to analyze state laws and with the American Bar Association to convince states to clarify and change those laws when necessary. This effort has paid dividends, with nine states adopting new policies ... to allow and encourage EPT, including a high-profile law passed by New York....

State-level advocates for EPT report that strong support from health care provider associations, local health departments, and frontline clinicians has been crucial to gaining legislative support even in conservative areas, such as upstate New York and states like North Dakota and Utah, both of which passed new laws.... High prevalence rates for chlamydia and gonorrhea have also turned heads: According to John Peller, director of government relations at the AIDS Foundation of Chicago, legislation to legalize EPT in Illinois has been boosted by the fact that Chicago's Cook County is "number one in the nation in gonorrhea rates and number two in chlamydia."...

Public health authorities and clinicians in states that have legalized EPT expect it to be a helpful new tool in their toolbox, particularly when partner tracing for many clients is impractical and local health departments are short staffed....

Nevertheless, no one tactic will be a silver bullet in stemming the STI epidemics. Some experts have promoted steps such as expanded coverage of STI screening in private insurance plans and the promotion of home testing kits for various STIs, to remove barriers related to access, embarrassment, and confidentiality. Sarah Stoesz, [president and CEO of Planned Parenthood Minnesota, North Dakota, South Dakota], . . . emphasizes the critical need for additional funding for outreach, education, and treatment. EPT itself is inexpensive, so it is not adding to clinicians' funding problems, but it will take some time for EPT to actually save public dollars by reducing the community's STI rates. "It's easy to pass EPT when there's no need for a budget behind it," she observes, asserting that securing additional state dollars to fight STIs is far more difficult, particularly in the current fiscal environment. . . .

Beyond the ever-present need for funding, advocates describe a need to treat the broader problems in the community. Hard-hit communities in cities like Minneapolis, Chicago, Baltimore, and New York appear to have reached a tipping point because STIs are so widespread. Reversing that trend is possible, but it is considerably more difficult to find and treat infected men and women than it is for STIs to spread. What is needed, says the AIDS Foundation's Peller, is to change the environment: "So many factors contribute to STIs, starting with the lack of access to health care in the community."

STDs at Record High

Centers for Disease Control and Prevention

LATEST U.S. DATA REVEAL THREAT TO MULTIPLE POPULATIONS

More than two million cases of chlamydia, gonorrhea, and syphilis were reported in the United States in 2016, the highest number ever, according to the annual Sexually Transmitted Disease Surveillance Report released [in 2017] by the Centers for Disease Control and Prevention (CDC).

The majority of these new diagnoses (1.6 million) were cases of chlamydia. There were also 470,000 gonorrhea cases and almost 28,000 cases of primary and secondary syphilis—the most infectious stages of the disease. While all three of these STDs can be cured with antibiotics, if left undiagnosed and untreated, they can have serious health consequences, including infertility, life-threatening ectopic pregnancy, stillbirth in infants, and increased risk for HIV transmission.

"Increases in STDs are a clear warning of a growing threat," said Jonathan Mermin, M.D., M.P.H., director of CDC's National Center for HIV/AIDS, Viral Hepatitis, STD, and TB Prevention. "STDs are a persistent enemy, growing in number, and outpacing our ability to respond."

Epidemic Accelerating in Multiple Populations—Impact Growing in Women, Infants, and Gay and Bisexual Men

While young women continue to bear the greatest burden of chlamydia (nearly half of all diagnosed infections), surges in syphilis and gonorrhea are increasingly affecting new populations.

Syphilis rates increased by nearly 18 percent overall from 2015 to 2016. The majority of these cases occur among men—especially gay, bisexual, and other men who have sex with men (MSM). However, there was a 36 percent increase in rates of syphilis among women and a 28 percent increase in syphilis among newborns (congenital syphilis) during this period.

More than 600 cases of congenital syphilis were reported in 2016, which has resulted in more than 40 deaths and severe health complications among newborns. The disease is preventable through routine screening and timely treatment for syphilis among pregnant women.

"Every baby born with syphilis represents a tragic systems failure," said Gail Bolan, director of CDC's Division of STD Prevention. "All it takes is a simple STD test and antibiotic treatment to prevent this enormous heartache and help assure a healthy start for the next generation of Americans."

While gonorrhea increased among men and women in 2016, the steepest increases were seen among men (22 percent). Research suggests that a large share of new gonorrhea cases is occurring among MSM. These trends are particularly alarming in light of the growing threat of drug resistance to the last remaining recommended gonorrhea treatment.

MSM also bear a great syphilis burden. MSM make up a majority of syphilis cases, and half of MSM diagnosed with syphilis were also living with HIV—pointing to the need to integrate STD and HIV prevention and care services.

Essential to Confront Most Urgent Threats, Upgrade Prevention Infrastructure

CDC uses STD surveillance data and other tools to detect and respond to these evolving threats and new challenges, directing resources where they can have the greatest impact. Targeted efforts include:

- Strengthening the congenital syphilis response with focused efforts to improve diagnosis and treatment of pregnant women and ensure prompt treatment of newborns at birth in the ten states hardest hit by congenital syphilis.
- Helping state and local health departments rapidly test for drug-resistant gonorrhea and quickly find and treat affected individuals, as part of the federal government's Combating Antibiotic Resistant Bacteria (CARB) Action Plan.
- Assisting state health departments and health clinics integrate STD prevention into care for people living with HIV.

Maintaining and strengthening core prevention infrastructure is also essential to mounting an effective national response to the STD epidemic. CDC provides support to state and local health departments for disease surveillance, disease investigation, and health promotion. CDC also issues and maintains testing and treatment guidelines for providers so individuals get the most effective care.

Turning back the rise in STDs will require renewed commitment from all players:

- State and local health departments should refocus efforts on STD investigation and clinical service infrastructure for rapid detection and treatment for people living in areas hardest hit by the STD epidemic.
- Providers should make STD screening and timely treatment a standard part of medical care, especially for pregnant women and MSM. They should also try to seamlessly integrate STD screening and treatment into prenatal care and HIV prevention and care services.

- Everyone should talk openly about STDs, get tested regularly, and reduce risk by using condoms or practicing mutual monogamy if sexually active.

"CDC uses its national-level intelligence to detect and respond to STD outbreaks while supporting the nation's on-the-ground workers who are spending each day protecting communities from STDs," Dr. Mermin stressed.

Source: Centers for Disease Control and Prevention, "STDs at Record High, Indicating Urgent Need for Prevention," 2017. https://www.cdc.gov/media/releases/2017/p0926-std-prevention.html.

VENEREAL DISEASE: SIN VERSUS SCIENCE

ELIZABETH FEE

Ways of perceiving and understanding disease are historically constructed. Our social, political, religious, and moral conceptions influence our perceptions of disease, just as do different scientific and medical theories. Indeed, these different elements often cannot be easily separated, as scientists and physicians bring their own cultural ideas to bear in the construction of scientific theories. Because these cultural ideas may be widely shared, their presence within medical and scientific theory may not be readily apparent. Often, such cultural conceptions are more obvious when reviewing medical and scientific theories of the past than they are in contemporary medical practice.[1]

Just as cultural conceptions of disease may be embodied in the framing of scientific theories, so these theories also influence popular perceptions of disease. At times such scientific theories may reinforce, or contradict, other cultural conceptions, such as religious and moral ideas or racial stereotypes.

In the case of the venereal diseases, it is clear that our attitudes embody a fundamental cultural ambivalence: are venereal diseases to be studied and treated from a purely biomedical point of view—are they infectious diseases like any others—or are they to be treated as social, moral, or spiritual afflictions?[2] As the name implies, venereal diseases are inevitably associated with sexuality—and therefore our perceptions of these diseases tend to be entangled with our ideas about the social meanings and moral evaluation of sexual behaviors. In the case of syphilis, a major killer in the first half of the twentieth century, health officials could decide that the true "cause" of syphilis was the microorganism *Treponema pallidum*, or they could define the "underlying cause" as "promiscuous sexual behavior." Each claim focuses on a different part of social reality, and each carries different messages of responsibility and blame. Each is part of a different language in which the disease may be described and defined. The first suggests the primacy of the medical clinic for treating disease; the second, the primacy of moral exhortation.

Throughout the twentieth century struggles have been waged over the meaning and definition of the venereal diseases. At times these diseases have been blanketed in silence, as though they belonged to a "private" realm, not open to public discussion. Wars, however, have tended to make venereal diseases visible, to bring them out of the private sphere and into the center of public policy discussions; this has highlighted the struggles over their proper definition and treatment. In World War I, for example, the American Social Hygiene Association consistently equated venereal disease with immorality, vice, and prostitution.[3] Its members thus tried to close down brothels and taverns, to arrest prostitutes, and to advocate continence and sexual abstinence for the soldiers. The Commission on Training Camp Activities tried to suppress vice and liquor and also to organize "good, clean fun":

sports events, theatrical entertainments and educational programs.[4] The Army, however, quietly issued prophylactic kits to the soldiers and made early treatment after possible exposure compulsory. Any soldier who failed to get treatment could face trial and imprisonment for neglect of duty. . . .

When dealing with major disease problems, we often try to find some social group to "blame" for the infection. During the war, educational materials clearly presented the fighting men as the innocent victims of disease; prostitutes were the guilty spreaders of infection. Indeed, prostitutes were often presented as implicitly working for the enemy against patriotic American soldiers.[5] In many communities prostitutes would be the focus, and often the victims and scapegoats, of the new attention to venereal infections. Prostitutes—the women responsible for the defilement of the heroic American soldier—would be regularly rounded up, arrested, and jailed in the campaign against vice.

The end of the war, however, brought a waning of interest in venereal disease and a return to "normal life," freed of the restrictions and regulations of military necessity. The energetic public discussion of venereal disease again lapsed into a public silence. Prostitutes and their customers were again permitted to operate without much official harassment; health departments quietly collected statistics on venereal disease but avoided publicity on the subject.[6]

This [reading] will examine the subsequent history of venereal disease, and especially syphilis, by focusing on a major industrial city, Baltimore, to see how the struggle between the moral and biomedical views of disease was played out in the context of city politics in the 1930s and 1940s. Although syphilis is no longer a significant public health problem, this account should be useful in helping us to reflect on the . . . problem of AIDS (acquired immune deficiency syndrome) today.

TREATMENT FOR VENEREAL DISEASE: THE PUBLIC HEALTH CLINICS

In Baltimore in the 1920s a great social silence surrounded the problem of syphilis. Since venereal diseases carried such negative social stigma, only a small proportion of cases were ever reported. Deaths from syphilis were often attributed to other causes as physicians endeavored to save patients and their families from possible embarrassment. A social conspiracy of silence resulted: patients did not talk about their diseases, physicians did not report them, the health department did not publicize them, and the newspapers never mentioned them. The diseases were thus largely invisible. Most hospitals and some physicians refused to treat patients with venereal diseases; some physicians specialized in these diseases and made a great deal of money from private patients.[7] Many patients, however, could not afford private medical care.

In the aftermath of the war, the city health department began quietly to treat venereal diseases in its public clinics. The first such clinic, opened in 1922, had 13,000 patient visits in its first year of operation. The clinic population grew so fast that the city soon opened a second clinic, and then a third. These patients, brought to the public clinics through poverty, were recorded in health department files as venereal disease cases. Like all the diseases of the poor, these cases attracted little public attention.

The venereal disease problem in Baltimore was, however, made publicly visible by a survey conducted by the United States Public Health Service in 1931.[8] The survey defined syphilis as a major problem in Baltimore, and as a problem of the black population. The reported "colored" rate was 22 per 1,000 males and 10 per 1,000 women; this contrasted with a reported white rate of 4 per 1,000 men and 1.3 per 1,000 women. Of course, whites were more likely to be seeing private physicians and thus less likely to have their disease reported to the health department. Syphilis, originally perceived as a disease of vice and prostitution, was now a black disease. . . .

THE DEPRESSION: RESTRICTING TREATMENT

During the Depression public clinics became more crowded than ever, with over 84,000 visits in 1932 alone. The city health department, already burdened with tight budgets and increasing health problems of every kind, complained that the hospitals in town were dumping poor patients on the city clinics.[9] . . .

In 1933 the problem of overcrowding became so acute that the city health department decided to treat only patients at the infectious stage of syphilis. They discontinued treatment to any patients who had received sufficient drugs to render them noninfectious to others, even though they had not been cured.[10] . . .

VENEREAL DISEASE AND RACISM

In the 1930s as today, health statistics were gathered by race but not by income. The statistics on venereal diseases confirmed the definition of syphilis as predominantly a black or "colored" problem. In fact almost all infectious diseases were far more prevalent among blacks than whites, reflecting the effects of poverty, poor housing, and overcrowding. . . .

While [Ferdinand] Reinhard [the head of the bureau of venereal diseases] described the black venereal disease problem as an effect of economics and social conditions, most whites saw venereal diseases simply as a question of sexual morality. Blacks were popularly perceived as highly sexual, uninhibited, and promiscuous. . . . White doctors saw blacks as "diseased, debilitated, and debauched," the victims of their own uncontrolled or uncontrollable sexual instincts and impulses.[11] . . . [H]ealth officials were certainly convinced that the main issue was sexual behavior, and they were equally convinced that it was the sexual behavior of the black population that had to be changed.

Since the problem was clearly understood as one of sexual behavior, the city health department began an energetic public education project aimed at changing sexual attitudes—by persuasion or by fear. In 1934 the department directed a new program on sex hygiene at the black population. They gave talks at the Colored Vocational School and the Frederick Douglass High School, and organized exhibits for Negro Health Week and for the National Association of Teachers in Colored Schools. They distributed nearly 14,000 pamphlets on venereal diseases. A "social hygiene motion picture" with the discouraging title *Damaged Lives* played in twenty-three theaters, thus reaching over 65,000 people, one-tenth of Baltimore's adult population.[12]

The main aim of this health propaganda was to stress the dangers of sexual promiscuity, but it also emphasized the need for early detection and treatment of disease. . . . Pamphlets distributed by the Social Hygiene Association and the city health department continued to urge chastity before marriage and sexual fidelity within marriage as the proper solutions to syphilis.

In 1935 syphilis was by far the most prevalent of the communicable diseases occurring in the city, with 5,754 reported cases; the next most prevalent disease was chickenpox—not a disease considered of much importance—with 3,816 reported cases.[13] . . . The facilities for actually treating syphilis were still completely inadequate.

Syphilis deaths were now running at between 110 and 150 per year. As Reinhard complained, "Any other group of diseases scattered throughout the community to this extent would be considered to have taken on epidemic proportions and would be cause for alarm on the part of health authorities."[14] . . .

Reinhard continued for several years to struggle against the partial treatment plan and to advocate extended clinic facilities, sufficient for all syphilis patients, and staffed with black physicians, nurses, and social workers. It seemed, at the time, to be a one-man campaign. Most physicians approved of the fact that the health department was not offering treatment, the proper domain of fee-for-service medicine. Particularly during the Depression years, when many physicians found it difficult to make a living on patient fees, the medical profession was antagonistic to efforts by public health officers to offer free treatments to any patients, whatever their illness.

SYPHILIS AS EVERYONE'S DISEASE: A NATIONAL CAMPAIGN

In 1936 Reinhard's "one-man campaign" against syphilis in Baltimore suddenly became part of a major national effort. Thomas Parran, Surgeon General of the United States Public Health Service, now lent the full weight of his authority to a campaign against venereal diseases. A forceful and dynamic man, Parran decided to break through the wall of silence and make the public confront the magnitude of the problem. To do this, he redefined syphilis as a diseases that struck "innocent" victims: the educated, respectable, white population. . . . Parran called syphilis "the great American Disease" and declared: "we might virtually stamp out this disease were we not hampered by the widespread belief that nice people don't talk about syphilis, that nice people don't have syphills, and that nice people shouldn't do anything about those who *do* have syphilis."[15] Parran's point was that nice people *did* have syphilis; he never tired

of pointing out that respectable physicians, innocent children, and heads of industry were among those infected.[16] . . .

Parran declared that half the victims of syphilis were "innocently infected": "Many cases come from such casual contacts as the use of [a] recently soiled drinking cup, a pipe or cigarette; in receiving services from diseased nursemaids, barber or beauty shop operators, etc., and in giving services such as those of a dentist, doctor or nurse to a diseased person."[17] Syphilis was just another contagious disease, although a highly threatening and dangerous one. The point was to find syphilis cases and to treat them; the state should be obliged to provide treatment, said Parran, and the patient should be obliged to endure it. Syphilis would be the next great plague to go—as soon as the public broke with the old-fashioned and pre-scientific notion that syphilis was "the wages of sin." . . .

[W]hile the city health department was consolidating the new biomedical approach to syphilis, it was suddenly challenged with a resurgent moral crusade against vice and prostitution, led by none other than the redoubtable J. Edgar Hoover.

MEDICAL TREATMENT OR CRUSADE AGAINST VICE?

"Captives Taken in Weekend Drive Against City's White Slave Traffic," declared the headlines of the *Baltimore Sun* on May 17, 1937.[18] . . . The raids generated great excitement and controversy, magnified when local prostitutes implicated a number of high level police officers and at least one state senator in Baltimore's "white slave trade."[19] The local newspapers took delight in reporting the activities of this organized racket, playing up Baltimore as a notorious center of vice and iniquity. . . .

State Senator Raymond E. Kennedy now implied that the city health department, like the police department, was implicitly involved in condoning vice. He demanded that all prostitutes being treated in city clinics be immediately incarcerated. Parran was called to appear as a witness before a Grand Jury investigation. On his arrival in Baltimore, however, Parran managed to turn this into a public relations coup for the health department. He announced a state survey of venereal diseases, suggested that Baltimore follow the successful Swedish model of disease control, including the provision of free drugs, and he declared to enthusiastic mass meetings that Maryland would take the lead in the fight against "social diseases."[20] . . .

Thanks to citywide publicity and political pressure on Mayor Jackson, [the health commissioner, Huntington] Williams was able to expand his budget and open the Druid Hill Health Center for black patients in west Baltimore—the first time that adequate public health facilities had been available in this area of the city.[21]

The city health department now tackled the problem of syphilis in industry. At the time, industrial workers were being fired (or never hired in the first place) if they were found to have positive blood tests for syphilis. Employers fired infected workers on the grounds that they were more likely to be involved in industrial accidents, and thus would increase the costs of workmen's compensation and insurance premiums. The health department started to provide free laboratory blood tests for industrial workers; the test results were kept confidential and those infected were referred for appropriate therapy. The health department followed individual workers to make sure they were receiving treatment but, at least in theory, no worker who accepted treatment could be fired. The fact that no guarantees were offered workers refusing therapy meant, however, that syphilis treatment was essentially made compulsory for industrial workers participating in the plan.[22] . . .

THE IMPACT OF WAR

In the late 1930s there were considerable grounds for optimism that the campaign against the venereal diseases was beginning to show results. The more open public health attitude toward syphilis as a problem of diseases rather than of morality seemed to be successful. . . . The numbers of reported cases of syphilis were decreasing each year, despite increased screening efforts and more effective reporting mechanisms. In 1938, 8,236 new cases were reported; in 1939, 7,509; and in 1940, only 6,213. . . . These records of syphilis incidence and prevalence may have been quite unreliable from an epidemiological point of view, but this was the first time that syphilis rates had even seemed to be declining; it was a natural conclusion that health department efforts were finally showing demonstrable results.

In the midst of this optimism, however, came the prospect of war and, with it, the fear that war mobilization and an influx of 60,000 soldiers would upset all previous gain.[23] In 1941, with the institution of selective service examinations, reported venereal disease rates began to climb. In Baltimore that year, 1.7 percent of the white enlistees had positive blood tests for syphilis, as had 24 percent of the black recruits.[24] Baltimore City won the dubious distinction of having the second highest syphilis rate in the country, second only to Washington, D.C. Baltimore's rate was 101.3 cases per 1,000 men examined, more than twice the national rate.[25] In an effort to justify these statistics, the city health department blamed the situation on the nonwhite population: the relatively high proportion of blacks to whites "explained" why Baltimore had the second highest venereal disease rate among the country's largest cities.[26] . . .

Such justifications were hardly likely to be sufficient for a country at war. With the war mobilization had come renewed national attention to protecting the health and fighting efficiency of the soldiers. As during World War I, the first concern was with the control or suppression of prostitution in the vicinity of army camps and with "social hygiene" rather than treatment programs. The May Act passed by Congress made prostitution a federal offense in the vicinity of military camps. . . .

[T]he Baltimore police seemed determined to prove their dedication to the attack on prostitution. By early 1943 they claimed to have closed most of Baltimore's brothels and to have driven prostitutes from the streets.[27] Police Commissioner [Robert] Stanton demanded statewide legislation to allow police officers to arrest prostitutes and force them to submit to medical examination and, if infected, medical treatment.[28]

Dr. Nels A. Nelson, head of the state venereal disease control program, declared that these arrests of prostitutes and compulsory medical examinations were completely ineffective: only a few prostitutes could be arrested at any one time, and as soon as they were treated and released, they would immediately return to the streets to become reinfected and to continue to spread infection until their next arrest. The only real control of venereal disease, concluded Nelson, depended on the complete "repression of sexual promiscuity."[29] Meanwhile, the reported cases of syphilis were rapidly increasing. In 1942 the selective service records showed that almost 3 percent of the white draftees and over 32 percent of the black soldiers had syphilis.[30] . . . Between 1940 and 1942 new cases of syphilis had almost doubled, from 6,213 to 11,293, and gonorrhea rates were also climbing. . . .

Nelson of the state health department had . . . abandoned the fight against prostitution. He was busily distributing free drugs for syphilis control to private physicians, while he publicly declared the city venereal disease clinics "little more than drug pumping stations in dirty, unattractive quarters."[31] Nelson

told the press he was tired of hearing the VD rate discussed as though it were only a Negro problem: "Negroes are plagued by venereal diseases because of their economic and social position."[32] . . .

The Army was also under attack for failing to organize an effective VD program.[33] Its programs and policies were plagued by contradictions; publicly, it advocated chastity, while privately, it provided prophylactics for the men. . . . The Army finally adopted a pragmatic approach and attempted to reduce the sources of infection as much as possible. The pragmatic approach lacked the fervor of a purity crusade, but tried to steer some middle course between laissez-faire attitudes and moral absolutism.

In Baltimore the new acting directors of the city's venereal disease program, Ralph Sikes and Alexander Novey, shared this pragmatic position. . . . Under their leadership health officers cooperated with the armed services in distributing prophylactic kits throughout the city: in police stations, fire houses, transportation terminals, hospitals, and clinics.[34] Implicitly, the VD control officers had thus accepted the idea that this was a campaign *against* disease, rather than a campaign *for* sexual morality; they concentrated on a fairly mechanical (if effective) approach to prevention while leaving the struggle around prostitution to social hygiene reformers, the police, and the courts.

SEX EDUCATION DURING THE WAR

During the war the city health department and a research group at the Johns Hopkins School of Hygiene and Public Health undertook a daring task—to teach "sex hygiene" in the public schools. They gave talks to groups of high school students (separated by sex), showed plaster models of male and female reproductive systems, and gave simple explanations of "menstruation, conception, pregnancy, nocturnal emissions and masturbation, but omitting intercourse and childbirth."[35] . . .

Having been assured that sex was both exciting and dangerous, students were then given a brief description of male reproductive physiology, ending with a caution against masturbation. Masturbation was not dangerous, students were told, merely unnecessary and possibly habit-forming. . . . A brief description of the female reproductive system was followed by a discussion of morals and ethics, warning of the need for judgment, but avoiding specific advice. . . . Students were urged to discuss their questions with parents and teachers and to read a social hygiene pamphlet on "Growing Up in the World Today."[36]

The third part of the presentation, on venereal diseases, emphasized the dangers of sex. Intimacy brought the germs of syphilis: sexual intercourse was the most threatening, but even kisses could carry disease. The best strategy was to avoid any possible contact with these sexual germs:

They can be caught only from an infected person and therefore, we should avoid intimate contact with an infected person. But we cannot tell by looking at a person whether he or she is infected or not; the answer is to avoid intimate contact with all persons except in marriage. This is the only sure way of avoiding these diseases.[37]

At least for these high school students, the link between sexual morality and venereal disease was clear: sexual intimacy led to syphilis and was therefore to be avoided except in marriage. Why marital sex should be "safe" was never explained, nor was congenital syphilis ever mentioned.

AFTER THE WAR: THE NEW PENICILLIN THERAPY

By the end of World War II, the problem of syphilis was beginning to recede, both in public consciousness and in statistical measures. Part of this was the normal relaxation in the immediate aftermath of war, the return to home and family, the desire for stability, and a reluctance to confront social and sexual problems or to dwell on their existence. Even more important, however, was the success of the new drug, penicillin: at last, venereal diseases could, it seemed, be quickly and effectively treated. Many felt it was only a matter of time before the venereal diseases were finally eliminated with the aid of modern medicine's "miracle cures."

By 1940 the new "miracle drug" penicillin had been discovered and purified: in 1943 it was first used against syphilis, but it was not yet generally available; supplies were still strictly rationed.[38] Soon, it would completely transform the old methods of treating venereal diseases. On December 31, 1944, the Baltimore City Hospitals opened the first Rapid Treatment Center for treating syphilis with penicillin. Penicillin doses for syphilis were given over eight days; since supplies of the drug were then very limited, only cases judged to be highly infectious were sent for "an eight-day cure, or what is for the present considered to be a cure."[39] From all initial reports the new experimental treatment was remarkably effective.

On June 20, 1945, Mayor Theodore R. McKeldin approved a new city ordinance making treatment for venereal diseases compulsory for the first time. Those suspected of having syphilis or gonorrhea were required to take penicillin therapy at the Rapid Treatment Center.[40] Those refusing treatment could be quarantined and isolated in the Baltimore city hospitals. . . .

The ordinance was, however, rarely invoked. Most patients were eager to go to the Rapid Treatment Center when diagnosed. In 1946 nearly 2,000 people with infectious syphilis received treatment; most were reported as completely cured. (Before penicillin, only an estimated 25 percent of patients completed the lengthy treatments considered necessary for a full cure.[41]) In 1947 the *Baltimore Sun* reviewed the city's experience with the new ordinance:

On the basis of this experience (over the last 16 months), it is clear that the protection of the public against persons carrying the disease and refusing to be treated more than outweighs the sacrifice of individual rights by so small a number. . . . Under the circumstances, the enactment of a permanent ordinance seems fully justified.[42]

The state health department in 1947 announced that "for the first time in history any resident of Maryland who contracts syphilis can obtain treatment resulting in prompt and almost certain cure."[43]

CONCLUSION: THE END OF THE STRUGGLE?

The biomedical approach to venereal diseases had apparently been stunningly successful. Diseases that only ten years before had been described as the most serious of all the infectious diseases had now been tamed by chemotherapy with a simple, safe, and effective cure. Diseases that twenty years previously had been guilty secrets, virtually unmentionable in the public press and quietly ignored by health departments, were now glorious examples of the triumph of modem medicine in overcoming ancient plagues. The ideological struggle between those who had seen the fight against venereal disease as a battle for sexual morality and those who had seen it as simply another form of bacteriological warfare was now over. The social hygiene reformers had to concede defeat to the public health officers, epidemiologists, and laboratory researchers. Or did they?

In 1947 the Maryland State Department of Health, announcing the success of the rapid treatment program, concluded its press bulletin with the warning: "To decrease the number of repeat patients and prevent venereal diseases it

will be necessary to reduce sexual promiscuity. If fear of disease is a less powerful restraining factor the problem must be attacked more strongly through moral training and suppression of prostitution."[44] . . .

Even those most committed to the bacteriological view of disease seemed uneasy about the decoupling of venereal disease from sin and promiscuity: How would sexual morality be controlled if not by the fear of disease? Would "rampant promiscuity" defeat the best efforts of medical treatment? . . .

As we have since discovered, the fear and underlying ambivalence toward sexuality were only lying dormant. Public concern, horror, and fear about AIDS have recently reignited the older social hygiene movement in a new form. The once prevalent description of the black population as sexually promiscuous, sexually threatening, and a reservoir of disease has now been applied to the gay male population. AIDS is popularly seen as "caused" by gay promiscuity and, even more broadly, as a punishment for unconventional or unapproved sexual behavior, rather than simply as the result of infection by a microorganism. Venereal disease is again perceived as the "wages of sin," or, as the Reverend Jerry Falwell says: "A man reaps what he sows. If he sows seed in the field of his lower nature, he will reap from it a harvest of corruption." . . .

Both the biomedical and moral perspectives on venereal disease highlight specific aspects of a complex social reality. Venereal diseases, like all other diseases, are experienced and reproduced in a social context. We may separate the biological and social aspects for analysis, but any complete understanding of a disease problem must involve both, as interrelated parts of a single social reality.

Social and cultural ideas offer a variety of ways in which diseases can be perceived and interpreted. The germ theory provides an explanation of disease that largely—but not completely—isolates it from this social context, robbing it of some of its social (and in this case, moral) meaning. But the purely "scientific" interpretation is never wholly victorious, for social and cultural meanings of disease reassert themselves in the interstices of science and prove their power whenever the biomedical sciences fail to completely cure or solve the problem. Only when a disease condition is completely abolished do social and cultural meanings cease to be relevant to the experience and perception of human illness.

NOTES

1. For a fascinating analysis of the history of cultural and scientific conceptions of syphilis, see Ludwig Fleck, *Genesis and Development of a Scientific Fact* (1935, rpt., Chicago: 1979).

2. For an excellent recent history of the controversies around venereal diseases in the United States, see Allan Brandt, *No Magic Bullet: A Social History of Venereal Diseases in the United States Since 1880* (New York: 1985).

3. National Academy of Sciences, *Scientific and Technical Societies of the United States and Canada,* 8th ed. (Washington, DC: 1968), 62.

4. Edward H. Beardsley, "Allied Against Sin: American and British Responses to Venereal Disease in World War I," *Medical History* 20 (1976): 194.

5. As one widely reprinted article, said to have reached eight million readers, described 'The Enemy at Home': "The name of this invisible enemy is Venereal Disease— and there you have in two words the epitome of all that is unclean, malignant and menacing. . . . Gonorrhea and syphilis are 'camp followers' where prostitution and alcohol are permitted. They form almost as great an enemy behind the lines as do the Huns in front." "V.D.: The Enemy at Home," as cited by William H. Zinsser, "Social Hygiene and the War: Fighting Venereal Disease a Public Trust," *Social Hygiene* 4 (1918): 519–20.

6. In 1920 William Travis Howard, a member of the city health department, complained: "The Baltimore health department has never inaugurated a single administrative measure directed at the control of the venereal diseases . . . the Baltimore health department has contented itself with receiving such reports as were made and with lending its power, when called upon, to force a few recalcitrant patients to appear at the venereal disease clinic established by the United States Government." Howard, *Public Health Administration and the Natural History of Disease in Baltimore, Maryland: 1797–1920* (Washington, DC: 1924), 154–55.

7. Baltimore City Health Department, Annual Report (1930).

8. Taliaferro Clark and Lida Usilton, "Survey of the Venereal Diseases in the City of Baltimore, Baltimore County, and the Four Contiguous Counties," *Venereal Disease Information* 12 (Washington, DC: 20 October 1931), 437–56.

9. Baltimore City Health Department, Annual Report (1932), 62.

10. Baltimore City Health Department, Annual Report (1933), 93.

11. James H. Jones, *Bad Blood: The Tuskegee Syphilis Experiment* (New York: The Free Press, 1981), 16–29.

12. Baltimore City Health Department, Annual Report (1934), 107.

13. Baltimore City Health Department, Annual Report (1935), 115.

14. Ferdinand O. Reinhard, "The Venereal Disease Problem in the Colored Population of Baltimore City," *American Journal of Syphilis and Neurology* 19 (1935): 183–95.

15. Thomas Parran, "Why Don't We Stamp Out Syphilis?" *Reader's Digest* (July 1936), reprinted in *Baltimore Health News* (August 1936): 3.

16. *E.g.* Parran, *Shadow on the Land: Syphilis* (New York: 1937), 207, 230.

17. Parran, "Why Don't We Stamp Out Syphilis?" *Reader's Digest*, 65–73.

18. "G-Men's Haul in Vice Raids Totals 47," *Baltimore Sun*, 17 May 1937.

19. "Vice Witness Names Police Lieutenant," *Baltimore Sun,* 18 May 1937; "Vice Arrests May Total 100; Bierman Named," *Sunday Sun,* 19 May 1937.

20. "Starts to Survey Venereal Disease," *Baltimore Sun,* 29 July 1937; "Venereal Disease Fight Is Planned," *Baltimore Sun,* 22 August 1937; "Fight Opens Here on Social Disease," *Baltimore Sun*, 25 August 1937; "Syphilis Control Unit Begins Work," *Baltimore Sun,* 21 October 1937; "Over 2,000 Attend Talks on Syphilis," *Baltimore Sun,* 26 October 1937.

21. Baltimore City Health Department, Annual Reports (1938), 159; (1939), 159.

22. Baltimore City Health Department, Annual Report (1938); 16; "21 Employers Asked in Drive on Syphilis," *Baltimore Sun,* 27 March 1938; "Syphilis Control Is Under Way Here," *Baltimore Sun*, 22 May 1938; W. M. P., "We Join the Anti-Syphilis Crusade," *The Kalends* (June 1938), reprinted in *Baltimore Health News* 15 (July 1938): 53–54; Baltimore City Health Department, "Syphilis in Industry" (Baltimore: n.d.).

23. Baltimore City Health Department, Annual Report (1940), 149–51.

24. Baltimore City Health Department, Annual Report (1941), 139.

25. "City Shown Second in Syphilis Survey," *Baltimore Sun*, 22 October 1941.

26. "High Syphilis Rate Laid to Race Ratio," *Baltimore Sun*, 26 October 1941.

27. "Says Vice Control Has Improved Here," *Baltimore Sun*, 27 January 1943.

28. "State Law Held Needed in War on Vice," *Baltimore Sun*, 28 January 1943.

29. "Stanton Idea for Examination of Prostitutes Is Denounced," *Baltimore Sun*, 29 January 1943.

30. "Venereal Picture Dark: Dr. Huntington Williams Says No Improvement Is Expected for Some Time," *Baltimore Sun*, 21 January 1943.

31. "Clinics Here Under Fire," *Baltimore Sun*, 30 March 1943.

32. "Venereal Disease Rate High in State," *Baltimore Sun*, 15 June 1943.

33. Parran and Vonderlehr, *Plain Words about Venereal Disease* (New York: Reynal or Hichcock, 1941), especially 96–120.

34. Baltimore City Health Department, Annual Report (1943), 148.

35. C. Howe Eller, "A Sex Education Project and Serologic Survey in a Baltimore High School," *Baltimore Health News* 21 (November 1944): 83.

36. Emily V. Clapp, *Growing Up in the World Today* (Boston: n.d.).

37. *Ibid.*, 14.

38. For the development of penicillin therapy, see Harry F. Dowling, *Fighting Infection: Conquests of the Twentieth Century* (Cambridge: Harvard University Press, 1977): 125–57.

39. Baltimore City Health Department, Annual Report (1945), 29.

40. Baltimore City Health Department, Annual Report (1945), 145–46; "Venereal Law Made Specific," *Baltimore Sun*, 26 August 1945.

41. "End of VD—Cure Center Seen as Calamity," *Evening Sun*, 12 June 1946.

42. "A Temporary Power Made Permanent," *Baltimore Sun*, 9 January 1947.

43. "Rapid Treatment," Press Bulletin No. 1043, Maryland State Department of Health, (27 January 1947), Enoch Pratt Library, Maryland Room, Baltimore.

44. *Ibid.*

HIV among People Aged 50 and Over

Centers for Disease Control and Prevention

People aged 50 and older account for an estimated 45% of Americans living with diagnosed HIV.

THE NUMBERS

HIV Diagnoses[1]

- People aged 50 and over accounted for 17% (6,725) of an estimated 39,513 HIV diagnoses in the United States in 2015. People aged 50 to 54 accounted for 45 percent (3,010) of the 6,725 diagnoses.
- Blacks/African Americans accounted for an estimated 43% of all new diagnoses among people aged 50 and over in 2015. Whites accounted for 36%, and Hispanics/Latinos[2] accounted for 17%.

- In 2014, 40% of people aged 55 and older were diagnosed with AIDS at the time of HIV diagnosis (i.e., diagnosed late in the course of the infection).

Living with HIV and Deaths

- In 2014, an estimated 45% of Americans living with diagnosed HIV were aged 50 and older, 27% were aged 55 and older, and 6% were aged 65 and older.

- Among people aged 55 and older living with HIV in 2014, 67% received HIV medical care and 55% received continuous HIV care.
- Of the 6,721 deaths from HIV in 2014, 2,610 (39%) were among people aged 55 and older.

PREVENTION CHALLENGES

Older people in the United States are more likely than younger people to be diagnosed with HIV infection late in the course of the infection, which results in their starting treatment late and possibly suffering more immune-system damage. Late diagnoses can occur because health care providers may not always test older people for HIV infection, and older people may not consider themselves to be at risk of HIV infection or may mistake HIV symptoms for those of normal aging and not consider HIV as a cause.

Many older people are sexually active, including those living with HIV, and may have the same HIV risk factors as younger people, including a lack of knowledge about HIV and how to prevent getting it, as well as having multiple sex partners. Older people also face some unique issues:

- Many widowed and divorced people are dating again. They may be less aware of their risks for HIV than younger people, believing HIV is not an issue for older people. Thus, they may be less likely to protect themselves.
- Women who no longer worry about becoming pregnant may be less likely to use a condom and to practice safer sex. Age-related thinning and dryness of vaginal tissue may raise older women's risk for HIV infection.
- Although they visit their doctors more frequently, older people are less likely than younger people to discuss their sexual habits or drug use with their doctors. And doctors are less likely to ask their older patients about these issues.

Stigma is a particular concern among older people because they may already face isolation due to illness or loss of family and friends. Stigma negatively affects people's quality of life, self-image, and behaviors, and may prevent them from seeking HIV care and disclosing their HIV status.

Aging with HIV infection also presents special challenges for preventing other diseases because both age and HIV increase risk for cardiovascular disease, thin bones, and certain cancers. Older HIV patients and their care providers need to maximize prevention efforts against these conditions and remain vigilant for early signs of illness. They also need to be careful about interactions between the medications used to treat HIV and those used to treat common age-related conditions such as hypertension, diabetes, elevated cholesterol, and obesity.

NOTES

1. *HIV diagnoses* indicate when a person was diagnosed with HIV, not when the person was infected.

2. Hispanics/Latinos can be of any race.

Source: Centers for Disease Control and Prevention, "HIV among People Aged 50 and Over," September 2017. https://www.cdc.gov/hiv/group/age/olderamericans/index.html.

DAMAGED GOODS:
WOMEN MANAGING THE STIGMA OF STDs

ADINA NACK

The HIV/AIDS epidemic has garnered the attention of researchers from a variety of academic disciplines. In contrast, the study of other sexually transmitted diseases (STDs) has attracted limited interest outside of epidemiology and public health.

. . . This [reading] focuses on how the sexual self-concept is transformed when the experience of living with a chronic STD casts a shadow of disease on the health and desirability of a woman's body, as well as on her perceived possibilities for future sexual experiences. The term *sexual self* means something fundamentally different from *gender identity* or *sexual identity*. Invoking the term *sexual self* is meant to conjure up the innately intimate parts of individuals' self-concepts that encompass how they think of themselves with regard to their experienced and imagined sensuality. Components of a sexual self may include the following: level of sexual experience, emotional memories of sexual pleasure (or lack thereof), perception of one's body as desirable, and perception of one's sexual body parts as healthy. . . .

To understand the individual-level experience of living with a chronic STD, it is important to take into account how these infections are symbolically constructed in American culture. The meanings that Americans give to being infected with an STD are intersubjectively formed during interactions. Individuals' experiences of health, illness, and medical care "are connected to the particular historically located social arrangements and the cultural values of any society" (Conrad and Kern, 1994: 5). Present American social values reflect the longstanding connections between sexual health and morality: Interactions with medical practitioners and lay people are the conduit through which the stigma of STDs is reinforced (Brandt, 1987). Pryce (1998) pointed to a critical gap—the "missing" sociology of sexual disease—and asserted that this application of sociology should focus on the social construction of the body as central in the medical and social iconography of STDs.

In answer to Pryce's (1998) challenge, this research . . . sociologically analyz[es] the impact of genital herpes and HPV on women's sexual selves. This study adds to this research area by examining sexual self-transformation, starting from the point of how individuals' sexual selves are transformed by the lived experiences of being diagnosed and treated for chronic STDs. Beginning from a premise that the majority of people grow up feeling sexually invincible, a variety of traumas have the capacity to disrupt a positive sexual self-concept (e.g., molestation, rape, and illness). Social-interactional traumas also transmit messages that can damage sexual selves: Some

From "Damaged Goods: Women Managing the Stigma of STDs," *Deviant Behavior*, Vol. 21, Issue 2, 2000, pp. 95–121. Copyright © 2000 Routledge, reprinted by permission of the publisher (Taylor & Francis Ltd, http://www.tandfonline.com).

physical bodies are undesirable; some sexual preferences are unacceptable; some levels of sexual experience are immoral.

SETTING AND METHOD

The motivation for this study stems from my personal experience with STDs. My "complete membership role" (Adler and Adler, 1987) stems from legitimacy and acceptance by other women with STDs as a member of this unorganized and stigmatized group. At 20, sexual health became the center of my world when I was diagnosed with mild cervical dysplasia, the result of an HPV infection. I began an informal self-education process that helped me manage the stress of my treatments. My commitment to managing my sexual health status would become the foundation for this research project and provide me with the personal insights needed to connect with others facing STDs and the clinical knowledge necessary to be a sexual health researcher.

As a campus sexual health educator, I began to question what sexual health services were not provided. Seeing that women and men were being diagnosed and treated for STDs without receiving follow-up education and counseling, I developed a women-only support group for individuals dealing with STDs. Because of the topic's sensitive nature, I chose a gender-segregated approach to the support group and, ultimately, to the research. . . .

Unfortunately, only one woman used the support group. Initially disheartened, I began to question why people flocked to other support groups that were based on shared stigma (e.g., eating disorders and alcoholism) but failed to use this sexual health support group. Even persons living with HIV and AIDS used support groups to collectively manage their stigma. . . .

To investigate the failure of this support group, I conducted a survey among patients using a local women's health care clinic. During a month chosen at random, clinic staff gave each patient who came in for an appointment an anonymous survey about a new service being offered: a women's sexual health support group. In all, 279 completed surveys were collected. . . . Owing to the population from which the sample was drawn, generalizability is restricted to the population of women who receive women's health care services from this clinic. . . .

I performed a multiple regression analysis on the data, the results of which supported the hypothesis that a person who has been diagnosed with an STD is less likely to be interested in a sexual health support group. . . . One of the most revealing findings was that only 23.3 percent of the women were definitely interested ("yes") in a sexual health support group. . . .

I interpreted this finding to reflect that the stigma of having an STD is so severe that the perceived cost of disclosing this sexual health status to strangers outweighs the possible benefits. Because there has yet to be a moral entrepreneurial campaign to destigmatize STDs in our society, the norm remains secrecy (Brandt, 1987). . . .

On the basis of these findings, I determined that in-depth interviews were my best chance for obtaining valid data. I constructed my research methods to reflect a reciprocal intention: As the women gave their stories to me, I would offer my support and resources as a sexual health educator. . . .

My first hurdle was to achieve approval from the campus Human Research Committee. . . . Because of the confidential nature of individuals' STD diagnoses, I was not allowed to directly recruit participants. Rather, they had to approach me, usually after hearing about my research project from other participants or women's health care practitioners with whom I had consulted. . . . I used snowball sampling to generate interviews.

I conducted 28 conversational, unstructured interviews with consensual participants, who ranged in age from 19 to 56. . . . I conducted the interviews in participants' preferred locations: their homes, my home, or other private settings. The interviews lasted from 1 to 2 hours and were tape recorded with the participants' permission. When appropriate, I concluded the interview with offers to provide sexual health information and resources, either in the form of health education materials or referrals to resources.

I then analyzed the data according to the principles of grounded theory (Glaser and Strauss, 1967). . . . With each interview, I started to cluster participants' experiences around particular stages to check the validity of my initial model. The six stages of sexual self-transformation [that emerged from the interviews] in chronological order, are as follows: sexual invincibility, STD suspicion, diagnostic crisis, damaged goods, healing/treatment, and integration. . . .

STIGMA AND THE SEXUAL SELF

For all but 1 of the 28 women, their STD diagnoses radically altered the way that they saw themselves as sexual beings. Facing both a daunting medical and social reality, the women used different strategies to manage their new stigma. Each stigma management strategy had ramifications for the transformation of their sexual selves.

Stigma Nonacceptance

Goffman (1963) proposed that individuals at risk for a deviant stigma are either "the discredited" or "the discreditable." The discrediteds'

stigma was known to others either because the individuals revealed the deviance or because the deviance was not concealable. In contrast, the discreditable were able to hide their deviant stigma. Goffman found that the majority of discreditables were "passing" as nondeviants by avoiding "stigma symbols," anything that would link them to their deviance, and by using "disidentifiers," props or actions that would lead others to believe they had a nondeviant status. Goffman (1963) also noted that individuals bearing deviant stigma might eventually resort to "covering," one form of which he defined as telling deceptive stories. To remain discreditable in their everyday lives, 19 of the women used the individual stigma management strategies of passing and/or covering. In contrast, 9 women revealed their health status to select friends and family members soon after receiving their diagnoses.

Passing

The deviant stigma of women with STDs was essentially concealable, though revealed to the necessary inner circle of health care and health insurance providers. For the majority, passing was an effective means of hiding stigma from others, sometimes even from themselves.

Hillary, a 22-year-old White college senior, recalled the justifications she had used to distance herself from the reality of her HPV infection and to facilitate passing strategies.

At the time, I was in denial about it. I told myself that that wasn't what it was because my sister had had a similar thing happen, the dysplasia. So, I just kind of told myself that it was hereditary. That was kinda funny because I asked the nurse that called if it could be hereditary, and she said "No, this is completely sexually transmitted"—I really didn't accept it until a few months after my cryosurgery.

Similarly, Gloria, a Chicana graduate student . . . was not concerned about a previous case of gonorrhea she had cured with antibiotics or her chronic HPV "because the warts went away." Out of sight, out of her sex life: "I never told anybody about them because I figured they had gone away, and they weren't coming back. Even after I had another outbreak, I was still very promiscuous. It still hadn't registered that I needed to always have the guy use a condom."

When the women had temporarily convinced themselves that they did not have a contagious infection, it was common to conceal the health risk with partners because the women themselves did not perceive the risk as real. Kayla, a . . . White college senior, felt justified in passing as healthy with partners who used condoms, even though she knew that condoms could break. Cleo, a White 31-year-old . . . , had sex with a partner after being diagnosed with HPV.

So at the time I had sex with him, yes, I knew but, no, I hadn't been treated yet. That gets into the whole "I never told him," and I didn't. Part of me thought I should, and part of me thought that having an STD didn't fit with my self-concept so much that I just couldn't disclose.

Francine, a White 43-year-old professional . . . , had never intended to pass as healthy, but she did not get diagnosed with herpes until after beginning a sexual relationship with her second husband.

I think there was all the guilt: What if I bring this on you? So, I felt guilt in bringing this into the relationship. Because he had not been anywhere near as sexually active as I had. . . .

Similarly, Tasha, a White graduate student, found out that she might have inadvertently passed as healthy when her partner was diagnosed with chlamydia. "I freaked out—I was like, 'Oh my God! I gave you chlamydia. I am so sorry! I am so sorry!' I felt really horrible, and I felt really awful." . . . Even if the passing is done unintentionally, it still brings guilt to the passer.

The women also tried to disidentify themselves from sexual disease in their attempts to pass as being sexually healthy. Rather than actively using a verbal or symbolic prop or action that would distance them from the stigma, the women took a passive approach. Some gave nonverbal agreement to putdowns of other women who were known to have STDs. For example, Hillary recalled such an interaction.

It's funny being around people that don't know that I have an STD and how they make a comment like "That girl, she's such a slut. She's a walking STD." And how that makes me feel when I'm confronted with that, and having them have no idea that they could be talking about me.

Others kept silent about their status and tried to maintain the social status of being sexually healthy and morally pure. . . . Putting up the facade of sexual purity, these women distanced themselves from any suspicion of sexual disease.

Covering

When passing became too difficult, some women resorted to covering to deflect family and friends from the truth. Cleo summed up the rationale by comparing her behavior to what she had learned growing up with an alcoholic father. " . . . I learned that's what you do. Like you don't tell people those things that you consider shameful, and then, if confronted, you know, you lie."

Hillary talked to her parents about her HPV surgery, but never as treatment for an STD. She portrayed her moderate cervical dysplasia as a precancerous scare, unrelated to sex. . . . When Tasha's sister helped her get a prescription for pubic lice, she actually provided the cover story for her embarrassed younger sister. "She totally took control, and made a personal inquiry: 'So, how did you get this? From a toilet seat?' And, I was like, 'a toilet seat,' and she believed me." . . . For Anne, a 28-year-old . . . graduate student, a painful herpes outbreak almost outed her on a walk with a friend. She was so physically uncomfortable that she was actually waddling. Noticing her strange behavior, her friend asked what was wrong. Anne told her that it was a hemorrhoid; that was only a partial truth because herpes was the primary cause of her pain. As Anne put it, telling her about the hemorrhoid "was embarrassing enough!"

Deception and Guilt

The women who chose to deny, pass as normal, and use disidentifiers or cover stories shared more than the shame of having an STD—they had also told lies. With lying came guilt. Anne, who had used the hemorrhoid cover story, eventually felt extremely guilty. Her desire to conceal the truth was in conflict with her commitment to being an honest person. . . . Deborah, a 32-year-old White professional . . . , only disclosed to her first sexual partner after she had been diagnosed with HPV; she passed as healthy with all other partners. Deborah reflected, "I think my choices not to disclose have hurt my sense of integrity." However, her guilt was resolved during her last gynecological exam when the nurse practitioner confirmed that after years of "clean" pap smear results Deborah was not being "medically unethical" by not disclosing to her partners. In other words, her immune system had probably dealt with the HPV in such a way that she might never have another outbreak or transmit the infection to sexual partners.

When Cleo passed as healthy with a sexual partner, she started "feeling a little guilty about not having told." However, the consequences of passing as healthy were very severe for Cleo:

No. I never disclosed it to any future partner. Then, one day, I was having sex with Josh, my current husband, before we were married, and we had been together for a few months, maybe, and I'm like looking at his penis, and I said, "Oh, my goodness! You have a wart on your penis! Ahhh!" All of a sudden, it comes back to me.

Cleo's decision to pass left her with both the guilt of deceiving and infecting her husband.

Surprisingly, those women who had unintentionally passed as being sexually healthy (i.e., they had no knowledge of their STD status at the time) expressed a similar level of guilt as those who had been purposefully deceitful. Violet, a middle-class, White 36-year-old, had inadvertently passed as healthy with her current partner. Even after she had preventively disclosed to him, she still had to deal with the guilt over possibly infecting him.

It hurt so bad that morning when he was basically furious at me thinking I was the one he had gotten those red bumps from. It was the hour from hell! I felt really majorly dirty and stigmatized. I felt like "God, I've done the best I can: If this is really caused by the HPV I have, then I feel terrible."

When using passing and covering techniques, the women strove to keep their stigma from tainting social interactions. They feared . . . rejection from their social circles of friends, family, and, most important, sexual partners. For most of the women, guilt surpassed fear and became the trigger to disclose. Those who had been deceitful in passing or covering had to assuage their guilt: Their options were either to remain in nonacceptance, disclose, or transfer their guilt to somebody else.

Stigma Deflection

As the women struggled to manage their individual stigma of being sexually diseased, real and imaginary social interactions became the conduit for the contagious label of damaged goods. Now that the unthinkable had happened to them, the women began to think of their past and present partners as infected, contagious, and potentially dangerous to themselves or other women. The combination of transferring stigma and assigning blame to others allowed the women to deflect the STD stigma away from themselves.

Stigma Transference

. . . Stigma is neither an emotion nor an impulse; rather, it is a formal concept that captures a relationship of devaluation (Goffman, 1963). Although the participants attributed their devalued relationship with sexual health ideals to real and imaginary others, they were not controlling unacceptable feelings. Rather, stigma transference manifests as a clear expression of anger and fear, and the women did not connect this strategy to a reduction in their levels of anxiety; in fact, several discussed it in relation to increased anxiety.

Cleo remembered checking her partner's penis for warts after her doctor told her that she could detect them by visual inspection. It became a habit for Kayla to check her partner for any visible symptoms of an STD. Gloria was more careful about checking future partners and asking if they had anything. Tasha explained, "I just felt like I was with someone who was dirty." In all four cases, the women were only sure of their own STD infections, yet in their minds these partners had become diseased.

Transference of stigma to a partner became more powerful when the woman felt betrayed by her partner. When Hillary spoke of the "whole trust issue" with her ex-partner, she firmly believed he had lied to her about his sexual health status and that he would lie to others. Even though she had neither told him about her diagnosis nor had proof of him being infected, she fully transferred her stigma to him. . . .

Kayla also transferred the stigma of sexual disease to an ex-partner, never confronting him about whether he had tested positive for STDs. The auxiliary trait of promiscuity colored her view of him: "I don't know how sexually promiscuous he was, but I'm sure he had had a lot of partners." Robin, a 21-year-old White undergraduate, went so far as to tell her ex-partner that he needed to see a doctor and "do something about it." He doubted her ability to pinpoint contracting genital warts from him and called her a slut. Robin believed that he was the one with the reputation for promiscuity and decided to trash him by telling her two friends who hung out with him. Robin hoped to spoil his sexual reputation and scare off his future partners. In the transference of stigma, the women ascribed the same auxiliary traits onto others that others had previously ascribed to them. . . .

In all cases, it was logical to assume that past and current sexual partners may also have been infected. However, the stigma of being sexually diseased had far-reaching consequences in the women's imaginations. The traumatic impact on their sexual selves led most to infer that future, as yet unknown partners were also sexually diseased. . . . They had already been damaged by at least one partner. Therefore, they expected that future partners, ones who had not yet come into their lives, held the threat of also being damaged goods.

For Hillary, romantic relationships held no appeal anymore. She had heard of others who also had STDs but stayed in nonacceptance and never changed their lifestyle of having casual, unprotected sex:

I just didn't want to have anything to do with it. A lot of it was not trusting people. When we broke up, I decided that I was not having sex. Initially, it was because I wanted to get an HIV test. Then, I came to kind of a turning point in my life and realized that I didn't want to do the one-night-stand thing anymore. It just wasn't worth it. It wasn't fun.

At this stage in her sexual self-transformation, Hillary imagined the world of possible partners having been polluted with contagion.

Anne's lesbian friends [told her] . . . future partners should be suspected of being dangerous. . . .

Anne recalled [one] friend's reaction. "Those rotten men! You should just leave them alone. It's clear that you should be with women, and it's safer and better that way. Women don't do this kind of thing to each other." Her friends' guidance was an overt attempt to encourage Anne to believe that only potential male partners bore the stigma.

Instead of going by gender, Gloria, a self-identified Chicana, made a distinction based on ethnicity as a predictor of sexual health status:

Now, if it was a White man, I made 'em wear a condom because I got it from a White man, and so I assumed that there had to be something with their culture—they were more promiscuous. But, one thing I do know culturally and with the times is that Chicano men were more likely to have a single partner.

These women felt justified in their newfound attitudes about sexual partners. What was only supposed to happen to "bad" women had happened to them. Overall, these women transitioned from blaming their own naivete to blaming someone else for not being more cautious or more honest.

Blame

The women's uses of stigma transference techniques were attempts to alleviate their emotional burdens. First, the finger of shame and guilt pointed inward, toward the women's core sexual selves. Their sexual selves became tainted, dirty, damaged. In turn, they directed the stigma outward to both real and fictional others. Blaming others was a way for all of the women to alleviate some of the internal pressure and turn the anger outward. This emotional component of the damaged goods stage externalized the pain of their stigma.

Francine recalled how she and her first husband dealt with the issue of genital warts. . . . Francine's husband had likely contracted genital

warts from his wild fraternity parties: "We really thought of it as, that woman who did the trains [serial sexual intercourse]. It was still a girl's fault kind of thing." By externalizing the blame to the promiscuous women at fraternity parties, Francine exonerated not only herself but also her husband. . . .

For Violet, it was impossible to neatly deflect the blame away from both herself and her partner.

I remember at the time just thinking, "Oh man! He gave it to me!" While he was thinking, "God, [Violet]! You gave this to me!" So, we kind of just did a truce in our minds. Like, OK, we don't know who gave it—just as likely both ways. So, let's just get treated. We just kind of dropped it.

Clearly, the impulse to place blame was strong even when there was no easy target.

Often, the easiest targets were men who exhibited the auxiliary traits of promiscuity and deception. Tasha wasn't sure which ex-partner had transmitted the STD. However, she rationalized blaming a particular guy. "He turned out to be kind of a huge liar, lied to me a lot about different stuff. And so I blamed him. All the other guys were, like, really nice people, really trustworthy." Likewise, when I asked Violet from whom she believed she had contracted chlamydia, she replied, "Dunno, it could've been from one guy, because that guy had slept with some unsavory women, so therefore he was unsavory." . . .

The actual guilt or innocence of these blame targets was secondary. What mattered to the women was that they could hold someone else responsible.

Stigma Acceptance

Eventually, every woman in the study stopped denying and deflecting the truth of her sexual health status by disclosing to loved ones. The women disclosed for either preventive or therapeutic reasons. That is, they were either motivated to reveal their STD status to prevent harm to themselves or others or to gain the emotional support of confidants.

Preventive and Therapeutic Disclosures

The decision to make a preventive disclosure was linked to whether the STD could be cured. Kayla explained,

Chlamydia went away, and I mean it was really bad to have that, but I mean it's not something that you have to tell people later 'cause you know, in case it comes back. Genital warts, you never know.

Kayla knew that her parents would find out about the HPV infection because of insurance connections. Before her cryosurgery, Kayla decided to tell her mom about her condition.

. . . [I]t was kind of hard at first. But, she wasn't upset with me. Main thing, she was disappointed, but I think she blamed my boyfriend more than she blamed me.

. . . Preventive disclosures to sexual partners, past and present, were a more problematic situation. The women were choosing to put themselves in a position where they could face blame, disgust, and rejection. For those reasons, the women put off preventive disclosures to partners as long as possible. For example, Anne made it clear that she would not have disclosed her herpes to a female sexual partner had they not been about to have sex. After "agonizing weeks and weeks and weeks before trying to figure out how to tell," Diana, a 45-year-old African American professional, finally shared her HPV and herpes status before her current relationship became sexual. Unfortunately, her boyfriend had a negative reaction: "He certainly didn't want to touch me anywhere near my genitals." . . .

For Summer, a 20-year-old Native American administrative assistant, and Gloria, their preventive disclosures were actually a relief to their sexual partners. Summer decided to disclose

her genital warts to a new boyfriend after they had been "getting hot n' heavy." Lying in bed together, she said, "I need to tell you something." After she disclosed, he lay there, staring at the ceiling for a couple of minutes before deeply exhaling, "I thought you were going to tell me you had AIDS." Similarly, one of Gloria's partners sighed in relief when she revealed that she had herpes; he thought she was going to say she was HIV positive.

Many of the therapeutic disclosures were done to family members. The women wanted the support of those who had known them the longest. . . . Tasha disclosed to her mother right after she was diagnosed with chlamydia.

My family died—"Guess what, mom, I got chlamydia." She's like, "Chlamydia? How did you find out you got chlamydia?" I'm like, "Well, my boyfriend got an eye infection." [laughter] "How'd he get it in his eye?" [laughter] So, it was the biggest joke in the family for the longest time!

. . . The women often unburdened their feelings of shame and guilt onto their close friends. Cleo shared her feelings with her roommate: "I told her that I was feeling weird about having had sex with this second guy, knowing that I had an STD." Kayla's therapeutic disclosure was reciprocal with her best friend. "At that time, she was also going through a similar situation with her boyfriend, so I felt okay finally to talk about it." . . . In Anne's case, her therapeutic disclosure to a friend was twofold: both to seek support and to apologize for initially having used the hemorrhoid cover story. Anne explained to her friend that she had felt too uncomfortable to tell the truth. . . .

Consequences of Disclosure

With both therapeutic and preventive disclosure, the women experienced some feelings of relief in being honest with loved ones. However, they still carried the intense shame of being sexually diseased women. The resulting emotion was anxiety over how their confidants would react: rejection, disgust, or betrayal. Francine was extremely anxious about disclosing to her husband. "That was really tough on us because I had to go home and tell Damon that I had this outbreak of herpes . . . I was really fearful—I didn't think that he would think I had recently had sex with somebody else—but, I was still really afraid of what it would do to our relationship." . . .

Overall, disclosing intensified the anxiety of having their secret leaked to others in whom they would never have chosen to confide. In addition, each disclosure brought with it the possibility of rejection and ridicule from the people whose opinions they valued most. For Gloria, disclosing was the right thing to do but had painful consequences when her partner's condom slipped off in the middle of sexual intercourse.

I told him it doesn't feel right. "You'd better check." And, so he checked, and he just jumped off me and screamed, "Oh fuck!" And, I just thought, oh no, here we go. He just freaked and went to the bathroom and washed his penis with soap. I just felt so dirty.

The risk paid off for Summer, whose boyfriend asserted, "I don't ever want to be *that guy*—the one who shuns people and treats them differently." He borrowed sexual health education materials and spent over an hour asking her questions about various STDs. Even in this best-case scenario, the sexual intimacy in this relationship became problematized (e.g., having to research modes of STD transmission and safe-sex techniques). Disclosures were the interactional component of self-acceptance. The women became fully grounded in their new reality when they realized that the significant people in their lives were now viewing them through the discolored lenses of sexual disease.

CONCLUSION

The women with STDs went through an emotionally difficult process, testing out stigma management strategies, trying to control the impact of STDs on both their self-concepts and on their relationships with others. . . .

Ironically, most of the women first tried to deny this deviant health status—one that was virtually secret through the protection of doctor–patient confidentiality laws. Although many used passing and covering techniques that relied on deceiving others, self-deception was impossible to maintain. The medical truth began to penetrate their sexual self-conceptions as soon as they fabricated their first lie. To strategize a successful ruse, it was necessary to know the scope of what they were trying to hide.

When guilt caught up with them, making it hard to pass as healthy, their goal shifted to stigma deflection. . . . However, this only delayed the inevitable—a deviant sexual self that penetrated the women's prior conceptions of their sexual selves.

After mentally transferring their stigma to real and imaginary others, all of the women finally accepted their tainted sexual health status through the reflexive dynamics of disclosure. . . . The women's sexual selves moved along a deviant career path by means of the interactive dynamics of their stigma management strategies.

. . . As the women made choices on which stigma management strategies to use, they grappled with the ramifications of internalizing this new label. Choosing passing and covering techniques meant they could remain in nonacceptance and put off stigma internalization. When they deflected the stigma onto others by means of stigma transference, the women glimpsed the severity of an STD stigma as reflected in the presumed sexual selves of real and imaginary others. Finally, the women's disclosures confirmed the new story of their tainted sexual selves.

. . . Unlike the stigma of HIV/AIDS—which carries the threat of life-changing illness, death, and contagion beyond the scope of sexual behaviors—the STD stigma lends itself to compartmentalization. The women were able to hide their shame, guilt, and fear (of further health complications, of contaminating others, of rejection, etc.) in the sexual part of their self-concept. They recognized that this part of their self-concept did not have to affect their entire identity. . . . If the impact of the STDs on their sex lives ever became too emotionally painful, the women could always decide to distance themselves from this role: choosing temporary or permanent celibacy. . . .

A narrative model of the self proposes that personal myths create the self and become "the stories we live by" (McAdams, 1996:266). I propose that we seek to understand the significance of the stories we choose not to live by. Personal STD "stories" are rarely told in American mass culture. McAdams (1996:22) proposed that "carrying on affairs in secret"—maintaining a discreditable stigma—is a way to keep stigmatizing stories from occupying center stage in people's personal myth. However, these data suggest that individuals manage identity transformations, especially transformations into deviant identities, by constructing and sharing self-narratives through disclosure interactions. Although the women do not maintain secrecy, they do keep their STD stories from center stage. . . .

REFERENCES

Ackerman, Sandra J. 1998. "HPV: Who's Got It and Why They Don't Know." *HPV News* 8(2):1; 5–6.

Adler, Patricia A., and Peter Adler. 1987. *Membership Roles in Field Research*. Newbury Park, CA: Sage.

Brandt, Allan M. 1987. *No Magic Bullet: A Social History of Venereal Disease in the United States since 1880*. New York: Oxford University Press.

Centers for Disease Control and Prevention. 1998a. "Genital Herpes." *National Center for HIV, STD & TB Prevention*. Retrieved from the World Wide Web February 4, 1998.

———. 1998b. "HIV/AIDS Surveillance Report." *National Center for HIV, STD & TB Prevention*. Retrieved from the World Wide Web February 4, 1998: URL.

Conrad, Peter, and Rochelle Kern, eds. 1994. *The Sociology of Health & Illness: Critical Perspectives*. 4th ed. New York: St. Martin's Press.

Glaser, Barney G., and Anselm L. Strauss. 1967. *The Discovery of Grounded Theory: Strategies for Qualitative Research*. Chicago: Aldine.

Goffman, Erving. 1963. *Stigma*. Englewood Cliffs, NJ: Prentice Hall.

McAdams, Dan P. 1996. *The Stories We Live By: Personal Myths and the Making of the Self*. New York: Guilford Press.

Pryce, Anthony. 1998. "Theorizing the Pox: A Missing Sociology of VD." Presented to the International Sociological Association.

Sandstrom, Kent L. 1990. "Confronting Deadly Disease: The Drama of Identity Construction among Gay Men with AIDS." *Journal of Contemporary Ethnography*, 19(3):271–94.

Siegel, Karolynn, and Beatrice J. Krauss. 1991. "Living with HIV Infection: Adaptive Tasks of Seropositive Gay Men." *Journal of Health and Social Behavior* 32(1):17–32.

Weitz, Rose. 1989. "Uncertainty and the Lives of Persons with AIDS." *Journal of Health and Social Behavior* 30(3):270–81.

HPV and Vaccines

Evelina Sterling and Wendy Simonds

Transmitted through intimate skin-to-skin contact, human papillomavirus (usually called HPV) is the most common sexually transmitted infection (STI). In fact, HPV infects about one in four people, mostly teens and young adults (Centers for Disease Control and

Prevention [CDC], 2016). There are more than 150 different HPV-related identified viruses now, and most people who become infected with HPV do not even realize they have it, as there are often no symptoms. In 90 percent of HPV cases, a healthy immune system will keep the virus in check, preventing any problems, and HPV infections will usually go away on their own within two years. For the other 10 percent, HPV lasts longer and can cause genital warts or lead to cervical cancer as well as other types of less common (but also serious) cancers that affect the vulva, vagina, penis, anus, tongue, throat, or tonsils. New research also suggests that HPV may even be linked to cardiovascular disease. While most people are exposed to HPV at some point in their lives, predicting whether an individual is at risk for developing any of these long-term and possibly life-threatening complications is impossible (CDC, 2016).

In 2006, the Food and Drug Administration (FDA) approved Gardasil, the first vaccine designed to prevent two types of HPV known to be associated with 70 percent of all cervical cancers, as well as two other HPV types associated with genital warts. Currently, the CDC recommend that all girls and young women and boys and young men between the ages of 9 and 26 receive the three-dose series of the vaccine to be fully protected against the HPV-linked cancers associated with the strains the vaccine covers. More recent research indicates that children under age 12 can receive only two doses. The vaccine, which now includes both Gardasil and Cervarix, is purported to be 100 percent effective against the strains of HPV they include. According to a CDC survey in 2013, only 38 percent of U.S. girls and 14 percent of boys aged 13 to 17 receive the recommended doses of the vaccine (CDC, 2014). Even with this low uptake of the HPV vaccine, HPV prevalence among young women has dropped significantly (National Institutes of Health [NIH], 2017).

Despite any benefits, the introduction of Gardasil was highly controversial, especially since its manufacturer, Merck and Co., actively lobbied states for mandates that would require the vaccine for all girls in order to attend school (Boston Women's Health Book Collective, 2011). Because the vaccine was found to be less effective if administered after exposure to HPV, guidelines targeted girls as young as nine in order to reach them before their first sexual experience (the initial guidelines were directed at girls only). (Once someone has HPV—and most sexually active individuals do, regardless of sexual orientation or number of partners—the HPV vaccine is much less effective.) Although many states have attempted to introduce legislation mandating HPV vaccines, only Virginia and the District of Columbia currently require the vaccine for girls entering the sixth grade. In July 2015, Rhode Island also announced a new requirement that all children entering seventh grade must receive the HPV vaccine. However, numerous exemptions exist for families wanting to opt out, making the requirements difficult to enforce (National Conference of State Legislatures [NCSL], 2017).

No doubt cancer is a serious health concern. More than 17,000 U.S. women are diagnosed with HPV-related cancers each year, most notably cervical cancer but also sometimes vaginal, vulvar, and mouth/throat cancers (CDC, 2016). The American Cancer Society (ACS) reports about 13,000 new cases of cervical cancer each year in the United States with about 4,000 women dying from the disease. However, about 80 percent of cervical cancer cases occur in developing nations, making cervical cancer the third most common cancer among women and the second most frequent cause of cancer-related deaths worldwide (NIH, 2017). Often it takes years for cervical or other HPV-related cancers to develop, and symptoms typically only become apparent when the cancer is quite advanced. But should the HPV vaccine be mandatory for all girls and young women in order to prevent cancer? The short answer: It's complicated. Most mandated vaccines are for diseases that spread easily from person to person during regular daily contact. HPV transmission is more difficult and can only be contracted through skin-to-skin contact during sexual activity. Furthermore, protection from HPV and its related complications is not guaranteed even with the vaccine.

As a result, a wide range of groups are voicing their concerns from all across the political spectrum, making it impossible to separate the potential benefits and risks of the HPV vaccine from gender, sexuality, and cultural politics. Religious and moral conservatives are adamantly opposed to mandating HPV vaccination. Strong proponents of abstinence-only sex education are afraid that lowering the risk of STDs will promote sex outside marriage. Health education experts also question the mandate, but for different reasons. Separating HPV prevention from comprehensive health education aimed at teaching adolescents to protect their sexual well-being could prove problematic. Perhaps this could give some kids a false sense of security about being protected from the many other STIs. Other critics feel parents should be encouraged to talk with their health care providers openly and honestly about what is right for their particular family, without any government intervention or industry influence.

Causing more concern, Gardasil was introduced to the public much more quickly than other previous vaccines and with limited research. Participants in clinical trials of Gardasil were primarily older girls and adult women, so there is still much to be learned about the most effective dosage and the long-term effects for younger girls, especially pre-teens. Although millions of young girls and boys have been vaccinated against HPV since 2006, the safety profiles of these drugs are just starting to become available. HPV vaccines are said to be as safe as or safer than other commonly used vaccines, but no vaccine is without risk. Common side effects reported with the HPV vaccines have included fainting, pain, swelling at the injection site, headaches, nausea, and fever. According to the CDC (2014), out of 90 million doses of HPV vaccines given in the United States between 2006 and 2016, it received 33,945 reports of adverse events; 7 percent were classified as "serious" (CDC, 2016). There have been deaths associated with HPV vaccines, but according to the CDC (2016), none was directly attributable to the vaccine.

Another important issue is that no other vaccines are directed toward one gender. Boys are as susceptible to HPV as girls are and are equally involved in transmitting the virus to others. Roughly 9,500 men are diagnosed with HPV-associated cancers each year, including cancers of the anus/rectum or penis as well as some head and neck cancers. There is neither a test to detect HPV in men nor one to detect early signs of HPV-associated cancers in men. Although the FDA and CDC both recommend the HPV vaccine for boys and young men between the ages of 9 and 21, the vaccine is not being promoted as heavily for boys, and boys are not specifically included in any proposed mandates, although this is starting to change (CDC, 2016). Much of the debate about whether boys should be vaccinated against HPV has focused solely on cost-effectiveness, not its impact on overall health (Bixler, 2011).

Eliminating HPV and associated cancers also requires addressing health disparities. Because the HPV vaccine must be administered in two to three separate doses during a specific age range and over a period of six months to be effective, it is unclear how a successful vaccine campaign aimed at preventing cervical cancer would be administered among individuals without access to regular health care or other prevention services. The HPV vaccine is also expensive; the current cost for the whole series is $400. Those women who are least likely to be able to afford or access HPV vaccines on their own are also at highest risk for developing cervical cancer due to limited access to health care. Most women who die of cervical cancer never had regular Pap tests, had false negative results, or did not receive proper follow-up (Boston Women's Health Book Collective, 2011: 616). Large differences exist in the rates of cervical cancer among women from different racial and ethnic groups. In the United States, rates of cervical cancer are 45 percent higher among black women and 65 percent higher among Hispanic women than among white women. Death rates from cervical cancer are the highest among black women, followed by Hispanic women (CDC, 2013).

When discussing HPV, women who have sex with women have been ignored. Many people falsely believe that the risk of HPV and other STIs is relatively low among women who have sex with women. As a result, many health care providers incorrectly assume that these women do not need to be screened, tested, or educated about HPV and other STIs. And scientific agencies omit people who identify as transgender or intersex in their discussions of HPV and vaccinations. Since anyone is at risk for contracting HPV if they have contact with the genitals of an infected person, everyone should have access to appropriate information and services regarding HPV prevention.

Informed consent is another complex topic associated with vaccinating young girls for HPV. How much involvement should minors themselves have in the decision-making process concerning whether to be vaccinated against HPV? Can 9-year-old children be part of informed health care decision-making, or should we depend solely on parents or government to decide what is right for young people's sexual health? With a mandate, some families

who don't want the vaccine would be pressured to have it anyway, but access to those with limited means would be greatly increased. Without a mandate, some adolescents would be prevented from getting the vaccine due to lack of parental consent, lack of access, and/or lack of financial resources. Adolescents are able to learn about their health options and make decisions about birth control and abortion services (though these rights are constrained in many states by parental notification requirements for abortion and decreased access for poor and rural women). As feminists, we strongly advocate that everyone be able to make informed choices about any decisions pertaining to their bodies, sexuality, or procreation. Why should HPV vaccine decision-making be treated differently from other sexual health issues?

Also troubling is the paternalistic framing of the issue of mandatory vaccines—and even heavy-handed recommendations. Casper and Carpenter (2008) further expand on the complexities of sexuality and sexual health among young girls:

On balance, the HPV vaccine controversy has reinforced prevailing understandings of women as responsible for controlling sexual activity and reproduction—and as sexually innocent and endangered. Yet a significant threat to young women—unwanted sex and abuse—is surprisingly absent from current debates; moral conservatives seem not to have recognized the need to protect "presexual" girls from assailant-transmitted HPV. (p. 896)

Indeed, discussions of the HPV vaccine and the surrounding controversy in public health and medical literature do not consider the gendered power dynamics that affect heterosexual adolescent (or adult) experiences.

Regardless of the arguments either supporting or opposing the vaccine, all experts agree that HPV vaccines are not 100 percent effective in preventing all types of HPV or its complications. In fact, 30 percent of cervical cancer cases are caused by HPV strains not covered by the vaccine. Thus, current cancer prevention strategies must continue. It is critical that all women have access to regular health screenings and Pap tests. The vast majority of cervical cancer cases and cervical cancer deaths occur in developing countries without access to Pap tests (NIH, 2017). Early screening is still the most effective method for preventing and identifying cancer. When found early, cervical cancer is one of the most successfully treated cancers, with a 92 percent survival rate (ACS, 2017). Additionally, the HPV vaccine does not eliminate the need for safer sex practices. Education and barrier methods of protection (such as condoms and dental dams) remain necessary to prevent HPV, other STDs, and unintended pregnancies.

REFERENCES

American Cancer Society. 2017. "What Are the Key Statistics about Cervical Cancer?" https://www.cancer .org/cancer/cervical-cancer/about/key-statistics.html.

Bixler, Jennifer. 2011. "CDC Committee Recommends Boys Receive HPV Vaccine." *CNN Health*. http://www .cnn.com/2011/10/25/health/hpv-vaccine/.

Boston Women's Health Collective. 2011. *Our Bodies, Ourselves*. New York: Touchstone. 616–17.

Casper, Monica J., and Laura M. Carpenter. 2008. "Sex, Drugs, and Politics: The HPV Vaccine for Cervical Cancer." *Sociology of Health and Illness*, 30: 886–99.

Centers for Disease Control and Prevention. 2013. "Cervical Cancer Rates by Race and Ethnicity. http:// www.cdc.gov/cancer/cervical/statistics/race.htm.

———. 2014. "Human Papillomavirus Vaccine Coverage among Adolescents, 2007–2013, and Post Licensure Vaccine Safety Monitoring, 2006–2014—United States." *Morbidity and Mortality Weekly Report*, 63(29): 620–24.

———. 2016. *Human Papillomavirus (HPV)*. https://www .cdc.gov/hpv/index.html.

Cervical Cancer Action. 2011. "Why Now? About Cervical Cancer." http://www.cervicalcanceraction.org/whynow /about.php.

National Conference of State Legislatures. 2017. *HPV Vaccine: State Legislation and Statutes*. http://www.ncsl .org/research/health/hpv-vaccine-state-legislation-and -statutes.aspx.

NIH. 2017. *Cervical Cancer*. https://report.nih.gov /nihfactsheets/viewfactsheet.aspx?csid=76.

Udesky, Laurie. 2007. "Push to Mandate HPV Vaccine Triggers Backlash in USA." *The Lancet*, 369 (March 24).

"PROPER SEX WITHOUT ANNOYING THINGS": ANTI-CONDOM DISCOURSE AND THE "NATURE" OF (HETERO)SEX

VIRGINIA BRAUN

In this [reading], I take a critical discursive perspective to analyse anti-condom discourse and interrogate the "nature" of (hetero) sex that is produced through this discourse. I take an anti-essentialist position, whereby this nature is understood as socially constituted, and contingent on time and place, rather than reflective of some core essence or truth about what (hetero)sex is.

CULTURAL NARRATIVES, SEXUALLY TRANSMITTED INFECTIONS AND THE PARADOX OF SAFER SEX

Condoms are important because they remain one of the key public and sexual health strategies to fight the transmission of sexually transmitted infections. . . . STIs are a major source of morbidity globally, with potential significant future impacts in terms of fertility and other aspects of sexual and reproductive health, and thus constitute a significant public health concern (World Health Organization, 2007). Most STIs are preventable by correct, consistent condom use. However, the research literature on condom use demonstrates that condoms are often not routinely or consistently used in sexual encounters (e.g., Abel and Brunton, 2005; Adolescent Health Research Group, 2003; De Visser and Smith, 2001; Fisher and Boroditsky, 2000; Grimley and Lee, 1997; Grunseit, 2004; Measor, 2006; Santelli et al., 1997; Tavory and Swidler, 2009; Wellings et al., 2001), even when there is a common understanding of the importance of condom use for sexual health (Mantell et al., 2011; Mashinini and Pelton Cooper, 2012; Williamson et al., 2009), and/or an intention or desire to use them (Gavey and McPhillips, 1999; Gavey et al., 2001). The persistence and even increase in STI incidence is an outcome of inconsistent use. While it might appear that condoms offer a simple prevention solution to STIs, and thus the failure effectively to implement this strategy within heterosexual communities represents a paradox, the problematic uptake and use of condoms are understandable if we consider the cultural narratives that exist around them (I focus on heterosexually related condom discourse; the situation with condom use within gay male communities is also complicated, and is an overlapping yet also different story). . . .

Condoms are typically viewed negatively by users—and non-users—(e.g., Chapman and Hodgson, 1988; Flood, 2003; Holland et al., 1998; Lowe, 2005; Mantell et al., 2011; Measor, 2006; Smith et al., 2012; Tavory and Swidler, 2009; Williamson et al., 2009; Winskell et al., 2011), and patterned negative meanings around condoms and condom use are remarkably persistent across time and also across different geographic locations, within, but also beyond, Anglo-western countries. Anti-condom discourse primarily falls into one or more of three main categories:

(1) pleasure/sensation; (2) intimacy/connection; and (3) spontaneity/interruption. Condoms are claimed to reduce the physical pleasure sensation experienced in sex, reportedly making sex like a "shower in a raincoat" (Chapman and Hodgson, 1988) or "'like eating a sweet in the wrapper" (Mashinini and Pelton Cooper, 2012; Tavory and Swidler, 2009). Such imagery evokes a massively reduced sensory experience for men (pleasure reduction is sometimes also reported by women). Condoms are also claimed to reduce or remove the intimacy of sex, and the sense of emotional connectedness possible, resulting in "fucking not making love" (Measor, 2006: 394). They are also disliked because they disrupt a smooth and insistent "trajectory" of (hetero)sex toward coitus, apparently "killing the moment" and making sexual spontaneity impossible.

. . . In this [reading], I aim to take the analysis of condom discourse further, by not only demonstrating the persistence of anti-condom discourse, but by examining the way a particular nature of heterosex is constructed in and through (anti-)condom discourse. I argue that this works to perpetuate ongoing resistance to condom use. In doing so, I examine Lowe's (2005: 75) contention of a "two-way relationship between contraception and heterosexual practices."

METHOD

The data for this [reading] come from a qualitative project on the social contexts of heterosexual STI transmission, which involved 15 focus groups with "lay" individuals aged below 35, as well as 32 individual interviews with professionals working in the area of sexual health (see Terry et al., 2012) in Aotearoa/New Zealand. . . .

Focus group participants were recruited through advertising, word of mouth, and snowballing. Two individuals were hired specifically to recruit participants from their broad networks. In total, 58 participants (38 female, 20 male) took part in 15 groups. Some groups were composed of strangers, and others of friends or acquaintances. Six were female only, four were male only, and the remaining five were mixed. The average age of participants was 25 (range: 16–36). Almost all participants identified as white, and most were working. The demographic profile of the participants does not reflect the ethnic/cultural diversity of residents of Aotearoa/New Zealand. . . .

All participants had had experiences of heterosexual sex and the vast majority identified as heterosexual. The average number of sexual relationships was six; the average number of sexual partners was over 12. At the time of data collection, 64% were in a relationship, and the average duration of these relationships was over three years; almost all were monogamous/exclusive. Seventy-five percent reported that they had engaged in casual sex at least once. Virtually all talked about engaging in "unsafe" sexual practices (e.g., intercourse without a condom, not knowing the STI status of partner or self) at some point, and 73% reported some sort of sexual health check-up (at least once). Twenty-five percent reported having had at least one known STI (of these, 27% reported more than one; 7% overall).

. . . Topics discussed included ideas and meaning around having sex; what sexual health is; knowledge of STIs and STI prevention; factors associated with unsafe sex; Aotearoa/New Zealand's STI statistics; and ideas about sexual health promotion. . . . Names and other identifying features have been changed. . . .

ANALYSIS

. . . Accounts of condoms that could be coded as "positive" were very rare in the data (only 17 extracts were coded as positive in any way across the entire dataset); most commonly, these related to a reassurance, lack of worry or "peace of mind" (Melanie . . .) related to risk of pregnancy or contracting an STI following sex. On two occasions, positive accounts related to making sex "nice and contained and unmessy" (Molly). . . . :

Melanie: I might sound like a prude I find it really like I I I I I like to use condoms and I actually find it quite gross not using them just I find—
?: Oh really?
Melanie: Like the whole semen in body thing quite weird. . . .

Here, Melanie's identity-amelioration work, her hesitation and multiple-repeats of the "I" signal "liking" condoms as uncommon, and as a perspective that's not easy to express. That this account is unexpected is reinforced by the repeated "oh really" response from one of her co-participants. Overall, then, positive accounts within the data were very rare, and potentially difficult to express, suggesting a widespread cultural norm of anti-condom sentiment.

In contrast, both anti-condom discourse and reports of condom-free "risky" sexual practices were prevalent. While reported relationships to condoms were complex, sometimes contradictory,[1] and certainly not uniform, a range of repeated and frequent negative meanings was evident, across both women's and men's accounts, in mixed- and single-sex groups. I begin by briefly outlining dominant accounts of condoms and "safe-sex" practice, to provide the broader context for making sense of discursive framings on condoms that follows.

"Safe Sex Is Condoms I Reckon" but "Condoms Suck"[2]

In line with public health discourse, the dominant account of "safe sex" was of condom use. . . . However, while condoms appear as the standard response to a question about what counts as safe sex, this was bounded and limited, with safer-sex discourse typically located only around vaginal intercourse.[3] The concept and practice of "protected" oral sex (both fellatio and cunnilingus) was rejected (as is common, see Stone et al., 2006):

VB: What would you think of you know as safe sex?
James: Um a condom usually. . . . That's about it.
VB: Mhmm.
Jason: I mean I gather that strictly speaking um you shouldn't even be having oral sex if it's going to be (mhm) protected but everyone does, so um.
Brandon: What's that what's that thing dental dam or something?
Jason: Exactly[.] I mean it's like it sounds that sounds like something esoteric. (laughs)
Brandon: And while I go down on, you you know—
Jason: (laughs) Yeah I'll just slip out my my gladwrap—
James: A condom for your mouth. (laughs)
. . . [ellipses in original]
Dylan: I wouldn't know about what you could get off the woman from her giving you oral sex[.] I'd have no idea I've heard some people say they reckon it's quite dangerous and . . . the general consensus seems to be you can't really catch anything.
VB: So you wouldn't wear a condom?
James: During what?
Jason: For a blowjob?
VB: For a blowjob.
Jason: No.
James: No no[;] try and avoid that one. (laughs)
Dylan: It's just not even worth it.

This extract demonstrates what could be called the "standard story" (Nairn and McCreanor, 1991) of safer heterosex: the use of condoms, but their containment to just vaginal (or anal) intercourse. Dylan's use of "just" in the final line provides a bottom-line position: the use of a condom renders fellatio not just less pleasurable, but "not even worth it." These participants normalise not using a condom or a dental dam during oral sex, through invocations of "consensus" and what "everyone does." While condom use (for coitus) simply is "safe sex," condom use for fellatio, or dental dam use for cunnilingus, do not form part of standard safer-sex discourse. Indeed, Brandon names the product, but then disclaims certainty of this knowledge—"dental dam or something"—while Jason reinforces non-normality with the adjective "esoteric." The use of language of "gladwrap" (clingfilm) or a (plastic) "shopping bag" (Jocelyn) similarly positions them outside the conceptual realm of sex. Such talk constructs the dental dam as an item not designed for the task in hand, as unerotic, and thus as categorically separate from sex. An evocation of "holding hands and wearing gloves" in relation to condom use for fellatio (George) does similar work: it invokes "unnaturalness" and "undesirableness"; the unstated desirable in these acts is skin-on-skin contact. Effectively, the idea of protected oral sex is framed as an unreasonable, excessive, and undesirable "demand"; such talk also constitutes an articulation of what "sex" should be about, which I develop further later in the [reading].

Despite a ready articulation of condoms for coitus as safe sex, condom-protected vaginal intercourse was similarly often framed as "unnatural" or less than natural by a number of participants. . . . This lack of "naturalness" was one of a range of offered motivations for why people might do "unsafe sex":

Kate: Pleasure, and doing it the most natural way, and feel good factor, and kind of what we said before about pleasing the guy, and you know, what as a girl, as a woman, knowing that guys hate condoms generally speaking, and wanting it to have, like, to be good for them.

This extract invokes many common features of anti-condom discourse (e.g., Flood, 2003). Across the dataset, the "safe sex is condoms" account coexisted with overwhelmingly dominant negative constructions of condoms, as negatively impacting across all aspects of sexual experience. Participants easily articulated dislike of condoms. . . . Kate associated "hating" condoms with men; like many other female participants, she also expressed her own "hatred" of them:[4] . . . "I think condoms are awful things[—]I wouldn't[—]I hate them."

Kate's language of hatred evokes a passionate, unequivocal and emotional response to condoms. The level of dislike of condoms, and the negative experience of sex with condoms, was often constructed as particularly intense through the use of such extreme language:

VB: So it's kind of why, you know, people have unsafe sex because?
Hermione: It's easy.
Gertrude: Condoms suck.
Bob: Condoms do take away all the feeling. . . .
Gertrude: It's so much more fun without one.
Bob: It is definitely better without one. . . .
Gertrude: I think it feels horrible.
Bob: Yeah definitely.
Gertrude: I can't stand them.

Alongside emotional evaluations, Bob's use here of an extreme case formulation about a loss of "all the feeling" works to produce a very negative reality for condom use. . . . Here, the "feeling" of sex is constructed in dichotomous terms: with a condom, you have no feeling; without a condom, you have full feeling. . . .

With the use of such language, it becomes inappropriate and even unreasonable to expect condoms to be routinely used in vaginal intercourse, particularly given the current dominant Western discourse which focuses on the right—indeed, obligation—to maximise sexual pleasure (Braun, 2005; D'Emilio and Freedman, 1997). If sex is about pleasure, and condoms remove, let alone just reduce, pleasure, they effectively remove the purpose of sex. These articulations reveal the entrenched way pleasure and safety remain competing sexual discourses in relation to heterosex (see Khan et al., 2004). . . .

The Condom-as-Killer

The condom-as-killer destroys an otherwise "natural" progression of sex, and the pleasures of it. Along with accounts of pleasure removal, condoms reportedly killed the mood of sex:

VB: Why do you think people do have, you know, unsafe sex then, why might they?
Samantha: Cos they'd say fuck it, it kills the mood putting on a condom.
Kevin: They're terrible.
Samantha: They're terrible things really.
Kimberly: They are actually.

This account is again characterised by extreme and maximising language (Potter, 1996), where the effects of condoms are brutal and final—death and destruction are not partial effects. As Edwards, Ashmore and Potter argued, "death" arguments invoke "the reality that should not be denied" (1995: 26, emphasis in original). The metaphor of the condom-as-killer appears to operate similarly, to invoke a (brutal) reality that should not be denied and, rhetorically, to invoke guilt (about the need for condom use, see Edwards et al., 1995, who claim the rhetorical effect of such death critiques is guilt induction). "Pleasing your male partner through very good sex" appears in (heterosexual) women's magazines as an important discourse, coexisting with a discourse of men as "naturally" inclined to cheat if the sex is not good enough, thus rendering male sexual pleasure an important concern for heterosexual women (Farvid and Braun, 2006).

Condoms were similarly talked about as killing the "moment":

François: I think it's also back to trust, 'cause if you gonna put a condom on, right, then you don't trust them, 'cause you trying to protect yourself from them, so I mean that can kill the moment, "hold on, we need to protect my—I need to protect myself from something you may have," so that while they're lying there things are running

through their mind, things are running through your mind, plus the time.

Here, the "sexual moment" is represented as a fragile thing, easily disruptable (see also Flood, 2003), and a moment/mood, which, it is suggested, requires a dislocation from "normal" (rational) concerns and thoughts. Others similarly described a loss of desire and a disruption to a presumed trajectory for sex with the introduction of a condom. . . .

Jason: It's just physiologically it just kills everything.
Brandon: It does.
Jason: And you're just like and the condom falls off and you're like "oh okay." (laughs)
James: Got another one.
Jason: (laughs) "I guess we're not having sex then."

. . . [I]n Jason's account, "sex" was obliterated by the physiological actions of his (formerly erect) penis, a response he blamed on the condom (see Measor, 2006, for more on men's stories around condom-induced erectile loss). In this account, the agency in his bodily change is given to the condom, rather than with his body, or his mind. . . . [T]he mind and "conscious thought" are located as a source of desire destruction, but activated by the condom and what it represents.

What is notable in these accounts is how fragile the supposedly robust and ever-present male sexual drive (Hollway, 1989) is. It is represented as something that can be eradicated by the mere hint of a condom (see also Vitellone, 2000). The metaphor of condom-as-killer endows the condom with agency within a sexual encounter (indeed, seemingly with more agency than the people involved, or their desires), and this agency is an ability actively to ruin a sexual encounter or experience. Rather than sexual manslaughter, this is sexual murder! The condom: tried, convicted and sentenced. As such, the metaphor works as a profoundly efficient and effective discursive resource for resisting condom use, and for perpetuating the negativity of much anti-condom discourse.

The metaphor was deployed to describe both the physical effects of a thin sheath, and also more symbolic, emotional or relational effects. For instance:

Stella: There can be something about sex that can be about becoming really intimate with someone and sharing something really special and when you have a piece of plastic between that, that's lost, you don't have that anymore, and it can also put up issues of trust. Like if you're in relationship when you're starting out you know, if you have to wear a condom it can be, it's kind of like a message to say I don't trust you, which is unhelpful.

. . . Intimacy and sharing—both emotional experiences and processes—are framed as hindered by this "plastic." The condom is positioned as an intimacy-killer, as well as a passion- and mood-killer. . . .

Alongside the explicit language and imagery of death and destruction that was prevalent in the data, the metaphor of condom-as-killer was also frequently evoked in a more "downgraded" form, through the language of "interruption":

Apollo: Yeah, it interrupts the heat of the moment. You've got to stop and fumble around in front of her and hopefully keep going.
Stella: It's all very unromantic.

The idea of "the heat of the moment," another common trope around sex, again invokes a "natural" trajectory for heterosex that is linear and cumulative (Lowe, 2005). Sex involves a build-up of passion (heat), and any disruption to this is thus a disruption to sex. Such accounts work to conceptually separate condoms from "desirable" sex; condoms are constructed as not synonymous with, or even oppositional to, things that sex is or should be about, such as passion, or romance. . . .

This metaphor of condom-as-killer invokes a closely related metaphor—of war or a battle—a (very hegemonically masculine) metaphor commonly deployed across domains as diverse as disease/immunology (Martin, 1989; Sontag, 1990) and the business world (Koller, 2004). If the condom (the bad guy) is attacking sex (the good guy), they must metaphorically battle it out. This works to construct sex and condoms in opposition to each other, and there must be a winner and loser. If the condom is the winner, sex (sexual sensation, the man, and even the relationship) is the loser; if sex is the winner, the condom is the loser (one does not get used). . . .

Adam, Eve, and the Nature of Heterosex

The metaphor of condom-as-killer and the evocation of a battle between sex and the condom construct a particular ideal form of heterosex, where sex should be a natural, continuous process, unimpeded by the "interruption" of a condom, following a linear trajectory toward penetration and ultimate pleasure (orgasm). It also re-articulates a particular "essential" nature of heterosex. . . .

The metaphor of condom-as-killer requires not only an opponent, but one that precedes the condom—something for it to kill, destroy or maim. The metaphor only makes sense if sex is positioned as separate from, but importantly also prior to, condoms. This evokes an essence or nature for what (hetero)sex is that conceptually excludes the condom. The model of sex that participants tended to articulate was one that did indeed exclude condoms. For instance . . . Oliver [said], "It's not like Adam and Eve, Adam and Eve didn't use condoms."

Reference to Adam and Eve provides a lovely example of how sex and condoms were conceptually separated. Through an invocation of a biblical past, and, in biblical terms, the origin of humanity and also of sex, sex necessarily precedes condoms. Condoms can only logically follow; they become the "unnatural" addition to the original ("natural") sexual act.[5]

In quite a different way, Jenna also positioned sex as naturally condomless:

Jenna: Yeah[,] they're just so annoying and like[,] you know[,] half the time they're just going to like come off or like rip or something it's just like why (laughs) if it's going to rip we may as well just not use one anyway and just have proper sex without annoying things.

Like Stella's earlier account of a piece of "plastic," the condom is here described in a way that positions it as inadequately designed for sex, and thus not really suitable for use in that context. But of primary analytic interest is Jenna's claim around "proper sex." If "proper sex" is what you do without a condom, a condom can only detract from sex in its pure form; condom-sex can only be "not proper sex." Such descriptions invoke a "natural" state of sex that is condomless, and implicitly contrast with an "unnatural" state of sex: sex that involves condoms (see also Lowe, 2005).

. . . To describe a condom as something that requires "stopping" sex, taking the actors out of that moment, requires a conceptualisation of sexual activity (and even a sexual mood) as something separate from a condom, again as something that precedes a condom. The not-sexual status ascribed to condoms is not inherent in the object itself; condoms are, alternatively, only a sexual object, as they have no purpose beyond sex. Indeed, if sex is constructed as a build-up toward ultimate pleasure, then the putting on of a condom could be seen as "anticipatory to further pleasure," rather than "destroying" the moment. But it was not. Instead, through accounts of stopping sex or killing the moment, the action of putting on a condom was framed as an essentially non-sexual event. . . .

CONCLUSIONS

. . . Within my data, the central account of sex as essentially condomless, and the metaphor of condoms-as-killer of the essence of sexual

activity and pleasure, work to produce a reality whereby heterosex exists conceptually separately to condoms, and where sex and condoms are oppositional, with condomless sex as the original, the pure and ideal form of sex, and condom sex as a poor imitation. Sex was almost entirely located within a discourse of passion and pleasure, the dominant, but relatively new, Western construction of (hetero)sex (D'Emilio and Freedman, 1997). In contrast, condoms were located within a discourse of sexual "safety," which is effectively constructed as a discourse of displeasure. Khan et al. (2004) and others have argued for the need to reconstruct condoms as part of the domain of heterosexual "pleasure" rather than "pain." How this can be done, and how safer heterosex can be eroticised, remains a crucial question (see Warr, 2001, also Allen, 2004). The tenacity of anti-condom discourse shows that challenge to be a deep one.

What I have argued here, however, is that it is important not just to interrogate and challenge anti-condom discourse for sexual health promotion, but to start to unpack and destabilise the foundational constructions of "sex" on which they rest. If we truly believe that sex is not a natural act (Tiefer, 2004), then this meaning is also up for contestation. Without contestation, it seems likely that anti-condom discourse will remain entrenched.

FUNDING

This research was funded by a University of Auckland Vice Chancellor's Research Excellence Award to Virginia Braun.

NOTES

1. . . . For instance, . . . Melanie then went on to say "like I think I me(unclear) from a sexual point like I think sex definitely feels better without a condom (VB: mm) and it's definitely more enjoyable but it's just kind of like mm it's just a bit icky."

2. First quotation from Jenna; second quotation from Gertrude.

3. Although anal intercourse was too rarely discussed to make conclusive comments, it was framed as desirable

to use a condom, but primarily because the anus was constructed as a "dirty" site, with potential for vaginal contamination if (unprotected) vaginal intercourse followed.

4. Although anti-condom discourse was expressed by almost all participants, regardless of gender, positioning and responsibility around sexual safety appeared gendered in certain ways in much of the data, with women in general (not necessarily the participants themselves) positioned as wanting condom use and men (both the participants and men in general) positioned as wanting to avoid condom use. Sex was often framed as an inherently non-communicative experience, but sex and safer sex (non) negotiations were often expressed in gendered terms, with safer sex something women were expected to want but often unable to express (e.g., see Gavey and McPhillips, 1999), and men as exploiting a knowledge of women's "vulnerability" around this. . . . Men's dislike of condoms was assumed, and women appeared often to expect to, or be expected to, engage in "work" to manage or accommodate this taken-for-granted truth. . . .

5. . . . The use of Adam and Eve (and the Bible) as the archetype of natural, acceptable or preferred behaviour has also been common in debates around lesbian and gay rights (e.g., Clarke, 2001).

REFERENCES

Abel G and Brunton C (2005) Young people's use of condoms and their perceived vulnerability to sexually transmitted infections. *Australian and New Zealand Journal of Public Health* 29(3): 254–60.

Allen L (2004) Beyond the birds and the bees: Constituting a discourse of erotics in sexuality education. *Gender and Education* 16(2): 151–67.

Braun V (2005) In search of (better) female sexual pleasure: Female genital 'cosmetic' surgery. *Sexualities* 8(4): 407–24.

Chapman S and Hodgson J (1988) Showers in raincoats: Attitudinal barriers to condom use in high-risk heterosexuals. *Community Health Studies* 12(1): 97–105.

Clarke V (2001) What about the children? Arguments against lesbian and gay parenting. *Women's Studies International Forum* 24(5): 555–70.

D'Emilio J and Freedman EB (1997) *Intimate Matters: A History of Sexuality in America*, 2nd ed. Chicago, IL: The University of Chicago Press.

De Visser RO and Smith AMA (2001) Inconsistent users of condoms: A challenge to traditional models of health behaviour. *Psychology Health & Medicine* 6(1): 41–46.

Edwards D, Ashmore M and Potter J (1995) Death and furniture: The rhetoric, politics and theology of bottom line arguments against relativism. *History of the Human Sciences* 8(2): 25–49.

Farvid P and Braun V (2006) 'Most of us guys are raring to go anytime, anyplace, anywhere': Male and female sexuality in Cosmopolitan and Cleo. *Sex Roles* 55(5–6): 295–310.

Fisher WA and Boroditsky R (2000) Sexual activity, contraceptive choice, and reproductive health indicators among single Canadian women aged 15–29: Additional findings from the Canadian contraception study. *The Canadian Journal of Human Sexuality* 9(2): 79–93.

Flood M (2003) Lust, trust and latex: Why young heterosexual men do not use condoms. *Culture, Health & Sexuality* 5(4): 353–69.

Gavey N and McPhillips K (1999) Subject to romance: Heterosexual passivity as an obstacle to women initiating condom use. *Psychology of Women Quarterly* 23(2): 349–67.

Gavey N, McPhillips K and Braun V (1999) Interruptus coitus: Heterosexuals accounting for intercourse. *Sexualities* 2(1): 35–68.

Gavey N, McPhillips K and Doherty M (2001) 'If it's not on, it's not on' – or is it? Discursive constraints on women's condom use. *Gender & Society* 15(6): 917–34.

Grimley DM and Lee PA (1997) Condom and other contraceptive use among a random sample of female adolescents: A snapshot in time. *Adolescence* 32(128): 771–79.

Grunseit AC (2004) Precautionary tales: Condom and contraceptive use among young Australian apprentices. *Culture, Health & Sexuality* 6(6): 517–35.

Holland J, Ramazanoglu C, et al. (1998) *The Male in the Head: Young People, Heterosexuality and Power*. London: The Tufnell Press.

Hollway W (1989) *Subjectivity and Method in Psychology: Gender, Meaning and Science*. London: SAGE.

Khan SI, Hudson-Rodd N, Saggers S, et al. (2004) Safer sex or pleasurable sex? Rethinking condom use in the AIDS era. *Sexual Health* 1(4): 217–25.

Koller V (2004) Businesswomen and war metaphors: 'Possessive, jealous and pugnacious'? *Journal of Sociolinguistics* 8(1): 3–22.

Lowe P (2005) Contraception and heterosex: An intimate relationship. *Sexualities* 8(1):75–92.

Mantell JE, Smit JA, Beksinska M, et al. (2011) Everywhere you go, everyone is saying condom, condom. But are they being used consistently? Reflections of South African male students about male and female condom use. *Health Education Research* 26(5): 859–71.

Martin E (1989) The cultural construction of gendered bodies: Biology and metaphors of production and destruction. *Ethnos* 54(3–4): 143–60.

Mashinini D and Pelton Cooper M (2012) HIV risk in a group of educated urban Black African women in South Africa: Private accounts of gendered power dynamics. *Feminism & Psychology* 22(2): 204–19.

Measor L (2006) Condom use: A culture of resistance. *Sex Education* 6(4): 393–402.

Nairn RG and McCreanor TN (1991) Race talk and common sense: Patterns in Pakeha discourse on Maori /Pakeha relations in New Zealand. *Journal of Language and Social Psychology* 10(4): 245–61.

Potter J (1996) *Representing Reality: Discourse, Rhetoric and Social Construction*. London: SAGE.

Santelli JS, Warren CW, Lowry R, et al. (1997) The use of condoms with other contraceptive methods among young men and women. *Family Planning Perspectives* 29(6): 261–68.

Smith J, Fenwick J, Skinner R, et al. (2012) Sex, condoms and sexually transmissible infections: A qualitative study of sexual health in young Australian men. *Archives of Sexual Behavior* 41(2): 487–95.

Sontag S (1990) *AIDS and its Metaphors*. London: Penguin.

Stone N, Hatherall B, et al. (2006) Oral sex and condom use among young people in the United Kingdom. *Perspectives on Sexual and Reproductive Health* 38(1): 6–12.

Tavory I and Swidler A (2009) Condom semiotics: Meaning and condom use in rural Malawi. *American Sociological Review* 74(2): 171–89.

Terry G, Braun V and Farvid P (2012) Structural impediments to sexual health in New Zealand: Key informant perspectives. *Sexuality Research and Social Policy* 9(4): 317–26.

Tiefer L (2004) *Sex is Not a Natural Act and Other Essays*, 2nd edn. Boulder, CO: Westview Press.

Vitellone N (2000) Condoms and the making of 'testosterone man': A cultural analysis of the male sex drive in AIDS research on safer heterosex. *Men and Masculinities* 3(2): 152–67.

Warr DJ (2001) The importance of love and understanding: Speculation on romance in safe sex health promotion. *Women's Studies International Forum* 24: 241–52.

Wellings F, Nanchahal K, Macdowall W, et al. (2001) Sexual behaviour in Britain: Early heterosexual experience. *The Lancet* 358(9296): 1843–50.

Williamson LM, Buston K and Sweeting H (2009) Young women and limits to the normalisation of condom use: A qualitative study. *AIDS Care* 21(5): 561–66.

Winskell K, Obyerodhyambo O and Stephenson R (2011) Making sense of condoms: Social representations in young people's HIV-related narratives from six African countries. *Social Science & Medicine* 72(6): 953–61.

World Health Organization (2007) *Global Strategy for the Prevention and Control of Sexually Transmitted Infections: 2006–2015. Breaking the Chain of Transmission*. Geneva: World Health Organization.

PrEP FOR HIV PREVENTION: COMMUNITY CONTROVERSY AND GENERATIONAL SEXUALITIES

GRIFF TESTER AND JENNIFER ROSEN

In the United States, rates of new human immunodeficiency virus (HIV) infections among gay men, other men who have sex with men (MSM), and transgender women are high (Dieffenbach and Fauci, 2011). In 2012, the U.S. Food and Drug Administration (FDA) approved a daily pill for people who are HIV negative but at high risk of infection that significantly reduces their chances of becoming infected. Despite this new treatment, called pre-exposure prophylaxis (PrEP), being a groundbreaking new development in HIV prevention, it generated very little media attention but quite a bit of controversy.

Damon L. Jacobs (2016), a licensed marriage and family therapist and self-described "PrEP Warrior," notes his surprise at the absence of media attention and lack of widespread celebration in queer communities. In an article published on an online HIV/AIDS resource webpage, The Body, Jacobs recounts the backlash he experienced when he began talking openly about using and advocating for PrEP. After starting an evidenced-based PrEP-focused Facebook group, he writes, "I received emails from strangers full of hate, venom, calling me a 'Truvada whore,' 'drug pusher,' 'sex addict,' 'corporate shill,' and one person even called me a 'passive murderer.'" Jacobs had expected community excitement but soon realized he underestimated "the persistent toxicity of fear" gay men feel about HIV, which is rooted in decades of sex-negativity, homophobia, and contradictory messages about and meanings attached to "safe sex." Indeed, the responses Jacobs received about his PrEP advocacy are not exceptional (see Belluz, 2014). Rather, they are illustrative of the current controversies in gay communities surrounding this new biomedical HIV-prevention approach.

In this reading, we first describe PrEP, the controversies surrounding it, and the biomedical and public health research related to the debates. Then, using the work of Ken Plummer (2010), a prominent sexuality scholar and founding editor of the journal *Sexualities*, we argue that a historical view is crucial to understanding the social context within which PrEP emerged and is currently situated and negotiated. Specifically, we maintain that the controversies surrounding PrEP are related to long-held biases about gay men, particularly as sexual actors who are incapable of making "appropriate" decisions about sexual health. In other words, the current PrEP controversies can be traced to beliefs that date back to the beginning of the epidemic, if not before.

RATES OF NEW HIV INFECTIONS

The Centers for Disease Control and Prevention (CDC) reported a 19 percent decline in the annual number of new HIV diagnoses between 2005 and 2014 in the United States (2016). Decreases among heterosexuals account for the bulk of the decline. During the same time, new diagnoses for gay and bisexual men increased by about 6 percent, particularly among young black and Latino men. This is consistent with other research suggesting that, in the United States, rates of new HIV infections are highest among gay men, other MSM, and transgender women, particularly impacting people of color (Dieffenbach and Fauci, 2011; van Griensven et al., 2009). While rates have remained high since 2014, they are stabilizing for gay and bisexual men in all racial and ethnic groups except Latinos (CDC, 2016).

WHAT IS PrEP?

In 2012, the FDA approved Truvada, an antiretroviral medication, for use by HIV-negative individuals. Oral Truvada contains two drugs that work together to prevent the virus from replicating in the body. PrEP is a prevention strategy that includes taking Truvada daily and making quarterly visits to a medical provider to monitor the impact of the medication on the kidneys and liver and to be tested for sexual transmitted infections (STIs). Truvada has few side effects,[1] and when the PrEP protocol is followed as prescribed, it is 99 percent effective at preventing HIV (Grant et al., 2010; Koester and Grant, 2015). Research shows that PrEP has proven effective for MSM, heterosexual men and women, and intravenous drug users (Baeten et al., 2012; Escudero et al., 2015). In a particularly informative study, researchers at Kaiser Permanente followed 650 MSM using PrEP for 36 months and found no new HIV infections (Volk et al., 2015).

In 2014, CDC issued a recommendation that anyone at "substantial risk" for HIV consider PrEP (CDC, 2014). Using data between 2007 and 2012, the CDC estimated that there are approximately 1.2 million adults in the United States who may benefit from PrEP, including 500,000 gay and other MSM (Smith et al., 2015). Research shows that as more at-risk individuals use PrEP, there will be benefits to the population more broadly. Predictions using mathematical models suggest that one-third of new infections in the United States can be prevented over the next ten years if 40 percent of

the people defined as high risk adhered to the PrEP protocol 62 percent of the time (Jenness et al., 2016). Increasing the number of PrEP users may also result in a significant decline in other STIs over time, since the PrEP protocol requires regular STI screening (Jenness, Weiss, et al., 2017).

Because gay and other MSM account for the bulk of new infections, public health officials have targeted these groups for PrEP. However, PrEP uptake across all groups has been slow (Krakower et al., 2012; Burns et al., 2014; Kirby and Thornber-Dunwell, 2014). Despite a dramatic increase in new prescriptions in the last few years, it is estimated that only 80,000 Americans are using PrEP (Rawlings et al., 2016), which is significantly lower than the number of estimated Americans who may benefit from it.

Research has shown that the slow uptake of PrEP is related to several factors, including a lack of awareness among potential users and primary-care providers and the cost of the medication, the required medical visits, and lab work (Grov et al., 2015; Horberg and Raymond, 2013). For many Americans, PrEP remains inaccessible, despite Truvada being covered by most insurance plans, the creation of programs in some states designed to improve access, and the drug manufacturer's insurance copay assistance program (Golub et al., 2013). According to Gilead Sciences, the drug manufacturer, most Truvada users are white men in their late 30s who are geographically concentrated in five states (i.e., California, New York, Texas, Florida, and Illinois) and nine cities (i.e., New York, San Francisco, Chicago, Washington, D.C., Los Angeles, Seattle, Boston, Atlanta, and Philadelphia) (Rawlings et al., 2016). While cost and knowledge are major barriers to the use of PrEP, the controversy surrounding and stigma attached to PrEP also help explain its slow uptake (Calabrese and Underhill, 2015; Gallagher et al., 2014).

THE "PrEP WARS"

While the widespread celebration initially envisioned by Damon Jacobs did not happen, many within gay communities and health institutions enthusiastically welcomed PrEP onto the prevention scene. Those who support PrEP acknowledge that it is not suitable for everyone, either because some people prefer and effectively use other prevention methods and/ or they lack access to the medical care necessary to use PrEP (Calabreze and Underhill, 2015). However, supporters call for expanded access because they believe it is a much-needed HIV-prevention tool for communities at high risk. Prior to PrEP, queer community and public health groups spent nearly three decades stressing individual-level behavioral change tactics for HIV prevention, particularly condoms for penetrative sex. As mentioned earlier, gay and other MSM continue to make up the bulk of new infections in the United States despite these messages. Research shows that gay men's condom use has been inconsistent, and that will likely continue (Dean, 2009; Grant and Koester, 2016).

Some men feel condoms impede sexual pleasure and intimacy (Calabreze and Underhill, 2015; Gamarel and Golub, 2015; Grant and Koester, 2016). While public health organizations increasingly acknowledge the relationship between sexual pleasure and well-being (Calabreze and Underhill, 2015; Grant and Koester, 2016; Race, 2016), mainstream prevention messages are generally aimed at simply providing health-related information, largely ignoring the role of sexual desire, sexual pleasure, and sexual meanings (Leonard, 2012; Race, 2016). PrEP provides a highly effective prevention option for people who desire barrier-free sexual intimacy and pleasure (Calabreze and Underhill, 2015; Gamarel and Golub, 2015; Grant and Koester, 2016).

In fact, by removing the fear and anxiety about HIV, PrEP may actually increase sexual pleasure and sexual agency (Calabreze and Underhill, 2015). Unlike other prevention tools, one partner does not have to convince the other to use a condom or wonder if they are accurately disclosing their HIV status. Likewise, if one's partner is HIV positive, they do not have to worry if they are consistently taking their antiretroviral therapy medications, which ensures that the virus cannot be passed (Gamarel and Golub, 2015; Grant and Koester, 2016). Additional empowerment comes from the fact that the decision to use PrEP takes place outside of the sexual moment, including those instances when alcohol or other substances are involved in decision making (Grant and Koester, 2016).

While research shows clear advantages to PrEP as a prevention strategy, opponents express concerns. The most commonly communicated fear is that PrEP will lead to gay men abandoning condoms, becoming more promiscuous, and, ultimately, increasing the rates of other STIs, which, at the individual level, Truvada does not protect against (Calabreze and Underhill, 2015; Duran, 2012; Spieldenner, 2016; Weinstein, 2015). Some PrEP critics, including some HIV-prevention leaders, have suggested that it is simply a "party drug" that enables promiscuity. In fact, PrEP-related "slut shaming" is widespread in gay spaces online (Belluz, 2014; Spieldenner, 2016). In the online comments section for an article published in the gay magazine *The Advocate*, posters called PrEP users "whores," "immature," and "undateable" (May 15, 2017). Another commenter remarked that drug companies were using PrEP to make money "off the backs of the gays" (Anderson-Minshall, 2017).

PrEP opponents maintain that long-standing behavioral strategies—such as remaining abstinent; practicing monogamy or minimizing the number of sexual partners; status disclosure;

always using condoms during sex; and regular HIV testing—are safer, cheaper, and more "respectable" (Dieffenbach and Fauci, 2011; Spieldenner, 2016). Additionally, as the comment above illustrates, opponents question the motivations of pharmaceutical companies (e.g., pushing profits over prevention or a cure).

There are queer interrogations of PrEP, too. Some queer scholars who may not necessarily oppose PrEP contend that "mass compliance with pharmaceutical mandates" has biopolitical side effects, such as viewing sex as simply a physical encounter that ignores the importance of pleasure, erotic fantasy, and how certain sexual acts, even risky sex, can be meaningful (Dean, 2015: 234; Race, 2016). Bailey (2016) is concerned that emphasizing biomedical prevention strategies benefits pharmaceutical companies and economically harms community-based organizations on the front lines in poor communities of color, where structural barriers (e.g., racism, homelessness, under- or unemployment, and hunger) to HIV prevention, testing, and treatment are high.

In addition to concerns about deemphasizing behavioral changes, opponents express concerns about the difficulties of daily adherence, a possible increase in other STIs, and the long-term side effects of Truvada (Spieldenner, 2016; U.S. Public Health Service, 2014: 24–26; Weinstein, 2015). However, studies show that adherence rates are generally good among gay men, especially among those who are at the highest risk of infection (Grant et al., 2014). Still, adherence is crucial. Like the birth control pill, to which PrEP is often compared, Truvada only works if users consistently take it. With this in mind, PrEP supporters suggest that public health officials and advocates in high-risk communities concentrate on developing ways to support adherence, rather than condemning PrEP and those who use or wish to use it (Calabreze and Underhill, 2015).

The existing biomedical and public health research suggests that gay men using PrEP may have more sexual partners, use condoms less often, and have other STIs more frequently than those not using PrEP (de Wit et al., 2015; Grov et al., 2015; Kojima, Davey, and Klausner, 2016; Marcus et al., 2013; Volk et al., 2015). However, questions remain about the relationship among using PrEP, condomless anal sex, and other STIs (Grant et al., 2014). Recent increasing rates of condomless anal sex and a resurgence of STIs among gay men predate PrEP (CDC, 2013; McCormack et al., 2014). There are currently no data on long-term patterns of sexual behavior after an individual begins using PrEP (Jenness, Akshay, et al., 2017). Likewise, without studies of gay men not using PrEP, we cannot know for sure whether PrEP use has caused increases in other STI rates. In addition, since STI testing is part of the PrEP protocol, users have more contact with medical providers, and test more frequently, than nonusers. Importantly, research also shows that gay men who are at the greatest HIV risk (e.g., those reporting receptive anal condomless sex before starting PrEP) are adopting PrEP at the highest rates (Grov et al., 2015; Grant et al., 2014). Leading HIV/PrEP researchers Kimberly Koester and Robert Grant (2015: 1605) suggest that, from a public health perspective, rising incidence of treatable STIs, in the context of decreased or no new HIV infections, is a "good problem to have" (2015: 1605).

Recognizing gay men's agency and resilience, and acknowledging the importance of history, they stress:

Trusting that PrEP users and their communities will respond to the threat of STIs can allow for novel and potentially more durable transformation of sexual health–promoting behaviors. For example, members of the gay community historically led the innovations around safer sex practices in the face of HIV/AIDS (Berkowitz, 2003). If the STI burden in the context of PrEP use become too great, communities can and will make course corrections. (Koester and Grant, 2015: 1605)

GENERATIONAL SEXUALITIES

Given PrEP's effectiveness, we have to ask why its adoption has been so controversial within gay communities. We argue that the best way to understand this is to apply Plummer's generational sexualities framework. Plummer (2010) contends that human sexuality is complex, contradictory, and contested, because it is constructed in social situations and layered in social contexts. He declares, "We are the storytelling, historical, political, ethical, symbolic, imaginative, memorializing sexual animal" (2010: 164). Part of the complexity of human life and sexuality stems from its generational character, or how life is shaped by social meanings saturated with historical and personal experiences (Plummer, 2010). As Plummer (2010: 165) explains, "At any moment of thinking about the sexual, we will usually find at least five generations helping shape that moment." Despite life's generational frames, Plummer emphasizes that generational experiences are never fully unified, because of social class, ethnicity, gender, sexuality, and the influence of other social forces. Indeed, "sexual practices (e.g., 'vanilla,' 'kinky,' 'raunchy'), sexual roles (e.g., 'top,' 'bottom,' 'versatile'), sexual types (e.g., 'bear,' 'daddy,' 'surfer,' 'cowboy'), and more recently serostatus ('HIV-positive,' 'HIV-negative') and sexual behaviors within the context of serostatus (e.g., 'safer sex only,' 'bareback sex')" create additional divisions within and across generations of gay men" (Yep, Lovaas, and Pagonis, 2002: 9).

Generational sexualities do not merely refer to chronological age or age cohorts but encompass *generational standpoints*, particular perspectives based on symbolic content experienced within a given time period and eventually communicated to subsequent age cohorts (Plummer, 2010). Generational standpoints emerge based on shared *critical sexual life events*—those critical moments, as cultures and sexual worlds shift, that create collective memories, identities, and new sexual worlds. They reveal the sexual attitudes, desires, and objects that are acceptable and visible, and those that are forbidden and hidden. As we consider below, the overlapping and clashing viewpoints about PrEP are shaped by the historic and enduring cross-generational sexual standpoints about gay men and gay sex that developed in response to the discovery of HIV/AIDS in 1981 and life-saving treatments in 1996.

Moreover, Plummer challenges the idea that a fully agreed upon dominant sexual culture exists, such as a prevailing "safe sex" ethos. Plummer maintains that if such a culture exists, or is invented, it must be understood in connection to other sexual cultures that are always present, even if they are located beneath the surface. These *sexual subterranean traditions* are the "lived sexual cultures that run against the grain, where any ideas of a dominant world or a hegemonic dominance are subverted, resisted, quietly ignored, or loudly challenged" (Plummer, 2010: 165). Like their conventional counterparts, rival sexual traditions have a range of generational forms and leave traces on successive generations. Plummer uses sex work as an example of a subterranean tradition that challenges the dominant view that sex is only appropriate in the context of traditional heterosexual marriage and for procreation.

Dominant and subterranean sexual cultures are evident in the PrEP Wars, too. Condoms have been a fundamental tool of HIV prevention for over 30 years and a sexual object uniquely embedded in gay men's sexual worlds (Chrimp, 1987; Spieldenner, 2016). Indeed, since the mid-1980s, "unprotected" sex meant anal sex without condoms, and, in the context of HIV/AIDS, mainstream public health models and society in general labeled gay men who did not always use condoms as mentally deficient or compulsive (i.e., pathological). PrEP's success has shaken the foundations of the prevailing condom-based notions of "safe/risky" and "protected/unprotected" sex (Auerbach and Hoppe, 2015; Dean, 2015; Koester and Grant, 2015; Spieldenner, 2016). What does unprotected sex mean for gay men in the era of PrEP? Many critics claim that an individual having condomless sex while using PrEP is not practicing "safe" sex, despite the clinical data suggesting otherwise, and they imply that gay men who use or wish to use PrEP are pathological. As this suggests, while PrEP is new, the standpoints framing the contentious debates about it are not. Indeed, noncondom-based HIV-prevention approaches (i.e., sexual subterranean traditions), which challenge mainstream positions about sex and risk and the presentation of gay men as sexual actors who are incapable of making "appropriate," healthy decisions, have deep roots stretching to the beginning of the epidemic. In the next section, we historically ground the current reactions to PrEP by exploring these origins.

GAY MEN, SEX, AND HIV RISKS

Constructing "Safe Sex"

Sparked by the threat of illness and death, and framed by a broader homophobic culture that regarded gay men and gay sex as deviant and pathological (i.e., a critical sexual event), gay communities created "safe sex," or what was later called "safer sex" (i.e., a sexual standpoint). Initially, this happened with little to no help from government or scientific and medical institutions (Epstein, 1996; Kippax and Race, 2003; Patton, 1996; Rofes, 1996). Rather, faced with the uncertainty of the disease and largely abandoned by medical and scientific establishments, gay communities developed and shared their own knowledge about their sexual experiences/health, ultimately producing their own set of behavioral changes aimed at prevention (Epstein, 1996; Kippax and Race, 2003; Patton, 1996; Rofes, 1996).

Early on, gay communities shared sex-positive and culturally based messages that attempted to engage with the social, symbolic, and biomedical complexities of sex and HIV. They used homoerotic imagery to situate condoms as part of the shared sexual and cultural norms of gay men, incorporating them as a way to attain pleasure in an epidemic (Leonard, 2012). For example, in 1982, a San Francisco–based activist group, the Sisters of Perpetual Indulgence, published a pamphlet that noted: "Mysterious forms of cancer and pneumonia are now lurking among us" (this was how the disease was first understood), and they made recommendations, such as using condoms, to remain healthy. In 1983, the year researchers at the Pasteur Institute in Paris isolated the virus that would later be named HIV (Barre-Sinoussi et al., 1983), members of the gay community in New York and their doctor published a pamphlet, *How to Have Sex in an Epidemic: One Approach*. Berkowitz (2003) contends that these two community-based sexually explicit publications are the foundations of "safe sex." In using sex-positive imagery, they empowered gay men to respond to the unknown illness by, at least in part, continuing to be sexually active while taking certain precautions (i.e., condoms) (Berkowitz, 2003).

Official U.S. public health HIV/AIDS education did not appear until 1986, and President Reagan did not publicly mention HIV/AIDS until 1987 (Patton, 1996). Like gay men who are using or considering PrEP now, gay men then found themselves in a "highly politicized position" (Race, 2016: 13). Mainstream health institutions eventually appropriated "safe sex" minus the queer aesthetic, which non-gay groups claimed was offensive and promoted homosexuality (Leonard, 2012). Mainstream health institutions utilized fear tactics and promoted monogamy and constant condom usage (Holt, 2014; Patton, 1996; Race, 2003; 2008). As is still the case with most dominant definitions of sexual health (Bailey, 2016), the focus of these early conventional codes was strictly on eliminating risks and reducing STIs, while ignoring issues of sexual meaning, desire, and pleasure (Halprine, 2007; Race, 2008; 2016; Rofes, 1998).

By the late-1980s, studies showed that most gay men were well informed about HIV/AIDS, and that they were increasingly using condoms for anal sex. However, these studies also showed that some gay men did not always or ever use condoms (Ames and Beeker, 1990; Hart et al., 1992). This research was limited and did not reflect the complexity of gay men's sexual lives. For example, researchers did not ask study participants about the types of relationships within which they had "protected" or "unprotected" sex, nor were they asked whether they knew their partners' HIV status before making sexual decisions (Hart et al., 1992). Nevertheless, the revelation that some gay men were not fully embracing the "condom ethic" (Race, 2008) sparked controversy within and outside of gay communities. Condomless anal sex, regardless of context, was—and, as the PrEP debates show, still is—viewed simply as "bad people" engaging in "bad behavior" (Holt, 2014; Race, 2003; Rofes, 2007). Based on this assessment, HIV-positive gay men became seen as the ultimate sexual deviant, an undesirable "other" against which HIV-negative gay men were defined (Román, 1997; Yep, Lovaas, and Pagonis, 2002).

Critiques of gay men and gay sex came from within gay communities, too, where some drew on society's morality-based sex-negativity, arguing that sexuality needed to be controlled (Patton, 1996; Rofes 1996; 1998; Race, 2016). They recycled stereotypes about the "unrestrained," abnormal, and immoral gay liberation culture of the 1970s, which linked gay emancipation to sexual freedom, labeling "gay liberation as a simple, selfish libertinism, a cause of AIDS," and gay men as fatalistic and sexually compulsive (Patton, 1996: 125). Rofes (1996) argued that some gay professionals at the helms of HIV/AIDS groups, which were becoming more institutionalized in the early 1990s, maintained rather than challenged the homophobic and oppressive sociopolitical system. Rofes (1996: 102) asserted that the relationship between the "gay masses" and some gay leaders replicated "a traditional pattern of interaction between marginalized groups and newly formed classes of 'professionals' and 'experts' who offer assistance"; his comment is relevant to PrEP in the current context.

Others in gay communities pushed back, maintaining a liberationist stance and challenging what they saw as enduring efforts to control sexuality (Patton, 1996; Rofes, 1996). Liberationists asserted that, to counter the persistent negative images of gay men, the history of gay men's resistance against psychological, medical, and social oppression, and their celebration of sex, had to be embraced, not condemned. They encouraged gay men to explore their own sexual meanings and experiences, and to understand safer sex as something to be constructed and reconstructed, not as a rigid practice without context (Patton, 1996; Rofes, 1996; Dean, 2009). Liberationists observed that, from the beginning of the epidemic, gay men have actively made sense of HIV within a homophobic sex-negative culture by embracing a stance that positioned gay men as capable of making "healthy" decisions that balanced risk, desire, and pleasure (Epstein, 1996; Race, 2016; Rofes, 2007; Spieldenner, 2014; 2016).

Subterranean Ideas about Sex and Risk

Like Plummer's (2010) view of sex, a queer sexual perspective comprehends the relationship between sex and risk as complicated and contextual. This relationship reflects power relations (i.e., risks are structured by homophobia, racism, poverty, HIV stigma, etc.), changing facts about HIV, and the lived sexual realities and cultural norms of various groups of queer people, including risk-taking *and* creativity, determination, and resilience in the face of adversity (Diaz and Ayala, 1999; Bailey, 2016; Carballo-Dieguez and Bauermeister, 2004; Peterson and Jones, 2009; Race, 2016; Rofes, 1996). Indeed, Rofes writes that "most of the gay men in their erotic adventures are not sick, immature, or vestiges of a bygone era rebuked by AIDS but instead brave innovators ever expanding the possibilities of intimacy and play, even and especially in the context of risk" (2007: v).

As discussed above, subterranean sexualities (i.e., sex without condoms) have existed since the beginning of the epidemic. After 1996, more raucously defiant underground sexual identities and practices, such as "barebackers" and "barebacking," or "the conscious and deliberate practice of unprotected anal intercourse" (Yep, Lovaas, and Pagonis, 2002: 4), became more visible in gay communities. In 1996, highly active antiretroviral therapies (HAART) were approved for treatment (Holt, 2014). HAART do not cure HIV but can reduce the quantities of the virus in the body to an "undetectable" level, resulting in a relatively normal healthy lifespan for people who are infected (May et al., 2014). Surely, the HAART breakthrough was a critical sexual event, shifting the epidemic from a deadly to a manageable chronic illness, particularly for resource-rich individuals and communities (Elford, 2006; Halkitis et al., 2004). Also, a person who is HIV positive and has an "undetectable" viral load is significantly less likely to transmit the virus to their HIV-negative sexual partners even when condoms are absent, which is why medical professionals see testing individuals at high risk and treating those who are as positive as an effective method of prevention (Cohen et al., 2011).

After HAART and throughout the late-1990s and into the 2000s, MSM of various ages, with various identities (e.g., "positive," "negative," and "gay" or "queer") and political positions (e.g., liberationist or assimilationist politics) attempted to make sense of the early AIDS crisis and the substantially altered, but ongoing, threat of HIV. This period was also marked by immense assimilationist gains in lesbian and gay rights (e.g., state and federal laws for marriage equality). However, unlike the increasing mainstream interest in most things gay, such as celebrities and heteronormative gay families, society still refused to acknowledge gay sexuality, or to have any meaningful discussions about the complexities of sex and risk (Dean, 2015; Race, 2008).

Despite the shadows cast by mainstream gay politics and an enduring refusal to acknowledge gay sex during this time, subterranean sexual behavior flourished, further highlighting the intricacies of sexuality and HIV prevention. Barebacking surfaced as a sexual and political identity among some gay men, and the fact that this behavior was deliberate, even celebrated, sparked more fervent debates within gay communities (Dean, 2009; 2015). Some queer scholars argue that barebacking is radical defiance to imposed norms of sex and health that have come from both within and outside of gay communities since the early 1980s (Dean, 2009; 2015; Rofes, 2007). Others suggest that barebacking reflects the structural vulnerabilities that some people face, particularly queer people of color (Bailey, 2016). Queer scholar Tim Dean (2009) situates barebacking on a continuum, distinguishing among barebacking with the desire to avoid HIV transmission, which appears to represent the motivations of the bulk of gay men who engage in condomless sex (Dawson et al., 2005; Grov and Parsons, 2006), barebacking with indifference to HIV, and barebacking with intention for viral transmission.

The practice of *serosorting* is a risk-reduction strategy, located on the "desire to avoid HIV" end of the barebacking range. Serosorting involves discussing HIV status with potential casual partners, and only having condomless sex with those who have the same status (Holt, 2014; Suarez and Miller, 2001). Romantic or regular sexual partners who agree to only having condomless sex with each other, and to always use condoms with casual partners, can reduce risks without always using condoms (Hart et al., 1992; Holt, 2014; Kippax et al., 1993). *Cum play*, or semen sharing, including "ejaculation over the anus, rubbing semen over the anus, or using semen as lubricant during masturbation or for digital and penile penetration," is another sexual behavior that defies the normative notion of "safe sex," since, because of HIV, semen has been characterized as "toxic" and "deadly," at least for gay men (Dean, 2009; Prestage, Hurley, and Brown, 2013: 1348). Barebacking, like cum play, can be practiced in a way that reduces risk (Prestage, Hurley, and Brown, 2013); and this behavior underlines the symbolic importance of semen as a normatively forbidden sexual "object."

Critics of serosorting question gay men's ability to effectively negotiate condomless sex, especially with casual partners, because it requires trusting that people accurately and honestly disclose their HIV status (Holt, 2014; Zablotska et al., 2009). Some even doubt gay men's ability to establish trust and honesty within sexual or romantic relationships, or to maintain sexual agreements (Ekstrand et al., 1993; Hoff and Beougher, 2010). Advocates acknowledge that these are risk-reducing, not risk-eliminating, approaches and argue that these strategies underscore gay men's agency, desires, and meanings (Holt, 2014). Writing about "desires of defiance," Rofes (2005: 123), like Plummer, reminds us that "for many, the forbidden becomes desired; taboo produces cravings; the return of the repressed is made corporeal and is experienced as an enormous hunger."

CONCLUSION

Given PrEP's incredible success at preventing new HIV infections, the lack of widespread celebration within gay communities might be surprising. However, when PrEP is considered within Plummer's generational sexualities framework, the controversy surrounding PrEP makes more sense. According to Plummer, and consistent with queer/liberationist perspectives, sexuality is complex, contradictory, and contested because it is constructed in social situations and layered in social-historical contexts. Critical events in the sexual histories of MSM, such as the discovery of HIV/AIDS and HAART, create and reinforce sexual standpoints that embody and reveal a society's cultural norms However, there were and still are, several—often opposing—sexual standpoints about gay men and gay sex, which are reflected in the overlapping and clashing viewpoints about PrEP.

The controversies surrounding PrEP have roots that even predate the early epidemic in the 1980s and reflect long-held biases about gay men, gay sex, and sexual health. These biases and the controversy they generated have likely shaped the slow uptake of this new prevention tool among gay men, which is significant considering the high rates of new HIV infections. Narratives of dominant and subterranean sexual cultures form the heart of this debate concerning the use of condoms during sex. The mainstream narrative has been (and continues to be) that the only gay sex that is "safe" is sex with condoms; but gay men's subterranean sexual worlds reveal that this narrative has never fully captured the lived experiences of all gay men and their divergent sexual norms. PrEP's success has reignited this debate and raised questions, once again, about what it means to have safe sex. In other words, while PrEP is new, the standpoints framing the contentious debates about it are not. Despite the evident need for HIV-prevention approaches that do not involve condoms, which PrEP provides, it is still a challenge to mainstream notions of sex and risk.

NOTE

1. Nausea, abdominal cramping, vomiting, dizziness, headache, and fatigue are possible short-term side effects of Truvada. For most people using the medication, these side effects occur during the first week or two of use and then go away. For a very small number of individuals, Truvada can also effect their renal function, or they can experience a loss of bone mineral density. These side effects are rare and reversed when the individual stops using the medication (Baeten et al., 2012; Grant et al., 2010). In a review of five major PrEP studies, Kojima and Klausner (2016) found that, as far as user safety, Truvada is comparable to aspirin.

REFERENCES

Ames, L. J., and C. Beeker. 1990. "Gay Men in Small Cities: How Risky Are They?" In *Sixth International Conference on AIDS*. June 20–24. San Francisco.

Anderson-Minshall, Jacob. May 15, 2017. "The New Gay Sexual Revolution." *The Advocate*. Retrieved June 14, 2017, from http://www.advocate.com /current-issue/2017/5/15/new-gay-sexual-revolution.

Auerbach, Judith D., and Trevor A. Hoppe. 2015. "Beyond 'Getting Drugs into Bodies': Social Science Perspectives on Pre-Exposure Prophylaxis for HIV." *Journal of the International AIDS Society*, 18(4 Suppl 3): 19983.

Baeten, Jared M., Deborah Donnell, Patrick Ndase, Nelly R. Mugo, James D. Campbell, Jonathan Wangisi, Jordan W. Tappero, et al. 2012. "Antiretroviral Prophylaxis for HIV Prevention in Heterosexual Men and Women." *New England Journal of Medicine*, 367(5): 399–410.

Bailey, Marlon. 2016. "Black Gay (Raw) Sex." In E. Patrick Johnson (ed.). *No Tea, No Shade: New Writings in Black Queer Studies*. Durham, NC: Duke University Press. 239–61.

Barre-Sinoussi, F., J. C. Chermann, F. Rey, M. T. Nugeyre, S. Chamaret, J. Gruest, and C. Dauguet. 2004. "Isolation of T-Lymphotropic Retrovirus from a Patient at Risk for Acquired Immune Defficiency Syndrome (AIDS)." *Science*, 220(4599): 868–71.

Belluz, Julia. 2014. "The Truvada Wars." *British Medical Journal*, 348–51. doi: 10.1136/bmj.g3811.

Berkowitz, R. 2003. *Stayin' Alive: The Invention of Safe Sex; a Personal History*. Boulder, CO: Westview Press.

Burns, David N., Cynthia Grossman, Jim Turpin, Vanessa Elharrar, and Fulvia Veronese. 2014. "Role of Oral Pre-Exposure Prophylaxis (PrEP) in Current and Future HIV Prevention Strategies." *Current HIV/AIDS Reports*, 11(4): 393–403.

Calabrese, Sarah K., and Kristen Underhill. 2015. "How Stigma Surrounding the Use of HIV Pre-Exposure Prophylaxis Undermines Prevention and Pleasure: A Call to Destigmatize 'Truvada Whores.'" *American Journal of Public Health*, 105(10): 1960–64.

Carballo-Diéguez, Alex, and José Bauermeister. 2004. "'Barebacking' Intentional Condomless Anal Sex in HIV-Risk Contexts: Reasons for and against It." *Journal of Homosexuality*, 47(1): 1–16.

Centers for Disease Control and Prevention. 2013. "HIV Testing and Risk Behaviors among Gay, Bisexual, and Other Men Who Have Sex with Men—United States." *Morbidity and Mortality Weekly Report*, 62(47): 958.

———. 2014. "Pre-exposure Prophylaxis for the Prevention of HIV Infection in the United States—2014: A Clinical Practice Guideline." 67. https://www.cdc.gov/hiv/pdf /guidelines/PrEPguidelines2014.pdf.

———. 2016. "Trends in US HIV Diagnoses, 2005–2014" (Fact Sheet). https://www.cdc.gov/nchhstp/newsroom /docs/factsheets/hiv-data-trends-fact-sheet-508.pdf.

Cohen, Myron S., Ying Q. Chen, Marybeth McCauley, Theresa Gamble, Mina C. Hosseinipour, Nagalingeswaran Kumarasamy, James G. Hakim, et al. 2011. "Prevention of HIV-1 Infection with Early Antiretroviral Therapy." *New England Journal of Medicine*, 365(6): 493–505.

Crimp, Douglas. 1987. "How to Have Promiscuity in an Epidemic." *October* [MIT Press], 43: 237–71.

Dawson, Alvin G., Jr., Michael W. Ross, Doug Henry, and Anne Freeman. 2005. "Evidence of HIV Transmission Risk in Barebacking Men-Who-Have-Sex-with-Men: Cases from the Internet." *Journal of Gay and Lesbian Psychotherapy*, 9(3–4): 73–83.

de Wit, J. B. F., D. A. Murphy, L. Lal, J. M. Audsley, N. Roth, R. Moore, B. K. Tee, T. Read, and E. J. Wright. 2015. "O19. 2 Pre-Exposure Prophylaxis and Risk Compensation: Evidence of Decreased Condom Use at Three-Month Follow-Up among Predominantly Gay Male Participants in the Vicprep Study. *Sexually Transmitted Infections*, 91(Suppl 2): A68.1–A68.

Dean, Tim. 2015. "Mediated Intimacies: Raw Sex, Truvada, and the Biopolitics of Chemoprophylaxis." *Sexualities*, 18(1–2): 224–46.

———. 2009. *Unlimited Intimacy: Reflections on the Subculture of Barebacking*. Chicago: University of Chicago Press. 97–100.

Diaz, Rafael M., and George Ayala. 1999. "Love, Passion and Rebellion: Ideologies of HIV Risk among Latino Gay Men in the USA." *Culture, Health and Sexuality*, 1(3): 277–93.

Dieffenbach, Carl W., and Anthony S. Fauci. 2011. "Thirty Years of HIV and AIDS: Future Challenges and Opportunities. *Annals of Internal Medicine*, 154(11): 766–71.

Duran, David. November 12, 2012. "Truvada Whores?" *Huffington Post*. Retrieved June 14, 2017, from http://www.huffingtonpost.com/david-duran/truvada-whores_b_2113588.html.

Ekstrand, Maria, Ron Stall, Susan Kegeles, Robert B. Hays, Michael DeMayo, and Thomas Coates. 1993. "Safer Sex among Gay Men: What Is the Ultimate Goal?" *AIDS*, 7(2): 281–82.

Elford, Jonathan. 2006. "Changing Patterns of Sexual Behaviour in the Era of Highly Active Antiretroviral Therapy." *Current Opinion in Infectious Diseases*, 19(1): 26–32.

Epstein, Steven. 1996. *Impure Science: AIDS, Activism, and the Politics of Knowledge*. Vol. 7. *Medicine and Society*. Berkeley: University of California Press.

Escudero, Daniel J., Thomas Kerr, Don Operario, Maria E. Socías, Omar Sued, and Brandon D. L. Marshall. 2015. "Inclusion of Trans Women in Pre-Exposure Phrophylaxis (PrEP): A Review." *AIDS Care*, 27(5): 637–41. doi: 10.1080/09540121.2014.986051.

Gallagher, Timothy, Lauren Link, Michael Ramos, Edward Bottger, Judith Aberg, and Demetre Daskalakis. 2014. "Self-Perception of HIV Risk and Candidacy for Pre-Exposure Prophylaxis among Men Who Have Sex with Men Testing for HIV at Commercial Sex Venues in New York City." *LGBT Health*, 1(3): 218–24.

Gamarel, Kristi E., and Sarit A. Golub. 2015. "Intimacy Motivations and Pre-Exposure Prophylaxis (PrEP) Adoption Intentions among HIV-Negative Men Who Have Sex with Men (MSM) in Romantic Relationships." *Annals of Behavioral Medicine*, 49(2): 177–86.

Golub, Sarit A., Kristi E. Gamarel, H. Jonathon Rendina, Anthony Surace, and Corina L. Lelutiu-Weinberger. 2013. "From Efficacy to Effectiveness: Facilitators and Barriers to PrEP Acceptability and Motivations for Adherence among MSM and Transgender Women in New York City." *AIDS Patient Care and STDs*, 27(4): 248–54.

Grant, Robert M., Peter L. Anderson, Vanessa McMahan, Albert Liu, K. Rivet Amico, Megha Mehrotra, Sybil Hosek, et al. 2014. "Uptake of Pre-Exposure Prophylaxis, Sexual Practices, and HIV Incidence in Men and Transgender Women Who Have Sex with Men: A Cohort Study. *The Lancet Infectious Diseases*, 14(9): 820–29.

Grant, Robert M., and Kimberly A. Koester. 2016. "What People Want from Sex and Preexposure Prophylaxis." *Current Opinion in HIV and AIDS*, 11(1): 3–9.

Grant, Robert M., Javier R. Lama, Peter L. Anderson, Vanessa McMahan, Albert Y. Liu, Lorena Vargas, Pedro Goicochea, et al. 2010. "Preexposure Chemoprophylaxis for HIV Prevention in Men Who Have Sex with Men. *New England Journal of Medicine*, 363: 2587–99.

Grov, Christian, and Jeffrey T. Parsons. 2006. "Bug Chasing and Gift Giving: The Potential for HIV Transmission among Barebackers on the Internet." *AIDS Education and Prevention*, 18(6): 490–503.

Grov, Christian, Thomas H. F. Whitfield, H. Jonathon Rendina, Ana Ventuneac, and Jeffrey T. Parsons. 2015. "Willingness to Take PrEP and Potential for Risk Compensation among Highly Sexually Active Gay and Bisexual Men." *AIDS and Behavior*, 19(12): 2234–44.

Halkitis, Perry N., David D. Zade, Michael Shrem, and Michael Marmor. 2004. "Beliefs about HIV Non-Infection and Risky Sexual Behavior among MSM." *AIDS Education and Prevention*, 16(5): 448–58.

Halperin, David M. 2007. *What Do Gay Men Want? An Essay on Sex, Risk, and Subjectivity*. Ann Arbor: University of Michigan Press.

Hart, Graham, Mary Boulton, Ray Fitzpatrick, John McLean, and Jill Dawson. 1992. "'Relapse' to Unsafe Sexual Behaviour among Gay Men: A Critique of Recent Behavioural HIV/AIDS Research." *Sociology of Health and Illness*, 14(2): 216–32.

Hoff, Colleen C., and Sean C. Beougher. 2010. "Sexual Agreements among Gay Male Couples." *Archives of Sexual Behavior*, 39(3): 774–87.

Holt, Martin. 2014. "Gay Men's HIV Risk Reduction Practices: The Influence of Epistemic Communities in HIV Social and Behavioral Research." *AIDS Education and Prevention*, 26(3): 214–23.

Horberg, Michael, and Brian Raymond. 2013. "Financial Policy Issues for HIV Pre-Exposure Prophylaxis." *American Journal of Preventive Medicine*, 44(1): S125–S128.

Jacobs, Damon. March 2, 2016. "The Persistence of HIV Fear in the Age of PrEP." *The Body*. Retrieved June 14, 2017 from http://www.thebody.com/content/77188/the-persistence-of-hiv-fear-in-the-age-of-prep.html.

Jenness, Samuel M., Steven M. Goodreau, Eli Rosenberg, Emily N. Beylerian, Karen W. Hoover, Dawn K. Smith, and Patrick Sullivan. 2016. "Impact of the Centers for Disease Control's HIV Preexposure Prophylaxis Guidelines for Men Who Have Sex with Men in the United States. *Journal of Infectious Diseases*, 214(12): 1800–07.

Jenness, Samuel M., Akshay Sharma, Steven M. Goodreau, Eli S. Rosenberg, Kevin M. Weiss, Karen W. Hoover, Dawn K. Smith, and Patrick Sullivan. 2017. "Individual HIV Risk versus Population Impact of Risk Compensation after HIV Preexposure Prophylaxis Initiation among Men Who Have Sex with Men." *PloS one*, 12(1): p.e0169484.

Jenness, Samuel M., Kevin M. Weiss, Steven M. Goodreau, Thomas Gift, Harrell Chesson, Karen W. Hoover, Dawn K. Smith, Albert Y. Liu, Patrick S. Sullivan, and Eli S. Rosenberg. "Incidence of Gonorrhea and Chlamydia Following Human Immunodeficiency Virus Pre-Exposure Prophylaxis among Men Who Have Sex with Men: A Modeling Study." *Clinical Infectious Diseases*, 65(5): 712–18.

Kippax, Susan, June Crawford, Mark Davis, Pam Rodden, and Gary Dowsett. 1993. "Sustaining Safe Sex: A Longitudinal Study of a Sample of Homosexual Men." *AIDS*, 7(2): 257–64.

Kippax, Susan, and Kane Race. 2003. "Sustaining Safe Practice: Twenty Years On." *Social Science and Medicine*, 57(1): 1–12.

Kirby, Tony, and Michelle Thornber-Dunwell. 2014. "Uptake of PrEP for HIV Slow among MSM." *The Lancet*, 383(9915): 399.

Koester, Kimberly A., and Robert M. Grant. 2015. "Editorial Commentary: Keeping Our Eyes on the Prize: No New HIV Infections with Increased Use of HIV Pre-Exposure Prophylaxis." *Clinical Infectious Diseases*, 61(10): 1604–05.

Kojima, Noah, Dvora Joseph Davey, and Jeffrey D. Klausner. 2016. "Pre-Exposure Prophylaxis for HIV Infection and New Sexually Transmitted Infections among Men Who Have Sex with Men. *AIDS*, 30(14): 2251–52.

Kojima, Noah, and Jeffrey D. Klausner. 2016. "Is Emtricitabine-Tenofovir Disoproxil Fumarate Pre-Exposure Prophylaxis for the Prevention of Human Immunodeficiency Virus Infection Safer than Aspirin?" *Open Forum Infectious Diseases*, 3(1): 1–5. doi: 10.1093 /ofid/ofv221.

Krakower, Douglas S., Matthew J. Mimiaga, Joshua G. Rosenberger, David S. Novak, Jennifer A. Mitty, Jaclyn M. White, and Kenneth H. Mayer. 2012. "Limited Awareness and Low Immediate Uptake of Pre-Exposure Prophylaxis among Men Who Have Sex with Men Using an Internet Social Networking Site." *PloS one*, 7(3): p.e33119.

Leonard, William. 2012. "Safe Sex and the Aesthetics of Gay Men's HIV/AIDS Prevention in Australia: From Rubba Me in 1984 to F** k Me in 2009." *Sexualities*, 15(7): 834–49.

Marcus, Julia L., David V. Glidden, Kenneth H. Mayer, Albert Y. Liu, Susan P. Buchbinder, K. Rivet Amico, Vanessa McMahan, et al. 2013. "No Evidence of Sexual Risk Compensation in the iPrEx Trial of Daily Oral HIV Pre-Exposure Prophylaxis." *PloS one*, 8(12): p.e81997.

May, Margaret T., Mark Gompels, Valerie Delpech, Porter Kholoud, Chloe Orkin, et al. 2014. "Impact on Life Expectancy of HIV-1 Positive Individuals of CD4+ Cell Count and Viral Load Response to Antiretroviral Therapy." *AIDS*, 28(8): 1193–202. doi: 10.1097 /QAD.0000000000000243.

McCormack, Sheena M., Mitzy Gafos, Monica Desai, and Myron S. Cohen. 2014. "Biomedical Prevention: State of the Science. *Clinical Infectious Diseases*, 59(Suppl 1): S41–S46.

McNeil, Donald. May 14, 2014. "Advocating Pill, U.S. Signals Shift to Prevent AIDS." *New York Times*. Retrieved May 31, 2017 from https://www.nytimes .com/2014/05/15/health/advocating-pill-us-signals-shift -to-prevent-aids.html?_r=0.

Patton, Cindy. 1996. *Fatal Advice: How Safe-Sex Education Went Wrong*. Vol. 147. *Series Q*. Durham, NC: Duke University Press.

Peterson, John L., and Kenneth T. Jones. 2009. "HIV Prevention for Black Men Who Have Sex with Men in the United States." *American Journal of Public Health*, 99(6): 976–80.

Plummer, Ken. 2010. "Generational Sexualities, Subterranean Traditions, and the Hauntings of the Sexual World: Some Preliminary Remarks." *Symbolic Interaction*, 33(2): 163–90.

Prestage, Garrett, Michael Hurley, and Graham Brown. 2013. "'Cum Play' among Gay Men." *Archives of Sexual Behavior*, 42(7): 1347–56.

Race, Kane. 2003. "Revaluation of Risk among Gay Men." *AIDS Education and Prevention*, 15(4: special issue): 369–81.

———. 2008. "The Use of Pleasure in Harm Reduction: Perspectives from the History of Sexuality." *International Journal of Drug Policy*, 19(5): 417–23.

———. 2016. "Reluctant Objects Sexual Pleasure as a Problem for HIV Biomedical Prevention." *GLQ: A Journal of Lesbian and Gay Studies*, 22(1): 1–31.

Rawlings, K. et al. 2016. "FTC/TDF (Truvada) for HIV Pre-Exposure Prophylaxis (PrEP) Utilization in the United States: 2013–2015." 21st International AIDS Conference, Durban. S. McCallister, presenting.

Rofes, Eric. 1996. *Reviving the Tribe: Regenerating Gay Men's Sexuality and Culture in the Ongoing Epidemic*. New York: Harrington Park Press.

———. 1998. *Dry Bones Breathe: Gay Men Creating Post-AIDS Identities and Cultures*. New York: Harrington Park Press.

———. 2005. *Radical Rethinking of Sexuality and Schooling: Status Quo or Status Queer?* New York: Roman and Littlefield.

———. 2007. "Thriving: Gay Men's Health in the 21st Century." Estate of Eric Rofes. http://citeseerx.ist.psu .edu/viewdoc/download?doi=10.1.1.694.2275&rep=rep 1&type=pdf.

Román, David. 1997. "Negative Identifications: HIV-Negative Gay Men in Representation and Performance." In Martin Duberman (ed.). *Queer Representations: Reading Lives, Reading Cultures*. New York: NYU Press. 162–76.

Smith, Dawn K., Michelle Van Handel, Richard J. Wolitski, Jo Ellen Stryker, H. Irene Hall, Joseph Prejean, Linda J. Koenig, and Linda A. Valleroy. 2015. "Vital Signs: Estimated Percentages and Numbers of Adults with Indications for Preexposure Prophylaxis to Prevent HIV Acquisition–United States 2015." *Morbidity and Mortality Weekly Report*, 64(46): 1291–95.

Spieldenner, Andrew. 2014. "Statement of Ownership: An Autoethnography of Living with HIV." *Journal of Men's Studies*, 22(1): 12–27.

———. 2016. "PrEP Whores and HIV Prevention: The Queer Communication of HIV Pre-Exposure Prophylaxis (PrEP)." *Journal of Homosexuality*, 63(12): 1685–97.

Suarez, Troy, and Jeffrey Miller. 2001. "Negotiating Risks in Context: A Perspective on Unprotected Anal Intercourse and Barebacking among Men Who Have Sex with Men—Where Do We Go from Here?" *Archives of Sexual Behavior*, 30(3): 287–300.

U.S. Public Health Service. 2014. *Preexposure Prophylaxis for the Prevention of HIV Infection in the United States—2014: A Clinical Practice Guideline*. Washington, DC: U.S. Public Health Service.

Van Griensven, Frits, Jan Willem de Lind van Wijngaarden, Stefan Baral, and Andrew Grulich. 2009. "The Global Epidemic of HIV Infection among Men Who Have Sex with Men. *Current Opinion in HIV and AIDS*, 4(4): 300–07.

Volk, Jonathan E., Julia L. Marcus, Tony Phengrasamy, Derek Blechinger, Dong Phuong Nguyen, Stephen Follansbee, and C. Bradley Hare. 2015. "No New HIV Infections with Increasing Use of HIV Pre-Exposure Prophylaxis in a Clinical Practice Setting." *Clinical Infectious Diseases*, 61(10): 1601–03.

Weinstein, Michael. 2015. "The War against Prevention." Retrieved May 17, 2017 from https://www.aidshealth.org/wp-content/uploads/2015/06/War-on-HIV-prevention.pdf.

Yep, Gust A., Karen E. Lovaas, and Alex V. Pagonis. 2002. "The Case of 'Riding Bareback': Sexual Practices and the Paradoxes of Identity in the Era of AIDS." *Journal of Homosexuality*, 42(4): 1–14.

Zablotska, Iryna B., John Imrie, Garrett Prestage, June Crawford, Patrick Rawstorne, Andrew Grulich, Fengyi Jin, and Susan Kippax. 2009. "Gay Men's Current Practice of HIV Seroconcordant Unprotected Anal Intercourse: Serosorting or Seroguessing?" *AIDS Care*, 21(4): 501–10.

AMERICA'S HIDDEN HIV EPIDEMIC

LINDA VILLAROSA

Early on a balmy morning last October, Cedric Sturdevant began his rounds along the bumpy streets and back roads of Jackson, Miss. Sturdevant, 52, has racked up nearly 300,000 miles driving in loops and widening circles around Jackson in his improvised role of visiting nurse, motivational coach and father figure to a growing number of young gay men and transgender women suffering from HIV and AIDS. Sturdevant is a project coordinator at My Brother's Keeper, a local social-services nonprofit. If he doesn't make these rounds, he has learned, many of these patients will not get to the doctors' appointments, pharmacies, food banks and counseling sessions that can make the difference between life and death.

Negotiating a maze of unpaved roads in Jackson in the company car, a 13-year-old Ford Expedition with cracked seats and chipped paint, he stopped to drop off HIV medication at a couple's home. One of the men was HIV-positive, the other negative; they lived in the neighborhood locals call the Bottom, where every fifth or sixth home is abandoned, with broken windows, doors hanging off hinges, downed limbs and dry leaves blanketing front yards. Sturdevant banged on the door of a small house, its yard overgrown with weeds, he knew not to leave the package on the doorstep, where it could be stolen. After a while a young man emerged, shirtless, shrugging off sleep. He had just gotten out of jail. Sturdevant handed him the package, shook his hand and told him to "stay out of trouble."

Sturdevant drove on another 15 minutes to pick up Marq (a shortened version of his name to protect his privacy), a teenager who was still reeling from the HIV diagnosis he received the previous spring. As they headed to and from a doctor's appointment and a meeting with a counselor, Sturdevant, slow-talking and patient, with eyes that disappear into his cheekbones when he smiles and a snowy beard, gently grilled him, reminding him to stay on his meds. The teenager slumped in the back seat, half listening, half checking his texts. He looked up briefly when Sturdevant told him, "You've come a long way. I'm proud of you." But Marq barely said goodbye as he jumped out of the car in front of a convenience store on an avenue scattered with a pawnshop, a liquor store and several Baptist churches, and he all but admitted he was planning to spend the afternoon smoking weed and looking at Instagram. "Knucklehead," Sturdevant whispered, as the teenager slammed the door. Pulling off his favorite Dallas Cowboys baseball cap and running a hand over his bald head, Sturdevant added softly, "Breaks my heart."

These patients of Sturdevant's are the faces of one of America's most troubling public-health crises. Thanks to the success of lifesaving anti-retroviral medication pioneered 20 years ago and years of research and education, most HIV-positive people today can lead long, healthy lives. In cities like New York and San Francisco, once ground zero for the AIDS epidemic, the virus is no longer a death sentence, and rates of infection have plummeted. In fact, over the past several years, public-health officials have championed the idea that an AIDS-free generation could be within reach—even without a vaccine. But in certain pockets of the country, unknown to most Americans, HIV is still ravaging communities at staggering rates.

Last year, the Centers for Disease Control and Prevention, using the first comprehensive national estimates of lifetime risk of HIV for several key populations, predicted that if current rates continue, one in two African American gay and bisexual men will be infected with the virus. That compares with a lifetime risk of one in 99 for all Americans and one in 11 for white gay and bisexual men. To offer more perspective: Swaziland, a tiny African nation, has the world's highest rate of HIV, at 28.8 percent of the population. If gay and bisexual African American men made up a country, its rate would surpass that of this impoverished African nation—and all other nations.

The crisis is most acute in Southern states, which hold 37 percent of the country's population and as of 2014 accounted for 54 percent of all new HIV diagnoses. The South is also home to 21 of the 25 metropolitan areas with the highest HIV prevalence among gay and bisexual men. Jackson, the capital of Mississippi, the country's poorest state, is best known for blues [and] barbecue. . . . It also has the nation's highest rate—40 percent—of gay and bisexual men living with HIV, followed by Columbia, S.C.; El Paso; Augusta, GA.; and Baton Rouge, LA. In Jackson, a small city of just over 170,000, half a dozen black gay or bisexual men receive the shock of a diagnosis every month, and more than 3,600 people, the majority of them black men, live with the virus.

The South also has the highest numbers of people living with HIV who don't know they have been infected, which means they are not engaged in lifesaving treatment and care—and are at risk of infecting others. An unconscionable number of them are dying: In 2014, according to a new analysis from Duke University, 2,952 people in the Deep South (Alabama,

Florida, Georgia, Louisiana, Mississippi, North Carolina, South Carolina, Tennessee and Texas) died with HIV as an underlying cause, with the highest death rates in Mississippi and Louisiana. Among black men in this region, the HIV-related death rate was seven times as high as that of the United States population at large.

Sturdevant, born and raised in Metcalfe, a tiny Mississippi Delta town of about 1,000, understands all too well the fear, stigma and isolation that can come with being a black gay man in the South. "Growing up, I was taught that God was not fixing to forgive a person who was homosexual," Sturdevant said. "The Bible supposedly said you're going straight to hell, automatically, there's no forgiveness. There were several times I thought about suicide. There were several times I wanted to get sick and die. Finally, my thought was, I just want to get out of here." He moved to Dallas, and then to Memphis.

When he learned he had HIV in 2005, Sturdevant knew little about the virus and was too depressed and ashamed to tell anyone at first. When his partner died the following year, he let the disease consume him. "I was weak, had a fever of 103, couldn't even keep down water," he recalled. Sturdevant has shared his story too many times to count, to let young men know that he has been there, too, and to help them understand that they can survive this plague. He also knows that many black gay and bisexual men have been rejected and discarded, and has wrapped his arms around as many as he can grab hold of, treating them like family. Sturdevant has two daughters from an early marriage and three grandchildren, but he says he feels just as strongly about his 16 or so unrelated "children," most of them living with HIV. He feeds them, sometimes houses them, but mostly listens to them. "Young black men feel abandoned and need someone they can believe in and who believes in them," Sturdevant said as he drove past fields of fluffy cotton, his hands resting lightly on the steering wheel. "I told God I want to be able to help guys like me, that didn't grow up with their father, and they started coming to me, wanting to talk. After a while, they would bring other people to me and say, 'Dad, can you help him, too?'"

Sturdevant moved his seat back, preparing for a long drive, and . . . headed to a small town 90 miles east of the city to visit Jordon, an HIV-positive 24-year-old. When Sturdevant himself was at his lowest point, he said, "I looked something like this boy we're going to see."

. . . [H]e turned down a dead-end street and pulled up in front of the one-story brick home where Jordon lived. "I'm real worried about him," Sturdevant said, lowering his voice as he walked up the driveway's cracked pavement toward the front door. Jordon had recently posted a photo of his skeletal frame on Facebook, asking friends to "pray for me."

As he stepped into Jordon's stuffy bedroom, Sturdevant's eyes scanned from a wheelchair leaning against the wall to a can of Ensure on the bedside table before settling on the young man. He was rubbing his feet, wincing from HIV-related neuropathy that caused what he described as "ungodly pain." Jordon's round, hooded eyes were sunk deep into his face. Gray sweatpants pooled around his stick-thin legs, so fragile they looked as if you could snap them in two. His arms were marked with scars from hospital visits and IVs. Over six feet tall, he weighed barely 100 pounds. He smiled slightly when he saw Sturdevant, dimples folding into his hollow cheeks. "Hey, Mr. Ced," he said, his voice raspy. . . .

With effort, Jordon sat up slightly, untangling himself from a jumble of sheets. Sturdevant asked how he was doing, and he cataloged a laundry list of what he called his "old man" ailments. "I've had everything—diarrhea, hemorrhoids, now this neuropathy," he said.

"My body hates me." Once a month, his mother or grandmother drove him to medical appointments in Jackson, to receive care from providers experienced in treating people living with HIV and to avoid the small-town gaze at the local facilities; there is no Gay Men's Health Crisis for him to visit in his small town, as there would be if he lived in New York. "Everybody knows everybody here," Jordon said. "At the hospital, they know my mom and my brother and my grandmother. I would rather be around people who don't know me." Too ashamed to admit that he had the virus, Jordon had told few friends about his diagnosis.

"Are you taking your medicine?" Sturdevant asked. For many young men, the HIV diagnosis and the illness are so overwhelming that maintaining a new and unfamiliar regimen of medication can be difficult. Jordon looked down. "Not as often as I should." When he saw Sturdevant's glare, he continued, sounding like a little boy. "I hate taking medicine; I hate it. I have to take six pills, now seven, eight, plus a shot—"

Sturdevant cut him off. "We all have to do this, Jordon. Don't you want to get better?"

Jordon let his head fall back on the pillow. "I know I can get better, Mr. Ced," he said, massaging his feet. "I just don't know how everything got so bad."

Given the advances in research, information and treatment, it seems inconceivable that someone living with the virus today, like Jordon, could look as if he had stepped out of the early years of the epidemic. And yet a series of fateful decisions and omissions, dating back to the discovery of the disease, have led to a present that looks like the past—but only for some.

History marks the beginning of the American AIDS epidemic as June 5, 1981, when an issue of the CDC's Morbidity and Mortality Weekly Report—the authoritative voice of the agency—highlighted five cases of pneumocystis pneumonia (PCP) in previously healthy men in Los Angeles. Healthy people do not contract a disease like PCP, which had been largely confined until then to patients on medication to suppress their immune systems for an organ transplant or cancer patients on chemotherapy. Though not stated explicitly, the language of the report, by omitting race, implied that its "five young men, all active homosexuals," were white, which they were. But there were two more documented cases, not mentioned in the notice, and these sixth and seventh cases were black—one of them a gay African American, the other a heterosexual Haitian.

Dr. Michael Gottlieb, the lead author of the report and a renowned physician specializing in HIV/AIDS, treated Rock Hudson before he died of AIDS complications in 1985 and still practices in Los Angeles. Gottlieb said he is often asked why he didn't include in that first report the documented case of the gay African American man, who had both PCP and cytomegalovirus, a virus that attacks the organs of patients with compromised immune systems. He explains that he discovered the case after the report was finalized. "Until recently, I wouldn't have thought it mattered," said Gottlieb, who said that he and others on the front line were grappling with an unprecedented and frightening medical mystery and largely working in the dark. "But in retrospect, I think it might've made a difference among gay black men."

Including gay black men in the literature and understanding of the origins of the disease and its treatment could have meant earlier outreach, more of a voice and a standing in HIV/AIDS advocacy organizations, and access to the cultural and financial power of the LGBT community that would rise up to demand government action. But 35 years of neglect, compounded by poverty and inadequate local health care infrastructure, have left too many black gay and bisexual men falling through a series of safety nets.

This has been true of even the most recent advances. In 2010, the Obama administration unveiled the first National HIV/AIDS Strategy, an ambitious plan that prioritized government research and resources to so-called key populations, including black men and women, gay and bisexual men, transgender women and people living in the South. With a mandate to "follow the epidemic," several pharmaceutical companies and philanthropic organizations also started projects to help gay black men, particularly in the Southern states. That same year, the Affordable Care Act and later the expansion of Medicaid in more than half of the country's states linked significantly more HIV-positive Americans to lifesaving treatment and care.

In 2011, HPTN 052, a study of 1,763 couples in 13 cities on four continents funded by the National Institute of Allergy and Infectious Diseases, found that people infected with HIV are far less likely to infect their sexual partners when put on treatment immediately instead of waiting until their immune systems begin to fall apart. This "test and treat" strategy also significantly reduces the risk of illness and death. The data [were] so persuasive that the federal government began pushing new HIV/AIDS treatment guidelines to health care providers the following year. And in 2012, the Food and Drug Administration approved the preventive use of Truvada, in the form of a daily pill to be taken as pre-exposure prophylaxis (commonly called PrEP). It has been found to be up to 99 percent effective in preventing people who have not been infected with HIV from contracting the virus, based on the results of two large clinical trials; an estimated 80,000 patients have filled prescriptions over the past four years.

But these measures have not extended to most black gay and bisexual men. A CDC report in February noted that only 48 percent of black gay and bisexual men effectively suppress the virus with consistent medication, and the numbers are even lower for these men in their late teens and 20s. In 2014, nearly one in five black gay men who had received a diagnosis of HIV had progressed to AIDS by the time they learned of their infection—which meant that they were generally very ill by the time they began treatment. Only a small percentage of black people use PrEP to prevent contracting the virus, accounting for only 10 percent of prescriptions; the vast majority of users are white. Many black gay and bisexual men either can't afford PrEP or don't know about it—they may not see a doctor regularly at all, and many medical providers haven't even heard of PrEP.

Turning things around would mean expanding testing and providing affordable treatment for those who are positive—to stop sickness and dying and also to block transmission of the virus. It would also require getting information and medication, including PrEP, to those most at risk. Even more challenging would be reducing the stigma, discrimination and shame that drive gay and bisexual men to hide their sexuality and avoid the health care system—and making sure providers have adequate resources and understand how to care for HIV patients.

"It's deeply troubling when 50 percent of African American gay men are expected to get HIV during their lifetime, but it's also been a clarion call for all of us to improve on what we're doing," said Dr. Jonathan Mermin, the director of the CDC's National Center for HIV/AIDS, Viral Hepatitis, STD and TB Prevention. "What we have been trying to do is ensure that we're having the greatest effect with the resources we're provided.". . .

For nearly two decades, the United States has focused money and attention on the HIV/AIDS epidemic elsewhere. Barbara Lee, the longtime United States representative from Northern California, has signed her name as a sponsor to every piece of major federal HIV/AIDS legislation since she was first elected in

1998. In 2003, she was a co-author of legislation that led to the President's Emergency Plan for AIDS Relief (Pepfar). The five-year, $15 billion global strategy provided prevention, treatment and care services to the countries most affected by the disease, almost exclusively in Africa. The largest international health initiative in history to fight a single disease, Pepfar is considered a success story by any measure and a crowning achievement of George W. Bush's presidency.

Black America, however, never got a Pepfar. Though the raw numbers were much lower than in Africa, parts of our country looked like the continent the program was created to save. Yet while buckets of money went overseas, domestic funding for HIV/AIDS remained flat, and efforts to fight the disease here were reduced to a poorly coordinated patchwork affair. "When we saw that the epidemic was out of proportion in the black community, we started calling for a domestic Pepfar that would bring new resources to the effort, create clear and ambitious objectives and rebuild health care infrastructure around the country," Lee said. "But we just couldn't get the administration to focus on a domestic plan.". . .

Beginning in the late '90s, the United States government funneled billions of federal dollars into abstinence-until-marriage programs here and abroad. In place of effective sex education, these programs often discouraged condom use while teaching abstinence as the only way to prevent the spread of AIDS—even as well-regarded research established that this kind of sex education does not lower the risk of contracting HIV and other sexually transmitted diseases.

During this time, many scientists, researchers and government administrators were afraid to speak openly about condoms, needle exchange and LGBT issues for fear of reprisal and loss of funding. Community organizations became targets of anti-gay crusades, subjected to intense scrutiny, including exhaustive audits, by federal agencies. "It is no coincidence that new rates of HIV infection among gay men, especially gay black men, began to spike sharply from 2000 on, because of an anti-science campaign that allowed for little or nothing to be done for a maligned community simply due to ideology and bigotry," Millett said. "The hostile environment made funding effective HIV-prevention programs, messages or research impossible for U.S. communities most impacted by HIV."

The election of Barack Obama brought renewed attention to the domestic epidemic and loosened the conservative grip on the federal government's prevention and research agenda. . . . On World AIDS Day in 2011, Obama directly addressed the HIV crisis among gay black men in a speech at George Washington University: "When new infections among young black gay men increase by nearly 50 percent in three years, we need to do more to show them that their lives matter."

But good intentions have not translated into enough funding and resources—from either the government or philanthropic organizations. Good intentions also have not counteracted the crippled medical infrastructure in states like Mississippi, which the Commonwealth Fund, an independent health-policy research foundation, ranks dead last in more than 40 measures of health-system performance. A 2014 study conducted by Dr. David Holtgrave of the Johns Hopkins Bloomberg School of Public Health found that to make any real progress in the HIV/AIDS crisis among black gay and bisexual men in the United States, the government would need to invest an additional $2.5 billion to address unmet testing, care, treatment and prevention needs. Despite the higher HIV diagnosis and death rates in the Deep South, the region received $100 less in federal funding per person living with HIV than the United States overall in 2015.

As the center of the epidemic has moved from New York and San Francisco to the smaller cities in the South, and from gay white men of means to poorer people of color, LGBT advocacy and fund-raising has shifted to marriage equality. In 2013, HIV activists persuaded 35 LGBT leaders to sign a statement and create a video imploring the greater gay community to recommit to the AIDS struggle. The message: "We need you to come back." But of $168 million in HIV/AIDS philanthropic dollars spent in the United States in 2015, $31 million was disbursed to the South, just 19 percent of total HIV philanthropy in the United States; only $26 million directly targeted African Americans, and just $16 million went directly to gay and bisexual men, according to the organization Funders Concerned About AIDS.

During Millett's decades in government and nonprofit organizations, he has combed through mounds of data about HIV/AIDS and black gay and bisexual men. Two years ago, he and his amfAR colleagues published a comprehensive report titled "HIV and the Black Community: Do #Black(Gay)Lives Matter?" When the calm, usually sunny Millett, known for his bookish blue glasses and ready smile, talks about what he calls this "perfect storm," his voice takes on a harder edge. "We are going to eventually end AIDS in the United States, but I fear it's not going to happen for black MSM," he said, referring to men who have sex with men. "We have waited too long. With so many black gay men already infected, the horse is already out of the barn."

Everybody knows everybody else in Jackson's small, tight-knit black gay community, and most men will find their sexual partners in this network. Most scientists now believe that risk of contracting HIV boils down to a numbers game rather than a blame game: If the virus is not present in your sexual network, you can have unprotected sex and not get infected. But if you are in a community, like Jackson, where a high percentage of gay and bisexual men are infected with HIV—and many don't know it and go untreated—any unprotected sexual encounter becomes a potential time bomb. This explanation of "viral load" helps dispel the stubbornly held notion that gay and bisexual black men have more sex than other men, a false perception embedded in the American sexual imagination and fueled by stereotypes of black men as hypersexual Mandingos dating back to slavery.

"Black men are not just out here having unprotected sex willy-nilly; the science disproves that," said Terrance Moore, deputy executive director of the National Alliance of State and Territorial AIDS Directors in Washington. He pointed to stacks of studies over the years, including a groundbreaking, exhaustive 2006 data dive led by Greg Millett that was published in *The American Journal of Public Health*. In this and other studies, Millett and his colleagues found that gay black men engage in risky sexual practices no more frequently, are as consistent about condom use, and have fewer sex partners than their nonblack peers. "It's that the viral load in communities of black gay men is higher, which puts them at disproportionate risk," Moore explained. "Plus, these are the same individuals that are dealing with structural barriers around lack of employment, lack of education and opportunities, transportation and, of course, very, very overt institutional racism."

An elevated viral load in a smaller sexual network (because most people still tend to have sex with people of the same race), amplified by the structural issues that Moore pointed to, also explains why HIV rates have always been disproportionately high in the black community overall. But in the first decades of the epidemic, these ideas and explanations had not been widely accepted to explain the growing body of data pointing to fast-rising numbers of HIV cases among black heterosexuals—in rates unmatched by those of white Americans. In fact, the African American community was largely in denial about the fact that HIV/AIDS was a black issue. Worse, most believed the disease was a conspiracy on the part of the federal government to kill off the race, God's punishment for homosexuality or simply not a subject for polite conversation, because the disease was thought to be connected to promiscuity and crack and heroin use.

The community's awakening came in 1991, when Magic Johnson tearfully announced, "Because of the HIV virus I have obtained, I will have to retire from the Lakers today," and warned, "It can happen to anyone." By 1994, AIDS had become the No. 1 killer of all African Americans ages 25 to 44. The virus was 16 times as common in black women as in their white counterparts—and the gap would widen over the next few years. . . .

. . . [C]oordinated efforts . . . started in the late '90s, when civil rights groups, politicians, clergy, fraternities and sororities and celebrities stepped up to encourage testing and distribute prevention information. All the major black publications collaborated in a highly visible campaign to spotlight the disease as a major health crisis. Black churches created AIDS ministries and offered HIV testing—and the number of congregations participating in the Black Church Week of Prayer for the Healing of AIDS ballooned to more than 10,000. . . .

Most of the lock-step mobilization efforts focused on preventing the disease in black women, who, for the most part, were contracting the virus through sex with male partners. Though the CDC and other agencies offered plenty of alarming statistics confirming the high and growing numbers of HIV cases and deaths among black women, there was a lack of empirical evidence to clearly explain why the rates were so high. Experts in academia and government researchers tried to unravel a knotted tangle of factors: Women were contracting the virus from bisexual men; higher rates of sexually transmitted infections among black women facilitated the spread of HIV; socioeconomic issues drove up the rates of all disease. The lack of research to create a coherent explanation was further confounded by a reluctance on the part of some scientists and activists to perpetuate the dangerous myth of black women as sexually promiscuous—another holdover from slavery.

Given the confusion, it was simplest to latch onto the most provocative idea: that black gay men, who we knew were also contracting HIV in high numbers, provided a "bridge to infection" to black heterosexual women. . . . As the theory went, closeted black gay men were using women as unsuspecting "cover girls" to hide their sexuality and then infecting them with HIV. . . . This idea made a certain amount of sense in the frustrating absence of scientific data.

In retrospect, the high rate of HIV infection among African American women was a result of a complicated combination of all these factors, as well as the reality that after decades of denial and neglect, the viral load piled up in black communities, making any unprotected sexual encounter with anyone a potential "bridge to infection." But two decades ago, in the midst of a very scary, fast-growing epidemic, the down-low brother became the AIDS boogeyman. . . .

In the end, the organized HIV outreach and education that proved successful to black women never translated to black gay men—and the excessive focus on the down low sucked away critical time, energy and resources. Between 2005 and 2014, new HIV diagnoses among African American women plummeted 42 percent, though the number of new infections remains unconscionably high—16 times as high as that of white women. During the same time period, the number of new HIV cases among young African American gay and bisexual men surged by 87 percent. . . .

The bias that black gay and bisexual men still face poisons the HIV picture in Mississippi and throughout the South. . . .

All too often, when people living with HIV in Jackson lack the support of their families, community and the church, they end up in Grace House, a homeless facility on a sleepy block in the midtown section of the city. A cluster of four suburban-looking houses, Grace House originally functioned as a hospice, where the sick came to die. Now that the infected are living longer—and the numbers of gay and bisexual men with the virus continue to creep up—more and more young men are seeking shelter.

Until recently, Justin Huff, a former Jackson State student, shared a room on the second floor of Grace House's main facility. He was infected with HIV a year and a half ago, when a man he met on Jack'd sexually assaulted him. He received his diagnosis just after his 21st-birthday celebration. "I was throwing up and couldn't eat anything for a few days; I thought it was from the drinking," Huff said. "When I went to the doctor, he was like, if I hadn't made it in the next two days, I would've been dead."

Frightened and overwhelmed, he eventually landed on the doorstep of Grace House. "I couldn't believe I was living in a shelter," said Huff, who is now couch-surfing, applying for jobs at fast-food outlets and retail shops and attending Sturdevant's support group, determined to stay healthy. "I felt like I had no one. Off and on, I got tired of living, because all I was doing was basically dying trying to stay alive."

Behind Grace House is a small, quiet makeshift graveyard that holds the cremated remains of 35 or so residents whose families did not pick up their bodies after they died. Ceramic angels, pieces of glasswork and other mementos left by friends in memory of the deceased dot the patch of earth at the base of a pecan tree. Stacey Howard, 47, the director of programs, remembers one of the last people buried there, a young man who was HIV-positive and addicted to crack, who had lived off and on at Grace House before he was found dead on the street in the spring of 2016.

"They had him at the local funeral home and were getting ready to turn his body over to the state, because no one would claim his remains," Howard explained as she leaned against the tree. "We got in touch with his family, who didn't want anything to do with him but at least signed the paperwork. I think it's part of our responsibility that when someone in our community passes away, we give them the dignity of a place to rest.". . .

Black gay and bisexual men and the organizations and activists that support them have come to the painful realization that the nation and society have failed them and that they must take care of themselves and one another. Their group names and slogans reflect a kind of defiant lift-as-we-climb self-reliance: My Brother's Keeper; Us Helping Us in Washington; the Saving Ourselves Symposium . . . ; Our People, Our Problem, Our Solution, the tag line of the Black AIDS Institute. Since last October, the young men in Sturdevant's orbit have been supported by the fragile scaffolding that "Mr. Ced" has constructed around them and with them. Jordon has gained weight and is up and walking. Marq has promised to stay on his meds and has begun calling Sturdevant "Dad."

But even Sturdevant knows he can't save everyone. A shadow passes over his face and his voice grows low when he talks about the one young man he couldn't save. He remains haunted by him. . . .

"Listen, I know I can't be there night and day for everyone. But at this point now, I feel like I can't lose another young man to this disease."

8

SOCIAL CONTROL

AN INTERVIEW WITH

AMIN GHAZIANI

Amin Ghaziani, PhD, is an associate professor of sociology and Canada research chair in sexuality and urban studies at the University of British Columbia. He is author or editor of four books: Sex Cultures *(Polity, 2017),* There Goes the Gayborhood? *(Princeton University Press, 2014),* The Dividends of Dissent *(University of Chicago Press, 2008), and* A Decade of HAART *(Oxford University Press, 2008). His articles have appeared in the* American Sociological Review, Annual Review of Sociology, City and Community, International Journal of Urban and Regional Research, Social Problems, *and* Theory and Society. *He has received fellowships from the Princeton Society of Fellows and the Institute for Advanced Studies at UBC, along with awards from the culture, social movements, and community/urban sections of the American Sociological Association. He is an editorial board member of the* American Sociological Review *and an active public intellectual who has contributed to conversations in the* New Yorker, American Prospect, Time *magazine,* Globe and Mail, USA Today, Los Angeles Times, New York Times, *and* Philadelphia Weekly, *among other outlets.*

What led you to begin studying sexuality?

The summer after my junior year in college in 1997, I signed up for a San Francisco Field Studies Program with Northwestern University's School of Education and Social Policy. NU offered an internship-based practicum as a way to apply analytical frameworks from an advanced research methods course to a worksite. I worked with Positive Resource Center (PRC), the first organization in the country dedicated to helping people living with HIV/AIDS return to work. Where once people were getting sick, leaving work, and embracing inevitable death, advances in antiretroviral medical technologies in the mid-1990s enabled them to renew their lease on life. Many of these people desired to go back to work. I worked with an incredible organization that was helping them do just that.

That summer changed my life. It ended with me writing a 20-page report for my class. PRC used my policy recommendations to restructure many of their programs, and then-Mayor Willie Brown even acknowledged them. I had been a progressive activist during my undergraduate years, but that summer taught me that I could also use my intellect to create social change. I knew then that I wanted to go to graduate school to study sexuality.

Of the projects you have done over the course of your academic career, which was most interesting and why?

After spending my first two years of undergraduate study at the University of Michigan in Ann Arbor, I felt intellectually restless and overwhelmed by the large student body. So I transferred to Northwestern—which was indeed rigorous and stimulating in the classroom—but my new campus felt politically apathetic and rife with non-reflexive privilege.

I had to shake things up. Drawing on progressive organizing skills that I had learned in Ann Arbor, I organized a Queer Kiss-In event on April Fool's Day. My idea was to have queer students meet in a central campus area and, at noon when many classes let out, to make out. Straight people often take for granted basic acts of intimacy and affection. Queer couples that hold hands or kiss in public risk hate speech and even violence.

A week prior to my event I did what any undergraduate student organizer would do: I taped fliers throughout the campus. I quickly discovered that the groundskeepers selectively removed my fliers. In response, the day before the Kiss-In, I purchased fabulous fuchsia paint for "The Rock," a large boulder at the center of campus where it is customary for students to paint messages and advertisements of social events. When I arrived at the site around three in the morning, a group of sorority women were already there painting the rock to advertise a party. They had also pitched a tent next to the rock to guard it so no one else painted over it. And so there I was with this gorgeous paint and an occupied rock! Bleary-eyed, I looked down on the ground in a sleepy haze—and that's when the proverbial "a-ha" moment struck. All over the ground were chalked messages and taped fliers. If chalk and tape were permissible, then why not paint? A fervent fury awoke within me, and I painted "QUEER POWER" across the entire plaza area.

The NU administration responded by threatening me with possible arrest for defacing private property because of the high cost of removing the graffiti, and I retaliated by defining their threat as a breach of my First Amendment rights. As fate would have it, I was taking a course titled "Problems and Principles in the First Amendment." I used what I learned in that class to write op-ed pieces for local papers and to give public radio interviews. Talk about knowledge in action! After much legal and political deliberation, the university compromised. In exchange for not pursuing a lawsuit, NU allowed me to revise their policy on the allowable "medium of expression" to advertise student activities.

What ethical dilemmas have you faced in studying sexuality?

I once did a research project on club drugs, risky sex practices, and sexually transmitted infections among self-identified gay and bisexual men who attended circuit parties. These are weekend-long dance events at which sexual activity and drug use are generally prevalent among several thousand revelers. As you might expect, my co-author Tom Cook and I had some trouble with the institutional review board. How do you ethically conduct an ethnographic study of drug use in a club context where you want party-goers to accept you into the fold of their friends—and where you are observing potentially illegal behavior of both drug use and sex?

We managed this problem in four ways. First, we secured a Certificate of Confidentiality from the National Institute on Drug Abuse that protected us from subpoena. Second, circuit parties attract an older demographic; you have to be at least 21 to get in the door. This resolved issues of interacting with minors. Third, when I engaged in participant observation, I deemed it necessary to appear as a partier and did not explicitly reveal my professional role. This enhanced the authenticity of my observations. And finally, because I was not going to take drugs like the majority of the attendees, I instead brought aspirin tablets with me into the party, which mimicked the appearance of ecstasy. Because much of the community interacts within smaller groups of friends who ritualistically consume drugs, there was a real issue of credibility that I had to confront if I was not a part of the ingesting group. In any case, the study was a big success. We published it in a medical journal, and it was picked up by more than forty international media outlets.

How do people react when you tell them you study sexuality?

The reactions are as varied as the diversity inherent in all human beings, of course, but one particular episode stands out in my mind. I struggled during my first round on the academic job market. As I sought to make sense of my unfavorable situation, one of my advisors shared with me a shocking assessment from a colleague who taught at a sociology department where I had applied for a tenure-track position. "What is his dissertation about?" asked the colleague in a private telephone conversation with my advisor, who proceeded to explain my topic of infighting in LGBT marches on Washington. "*And* he's gay?" the colleague retorted. Although puzzled by the question, my advisor nonetheless replied, "Yes. So what?" Then the curtains were lifted: "Well, that's the problem: he's narcissistic."

I choose to remember this offensive and homophobic remark as an isolated incident, rather than how sociologists in general react when I tell them what I study. But it still stung. It taught me that bias operates at all levels, even among highly educated people. To be gay and to care about gay issues is somehow narcissistic. The personal is always political, yes, but sexuality penetrates into our imagination in unique ways.

Why is sex research important? How does your work on LGBTQ social movements relate to everyday life?

Sex research is important for so many reasons, but I'll just share the first two that come to my mind. One of society's favorite myths about gay people is that we're all alike. Social psychologists call this the "out-group homogeneity effect," a majority-group perception that minority group members are fairly similar to one another. Sex research enables us to debunk this pervasive bias about LGBTQ individuals. From a personal perspective, part of what makes studying sexuality right now so exciting is that we're living with a generation of scholars who have pioneered the writing of our history. Unlike other minority groups, queer people have a comparatively weaker sense of our own heritage and history. Sex research is important because we still have much about queer lives that needs to be collectively remembered and preserved. There are many more stories to tell.

If you could teach people one thing about sexuality what would it be?

The world appears and feels so much more effervescent when passion and pleasure accompany the pursuit of your craft. It's important to love what you do. Studying sexuality offers opportunities for intense intellectual stimulation and unbridled pleasures in the process of doing it.

THE NEW PARIAHS:
SEX, CRIME, AND PUNISHMENT IN AMERICA

ROGER N. LANCASTER

Narratives of sexual danger are older than the republic itself. Indeed, the drama of protection—what Susan Faludi calls "the guardian myth"—serves as something of a foundational national story line about the wresting of white civilization from sexual savagery.[1] During the colonial, antebellum, Jim Crow, and Progressive eras, white Americans were variously preoccupied with tales of sexual danger to white women and children. The retrograde racial and gender politics involved in guardianship could not be clearer. Historically, the guardian myth cast white men as protectors of white women and children; the villains of the piece were depraved red, black, brown, or yellow men. But Depression and McCarthy-era paranoias put a new spin on this old story line. With the decline of lynch law in the 1930s, the focus of white middle-class sexual anxieties shifted from external threats to internal deviations, and a new species of sexual monster—the "sexual psychopath" who was raced and sexed as homosexual—lurched onto the historical stage.[2] After a brief hiatus during the 1960s, he resumed his stalking of children in the wake of gay liberation—at about the same time that Americans started to repeal sodomy laws while getting tough on crime. . . . The sexual psychopath eventually would morph into the modern pedophile just in time for new plot twists, such as stories about satanic ritual abuse, stranger danger, and a host of subsequent perils to children.[3] . . .

Keeping in view the wide sweep of these trends and motifs, I shall try to take a step beyond existing analyses of what is now well established: mass incarceration's roots in racial domination. . . . Repression, too, is only one of the mechanisms in play. Increasingly, subject citizens are primed to crave the new techniques of supervision—for their own "good," even for their own sense of freedom—which are silently disseminated across a rebuilt landscape.

The (implicitly white) sexual predator has played an important role in the production of this wider system. His crimes are understood as being both uniquely horrific and uniquely widespread; they are thus to be constantly anticipated and guarded against. Because his predations occur in secret, and because they often invade otherwise safe spaces, they must be constantly flushed out and exposed. The merest suspicion of the predator's presence justifies, even demands, the laying of traps, the deployment of decoys, the staging of "stings," the application of surveillance technologies at new sites. . . .

The emotions he stirs have played a crucial part in stoking public outrage, in mobilizing an inflamed citizenry, and in cementing the prevailing tabloid story line around innocence, vulnerability, and victimization.

"Innocence," of course, is an especially precarious concept, never more so than when it is imagined as "sexlessness," and it would appear that the sexual predator is an absolutely indispensable element in underwriting this concept: it is ultimately he who secures the existence of innocence . . . by threatening to snatch it away.

In the mutually constitutive interplay between innocent sexlessness and sexual evil, innocence serves as a stand-in for health, not only for the child but for the species as well: its preservation, up to a certain unclear age, points to a happy, well-adjusted future. Correlatively, the predator's pernicious sexuality constitutes a kind of disease: the perils he poses circumscribe the normal, desired state, and their intrusion into the closed world of childhood—more so than poverty, neglect, or violence—is deemed uniquely capable of diverting the child from the proper developmental path. This dialectic between innocence and its despoilation has given rise to a biopolitical system every bit as expansive as any variant of nineteenth-century sexual hygienics, replete with corps of specialists, advocates, and disciplinarians. The most successful new social movement of the late twentieth century, the victims' rights movement, could scarcely have staged so many notable triumphs in the fields of law, policing, and court procedures without the help of that massive new hygienic infrastructure and without invoking, as its foil, the ignominious figure of the sexual predator. Expansive new cadres of professional child protectors could scarcely have occupied an increasingly crowded field except in the shadow of his outsized existence.

A dark suspicion begins to form: Might we think that in a society committed both to a war on crime (with its mass incarceration of black men) and to ridding itself of racism (through formal adherence to a regime of civil rights), the feared figure of the white pedophile is necessary? Might we wonder whether part of the psychosocial work he performs is to absolve the guilty conscience of racism at a time when so many fears are focused on the black gang-banger or the brown border menace? Perhaps. Facts in evidence: Penalties for a variety of sex crimes have continued to intensify, even as drug crime laws have been relaxed. The population administered by sex laws continues to grow, even as the prison population has stabilized.

I therefore venture a working hypothesis. Sexual fears and strategies for the containment of sexual dangers are key threads of the new reticulum. They figure prominently in ongoing redefinitions of norms of governance. They provide a reusable template, suitable for application in other domains. If we want to see what social control could look like over the course of the twenty-first century, we should look to the sex offender.

SEX OFFENDER LAWS

America's current sex offender laws have smaller-scale precedents in mid-twentieth-century sex panics, when, in the name of child protection, thirty states devised civil commitment procedures for sexual psychopaths and a trickle of states imposed sex offender registries. With the sexual and due process revolutions of the 1960s, some of these statutes were modified or retired. But then a new series of sex panics began in the 1970s, and by the 1980s some states were passing sex offender laws that resembled those of the McCarthy era. Still, as late as 1993, only twelve states had sex offender registries.

This picture changed dramatically in 1994, when Congress passed and President Bill Clinton signed into law a federal statute named for Jacob Wetterling, an eleven-year-old Minnesota boy who was abducted by a masked gunman in 1989. Although nothing was known of Wetterling's fate or his abductor's identity for the better part of 27 years, activists and reporters generally—and, it turns out, correctly—interpreted the tragedy as an instance of abduction, rape, and murder. The Wetterling Act required convicted sex offenders to register with authorities upon release, parole, or probation. It mandated annual registration for a ten-year period for some offenses (any sexually violent offense and certain criminal offenses against a victim who was a minor) and lifetime registration on a quarterly basis for persons determined to be "sexually violent predators." It also required local authorities to transmit registry information to state law enforcement and the FBI.

Then, under a 1996 amendment to the Wetterling Act, all states were required to adopt statutes collectively known as Megan's Law, named for Megan Kanka, a seven-year-old girl who was raped and murdered in New Jersey in 1994. This amendment required local law enforcement authorities to notify neighbors about a sex offender's presence in their community. Although registration and notification requirements varied, all states came to post searchable online lists of at least some categories of registered sex offenders.

More recently, the 2006 Adam Walsh Act enhanced and systematized registry and notification requirements. Named for the abducted and murdered son of John Walsh, who went on to become the host of Fox Broadcasting Company's America's Most Wanted, the legislation was expressly drafted "in response to the vicious attacks by violent predators" against seventeen other named victims who died over a sixteen-year period. The act's preamble cites these anomalous child murders as evidence of "deadly loopholes" in the antecedent Wetterling Act and Megan's Law. (There is no evidence that sex was involved in Walsh's kidnapping and murder, but as in the Wetterling case, this was the motive assumed by family members, advocates, and reporters.) And so the Walsh Act tightened sex offender registration requirements and established a three-tier system based on the type of offense committed (a break with earlier classifications that purported to be based on the risk of recidivism): Tier 1 offenders are subject to annual registration for a period of fifteen years; Tier 2 offenders must update their registration every six months for twenty-five years; and Tier 3 registrants are required to register their whereabouts every three months for life.

In addition to enhancing penalties for an array of sex crimes, the legislation established a national public sex offender database (over and above existing state registries) and made failure to register or update one's registration a felony. Other sections of the act, each named for a different child victim, contain provisions for DNA collection and, in a striking display of petty punitiveness, make it more difficult for the relatives of anyone ever convicted of a sex offense to obtain green cards. Ex post facto law is usually viewed as inimical to democratic norms, but the Walsh Act also gives the U.S. attorney general the authority to apply its provisions retroactively.

The marking and tracking of sex offenders leapt beyond national borders with the enactment of International Megan's Law. Passed by the House in a unanimous voice vote . . . the bill was signed into law by President Obama in 2016. The new law purports to allow authorities to preempt sex tourism and child exploitation: it requires registered sex offenders convicted of crimes involving minors to pre-report all international travel, and it provides for a newly created Angel Watch Center to share these travelers' itineraries with foreign governments. The law also requires a "visual designation affixed to a conspicuous location on the passport indicating that the individual is a covered sex offender."

One might well hope for a legal classification system that distinguishes menace from nuisance, with nuanced criteria for sorting violent repeat offenders, who belong in prison or require supervision, from nonviolent or one-time offenders. But as Gayle Rubin observed in her indispensable essay on sex panics, American thinking admits little nuance or proportion when it comes to sex.[4] This lack of nuance is not merely a cultural legacy of Puritanism; it is constantly stoked in raw, emotional campaigns by victims' rights and child advocacy groups, crusading journalists, and opportunistic politicians. Every victim-named law tells the story of an elaborate institutional collaboration to exaggerate risk and to conflate categories of harm: its naming commemorates the true story of a helpless child who suffered a terrible death at the hands of a hardened criminal; its legislative content applies stringent measures against a host of minor, first-time, and nonviolent offenders. . . .

The most intense form of public dread is directed at the lurking stranger, the anonymous repeat offender. In fact, the crimes that most spur public outrage—the abduction, rape, and murder of children—are exceedingly rare. In a nation whose population includes roughly 74 million minors, about one hundred high-risk abductions of children by strangers occur every year, and about half end in murder. Statistically, then, a child's risk of being killed by a sexual predator who is a stranger (1 in 1,480,000) is lower than the chance of being killed by lightning (1 in 1,200,000). Most perpetrators of sexual abuse are family members, close relatives, or friends or acquaintances of the victim's family. And in 70 to 80 percent of child deaths resulting from abuse or neglect, a parent is held responsible.[5]

Advocates for laws to register, publicize, and monitor sex offenders after their release from custody typically assert that those convicted of sex crimes pose a high risk of sex crime recidivism. But studies by the Justice Department and other organizations show that recidivism rates are significantly lower for convicted sex offenders than for burglars, robbers, thieves, drug offenders, and other convicts. And only a tiny portion of sex crimes are committed by repeat offenders, which suggests that current laws are misdirected and ineffective. A federally financed study of New Jersey's registration and notification procedures found that sex offense rates were already falling before the implementation of Megan's Law; the study also found no discernible impact on recidivism and concluded that the growing costs of the program might not be justifiable. Other studies have suggested that public registries actually promote recidivism by relegating registrants to a status of permanent social exclusion, thus depriving them of any interest in their own rehabilitation.[6]

The "typical" sex offender is a less exceptional figure than official narratives suggest. Contrary to the common belief that burgeoning registries provide lists of child molesters, the victim need not have been a child and the perpetrator need not have been an adult. Child abusers may be minors themselves. (Up to 41 percent of child sex abuse perpetrators are said to be juveniles.[7])

First-degree rape is always a registry offense. Statutory rapists—who are not rapists at all, insofar as their crimes involved neither coercion nor violence—are variously covered in many states. Some states require exhibitionists and "peeping Toms" to register. Louisiana once compelled some prostitutes to do so. "Forcible touching" is a registry offense, and this designation may apply even to adolescent boys who "copped a feel," as it was called on my junior high playground. (In New Jersey a neurologically impaired twelve-year-old boy who groped his eight-year-old brother in the bathtub was required to register as a sex offender.[8]) Fully two-thirds of the North Carolina registrants sampled in a 2007 study by Human Rights Watch had been convicted of the nonviolent offense of "indecent liberties with a minor," which does not necessarily even involve physical contact. (Virtually all of the five hundred registrants randomly sampled—98.6 percent—were one-time offenders; that is, the offense for which they were registered was their first and only conviction for a sex offense.[9]) Culpability and harm vary greatly in these offenses. Some are serious. Some would not be classified as "criminal" under European laws, which set lower ages of consent than do American laws. Some defy common sense. And because sex crimes are broadly defined and closely monitored, the number of people listed in sex offender registries has grown rapidly: 843,680 at latest count, more than the population of San Francisco (currently the thirteenth largest city in the country).[10]

Talk about "risk" was ubiquitous in deliberations around registry requirements. Risk assessment models usually purport to provide calibrated calculations and bias-free assessments of probability. But applied to sex offenders, actuarial logic has deteriorated into something else: panicky risk-aversion, arbitrary judgments, and a rapid expansion of sanctions targeting broad populations for registration and other forms of "waste management."[11] Registry procedures involve not one but two leaps of actuarial logic. First, the recidivism of some becomes tantamount to the recidivism of all, with the result that "there can be no such thing as an 'ex-offender'—only offenders who have been caught before and will strike again," as David Garland succinctly puts it. Under this distorted logic, "criminals" will "have few privacy rights that could ever trump the public's uninterrupted right to know."[12] Second, since the commission of lower-level sex offenses with willing participants is understood to be preliminary to the commission of horrendous, brutal crimes, this anticipated escalation must be deterred by escalating penalties. Thus, gradations that were first haltingly elaborated to distinguish degrees of risk or harm subsequently have become the basis for blurring those very distinctions, and in many locales mid- and lower-level nonviolent offenders have become subject to invasive, onerous notification procedures: web listings, the distribution of electronic notices or paper flyers, to say nothing of increasingly punitive federal rules.

This is associative logic—or magical thinking, as the anthropologists would have it: the logic of panic.[13] It aligns not with "science" in any meaningful sense of the word, much less with rational risk assessment, but with much older ideas about danger, taboo, and ritual pollution. It has the force of an irrefutable argument; it takes the form of extortion; and it gathers like an unstoppable wave: Who but a moral monster would oppose a law, no matter how draconian, named for a murdered child?

Registration and notification rules violate basic legal principles and amount to an excessive and enduring form of punishment. They render registrants all but unemployable and unhousable. But these are only the beginning of added-on penalties and collateral measures. Other laws go much further. At last count, forty-one states and the District of Columbia have passed laws that require some sex offenders to be monitored—sometimes for life—with electronic ankle bracelets that use radio frequency or global positioning systems (GPS). The Walsh Act includes a federal pilot program to use global positioning to keep an eye on sex offenders. Nine states either allow or require chemical castration for some categories of sex offenders. In addition, new civil commitment laws in twenty states and the District of Columbia resurrect that odd institution from the 1950s, allowing for the indefinite detention of sex offenders after the completion of their sentences. . . . The Walsh Act created a federal civil commitment program. Civil libertarians oppose civil confinement on principle: it violates due process, it represents a form of double jeopardy, and it is tantamount to indefinite preventive detention. The Supreme Court has repeatedly swatted aside these objections: civil confinement is not deemed punitive if psychological treatment is provided. Such a rationale for civil commitment would seem to display an inherent illogic: the accused is deemed mentally fit for trial and sentencing but mentally unfit for release.[14] Moreover, psychological treatment for civilly confined sex offenders is largely unscientific, based more on therapeutic fad and conjecture than on any body of informed evidence or double-blind studies. Still, inmates are presented with a legal catch-22: One condition of release from civil commitment is the successful completion of psychological therapy. But since therapy typically requires a complete recounting of past crimes—including those unknown to authorities—and since the number of crimes committed is a factor in determining whether the detainee is subject to civil commitment, many logically refuse therapy and do so on the advice of counsel.[15]

In theory, these procedures are applied against the worst of the worst: violent repeat offenders. In practice, civil commitment is applied to a mixed group that sometimes includes minors and nonviolent offenders such as exhibitionists but not violent, garden-variety rapists. One detainee shared his story with me in a letter: When he was eighteen, he was charged with sending pornographic material via email to a respondent he believed to be his fourteen-year-old male cousin. The recipient was actually a decoy, planted by an aggressive prosecutor. And because this was the young man's second offense—his first offense had involved voluntary relations with a same-sex partner when he was fifteen and the younger partner was thirteen—he was classified as a "violent sexual predator" and sent directly to civil commitment. Such are the judgments that can go into designating a violent sexual predator.

The most recent survey of sex offender civil commitment programs, dating to 2013, found 5,640 detainees.[16] Meanwhile, laws in more than twenty states and hundreds of municipalities restrict where a sex offender can live, work, or walk. Where a sex offender lives has no bearing on whether he will commit new crimes. But residency restrictions have proved popular, promoted by citizens' groups, victims' rights advocates, crusading journalists, and politicians in a wide variety of settings. California's Proposition 83 prohibits all registered sex offenders (felony and misdemeanor alike) from living within two thousand feet of a school or park, effectively evicting them from the state's cities, rendering them homeless, or scattering them into isolated rural areas. The law also mandates lifelong electronic tracking of all felony sex offenders, whether deemed dangerous or not, through GPS.

A lawyer describes his client's shattered life in 2008: the uprooted offender perpetually circulates through the streets of the Bay Area, where there are no places he can live. He and his wife must move their trailer constantly to avoid violating a rule tacked on by the Department of Corrections and Rehabilitation, which prohibits sex offenders from being in the same noncompliant place for two hours.

His original registry offense was indecent exposure: mooning his sister-in-law during a family argument.[17]

There are signs of corrective movement on some of the most excessive "child safety zone" laws. California courts have scaled back the statewide law in a succession of rulings, a U.S. District Court judge has thrown out Michigan's one-thousand-foot buffer zone, and the Massachusetts Supreme Judiciary Court has broadly ruled residency restrictions an unconstitutional form of "banishment." A few states and municipalities have modified their laws in the wake of chaotic displacements. Still, lawmakers are loath to appear "soft" on sex crime, so these modifications usually give something with one hand and take away something with the other. . . .

CONTINUOUS CONTROL

. . . Digital scarlet letters, electronic tethering, and practices of banishment have relegated a growing number of people to the logic of "social death," a term introduced by the sociologist Orlando Patterson, in the context of slavery, to describe a condition of permanent dishonor and exclusion from the wider moral community.

The creation of a pariah class of unemployable, uprooted criminal outcasts largely escaped the notice of academic queer theorists, who in their heyday supposedly earned their keep by accounting for such phenomena. But it has drawn the attention of human rights activists, and even a journal as staid as the *Economist* has decried U.S. sex offender laws as harsh and ineffective.[18]

This business should worry us more than it apparently does, in part because the techniques used for marking, shaming, and controlling sex offenders have come to serve as models for laws and practices in other domains. Electronic ankle bracelets and techniques of house arrest are being applied to an expanding list of offenders and defendants—including undocumented immigrants who have been released from custody to await processing (on civil, not criminal charges). It is estimated that a quarter of a million people are currently manacled to some form of electronic monitoring.[19] Public registries, which make visible any stain on a person's record, have proved especially popular with government agencies, civic organizations, and private vigilante groups. A victims' rights clearinghouse in New Mexico posts an online database of everyone convicted in the state of driving while intoxicated. Several states publish online listings of methamphetamine offenders, while lawmakers in Texas, Nevada, and California have introduced initiatives to create public registries of those convicted of domestic violence. Gregory Tomso discusses the website STDcarriers.com, for example, [which] publishes the names and photographs of thousands of people worldwide who have tested positive for STIs or who have been prosecuted for criminal HIV transmission."[20] Mimicking Megan's Law, Florida maintains a website that gives the personal details (including photo, name, age, address, offenses, and periods of incarceration) of all prisoners released from custody. Some other states post similar public listings

of paroled or recently released ex-convicts. It goes without saying that such procedures work against rehabilitation and reintegration.

Other things merit saying, however. Costly and inefficient as they are, such techniques of supervision are cheaper than incarceration. They invite adoption in a time of budget shortfalls and ever-less-expensive digital technologies. They resonate well with public opinion, which would like to see fewer people in prison but also favors putting all ex-convicts under some form of supervision, if recent survey results are any guide.[21] And they satisfy liberal urges to look for supposedly more humane alternatives to mass incarceration. . . .

Anxiety (Dis)Order

. . . Crime-conscious routines and surveillance technologies purport to make us feel safer, but there is good reason to think that they have the opposite effect: they produce subject citizens who are always thinking about crime. . . .

Judith Levine, Janice Irvine, and other sex-positive feminists have argued that the established culture of child protection—with its fetishization of virginity and its constant battery of alarmist messages that equate sex with risk and danger—actually harms children and impedes their social development.[22] A lifeworld dominated by sexual fear certainly discourages experimentation, pleasure, and autonomy. More than that, it tacitly redefines sex, like smoking, as a form of harm, permitted only to adults (who are allowed to accept responsibility for their own decisions). James Kincaid goes further to suggest that in the prevailing story line about harm, "innocence" itself has been eroticized: the purer the child is imagined to be, the greater the danger of his or her defilement—and the greater the thrill some adults will experience in performing rites of protection.[23] Speculations along these lines purport to delve into the nether regions of the psyche.

But what if what lurks in the closet and stirs anxieties there is more literal than figurative? The kinds of laws that I have been enumerating are themselves logical sources of anxiety. Harvey Silverglate has suggested that the average American unwittingly commits three felonies per day. Or, more accurately put, expansive, vaguely written laws give prosecutors great leeway in pinning raps, and America's sex laws supply prosecutors with a veritable trove of actionable material. What sort of leeway? Silverglate gives the example of a respected lawyer who was charged with obstruction of justice when he destroyed a hard drive containing images of naked boys that were discovered on his client's—an Episcopal church's—computer. The attorney acted in good faith: he recommended immediately firing the church's organist (who had stored the images) and he destroyed the hard drive without any knowledge that the feds had begun an investigation of the organist. Many attorneys would have done the same. Child pornography "is illegal to possess ('contraband') and therefore holding, rather than destroying it, arguably would be criminal."[24] The lawyer's dangerous predicament illustrates a recurring dilemma in modern sex laws: the difference between licit and illicit behavior becomes so slight as to be a matter of point of view.

. . . Arrests for "public" sex, for example, typically target men who "[believe] they are alone or out of view," but who are observed by police using peepholes or hidden cameras, or who are responding to overtures from police decoys.[25] Lawyers and researchers tell me that a large percentage of defendants in statutory rape cases credibly believed that they were involved with a partner who was above the age of consent. (Many states do not allow defendants to argue that the minor impersonated an adult.) Of course, mature adults have no monopoly on misjudgments, momentary lapses, indiscretions, or reckless passions. Many young people do not realize that they are violating their states' consent or abuse laws when they engage in standard routines of courtship and seduction. Cell phones put the tools for serious lawbreaking—"sexting" among underage teens, which violates child pornography laws—in everyone's hands. (A recent survey finds that nearly 20 percent of teens under the age of eighteen have sent a sexually explicit picture of themselves via cell phone; nearly 40 percent had received such images, with a substantial number of those forwarding them on to others.[26])

In view of rampant legal hazards it is unclear just where the search for "monster" might lead us. Tabloid scandals give hints. A headline, typical of its genre, announces a citizenry's shock and consternation: "Town Is Shaken after Prosecutor's Arrest in a Child-Sex Sting." The first line of a story in *USA Today* reads, "A Bible camp counselor and a Boy Scout leader were among 125 people arrested nationwide in an Internet child pornography case." An article on a lawsuit against Richard Roberts, then president of Oral Roberts University, obliquely refers to cell phone text messages sent to "under-age males."[27]. . . The monster, we are told, is hiding in plain sight!

Such narratives ricochet and whiplash in the culture at large. . . . Sad stories about fallen figures or exposed pretenders trade in schadenfreude: they allow tellers and listeners to revel in exposing the hypocrisy of others; and in this telling, they reveal the capacity for recursive regression in sex panics. That is, whenever those who have been most zealous about protecting innocence find themselves caught up in scandal, the result is not a reconsideration of the ground from which this business started—inflated notions of harm, the politics of protection—but instead, remorse on the part of the fallen and panicked calls for greater zeal, tighter laws, tougher enforcement, more continuous control. . . .

NOTES

1. Susan Faludi, *The Terror Dream: Fear and Fantasy in Post-9/11 America* (New York: Metropolitan, 2007), 215–16, 262, 289. . . .

2. Estelle B. Friedman, "'Uncontrolled Desires': The Response to the Sexual Psychopath, 1920–1960," *Journal of American History* 74 (1987): 83–106; Neil Miller, *Sex Crime Panic: A Journey to the Paranoid Heart of the 1950s* (Los Angeles: Alyson Books, 2002). . . .

3. Debbie Nathan and Michael Snedeker, *Satan's Silence: Ritual Abuse and the Making of a Modern American Witch Hunt* (New York: Basic, 1995); Richard Ofshe and Ethan Watters, *Making Monsters: False Memories, Psychotherapy, and Sexual Hysteria* (Berkeley: University of California Press, 1996); Philip Jenkins, *Moral Panic: Changing Concepts of the Child Molester in Modern America* (New Haven: Yale University Press, 1998).

4. Gayle Rubin, "Thinking Sex: Notes for a Radical Theory of the Politics of Sexuality," in *Pleasure and Danger: Exploring Female Sexuality*, 2nd ed., ed. Carole S. Vance (London: Pandora, 1992), 267–319.

5. I derive these numbers from various studies produced by the Office of Juvenile Justice and Delinquency Prevention and published in *National Incidence Studies of Missing, Abducted, Runaway, and Thrownaway Children* (NISMART), U.S. Department of Justice, Washington, D.C., as well as from the U.S. Department of Health and Human Services Child Maltreatment Annual Reports.

6. Patrick A. Langan, Erica L. Schmitt, and Matthew R. Durose, "Recidivism of Sex Offenders Released from Prison in 1994," U.S. Department of Justice, 2003; . . . Patrick A. Langan and David Levin, "Recidivism of Prisoners Released in 1994," U.S. Department of Justice, 2002. . . .

7. Emily M. Douglas and David M. Finkelhor, "Childhood Sexual Abuse Fact Sheet," Crimes against Children Research Center, May 2005, http://www.unh.edu/ccrc/factsheet/pdf/childhoodSexualAbuseFactSheet.pdf.

8. Judith Levine, *Harmful to Minors: The Perils of Protecting Children from Sex* (New York: Thunder's Mouth, 2003), 47.

9. "No Easy Answers: Sex Offender Laws in the U.S.," *Human Rights Watch* 19, no. 4G (September 2007): 31–32.

10. According to statistics compiled from state registries by the National Center for Missing and Exploited Children, http://www.missingkids.com/en/US/documents/SexOffendersMap2015.pdf (accessed Feb. 8, 2016).

11. See Malcolm M. Feeley and Jonathan Simon, "The New Penology: Notes on the Emerging Strategy of Corrections and Its Implications," *Criminology* 30, no. 4 (1992): 449–74. . . .

12. David Garland, *The Culture of Control: Crime and Social Order in Contemporary Society* (Chicago: University of Chicago Press, 2001), 180–81.

13. See . . . Roger N. Lancaster, *Sex Panic and the Punitive State* (Berkeley: University of California Press, 2011), 7, 41, 81, 237–38.

14. Kansas v. Hendricks, 521 U.S. 346 (1997); Allison Morgan, "Civil Confinement of Sex Offenders: New York's Attempt to Push the Envelope in the Name of Public Safety," *Boston University Law Review* 86 (2007): 1034.

15. Monica Davey and Abby Goodnough, "For Sex Offenders, Dispute on Therapy's Benefits," *New York Times*, March 6, 2007: Al.

16. Deirdre D'Orazio, Rebecca Jackson, Jennifer Schneider, and Alan Stillman, "Annual Survey of Sex Offender Civil Commitment Programs 2013," October 28, 2013. Presented at the Annual Conference for Sex Offender Civil Commitment Programs Network, Chicago, IL.

17. Marc Gardner, a defense attorney living in the Bay Area, has written about this case: "When Mooning Is a Sex Crime," *Counterpunch*, November 18, 2008, http://www.counterpunch.org/2008/n/18/when-mooning-is-a-sex-crime.

18. . . . Georgia Harlem, "America's Unjust Sex Laws," *Economist*, August 6, 2009: 9. . . .

19. This estimate was given by Robert Gable, a student of B. F. Skinner who co-designed the first electronic monitoring system with the aim of providing positive social support for the rehabilitation of offenders and parolees. Instead, laments Gable, the tool is being (mis)used "almost exclusively as an information system to document rule violations." . . .

20. Gregory Tomso, "HIV Monsters: Gay Men, Criminal Law, and the New Political Economy of HIV," in *The War on Sex*, ed. David Halperin and Trevor Hoppe (Durham, NC: Duke University Press, 2017), 353–77.

21. Public Opinion Strategies and the Mellman Group, "Public Opinion on Sentencing and Corrections Policy in America," March, 2012.

22. Levine, *Harmful to Minors*; Janice M. Irvine, *Talk about Sex: The Battles over Sex Education in the U.S.* (Berkeley: University of California Press, 2004).

23. James R. Kincaid, *Erotic Innocence: The Culture of Child Molesting* (Durham, NC: Duke University Press, 1998), esp. 14–16, 54–55, 102–06.

24. Harvey Silverglate, *Three Felonies a Day: How the Feds Target the Innocent* (2009; repr. New York: Encounter, 2011), see esp. 159–66.

25. Robert L. Jacobson, "'Megan's Laws' Reinforcing Old Patterns of Anti-Gay Police Harassment," *Georgetown Law Journal* 81 (1998–1999): 2456.

26. Donald S. Strassberg, Ryan K. McKinnon, Michael A. Sustaita, and Jordan Rullo, "Sexting by High School Students: An Exploratory and Descriptive Study," *Archives of Sexual Behavior* 42, no. 1 (January 2013): 15–21.

27. Abby Goodnough, "Town Is Shaken after Prosecutor's Arrest in a Child-Sex Sting," *New York Times*, September 29, 2007: A8; "Feds Arrest 125 People Nationwide in Child-Porn Investigation," *USA Today*, October 19, 2006, http://usatoday30.usatoday.com/news/nation/2006-10-19-child-porn-arrests_x.htm; Ralph Blumenthal, "Professors Sue Oral Roberts President," *New York Times*, October 11, 2007: AJ2.

Too Young to Consent?

Elizabeth Cavalier and Elisabeth O. Burgess

In contemporary U.S. society, adolescents are engaging in sexual activity. Data from the Centers for Disease Control and Prevention (CDC) show that 41 percent of high school students have had sexual intercourse (CDC, 2015). Most sexual activity, especially first sexual activity, is between two people of similar ages. Approximately 74 percent of the first male sexual partners of adolescent females are the same age or one to three years older, and only 8 percent of teen females have first partners 6 or more years older (Abma et al., 2004). But the legal and cultural significance of age difference varies across the life course. A 15-year gap between a 55-year-old man and his 40-year-old wife is less significant than the three-year age difference between an 18- and 15-year-old having sex when they are high school students. In some states, that 18-year-old could be arrested for statutory rape, even if both parties agree the sex was consensual. However, an 18-year-old engaging in sex acts with a 10-year-old would violate cultural norms about sex in contemporary America. Most people in the United States would agree that 10 is too young to consent to sex. So where do we draw the line? Who gets to decide and why? How are these moral values legislated and prosecuted?

England developed the first known laws prescribing a minimum age of 12 for consent to sexual activity in 1275. By 1576, the age of consent was codified at 10 years old, and sex between individuals above and below the age of consent became a felony. Colonial America adopted these laws, defining ages of consent ranging from 7 to 12 (Cocca, 2004). Traditionally, these laws were enacted to protect virginity and were only enforced if the victim was a white female who was a virgin prior to the sexual act in question. These crimes were prosecuted as property crimes against the girl's household; premarital virginity was treated as a valuable commodity.

Since colonial times, laws about age of consent[1] have become more complicated, the age of consent has steadily risen, and the statutes have expanded to include both female and male victims. Regulations around adolescent sexual activity in modern history have generally been couched in three different, and sometimes overlapping, areas of social concern: a concern about potentially coercive sex between older adults and younger adolescents, a concern about sex between unmarried partners, and an economic argument that adolescent out-of-wedlock births pose a drain on society via the welfare system

(Cocca, 2004). Since the 1970s, the United States has seen a steady tightening of control around issues of adolescent sex and age of consent. On a global scale, some countries have recently increased the age of sexual consent: Uganda raised the age of consent for girls from 14 to 18, purportedly to protect them from exposure to HIV from older men (Parikah, 2012). In 2008, Canada raised the age of consent from 14 to 16 as part of the Tackling Violent Crime Act in an attempt to protect children from Internet predators (Hunt, 2009). Legislative approaches to adolescent sexuality have shifted from a *consent* model to one of *protection*.

Currently, the majority of U.S. states (32 including the District of Columbia) use 16 as the age of consent.[2] However, in the United States, the laws vary widely and can be based on a number of factors, including age of consent, minimum age of victim, age difference between victim and perpetrator, and minimum age of defendant in order to prosecute. Most age-of-consent laws focus on sexual intercourse; the laws about sexual contact (including oral and anal sex) are more complicated and unevenly enforced. Such variety in laws and enforcement creates a problem whereby sexual activity between consenting adolescents and young adults may be legal in one state, a misdemeanor in another, and a felony in a third state. In addition to legal disparities across states, enforcement differs based on the sex of the victim and defendant, the race of the victim and defendant, the type of relationship (romantic, acquaintance, or stranger), and the type of sexual activity in question (oral and anal sex rather than intercourse or heterosexual sex rather than homosexual sex). Though rarely reported, same-sex statutory rape incidents are far more likely to result in an arrest than cross-sex cases (Chaffin, Chenoweth, and Letourneau, 2016).

Public perception and media coverage of age-of-consent cases do not coincide with actual rates of crime, particularly concerning the sex of perpetrators and victims. The National Incidents Based Reporting System (NIBRS) reports that 95 percent of victims in statutory rape cases are female and 99 percent of offenders of female victims are male (Troup-Leasure and Snyder, 2005). Yet popular press reports emphasize female perpetrators (often teachers) with younger male victims, such as the case of Mary Kay Letourneau, who had two children with a student she began a sexual relationship with when she was a married 34-year-old and the student was 12 (Cavanaugh, 2007). Despite representing less than 5 percent of the cases of statutory rape and significantly less of the prosecutions (Cocca, 2004), female perpetrator/male victim statutory rape cases are sensationalized on the news and talk shows. This media coverage perpetuates the myth that there is an epidemic of older women preying on younger adolescent boys, and much of the rhetoric surrounding these cases treats the male as experiencing a "hot for teacher" fantasy rather than being victimized by a sexual predator. The language that is used in coverage of these crimes glorifies and glamorizes the incidents and incites a culture of sexual panic that further reinforces norms of appropriate sexual partners and behaviors (Cavanagh, 2007). The disproportionate coverage of male victims is especially ironic considering that statutory rape laws were originally enacted to protect young girls. It was not until the early 1990s that the language of statutory rape laws was changed to include gender-neutral language, allowing for the potential for male victims (Cocca, 2004). From the 1960s to the 1990s, public debate around legal and social policies about statutory rape often centered on rhetoric about protecting young girls from predatory older men. Adolescents, girls in particular, were seen as not having the legal capacity or emotional maturity to consent to sexual activity. Yet, during the same time period, the juvenile justice system was also undergoing a profound shift, seeing a steady decline in treating defendants, primarily males, as juveniles and instead prosecuting them as adults, particularly for violent crimes (Schaffner, 2005). This sexual double standard illustrates a peculiar dichotomy whereby girls are treated as innocent, virginal children without the ability to be autonomous decision-makers about their sexual lives, while boys are treated as adults with the intellectual capacity to commit a crime and be held legally culpable.

Race of the victim and perpetrator is the second area where there are significant disparities in enforcement of statutory rape laws. Similar to other crimes, men of color, particularly African American men, are more likely to be arrested and prosecuted and disproportionately sentenced (Criminal Justice Policy Foundation, 2005). The case of Marcus Dixon, a black 18-year-old male who had consensual sex with a white girl who was three months shy of her 16th birthday, received national coverage and illustrated a major problem with existing laws. Although he was acquitted of rape, battery, assault, and false imprisonment, he was convicted of statutory rape, and because of the girl's age, aggravated child molestation. He was sentenced to 10 years in prison, but his sentence was overturned and he was released a year later after public outcry about the case (Melby, 2006). Likewise, the case of Genarlow Wilson, a 17-year-old black male who had consensual oral sex with a 15-year-old female, drew international attention when he was convicted of aggravated child molestation and sentenced to 10 years in prison. He served over two years before his conviction was overturned by the Georgia State Supreme Court. In a letter to the state attorney general, former president Jimmy Carter wrote, "The racial dimension of the case is likewise hard to ignore and perhaps unfortunately has had an impact on the final outcome of the case" (Jarvie and Fausset, 2007). Disproportionate prosecuting and sentencing of black

men for statutory rape reflect remnants of historical racism predicated on white fears about black men having sex with white women.

The Genarlow Wilson case also illustrates a third area of differential enforcement of consent laws based on types of sexual behavior. Had he been convicted of sexual intercourse with the 15-year-old, rather than oral sex, a child molestation charge would not have applied. More often, the differential enforcement of laws based on behavior involves disparities between heterosexual and homosexual sexual activity. Matthew Limon was released from prison in 2005 after serving almost six years in prison for consensual gay sex when he had just turned 18 and his partner was 14, nearly 15. He was convicted of criminal sodomy because Kansas's "Romeo and Juliet" law, which reduced penalties for consensual sex between two teenagers, only applied to heterosexual sex. He was sentenced to 17 years in prison but would have only been sentenced to 15 months had his partner been female. The case went all the way to the U.S. Supreme Court, which overturned the conviction, but by that time Limon had served nearly six years in prison (Melby, 2006).

A final area where adolescent sexual agency has intertwined with the legal system has been through attempts to control use of social media, especially the phenomenon of "sexting" between young people of similar ages (which involves sending sexually explicit material, including photos, through various social media platforms). The moral outrage surrounding sexting behavior frequently focuses on protecting and/or controlling adolescent girls and avoids issues of consent and sexual agency (Hasinoff, 2015). As of [2017, 25] U.S. states have enacted "sexting" laws, which clarify and attempt to differentiate between the dissemination of child pornography between adults and the dissemination of sexually explicit pictures between adolescents. In some states, "sexting" laws are rigidly enforced; in others, they are only in place when sexually explicit material is distributed to others as a form of revenge (Cyberbullying Research Center, 2015). In states where there are no specific laws about "sexting" or revenge porn, a teenager sending a scantily clad photo of himself or herself to his or her significant other could be prosecuted for child pornography and forced to register as a sex offender if convicted. For example, an "explicit selfie" sent to a male friend on Snapchat by a Minnesota girl was saved and forwarded by classmates. The 14-year-old girl is now facing felony sex crime charges for child pornography (Burns, 2018). The criminal justice system has continued to struggle with differentiating between consensual sexual behavior between teenagers and exploitation of minors by older adults. It has proven difficult to draw clear boundaries between the two and to determine the extent to which adolescent sexual agency should be respected.

Age of consent and statutory rape laws are not designed to catch and punish persistent child sexual offenders; states have separate legislation that prohibits child molestation and pedophilia. Statutory rape laws, with their uneven and often discriminatory enforcement, have primarily served to criminalize adolescent sexual exploration. NIBRS (2005) reports that 3 out of 10 reported cases of statutory rape regarding juveniles involve people who considered themselves "boyfriend/girlfriend," and 6 out of 10 involve people who considered each other "acquaintances or friends" (Troup-Leasure and Snyder, 2005). The legislation, punishments, and moral panic around age of consent do not prevent adolescents from having sex, but they deny their sexual agency and limit their sexual partners (Cavanagh, 2007; Hunt, 2009). The CDC (2015) reports that by ninth grade 20.7 percent of girls have ever engaged in sexual intercourse, and by twelfth grade that percentage increases to 57.2 percent. For boys, 27.3 percent haved engaged in

sexual intercourse by ninth grade, but the percentage increasesd to 59.0 percent by twelfth grade. The CDC also reports that nearly half (46 percent) of high school seniors have been sexually active in the past three months, and nearly 20 percent have had more than four partners in their lifetime by their senior year. Adolescents are having sex; the threat of criminal prosecution for sexual exploration adds unnecessary fear and anxiety into the process over something that even adults disagree on (as evidenced by the wide disparity across states in age-of-consent laws and differential enforcement of these laws). Perhaps we should instead focus our attention on defining and enforcing laws that address coercive sexual behavior.

NOTES

1. Age of consent laws traditionally define the age below which you are too young to consent to sexual behavior. These laws may also stipulate exceptions to the law. Statutory rape laws (or related statutory offenses) define the criminal punishmend for those who engage in sexual behavior that violates age of consent laws.

2. State by state information about age of consent can be found at https://www.ageofconsent.net/ and https://www.legalmatch.com/law-library/article/age-of-consent-by-state.html.

REFERENCES

Abma, J. C., G. M. Martines, W. D. Mosher, and B. S. Dawson. 2004. "Teenagers in the United States: Sexual Activity, Contraceptive Use, and Childbearing, 2003." National Center for Health Statistics. *Vital Health Stat*, 23(24).

Ageofconsent.net. 2017. "Age of Consent and Sexual Abuse Laws around the World." Retrieved December 18, 2017 (https://www.ageofconsent.net/).

Burns, Janet. 2018. "14-year-old Charged with Felony Sex Crime for Sending a Dirty Selfie." *Forbes* (January 3). Retrieved January 2018 (https://www.forbes.com/sites/janetwburns/2018/01/03/14-year-old-charged-with-felony-sex-crime-for-sending-a-dirty-selfie/#485fee254cbf).

Cavanagh, Sheila L. 2007. *Sexing the Teacher: School Sex Scandals and Queer Pedagogies*. Vancouver: University of British Columbia Press.

Centers for Disease Control and Prevention. 2015. "Youth Risk Behavior Surveillance System–United States

1991–2015." Retrieved December 3, 2017 (https://nccd
.cdc.gov/youthonline/App/Default.aspx).

Chaffin, M., S. Chenoweth, and E. J. Letourneau. 2016.
"Same-Sex and Race-Based Disparities in Statutory
Rape Arrests." *Journal of Interpersonal Violence*, 31(1):
26–48.

Cocca, Carolyn. 2004. *Jailbait: The Politics of Statutory Rape
Laws in the United States*. Albany: State University of
New York Press.

Criminal Justice Policy Foundation. "Sentencing Policy."
2005. Retrieved January 13, 2009 (http://www.cjpf.org
/sentencing/racialdisparity.html).

Cyberbullying Research Center. 2015. "State Sexting
Laws." Retrieved December 3, 2017 (https://
cyberbullying.org/state-sexting-laws.pdf).

Hasinoff, Amy A. 2015. *Sexting Panic: Rethinking
Criminalization, Privacy, and Consent*. Urbana: University
of Illinois Press.

Hines, D. A., and D. Finkelhor. 2007. "Statutory Sex
Crime Relationships between Juveniles and Adults: A
Review of Social Scientific Research." *Aggression and
Violent Behavior*, 12: 300–14.

Hunt, Kalev. 2009. "Saving the Children: (Queer) Youth
Sexuality and Age of Consent in Canada." *Sexuality
Research and Social Policy*, 6(3): 15–33.

Jarvie, J., and, Richard Fausset. 2007. "After Teen
Sex Reading, He's Free." *Los Angeles Times*,
October 27: A9.

LegalMatch. 2017. "Age of Consent by State." Retrieved
December 18, 2017 (https://www.legalmatch.com
/law-library/article/age-of-consent-by-state.html).

Melby, Todd. 2006. "When Teens Get Arrested for
Voluntary Sex: Laws Designed to Punish Adult
Offenders Sometimes Trap Kids." *Contemporary
Sexuality*, 40(2): 1–6.

Parikh, Shanti A. 2012. "They Arrested Me for Loving
a Schoolgirl: Ethnography, HIV, and a Feminist
Assessment of the Age of Consent Law as a Gender-
Based Structural Intervention in Uganda." *Social
Science & Medicine*, 74(11): 1774–82.

Schaffner, Laurie. 2005. "Capacity, Consent, and the
Construction of Adulthood." In *Regulating Sex: The
Politics of Intimacy and Identity*, eds. Elizabeth Bernstein
and Laurie Schaffner. New York: Routledge. 189–205.

Troup-Leasure, Karyl, and Howard N. Snyder. 2005.
"Statutory Rape Known to Law Enforcement." Juvenile
Justice Bulletin No. NJC 208803. Washington, D.C.:
Office of Juvenile Justice and Delinquency Prevention.
Retrieved January 13, 2009 (http://www.ncjrs.gov
/pdffiles1/ojjdp/208803.pdf).

SICK SEX

ELROI J. WINDSOR

hat is sick sex? In other words, what aspects of sexuality qualify as psychologically "unhealthy"? If a man has problems getting erections, or if a woman has never had an orgasm, are they dysfunctional? Do they have mental health problems? What about people who fantasize about raping or being raped? Or those who enjoy being handcuffed or tying up their partners during sex? Are they "sick" individuals? How about if a person has the most amazing, mind-blowing orgasms when "yiffing" (i.e., having sex) in an elaborately designed wolf fursuit?[1] Is that person clinically ill? Among all these people, who might have a diagnosable mental disorder? Some of these examples are common occurrences; others may strike you as more peculiar. All of these different scenarios, however, challenge the parameters of what counts as "normal" sexuality. Although humans report a wide range of fulfilling sexual fantasies and behaviors,[2] psychomedical institutions classify some of these sexual fantasies, urges, and behaviors as mental disorders.

The *Diagnostic and Statistical Manual of Mental Disorders* (DSM) is the official guidebook for mental health professionals who practice in the United States. This massive text of diagnoses is published by the prestigious American Psychiatric Association (APA). The most recent version of the DSM—the fifth edition, or DSM5—was published in 2013.[3] The DSM5 devotes two sections to sexual issues.[4] Here, sexual behaviors ranging from premature ejaculation to pedophilia receive official classification as disordered. But categorizations of sexual "dysfunctions" and "disorders" are rife with controversy.

DEFINING "SICK" SEX: SEXUAL DYSFUNCTION AND PARAPHILIAS

The process of classifying human behavior as evidence of mental illness has a long and troubled history. From ascribing the "hysteria" label to anxious women to creating a disease category for enslaved African Americans who wanted to run away, the field of mental health has suffered through some embarrassing times. The most recent edition of the DSM signifies expansive new evolutions in mental disorders. For example, the DSM grew from 132 pages in its original 1952 version[5] to nearly 1,000 pages in the current edition. And between the fourth and fifth editions, the number of diagnostic classes rose from 16 to 21.[6]

These dramatic increases have provoked skepticism regarding the validity of the categorization process: Are people in the United States becoming increasingly mentally ill? Are psychomedical professionals perfecting their craft? Are clinicians creating more categorizations to aid insurance reimbursement for treatments, including costly pharmaceutical interventions? Classifying human conditions as mental disorders is a subjective process[7] often fraught with political tension.[8] The diagnoses in the DSM are also not easily transferable across cultures,[9] illustrating their socially constructed nature.[10] Yet, as a diagnostic tool, the DSM has incredible power.[11] A mental illness label carries tremendous stigma, which can result in employment discrimination, loss of voting rights and custody privileges, forced sterilization and institutionalization, and, iron-ically, inadequate access to medical services.[12] Worse, psychiatric labeling has been unevenly leveled against already disadvantaged groups, including women and racial minorities,[13] and diagnoses have been used to legitimize the political oppression of sexual minorities.[14]

Given this history of psychiatric labeling, what do we know about "abnormal" sexuality today? The DSM5 lists two types of mental disorders related to sexuality: sexual dysfunc-tions and paraphilic disorders. Sexual dys-functions "are characterized by a clinically significant disturbance in a person's ability to respond sexually or to experience sexual pleasure."[15] The DSM5 lists ten sexual dys-functions that categorize problems related to sexual desire and arousal, orgasm, and pain. Disorders related to sexual desire and arousal are grouped by sex (male or female), and include "Female Sexual Interest/Arousal Dis-order" and "Male Hypoactive Sexual Desire Disorder" (lack of or low sexual interest or arousal). Another disorder of arousal is "Erec-tile Disorder," and is used in diagnosing males only. Disorders dealing with orgasms are also sex-based and include "Delayed Ejaculation," "Premature (Early) Ejaculation," and "Female Orgasmic Disorder" (absent, infrequent, or delayed orgasm in women). The disorder based on genital pain, "Genito-Pelvic Pain/Penetra-tion Disorder," is reserved for women only and refers to pain during vaginal penetration, or pain in vulvovaginal and pelvic areas. Two of the remaining three sexual dysfunctions are less specific: "Other Specified Sexual Dys-function," "Unspecified Sexual Dysfunction," and "Substance/Medication-Induced Sexual Dysfunction,"[16] which refers to dysfunctions related to substances. In order for a diagno-sis to be made, people who experience these issues must also feel "clinically significant dis-tress."[17] The DSM5 advises clinicians to use discretion in diagnosing so that a person's age,

culture, and life circumstances are taken into account.[18]

Classifications of sexual dysfunctions refer to issues that infringe upon the normative sex-ual response cycle or sexual intercourse. In con-trast, paraphilic disorders refer to desires and practices considered out of the norm that cause distress to the individual experiencing them or cause harm to others. Unlike in previous edi-tions, where the existence of unusual desires or practices was sufficient for a diagnosis, the DSM5 differentiates between desires and prac-tices when determining what might qualify as a disorder.[19] The DSM5 defines "paraphilia" as "any intense and persistent sexual interest other than sexual interest in genital stimulation or preparatory fondling with phenotypically normal, physically mature, consenting human partners."[20] In other words, exhibiting a strong interest in sexual behaviors beyond conven-tional practices, or with unacceptable partners, is considered a paraphilia. But the "paraphilic disorder" diagnosis is reserved for people who have "a paraphilia that is causing distress or impairment to the individual or a paraphilia whereby satisfaction entail[s] personal harm, or risk of harm, to others."[21]

The ten paraphilic disorders named in the DSM5 relate to "anomalous" "erotic activities" (what a person does) and "erotic targets" (who or what a person interacts with sexually).[22] There are two types of paraphilic disorders based on anomalous erotic activities. One type is based on "courtship practices" with nonconsenting or unsuspecting persons and includes "Voyeuris-tic Disorder" (watching an unsuspecting per-son who is undressing, naked, or engaging in sex), "Exhibitionist Disorder" (exposing one's genitals to an unsuspecting person), and "Frot-teuristic Disorder" (when a person touches or rubs against a nonconsenting person). The second type of paraphilic disorders based on erotic activities refers to practices involving pain and suffering and includes "Sexual Sadism

Disorder" (sexual arousal from causing another physical or psychological suffering) and "Sexual Masochism Disorder" (one's own sexual arousal from suffering, including being humiliated, beaten, or bound).[23] The DSM5 lists three paraphilic disorders that relate to anomalous erotic targets. One, "Pedophilic Disorder," refers to orientations toward children and is characterized by "recurrent, intense sexually arousing fantasies, sexual urges, or behaviors involving sexual activity with a prepubescent child or children (generally age 13 years or younger)."[24] The other two refer to nonhuman erotic targets. "Fetishistic Disorder" describes intense sexual arousal from objects or nongenital body parts, and "Transvestic Disorder" refers to sexually arousing crossdressing. The remaining two paraphilic disorders are nonspecific: "Other Specified Paraphilic Disorder" and "Unspecified Paraphilic Disorder."

The DSM5 categorizations of specific sexual dysfunctions and paraphilias outline precisely which sexual behaviors and fantasies qualify as disordered, "abnormal" sexuality. However, these taxonomies of disorder raise important questions about the boundaries between "normal" and "abnormal" sexual practices.

IS SICK SEX SICK?

Several issues mar the sexual pathology classifications in the DSM5. One major problem is that the DSM5's criteria for "dysfunctional" and "anomalous" are subjective and informed by sociocultural norms. Similarly, requiring clinically significant distress before issuing a diagnosis presents challenges for providers with varying perspectives on sexuality. The DSM5 is also inconsistent in how it considers consent in diagnoses. Another problem is that some sexual disorders only apply to, or are most often found in, certain demographics of people. Finally, diagnostic criteria lead to gender and sexual inequalities in treatment.

Subjective Classifications of Pathology

A problem with sexual disorder classifications is the cultural relevancy that distinguishes between "functional" and "normal" versus "dysfunctional" and "anomalous." What counts as disordered sex? Regarding fetishism, some inanimate objects are more acceptable than others. High-heeled boots, lacy lingerie, feathers, candles, and rose petals are often integrated into dominant narratives of "sexy" encounters. The popularity of these items in late-night television and romance novels confirms for these people that attaching erotic meaning to these objects is ordinary. In addition, many people take pleasure in a wide variety of toys designed for sexual stimulation, and some women report only being able to orgasm when using a vibrator.[25] Would fetishistic disorder be an appropriate diagnosis for people who rely on these objects, or is the disorder reserved for objects that are not considered "sexy"? And what about people who lust for nongenital body parts? Some people lavish bountiful attention on breasts and buttocks during sex. Their desire for interacting with these parts may be more exciting than genital stimulation. According to the DSM5, excessive attention to these nongenital areas can be troublesome and diagnosable—if it causes clinically significant distress. But cultural standards can affect the way we perceive our interests. Fetishistic disorder depends on socially constructed standards of "acceptable" sexual objects. Some of the inanimate objects used during sex become props that mark the normative sex scene. But other inanimate objects—flip-flops, thermal underwear, flashlights, and jack-o'-lanterns—are not readily coded as "sexy" and so may provoke distress in individuals who find them arousing. Similarly, some body parts are more acceptably "fetishized" than others. If someone described himself as "an ass man," few people would bat an eye. But if he admitted to being "an elbow man," his disclosure would probably evoke suspicion. Ultimately, "fetishistic disorder" illustrates the social construction of appropriate sexualities. Some inanimate objects, and some body parts, are more acceptable to include in the trappings of sex than others.

The subjectivity embedded in sexual disorder classifications is evident when comparing the most recent edition of the DSM. For example, the previous edition of the DSM, published in 2000, listed sexual sadism and sexual masochism as disorders regardless of whether sadomasochist fantasies or behaviors caused a person distress.[26] That meant that individuals who fantasized about or engaged in BDSM—bondage, discipline, domination, submission, sadism, and masochism—qualified as disordered. But the current DSM5 acknowledges that these practices are not necessarily disorders if they are done between consenting partners or if the person is unbothered by their interests. What changed in the 13 years between the editions? Perhaps the existence of established BDSM and "kink" communities garnered more legitimacy. After all, the erotic novel *Fifty Shades of Grey* sold over 20 million copies in the United States, titillating countless readers and bringing sadomasochistic romance to the Hollywood screen.[27] Long before *50 Shades* popularized kink, BDSM practitioners had been stressing the central tenets of their practices as safe, sane, and consensual.[28] They objected to classifying erotic pain and suffering as inherently pathological. They noted that pain is acceptable, even expected, in other parts of life that many people find enjoyable, such as boxing, long-distance running, and ballet.[29] With the publication of the DSM5, all those previously diagnosable BDSM practitioners suddenly became sexually healthy. Clearly, society had changed and consensual BDSM was no longer considered a sexual disorder. This case illuminates the power of sociocultural norms to influence what gets counted

as disordered sexuality. These classifications expose "an underlying moral conception that continues to sanction socially reprehensible behaviors, pathologizing these as a way of maintaining/protecting public morality."[30]

Challenges in Assessing Distress

Another related problem with the DSM5 is that it directs clinicians to diagnose based on clinically significant distress, accounting for other life factors that may afflict a person. At first blush, this recommendation appears fair. If a person is not bothered by a lack of sexual desire, for example, why burden him with a diagnosis? And if someone is only upset about her inability to orgasm because her partner has shamed her, then surely she would not be the one with the problem.

But the challenge with determining what counts as clinically significant distress is that it relies on subjective assessments, not standardized tests or objective measures. In practice, clinicians may impose their own sexual standards and expectations. For example, a general practitioner may feel that a man's persistent lack of sexual desire is a major problem due to his own biases about male sexuality, whereas a certified sex therapist may have more comprehensive sexuality-specific training and experience that would not necessarily pathologize this client's behavior. Reliable diagnosing is challenging, even for psychotherapists using the same diagnostic criteria.[31]

The Inconsistent Criterion of Consent

On the topic of consent, the DSM5 is noticeably silent on a sexual problem that plagues the United States—rape. Sexual violence is widespread. According to the Bureau of Justice Statistics, the sexual assault rate for 2016 was 1.2 per 1,000 people.[32] Despite ample empirical evidence detailing the harms of sexual assault, and its nonconsensual nature, forcing someone to perform sexually is not considered pathological.

Some clinical researchers have advocated for including "rapism" or "coercive paraphilia" in the DSM.[33] This classification would align with other nonconsensual acts that are listed as paraphilic disorders. But historically, the DSM has excluded rape from its list of mental disorders[34] due to fears of misusing the diagnosis as a backdoor legal strategy that would aid criminal offenders.[35] This omission is remarkable, given that the DSM5 does include other nonconsensual acts that are also criminal behaviors: voyeurism, exhibitionism, frotteurism, and pedophilia. In practice, for example, pedophiles do not receive shorter prison sentences due to having a diagnosable mental illness. In fact, states with special provisions for sexually violent criminal offenders may impose additional requirements *after* offenders complete their prison sentences, such as mandatory commitment to mental health institutions.[36] Worry over potential unintended legal consequences of psychiatric labeling is unwarranted and arbitrarily applied. These problems situate psychiatry as a science that is at odds with the legal system.

Demographic Differences in Diagnosing

Another glaring issue with sexual disorder classifications relates to *who* is diagnosable. Although the DSM5 considers age as a factor related to sexual dysfunctions and paraphilic disorders, one diagnosis involves specific age classifications. For a person to receive the diagnosis of "pedophilic disorder," they must be at least 16 years old and at least five years older than the child.[37] Clinically speaking, a 15-year-old who has sex with a four-year-old child cannot be diagnosed with pedophilic disorder.[38] The DSM5 also states that people with pedophilic disorder sexually objectify youth who are "generally age 13 years or younger."[39] A 75-year-old man who has sex

with a 14-year-old teen is not diagnosable according to these guidelines. These rigid age parameters delineate disordered conduct. Once again, the DSM5's clinical criteria clash with codes established by legal authorities.[40] In the United States, the legal age at which a person can consent to sex ranges from 16 to 18.[41] Thus, the aforementioned 75-year-old man may be criminally liable for his conduct, but intact psychologically, according to the DSM5. These different age-based classifications create an ideological chasm between psychomedical and legal professionals concerning "unacceptable" behavior.

Another demographic pattern in sexual disorders relates to gender. In the previous edition of the DSM, "transvestic disorder" was termed "transvestic fetishism" and required the person diagnosed to be a heterosexual male. Prior to the current 2013 version, gay and bisexual men, as well as women of all sexualities, were ineligible to receive the diagnosis.[42] Now, the DSM5 has embraced a gender-egalitarian model that does not limit the diagnosis to a single group. However, the DSM5 notes that most people with transvestic disorder are heterosexual males.[43] Indeed, the DSM5 notes that most paraphilias are present almost exclusively in cisgender men.[44] The high occurrence of paraphilic sexual disorders in men begs questioning. Perhaps some observers of the trend might conclude that there is something innately wrong with male sexuality. But a more sociological interpretation would examine the sociocultural norms and institutional constraints that affect the ways men express their gender and sexuality. In the United States, boys and men are taught to adhere to narrow standards of hegemonic masculinity or risk being ostracized from society.[45] In contrast, women are afforded more flexibility in gender and sexual expression.[46] For example, it is much more acceptable for women to don men's attire than the reverse. And if a woman sleeps in her boyfriend's boxers, she can usually do so without having her gender or sexuality called into question. But how acceptable is it for men to wear women's silk panties to bed? The prevalence of heterosexual males among paraphilic classifications may say more about the nature of our social norms than the nature of an entire gender group. Social norms also help explain why the DSM5 classifies pain-based sexual dysfunction as something only women experience. If we consider how vaginas are depicted in society, we can see that their sociocultural meanings involve passivity, vulnerability, abuse, and a general inferiority to the penis.[47] Is it any surprise, then, that women are more likely to fear the possibility of pain during penetration?

Inequalities in Treatment

Finally, it is important to understand the gender and sexual biases inherent in the DSM5. Diagnostic labeling is not the ultimate objective of mental health care; it is a means for treatment. The treatments for sexual dysfunction highlight "blindspots of medical discourse"[48] that rely on sociocultural norms about gender and sexuality. For example, sexual dysfunctions for males rely on the penis's ability to become erect when stimulated, maintain an erection for a reasonable amount of time, and ejaculate—not too soon and not too late. Besides relying on unclear ideas about appropriate times for erection and ejaculation, these diagnoses limit men's sexual responses to a single body part. They ignore other avenues for sexual pleasure for males, such as prostate stimulation,[49] or the orgasmic potential of "edging" (withholding or delaying ejaculation to increase orgasmic response). In examining Genito-Pelvic Pain/Penetration Disorder, a pain-based sexual dysfunction reserved for females, the American Psychiatric Association is clearly most interested in pain associated with penile–vaginal penetration.[50] According to

this classification, pain associated with the clitoris or G-spot ejaculation is irrelevant.[51] These issues underscore a heteronormative standard of penile–vaginal intercourse in the DSM5 and ignore countless other acts that are pleasurable and potentially painful. These standards then inform the ways therapists recommend treatments for their clients.

Another inequality in treatment relates to gender. Women are diagnosed with sexual dysfunction more often than men—estimates range "from 10% to 52% of men and 25% to 63% of women."[52] Treatments for sexual dysfunction often do not differentiate between women and men's sexual responses. For example, Viagra has been prescribed as an off-label treatment for women with low arousal responses,[53] even though women's sexual arousal involves parts of the body that Viagra does not affect. Prescribing Viagra to women, then, suggests that health care providers view this drug as a cure-all treatment. Other treatments for sexual dysfunction are designed to help women accommodate penises, such as vaginal-tightening "rejuvenation" surgery or labiaplasty.[54] Phallocentric medical approaches privilege men's sexual pleasure,[55] ignoring the role of the clitoris in women's erotic response. These treatment trends also challenge whether higher rates of sexual dysfunction among women can be attributed to cultural gender and sexuality norms, rather than to some innate problem in female sexuality.

In addition, women are not the only gender targeted by normative medical gazes. Treatments for sexual dysfunction also reify hegemonic masculinity standards. The widespread use of Viagra to treat men reinforces imperatives that a man should be able to get it up and keep it up, regardless of his desire for sex. Men's sexuality, then, becomes manageable by external medication and is reduced to the penis.[56] The medicalization of men's sexuality reinforces masculinity standards and avoids a whole-body approach to understanding sexuality.[57] These critiques of biases in the DSM5 are not exhaustive. But they present some challenges to the ways psychomedical institutions construct boundaries between "normal" and "abnormal" sex.

PROGNOSIS

Although the DSM5 specifies a range of pathologized sexual desires and behaviors, it never actually describes what counts as *healthy* sexuality.[58] Based on the characteristics identified as dysfunctional or paraphilic, we can deduce what healthy sex entails. So, based on these standards, how many people have healthy sex 100 percent of the time? To return to the first paragraph of this reading, the DSM5 classification system means that the man who had erection problems and the woman who never had an orgasm might be considered dysfunctional. The people who engaged in bondage might be evaluated for a paraphilic disorder diagnosis. But the people fantasizing about rape and orgasming while yiffing would not present with desires or behaviors denoted as diagnosable. I offer these specific cases to illustrate the arbitrary ways the DSM5 creates boundaries between sexual "health" and "pathology"; they are not an endorsement of a need for continued or more expansive pathologizing.

Ultimately, the problems with DSM5 diagnoses illustrate how distinguishing between "sick" and "healthy" is tricky. Categorizations of "disorder" are informed by sociocultural norms. They are partial to political and historical trends. The evolution of "sick" sexuality illustrates how meanings of sexual pathology change over time, such as the landmark transformation brought by the removal of homosexuality from the DSM in 1973.[59] Sexual disorders are social constructions. Given that, are the sexual preferences currently delineated in the DSM5 truly pathological, or are they part of normal human variation? Some clinicians are highly critical of the classification system: "Non-clinical studies of individuals with unusual sexual interests demonstrate that these individuals are indistinguishable from those with 'normophilic' (i.e., conventional) sexual interests."[60] Unusual sexual fantasies commonly enter the imaginations of all people,[61] and research shows that nonoffenders have just as "deviant" fantasies as sex offenders.[62] Even the gold standard of sexual normativity—heterosexuality—could seem pathological based on the DSM5's classification system. For example, given the high rate of sexual dysfunction among heterosexuals—distress and impairment related to types of sexual practices and frequency of sexual activity, as well as sexual insecurity, substance abuse, and violence that interfere with social relationships—this sexuality meets the same flawed diagnostic criteria already in use in the DSM5.[63] This assertion appears ludicrous, but it epitomizes a central problem with the DSM5: "Sick" sex is more of a subjective designation.

Will the current list of sexuality disorders stand the test of time? Debates about the current classifications are underway. Scholars have even questioned the scientific basis of the sexual disorders and paraphilias in the DSM5.[64] These questions are important because they transcend mere theoretical or intellectual exercises. The classifications in the DSM5 raise important questions about how psychomedical institutions manage sexuality. Furthermore, the social control of sexuality can have serious personal and political effects.[65] People can feel intense shame and disgust based on how professionals categorize them. Their sexual relationships can be strained and unfulfilling. And when classification systems regulate "appropriate" behavior, people with diagnosable sexual conditions can experience great loss. They can lose their jobs, their children, and their freedom. They can feel condemned morally and spiritually. In short, people can be made to feel sick.

When the next edition of the DSM is released, new diagnostic criteria will mark different parameters of mental illness. This text will change the mental health statuses of countless people simply through its publication. Take stock of the sexual repertoire listed in this next edition to assess what psychomedical professionals have decided. What desires and acts will be depathologized, and what will continue to be called "sick" sex?

NOTES

1. Explanations of the word "yiff" can be found at http://en.wikifur.com/wiki/Yiff, and a description of fursuits can be found at http://en.wikifur.com/wiki/Fursuit.

2. Rye, B. J., and Glenn J. Meaney. 2007. "The Pursuit of Sexual Pleasure." *Sexuality and Culture*, 11: 28–51. Also in Chapter 6 of this book.

3. American Psychiatric Association. 2013. *Diagnostic and Statistical Manual of Mental Disorders*, 5th edition. Arlington, VA: American Psychiatric Publishing.

4.The DSM5 has a section titled "Gender Dysphoria," which includes issues faced by people whose bodies are not aligned with their internal gender identities. However, I do not discuss these classifications here, as they relate to gender and gender identity, not sexuality. Note that "gender dysphoria" is contested as pathologizing gender variance. For a brief essay on this issue, see Cabral, Mauro. 2018. "I Am Transgender and Being Myself Is Not a Disorder." *The Guardian*. Retrieved January 10, 2018 from https://www.theguardian.com/global-development -professionals-network/2017/feb/24/im-transgender-why -does-the-who-say-i-have-a-mental-disorder.

5. Shorter, Edward. 1997. *A History of Psychiatry: From the Era of the Asylum to the Age of Prozac*. New York: John Wiley and Sons.

6. Rodríguez-Testal, Juan Francisco, Cristina Senín-Calderón, and Salvador Perona-Garcelán. 2014. "From DSM-IV-TR to DSM-5: Analysis of Some Changes." *International Journal of Clinical and Health Psychology*, 14: 221–31.

7. Rosenhan, David L. 1973. "On Being Sane in Insane Places." *Science*, 179: 250–58.

8. Spiegel, Alix. 2005. "The Dictionary of Disorder: How One Man Revolutionized Psychiatry." *The New Yorker*, January 3: 56–63.

9. Andary, Lena, Yvonne Stolk, and Steven Klimidis. 2003. *Assessing Mental Health across Cultures*. Bowen Hills, QLD: Australian Academic Press Pty. Ltd. For several examples of culture-specific diagnostic guides, see the Third Cuban Glossary of Psychiatry, the Latin American Guide for Psychiatric Diagnosis, and the World Health Organization's International Classification of Diseases.

10. Cooksey, Elizabeth C., and Phil Brown. 1998. "Spinning on Its Axes: DSM and the Social Construction of Psychiatric Diagnosis." *International Journal of Health Services*, 28(3): 525–54.

11. Conrad, Peter. 2007. *The Medicalization of Society: On the Transformation of Human Conditions into Treatable Disorders*. Baltimore: Johns Hopkins University Press.

12. Hinshaw, Stephen P. 2009. *The Mark of Shame: Stigma of Mental Illness and an Agenda for Change*. New York: Oxford University Press.

13. Ali, Alisha. 2004. "The Intersection of Racism and Sexism in Psychiatric Diagnosis. In Paula J. Caplan and Lisa Cosgrove (eds.). *Bias in Psychiatric Diagnosis*. New York: Rowman and Littlefield. 71–75.

14. Moser, Charles, and Peggy J. Kleinplatz. 2005. "DSM-IV-TR and the Paraphilias: An Argument for Removal." *Journal of Psychology and Human Sexuality*, 17(3/4): 91–109.

15. Ibid., supra 3, 423.

16. Ibid. See pages 423–50 in the DSM5 for detailed explanations of each sexual dysfunction.

17. Ibid., 423–50.

18. Ibid.

19. Sorrentino, Renee. 2016. "DSM-5 and Paraphilias: What Psychiatrists Need to Know." *Psychiatric Times*. Retrieved January 11, 2018 from www.psychiatrictimes .com/dsm-5-0/dsm-5-and-paraphilias-what-psychiatrists -need-know.

20. Ibid., supra 3, 685.

21. Ibid., supra 19.

22. Ibid., supra 3, 685.

23. Ibid., 685–705.

24. Ibid., 697.

25. Hite, Shere. 2004. *The Hite Report: A Nationwide Study of Female Sexuality*. New York: Seven Stories Press.

26. Ibid., supra 3.

27. Grinberg, Emanuella. 2017. "Explaining 'Fifty Shades' Wild Success." *CNN*. Retrieved January 11, 2018 from www.cnn.com/2012/07/13/living/fifty-shades-buzz-50 -shades-success/index.html.

28. Wright, Susan. 2006. "Discrimination of SM-Identified Individuals." *Journal of Homosexuality*, 50(2–3): 217–31.

29. Kleinplatz, Peggy J., and Charles Moser. 2005. "Is SM Pathological?" *Lesbian and Gay Psychology Review*, 6(3): 255–60.

30. Giami, Alain. 2015. "Between DSM and ICD: Paraphilias and the Transformation of Sexual Norms." *Archives of Sexual Behavior*, 44(5): 1127–38, at 1136.

31. Spiegel, Alix. 2005. "The Dictionary of Disorder: How One Man Revolutionized Psychiatry." *The New Yorker*, January 3: 56–63.

32. Morgan, Rachel E., and Grace Kena. 2016. "Criminal Victimization, 2016." U.S. Department of Justice, Office of Justice Programs, Bureau of Justice Statistics. Retrieved January 12, 2018 from https://www.bjs.gov/content/pub /pdf/cv16.pdf.

33. Stern, Paul. 2010. "Paraphilic Coercive Disorder in the DSM: The Right Diagnosis for the Right Reasons." *Archives of Sexual Behavior*, 39(6): 1443–47.

34. Frances, Allen J. 2011. "DSM 5 Rejects Coercive Paraphilia." DSM5 in Distress, *Psychology Today*, May 26. Retrieved January 11, 2018 from www.psychologytoday .com/blog/dsm5-in-distress/201105/dsm-5-rejects-coercive -paraphilia.

35. Frances, Allen, Shoba Sreenivasan, and Linda E. Weinberger. 2008. "Defining Mental Disorder When It Really Counts: DSM-IV-TR and SVP/SDP Statutes." *Journal of the American Academy of Psychiatry and the Law Online*, 36(3): 375–84. Retrieved January 11, 2018 from http://www.jaapl.org/content/36/3/375.full.

36. Ibid.

37. Ibid., supra 3, 697.

38. Legal classifications of sexual misconduct, however, are another matter. For an analysis of tensions between crimes and mental disorders, see Walvisch, Jamie. 2017. "Defining 'Mental Disorder' in Legal Contexts." *International Journal of Law and Psychiatry*, 52: 7–18.

39. Ibid., supra 3, 697.

40. Moser, Charles. 2009. "When Is an Unusual Sexual Interest a Mental Disorder?" *Archives of Sexual Behavior*, 38: 323–25.

41. Robinson, Paul H., and Tyler Scot Williams. 2017. *Mapping Criminal Law: Variations across the Fifty States*. Ch. 20: *Statutory Rape*. Retrieved January 11, 2018 from https:// poseidon01.ssrn.com/delivery.php? ID=038100029123011 00909107409500112608506307404804403008807602300 70230910931260661221190021230330630230550350741 04027103100080121049087078093002003088101098102 21220280290620861050701210841050810890820220002 03107101307200509310109609211012512210010306 4017&EXT=pdf. For a discussion of age of consent laws, see Cavalier and Burgess's "Too Young to Consent?" in Chapter 8 of this book.

42. American Psychiatric Association. 2000. *Diagnostic and Statistical Manual of Mental Disorders,* 4th edition, Text Revision (DSM-IV-TR). Arlington, VA: American Psychiatric Association.

43. "Cisgender" refers to non-transgender status, or people whose assigned sex at birth is congruent with their gender identity. On the issue of the disproportionate number of cisgender men who have paraphilias, see Kennedy, Harry. 2001. "Do Men Need Special Services?" *Advances in Psychiatric Treatment*, 7: 93–99. Retrieved January 11, 2018 from http://apt.rcpsych.org /content/7/2/93.full.pdf.

44. For an insightful sociological study on this phenomenon, see Pascoe, C. J. 2012. *Dude, You're a Fag: Masculinity and Sexuality in High School*. Berkeley: University of California Press.

45. Kivel, Paul. 1999. *Boys Will Be Men: Raising Our Sons for Courage, Caring, and Community*. Gabriola Island, BC, Canada: New Society Publishers.

46. For example, see Budnick's "'Straight Girls Kissing'? Understanding Same-Gender Sexuality beyond the Elite College Campus" in Chapter 1 of this book.

47. Braun, Virginia, and Sue Wilkinson. 2001. "Socio-Cultural Representations of the Vagina." *Journal of Reproductive and Infant Psychology*, 19(1): 17–32.

48. Mollenhauer, Whitney F. 2011. "Female Sexual Dysfunction: History, Critiques, and New Directions" (p. 3). Thinking Gender Papers, UCLA Center for the Study of Women. Retrieved January 18, 2012 from http://escholarship.org/uc/item/8jh824nc.

49. Silverberg, Cory. 2017. "Your Guide to Prostate Stimulation." Retrieved January 12, 2018 from www.liveabout.com/how-to-find-and-stimulate-the -prostate-2982400.

50. Ibid., supra 3. See Criterion A (p. 437) for descriptions of the four pain areas associated with this disorder.

51. For a detailed discussion of cisgender female orgasmic responses, including G-spot ejaculation, see "The G-Spot and Other Mysteries" in Chapter 5 of this book.

52. Heiman, Julia R. 2002. "Sexual Dysfunction: Overview of Prevalence, Etiological Factors, and Treatments." *Journal of Sex Research*, 39(1): 73–78, at 73.

53. Hartley, Heather. 2006. "The 'Pinking' of Viagra Culture: Drug Industry Efforts to Create and Repackage Sex Drugs for Women." *Sexualities*, 9(3): 363–78.

54. Braun, Virginia. 2005. "In Search of (Better) Sexual Pleasure: Female Genital 'Cosmetic' Surgery." *Sexualities*, 8(4): 407–24.

55. Drew, Jennifer. 2003. "The Myth of Female Sexual Dysfunction and Its Medicalization." *Sexualities, Evolution, and Gender*, 5(2): 89–96.

56. Marshall, Barbara L. 2002. "'Hard Science': Gendered Constructions of Sexual Dysfunction in the 'Viagra Age'" *Sexualities*, 5(2): 131–58.

57. Low, Meika. 2004. *The Rise of Viagra: How the Little Blue Pill Changed Sex in America*. New York: New York University Press.

58. Ibid., supra 14.

59. Cooper, Rachel. 2004. "What Is Wrong with the DSM?" *History of Psychiatry*, 15(1): 5–25.

60. Ibid., supra 14.

61. Renaud, Cheryl A., and E. Sandra Byers. 1999. "Exploring the Frequency, Diversity and Content of University Students' Positive and Negative Sexual Cognitions." *Canadian Journal of Human Sexuality*, 8(1): 17–30.

62. Langevin, Ron, Reuben A. Lang, and Suzanne Curnoe. 1998. "The Prevalence of Sex Offenders with Deviant Fantasies." *Journal of Interpersonal Violence*, 13(3): 315–27.

63. Moser, Charles, and Peggy J. Kleinplatz. 2005. "Does Heterosexuality Belong in the DSM?" *Lesbian and Gay Psychology Review*, 6(3): 261–67.

64. Moser, Charles. 2016. "DSM-5 and the Paraphilic Disorders: Conceptual Issues." *Archives of Sexual Behavior*, 45: 2181–86.

65. Ibid.

BIRTHRIGHT: A HISTORY OF PLANNED PARENTHOOD

JILL LEPORE

The fury over Planned Parenthood is two political passions—opposition to abortion and opposition to government programs for the poor—acting as one. . . . Margaret Sanger opened that first clinic in Brooklyn four years before the passage of what was called, at the time, the Susan B. Anthony Amendment: "The right of citizens of the United States to vote shall not be denied or abridged by the United States or by any State on account of sex." Women had only just got the right to vote when the Equal Rights Amendment, written by Alice Paul, was introduced to Congress: "Men and women shall have equal rights throughout the United States." Revisions were introduced in every session from 1923 to 1971. In 1972, the ERA passed and went to the states for ratification. Its eventual defeat was accomplished by conservatives led by Phyllis Schlafly, who opposed the women's rights movement and supported a human-life amendment. . . .

The first birth-control clinic in the United States opened on October 16, 1916, on Amboy Street in Brooklyn. There were two rooms, and three employees: Ethel Byrne, a nurse; Fania Mindell, a receptionist who was fluent in Yiddish; and Byrne's sister, Margaret Sanger, a thirty-seven-year-old nurse and mother. Sanger and her sister came from a family of eleven children, one of whom Sanger helped deliver when she was eight years old. When Sanger began nursing poor immigrant women living in tenements on New York's Lower East Side, she found that they were desperate for information about how to avoid pregnancy. These "doomed women implored me to reveal the 'secret' rich people had," Sanger wrote in her autobiography.

(A study conducted in New York at the time found that 41 percent of women who received medical care through clinics operated by the city's department of health had never used contraception and, of those, more than half had had at least one abortion; they averaged almost two apiece.)

Between 1912 and 1913, Sanger wrote a twelve-part series for *The Call*, the socialist daily, titled "What Every Girl Should Know." Because any discussion of venereal matters violated the Comstock law, Sanger's final essay, "Some Consequences of Ignorance and Silence," was banned on the ground of obscenity. By way of protest, *The Call* ran, in place of the essay, an announcement: "'What Every Girl Should Know'—NOTHING!"

Sanger wasn't the only person to hand out literature about contraception—Emma Goldman once spent fifteen days in the Queens County jail for doing the same thing—but she was the first to make it a movement. In 1914, Sanger began publishing *The Woman Rebel*, an eight-page feminist monthly, in which she coined the term "birth control." Six of its seven issues were declared obscene, and were suppressed. Indicted, Sanger fled the country. When she returned, in 1915, the charges against her were dropped. One of her three children, a five-year-old daughter, had just died of pneumonia, and the prosecution decided that bringing a grieving mother to trial for distributing information about birth control would only aid her cause.

Determined to have her day in court, Sanger rented a storefront from a landlord named Rabinowitz, who lowered the rent when she told him what she was going to use the space for. She wrote a letter informing the Brooklyn District Attorney of her plan. Then she posted handbills in English, Italian, and Yiddish:

MOTHERS!
Can you afford to have a large family?
Do you want any more children?
If not, why do you have them?
DO NOT KILL, DO NOT TAKE LIFE, BUT PREVENT
Safe, Harmless Information can be obtained of trained nurses at 46 AMBOY STREET.

On the day the clinic opened, Jewish and Italian women pushing prams and with toddlers in tow lined up down the street, Sanger recalled, "some shawled, some hatless, their red hands clasping the cold, chapped, smaller ones of their children." They paid ten cents to register. Then Sanger or Byrne met with seven or eight at once to show them how to use pessaries.

Nine days later, an undercover policewoman came, posing as a mother of two who couldn't afford any more children. Mindell sold her a copy of "What Every Girl Should Know." Byrne discussed contraception with her. The next day, the police arrived, arrested Sanger, confiscated an examination table, and shut down the clinic.

Mindell and Byrne were also arrested. Mindell was convicted on obscenity charges; her conviction was eventually overturned. Byrne and Sanger were charged with violating a section of the New York State Penal Code, under which it was illegal to distribute "any recipe, drug, or medicine for the prevention of conception." (The fear was that contraception would promote promiscuity.) Byrne's lawyer argued that the penal code was unconstitutional because it infringed on a woman's right to the "pursuit of happiness." She was found guilty.

Sentenced to thirty days, she went on a hunger strike and nearly died. An editorial in the New York *Tribune* begged the governor to issue a pardon, threatening him with the judgment of history: "It will be hard to make the youth of 1967 believe that in 1917 a woman was imprisoned for doing what Mrs. Byrne did."

At Sanger's trial, during which the judge waved a cervical cap from the bench, Sanger hoped to argue that the law preventing the distribution of contraception was unconstitutional: exposing women, against their will, to the danger of dying in childbirth violated a woman's right to life. But the judge ruled that no woman had "the right to copulate with a feeling of security that there will be no resulting conception." In other words, if a woman wasn't willing to die in childbirth, she shouldn't have sex. Sanger went to Queens County Penitentiary. She was sentenced to thirty days.

From the start, the birth-control movement has been as much about fighting legal and political battles as it has been about staffing clinics, because, in a country without national health care, making contraception available to poor women has required legal reform. When Sanger appealed her conviction, the judge ruled that doctors could prescribe contraception, which is what made it possible, subsequently, for Sanger to open more clinics. In 1921, Sanger founded the American Birth Control League. She received stacks of letters. "I have Ben married 4 years the 25 december and I have all Redy given Birth to 3 children and all 3 of my children ar Boys and I am all most Broken down and am only 24 years old," a Kentucky woman wrote in 1922. "mrs sanger I do want you to write me an Return mail what to do to keep from Bring these Little one to this awfel world." Mailing her that information would have broken the law. In 1926, Sanger and her colleagues went to Washington and met with sixty senators, twenty congressmen, and seventeen members of the Judiciary

Committee. (Mary Ware Dennett, of the Voluntary Parenthood League, had pointed out, when she lobbied the New York State Legislature in 1924, that the very men who refused to change the law had wives who broke it: congressional families had an average of 2.7 children.) They didn't make much headway. Senator James Reed, of Missouri, told the lobbyists that "Birth Control is chipping away the very foundation of our civilization," that "women should have many children and that poverty is no handicap but rather an asset." Henry Ashurst, a senator from Arizona, said that he "had not been raised to discuss this matter with women." . . .

During the Depression, when more and more people were interested in having fewer children, Gallup polls found that three out of four Americans supported the legalization of contraception. In 1931, a committee of the Federal Council of Churches of Christ, chaired by Reinhold Niebuhr, issued a report endorsing contraception, arguing that, by separating sex from reproduction, it promoted marital love. In 1936, a federal appellate court heard *U.S. v. One Package of Japanese Pessaries*—a test case engineered by Sanger—and removed contraception from the category of obscenity. Not long after that, the American Birth Control League merged with Sanger's Birth Control Clinical Research Bureau to become the Birth Control Federation of America. Sanger, however, did not have much of a role in the new organization, whose leaders deemed the words "birth control" too radical; in 1942, despite Sanger's strenuous objection, the organization became the Planned Parenthood Federation of America.

During the Second World War, Planned Parenthood touted controlling family size as part of the war effort. Birth control continued to gain religious support. In 1946, more than 3,200 Jewish and Protestant clergy signed a resolution in support of Planned Parenthood.

In the 1950s, the organization was run primarily by men interested in population control. Barry Goldwater was an active supporter of Planned Parenthood, and his wife served on the board in Phoenix. In 1956, Sanger, who had retired, wrote to a former national director, "If I told or wrote you that the name Planned Parenthood would be the end of the movement, it was and has proven true. The movement was then a fighting, forward, no fooling movement, battling for the freedom of the poorest parents and for women's biological freedom and development. The PPF has left all this behind." Sanger was bitter, but she was right. Birth control, as the historian David Kennedy once argued, was a liberal reform often turned to conservative ends.

Planned Parenthood began to wrestle with the subject of abortion in 1955, at the urging of Mary Steichen Calderone, a public-health physician who served as its medical director. (It was during Calderone's tenure that Planned Parenthood clinics began to administer Pap smears.) Abortion had been legal until 1821, when Connecticut became the first state to make abortion after quickening—at about four months—a crime. By the middle of the twentieth century, with limited exceptions, abortion had become illegal in most states. It was, nevertheless, widely practiced. "If there was even a communicable disease that affected that many people in this country, we would do something about it," Calderone said. She organized a conference and conducted a study. In an article published in 1960, she remarked on the difference between a legal abortion and an illegal one: three hundred dollars and knowing the right person.

Calderone left Planned Parenthood in 1964 to found the Sex Information and Education Council of the United States. She wanted to teach people how to talk about sex, because, as she once said, "People don't have much of a vocabulary. Or a concept of anything, except fucking." Alan F. Guttmacher, the chief of obstetrics at Mount Sinai Hospital and a clinical professor of obstetrics and gynecology at Columbia, had become the president of Planned Parenthood in 1962. Guttmacher had three priorities: improving Planned Parenthood's relationship with the black community, securing federal support for family-planning programs for the poor, and liberalizing abortion law.

The Birth Control Federation of America had established a National Negro Advisory Council and a Division of Negro Service: black doctors and public-health officials who wanted to reduce black maternal-death and infant-mortality rates through child spacing. Guttmacher hoped to strengthen these alliances, build new ones, and counter the accusation that the organization was racist. In 1962, the director of the Planned Parenthood clinic in Harlem (over whose opening, three decades earlier, W. E. B. DuBois had presided) met with Malcolm X. Malcolm X said that he thought it would be better if the organization called its service "family planning instead of birth control." (The meeting notes, sent to Guttmacher, read, "His reason for this was that people, particularly Negroes, would be more willing to plan than to be controlled.") In 1966, Martin Luther King, Jr., who, as a young minister, had joined a Planned Parenthood committee, was given the Margaret Sanger Award. In his acceptance speech, he drew parallels between the birth-control and civil-rights movements—"There is a striking kinship between our movement and Margaret Sanger's early efforts"—and celebrated Sanger for having "launched a movement which is obeying a higher law to preserve human life under humane conditions." In 1967, after a leader of the Pittsburgh branch of the NAACP said that Planned Parenthood was holding down the black birth rate, the assistant executive director of the national organization clarified that the NAACP supported family

planning. In 1968, a clinic in Cleveland was set on fire.

Before the mid-1960s, birth control had largely been privately funded; clinics affiliated with Planned Parenthood ran on donations, grants, and fees for service. "I cannot imagine anything more emphatically a subject that is not a proper political or governmental activity or function or responsibility," Dwight Eisenhower said in 1959. "That's not our business." But by 1965, as concerns about overpopulation, worldwide, began to dominate policy debates, Eisenhower had reversed his position on family planning, serving with Harry Truman as co-chairman of a Planned Parenthood committee. Meanwhile, the last legal obstacles to contraception were overcome. After Estelle Griswold, the executive director of Planned Parenthood of Connecticut, opened a birth-control clinic in New Haven, she was arrested and fined under the provisions of a Connecticut statute banning the use of contraceptives; in 1965, the Supreme Court declared that ban unconstitutional. The next year, Guttmacher testified before Congress, "We really have the opportunity now to extend free choice in family planning to all Americans, regardless of social status, and to demonstrate to the rest of the world how it can be done. It's time we get on with the job."

In 1968, Paul Ehrlich's "Population Bomb" was published, the Pope issued "Humanae Vitae," reiterating the Church's prohibition on both abortion and contraception, and Lyndon Johnson appointed a Committee on Population and Family Planning. The next year, Richard Nixon pushed Congress to increase federal funding for family planning. In the House, Representative George H. W. Bush, of Texas, said, "We need to make family planning a household word. We need to take the sensationalism out of the topic so it can no longer be used by militants who have no knowledge of the voluntary nature of the program, but rather are using it as a political stepping stone." In 1969, Nixon told Congress, "No American woman should be denied access to family planning assistance because of her economic condition." The following year, he signed Title X into law. . . .

. . . [In 1967], Alan Guttmacher edited a book called *The Case for Legalized Abortion Now.* As a young intern in the 1920s, Guttmacher had watched a woman die of a botched abortion, and had never forgotten it. At Mount Sinai, he performed abortions until the hospital told him to stop. Laws liberalizing abortion in the 1960s and early 1970s were urged by doctors and lawyers and supported by clergy. Between 1967 and 1970, some restrictions on abortions were lifted by legislators in Alaska, Arkansas, California, Delaware, Georgia, Hawaii, Kansas, Maryland, New Mexico, New York, North Carolina, Oregon, South Carolina, Virginia, and Washington. Governor Ronald Reagan signed the California law. By 1970, the Clergy Consultation Service on Abortion, established to help women find doctors who could conduct abortions safely, was offering services in 26 states.

Women were not much involved in any of this agitation. Betty Friedan endorsed the liberalization of abortion laws at a meeting of the National Organization for Women in 1967, but women's-rights activists really began to join this effort only in 1969, the year the abortion-rights group NARAL was founded, at a conference in Chicago during which Friedan declared, "There is no freedom, no equality, no full human dignity and personhood possible for women until we assert and demand the control over our own bodies, over our own reproductive process.". . . [T]en months after *Roe*, Guttmacher described having shown up at Brigham and Women's Hospital, in Boston, to give a lecture, only to be confronted by a protester wearing a surgeon's gown spattered with red paint, crying "Murderer." Guttmacher wrote in the *Reader's Digest* that "those who oppose

and those who favor legalization of abortion share a common goal—the elimination of *all* abortion," through better, safer, cheaper contraception, because, as he saw it, "each abortion bespeaks medical or social failure." This earned him plenty of hate mail. He died not long afterward. . . .

In 1969, in "The Emerging Republican Majority," the Nixon strategist Kevin Phillips offered a blueprint for crushing the Democrats' New Deal coalition by recruiting Southerners and Catholics to the GOP. At the time, prominent Democrats, including Edward Kennedy, were vocally opposed to abortion. Nixon's advisers urged him to reconsider his position on abortion and family planning. In 1970, the year Nixon signed Title X, the Department of Defense adopted a policy that doctors on military bases could in some instances perform abortions. In 1971, Patrick Buchanan wrote a memo recommending that the President reverse that policy, as part of a strategy to insure that George McGovern (the candidate Nixon wanted to run against) would defeat Edmund Muskie for the Democratic nomination. Observing that abortion was "a rising issue and a gut issue with Catholics," Buchanan wrote, "If the President should publicly take his stand against abortion, as offensive to his own moral principles . . . then we can force Muskie to make the choice between his tens of millions of Catholic supporters and his liberal friends at the *New York Times* and the *Washington Post.*" A week later, in a statement to the Department of Defense, Nixon borrowed the language of the Catholic Church to speak of his "personal belief in the sanctity of human life—including the life of the yet unborn.". . .

Abortion wasn't a partisan issue until Republicans made it one. In June of 1972, a Gallup poll reported that 68 percent of Republicans and 59 percent of Democrats agreed that "the decision to have an abortion should be made solely by a woman and her physician."

Fifty-six percent of Catholics thought so, too. [Justice Harry] Blackmun clipped the *Washington Post* story reporting this survey and put it in his *Roe* case file.

Nixon was reelected in November of 1972. Eight days after the Supreme Court issued its ruling on *Roe*, in January of 1973, a right-to-life amendment was introduced to Congress. "This poses real strategy problems," a former president of Planned Parenthood said in an interview, "because to the degree that any of us fight to keep that out of the Constitution, it brands Planned Parenthood as pro-abortion." Gerald Ford's wife and his Vice-President, Nelson Rockefeller, supported abortion rights. In 1976, the year Congress passed the Hyde Amendment, [former Texas governor] Ann Richards ran for office for the first time, and [her daughter] Cecile Richards, a student at Brown, . . . got her birth control at Planned Parenthood in Providence.

In the late 1970s, the Republican strategists Richard Viguerie and Paul Weyrich, both of whom were Catholic, recruited Jerry Falwell into a coalition designed to bring together economic and social conservatives around a "pro-family" agenda, one that targeted gay rights, sexual freedom, women's liberation, the ERA, child care, and sex education. Weyrich said that abortion ought to be "the keystone of their organizing strategy, since this was the issue that could divide the Democratic Party." Falwell founded the Moral Majority in 1979; Paul Brown, the founder of the American Life League, scoffed in 1982, "Jerry Falwell couldn't spell 'abortion' five years ago.". . .

Meanwhile, opposition to abortion grew violent. In 1985, pro-life protesters picketed at 80 percent of clinics that provided abortions. Linda Gordon, in her history of the birth-control movement, reckoned the toll between 1977 and 2001: "3 doctors, 2 clinic employees, 1 clinic escort, and 1 security guard were murdered. There were also 17 attempted murders, 41 bombings, 165 arson attacks, 82 attempted bombings or arson attacks, and 372 clinic invasions."

In 1983, Planned Parenthood added to its legal department a new arm, headed by Roger Evans, to handle a growing body of litigation. Evans has served as counsel for most of the major reproductive-rights cases of the past quarter century, including *Planned Parenthood v. Casey*. "People opposed to abortion have spent decades trying to make it more and more difficult for women to get to an abortion by placing hurdles in their path," he says. "And I think they have learned that that is a largely ineffective approach; it's more like torture." But it did have an effect: fewer and fewer places were willing to provide abortions, which made Planned Parenthood, in many parts of the country, the last abortion provider left standing. Today, more than a quarter of all abortions conducted in the United States take place in clinics affiliated with Planned Parenthood. . . . Republicans established the very federal family-planning programs that Republican members of Congress and the GOP's Presidential candidates are . . . pledging so vigorously to dismantle. Republicans made abortion a partisan issue—contorted the GOP to mold itself around this issue—but Democrats allowed their party to be defined by it. And, as long as Planned Parenthood hitches itself to the Democratic Party, and it's hard to see what choice it has, its fortunes will rise and fall—its clinic doors will open and shut—with the power of the Party. Much of the left, reduced to a state of timidity in the terrible, violent wake of *Roe*, has stopped talking about rights, poverty, decency, equality, sex, and even history, thereby ceding talk of those things to the right. Planned Parenthood, a health-care provider, has good reason to talk about women's health. But, even outside this struggle, "health" has become the proxy for a liberal set of values about our common humanity. And it is entirely insufficient.

Meanwhile, however divided the electorate may or may not be over abortion, as long as Planned Parenthood is the target, the GOP stands only to gain by keeping up the attack. . . .

EDITOR'S NOTE

Since the previous edition of *Sex Matters*, Republicans' calls for the elimination of Planned Parenthood have continued. In 2014 and 2015, working for an anti-abortion group called "the Center for Medical Progress," David R. Daleiden and Sandra S. Merritt secretly recorded Planned Parenthood officials and employees from "other groups that perform abortions and a business that supplies fetal tissue for research" (Pérez-Peña, 2017). Their falsified videos led to a congressional investigation of Planned Parenthood. Daleiden and Merritt "claimed to have gathered evidence that abortion providers and others were selling tissue from aborted fetuses for profit, which is illegal, but subsequent investigations failed to find evidence of that" (Pérez-Peña, 2017). Felony charges (conspiracy and 14 counts of illegal recording) against Daleiden and Merritt were filed in California in March of 2017 (Pérez-Peña, 2017).

Pérez-Peña, Richard. 2017. "Anti-Abortionist Activists Charged in Planned Parenthood Video Case." *New York Times* (March 29). https://www.nytimes.com/2017/03/29/us/planned-parenthood-video-charges.html (accessed January 6, 2018).

From Contraception to Abortion: A Moral Continuum

Wendy Simonds

I've done a lot of research over the course of my career that centers on ways that women avoid procreation. These methods include abortion (both surgical and "medical"—with mifepristone) and emergency contraception (higher dosages of the same drugs in birth control pills, which, when taken within 72 hours of unprotected heterosex, can be 80 percent effective at preventing a pregnancy) (Simonds and Ellertson, 2004; Simonds et al., 1998; Simonds, 1996; Simonds, 1991; Ellertson et al., 1999).

I've studied the ways in which health care workers and the women they serve think and speak about abortion and contraception as a moral issue, within a politicized climate in which anti-abortionists and pro-choice activists do rhetorical battle over women's rights and fetal status. These terms have changed very little over the course of my career as a procreative justice scholar.

Each side refutes the other's language: anti-abortionists call themselves "pro-life" and refer to their enemies as "pro-abortion," whereas those who support abortion rights counter with "pro-choice" and refer to their opponents as "anti-choice" or, more simply, as "antis." Each side seeks to ally itself with what the general public defines as truly moral, offering judgments about what the opposing value system threatens. Pro-choice activists proclaim the endangerment of individual rights, especially those of women. Anti-abortionists predict the destruction of the patriarchal heterosexual family unit by selfish (or sadly misguided) aborting women and evil profit-mongering doctors and clinic workers—all of whom they label "baby killers" (see, e.g., Ginsburg's 1989 and Luker's 1984 ethnographies of activists on both sides of the issue).

Carole Joffe writes that early anti-abortionist rhetoric in the United States in the late nineteenth century included the views that "abortion represents a threat to male authority and the 'traditional role' of women; abortion is a symbol of uncontrolled female sexuality and an 'unnatural' act. Above all, the aborting woman is selfish and self-indulgent" (1995: 29). In 1871, the AMA Committee on Criminal Abortion wrote of "the" aborting woman: "She becomes unmindful of the course marked out for her by Providence. . . . She yields to the pleasures—but shrinks from the pains and responsibilities of maternity" (cited in Joffe, 1995: 29). Today, with the popularization of sonography and high-tech enhanced medical photography techniques (like Lennart Nilsson's film *The Miracle of Life*), embryonic and fetal images have become ubiquitous; anti-abortionists take advantage of this technology in their quest to personify the fetus. This relatively recent fetal fetish means that women are increasingly absent from quite a lot of anti-abortion visual rhetoric (see, e.g., Petchesky, 1987), and their absence may well go unnoticed the more accustomed people become to this manner of seeing fetuses. At this writing (January 2018), 14 states mandate that abortion providers do sonograms on all women seeking abortions (in three of these states, providers must "show and describe the image" to each woman, and in nine of these states, they are required to "offer [each] woman the opportunity to view the image"; seven more states require that providers offer each woman "the opportunity to view a sonogram image" (Guttmacher Institute, 2017).

Pro-choice rhetoric and representations, in contrast, are distinctly woman-centered. Legal framing of the issue is more neutral: defining the right to abortion as a right to privacy, though sexual privacy remains another deeply contested issue in our culture. Pro-choice rhetoric draws on both liberalism and capitalism: As Barbara Katz Rothman (1989) points out, women are portrayed as individual self-owners entitled to control over our bodies. If I "own" my body, it is mine; anything within it counts as my property, thus abortion becomes an exercise in unarguably justifiable individualism. This rhetoric sidesteps an overt discussion of sexuality, but viewing sexuality through this lens clearly means seeing women as free choosers of what they want.

Pro-choice rhetoric includes endorsements of motherhood as a chosen activity; the decision to abort serves as testimony to how seriously women take motherhood. As Elizabeth Karlin writes, "I am an abortion practitioner because of my utmost respect for motherhood, which I refuse to believe is punishment for a screw. I do what I do because I am convinced that being a mother is the hardest job there is" (1998: 287). In years spent talking with health care workers and their clients, I've found that a particular moral continuum emerges that shows how anti-abortionist views of sex as shameful and women as frivolous shape aspects of the pro-choice view, too. This moral continuum is particular to our time: Bear in mind that it is only recently (the late twentieth century) that contraception has not shared the same stigma as abortion, and that abortion was not considered a moral issue until the mid-1800s. On "our" current moral continuum, late abortion is the worst, and responsible heterosex is the best. (No sex is another matter altogether: the anti-abortionists' ultimate moral category for unmarried women, seen as unrealistic or nonsensical by pro-choice activists.) Women who have heterosex should be "responsible"—this means, basically, that they should use contraception. So an unanticipated pregnancy that happens because a condom breaks is morally superior to an unanticipated pregnancy that occurs without any contraception; using contraception during actual sex is better than using emergency contraception the next day or the day after that; having an abortion in the first trimester is better than having one later on; and so forth. Yet at least one dominant cultural script for sex endorses being carried away (especially for women wooed by men) and another discourages women from planning for sexual encounters, because to do so indicates slutty intent (according to the script, to be prepared equates to being "loose").

Poll data show that many people buy the moral dilemma approach promulgated by anti-abortionists. According to various polls, public support for first-trimester abortion is strongest (ranging between 60 and 70 percent). "Americans are closely divided between those calling themselves 'pro-choice' and . . . 'pro-life'; now 49 percent and 45 percent, respectively. . . . It is the first time since 2008 that the 'pro-choice' position has had the numerical advantage," in Gallup polling, writes Lydia Saad (2011a). Poll data show that support for limits on legal abortion has grown since the 1989 *Webster* decision gave states the right to impose various limitations on abortion (Goldberg, 1999; Polling Report, 2011; Saad, 2011a). Currently, the most popular restrictions favored by Americans, according to recent poll data, are parental consent restrictions, mandatory "information" sessions (with varying content about risks and fetal development), and waiting periods (Saad, 2011b). A large majority supports abortion when a pregnant woman's life is endangered by the pregnancy, when her pregnancy resulted from rape or incest, or when the fetus is "defective." Support wanes (ranges from less than half to one quarter of those polled) if a woman "cannot afford any more children"; if she "does not want to marry the man"; and if the "pregnancy would interfere with [her] work or education." These poll data indicate the power of cultural attitudes about sexually active women as untrustworthy and immoral. Anti-abortionists perpetuate these attitudes in their legal assaults on abortion rights. 2011 saw an unprecedented number of restrictions introduced and enacted around the United States (Guttmacher Institute, 2011). Restrictions, of course, are most onerous for young women and poor women. The *Gonzales v. Carhart* 2007 Supreme Court decision made a particular late-term abortion procedure illegal. The procedure, called "intact dilation and extraction" by doctors and "partial-birth abortion" by anti-abortionists, accounted for less than 1 percent of all abortions in the United States. In sum, depending on societal attitudes about women's sexuality, the freedom to use contraception and abortion may be conceptualized as dangerous and immoral or as an essential aspect of individual liberty. Both the legal and moral future of abortion—and other methods of limiting procreation—remain at stake.

AUTHOR'S NOTE

At this writing, in January 2018, Donald Trump is president, and he has continually announced his contempt for procreative justice. The record of Trump's vice president, Mike Pence, demonstrates a similar misogynist contempt toward procreative justice. Trump's reactionary regime has given hope to anti-choice groups, which remain dedicated to controlling women's bodies. Thus far, Trump's regime has reinstated the "global gag rule," which denies U.S. funding to any nongovernmental agency worldwide that provides abortion, and nullified a rule that "effectively barred state and local governments from withholding federal funding for family planning services related to contraception, sexually transmitted infections, fertility, pregnancy care, and breast and cervical cancer screening . . . regardless of whether they also performed abortions" (Hirshfield Davis, 2017).

REFERENCES

Ellertson, Charlotte, Wendy Simonds, Kimberly Springer, and Beverly Winikoff. 1999. "Providing Mifepristone-Misoprostol Medical Abortion: The View from the Clinic." *Journal of the American Women's Medical Association*, 54 (Spring): 91–96, 102.

Ginsburg, Faye D. 1989. *Contested Lives: The Abortion Debate in an American Community*. Berkeley: University of California Press.

Goldberg, Carey, with Janet Elder. 1998. "Public Still Backs Abortion, But Wants Limits, Poll Says." *New York Times* (January 16): A1, A16.

Guttmacher Institute. 2011. "States Enact Record Number of Abortion Restrictions in First Half of 2011." (July 13): http://www.guttmacher.org/media/inthenews/2011/07/13/index.html.

———. 2017. "Requirements for Ultrasound." (Dec. 1): https://www.guttmacher.org/state-policy/explore/requirements-ultrasound.

Hirschfield Davis, Julie. 2017. "Trump Signs Law Aimed at Planned Parenthood Funding." *New York Times* (April 13). https://www.nytimes.com/2017/04/13/us/politics/planned-parenthood-trump.html (accessed January 6, 2018).

Joffe, Carole. 1995. *Doctors of Conscience: The Struggle to Provide Abortion before and after* Roe v. Wade. Boston: Beacon.

Karlin, Elizabeth. 1998. "'We Called It Kindness': Establishing a Feminist Abortion Practice." In *Abortion Wars: A Half Century of Struggle, 1950–2000*, ed. Rickie Solinger. Berkeley: University of California Press.

Luker, Kristin. 1984. *Abortion and the Politics of Motherhood*. Berkeley: University of California Press. 1984.

Petchesky. Rosalind Pollack. 1987. "Fetal Images: The Power of Visual Culture in the Politics of Reproduction." *Feminist Studies*, 13(2): 263–92.

Polling Report. "Abortion and Birth Control." http://www.pollingreport.com/abortion.htm (accessed January 2011).

Rothman, Barbara Katz. 1989. *Recreating Motherhood: Ideology and Technology in a Patriarchal Society*. New York: W. W. Norton.

Saad, Lydia. 2011a. "Americans Still Split along 'Pro-Choice,' 'Pro-Life' Lines." Gallup (May 23). http://www.gallup.com/poll/147734/americans-split-along-pro-choice-pro-life-lines.aspx.

———. 2011b. "Common State Abortion Restrictions Spark Mixed Reviews." Gallup (July 25). http://news.gallup.com/poll/148631/Common-State-Abortion-Restrictions-Spark-Mixed-Reviews.aspx.

Simonds, Wendy. 1991. "At an Impasse: Inside an Abortion Clinic." In *Current Research on Occupations and Professions*, 6, ed. Helena Z. Lopata and Judith Levy. Greenwich, CT: JAI Press, 99–116.

———. 1996. *Abortion at Work: Ideology and Practice in a Feminist Clinic*. New Brunswick, NJ: Rutgers University Press.

Simonds, Wendy. and Charlotte Ellertson. 2004. "Emergency Contraception and Morality: Reflections of Health Care Workers and Clients." *Social Science & Medicine*, 58: 1285–97.

Simonds, Wendy, Charlotte Ellertson, Kimberly Springer, and Beverly Winikoff. 1998. "Abortion, Revised: Participants in the U.S. Clinical Trials Evaluate Mifepristone." *Social Science & Medicine*, 46: 1313–23.

Choice or Coercion? Abortion and Black Women

Zakiya Luna

Abortion is a controversial subject that is debated every national election year and at many points in between. While contentious, abortion is a common procedure; some sources suggest that one-third of U.S. women will receive one in their lifetime (Guttmacher Institute, 2011). Conflicts in the "abortion wars" are polarized between "pro-choice" and "pro-life" activists, groups holding increasingly dissimilar beliefs that make finding a middle ground difficult (Ginsberg, 1998; Luker, 1985; Munson, 2008; Tribe, 1992).[1] One recent "skirmish" between these activists concerned the "Endangered Species" anti-abortion billboard campaign of 2010.

Social scientists analyze the debate over campaigns such as these because we have long recognized that attitudes and activism around abortion are useful sites through which to analyze larger social anxieties about gender, sexuality, and morality (Ginsberg, 1998; Luker, 1985). The visible groups on both sides of the abortion debate emphasize gender, sexuality, and morality concerns, but because racial minorities are not represented as having a stake in this debate, race remains largely undiscussed. Yet, black and Hispanic women are more likely than white women to obtain an abortion (Guttmacher Institute, 2011), and historically, there have been African American groups both in support (Nelson, 2003) and in opposition to abortion rights (Prisock, 2003).

THE ORGANIZATIONS IN OPPOSITION

The pro-life Radiance Foundation was founded in Atlanta in 2009. Its director, Catharine Davis, had been active in pro-life politics for decades before the billboard campaign. National Right to Life is a major organization in the anti-abortion effort, and Georgia Right to Life is a state affiliate. GRTL hired Davis, an African American woman, in 2009 to assist with its minority outreach program. Radiance identifies as an "educational life-affirming organization" with a mission to "educate audiences about pressing societal issues and how they impact the understanding of God-given Purpose. We motivate people to positively affect their families, their schools and their communities. Our combination of powerfully designed media content, thorough research and personal experiences, is unmatched and connects with people cross-culturally and cross-generationally" (Radiance Foundation, "Our Vision and Mission").

The pro-choice SisterSong Women of Color Reproductive Justice Collective was founded in Atlanta in 1997. This national coalition of 80 organizations aims to "amplify and strengthen the collective voices of Indigenous women and women of color to ensure reproductive justice through securing human rights" (Sister-Song, "Our Story"). Reproductive justice goes beyond abortion rights advocacy and includes "the right to have children, not have children,

and to parent the children we have in safe and healthy environments" (SisterSong, "Our Story"). Loretta Ross, an African American woman, serves as the national coordinator and has been active in the women's movement for decades. SisterSong coordinated the response to the "Endangered Species" campaign that included various reproductive justice organizations such as SPARK Reproductive Justice Now, a Southern reproductive justice organization, and allied organizations.

THE CONTROVERSIAL CAMPAIGN AND RESPONSE

The controversy began when Radiance placed 80 billboards throughout Atlanta in February 2010. The billboard image featured the face of an African American child under the text "Black Children Are an Endangered Species." At the bottom of the billboard was the Web address for Radiance's campaign "Too Many Aborted." The TMA website listed the mission of the campaign: "We strongly encourage adoption and provide connections to local resources. Through speaking events and media campaigns, we expose the distortion and destruction of Planned Parenthood and its abortion advocates" (TMA, "Our Vision and Mission").

While Radiance opposed abortion generally, the TMA campaign focused on one abortion provider specifically: Planned Parenthood Federation of America. Radiance claimed that black children were endangered because Planned Parenthood coerced black women to obtain abortions. Ninety-year-old Planned Parenthood has been dogged by charges of racism for decades because its founder, Margaret Sanger, was allied with supporters of the eugenics movement, a movement dedicated to the practice of selective encouragement and discouragement of some populations (Planned Parenthood, 2004; Roberts, 1998). While present-day Planned Parenthood leaders explicitly state that the organization does not support eugenics, its founder's beliefs leave the health care provider vulnerable to suspicion.

In response to the billboards, SisterSong and the coalition it later headed, Trust Black Women, wanted to shift attention away from a specific abortion provider to a more general emphasis on black women's reproductive experiences. They disagreed that black women were targets of abortion providers. They insisted that not only should women have the right to control their bodies, but that black women should not be blamed for their reproductive choices (Trust Black Women, 2010).

Radiance understood its activities as part of its mission "to eliminate the destruction of Life by focusing on solutions that empower women, men and children (born and unborn)" (Too Many Aborted, "Our Vision and Mission"). SisterSong countered, explaining that "[t]he mere association between the born and unborn with endangered animals provides a disempowering and dehumanizing message to the Black community, which is completely unacceptable" (SisterSong, "SisterSong Collective Opposes HB 1155"). The controversy gained both local and national media attention. SisterSong and SPARK hosted a press conference at the Georgia state capitol. Their representatives, and other coalition partners such as Planned Parenthood, local residents, and legislators, denounced the billboards as racist and sexist.

Radiance took a typical pro-life stance, identifying abortion as the cause of many social ills:

Since the legalization of *Roe v. Wade*, the black community has been hit hardest with its aftermath. Urban decay has been accelerated due to rampant sexual irresponsibility, increasing single-parent poverty, fatherlessness that exceeds 70 percent, and the continuing deterioration of stable (two-parent) black families. Abortion hasn't mitigated ANY of these factors. All of these societal conditions (as evidenced in U.S. Census Bureau and CDC reports) have all risen in direct correlation with increased prominence of Birth Control policies and legalized abortion. (Too Many Aborted, "The Truth in Black and White")

On the surface, sexuality plays a role in this objection to abortion, as Radiance argued that abortion encourages "rampant sexual irresponsibility." However, Radiance's objection has a particularly racialized tone to it by linking abortion to "urban decay."

Early on, SPARK suggested that the billboards were a direct attack on the bodies and sexuality of black women: "The goals of these billboards are to shame, demonize and blame black women, their bodies, sexualities, and capacity to make informed decisions about their bodies" (SPARK newsletter, February 11, 2010). Reproductive justice supporters like SisterSong and SPARK were taking a different approach to opposing anti-abortion activity. In their view, black women chose to have abortions without any coercion by providers. Black women's reproductive choices were instead constrained by lack of access to health care, proper sexuality education, jobs that provided wages on which to support a family if desired, and other effects of institutional racism.

EXPANDING THE DEBATE INTO THE LEGISLATIVE ARENA

Georgia Right to Life, Radiance's sponsor in developing the "Endangered Species" billboards, gained a sponsor for Georgia House Bill 1155, the Prenatal Non Discrimination Act, which would have prohibited women from being coerced into having an abortion due to the race or sex of the fetus. Critics such as SisterSong argued that this was a roundabout way to prohibit abortion. The legislation was eventually defeated.

The debate then expanded geographically, as Radiance's billboard campaign extended to different states through its partnerships with local pro-life organizations. Similar billboards were erected in other cities by pro-life organizations not associated with Radiance. For example, Spanish-language billboards with the same message of "endangerment" were erected in California. They too gained public attention, although Radiance's initial billboards were given the most media attention. In December 2011, Representative Trent Franks (R-Arizona) proposed a federal anti-abortion bill similar to the Georgia bill, named the Susan B. Anthony and Frederick Douglass Prenatal Nondiscrimination Act. Various civil rights organizations and their supporters objected to the use of these two figures in the name of anti-abortion activism. The act progressed to committee markup in February 2012 and died in May 2012.[2]

CONCLUSION

This controversy highlights how abortion crystallizes concerns about gender, sexuality, and race. Pro-life activists argued that sexual freedom was creating conditions that increased the instability of black families by promoting permissive sexual activity. Further, this activity resulted in pregnancies that abortion providers would profit from terminating, hence their supposed targeting of black women. Reproductive justice activists argued that this anti-abortion campaign was not about supporting black women and their children, but instead about restricting all women's reproductive options. In their view, to support black women would mean to support legislation that expanded health care or improved education for their children.

The "Endangered Species" campaign also raised questions of how reproductive justice advocates could best support abortion rights while remaining focused on addressing a wide range of reproductive issues, a question that will continue to be raised. Readers may wonder

if abortion is a simple matter of choice; if analysis of gender, race, and sexuality can ever be separated from one another; and if the two opposing sides in the abortion war that are commonly represented in the media (pro-life and pro-choice) are missing important perspectives. The expansion of this billboard campaign, responses by pro-choice organizations, and legislation proposed at the state and federal levels suggest that the race-inflected aspect of the abortion controversy will continue to command attention and perhaps require us all to think differently about what is at stake in the abortion war.

NOTES

1. I use the labels the larger movements choose for themselves. It would be more accurate to refer to SisterSong as "pro-reproductive justice," but I use the term "pro-choice" for simplicity. As described shortly, reproductive justice focuses on more than abortion rights, which is typically what people associate with the phrase "pro-choice" (see Luna, 2011; Nelson, 2003; Silliman et al., 2004).

2. *Editor's Note:* Parts of this proposed act have recurred in recent efforts to restrict abortion, including former Indiana Governor Mike Pence's anti-abortion law, struck down by a federal judge in 2017.

REFERENCES

Ginsberg, Faye D. 1998. *Contested Lives: The Abortion Debate in an American Community*. Berkeley: University of California Press.

Guttmacher Institute. 2011. "Facts on Induced Abortion in the United States." http://www.guttmacher.org/pubs/fb_induced_abortion.html.

Luker, Kristin. 1985. *Abortion and the Politics of Motherhood*. Berkeley: University of California Press.

Luna, Zakiya. 2011. "'The Phrase of the Day': Examining Contexts and Co-optation of Reproductive Justice Activism in the Women's Movement." *Research in Social Movements, Conflicts and Change*, 32: 219–46.

Munson, Ziad W. 2008. *The Making of Pro-Life Activists: How Social Movement Mobilization Works*. Chicago: University of Chicago Press.

Nelson, Jennifer. 2003. *Women of Color and the Reproductive Rights Movement*. New York: New York University Press.

Planned Parenthood Federation of America. 2004. "Opposition Claims about Margaret Sanger." http://www.plannedparenthood.org/files/PPFA

/OppositionClaimsAboutMargaretSanger.pdf (accessed February 1, 2012).

Prisock, Louis. 2003. "'If You Love Children, Say So': The African American Anti-Abortion Movement." *The Public Eye*, 17(3). http://www.publiceye.org/magazine/v17n3 /v17n3.pdf.

Radiance Foundation. http://www.theradiancefoundation .org (accessed February 2, 2012).

Roberts, Dorothy. 1998. *Killing the Black Body: Race, Reproduction and the Meaning of Liberty.* New York: Vintage Books.

Silliman, Jael, Marlene Gerber Fried, Loretta Ross, and Elena Gutiérrez. 2004. *Undivided Rights: Women of Color Organizing for Reproductive Justice.* Boston: South End Press.

SisterSong. http://www.sistersong.net (accessed February 1, 2012).

Too Many Aborted. http://www.toomanyaborted.com/ (accessed February 1, 2012).

Tribe, Laurence H. 1992. *Abortion: The Clash of Absolutes.* New York: W. W. Norton.

Trust Black Women. "Our Story." http://www.trustblackwomen .org/about-trust-blackwomen/our-story (accessed February 1, 2012).

NO BROKEBACK FOR BLACK MEN: PATHOLOGIZING BLACK MALE (HOMO)SEXUALITY THROUGH DOWN LOW DISCOURSE

C. WINTER HAN

In the fall of 2003, *The New York Times Magazine* ran an article titled "Double Lives on the Down Low," in which the author, Benoit Denizet-Lewis, took readers on a whirlwind journey through the not-quite-gay underground world of down low men, those who have sex with other men while leading supposedly "straight" lives. After navigating through bathhouses in Cleveland, nightclubs in Atlanta, the headquarters of an X-rated website, and other sexual romps, the author arrived at the conclusion that

today, while there are black men who are openly gay, it seems that *the majority of those having sex with men still lead secret lives*, products of a black culture that deems masculinity and fatherhood as a black man's primary responsibility, and *homosexuality as a white man's perversion*. (Denizet-Lewis, 2003, emphasis added)

Stereotypes of closeted black men aside, the article further insinuated that unsafe sex is rampant among black down low men, who not only refuse to get tested for HIV but also refuse to use condoms, as doing so would somehow threaten their sense of masculinity. In case there was any doubt that the down low was exclusively a "black" phenomenon, Denizet-Lewis followed up his earlier piece with an article in the online magazine *Slate* called "Get Out of My Closet: Can You Be White and on the 'Down Low'?" in which he wrote:

Men of all races have long had secret sexual and romantic male relationships, complete with the usual accessories of a double life: lies, deception, and shame. But the *Down Low was a uniquely*

African-American creation. If the closet is a stifling, lonely place for white guys who realize they're gay but aren't ready to admit it publicly, the Down Low is a VIP party for 'masculine' black men who will never admit to being homosexual—because they don't see themselves that way. (Denizet-Lewis, 2006, emphasis added)

The above quote may, perhaps, much better illustrate the lived experiences of black men who purport to be on the down low. Certainly, there are an uncountable number of men of all races who have secret sexual and romantic relationships with other men. Yet the down low, at least at the time of Denizet-Lewis's writing, was a uniquely black phenomenon in that closeted non-black men were rarely likely to self-identify as being on the down low. More importantly, public discussions about white men who were engaging in clandestine sexual behaviors with other men were rarely characterized as down low, nor was it likely to be marked with the negative connotations attached to that label. However, this portrayal of the down low leads to other questions. First, how "closeted" are these men if they, as Denizet-Lewis notes, are attending metaphorical VIP parties where sex with other men is the widely acknowledged intent for the "party"? More importantly, why

From "No brokeback for black men: pathologizing black male (homo)sexuality through down low discourse," *Social Identities: Journal for the Study of Race, Nation and Culture*, Vol. 21, No. 3, 2015, pp. 228–43. Copyright © 2015 Taylor & Francis Group, LLC, reprinted by permission of the publisher (Taylor & Francis Ltd, http://www.tandfonline.com).

would these men accept and adopt a label that is openly understood as a euphemism for "a man who has sex with men" if their primary goal were to hide their clandestine sexual activities? Clearly, these men "don't see themselves that way," but what "way" is it that they don't see themselves? It would appear that if the primary goal of being on the down low is to hide sexual activity with other men, then actually being on the down low seems to be one of the worst ways to do so.

Given these questions, it seems too simplistic to argue that the down low is just a way for black men to remain in the closet or a way of denying to themselves that they are men who have sex with men, as their public actions don't seem to indicate a strong desire to hide their sexual behaviors from others or the "lies, deception, and shame" often associated with the inability to accept oneself as having same-sex attractions. If not a way of hiding one's sexual behaviors or an act of mental gymnastics that would allow one to self-deny one's "true" identity, then what exactly is the down low?

The idea of being "on the down low" has a long history in the black community, and other writers have written about the down low phenomenon before Denizet-Lewis. While the exact origin of the phrase is unknown, it was originally used to refer to any type of behavior that was meant to be kept secret. While straight men having extramarital relationships also used the term, it was not uniquely related to sexual activities. By the time Denizet-Lewis wrote his article, many black men were using the term to describe same-sex sexual behaviors that they wished to keep hidden. However, the years following the publication of Denizet-Lewis' article have been marked by an exponential increase in attention by the mainstream media on the down low phenomenon, particularly as an explanation for the rising rates of HIV infection among black women, and have led to the term becoming entirely linked to

black men's sexual behaviors, specifically clandestine same-sex sexual behaviors. Also, the tone and cadence of the "new" discourse on the down low shifted from an earlier emphasis on the exploration of alternative forms of sexual expression among blacks, both men and women, to outright demonization of black men who engage in homosexual activity. On 16 April 2004, Oprah Winfrey called the phenomenon a "shocker" when she hosted author J. L. King on her wildly popular syndicated daytime talk show by introducing him as one man who "blows the lid off this sexual underground." King, who had recently authored a bestselling book titled *On the Down Low: A Journey into the Lives of "Straight" Black Men Who Sleep with Men*, was invited to the show to discuss the issue of the down low "lifestyle," which had already caught the national imagination and spawned a number of newspaper and magazine articles throughout the country. Calling the episode "A Secret Sex World: Living on the 'Down Low,'" Winfrey largely followed the narrative arc brewing among mainstream popular press that black men having sex with men, while in an intimate relationship with women, were endangering the lives of these women by putting them at risk of HIV infection, a trope being echoed among academic articles that men on the down low may be acting as a "bridge" for the spread of HIV between gay men and straight women.

Even prior to his appearance on the *Oprah Winfrey Show*, King had been working the media circuit promoting his book, which he described as an attempt "to facilitate a movement and awareness campaign" (Scott, 2004) about the down low phenomenon, which he himself blamed as the cause of black women contracting HIV at "alarming rates." Revisiting this same topic in her final season, Oprah told her audience to "imagine finding out [that] your soul mate, the man you share your life with, and your bed with, is sneaking out and having sex with other men." While sensationalistic, Winfrey was hardly alone in pointing the finger of blame toward black men who were allegedly in the closet and engaging in clandestine sex with other men while simultaneously leading publicly "straight" lives and putting black women in mortal danger.

Movies and television programs were no better with the down low, even making the topic a now infamous "ripped from the headlines" featured story line on an episode of *Law and Order: Special Victims Unit*. As early as 1998, with the release of the movie *How Stella Got Her Groove Back*, based on Terry McMillan's fictionalized accounts of her own personal experience being married to a gay man, the theme of a down low black man was being explored in mainstream media outlets. In the movie *For Colored Girls*, written and directed by Tyler Perry based on the play *For Colored Girls Who Have Considered Suicide When the Rainbow Is Enuf* by Ntozake Shange, Omari Hardwick plays Carl, a successful and masculine black man married to Joanna, played by Janet Jackson, who infects her with HIV after engaging in clandestine sex with other men. After finding out that she contracted HIV, Joanna confronts Carl with the diagnosis. Upon hearing this news, Carl tells her that he has never been with another woman since they have been together. When Joanna asks, "What about a man?" Carl angrily, but calmly, slurs out, "What the fuck did you just ask me?" As the conversation progresses, Joanna asks Carl if he is gay, to which he replies, "How you gonna ask me a question like that?" to which Joanna responds with, "How did you marry a woman and then turn around and let a man bend you over?" At this, Carl grows increasingly agitated and angry, leading him to justify his behavior with the statement that "I don't wake up holding another man, walking down the streets holding some man's hands, that's gay, okay? That ain't me." When Joanna tells him that he's "sayin' a lie,"

Carl continues to explain that "your husband is a man. I'm a man every day of the week. I'm a man. I'm just a man who enjoys having sex with another man, Jo. No attachments, no fucking . . . no relationships, just sex." While it's true that Carl is clearly attempting to hide his clandestine sexual behavior with men from Joanna, his rationale for not considering himself "gay" is not that he's trying to hide that behavior but that he's a "man" who does not hold another man's hand or walk down the street holding a man's hand. Here, it's clear that Carl defines sexuality not by the gender of his sexual partner but by his emotional, or lack of emotional, attachment to men and his unwillingness to share nonsexual intimacies with other men. Here, down low is not about sex at all but about a gender identity as a man.

As Denizet-Lewis noted in his article about down low black men in general, Carl is a black man who will never admit to being homosexual because he doesn't see himself that way. But Carl's unwillingness to identify as a "gay" man is not based on his inability to acknowledge and accept himself as a man who has sex with other men. Rather, for Carl, "being gay" is defined as waking up with and holding the hand of another man rather than by bending over, or being bent over by, another man. Because he does not form attachments to other men or have relationships with them, he can still claim the "heterosexual" label. But more importantly, he can claim the more prized label of "man." As long as he does not wake up with another man in his arms or walk down the street holding another man's hand, and as long as he avoids romantic attachments with another man, he is not "gay" but just "a man who enjoys having sex with another man." In Carl's mind, there is a clear disconnect between being "gay" and being a "man." More importantly, having sex with men does not define one as "gay." So it isn't that Carl fails to see himself as gay or that he is engaging in mental gymnastics that would allow him to delude his "true" self, as he clearly can acknowledge and accept that he is a "man who has sex with other men." Rather, the definition of "gay" for Carl does not necessarily include sex with other men, but is almost exclusively defined by a gendered presentation of self. Using that definition, Carl is not "gay" but rather a "man who likes to have sex with men."

SHIFTING BLAME DOWN LOW

As noted earlier, the mainstream media's focus on the down low phenomenon largely focused around the phenomenon as an explanation for the increasing rates of HIV among black women. Laying the blame squarely on the shoulders of black men who supposedly lead down low lives, Jason B. Johnson (2005) wrote in the *San Francisco Chronicle* that "secret gay encounters of black men could be raising women's infection rate." As the author contended, these secret sexual practices "have raised concerns that [black men who have sex with men and women] pass HIV to unsuspecting wives and girlfriends." While offering no scientific evidence, the article simply mimicked Winfrey's earlier contention on her show that black men living on the down low is "one of the big reasons why so many women are getting AIDS." This article followed on the heels of a *New York Times* article, "AIDS Fears Grow for Black Women," which ran on 5 April 2004. In it, the author Linda Villarosa interviewed five women who had recently gone to see *Not a Day Goes By*, a musical about black men on the down low, and noted that the down low phenomena was a subject of "increasing urgency" for these women and, by default, for all black women. Despite lip service that the down low could potentially be a concern for all women, media portrayals were nearly uniformly centered on black men.

Even the supposedly positive-friendly *POZ* magazine ran an article in the summer of 2003 called "Undercover Brothers" that began:

Just as afternoon is waning, you'll find Jamal in a secluded section of Prospect Park, Brooklyn—young and good looking, rocking a navy down coat, baggy jeans and a white do-rag. He's waiting, like the other men idling on the edge of this wooded area, for the sun to go down. After dark, he'll follow them down paths into dense bushes to have anonymous and, in many cases, unprotected sex. But by day, Jamal is in a relationship with a woman with whom he has a 2-year-old daughter. Stacie doesn't know about Jamal's quick tryst in the shadows. (Cited in Bell, 2012: 129)

The narrative arc of the *POZ* magazine article reflected the "new" discourse surrounding the down low as it shifted from an earlier emphasis on the exploration of alternative forms of sexual expression among blacks that was a way for them to self-identify as "not straight" within a cultural and racial universe that was more relevant to their own experiences; the new thrust of interest was on the outright demonization of black men. More importantly, placing "Jamal," a "baggy jeans and white do-rag"–wearing young man as the protagonist of the clandestine sexual tale . . . , the article managed to put a black face on a race-neutral phenomenon. In the world of clandestine sexual undergrounds, the actors aren't white men named "Larry" wearing business suits or "Ted" giving sermons at all-white churches; clandestine sexual actors are all "Jamals" wearing baggy jeans and do-rags who are hiding in the bushes.

The problem, as even these media outlets have grudgingly noted while simultaneously pointing the finger at black men on the down low, is that little is really known about the down low phenomenon among black men outside of anecdotal accounts, innuendos, and conjectures. In fact, recent scholarly evidence seems to point to inconclusive findings regarding the sexual risk behaviors among men who may be considered on the down low, or self-label as being on the down low, with some reporting higher risk and others reporting lower risk for HIV transmission among members of this group (Millett, Malebranche, Mason, and Spikes, 2005; Wolitski, Jones, Wasserman, and Smith, 2006).

Yet despite the lack of academic evidence about the impact of men on the down low on the rising HIV rates among black women, popular press coverage has been an unrelenting cycle of blame and denunciation of black men who engage in homosexual activity. Rather than leading to an increase in available information to combat HIV/AIDS, Layli Phillips (2005: 8) argues that the media discourse surrounding the down low phenomenon may actually aid and abet the spread of HIV/AIDS in the black community by "standing as a scapegoat for the HIV/AIDS phenomenon." More importantly, the down low discourse also feeds a neo-racist agenda by keeping black women and men at odds with each other, making spectacles of blacks, and reinforcing the stereotype of black hypersexuality. Not only does the down low discourse completely erase the actual causes of the spread of HIV, it demonizes black men who have sex with men by shifting the blame on them and therefore increases homophobia in the black community (Phillips, 2005). In fact, current research into the alleged down low phenomena among black men has led to inconclusive findings. In a recent study, Bond et al. (2009) found that black men who self-identify as being on the down low were no more likely to engage in unsafe sex than black men who did not. Also, media coverage of the down low phenomenon further perpetuates the misguided belief that only gay men have HIV, that bisexual men only contract HIV through homosexual contact, and that women only contract HIV through sex with bisexual men, while virtually ignoring other factors such as poverty, lack of access to sexual education, and, most importantly, injection drug use. As Angela Bronner Helm (2010) of the Black AIDS Institute noted:

Talking about injection drug use is not as sexy as discussing DL black men. And those addicted to heroin, cocaine or other injection drugs are not in a position to advocate for themselves. So black America remains ignorant about, and powerless against, this missing link to high HIV rates in our communities.

In fact, the down low discourse in the popular media has become so vitriolic that at least one HIV researcher has labeled the media coverage as "racist slander" (Dixon, 2005). This is especially unfortunate as most of what the general public "learns" about the HIV epidemic comes from popular media sources (Henry J. Kaiser Foundation, 2003).

Complicating the debate further has been the lack of scholarly evidence about black men who have sex with men and women. Although studies have shown that a bigger percentage of black men who have sex with men also report having sex with women than white men who have sex with men, only a minority of black men who have sex with men report having sex with women. So while mainstream media makes claims such as "the majority of [black men] having sex with men still lead secret lives," the academic data simply does not support such a claim. [While] there are a great number of black men who have sex with men and women while hiding their homosexual activities, . . . there are also many white men, and men of every race, who do just the same. Despite the recognition in the academic literature that men of all races engage in what can be considered down low behaviors, black men seem to take an especially harsh hit from the mainstream press (Phillips, 2005).

So sparse is the data on the impact of HIV risk for black women as the result of black men engaging in sex with other men that the Centers for Disease Control noted that "there are no data to confirm or refute publicized accounts of HIV risk behavior associated with these men" (CDC, 2006). While recent work has begun to shed some light on the down low phenomenon, findings have been mixed at best.

THE CONSTRUCTION OF BLACK MALE (BI)SEXUALITY

The construction of the black man as being on the down low is much more than just about finding a scapegoat for rising rates of HIV among black women. Rather, it is deeply embedded in the American tradition of creating black sexuality as one that is fundamentally different from the supposedly "normal" white sexuality. In this tradition, black sexuality is, by essence, hypersexual and deviant (Collins, 2004). And as Segal has noted, "black is the color of the 'dirty' secrets of sex" (1990: 176). Nowhere is the characterization of black sexual behavior as a "dirty secret" more evident than in the way the mainstream media covered clandestine (homo)sexual behavior of white men who are married to women compared with that of black men. For example, media coverage of Larry Craig, a married, anti-gay United States senator from Idaho, following his arrest at the Minneapolis–St. Paul International Airport on suspicion of lewd conduct was void of the potential risk of sexually transmitted diseases and the "danger" that he posed to his wife of nearly three decades. Perhaps this discrepancy is most evident in the different media coverage about bisexual white men following the release of the film *Brokeback Mountain*, a movie about two married cowboys who carry on a clandestine sexual affair, and that of black men on the down low. In examining over 170 articles written between 2001 and 2006, Richard Pitt (2006) found that white bisexuality is described using pitying language, garnering sympathy for white men who are in the closet, while black

bisexuality is described using pejorative language, painting black men as a "threat" to black women. Pitt noted magazine and newspaper articles about bisexual black men had titles like "The Stunned Wife: Preacher Husband Infected Her with HIV—Knowingly," "Deadly Deception," and "A Down Low Dirty Shame," while articles about white bisexuality are given titles like "Many Couples Must Negotiate Terms of 'Brokeback' Marriages." Pitt cites one newspaper article that quotes a black woman as having said:

If it looks like a duck, and it walks like a duck, then it's a duck. Who do these men think they are fooling? I get it, you can sleep with another man for sex, but you run back home to your wife, or girlfriend, and you say, "Oh, I'm not gay!" Yeah right! This whole situation is a hot mess.

Following this theme, another black woman is quoted as saying:

This DL crap is ridiculous because they are not responsible and it is killing black women and they don't want to admit they are GAY, GAY, GAY, AND . . . GAY!

Compare this with the *New York Times* article about bisexual white men that included an image of former New Jersey Governor James McGreevey, whose sexuality was exposed in an article in the *Record*, a newspaper based in Bergen County, New Jersey. In that article, the author notes:

On the whole these marriages are not marriages of convenience or cynical efforts to create cover. Gay and bisexual men continue to marry for complex reasons, many impelled not only by discrimination, but also by wishful thinking, the layered ambiguities of sexual love and authentic affection. (Butler, 2006)

More importantly, a professional social worker who has counseled "hundreds of gay married men" is quoted numerous times in the *New York Times* article being sympathetic to married men who are still in the closet and living double lives. According to the social worker:

These men genuinely love their wives. . . . They fall in love with their wives, they have children, they're on a chemical high, and then after about seven years, the high falls away and their gay identity starts emerging. . . . *They don't mean any harm.* (Butler, 2006, emphasis added)

As the above quotes demonstrate, white men who are in the closet are there because of many "complex reasons," including discrimination from others. More importantly, closeted white men who marry women, have children, and then carry on clandestine sexual affairs "don't mean any harm." They are portrayed as men who have tried their best to keep their sexuality suppressed in order to meet society's expectations and have struggled with their feelings. Because they mean no harm, they are deserving of our sympathy. . . . Generally, the men are portrayed as having struggled and having made difficult choices in their lives. Black men, on the other hand, are simply "ridiculous" and a "hot mess," having little regard for the lives of others. As one *Washington Post* article stated:

Such men, Nall said, sometimes use women as a front. "They bring women to the company Christmas parties. They introduce them to their families. But the women are just that—a front," she said. "And when everything comes spiraling down, when these women find out what's really going on, they can't help but feel used." (Vargas, 2003)

What is perhaps most surprising is that the above article, critical of black men who engage in clandestine sex with other men, was written by the same author who, when the lens was turned to white men a year later, somehow managed to find sympathy and compassion for their plight. If presenting them as simply using women as fronts to hide their clandestine sexual behaviors was not enough, a *Washington*

Times editorial resorted to near name-calling of black men by noting:

This dangerous nonsense just indicates how greedy, selfish and foul folks can make up all kinds of excuses and explanations to divorce themselves from the truth and their questionable and foolish behavior. (Washington, 2005)

This theme of dangerous black men is repeated numerously by various media outlets, not only by major newspapers on the coasts, but by smaller papers inland. In one editorial that appeared in the *Cleveland Plain Dealer*, the paper's associate editor had this to say:

Men who have sex with other men and go home to a woman are a health danger, even if the woman is informed. Men who have sex with men, go home to a woman and deny that they have engaged in gay sex are not only dangerous—they are dangerous, self-deluded liars. (Morris, 2004)

Morris's editorial is interesting particularly because it robs individuals of any sexual agency. He notes that men who have sex with men and women are "dangerous" even with a female partner who is informed of his sexual activities. For Morris, it isn't even the clandestine nature of these sexual behaviors, but simply the fact that these are black men having sex with other men that makes them dangerous.

So unlike the white men who genuinely love their wives, black men are portrayed as simply using these women for their own selfish reasons. Rather than a loving spouse who feels guilt and struggles with his deception, black men are simply users who have little regard for the feelings of others. Unlike white men who are still in the closet due to "complex reasons" such as discrimination, black men simply "refuse" to admit that they are gay because they are simply "not responsible." Whereas white men are struggling with their sexuality and attempting to maintain society's expectations of normative behavior by "sacrificing" their own desires, black men are simply greedy and selfish.

It's not just black men but also black women who are being constructed. It's obvious from the media coverage of the down low that black women are being presented as being scared and suspicious of black men. More importantly, the women are angry. For example, a *Washington Post* article about married black men who have clandestine sex with other men quoted one black woman as stating:

If only he told me he preferred men over women. If only he came out with it. We could have been just friends. . . . I'm very angry, I'm very hurt. This is someone who killed my child. I want revenge. Should I kill him? Sue him? (Vargas, 2003)

Compare this with the way white women are presented. In the *New York Times* article noted above, white women are presented as more sympathetic, more understanding, and more committed to their cheating husbands and their families. One woman who decided to remain married to her husband is quoted as stating:

He tried to go back in the closet, but the more research I did on the subject, the more I realized this is an integral part of the person. You can't just turn it off like a light switch. My husband is the man of my dreams, and I could not face the rest of my life with the man of my dreams being miserable and guilt ridden over being gay. (Butler, 2006)

Compare her statement of support for her husband with that of the black women and an entirely different type of appropriate female gender role becomes evident. Where the black woman feels anger toward the man who "killed [her] child," and is eager to abandon her husband, the white woman is sympathetic to the misery and guilt that her husband must have felt over being gay and determined to not only support her husband but to maintain the family. In these narratives, white women better fit the societal image of the "good wife" who supports her husband and maintains the sanctity of marriage, even at great expense. More importantly, she is compassionate toward the

"struggle" that her husband endures. Yet black women are eager to abandon the men they supposedly love and seem to have no issues dissolving the family unit without regard to the sufferings of their husbands.

More significantly, black men are portrayed as having consciously kept a secret from the women they married. Based on the narratives presented above, we are to assume that the black men "knew" that they were gay but chose consciously not to disclose this to their wives, thus engaging in active deception. White men, however, are presented as "truly loving" their wives but "confused" over their feelings. Only after "years" of trying to suppress their feelings, being relatively unaware and/or unable to confront their true feelings, does the chemical high of being married and having kids fade, leading to these gay feelings "developing." Presented this way, white men are not engaging in active deception when they propose marriage, get married, have kids, and build a life with a woman. Rather, their feelings and situations change slowly over time, and the white man is caught equally surprised as his wife.

DOWN LOW AS MORAL PANIC

Despite the alarm raised by the popular press, there is little evidence that black men's clandestine sexual behavior is impacting the rates of HIV among black women. In fact, saying the evidence is mixed is a rather generous appraisal. As Goode and Ben-Yehuda (1994) have noted, a social problem can be approached from either an objectivist or a constructionist perspective. . . . Within this frame, a "moral panic" includes an overheated reaction by various social institutions, including the media, in presenting a constructed "problem" as a grave concern for the general population. As Cohen stated, during a moral panic

a condition, episode, person or group of persons emerges to become defined as a threat to societal values and interests; its nature is presented in a stylized and stereotypical fashion by the mass media; the moral barricades are manned by editors, bishops, politicians and other right-thinking people; socially accredited experts pronounce their diagnoses and solutions; ways of coping are evolved. . . . Sometimes the subject of the panic is quite novel and at other times it is something which has been in existence long enough, but suddenly appears in the limelight. (Cohen, 1972: 9)

. . . [D]uring a moral panic, the over-reaction of various social institutions, including the media, to relatively insignificant or nonexistent threats, leads to the creation of those perceived to be responsible for the threat as deviants and their behaviors as being marked as being deviant. While black male sexuality has always been pathologized not only as being deviant from the norm but as dangerous to the innocence, and by extension purity, of white sexuality (Ferguson, 2003), the increase in media attention specifically to the down low phenomenon following the rash of publications in the mid-2000s certainly turned black male sexuality from a hovering threat to an outright moral panic.

. . . [T]he perceived threat of black sexuality, both male and female, can be traced with its roots extending beyond pre-colonial history. . . .

Needless to say, the down low narrative fits neatly into the already existing discourse of a dangerous black sexuality that poses a grave threat to the larger moral order. For example, a *USA Today* article published on March 15, 2001, began:

Black women think he's Prince Charming: well-paid, well-educated, nicely dressed, active in church and devoted to family. Yet, there's something the women don't know and maybe never will: he's secretly having sex with men. What's more, he might bring home an unwelcome guest—HIV, the AIDS virus. (Sternberg, 2001)

As the above quote demonstrates, in addition to the heightened level of concern and hostility toward those who are perceived to be the cause of the problem, the moral panic discourse surrounding the down low phenomenon adds yet another dimension, that of a hidden secret lurking just beneath the surface, ready to impact anyone. In this imagining of the down low, the biggest threat is that it presents itself as something noble and good, like the proverbial wolf in sheep's clothing. . . . As if presenting the down low as a dark and sinister secret ready to pounce on unsuspecting victims is not enough, the same *USA Today* article explained that "some of those on the 'down low' apparently learned to like sex with men in prison and began dual sex lives after being released." In adding this statement, the article attempts to equate black male sexual behavior with other forms of deviance and link those who engage in these behaviors with other types of deviant behavior. No attempt is made to explain or explore why then white men who may have also engaged in homosexual behaviors during incarceration are not implicated in the down low phenomenon. By adding the element of criminality, black sexuality is given yet another dimension of abnormality and brutality.

Like all moral panics, the down low is also a danger to the larger society as evidenced by two editorials that appeared in the *Washington Times* in 2004. As evidenced by their titles, "Menace to Society: The Low Down on the 'Down Low,'" and "Menace to Society II: Not Being Up and Up on the 'Down Low,'" it isn't just the people involved who are affected but society as a whole (Simmons, 2004a, 2004b). For example, in the first part of the two-part editorial, the author cites federal statistics of Americans living with HIV, making sure to note that 51.7 percent of all estimated cases of HIV diagnosed in 2002 were among blacks. Yet, she makes no effort to discuss other factors that may influence higher rates of HIV infection among blacks, such as lack of access to sexual health information, lack of education regarding sexual health, higher rates of injection drug use, etc., but instead lays the entirety of blame on allegedly down low men. In fact, discussing these statistics, which can be attributed to all manner of infection, she writes:

Those are the cold realities of mostly unconscionable behavior and statistics driven by the sinister lifestyle called the "down low" and something called denial. . . . Many of them engage in unprotected sex, switch hitting and preying on unsuspecting male and female partners. (Simmons, 2004a)

So the author engages in a bit of sleight of hand to paint the down low as a "public health crisis." Using statistics that cover all manner of HIV infections, she twists the argument to place the blame entirely on down low men. It's interesting to note that the articles are named after the 1999 movie *Menace II Society* about the life of a gangster named Caine Lawson that attempted to highlight teenage life in contemporary Watts but only succeeded in offering violent stereotypes about black youths and the "problem" they pose to contemporary America.

SO WHAT EXACTLY IS THE DOWN LOW?

Like many things, the down low is a much more complex phenomenon to explain than newspaper or magazine articles might lead us to believe. In fact, there isn't even a consensus of what living on the down low entails, or what it means for these men to identify as being on the down low (Millett et al., 2005). Likewise, the definition of bisexuality is often confusing and muddled, particularly as it relates to black men (Lichtenstein, 2000). To date, there has been only one article in the academic literature that specifically asked black men who have sex with men and women how they define what it means to be on the down low. In their exploratory study, Martinez and Hosek (2005) found that the definition of being on the down low is not only contentious but also resisted by the

men that the mainstream media might consider to be on the down low. According to one of the informants in their study who self identifies as "straight":

I'm not insecure with myself. I just don't consider myself to be gay. I don't like the label (down low). I just feel like I do what I do.

While the men in their study indicated an overall rejection of labels, some labels were more problematic for them than others. As another informant said:

I don't like any of them [labels] to be honest with you. I don't know what to call myself. I don't like "gay," I don't like "bisexual," and I don't like "straight." But I'll choose "straight" before any of the others.

More importantly, when men are asked, they give a number of different reasons for being on the down low. Yet the most common reason seems to be in order to avoid the label of being "gay." For example, one of their informants stated:

I don't speak of myself as being gay, because I'm not gay. I don't speak of myself as being bisexual, because I'm not bisexual. Now, if I choose to be with a male, then I choose to be with a male, but I'm not gay. I don't speak about being gay, and I don't intend to be gay. Actually, I don't even want to think about it; it's discouraging to me.

The reasons for not wanting to self-identify as "gay" are numerous. As Martinez and Hosek (2005) note, many black men who have sex with men simply don't feel comfortable in the gay community, which they perceive as predominantly white and "feminine."

. . . [R]acism in the gay community is well documented in both the mainstream and academic press (Choi, Han, Paul, and Ayala, 2011; Diaz, Bein, and Ayala, 2006; Han, 2007; Teunis, 2007). More importantly, "gay culture" has been largely constructed as white, leading men and women of color to see the "gay community" as unresponsive to their needs and unrepresentative of their personal experiences (Bérubé, 2001). As Robinson and Vidal-Ortiz (2013) note, the racism in the gay community and the construction of "gay culture" as being largely white may lead to homosexuality not being perceived as black. . . . In fact, in many urban areas, there exists a thriving black gay subculture marked by events such as "Black Pride" in cities as diverse as Philadelphia and Atlanta. In many cases, gay black men have created elaborate underground club scenes largely invisible to gay white men as well as developing their own social and cultural organizations (Bailey, 2013; Hawkeswood, 1996). Thus accusations that gay black men who remain outside the larger gay "community" do so in order to remain closeted say more about the rather white-centric beliefs about what it means to be "gay" than about black men (or any other men) who self-identify as being on the down low. . . .

The belief that "gay" is equated with "feminine" also seems to be a common theme among black men who are on the down low. For example, one of my informants for a different study stated that he did not identify as "gay" because

they're flaming, openly gay, switching and clicking. You know, the whole thing. You know, it's just you know, it's not necessary. Really, it's not necessary at all to carry on like that just because you're gay.

This theme was echoed by another informant in my study who noted that

I mean, like you can be a man havin' sex with men. It's the way you carry yourself. If you don't, if people respect you, like before they knew you were [having sex with men], you know what I mean, gay or bisexual or whatever may have you, they'll respect you long as you don't cross those boundaries and stuff.

For this non–gay identified black man, the boundaries that cannot be crossed are not those involving sex with other men but the public presentation of gender. For many black men on the down low, "gay" identity involves certain types of stereotypical feminine behaviors, which they choose to not perform. The important thing here is to note that for many of these men, being gay involves a series of public gendered performances that they actively choose not to perform, and therefore, self-identifying as gay is more about a gender performance than a sexual act. . . .

But it's even more than that. For some black men, taking on the down low label is an implicit understanding of their position in the larger social structure. As one gay black man stated:

I was gonna say in Philadelphia and a lot of other cities, I think the DL is attributed to financial status and things like that because a lot of people aren't gonna disclose what they do and how they do it if they're in a certain income bracket 'cause there's a lot of people lookin' at you that can kinda bring you down a little faster. And when you're, you know, usually a little bit more independently wealthy, you can usually act out and do what you want to do because you don't have to worry about certain people tearing you down as fast, you know. It's just like anything else. Money rules the world.

The above statement demonstrates how some black men may see the world and their place in it. For some men, the recognition that they are lower on the socioeconomic ladder, coupled with their recognition that there is a clear and identifiable racial hierarchy in the U.S., leads them to be more hesitant in adding yet another disadvantaged status marker to themselves.

Given these recent discussions, it is quite possible that the down low is not an attempt to "hide" their sexual behaviors from women but something else entirely (Han, Rutledge, Bond, Lauby, and LaPollo, 2014). More importantly, trying to argue that the down low is simply a way for black men, or any men, to hide clandestine sexual activity is problematic along a number of different axes. At the same time, why then do these men adopt these identities when there are so many negative connotations attached to them? As Essig (2008: 862) has pointed out in describing David Valentine's

Imagining Transgender, "categories are messy and difficult to point out." But the central point of Valentine's (2007) work on transgender identities is that while people may refuse the categories imposed on them by others, they nonetheless recognize that some aspects of those categories do, in fact, serve some function in helping them meet their identificational needs.

Certainly, there are many black men who self-identify as gay, queer, same gender loving, or a number of other ways that one can mark oneself as being "not straight." Nor are these ways of self-identifying mutually exclusive. It is highly likely, given the discussion above, that life for some of the men who self-identify as being on the down low is fraught with tensions, and for many of them, the down low is clearly not about hiding clandestine sexual behaviors. Rather, the down low provides some men an opportunity to acknowledge their sexual behaviors and their sexual realities in a way that is different from their perspectives about what it means to adopt a "gay" identity. For them, it is both an action and an identity, embedded in their cultural understanding of the world they inhabit. Problematizing and vilifying the down low as an inability to accept oneself as a "gay man" . . . is to further promote the untenable argument that there is only one true way of "being gay" or that there is only one way of interpreting sexual behaviors and that all other ways are somehow invalid. Such an argument erases the true experiences, beliefs, and values of those who would, for reasons having little to do with shame and deceit, think otherwise.

REFERENCES

Bailey, M. M. 2013. *Butch queen up in pumps: Gender, performance, and ballroom culture in Detroit.* Ann Arbor, MI: University of Michigan Press.

Bell, C. (Ed.) 2012. *Blackness and disability: Critical examinations and cultural interventions.* Lansing, MI: Michigan State University Press.

Bérubé, A. 2001. How gay stays white and what kind of white it stays. In B. B. Rasmussen, E. Klinenberg, I. J. Nexica, and M. Wray (Eds.), *Making and unmaking of whiteness.* Durham, NC: Duke University Press. 234–65.

Bond, L., Wheeler, D. P., Millett, G. A., LaPollo, A. B., Carson, L. F., and Liau, A. 2009. Black men who have sex with men and the association of down-low identity with HIV risk behavior. *American Journal of Public Health,* 99(S1), S92–S95. doi:10.2105/AJPH.2007 .127217.

Butler, K. 2006, March 7. Many couples must negotiate terms of "brokeback" marriages. *The New York Times.* Retrieved from http://www.nytimes.com/2006/03/07 /health/07broke.html?pagewanted=print&_r=0.

Centers for Disease Control and Prevention. 2006. Questions and answers: Men on the down low. http://www .cdc.gov/hiv/topics/aa/resources/qa/print/downlow.html.

Choi, K-H., Han, C., Paul, J., and Ayala, G. 2011. Strategies for managing racism and homophobia among U.S. ethnic and racial minority men who have sex with men. *AIDS Education and Prevention,* 23: 145–58. doi:10.1521/aeap.2011.23.2.145.

Cohen, S. 1972. *Folk devils and moral panics: The creation of the mods and rockers.* London: MacGibbon and Kee.

Collins, P. H. 2004. *Black feminist thought: Knowledge, consciousness, and the politics of empowerment.* New York, NY: Routledge.

Denizet-Lewis, B. 2003, August 3. Double lives on the down low. *The New York Times.* Retrieved from http:// www.nytimes.com/2003/08/03/magazine/double-lives -on-the-down-low.html.

Denizet-Lewis, B. 2006, August 11. Get out of my closet: Can you be white and "on the down low?" *Slate Magazine.* Retrieved from http://www.slate.com/articles /news_and_politics/hey_wait_a_minute/2006/08/get _out_of_my_closet.html.

Diaz, R. M., Bein, E., and Ayala, G. 2006. Homophobia, poverty, and racism: Triple oppression and mental health outcomes in Latino gay men. In A. Omoto and H. Kurtzman (Eds.), *Sexual orientation and mental health: Examining identity and development in lesbian, gay, and bisexual people.* Washington, DC: American Psychological Association.

Dixon, B. 2005, September 8. The low down on the down low: Looking for HIV/AIDS in all the wrong places. *The Black Commentator.* Retrieved from http:// www.blackcommentator.com/149/149_cover_lowdown _downlow.html.

Essig, L. 2008. Review of imagining transgender: An ethnography of a category. *American Journal of Sociology,* 114: 862. doi:10.1086/597449.

Ferguson, R. A. 2003. *Aberrations in black: Towards a queer of color critique.* St. Paul: University of Minnesota Press.

Goode, E., and Ben-Yehuda, N. 1994. Moral panics: Culture, politics, and social construction. *Annual*

Review of Sociology, 20: 149–71. doi:10.1146/annurev .so.20.080194.001053.

Han, C. 2007. They don't want to cruise your type: Gay men of color and the racial politics of exclusion. *Social Identities*, 13(1): 51–67. doi:10.1080/13504630601163379.

Han, C., Rutledge, S. E., Bond, L., Lauby, J., and LaPollo, A. B. 2014. You're better respected when you carry yourself as a man: Black men's personal account of the down low "lifestyle." *Sexuality & Culture*, 18(1): 89–102. doi:10.1007/s12119-013-9192-3.

Hawkeswood, W. G. 1996. *One of the children: Gay black men in Harlem*. Berkeley: University of California Press.

Helm, A. B. 2010. Injection drug use fuels black HIV rates: Why don't we talk about it? The Black AIDS Institute. Retrieved from https://www.blackaids.org/news-2010 /669-injection-drug-use-fuels-black-hiv-rates-why-dont -we-talk-about-it.

Henry J. Kaiser Foundation. 2003. *National survey of adolescents and young adults: Sexual health knowledge, attitudes and experiences*. Menlo Park, CA: The Kaiser Family Foundation.

Johnson, J. B. 2005, May 1. Secret gay encounters of black men could be raising women's infection rate. *The San Francisco Chronicle*. Retrieved from http://www .sfgate.com/health/article/Secret-gay-encounters-of -black-men-could-be-2637689.php.

Lichtenstein, B. 2000. Secret encounters: Black men, bisexuality, and AIDS in Alabama. *Medical Anthropology Quarterly*, 14: 374–93. doi:10.1525 /maq.2000.14.3.374.

Martinez, J., and Hosek, S. G. 2005. An exploration of the down-low identity: Nongay-identified young African-American men who have sex with men. *Journal of the National Medical Association*, 97: 1103–12.

Millett, G., Malebranch, D., Mason, B., and Spikes, P. 2005. Focusing "down low": Bisexual black men, HIV risk, and heterosexual transmission. *Journal of the National Medical Association*, 97: 52S–59S.

Morris, P. 2004, February 17. Irresponsible men on the down low put women at risk. *Cleveland Plain Dealer.*

Phillips, L. 2005. Deconstructing the "down low" discourse: The politics of sexuality, gender, race, AIDS, and anxiety. *Journal of African American Studies*, 9(2): 3–15. doi:10.1007/s12111-005-1018-4.

Pitt, R. N. 2006. Downlow mountain? De/stigmatizing bisexuality through pitying and pejorative discourse in media. *Journal of Men's Studies*, 14: 254–58.

Robinson, B. A., and Vidal-Ortiz, S. 2013. Displacing the dominant "down low" discourse: Deviance, same-sex desire, and craigslist.org. *Deviant Behavior*, 34: 224–41. doi:10.1080/01639625.2012.726174.

Scott, M. 2004, June 10. Invisible lives: The author of a best seller about black men who secretly sleep with other men says he's trying to protect women. Critics say he's trying to make a buck. *St. Petersburg Times.*

Segal, L. 1990. *Slow motion: Changing masculinities, changing men*. New Brunswick, NJ: Rutgers University Press.

Simmons, D. 2004a, April 23. Menace to society: The low down on the down low. *The Washington Post.*

Simmons, D. 2004b, April 30. Menace to society II: Not being up and up on the down low. *The Washington Post.*

Sternberg, S. 2001, March 15. The danger of living "down low": Black men who hide their bisexuality can put women at risk. *USA Today.*

Teunis, N. 2007. Sexual objectification and the construction of whiteness in the gay male community. *Culture, Health and Sexuality*, 9: 263–75. doi:10.1080/13691050601035597.

Valentine, D. 2007. *Imagining transgender: An ethnography of a category*. Durham, NC: Duke University Press. doi:10.1215/9780822390213.

Vargas, J. A. 2003. HIV-positive, without a clue: Black men's hidden sex lives imperiling female partners. *The Washington Post.*

[. . .]

Villarosa, L. 2004, April 5. AIDS fears grow for black women. *The New York Times.*

Washington, A. T. 2005, August 12. District's AIDS epidemic deserves public debate. *The Washington Times.*

Wolitski, R. J., Jones, K. T., Wasserman, J. L., & Smith, J. C. 2006. Self-identification as "down low" among men who have sex with men (MSM) from 12 US cities. *AIDS and Behavior*, 10: 519–29. doi:10.1007/s10461 -006-9095-5.

UNEQUAL PLEASURES

LISA WADE

Women in college, like American women more generally, have fewer orgasms than their male counterparts. The numbers vary but, in general, women have one or two orgasms for every three that men enjoy. The data on college students reflect this pattern. The Online College Social Life Survey results show that in hookups men are more than twice as likely as women to have an orgasm.

Myths about men's and women's bodies suggest that this gap is a biological inevitability. Men's orgasms are easy to elicit, we are told. If anything, they arrive too effortlessly. The female orgasm, in contrast, is portrayed as finicky. If women don't have orgasms, the narrative suggests, it's because the clitoris is hard to find and difficult to operate. Even when conditions are ideal, an orgasm often fails to show. It's a mystery, we shrug. We tell ourselves that women are physiologically different—not as sexual as men—and so we presume that release is less important to them anyway.

Today's college students generally buy into these ideas. When sociologists Jess Butler asked students at the University of Southern California what accounted for gender difference in rates of orgasm, "by far," she said, "the most common explanation . . . was 'it's biological.'" Her students believed that orgasm was "harder" for women and "takes longer," but "just happens" for men. Given this sense of the nature of things, she said, her students were "unfazed" by statistics demonstrating that men were getting off more often than women.

The idea that the orgasm gap is natural, though, is wrong. Some countries, such as the United States and Russia, have up to twice as large a gap as others, such as Brazil and Japan. Among Americans, lesbian women report two to three times as many orgasms as heterosexual ones—as many, in fact, as heterosexual men. In masturbation, orgasms come easily and quickly to both sexes; on average, each requires just four efficient minutes to reach climax. Even women who never have orgasms with male partners often do regularly when they're alone.

The orgasm gap is not a biological fact; it's a social one, which reflects on what people choose to do in bed together. Among college students for example, the likelihood of a woman having an orgasm in a hookup with a man varies from 15 to 63 percent, depending on whether he performs oral sex, they engage in intercourse, she self-stimulates, or they do some combination of those things. In relationships, if couples engage in all three activities, women's likelihood of having an orgasm is 92 percent. Not so finicky, it turns out.

If hookup culture has an orgasm gap—and it does—then the question isn't what might be wrong with women's bodies, but the extent to which the female orgasm is made a priority. What we should be asking is whether men and women care enough about female orgasm to give it the ol' college try. . . .

In fact, many of my female students, and especially the heterosexual ones, had internalized a "general disgust" toward their genitals. . . . Women overheard men saying that "vaginas were dirty" and that women who "squirt" are "disgusting." One woman's friend announced that he would never go down on a girl "unless she was completely shaven and I saw her clean her vagina out." Another girl sat at dinner with a guy who complained that their Vietnamese spring roll appetizer tasted like "cooter." All of this was pretty hard for women to disregard, even if most men didn't feel the same.

For some lucky women, fantastic experiences with men who enjoyed performing oral sex turned the tide—"it really impresses most girls," boasted one cunnilingus-loving guy—but most women remained ambivalent, at best, about whether it was a good idea to let a guy go down on them. Even women who believed that the negative characterization of female genitals was unfair had a hard time shaking off their worries. "I tend to be more self-conscious about the way I taste or smell," wrote one, "even though I know I'm very clean and it's really his problem if he doesn't like it."

Izzy felt the same: "I think the act that has been the most touchy for me is cunnilingus, because it's considered to be so intimate and possibly unpleasant for the person doing it." She discussed overhearing people saying, "Oh, it's smelly down there, it tastes bad, it takes forever.". . . Likewise, sexually audacious Celeste, despite being experienced and adventurous, wasn't immune to these comments. Only one of the twelve guys she had hooked up with had performed oral sex, and this was maddening—but it was a relief, too. Using the term most common among my students, she admitted that "many girls are a little uncomfortable and insecure about being eaten out, including myself. We women are afraid of being judged and talked about as being smelly or whatever."

Interested in women's discomfort with cunnilingus, sociologist Laura Backstrom and her colleagues interviewed women at Stanford and Indiana University about their thoughts on receiving oral sex. Just over a quarter of the women had strongly negative views of the practice, using words like "weird," "bizarre,"

"dirty," and "nasty" to describe it. The rest had positive feelings about cunnilingus, but only a few felt comfortable asking for it from men, especially in hookups. Some expressed the familiar idea that cunnilingus is somehow a "bigger deal" than fellatio. "It feels like a guy going down on you is a bigger step than you going down on a guy," said one, "which is probably unfair." "I think I felt kind of guilty almost," said another woman of the men she hooked up with, "like I felt like I was kind of subjecting people to something they didn't want to do and I felt bad about it."[1] Women seem convinced that men don't like it. . . .

Men—at least men who are attracted to women—put extraordinary amounts of effort into getting into the vagina. . . . And, in real life, there are lots of men who love cunnilingus. This is something that my female students, and the ones at Stanford and Indiana, are wrong about. In fact, according to the National Health and Social Life Survey, one of the largest, most comprehensive, and well-designed studies of American sexuality ever completed, men like performing cunnilingus even more than women like receiving it.

So, what is this cultural disgust at women's bodies really about? It's quite obviously not about whether cunnilingus is gross. It's certainly not any grosser than fellatio. I can still recall the moment that a male friend of mine first encountered the idea of receiving such a "genital kiss." We were first-year college students, he from a very conservative Mormon background, and his immediate reaction was disgust. "But you pee through that thing!" he said incredulously. It's true. Men pee through that thing. And there are other reasons why someone might find fellatio unappetizing: the smell of a man's genitals after being confined in a pair of pants all day, the difficulty of getting a penis in one's mouth, pubic hairs caught in teeth, the effort to create suction that strains the muscles underneath the jaw, difficulty catching one's breath, and the taste of precum and semen. In fact, when Jess Butler asked female students at the University of Southern California whether they liked fellatio, none of the more than two dozen she talked to claimed to enjoy it. As one said, "I'd rather not have to do it ever again in my life, but I feel like I have to." "It's gross," said another. "Nobody likes it," insisted a third in response.[2] A person can truly and emphatically enjoy giving a blow job, but one has to be in the right frame of mind. Ditto for cunnilingus.

Yet, while the potential downsides of cunnilingus are front and center in the minds of heterosexual students of both sexes, the similar downsides of fellatio are almost never discussed and are generally considered irrelevant. "No one," a student observed, "ever talks about what a penis is supposed to smell like or what 'cum' is supposed to taste like." Noting that "scented tampons and 'feminine sprays' line the aisles of drug stores," one pointed out, rightly, "Guys don't have to make sure their junk smells like jasmine." The potentially unpleasant things about fellatio are never used to suggest that women would be justified in refusing to do it. And men never seem to mention the possibility that fellatio might be "gross" as a reason to fear blow jobs.

If it was just about being gross, our attitudes toward cunnilingus and fellatio would still be symmetrical. They're not. So, the idea that vaginas are gross is not really about women's bodies at all. It's about what we do with their bodies. That is, do we use them for getting men off or getting women off? For his orgasm or for hers? Heterosexual students seem to take to the former just fine, but the latter—the privileging of female pleasure through cunnilingus—makes some uncomfortable. That's why they laugh. They're nervous.

Men have more orgasms than women in hookup culture, then, because the culture doesn't promote reciprocity. It's specifically designed for men's orgasm. Female orgasm is acceptable, even ideal, but it's not what it's about. A bisexual man I spoke to at a campus visit put this in stark perspective, observing sheepishly that he prioritized his partner's orgasm when he hooked up with men and his own when he hooked up with women. A guy at Stanford put it equally plainly: "I don't think hookup culture is based on mutual orgasm, it's really just based on an orgasm for me."[3]

This will not be a surprise to college women anywhere. "Hookup culture" really means "three years of bad sex," concluded a student at Duke who'd had just about enough.[4] He "didn't even care," said a woman at Brown about her most recent hookup. "I don't think he tried at all."[5] "I think very few guys really care," a student enrolled at the University of Southern California reported. Women are "literally just there to let the guy get off."[6]

My female students sang the same tune. They talked about desire, but it was rare for them to mention orgasm, or even physical pleasure more generally, as an outcome of hooking up. They often echoed Celeste when she complained about being a "masturbation toy." "I was just a warm body being used to give a guy an orgasm," wrote one. Men "treat me like two hands and three holes," grumbled another. "Ultimately," wrote a third, "it's about allowing the male to use your body." "The idea of being 'used' for sex like a masturbatory device," observed a guy about his female friends, "is a common complaint."

A complaint perhaps; but women, too, tend to prioritize male orgasm. "Most of the time we don't ask for anything in bed," Celeste admitted, "or at least I don't." Her priority was to impress her partners. "I want to kind of blow him out of the water," she explained. "If they attempt to do the same for me, that's great, though most of the time that does not happen." Other women agreed that they focused on giving orgasms instead of seeking them. "I don't feel like I've had a sexual experience if the guy doesn't come," wrote one. Male orgasm was paramount: "I will do everything in my power," insisted another, "to get [him] off." Another said that she would "focus completely" on her partner's orgasm. Their own pleasure was beside the point. "My sexuality was filled with anxiety and my need to please the guy instead of worrying about my own pleasure," wrote one student. "Even if I was in charge," another revealed, "I did not make sure I was being pleased."

Some women feel that expecting an orgasm from a male hookup partner is demanding or rude. The women at the University of Southern California did as well. They told Butler that women "cater to guys," "want men to be happy," and "wanna make the guy feel good about himself." Said one interviewee, "We want them to be happy with the hookup, with the orgasm or whatever, and with us. And our ability to create that for them."

If women deprioritize their own orgasm, it might be because they suspect that it's pointless to do otherwise. Some then, like the Stanford guy above, willingly admit that they're not interested in giving women pleasure. "I don't think [her orgasm] matters as much to the guy," said another. "Say they meet a girl at a party and it's a one-night thing," explained a third about guys in general, "I don't think it's gonna matter to them." When asked about the importance of female orgasm, another male student retorted, "I don't give a shit."

Importantly, men aren't uniformly uninterested in female orgasm; they are specifically disinterested in the orgasms of women they're hooking up with. The guy who didn't "give a shit" about women's orgasms, for instance, followed up to clarify that he was "all about" orgasm if the woman was his girlfriend. Differentiating between sex with girlfriends and hookups, it turns out, is common: "I think if you're in a long-term relationship," said another

guy, "it's essential that she has an orgasm during sexual activity." Short-term relationships, he specified, were entirely different.

Men generally agreed that a woman's orgasm is "more important if it's in a relationship than if it's a one-night stand" or if "it's somebody I care about." Another man explained the expectation that he gives his girlfriends orgasms like this:

Now that I'm in a relationship, I think [her orgasms are] actually pretty important. More important than I think the hookup because you have more invested in that person. . . . It's more a reciprocal thing.

Invoking the ideas of care and reciprocity to differentiate hookup sex from relationship sex is consistent with Mimi Schippers's idea that students think that relationships are a site for interpersonal kindness, but hookups are not. Many men think of relationships as a meeting of equals in which they're accountable for treating the other person with respect. Another guy made it explicit: "In a relationship," he said, "there's much more expected as far as like equality-wise, like give and take sexually."[7]

The data on orgasm reveals this dynamic clearly. Women in relationships are having almost seven times as many orgasms as women hooking up for the first time,[8] and the orgasm gap between men and women shrinks by half. Many men want to give orgasms to their girlfriends—whom they care about, want to please, and believe should be treated as equals—but feel little need to do their hookup partners the same courtesy.

Men, then, aren't uniformly dismissive of women's pleasure, just that of the women they're hooking up with. That's because men in committed relationships aren't playing by the rules of hookup culture. The guys who are hooking up, though, often are. And while the rules of heterosexual relationships are at least a little influenced by what women want, the rules that men play by when you're just looking to hook up are made and enforced, first and foremost, by other men. In this game, women's pleasure isn't a bonus at all; it's a bargaining chip. . . .

So yeah, there's an orgasm gap on college campuses. It favors heterosexual men, and there's nothing natural about it. It reflects a privileging of male sexual pleasure, a focus on his orgasm on the part of men and women alike, and a narrative that justifies an aversion to giving women pleasure, one that many women internalize. . . .

. . . [M]ore than half of the women who completed the Online College Social Life Survey felt disrespected by at least one guy they'd hooked up with. Some of this may just be anxiety about what men think of women who have casual sexual encounters—because they know that some men call women "nasty"—but much of it is also likely attributable to how they were treated. They notice when men are brusque or bullying. They notice when they are selfish, when they pay no attention, when they don't ask. They notice when they get treated like shit. And they notice when they don't have orgasms. We know that because, when they do have an orgasm, they're six times as likely as women who didn't to say that they enjoyed their last hookup "very much."[9]

"Good sex is so hard to come by," complained a student named Veronica about women's experience in hookup culture, "that we can be sure sexual satisfaction is not the primary motivation for girls engaged in hooking up." She didn't understand why so many women, herself included, continued to actively seek out men to hook up with, writing:

I can think of several examples of my friends repeatedly hooking up with the same guys, unable to provide an explanation for why. Beautiful, interesting, seemingly self-respecting girls, . . . It's not the sex and it's certainly not the emotional connection they're pursuing.

Veronica is right to notice that women actively pursue opportunities to hook up with men, and probably not primarily for pleasure or emotional satisfaction, but she'd likely be surprised to discover that the majority say they enjoy their experiences. Of the women who filled out the Online College Social Life Survey, for example, 84 percent reported that they enjoyed their last hookup at least "somewhat."[10]

In fact, when I've asked women around the country what they are getting out of hookups, they string together a long list of pleasures. Alongside the occasional orgasm, women enjoy the simple pleasure of being turned on, the exhilaration of firsts, and the satisfaction that comes with honing sexual skills. They describe the uneasy thrill of exploring a sexual identity tentatively and the joy of embracing it wholeheartedly. And, since they never know if a hookup will turn into romance, some experienced the pleasure of hope and anticipation, too.

Veronica herself would recognize some of these. Elsewhere she described hooking up as an "adrenaline rush." "Being young and having this sexual appetite and being horny and knowing that you're getting closer to scratching that itch by being physical with boys," she wrote, was intoxicating. It was, she said, "a desperately sexually frustrating time," but it felt good, too. There is pleasure to be had for women even in the face of hookup culture's deficiencies, to be sure.

Yet, in my discussions with students and in the pages of their journals, one type of pleasure stood out as especially common and strongly motivating for women. It was a real pleasure—but a troubled one—maybe, even, a dangerous one. . . . It was the pleasure of being chosen.

NOTES

1. Backstrom, Laura, Elizabeth Armstrong, and Jennifer Puentes. 2012. "Women's Negotiation of Cunnilingus in College Hookups and Relationships." *Journal of Sex Research*, 41, 1: 1–12.

2. Butler, Jess. 2013. "Sexual Subjects: Hooking Up in the Age of Postfeminism." Ph.D. dissertation, University of Southern California.

3. Media Education Foundation. 2011. *Understanding Hookup Culture: What's Really Happening on College Campuses.* Northampton, MA: Media Education Foundation.

4. Reed, Lillie. 2013. "The Best Four Years, Study Shows." *Chronicle* (August 28).

5. Kitroeff, Natalie. 2013. "In Hookups, Inequality Still Reigns." *New York Times* (November 11).

6. Butler, 2013.

7. Armstrong, Elizabeth A., Paula England, and Alison C. K. Fogerty. 2012. "Accounting for Women's Orgasm and Sexual Enjoyment in College Hookups and Relationships." In Barbara Risman and Virginia Rutter (eds.) *Families as They Really Are*, 2nd ed. New York: W. W. Norton.

8. Ford, Jessie, and Paula England. 2015. "What Percent of College Women Are Sexually Assaulted in College?" *Contexts* (January 12).

9. Ibid.

10. Ibid.

"HOW YOU BULLY A GIRL": SEXUAL DRAMA AND THE NEGOTIATION OF GENDERED SEXUALITY IN HIGH SCHOOL

SARAH A. MILLER

Over the past decade, sexual rumor-spreading, slut-shaming, and homophobic labeling have become central examples of bullying among young women. Between 2006 and 2016, the U.S. media covered the suicides of 24 adolescent girls[1] who were the subjects of sexual rumors or labeled "sluts," "whores," or "lesbians" in the months prior to their deaths. While these tragedies had many contributing factors, they were often reported as examples of "bullycide" (Bazelon 2013), a contemporary "youth crisis" garnering widespread media attention. These cases have placed the intersecting gendered and sexualized dimensions of girls' conflicts at the forefront of national campaigns against bullying (The Unslut Project 2013), as well as at the center of debates about its criminalization (Marcus 2010). However, while these tragedies made their mark in U.S. consciousness, we empirically know little about the role sexual bullying practices play in girls' relational lives.

While adults increasingly classify this form of youth conflict as "bullying," girls are more likely to identify it as "drama": conflict involving a variety of relationally aggressive practices that vary in severity, often with an audience both live and online (boyd 2014; Marwick and boyd 2014). This [reading] explores girls' experiences with sexual forms of drama, which involves a constellation of behaviors, including sexualized rumor-spreading and gossip, slut-shaming, homophobic labeling, and targeted avoidance tactics. Through interviews with 54 class and racially diverse late adolescent girls, I ask what this conflict does: what meanings does it make,

what functions does it serve, and why is it useful to young women? I find that while they reproduce inequality through these practices, sexual drama is a resource for girls: one that is valuable for making claims to, and sense of, gendered sexuality within the constraints of high school—an institutional setting that often reinforces traditional gender norms and limits sexuality information.

BULLYING AND GENDERED/SEXUAL HIERARCHIES

Bullying[2] is both a gendered practice and a gendering process. Contrary to dominant binary ideologies, boys and girls often resort to similar bullying strategies, including insults and rumors (Orpinas, McNicholas, and Nahapetyan 2015; Underwood 2003). However, their practices are routinely characterized as distinct. Boys' bullying is often described as physical and direct (Wang, Iannotti, and Nansel 2009), while girls' is often labeled "relational aggression"—an indirect form of conflict, including rumor-spreading, gossip, name-calling, and social exclusion (Brown 2005; Grotpeter and Crick 1996). These practices help youth negotiate status within their social spheres (Faris and Felmlee 2011, 2014). They also police and produce meanings about gender norms and expectations (Pascoe 2013), informing teens how gender should—and should not—be "done" (West and Zimmerman 1987). Sexuality plays a significant role in many teens' experiences with bullying (Duncan 1999; Rivers and Duncan 2013). Among boys, the intersection of bullying, sexuality, and gender regulation has been widely documented (Klein 2012; Messerschmidt 2012; Pascoe 2007, 2013). For instance, both Pascoe (2007) and Chambers, Tincknell, and Van Loon (2004) find that homophobic and misogynistic verbal abuse function as mechanisms for boys' collective construction and regulation of masculine gender identities. Girls' bullying practices are also often mediated through discourses about gendered sexuality, including slut slander (Payne 2012) and homophobic slurs (Poteat and Rivers 2010). Girls are also more likely to be targets of bullying when they fail to conform to normative sexual behaviors and feminine gender presentations (Messerschmidt 2012). However, while much has been published recently in the popular press about the intersections of gender and sexuality in girls' experiences with bullying (Cappiello et al. 2015; Lindin 2015; Sales 2016; Tanenbaum 2015), academic studies have largely left unexplored how this conflict contributes to girls' gendering processes.

While bullying is often conceptualized as a "youth problem," its content often reflects attitudes and ideologies pervasive among adults (Bazelon 2013; Klein 2012). Teens' engagement with this content reflects what Corsaro (1992) calls "interpretive reproduction," a means through which children become part of adult culture by creatively appropriating information from the adult world within their peer groups. Thus, rather than blaming them for their participation, it is essential to contextualize teens' bullying practices within broader adult culture and examine closely the institutionally situated meanings they produce and reinforce (Pascoe 2013; Payne and Smith 2013). As Pascoe argues, researchers should be attending "to the way

bullying often reflects, reproduces, and prepares young people to accept inequalities embedded in larger social structures" (2013, 9). To do so, we need to pay closer attention to the *content* youth share through these practices. This content illustrates how teens collectively make meaning through conflict—meanings that both reflect and reproduce structural inequalities.

RUMORS, AGENCY, AND GENDER CONSTRAINT

Rumor-spreading is the most common form of bullying between girls (Lessne and Cidade 2015). However, we currently know little about the content of girls' rumors and the gossip that surrounds them, and even less about how this content contributes to their constructions of femininity and sexuality. Scholars have long documented the many social functions of rumor and gossip in everyday life. People's use of rumor and gossip often have agentic, though constraining, qualities: both provide a source for connection and the strengthening of group bonds (Fine 1985; Gluckman 1963), and a means of projecting a positive self-image by discrediting others (Paine 1967). Both are also mechanisms through which moral standards are established (Fine 1985) and function as a form of social control by establishing and reinforcing group norms (Eder and Enke 1991).

Rumors and gossip are particularly useful among youth, for whom other resources for attaining social power are limited. As children do not have access to objects or autonomy the way adults do, they develop their own economies within their peer groups (Thorne 1993). These rhetorical strategies have transactional value (Rosnow and Fine 1976) that young people use to develop and reinforce gender ideologies (Chambers, Tincknell, and Van Loon 2004; Eder, Evans, and Parker 1997). Among teens, sharing rumors is a form of currency, a means of exchanging stories for acceptance, connection, and recognition (Marwick and boyd 2014). Yet increasingly, this form of adolescent tender is traded in virtual spaces, as rumors are now spread via text messages and social media. These "networked publics" make rumors more virulent, given their potential to be searchable, replicable, and visible to invisible audiences (boyd 2014). Because of these properties, rumors have the potential to spread further for today's youth than those of earlier eras.

Sexual rumors are nothing if not delicious stories—stories that reflect the institutional contexts of their telling (Plummer 1995). In the accounts that follow, girls' rumors often reflect dominant and negative cultural narratives about women's sexuality that circulate in the media, their schools, and communities. Many studies have captured these narratives and have shown how sexual double standards (Crawford and Popp 2003; Kreager and Staff 2009), along with slut-shaming, homophobic labeling, and other gendered discourses on sexual morality, impact girls' relational lives. These narratives also profoundly shape and constrain girls' sexual subjectivities: their experiences of themselves as sexual beings and their abilities to make sexual choices founded on their entitlement to sexual safety, pleasure, and agency (Martin 1996; Schalet 2009; Tolman 2002).

SLUTS, LESBIANS, AND PEER REGULATION

Rated the worst possible pejorative among girls, and one of the most common among teens (Tanenbaum 2015; Thurlow 2001), the specter of the "slut" has been widely recognized as an organizing principle (Attwood 2007) and a key site where girls engage in boundary-work (Fjaer, Pedersen, and Sandberg 2015; Wilkins 2008). Much like the figure of the "fag" among boys (Pascoe 2007), the "slut" achieves its rhetorical power through abjection (Butler 1990), allowing girls to claim

their own normative femininities by repudiating others for their sexual deviance. While boys and men have long used slut talk to discipline girls and women (Cappiello et al. 2015), it is also a discourse used between girls as they negotiate gendered status hierarchies (Armstrong et al. 2014).

Slut-shaming is not only a gendered and sexualized discourse, but one that also reflects existing racialized and classed hierarchies (Bettie 2003; Wilkins 2008; Wilkins and Miller, forthcoming). These hierarchies are reinforced through a history of "controlling images" that position white, middle-class women as sexually "pure" in comparison to low-income whites and women of color (Collins 1990). However, slut-shaming is not solely useful to those most advantaged. Low-income girls and young women of color also employ talk about other women's sexual morality to reject racist and classist sexual stereotypes about their "inherent promiscuity" (Froyum 2010; Garcia 2012), claiming a superior morality to that of "loose" white girls (Das Gupta 1997; Espiritu 2001), or "rich, bitchy sluts" (Armstrong et al. 2014). Importantly, this body of literature shows how judgmental talk about other girls' sexual behavior is *useful* within the context of girls' particular social location.

The "slut" is not the only sexual specter that threatens young women. They are also regulated by, and reinforce social hierarchies through, homophobic talk, judgment, and avoidance tactics (Poteat and Rivers 2010; Renold 2002). For example, Chambers, Tincknell, and Van Loon (2004) find that adolescent girls collectively define femininity by labeling deviant girls as both "sluts" and "lesbians" through gossip rituals, while Hamilton (2007) and Stone and Gorga (2014) find that heterosexual college women distance themselves from lesbian peers. Like slut-shaming, homophobic labeling also functions to shore up race and class boundaries. Froyum (2007) finds that low-income Black girls (and boys) use homophobic strategies to assert their heterosexual superiority to access privilege in ways they otherwise lack. Further, the specters of sluts and lesbians, or what Schippers (2007) calls "pariah femininities," often overlap for young women. In Lees's (1993) study, girls who contest the slut label are often labeled lesbians, while Payne (2010) finds that lesbian adolescents are subjected to *both* homophobic slander and slut-shaming.

Though they often have different outcomes, sexual criteria determining women's morality and worth are persistent in young women's lives, across social location. These criteria often give the sexual elements of girls' conflict substantial power, practices where stories about "sluts" and "lesbians" function to keep girls from deviating from race, class, gender, and sexual norms. This [reading] explores the social and institutional mechanisms that make sexual drama *useful* to young women. While some of their experiences clearly constitute bullying, and some do not, their accounts indicate that sexual drama functions along a continuum that girls regularly have to negotiate within their peer groups. Ultimately, this conflict constrains girls' sexual subjectivities while informing their gendering processes as they collectively negotiate gender and sexual norms.

METHODS AND DATA

This analysis draws on 54 semistructured in-depth interviews with cisgender women, aged 18 to 20, conducted between 2011 and 2014. Participants were recruited from five geographically proximate schools in the Northeast: an elite women's college, an urban and a rural community college, a private urban liberal arts college, and a large public university. Initial participants were sampled through a pilot study at the women's college, while the majority were sampled through introductory courses that fulfilled general education requirements across disciplines. I did not sample for individuals who had been "bullied," but rather I recruited by asking for young women willing to talk about their friendships.

This sampling strategy yielded a diverse pool of participants who had recently attended high school in 13 states across five regions of the United States. Nearly half were working class or poor and nearly half identified as women of color. As participants were late adolescents, class was assessed based on family of origin, including parents' occupations and highest levels of education (if known). However, as all of these young women were college students at the time of interview, they also were upwardly mobile. Forty-four participants identified as heterosexual, one as queer, two as lesbian, two as asexual, and five as bisexual.

All interviews were conducted on campus and ranged from 45 minutes to three hours. Interviews contained questions about friendships, status, sexuality education, conflict, and schooling. After conducting and transcribing the interviews, I used an inductive process to analyze the data (Wolcott 1994). Upon review, I generated initial themes and identified common patterns that were refined in the analysis and writing process.

This paper focuses on young women's retrospective accounts of high school, as sexual drama was most prevalent during that period of their lives. The most common form was sexual rumor-spreading. In some cases, girls describe drama that circulated less than four months prior to their interview, in others, a few years. While the retrospective nature of the data limits my ability to analyze interactions, their accounts offer insights on the meanings girls made through these experiences. These young women's stories indicate that sexual drama was an instructive element of their adolescence, as they developed attitudes and understandings about gendered sexuality.

"LIKE TRYING TO CATCH SMOKE": THE PERVASIVENESS OF SEXUAL DRAMA

Early in our interview, Gaby,[3] a working-class, heterosexual Latina, told me: "That's how you bully a girl, that's how you just get her. You get her by spreading a rumor about her. . . . Trying to stop bullying is like trying to catch smoke with your bare hands." Gaby's adamancy on this point is connected to her personal experience. During the beginning of her junior year of high school, a rumor was spread by a girlfriend that Gaby had given a blow job to a boy in the theater prop room. She recalled, "It was just horrible, like *horrible* . . . to have orally done something in the basement of our school?! Like—I'm a good girl!" Gaby's emphasis on being a "good" girl is indicative of why sexual drama matters to young women. As their narratives will show, these practices are both threatening and useful to girls because they often contain information about the intertwined boundaries of femininity, sexuality, and identity.

Gaby's experience is unfortunately not unique. The young women in this study attended 52 different high schools in five regions of the country, ranging from Catholic, single-sex, Waldorf, charter and tech schools, to magnet math and science academies, elite boarding schools, and urban, suburban, and rural public schools. Some graduating classes were as small as 35, while others came close to a thousand. Across contexts, all women had stories to share about their experiences with sexual drama in their high schools, and nearly a third (n = 16) had been the subject of a rumor about their own sexual actions and/or orientations. All but one of the girls targeted described significant disruption in their social lives and academic trajectories as a result of the rumors, including depression, changing courses, losing friendships, quitting extracurricular activities, or leaving school altogether. In all, participants recalled a total of 213 rumors, 201 of which were both sexual and about a girl.[4] Though not all girls interviewed ended up subjects of a rumor, and many were simply bystanders, their direct and indirect experiences with sexual drama were common, and nearly always perpetrated by girls.

Unlike Gaby, many rejected the notion that they had experienced or participated in "bullying." Instead, more than half (n = 35) called these experiences "drama." For example, Helen, a white, upper-middle-class, heterosexual young woman, was often the target of girls' slut rumors both online and live, resulting in isolation and unwanted sexual advances from boys. Yet she did not think she experienced bullying: "I know that it fits [the definition] but like what I see, girls like being mean and talking about other girls, it's girls being girls. I don't see it as bullying, I just see it as drama." This discursive move from "bullying" to "drama" both normalizes girls' behaviors while making them seem inconsequential and unreflective of inequality. Note this rhetorical strategy is also gendered: in their accounts, drama was uniformly described as "a girl thing" or "girls being girls." Yet, while young women's use of this rhetoric reinforces gender norms that undervalue girls (Chesney-Lind and Irwin 2008; Ringrose 2006), its use can also be read agentically. If what they are experiencing is just "drama," then girls are better capable of distancing themselves from being labeled both "bullies" and "victims": adult-defined positionalities (Marwick and boyd 2014) signaling victimization, and increasingly criminality, that youth are understandably invested in avoiding. Further, young women's insistence that these practices are "girl" behaviors is instructive. If sexual drama is a "girl thing," what is it telling girls about girlhood?

NEGOTIATING WHAT'S "NORMAL"

The content of sexual drama is most visible in young women's accounts of rumors and the gossip that surrounded them. Examined closely, sexual rumors are case studies girls use to negotiate both sexuality and gender norms. As Zoey, a white, upper-middle-class, queer young woman observed, the subjects of rumors "were girls who people knew . . . had done things that weren't considered normal." In these stories, both girls' heterosexual and homosexual activities warranted other girls' gossip and judgment. The 201 sexual rumors participants recalled delineated gendered sexual norms through stories about a girl's sexual orientation, the sex acts she participates in (e.g., masturbation, oral or anal sex), the context in which she has sex (e.g., while drunk, in public), the sexual partners she has (e.g., their or someone else's partner, authority figures), the quantity of sexual partners she has (e.g., multiple boys, an entire team), or sexual consequences (e.g., abortion, STIs). Notably, these rumors were often unrelated to knowledge of a peer's actual identity or behaviors. In what follows, I offer an analysis of the two central typologies of sexual rumors: lesbian/bisexual (n = 34) and slut (n = 167) rumors. Throughout, I argue that both types of rumors help young women collectively make meaning about normative sexuality *and* normative femininity.

LESBIAN/BISEXUAL RUMORS

Half of the young women described rumors about girls' nonheterosexual actions or orientations (n = 34). These rumors often focused on a girl either having too much and/or the wrong kind of desire. For instance, Torielle, a Black, poor, heterosexual young woman, told me: "If we heard a rumor that a girl was bisexual in my high school, we considered them a whore. Because we felt like they just . . . wanted both

worlds, they were a whore." For Torielle and her friends, bisexual rumors offered sites to make claims about the kind and quantity of desire that is, and is not, normative for girls. Likewise, Lisa, who is white, middle class, and heterosexual, described her friends spreading a rumor about a peer they called "troll girl":

We wouldn't say anything to her but we all talked about it behind her back. . . . We were just saying how gross it was that she was a lesbian . . . about how oh, it's nasty, carpet— whatever that word is? Carpetmuncher? Yeah, you know, like how gross she is.

Lisa recalled how "fun" this gossip was for her friend group at the time. By collectively marking certain sexualities "gross," they implicitly made claims about their own "normative" identities and desires.

Lesbian rumors also were often about the violation of gender presentation norms. As Charlotte, an upper-middle-class, heterosexual young woman, explained: "in my town, if you weren't a girlie girl, you were called a lesbian." Girls focused on targeted girls' outward appearance and mannerisms, which were understood to be implicit of their homosexuality. For instance, Mary, a working-class, heterosexual Latina, told me about Jacinda, an openly lesbian peer who was the target of homophobic rumors spread by girls in their high school:

[They] would never have the guts to say anything to her face but I know they would just be like grossed out by it. She didn't look like a girl, she didn't have the feminine ideal, so it wasn't okay. . . . I mean I don't think anyone really like *enjoyed* Jacinda and her outness. . . . People didn't even like give [her] the time of day.

According to Mary, the focus on Jacinda was as much about her appearance as it was about her attraction to women. Girls' response was to gossip about and avoid her. Likewise, Toni, a white, poor lesbian, who was frequently the subject of girls' rumors, told me girls talked about her because "I was an outlier in the ways that they felt were most important at the time. . . . I didn't look like them, I didn't dress like them, I didn't have any interests that they did." Toni emphasizes how much her experience of girls' homophobia was about being an "outlier" in both her gender presentation and sexual orientation (see also Horn 2007). In both Toni's and Jacinda's cases, girls' homophobic rumors reinforced to those sharing them the importance of conforming to normative feminine ways of dressing and acting.

These young women's accounts also indicate that girls' negotiation and regulation of gendered sexual norms was consequential to their friendships. Through lesbian/bisexual rumors, girls bonded over their (presumed) heterosexualities while distancing themselves from their peer and from homosexuality in general. For example, Kaya, a mixed-race, upper-middle-class, heterosexual young woman, recalled spreading a rumor with her girlfriends about Jackie, a peer they claimed was having sex with a lesbian teacher. "It was definitely a source of humor for us. . . . Sometimes it was easy to get caught up with it and make fun of her. It was ridicule definitely. . . . It was made to humiliate her, and to make her the butt of jokes." Kaya described this talk as compelling for her friend group, a means of fitting in. She told me, "I guess I really wanted to fit in too. . . . It was definitely easier to pick on her and talk about her." While talk about other girls' purported homosexual exploits was described as "fun" for Lisa's friends and a "source of humor" for Kaya's, these narratives served to bond girls while repelling others through the collective marking of gendered sexual boundaries.

Girls at the center of these rumors were well aware of this function. Toni told me girls targeted her "to feel like they were all on the same side about something. That they have something to connect about. To feel a part of

something." To make sense of what happened to her, Toni suggested that her peers bonded through the process of drawing boundaries against her. However, this bonding process also isolated targeted girls, with lasting effects. Toni eventually left her high school to pursue a GED, in large part due to girls' homophobic ridicule. While Toni was the only participant to leave school, many targeted girls, regardless of their sexual orientation, described isolation after rumors spread about their sexuality.

This was the case for Charlotte, who is heterosexual but was the subject of a lesbian rumor: "It bothered me. . . . I didn't put myself out there to try and be friends with people. I just kind of like internalized everything people said and just like blocked everyone out." Charlotte intentionally isolated herself after the rumor spread, "blocking everyone out" by smoking pot every day before school. She also described this isolation and fear of girls' judgment lasting into college:

It makes me really uncomfortable like even now . . . like, if you're watching a movie, you're laying on someone . . . I always feel like I can't do that because they would be like, "Charlotte was like cuddling me, she must be a lesbian."

Like Toni, Charlotte also described the lasting impact of homophobic rumors, which not only shaped her relationships with other girls but also her ability to succeed in school. Yet Charlotte's case also captures the regulatory work homophobia performs on heterosexual girls. She concludes, "You'd much rather be a slut than a lesbian in my town."

Ultimately, "lesbian" and "bisexual" rumors function similarly to "slut" rumors. They often operate like magnets: invigorating connections between some girls, while repelling others through their negotiations of "normative" feminine sexuality. Their content centers not just on *what* a girl does, but *who* she is, and *what it means* to occupy an abject position. It also emphasizes, through repudiation, what it means to be a "normal" girl. However, while girls use lesbian and bisexual rumors to mark and make sense of gendered sexual norms in many of the same ways they do heterosexual rumors, the outcomes are different. Being labeled a slut still offers a girl heterosexual privilege, just not the attendant acceptance or invisibility. Further, lesbian and bisexual rumors were key sites where girls talked about other girls' *desires*. Ironically, this was largely *not* the case in their stories about sluts.

SLUT RUMORS

All 54 participants recalled some version of a slut rumor—rumors that illustrate the boundaries of both femininity and heterosexuality. The young women shared 167 accounts of this form of drama. Slut-shaming and slut rumors were, as Miranda recalled, "the most powerful thing you could say about a girl at the time" because they threatened a girl's desirability and her femininity. Lisa told me that spreading rumors about girls' "slutty behavior" is "definitely degrading a woman's femininity, them being feminine, because if you're nasty, who wants you?" Here, Lisa alludes to the notion that being feminine is about being wanted (by men), not *wanting*. According to her logic, for girls to effectively perform (hetero)normative femininity and not be seen as sluts, they should be desired by boys but not openly desire sex themselves.

However, the subjects of slut rumors were rarely described as agents of their own desires, but rather as passive recipients of boys'. Many girls who ended up in the limelight were those who other girls believed "let boys use" them (see also Wilkins and Miller, forthcoming). Cailyn, who is Black, upper middle class, and lesbian, told me that rumors in her high school were "often about girls being complacent to guys." Likewise, Emma, a white, upper-middle-class,

heterosexual young woman, recalled gossiping with friends about Allison, who was often the target of girls' slut rumors in high school because "she would like be *used* by a lot of guys [pause] for sex. . . . I would have to go pick her up from like guys' houses because they refused to drive her home once they were like [pause] *done* with her." Emma's narrative speaks to the complexities of being a teenage girl navigating unequal power dynamics in sexual encounters with boys, and yet she and her friends did not empathize with Allison. Instead they judged her "willingness" to "let herself be used." Sharing stories about Allison offered Emma's friend group the ability to collectively claim their own sexual choices as normal, while asserting that they would never be the kind of girls who would "let" themselves be treated badly by boys.

Slut rumors thus emphasize the notion that "normal" heterosexual girls are simultaneously not supposed to show or act on their own desires, nor submit to the desires of boys. Social media provided a broad audience to reinforce this expectation. Davina, a Black, middle-class, heterosexual young woman, told me about multiple "exposure" cases on Twitter, when a girl sends a nude picture to a boy who requests it, who subsequently posts the picture publicly. According to Davina, girls often used boys' exposure practices to slut-shame other girls on the social media site, which led to rumors spreading in her high school:

I remember this one girl, she was arguing [online] with another girl who got exposed and she was like "You're such a whore. Don't forget where you came from." And then she like put the picture in the tweet. Girls, I think, are meaner than guys are.

Here, a boy's offense offers an opportunity for girls to shame other girls, both for being sexual and for trusting boys.

In all, 13 young women offered stories of girls using boys' exposure practices to spread sexual rumors and slut-shame their peers, and most were not critical of this practice. For example, Lee, an upper-middle-class, heterosexual, Asian young woman, described feeling justified for participating in a rumor about an exposed girl:

You put yourself into the situation . . . you're just asking for it. Like rumors were spread around because . . . you put yourself up there. If you don't want rumors spread around [pause], I mean like that's your own fault.

Like many young women who recalled these cases, Lee is clear that when a girl gets exposed, it is both her fault, and other girls' right, to publicly shame her for her sexual actions and poor judgment.

Slut rumors routinely reinforced gender inequality by positioning girls as culpable yet passive actors while rendering boys' choices and actions invisible. As Janelle, a mixed-race, middle-class, heterosexual young woman, explained: "Most rumors had to do with sex. I mean obviously a guy would be involved, but it was like the big thing was that it was the girl." In their accounts, the young women always remembered the girl in question, but often couldn't remember anything about the boy(s) involved in the story. For example, Carmen and Noelia, both heterosexual, poor Latinas, told me nearly identical stories from their different high schools about "slutty" girls who were caught "giving someone a blow job" on school property. The girls' identities were clear—both remembered their names and what happened to them after the rumor spread. But when asked who was receiving oral sex, Noelia was unsure, while Carmen replied with a shrug, "I don't know, just some dude." These responses are indicative of how girls and boys encounter different standards in their experiences of adolescent sexuality (Crawford and Popp 2003). However, they also demonstrate that because of their awareness of these standards, girls are paying attention to the girls—not the boys—in these stories to help make sense of what is and is not permissible sexual behavior for *themselves*.

This was the case for Heather, a white, upper-middle-class, heterosexual young woman, who described a rumor about a girl at a high school scavenger hunt:

On that list it would be things like "have sex with a freshman or get head from a freshman" or like all this nasty stuff, like "have a threesome," like disgusting, disgusting, terrible, horrible, evil things. . . . I was just like, "eeew." . . . But this girl, like, was one of the girl freshmen in the pictures of things that seniors needed [pause] *to do.* . . . Like we did not hesitate to make fun of [her], because I was just like "you literally don't care about yourself, you're so pathetic and it's hilarious."

Heather is making meaning here about *girls'* sexuality. The "we" in the narrative refers to her girlfriends, who she recalls collectively making fun of the girl, but notably *not* the boys in the story. The sexual activities are described as "nasty," outside the boundaries of what Heather felt was normative, while the blame rests on the girl, because she "doesn't care" about herself. Meanwhile, Heather ignores the power differentials embedded in the position of being the 14-year-old girl that a group of 17- and 18-year-old boys "needed to do." She then uses gossip to position herself and her friends as the kind of girls who would never put themselves in such a position. Here, the rumor makes visible the many inequities young women encounter navigating adolescent heterosexuality, while simultaneously reinforcing them.

Unfortunately, in some cases, boys' "use" of girls in these stories blended into unacknowledged *abuse*. Nine young women recounted "train rumors," where an intoxicated girl allegedly has sex with many boys sequentially in one setting. For example, Miranda, a white, middle-class, heterosexual young woman, recalled hearing a rumor about two tenth-grade girls who were "wicked drunk" at a party and "had a train run on them" by a group of boys: "I was like, 'Oh boy! Ok. Well, these girls are way into some crazy stuff.' . . . I can't deal with this. Like these girls are sluts." At no point in the interview does Miranda acknowledge that the girls likely could not have given consent that night, let alone to a group of boys. Rather than expressing concern for their well-being, she focuses on what she believes to be their "choices," reinforcing that those are not the kind of choices *she* makes. Miranda was not the only participant to recall a story like this. Mel, who is white, upper middle class, and bisexual, recalled a rumor about a girl nicknamed "poopy pants" who got intoxicated at a party and ended up "peeing and pooing and vomiting all over herself" as a boy was having sex with her. Mel told me, in retrospect, "You know in some levels I feel really bad for her. . . . I don't know. It sucks to be called 'poopy pants' in high school. But at the same time, on some level, I want to believe that she deserved it."

In addition to marking the boundaries of what is "normal" feminine sexual behavior, the kind of slut rumors Mel and Miranda tell offer girls an opportunity to distance themselves from the sexual violence that may be taking place in their communities, as well as their own vulnerability. These stories reinforce the normalization of sexual violence among young women (Hlavka 2014) by making these experiences seem commonplace, nonviolent, and commonsensically the girls' fault. If it's a girl's "choice" to "let herself be used," then, the logic goes, she should obviously not be the sort of girl who makes those kinds of choices. If you are the sort of girl who does, you "deserve" the consequences. Because slut rumors always focus on girls' choices, they render *boys'* choices invisible. The normalizing quality of these stories, as well as the naturalized judgments embedded within them, help make existing with the threat of (hetero) sexual violence *within their peer groups* feel less dangerous for young women (see also Armstrong, Hamilton, and Sweeney 2006).

While only some slut rumors alluded to sexual violence, most reinforced the gender inequities that often exist for girls engaged in heterosexual encounters. Notably, these inequities are embedded in the gendered sexual norms girls enforce among themselves. Though some of the inherent cruelness in these stories may be hard to digest, it is important to not blame young women for their engagement with this kind of drama. Girls talk about other girls' sexual "choices" because these conversations offer a crude road map for navigating gendered (hetero)sexuality while avoiding emotional, social, or physical harm. Ironically, girls were far more likely to receive this kind of information in high school through the rumor mill than through a lesson plan.

FILLING A VOID

As we have seen, talk about *other* girls' sexualities was common in girls' accounts of adolescence. Notably, talk about *their own* was not. For example, Ebony, a Black, middle-class young woman, told me that talk about her and her friends' heterosexual experiences "was sort of like forbidden territory almost in high school." Mel recalled not talking about her bisexual curiosities with her friends because "I felt like it's a really . . . taboo thing." Mariame, a Black, working-class, young woman who identifies as bisexual, remembered about her friends, "We talked about guys a lot. . . . Sex? Not so much. I think that was a little bit uncomfortable, but you did know the girls who were having sex. Like you'll hear rumors." And Kaya told me: "I didn't talk about sex with my friends at all. I remember talking about other girls' sex lives, though. Just about different sluts in school." These kinds of responses were surprisingly common among women across race, class, and sexual orientations. While many felt like they couldn't share their personal sexual experiences and curiosities with their peers, sexual drama offered girls a site to *acceptably* talk about sex and sexuality during high school.

In many young women's narratives, talk about personal experiences with sexuality was described as a liability, even among friends. This was true for talk about sexual encounters *and* orientations. For example, Lindsay, who is upper middle class and white, refused to tell her high school friends that she is bisexual: "It would have definitely gotten around. . . . It just was never okay to really even question it or to think about it, and certainly not to talk about it . . . 'cause of like, the whole atmosphere." Likewise, Casey, who is white and poor, told me that she would never share information about her own heterosexual encounters because it was powerful information:

I'm not telling. . . . I don't need the whole school knowing my business. I'm sorry. And you knew that. You tell somebody something, it doesn't matter who that person is, and how best of a friend that person says they are, it's gonna go around. . . . *It's money! It's like money!* [emphasis mine]

It's noteworthy that Casey likens this information to currency (Rosnow and Fine 1976), a commodity to be exchanged for inclusion, attention, or status. However, this form of "currency" is valuable to young women because of the constraints of the "atmosphere" in which it is exchanged. This phenomenon has to do with what girls officially learn about gendered sexuality. Priya, an Asian, working-class, heterosexual young woman, told me, "Girls aren't supposed to talk about their sexual conquests. They're supposed to be, I don't know, contained. . . . This is just what I've learned." Likewise, Lindsay posited: "There's . . . a taboo about exploring your body and your sexual needs. . . . It's all about the men's sexual desire, not about the women's. Especially in high school." Both Lindsay and Priya describe common perceptions about gendered sexuality that circulate

among teens and are reinforced in schools. In both comprehensive and abstinence-based sex education classes, sex often *is* all about men's desire and not women's, and also is frequently discussed solely in heterosexual terms (Bay-Cheng 2003; Fields 2008). Girls learn far more about the responsibilities of being an *object* than the experiences of being the *subject* of desire in school settings (Fine and McClelland 2006), a phenomenon further reflected in the media and surrounding culture. This was the case for nearly all of the young women in this study. Few reported learning anything about women's sexuality beyond information about STIs and pregnancy. Most recalled learning nothing about nonheterosexual sexualities, and only two reported hearing anything about women's desire or pleasure. Further, multiple young women recalled their teachers telling girls to avoid "acting slutty" and participating in sexual rumors themselves, further reinforcing judgmental gendered messages about girls' sexualities.

Given this context, it is not surprising that the sexual rumor economy is valuable to girls: it fills a void. In the absence of positive and diverse sexuality and gender education, rumors offer information about girls' sexuality in a socially acceptable discursive package. Tales about "the blow job girl," "the slut," "the dyke," "the girl who had a train run on her" are *useful* to girls because they help define their own sexualities as normative in a respectable way. Yet, this is because they have little institutional and social support to do so in other ways. It is not that girls never talked positively about their own sex lives in high school—indeed, some told jovial stories about sharing the details of their virginity loss, coming out, and hookups with their close friends—but most also noted that there was more risk when they did. In sum, girls articulated feeling far more licensed to talk about their sexual standards than their sexual experiences, a message often reinforced through the formal and informal information they received about gendered sexuality at school.

CONCLUSION

Sexual drama flourished in participants' experiences of high school—an institutional setting where girls are given limited sexual information and are rarely supported to talk about their own sexual experiences or curiosities. In this context, sexual rumors offered girls the opportunity to collectively negotiate and make meaning about gendered sexuality. This process likely sounds familiar to gender scholars. Much research on masculinity has shown that bullying offers sites for collective gendered meaning-making, as well as opportunities for boys to define their own sexual selves in relation to the ever-fluctuating boundary of what is "normal" (Pascoe 2007, 2013; Rivers and Duncan 2013). As we have seen, girls have similar strategies, with similar outcomes: sexual drama is a vehicle for girls to make claims about their own femininities. However, this process is useful to girls for different reasons, as girls experience more limitations in making claims about desire and sexual experiences in adolescence (Eder, Evans, and Parker 1997; Martin 1996). Thus, in order to make respectable sexual claims about the self, girls are left to make claims about *other* girls' sexualities—naming what *kind* of girl they are by naming what *kind* of girl they are not.

This paradox has to do with constraints on girls' sexual subjectivities. Feminist scholars have documented the many barriers young women experience as they navigate desire and their development of sexual subjectivity, emphasizing the roles that schools, families, the media, and politics play in shaping these constraints (Bell 2013; Fine 1988; Fine and McClelland 2006; Martin 1996; Schalet 2011; Tolman 2002). My findings indicate that these barriers are also connected to girls'

relationships with each other. Collectively, these young women's accounts document how girls' conflicts both constrain and shape their sexual subjectivities and their ability to discuss their own sexual desires and experiences. While structural barriers create the context that makes sexual drama a problematic yet potent resource for young women, we might better support them if we also acknowledge the role that girls themselves play in reinforcing their own "dilemmas of desire" (Tolman 2002). To do so, adults must interrogate and adjust their institutional practices to better support girls in developing healthy sexual subjectivities as well as critical consciousness about gendered sexuality.

This [reading] focused on the commonalities of girls' use of sexual drama in order to explore its functions among them. Across race, class, and sexual orientations, girls told surprisingly similar stories about their experiences with this kind of conflict in their very different high schools. However, in the interest of space, this paper has not explored the significant distinctions that existed between differently positioned girls in its use and outcomes. As documented by other scholars (Armstrong et al. 2014; Das Gupta 1997; Espiritu 2001; Froyum 2007; Wilkins 2008), girls across positionalities in this study also used slut-shaming, rumors and gossip, and, to a lesser degree, homophobic slander to shore up classed and racialized boundaries, compete for status, and make claims about themselves in contrast to girls who were not similarly positioned. Further, in some cases, drama appears to be a luxury. For example, some low-income girls and young women of color described resisting involvement in sexual drama in high school because they wanted to avoid being stereotyped or criminalized, or had "bigger things to worry about," including physical and financial insecurity. Meanwhile, privileged girls' accounts often illustrated greater access to drama, as they had more leisure time and were less concerned about how their behavior would reflect on their families, communities, or academic records. These findings complicate girls' experiences with sexual drama. Still, the commonalities that exist among this diverse sample of young women illustrate the pervasive role the conflicts described here play in girls' gendering processes across social locations.

While sexual drama was most prevalent in these young women's accounts of high school, sexual judgment still persisted in early adulthood for some. This is not unlike the findings of Armstrong et al. (2014), Hamilton (2007), and Wilkins (2008). Yet, I found that the volume of sexual rumor-spreading, reputational slander, and avoidance of girls perceived as doing sexuality "wrong" was markedly less in participants' accounts of college as compared to high school. This finding could be an outcome of the interview process. Participants may have felt compelled to present their current experiences as better than those in the past, sharing accounts of either reformation or liberation in order to claim agency and position themselves in a more positive light.

However, I believe that sexual drama is an institutionally linked phenomenon. Nearly all of the young women narrate a significant change in their and others' engagement with this kind of conflict at college. Across the different colleges they attended, participants described similar shifts in their social landscape: sexual information flows more freely, LGBQ sexual orientations become less stigmatized, and sex evolves from something only some girls take part in to an activity that all girls are expected to engage in. In most of their accounts of college, young women's sexualities are normalized, rendering conflicts that focus on who and what is sexually "not normal" less useful. While some of the underlying attitudes and judgments persist, the function, outcomes, and social reinforcement of these ideas transformed in similar ways across college contexts.

Meanwhile, what their narratives collectively indicate is that U.S. high schools—regardless of size, location, or kind—provided an institutional setting for this kind of conflict to flourish.

Sexual drama illustrates how young women connect through the reproduction of inequality (see also Pascoe 2013). However, rather than pathologizing their behaviors, girls will be better served if we critically acknowledge the contexts in which these behaviors take place. Sexual drama is a powerful social currency that maps onto the closed network structure, limited sex education, and restrictive gender norms that make up many U.S. schools (Bay-Cheng 2003; Eder, Evans, and Parker 1997; Faris and Felmlee 2011; Fields 2008; Klein 2012). In this context, this currency is a resource girls use to compete for status while navigating the gendered peer hierarchies that schools themselves reinforce (Armstrong et al. 2014). Schools are also embedded in a culture where teen girls are hypersexualized in the media (APA 2010), receive limited and constrained sexuality information at home (Elliott 2012; Schalet 2011), often experience unequal power dimensions in heterosexual relationships (Holland et al. 2004), and are subjected to the persistent threat of sexual violence (Hlavka 2014; Phillips 2000). Given these constraints, girls' use of this kind of conflict is better understood as a *reasonable* reaction to the often sexist, misogynistic, and homophobic culture that surrounds them.

As Gary Alan Fine argues, "A society where rumors spread is characterized by institutional breakdown: either institutions are not communicating, or they are not believed to be providing accurate, fair or necessary information" (2009, 192). When young women are given limited and contradictory information about gendered sexuality, it is no wonder they use sexual drama to make sense of and negotiate its complicated terrain. In lieu of being institutionally and culturally supported in articulating sexual stories that are positive or agentic, girls are left to talk about what they are not supposed to do, what they are not supposed to say, and what "kind of girl" they are not supposed to be. Trying to stop these practices should not be, as Gaby tells us, "like trying to catch smoke." Yet, given the institutional and cultural contexts girls inhabit, it is currently an uphill battle. Young women have the capacity to share different, positive sexual stories. In order to support them in doing so, adults need to provide them with more information and better templates.

NOTES

1. Cases include July Barrick, Sarah Butler, Amber Caudel, Ashlynn Conner, Amber Cornwell, Amanda Cummings, Rachel Ehmke, Felicia Garcia, Angel Green, Carla Jamerson, Samantha Johnson, Hailee Lamberth, Jessica Laney, Jessie Logan, Gabrielle Molina, Alyssa Morgan, Alexis Pilkington, Phoebe Prince, Meredith Rezak, Ashley Rogers, Rebecca Sedwick, Amanda Todd, Sladjana Vidovic, and Hope Witsell.

2. Definitions of bullying vary. The U.S. Department of Justice assesses bullying by asking "whether another student had made fun of you, called you names, or insulted you; spread rumors about you; threatened you with harm; pushed or shoved you; forced you to do something you did not want to do; excluded you from activities; or destroyed your property" (DeVoe and Bauer 2011). Definitions also often involve repetition (Kann et al. 2014) and an imbalance of power (Olweus 1993). However, scholars have called these qualifiers into question (Faris and Felmlee 2011) and argued that current definitions are too narrow (Finkelhor, Turner, and Hamby 2012).

3. All identifying information has been changed.

4. The 12 unrelated rumors focused on drug use, physical fights, or on a boy's purported homosexuality.

REFERENCES

APA (American Psychological Association). 2010. *Report of the APA task force on the sexualization of girls*. Washington, DC: APA.

Armstrong, Elizabeth A., Laura T. Hamilton, Elizabeth M. Armstrong, and J. Lotus Seeley. 2014. Good girls. *Social Psychology Quarterly* 77 (2): 100–22.

Armstrong, Elizabeth A., Laura Hamilton, and Brian Sweeney. 2006. Sexual assault on campus. *Social Problems* 53 (4): 483–99.

Attwood, Fiona. 2007. Sluts and riot grrrls? *Journal of Gender Studies* 13 (3): 231–45.

Bay-Cheng, Laina. 2003. The trouble of teen sex. *Sex Education* 3 (1): 61–74.

Bazelon, Emily. 2013. *Sticks and stones*. New York: Random House.

Bell, Leslie. 2013. *Hard to get*. Berkeley: University of California Press.

Bettie, Julie. 2003. *Women without class*. Berkeley: University of California Press.

boyd, danah. 2014. *It's complicated*. New Haven, CT: Yale University Press.

Brown, Lyn Mikel. 2005. *Girlfighting*. New York: New York University Press.

Butler, Judith. 1990. *Gender trouble*. New York: Routledge.

Cappiello, Katie, Meg McInerney, Jennifer Baumgardner, and Carol Gilligan. 2015. *SLUT*. New York: Feminist Press.

Chambers, Deborah, Estella Tincknell, and Joost Van Loon. 2004. Peer regulation of teenage sexual identities. *Gender & Education* 16 (3): 387–415.

Chesney-Lind, Meda, and Katherine Irwin. 2008. *Beyond bad girls*. New York: Routledge.

Collins, Patricia Hill. 1990. *Black feminist thought*. New York: Routledge.

Corsaro, William. 1992. Interpretive reproduction in children's peer cultures. *Social Psychology Quarterly* 55 (2): 160–77.

Crawford, Mary, and Danielle Popp. 2003. Sexual double standards. *Journal of Sex Research* 40 (1): 13–26.

Das Gupta, Monisha. 1997. What is Indian about you? *Gender & Society* 11 (5): 572–96.

DeVoe, Jill, and Lynn Bauer. 2011. *Student victimization in U.S. schools*. Washington, DC: U.S. Department of Education NCES 2012-314.

Duncan, Neil. 1999. *Sexual bullying*. London: Routledge.

Eder, Donna, and Janet Enke. 1991. The structure of gossip. *American Sociological Review* 56 (4): 494–508.

Eder, Donna, Catherine Evans, and Stephen Parker. 1997. *School talk*. New Brunswick, NJ: Rutgers University Press.

Elliott, Sinikka. 2012. *Not my kid*. New York: New York University Press.

Espiritu, Yen Le. 2001. We don't sleep around like white girls do. *Signs* 26 (2): 415–40.

Faris, Robert, and Diane Felmlee. 2011. Status struggles. *American Sociological Review* 76 (1): 48–73.

Faris, Robert, and Diane Felmlee. 2014. Casualties of social combat. *American Sociological Review* 79 (2): 228–57.

Fields, Jessica. 2008. *Risky lessons*. New Brunswick, NJ: Rutgers University Press.

Fine, Gary Alan. 1985. Rumors and gossiping. In *Handbook of discourse analysis*, edited by Teun Van Dijk. London: Academic Press.

Fine, Gary Alan. 2009. Does rumor lie? In *Deception*, edited by Brooke Harrington. Stanford, CA: Stanford University Press.

Fine, Michelle. 1988. Sexuality, schooling, and adolescent females. *Harvard Educational Review* 58 (1): 29–53.

Fine, Michelle, and Sara McClelland. 2006. Sexuality education and desire. *Harvard Educational Review* 76 (3): 297–338.

Finkelhor, David, Heather Turner, and Sherry Hamby. 2012. Let's prevent peer victimization, not just bullying. *Child Abuse & Neglect* 36 (4): 271–74.

Fjaer, Eivind Grip, Willy Pedersen, and Sveinung Sandberg. 2015. I'm not one of those girls. *Gender & Society* 29 (6): 960–81.

Froyum, Carissa. 2007. At least I'm not gay. *Sexualities* 10 (5): 603–22.

Froyum, Carissa. 2010. Making "good girls." *Culture, Health and Sexuality* 12 (1): 59–72.

Garcia, Lorena. 2012. *Respect yourself, protect yourself*. New York: New York University Press.

Gluckman, Max. 1963. Gossip and scandal. *Current Anthropology* 4 (3): 307–16.

Grotpeter, Jennifer, and Nicki Crick. 1996. Relational aggression, overt aggression, and friendship. *Child Development* 67: 2328–38.

Hamilton, Laura. 2007. Trading on heterosexuality. *Gender & Society* 21 (2): 145–72.

Hlavka, Heather. 2014. Normalizing sexual violence. *Gender & Society* 28 (3): 337–58.

Holland, Janet, Caroline Ramazanoglu, Sue Sharpe, and Rachel Thompson. 2004. *The male in the head*. London: Tufnell Press.

Horn, Stacey. 2007. Adolescents' acceptance of same-sex peers based on sexual orientation and gender expression. *Journal of Youth & Adolescence* 36: 363–71.

Kann, Laura, Steve Kinchen, Shari Shanklin, Katherine H. Flint, Joseph Hawkins, William A. Harris, Richard Lowry, Emily O'Malley Olsen, Tim McManus, David Chyen, Lisa Whittle, Eboni Taylor, Zewditu Demissie, Nancy Brener, Jemekia Thornton, John Moore, and Stephanie Zaza. 2014. *Youth risk behavior surveillance—United States, 2013*. 63(4). *MMWR Surveillance Summaries*. Atlanta, GA. Centers for Disease Control and Prevention.

Klein, Jessie. 2012. *The bully society*. New York: New York University Press.

Kreager, Derek, and Jeremy Staff. 2009. The sexual double standard and adolescent peer acceptance. *Social Psychology Quarterly* 72 (2): 143–64.

Lees, Sue. 1993. *Sugar and spice*. New York: Penguin.

Lessne, Deborah, and Melissa Cidade. 2015. *Student reports of bullying and cyberbullying: Results from the 2013 School Crime Supplement to the National Crime Victimization Survey. NCES 2015-056. National Center for Education Statistics*. Washington, DC: US Department of Education.

Lindin, Emily. 2015. *UnSlut*. San Francisco, CA: Zest.

Marcus, Ruth. 2010. Should we be criminalizing bullies? *The Washington Post*, 7 April.

Martin, Karin. 1996. *Puberty, sexuality, and the self*. New York: Routledge.

Marwick, Alice, and danah boyd. 2014. It's just drama. *Journal of Youth Studies* 17 (9): 1187–204.

Messerschmidt, James. 2012. *Gender, heterosexuality, and youth violence*. Lanham, MD: Rowman & Littlefield.

Olweus, Dan. 1993. *Bullying at school*. Oxford: Wiley-Blackwell.

Orpinas, Pamela, Caroline McNicholas, and Lusine Nahapetyan. 2015. Gender differences in trajectories of relational aggression perpetration and victimization from middle to high school. *Aggressive Behavior* 41: 401–12.

Paine, Robert. 1967. What is gossip about? *Man* 2 (2): 278–85.

Pascoe, C. J. 2007. *Dude, you're a fag*. Berkeley: University of California Press.

Pascoe, C. J. 2013. Notes on a sociology of bullying. *QED* 1 (1): 87–104.

Payne, Elizabethe. 2010. Sluts. *Educational Studies* 46 (3): 317–36.

Payne, Elizabethe. 2012. Slut. *The Huffington Post*. http://www.huffingtonpost.com/elizabethe-c-payne/slut-gender-policing-as-bullying-ritual_b_1952205.html.

Payne, Elizabethe, and Melissa Smith. 2013. LGBTQ kids, school safety, and missing the big picture. *QED* 1 (1): 1–36.

Phillips, Lynn. 2000. *Flirting with danger*. New York: New York University Press.

Plummer, Kenneth. 1995. *Telling sexual stories*. London: Routledge.

Poteat, V. Paul, and Ian Rivers. 2010. The use of homophobic language across bullying roles during adolescence. *Journal of Applied Developmental Psychology* 31 (2): 166–72.

Renold, Emma. 2002. Presumed innocence. *Childhood* 9 (4): 415–34.

Ringrose, Jessica. 2006. The new universal mean girl. *Feminism & Psychology* 16 (4): 405–24.

Rivers, Ian, and Neil Duncan. 2013. *Bullying*. New York: Routledge.

Rosnow, Ralph, and Gary Alan Fine. 1976. *Rumor and gossip*. New York: Elsevier.

Sales, Nancy Jo. 2016. *American girls*. New York: Knopf.

Schalet, Amy. 2009. Subjectivity, intimacy, and the empowerment paradigm of adolescent sexuality. *Feminist Studies* 35 (1): 133–60.

Schalet, Amy. 2011. *Not under my roof*. Chicago: University of Chicago Press.

Schippers, Mimi. 2007. Recovering the feminine other. *Theory and Society* 36 (1): 85–102.

Stone, Amy, and Allison Gorga. 2014. Containing pariah femininities. *Sexualities* 17 (3): 348–64.

Tanenbaum, Leora. 2015. *I am not a slut*. New York: Harper Perennial.

Thorne, Barrie. 1993. *Gender play*. New Brunswick, NJ: Rutgers University Press.

Thurlow, Crispin. 2001. Naming the "outsider within." *Journal of Adolescence* 24: 23–38.

Tolman, Deborah. 2002. *Dilemmas of desire*. Cambridge, MA: Harvard University Press.

Underwood, Marion. 2003. *Social aggression among girls*. New York: Guilford.

The Unslut Project. 2013. http://www.unslutproject.com.

Wang, Jing, Ronald Iannotti, and Tonja Nansel. 2009. School bullying among U.S. adolescents. *Journal of Adolescent Health* 45 (4): 368–75.

West, Candace, and Don Zimmerman. 1987. Doing gender. *Gender & Society* 1 (2): 125–51.

Wilkins, Amy. 2008. *Wannabes, Goths, and Christians*. Chicago: University of Chicago Press.

Wilkins, Amy, and Sarah Miller. Forthcoming. "Secure girls." *Sexualities*.

Wolcott, Harry. 1994. *Transforming qualitative data*. Thousand Oaks, CA: Sage.

OUT IN THE COUNTRY

MARY L. GRAY

The Highland Pride Alliance (HPA), a community-based social support group for [rural Eastern Kentucky] area lesbian, gay, bisexual, and transgender (LGBT) people and their straight allies, usually met at a member's house or in the basement of a local public county library. Only a few members had homes with the space and welcoming families to accommodate the six to ten regular attendees. No one could host this particular week and another community group had booked the library's meeting room. So, the HPA gathered at Dolly's House, the Christian bookstore across the county line.

Recently, the owner had decided to put some green plastic lawn chairs around carafes of flavored coffee in the store's entryway and call it a café. Dolly's House quickly became a popular youth hangout. Take a few steps past the coffee and you were in the bookstore—a room with several racks of greeting cards, books on tape, and "ready-to-order personalized Bibles." Because this was one of the Wednesday evenings when Dolly's owner closed up early to attend church, the members of the HPA shuffled their meeting to the Gas-n'-Go farther down the highway that cut through the deep river valley they routinely traversed. It was the only place open after 9 P.M. on this stretch of road where the closest town was a mile off the highway exit and had less than 3,000 people. . . .

This time, Shaun, HPA's co-chair and my main contact, was the first of his friends to arrive at the donut shop attached to the Gas-n'-Go. Shaun called to let me know that the meeting had moved and invited me to join them at the new rendezvous point. The talk of next month's HPA Halloween fundraiser turned to casual gossip and chatter regarding this evening's after-meeting plans. They could go back to Tim's place and watch some movies. That was quickly rejected. They spent hours at Tim's last night watching the then recently released (U.S. version of) *Queer as Folk* First Season collection on DVD. Other possibilities were bandied and then dismissed as "too boring" or "too far away." Joe tossed out the idea of heading over to neighboring Springhaven—20 minutes due south—to do some drag at the Wal-Mart. He was dying to try out the fake eyelashes he had bought at the Dollar Tree last weekend. The group's collective uproar of affirming whoops and laughter drew the eyes of two bleached blond–haired women in their mid-twenties listlessly tending to the donut display case and coffee hot plates. Shaun met their tentative smiles with a large grin and a small princess-atop-a-float wave. Turning back to the group, he giggled and said softly, "Now, settle it down, y'all."

This would not be the group's first foray to the Wal-Mart Supercenter located in the county seat, population just more than 10,000. Within a few months of the Supercenter's grand opening, the HPA had reappropriated Wal-Mart, turning it into a regular gathering spot for their post-meeting social activities. At one point, the HPA website even featured photos snapped of members posing in their most memorable outfits amid Wal-Mart's aisles. The HPA had turned Wal-Mart into a meeting space, drag revue, and shopping excursion all rolled into one.

"From Wal-Mart to Websites" from *Out in the Country: Youth, Media, and Queer Visibility in Rural America* by Mary L. Gray, Copyright © 2009 by New York University. Reprinted by permission of New York University Press.

That these boisterous LGBT-identifying rural young people and their allies move among house parties, public libraries, Christian bookstores, gas stations, Wal-Mart, and websites may seem surprising. I will admit, it surprised me. I had assumed they met exclusively in friends' houses to avoid trouble or hostility from locals. But as I would learn again and again, the everyday lives of rural youth I met complicate simple dichotomies of rural and urban experience or private versus public experiences of queer visibility. I hope that by detailing the work of responding to the expectations a politics of LGBT visibility poses, particularly in an era saturated by gay visibility in the media and via the Internet, I can show that, for the people who live in them, rural communities are more than backdrops or landscapes to late-modern queer subjectivities. If, as feminist geographer Doreen Massey argues, "the social is inexorably also spatial" (Massey 1994, 265), we cannot examine the social relations of power that produce the meaning of LGBT identities without a careful consideration of how locations, rural locales in this case, matter to those relations.[1] . . .

These young people live in communities that lack the human, social, and financial capital to maintain the gay neighborhoods, bookstores, and coffeehouses found in urban settings such as the Castro in San Francisco, New York City's Christopher Street, Chicago's Boystown, or Dupont Circle in Washington, D.C. Nearly all of them live in "dry counties" where alcohol cannot even be sold let alone served in a gay bar. These youth can (and regularly do) travel to gay enclaves in Louisville, Lexington, and Nashville. But they cannot produce in their rural daily lives the sustained infrastructure of visibility that defines urban LGBT communities. Instead, they travel to each other's houses and caravan roundtrip to a larger city with a gay bar or gay-affirming church several hours away. In other words, much as historian John Howard

found in his history of queer community formation in rural Mississippi of the 1940s–1980s, rural queer and questioning youth make up for their lack of local numbers and gay-owned spaces by using a strategy of circulation rather than congregation (Howard 1999, 78).[2]

IMAGINING RURAL QUEERNESS

. . . Even historical accounts of the recent rural past paint private house parties as the primary location of queer possibility and community—if any community is imagined possible at all.[3] Drawing on popular documentaries screened at LGBT film festivals in the first few years of the twenty-first century, historian John Howard argues that rural LGBT lives are marked not by violence or isolation, but by "mundane, everyday trade-offs" such as "fewer public displays of affection, a greater feeling of rootedness, less pride in outness, more of a sense of safety" (Howard 2006, 101–2). As Howard notes, hate crimes directed at LGBT people are more often perpetrated by groups of men who use the safety of their numbers to single out victims living in dense urban areas (Howard, 2006, 101–2). Although LGBT-related hate crimes are not nationally recorded and systematically tracked, studies of rural crime patterns suggest that violence directed at queer difference in rural spaces (an issue I will return to at the end of this [reading]) is different from, though statistically no greater than, the violence cities exact.[4] Contrary to popular representations and presumptions drawn from historical accounts, today's rural youth do not (arguably cannot) privately suffer an endemic estrangement or isolation from queer subjectivities. The trickle of denigrating national press accounts of "the homosexual lifestyle" that began in the mid-1960s presaged a veritable flood of gay visibility.[5] Rural youth in the United States have unprecedented access to national media markets. These markets saturate them in a politics of LGBT visibility that demands public recognition. Seeking acknowledgment as lesbian, gay, bisexual, or transgender means grappling with these demands no matter where one lives. Rural youth must respond to the call for LGBT visibility that structures their feelings of authenticity amid vastly underfunded, rural public spaces that prioritize allegiance to familiarity and solidarity over public claims to difference of any kind. . . .

Dragging It Up at Wal-Mart

A bright, neon archway flickering "always low prices, always food center" hovers above the entrance to the Springhaven, Kentucky, Wal-Mart Supercenter. The blue-trimmed, one-story building starts at stoplight 14 and spans an eroding stretch of state highway that bisects the town. On this Sunday evening, young men and women hold hands and roam through the aisles. Aside from a few young Latino families, most customers are white and speak with the low, slow drawl of Southern accents.

The Supercenter has nearly 100 aisles, from a full grocery on one end to pet supplies and beauty products on the other. Rows of fabric bolts spill out of their display bins. A range of household appliances, an electronic wedding registry kiosk, floor rugs, and an extensive work-boot collection crowd the West Entrance. Monitors above the aisles blare advertisements from the DisneyHealth Network produced for Wal-Mart hawking products in between snippets of music videos. University of Kentucky logo-wear easily fills a 9-foot-by-12-foot space. There's an eatery to the right of the automated superstore double doors. Smokers fill the red and white tables, savoring their last cigarette drags before entering the smoke-free discount merchandiser that has been in this strip mall for 18 months.

The Springhaven Wal-Mart is the only business open 24 hours within an 80-mile radius. I found out about the popularity of this Wal-Mart when I asked Clay, a local teen, what he and his friends did for fun. "Most gay people around the county, we all go to Hardee's or the new Backyard Burgers." He added casually, "And then most people all haul up together in big carloads, put on some drag, runway walk the Super Wal-Mart in Springhaven and walk around for about five hours with people almost having heart attacks and conniption fits cause we're running around. . . . We take pictures of us all, post them to the website, and have fun with our little getaway from living in rural Kentucky."

When I asked other area youth about their experiences at Wal-Mart, they confirmed that performing drag in the superstore's aisles was a rite of passage for those entering the local gay scene. Joe recalled his initiation this way: "The first time I was with them, we all put on these furry jackets and we was walking through the aisles. That was fun. Me and all my friends, we all gather up several cars all the time, and now we go once or twice a month. We all just huddle up together and run up there." With the exception of a few young people working night shifts at factories or fast-food chains, Highland Pride Alliance members attended drag nights at Wal-Mart as regularly as they attended the group's more formal organizational meetings.

When asked to describe why they chose Wal-Mart, most of the young people couldn't remember, nor did they understand my surprise. To them, the Wal-Mart Supercenter seemed an obvious place to hang out. As Shaun put it, "Why wouldn't we go there?! It's the best place to find stuff to do drag. They've got all the wigs and makeup and tight clothes and stuff." Then he added, "Besides, no matter how much we bug people doing what we're doing, we're still customers too. And we have friends who work there who won't let nothing happen to us if they see any trouble start." Contrary to the anonymity Wal-Mart and other so-called big box stores might provide in the suburbs of metropolitan areas, HPA members do not experience this space as anonymous. It is their own backyard after all, and there are few options this close to where they live.

Beyond the makeshift runways and basic drag gear found in Wal-Mart's aisles, the megachain's national guidelines that situate its customers as "guests" also facilitate youth doing drag in its stores. As long as these young people are still readable as consumer citizens, the logic of capital cannot bar them from this queer twist on the public square. Plus, Wal-Mart's (then recent) instatement of domestic-partner benefits for employees signaled that Wal-Mart was, as Clay put it, "a tolerant place where they could expect to be accepted." Unlike their public school experiences, which were described by many as a "living hell," Wal-Mart stood out as a safe public space where they would be protected.

Part of Something Bigger

Gay rights organizations dot the rural landscape. One finds chapters of nationally organized nonprofits, like PFLAG and the Gay, Lesbian, and Straight Education Network. . . . One also finds statewide and regionally based groups, such as the Kentucky Fairness Alliance (KFA) and the Highland Pride Alliance. Each organization draws capital investments from donors and then circulates resources in time, training, and visibility to local residents—including youth in this study—interested in connecting to a broader community of organizers.

Rural youth seeking terrain for their queer-identity work can find fertile ground in not-for-profit organizations. . . . As one 17-year-old gay-identifying man put it, "Going to PFLAG or KFA's Lobby Days in [the State Capitol in] Frankfort and meetings and stuff like that makes me feel like I've got a whole big gay extended family out there . . . like I'm part of something bigger even when nothing's really happening in my own town." For

many youth this means taking advantage of a ready-made structure that includes things like banners, e-mail addresses, listings on national websites and directories, and an imagined network of like-minded allies and friends.

Locally grown groups with overlapping membership in these offshoots and branches of national or regional organizations are equally important. The Highland Pride Alliance, for example, has existed for nearly a decade.[6] Most members are white, gay or nonidentifying and range in age from late teens to forty-something men. All of them come from four surrounding counties. Some members found out about the group from someone they met while hanging out (or cruising) at the local state park. Others were clued in by the group's reputation or, increasingly, the group's website.

When I met Shaun, he was the driving force behind the group. When he joined the HPA two years earlier, it consisted mostly of local white men interested in quiet social gatherings. Period. They met at each other's homes and did their best to keep out of the public eye. But Shaun was 17 and stinging from harassment in public high school. He wasn't about to "go back to meeting secretly." "What was the point?" he said. In his town of 2,100, everyone knew he was gay. If they didn't know it from the common gossip of the schoolyard, they heard it from a popular Baptist minister who was once a close friend of Shaun's. . . .

Shaun instigated many of HPA's activities, such as meetings at the public library, involvement in rallies supporting a distant rural high school's efforts to form a Gay–Straight Alliance, and plans to bring the first "Meals on Wheels" service for people with AIDS to the region with support from AIDS Volunteers of Lexington. Shaun saw the building up of the HPA and its relationships to statewide groups as vital to creating opportunities for all local LGBT people. . . .

Bashing at the Wal-Mart

What follows is an account of drag gone awry in Springhaven. HPA members noted that turning the aisles of a regional Wal-Mart Supercenter into a boundary public for drag performance was fun and, to them, safe. They felt their status as "guests" could shield them from any direct harassment. They also presumed that friends who worked at Wal-Mart would intervene and protect them by asserting their positions as the default authority of this milieu. But there was also a sense of belonging that permeated their temporary occupations of these privatized zones. "This is my hometown," Clay commented. "I know a lot of the folks coming in and out of the store already. . . . I know who to steer clear of.". . .

"Maybe they thought my lipstick was too loud," Shaun giggled. "I mean really, why should they care? I wasn't hurting anyone." A month earlier, a dozen or more HPA members and their friends—ranging from 16-year-old Chris to Phillip, who had just celebrated his twenty-third birthday—sashayed through the Wal-Mart like they had on so many nights before. Typically, HPA drag nights elicited no more than occasional stares, but this time things were different.

After trying on a tight girl's T-shirt glittered with the words "Star Gazer" across the chest, Shaun walked out of the men's fitting room to find himself face-to-face with a boy from his old high school. Sneering, the boy growled, "What are you doing in the wrong dressing room, faggot?" Shaun pushed past the boy, as he had so many times before in the school hallways, rolling his eyes and clicking his tongue, "Tisst! Whaaat . . . evverr!" while nervously scanning the aisle for his friend, Clay, whom he found in the makeup section "trying on 'Shades of Passion' for the umpteenth time." Shaun and Clay gathered up as many HPA folks as they could find and headed for the checkout counter. They assumed one of their friends was working her usual shift but were informed by the young man staffing her register that she had unexpectedly taken the night off.

Shaun and Clay's voices filled with frustration and exhaustion as they recalled what happened next. "He was just a big ol' redneck with nothing better to do than give us a hard time, that's all," Clay said. Shaun added, "It wasn't anything that wouldn't or didn't happen at school . . . difference was, I thought my friend was working that night . . . she would've put him in his place." Instead, the 17-year-old boy followed the HPA youth out to the parking lot and yelled every epithet he could conjure. An older man exiting the store told the harasser to settle down, but the young man paid no attention. No one from the store intervened. Shaun yelled, "We're not hurting no one!" and then saw two more of his old high school nemeses approaching. Rather than continue the exchange, Shaun and his-friends sauntered to their cars and piled in to them for the drive home.

The next day, Shaun took down the photos of HPA's Wal-Mart drag extravaganzas, as well as pictures of equally fabulous outings to the town square, from the group's website. When I asked him why he no longer wanted the photos of his friends in their tight minis and platinum wigs on the HPA homepage, he paused and said, "I just don't know if it's safe to have those up there. Someone we don't know could see them. . . . I guess I don't want anyone getting bashed because some narrow-minded homophobe from out of town saw a picture of us up there and thought we had taken things too far."

Some could read the HPA members' initial feelings of entitlement to their surroundings as an implicit assertion of their racial privilege as white young men. They anticipate moving through their surroundings without the scrutinizing that might, say, be cast on the one Latino youth who was new to the HPA.

Members of the HPA see their harassment as a response to the ways they trouble expectations and norms of their male privilege. They categorically liken it to the chiding young women receive for walking through the stores: "I know I've seen girls given a hard way because they don't dress all proper and they might be having fun, being loud. If someone's mad at me, it's because I'm being too girly—that's what being gay means to them anyways . . . that I'm being a girl." The notion of homosexuality as gender inversion persists in these communities much as it does in popular culture despite generations of gay and lesbian organizing to distance itself from the intersectionality of sexuality and gender.[7] Publicly disrupting normative gender expectations arguably remains as, if not more, contentious than homoerotic desires.

HPA youth threaten an unspoken agreement to "live and let live" when they visibly assert themselves as readable gay subjects. But they seem to break tentative, unspoken rules of occupying the boundaries of public spaces when they visibly stray too far afield from their status as familiar gay locals and become ambiguous queer objects that undo expectations of what it means to be a young man in the community. Their tentative feelings of safety are rattled more by how they challenge gender norms than by the implicitness of their sexual identities.

The mixed-class backgrounds of these youth, which range from white collar to working poor, also complicate access to a presumed privilege. The youth felt dragging it up at the Wal-Mart was more of a right than a risk. But several youth were aware that their status as "gay" would be compromised if they actually admitted to shopping for clothes at Wal-Mart, even though it's what they could afford. As Dale, a 21-year-old from Eastern Kentucky, put it, shopping at Wal-Mart is "just not gay enough." He is a student at a small Christian college. He is on financial aid and works part-time to help

support his mother and younger sister. He can only afford to buy clothes at Wal-Mart. "Sometimes it's such a burden to be gay nowadays," he lamented:

. . . because you're expected to know everything. They [his straight-identifying college friends] come to you. Well, you're gay, what do you think about this outfit? I'm, like, "I'm not that kind of gay! I may sound like I'm that kind of gay." I'm, like, "Look at me! I'm wearing Wal-Mart clothes! My entire outfit comes from Wal-Mart! Everything! I did not spend 40 bucks on this entire thing, and you're asking me about fashion!" They're, like, "But you're gay!" I'm, like, "So?! I'm a badly dressed gay man. I admit it. I embrace it. Leave me alone. Let me do my clearance aisles at Wal-Mart."

. . . Not being able to afford the consumptive markers of gay identity left Dale and his working-class peers shaken in their sense of self-identity. Alongside vicious verbal attacks lobbed in store parking lots or in school classrooms, LGBT visibility's commodification and its demanding consumer pressures posed considerable challenges to the queer-identity work of working-poor kids like Dale. . . .

NEW MEDIA LANDSCAPES

. . . It is tempting to assume that the Internet and other digital media offer something entirely new to rural queer and questioning youth. But the experiences of rural youth indicate a different direction for such analyses. For these young people, new media were imagined as both a supplement to local queer-identity work and an integrated part of this local occupation. Youth didn't use new media as hideouts from the real world. . . .

As discussed earlier, Shaun quickly took down photos chronicling HPA's drag excursions after what members referred to as "the bashing at Wal-Mart." He was sad and reluctant to remove the pictures at first. Shaun was proud that he had not only taken the snapshots but also learned how to crop the images and post them to the HPA website. But after the HPA received hate e-mail through the website's interactive guestbook a few days after the heated exchange in the Wal-Mart parking lot, he thought it needed to be done.

As the person responsible for sifting through e-mail coming in from the website, Shaun bore the brunt of these comments. One was the ALL CAPS standard, "I HATE FAGGOTS. KISS MY STRAIGHT ASS." The other told the HPA that they "were welcome to have their sexuality but it was disrespectful to hang all over each other and put pictures up on the website of this" (referring to photos on the HPA website of the group dragging it up at the Springhaven Wal-Mart and around the town square a different weekend). The e-mail went on to say "they should have some respect for the county."

Although there was no need for more than one person to monitor the HPA account, Shaun wished someone else would have read the e-mails first. "It just made me so mad and sad all over again! . . . I know these people are probably the same ones we ran into—and that means it's my fault that we're getting these hate mails." Both e-mail messages referenced Rust Falls—Shaun's hometown—building his suspicion that they were likely connected to the young men from high school he confronted that night. The irony is perhaps that the author/s of these e-mails saw the HPA website as reflective of their community and a kind of public that needs monitoring. The e-mails also suggest there is room for the HPA's sexuality, indicating the quiet, if begrudging, acceptance Shaun and his friends felt in their communities. . . .

CONCLUSION

Media coverage of the 1993 New Year's Eve murder of Brandon Teena, a young female-to-male transperson, in rural Nebraska and the even greater swell of reporting and public

outrage that followed the 1998 killing of a young gay man named Matthew Shepard in Wyoming emphasized the brutality of their deaths against a backdrop of the rural communities in which they were killed.[8] As Judith Halberstam observes, "The varied responses to the tragic murders of these two young white, rural queers have much to tell us about selective memorialization and political activism, space and sexual identity, and the mobilization of trauma" (Halberstam 2005, 17). There is much to unpack regarding the different treatments and degrees of culpability placed on these young people's bodies, most notably the relative political silence in 1993 around Brandon Teena's rape and murder compared to national vigils and outcries for gay-inclusive hate crime reforms that immediately followed Shepard's brutal murder. However, in both cases, news and film narratives placed Brandon and Matthew as young queers in the wrong place at the wrong time. Small-town, working-poor America was put on trial as horrific scenes of intolerance.[9] . . .

Ethnographic studies of queerness in rural communities suggest that cities and rural areas are differently (incomparably perhaps) intolerant toward queer difference. Shaun and other HPA members are constant reminders to their fellow rural residents that structures of familiarity are vulnerable as much from locals as from strangers. Rural communities manage the perceived threats of difference in myriad ways. They may attempt to excise queer difference, as in the case of threats of violence to HPA members outside Wal-Mart . . . or the bombardment of the HPA website with hate e-mail. Alternatively, community members might make appeals to the local status of their queerly different neighbors in an effort to maintain the fragile structures that organize the mythos of familiarity in rural life.

Lest I seem to offer a rosy picture of the oppression of queer difference in rural areas, let me reiterate: the examples of harassment explored above reflect the realities of violence in rural communities. But this violence is notably most often experienced as intimate, exacted by those these youth presume they know rather than the random acts of property destruction or "stranger danger" that pervades the psyches of most queer urban dwellers bashed outside populous city nightclubs.[10] The one critical advantage Shaun saw to the distinct quality of violence that permeates his community was that, as he put it, "I know who I need to avoid. I've been working to steer clear of those people all my life." Years later, Shaun underscored this point in a conversation with me about media representations of gay people living in rural places and, specifically, the movie *Brokeback Mountain.*

Shaun felt a certain dissonance watching Hollywood depictions of foreboding rural communities and their hapless queer inhabitants. He found Ang Lee's Academy Award–winning 2005 film about rural Wyoming cowboy lovers (Jack and Ennis) in particular "just ridiculous." When I asked him why, he seemed exasperated that he had to explain what seemed so obvious to him. "It just didn't make any sense! People in small towns don't go around killing people who have lived there all their lives [referring to the plotline that connects Ennis' fear of living with Jack to childhood memories of the brutal murder of male lovers in his hometown and, later, Jack's murder by a faceless mob]." Shaun then added, "Jack and Ennis could have lived together quietly . . . anyone who lives in a small town knows about couples or relatives like that. You know how to avoid trouble if you've lived in a place long enough." Ultimately, it was *Brokeback Mountain*'s representation of isolation and unpredictable mob violence lurking around the bend that seemed most at odds with Shaun's own sense of conditional safety traveling around the boundaries of his community. It wasn't that violence couldn't happen. Indeed,

Shaun had experienced persistent verbal and sometimes physical harassment through much of his high school years at the hands of longtime, childhood friends. But for Shaun, it seemed unfathomable that such extreme violence would be exacted by a mob of people you considered neighbors. Violence inflicted by loved ones was a much more familiar scenario but, through its familiarity, seemed easier to predict and circumvent. Violence wrought by strangers in rural communities would not go unnoticed or unchecked and therefore seemed more out of place.

In the end, Shaun decided to remove HPA's photos of drag at the Wal-Mart not because he feared retribution from local "troublemakers." In fact, much like the folk belief that the most vehement homophobes are queers in disguise, Shaun assumed anyone he knew "making hay was probably gay." His greater concern was that strangers might happen to find the photos and zero in on the HPA as an easy target. . . .

. . . The study of how rural youth put new media technologies to use illustrates that what counts as public and private is evolving and shifting. In looking at this disruption, we also see the politicization of what is relegated to the realm of the public sphere and what is considered the domain of private matters. When sexualities and gender identities are framed as matters of privacy, we are prone to overlook the realities of how people use public spaces for the expressions of their private selves. Publics are vital to our experiences of the private. Rural places send up the realities of this intermixture because there is so little public infrastructure to work with, so little raw material with which to parse out the private from the public. . . .

Youth have very different access to publics and therefore relationships to privacy. Queer youth do make space for themselves. Doing so is a necessary part of their identity work as they attempt to meet the expectations of the politics of visibility that demand public recognition. This work can and does happen in surprising places in rural communities. The above examples illustrate how rural youth who identify as lesbian, gay, bisexual, and transgender or question sexual and gender norms craft a tentative yet often vibrant sense of visibility. . . . Their move . . . is a complicated response to an overall lack of public spaces in rural communities that cannot be flattened into a more personal, psychological need or desire to "be closeted" or to some imagined sense that rural communities are inherently more hostile to queer identities. Yes, they accomplish this through the use of websites and other new media technologies, but they also commandeer publics available to them. Websites, Wal-Mart, punk music, listservs, public library meeting rooms, and church skate parks are the resources available to them. They make do. They get by. . . .

NOTES

1. Doreen Massey, *Space, Place, and Gender* (Minneapolis, MN: University of Minnesota Press, 1994).

2. John Howard, "Of Closets and Other Rural Voids," *GLQ: A Journal of Gay and Lesbian Studies* 13, no.1 (2006).

3. James T. Sears, *Rebels, Rubyfruit, and Rhinestones: Queering Space in the Stonewall South* (New Brunswick, NJ: Rutgers University Press, 2001); Will Fellows, *Farm Boys: Lives of Gay Men from the Rural Midwest* (Madison: University of Wisconsin Press, 1996); and for an important exception and complication, see John Howard, *Men Like That: A Southern Queer History* (Chicago: University of Chicago Press, 1999).

4. On rural crime rates that report that "intimate violence"—between relatives and longtime acquaintances—is more consistent with rates of random violence in urban centers whereas rural communities report far less crime around property, see the work of Cynthia Barnett and F. Carson Mencken, "Social Disorganization Theory and the Contextual Nature of Crime in Nonmetropolitan Counties," *Rural Sociology* 67, no.3 (2002): 372–93; and Matthew R. Lee, Michael O.Maume, and Graham C. Ousey, "Social Isolation and Lethal Violence across the Metro/Nonmetro Divide: The Effects of Socioeconomic Disadvantage and Poverty Concentration on Homicide," *Rural Sociology* 68, no. 1 (2003): 107–31.

5. See Larry P. Gross, *Up from Invisibility: Lesbians, Gay Men, and the Media in America*, Between Men—Between Women (New York: Columbia University Press, 2001),

233; Suzanna Danuta Walters, *All the Rage: The Story of Gay Visibility in America* (Chicago: University of Chicago Press, 2001); Katherine Sender, "Sex Sells: Sex, Class, and Taste in Commercial Gay and Lesbian Media," *GLQ: A Journal of Gay and Lesbian Studies* 9, no. 3 (2003): 331–65; and Katherine Sender, *Business, Not Politics: The Making of the Gay Market*, Between Men—Between Women (New York: Columbia University Press, 2004). See also Martin Meeker, *Contacts Desired: Gay and Lesbian Communications and Community, 1940s–1970s* (Chicago: University of Chicago Press, 2006).

6. There is a rich scholarly literature in anthropology and sociology that examines peer networks and their role in the social construction and expansion of gay and lesbian "communities." For example, see Murray on the meaning of "community" and his convincing argument that if "community" is a sociologically viable category, gays and lesbians typify it through their collective action, shared sense of territoriality, and reliance on friends as a primary group. In Stephen O. Murray, *American Gay*, Worlds of Desire (Chicago: University of Chicago Press, 1996), 182–214. On friendship networks and their role as fundamental units of support, see David Woolwine, "Community in Gay Male Experience and Moral Discourse," *Journal of Homosexuality* 38, no. 4 (2000): 5–37.

7. See Susan Stryker on the history of this effort by early and contemporary gay- and lesbian-rights organizing in San Francisco, in particular in "Transgender History, Homonormativity, and Disciplinarity," *Radical History Review* 100 (Winter 2008): 150. See also David Valentine's recent critique of gay and lesbian social-service organizations that maintain a policing among categories of gay, lesbian, bi, and trans, often denying clients' sense of the interconnectedness of their gender and sexual modalities. In David Valentine, *Imagining Transgender: An Ethnography of a Category* (Durham, NC: Duke University Press, 2007).

8. In fact, the U.S. House of Representatives voted to pass legislation called the Matthew Shepard Act to expand existing federal hate-crime laws authorizing the Department of Justice to investigate and prosecute bias-motivated crimes based on the victim's actual or perceived sexual orientation, gender, gender identity, or disability. Current law only includes race, color, religion, or national origin; eliminates the restrictions currently in place that limit federal involvement to cases in which a victim of a bias-motivated crime was attacked because he/she was engaged in a specified federally protected activity such as voting, serving on a jury, or attending school; and adds "gender" and "gender identity" to the Hate Crimes Statistics Act to keep national statistics on LGBT-related hate crimes. For more on the discussion of hate crimes, see Judith Butler, *Excitable Speech: Contemporary Scenes of Politics* (New York: Routledge,

1997); for reading on hate crimes and their relationship to the Shepard murder, see Beth Loffreda, *Losing Matt Shepard: Life and Politics in the Aftermath of Anti-Gay Murder* (New York: Columbia University Press, 2000).

9. See Lisa Henderson, "The Class Character of *Boys Don't Cry*," *Screen* 42, no. 3 (2001): 299–303; and Judith

Halberstam, *In a Queer Time and Place: Transgender Bodies, Subcultural Lives*, Sexual Cultures (New York: New York University Press, 2005), 22–46.

10. Again, see the work of Barnett and Mencken, "Social Disorganization," 372–93; and Lee, Maume, and Ousey, "Social Isolation and Lethal Violence," 107–31.

LGBTQ Politics in America: An Abbreviated History

Marik Xavier-Brier and Chet Meeks

The lesbian, gay, bisexual, transgender, queer (LGBTQ) community has been the target of systematic, institutionalized forms of regulation in American society since at least the middle of the twentieth century. This means that LGBTQ people are not merely discriminated against by particular individuals, but that a social norm making heterosexuality superior is embedded in and informs the logics of all of America's core social institutions: the state, the criminal justice system, the media, education, and the family. American social institutions have worked to make any sexuality deviating from the heterosexual norm criminal and deviant. When a group of individuals is systematically regulated in such a way, they sometimes organize to create social changes in the areas of law, public opinion, or social policy. Sometimes they try to revolutionize how we think of and practice sex itself. This is what we mean by "sexual politics," and here we offer an abbreviated history of LGBTQ politics in America.

The first rumblings of LGBTQ resistance could be felt in the 1950s. Harry Hay and Rudi Gernreich organized a group called the Mattachine Society, which primarily focused on the interests of gay men. At almost the same time, Del Martin and Phyllis Lyon organized the Daughters of Bilitis, which primarily focused on the needs of lesbians. Some other groups were ONE and the Society for Individual Rights. These early groups called themselves "homophile" organizations. They emerged in response to the state-sponsored harassment and criminalization of homosexuality in America. America in the 1950s was a place where homosexuality, like communism, had come to be associated with evil and moral bankruptcy. Homophile organizations were fledgling groups and only ever partially visible in the mainstream public sphere. They spoke through heterosexual proxies, like tolerant doctors or lawyers, in order to make their case about a given issue. Homophile groups had some successes, though. For example, ONE sued the American postal service in 1958 for refusing to mail their monthly magazine. But a strong, vocal, and truly organized LGBTQ politics did not really get underway until the late 1960s.

On June 28, 1969, a brawl broke out between New York City police officers and some drag queens at a Greenwich Village bar called the Stonewall Inn. The Stonewall riots marked the beginning of a new era in LGBTQ politics. From the spirit of rebellion at Stonewall, two LGBTQ organizations were born: the Gay Liberation Front (GLF) and the Gay Activist Alliance (GAA). Although these organizations are no longer around, the spirit and worldview that animated their respective political actions remain very much present in contemporary forms of LGBTQ struggle.

The GLF was organized by Martha Shelley, Craig Rodwell, and Jim Fourrat three weeks after the Stonewall riots. As their name suggests, the GLF espoused a liberationist worldview. According to liberationists, America is a society that systematically demonizes, criminalizes, and ghettoizes all forms of sexual and gender expression that do not conform to a very narrow standard of heterosexual "normality." Struggle and resistance, in a world like this, cannot be limited to demanding civil rights, reform, or tolerance. Rather, revolution—sexual revolution in particular—is the only viable option. Borrowing an idea from feminism, liberationists argued that "the personal is political," and they believed that only by transforming sexuality could the broader social fabric be revolutionized. They encouraged their members to experiment with new forms of "liberated" sexuality and social relationships—like nonmonogamy and communal living. Liberationists, moreover, viewed the plight of LGBTQ people as indelibly linked to the problems faced by black Americans, "third world" people and refugees, victims of American and European military aggression, and members of the working class. They struggled alongside the Black Panthers and critics of the Vietnam War, demanding justice for all oppressed people.

Although the GAA emerged at nearly the same time and in the same political climate as the GLF, they possessed a worldview that was very different from that of the liberationists. They did not believe that the plight faced by lesbians and gay men was necessarily linked to other forms of oppression, like race or class status. Neither did they believe that American society was systematically anti-queer, in the way suggested by liberationists. Rather, they believed that, at its core, America was a tolerant and just society, one that had successfully integrated a large number of minority groups. American institutions, they argued, are copious and open to change. The problem was that this tolerance had not yet been extended to lesbians, gay men, transgender people, and bisexuals.

Sexual revolution was not the answer, according to the GAA. They were not liberationists, but assimilationists. They believed that tolerance and respect for LGBTQ people had to be won through the slow, incremental reform of existing institutions. Assimilationists believe rights are granted through respectability and espouse ideas of "we're just like you" to the heterosexual community. They believe that, just as black Americans and women had fought to gain civil rights reforms in the 1960s and 1970s, lesbians and gay men must fight to be recognized as respectable Americans. They fought to pass civil rights ordinances in cities like New York. Unlike the liberationists, they focused much less on the sexual lives of activists themselves, and they eschewed attempts to connect lesbian and gay justice to the struggles of other groups.

The liberationist worldview was reborn in the radical sexual politics of the 1980s and 1990s, in groups like Act-Up and Queer Nation. The Reagan Administration of the 1980s had largely ignored the growing AIDS epidemic, mainly because gay men were the most visible victims of the disease. Also, large pharmaceutical companies were making the drugs used to treat AIDS symptoms so expensive that only the very wealthy could afford them. Against this stifling climate, Act-Up shouted, "Silence Equals Death," and against the growing stigmatization of gay and queer people due to AIDS, Queer Nation shouted, "We're Here, We're Queer, Get Used to It!" Like their assimilationist counterparts, Act-Up and Queer Nation linked notions of social revolution to self-transformation. Yet they believed that nothing would ever truly change until queer people had put an end to "straight tyranny," which has become known as heteronormativity. Heteronormativity sets heterosexuality as normative. It establishes same-sex relationships as bad or deviant and restricts gender identity, gender roles, and sexuality. Heteronormative culture is one that fosters a climate of discrimination against LGBTQ people in all social institutions.

While the GAA no longer exists, their goal of assimilation remains central to many of the most visible contemporary LGBTQ organizations. Coming to power largely in the 1990s, the Human Rights Campaign (HRC), the Lambda Legal Defense and Education Fund (Lambda), and the Gay and Lesbian Alliance against Defamation (GLAAD) all borrow from the worldview of the GAA. The Human Rights Campaign has become an extremely successful lobbying organization in Washington, DC. It has over one million members and supporters, and the organization lobbies Congress continually for federal hate crime legislation and other legal reforms to make LGBTQ people safe and equal citizens. Both the HRC and Lambda have been making inroads in the fight toward lesbian and gay equality in the arena of marriage. In 1993, Lambda was the first organization to successfully take a marriage lawsuit to a state Supreme Court in the famous *Baehr v. Lewin* case in Hawaii. In response, a few years later, Congress passed the Defense of Marriage Act (DOMA), defining marriage as limited to one man and one woman, with no state having to recognize a same-sex marriage that was performed in another state. In 2004, Massachusetts became the first state to recognize same-sex marriage, and finally in 2015 in *Obergefell v. Hodges*, the Supreme Court of the United States legalized same-sex marriage for all LGBTQ couples. However, despite gaining the right to marry, the fight for equality is far from over.

In terms of the media, GLAAD was declared by *Entertainment Weekly* one of the most successful media organizations in the country. GLAAD came into existence in an era when LGBTQ people were only vilified on television and in the media, when they were represented at all. Today, the GLAAD awards (given for fair, accurate, and positive portrayals of LGBTQ people) are coveted by many of Hollywood's most elite actors, actresses, directors, and producers. Mainstream LGBTQ organizations were also successful in overturning the U.S. military's longstanding "don't ask, don't tell" policy, so now gays and lesbians can serve openly in the military. However, in 2017, President Donald Trump attempted to repeal the right for transgender service members to enlist in the armed forces.

Counter to the goals of assimilation, LGBTQ people who take a more liberationist stance have recently been arguing that assimilationists are colluding with the structures of heteronormativity; these liberationists use the term *homonormativity* to describe gays and lesbians that focus on monogamy, procreation, and traditional gender identity. Liberationists speak out against mainstream politics and seek to destabilize social institutions, power structures, and the gender binary. This split inevitably establishes a hierarchy within the gay community that is centered on the level of subscription to a mainstream presentation and values. We see that today, even while there are still debates about how the LGBTQ community believe they should be granted rights (whether through assimilationist or liberationist methods), ultimately both groups are striving for the same outcome—the end of discrimination and prejudice that keeps LGBTQ people second-class citizens.

A lot has changed in American society since the 1950s and 1960s, when the postal service refused to carry LGBTQ publications, when cities like New York still had laws requiring that everyone wear at least "three articles of gender appropriate clothing," and when police would frequently raid bars like the Stonewall Inn in order to harass their patrons. We live in a world where we see more gay characters on television, more "out" gay members in government, and court cases overturning unconstitutional laws. A 2016 Gallup survey found that 4.1 percent of U.S. adults self-identify as LGBT, up from 3.5 percent in 2012. This means there are an estimated 10 million adults who now identify as LGBT in the United States, which is approximately 1.75 million more individuals than in 2012 (Gates, 2017).

LGBTQ inequality nonetheless persists, as does heteronormativity, even if in more subtle forms. LGBTQ people still face violence in their everyday lives and second-class status in most areas of social policy. According to the Federal Bureau of Investigation (2017), in 2016 law enforcement agencies reported 1,218 hate crime offenses based on sexual orientation, and an additional 130 were based on gender identity. And antidiscriminatory policies such as the Equality Act (formerly known as the Employment Non-Discrimination Act) remain unpassed and stuck in congressional committees, despite estimates from the National LGBTQ Taskforce that there are at least 5.4 million LGBTQ workers in the United States. Studies have found that anywhere from 21 to 47 percent of LGBTQ adults faced employment discrimination because they were gay or transgender. More staggering, 90 percent of transgender employees report experiencing some form of harassment or mistreatment on the job. Currently, only 20 states and the District of Columbia have policies protecting employees from discrimination on the basis of sexual orientation and gender identity, and only an additional two states have laws prohibiting discrimination based on sexual orientation.

It will be up to tomorrow's LGBTQ political organizations to tackle these problems—but in doing so, they will likely borrow from the tactics and worldviews of their historical predecessors.

REFERENCES

Federal Bureau of Investigation. 2017. "Hate Crime Statistics, 2016." Retrieved from https://ucr.fbi.gov/hate-crime/2016/topic-pages/incidentsandoffenses.pdf.

Gates, Gary J. 2017. "In U.S., More Adults Identifying as LGBT." *Gallup*, January 11. Retrieved from http://news.gallup.com/poll/201731/lgbt-identification-rises.aspx.

"HOW COULD YOU DO THIS TO ME?" HOW LESBIAN, BISEXUAL, AND QUEER LATINAS NEGOTIATE SEXUAL IDENTITY WITH THEIR FAMILIES

KATIE ACOSTA

Latina/o studies scholars have explored the role of sexuality in Latina/o familial relationships (Espin, 1997; Hurtado, 2003; Gonzalez-Lopez, 2005; Zavella, 2003). Yet this work has predominantly focused on familial tensions regarding heterosexual sexuality and virginity. In this [reading], I explore the unique tensions that sexual nonconformity creates in Latina families by exploring the complex relationships that lesbian, bisexual, and queer (LBQ) Latinas have with their families of origin. I describe how disclosure and nondisclosure of one's sexual identity changes these women's relationships with their families. The questions driving this [reading] are: What strategies do first- and second-generation Latinas use when negotiating sexual nonconformity with their families? How do age, economic autonomy, and geographic location affect these relationships? How do these women minimize the risk of rejection from families?

I propose that sexually nonconforming Latinas' relationships with family cannot be placed into simple categories of acceptance or rejection. I offer three distinct interaction strategies that study participants report engaging in with their families of origin: (1) erasure of nonconformity, (2) sexual silencing, and (3) avoidance after disclosure. *Erasure of nonconformity* occurs when the respondent discloses her lesbian, bisexual, or queer identity to her family and they in turn try to erase it by using control and manipulation tactics. *Sexual silencing* is a strategy used by respondents who chose not to disclose their sexuality and instead are com-plicit with their family members in pretending their relationships with women are platonic friendships. Even though there is no disclosure with the silencing strategy, respondents believe everyone is silently aware of their same-sex relationships. Last, the *avoidance after disclosure* strategy occurs when the respondents do disclose their lesbian, bisexual, or queer identity to family members and then become complicit with them in rendering the disclosure unheard. With this strategy, families and participants choose to separate the sexual nonconformity completely from family life. This strategy is different from the silencing strategy because it involves direct communication about the sexual nonconformity followed by a clear rejection. This strategy is also distinct from the erasure strategy because with avoidance, the respondents and their families are complicit in separating the lesbian, bisexual, or queer self from family life whereas with the erasure strategy the participants do not have that choice. . . .

FAMILISM AND NEGOTIATING SEXUALITY IN *LA FAMILIA*

Scholars have established that familism, a concept that emphasizes loyalty, solidarity, and interdependence with family, is very important for

Mexican populations and vital to their survival as immigrants in the United States (Baca-Zinn, 1982). Familism has been recognized as a core value for other Latino groups as well (Vega, 1995). However, Latinos are not monolithically familistic in their values, and familism is not unique to Latina/o populations. The values of familism may vary greatly according to class, generation in the United States, and immigrant status. . . .

The values of familism are (1) familial support, the belief that one must support family in their time of need; (2) familial interconnectedness, the belief that family must remain physically and emotionally close when possible; (3) familial honor, the belief that the individual is responsible for preserving the family name; and (4) subjugation of self for family, the belief that an individual must respect family rules (Lugo-Steidel and Contrerars, 2003). *La familia*, however, does not just consist of a mother, father, and children but very often includes aunts and uncles, grandparents, compadres/coparents, and padrinos/godparents (Suarez-Orozeo, 2002). *La familia*, then, is crucial in shaping experience. When it comes to sexuality, the role of *la familia* is particularly vital. The family has the ability to control and shape Latinas' sexual or romantic relationships, and mothers in particular are the enforcers of sexual morality and heterosexuality (Gonzalez-Lopez, 2005).

Latinas sometimes grow up experiencing silence regarding sexuality, changes in their bodies, and same-sex attractions (Carillo, 2002; Zavella, 2003). What messages they do receive are heteronormative in nature, emphasizing virginity, purity, and saving oneself for marriage (Espin, 1997; Hurtado, 2003). In a study of Puerto Rican and Dominican families, Diane Mckee and Allison Karasz (2006) found that while both mothers and daughters valued two-way open communication regarding sex, sexuality, and nurturing *confianza*, both were apprehensive about participating in these conversations (Mckee and Karasz, 2006). Their hesitancy to initiate these conversations resulted in

sexual silencing. Among some Latina groups, sexual silences are combined with messages of empowerment through education and independence from men (Ayala, 2006). Still, while some Latinas are encouraged to empower themselves and not become distracted by the needs of men, the silences around relationships with women prevail. Socially acceptable intimacy among Latinas can include sharing *consejos* or advice and care work and physical displays of affection. Yet while these intimate female bonds are encouraged, lesbianism is still stigmatized (Espin, 1997; Zavella, 1997). . . .

THEORETICAL FRAMEWORK

This [reading] utilizes a dramaturgical perspective to analyze lesbian, bisexual, and queer Latinas' social interactions with their families. Erving Goffman notes that in our everyday lives we present ourselves to others based on our internalized understandings of cultural values and social expectations in order to gain acceptance from others. In this way, we manage the impressions of ourselves that we give off to others and behave as performers of a role. Others, however, are also engaging in this performance by going along with our presentations and by managing their own impressions (Goffman, 1959). The interactional strategies that lesbian, bisexual, and queer Latinas engage in with their families demonstrate this process in action. . . .

METHODS

The data for this study consist of in-depth interviews and participant observations that were carried out between 2006 and 2008. There were forty formal interviews conducted in addition to numerous informal conversations that I engaged in at LGBTQ events as part of the participant-observation process. The interviews were conducted in Massachusetts, Connecticut, New York, and New Jersey, and the participant observation took place primarily in New York City. As of 2000, New York, New Jersey, and Massachusetts were among ten states with the largest Latin American immigrant populations. Massachusetts, Connecticut, New York, and New Jersey are also among the ten U.S. states with the largest Caribbean population (Migration Policy Institute, n.d.). The high concentration of immigrants of Latin American or Caribbean descent in this region made it an appropriate area to conduct this research.

All formal interviewees self-identified as lesbian, bisexual, or queer Latinas, were at least 18 years of age, and lived in the geographic northeast. Participants ranged in age from 19 to 54. Eighteen of the participants were first-generation Latinas, and 22 were second-generation Latinas. . . . The study consisted of 11 Puerto Ricans, seven Dominicans, six Mexicans or Chicanas, six Peruvians, three Colombians, three Nicaraguans, two Cubans, one Guatemalan, and one Ecuadorian. Their class backgrounds varied greatly. The second-generation Latinas were predominantly raised working-class although many are currently middle-class due to achievements in higher education. In contrast, the first-generation Latinas were predominantly raised middle- to upper-class in their countries of origin. Half of these women suffered downward social mobility after migrating to the United States; the other half were mostly Puerto Rican migrants whose class level either elevated or remained the same after migration. . . . Thirty of the study participants identified as lesbian, three as queer, and seven as bisexual. . . .

ANALYSES

When I asked the interviewees to tell me about their relationships with their families of origin, they often shared with me their struggles with their mothers. Consistent with previous findings, study participants' mothers were overwhelmingly the major enforcers of sexual morality and heterosexuality in their lives (Gonzalez-Lopez, 2005). Study participants report having received more resistance and nonacceptance from their mothers than from any other member in their families. The participants report their mothers reacting to their disclosure with questions like "how could you do this to me?" or "I raised you better than that." The participants believe their mothers saw their sexual nonconformity as a reflection on their parenting and as an outcome to their failure to effectively teach normative sexuality. None of the forty study participants were disowned by family members for their sexual nonconformity. Families were often not accepting of Latinas' same-sex relationships and/or sexual orientations, but they did not rebuke these women entirely. Nonetheless, familial reactions caused guilt in the study participants and led them to engage in the invisible work of appeasing these relationships.

Erasing Nonconformity

The erasure strategy was commonly used by families as a way of rejecting their daughters without disowning them. Erasure of nonconformity predominantly occurred between very young study participants (women between the ages of 19 and 25) and those who were economically dependent on their families. The participants' young age and financial dependency made them most susceptible to the erasure strategy. Families engaging in the erasure strategy gain leverage against their loved ones because of their lack of autonomy as well as because of their respect for family values. The erasure strategy is premised on hypermanipulation and control, and families engaging in this strategy attempt to force their daughters out of dating other women. When Mariela was 16 years old, someone caught her kissing her girlfriend Alisa. Her mother confronted her, and thereafter their relationship was greatly compromised. Her experience represents the kind of familial rejection that was common with the erasure strategy. Mariela is a second-generation Colombian. She described her situation in the following ways:

So my mom approached me about it and said "oh what is this all about? How dare you? How could you do this to me? Haven't I taught you better? I told you she [Alisa] was a bad influence on you." My mom said this is going to *end right now.* She was in such a shock that all she did was yell and beat me up. But I tried to tell her this is something I chose to do. It's not because I felt influenced by anybody. But she didn't believe me. One of [the] things my mom didn't do is tell my dad. She would never tell him because she thinks he'd commit suicide if he ever found out. So she made me promise her that night that I would never tell him either.

Several years after this altercation with her mother, Mariela has kept her promise to not come out to her father. By saying that her father would commit suicide if he knew about her lesbianism, Mariela's mother is manipulating her daughter's emotions and heightening her control over her on the basis of the secret they share. Mariela's behaviors inside and outside the home are premised on the fact that she promised to keep her lesbian self a secret from her father. Latinas' subjugated position in patriarchal societies has compromised their ability to negotiate sexual nonconformity with family members. Their value on *"no faltar el respeto"* or to not be disrespectful makes them susceptible to hypercontrol as the women in their families enforce patriarchy. . . .

The study participants who engaged in erasure strategies with their parents overwhelmingly report feeling the burden of having to fulfill their parents' dreams. They bear the burden of accomplishing not only their goals but also the goals that their parents could not accomplish on account of a lack of opportunities. They overwhelmingly report taking pride in having always been "good girls" who excelled in school and carried their family's hopes and dreams proudly. Coming out to their families as women who love other women often means shattering the dreams their families had for them in order to pursue their own desires. . . .

Families engaging in erasure strategies often defer to religion as a way of rationalizing their rejection. This was the case even for families that were not otherwise very religious. In some ways, for families that are uncomfortable with their daughters' choices, religion becomes a shield that protects them from the things that make them uneasy. Kayla, a second-generation Puerto Rican who identifies as a lesbian, met her first female partner while attending college. When Kayla told her mother that she was in a relationship with another woman, her mother immediately pointed her in the direction of the church. Kayla recounts this experience below:

My mother said you need to go speak to a priest. The next day I went and found where the priest lives on campus. Father John answered the door. And I started crying right there in the doorway. He sits me down in this little area that they have right by the door and asks, "What's the matter?" And I said, "I just told my mom that I'm in a relationship with a woman. I told her that I'm gay." And then he said something that set me free. He said, "You know what, there's nothing wrong with giving your love to another human being, and that's all that you are doing." I asked specifically, "Am I going to be kicked out of the church?" He's like no, no. I said, "Can I tell my mom that?" He said yes.

Kayla's parents sent her to see a priest because they wanted her to confess her "sin." She went to this church full of anxiety and half expecting to be rejected yet again. Instead, Father John gave her the ammunition she needed to take down her parents' protective shield. By telling her that she was still welcome in the church and that she was not committing a sin, Father John gave Kayla what she needed to confront her parents. In her eyes, they could no longer use religion as an excuse to not accept her.

Respondents whose families engaged in erasure strategies often had self-esteem issues. For these women more so than for any other Latinas in this study, erasure created insecurities, vulnerability, and sometimes internal self-hate. These women were more likely than those in any other group to be manipulated by family members because of their age and financial dependency. Furthermore, they were ill-equipped to handle a world without familial support.

Silencing Strategies

Not all the study participants' families engaged in erasure strategies. Some participants engaged in silencing strategies with their families. Among the migrant Latinas, it was common for participants to never have had candid conversations with their parents about their sexual nonconformity. Nor have their parents ever confronted them about it. Rather, both the study participants and their families have taken to silencing this aspect of their lives altogether.

The study participants and their families have found protection in strategies of sexual silence. Sexual silence is a way for families to tacitly accept sexual nonconformity without ever directly acknowledging it. This strategy has also been referred to as *"un secreto a voz"* or an open secret (Zavella, 1997). It allows individuals to meet the expectations of normalcy because no one acknowledges or verbalizes the transgressions. Study participants rationalize sexual silencing strategies as their way of remaining respectful of their families. These relationships resemble a tacit agreement in which the families do not meddle in their daughters' personal lives and in return the

daughters conduct themselves respectfully and discreetly. Scholars have found that among Latino gay men and men who have sex with men (MSM), *"de eso no se habla"* is a tacit agreement that allows individuals to engage in same-sex behavior outside of the home and away from their families and in return their families turn a blind eye on these activities (Carillo, 2002; Lumsden, 1996). However, the dynamic taking place between these Latina women who love women and their kin is slightly different. This is not something that occurs away from the home but something that occurs in the home when no one is looking. The families do not pressure their daughters to have relationships with men, to get married, or to have children, and the daughters lead everyone to believe that their female lovers are just *"amigas"* or friends who sleep over on the weekends.

Angelica lived in her parents' home until she immigrated to the United States from the Dominican Republic in her thirties. She had several lovers while living with her parents. She describes the agreement in her home in the following ways:

They always preferred to think that I was a very studious girl, than to see the reality, which was that I didn't have a boyfriend. That the few people that I brought home were women. What they have always seen in me is female friendships. And they have met my partners without knowing they are my partners. Because the ones that I've had stable relationships with have come to my house. They've met my parents and have established relationships with them. But I've never actually come out and said I'm gay. The partner that I have now, I've been with her for five years. When I lived in Santo Domingo and she lived here [in the United States], she would come on vacation and she would stay in my house. If [my family] didn't see it, it's because they didn't want to see it.

Here, Angelica describes the avoidance strategy she engages in with her family. The difference between this type of sexual silencing and *de eso no se habla* is that Angelica's parents always knew her partners. They developed relationships with these partners and welcomed them into their home as their daughter's "*amigas*" or friends. For them, then, sexual silence is not about keeping same-sex intimacy outside the home but about engaging in such relationships under the guise of platonic friendship. . . .

. . . The utility of sexual silencing strategies is that they allow families to avoid shame in their communities. So long as lesbian, bisexual, and queer Latinas do not openly display their sexual transgression, the families are allowed to save face with the community. For this reason, these families continuously ignore Latinas' intimacy with "*amigas*" and their lack of interest in men. Family members and study participants are complicit in maintaining sexual silence because it allows them to preserve their familial bond and deflect the tumultuous complications that can come with disclosure. Participants engaging in silencing strategies were fortified by the belief that their families did accept them even if only tacitly, which is something that Latinas engaging in erasure strategies or avoidance strategies did not get. . . .

Sometimes silencing strategies were not just about pretending that participants' lovers were just *amigas*. In an effort to minimize rejection, sometimes participants took silencing strategies even further by pretending that they were in relationships with men. Some of the sexually nonconforming women who engaged in silencing strategies with their families pretend to have relationships with gay male friends in order to help keep up the ruse. . . .

The Latinas who held this type of agreement with their families report not wanting to bring them shame. They internalized the importance of maintaining familial honor by being discreet about their transgressions. They were greatly concerned with how their parents would be treated in the community as well as by other family members if the sexual silence was broken. In the event that disclosure did happen, mothers tried to hide this information from other family members and friends. In these instances, however, families sometimes shift from maintaining sexual silence to the avoidance after disclosure strategy.

Avoidance after Disclosure

The third arrangement that study participants reported engaging in with their families is avoidance after disclosure. This strategy can occur when participants disclose or are forced to disclose their sexual nonconformity to families but later choose with their families to render the disclosure unheard altogether. With avoidance after disclosure, it is no longer okay for Latinas to bring *amigas* home. By verbalizing the sexual transgression, new guidelines must be established whereby what Latinas do must remain unknown or out of sight. This is because after verbalization, acceptance is no longer possible.

Study participants and their families can maintain seemingly ordinary relationships by not ever acknowledging their romantic dealings with women and pretending the disclosure never occurred. Diana is a young graduate student at a prestigious university. A second-generation Dominican, she was raised by a single mother in New York City. She lives on her college campus during the school year and comes home to her mother in the summer. When Diana's mother learned she was dating women, she panicked. She entered a state of denial and tried to find a therapist to "cure" her daughter. She convinced herself that her daughter's dealings with women were part of a phase. Since this time, Diana and her mother have found a way to maintain their relationship by never discussing her queer existence. Diana describes this avoidance strategy: "It was tense for a long time. She didn't know who I was. She didn't know who she was dealing with. But we're really, really close so we got back into the swing of things and kind of, you know, we didn't talk about it, didn't really mention it. We are pretending like nothing really exists when it comes to that [the disclosure of her queer identity]." Diana's arrangement with her mother allows her to maintain two separate lives. She has the life that she shares with her lovers and LGBTQ friends and another life that she shares with her family of origin. Because her relationship with her family is contingent upon everyone pretending the disclosure never happened, these two worlds do not coexist or overlap as they do with families utilizing the silencing strategies.

Sometimes, for participants, the separation of these two worlds is maintained through geography. Maritza immigrated to the United States because her mother discovered that Lourdes, a woman she accepted in her home as her daughter's *amiga*, was in fact her lover. Once her mother learned this information, the relationship between Maritza and her family became poisonous. Immigrating to the United States became a way for Maritza to create distance between them, and over time the family came to engage in avoidance after disclosure. This separation allows Maritza and her family to maintain their bond in a way that may not have been possible in Peru.

Like all the other strategies, avoidance after disclosure comes at a price. The erasure, silence, or avoidance of Latinas' lesbian, bisexual, or queer selves can often result in their isolation. These Latinas were often raised to keep their problems within the family and to only share their struggles with their parents and siblings and not with friends or psychologists. Given this, when family members render their same-sex relationships unheard or try to erase or silence them, Latinas can be left with no one to turn to in grappling with the difficulties of their same-sex relationships. . . .

This experience speaks to how vulnerable these Latinas can be when their families are not fully accepting of their sexual nonconformity. It often leaves these women with no one to turn to in the event of physical or emotional abuse. . . .

Despite the fact that family members try to erase, silence, or avoid an important part of their selves, these women have not given up on their kin. On the contrary, they have rationalized their family's hurtful reactions and healed their own wounds in their efforts to forgive their families. In many ways, they continue to subject themselves to familial abuse because they have such a strong sense that family is central to their happiness. . . . The study participants were not judgmental of their families for rejecting them, and they did not turn away from their families even when their families gave them reason to do so. Instead, they have found ways to remain hopeful that their families would eventually move toward acceptance.

DISCUSSION AND CONCLUSIONS

This [reading] highlights the interactional strategies LBQ Latinas engaged in with family members at first disclosure, but this is just a small segment of their relationships. These options do not exhaust the possibilities, nor are they static interactions. Participants' relationships with their families often changed over time. Sometimes they became healthier as the respondents and their family members had more time to change their outlooks and embrace their fears. . . .

The strategies that study participants engaged in cannot be reduced to a narrative of remaining in the closet. One cannot simply look at the closet as something that you are either in or out of. These women negotiate very complex arrangements with their families and lovers. As Decena notes, the closet is a coproduction. The family is just as complicit as the individual in maintaining the strategies described in this [reading]. Arguably, those who had never disclosed and used a silencing strategy were the most successful in combining their sexual lives with their family lives. Those who had engaged in verbal disclosures were less able to combine these two aspects of the self. Therefore, the Western notion of "coming out of the closet" did not really exist for these participants in the way that we presume it does for non-Latinos. . . .

REFERENCES

Ayala, Jennifer. 2006. "Confianza, Consejos, and Contradictions: Gender and Sexuality Lessons between Latina Adolescent Daughters and Mothers." In *Latina Girls: Voices of Adolescent Strength in the United States.* Jill Denner and Bianca Guzman (eds.), 29–43. New York: New York University Press.

Baca-Zinn, Maxine. 1982. "Familism among Chicanos: A Theoretical Review." *Humboldt Journal of Social Relations* 10 (1): 224–38.

———.1998. "Race and the Family Values Debate." In *Challenges for Work and Family in the 21st Century,* Danna Vannoy and Paula Dube (eds.), 49–62. Piscataway, NJ: Aldine Transaction.

Carillo, Héctor. 2002. *The Night Is Young: Sexuality in Mexico in the Time of AIDS.* Chicago: University of Chicago Press.

Espin, Oliva. 1997. *Latina Realities: Essays on Healing, Migration, and Sexuality.* Boulder. CO: Westview.

Goffman. Erving. 1959. *The Presentation of Self in Everyday Life.* New York: Anchor.

Gonzalez-Lopez, Gloria. 2005. *Erotic Journeys: Mexican Immigrants and Their Sex Lives.* Berkeley: University of California Press.

Hurtado, Aida. 2003. *Voicing Chicana Feminism: Young Women Speak Out on Sexuality and Identity.* New York: New York University Press.

Lugo-Steidel, Angel, and Josefina Contrerars. 2003. "A New Familism Scale for Use with Latino Populations." *Hispanic Journal of Behavioral Sciences* 25 (3): 312–30.

Lumsden, Ian. 1996. *Machos, Maricones, and Gays: Cuba and Homosexuality.* Philadelphia: Temple University Press.

Mckee, Diane, and Allison Karasz. 2006. "You Have to Give Her that Confidence: Conversations about Sex in Mother-Daughter Dyads." *Journal of Adolescent Research* 21 (2): 158–84.

Migration Policy Institute. http://www.migrationpolicy.org (accessed August 3, 2009).

Suarez-Orozco, Carola. 2002. "Commentary." In *Latinos Remaking America,* Marcelo Suarez-Orozco and Mariela Paez (eds.), 302–05. Berkeley: University of California Press.

Vega, William. 1995. "The Study of Latino Families: A Point of Departure." In *Understanding Latino Families: Scholarship, Policy, and Practice.* edited by Ruth Zambrana, 3–17. Thousand Oaks, CA: Sage.

Weston, Kath, 1991. *Families We Choose: Lesbians, Gays. Kinship.* New York: Columbia University Press.

Zavella, Patricia. 1997. "Playing with Fire: The Gendered Construction of Chicana/Mexicana Sexuality." In *The Gender/Sexuality Reader: Culture, History, Political Economy,* Roger Lancaster and Micaela di Leonardo (eds.), 392–410. New York: Routledge.

———. 2003. "Talkin' Sex: Chicanas and Mexicans Theorize about Silences and Sexual Pleasures." In *Chicana Feminisms: A Critical Reader,* Gabriela Arredondo, Aida Hurtado, Norma Klahn, Olga Najera-Ramirez, and Patricia Zavella (eds.), 228–53. Durham, NC: Duke University Press.

SEXUAL VIOLENCE

AN INTERVIEW WITH

KEVIN SWARTOUT

Kevin Swartout is an associate professor of psychology and public health at Georgia State University. His research interests are trajectories and social correlates of violence and victimization, as well as measurement and data analysis issues specifically related to violence research. Dr. Swartout has received early-career awards from the International Society for Research on Aggression, the Southeastern Psychological Association, and Georgia State University.

What led you to study sexuality, and sexual violence in particular?

It might seem cliché, but I was shocked when, as a first-year doctoral student, I first learned that one in five women will experience sexual assault by the time they graduate college. This was before conversations about women's experiences with violence and harassment entered our general public discourse. At the time I probably would have guessed that the rate was less than 5 percent. I remember thinking: "How could I have missed this?" and "Does everyone know about this?" I asked some of my friends, most of whom were as shocked as I was. The knowledge that women experience sexual assault at epidemic-level incidence rates—and that those outside of academia were largely oblivious at the time—compelled me to devote my career to help better understand and ultimately prevent sexual violence.

I was very fortunate to be mentored as a graduate student by Dr. Jacquelyn White—a pioneering feminist psychologist. She had studied violence against women for over 35 years by the time I came to work with her. Through her mentorship, I focused my research on sexual violence perpetration to inform primary prevention approaches. Together, we began to question our fundamental understanding of the men who perpetrate sexual violence, with an emphasis on college men who perpetrate. We soon developed a more nuanced understanding of these men in regard to when they are likely to perpetrate as well as risk and protective factors for perpetration. It was exciting to contribute to such an important literature at that early stage of my career. Even better: the thought that my research might ultimately contribute to reducing sexual violence rates.

How do people respond when they hear about your research?

In general, people are surprised to learn that my research is focused on sexual violence, which is traditionally thought of as a *women's issue*. It's obviously a human rights issue, but old ideas die hard. People seem quite interested once they get past this initial cognitive dissonance, though. Nowadays, most people I talk with about my research already know the "one in five" statistic, so I typically have no trouble conveying the significance of my work. And audiences typically have no trouble applying my research findings to their understanding or experiences related to sexual violence.

It has been a slightly different story outside of academic settings. I spent a lot of time in coffee shops while writing my dissertation, which focused on how college men's social networks influence their sexual violence perpetration. I liked to set up in a quiet corner of the shop, organize my articles on the table, and sometimes stay there for the better part of a day. On one such day, I kept noticing people giving me funny looks, almost sneers. This made me very self-conscious. Was I taking up too much space? Was I making too much noise as I typed? It took me a while to realize that people were likely reacting to the book I had propped in front of my face the entire morning, with the prominently inscribed title *The Handbook of Sexual Assault*. I can only imagine the attributions others in the coffee shop made about me that day; based on their responses, few assumed I was a doctoral student pushing forward on my dissertation literature review.

Which of your research projects (involving sexuality) have you found most interesting? Why?

Sexually violent college men and victimized college women have traditionally both been considered homogeneous groups. My research has revealed they are not. I have conducted a series of research projects that describe heterogeneity among either aggressors or victims. For example, one study described trajectories of college men's rape perpetration across their pre-college and college years (Swartout, Koss, White, Thompson, Abbey, and Bellis, 2015). I analyzed the two largest longitudinal data sets of college men's sexually violent behavior available at the time and uncovered three cohesive trajectories: men who had a low or time-limited, decreasing, or increasing likelihood of perpetrating rape. This pattern of findings contradicted the prevailing notion at the time that most college men who perpetrate rape are consistent offenders.

A more nuanced picture emerges when using a broader operationalization of sexual violence—nonconsensual sexual behavior that does not necessarily meet legal definitions for rape. In two studies where I used this operationalization, I found evidence for four trajectories of college men's sexual violence perpetration (Swartout, Swartout, Brennan, and White, 2015; Thompson, Swartout, and Koss, 2013). There was a class of men that consistently perpetrated acts of sexual violence in both of these studies, although follow-up analyses revealed that the sexual violence these men were likely to perpetrate did not meet definitions of rape or attempted rape; rather, it constituted unwanted sexual contact or verbal coercion.

I have also uncovered heterogeneity of college women's sexual violence victimization patterns (Swartout, Swartout, and White, 2011). Taken together across all of these studies of college students' violence and victimization trajectories, many of the students who will perpetrate or experience violence before or during college tend to either decrease or increase in risk soon after college matriculation. This robust finding suggests that one or more elements involved with either the transition to college or the college environment affects students' risk for perpetrating or experiencing violence. The results of these studies are interesting and important because they signal the need for sexual violence prevention and risk reduction programming that begins earlier than college matriculation and extends throughout students' college experiences.

Can you describe some of the findings from your recent research?

Along the lines of the research described above, my lab recently conducted a study on profiles of sexually violent college men. Our main goal in this study was to determine whether or not there are cohesive subgroups of college men in regard to the types of sexually violent behaviors they engage in. Our analysis yielded three groups of college men: a large group that is not likely to perpetrate any sexual violence; a smaller group likely to perpetrate sexual violence using verbal coercion or victim intoxication but not threats or physical force; and finally a group relatively likely to perpetrate the full range of sexually violent behaviors, including threats and physical force. These findings are important because they continue to support the notion that there are multiple subgroups of college men who perpetrate sexual violence and underscore the need for more tailored prevention programming on college campuses focused on different types of offenders.

What ethical challenges or concerns have you faced in your research on sexuality and sexual violence?

Sexual violence is a highly sensitive and personal topic and, to borrow the title of Carol Hanisch's groundbreaking paper, *The Personal Is Political*. The personal and political nature of this topic is especially apparent when I discuss my findings—I have had conversations about my research with a wide variety of people, from sexual assault survivors to university presidents and politicians. It is common for researchers to *spin* their findings to maximize their impact on the field. I try to guard against those urges and to offer interpretations and recommendations that are solidly supported by my data.

If you could teach people one thing about sexuality, what would it be?

I subscribe to the belief that as a society we do not talk enough about what constitutes healthy, consensual sex. Sometimes people draw false parallels between consensual sexual behavior and nonconsensual behaviors that amount to sexual harassment or violence. This can lead to either demonizing all forms of sexual interaction or permitting harassment and violence.

An example of the latter: a popular rape myth asserts that a woman who agrees to go back to a man's residence after their date is to some degree obliged to have sex with him. Women who are harassed or sexually assaulted in these scenarios are often perceived to be at fault, at least to some degree. People typically defend this opinion by asserting that women "know what they are getting into" in these situations. There are several logical errors at play in this myth. First, why would anyone assume someone else would harass or assault them, especially immediately after a cordial date? It might be fair to assume that a man would request to have sex after they got to his place; a request the woman would be free to deny, and that would be it. Many couples agree to have sex during or after dates—it is condescending to suggest that women who are assaulted do not know this. But the key component that seems to get lost here is a woman's right to say no, and her decision should be respected by her date. There is also an element of hindsight bias in this myth: knowing that the date ended in sexual assault leads people to read risk into situations and decisions made leading up to the assault. For a woman to really "know what she was getting into," she would have to know that her date had some proclivity toward sexual violence.

Social conversations about healthy sex and the importance of consent can help address some of these misconceptions, highlighting rape myths when they arise and providing people with alternative narratives to blaming the victim. To change the way that people are socialized to think about sex, sexual violence, and consent, we have to begin early—teaching young boys and girls about bodily autonomy and respect. My hope is that moving forward, people will begin to understand that the critical decision in the scenario above was *not* the woman choosing to go to the man's apartment—it was the man choosing to pursue sexual activity without the woman's consent.

REFERENCES

Swartout, Kevin M., Mary P. Koss, Jacquelyn W. White, Martie P. Thompson, Antonia Abbey, and Alexandra L. Bellis. 2015. "Trajectory analysis of the campus serial rapist assumption." *JAMA Pediatrics* 169(12): 1148–54.

Swartout, Kevin M., Ashlyn G. Swartout, Carolyn L. Brennan, and Jacquelyn W. White. 2015. "Trajectories of male sexual aggression from adolescence through college: A latent class growth analysis." *Aggressive Behavior* 41(5): 467–77.

Swartout, Kevin M., Ashlyn G. Swartout, and Jacquelyn W. White. 2011. "A person-centered, longitudinal approach to sexual victimization." *Psychology of Violence* 1(1): 29–40.

Thompson, Martie P., Kevin M. Swartout, and Mary P. Koss. 2013. "Trajectories and Predictors of Sexually Aggressive Behaviors during Emerging Adulthood." *Psychological Violence* 3(3): 247–59.

"I WASN'T RAPED, BUT . . .": REVISITING DEFINITIONAL PROBLEMS IN SEXUAL VICTIMIZATION

NICOLA GAVEY

When a woman says she wasn't raped but describes an experience of forced, unwanted sexual intercourse, what are we to think? Was she "really" raped, despite disowning that label for her experience? Or does her refusal of the label suggest that her interpretation of the experience as other than rape makes it so? And what does it say about our culture(s) that there can be so much ambiguity over the differential diagnosis of rape versus sex? How should we conceptualize and judge the myriad coercive sexual acts that lie somewhere between rape and consensual sex? Finally, is being the object of violence or coercion always the same thing [as] being the *victim* of such violence or coercion?

In this [reading] I begin to explore some of the convoluted layers of issues in which such questions are embedded. . . . In thinking through and around these questions, I find I can't settle comfortably into a straightforward, unitary position from which to craft an argument. . . . I have concluded . . . that there are indeed murky issues at the interface between (hetero)sex and sexual victimization. Even at the most basic level, I want to talk about and against rape and sexual victimization (as though these are straightforward terms) at the same time as I destabilize these categories, in the belief that this is an important part of the same fight at a different level.

I trace some of the changes in research on rape and sexual victimization over the past two decades and consider some of the implications of the new feminist social science approach. In particular, I consider three points that raise the need to revisit current conventions for conceptualizing sexual victimization. These points concern the concept of the unacknowledged rape victim, the loose distinction between rape and attempted rape, and the use of the term *sexual victimization* to refer to a broad range of arguably normative coercive heterosexual practices. . . .

A STARTING POINT

In the title of this [reading], I refer back to Martha Burt and Rhoda Estep's 1981 paper "Who Is a Victim? Definitional Problems in Sexual Victimization." In their . . . article, Burt and Estep mapped the nascent influence of 1970s feminism on a redefinition and reconceptualization of sexual assault. They endorsed the more inclusive definition of sexual assault that was emerging from feminism at the time, drawing attention to the similarity between rape and other coercive sexual practices. Moreover, they argued strongly for the benefits for all women who have been sexually assaulted to claim the victim role. Although aware of what they called the "negative social value" and the "obligations" of the victim role, they proposed that the benefits would include "the right to claim assistance, sympathy, temporary relief from other role responsibilities, legal recourse, and other similar advantages" (p. 16).

. . . [Using] the language of victimization was imposed as a way of making sense of and opposing the moral injustice of women's oppression in the forms of violence and harassment.

THE "NEW" FEMINIST RESEARCH ON SEXUAL VICTIMIZATION

Since 1981, . . . both feminist activism and feminist social science have been instrumental in promoting a major rethinking of rape—and sexual victimization in many western societies. . . . In a very short time we moved from a climate in which rape was widely regarded as rare to one in which rape is regarded as a widespread social problem. . . .

. . . [F]eminist empirical research was specifically designed to overcome the limitations of previous estimates of rape prevalence (which relied on reports of rape to the police or reports in national crime surveys). . . . This work introduced an important methodological point of departure from any previous attempts to measure the scope of rape. Women were asked not whether they had been raped[1] but rather whether they had had any experiences that matched behavioral descriptions of rape. For example, they were asked whether they had ever had sexual intercourse when they didn't want to because a man threatened or used some degree of physical force to make them do so (e.g., Koss et al., 1987). Moreover, this question was one among many such specific questions that women would be asked about a range of coercive sexual experiences. Such methodological refinements were designed to be sensitive to women's reluctance to report rape. They were seemingly successful, and the body of research produced shocking new data showing widespread rape and sexual victimization.

At the same time, two other important changes to the picture of rape emerged from this research. First, Diana Russell (1982; 1984)—and later, others—showed that women were far more likely to be raped by husbands, lovers, boyfriends, and dates than by strangers. Not only were the cultural blinkers that had enabled this to be regarded as "just sex" lifted, but it was found that such rapes were far more common than the stereotypical rape by a stranger. Second, . . . while rape [was] the extreme act, it [was] regarded as being on a continuum with more subtle forms of coercion, from an unwanted kiss to unwanted sexual intercourse submitted to as a result of continual verbal pressure. . . .

[These changes] have two important effects: (1) They construe experiences that would have previously fallen within the realm of sex as forms of sexual *victimization;* and (2) they implicitly invite a critical examination of the whole realm of normal heterosexual practice. . . .

Against a backdrop where rape was considered to be rare—and where complaints of rape were commonly regarded to be lies, distortions of normal sex, harmless, or provoked by the victim—the call to broaden the definition of sexual assault and victimization has been an important feminist move. Similarly, the way in which we have elaborated on the understanding of rape as a form of *victimization* has arguably contributed to more widespread concern about rape as a serious social problem. These moves [were] one part of increased focus during the 1980s on many forms of victimization, and of widespread social concern for understanding their extent and dynamics and for ameliorating and preventing their harm.

"VICTIMIZATION" IN CRISIS

[By] the late 1990s, the concept of victimization [was] arguably in crisis. Joel Best (1997) opened a . . . *Society* commentary with the unfavorable verdict that "victimization has become fashionable" (p. 9). As Richard Feldstein (1997) . . .

observed, the term *victim* . . . has been targeted for critique by neoconservatives in the United States. . . . As part of more general conservative campaigns against research and services relating to victimization, there has been critical dispute over the new feminist research on rape—especially that on "date rape." It has been claimed that the issue has been exaggerated or that it has no validity as a concept (e.g., Gilbert, 1994; Paglia, 1992; Roiphe, 1993; see also Denfeld, 1995; Sommers, 1994; Newbold, 1996). . . .

ARE VICTIMS CREATED BY A VICTIMIZATION FRAMEWORK?

There are many ways to victimize people. One way is to convince them that they are victims.
—(Hwang, 1997, p. 41)

One strand of public concern at the moment is the fear that talk about victimization is needlessly creating victims. Moreover, critics of the movement against date rape have implied that it violates "assumptions of women's basic competence, free will, and strength of character" (Roiphe, 1993, p. 69; see also Paglia, 1992). . . .

There are various ways in which the language of sexual victimization can have material cultural effects. . . . For example, it may reinforce and perpetuate images of women as weak, passive, and asexual and images of men as sexually driven, unstoppable, and potentially dangerous. These gendered ways of being may be further enhanced by the exacerbation of women's fears about rape through media reportage and through warnings about violent sexual attacks that emphasize women's vulnerability to rape over their potential for resistance. . . . A rapist's moral infringement prescribes an experience of victimization for the rape *victim* . . . [and a] particular psychological outcome is preconfigured by calling the violence "victimization."

. . . [H]ow valid is the sort of seductive public warning in Karen Hwang's point [quoted above]? Are victims really created out of thin air? When feminists and other social critics name certain practices as victimization, they are drawing attention to the relationships of power that systematically privilege the experiences of some groups of people over those of others. Is the hysterical anxiety behind the suggestion that talking about victimization creates victimization a sort of head-in-the-sand approach to unpleasant social conditions—a naive hope that if a phenomenon is not seen and not heard, then it does not exist? . . . [C]ommentators such as Katie Roiphe suggest that "prior to the discourse of date rape, the experience itself did not occur, or at least not with such traumatizing after-effects as we now associate with rape" (p. 16). . . .

In light of the backlash crisis of representation of victimization . . . , it is perhaps time to revisit Martha Burt and Rhoda Estep's (1981) contention that it is in a woman's best interests to be perceived as a victim when she has experienced sexual coercion or violence. It is difficult to know how to evaluate this claim, and our attempts may benefit from some empirical analysis of women's accounts of their experiences of coercion, abuse, and violence. Few would deny that what we refer to as rape, sexual assault, sexual coercion, and sexual abuse can be victimizing. That is, they can be horrific events that traumatize women[2] and produce victims. Moreover, abusive and coercive practices can produce victims in more subtle and less horrific ways, through undermining a woman's confidence and eroding her agency over time. In the fight against rape, public feminist rhetoric has tended to privilege one of the many contradictory broader cultural meanings of rape—that is, its power to cause severe and irrevocable psychological harm to the victim. Those of us drawn to activism against rape often have firsthand knowledge of the effects of rape on friends, family members, women we have worked with, or ourselves. The potential trauma and devastating harm of rape, silenced and hidden for so many years, have now come to be almost automatically signified by the term *rape* (although not without exceptions). . . .

UNACKNOWLEDGED RAPE VICTIMS

As discussed earlier, the new research on rape has tended not to rely on asking women whether or not they have ever experienced "rape." Some studies have included this direct question along with the more specific behavioral questions about forced, unwanted sex. It has been found that only around 30 to 50 percent of women who affirm they have had an experience that meets a narrow definition of rape identify that they have experienced "rape" (e.g., Koss, 1988; Gavey, 1991a; 1991b). . . . [T]his research paradigm has . . . categorize[d] women as victims of rape if they report having had an experience consistent with the predetermined behavioral description that researchers define as rape when the questionnaires or structured interview data are analyzed. If these women do not report that they have experienced "rape" (when asked directly), then they are considered "unacknowledged" rape victims by the researchers (e.g., Koss, 1985). . . .

 . . . [S]ocial critics have targeted this feature of the feminist empirical work on rape prevalence as a major weakness of the whole body of research.[3] Neil Gilbert (1994), for example, cites as a problem of Koss's rape prevalence estimates that "almost three-quarters of the students whom Koss defined as victims of rape did not think they had been raped" (p. 23). . . . Ironically, this methodological approach is totally consistent with the positivist conventions of social and behavioral psychology . . . , where it is considered good research practice to use operational definitions for specifying precise categories of behavior that can be reliably measured. . . . For instance, it would be considered valid to classify a person as "depressed" if he or she answered a range of questions on a depression inventory in the predicted ways, even if the individual did not affirm the statement "I am depressed."

Let us consider an example of the sort of experience that could be described as an unacknowledged rape. One woman I interviewed described an experience, which occurred when she was nineteen, of waking to find her thirty-year-old male apartment mate in her bed, "groping" her (Gavey, 1990; 1992). She had no prior sexual or romantic relationship with this man, but on this night he got into her bed while she was asleep and had intercourse with her, with no apparent consideration of her lack of interest. She explained:

Ann: . . . it all happened quite quickly really, but I remember thinking quite clearly, "Well, if I don't— If I try and get out of the bed, perhaps if I run away or something . . . he might rape me [pause] so I had better just . . ."
Nicola: If you try and run away you mean?
Ann: If I tried it, if I'd resisted, then he might rape me, you know. So he did anyway, sort of thing, really, when you think about it, when I look back.

This man was rough and left her bleeding. Later, she was frightened, "confused," "nervous within the house," and hypervigilant about making sure she was never asleep before he'd gone to bed. . . . Nevertheless, Ann did not conceptualize this event as rape at the time.

Technically, this encounter may not count as rape in a narrow legal sense, because it is unclear how explicitly Ann communicated her nonconsent. Most feminist analyses, however, would point out the restraints on her being able to do this, such as being only just awake and fearing that her resistance might lead to worse treatment. Feminists would also highlight the absence of reasonable grounds for this man assuming consent (e.g., Pineau, 1989). That is . . . it [is not] reasonable for a man to assume that a woman approached when she is asleep in her own bed by a man with whom she had no prior sexual or romantic relationship would be consenting to sex, in the absence of some active communication of this consent. Consequently, many feminists would describe this incident as rape or, at the very least, sexual assault. Clearly, in spite of Ann's resistance to the identity of rape victim, the experience had a negative psychological impact on her. It is impossible to know how, if at all, the effects would have been different had she viewed what happened as rape. There is some indication in her account that to have had an experience she would have called "rape" would have been worse—"if I'd resisted, then he might rape me." Indeed, it would have been a different experience and one that may have more powerfully signaled her lack of control and her vulnerability. Psychologically, she perhaps maintained more control (a meager but significant amount) and risked losing less by choosing not to "run away or something" than if she had resisted as hard as she could and been raped anyway.

During our interview several years after this incident, Ann moved toward retrospectively understanding it as rape—after explaining that she did not resist because "he might rape me," she said "So he did anyway, sort of thing . . . when I look back." . . . [I] struggled with the validity and ethics of labeling Ann a "rape victim" at the time when she did not choose this label herself. However, . . . ambiguity . . . arises in talking about Ann's experience and how to make sense of it in the research context. . . . If this woman's experience is not considered to be rape or some form of sexual assault very close to rape (by her *or* by the man involved *or* by police, judges, and juries *or* by researchers and social theorists), then what is it? Sex? If it can be accepted as just part of the realm of sex, then it redirects a critical spotlight onto heterosexuality itself.

It is worth noting that although Ann "resisted" seeing herself as a rape victim, this did not enable her to resist the assault physically. This illuminates how it would be misleading to assume that *not* being positioned in an overt discourse of rape or victimization somehow protects a woman from sexual assault. In a situation such as that Ann faced, the mark of gender difference imposed on what is a physical contest of sorts already incites certain responses, such as immobility and fear, that aid a rapist in his attack. . . . [T]his suggests that [we need] . . . ways of understanding heterosex that don't leave room for ambiguity over a woman's entitlement to refuse unwanted sex.

A FEMINIST RESPONSE—THE METHODOLOGY

With critical reflection on the research strategy of classifying some women as unacknowledged rape victims, what do we want to say in response to the critics but also as part of ongoing . . . research practice? There is probably no straightforward answer, but I think it is important that we approach it as an open question rather than with formulaic answers. Why do so many women who have bad experiences consistent with a legal definition of rape resist the label of "rape victim" (e.g., Koss, 1985)? And how should feminist research respond to these women's rejection of the "rape" label? These questions raise complicated issues that are at the heart of feminist theory about research practice. If we see our role as giving women voice, then it may not be legitimate to "put words in their mouths," to describe experiences as rape that women themselves do not describe in that way. However, feminist research increasingly seeks to go beyond giving women voice and reporting on women's experiences, to offer analyses and critiques that help make sense of women's experiences as they are shaped and constrained by power relations in social contexts. When women's voices don't always tell "our story," it can be troubling to know how to proceed. (See also Fine, 1992; Kitzinger and Wilkinson, 1997.)

Evaluated in this light, the feminist empirical research on rape prevalence occupies an interesting position. In its use of traditional methods to produce conventional data dressed in the language of science rather than that of feminist politics, this research has been an important part of wider feminist action. This action has had some important successes—most notably, changes to rape laws, in many English-speaking countries and in portions of the United States, to recognize rape within marriage as a crime. Widespread publicity about date rape has also led to rape prevention programs on many university campuses. Despite the limited effectiveness of these changes so far (for instance, convictions for wife rape are extremely rare), this body of research has nevertheless had a subversive and transformative role in the changing representations of rape. It has generated a profound shift in the meaning of rape, to the extent that it is no longer impossible to think of a man raping his wife or a sporting hero raping a woman he dated (although this possibility is still more likely to be readily accepted if the man is black). . . .

RESEARCH AND COMPLEXITY

. . . [R]esearch . . . has yielded the findings discussed above at a cost. It has forced closure on definitions of various forms of victimization and classified women's experiences into ready-made categories of victims. This style of methodology necessitates disregard for nuanced and possibly contradictory meanings. Moreover, researchers seem to find it reasonably unproblematic that answers to such basic questions as whether or not a particular experience counts as "rape" are constructed through the research process. The resulting certainty that can be projected about the extent and nature of rape and sexual victimization may eventu-

ally undermine the authority of the findings, when it is found that the reductive and universalizing features of this style of research don't "speak to" the experience of all women whom it ostensibly represents. Not only are decisions about who is and who is not a rape victim not always straightforward, but the partiality of new truths about the effects of rape is sometimes overlooked.

In some instances, women's reactions may be contradictory and not consistent with either dominant traditional or dominant feminist constructions of rape. One woman participating in my research (Gavey, 1990) described a situation with her boyfriend, whereby she said she wanted to say to him, "The very first time we had sex you raped me." However, she didn't always view the forced sex as rape, and she continued her relationship with this man for more than two years. She detailed a complex set of contradictory, ambivalent, and changing reactions to this and other coercive sexual experiences in the relationship. She also discussed how the usual feminist analyses of rape, such as those she later encountered at a rape crisis center, were not entirely helpful. Her reactions were not consistent with what she was hearing about how women respond to rape—because she loved the man who raped her, remembered some of their sex as "wonderful," and so on—she went through a stage of feeling that she must be a "sick" and "masochistic" person. . . .

Feminist accounts of rape need to be able to take account of such women's experiences without, in effect, dismissing them as the result of false consciousness. Carefully listening to and theorizing such ambivalent and confusing experiences may illuminate the complex relationship between heterosexuality and rape. Moreover, it may produce feminist analyses of rape that are sympathetic to all women who are raped, no matter how they experience it.

Although there may be short-term political costs, embracing a more complex and less certain position on the ways in which rape can and does affect women may ultimately be an effective political strategy. By this I mean that psychologists, therapists, and activists should continue to work on understanding, helping, and speaking about the trauma of rape but at the same time be open to accepting, for example, that not all women are traumatized by rape. . . . The notion that it may be possible to experience rape and suffer no lasting devastating psychological effects is less often articulated than is the discourse of harm. But this "finding" about the effects of rape begs the question of whether such research, which once again must compress and order experience into finite categories, is adequate to perceive more subtle, idiosyncratic, and unpredictable psychological effects of rape. . . .

IS ATTEMPTED RAPE SOMETIMES VERY DIFFERENT FROM COMPLETED RAPE?

While some experiences of sexual coercion (and presumably most, if not all, experiences of sexual coercion that fit a narrow definition of rape) are surely victimizing, some possibly are not. Is it possible that our framework for conceptualizing *all* instances of sexual assault, and many instances of unwanted sex, as victimization actually helps constitute some of these experiences as victimizing, when they might otherwise have had effects that were less disabling? Although this question shares the anxiety typical of the backlash positions, it is an important question for feminists. In particular, are experiences of attempted rape and attempted sexual assault *sometimes* very different from actual experiences of rape and sexual assault?

I can think of a personal experience, when I was sixteen, that was probably attempted rape. This episode involved being tricked into stopping at an older male co-worker's place

on the way to a party after we had finished work past midnight on New Year's Eve. I was thrown onto a bed that was just across from the front door of the flat, and he proceeded to jump on top of me and attempt to remove my pants. He was a relatively small man, and I was relatively physically strong from sports, and I remember having to struggle as hard as I could to prevent him [from] removing my pants, with the intention (it seemed to me at the time) of having intercourse with me. (This point also reminds me how it is difficult to judge when a man's actions become "attempted rape" when a man and woman are acquainted and, at some stretch of the imagination, a mutual sexual encounter could be appropriate.) Despite the fact that both of us had been drinking alcohol with other workers at the restaurant where we worked before we left, I was never in any doubt as to my lack of sexual interest in this man—at all, let alone on this occasion. I was not ambivalent in my communication with him and told him clearly, verbally, that I did not want to have sex with him, and I resisted him physically as hard as I could. Yet he seemed to have one goal on his mind, which was unchanged by my refusal. I think it was my relative physical strength that enabled me to resist him vigorously and successfully, to the point that he possibly decided not to keep trying.

Ten years later, when I was working at a sexual abuse counseling agency, the subcultural milieu encouraged me to think back on and identify this experience as attempted rape and to wonder about its negative effects on me. While this was not a totally new way of interpreting this experience, it did [cement] it with more certainty. And it did induce me to scrutinize my past to look for psychological effects of this experience. I recall that I was subsequently worried about this man's "interest" in me and arranged for my mother to pick me up from work on some of the following nights. I also recall that being able to successfully prevent a forceful attempt at unwanted sex left me feeling strong, determined, and invulnerable. Although I can't remember enough of the detail of what followed to be sure there were not also subtle negative effects on my identity and sexuality, it strikes me that such experiences of attempted rape that is successfully repelled are extremely different from experiences of completed rape, in terms of their effect on women. In my case, I did not feel like a victim. I despised his actions, but I did not feel I had been harmed. To the contrary, the effects of his attempt had probably been as empowering as they were disempowering. Was what happened "victimization"? Or is there a better way of describing it that recognizes and celebrates the power of this kind of physical resistance, of fighting back . . . ?

. . . [A]t the time I was imagining the possibility of identifying as an attempted rape victim, it seemed important to join together with women who had been sexually victimized by men, in part to make a political show of solidarity in the face of oppressive acts of male sexuality. However, I never really felt like I properly "belonged," in the sense that I didn't share the legacy of pain that some of the women around me had suffered. Moreover, it backed me into a speaking position that did not fully represent my recollected experience. That adopting an identity as an attempted rape victim would have silenced my different kind of story, which included traces of empowerment, seemed (and still seems) a relatively trivial concern in relation to the political and interpersonal importance of standing alongside women who *had* been harmed. However, perhaps there is more at stake here than some notion of making room for the "authenticity" of experiences like my own. Perhaps there is some political advantage in being able to tell lots of different stories about diverse experiences of sexual violence. In making room for a respectful plurality, we may be able to acknowledge the oppressiveness and potential pain of rape at the same time as igniting discourses that disrupt the possibilities of rape. . . .

Clearly, not all attempted rapes are the same. Some experiences will involve violent and terrifying attacks, where a woman may literally fear for her life. However, the use of behavioral descriptions in surveys to measure the extent of sexual victimization does not distinguish these discrepant possibilities.

EMPHASIZING WOMEN'S STRENGTH

. . . [T]he normative practices of therapy for rape and sexual abuse victims may inadvertently help reinforce some of the effects of victimization through their concern with trauma, recovery, and healing. Again, a particular kind of psychological subject is assumed by such therapy approaches, and arguably, this "recovering" subject is always already constituted as lacking and in need of "betterment."

. . . Sharon Marcus (1992) considers how particular constructions of rape affect the very possibility of rape. . . . Marcus argues that in order to resist rape culture, we need to deny a necessary conflation between the act of rape and irrevocable harm. Marcus's feminist approach to rape is radically different from the approach of Susan Brownmiller's (1975) classic feminist analysis of rape. Marcus (1992) considers that "such a view takes violence as a self-explanatory first cause and endows it with an invulnerable and terrifying facticity which stymies our ability to challenge and demystify rape" (p. 387). She, in contrast, argues that

in its efforts to convey the horror and iniquity of rape, such a view often concurs with masculinist culture in its designation of rape as a fate worse than, or tantamount to, death; the apocalyptic tone which it adopts and the metaphysical status which it assigns to rape implies that rape can only be feared or legally repaired, not fought. (p. 387)

Marcus instead argues for the need to "envision strategies which will enable women to sabotage men's power to rape, which will empower women to take the ability to rape completely out of men's hands" (p. 388). It is sometimes difficult to understand exactly how this sort of transformation could take place, but Marcus's . . . argument is at least suggestive that it may be possible to conceptualize rape differently, in a way that somehow renders it less powerful without trivializing it.

I suggest that a small step in this sort of transformative direction would be the opening up of all sorts of narratives of resistance—by making room for stories about how potential rape was successfully fought, about how some women who are raped do not experience overwhelming psychological despair, and so on. As I suggested earlier, the potential cost of this strategy is that it may do violence to the experience of women who are victimized and traumatized by rape. Sensitivity to this possibility is necessary so that stories of particular kinds of resistance don't come to be privileged in ways that contribute once again to a silencing of women's experiences of victimization.

Apart from concern about the . . . effects of the language of victimization, there are other questions that should be on the minds of feminists. . . . [W]e may need to observe critically the effects of backlash discourse around "victimization." In the ensuing battle over the meaning of victimization, we may need to question which sorts of tactics are most likely to be effective in the political fight against rape. For instance, will the . . . strategy of simply speaking a victim-advocacy position more loudly be sufficient, or will we need to . . . contest the very terms of the debate? . . . [Moreover,] I suggest that an unwanted kiss or touch doesn't always make a *victim,* and the effect of this rhetorical excess in the context of backlash activity may be to weaken the whole struggle against rape by acquaintances, dates,

husbands, and so on. . . . [We must recognize that we live in] a culture of heterosexuality in which power is allowed to infuse sex in different ways for women and men—ways that consistently foreground men's rather than women's rights and desires. . . .

Another problem with the way the framework of victimization is used is that it may implicitly require us to establish psychological harm in order to take a moral stand against violence and against heterosexual practice that is offensive or disrespectful without necessarily being violent (in the usual sense). That is, the injustice of sexual coercion and sexual violence may become too closely tied with the "proof" of psychological damage. . . .

SUPPLEMENTING THE LANGUAGE OF VICTIMIZATION

The new feminist research has come a long way since Burt and Estep's article (1981) in describing the widespread problem of sexual victimization. But has it both gone too far and not gone far enough? Positivist methodologies have required us to iron out complexity, ambivalence, and contradiction. Public expectations of science have reinforced this drive for certainty in the form of concrete, definitive "findings." But when we peep behind the positivist mask, all sorts of discomforting questions arise: Are all instances of sexual coercion always victimizing? Do they always cause harm? For instance, in the arena of attempted sexual assaults, are women sometimes warriors, fighters, heroes? What are the effects of using these different kinds of language? Are the more subtle forms of sexual coercion, argued to be contiguous with rape by some feminists, best conceptualized on a continuum of sexual victimization? Or are there other ways of critiquing heterosexual practice, which routinely privileges men's sexual interests over women's? Or should both strategies be adopted simultaneously?

In case I've overstated my concerns about the language of victimization, I emphasize that I am not arguing for an abandonment of the victimization framework. Rather, I am suggesting that we need to question whether it is always appropriate or wise to talk about all the different forms and occasions of sexual coercion, sexual assault, sexual abuse, and sexual violence as *victimization*. Making connections between everyday sexual practices (such as sexual pressure in a marriage) and sexual violence has been important for highlighting the role of normative culture in sustaining problems such as rape. However, we have not always maintained a distinction between the theorization of, say, a continuum of sexual victimization and the implications for how we then understand men's and women's actions and experiences at the more normative end of the continuum. Using the language of victimization to discuss this territory of the continuum may be theoretically valid yet at the same time (wrongly?) give the impression that we believe every act that falls along the continuum is an act of "victimization," that it makes "victims." I don't think I want to insist every time a woman experiences some unwanted sexual contact, it is an experience of victimization. But far from dismissing such experiences, it seems to me the challenge is to find different ways of critiquing the ways in which our culture(s) can tolerate all sorts of injustices, inequalities, and plain unfairness in the name of normative heterosexuality.

I close this [reading] in a mood of uncertainty. I worry that my questions could lead to unnecessary and undermining problems for the feminist analyses of rape and sexual coercion that I value. Yet I raise these points in a desire to help strengthen and sharpen our critique of victimizing forms of sexual coercion, in ways that help prevent victimization and ameliorate the effects of potentially victimizing acts for individual women. If we don't ask these questions about the victimization framework, I sense we may risk leaving a fertile gap for backlash discourse to take hold. At the same time, this kind of move should create spaces for developing supplementary ways to critique both normative and violent forms of heterosexual practice—without losing sight of the possibility for both rape and more normative forms of sexual coercion to be victimizing. That is, it may enable us to issue new and more varied moral arguments against the cultural acceptance of a form of heterosexual practice in which it can be hard to tell the difference between "just sex" and rape.

NOTES

1. In some of Koss's studies women were asked this direct question in addition to many more of the specific behavioral questions.

2. Of course, men are also raped and sexually abused, but not usually by women. As I am writing largely about the rape and sexual coercion of women in heterosexual relationships, I refer to those who rape as men and those who are raped as women.

3. Another common criticism of this work centers on the ambiguity of questions about unwanted sexual intercourse and unwanted attempts that occurred "because a man gave you alcohol or drugs." Due to the ambiguity of the question, the validity of scoring affirmative responses as "rape" has been questioned. Discussion of this problem with the research is beyond the scope of this [reading].

REFERENCES

Best, J. May/June 1997. Victimization and the victim industry. *Society*, 9–17.

Brownmiller, S. 1975. *Against our will: Men, women and rape.* Harmondsworth: Penguin.

Burt, M. R., and Estep, R. E. 1981. Who is a victim? Definitional problems in sexual victimization. *Victimology: An International Journal* 6, 15–28.

Denfeld, R. 1995. *The new Victorians: A young woman's challenge to the old feminist order.* New York: Warner Books.

Feldstein, R. 1997. *Political correctness: A response from the cultural left.* Minneapolis: University of Minnesota Press.

Fine, M. 1992. *Disruptive voices: The possibilities of feminist research.* Ann Arbor: University of Michigan Press.

Gavey, N. 1990. Rape and sexual coercion within heterosexual relationships: An intersection of psychological, feminist, and postmodern inquiries. Unpublished doctoral thesis, University of Auckland.

———. 1991a. Sexual victimization prevalence among Auckland university students: How much and who does it? *New Zealand Journal of Psychology* 20: 63–70.

———. 1991b. Sexual victimization prevalence among New Zealand university students. *Journal of Consulting and Clinical Psychology* 59: 464–66.

———. 1992. Technologies and effects of heterosexual coercion. *Feminism and Psychology* 2: 325–51.

Gilbert, N. 1994. Miscounting social ills. *Society* 31 (3): 18–26.

Hwang, K. 1997. Excerpt from *The Humanist,* July/August 1997. Cited in Talking stick. *Utne Reader,* (84): 41.

Kitzinger, C., and Wilkinson, S. 1997. Validating women's experience? Dilemmas in feminist research. *Feminism and Psychology* 7: 566–74.

Koss, M. P. 1985. The hidden rape victim: Personality, attitudinal, and situational characteristics. *Psychology of Women Quarterly* 9: 193–212.

———. 1988. Hidden rape: Sexual aggression and victimization in a national sample of students in higher education. In A. W. Burgess (ed.), *Rape and sexual assault,* Vol. 2 (pp. 3–25). New York and London: Garland.

Koss, M. P., Gidycz, C. A., and Wisniewski, N. 1987. The scope of rape: Incidence and prevalence of sexual aggression and victimization in a national sample of higher education students. *Journal of Consulting and Clinical Psychology* 55: 162–70.

Marcus, S. 1992. Fighting bodies, fighting words: A theory and politics of rape prevention. In J. Butler and J. W. Scott (eds.), *Feminists theorize the political* (pp. 385–403). New York: Routledge.

Newbold, G. 1996. Commentary on Professor Mary Koss's keynote address: Redefining rape. In J. Broadmore, C. Shand, and T. Warburton (eds.), *The proceedings of 'Rape: Ten years' progress? An interdisciplinary conference,* Wellington, New Zealand, 27–30 March 1996 (pp. 144–46). Doctors for Sexual Abuse Care.

Paglia, C. 1992. *Sex, art, and American culture.* New York: Vintage Books.

Pineau, L. 1989. Date rape: A feminist analysis. *Law and Philosophy* 8: 217–43.

———. 1996. A response to my critics. In L. Francis (ed.), *Date rape: Feminism, philosophy, and the law* (pp. 63–107). University Park, PA: Pennsylvania State University Press.

Roiphe, K. 1993. *The morning after: Sex, fear, and feminism.* London: Hamish Hamilton.

Russell, D. E. H. 1982. *Rape in marriage.* New York: Macmillan.

———. 1984. *Sexual exploitation: Rape, child sexual abuse, and workplace harassment.* Beverly Hills: Sage.

Sommers, C. H. 1994. *Who stole feminism? How women have betrayed women.* New York: Simon & Schuster.

RAMPANT OR RARE? THE CONUNDRUM OF QUANTIFYING RAPE AND SEXUAL ASSAULT ON COLLEGE CAMPUSES AND BEYOND

MEGAN M. TESENE

We know the numbers: one in five of every one of those women who is dropped off for that first day of school, before they finish school, will be assaulted, will be assaulted in her college years.

—Vice President Joe Biden speaking
on sexual assault, April 29, 2014

Nearly one in five women in America has been a victim of rape or attempted rape.

—President Barack Obama, February 8, 2015

One in five. Chances are, if you've heard any politician, political analyst, or media pundit discuss the issue of sexual assault—particularly in reference to women on college campuses—you've heard this statistic. It is one of the most oft-cited statistics when it comes to college women's experiences with rape and sexual assault (Krebs and Lindquist, 2014; Nelson, 2014a; New, 2015, 2016). It has also been highly contested by critics in terms of its accuracy and representativeness (Kessler, 2014; New, 2015, 2016). Indeed, even the lead researchers of the study have repeatedly refuted the generalizability of their findings (Krebs and Lindquist, 2014). The statistic came from a random sample of 5,446 undergraduate women in their senior year at just two large public universities (Kessler, 2014; Krebs et al., 2007; Krebs and Lindquist, 2014). As such, Krebs and Lindquist (2014) argue that the study is not representative of all college campuses, and certainly not of all women residing in the United States. They further clarify that the one-in-five statistic combines victims of rape and of other types of sexual assault (Krebs et al., 2007; Krebs and Lindquist, 2014).

Does this mean that these findings should be discounted? Not quite. Rather, it reminds us to be diligent in understanding where such information comes from, the context from which it originates, and if and when it can be applied more broadly. Although the 2007 study cannot be understood to represent the scope and nature of sexual assault on college campuses throughout the United States, the one-in-five statistic *has* been replicated in other campus climate studies (Association of American Universities, 2015; Krebs et al., 2016), giving credence to its reliability. For example, the Association of American Universities (AAU) conducted a climate survey of over 150,000 students at 27 universities (AAU, 2015; New, 2015). The study found that approximately 11.7 percent of students—both male and female—experienced nonconsensual sexual contact via physical force, threats of physical force, or incapacitation. On average, female students had higher rates of incidence, with approximately 23 percent of female subjects reporting such experiences (AAU, 2015; New, 2015). In a follow-up to the 2007 one-in-five study, climate surveys were administered to over 23,000 students across nine universities (Krebs et al., 2016). Again researchers found that approximately 21 percent of female undergraduates indicated they had been sexually assaulted during their time in college (Krebs et al., 2016; New, 2016).

Researchers have identified similar trends at the national level, as denoted by former President Obama's above quote. His "one in five" statement references the 2011 National Intimate Partner and Sexual Violence Survey (NISVS), conducted by the Centers for Disease Control and Prevention, which identified a 20 percent lifetime risk of rape or attempted rape for adult American women (Breiding et al., 2014). That is, one in five American women are likely to be raped within their lifetime. Those findings echo an earlier nationally representative survey conducted by the United States Department of Justice (DOJ) wherein the researchers determined that approximately 18 percent of women in the United States have been raped within their lifetime (Kilpatrick et al., 2007). While these studies seem to confirm the one-in-five statistic regarding women's experiences at both the collegiate and national levels, it is not always clear as to what behaviors or actions are included within this oft-cited statistic. Whether researchers examine sexual assault, rape, attempted rape, or nonconsensual sexual contact, it is necessary to understand precisely what is meant by those terms. Only then can we make sense of the meaning of research findings and their applied value.

DISTINCTIONS IN TERMINOLOGY

For the sake of clarity here, it is necessary to provide basic definitions to identify the nuances among key terms. As you review these terms, remember that a major barrier to documenting the scope and frequency of sexual violence is a failure to apply clear, consistent definitions across the numerous agencies and institutions that manage and research sexual violence. Ultimately, while these definitions are accurate and ground us with a basic understanding of the different types of sexual violence, they may differ from those implemented elsewhere. The

National Institute of Justice (NIJ) (2017) uses the following definitions:

Sexual violence "refers to a specific constellation of crimes including sexual harassment, sexual assault, and rape. The perpetrator may be a stranger, acquaintance, friend, family member, or intimate partner" (2017: para. 1).

Sexual harassment consists of a range of behaviors such as "degrading remarks, gestures, and jokes to indecent exposure, being touched, grabbed, pinched, or brushed against in a sexual way" (2017: para. 2).

Sexual assault "covers a wide range of unwanted behaviors—up to but not including penetration—that are attempted or completed against a victim's will or when a victim cannot consent because of age, disability, or the influence of alcohol or drugs. Sexual assault may involve actual or threatened physical force, use of weapons, coercion, intimidation, or pressure" (2017: para. 3).

Rape can be understood as "nonconsensual oral, anal, or vaginal penetration of the victim by body parts or objects using force, threats of bodily harm, or by taking advantage of a victim who is incapacitated or otherwise incapable of giving consent" (2017: para. 4).

Incapacitation "may include mental or cognitive disability, self-induced or forced intoxication, status as minor, or any other condition defined by law that voids an individual's ability to give consent" (2017: para. 4).

At the foundation of each of these crimes is a lack of consent. While precise definitions of **consent** may vary by state and from institution to institution (Tracy et al., 2012), here it is understood as "words or overt actions by a person who is legally or functionally competent to give informed approval, indicating a freely given agreement to have sexual intercourse or sexual contact" (Basile et al., 2014: 11). Further, the **inability to consent** arises when "a freely given agreement to have sexual intercourse or sexual contact could not occur because of the victim's age, illness, mental or physical disability, being asleep or unconscious, or being too intoxicated (e.g., incapacitation, lack of consciousness, or lack of awareness) through their voluntary or involuntary use of alcohol or drugs" (Basile et al., 2014: 11).

DIFFERENCES IN RESEARCH: CRIMINAL JUSTICE VS. PUBLIC HEALTH APPROACHES

While some studies indicate that rape and sexual assault are widespread on college campuses, others point to significantly lower rates (Wong, 2016). In fact, the American Association of University Women (AAUW) recently reported that 91 percent of colleges and universities documented *zero* incidences of rape in 2014 (AAUW, 2015; Wong, 2016). Similar discrepancies exist in research at the national level. For instance, while the National Intimate Partner and Sexual Violence Survey estimated that 1.9 million women were raped in 2011 (Breiding et al., 2014), the 2012 National Crime Victimization Survey documented just 347,000 cases of rape and sexual assault among both men *and* women (Truman and Langton, 2014). How is it possible that the leading studies on the issue of rape and sexual assault in the United States find such disparate numbers? Furthermore, what is one to make of these seemingly contradictory statistics? As it turns out, quantifying the frequency of rape and sexual assault is not so simple. Issues such as definition, reporting, and measurement complicate the effort to create a clear picture of the prevalence and nature of these crimes. Determining accurate statistics on rape and sexual assault is paramount to developing policies that can effectively respond to and deter these forms of sexual violence (Kilpatrick et al., 2007).

To better understand the variance in reported rates of rape and sexual assault, it is necessary to explore the methodology behind the research. There are two main approaches to researching rape and sexual assault: criminal justice and public health (Kessler, 2014; Kilpatrick, 2004; Sinozich and Langton, 2014). The data collected within these approaches are quite different (Kessler, 2014; Kilpatrick, 2004; New, 2015; Sinozich and Langton, 2014). Whereas a criminal justice approach uses narrow definitions to document reported crimes and criminal victimization, a public health approach adopts expansive language to identify a range of behaviors that fall both inside and outside of legal definitions of rape and sexual assault that may have occurred but were not necessarily reported. As a result, criminal justice approaches offer rates of occurrence that are relatively low, while public health approaches document frequencies that are much more alarming. Neither of these approaches is "wrong" per se; they simply document different aspects of rape and sexual assault. The key is understanding what data were collected and the context in which they can be understood. Problems arise when research is misused, misinterpreted, or applied inaccurately.

In recording incidences that constitute a crime, criminal justice studies examine only those situations that meet legal definitions of rape or sexual assault. A complication of this approach is that local, state, federal, and tribal laws differ in how they define these crimes (Kilpatrick, 2004). Inconsistencies in definitions lead to inconsistencies in the reporting and handling of cases. For instance, while the Federal Bureau of Investigation (FBI) recently updated its definition of rape to be more inclusive, some state and local agencies have not made or implemented those changes (FBI, 2013; Hurtado, 2017). Prior to 2012, the FBI defined rape as "the carnal knowledge of a female forcibly against her will" (FBI, 2013: para. 2). The definition was incredibly narrow, excluding male rape victims, oral and anal rapes, and those rapes that do not clearly involve the use of force (FBI, 2013; Tesene, 2014). To address the limitations and inadequacies of this outdated definition, the formal definition was changed to "the penetration, no matter how slight, of the vagina or anus with any body part or object, or oral penetration by a sex organ of another person, without consent of the victim" (FBI, 2013: para. 2). While the intent was to implement a comprehensive and consistent definition across the myriad of law enforcement agencies, several state and local agencies continue to use outdated or varied definitions (FBI, 2013; Hurtado, 2017). Although the FBI's new definition is more inclusive, it lacks widespread implementation, and as of yet, there is no evidence that the change in definition has had an effect on reporting or documentation.

Another issue with the criminal justice approach is that it generally only records those instances that were formally reported—either to law enforcement or to the appropriate institutional authorities, such as the administration at a university or within the military. Considering that the majority of rapes and sexual assaults go unreported (AAU, 2015; Hefling, 2014; NIJ, 2008; Sinozich and Langton, 2014), criminal justice studies are inadequate in terms of accurately framing the prevalence of these forms of sexual violence. For example, the statistic that 91 percent of colleges and universities reported zero rapes in 2014 is based on annual reporting for the Clery Act, which includes only those rapes that were formally reported in the previous year (Clery Center, 2017; Pauly, 2015; Wong, 2016). The fact that 91 percent of these institutions of higher education reported zero rapes does not mean that no rapes occurred that year. Rather, it indicates that the institutions themselves may have barriers in place—both structural and cultural—that prevent students from reporting (Pauly, 2015; Wong, 2016).

While there are several reasons why someone might avoid reporting a rape or sexual assault, fear is perhaps one of the most significant barriers. When asked why they did not report a rape or sexual assault, victims cite fears of mistreatment and re-victimization; they fear their case will be mishandled or that they won't be taken seriously; they fear that others will blame them for what happened or that the authorities will altogether dismiss their claims; they fear facing reprisal or retaliation at the hands of their peers or by the governing institution (e.g., college or military agency); and they fear that their perpetrators will not face any sort of justice (Hefling, 2014; Rhode, 2016). Indeed, cases of rape and sexual assault rarely result in a conviction (Dripps, 2010; Rhode, 2016; Lonsway and Archambault, 2012; Seidman and Vickers, 2005) and in some cases, the perpetrators are protected while victims are punished for making a report (Rhode, 2016).

For instance, the U.S. Department of Defense reports that 62 percent of service members *who reported an assault* faced some type of retaliation—either social or professional (Childress, 2015; RAND Corporation, 2014; Rhode, 2016). Meanwhile, those armed services members who were accused of sexual assault had just an 8 percent chance of facing a court martial (Rhode, 2016). Civilian cases also fare poorly, with less than 10 percent of reported incidences resulting in a conviction (Dripps, 2010; Rhode, 2016) and less than 1–2 percent serving any actual jail or prison time (Lonsway and Archambault, 2012). As for college campuses, an analysis of Department of Justice data found that less than a third of students who are found to be responsible for sexual assault are expelled (Kingkade, 2014a, 2014b). For many, reporting a rape or sexual assault under these circumstances simply isn't worth the trouble (Hefling, 2014; Kilpatrick, 2010; Rhode, 2016).

Cultural beliefs about what constitutes rape or sexual assault can also shape reporting. The image of an unknown violent predator, aggressively and clearly using force, permeates the cultural psyche (New, 2015; Rhode, 2016). The ubiquity of this image persists even though the vast majority of assaults are enacted by perpetrators known to the victim, often in spaces considered "safe," and where the threat of explicit violence may not be overt (Hefling, 2014). Those incidences that fall outside the dominant narrative may be viewed by victims as "not that serious," even when the circumstances clearly fall under the formal definition of rape or sexual assault (Hefling, 2014; Kilpatrick, 2010; Nelson, 2014b). When individuals don't recognize what happened to them as a rape, or if they don't identify with the victimization framework often employed in formal reporting, they may avoid making a report (Karjane et al., 2002; Kingkade, 2014c; Nelson, 2014b; NIJ, 2008; Sinozich and Langton, 2014). Understanding that a rape or sexual assault has occurred is vital to documenting and responding to these crimes. Although researchers at the National Sexual Violence Resource Center (NSVRC) recently documented a high level of awareness among U.S. adults in recognizing which behaviors constitute sexual violence, they found that young adults and men exhibited lower levels of awareness than older adults and women (NSVRC, 2017). While these findings are promising, they point to a need to improve education and increase understanding about sexual violence and consent (NSVRC, 2017).

Public health studies have attempted to address some of the aforementioned concerns. Rather than only documenting those incidences that were formally reported to an institution or to authorities, these studies typically consist of anonymous, randomized surveys of a target population. Given the prevalence of underreporting, these surveys directly ask individuals whether they have experienced situations that would qualify as rape or sexual assault.

Oftentimes, this type of research avoids explicitly using the words *rape, sexual assault,* or *victim* (Nelson, 2014b). By avoiding these terms, public health researchers hope to detect those incidences that count as rape or sexual assault, but wherein the individual does not necessarily identify with that terminology or as a victim of those crimes (Nelson, 2014b). Critics note that such an approach requires the researchers to determine whether an incident qualifies rather than relying on self-reporting (Kessler, 2014). However, a significant portion of individuals who have experienced incidences that meet the criteria of rape or sexual assault do not view those incidences as such (Karjane et al., 2002; NIJ, 2008; Rhode, 2016; Sinozich and Langton, 2014). Therefore, it becomes difficult for researchers to identify the frequency of rape and sexual assault when relying solely on self-reporting. Perhaps there is much to be learned from such discrepancies—potentially offering insights on the complexities of sexual violence in general.

A public health approach may also use expansive language that includes a variety of behaviors that constitute sexual assault or rape yet may not fall under varying legal definitions.

This tendency of public health–based research to rely on broad, inclusive definitions has served as a criticism by those who argue that such measures may lead to an overestimation when determining the frequency of rape and sexual assault (Kessler, 2014; NIJ, 2008; New, 2015; Taylor, 2015). Sexual violence includes a constellation of behaviors or acts that can overlap. The lines between categorization can be blurry and complicated (e.g., where is the line between sexual harassment and sexual assault, or between sexual assault and rape?). Consider the lack of consensus in defining various forms of sexual violence among the agencies and researchers who work in this area. That lack of clarity exists among members of the general public as well, with many people conflating sexual assault with rape (Krebs and Lindquist, 2014) or simply being ill-informed about what constitutes sexual violence more generally (NSVRC, 2017). By providing a list of detailed items that respondents can mark "yes" or "no" to indicate whether they've had that particular experience, researchers hope to capture the wide range of sexual violence taking place. This approach doesn't require that respondents adhere to a particular understanding of rape or sexual assault; they need not identify themselves as victims or as having experienced a crime. They merely need to indicate whether they've had certain experiences as outlined in the survey or questionnaire. As critical consumers of research, it is necessary to understand what those items are and how they've been operationalized by researchers.

CAMPUS SEXUAL ASSAULT: UNDERSTANDING CLERY, TITLE IX, AND MANDATORY REPORTING

Both criminal justice and public health approaches have been implemented to research and track the scope and frequency of campus rape and sexual assault. Perhaps you have participated in a campus or workplace climate survey. These surveys are generally anonymous and target a specific population (e.g., an entire college campus or workplace) to gauge and improve the climate, should there be documented problems or concerns. Climate surveys are typically structured on a public health–research approach, identifying a variety of behaviors or incidents and allowing respondents to anonymously indicate the level of intensity and frequency of occurrence. Incidents need not be formally reported to the institution for inclusion. The goal of such studies is to glean the most accurate understanding of a campus's climate and student experiences with respect to a particular issue—in this case, sexual violence. By understanding the extent of the problem through data, organizations can institute

policy to help remedy or prevent sexual violence (Kilpatrick et al., 2007).

However, it is worth noting that by identifying the extent of sexual violence on campuses, some universities could be negatively affected (Kitchener, 2014; Wong, 2016). While colleges and universities can suffer via reputation and federal sanctions for failing to appropriately handle sexual violence on campus due to their Title IX obligations, as discussed below (Kitchener, 2014; Rhode, 2016), there may be disincentives to identifying and reporting the full extent of these incidences (Wong, 2016; Yung, 2015). When colleges or universities collect data on rape and sexual assault on their campuses, they might find that the prevalence and frequency are higher than they'd like. Institutions of higher education want to project an image that reflects positively on their school, campus, and administration. Anything that will essentially make a school look bad—whether it is poor student outcomes or an unsafe campus environment—can severely influence an institution's reputation, recruitment efforts, and potential funding sources (Kitchener, 2014; Wong, 2016). Being transparent and investing in resources that are meant to facilitate the reporting of sexual assault open institutions of higher education up to negative publicity and potential sanctions, should they be found to be creating or supporting a hostile campus environment. Ultimately, some universities may be motivated to underreport rates of sexual assault (Kitchener, 2014; Wong, 2016; Yung, 2015).

The Clery Act requires any college or university receiving federal funding to submit annual reports on campus crime statistics (Clery Center, 2017; Yung, 2015). Criminal offenses, such as rape and sexual assault, must be reported to the U.S. Department of Education each October (Clery Center, 2017). Further, universities must also indicate what efforts are being made on campus to improve safety (Clery Center, 2017). The annual reporting from Clery requires that formal reports be made to the institution; therefore, Clery reporting falls under the criminal justice approach. Analyzing sexual assault data of universities that were audited for Clery Act violations, Yung (2015) found discrepancies in annual reporting where universities reported higher rates of sexual assault in audit years. Yung contends that the discrepancy between audit and nonaudit years serves as evidence that universities are likely underreporting sexual assault. That is, when being more closely monitored, universities may more effectively report campus sexual assault.

In addition to the Clery Act, colleges and universities receiving federal dollars are required to adhere to Title IX. Title IX states: "No person in the United States shall, on the basis of sex, be excluded from participation in, be denied the benefits of, or be subjected to discrimination under any educational program or activity receiving Federal financial assistance" (USDOJ, 1972: Sec. 1681a). The law has been broadly interpreted to include sexual harassment and sexual violence on college campuses (National Women's Law Center, 2016; Office for Civil Rights [OCR], 2015). According to the Office for Civil Rights (OCR) (2014: 1), students' rights are violated when:

(1) the alleged conduct is sufficiently serious to limit or deny a student's ability to participate in or benefit from the school's educational program, i.e., creates a hostile environment; and (2) the school, upon notice, fails to take prompt and effective steps reasonably calculated to end the sexual violence, eliminate the hostile environment, prevent its recurrence, and, as appropriate, remedy its effects.

Under these policies, schools are required to address and prevent sexual violence and harassment on their campuses, regardless of whether police are investigating a particular case (Know Your IX, 2017; National Women's Law Center, 2016).

In recent years, many colleges and universities have taken more aggressive approaches to ensure they adhere to Title IX by instituting mandatory reporting by university faculty and staff (Deamicis, 2013; Flaherty, 2015; Sokolow, 2013). Under this policy, any "responsible employees" must report any incidents of sexual violence and misconduct of which they become aware—regardless of whether a student wanted to formally make a report (OCR, 2014; Deamicis, 2013; Flaherty, 2015). While "responsible employees" may vary across institutions, most university faculty have found themselves placed within this category (OCR, 2014; Deamicis, 2013; Flaherty, 2015). Only those university employees who qualify as "confidential" or "privileged" employees (e.g., counselors, health care providers) may refrain from reporting. The policy has garnered much debate, particularly by university faculty and sexual assault advocates, who worry that such policies will harm students, negatively affect faculty–student relationships, and prevent students from making a report or seeking out assistance (Deamicis, 2013; Flaherty, 2015). Such policies are often in flux. Indeed, the Department of Education, with oversight from President Trump's secretary of education, Betsy DeVos, is currently reviewing various Obama-era policies with the aim of making significant changes (Saul and Goldstein, 2017; Svrluga, 2017; Yoffe, 2017). The finality of these changes is not yet known; however, shifts are expected around the level of evidence required to make formal charges, as well as the rights of the accused to have due process (Saul and Goldstein, 2017; Svrluga, 2017).

BEYOND THE COLLEGIATE EXPERIENCE

Much of the public discourse surrounding rape and sexual assault centers around college campuses. Addressing and dealing with campus sexual assault is both important and necessary; however, it should not prevent conversations or efforts to confront sexual violence in other contexts. For instance, women aged 18–24 who are *not* college students report slightly higher rates of rape and sexual assault than do college women in this same age group (Rennison, 2014; Sinozich and Langton, 2014). Educational attainment is directly related to the risk of sexual violence (Rennison, 2014). Women without a high school diploma were found to have rates of sexual victimization 53 percent higher than women with high school diplomas or some college (Rennison, 2014). Compared to women with a bachelor's degree or higher, that rate increases to over 400 percent greater (Rennison, 2014). Researchers have found that rates of sexual violence are the greatest among the most disadvantaged communities—particularly when considering key socioeconomic factors such as income level or homeownership (Planty et al., 2013; Rennison, 2014). The highest rates of sexual violence were identified among those with lower income levels and those lacking homeownership (Rennison, 2014). Because racial inequality cannot be disentangled from socioeconomic inequalities, communities of color are disproportionately represented among those most at risk. Whereas the 2011 National Intimate Partner and Sexual Violence Survey found that 19.3 percent of all U.S. women would be raped within their lifetime (Breiding et al., 2014), rates varied by racial group: 32.3 percent for multiracial Americans, 27.5 percent for American Indian/Native, 21.2 percent for non-Hispanic blacks, 20.5 percent for non-Hispanic whites, 13.6 percent for Hispanics (Breiding et al., 2014).

Sexual violence research and public discourse also tend to center the experiences of heterosexuals, further disadvantaging those in the LGBTQ community. Rates of reporting are notoriously low for rape and sexual assault in general (Hefling, 2014; NIJ, 2008; Sinozich and Langton, 2014). Yet the LGBTQ community must also contend with the additional stigmas of homophobia and transphobia, typically accompanied by a lack of understanding about LGBTQ sexuality (Men against Abuse Now, 2017; Quinlan, 2013). Oftentimes, when members of the LGBTQ community report crimes, they are mistreated by police and other authority figures (Grant et al., 2011; Men against Abuse Now, 2017; Quinlan, 2013). Gay men may face hostility and a unique form of victim blaming that views gay men as at fault for sexual violence (White and Robinson Kurpius, 2002). Dominant ideologies regarding masculinity and sexual victimization prevent men from reporting sexual violence in the first place; the mistreatment by authorities of those men who do come forward is also rooted in this troublesome ideology (Men against Abuse Now, 2017; Walker et al., 2014).

Women who experience sexual violence at the hands of other women may experience a different kind of barrier. Our culture's prioritization of penile penetration as a defining trait of sexual intercourse, and the myth that women cannot rape, can prevent LBQ women from having their experiences treated as legitimate or serious (Men against Abuse Now, 2017; Quinlan, 2013; Walker et al., 2014). The transgender community also fares poorly when reporting sexual violence (Grant et al., 2011; James et al., 2016). Trans individuals commonly face verbal harassment, physical assault, and hostile mistreatment at rape crisis centers, in domestic violence shelters, and by police and medical practitioners (Grant et al., 2011). They may further find that they are not believed when reporting sexual violence, especially since our society has framed transgender bodies as undesirable or unworthy of sexual attention in general (McBride, 2017).

As noted earlier, the development of rape definitions that go beyond traditional heterosexual penile–vaginal intercourse is relatively new (FBI, 2013; Tesene, 2014). However, even if the federal definition of rape has become more inclusive, that doesn't mean that those changes have been made or are being implemented at the local, state, or regional levels (FBI, 2014; Hurtado, 2017; Kilpatrick, 2004; Quinlan, 2013). Policies within higher education have also changed recently. For instance, the U.S. Department of Education now mandates that same-sex incidents of campus sexual violence be managed by the same policies and standards as all sexual violence complaints (Shapiro, 2014; OCR, 2014). Although, given the dysfunction and inability of institutions of higher education or the criminal justice system to effectively deal with sexual violence in general, these updates offer few assurances.

CONCLUSION

Sexual violence is a multifaceted issue, shaped by a myriad of individual, interactional, and institutional mechanisms that are continuously evolving. It follows that researching sexual violence in its many forms may face complications. However, at the very least, it is necessary to clearly and consistently define what constitutes sexual violence and its various underlying categories. If documenting the frequency and scope of sexual violence is key to developing strategic policies that can effectively prevent or respond these crimes (Kilpatrick et al., 2007), it is paramount that we develop comprehensive, accurate, and consistent measurements. The quality of sexual violence research and the ability of our criminal justice system to respond to these crimes are dependent upon this task.

As for making sense of the existing research on sexual violence, it is important to understand the methodology and the measurements behind the numbers being reported. When confronted with statistics on rape and sexual assault, individuals must ask themselves a variety of questions: Who conducted this research? How did they go about conducting it? How and why did they measure variables in a particular manner? Are those measurements valid? Are the findings reliable in that they have been or can be replicated? Who was the target population and how were data collected? In asking such questions, individuals may better infer the significance and applicability of those findings. Knowing that a reported study took place at just a handful of colleges or within a single branch of the military provides context and meaning. It also helps a critical consumer of information deduce that those findings are not generalizable to the national population but are nonetheless useful. Each study can be used to make changes within an institutional setting, but it also adds to a growing body of research on an incredibly complex issue. As researchers, policymakers, activists, and advocates make headway on collecting data from diverse populations in a multitude of settings, we can better move forward in making sense of and preventing sexual violence.

REFERENCES

American Association of University Women. 2015. "91 Percent of Colleges Reported Zero Incidents of Rape in 2014." Retrieved April 12, 2017 from www.aauw.org /article/clery-act-data-analysis/.

Association of American Universities. 2015. "AAU Climate Survey on Sexual Assault and Sexual Misconduct." Retrieved April 18, 2017 from www.aau.edu/key -issues/aau-climate-survey-sexual-assault-and-sexual -misconduct?id=16525.

Basile, Kathleen, Sharon Smith, Matthew Breiding, Michele Black, and Reshma Mahendra. 2014. *Sexual Violence Surveillance: Uniform Definitions and Recommended Data Elements, Version 2.0.* National Center for Injury Prevention and Control. Atlanta, GA: Centers for Disease Control and Prevention. Retrieved August 26, 2017 from www.cdc.gov/violenceprevention /pdf/sv_surveillance_definitionsl-2009-a.pdf.

Breiding, Matthew, Sharon Smith, Kathleen Basile, Mikel Walters, Jieru Chen, and Melissa Merrick. 2014. *Prevalence and Characteristics of Sexual Violence, Stalking, and Intimate Partner Violence Victimization—National Intimate Partner and Sexual Violence Survey, United States, 2011.* Atlanta, GA: Centers for Disease Control and Prevention.

Childress, Sarah. 2015. "How the Military Retaliates against Sexual Assault Victims." *Frontline* (PBS). Retrieved April 12, 2017 from www.pbs.org/wgbh /frontline/article/how-the-military-retaliates-against -sexual-assault-victims/.

Clery Center. 2017. "Summary of the Jeanne Clery Act: A Compliance and Reporting Overview." Retrieved May 31, 2017 from https://clerycenter.org/policy -resources/the-clery-act/.

Deamicis, Carmel. 2013. "Which Matters More: Reporting Assault or Respecting a Victim's Wishes?" *The Atlantic*. Retrieved October 20, 2017 from www.theatlantic.com /national/archive/2013/05/which-matters-more -reporting-assault-or-respecting-a-victims-wishes/276042/.

Dripps, Donald. 2010. "Rape, Law and American Society." In Clare McGlynn and Vanessa Munro (Eds.). *Rethinking Rape Law: International and Comparative Perspectives*. New York: Routledge. 224–36.

Federal Bureau of Investigation. 2013. "Crime in the United States, 2013: Rape Addendum." Retrieved March 10, 2017 from https://ucr.fbi.gov/crime-in -the-u.s/2013/crime-in-the-u.s.-2013/rape-addendum /rape_addendum_final.

Flaherty, Colleen. 2015. "Faculty Members Object to New Policies Making All Professors Mandatory Reporters of Sexual Assault." *Inside Higher Ed*. Retrieved October 20, 2017 from www.insidehighered.com/news/2015/02/04 /faculty-members-object-new-policies-making-all -professors-mandatory-reporters-sexual.

Grant, Jaime, Lisa Mottet, Justin Tanis, Jack Harrison, Jody Herman, and Mara Keisling. 2011. *Injustice at Every Turn: A Report of the National Transgender Discrimination Survey*. Washington, DC: National Center for Transgender Equality and National Gay and Lesbian Task Force.

Hefling, Kimberly. 2014. "Justice Department: Majority of Campus Sexual Assault Goes Unreported to Police." *Frontline* (PBS). Retrieved April 30, 2017 from www.pbs .org/newshour/rundown/four-five-acts-campus-sexual -assault-go-unreported-police/.

Hurtado, Fernando. 2017. "The FBI Changed Its Definition of Rape, but Some States Still Don't Recognize Male Victims." *Circa News*. Retrieved May 9, 2017 from http://circa.com/politics/issues/fbi-changed -definition-of-rape-but-some-states-still-dont-recognize -male-rape.

James, Sandy, Jody Herman, Susan Rankin, Mara Keisling, Lisa Mottet, and Ma'ayan Anafi. 2016. *The Report of the 2015 U.S. Transgender Survey*. Washington, DC: National Center for Transgender Equality.

Karjane, Heather, Bonnie Fisher, and Francis Cullen. 2002. *Campus Sexual Assault: America's Institutions of Higher Education Respond: Final Report*. NIJ Grant # 1999-WA-VX-0008. Newton, MA: Education Development Center, Inc.

Kessler, Glenn. 2015. "Obama's Claim that One in Five American Women Has Been a Victim of Rape or Attempted Rape." *The Washington Post*. Retrieved April 24, 2017 from www.washingtonpost.com/news /fact-checker/wp/2015/02/12/obamas-claim-that -one-in-five-american-women-have-been-raped /?utm_term=.109ea16fa794.

Kilpatrick, Dean. 2004. "What Is Violence against Women? Defining and Measuring the Problem." *Journal of Interpersonal Violence*, 19(11): 1209–34.

———. 2010. "Rape in the United States: The Chronic Failure to Report and Investigate Rape Cases." Committee on the Judiciary, United States Senate. Retrieved April 19, 2017 from www.judiciary.senate.gov /imo/media/doc/10-09-14KilpatrickTestimony.pdf.

Kilpatrick, Dean, Heidi Resnick, Kenneth Ruggiero, Lauren Conoscenti, and Jenna McCauley. 2007. *Drug-facilitated, Incapacitated, and Forcible Rape: A National Study*. Washington, DC: U.S. Department of Justice.

Kingkade, Tyler. 2014a. "Fewer than One-Third of Campus Sexual Assault Cases Result in Expulsion." *Huffington Post*. Retrieved October 21, 2017 from www.huffingtonpost.com/2014/09/29/campus-sexual -assault_n_5888742.html.

———. 2014b. "Sexual Assault Sanctions from Department of Justice FY 2011-2013." *Huffington Post*. Retrieved October 21, 2017 from www.huffingtonpost .com/2014/09/29/campus-sexual-assault_n_5888742 .html.

———. 2014c. "Sexual Assault Statistics Can Be Confusing, but They're Not the Point." *Huffington Post*. Retrieved April 12, 2017 from www.huffingtonpost .com/2014/12/15/sexual-assault-statistics_n_6316802 .html.

Kitchener, Caroline. 2014. "When Helping Rape Victims Hurts a College's Reputation." *The Atlantic*. Retrieved September 21, 2017 from www.theatlantic.com /education/archive/2014/12/when-helping-rape -victims-hurts-a-universitys-reputation/383820/.

Know Your IX. 2017. "Why Schools Handle Sexual Violence Reports." Retrieved October 20, 2017 from www.knowyourix.org/issues/schools-handle-sexual -violence-reports/.

Krebs, Christopher, and Christine Lindquist. 2014. "Setting the Record Straight on '1 in 5.'" *Time* magazine. Retrieved March 10, 2017 from http://time .com/3633903/campus-rape-1-in-5-sexual-assault-setting -record-straight/.

Krebs, Christopher, Christine Lindquist, Marcus Berzofsky, Bonnie Shook-Sa, and Kimberly Peterson. 2016. *Campus Climate Survey Validation Study: Final Technical Report*. Bureau of Justice Statistics, Research and Development Series. Washington, DC: U.S. Department of Justice.

Krebs, Christopher, Christine Lindquist, Tara Warner, Sandra Martin, and Bonnie Fisher. 2007. *The Campus*

Sexual Assault (CSA) Study: Final Report. National Institute for Justice. Washington, DC: U.S. Department of Justice.

Lonsway, Kimberly, and Joanne Archambault. 2012. "The 'Justice Gap' for Sexual Assault Cases: Future Directions for Research and Reform." *Violence against Women*, 18(2): 145–68.

McBride, Sarah. 2017. "Why I'm Not Staying Silent about Being a Trans Woman Who Was Sexually Assaulted." *BuzzFeed*. Retrieved November 4, 2017 from www .buzzfeed.com/sarahemcbride/why-its-so-hard-for -trans-women-to-talk-about-sexual-assault?utm_term =.ihg6vMAPY#.lxy5g0Ako.

Men against Abuse Now. 2017. "Same-Sex Rape and Sexual Assault." Stanford University. Retrieved September 17, 2017 from https://web.stanford.edu /group/maan/cgi-bin/?page_id=313.

National Institute of Justice. 2008. "Sexual Assault on Campus: Measuring Frequency." Retrieved April 24, 2017 from www.nij.gov/topics/crime/rape-sexual -violence/campus/pages/measuring.aspx.

———. 2017. "Rape and Sexual Violence." Retrieved August 26, 2017 from www.nij.gov/topics/crime/rape -sexual-violence/Pages/welcome.aspx.

National Sexual Violence Resource Center. 2017. "New Data Reveals High Awareness among U.S. Adults on What Constitutes Sexual Assault." Retrieved April 23, 2017 from www.nsvrc.org/news/press-releases/new -data-reveals-high-awareness-among-us-adults-what -constitutes-sexual-assault.

National Women's Law Center. 2016. "Title IX Requires Schools to Address Sexual Violence." Retrieved September 17, 2017 from https://nwlc.org/resources /title-ix-requires-schools-to-address-sexual-violence/.

Nelson, Libby. 2014a. "'1 in 5': How a Study of Two Colleges Became the Most Cited Campus Sexual Assault Statistic." *Vox*. Retrieved March 15, 2017 from www.vox.com/2014/12/11/7377055/campus-sexual -assault-statistics.

———. 2014b. "Why Some Studies Make Campus Rape Look Like an Epidemic While Others Say It's Rare." *Vox*. Retrieved March 10, 2017 from www.vox .com/2014/12/11/7378271/why-some-studies-make -campus-rape-look-like-an-epidemic-while-others.

New, Jake. 2015. "Students and Violence: Differing Definitions." *Inside Higher Ed*. Retrieved April 30, 2017 from www.insidehighered.com/news/2015/09/02/rutgers -survey-using-broad-definition-finds-1-5-female -students-have-experienced?utm_source=slate&utm _medium=referral&utm_term=partner.

———. 2016. "Justice Department: 1 in 5 Women Sexually Assaulted in College." *Inside Higher Ed*. Retrieved April 25, 2017 from www.insidehighered.com/quicktakes /2016/01/21/justice-department-1-5-women -sexually-assaulted-college.

Office for Civil Rights. 2014. *Questions and Answers on Title IX and Sexual Violence*. Office for Civil Rights. Washington, DC: U.S. Department of Education. Retrieved October 19, 2017 from www2.ed.gov/about /offices/list/ocr/docs/qa-201404-title-ix.pdf.

———. 2015. *Title IX and Sex Discrimination*. Office for Civil Rights. Washington, DC: U.S. Department of Education. Retrieved October 23, 2017 from www2 .ed.gov/about/offices/list/ocr/docs/tix_dis.html.

Pauly, Madison. 2015. "Here's What's Missing from the Stats on Campus Rape." *Mother Jones*. Retrieved March 10, 2017 from www.motherjones.com/politics/2015/10 /campus-crime-statistics-undercount-sexual-assaults.

Planty, Michael, Lynn Langton, Christopher Krebs, Marcus Berzofsky, and Hope Smiley-McDonald. 2013. *Female Victims of Sexual Violence, 1994–2010, Special Report*. Bureau of Justice Statistics. Washington, DC: U.S. Department of Justice.

Quinlan, Casey. 2013. "When Women Rape: Everything We're Not Talking About." *Autostraddle*. Retrieved September 17, 2017 from www.autostraddle.com/when -women-rape-everything-were-not-talking-about-185931/.

RAND Corporation. 2014. "Initial Results from Major Survey of U.S. Military Sexual Assault, Harassment." Retrieved April 12, 2017 from www.rand.org/news /press/2014/12/04.htm.

Rennison, Callie Marie. 2014. "Privilege, among Rape Victims." *The New York Times*. Retrieved September 20, 2017 from www.nytimes.com/2014/12/22/opinion/who -suffers-most-from-rape-and-sexual-assault-in-america .html.

Rhode, Deborah. 2016. "Rape on Campus and in the Military: An Agenda for Reform." *UCLA Women's Law Journal*, 23(1): 1–27.

Saul, Stephanie, and Dana Goldstein. 2017. "Betsy DeVos Says She Will Rewrite Rules on Campus Sex Assault." *The New York Times*. Retrieved October 23, 2017 from www.nytimes.com/2017/09/07/us/devos-campus-rape .html.

Seidman, Ilene, and Susan Vickers. 2005. "The Second Wave: An Agenda for the Next Thirty Years of Law Reform." *Suffolk University Law Review*, 38: 467–91.

Shapiro, Joseph. 2014. "Campus Sexual Assault Law Now Includes Language on Same-Sex Violence." *National Public Radio*. Retrieved September 17, 2017 from www .npr.org/2014/10/01/352757107/campus-sexual-assault -law-now-includes-language-on-same-sex-violence.

Sinozich, Sofi, and Lynn Langton. 2014. *Rape and Sexual Assault Victimization among College-Age Females, 1995–2013, Special Report*. Bureau of Justice Statistics. Washington, DC: U.S. Department of Justice.

Sokolow, Brett. 2013. "Mandatory Reporting for Title IX: Keep It Simple." *The Chronicle of Higher Education*. Retrieved October 17, 2017 from www.chronicle.com /article/Mandatory-Reporting-for-Title/141785.

Svrluga, Susan. 2017. "Transcript: Betsy DeVos's Remarks on Campus Sexual Assault." *The Washington Post.* Retrieved October 23, 2017 from www.washingtonpost .com/news/grade-point/wp/2017/09/07/transcript-betsy -devoss-remarks-on-campus-sexual-assault/?utm_term =.d0078887f0fc.

Taylor, Stuart. 2015. "The Latest Big Sexual Assault Survey Is (Like Others) More Hype than Science." *The Washington Post.* Retrieved April 11, 2017 from www .washingtonpost.com/news/grade-point/wp/2015/09/23 /the-latest-big-sexual-assault-survey-is-like-others-more -hype-than-science/?utm_term=.af35b4e4f082.

Tesene, Megan. 2014. "The Changing Definitions of Rape." In Mindy Stombler, Dawn Baunach, Wendy Simonds, Elroi Windsor, and Elisabeth Burgess (Eds.). *Sex Matters: The Sexuality and Society Reader,* 4th edition. New York: W. W. Norton. 593–94.

Tracy, Carol, Terry Fromson, Jennifer Gentile Long, and Charlene Whitman. 2012. *Rape and Sexual Assault in the Legal System.* Bureau of Justice Statistics, National Research Council Panel on Measuring Rape and Sexual Assault. Washington, DC: U.S. Department of Justice. Retrieved October 13, 2017 from http://jpp.whs.mil /Public/docs/04Meetings/sub20150507/03_Rape _SexAsslt_LegalSystem_WLP_AEQuitas_20120605.pdf.

Truman, Jennifer, and Lynn Langton. 2014. *Criminal Victimization, 2013.* Bureau of Justice Statistics. Washington, DC: U.S. Department of Justice.

Retrieved April 24, 2017 from www.bjs.gov/index .cfm?iid=5111&ty=pbdetail.

U.S. Department of Justice. 1972. "Discrimination Based on Sex or Blindness." In *Title IX of the Education Amendments of 1972.* Washington, DC: U.S. Department of Justice.

Walker, Jayne, John Archer, and Michelle Davies. 2014. "Effects of Rape on Men: A Descriptive Analysis." In Mindy Stombler, Dawn Baunach, Wendy Simonds, Elroi Windsor, and Elisabeth Burgess (Eds.). *Sex Matters: The Sexuality and Society Reader,* 4th edition. New York: W. W. Norton. 628–29.

White, Bradley, and Sharon Robinson Kurpius. 2002. "Effects of Victim Sex and Sexual Orientation on Perceptions of Rape." *Sex Roles,* 46(5–6): 191–200.

Wong, Alia. 2016. "Why the Prevalence of Campus Sexual Assault Is So Hard to Quantify." *The Atlantic.* Retrieved March 10, 2017 from www.theatlantic.com/education /archive/2016/01/why-the-prevalence-of-campus-sexual -assault-is-so-hard-to-quantify/427002/.

Yoffe, Emily. 2017. "The Uncomfortable Truth about Campus Rape Policy." *The Atlantic.* Retrieved September 20, 2017 from www.theatlantic.com/education /archive/2017/09/the-uncomfortable-truth-about-campus -rape-policy/538974/.

Yung, Corey Rayburn. 2015. "Concealing Campus Sexual Assault: An Empirical Examination." *Psychology, Public Policy, and Law,* 21(1): 1–9.

I Was Raped by a Woman

Caroline Catlin

I was supposed to fear the boys. The men. The frat guys, you know, those guys.

I wasn't supposed to fear you.

You, the queer woman, the cool senior girl, the dark haired and bold, the captivating comic, the body positive. The sex positive.

You were supposed to represent the other side. Or at least, whatever side I was on. An emblem of a community where sex is a conversation, where gender is on the way out, where we are somehow better than the

heteropatriarchal bullshit that everyone else experiences. We, the queer ones, the rule breakers rewriting the rules.

You were supposed to be safe.

And yet, today a man whistled at me and I remembered your fists inside of me. Today, I dissociated for 30 seconds in a parking lot because one night, three years ago, you violated and assaulted me in your bedroom. Today, I did the breathing exercises I have been taught, walked through the PTSD grounding techniques, and cried in my car because you, a queer woman, were not safe.

Here are the facts, in case you've forgotten: One Friday night in September I went home with you, consented to sex, and stopped consenting after it got violent. You did not ask my permission before penetrating me. You choked me, left bruises on my arms and chest, and bit a dark circle into my inner thigh. You pushed me into walls, pulled my hair, and fingered me while I slept. Later, when I asked you why, you told me you thought it was hot and fun.

If I speak of this without gender attached, people are sympathetic and kind and sad. If I assign male pronouns to the story, people are angry, and protective, and most feel solidarity. Men, other survivors say, they're monsters. And when I speak the truth, when I say a queer woman did these things, made me bleed, left me limping—people get quiet. Or awkward. Or uncomfortable. They say things like are you sure and did you say no and so it wasn't like, a rape thing.

I am writing to you because queerness and femininity do not make anyone exempt from the rules of consent. Because violence is not sexy if you don't ask first. Because somewhere out in the world, you, perpetrator, are still having sex and I need you to know that one yes does not give you an all-access pass.

And I am writing, because somewhere, someone reading this letter just began to write one of their own. Because it took me finding a letter like this to know it was okay to call this assault, even though you're a woman, and I'm a woman, and somehow we're supposed to be on the same team.

Because I needed this truth when you first did this to me, and my guess is somewhere, someone else does too.

So for the last bit of my letter, I am going to address that someone, and I hope you, perpetrator, listen as well:

Dear survivor, rape is still rape, no matter the pronoun. Your body is still yours, until permission is explicitly given. There is no in-between here, no excuse based on a shared gender, or uncertain gender, or complicated relationship history. Here is your permission slip to believe yourself. Your body is yours is yours is yours, a thousand times over, and no amount of queerness makes that untrue. I promise.

THE RAPE-PRONE CULTURE OF ACADEMIC CONTEXTS: FRATERNITIES AND ATHLETICS

PATRICIA YANCEY MARTIN

About two decades ago, feminist sociologists stopped focusing on rape and sexual assault, even though rapes and their destructive toll on girls and women did not end. Rape did not diminish appreciably and neither did the legal justice system dramatically improve its treatment of victims. Perhaps this is why 80 percent of women college students and 67 percent of non-college women fail to report being raped to the police (Langton and Siznocich 2014, citing National Crime Survey data). We now know that the great majority of rapes in the United States—about 80 percent—are perpetrated by someone known to the victim, not by a stranger who jumps out of the bushes. This pattern suggests that rape often is not a random event but, in many cases, a planned one. While some men are more apt than others to commit rape, some *social contexts* also are more amenable to rapes. Two such contexts that inhabit U.S. academic institutions—men's social fraternities and athletic programs—are the focus of this essay. These contexts can be understood only within the wider parent institution—the contemporary college or university (Stotzer and MacCartney 2015). Thus, the qualities and dynamics of multiple contexts must be addressed. . . .

The thesis of this [reading] is that the dynamics of particular social contexts make them more probable sites for sexual assaults, irrespective of individual men's attitudes or beliefs. Among such contexts are military units; street, drug, and motorcycle gangs; elite schools; college[1] fraternities; and men's athletic programs (see Harkins and Dixon 2010 for a review of sexual assaults by groups of men or boys). As with other aspects of sexual assault, rape on U.S. campuses received extensive attention earlier (Martin and Hummer 1989; Sanday 1990) and now, after two decades, the issue is salient again. Carey et al. (2015) claim that today's college women are five times more likely than other women to be sexually assaulted.

CAMPUS CONTEXTS

Two levels of contexts are at play in the crime of sexual assault/rape on campus: an *external environment* composed of the academic institution as a particular kind of social, cultural, political, and economic context; and an *internal environment* composed of affluent (fraternity) and/or venerated (athletes) men (Messner 2002). These men are students whose organizational cultures and practices reward competition, aggression, and the sexual exploitation of women (Martin and Hummer 1989; Murnen and Kohlman 2007; Stombler 1994). In concert with Connell (2005), I view violence by men as a collective privilege, not an individual aberration (cf. Messerschmidt 2000), and sexual coercion as part of that privilege (Hlavka 2014). Fraternities and intercollegiate athletic programs actively encourage the kinds of masculinity that make their involvement in sexual assaults of women more probable (Harkins and

Dixon 2010; Martin and Hummer 1989; Sanday 1990, 1996).

The Political Economy of the Campus Context(s)

Renzetti (1996) states that academic institutions regularly turn a blind eye to men's sexual assault of women, a practice, I suggest, that reflects contextual conditions. With many issues on their plate, academic administrators have conflicting priorities. While they no doubt want women students to be safe from sexual assault, their dedication to this issue is constrained. Colleges and universities strive to please many external constituents—alumni; accrediting bodies; corporations; granting agencies; community, state, and national officials/governments; athletics supporters; the media; and the public. Not surprisingly, the expectations of some of these groups contradict the expectations of others. For example, sports enthusiasts may be more interested in winning competitions than in SAT scores, federal grant dollars, or faculty honors. They are not shy about promoting their agendas and may withdraw contributions if a star athlete is sidelined. Fraternity alumni who believe boys have "a right to be boys" by drinking to excess and having sex with as many girls as possible may pressure a president to hold back on punishing accused fraternity members. Public opinion often sides with alleged rapists over victims (Chancer 1987), thus giving administrators an out if they want one. Letters to the newspaper often urge administrators to "go easy" on accused "bad boys."

Other constituents also protect the institution in ways that work against the interests of rape victims. Police officers, district attorneys, and even judges may resist lodging criminal charges against star athletes or affluent fraternity boys. Officials who are graduates may protect "their" institution by dragging their feet when investigating or by framing an alleged rape in ways that fail to justify criminal charges.

Powerful fraternity alumni may pressure administrators to excuse a member accused of having perpetrated a sexual assault. Even more distressing, powerful constituents may discourage university officials from taking action against athletes and fraternity members even *after* official judicial proceedings have found them guilty of sexual assault. The documentary film *The Hunting Ground* (2015) reports examples of this practice in several U.S. institutions.

Fraternities and Intercollegiate Athletic Teams: Rape-Prone Contexts[2]

. . . Men's social fraternities are regularly implicated in rapes on campus. Martin and Hummer (1989) noted that unless fundamental changes were made in social fraternities, their treatment of women would not improve. These changes have not occurred. Contextual conditions that facilitated the sexual assaults of women by fraternity members in earlier years also exist today (see DiMaria 2014; Flanagan 2014; Kennerly 2014). The at-odds relationship between university and fraternity, along with the homogeneity of members, a stress on loyalty and secrecy, and extensive alcohol use, contribute to a *rape-prone culture* in fraternity contexts (Decker and Baroni 2011; Harkins and Dixon 2010; Sanday 1996).

In a meta-analysis of research, Murnen and Kohlman (2007) found that multiple features of fraternity (and athletic) contexts lead to higher odds of involvement in sexual assaults. Historian Helen Horowitz (1987) helps us understand why. A founding principle of men's fraternities was to oppose authority—both faculty and administration. According to Peggy Sanday (1996), groups that live in harmony with their environment are more likely to treat women respectfully and to value women's contributions; they are more apt to be "rape-free" than "rape-prone." Unfortunately, fraternities are seldom in harmony with their environments;

members often treat women disrespectfully and rarely do they value women's contributions (Decker and Baroni 2011; Martin and Hummer 1989; Sanday 1990; Stombler 1994). Boswell and Spade (1994) found that men in rape-prone fraternities use loud music (too loud for talking), low lighting (one cannot see across a room), and the plying of alcohol to women to enhance their odds of sexual compliance. Furthermore, they discourage members from having girlfriends (Boswell and Spade 1994). Instead of treating women with respect and valuing their contributions, they view them as fodder in competitions to prove their masculinity (Sanday 1990). Of course, all fraternities do not behave this way, but research and journalistic/media reports indicate that many do (see Bidgood and Motoko 2015 on similar dynamics among boys at an elite high school).

Homogeneity in terms of gender, age, race/ethnicity, and social class also contribute to rape-proneness. Fraternity members are males of a similar age (18–23) and typically the same race/ethnicity, such as white or black or Jewish (Martin and Hummer 1989). Homogeneity means that people with different qualities become fodder for scapegoating and ridicule—women, homosexuals, other racial/ethnic groups. One example is the University of Oklahoma Sigma Alpha Epsilon fraternity chapter that taught its members a song using the N-word for African Americans (Svrluga 2015). In addition, economic affluence fosters assumptions of privilege and a belief that those with privilege stand above (or outside) formal authority (see Kahn 2011 on privilege among boys at an elite school). This situation was in evidence 27 years ago when a Pi Kappa Alpha chapter refused to provide its membership list to the state prosecutor after a gang rape (Martin and Hummer 1989). One fraternity member said his father had "hired" the university president and could fire him, too, so there was no worry about a legal case.[3]

Fraternities insist upon in-group loyalty and secrecy, practices that protect the organization from public exposure and lawsuits (Kennerly 2014; Martin and Hummer 1989; Sanday 1990). The loyalty standard requires members to remain silent even when they know actions are illegal or when they personally disapprove. They must not tell. Additionally, members use alcohol as a weapon to gain women's sexual compliance (Crosset 1999; Martin and Hummer 1989). Sanday (1990) concludes that excessive alcohol use by fraternities is a major contributor to their "rape-proneness," a point with which journalist Caitlin Flanagan (2014) agrees. Her case study of a gang rape on an East Coast campus revealed that members use alcohol to "work out a yes" from women who resist having sex (Sanday 1990). Claire Renzetti (1996) reports a similar practice elsewhere. . . .

Alcohol use by fraternity members is facilitated by two factors: (1) many fraternity houses are private residences, and (2) student residents lack adult supervision. Formerly, "house mothers" lived onsite to oversee meals and budgets, and ensure decorum and keep the boys in line. When fraternities became too obstreperous, they quit. Today's typical *house manager* is a fraternity alumnus, marginally older than the students. Police cannot enter fraternity houses without permission or a warrant, for example, to check for underage drinking or sexual assaults. Insurance companies view fraternities as too high risk to insure; thus, the national chapter or a consortium of 32 national fraternities called the Fraternity Risk Management Trust insures them (DiMaria 2014).

Flanagan (2014), after a yearlong study of fraternities, views alcohol use by fraternity men as *the* major cause of their legal culpability. She writes that taking alcohol out of the fraternity house would lower the legal claims against it by 85 percent and the dollar amount of claims by 95 percent. . . .

. . . [A]lthough resembling fraternities in some ways, organized athletic contexts are also distinct. They exist across the nation—in rural areas, small towns, large cities—and countless U.S. boys and men participate in them—in middle or high school (or earlier), college, and professional arenas. Boys and men who do not participate are often eager fans. The rewards for athletic stardom are great (Messner 1992). For example, at the professional level, they may entail exorbitant signing bonuses and salaries, access to national leaders or film and television stars, and, central to this essay, access to women and sex. Even in less elevated realms, boys and young men are touted, praised, and treated as special because of their performance in sports (Messner 1992).

College-level athletes are often treated as heroes, as special people with special qualities. Their peers—and faculty and administrators— may allow them to do things they decry in others. College athletics are, like fraternities, gender-segregated contexts with a culture that denigrates women and femininity (Curry 1991; McCray 2015). Loyalty and secrecy are emphasized by coaches and "handlers" (tutors, supervisors, trainers), in the interest of preventing secrets—plays, scandals, etc.—from being shared. Athletes are told to keep negative comments to themselves lest they harm the program by casting it in a bad light or risk losing their athletic scholarship status or position on the team.

Scholarship athletes are often housed separately from other students and assigned other athletes as roommates. On many campuses, they are fed communally, away from other students. Practice, weight training, study sessions, and classes fill their time and prevent them from participating in other campus activities or interacting with nonathletes. Television and newspaper reporters pay extensive attention to them and regularly ask them to pose for photos and offer comments. Athletes are extensively "observed" when they go into the community to eat, drink, or engage in other activities. Because of special treatment, they may come to believe that the rules of ordinary social intercourse do not apply to them. Women (and girls) may flock to them and make themselves available for sex. In such a context, any woman's refusal to have sex may be interpreted as an affront to the man's "right" to her sexual compliance.[4] Being around mostly other athletes and having limited opportunity to interact with "regular students," particularly women, may foster misunderstanding of everyday social norms.

CAN CAMPUSES BE FIXED?

. . . Can anything be done? Perhaps, but monumental effort will be required. Perhaps the Title IX complaints that women students have lodged against 129 U.S. universities or colleges will have tangible effects. The complaints, some of which are also lawsuits, accuse institutions of allowing women students to be sexually assaulted while doing nothing to respond to or prevent it. End Rape on Campus (EROC) is a grassroots organization founded by two young women at the University of North Carolina at Chapel Hill who were raped in their first days on campus and who received no support from the institution. They eventually found each other and started EROC with the goals of providing "direct support for survivors and their communities; prevention through education; and policy reform at the campus, local, state, and federal levels" (endrapeoncampus.org website, August 17, 2015). The attention their efforts have drawn—particularly in the documentary *The Hunting Ground*—has arguably started a new grassroots mobilization against campuses that tolerate rapes of women students.

One strategy is to ban fraternities from campus, but less drastic measures are more feasible. For example, fraternity members could be prohibited from residing in a private house owned by the fraternity. If a fraternity already owns one (as many do), members could be allowed only to hold meetings and events in it, and not to reside there. Colleges could require (and if necessary provide) adult residential supervision at every fraternity residence and social event. Restricting the ability of sports boosters to influence athletes and athletic programs is a high priority. Administrators can say no to powerful constituents who favor sports over academics and the principles of institutional integrity. Colleges also could develop meaningful ways of sanctioning fraternity men and athletes who assault women. Taking away scholarships and expelling from school men who behave inappropriately would send a powerful message. An internal judicial process that takes principled action on rape allegations without waiting for formal legal proceedings to conclude is an essential practice as well. . . .

NOTES

1. I use the terms *colleges* or *campuses* to refer to both university and undergraduate institutions.

2. Rape-prone is a concept anthropologist Peggy Sanday (1981) coined in comparing a sample of "primitive" societies to identify which cultures/societies were more apt to have higher rape rates. She found that "rape is part of a cultural configuration which includes interpersonal violence, male dominance, and sexual separation" (p. 5).

3. This case was so exceptional that the prosecutor charged the perpetrators with felonies and prosecuted them. According to the state's attorney, it was the first gang rape case in the United States to be prosecuted. One theory as to why prosecution went forward was the egregious way the rapists treated the victim. They wrote on her unconscious body and dumped her in the hallway of another fraternity house. The wealthy family of the lead perpetrator hired an experienced out-of-town defense attorney and, in a settlement just before the trial was to begin, the lead assailant was sentenced to 364 days in county jail and 20 years' probation. Another perpetrator was placed on five years' probation and two more were placed on probation for a shorter time.

4. Messerschmidt's (2000) study of nine boys, six of whom were violent sexually or otherwise and three of whom were not, argues that *violence is a masculine resource* for boys and men. Society gives them a right to use violence when other

strategies fail, whereas girls lack such legitimacy. Boys grow up being taught that they "have a right" to girls' sexual compliance and can touch girls' bodies with impunity (Hlavka 2014).

REFERENCES

Bidgood, Jess, and Rich Motoko. 2015. Rape trial puts focus on culture of a school. *New York Times*, 19 August, A12, 17.

Boswell, Ayres, and Joan Z. Spade. 1996. Fraternities and collegiate rape culture: Why are some fraternities more dangerous places for women? *Gender & Society* 10: 133–45.

Carey, Kate B., Sarah E. Durney, Robyn L. Shepardson, and Michael P. Carey. 2015. Incapacitated and forcible rape of college women: Prevalence across the first year. *Journal of Adolescent Health* 56 (6): 678–80.

Chancer, Lynn. 1987. New Bedford Massachusetts: March 6, 1983, March 22, 1984: The before and after of a group rape. *Gender & Society* 1 (3): 239–60.

Connell, Raewyn. 2005. *Masculinities*, 2nd ed. Berkeley: University of California Press.

Crosset, Todd W. 1999. What do we know and what can we do about male athlete violence against women? A critical assessment of the athletic affiliation and violence against women debate. *Quest*, August.

Crosset, Todd W., James Ptacek, Mark A. McDonald, and Jeffrey R. Benedict. 1996. Male student athletes and violence against women. *Violence against Women* 2 (2): 163–79.

Curry, Tim J. 1991. Fraternal bonding in the locker room: A pro-feminist analysis of talk about competition and women. *Sociology of Sports Journal* 8: 119–35.

Decker, John F., and Peter G. Baroni. 2011. "No" still means "Yes": The failure of the "non-consent" reform movement in American rape and sexual assault law. *Journal of Criminal Law & Criminology* 101 (4): 1081–169.

DiMaria, Frank. 2014. Lawsuits against fraternities reveal risks and responsibilities. *Insurance News Net*, 25 July. http://insurancenewsnet.com/oarticle/2014/07/25 /Lawsuits-Against-Fraternities-Reveal-Risks-and -Responsibilities-a-535697.html.

End Rape on Campus. http://endrapeoncampus.org/.

Flanagan, Caitlin. 2014. The dark power of fraternities: A year-long investigation of Greek houses reveals their endemic, lurid, and sometimes tragic problems—and a sophisticated system for shifting the blame. *The Atlantic*, March.

Harkins, Leigh, and Louise Dixon. 2010. Sexual offending in groups: An evaluation. *Aggression and Violent Behavior* 15: 87–99.

Hlavka, Heather R. 2014. Normalizing sexual violence: Young women account for harassment and abuse. *Gender & Society* 28 (3): 337–58.

Horowitz, Helen Lefkowitz. 1987. *Campus life*. New York: Alfred A. Knopf.

The Hunting Ground, written and directed by Kirby Dick and produced by Amy Ziering. New York: RADius-TWC/Weinstein Co., 2015, documentary.

Kahn, Shamus R. 2011. *Privilege: The making of an adolescent elite at St. Paul's School*. Princeton, NJ: Princeton University Press.

Kennerly, Maxwell S. 2014. The fraternity mindset: Why be responsible when you can dodge responsibility? Litigation & Trial: The Law Blog of Plaintiff's Attorney Max Kennerly. The Beasley Firm, LLC, 4 March. www.litigationandtrial.com/2014/03/articles/attorney/personal-injury-1/fraternity-responsibility/.

Langton, Lynn, and Sofi Sinozich. 2014. *Rape and sexual assault among college-age females, 1995–2013*. U.S. Bureau of Justice Statistics. National Crime Victim Survey, December. www.bjs.gov/index.cfm?ty=pbdetail&iid=5176.

Martin, Patricia Yancey, and Robert Hummer. 1989. Fraternities and rape on campus. *Gender & Society* 3: 457–73.

McCray, Kristy L. 2015. Intercollegiate athletes and sexual violence: A review of literature and recommendation for further study. *Trauma, Violence, and Abuse* 16 (4): 438–43.

Messerschmidt, James W. 2000. *Nine lives: Adolescent masculinities, the body, and violence*. Boulder, CO: Westview.

Messner, Michael A. 1992. *Power at play: Sports and the problem of masculinity*. Boston, MA: Beacon Press.

Messner, Michael A. 2002. *Taking the field: Women, men, and sports*. Minneapolis: University of Minnesota Press.

Murnen, Sarah K., and Marla H. Kohlman. 2007. Athletic participation, fraternity membership, and sexual aggression among college men: A meta-analytic review. *Sex Roles* 57: 145–57.

Renzetti, Claire. 1996. Editor's introduction. *Violence against Women* 2 (2): 131–33.

Sanday, Peggy Reeves. 1981. The socio-cultural context of rape: A cross-cultural study. *Journal of Social Issues* 37 (4): 5–27.

Sanday, Peggy Reeves. 1990. *Fraternity gang rape: Sex, brotherhood, and privilege on campus*. New York: New York University Press.

Sanday, Peggy Reeves. 1996. Rape-prone versus rape-free campus cultures. *Violence against Women* 2 (2): 191–208.

Stombler, Mindy. 1994. "Buddies" or "slutties": The collective sexual reputation of fraternity little sisters. *Gender & Society* 8 (3): 297–323.

Stotzer, Rebecca L., and Danielle MacCartney. 2015. The role of institutional factors on on-campus reported rape prevalence. *Journal of Interpersonal Violence* 31, no. 16 (2015): 2687–707.

Svrluga, Susan. 2015. OU: Frat members learned racist chant at national SAE leadership event. *Washington Post*, 27 March. www.washingtonpost.com/news/grade-point/wp/2015/03/27/ou-investigation-sae-members-learned-racist-chant-at-national-leadership-event/.

Sexual Coercion among Athletes

Jake New

Driven by negative attitudes toward women and misperceptions about rape and consent, more than half of male college athletes surveyed for a new study say they have pressured women—through physical and verbal threats—into having sex with them.

And sexual coercion, which is defined as "any unwanted oral, vaginal or anal penetration as a result of verbal or physical pressure, including rape," is not just prevalent among big-time basketball and football players. The athletes included in the study were mostly those who play recreational, not intercollegiate, sports.

"What we see in this study speaks to a larger issue than just the high-profile and sensational reports we hear about," said Sarah Desmarais, an associate professor of psychology at North Carolina State University and the study's co-author. "There are some attitudes and beliefs prevalent among all kinds of male athletes that seem to be leading to high levels of sexually coercive behavior."

The study is based on an online survey of 379 male undergraduate students at a large public university in the National Collegiate Athletic Association's Division I. Students were asked questions about their sexual behaviors, attitudes toward women and belief in what are called rape myths—a series of commonly held but inaccurate assumptions about sexual violence.

The authors of the study said they decided to conduct the survey after noticing there was a dearth of research on the prevalence of sexual assault among athletes. A 1995 survey of 30 NCAA Division I institutions found that while athletes only represented 3 percent of students, they accounted for 19 percent of sexual assaults, but there's been little published research on the subject since that study.

"Despite the ongoing, high-profile cases of violence against college women by male intercollegiate athletes, research on this phenomenon has been stagnant," the researchers wrote. "This present study not only adds to the paucity of research on intercollegiate athletes, but also widens the scope to include recreational athletes."

The researchers define recreational athletes as students who train up to four times per week but don't compete nationally and are not members of any intercollegiate team. They surveyed 29 intercollegiate athletes and 159 recreational athletes, as well as 191 nonathletes, all of whom were men.

More than 54 percent of the athletes said they had engaged in sexually coercive behaviors, compared to 37 percent of the nonathletes. There was no difference between intercollegiate and recreational athletes.

"I think we were somewhat surprised at first that there was no difference," Desmarais said. "But when we really thought about the findings, they made a lot of sense. Those participating in recreational athletics were likely involved in team and varsity sports in high school or middle school, and they arrive at college with many of the same beliefs as those who continued to play the sport for a college team. It makes a lot of sense that there would be similar issues between those two groups."

The survey included questions about common rape myths, such as "if a woman is drunk or doesn't fight back, then the encounter is not rape." Athletes were more likely to believe those myths than nonathletes, the researchers found.

Using a survey tool called the Attitudes Toward Women Scale, the study also examined what kinds of beliefs male students had about women and their role in society. For example, the students were asked to say how much they agreed that "women should worry less about their rights and more about becoming good wives and mothers."

Athletes in the study were more likely than nonathletes to have traditional, and often negative, views of women, the study concluded. An analysis of the prevalence of these beliefs and the prevalence of sexual coercion among athletes indicated that "the effect of athletic status on likelihood of sexual coercion may be attributable to group differences in attitudes toward women and rape myth acceptance," the researchers wrote.

"This study shows how important it is to change these attitudes," Desmarais said. "The Attitudes Toward Women Scale used in the study was created in the 1970s and includes some truly archaic, sexist items, and we still see these results today. That shows you how far we still have to go. The hope is that this research provides some concrete targets that prevention programs can look at."

While the . . . authors of the study take care to note that this study represents athletes at just one institution, research published earlier this year by the NCAA also suggests many male athletes hold problematic beliefs about sexual assault.

A survey of 923 students found that male athletes struggled to understand consent more than nonathletes did. Nearly two-thirds of male athletes said they agreed that "it is OK to take it to the next level unless you get a definite no," compared to 47 percent of nonathletes.

"The results of these surveys are not all that surprising," said John Foubert, a professor of higher education and student affairs at Oklahoma State University and founder of the sexual assault prevention program One in Four. "Hostile masculinity is a predictor of sexual violence, and you're more likely to see that on an athletic team. If you have a norm among a group of men that is negative toward women, there can be an effect where they all drop to that lowest common denominator. If you have a few vocal, popular members of a football team, and they're saying noncomplimentary things toward women, it can impact the team's culture."

Source: "More than half of athletes in study say they engaged in sexual coercion," *Inside Higher Ed*, June 3, 2016. Reprinted by permission of Inside Higher Ed.

THE SEXUAL VICTIMIZATION OF MEN IN AMERICA: NEW DATA CHALLENGE OLD ASSUMPTIONS

LARA STEMPLE AND ILAN H. MEYER

We assessed 12-month prevalence and incidence data on sexual victimization in 5 federal surveys that the Bureau of Justice Statistics, the Centers for Disease Control and Prevention, and the Federal Bureau of Investigation conducted independently in 2010 through 2012. We used these data to examine the prevailing assumption that men rarely experience sexual victimization. We concluded that federal surveys detect a high prevalence of sexual victimization among men—in many circumstances similar to the prevalence found among women. We identified factors that perpetuate misperceptions about men's sexual victimization: reliance on traditional gender stereotypes, outdated and inconsistent definitions, and methodological sampling biases that exclude inmates. We recommend changes that move beyond regressive gender assumptions, which can harm both women and men.

The sexual victimization of women was ignored for centuries. Although it remains tolerated and entrenched in many pockets of the world, feminist analysis has gone a long way toward revolutionizing thinking about the sexual abuse of women, demonstrating that sexual victimization is rooted in gender norms[1] and is worthy of social, legal, and public health intervention. We have aimed to build on this important legacy by drawing attention to male sexual victimization, an overlooked area of study. We take a fresh look at several recent findings concerning male sexual victimization, exploring explanations for the persistent misperceptions surrounding it. Feminist principles that emphasize equity, inclusion, and intersectional approaches;[2] the importance of understanding power relations;[3] and the imperative to question gender assumptions[4] inform our analysis.

To explore patterns of sexual victimization and gender, we examined 5 sets of federal agency survey data on this topic (Table 52.1). In particular, we show that 12-month prevalence data from 2 new sets of surveys conducted, independently, by the Centers for Disease Control and Prevention (CDC) and the Bureau of Justice Statistics (BJS) found widespread sexual victimization among men in the United States, with some forms of victimization roughly equal to those experienced by women.

Despite such findings, contemporary depictions of sexual victimization reinforce the stereotypical sexual victimization paradigm, comprising male perpetrators and female victims. As we demonstrate, the reality concerning sexual victimization and gender is more complex. Although different federal agency surveys have different purposes and use a wide variety of methods (each with concomitant limitations), we examined the findings of each, attempting to glean an overall picture. This picture reveals alarmingly high prevalence of both male and female sexual victimization; we highlight the underappreciated findings related to male sexual victimization.

From "The Sexual Victimization of Men in America: New Data Challenge Old Assumptions," *American Journal of Public Health* Vol. 104, No. 6, pp. e19–e26. Reprinted by permission of The Sheridan Press.

TABLE 52.1 US Federal Agency Surveys of Sexual Victimization Using Probability Samples

STUDY	YEAR OF STUDY	CONDUCTED BY	SAMPLE	NO.
National Intimate Partner and Sexual Violence Survey (NISVS)	2010	Centers for Disease Control and Prevention	Nationally representative telephone survey of 12 mo and lifetime prevalence data on sexual violence, stalking, and intimate partner violence	16,507
National Crime Victimization Survey (NCVS)	2012	Bureau of Justice Statistics	Longitudinal survey of US households	40,000 households; 75,000
Uniform Crime Report (UCR)	2012	Federal Bureau of Investigation	NA (UCR is a cooperative statistical effort whereby 18,000 city, university, and college, county, state, tribal, and federal law enforcement agencies report data on crimes brought to their attention.)	NA
Sexual Victimization in Prisons[a] and Jails Reported by Inmates	2011–2012	Bureau of Justice Statistics	Probability sample of state and federal confinement facilities and random sampling of inmates within selected facilities	92,449
National Inmate Survey (NIS 2011–12) Sexual Victimization in Juvenile Facilities[a] Reported by Youth; National Survey of Youth in Custody (NSYC 2012)	2012	Bureau of Justice Statistics	Multistage stratified survey of facilities in each state of the United States and random sample of youths within selected facilities	8,707

Note: NA = not available.

[a]In these reports, 12-month prevalence refers to 12 months, or shorter if the respondent has been in the facility for less than 12 months.

For example, in 2011 the CDC reported results from the National Intimate Partner and Sexual Violence Survey (NISVS), one of the most comprehensive surveys of sexual victimization conducted in the United States to date. The survey found that men and women had a similar prevalence of nonconsensual sex in the previous 12 months (1.270 million women and 1.267 million men).[5] This remarkable finding challenges stereotypical assumptions about the gender of victims of sexual violence. However unintentionally, the CDC's publications and the media coverage that followed instead highlighted female sexual victimization, reinforcing public perceptions that sexual victimization is primarily a women's issue.

We explore 3 factors that lead to misperceptions concerning gender and sexual victimization. First, a male perpetrator and female victim paradigm underlies assumptions about sexual victimization.[6] This paradigm serves to obscure abuse that runs counter to the paradigm, reinforce regressive ideas that portray women as victims,[7] and stigmatize sexually victimized men.[8] Second, some federal agencies use outdated definitions and categories of sexual victimization. This has entailed the prioritization of the types of harm women are more likely to experience as well as the exclusion of men from the definition of rape. Third, the data most widely reported in the press are derived from household sampling. Inherent in this is a methodological bias that misses many who are at great risk for sexual victimization in the United States: inmates, the vast majority of whom are male.[9,10]

We call for the consistent use of gender-inclusive terms for sexual victimization, objective reporting of data, and improved methodologies that account for institutionalized populations. In this way, research and reporting on sexual victimization will more accurately reflect the experiences of both women and men.

MALE PERPETRATOR AND FEMALE VICTIM PARADIGM

The conceptualization of men as perpetrators and women as victims remains the dominant sexual victimization paradigm.[11] Scholars have offered various explanations for why victimization that runs counter to this paradigm receives little attention. These include the ideas that female-perpetrated abuse is rare or nonexistent,[12] that male victims experience less harm,[8] and that for men all sex is welcome.[13] Some posit that because dominant feminist theory relies heavily on the idea that men use sexual aggression to subordinate women,[14] findings perceived to conflict with this theory, such as female-perpetrated violence against men, are politically unpalatable.[15] Others argue that researchers have a conformity bias, leading them to overlook research data that conflict with their prior beliefs.[16]

We have interrogated some of the stereotypes concerning gender and sexual victimization, and we call for researchers to move beyond them. First, we question the assumption that feminist theory requires disproportionate concern for female victims. Indeed, some contemporary gender theorists have questioned the overwhelming focus on female victimization, not simply because it misses male victims but also because it serves to reinforce regressive notions of female vulnerability.[17] When the harms that women experience are held out as exceedingly more common and more worrisome, this can perpetuate norms that see women as disempowered victims,[7] reinforcing the idea that women are "noble, pure, passive, and ignorant."[13(p. 1719)]

Related to this, treating male sexual victimization as a rare occurrence can impose regressive expectations about masculinity on men and boys. The belief that men are unlikely victims promotes a counterproductive construct of what it means to "be a man."[18] This can reinforce notions of naturalistic masculinity long criticized by feminist theory, which asserts that masculinity is culturally constructed.[19] Expectations about male invincibility are constraining for men and boys; they may also harm women and girls by perpetuating regressive gender norms.

Another common gender stereotype portrays men as sexually insatiable.[13] The idea that, for men, virtually all sex is welcome likely contributes to dismissive attitudes toward male sexual victimization. Such dismissal runs counter to evidence that men who experience sexual abuse report problems such as depression, suicidal ideation, anxiety, sexual dysfunction, loss of self-esteem, and long-term relationship difficulties.[20]

A related argument for treating male victimization as less worrisome holds that male victims experience less physical force than do female victims,[21] the implication being that the use of force determines concern about victimization. This rationale problematically conflicts with the important feminist-led movement away from physical force as a defining and necessary component of sexual victimization.[22] In addition, a recent multiyear analysis of the BJS National Crime Victim Survey (NCVS) found no difference between male and female victims in the use of a resistance strategy during rape and sexual assault (89% of both men and women did so). A weapon was used in 7% of both male and female incidents, and although resultant injuries requiring medical care were higher in women, men too experienced significant injuries (12.6% of females and 8.5% of males).[23]

Portraying male victimization as aberrant or harmless also adds to the stigmatization of men who face sexual victimization.[8] Sexual victimization can be a stigmatizing experience for both men and women. However, through decades of feminist-led struggle, fallacies described as "rape myths"[24] have been largely discredited in American society, and an alternative narrative concerning female victimization has emerged. This narrative teaches that, contrary to timeworn tropes, the victimization of a woman is not her fault, that it is not caused by her prior sexual history or her choice of attire, and that for survivors of rape and other abuse, speaking out against victimization can be politically important and personally redemptive. For men, a similar discourse has not been developed. Indeed contemporary social narratives, including jokes about prison rape,[25] the notion that "real men" can protect themselves,[8] and the fallacy that gay male victims likely "asked for it,"[26] pose obstacles for males coping with victimization. A male victim's sexual arousal, which is not uncommon during nonconsensual sex, may add to the misapprehension that the victimization was a welcome event.[27] Feelings of embarrassment, the victim's fear that he will not be believed, and the belief that reporting itself is unmas-culine have all been cited as reasons for male resistance to reporting sexual victimization.[28] Popular media also reflects insensitivity, if not callousness, toward male victims. For example, a 2009 CBS News report about a serial rapist who raped 4 men concluded, "No one has been seriously hurt."[29]

The minimization of male sexual victimization and the hesitancy of victims to come forward may also contribute to a paucity of legal action concerning male sexual victimization. Although state laws have become more gender neutral, criminal prosecution for the sexual victimization of men remains rare and has been attributed to a lack of concern for male victims.[30] The faulty assertion that male victimization is uncommon has also been used to justify the exclusion of men and boys in scholarship on sexual victimization.[31] Perhaps such widespread exclusion itself causes male victims to assume they are alone in their experience, thereby fueling underreporting.[32]

Not only does the traditional sexual victimization paradigm masks male victimization, it can obscure sexual abuse perpetrated by women as well as same-sex victimization. We offer a few counterparadigmatic examples. One multiyear analysis of the NCVS household survey found that 46% of male victims reported a female perpetrator.[23] Of juveniles reporting staff sexual misconduct, 89% were boys reporting abuse by female staff.[33] In lifetime reports of nonrape sexual victimization, the NISVS found that 79% of self-reported gay male victims identified same-sex perpetrators.[34]

Despite such complexities, as recently as 2012, the National Incident Based Reporting System (a component of the Uniform Crime Reporting Program [UCR]) included male rape victims but still maintained that for victimization to be categorized as rape, at least 1 of the perpetrators had to be of the opposite sex.[35] Conversely, under the NISVS definitions, for a female to fall into the "made to penetrate" category, the perpetrating receptive partner must also be female.[5] ("Made to penetrate" includes anal penetration by a finger or other object, and a female could therefore be made to penetrate a male.) Additional research and analysis concerning female perpetration and same-sex abuse is warranted but is beyond the scope of this [reading]. For now we simply highlight the concern that reliance on the male perpetrator and female victim paradigm limits understandings, not only of male victimization but of all counterparadigmatic abuse.

DEFINITIONS AND CATEGORIES OF SEXUAL VICTIMIZATION

The definitions and uses of terms such as "rape" and "sexual assault" have evolved over time, with significant implications for how the victimization of women and men is measured. Although the definitions and categorization of these harms have become more gender inclusive over time, bias against recognizing male victimization remains.

When the Federal Bureau of Investigation (FBI) began tracking violent crime in 1930, the rape of men was excluded. Until 2012, the UCR, through which the FBI collects annual crime data, defined "forcible rape" as "the carnal knowledge of a female forcibly and against her will" (emphasis added).[36] Approximately 17,000 local law enforcement agencies used this female-only definition for the better part of a century when submitting standardized data to the FBI.[37] Meanwhile, the reform of state criminal law on rape, which began in the 1970s and eventually spread to every jurisdiction in the country, revised definitions in numerous ways, including the increased recognition of male victimization. Reforms also broadened definitions to address nonrape sexual assault.[38]

These state revisions left a mismatch with the limited UCR definition, forcing agencies to send only a subset of reported sexual assault to the FBI. Some localities eventually refused to parse their data according to the biased federal categories. For example, in 2010 Chicago, Illinois, recorded 84,767 reports of forcible rape under UCR, but because they refused to comply with the UCR's outdated categorization, the FBI did not include Chicago rape data in its national count.[39]

In 2012 the FBI revised its 80-year-old definition of rape to the following: "the penetration, no matter how slight, of the vagina or anus with any body part or object, or oral penetration by a sex organ of another person, without the consent of the victim."[40] Although the new definition reflects a more inclusive understanding of sexual victimization, it appears to still focus on the penetration of the victim, which excludes victims who were made to penetrate. This likely undercounts male victimization for reasons we now detail.

The NISVS's 12-month prevalence estimates of sexual victimization show that male victimization is underrepresented when victim penetration is the only form of nonconsensual sex included in the definition of rape. The number of women who have been raped (1,270,000) is nearly equivalent to the number of men who were "made to penetrate" (1,267,000).[5] As Figure 52.1 also shows, both men and women experienced "sexual coercion" and "unwanted sexual contact," with women more likely than men to report the former and men slightly more likely to report the latter.[5]

This striking finding—that men and women reported similar rates of nonconsensual sex in a 12-month period—might have made for a newsworthy finding. Instead, the CDC's public presentation of these data emphasized female sexual victimization, thereby (perhaps inadvertently) confirming gender stereotypes about victimization. For example, in the first headline of the fact sheet aiming to summarize the NISVS findings the CDC asserted, "Women are disproportionally affected by sexual violence." Similarly, the fact sheet's first bullet point stated, "1.3 million women were raped during the year

FIGURE 52.1   12-Month Sexual Victimization Prevalence among Adult Population (Noninstitutionalized)

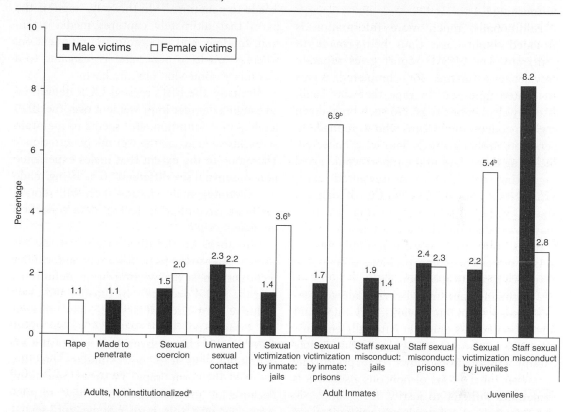

[a]Among the 5 federal agency surveys we reviewed, only NISVS collected lifetime prevalence, limiting our ability to compare lifetime data across surveys. It found lifetime prevalence for men as follows: made to penetrate = 4.8%, rape = 1.4%, sexual coercion = 6.0%, and unwanted sexual contact = 11.7%. For women: rape = 18.3%, sexual coercion = 13.0%, and unwanted sexual contact = 27.2%.

[b]Female detainees are significantly more likely to be sexually victimized by fellow detainees than are males; a presumably same-sex pattern of abuse that runs counter to the male perpetrator/female victim paradigm.

Source: From *National Intimate Partner and Sexual Violence Survey 2010*; among adult and juvenile detainees, *National Inmate Survey 2011–2012* and *National Survey of Youth in Custody, 2012: United States.*

preceding the survey." Because of the prioritization of rape, the fact sheet failed to note that a similar number of men reported nonconsensual sex (they were "made to penetrate").[41]

The fact sheet paints a picture of highly divergent prevalence of female and male abuse, when, in fact, the data concerning all nonconsensual sex are much more nuanced. Unsurprisingly, media outlets then emphasized the material the CDC highlighted in its summary material. The *New York Times* headline read,

"Nearly 1 in 5 Women in U.S. Survey Say[42(p .A32)] They Have Been Sexually Assaulted."

In addition, the full NISVS report presents data on sexual victimization in 2 main categories: rape and other sexual violence. "Rape," the category of nonconsensual sex that disproportionately affects women, is given its own table, whereas "made to penetrate," the category that disproportionately affects men, is treated as a subcategory, placed under and tabulated as "other sexual violence" alongside lesser-harm categories such as "noncontact unwanted sexual experiences," which are experiences involving no touching.[5]

Additionally, much more information is provided about rape than being made to penetrate. The NISVS report gives separate prevalence estimates for completed versus attempted rape and for rape that was facilitated by alcohol or drugs. No such breakdown is given concerning victims who were made to penetrate, although such data were collected. Including these data in the report would avoid suggesting that this form of unwanted sexual activity is somehow less worthy of detailed analysis.[1] These various reporting practices may draw disproportionate attention to the sexual victimization of women, implying that it is a more worrisome problem than is the sexual victimization of men.

Prioritizing rape over being made to penetrate may seem an obvious and important distinction at first glimpse. After all, isn't rape intuitively the worst sexual abuse? But a more careful examination shows that prioritizing rape over other forms of nonconsensual sex is sometimes difficult to justify, for example, in the case of an adult forcibly performing oral sex on an adolescent girl and on an adolescent boy. Under the CDC's definitions, the assault on the girl (if even slightly penetrated in the act) would be categorized as rape but the assault on the boy would not. According to the CDC, the male victim was "made to penetrate" the perpetrator's mouth with his penis,[5(p. 17)] and his abuse would instead be categorized under the "other sexual violence" heading. We argue that this is neither a useful nor an equitable distinction.

By introducing the term "made to penetrate," the CDC has added new detail to help understand what happens when men are sexually victimized. But the distinction may obscure more than it elucidates. In contrast to the term "rape," the term "made to penetrate" is not commonly used. The CDC's own press release about the survey, for example, uses the word "rape" (or "raped") 7 times and makes no mention of "made to penetrate."[43] In this way, "rape" is the harm that ultimately captures media attention, funding, and programmatic intervention, whereas "made to penetrate" is relegated to a secondary, somewhat obscure harm.

Similarly, the FBI's revised UCR definition, although a distinct improvement over the 1929 female-only definition, still seems to maintain an exclusive focus on the victim's penetration.[40] Therefore, to the extent that males experience nonconsensual sex differently (i.e., being made to penetrate), male victimization will remain vastly undercounted in federal data collection on violent crime.[5]

This focus on the directionality of the act runs counter to the trend toward greater gender inclusivity in sexual victimization definitions over the past 4 decades. The broader and more inclusive term "sexual assault" has replaced the term "rape" in at least 37 states.[44] Not only has this change been widespread in legal definitions, but it is now standard practice to avoid the term "rape" in survey questions because of inconsistencies in how respondents perceive this term.[21] Some anti–sexual violence activists may resist movement away from a term as compelling and vivid as "rape," but others have noted that victims who choose another label may do so as a legitimate coping strategy.[45]

We recognize that when it comes to the impact of sexual victimization, men and women may indeed experience it differently.[21] But categorizing the forms of sexual victimization that men typically experience as different and lesser than the forms of victimization that women typically experience would require considered justification. The reasons for continuing such practices would need to outweigh the drawbacks we have enumerated. We do not believe that such justification has been offered in the literature.

We therefore urge federal agencies to use care when collecting and reporting data on sexual victimization to avoid biased categorization. This does not mean that we suggest treating all sexual victimization identically. Nonconsensual penetrative acts (regardless of directionality) may be legitimately distinguished from acts that do not involve penetration. Likewise, harms that do not involve any genital contact whatsoever, such as unwelcome kissing, flashing, and sexual comments, although harmful for some victims, are categorically distinguishable because they do not involve contact with socially inviolable and physically sensitive reproductive parts of the body.

Without seeking to outline an entirely new classification scheme, we posit that "rape" as currently defined by the CDC and the FBI will continue to foster the underrecognition of the extent of male victimization. Terms such as "sexual assault" and "sexual victimization," if defined in gender-inclusive ways, have the potential to capture the kind of abuse with which federal agencies ought to be concerned. They can be used more consistently and with less gender and heterosexist bias across crime, health, and other surveys. This would facilitate important cross-population analyses that inconsistent definitions now limit.

SAMPLING BIAS

In population-based sexual victimization studies, as in many other areas, researchers use a sampling frame that is restricted to US households. This excludes, among others, those held in juvenile detention, jails, prisons, and immigration detention centers. Because of the explosion of the US prison and jail population to nearly 2.3 million people[46] and the disproportionate representation of men (93% of prisoners[9] and 87% of those in jail[10]) among the incarcerated, household surveys—including the closely watched NCVS—miss many men, especially low-income and minority men who are incarcerated at the time the household survey is conducted.

Opportunities for intersectional analyses that take race, class, and other factors into account are missed when the incarcerated are excluded. For instance, characteristics such as sexual minority and disability status, including mental health problems, place inmates at risk: among nonheterosexual prison inmates with serious psychological distress, 21% report sexual victimization.[47]

Of course, surveys of inmate and juvenile populations present a host of ethical, legal, and logistical challenges for surveyors. Sexual victimization in particular is risky for inmates to disclose; those who report abuse may be targeted for retaliation. The challenges of including vulnerable populations are very real, but because inmates are at great risk, their exclusion is especially likely to skew the public understanding of sexual victimization. For example, the NCVS's household data on rape and sexual assault are widely reported in the media each year but typically without mention of the impact of excluding incarcerated individuals (or other institutionalized or homeless persons).

Recognizing the lack of data concerning incarcerated persons, the 2003 Prison Rape Elimination Act mandates that BJS conduct a regular comprehensive survey about sexual victimization behind bars.[48] These results help fill the gap in knowledge concerning sexual victimization in the United States. We reviewed 2 of the recently released reports (Table 52.1), which provide results from the National Inmate Survey 2011–2012 and the National Survey of Youth in Custody 2012.

These 2 surveys demonstrate that male and female detainees both experience sexual victimization committed by staff and other inmates and that the prevalence differs by sex

(Figure 52.1). The National Inmate Survey 2011–2012 shows that slightly more men than women in jails and prisons reported staff sexual misconduct, which includes all incidents of sexual contact with staff (12-month prevalence for men in jails = 1.9%, men in prisons = 2.4% vs 1.4% and 2.3%[47] for women, respectively). Women in jails and prisons reported more inmate-on-inmate abuse than did men (women in jails = 3.6%, women in prisons = 6.9% vs 1.4% and 1.7% for men, respectively).

In the National Survey of Youth in Custody 2012, about 9.5% of male and female juvenile detainees reported sexual victimization in the 12 months before the interview (or since detained, if < 12 months).[33] But gender differences were observed: females were more likely than were males to report sexual victimization by other youths (5.4% vs 2.2%), and males were more likely than were females to report sexual victimization by facility staff (8.2% vs 2.8%).[33]

The examination of data from prisons, jails, and juvenile detention institutions reveals a very different picture of male sexual abuse in the United States from the picture portrayed by the household crime data alone. This discrepancy is stark when comparing the detainee findings with those of the NCVS, the longitudinal crime survey of households widely covered in the media each year. The 2012 NCVS's household estimates indicate that 131,259 incidents of rape and sexual assault were committed against males.[49] Using adjusted numbers from the detainee surveys, we roughly estimate that more than 900,000 sexual victimization incidents were committed against incarcerated males (Figure 52.2).

Comparability is limited, as the inmate surveys include a much broader range of victimization, such as sex between staff and inmates that inmates report as "willing." When guards and other staff engage in sexual activity with inmates in their care, it occurs in the context of an extreme power imbalance and is a criminal offense in all 50 states. We therefore find it worthy of inclusion. Moreover, more than half of both male and female prison and jail inmates who report staff sexual misconduct indicate that at least some of the sexual activity was "pressured"; more than one third indicate that some of it was accomplished with "force or threat of force."[50]

We have presented these figures not to offer a precise overall estimate of sexual victimization in the United States but to suggest that relying solely on NCVS household surveys vastly underrecognizes sexual victimization incidents that occur among men. (Prevalence data from the NISVS serve as further evidence of the NCVS's undercount of male and female victimization; Figure 52.1.)

We understand the reasons for using household surveys, and we acknowledge the complexities inherent in surveying vulnerable populations, which include not only the incarcerated but also homeless persons and those in care facilities, such as nursing homes. We underscore, however, that exclusive reliance on household methods may paint a misleading picture of sexual victimization in the United States by missing those at enormous risk. In addition to advocating greater awareness about such bias, we recommend the development of methods that would derive population estimates from the results of both household surveys and surveys of institutionalized individuals.

ADDITIONAL METHODOLOGICAL LIMITATIONS

We find it noteworthy that the newer NISVS and the BJS detainee surveys show less disparity between male and female reports of sexual victimization than does the longstanding crime survey, NCVS (Figures 52.1 and 52.2). In 2012, male victims experienced 38% of incidents, but the previous 5 years of NCVS data show even greater gender disparity. The percentage of rape and sexual assault incidents committed against

FIGURE 52.2   Annual Incidents of Sexual Victimization

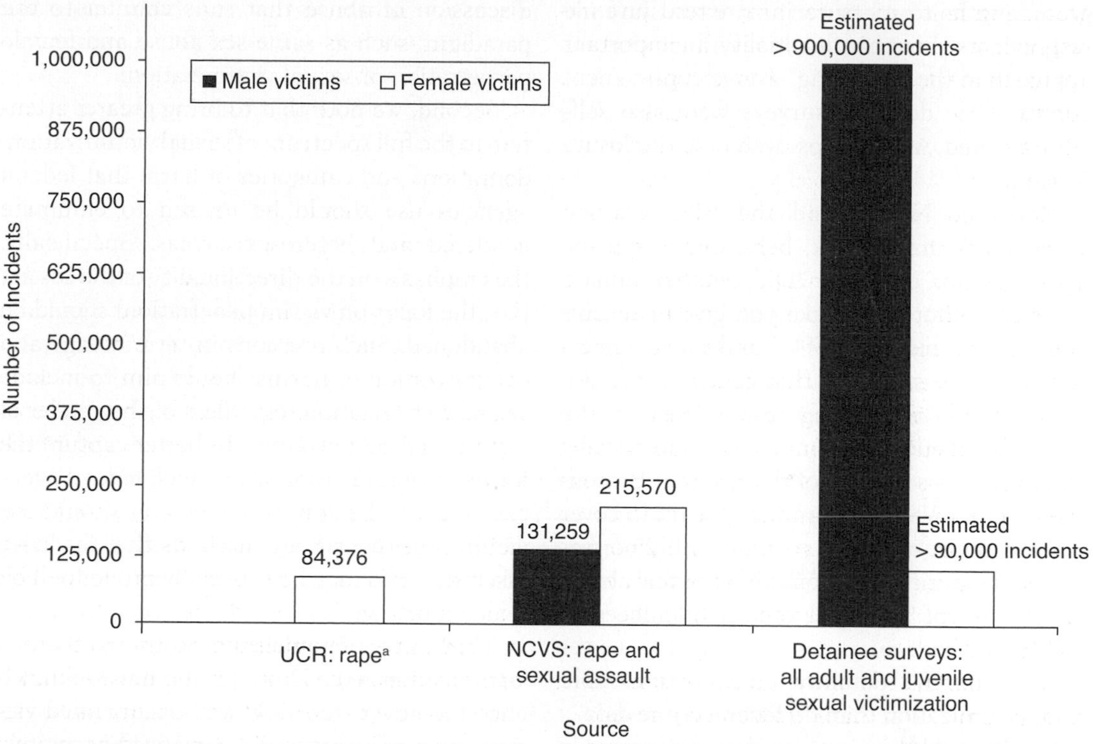

[a]Men were excluded from the definition of rape.

Note: We calculated the sex of victims in NCVS using the publicly available Victimization Analysis Tool www.bjs.gov/index.cfm?ty=nvat. We generated a rough estimate of the number of annual incidents of sexual victimization in jails, prisons, and juvenile detention facilities by sex, using the 2008–2009 data, the most recent publicly available data on repeat incidents.[50,54] (Repeat incidents were not reported in detail in 2011–2012.) To arrive at this, we multiplied a flow-adjusted number of detainees who reported at least one sexual victimization incident by the mean number of incidents of sexual victimization reported per victimized detainee. The flow-adjusted number of victims corrects for persons moving in and out of facilities during the 12-month sampling. The US Department of Justice Regulatory Impact Assessment of PREA[55] provides a flow-adjusted prevalence estimate of sexual victimization. The NIS-2 and NSYC report on the number of incidents of victimization as a range; we used the middle of the range. NISVS findings are not included because data on number of incidents have not been made public.

Source: From *Uniform Crime Report (UCR)* and *National Crime Victim Survey (NCVS), 2012*; *National Inmate Survey-2, 2008–2009*; and *National Survey of Youth in Custody 2008–2009: United States.*

males ranged from only 5% to 14% from 2007 to 2011.[49] Because NCVS is an omnibus crime survey, rather than a survey focused specifically on sexual victimization, one would anticipate lower reporting overall. But what explains the marked gender disparity in reporting among these federal surveys?

Perhaps because NCVS is focused on crime, rather than on health or sexual victimiza-

tion specifically, men are less likely to report unwanted sex (particularly with a female abuser) as criminal, thus leading to a greater gender disparity in the NCVS than in noncrime surveys. Additionally, the victim-sensitive survey methods used more recently in the NISVS and the BJS detainee surveys may be especially useful for eliciting male disclosure. For example, CDC researchers used graduated informed consent and frequent check-ins to build rapport and ensure participant comfort. BJS went to great lengths to reassure inmate and juvenile respondents about confidentiality, an important approach in the "snitching"-averse confinement context. The detainee surveys were also self-administered, which helps overcome disclosure resistance.

Both the NISVS and the BJS detainee surveys ask many frank, behaviorally specific questions, for example, "Did another inmate use physical force to make you give or receive oral sex or a blow job?"[47(p. 41)] and more numerous questions, strategies that generally increase reporting by acclimating respondents to the topic, desensitizing them (perhaps especially men) to the discomfort of disclosure.[51] By contrast, the NCVS, an instrument meant to cover a broad range of crimes, contains only nonbehaviorally specific questions about sexual abuse. These (and perhaps still other) differences in survey methods may explain why the newer NISVS and BJS detainee data capture more male victimization than do federal crime data.

Crime and health surveys do not necessarily intend to measure the same events. But to the extent that the newer victim-sensitive methods increase the reporting of the types of sexual victimization experiences with which crime surveys ought to be concerned, such methods should be considered for the NCVS to increase the reporting of sexual crimes among women and men.

CONCLUSIONS

While recognizing and lamenting the threat that sexual victimization continues to pose for women and girls, we aim to bring into the fold the vast cohort of male victims who have been overlooked in research, media, and governmental responses. In so doing, we first argue that it is time to move past the male perpetrator and female victim paradigm. Overreliance on it stigmatizes men who are victimized,[8] risks portraying women as victims,[52] and discourages discussion of abuse that runs counter to the paradigm, such as same-sex abuse and female perpetration of sexual victimization.

Second, we note that to bring greater attention to the full spectrum of sexual victimization, definitions and categories of harm that federal agencies use should be revised to eliminate gendered and heterosexist bias. Specifically, the emphasis on the directionality of the sex act (i.e., the focus on victim penetration) should be abandoned. Such revisions in terminology and categorization of harms should aim to include sexual victimization regardless of the gender of victims and perpetrators. To better capture the forms of victimization with which federal agencies ought to be concerned, studies should use victim-sensitive survey methods that facilitate disclosure and may be especially prone to illicit male reporting.

Third, any comprehensive portrayal of sexual victimization in the United States must acknowledge the now extensively well-documented victimization of incarcerated persons to accurately reflect the experiences of large numbers of sexually victimized men. Because the United States disproportionately incarcerates Black, Hispanic, low-income, and mentally ill persons, accounting for the experience of the incarcerated population will help researchers and policymakers better understand the intersecting factors that lead to the sexual victimization of already marginalized groups. Homeless persons and other institutionalized individuals may be similarly vulnerable. To arrive at better estimates of sexual victimization, analytic approaches that combine data from households and nonhousehold populations are necessary.

Finally, a gender-conscious analysis of sexual victimization as it affects both women and men is needed and is not inconsistent with a gender-neutral approach to defining abuse.[53] Indeed, masculinized dominance and feminized subordination can take place regardless of the biological sex or sexual orientation of the actors. We therefore advocate for the use of gender-conscious analyses that avoid regressive stereotyping, to which both women and men are detrimentally subject. This includes an understanding of how gender norms can affect the sexual victimization of all persons.[53]

ABOUT THE AUTHORS

Lara Stemple is with the Health and Human Rights Law Project, University of California, Los Angeles School of Law. Ilan H. Meyer is with the Williams Institute for Sexual Orientation Law and Public Policy, University of California, Los Angeles School of Law.

Correspondence should be sent to Lara Stemple, UCLA Law, 405 Hilgard Ave., Los Angeles, CA 90095-1476 (e-mail: stemple@law.ucla.edu). Reprints can be ordered at http://www.ajph.org by clicking the "Reprints" link.

This article was accepted February 13, 2014.

CONTRIBUTORS

L. Stemple and I. H. Meyer contributed to the conceptualization of this article, the interpretation of data, and the drafting and revision of content.

ACKNOWLEDGMENTS

Work on this article was supported, in part, by a grant from the Ford Foundation to the Williams Institute (grant 0130-0650).

The authors wish to thank Christina Kung, Tiffany Parnell, and Brad Sears.

Human Participant Protection

Institutional review board approval was not necessary, as we analyzed data in previously published reports.

REFERENCES

1. Fitzpatrick J. *The Use of International Human Rights Norms to Combat Violence against Women.* Human Rights of Women: National and International Perspectives. Philadelphia, PA: University of Pennsylvania Press; 1994.
2. Crenshaw KW. Mapping the margins: intersectionality, identity politics, and violence against women of color. *Stanford Law Rev.* 1991; 43(6): 1241–99.
3. MacKinnon CA. *Feminism Unmodified: Discourses on Life and Law.* Cambridge, MA: Harvard University Press; 1987.
4. Millett K. *Sexual Politics.* Garden City, NY: Doubleday; 1970.
5. National Center for Injury Prevention and Control. The National Inmate Partner and Sexual Violence Survey. 2011. Available at: http://www.cdc.gov /ViolencePrevention/pdf/NISVS_Report2010-a.pdf. Accessed September 28, 2012.
6. Copelon R. Surfacing gender: reengraving crimes against women in humanitarian law. In: Nicole Ann Dombrowski, ed. *Women and War in the Twentieth Century: Enlisted with or without Consent.* New York, NY: Garland; 1990: 245–66.
7. Kapur R. *The Tragedy of Victimization Rhetoric: Resurrecting the Native Subject in International/ PostColonial Feminist Legal Politics.* London, UK: Routledge; 2002.
8. Scarce M. *Male on Male Rape: The Hidden Toll of Stigma and Shame.* New York, NY: Insight Books; 1997.
9. US Department of Justice. Prisoners in 2012—advance counts. 2013. Available at: http://www.bjs.gov/content /pub/pdf/p12ac.pdf. Accessed January 19, 2014.
10. US Department of Justice. Jail inmates at midyear 2012—statistical tables. 2013. Available at: http://www .bjs.gov/content/pub/pdf/jim12st.pdf. Accessed January 19, 2014.
11. Denov MS. The myth of innocence: sexual scripts and the recognition of child sexual abuse by female perpetrators. *J Sex Res.* 2003; 40(3): 303–14.
12. Mendel MP. *The Male Survivor: The Impact of Sexual Abuse.* Thousand Oaks, CA: Sage; 1995.
13. Smith, B. V. Uncomfortable places, close spaces: female correctional workers' sexual interactions with men and boys in custody. *UCLA Law Rev.* 2012; 59(6): 1690–745.
14. Brownmiller S. *Against Our Will: Men, Women and Rape.* New York, NY: Simon and Schuster; 1975.
15. Gelles RJ. The politics of research: the use, abuse, and misuse of social science data—the cases of intimate partner violence. *Fam Court Rev.* 2007; 45(1): 42–51.
16. Dutton DG, Nicholls, T. L. Gender paradigm in domestic violence research and theory: Part 1—The conflict of theory and data. *Aggress Violent Behav.* 2005; 10(6): 680–714.
17. Miller AM. Sexuality, violence against women, and human rights: women make demands and ladies get protection. *Health Human Rights J.* 2004; 7(2): 16–47.
18. Gear S. Behind the bars of masculinity: male rape and homophobia in and about South African men's prisons. *Sexualities.* 2007; 10(2): 209–17.
19. Kimmel MS. Masculinity as homophobia: fear, shame, and silence in the construction of gender identity. In: Gergen MM, Davis SN, eds. *Toward a New Psychology of Gender.* New York, NY: Routledge; 1997: 223–24.
20. Struckman-Johnson C, Struckman-Johnson D. Acceptance of male rape myths among college men and women. *Sex Roles.* 1992; 7(3/4): 85–100.

21. Koss MP, Abbey A, Campbell R, et al. Revising the SES: a collaborative process to improve assessment of sexual aggression and victimization. *Psychol Women Q*. 2007; 31(4): 357–70.

22. Clay-Warner J, Burt CH. Rape reporting after reforms: have times really changed. *Violence against Women*. 2005; 11(2): 150–76.

23. Weiss KG. Male sexual victimization: examining men's experiences of rape and sexual assault. *Men Masc*. 2010; 12(3): 275–98.

24. Lonsway KA, Fitzgerald LF. Rape myths: in review. *Psychol Women Q*. 1994; 18(2): 133–64.

25. Stemple L, Qutb S. Just what part of prison rape do you find amusing? *San Francisco Chronicle*. 2002. Available at: http://www.sfgate.com/opinion/article/PRISONS-Selling-a-Soft-Drink-Surviving-Hard-2811952.php. Accessed April 10, 2014.

26. Wakelin A, Long KM. Effects of victim gender and sexuality on attributions of blame to rape victims. *Sex Roles*. 2003; 49(9/10): 477–87.

27. National Center for Victims of Crime. Male rape. 2008. Available at: http://www.nsvrc.org/publications/articles/male-rape. Accessed October 12, 2012.

28. Groth AN, Burgess AW. Male rape: offenders and victims. *Am J Psychiatry*. 1980; 137(7): 806–10.

29. CBS. Male-stalking rapist puzzles experts. 2009. Available at: http://www.cbsnews.com/news/malestalking-rapist-puzzles-experts. Accessed September 28, 2012.

30. Capers B. Real rape too. 2011. Available at: http://www.californialawreview.org/assets/pdfs/99-5/02-Capers.pdf. Accessed September 28, 2012.

31. Posner RA. *Sex and Reason*. Cambridge, MA: Harvard University Press; 1992.

32. Mezey G, King M. The effects of sexual assault on men: a survey of 22 victims. *Psychol Med*. 1989; 19(1): 205–09.

33. Beck AJ, Cantor D, Hartge J, Smith T. Sexual victimization in juvenile facilities reported by youth, 2012. Available at: http://www.bjs.gov/content/pub/pdf/svjfry12.pdf. Accessed December 18, 2013.

34. National Center for Injury Prevention and Control. The National Inmate Partner and Sexual Violence Survey: 2010. Findings on victimization by sexual orientation. 2013. Available at: http://www.cdc.gov/violenceprevention/pdf/nisvs_sofindings.pdf. Accessed August 28, 2013.

35. US Department of Justice. National Incident-Based Reporting System (NIBRS) Technical Specification. 2012. Available at: http://www.fbi.gov/aboutus/cjis/ucr/nibrs_technical_specification_version_1.0_final_04-16-2012.pdf. Accessed January 15, 2014.

36. US Department of Justice. Crime in the United States: forcible rape. Available at: http://www.fbi.gov/about-us/cjis/ucr/crime-in-the-u.s/2012/crime-in-the-u.s.-2012/violentcrime/rape/rapemain.pdf. Accessed December 18, 2013.

37. US Department of Justice. Uniform Crime Reporting Handbook. 2004. Available at: http://www2.fbi.gov/ucr/handbook/ucrhandbook04.pdf. Accessed January 18, 2014.

38. Berger RJ, Neuman WL, Searles P. Impact of rape law reform: an aggregate analysis of police reports and arrests. *Crim Justice Rev*. 1994; 19(1): 1–23.

39. Savage C. US to expand its definition of rape in statistics. 2012. Available at: http://www.nytimes.com/2012/01/07/us/politics/federal-crime-statistics-toexpand-rape-definition.html?_r=1&. Accessed September 28, 2012.

40. US Department of Justice. Attorney general Eric Holder announces revisions to the uniform crime report's definition of rape. 2012. Available at: http://www.fbi.gov/news/pressrel/press-releases/attorney-general-ericholder-announces-revisions-to-the-uniform-crimereports-definition-of-rape. Accessed September 28, 2012.

41. National Center for Injury Prevention and Control. The National Inmate Partner and Sexual Violence Survey: fact sheet. 2011. Available at: http://www.cdc.gov/ViolencePrevention/pdf/NISVS_FactSheet-a.pdf. Accessed September 28, 2012.

42. Rabin RC. Nearly 1 in 5 women in US survey say they have been sexually assaulted. 2011. Available at: http://www.nytimes.com/2011/12/15/health/nearly1-in-5-women-in-us-survey-report-sexual-assault.html?_r=1&scp=2&sq=centers%20for%20disease%20control%20and%20prevention%20rape&st=cse. Accessed September 28, 2012.

43. Centers for Disease Control and Prevention. Sexual violence, stalking, and intimate partner violence widespread in the US. 2011. Available at: http://www.cdc.gov/media/releases/2011/p1214_sexual_violence.html. Accessed December 17, 2013.

44. McMahon-Howard J. Does the controversy matter? Comparing the causal determinants of the adoption of controversial and noncontroversial rape law reforms. *Law Soc Rev*. 2011; 45(2): 401–34.

45. Kahn AS, Jackson J, Kully C, Badger K, Halvorsen J. Calling it rape: differences in experiences of women who do or do not label their sexual assault as rape. *Psychol Women Q*. 2003; 27(3): 233–42.

46. Walmsley R. *World Prison Population List*. 9th ed. London, UK: International Center for Prison Studies; 2012.

47. Beck AJ, Berzofsky M, Caspar R, Krebs C. Sexual victimization in prisons and jails reported by inmates, 2011–12. 2013. Available at: http://www.bjs.gov/content/pub/pdf/svpjri1112.pdf. Accessed December 18, 2013.

48. The Prison Rape Elimination Act of 2003. Pub. L. No. 108-79, 42 U.S.C. §§15601–15609.

49. Truman J, Langton L, Planty M. Criminal victimization, 2012. 2013. Available at: http://www.bjs.gov/content/pub/pdf/cv12.pdf. Accessed January 21, 2014.

50. Beck AJ, Harrison PM. Sexual victimization in prisons and jails reported by inmates, 2011–12. 2010. Available at: http://www.bjs.gov/content/pub/pdf/svpjri0809.pdf. Accessed January 19, 2014.

51. Sorenson SB, Stein JA, Siegel JM, Golding JM, Burnam MA. The prevalence of adult sexual assault: the Los Angeles Epidemiologic Catchment Area Project. *Am J Epidemiol.* 1987; 126(6): 1141–53.

52. Stemple L. Human rights, sex, and gender: limits in theory and practice. *Pace Law Rev.* 2012; 31(3): 823–36.

53. Stemple L. Male rape and human rights. *Hastings Law J.* 2009; 60(605): 628.

54. Beck AJ, Harrison PM, Guerino P. Sexual victimization in juvenile facilities reported by youth. 2010. Available at: http://www.bjs.gov/content/pub/pdf/svjfry09.pdf. Accessed January 19, 2014.

55. US Department of Justice. Regulatory impact assessment for PREA final rule. 2012. Available at: http://www.ojp.usdoj.gov/programs/pdfs/prea_ria.pdf. Accessed January 17, 2014.

EVERYTHING YOU NEED TO KNOW ABOUT CONSENT THAT YOU NEVER LEARNED IN SEX ED

ZHANA VRANGALOVA

Over the past couple of years, we have started emphasizing the importance of sexual consent more than ever before in U.S. history. But what often gets left out of these discussions is how exactly you go about the business of obtaining and providing consent in real-life sexual situations. And especially, how to do it without the much-feared "ruining of the mood."

There's more than one way to approach consensual sex. The debate is still raging over where exactly the line of consensual sex versus sexual assault should be drawn: Some insist that the old "only no means no" approach is adequate, which is the idea that unless you explicitly say "no," you are implicitly consenting to whatever is being done to your body. Others argue that we need a new standard of "only yes means yes," which is the idea that unless you explicitly say "yes," you are not giving consent. But regardless of where you think the *legal* lines should be drawn, we can all agree that we want both ourselves and our partners to be enthusiastic about any sexual encounter. That is to say that every sexual encounter is ideally met with *enthusiastic* consent, rather than a situation where someone feels obligated or pressured to say yes, despite not being totally excited about participating.

There is no single approach for negotiating enthusiastic consent that will work for every person in every situation, but here are some things you can do to ensure that both you and your partner will be happy and comfortable with the physical activity you engage in.

OBTAINING ENTHUSIASTIC CONSENT

The person initiating the sexual encounter, or initiating the escalation of sexual intimacy in the sexual encounter, has a lot of responsibility in making sure the other person feels safe, comfortable, and is truly enjoying themselves. Here's what you need to know about obtaining enthusiastic consent.

Avoid Partners Who Are Vulnerable

When people are intoxicated, sexually inexperienced, in a new situation, or acting recklessly or immature, their physical and/or mental capacity to make informed sexual decisions is impaired or limited. The more vulnerable they are—and the more vulnerable than you they are—the greater the risk they will feel coerced or regretful the next day. If they are particularly vulnerable (like heavily intoxicated, asleep, unconscious, or not of legal age), they are not legally capable of providing consent, and sex with them is by default sexual assault, no matter how eager they seem.

Establish Reciprocal Interest before You Start Thinking about Physical Touch

Part of this is the good old art of flirting and building erotic tension: Are they making eye contact, smiling at you, leaning in, chatting excitedly? . . . Don't just come up to someone out of nowhere and ask them if you can kiss them, or worse, touch them. The other part of this has to do with trying to ensure your partner's intentions and expectations of the sexual encounter are in line with yours. If you just want a casual hookup, but they are hoping for a relationship, try to find out if they'd be OK with it.

Negotiate Consent Verbally

Explicitly *asking for permission* is the most obvious way to escalate to physical touch, and the one most commonly discussed when enthusiastic consent is brought up: "May I kiss/touch/take your shirt off? . . ." "Is it OK if I _____?" For safest results, it's good to ask permission for any escalation in intimacy, so a permission to kiss someone is not an automatic permission to touch them below the belt. This is an effective method that is preferred by some people, but it is also the one many people feel is a potential mood-killer.

Luckily, there are other ways to verbally obtain consent. Instead of asking for permission, you can offer your partner something you'd like to do for them. "I would love to kiss you/give you a massage/take your shirt off. . . . Would you like that?" Or, alternatively, *you could invite them to do something to/for you*: "I'd love a massage. Would you like to give me a back rub?"

Another way to do this is to tell your partner what you plan on doing for/with/to them before you actually do it, an approach known as safe-porting. That gives them a chance to process that info and decide whether they are on board with your ideas. For example, if you're making out with your clothes on, you can say, "I'm gonna slide my hand underneath your shirt . . . ," then wait for their reaction—verbal or nonverbal—before you decide whether you should actually do it or not.

Establish "Blanket Consent" Ahead of Time

One strategy for people who are more experienced is what sex educator Kenneth Play calls "blanket consent": explicitly agreeing on an "only no means no" policy. At some point—either before you start anything physical or after you've already obtained consent for a few individual acts—tell your partner something like, "I'd like the freedom to hook up without continually asking permission for each individual act. But consent is really important to me, so I'd like you to tell me if something doesn't feel good, if you want me to slow down or stop. Does this work for you? Do you feel comfortable saying 'no' when you want to say 'no'? Or would you rather me check in with you more regularly? Totally cool either way."

This is for people who are more sexually experienced, because it assumes that both partners know exactly what they (don't) want and are assertive enough to communicate that. While this is an ideal we should all strive toward, in reality, many people are not ready for an agreement like this. I would caution against taking a blanket consent approach with partners who are in any way vulnerable. Remember that at any point, no matter what you agreed to, you or your partner can say no or change your mind about what you already established.

Negotiate Consent Nonverbally

Some people argue that consent must always be verbal, that trying to decipher body language is just too uncertain, [leaving] too much room for error. Indeed, trying to negotiate consent without any words is riskier: Unlike spoken language, not everybody is good at reading body language, and not everyone is good at "speaking" body language.

That said, there are some partners and some situations where you can successfully negotiate consent nonverbally, but it requires a lot more experience, carefulness, and perceptiveness.

The basic rule is to build it up slowly, and get continued, reciprocated, and enthusiastic responses before you escalate to each subsequent intimate act. Like, don't just grab someone's butt or thigh right away; start with touch that is noninvasive, like briefly touching their hand, patting their back or arm, lightly grazing their knee with yours (and all of these should come only after you've already established basic mutual interest). Then, *and this is absolutely critical*, read their body language (or verbal response) very carefully. Are they responding with a smile, leaning in closer, letting out a little sigh, reciprocating with a similar touch, saying, "your hand feels so soft"? If so, that usually means "yes, continue."

Are they pulling away, freezing in fear, do they seem uncomfortable, or do they not respond in any sort of way? Those are all the nonverbal equivalent of a "no" and you should stop touching them. If their body language is ambiguous, or if you're not quite sure what it is saying, don't assume it's saying what you want it to be saying! Defer to one of the verbal consent options instead. And in general, for best and safest results, combine nonverbal consent with verbal consent options.

Encourage Your Partner to Say "No" (as Well as "Yes") at Any Point

Regardless of the primary method of obtaining consent you choose to take, you can always add this to the mix. Some time early in the physical encounter, pause for a moment and say something like what author Michael Ellsberg says: "I want you badly, but I'm also committed to you feeling totally safe and comfortable with me. So if anything I do with you makes you feel even slightly uncomfortable, I want you to say 'stop' or 'slow down' immediately and I'll stop or slow down."

Err on the Side of Caution

If you're not sure whether your partner is providing enthusiastic consent, err on the side of caution—especially if you're hooking up with a new partner, or someone more vulnerable than you. General rules of thumb: Only take an enthusiastic "yes" (either verbal or nonverbal) as "yes." Take "no," "maybe," and doing nothing at all as no; even take a hesitant "yes" as no. If they seem hesitant, give them time and space to make a decision without pressure. Say something like, "You seem hesitant right now. Why don't you think it over and maybe we'll do that next/some other time." There will be other opportunities.

PROVIDING ENTHUSIASTIC CONSENT

Most of the conversations around consent revolve around obtaining consent, placing all the responsibility in the hands of the person initiating the action. But in every sexual encounter, each of us has just as much responsibility to provide continuous enthusiastic consent as we have to obtain it. It is important to let your partner know you are really into it—and you have to be completely honest about it. You must own your "yes" as well as your "no."

Share Your Intentions and Limitations

What are you looking for in this scenario? If you wouldn't be hooking up unless this had potential to be more than a hookup, let your partner know. If you wouldn't be doing this if they had another partner, ask them whether they're single. Don't assume that just because you want or don't want something that the other person is on the same page.

Let Your Partner Know What Kind of Consent Works for You

And do this before or as soon as things start turning sexual. Are you the kind of person who likes to take things slow, be asked verbally before any escalation of physical closeness, and checked in with often? Tell them that. If you're new to sex, or with a new partner, this might be the way to go. Or do you prefer the more traditional "only no means no" approach? Say, "Feel free to explore my body without asking. I'll let you know if something is uncomfortable." But keep in mind, giving people this type of blanket consent carries the responsibility of actually saying "no" when you want them to stop.

Provide Continuous Positive Feedback

Provide continued "yes" feedback. You can do this verbally, by saying things like "yes," "that feels good," "I like that," and by telling your partner how and where to touch you. Or you can do it nonverbally, by touching your partner, returning their kisses, taking their clothes off, and showing them how and where to touch you.

Learn How to Convey "No" Effectively and Get Comfortable Doing It

Saying "no" is not easy; it can be awkward, uncomfortable, anxiety-provoking. But you are your own first line of defense: Research shows there are far more people out there willing to disregard a lack of enthusiastic "yes" than there are people willing to push through a strong "no." You can say "no" gently (but firmly), either nonverbally (by moving away, moving their hand away) or verbally (e.g., "I'm not interested, thanks for asking," "I don't like _____."). If people aren't getting more subtle signs, you can move on to saying "no" more forcefully. Doing nothing is NOT a very clear "no."

Err on the Side of Caution

If you're not sure what you want, err on the side of caution and say "no." Especially with new partners you don't know well or when you're feeling vulnerable. You can always change your mind to a "yes" later.

Keep in mind, there is no one type or form of consent that works for everyone in every situation. Which approach you take will depend on who you are, who your partners are, and what the situation is. Also keep in mind that no one was born knowing how to negotiate these situations. We're all always learning and improving, and making mistakes. When you screw up, make amends (as much as possible), then learn from your mistakes and don't repeat them. And remember, like with many things in life, practice makes perfect.

Sex Workers Don't Deserve to Be Raped

Jillian Keenan

At the peak of her career as a high-end escort, Veronica Monet got a call. A new client wanted to hire her at the usual rate: $500 for one hour.

At first, Monet hesitated. His address was in a poor part of Oakland. It wasn't the kind of neighborhood where clients could typically afford her services. Not wanting to discriminate against low-income clients, though, she scheduled the appointment. And when Monet arrived at his house, her earlier concerns disappeared. She liked him. He spoke movingly of his work with a church choir and of his history in the U.S. Army. Then things changed. When Monet asked for the money they'd agreed on, the client became threatening and aggressive. He told her that she was going to take a check, although they had previously agreed on a cash payment. Monet decided to leave. But she couldn't.

"I realized that his house was a cage—there were bars on the windows, bars on the doors, and everything was locked with a key," Monet said. "There was no way to get out. I was trapped." So when the man grabbed her and threw her onto the floor, Monet went into survival mode. She decided that the most important thing was to get out alive. The physical wounds from the attack left her torn and bleeding.

Monet knew how the police would treat her if she tried to report the assault, so she fought back the only way she knew how: she spoke to her friends and colleagues in the sex work community, warning them to stay away from the man who had raped her. But the warning didn't travel quickly enough. Three weeks later, the same man raped another sex worker. But that time it was different: The woman fought back. He stabbed her in the face.

"We tried to convince her to report it because we thought the police would take her more seriously than the rest of us—and it turned out there were a lot of us," Monet says. "But she was 18. She was terrified of the police." The second victim didn't report her rape either. Monet said the girl disappeared, and she doesn't know what happened to the man who raped them. She assumes he's probably still out there, waiting for his cage house to trap its next victim. . . .

"We need prostitutes to be able to report these things, because the bad guys prey on prostitutes first," Monet said. "When sex workers are afraid of the police, it makes the world a more dangerous place for every single woman."

Sex workers' fears are grounded in the realities of a justice system that criminalizes their livelihood. Prostitutes who report sexual assault to police can be laughed at, ignored, accused of lying, arrested, or worse—even when the assault didn't necessarily happen on the job. "If a woman [sex worker] tries to bring charges against a partner who has raped her, chances are they're going to use her job against her in court," Audacia Ray, whose New York City–based Red Umbrella Project supports current and former sex workers. "It's the chilling effect of knowing that the law is not with us."

Reliable statistics about rape and prostitution are nearly impossible to find, since a huge number of survivors don't report their assaults, but one recent study[1] found that sex workers have a 45 to 75 percent chance of experiencing sexual violence at some point in their careers. Our criminal justice system's explicit bias against sex workers only compounds the problem. In 2007, a judge in Philadelphia dismissed rape charges against a man who organized the gang rape of a prostitute at gunpoint, saying that his crime was merely "theft of services."[2] New York State's 1975 rape shield law—which protects rape victims from having their sexual histories used against them in criminal proceedings—explicitly does not apply to anyone with a prostitution conviction on her record in the past three years.[3] And when another Oakland sex worker, who goes by the name Ms. R, applied for state-funded victim compensation after the serious injuries from a rape left her unable to return to work immediately, she was denied support on the grounds of her job. The police and criminal justice systems treat sex workers as though rape were a mere "occupational hazard" of their work—an accusation that would never be thrown at a bank teller who survived a robbery.

"Sex workers are seen as 'criminals,' so it allows a whole section of society to not care if we're attacked," said Mariko Passion, an activist and current sex worker who said the police made fun of her when she tried to report a rape. "Criminalization allows people to imagine that we don't have boundaries, voices or labor rights. It allows them to forget that we can say 'no,' too."

The criminalization of sex work leaves women in that industry without the basic protections and labor standards that apply to people in other risky professions. But another problem—which may be harder to erase—is the stigma: even legal sex workers, such as exotic dancers and phone sex operators, told me they feel afraid to report rape and assault. And while some sex workers turn to advocacy groups, even rape support organizations sometimes perpetuate stigma. After Ms. R's attack, she sought help from Bay Area Women Against Rape, San Francisco Women Against Rape, and the California Coalition Against Sexual Assault—all three of which turned her away when they learned about her job. A male employee at Bay Area Women Against Rape even drove Ms. R to tears when he told her that she was "responsible" for the assault against her.

It's shocking to hear stories of victim-shaming within the world of advocacy organizations, but that attitude is common to all sexual assault survivors. A recent *Washington Post* column, for example, mocked a rape victim for having previously "hook[ed] up" with her attacker, and social media rushed to declare the Steubenville rape survivor a "slut" or "prostitute" after her assault.[4] So when our culture rushes to discredit all rape survivors with the implication that they are figurative "prostitutes," what happens to victims of sexual assault who are literal sex workers?

"I wanted to call the police," says a soldier in the U.S. Army Reserves who works as, in her words, "a massage-centered companion." "But what could I tell them? That I'm a prostitute and he anally raped me, even though I screamed at him to stop? I knew exactly what they would say. I knew no one would help me."

In lieu of legal protections or even support from anti-rape NGOs, some sex workers turn to organizations that specifically campaign for their rights. When Ms. R learned that her victim's compensation claim had been denied, she reached out to the U.S. PROStitutes Collective, the Erotic Service Providers Union, and the ACLU. They took on her case, and successfully campaigned to have California's discriminatory prohibition overturned.[5] It was a huge—but rare—victory for sex worker rights.

For many, the fundamental problem remains that as long as sex workers fear they might be arrested for doing their jobs—or merely for trying to report an assault—they are driven even deeper underground, where violence and rape thrive unchecked. Hawk Kinkaid, the president of HOOK, the nation's only grassroots organization that specifically supports male sex workers, said that in most parts of the United States, former prostitutes can be fired for having previously worked in the sex industry. In other words, the criminalization of prostitution makes it difficult for sex workers to change jobs—even when they want to.

A recently leaked policy document from Amnesty International agreed that the criminalization of prostitution leaves sex workers vulnerable to "violence and abuse by police and clients."[6] Even the criminalization of sex workers' clients—the so-called Nordic Model, which decriminalizes prostitutes but criminalizes their customers—has been "proven to drive those engaged in sex work underground, increasing the risk of violence and abuse."

Many sex worker advocates also argue that anti–human trafficking initiatives that focus specifically on sex workers depress human rights and labor standards for women who are consensually involved in the erotic industries.[7] They point out that forced labor exists in many industries—in fact, the International Labour Organization estimates that people trafficked into "forced sexual exploitation" make up only roughly one-quarter of all people trafficked into forced labor worldwide.[8] The agriculture industries, for example, have some of the highest rates of forced labor in the United States, but it's hard to imagine that police would arrest an Alaskan crab fisherman to "protect" him from the risk of trafficking.[9] This double standard puts willing sex workers in danger.

There is some strong evidence to suggest that decriminalization can protect sex workers, and all women, from violent crime. According to a recent paper from the Bureau of Economic Research, rates of rape dropped dramatically after the state of Rhode Island decriminalized indoor prostitution for six years. (In fact, the 31 percent drop in the number of reported rapes was so significant that the researchers re-confirmed the data with three separate statistical methods.)[10] After Germany and New Zealand decriminalized sex work, rates of violence against sex workers in those countries similarly decreased.[11]

Several theories explain these trends. First, legal sex workers in frightening situations can threaten to call the police, which may discourage violent escalation. Open and transparent transactional markets also make it easier for sex workers to share information and vet potential clients. And many point out that the criminalization of any field, such as the prohibition of alcohol, has historically allowed criminal organizations (and their resulting violence) to dominate industries.

"No system works 100 percent, but we do know that decriminalization is the number one thing we have to do first," said Kinkaid. "It's the only way to have a productive, adult conversation about how to protect people who consciously make a decision to work in this industry."

NOTES

1. *American Journal of Public Health*. 2014 May; 104(5): e42–54. doi: 10.2105/AJPH.2014.301909. Epub 2014 March 13.

2. http://abcnews.go.com/TheLaw/story?id=3801167.

3. http://www.anusha.com/nyshield.htm.

4. https://www.washingtonpost.com/opinions/george-will -college-become-the-victims-of-progressivism/2014/06/06 /e90e73b4-eb50-11e3-9f5c-9075d5508f0a_story.html.

5. http://www.dailynews.com/2013/12/12/california -prostitutes-win-victim-compensation/.

6. https://www.scribd.com/doc/202126121/Amnesty -Prostitution-Policy-document.

7. https://www.nytimes.com/2014/05/30/opinion/the-price -of-a-sex-slave-rescue-fantasy.html?_r=1.

8. http://www.ilo.org/global/topics/forced-labour/lang–en /index.htm.

9. https://www.unodc.org/unodc/en/human-trafficking/faqs .html.

10. https://www.nber.org/papers/w20281 and https://www .washingtonpost.com/news/wonk/wp/2014/07/17/when -rhode-island-accidentally-legalized-prostitution-rape-and -stis-decreased-sharply/?utm_term=.70b0f07efe0c.

11. http://www.fairobserver.com/region/europe/german -prostitution-model-reducing-violence-against-sex-workers/.

RAPE AND WAR:
FIGHTING MEN AND COMFORT WOMEN

JOANE NAGEL

Sexuality has always been an important, though often disregarded, aspect of all militaries and military operations. Throughout history women have been among "camp followers" providing services such as laundry, nursing, companionship, and sex to soldiers on military missions during peace and war.[1] Sometimes these women have been wives, relatives, or girlfriends, but always among their ranks have been prostitutes as well. Women who have had sex with servicemen around the world, however, have not always been volunteers. Throughout history local women have been involuntarily "drafted" in the sexual service of militaries as rape victims and sexual slaves.[2]

Rape in war is at its core an ethnosexual phenomenon. Whether a war is fought across national borders or inside state boundaries, the military front is typically an ethnosexual frontier. Differences in nationality, race, or ethnicity separate the combatants and identify the targets of aggression in military operations. Whether violence in war is from combat or sexual attack, and whether it is guns or bodies that are used as weapons, those who are physically or sexually assaulted almost always are different in some ethnic way. . . .

Sexual exploitation and abuse are important weapons of war, and rape is perhaps the most common component of war's sexual arsenal. Susan Brownmiller documents the routine practice of rape, especially gang rape, in war.[3] Moving or occupying armies use the rape of "enemy" women and girls as both a carrot and a stick: raping local women is a spoil of war for the troops to enjoy, and rape is also a technique of terror and warfare designed to dominate and humiliate enemy men by sexually conquering their women. Rape in war, as in many other ethnosexual settings, is best understood as a transaction between men, where women are the currency used in the exchange. Sexually taking an enemy's women amounts to gaining territory and psychological advantage. In countries around the world, rape often is defined as a polluting action, a way to soil the victim, her kin, and her nation physically and symbolically. Sexual warfare can extend beyond the moment of violation in situations where victims are reputationally smeared, physically mutilated, or when pregnancies or births result from sexual assaults. For instance, the widespread rape of mainly Muslim and some Croatian women by Serbian men in Bosnia in the early 1990s was partly intended to impregnate the women so that they would bear Serbian babies, "little Chetniks."[4] In order to guarantee that these rape victims could not obtain abortions, the Serbs set up concentration camps where pregnant women were imprisoned until they gave birth.[5]

Probably the best-known instance of rape in war is the so-called Rape of Nanking that occurred during the Japanese invasion of China in the winter and spring of 1938–1939,

From "Rape and War: Fighting Men and Comfort Women," *Race, Ethnicity, and Sexuality: Intimate Intersections, Forbidden Frontiers* by Joane Nagel, pp. 181–87. © Oxford University Press, Inc. 2003. By permission of Oxford University Press, USA.

when Japanese soldiers raped an estimated eighty thousand Chinese women and girls.[6] A less well-known instance of Japanese wartime sexual exploits was the sexual enslavement of thousands of mainly Asian women by the Japanese Imperial Army during World War II. Sexual slavery in war is a variation on the theme of wartime rape. Slavery extends the tactic of rape as a short-term strategy of a military mission into a permanent feature of military operations. The Japanese military established camps of so-called military comfort women (*Jugun Ianfu*) in Japan and other countries where Japanese troops were stationed. While there were some mainly lower-class Japanese women forced into sexual slavery, most of the estimated 200,000 women enslaved by the Japanese army were ethnic or national. Others were brought from Korea, China, Taiwan, Indonesia, Malaysia, and the Philippines to sexually service the troops.[7] Kazuko Watanabe reports that in such settings a woman's worth as a sexual commodity was based on her class and her ethnicity:

The Japanese Imperial Army divided comfort women into a hierarchical order according to class, race, and nationality. . . . Korean and most other Asian women were assigned to lower-class soldiers. Japanese and European women went to high-ranking officers. Most of the European women were Dutch [often of mixed ancestry] who were imprisoned in a prisoner of war camp in the Netherlands East Indies.[8]

Soldiers' rankings of and preferences for women of particular races and nationalities enslaved in rape camps were not unique to the Japanese military.[9] Japan was not the only country that established large-scale organized operations of forced sexual servitude during World War II. The Nazis used concentration camps in Germany and other occupied countries for more than industrial and war-related labor, their program of genocide against the Jews, and the mass deportation and killing of Roma (gypsies) and other "non-Aryan"

peoples. Sexual labor was also demanded of women internees, and both men and women prisoners were used for sexual experimentation by Nazi scientists and physicians. German concentration camps were sites of forced prostitution and sexual assault, and as was the case with Japan, not all women in the German camps were treated as "equal" when it came to sexual abuse. A woman's age, youth, and physical appearance made her more or less likely to be the target of Nazi sexual aggression.[10] And, as in so many areas of social life, even (especially) in wartime concentration camps, ethnicity mattered. There were official prohibitions against German soldiers having sex with Jewish women, though these rules often were not enforced. Many Jewish women survivors reported extensive sadistic sexual torture, as well as rape, and these assaults often were accompanied by a barrage of racial and anti-Semitic verbal abuse.[11]

The Allies also were involved in sexual violence and exploitation during World War II. Some was in the form of mass rapes, such as those committed against German women by the Soviet army.[12] In other cases, sexual abuse and exploitation resulted when military personnel capitalized on the vulnerability of women who faced economic hardship, malnourishment, or starvation because of the war's disruption of local economies and food production. Many women in occupied or liberated countries found sexual liaisons or prostitution preferable to the grim alternatives available for themselves and their dependent families. U.S. troops also committed rapes during the war and the occupation that followed. In her examination of U.S. Army records, Brownmiller found 947 rape *convictions,* not simply charges or trials of American soldiers in Army general courts-martial during the period from January 1942 to July 1947.[13]

Wartime rape did not stop at the end of World War II, nor did its ethnosexual character change after 1945. The practice of rape in war extended into major and minor conflicts during the second half of the twentieth century—in civil wars, wars of independence, and military invasions, interventions, and operations in countries and regions around the world including Bangladesh, Vietnam, Iraq, Kuwait, Bosnia, Croatia, Serbia, Rwanda, Liberia, Kashmir, and Sierra Leone.[14] The logic of rape in war is always the same: rapes are committed across ethnosexual boundaries, and rape is used by both sides for the familiar time-honored reasons—to reward the troops, to terrorize and humiliate the enemy, and as a means of creating solidarity and protection through mutual guilt among small groups of soldiers. Ethnic loyalty and ethnic loathing join hands in rape in war.

In the post–Soviet era East European nationalist conflicts, the use of rape as a weapon of war has begun to move from the shadows more fully into view. For instance, during the 1990s warfare occurred along a number of ethnic and national borders in the former Yugoslavia—between Croats and Serbs, Christians and Muslims, and against Roma, among others. The most notorious of these ethnic conflicts was in Bosnia; the conflict's notoriety stemmed in part from its sexual character, especially the mass rape of Bosnian Muslim women by Orthodox Christian Serbian men. Many of these men and women were former neighbors. Muslims and Christians had lived side by side in the city of Sarajevo and elsewhere in Bosnia for decades and many had intermarried. That peace was shattered in 1992 when "ethnic cleansing" began.

Ethnic cleansing, or the removal of one ethnic group from a territory claimed by another, followed a common pattern across the region. Groups of armed Serbian men (sometimes uniformed troops and sometimes "irregulars" who were not officially in the military and not in uniform) roamed Bosnian towns and villages in groups, opportunistically looting and pillaging houses and businesses, raping and killing mainly unarmed Muslims they encountered along the way. Survivors reported that the Serbs came through the same towns several times in waves. During the first wave, typically, some of the Muslim men were killed and the rest were rounded up to be killed later or to be interned in concentration camps. Muslim women, children, and the elderly were left behind. It was during the next waves of Serbs passing through the towns that they raped local non-Serbian girls and women.

Munevra was a forty-eight-year-old widow with three sons ranging in age from fourteen to twenty-four, ages that made them targets for the Serbs to kill or deport to concentration camps. She kept the young men hidden in the cellar as small groups of armed Serbian men repeatedly came through the town. In the spring of 1992, two men came to her house and sexually assaulted her. . . .

I was afraid my sons would hear me. I was dying of fear 'cause of my sons. They're decent people. . . . Then this man touched my breasts. He pulled up my blouse and took out my breasts. . . . He said, "For a woman your age your breasts aren't bad." Then they brought me to the other room. . . . I begged him and cried, and I crossed my legs. Then he took out his thing, you know, and he did it and sprayed it on me. When he was done the other one came and did the same thing. . . . When they left, my sons came out and . . . they asked me what happened: "What'd they do to you?" I said, "Nothing." I couldn't tell them about it. . . . I'd rather die than have them find out about it.[15]

Women's and families' shame about such incidents were part of the process of victimization and violations.[16] Munevra's experience occurred relatively early in the nationalist conflict; far worse sexual violations were in store for women as the war escalated.

The scene in Serbian so-called rape camps was a longer, more brutal nightmare for Muslim and other non-Serbian women and girls. Twenty-six-year-old Ifeta was arrested by Serbian soldiers, most of whom she knew, and taken to a women's camp in Doboj:

Three drunken [Serbian army] soldiers . . . dragged her into a classroom . . . here she was raped by all three men "at the same time," says Ifeta, pointing to her mouth and backside. "And while they were doing it they said I was going to have a baby by them". . . . After that the rapes were a part of Ifeta's daily life. . . . It was always a gang rape, they always cursed and humiliated her during it, and the rapists very frequently forced her to have oral sex with them.[17]

Another camp internee, Kadira, described the weeks she spent at Doboj:

"They pushed bottle necks into our sex, they even stuck shattered, broken bottles into some women. . . . Guns too. And then you don't know if he's going to fire, you're scared to death." . . . Once she was forced to urinate on the Koran. Another time she and a group of women had to dance naked for the Serbian guards and sing Serbian songs. . . . She has forgotten how many times she was raped.[18]

The same pattern of sexual terror, torture, and rape used by the Serbs in their campaigns of ethnic cleansing and warfare in Bosnia was repeated in Kosovo, Yugoslavia, in 1998–1999. Once again groups of Serbian men—police, soldiers, irregulars—swept through villages invading homes and raping Kosovar Albanian (mainly Muslim) female occupants, sexually attacking Kosovar Albanian women refugees fleeing combat zones, and sexually assaulting Kosovar Albanian women who were being held hostage or detained. The Kosovo conflict ended when NATO troops entered Kosovo in June 1999.[19]

In spring 2000, the UN convened the International Criminal Tribunal for the Former Yugoslavia in The Hague, Netherlands, to investigate and prosecute those ordering mass killing and mass rape in the various ethnic conflicts in the former Yugoslavia.[20] This investigation raised the issue of whether rape and sexual slavery are "crimes against humanity." Enloe argues that this question reflects a new awareness and public airing of what has been a long hidden history of sexual assault, torture, and exploitation of women during war:

[T]he rapes in Bosnia have been documented by women's organizations . . . [that] have helped create an international political network of feminists who are making news of the Bosnian women's victimization not to institutionalize women as victims, not to incite men to more carnage, but to explain anew how war makers rely on peculiar ideas about masculinity. . . . [F]eminist reporters are using news of wartime sexual assaults by male soldiers to rethink the very meanings of both sovereignty and national identity. . . . If they succeed, the construction of the entire international political arena will be significantly less vulnerable to patriarchy.[21]

As the reports of human rights hearings and organizations document every year, it is not only enemy women who are the targets of sexual abuse and torture in war. I have not seen reported the establishment of rape camps with men as sexual slaves, however, men often are assaulted sexually as part of intimidation, torture, and combat in international conflicts and wars, as well as in military or paramilitary operations against internal political or ethnic insurgents. For instance, in Bosnia, there were numerous reports of cases in which Muslim and Croatian men were castrated or forced to castrate one another:

In villages, towns, cities, the countryside, and concentration camps, male and female adults and children are raped as part of more extensive torture. Many of the atrocities committed are centered on the genitalia. . . . [T]estimonies of castrations enforced on Bosnian-Herzegovinian and Croatian prisoners, and in particular of orders under threat of death that they castrate each other with various instruments and at times with their teeth, are widely available, as the [United Nations] Bassiouni Report makes clear.[22]

Men also can be vulnerable to sexualized warfare in more indirect ways. In her critique of Japan's patriarchal Confucianist view of all women and racist treatment of non-Japanese men and women, Kazuko Watanabe also identifies a danger for men. She argues that in many countries men are trapped in masculinist roles, and forced to act out patriarchal and sexual scripts that commodify and endanger them as well as the women they victimize:

Men's bodies and sexualities are also victims of militarist and consumerist capitalist societies. Men are, supposedly, unable to control their sexual impulses and are in need of prostitutes. [In World War II] Male soldiers were dehumanized to make them good fighters then stimulated by sexual desire that was fulfilled by comfort women. . . . Both the soldiers who were forced to die for the emperor on the battlefields and today's businessmen who die for their companies from karoshi (overwork) have often been rewarded with prostitutes.[23]

Watanabe's analysis suggests that although they are perpetrators of the rape and sexual abuse of both women and other men in times of war, men pay a psychological, social, and physical price for their complicity in patriarchal masculinist systems of sexual and ethnosexual violence. For instance, many soldiers display varying degrees of post-traumatic stress or "shell shock" following combat. Michael Kimmel reports that during World War I officers and doctors tended to view such disorders as "failures to conform to gender demands":

Most psychiatric treatments for shell shock involved treating the disease as the result of insufficient manliness. T. J. Calhoun, assistant surgeon with the Army of the Potomac, argued that if the soldier could not be "laughed out of it by his comrades" or by "appeals to his manhood," then a good dose of battle was the best "curative."[24]

Although modern-day soldiers suffering from post-traumatic stress are viewed with more sympathy than their historical counterparts, many, including those working in the health care industry, still view soldiers exhibiting

symptoms arising from combat and military operations with some suspicion, as malingerers, frauds, or weaklings.[25]

High rates of post-traumatic stress disorder (PTSD), including suicide, among male and female soldiers in the early twenty-first-century U.S. wars in Iraq and Afghanistan led the U.S. military to try to understand the causes and treat the consequences of PTSD for an estimated one-fifth of U.S. troops.[26] Sexuality plays a role in PTSD for both men and women. Military sexual assault or "military sexual trauma" (MST) among U.S. troops was revealed to be a major cause of PTSD in the U.S. armed forces. The U.S. Department of Veterans Affairs found that 1 in 5 women and 1 in 100 men treated for PTSD at veterans hospitals reported being victims of MST.[27] From 2007–2010, the Department of Defense (2010) received over 11,000 reports of military sexual assaults.[28] A 2010 U.S. Air Force survey found that 18.9 percent of women and 2.1 percent of men reported experiencing some form of sexual assault while in the Air Force. Civilian studies of military sexual assault report much higher rates; some find as high as one-quarter of service women are sexually assaulted during their military service with many more reporting sexual harassment.[29]

Military sexual assault is only one of several faces of "sex and war" unveiled during the U.S. wars in Iraq and Afghanistan when the percent of women in the U.S. Armed Forces rose to 15 percent (from 1 percent in 1970). The increased presence of women in the U.S. military did not undermine the military's masculinist culture and mission. Studies of the two wars found that the military capitalized on its new feminine resources and developed new strategies for incorporating femininity and women's presence into its mission.[30] In the Iraq war, women soldiers were deployed not only as supply clerks, cooks, mechanics, nurses, doctors, and pilots, they also were enlisted in a variety of gender and sexual roles above and beyond the call of duty—as wives and lovers of service personnel, as targets of sexual harassment and assault, as weapons of war, and as symbols for enactments of masculine bravery. The infamous pictures of prisoner abuse in Iraq's Abu Ghraib prison prominently featured servicewomen as instruments of torture (holding leashes around the necks of Iraqi men, posing behind piles of naked male prisoners, placing their underwear on prisoners' heads). Service women also provided convenient opportunities to display male soldiers' and the military's bravery and gallantry. The staged rescue of Private Jessica Lynch from an Iraqi hospital early in the war was the subject of much media attention and multiple books and films which publicized another role for servicewomen: the damsel in distress saved by heroic men in arms.

NOTES

1. See, for instance, Anne M. Butler, *Daughters of Joy, Sisters of Misery: Prostitutes in the American West, 1865–90* (Chicago: University of Illinois Press, 1985).

2. For a recent overview, see Anne Llewellyn Barstow, *War's Dirty Secret: Rape, Prostitution, and Other Crimes against Women* (Cleveland: Pilgrim Press, 2000).

3. Susan Brownmiller, *Against Our Will: Men, Women, and Rape* (New York: Ballantine Books, 1975).

4. Beverly Allen, *Rape Warfare: The Hidden Genocide in Bosnia-Herzegovina and Croatia* (Minneapolis: University of Minnesota Press, 1996), 96.

5. Ibid., 96.

6. See Iris Chang, *The Rape of Nanking: The Forgotten Holocaust of World War II* (New York: Basic Books, 1997); James Yin and Shi Young, *The Rape of Nanking: An Undeniable History in Photographs* (Chicago: Innovative Publishing Group, 1997).

7. Japan has yet to make satisfactory restitution to Korean and Filipina "comfort women" who were sexually enslaved during World War II, and some former victims have come forward to demand a public apology and accounting for their treatment; see Seth Mydans, "Inside a Wartime Brothel: The Avenger's Story," *New York Times,* November 12, 1996:A3; Maria Rosa Henson, *Comfort Woman: A Filipina's Story of Prostitution and Slavery under the Japanese*

Military (Lanham, MD: Rowman and Littlefield Publishers, 1999); Sangmie Choi Schellstede, *Comfort Women Speak: Testimony by Sex Slaves of the Japanese Military* (New York: Holmes and Meier, 2000); for discussions of Japan's system of brothels, see George L. Hicks, *The Comfort Women: Japan's Brutal Regime of Enforced Prostitution in the Second World War* (New York: W. W. Norton, 1995); Keith Howard, *True Stories of the Korean Comfort Women* (London: Cassell, 1995); Sayoko Yoneda, "Sexual and Racial Discrimination: A Historical Inquiry into the Japanese Military's 'Comfort' Women System of Enforced Prostitution," in *Nation, Empire, Colony: Historicizing Gender and Race,* ed. Ruth Roach Pierson and Nupur Chaudhuri (Bloomington: Indiana University Press, 1989), 237–50; for a discussion of restitution in general and specifically as it relates to the women enslaved by Japan during World War II, see Elazar Barkan, *The Guilt of Nations: Restitution and Negotiating Historical Injustices* (New York: W. W. Norton, 2000), especially chapter 3.

8. Kazuko Watanabe, "Trafficking in Women's Bodies, Then and Now: The Issue of Military 'Comfort Women,'" *Peace & Change* 20, no 4 (1995): 503–04.

9. Both sexual and nonsexual labor were also demanded of women enslaved by the Japanese (ibid., 503); the Japanese also used rape as an instrument of terror and domination; most infamous is the "rape of Nanking" in which thousands of women were raped and killed; see Brownmiller, *Against Our Will,* 53–60.

10. Susan Brownmiller, *Against Our Will: Men, Women, and Rape* (New York: Ballantine Books, 1975), 61–62.

11. For firsthand accounts of women's treatment in the camps, see Sarah Nomberg-Przytyk, *Tales from a Grotesque Land* (Chapel Hill: University of North Carolina Press, 1985), 14–20; Livia E. Bitton Jackson, *Elli: Coming of Age in the Holocaust* (New York: Times Books, 1980), 59–61; Cecile Klein, *Sentenced to Live* (New York: Holocaust Library, 1988), 73–77; Lore Shelley, *Auschwitz: The Nazi Civilization* (Lanham, MD: University Press of America, 1992).

12. See Cornelius Ryan, *The Last Battle* (New York: Simon and Schuster, 1966); Anne Llewellyn Barstow, *War's Dirty Secret: Rape, Prostitution, and Other Crimes Against Women* (Cleveland: Pilgrim Press, 2000).

13. Susan Brownmiller, *Against Our Will: Men, Women, and Rape* (New York: Ballantine Books, 1975), 76–77; these 947 convictions are only part of a much greater universe of sexual assault by U.S. troops for several reasons: most rape is not reported and when it is, convictions are relatively rare even today, much less back in the 1940s during a state of war and/or military occupation; further, these were *convictions* where the soldier was found guilty, and did not include what could only have been a much larger number of charges filed and trials conducted; further still, these

records were only for convictions of Army and Air Force personnel, and did not include data on the U.S. Navy or Marine Corps; finally, these records did not include information on charges, trials, or convictions for lesser sexual crimes than rape, such as sodomy or assault with the intent to commit rape or sodomy.

14. See Americas Watch and the Women's Rights Project, *Untold Terror: Violence against Women in Peru's Armed Conflict* (New York: Americas Watch, 1992); Asia Watch and Physicians for Human Rights, *Rape in Kashmir: A Crime of War* (New York: Asia Watch, 1993); Ximena Bunster, "Surviving beyond Fear: Women and Torture in Latin America," in *Women and Change in Latin America,* ed. June Nash and Helen Safa (South Hadley, MA: Bergin & Garvey, 1986), 297–325; Samir al-Khalil, *Republic of Fear: The Politics of Modern Iraq* (Berkeley: University of California Press, 1989).

15. Alexandra Stiglmayer, "The Rapes in Bosnia-Herzegovina," in *Mass Rape: The War against Women in Bosnia-Herzegovina,* ed. Alexanda Stiglmayer (Lincoln: University of Nebraska Press, 1994): 101.

16. See Elizabeth Bumiller, "Deny Rape or Be Hated: Kosovo Victims' Choice," *New York Times,* June 22, 1999:1; Peter Finn, "Signs of Rape Sear Kosovo; Families' Shame Could Hinder Investigation," *Washington Post,* June 27, 1999:1.

17. Alexandra Stiglmayer, "The Rapes in Bosnia-Herzegovina," in *Mass Rape: The War against Women in Bosnia-Herzegovina,* ed. Alexanda Stiglmayer (Lincoln: University of Nebraska Press, 1994): 117–18.

18. Ibid., 118–19.

19. Human Rights Watch reports that although both sides committed sexual assault during the conflict, rates of rape by Serbian men far outnumbered instances of sexual abuse by Kosovar Albanian men during the conflict; see Human Rights Watch Report, "Kosovo: Rape as a Weapon of 'Ethnic Cleansing'" (March 21, 2000); my thanks to Hsui-hua Shen, Department of Sociology, University of Kansas, for bringing this report to my attention.

20. For early reports on the hearings and judgments of that tribunal, see Marlise Simons, "Bosnian Serb Trial Opens: First on Wartime Sex Crimes," *New York Times,* March 21, 2000:3; John-Thor Dahlburg, "Bosnian Witness Says She Endured Series of Rapes; Courts: Victim No. 50 Testifies in The Hague," *Los Angeles Times,* March 30, 2000:1; Chris Bird, "UN Tribunal Told of Bosnian Rape Camp Horrors," *Guardian,* April 21, 2000:1; Roger Thurow, "A Bosnian Rape Victim Suffers from Scars that Do Not Fade," *Wall Street Journal,* July 17, 2000:18.

21. Cynthia Enloe, "Afterword: Have the Bosnian Rapes Opened a New Era of Feminist Consciousness?" in Alexandra Stiglmayer (ed.), *Mass Rape: The War against*

Women in Bosnia and Herzegovina (Lincoln: University of Nebraska Press, 1994), 219–30; progress continues to be made, slowly, in the shift toward defining rape as a human rights violation and in the prosecution of those responsible for the sexual assaults in the former Yugoslavia: on June 29, 2001, the Serbian government turned over former Yugoslavian president Slobodan Milosevic to the United Nations war crimes tribunal in The Hague, Netherlands; Marlise Simons with Carlotta Gall, "Milosevic Is Given to U.N. for Trial in War-Crime Case," *New York Times,* June 29, 2001:1; it is important to note that at about the same time the rapes and killings were happening in Yugoslavia and Bosnia, millions of men, women, and children were being raped, mutilated, and murdered in Rwanda; while Western governments dithered and delayed responding to both the Yugoslavian and Rwandan massacres and atrocities, and while an international tribunal was established in 1994 to prosecute Rwandans for their war crimes, the issue of rape as a war crime came to the fore in Yugoslavia, but not in the much larger-scale Rwandan case; perhaps it required reports of the mass rapes and sexual enslavement of white women, albeit Muslim white women, for the "civilized" world to take notice of ethnosexual violence in war.

22. Beverly Allen, *Rape Warfare: The Hidden Genocide in Bosnia-Herzegovina and Croatia* (Minneapolis: University of Minnesota Press, 1996), 78; the "Bassiouni Report" is the result of an October 1992 decision by the Secretary-General of the United Nations to appoint a commission of experts "to examine and analyze information gathered with a view to providing the Secretary-General with its conclusions on the evidence of grave breaches of the Geneva Conventions and other violations of international humanitarian law committed in the territory of the former Yugoslavia" (ibid., 43).

23. Kazuko Watanabe, "Trafficking in Women's Bodies, Then and Now: The Issue of Military 'Comfort Women,'" *Peace & Change* 20, no 4 (1995): 506–07.

24. Michael Kimmel, *Manhood in America* (New York: Oxford University Press, 1998): 133–34.

25. Ibid.

26. In a 2008 study the Rand Corporation found that 14 percent of the 1.64 million service members deployed in Operation Iraqi Freedom and Operation Enduring Freedom in Afghanistan were positively screened for PTSD and one-third of service members suffered from PTSD, major depression, or traumatic brain injury (Tanielian and Jaycox, 2008:7 at http://www.rand.org/content/dam /rand/pubs/monographs/2008/RAND_MG720.sum.pdf accessed January 8, 2012). Seal et al. (2009) reported that 40 percent of Iraq and Afghanistan veterans receiving health care from VA hospitals between 2002 and 2008 were diagnosed with one or more mental disorders, including

22 percent diagnosed with PTSD (at http://www.rand
.org/content/dam/rand/pubs/monographs/2008
/RAND_MG720.sum.pdf accessed January 8, 2012).

27. Military Sexual Trauma (MST) is "psychological
trauma, which in the judgment of a VA mental health
professional, resulted from a physical assault of a sexual
nature, battery of a sexual nature, or sexual harassment
which occurred while the Veteran was serving on active
duty or active duty for training" (at http://www.ptsd.va.gov
/public/pages/military-sexual-trauma-general.asp accessed
January 8, 2012).

28. This is a conservative estimate since it involves
official reports to the DOD; in random sample surveys
servicewomen and military academy cadets report much
higher rates of sexual harassment and assault. The
U.S. Army has instituted the SHARP program (Sexual
Harassment/Assault Response & Prevention) to address
these high levels of MST, but its effectiveness has not been
established; see http://www.sexualassault.army.mil
/index.cfm. Despite recurrent exposés, investigations, and
prevention programs, the problem persists; for instance,
the DOD found a 63 percent increase in sexual assaults at
U.S. military academies between 2010 and 2011
(at http://www.military.com/news/article/dod-reported
-sexual-assaults-up-at-service-academies.html accessed
January 8, 2012).

29. For an overview see *New York Times* series "Women
at Arms: A Trust Betrayed," especially the article,
"A Peril in War Zones: Sexual Abuse by Fellow GIs"
(at http://www.nytimes.com/2009/12/28/us/28women
.html?ref=womenatarms accessed January 8, 2012) and
Corbett (2007).

30. Kampfner (2003); Eisenstein (2007); Greenberg and
Dratel (2005); Karpinski (2006); Feitz and Nagel (2008);
Nagel and Feitz (2007); Massad (2004).

REFERENCES

Corbett, Sara. 2007. "The Women's War." *New York Times Magazine* (March 18).

Eisenstein, Zillah. 2007. *Sexual Decoys Gender, Race and War in Imperial Democracy.* New York: Zed Books.

Feitz, Lindsey, and Joane Nagel. 2007. "The Militarization of Gender and Sexuality in the Iraq War," pp. 201–25 in *Women in the Military and in Armed Conflict,* ed. C.H. Carreiras & G. Kümmel Wiesbaden, Germany: VS Verlag für Sozialwissenschaften.

Greenberg, Karen J., and Joshua L. Dratel. 2005. *The Torture Papers: The Road to Abu Ghraib.* New York: Cambridge University Press.

Kampfner, John. 2003. "Saving Private Lynch Story 'Flawed.'" *BBC News* (5/15) at http://news.bbc.co.uk/2
/hi/programmes/correspondent/3028585.stm accessed July 19, 2005.

Karpinski, Janis. 2006. *One Woman's Army: The Commanding General of Abu Ghraib Tells Her Story.* New York: Miramax Books.

Massad, Joseph. 2004. "Imperial Mementos." *Al-Ahram Weekly* (May 20–26, No. 691):1.

Nagel, Joane, and Lindsey Feitz. 2007. "Deploying Race, Gender, Class, and Sexuality in the Iraq War." *Race, Gender & Class* 14(3/4):28–47.

Seal, Karen, Thomas J. Metzler, Kristian S. Gima, Daniel Bertenthal, Shira Maguen, and Charles R. Marmar. 2009. "Trends and Risk Factors for Mental Health Diagnoses among Iraq and Afghanistan Veterans Using Department of Veterans Affairs Health Care, 2002–2008." *American Journal of Public Health* 99 (9):1651–58.

Tanielian, Terri, and Lisa H. Jaycox. 2008. *Invisible Wounds of War: Psychological and Cognitive Injuries, Their Consequences, and Services to Assist Recovery.* Santa Monica, CA: Rand Corporation.

U.S. Department of Defense. 2011. Department of Defense Annual Report on Sexual Assault in the Military, FY2010 at http://www.sapr.mil/media/pdf /reports/DoD_Fiscal_Year_2010_Annual_Report_on _Sexual_Assault_in_the_Military.pdf accessed January 8, 2012.

EDITOR'S NOTE

Nagel's work demonstrates the continued use of
rape as a tool of war. The use of that tool continues.
More recently rape has been used by Boko Haram, a
jihadist group in Nigeria that began its attacks in 2009.
Members of Boko Haram have abducted thousands
of women and girls—many of them raped.[1] Girls who
managed to escape described daily rapes by multiple
men. Journalists have shared accounts of young boys
being trained to rape captive women, partly as a reward
for participation in combat missions.[2] And former
captives and their children born as a result of rape
are often not welcomed home, following release or
escape.[3] Women and girls who survived Boko Haram
have even faced sexual violence by government officials
and other authorities in internal displacement camps.[4]
Non-governmental organizations and journalists have
also documented the military's widespread use of rape
and sexual violence in Myanmar (formerly Burma), a
nation currently embroiled in civil war.[5] Since 2010,
the Women's League of Burma (WLB) has documented
over 100 crimes of ethnosexual violence, including
47 gang rapes perpetrated by the military against
ethnic minorities in Myanmar. The WLB "is urging an
immediate end to these atrocities," pointing to a military
system that fails to prosecute perpetrators.[6] Meanwhile,
ISIS (or ISIL) continues to rape and sell thousands of

women and girls into sexual slavery in Iraq, primarily those from the Yezidi community.[7] Since 2014:

> the systematic rape of women and girls from the Yazidi religious minority has become deeply enmeshed in the organization and the radical theology of the Islamic State in the year since the group announced it was reviving slavery as an institution. . . . A total of 5,270 Yazidis were abducted [in 2014], and at least 3,144 are still being held, according to community leaders. To handle them, the Islamic State has developed a detailed bureaucracy of sex slavery, including sales contracts notarized by the ISIS-run Islamic courts. . . . A growing body of internal policy memos and theological discussions has established guidelines for slavery, including a lengthy how-to manual issued by the Islamic State Research and Fatwa Department. . . . Repeatedly, the *ISIS* leadership has emphasized a narrow and selective reading of the Quran and other religious rulings to not only justify violence, but also to elevate and celebrate each sexual assault as spiritually beneficial, even virtuous.[8]

It is clear, based on these three current examples, that the patterns of behavior described by Nagel and their rationales continue to hold today, with only slight nuances, as rape and war are wholly intertwined.

1. Nwaubani, A. T. (2016, July 5). "Bad blood" fears fuel abuse of children born of Boko Haram rape. Retrieved November 13, 2017, from http://www.reuters.com /article/us-nigeria-boko-haram-women/bad-blood -fears-fuel-abuse-of-children-born-of-boko-haram-rape -idUSKCN0ZL0TC?il=0.

2. Obaji, Philip, Jr. (2016, December 27). Boko Haram teaching child soldiers to rape. Retrieved November 13, 2017, from https://www.thedailybeast.com/boko-haram -teaching-child-soldiers-to-rape.

3. Nwaubani, 2016.

4. Nigeria: Officials abusing displaced women, girls. (2017, April 10). Retrieved November 13, 2017, from https://www.hrw.org/news/2016/10/31/nigeria-officials -abusing-displaced-women-girls.

5. Mass rapes to mass protests: Violence against women in 2016. (2016, November 28). Retrieved November 13, 2017, from https://www.hrw.org/news/2016/11/28/mass -rapes-mass-protests-violence-against-women-2016.

6. Women's League of Burma (WLB). Retrieved November 13, 2017, from http://womenofburma.org/same-impunity -same-pattern-report-of-systematic-sexual-violence-in -burmas-ethnic-areas/.

7. Report on the Protection of Civilians in the Armed Conflict in Iraq: 1 May–31 October 2015. (n.d.). Retrieved November 13, 2017, from http://www.ohchr.org /Documents/Countries/IQ/UNAMIReport1May31 October2015.pdf.

8. Callimachi, R. (2015, August 13). ISIS enshrines a theology of rape. Retrieved November 13, 2017, from https://www.nytimes.com/2015/08/14/world/middleeast /isis-enshrines-a-theology-of-rape.html.

10

COMMERCIAL SEX

AN INTERVIEW WITH

KARI LERUM

Kari Lerum, PhD sociology, is an associate professor in cultural studies and gender, women, and sexuality studies at the University of Washington–Bothell. Her research focuses on the intersections of sexuality, power, and context. Her current work focuses on domestic and international policies about sex work and human trafficking. Her scholarship has also critically evaluated popular discourses about the "sexualization of girls," sexuality education, and carceral strategies for racial, economic, gender, and sexual justice.

What led you to study sexuality?

I became intrigued with questions about sexuality at a young age. Growing up in a religious community, I especially wanted to understand why sexual expressions were so often policed through religious traditions, especially for girls and women. When

I started graduate school in the 1990s, the "feminist sex wars" were well underway. By then I identified as a feminist myself but was confused about why some feminists seemed to be taking the side of religious conservatives when it came to issues like sex work. This puzzle led me to investigate the meaning of sex work from a variety of positionalities and perspectives, including women working in different parts of the sex industry, police officers, and social workers. This first graduate school study set the stage for a career in investigating and theorizing sexual power and politics across interpersonal, institutional, and cultural levels.

How do people respond when they hear about your research?

It depends on who is listening and how much time we have. The dominant cultural discourse in the United States has long produced a shallow, sensationalistic, and moralistic understanding of sexuality, particularly when it is commodified. After the turn of the twenty-first century, the term *human trafficking* became a popular way to channel discomfort with sex work by allowing some to write it all off as "sex trafficking." If the person I am speaking with is open to it, I will explain the differences between criminal justice vs. social justice approaches to helping individuals in the sex trade. The former focuses on "rescuing" young (white) cis women from the sex trade (whether they want to be rescued or not) and criminalizing black and brown men and women, trans and queer individuals, and poor communities. In contrast, a social justice approach focuses on economic, racial, and gender rights and empowerment for all. I find that white, middle-class, straight folks have the hardest time with this explanation. In contrast, individuals whose families and communities have been policed due to their race, gender expression, or economic status tend to understand this distinction very well.

Which of your research projects (involving sexuality) have you found most interesting? Why?

For my dissertation research, I conducted a comparative ethnographic analysis of sexual power dynamics across three customer service organizations, all jobs involving the serving of food and/or drink. Over the course of a year and a half, I worked as a waitress in a fine dining restaurant, a family diner, and a strip club. In many ways, this experience was very humbling: I was working long hours on my feet, learning to navigate a range of dynamics with customers, co-workers, and bosses, while also making poverty-level wages at times. Yet simultaneously, my time in the field was illuminating and even personally empowering: I observed the ways that sexual banter in each workplace served a variety of functions, and not always in a negative way. I also learned an extraordinary amount about resilience and interpersonal confidence from my co-workers, especially at the strip club. Overall, this project gave me deep respect for service workers, as well as insights into how the culture of a workplace combined with its organizational structure can affect workers' sense of creative freedom, camaraderie with other workers, and job satisfaction.

Can you describe some of the findings from your recent research?

Over the past several years I have regularly conducted Internet image searches for the generic legal term *human trafficking* (as opposed to *sex trafficking* or *sexual slavery*); these searches have produced an archive of images that predominately features women in symbolic slave poses (hands bound by ropes or chains; fingers clutching bars or barbed wire; mouths taped or bound shut). Most of these symbolic slaves are white, young, and slim, often with manicured fingernails; sometimes their hands are clutched as if in prayer. When men appear in these images, they usually play the role of villains, holding their hands (which often appear to be artificially darkened) over the mouths of white girls and women. These racialized, gendered, and often erotized images illustrate a sexual morality tale featuring girls' stolen innocence and complete lack of agency. In contrast, the dominant images and stories told about human trafficking feature men making evil, good, or heroic choices. I argue that the success of contemporary U.S.–based movements against human trafficking rests on a storytelling framework that deploys deep religious and cultural tropes, deeming irrelevant for many consumers the lack of overlap with empirical evidence.

What ethical dilemmas or challenges have you faced in your research on sexuality?

When I first decided to study the sex industry, my models for how to approach sex workers were undercover cop shows and sociological studies of deviance. The latter were more academic and empathetic than the former, but both treated sex workers as outsiders to society, either as inherently problematic or as curiosities for the "civilized" world. Fortunately, since then, I have learned far more ethical and respectful methods of working with sex workers. At the center of my ethics is a commitment to allyship with sex worker communities. I regularly work with sex worker–led coalitions and take their lead in directing the kind of research and public scholarship that is needed to reduce the oppression of individuals in the sex trade (such as documentation of police violence against sex workers). My ongoing challenge in this work is offering my research expertise and status as a tool for elevating the voices and needs of sex workers without speaking for sex workers. Sometimes this just means staying quiet and listening more than speaking.

If you could teach people one thing about sexuality, what would it be?

Sexuality is a topic that can evoke strong emotional and political reactions. For many, this is especially true when it pertains to imagining anything outside of adult monogamous heteronormative relationships, or what Gayle Rubin calls the "charmed circle." But even inside this "charmed circle" of societal privilege, people often have a range of unsettling reactions to, and questions about, their own sexuality. As a way of unpacking the "meaning" of sexuality, I ask my students to reflect on the ways that their life experiences and cultural messages have contributed to their own sexual assumptions. For example, in what ways have shame, secrecy, fear, trauma, pleasure, thrill, connection, disability, racism, sexism, or any number of other experiences shaped their sexuality up to this point in their lives? This reflective work is key, I believe, to constituting a more empathetic understanding of one's own sexuality, as well as more empathy and respect for individuals with different sexual stories from one's own.

WHAT MALE-FOR-MALE INTERNET ESCORTS SAY ABOUT WHAT THEY DO

KEVIN WALBY

This [reading] examines how the work of male-for-male Internet escorting is organized. Escorting as self-employment has been shaped in part by the availability of computer and Internet technologies, which have fused commercial sex with entrepreneurial e-business. . . .

. . . I analyze the narratives of male Internet escorts. I discuss elements of labor process such as entering the trade, work conditions, tasks, advertising, and pricing. I focus on escorts' narratives as a way of understanding how their work is organized. . . . One paradox of what male escorts say about what they do is that some of the men reject the idea of sex worker solidarity while using labor vocabulary. Male-for-male Internet escorts manifest diverse understandings of sex work, but few locate themselves in the sex work paradigm, thus raising questions about sex work organizing and solidarity.

LABOR PROCESS AND MALE-FOR-MALE INTERNET ESCORTING

I have had regular jobs. I plan to again. But for now it is nice not having a retail store manager telling me what to do. I do not have to deal with crap. I was a call center phone operator, a grocery store clerk. Dealing with clerks, 20 customers, learning about the whole organization and the whole goddamn store. My work is different. I am awkward around some straight people, but with gay men I'm in my element. I can be the life of the party in gay spaces. In this job, I work with gay men or closeted gay men, in their homes or hotel rooms. I know how to talk to them, and I know how to please them. One at a time in a private space. This suits my skills and talents better than a straight desk job. (*Frank, Toronto*)

Frank's narrative indicates how male-for-male Internet escorts make sense of their work in relation to other jobs they have had as well as jobs they hope to have in the future. Some sex workers select commercial sex over the labor process of service-sector work, and Frank's narrative certainly underscores the difference between escorting work and work in a retail store, a grocery store, a call center or a "straight desk job.". . .

. . . [W]hat kind of work is sex work? . . .

Work is conventionally conceived of as full-time and related to manufacturing, yet this kind of work is increasingly rare. There exist many ways of categorizing new nonstandard work, including "nonconventional" and "atypical." Male-for-male Internet escorting is nonstandard work. Escorts are not represented by agencies and are largely unaware of each other as "competitors," meaning that Internet escorting operates according to an individuated labor process and is similar to "self-employment" and "dependent self-employment.". . . Self-employment refers to work in which the worker makes decisions autonomously but has no office support. Dependent self-employment signals work that ties the worker to an agency or a clientele, where the cost of switching from the client pool would be a burden. Some escorts use this labor vocabulary in describing what they do:

You're self-employed, and you're also not self-employed. . . . You're dependent on whether or not someone is interested in you, whether or not they want to see you again, whether or not they like your pictures online, whether or not they liked what you had to say in an email. (*Claude, Montréal*)

. . . Male-for-male Internet escorting is distinctive in placing the sexualized male body at the center of the labor process, thereby troubling conventional understandings of masculinity and work in which men's work is generally associated with manual labor. Indeed, working men's bodies are thought to represent a working-class habitus and are assumed to be heterosexual. Men's work has also been tied to family through the notion of "breadwinning," construed as a man's ability to bring home money to pay for family expenses. Yet heterosexual, breadwinning masculinity is less and less associated with nonstandard work. Male-for-male escorting involves aesthetic labor, where escorts are pressed to work on the body's appearance for pay. Male-for-male escorting is also a form of body work . . . that involves men erotically touching the bodies of other men. Male-for-male escorting erodes the link between heterosexual masculinity and work as breadwinning masculinity is replaced by the fluidity of queer sexuality, and the escort's body is sexualized as a matter of labor process. . . .

WHAT MALE-FOR-MALE INTERNET ESCORTS SAY ABOUT ENTERING THE TRADE

Getting Started

These men's stories about their entry into escorting challenge common stereotypes about sex workers. David Luckenbill (1985) argues that entry into male sex work occurs as a solution to desperate living or as an exciting adventure. By contrast, these men's stories suggest that escorting and other forms of work share the same impetus: the need to exchange one's labor power under capitalism. For instance, before becoming an Internet escort in Canada, Sam from Ottawa advertised his abilities as a manual laborer in a local newspaper somewhere in the Caribbean. He began receiving inquiries from potential clients about whether he conducted erotic massage:

At first, I was a bit scared. You know how people think about this job. So, at the beginning I said no. But it kept coming with every ad. There would be a call now and then, because I was putting my phone number in the ad. I was not ashamed to be looking for work. (*Sam, Ottawa*)

Sam found that erotic massage (and then escorting) did not subject him to external rules or employer surveillance. He perceived entering the trade as a decision to secure the best income available to him at the time: "People were offering me money to do the work for them. I came to find myself in a position where I am making rules." Unlike Sam, some escorts start out in escorting agencies. Sex workers in Luckenbill's (1985) study either left the escort agency they worked at because they felt controlled by management or they were fired because they did not follow the rules. Whitaker (1999) also discusses some of the ups and downs that come from working for agencies. A few of the escorts I spoke with had quit agencies because of pressure from the employer:

My first client in Ottawa was through an agency. There was added security. The agency knew the guy and his place and contact number; if anything happened, there would be a safe out. But the guy running the agency was an asshole. He made me sick to my stomach. I did not stay there for long because I felt degraded. . . . I felt like I was a number. They were not respecting my existing work schedule. (*Tyler, Ottawa*)

After getting into Internet escorting, these men found that the lack of employers' rules was a welcome change compared with other work—and other forms of sex work, too. . . .

Consistent with sociological claims about conventional working lives being replaced by erratic postindustrial job changes, . . . some men entered escorting after losing other jobs. Frederico moved to Ontario from Mexico a few years before I interviewed him. He had been working in the automotive sector near Toronto. When the manufacturing plant where he was working closed, he found himself without income and with credentials valued only by an ailing industry. Frederico had always been interested in sex with men but had never considered commercial sex relations prior to being laid off. "These times are difficult for manufacturing," he says. Frederico continues to look for other work while living off escorting during this transition. . . . Other men sought a second job, indicating that escorting is, for some, temporary work. Some men start escorting merely to supplement their income:

I started this when I was 46. My regular job, I make $80,000 a year, and my first year of escorting I made in excess of $10,000. . . . I didn't rely on that as my primary, but it was a good supplement, good part-time work that didn't require as many tedious hours as a part-time job at a bookstore. (*Donald, New York*)

While some men become involved in escorting when they are older and have a steady income, other men started out in the more perilous business of on-street propositioning:

When I was 18 was probably the first time on the street; I was propositioning. Then it became a little more structured. The difference would be post-Internet; it created more professionalism with people who have websites. They go to the gym. They are into fitness. They do porn. I don't do any of that. Their website is slick. They charge a lot of money and are more like a companion. I fall in the middle. I'm not a pro, but I'm not a scam artist. I do it for extra money. It doesn't pay my rent. (*Conrad, Toronto*)

The men I spoke with are employed in other jobs, have Internet access, and accept clients depending on income, resonating with what Bernstein (2007) refers to as "middle class sex work." Commercial sex is now accepted as a way to make money due to a shift to "a recreational model of sexual intimacy" (p. 141), creating new possibilities for the sexualization of men's bodies. The men I interviewed seek out the best earnings/hours-worked ratio.

It's an efficient way to make money. Rather than working four hours and coming home with $45 like at my day job, plus my commute, I can work for about an hour and fifteen minutes, come home, and I've got 200 bucks. (*Frank, Toronto*)

What makes escorting so efficient is the Internet. The hardware and software required to communicate with clients are the "instruments" of the labor process for self-employed sexual entrepreneurs. The profiles created by escorts are searchable based on city location and aesthetic features of the escort, meaning that clients sort escorts based on categories of sexuality and body type. Escorts accentuate certain parts of their bodies using pictures to leverage a competitive advantage.

WORK TASKS AND CONDITIONS: ESCORTS AS SEXUAL ENTREPRENEURS

Male-for-male Internet escorting is not tied to any formal organization, but it is organized according to the anonymous, just-in-time relations enabled by the Internet. Thompson and Smith (2009) contend that communication technologies like the Internet make possible work that is no longer tied to a particular locale. Male-for-male Internet escorting is part of the circuit of global capital enabled by such technologies. Escorts' clients are often traveling members of the transnational capitalist class, such as chief executives, looking for a one-night mate in each new city.

Establishing a connection with a client requires hours in front of a computer creating online advertisements or finding clients in online chat rooms. Whether escorts use specialty sites or chat rooms, the escort controls when work happens: "When I am not available, I am not available. I am on a couple of gay sites. When I am online, I am available. Guests who come a second time usually have my number" (*Sam, Ottawa*). While a "new breed of e-pimps" (Kilvington et al. 2001:90) may have emerged in other online sectors of commercial sex, this is not the case with male-for-male Internet escorting. Escorts select clients based on email correspondence. Screening occurs via the process of reading correspondence and looking for cues to ensure the other person is a serious client, not a police officer or a time waster: "I screen based on gut feeling. When I talk to someone on the phone, or by email, if the language and the words do not sound right, they are screened right away" (*Tyler, Ottawa*). Working at a computer and dealing with emails are constant tasks among online escorts. Indeed, this clerical activity of booking clients is the foremost task in online escorting.

. . . For male-for-male Internet escorts, the timing of the work is undisciplined and no formal organization regulates the work. But some of these men are "on call" at the whim of clients. Clientele surges, for example, during the week of Gay Pride celebrations, yet over time the number of clients rises and falls:

I'll have a day or two where my phone is ringing off the hook and I'm seeing four or five clients in a day, then I don't get a call for a week . . . either everybody wants to get laid or nobody wants to get laid. . . . I always had jobs where I worked specific days of the week before. I thought, I'll book one or two clients today, one or two clients tomorrow, one or two clients the next day, you know, have a couple of days off. It doesn't work like that. (*Claude, Montréal*)

Rather than having a boss or manager dictate work tasks, escorts provide on demand the kind of sexual event that clients want. The escort owns his sexualized body and labor power until he negotiates their sale to the client. Not only is the work unsteady, but the rapport the escort attempts to create with the client does not always lead to that client becoming a repeat client. Repeat clients allow escorts to build up a clientele and to start escorting full-time. This uncertainty about clientele parallels the labor uncertainty faced by independent contractors.

Further signaling an individuated labor process, escorts tend not to know one another. One escort from Ottawa (the smallest city in this study at one million people) mentioned that he knows a couple of escorts and they occasionally meet to discuss clients: "It's a small community here and so we compare notes every once in a while. If a client is an asshole it gets out" (*Bob, Ottawa*). In Ottawa, the small number of escorts and the limited clientele make for a competitive market: "summer gets rough, all the kids come in and it can get competitive. When I started there were two in a chat room, now there's 20" (*Bob, Ottawa*). . . .

Most male-for-male Internet escorts tend, however, not to know one another unless they are "co-workers" who facilitate group encounters to make more money. Only one escort I interviewed knew several other escorts. He referred clients to other escorts by email or phone:

I got business cards. Whenever I go to a new city, Las Vegas, San Antonio, that is how I get other guys to work for me. I try to get Latin guys or dark-haired guys, a dark complexion and tight body like mine. I have an ad with more than one city on it, so with those cities if someone calls but I am not there I can give it to my friends. Get a kickback. I have not seen many guys in the last two years cause I do more referrals. (*Byron, Houston*)

. . . Because Internet escorts are not represented by agencies, they must be entrepreneurial in order to make money. An entrepreneur assumes the risk of an initiative to make profit. The risk for male-for-male Internet escorts is that they will not locate clientele interested in their bodily features. . . . Key aspects of sexuality for Internet escorts, then, include signaling their sexual persona, suggesting what sexual activities they will engage in, and fashioning their bodies to be fit for these activities. In this way, client demands compel the escort's working sexuality. . . .

Since pictures are crucial for attracting clients, Garry from Toronto says he will "play with pictures. I've learned how to Photoshop. It's tedious and a bit soul destroying to alter your own pictures, but I'm good at it." Aligning their physical features with a "cyber-type" (Nakamura 2002), an innovative display of the online self, is an effective way for Internet escorts to signal what niche sexual market they cater to.

These narratives about self-appearance suggest the centrality of aesthetic labor to escorting. Warhurst and Nickson (2007) define aesthetic labor as the positioning of workers in the labor process based on bodily appearance. However, escorts engage in aesthetic labor not for the competitive advantage of an employer but to leverage competitive advantage as sexual entrepreneurs. Aesthetic labor requires plucking, trimming, waxing, and shaving. Rather than an employer choosing which bodily features to value, this aesthetic aspect of the escort labor process is individuated. This work on self-appearance to fulfill clients' sexual demands demonstrates that escorts' appearances are crucial for obtaining and continuing work as an escort.

Escorts have no professional association through which they locate clients or work-related support. Nor do many escorts advocate such an association. Escorts rarely correspond with one another because of how clandestine escorting can be in some cities: "people I see, one's an admiral, one's a high-ranking judge, I could get in trouble if it ever came out. It's incredibly discreet" (Bob, Ottawa). Some activists and scholars consider the requirement of anonymity as a barrier to sex workers' activism. . . . Certainly, male sex workers can be stigmatized if they do

not keep their work quiet, . . . but escorts can be more "out" in particular cities. The important point here is that successful escorts must be skilled at something other than keeping secrets. Escorts catering to the transnational capitalist class need to know how to operate in elite settings:

Escorting is not just about having a nice cock and a nice ass, it is about knowing what people want and marketing it well. If you are a traveling escort like I am, you need to know how to conduct yourself in a five-star hotel, how to eat at a restaurant with five forks. (Ben, London)

Some authors have claimed that the sex work skill set is similar to that of service economy jobs, including surface acting or "putting on" a face to engineer a feeling for customers. . . . But the specific skill set of escorts depends on their clientele. Rather than a labor process marked by routinization of various social competencies, as in service economy jobs, escorts' work tasks are "not unlike those of self-employed individuals or other small business owners" (Parsons et al. 2007:238). Similar to the stories that female sex workers shared with Jeffrey and MacDonald (2006), these men's narratives suggest that they prefer escorting because it differs from service-sector work. . . . If commercial sex is a way of earning an income without participating in the minimum-wage service sector, then sex work may be thought of as a way of maximizing control over the labor process. . . .

Advertising

Escorts advertise on specialty websites, just as other self-employed workers do. Ads allude to which sexual services the escort offers. The wording of ads must be precise if escorts are targeting a niche market, such as bondage. Profiles include notes about penis size and body hair, which constitute sexualized features of the escort body. Commercial sex profiles must account for many details, including a description of the services offered:

When I went on Gay.com in the summer of 2007 for the first time, I placed a very nice ad. Age, weight, height, with details about what I do during my massage. When I go online, I put in my bio something like Magic Blacks Hands, commercial massage, for generous gents. (*Sam, Ottawa*)

Pictures of the body are important for alluring clients, and email correspondence between client and escort often pertains to this body. The displayed body and the sexualized body: these are what the client is keen to see and to touch. Body type influences the escort's sex work persona and marketing:

If someone's skinny and they don't have muscle, they can't market themselves as a jock. The thing about escorting is it's a market where anybody could be an escort. A 90-year-old grandmother could be. It's a matter of marketing yourself. (*Steve, Toronto*)

Placement of an ad is no guarantee that the escort will develop a clientele. Clients post reviews of escorts and rate them with a score, which determines where the escort's profile will be positioned in the hierarchy of profiles: "If you are not in the first 10 pages, forget about it. People get bored, and they're going to find people before you. You move up through the pages based on reviews" (*Gabe, Toronto*). If one escort offers a talent that impresses the client and the client writes a glowing review, this difference can catapult the escort ahead in the rankings. Clients rank escorts on their sexual performance, overall charm, conversational skills, knowledge of a city, and the provision of temporary companionship. . . .

The role of online client reviews in determining escort access to the client pool demonstrates how the escort labor process is tied to the Internet. Internet technology enables certain relations between escort and client but also constrains escorts in various ways. The websites allow clients to search easily and to contact escorts in any city, but the websites also sort escorts based on reviews, making it harder for some escorts to find clients because their profiles move down the list and get buried. Depending on the city, escorts may use print advertisements. Few escorts in Canada advertise in magazines or newspapers, but this type of advertising is more popular in the United States and England. . . .

The costs of advertising, sex toys, and condoms add up. As Sean from Toronto puts it, "you have to spend some money to get some." Ads are a costly necessity for the sexual entrepreneur, whose sexualized bodily features must be known in order to be enticing.

Getting Paid

Some days are long and boring. I have taken clients where I did not feel like doing it, but I knew it was going to be $120 or more, or I have taken an exhausting client, but it pays $100 a hour for ten hours because he likes to do ecstasy and jerk off to porn and all he wants you to do is jerk him off. There are times when I am like "not tonight," but the client has called three times and he cums in 15 seconds and is out the door. Nobody makes that kind of money in so little time. (*Tyler, Ottawa*)

Escorts develop informal strategies for getting paid and negotiating fees. There are no paychecks. There are no contracts. Some escorts maintain nonnegotiable set fees, while others exercise greater flexibility in pricing. Tyler from Ottawa charges repeat clients less, a common practice among the self-employed:

People who meet me once a week get discounted in a major way because in the long run after four weeks or five weeks I see the benefit of not charging them the same price I charge one-time customers. It makes business sense.

Being an independent sex worker can create certain "leverage points" (Gall 2006:34), since Internet escorts control pricing to a certain extent. But, because escorts are not subject to formal pricing regulations, there remains the possibility of undercutting other escorts. Escorts express animosity for other escorts who pull the prices down and create an expectation among clients that certain services can be had cheaply:

I do not give $20 blow jobs. I will judge you if you give a $20 blow job. You are taking my business away selling it cheap. I hate people who undercut. If everyone were to ask for the same prices, it would raise the playing field. (*Tyler, Ottawa*)

Most Internet escorts set their prices high and feel that advertising higher prices makes them appear more professional: "You hire a lawyer that charges $500 an hour, you're going to expect a lot more of them than a lawyer who charges $250. Escorting is the same" (*Claude, Montréal*). Prices are set to maximize the income earned per meeting with a client:

You can do five calls at $300 and get $1500 or five calls at $150 and get half that. It makes sense to get more every time you see someone because if you are good looking and have youth to yourself and have a nice body, it is easy to get that amount. We call them professional tricks, they want to see everyone. So if you only see them once and then they see others, you might as well get as much as you can. (*Byron, Houston*)

Escorts treat what they do as a way of earning an income, and their pricing reflects this attitude. As Oscar from London remarks, "I try to keep it like any other business." Most escorts set prices high so that they can generate and retain surpluses for themselves.

Thinking of Calling It Quits

Some escorts feel pressure to abandon escorting. Their reasons include loss of repeat clients who provide a steady income but are hard to come by, desire for a secure job, lifestyle changes, and lack of sexual interest: "There is no victim here. It has never been an issue for me legalizing or not legalizing. This is not something I want to do for the rest of my life. I want to find a good man and move along" (*Sam, Ottawa*). Some escorts do not want to leave the trade but do want to enjoy upward mobility; they want to see fewer but "better quality clients" who are willing to pay more money per hour. Upward mobility in the industry requires a shift in persona to attract a new clientele:

I'm going to get more professional and higher-end clients . . . shift more toward like business travelers basically who are the best ones who come to the city for a weekend and plan it ahead. They pay more money. (*Conrad, Toronto*)

One issue that differentiates male-for-male Internet escorts from other kinds of sex workers is that this work is often conducted as an extension of their sex life. Sometimes escorts feel like leaving escorting because other opportunities have come along or because they are frustrated with the demands escorting places upon them:

My career is almost over. I am establishing a training business here in London. I have been here for three months, and it is going really well. Once the personal trainer business picks up, escorting will drop off. (*Mark, London*)

For the most part, escorts express no overarching theme of exiting the industry because of violence, poverty, or drugs. Entrepreneurialism marks these men's orientation—a curious feature given their general reluctance to embrace the term "sex work" as a way of valorizing what they do. Most escorts narrate their exit from this work as a life course shift or a transition into other forms of work.

DISCUSSION

The male-for-male Internet escorts that I interviewed consider their sex work to provide serious income despite the lack of a social context that would legitimize it as work. Male-for-male

Internet escorting does not have ties to organizations, although the work is organized by parameters set out by the Internet (e.g., the ranking of escorts based on client reviews). . . . Since the work of male-for-male Internet escorting is largely clerical, taking place in front of a computer, the labor process is individuated. Escorting involves the sexual entrepreneurialism of aesthetic labor, as escorts manage their bodily appearance to attract and maintain clients. Because escorting also concerns men's bodies touching together, it constitutes a form of body work that makes central the sexualization of men's bodies in the labor process. . . .

One purpose of this [reading] is to understand how male-for-male Internet escorts make sense of the idea of sex work. Sex work discourse includes two fundamental ideas: First, that sex work should be decriminalized; and second, that sex workers should organize as a community because of their ostensibly shared labor process. However, few of those escorts I interviewed explicitly associated themselves with the idea of sex work. When I asked Byron from Houston, "Do you wish your work was decriminalized?" he responded bluntly, "No, 'cause if it was, everyone would be doing it and I would not make as much money." When I asked Josh from Toronto, "Do you feel like you have an escort community?" he responded, "I don't, nor do I want that." Some of the escorts felt connected to other escorts, but most felt entirely disconnected and were fine with that: "I do not know the market, 'cause everyone works for themselves. People do not talk about what they do with each other, workers do not know the other workers" (*Sam, Ottawa*). Escorts describe themselves as entrepreneurs or self-employed as opposed to service-economy workers, who are compelled to toil under management's thumbs. At the same time, many escorts use labor vocabulary to narrate their touching encounters with other men while disavowing the sex work discourse. Their narratives substantiate Gregor

Gall's (2006) point that many escorts do not identify with sex work discourse. This remains a complicated issue, however. Since the decriminalization of sex work would mean greater regulation of their income, some male escorts reject the subject position "sex worker" and the sex work movement as a whole; other male escorts support the movement for political reasons; and some identify as "sex workers" despite differences in labor process. The "sex worker" subject position may fragment support among escorts, but this fragmentation has not necessarily damaged the movement. If movement organizers are interested in growing the movement's base and reaching out to sex workers with highly individuated labor processes, however, then other recruitment and promotional strategies may be necessary to increase solidarity. . . .

REFERENCES

Bernstein, E. 2007. "Sex Work for the Middle Classes." *Sexualities* 10(4): 473–88.

Gall, G. 2006. *Sex Worker Union Organizing: An International Study.* Basingstoke: Palgrave Macmillan.

Jeffrey, L., and G. MacDonald. 2006. *Sex Workers in the Maritimes Talk Back.* Vancouver: University of British Columbia Press.

Kilvington, J., S. Day, and H. Ward. 2001. "Prostitution Policy in Europe: A Time of Change?" *Feminist Review* 67: 78–93.

Luckenbill, D. 1986. "Deviant Career Mobility: The Case of Male Prostitutes." *Social Problems* 33(4): 283–96.

Nakamura, L. 2002. *Cybertypes: Race, Ethnicity, and Identity on the Internet.* New York: Routledge.

Parsons, J., J. Koken, and D. Bimbi. 2007. "Looking beyond HIV: Eliciting Individual and Community Needs of Male Internet Escorts." In *Male Sex Work: A Pleasure Doing Business,* ed. T. Morrison and B. Whitehead. New York: Haworth Press.

Thompson, P., and C. Smith. 2009. "Labor Power and the Labor Process: Contesting the Marginality of the Sociology of Work." *Sociology* 43(5): 913–30.

Warhurst, C., and D. Nickson. 2009. "'Who's Got the Look?': Emotional, Aesthetic, and Sexualized Labor in Interactive Services." *Gender, Work, and Organization* 26(3): 385–404.

Whitaker, R. 1999. *Assuming the Position: A Memoir of Hustling.* New York: Four Walls Eight Windows.

CAN WE "CURE" THE MEN WHO PAY FOR SEX?

BROOKE JARVIS

The men[1] cross their arms, slouch, and spread their feet wide—and you've never felt anything quite like the overwhelming awkwardness, the tangible defensiveness, that surrounds them. All eight have been busted for trying to buy sex. They've paid fines or spent time in jail or, in some cases, been forced to register as sex offenders. And now they're here, in this beige classroom, for the final, and most unusual, part of the punishment meted out by King County, Washington.

For the next couple of months, they'll be required to think deeply about what led them to the parking lots and motels where they were arrested. They'll be asked to plumb their emotions and to contemplate their place in the patriarchy. It's a modest experiment with a rather immodest goal: to solve the sex trade by changing the lives of the men who perpetrate it.

I wanted to see what on earth this might look like in practice. An eight-week court-ordered course meant to teach so-called johns about empathy and healthy relationships, about gender socialization and victim-blaming and toxic masculinity? When I asked for a closer look, the men in a recent course were invited to vote on whether they'd be okay with a female reporter quietly observing it all from the back of the room. Remarkably, they said yes.

And so, on a Thursday evening, I shook hands with the men, one by one, as they trickled in, took their seats, and slumped in silence. The usual small talk was clearly moot here. What would they say? Each man already knew at least the outline of how the others had ended up in that room, because it was the same way he had ended up there.

For Akio, who's 40 but has a shyness that makes him seem much younger, it was a first-time lark. He made a point of calling it "hanging out" when he asked how much he and a friend would be charged for an hour with a woman at a Ramada Inn.

Steve, 60, divorced, fresh from stalking allegations and more than one restraining order, had responded to a daddy-daughter deal on a fetish site.

Jason, a 22-year-old Mormon just back from a two-year mission—during which spending time with the opposite sex was strictly off-limits—arranged for a $70 blow job from a girl (she made a point of telling him she was a minor, though he swears he didn't go looking for that). She told him to meet her in the parking lot between a bank and a McDonald's.

David, 51 and fairly new to the computer, was on Craigslist looking for deals on auto parts when he noticed there were other ads there, too, ads for young women. Back in his military days, he'd bought sex on the street pretty regularly—"I treat 'em just like a human," he told me later. He clicked on one of the ads and got an answer back from someone who gave her name as Jen. "What if I'm under 18?" she asked him. David went to meet her at a 7-Eleven, but when he got there, there was no Jen. There never had been. There was only the police waiting for him.

Man after man, the details differed but the denouement was the same: They went to a parking lot or to a motel or to some other rendezvous expecting sex, and got something

From "Can We 'Cure' the Men Who Pay for Sex?" GQ, February 2, 2017. Copyright Condé Nast. Reprinted by permission.

else. The blood drains, the stomach drops, and instead of the woman he arranged to meet, there's a police detective standing in the doorway or stepping out of the car. Some of what followed was predictable: the trips to court, the heavy fees, to say nothing of the shame that must be borne before wives, bosses, pastors.

But ending up here in this classroom was far less expected. The idea for the course came from Peter Qualliotine, a co-founder of the Seattle-based Organization for Prostitution Survivors, who had worked for years with women caught up in the sex trade. But long ago, Peter became convinced that his best chance for combating the harms of the sex trade depended on working with the men— with those trying to pay for sex.

In plenty of cities and counties around the country, men busted for buying sex get sent to a class known as "john school"—usually just a scared-straight afternoon with lectures about STDs and jail time and the harms of prostitution. It's the sex-work version of traffic school; in some places, the whole thing consists of a 15-minute video. Peter had taught those classes and didn't think much of their effectiveness. He had something grander in mind.

"My pitch for the men is: Patriarchy hurts you, too," Peter told me when I first contacted him about the singular experiment he's launched in King County. "You deserve a healthy relationship that makes you happy." Laughing, he offered another way to put it: "We're trying to teach them how to love." Then he stopped laughing and said, "For real."

On the first day of class, Peter stood at the whiteboard and wrote the phrase "Act Like a Man." He then asked the class to give him examples of what the phrase meant to them, writing down the answers they called out: *strong, tough, good at sports, lots of sex, fighting, devoid of emotion, disciplined.*

Then he drew a box around the list and suggested that these notions created a rather impossible standard for guys, a standard that excludes important things like empathy and vulnerability and gets in the way of deep relationships. He asked them to think about what it would take, in their own lives, to fit within the box he'd drawn, what names they'd get called if they strayed outside it. The men offered up "sissy" and "queer" and other words that questioned their sexuality.

Steve, the man who'd responded to the daddy-daughter ad, told me later that he regarded the activity as just an icebreaker—kind of a fun get-to-know-you exercise. He was sure it didn't have anything to do with the point of the class or the notion of sexual exploitation or why he might have done the things that landed him there. Instead, when I met him outside of class to chat (he'd suggested we get together at a Starbucks right next to the county line, which he said he wasn't allowed to cross without permission), he tried to explain away, in an almost unstoppable monologue, the restraining order, the domestic violence arrest, the tracking device he put on his ex-girlfriend's truck, the stalking allegations that got him effectively banned from a hospital and an entire small city, and especially his conviction for trying to buy sex from a person he was told was a 15-year-old girl.

It was clear from the start that Peter would have his work cut out for him. In class, throughout those first weeks, a number of the men showed with their body language that they thought the whole exercise was bullshit, a waste of their time. Several maintained that their arrests had been misunderstandings, and several, including Steve, made it clear that they thought it was nonsense that prostitution was a crime at all. He was already turned off by the class's official title, Stopping Sexual Exploitation: A Program for Men, because of the word *exploitation:* "It kind of gives you an indication of what their position is."

In fact, Peter does nothing to hide his position or his ideas about how best to combat prostitution—notions that stem from years of working with men and women on both sides of the sex trade. In an age when new ideas are flourishing about the role of sex work in society, Peter stands apart from those who'd like to decriminalize it; he disagrees with activists who argue that regulating prostitution can make it safer. To Peter, decriminalizing sex work won't strip it of its danger and its tendency toward exploitation. He'd like to see more johns prosecuted for buying sex, but also new attention paid to preventing it.

Over years spent talking to johns, Peter says, he's realized that most men feel, at best, conflicted about prostitution. The problem, he believes, is bigger than sex and boils down to "men not having the social and emotional learning to deal with our shit." And so, in a bid to solve some of that, he envisioned a course that attacked what he considered to be the roots of the issue: patriarchy, male privilege, and the social barriers that stand in the way of healthy relationships.

During the 1990s, Peter, who lived in Portland, Oregon, then, pitched a version of the class he imagined—but it was always turned down as too political. It wasn't until 2012, after he had moved to Seattle, that his ideas began to find some traction. That's when Peter met Valiant Richey, a King County prosecutor who had been waging his own battle against prostitution—targeting pimps and traffickers but watching in frustration as the area's sex trade grew. Analysis had concluded that his office was, as he put it recently, "overwhelmingly and disproportionately prosecuting the wrong people." As was—and still is—the case in many jurisdictions throughout the country, the large majority of prostitution-related arrests were of women.

In 2009, Richey's unit charged more than 50 juveniles—including many girls who couldn't even legally consent to sex—with criminal prostitution. Meanwhile, the unit prosecuted just two buyers that year. (Peter heard stories of arresting officers handing the john his money back before sending him on his way and taking the sex worker to jail.) "It was not," Richey says now, "a proud time for us." Like Peter, Richey was interested in trying something different.

The two teamed up on a new approach and began by persuading police to go after buyers—a strategy so unusual that it's known as a "reverse sting." Detectives in King County began posting online ads (they often included words like "fresh" and "young" in order to find men who looked for minors); they'd get hundreds of responses within an hour. Soon they'd flipped their proportions, charging more buyers than sellers by a ratio of three to one. And the men they arrested were ordered by the courts to attend the very course that Peter had once imagined—a novel class he would design and implement.

During the course that I sat in on, Peter was assisted by a co-facilitator, Juan—a young ponytailed physician who'd been caught in a sex-buying sting himself, then been so captured by the ideas in the class that he voluntarily took it three more times. The goal of the class, Juan told me, was "to turn the lights on to those questions that men hate to ask themselves." These eight men were his first students, and he was anxious about whether he'd be able to lead them to some of the same kinds of discoveries he'd made about himself during all those classes—discoveries that came from exploring what he called "a place of discomfort inside me." But many of the students, he was afraid, were just as happy to leave the lights out and the uncomfortable places alone.

During the third class, Peter drew a slanted line on the whiteboard and wrote "Gary Ridgway"—better known as the Green River Killer, who confessed to taking the lives of more than 70 women, many of them underage prostitutes and runaways, in and around King County in the '80s and '90s. The men looked a little shocked; clearly no one in this room was on par with Gary Ridgway. For years, Peter had worked with women and girls who told him shattering stories about being vulnerable young runaways, being manipulated and abused by pimps, being assaulted, raped, kidnapped. By invoking a serial killer, he told the men, he wanted them to think about the kinds of violence that women face, how much higher the risks are for women in sex work—and how lesser forms of harassment are linked to real violence.

The men stared silently back at him.

"Let's back way, way, way up," said Peter. From the murderer's name, he followed the diagonal line to the bottom, where he wrote the words "catcall" and "rape joke." David clearly couldn't believe the comparison he was seeing develop between killing and catcalling— "That's the most standard pickup line at the bar!" he said. Put yourself in the woman's shoes, Peter responded. You might not *mean* to scare her, but that doesn't mean you're not. When David defended "complimenting" a stranger by wolf-whistling at her, it was another student, Anthony, a burly, tattooed guy from the Philippines, who chided him: "If she wanted to know what you thought, she'd ask you."

With a few jarring exceptions, most of the men in the class seemed to be more clueless than abusive or predatory. Many of them were likable, earnest men. There was Musa, from the Gambia, who told the room about fleeing a domineering father; José, from Mexico, whose eyes were wet when he talked about his fear that after his arrest his wife might no longer trust him. Jason, the young, nervous Mormon, seemed to feel more shame about sex than entitlement.

I asked Valiant Richey about this, and he agreed that while some men he prosecuted were genuinely dangerous (and those men are generally sent not to Peter's class but to "deviancy treatment"), most really aren't predators but instead "lonely, emotionally stunted, challenged about how to act in the world." Still, he said, all the men had broken the law, and their actions had helped propagate a system that regularly exploits women and girls; even if they were "nice guys," the result of their behavior, on a mass scale, was a lot of damage to a lot of vulnerable people. That was what interested him about attempting to change behavior with the class: "We could arrest until the end of time and never get a grip on this problem." And, as far as he was concerned, most men—whether they are sex buyers or not—could probably benefit from the class. He felt he had, just from talking to Peter. "As a human—not just a prosecutor—I'm fascinated by how much this has overhauled my life," he told me. "I really have had my eyes opened to the scope of gender inequality in our society."

Before long, the diagonal line on the whiteboard filled up with examples of sexual harassment and coercion. Anthony told a story of a date his sister had gone on, where a man had taken her to a restaurant: "He said, 'If you're not sleeping with me tonight, you're paying for that.' I shit you not! And she's a vegetarian, so it didn't even cost that much!" Then Peter began to discuss outright violence. The room went quiet. He asked the men what they did to prevent being raped; they stared back at him like he was nuts. If the classroom was full of women, he told them, correctly, it would be full of strategies. . . .

The next week, Peter asked some of the men to role-play a transaction. Anthony volunteered to play a sex worker (he was handed a few details to help him form his character, whom he called Destiny), and a protesting, red-faced Jason was chosen to be the john, after insisting, again, that due to the sting, he'd never actually met a sex worker in person and didn't know how it was supposed to work. Finally, he offered $40 and a meal at Taco Bell.

"You're terrible at this," Anthony told him.

Peter pushed them to empathize with their characters, to consider what they had in common, whether they were afraid or in control. He asked them to think about the mystery of the other person's intentions and history, what that felt like. "I was thinking, *I'm a nice guy*." Jason said. "But this shows it's still scary for her."

Anthony handed back the piece of paper with details of his role as a sex worker. "I don't need *this* in my pocket if I get pulled over," he said.

The weeks multiplied and the discussions grew more intense. There was a session called Power and Violence, about the difference between domination and partnership. The men squirmed visibly as the talk turned to destructive relationships. José shared that his father had abused his mother but she hid it from her son, telling only José's sister. Peter shared with the men a story about a past student who'd treated the class as a bunch of useless nonsense until he complained about it to his wife and she stopped him to say, "You should listen to those guys." She'd been sexually assaulted more than once, she told him, but had never felt that he was a safe person to tell. The man was stunned, he told Peter the next week; afterward, his whole attitude toward the class, down to his body language, was different.

Slowly, I watched as the men built a strange camaraderie. They laughed more, shared more. Jason finally told the other men about his religious upbringing and his recent disillusionment. In week seven, he announced that he'd had a kind of breakthrough: He'd hated himself for trying to buy sex; he felt like a monster afterward for disappointing his parents and church elders, and could never explain why he'd done it. Now he found it meaningful that he had arranged the meet-up that got him arrested not long after he'd discovered that a woman he'd been seeing was married. "That's, like, the second-worst thing you can do in my parents' religion, after murder," Jason said. "It festered, and one thing led to another."

"I always feel so damn sensitive after I leave this class on Thursdays," Anthony said one night. "It's like I have to go drink a beer and scratch myself. Y'all are gonna see me on *Oprah*."

Another night he told Peter, "When I hear you talk, I think, 'His wife must love him so much!'" Peter laughed and told the guys that his wife had once threatened to follow him to the class and tell everybody what a damn hypocrite he could be.

Outside of class, Peter talked with me about how he sometimes felt he had to walk a razor's edge between holding the johns accountable and empathizing with them. In the early days, he'd felt more anger toward the men in his classes—"I used to feel like I was talking to my father," an abuser. Lately, he'd been seeing them more compassionately, as victims of a sexist society. "Now," he said, "it's like I'm talking to myself."

During week seven, David—whose discomfort with emotions had by then become a class joke—suddenly came alive with feeling. The discussion topic was vulnerability and shame, which Peter asked the men to discuss. David was the first to speak up, defining it as "a deep-down gut feeling. To me it's like a sickness."

For weeks, he'd belligerently stood up for the rightness of his behavior, but now, reflecting on his arrest, he said, "I haven't done many shameful things, but this takes the cake: to use your one phone call late at night to call your wife and tell her you won't be coming home."

Peter said that his goal was to get the guys to move from shame, which can be crippling, to responsibility and vulnerability. "I take responsibility," said David, for the first time. "I did do it." He was at least glad, he said, that the arrest "made me and the wife communicate more." He stared at the floor, nodding to himself, and said, almost silently: "We'll get through it."

Akio, who'd spoken before about how much he struggled to connect with other people, said that he'd avoided telling almost anyone he knew about his arrest. "I'm good at hiding these things from everybody," he said. "That's kind of my life so far. Does that sound sad?" Later he told me he was making an effort to deepen his relationships with his roommates and co-workers, practicing what he'd learned in the class about listening.

Jason told me that the class on vulnerability was big for him, too. He finally stopped thinking of himself as a monster, reached out to friends and family that he'd been avoiding since the arrest, and he even had a new girlfriend. On a date, under the stars, he told her about his arrest and the things he'd learned since—the first person he'd confided in without being mandated by King County.

There have been no studies yet of any long-term effect that the course has on its students or on sex buying—and even Peter is careful to avoid claiming that the program provides unequivocal results. He is adamant that his course should not replace other forms of conventional punishment. But he's encouraged by what he sees. He's hopeful that its graduates will discuss what they've learned with other men they know, and that slowly the ideas will spread. A few men have been re-arrested; some have stayed in close touch with Peter and the program. It's a process, he acknowledges. A slow one.

On the last night, Peter taught the promised class on love—not just sexual or romantic love but the three other types that the Greeks talked about: familial empathy, respect between equals, and *agape*, which Peter described as the feeling of being a part of something bigger than yourself. They talked about the danger of relying on toxic, substitute versions of these emotions, and Peter asked the men to reflect aloud on the needs that weren't being met in their own lives and what they could do about it.

"As you've started to realize, this class is about a lot more than prostitution," he said, to laughter.

Before the men left, they filled out anonymous evaluations, and I looked through them for the anger and resistance that was no longer obvious in the classroom. Instead, over and over, I saw gratitude.

Even Steve told me he'd learned from the class—and though I hoped in some ways he had, it was certainly hard to see evidence. When he was asked by Peter to reflect on shame, he proudly told the story of the tracking device, yet again. "I get the sense that this particular section is really not landing with you," Peter told him. Week after week, though, he was an eager participant in discussions—he gave the impression he didn't have a lot of other people to talk to—Steve stuck to his attitudes of righteousness and victimhood. He kept making sexist jokes, even after the other men began to greet them with silence.

But I never heard Peter give up on anyone as irredeemable. If anything, resistance seemed to make him try harder, to believe more fervently in the possibility of eventually breaking through.

A few months later, I got an e-mail from Peter. He was headed to the second meeting of a whole new class of men, and the first meeting had not gone well. Several of the attendees were unusually challenging; one had casually declared that "some women like to get beaten." Peter found himself dreading the upcoming classes. It was difficult to hear men talk like that. But it didn't make him doubt his approach—or the power of his program. If anything, it inspired him to push harder. "I wish," he wrote, "I could send the men like him to a longer-term program."

NOTE

1. Offenders' names have been changed throughout.

Strip Clubs and Their Regulars

Katherine Frank

Sexual services and products have long been a part of the U.S. entertainment and leisure industries. In a 1997 article for *U.S. News & World Report,* Eric Schlosser reported that in the prior year Americans spent "more than $8 billion on hard-core videos, peep shows, live sex acts, adult cable programming, sexual devices, computer porn, and sex magazines." The number of major strip clubs catering to heterosexually identified men nearly doubled between 1987 and 1992, and an estimate for late 1998 puts the number of clubs at around 3,000 with annual revenues ranging from $500,000 to more than $5 million.

While some men dislike strip clubs or find them boring, there is a significant population of heterosexual American males who are willing to spend their money on the kind of public, voyeuristic (although interactive) fantasy available in a no-contact strip club. Despite popular beliefs to the contrary, strippers are generally not selling sex to their customers in this type of club—although they are selling sexualized and gendered services. Rather than fulfilling a biological need for sexual release, as some pop sociobiological accounts suggest, or serving a masculine need for domination, strip clubs provide a kind of intermediate space (not work and not home, although related to both) in which men can experience their bodies and identities in particular pleasurable ways. . . .

Strip clubs are stratified in terms of luxury, status, and other distinguishing features. Whereas strip clubs were once primarily located in "red light" areas of towns and cities associated with crime and prostitution, the upscale clubs are now often quite visible and work to develop reputations for safety, comfort, and classiness. Drawing on cultural markers of status—such as luxury liquors, fine dining, valet parking, and private conference rooms—upscale clubs advertise themselves as places for businessmen to entertain clients or for middle-class professionals to visit after work. Dancers may be advertised as refined, well-educated women. Sophisticated sound and lighting equipment, multiple stages, large video screens, and multimillion-dollar construction budgets make many contemporary strip clubs into high-tech entertainment centers. This is not to say that smaller or "seedier" clubs have disappeared. The clubs in any locale, however, are categorized through their relationships to one another and this system of relationships helps inform both the leisure experiences of the customers and the work experiences of the dancers.

The proliferation and upscaling of strip clubs during the 1980s needs to be situated in late capitalist consumer culture as well as within a variety of social changes and developments. In many ways it makes sense that strip clubs should multiply during the last several decades, along with the panic about AIDS and fears about the dissolution of "the family." The process of upscaling in strip clubs, with a promise of "clean" and respectable interactions, alleviated fears about contamination and disease. The fact that sexual activity is not generally expected or offered in strip clubs also fit well with a growing emphasis on monogamy and marriage for heterosexuals after the sexual experimentation (and ensuing disillusionment for many) of the 1970s. There are other social changes that may be influencing this rapid increase in strip clubs as well: women's increased presence in the workforce; continuing backlashes against feminism; ongoing marketing efforts to sexualize and masculinize particular forms of consumption ("sports, beer, and women," for example); changing patterns of mobility, which influence dating practices and intimate relationships; and increased travel for businessmen and more anonymous opportunities to purchase commodified sexualized services, to name just a few.

Despite their prevalence and popularity, strip clubs are still often the subject of intense public scrutiny. Local ordinances have been drafted across the nation to harass, limit, or eradicate strip clubs—often citing "adverse secondary effects" such as increased crime and decreased property values in neighborhoods that house such venues as justifications for these legislative actions. Many such ordinances seem to be based on conjectures about just what the men (and women) are up to when they set foot in a strip club. There is endless speculation about drug use, prostitution, and crime— by customers, lawmakers, and people who have never even entered a strip club. . . . While these activities surface at times, in often scandalous ways—as they do in many industries—I came away from my research with a belief that most of the customers were in search of something completely different through their interactions.

Media and scholarly attention to the customers of strip clubs has been far less pervasive than that focused on the dancers or the clubs themselves. But what is it, exactly, that the customers are seeking in these venues? After all, without enough men willing to open their wallets each night the industry would cease to exist. As a cultural anthropologist dedicated to participant observation—that is, becoming immersed in the community you study— I selected five strip clubs in one city, sought employment as an entertainer, and interviewed the regular male customers of those clubs. For regulars, visits to strip clubs are a significant sexualized and leisure practice; these are not men who have wandered into a club once or twice or visit only for special occasions like bachelor parties. The majority of the regulars were men middle-aged or older with enough disposable income and free time that they could engage in this relatively private and often expensive leisure practice. I also interviewed dancers, club managers and other club employees, advertisers, and men who preferred other forms of adult entertainment.

Most of the regular customers claimed that they knew where to get sex if they wanted it, and that they chose no-contact strip clubs (or clubs that offered table dancing rather than lap dancing) precisely because they knew that sex would not be part of the experience. While watching the dancers perform on the stages was certainly appealing, many of the regulars were also interested in the conversations that they could have with dancers. Unlike burlesque performers of years past, contemporary exotic dancers "perform" not just onstage but individually for the customers as they circulate among the crowd selling table dances. Dancers are thus also selling their personalities, their attentions, and conversation to the customers. Some of the regulars returned repeatedly to see a particular dancer; others enjoyed briefer interactions with a number of dancers. Either way, talk was one of the important services being provided and conversations would focus on work, family, politics, sports, sexual fantasies, or any number of other topics.

Whether visiting a small neighborhood bar or a large, flashy gentleman's club, the customers repeatedly told me that they visited strip clubs to relax. Part of the allure of strip clubs for their patrons lies in their representation as somewhere out of the ordinary, somewhere proscribed and perhaps a bit "dangerous"—yet as a safe space of play and fantasy where the pressures, expectations, and responsibilities of work and home can be left behind.

In many ways, then, strip clubs were seen as relaxing because they provided a respite from women's demands or expectations in other spheres, as well as the possibility (not always actualized) of avoiding competition with other men for women's attention. Strip clubs also offered the customers an opportunity for both personal and sexual acceptance from women, a chance to talk about their sexual desires without reproach or to fantasize that they were attractive enough to gain the interest of a dancer regardless of whether they paid her. Some customers wanted an ego boost. As one man said: "It's just absolutely an ego trip because you go in there, and if you're a warthog, bald, and got a pot belly, some good looking girl's gonna come up and go, 'Hey, do you want me to dance for you?' Seducing women is something all men wish they were better at. . . . This seems like you're doing it, and it's easy!"

Strip clubs were also relaxing because they provided a safe space in which to be both married or committed and interacting with women in a sexualized setting, and the services offered fit well with these particular men's desires to remain sexually monogamous. Customers are also not expected to perform sexually or to provide any pleasure to the dancer (beyond paying her for her time), and this was also seen as relaxing by many of the men. . . .

However, because they provided a space in which many everyday expectations are inverted (by featuring public nudity, for example), the clubs were still seen as "taboo," as dangerous and exciting, by the regulars as well as safe and predictable. Many of the interviewees discussed their experiences in the language of "variety," "travel," "fun," "escape," and "adventure," and described themselves as "hunters" or "explorers" despite the fact that their experiences in the clubs were highly regulated by local ordinances, club rules, and club employees. Some customers enjoyed the fact that their visits to strip clubs took them to marginal areas of the city. Further, visits to the clubs often were unacceptable to the married regulars' more "conservative" wives or partners. Significantly, then, strip clubs are also dangerous enough to be alluring, a bit "less civilized" and rowdier than the places these middle-class customers would ordinarily enter. This balance between safety and excitement was very important, for if strip clubs lose their edge for a particular customer or, conversely, become too transgressive, he may lose interest and seek a different form of entertainment.

Understanding the motivations of the men who frequent no-contact strip clubs can help quell some of the fears that tend to drive oppressive regulation. There are indeed problems with strip clubs as they currently exist, often rooted in material inequalities between different classes of laborers, in the poor working conditions found in many clubs, in the stigma that surrounds sex work, and in double standards for men's and women's sexualities, for example. However, eradicating or more tightly regulating strip clubs does little to combat these problems, which are related to the organization of labor in late capitalism, to systemic inequalities and prejudices, and to the stigmatization and fear that still surround issues of sex and sexuality in the United States.

Source: "Strip Clubs and their Regulars," *American Sexuality Magazine*, Vol. 1, No. 4, 2003. Copyright 2003, National Sexuality Resource Center. Reprinted by permission of the author.

OVERCOME: THE MONEY SHOT IN PORNOGRAPHY AND PROSTITUTION

LISA JEAN MOORE

For a few years in the early 1990s, I worked on a national sex information switchboard. Much to my surprise, a majority of the callers were men, and their two most common questions were "What is the normal penis size?" and "Where is the clitoris?" Trained to provide anonymous, nonjudgmental, and accurate information to callers, I would respond that most penises, when erect, were between 5 and 7 inches. I would receive immediate thanks for this information, and as they hung up I remember thinking their relief was palpable. Their penises, presumably, were "okay."

As for the clitoris question, I instructed callers to place their hands in a praying position, bend their knuckles slightly and imagine this as the vagina. If the area between the thumbs was the vagina opening, the clitoris was roughly located in the place above the tips of their thumbs, in the triangular area. This answer was not as successful as the first. Many callers fumbled with or even dropped the phone while trying to follow my instructions. Some callers were clearly confused by the model itself, asking, "So it's a hole?" or "But what does the vagina really look like?" Furthermore, I was increasingly alarmed by the steady stream of female callers who asked for instructions on how to find their own clitorises or, somewhat paradoxically, wanted suggestions on how to experience orgasms exclusively through vaginal penetration. "Is there something wrong with me?" they inquired when discussing their dissatisfaction with penis-vagina penetration, often explaining that they had never experienced an orgasm during sex. Clearly, there is something baffling and mysterious about the clitoris. Even though size

doesn't matter, location and purpose do. Where is it? What does it do? These callers rarely hung up with the same sense of relief as the first set of callers. The former found answers; the latter continued to question.

I use these examples to illustrate the conventional wisdom on male and female anatomy and sexual responses. In contrast to women, and whether or not each man experiences it to be true, conventional wisdom holds that men's sexuality is fairly simple. It isn't difficult to make men come, and it isn't difficult to know whether or not they have come. The phenomenon of men faking orgasm, though possible, doesn't often get discussed. Semen is, of course, the reason for this; it is thought to be the irrefutable evidence.

Although male callers rarely asked about their semen, in our training, we were instructed to provide them with these facts. Spermatogenesis, or the production of the sperm cell, takes approximately 72 days. Both Cowper's and Littre's glands, which are located in the genital area, contribute secretions in the processes of ejaculation. The prostate also adds fructose and liquefying enzymes.[1] When a man comes, a range of 2–10 milliliters of fluid is produced through his ejaculation at about 10 miles per hour. Between 200 and 500 million sperm cells are contained in most ejaculates, the equivalent of about 5–15 calories. It is estimated that a man ejaculates 5,000 times in his lifetime.[2] Theoretically any man could repopulate the United States with just a few ejaculates (and the participation of 290 million women, or less if multiple births occur).

GROWING UP: FROM INNOCENCE TO DEBAUCHERY

. . . Ejaculation is taken as external proof that a man has experienced an orgasm, despite evidence that men can ejaculate without orgasm, technically known as anorgasmic ejaculation.[3] The physical presence of the ejaculate, the seminal fluid, is a material reality that confirms men's pleasure.[4] Most pornographic entertainment reinforces this belief, as ejaculation, or the "money shot" in porn parlance, is the raison d'être of sexual encounters. The money shot signals the end of the male sexual act—cue the drum roll, he has come. Cindy Patton, an activist and scholar of human sexuality, points out that in Western culture male sexual fulfillment is "synonymous with orgasm" and that the male orgasm is "an essential and essentialist punctuation of the sexual narrative. No orgasm, no sexual pleasure. No cum shot, no narrative closure."[5] In other words, the cum shot is the period at the end of the sentence. Case closed. Alternatively, with the rare exception of anorgasmic ejaculation, both the female anatomy and orgasm are more complex, even elusive—for both men and women. That being the case, in pornography the sex act itself is centered around the male penis and orgasm. Only when that happens does conventional wisdom tell us that sex has occurred.[6]

There is an entire lexicon for the release of semen from the body; terms like ejaculation, premature ejaculation, nocturnal emissions, wet dreams, and shooting your wad are just a few. With such a wide variety of ways to describe ejaculates and the act of ejaculating, it would seem that many men are preoccupied with ejaculation, and especially measurements

of it. From the record books to website legends, claims about the feats of men and their ejaculations abound. For example, the world record for number of male orgasms is 16 in one hour. According to several unsubstantiated reports on websites, the greatest distance of an ejaculate is 18 feet 9 inches, which was achieved by Horst Schultz, who apparently also holds the record for the greatest height of ejaculate (12 feet 4 inches).

Not all ejaculates are created equal. Each time ejaculation occurs, semen contains varying proportions of ingredients. These variations are affected by diet, age, how the ejaculation was achieved (through masturbation or partner sexual stimulation, whether anal, oral, or vaginal), level of arousal, physical fitness, and number of ejaculations in the past 72 hours. The age of first conscious ejaculation, known as "oigarche," is generally between 10 and 15 years old. Nocturnal emissions, or wet dreams that are generally erotic or sexual, are accompanied by the release or ejaculation of semen. Roughly 50 percent of boys between the ages of 10 and 20 experience wet dreams, possibly as a way for the reproductive system to get rid of excess semen, although most agree that semen is reabsorbed back into the body.

But sometimes men are not physiologically in control of when and how their semen emerges. Premature ejaculation, recently renamed "rapid ejaculation" . . . is increasingly considered a medically diagnosable condition for men under 40. It is defined as ejaculation prior to the desires of both sexual partners. Although rapid ejaculation may be underreported, the National Health and Social Life Survey suggests that its prevalence is roughly 30 percent. Sex therapy, antidepressants, and lidocaine cream or related topical anesthetic agents have all demonstrated success at treating rapid ejaculation.

Regardless of the quantity of semen or the quality of its delivery during ejaculation, in the world of sex entertainment the release of semen signifies the successful conclusion of the sex act. The appearance of semen is the proof of sexual fulfillment, so the more the better, right? It turns out that the equation is not so simple when we consider the layered meanings of sperm and semen across the worlds of pornography, prostitution, and popular culture.

FETISHIZING SEMEN

Members of the specifically heterosexual[7] sex entertainment industry, sex workers and pornographic filmmakers in particular, contribute to our understanding of sperm in important ways. From ideas about what constitutes sex or sex acts to what is considered sexy, to how men and their penises can perform, the sex industry—even if covertly—has greatly influenced popular notions of sex. Pornographic filmmakers specialize in representing a variety of techniques to animate ejaculation and semen, thereby fetishizing it. Within sex entertainment settings, semen is worshiped as a magical substance of both supernatural arousal and erotic achievement. It is depicted in films and printed media as a substance that has extraordinary power over humans. The male actors seem repeatedly shocked by the force, volume, and desirability of their semen, while the female actors can't control themselves in the presence of this semen and must slather it all over their bodies, even drink it down as if dying of thirst. Different cultures vary the themes of seminal ejaculate in their pornography. For example, in the late 1990s, *bukkake,* a style of pornography that was popularized in Japan, depicts multiple men ejaculating on a woman or group of women.[8] The use of ejaculation is part of a humiliation ritual and generally does not involve any of the female characters experiencing orgasm.

So although semen is presented as the end product of a sexual experience, it is also an object manipulated by the directors, cameras, lighting, scripts, and actors to elicit arousal. The camera lens focuses on the glory of seminal expression and encourages the viewer to witness the money shot as the reward of spectatorship. . . .

But semen does not exist in a vacuum; rather, it is a bodily fluid that is deeply implicated in history and epidemiology. At least for the past 30 years, unprotected seminal ejaculation brings to mind disease transmission—including HIV, hepatitis B and C, and sexually transmitted diseases (STDs). Being such a dangerous vector of infection, semen has become increasingly seen as grotesque—something feared and unwanted. Unprotected seminal ejaculation during vaginal or anal sex is not the only dangerous practice; semen ejaculated into the mouth, eyes, and nose can transmit herpes, chlamydia, syphilis, and gonorrhea.

As a result of these risks, exposure to semen is evermore regulated within the sex entertainment industry. California's Division of Occupational Safety and Health (CAL-OSHA) oversees and regulates workers in the adult-film industry; most porn films are produced in southern California. The agency provides adult-film workers with safety guidelines and employment protection from work practices that might expose them to blood and "other potentially infectious material (OPIM)."[9] According to CAL-OSHA's website, "semen and vaginal fluid are always considered OPIM." The website also provides examples of "engineering and work practice controls" used in the adult film industry. . . .

In the sex entertainment industry, some film studios demand regular HIV tests. Adult Industry Medical Health Care Foundation (AIM), a nonprofit health-care foundation concerned with sex worker mental and physical health, provides on-site testing services for performers and encourages the responsible sharing of test results between working partners. Yet there have been HIV transmission cases within the pornography industry. As reporter Ann Regentin explains:

In 1986, John Holmes contracted the virus and continued to work without telling anyone until 1988, when he died of AIDS. In 1998, a rash of HIV cases seemed to point to Marc Wallice, who tested positive for the virus and had been caught working with faked HIV test results. In 1999, Tony Montana tested positive and immediately stopped working. As far as anyone knows, he did not infect anyone else.[10]

On April 12, 2004, porn star Darren James, who contracted the virus while shooting in Brazil, infected others through work, leading to a brief shutdown of production within the San Fernando Valley. Clearly, there are occupational risks to working in the porn industry, but these can be mitigated through precautions and regulations. Within the sex entertainment industry, then, this bodily fluid straddles the line between being supremely erotic and a lethal weapon.

Each sex worker must develop methods, practices, and professional expertise to avoid exposure to potential diseases or lethal toxins. Furthermore, fertile female sex workers must also try to limit their risk of pregnancy, an occupational hazard of frequent contact with semen. As one of my informants related to me, sex work includes aspects of "hazardous waste material" management. There are different risks associated with exposure to semen by sex workers in the porn industry. Reviewing a working partner's HIV tests is one industry standard. With the advantage of not performing sex in real time, actors and actresses in the porn industry are able to manipulate some exposure to seminal ejaculation. For example, a porn star can appear to swallow ejaculate without actually doing so. During an interview, Raylene, a porn star, stated, "I don't swallow that often because I really don't like the taste. I mean I have, but I don't really like it."[11] . . .

THE MONEY SHOT

Some recent mainstream films use semen in a different way: as props for gags or as symbols of alienation. The actual appearance of sperm in mainstream films is a relatively new phenomenon and perhaps can be seen, in some ways, as an extension of the increasingly graphic and "realistic" images of the body that are so commonplace today, especially in television crime and medical dramas. Here severed limbs, burnt bodies, and gaping wounds are regularly featured, but we often even "go inside" the body to see the actual source of the disease, parasite, or infected organ.

Given the intensely graphic nature of such shows, and given that sperm has long been readily seen and featured in pornographic films, it is perhaps not surprising that the once-taboo substance now makes its appearance in mainstream movies. In the film *Magnolia*, for example, protagonist Frank Mackey (played by Tom Cruise) is a motivational speaker for a seminar series, "Seduce and Destroy," which includes a session entitled "How to turn your 'friend' into your sperm receptacle," encouraging insecure men to use their sperm as a means of conquering and depositing waste into the female body. Taking this a step further, films like *There's Something About Mary* and *The Squid and the Whale* use sperm as, in the former, hair gel and, in the latter, a means for acting out adolescent angst. Such material would once have been considered obscene but is now enough of a novelty in mainstream film that it is capable of grabbing the audience's attention and eliciting somewhat shocked laughs. . . .

Such treatment of semen is a far cry from its standard depiction in pornographic films. Far from providing comedic relief, semen . . . often has a starring and very important role to play in these features. . . . The man's ejaculation is the raison d'être for these films. The money shot, where a man ejaculates on screen, is the compulsory display of semen in most pornographic films and a number of pornographic magazines as well. Ejaculation, the release of seminal fluid often with astounding force, authenticates the pornographic film in that the sexual desire, the arousal, and the performance are seemingly based on "real" desire. As a male friend quipped to me during a more explosive money shot, "Now you can't fake that." The cum shot is typically defined where a man ejaculates onto a woman, usually onto her face (referred to as a facial) or sometimes onto her sex organs. To be classified as a money shot, the semen must be clearly visible. The "money" refers to the money the actor receives as payout for making the film, which sometimes includes a bonus for the act of ejaculation. . . .

When seminal ejaculation is the denouement of a film, there is a presumption about those watching the film. As Patton states, "Even though not everyone in this culture has a penis, the cinematic conventions which position the viewer as the person coming are fairly seamless, and it is quite easy to imagine that this is your penis, regardless of your anatomical configuration."[12] In the porn film, we are each beckoned to identify with that penis and to experience the rush of relief as ejaculate spews forth. Furthermore, Patton has argued that after the wild abandon of pornographic sex, seminal ejaculation enables the man to be responsible for the restoration of sexual order.[13] The stylized repetition of money shots is alluring in that it signals release of control, pleasure, achievement, and success.

It is not clear at what historical moment the money shot emerged as a cinematic convention, but Patton suggests that it has at least existed in the United States since the 1930s as "handmade gay male pornographic drawings from the interwar years."[14] The male orgasm demonstrated through ejaculation indicates the completion of a sex act, the scene, the movie, the book, and the encounter. It instructs the audience that the activity is over and has been successful. As an industry standard of pornographic films, the money shot was fairly commonplace after World War II.[15] . . .

GIRLS GONE WILD FOR SPERM

There is a new niche market of seminal ejaculate films that expand on the glorification of men's ejaculate. Unlike other pornographic genres, these movies focus on semen as the central theme of the narrative and the action, not solely the denouement. Titles such as *Semen Demons, Desperately Seeking Semen, The Cum Cocktail, We Swallow, Sperm Overdose* (volumes 1–6), *Sperm Dreams, Sperm Burpers* (volumes 1–5), *A Splash of Sperm,* and *Feeding Frenzy* (volumes 1–3) venture beyond the money shot toward eroticizing seminal ingestion. The contents of the promotional descriptions of the videos, as well as the videos themselves, depict a variety of women drinking and bathing in semen from diverse male partners. Women appear to be insatiable and competitive about their desire for ingesting the semen as they rush to get to the ejaculating penis, the full shot glass, or residual ejaculate on a sheet. What does it mean to see women completely overcome with their desire to drink semen? To smear it all over their bodies? What does this say about male desire and masculinity? Here is a sampling of promotional descriptions of a few films:[16]

Promo for the movie Semen Shots 2

There's nothing that a pretty girl likes more at the end of a sexual encounter than to drink her lover's cum out of a shot glass. That's the premise behind this developing series, anyway. Delilah Strong entertains five young men and takes two cocks in her pussy before swigging multiple shots of their hot spunk. Jasmyn Taliana whimpers a lot before downing her two shots. Mason Storm enjoys a bit of anal before laughing her way through two fingers of warm sperm. Rio Mariah takes a double penetration and then squeezes the contents of her pussy and ass into a glass for savoring. Monica Sweetheart looks pretty in a sheer nightie with sparkly flowers during her anal and still looks cute while tossing back some of Brian Pumper's love cocktail. . . .

Promo for Wad Gobblers, Volume 13
This video begins with an amazing wild montage of twelve or fourteen chicks all taking it in the face with gobs of splashing semen, a dozen or more beauties being blasted with emissions so powerful it shoots up their nostrils. Their tongues snake out to lap up every drop and the overflow bubbles like lava out of their mouths.

These descriptions of money shots use sensational linguistic cues to entice the reader to purchase or rent these videos. It is obvious that seminal ejaculation is the main attraction in each video, the star of the show. Women's bodies are the surfaces for seminal display or the containers to ingest semen. Using the props of shot glasses and cocktail accessories, women literally become drunk on semen, often losing control in the presence of such powerful and intoxicating fluids.

Ironically, this genre of pornography is being produced against a cultural backdrop in which semen is directly associated with risk. Warnings about HIV/AIDS and STDs are plastered on bus stops, broadcast through public service announcements on radio and television, and echoed in health-care interactions. We are told to avoid semen to lessen our risk of pregnancy, disease, and death. Some industries, such as health care and forensics, have worked to imbue the raw material of semen with risk. Similarly, fertility enterprises and spouse or partner surveillance companies market their services by both reminding us of the risk of seminal ejaculate and claiming to mitigate that risk for us.

But the constant messages about risk and danger from seminal ejaculate have likely affected men's own relationship to their semen, as well as amplified a sense of it as forbidden. These pornographic videos then capitalize on recovering and eroticizing the raw material

of semen as safe, natural, organic, whole. The commodification of semen in these videos relies on a specific form of consumption in the narrative arc. Taking the action a moment beyond the money shot, the triumph of these videos is actually the expression of reverence for semen as it is placed either in a shot glass or on a woman's face, buttocks, or breasts. The absence of, or disregard for, risk is also a saleable dimension of these videos. They sell the image of sperm as not embodying risk or, even if risky, then certainly worth that risk. In these films, these female actors are depicted as willing to debase themselves, put themselves at risk, and even become sick in order to please their men. . . .

. . . [T]he taste of semen [is not necessarily] as delicious as the videos portray. Some have compared the scent of semen to bleach, household cleanser, or swimming pool water. The taste has been described as salty and bitter, which may explain why Semenex, a patented, all-natural powder drink has been created to sweeten semen. Semenex, with an advertised price of $54.95 for a 30-serving container, relies on testimonials similar to this one: "Tasty! I've never really had a problem with semen, except when it gets really bitter, but this product really makes drinking a man down a treat!" so says, Jenni from Mesa, Arizona. As an online ad in *Maxim* magazine claims, "Semenex is where to go for delicious sperm guaranteed. Finally, an answer to the 'I don't like the taste' argument."[17] Interviewed as part of the 2005 documentary *Inside Deep Throat* about the infamous porn movie, Helen Gurley Brown, *Cosmopolitan* editor in chief and author of the 1962 best seller *Sex and the Single Girl,* extols the benefits of semen, saying, "Women have known for years that ejaculate is good for the skin because it is full of babies. . . . It's full of protein. Just rub it all over your face, and skin and chest."

While semen may get mixed reviews from actual women, in the world of pornographic films semen is no longer something that is gross, yucky, smells bad, or brings disease—rather, it is something delicious, desired, and needed. Perhaps only the bold fantasy of a world dominated by men, and their need for sexual pleasure, could provide the scenario where women actually fight with each other for the pleasure of guzzling down ounces of semen. . . .

Within the sex industries of prostitution and pornography, sperm maintains contradictory meanings. It is referred to as a dangerous, if not lethal, weapon and, alternatively, as the crowning achievement of human interaction. For sex workers who perform sex acts with actual people (as opposed to pornography film actors), seminal ejaculation is a hazardous waste material to be managed and avoided for fear of pregnancy or disease. Sex workers do not have the benefit of reviewing their partners' HIV test results before a scene. Nor are there multiple takes to "get it right." And since many male clients are socialized by pornographic videos that do not depict safe sex, many sex workers find that, while they must use latex devices to protect themselves, at the same time they must eroticize their safe sex practices or risk failing to perform the job they are being paid for.

"DEALING WITH THE JIZZ": STORIES FROM SEX WORKERS

Most sex workers handle men as if they are dangerous; they can be violent, deceiving, and vectors of disease. Despite this belief about men, most sex workers will take on the risk of intimate physical contact as long as the men have the money to pay for it. This, of course, assumes that men can afford an average $200- an-hour sexual experience. In an ironic twist, sex workers and sperm banks have an inverse relationship with regard to sperm and money. Men pay sex workers for their services, which includes managing their potentially dangerous semen, while people pay sperm banks to store or purchase

certifiably healthy semen. Semen banks pay donors between $40 and $60 per ejaculate. Each ejaculate can be divided up into between two and three vials, which cost roughly $150 each. So one ejaculate divided into two samples is $(150 \times 2) - 60 = \$240$ profit per ejaculate. This is $40 more than the typical sex worker makes.

The analysis that follows is based on interviews conducted over a five-year period (1991–1996) with well-paid, in-call, consenting sex workers. Sex workers occasionally reject clients who use heavy drugs or alcohol, are on the bad trick list, or simply give them the creeps. A bad trick list circulates within communities of sex workers and has the names and descriptions of previously delinquent or violent male clients. Perhaps through personal stigma and immersion in an AIDS/HIV culture, sex workers view all bodily products as having degrees of toxicity. In the pursuit of self-preservation and profit, semen is treated as a carrier of pathogens, germs, and sperm that may debilitate, kill, or impregnate the worker. All sex workers interviewed about their safer sex practices stated they always use a condom for each act of vaginal and anal intercourse. Here are some of their comments about men and their sperm:

I personally do not want to have any contact with fluids that come out of a man's dick. So like today I saw somebody who had a little pre-ejaculate on his belly and what I do is I take a piece of tissue and I wipe it off, then I take another piece of tissue and I apply nonoxynol nine. (Bonny, 54; 20-year professional dominant) . . .

My party line is rubbers for fucking and rubbers for sucking. I have always been strict about it. (Hadley, 55; 25-year veteran stripper, prostitute, professional dominant) . . .

Men and their semen are viewed here as universally dangerous, distrustful, and dirty. Semen is something that must be managed. No matter how it is represented, as good or bad, or somewhere in between, at the time of its ejaculation, semen has to be dealt with. As Quincy, a 45-year-old sex worker who has been in the industry since her late 20s, states,

The guys want me to really like their cum. I think many of them would like to see me roll around in it and drink it and basically bathe in it. Maybe like they see on the movies they watch. But, I can't really do that. So I just sort of pretend. There would be something nice about being able to wallow in body fluids but I am not even going to go there.

As discussed, this desire to "wallow in body fluids" is promoted in almost all pornographic videos, but it is only risk-free for the jizzee, not the jizzed upon. Quincy empathizes with her clients about semen, telling them, "I really love sperm and I wish I could swallow it. But we can pretend and I bet you will not even notice the difference." In her sex work career and as a practitioner of latex devices, Quincy claims that men do not know the difference between safer sex and unprotected sex when things are done by a professional. She claims when safer sex is seamlessly accomplished, her male clientele (and perhaps men in general) accept its use: "So it's like a Pavlovian trick to get people more comfortable with and more turned on to the possibility of safe sex. The snap of the glove or smell of condoms means something fun is going to happen."

Sex workers create safety standards for dealing with semen. They use male and female condoms, gloves, and finger cots (small latex coverings for individual fingers), as actual physical barriers that inhibit the semen from making contact with exposed body surfaces. Safer sex, as a collection of symbols, practices, and technological innovations, both protects sex workers from contamination and assures clients of standard operating procedures that reduce their own exposure to the "hazardous waste material" of previous clients. As Michelle, a 38-year-old petite blonde, states, "When my clients get a little strange about my safer sex stuff, I will say, 'Well, this might bug you a little bit,

but I promise to keep you safe' and then I will smile all sweet."

In addition to manipulations for safety purposes, sex workers have crafted techniques to make semen perform more predictably, to make this recalcitrant substance more workable. Sex workers train their clients in techniques for semen control and manipulation. For example, many sex workers instruct their clients on how to put on a condom. They can instruct men in how to maintain erections and delay ejaculation through practicing sex acts and talking about their bodies. By bringing an erect man close to orgasm and then delaying the ejaculation, sex workers talk about building a man's endurance and self-control during sex acts. They work with their clients, talking to them and coaxing them to understand their own bodies and sexual responses. Several of the women I interviewed have developed symbolic rituals of performance to promote pleasurable semen control. They place a variety of male condoms in special places on a night table or at an altar with candles and incense, "To honor the act they know will be coming soon," as Olivia put it. Most sex workers opened up male condoms during our interviews to demonstrate different techniques for placing condoms on imaginary penises using their mouth and hands, coaching men through the safer sex requirements with statements like, "Now comes the fun part," and, "I can't wait. Can you?"

When I was interviewing Michelle at her apartment, she invited me to look at an album of erotic photographs of herself in full makeup and dressed in lingerie. "This is how I look when my clients come over," she explained as we explored the ironies of attempting to be sexy and available while assiduously managing men's ejaculate. Michelle knows that in her work she cannot use the universal precautions of the health-care industry to protect herself. Rather, she must maintain her sexy, available, and pleasurable image while ensuring her survival:

I mean going to see my dentist becomes—I feel like a hazardous waste material myself. First he had some new goggles, well then he got a shield, you know, and next I expect him to come in just like—you know, a space suit next time. It's so funny. But that's what we're having to do. See, the medical profession has the luxury of looking like they're in this space suit. I can't look like I'm in a space suit. I have got to look like I'm being very intimate and everything, and yet really I am trying to have my own little space suit going on here.

Ana, a 38-year-old petite, brunette sex worker, explained one of the ways she flatters men while retrieving used condoms:

It's funny because I started doing this thing with the condoms. When I take them off the guy, before I throw them away or flush them down the toilet, I show them to the guy. . . . I mean most guys because a couple of my guys might be out the door before I get a chance. But when I show them to the guy, I say something like, "Wow you must really like me a lot" or "I have never seen this much before." Lots of guys seem to really like that when you tell them that they have a lot [of semen]. They kind of get off on it.

This verbal acknowledgement and visual display of seminal volume echoes the penis size concerns explored at the beginning of this [reading]. Ana is exploiting a man's concern with size, density, and volume as a way to praise men and continue the pleasurable (safer) sexual experience. If seminal ejaculate were not contained in a condom, how else might a man know how virile he apparently is?

In spite of the acknowledged risks, sex workers are handling semen and managing men. In many instances, sex workers innovate containment strategies to limit exposure to semen while also making men feel good about their semen and their expressions of masculinity. Through the use of flattery, men are encouraged to believe they measure up to or exceed other men's performances and bodies. Sex workers' (like Ana's) use of male condoms enables them to capture semen. In this context, semen is used to compliment a man on his potency. By empathizing with men about the "good old days," sex workers can enforce rules about seminal exposure, while making men feel that their semen is not hazardous. Sex workers' expertise at using latex devices enables them to make men feel taken care of, while assuring their own safety from exposure.

THE ESSENCE OF (EVERY)MAN

With the proliferation of movies and videos that glorify the money shot, the sex entertainment industry provides an avenue for men to be spectators in the celebration of unprocessed, carnal, natural semen. Unlike other industries that manage semen, such as scientific laboratories, fertility clinics, and forensics enterprises, male bodily products do not need to be technologically enhanced or scientifically manipulated to be useful or understood. Unlike the workers in these industries, porn stars do not use universal precautions of covering their bodies with latex gloves, goggles, and face masks when handling semen. In real life, most sex workers, particularly the successful ones, are not entirely cloaked in thin layers of plastic, rigidly carrying out state-regulated mandates for handling body fluids. Sex workers, in films and real life, are either very minimally dressed or naked and do not shrink away from intimate contact with seminal fluid.

As other industries that manage sperm have established, not all men are created equal. For example, a majority of men who attempt to donate sperm are rejected from sperm banks. And even outside of the fertility clinics, there are multiple reminders that most men produce semen that is gross, diseased, genetically inferior, incompetent, lazy, and unwanted. To some extent, then, the pornography industry produces images that address the needs and desires of these men. That is, since men are socialized to believe that their semen is undesirable and even disgusting to women, and possibly perceived as a health hazard, it is a relief to see representations of their semen as cherished. The raw material of male desire, seminal fluid, is produced directly from the source, and it is wanted and desperately desired in its purest form.

In these videos, there is still power associated with the man's characteristics, but power and social desirability are also assigned to the color, amount, and image of the semen itself—and the woman's positive reaction to it. No one is running to the bathroom to spit out the ejaculate, and everyone swallows with a smile. Semen, in these videos, is not abstracted into a characterization— it is not anthropomorphized—yet it is still desirable. Furthermore, the fairly recently established niche genres that focus on the consumption of semen depict women who can't get enough. They have no fear and no disgust for the substance in its natural state. No technological manipulation of semen is necessary.

While this process of appreciating everyman's sperm may seem liberating, it is still occurring within systems of male domination. The forces of hegemonic masculinity act to subjugate some men to the control of other men deemed more worthy, esteemed, or powerful. These fantasies about seminal consumption sell subjugated men the belief that they are the epitome of traditionally masculine power when they may rank quite low. While some men may opt out of a traditionally masculine set of behaviors and work to redefine masculinity, other men will literally buy into the images and tropes of pornography. Those men who are still participating in and consenting to a process that de-values them become perfect consumers of films that bolster the story of male dominance. This means that, even though these men may not directly benefit from hierarchal relations of masculine power, they will support films that depict male domination because they identify with the male protagonist. Porn becomes one of the many opiates of the wimpy men who cannot take a stand against the ultimate nonconsensual subordination of others because they themselves are so subordinated. In this way, hegemonic masculinity maintains its dominance by providing commodities that work to placate those oppressed by activities that are in reality disempowering.

My analysis of semen as represented, consumed, and manipulated within industrial and commercial sex markets further establishes sperm's elasticity of meaning. While individual men may be aware of their social worth as subordinate to other men, commercial sex work is one arena in which men can retain hope that their seminal ejaculate, their essence of manhood, is enjoyed, powerful, and spectacular.

NOTES

1. Vivien Marx, *The Semen Book* (London: Free Association, 2001).

2. Caroline Aldred, *Divine Sex: The Art of Tantric and Taoist Arts of Conscious Loving* (San Francisco: HarperCollins, 1996).

3. For recent scientific explorations of ejaculatory disorders, see David J. Ralph and Kevan Wylie, "Ejaculatory Disorders and Sexual Function," *British Journal of Urology* 95:9 (2005): 1181–86.

4. Kalyani Premkumar, *The Massage Connection: Anatomy and Physiology* (Philadelphia: Lippincott, Williamson and Wilkins, 2004: 436).

5. Cindy Patton, "Hegemony and Orgasm: Or the Instability of Heterosexual Pornography," *Screen* 30:4 (1989): 1–34.

6. For example, Laura M. Carpenter, *Virginity Lost: An Intimate Portrait of First Sexual Experiences* (New York: New York University Press, 2005).

7. Due to methodological constraints, this [reading] primarily relies on heterosexually produced pornography and heterosexually oriented sex workers. That is not to say that viewers or participants in these industries are heterosexual, but it is to bracket the data as produced primarily for a presumed heterosexual audience. Clearly, gay porn or porn featuring men who have sex with men would be a robust site for research about semen and the eroticization of ejaculation.

8. Pamela Paul, *Pornified: How Pornography Is Transforming Our Lives, Our Relationships and Our Families* (New York: Holt, 2005).

9. *Vital Information for Workers and Employers in the Adult Film Industry,* CAL-OSHA, 2003, available at http://www .dir.ca.gov/dosh/adultfilmindustry.html (accessed October 14, 2006).

10. Ann Regentin, *What We're Really Watching,* May 26, 2004, available at http://www.cleansheets.com/articles /regentin_05.26.04.shtml (accessed October 14, 2006).

11. Interview with Raylene by Max Gunner, "Seven Inches of Pleasure," *Popsmear Online Magazine,* available at http://www.popsmear.com/lovemaking/seveninches/15.0 /index.html (accessed October 14, 2006).

12. Patton, "Hegemony and Orgasm," 105.

13. Cindy Patton, "The Cum Shot: Three Takes on Lesbian and Gay Studies," *Out/Look* 1:3 (1988): 72–76.

14. Ibid., 106.

15. For a history of pornography in the United States, see Joseph Slade, *Pornography in America: A Reference Handbook* (Santa Barbara, Calif.: ABC-CLIO, 2000). As Slade states on page 323: "After the war, the cum shot, the penis ejaculating out of the vagina, became nearly universal."

16. These are a collection of descriptions taken from *Reviews,* 2004, available at www.avn.com (accessed October 14, 2006).

17. *Come Again, and Again . . .* , available at http://www .semenex.com/maximwebguide4th.jpg (accessed October 14, 2006).

AUTONOMY AND CONSENT IN SEX WORK

KIMBERLY KAY HOANG

Western men hear about girls who are sold and forced to sell their bodies, but no one here is forced to do anything. I come to the bar to work, . . . and if I want to have sex with a client, I have sex with him. If I don't, then I won't. No one forces me to do anything I don't want to do. [NGO workers] come here trying to give us condoms or save us, [but] how can they help me when I make more money than them?

> —Vy, twenty-two-year-old hostess
> in Naughty Girls

Can you go back to America and tell all your friends that I do NOT want to be rescued? All these Americans and Viet Kieus who come here thinking that they need to save us are so stupid. If you had to choose between working in a factory for twelve hours a day with bosses who don't let you rest and [who] look at you like they are raping you with their eyes, or working in a bar where you have a few drinks and sometimes spread your legs for a man, which would you choose? Why don't people go rescue factory workers? We are the ones who were not scared to leave factory work for sex work. We are smart hustlers [nguoi chen lan], not dumb, scared factory workers!

> —Trinh, twenty-four-year-old hostess
> in Lavender

In the U.S. popular media, advocates like Nicholas Kristof and Sheryl WuDunn (2010) frequently suggest training in factory work as a form of rescue for women they view as either trafficking victims forced into sex work or coerced, impoverished women without training or options for their labor. . . . However, the women in my study asserted the opposite. These women experienced sex work as an escape from the low pay and harsh working conditions in other sectors of Vietnam's economy. Remarkably, given the negative tone in many previous studies, all fifty-six of the female workers I spoke with in 2006–2009, along with the ninety women I later interviewed in 2009–2010, described their relationships with their mommies and bosses in a positive light. That is because, in these bars, the actual practice of sex work operated according to strict moral codes oriented toward freedom and consent rather than forced labor. Their work in the sex industry allowed women workers to imagine themselves as citizens of a vibrant contemporary political economy in Ho Chi Minh City, rather than as poor Third World victims.

Several studies suggest that bar owners and the madams who run the bars exploit their workers. . . . However, recent works by Christine Chin (2013), Rhacel Parreñas (2011), and many others analyze the complex social structures that shape the range of choices available to women in their relationships with clients, club owners, and brokers. . . . Rather than treat women as victims of global poverty who are kidnapped and forced, or duped, into the sex industry, sex workers across all four markets offer a different perspective from which to examine the sex industry. Like Vy and Trinh quoted [above], many sex workers were frustrated with media images and NGO narratives about trafficked victims, because they saw themselves as fearless women who stepped out

From "Autonomy and Consent in Sex Work," in *Dealing in Desire: Asian Ascendancy, Western Decline, and the Hidden Currencies of Global Sex Work.* © 2015 by Kimberly Kay Hoang. Reprinted by permission of University of California Press.

of the factories and into sex work, where they had much more autonomy over their labor and their bodies. . . .

. . . [T]he sexual commerce that took place [at Khong Sao Bar, Lavender, Secrets, and Naughty Girls] hinged on a strict moral code that inhibited the bar owners and madams from forcing a woman to have sex against her will. To illustrate this process, I draw on Erving Goffman's concepts of "frontstage" and "backstage," which describe the roles *social* actors (that is, individuals in everyday life) play in relation to various audiences. According to Goffman (1959), one's performance on a frontstage is open to judgment, and actors perform there in a way that adheres to conventions that have meaning to the audience. Meanwhile, the backstage is a place where the audience is absent and actors can let their guard down and discuss or refine their performances without revealing these strategies to their audience. . . .

"GO SAVE FACTORY WORKERS!"— CONSENSUAL LABOR IN SEX WORK

One afternoon when the bar did not have many customers, three NGO workers walked into Naughty Girls with pamphlets informing the workers of centers where they could get tested for HIV/AIDS and packets of information on local NGOs working to save victims of sex trafficking. All three of the aid workers were local Vietnamese women hired by an international organization to target sex workers and drug users. As the aid workers walked through the bar, the hostesses openly mocked their looks and commented that they wished the NGOs would simply leave them alone. After the outreach workers left, Truc, a twenty-nine-year-old hostess, told me,

I got arrested three times after the police found me making a deal with a client. The second time, I was

sent to this [detention] center for eighteen months, and they made me learn how to sew. I told them that I worked in a factory for two years before working in the bar, and that I already knew how to sew, but they didn't care. The third time, they told me that if I told people I was forced to sell sex, I could leave and go to a rehabilitation center. . . . A Viet Kieu woman from the United States ran that center. That place wasn't any better. There was a strict curfew, and she wouldn't let us leave at night. We couldn't call anyone, and we spent our days taking English lessons or learning how to sew or cook.

For Truc, the training that she was forced to go through in both the detention center and the rehabilitation center was isolating and demoralizing. She could not understand why these places were so focused on teaching the workers skills in the very trades that they were trying to escape. Life in the factories, she told her coworkers, was much worse than life in the bars.

In that same conversation, Mai-Lan, a twenty-eight-year-old hostess, turned to me and asked, "Do those Western and Viet Kieu women who come here thinking that they are going to help us know that we are sleeping with their husbands? We are not the ones they should save." Vy-Van added, "When you go home [to America], tell people that this is a job just like any other job." Truc jumped in, saying, "Tell [the NGO workers] they should go save factory workers who are forced to work long hours for little pay, [are] beat by their bosses, and [who] sometimes have to offer sexual [favors] to get higher pay."

Sex workers made a clear distinction between force and choice and were incredibly articulate about the paternalistic approach of the state's rehabilitation centers and NGOs looking to "rescue" them. Because organizations needed to show their donors that they were indeed "rescuing and reintegrating" trafficked victims, they often ended up working with women who had been free agents and who were arrested on the streets. NGOs required these sex workers to reframe themselves as "trafficked victims" in need of aid, rather than as "criminals" who engaged in illicit sex-for-money exchanges, before they could get out of the detention centers. Though the sex workers did not see themselves as in need of rescue, they often capitulated, adopting NGO narratives to avoid the eighteen-month sentence in a detention center. These arrests, though rare in the bars where I did my research, demonstrate the contemporary frictions within the state, which attempts to appeal to the interests of NGOs and the U.S. Department of State while simultaneously turning a blind eye to critical spaces of entertainment for Western tourists. . . .

. . . [M]any of the women in my study described domestic work or factory work as far more abusive and less autonomous when compared with sex work. As maids, not only did the workers have to work long hours, but some were also vulnerable to rape by their bosses. As factory workers, women often felt coerced into performing undesirable labors at impossible speeds and were victims of wage theft, making them feel less free or less in control of their labor. Thuyen, a twenty-five-year-old worker at Naughty Girls, told me that her friends who also worked as maids never told anyone about their sexual relations with their bosses, because they were afraid that they would lose their jobs or, worse, their places to live in the big city. In the factories, workers were constantly racing to produce goods in a timely manner. If they could not keep up, their bosses did not hesitate to publicly humiliate them or physically abuse them. . . .

In the conversations that I had with the women about why they entered into sex work, many described their sense of freedom and the relationships of intimacy built on trust and consent that enabled them to be innovative and flexible in their work. The madams were key to supporting this trust and consent because they made sure that sexual relationships between clients and workers were consensual. These mommies felt morally bound to support workers' desire to fight back at moments when clients overstepped the women's boundaries.

LABOR AND THE MORAL ORDER OF MOMMIES AND BAR OWNERS

Over the year and a half (2009–2010) I spent in Khong Sao Bar, Lavender, Secrets, and Naughty Girls, I learned that the relationships between mommies and bar owners and the hostesses who worked in the bars were guided by a strict moral code entrenched in a labor system that relied on free or cheap labor. The women in Khong Sao Bar and Lavender all earned their money through client tips and sex work. As a result, they were essentially a pool of free labor for the bar owners and the madams in those bars. While workers were required to drink, sing, and dance, none of the women I worked with were ever forced to have sex with a client. Hanh, the head mommy in Khong Sao Bar, described the moral order that governed her relations with workers in the bar in this way:

If you have *dao* [faith or religion] without *duc* [morals], you have nothing. You have to have both *dao* and *duc*. If you decide to have sex with someone for money outside the bar, you can. I will never take any money from what you make from having sex—it is not moral to take that money. I do not want to live with those sins when I die. When a client asks if they can take a girl out of the bar, I always say that they have to ask the girl and negotiate with the girl themselves. I am just here to help the ones who are having a hard time getting clients.

. . . In my time at Khong Sao Bar, Hanh held firm to the principle of not forcing workers to have sex with any particular client. For example, on one of several occasions when a worker refused to leave the bar with a client, I watched the client turn to Hanh and urge her to convince the woman to leave with him. Hanh responded by smiling and saying, "All I can do is make sure that you are having a good time in the bar with the girls here. I cannot control what happens outside the bar. If something goes wrong, I don't want to be responsible for it. It is her choice. I cannot force any of them to go, because I do not want to worry about them outside of this bar."

After this, Hanh walked to the back room where the women sat when they were not at a client's table. She pointed to the cross that hung on her necklace and said, "I have morals. These men think that they can push me to make you go with them. I will not do it. If I do it one time, for one person, they will think that I treat some people more specially than others. God will never forgive me if I do that." Hanh stood firm in her belief that forcing women to have sex with clients was a sin and even actively defended her workers against customers who tried to insist on taking women out of the bar against their will. However, it was not simply Catholicism or Hanh's religious beliefs that drove her to take a moral stance. Rather, her religious beliefs reinforced a labor process here, where the need for worker consent also pushed her to adopt this morality. Neither she nor the bar owner paid the workers a wage for working in the bar; if she did not cultivate a trusting relationship with her workers by making them feel completely free and in control of their labor, she would lose their consent to her management. . . .

The bar owners and madams at all four bars believed that they had a duty to care for their employees. By ensuring that workers felt they had complete autonomy over their sexual labor, as well as protection against aggressive clients, the mommies established a sense of community in the bars. This maternal care was bound within a labor structure that relied heavily on the mommies' and bar owners' ability to ensure that workers felt they had control over their own bodies, and that they could rely on the mommies to offer them an extra layer of protection against aggressive clients. Workers' consent was crucial to the social and moral order within the bars. It was the key factor that made sex work seem like a viable option, in sharp contrast to the beatings and the withholding of wages that workers experienced in factories. . . .

While the moral compasses and religious beliefs of the owners and mommies guided their relationships with their workers, their maternal acts of care were not simply acts of generosity. In all four niche markets, meeting their moral obligations was central to the mommies' management of the labor process. If the mommies could not provide a safe working space and allow the workers freedom to manage what happened to their own bodies in relation to the clients, the workers would not consent to providing free labor in Khong Sao Bar, Lavender, and Naughty Girls or cheap labor in Secrets. The mommies' moral obligations and maternal duty to care for their workers ultimately kept the bars open and their workers readily available to meet their clients' desires.

FRONTSTAGE BONDS: MATERNAL DUTY TO DEFEND WORKERS' CONSENT

The positive relationships between mommies and hostesses fostered a dynamic of respect and mutual reciprocity among hostesses. In each bar in which I worked, the mommy regulated the work atmosphere by making it very clear that if a worker violated these norms, she would be fired. On the frontstage, workers brought each other along to tables or introduced their coworkers to clients. At Khong Sao Bar, if a woman was left behind, the other workers would try to get her seated at a table or set her up with new clients who entered at the end of the night. Workers also collectively shared responsibilities related to drinking and serving the clients. Women who served clients drinks and food often did so to free up other workers who were strong performers to sing or dance. In all four bars, workers established a shared culture related to drinking. Each time a woman poured a shot, she poured one for each person at the table, so that no worker had to consume more alcohol than another at the table. And each time a woman raised a glass to her clients, the other women also raised a glass, so that each woman matched her drinking pace to that of the other women at the table. This way, no worker drank more than any of the other workers. In sharing the work of drinking, the women also actively protected each other from sexually aggressive clients or clients who became belligerent after they had too much to drink.

One evening, a group of men became aggressive in Khong Sao Bar after two hours of drinking, and a client began to grab Nhung's breasts; he then sat on top of her and pressed her against the couch. Almost immediately, Tram, one of her coworkers, picked up her glass and insisted on toasting the client to distract him. He drank with her while the other workers turned on loud techno music, pulled Nhung onto the dance floor, and began dancing to distract the men in his group. As everyone danced, the women signaled to each other that they were going to begin drinking quickly and heavily in order to push the bar tab up so the men would leave. When the table had almost finished its fourth bottle of whiskey, another aggressive client asked Nhung to go home with him. She politely refused by smiling and telling him that she had to work. When the client refused to take no for an answer, the other workers chimed in and said that Nhung had to attend her brother's birthday party later that night. After he continued to insist, the workers called on the mommy.

Hanh walked into the room, picked up a glass, and began toasting the men. They all drank with her, and then she turned on the karaoke machine to sing a song for them.

Everyone listened as Hanh sang, and when the song was over she had the service workers bring in the bill. The client told Hanh that he wanted Nhung to leave with him, and Hanh firmly supported Nhung's decision to remain in the bar. The client got upset and decided that he was not going to tip Nhung or Hanh. Hanh turned to him and said, "I have never had to deal with someone as aggressive as you. This is a high-class bar with respectable women. You need to treat them with respect." The man turned and grabbed Hanh's breasts in front of everyone. She responded by slapping him twice. He was stunned and ashamed in front of his friends, so he tried to slap her back, but his friends stopped him and apologized profusely. Finally, his friends tipped Hanh on behalf of the aggressive client before they left the bar.

This interaction illustrated the solidarity that workers shared on the frontstage. By singing and dancing, workers were able to distract clients from touching hostesses' bodies in ways that made the workers feel uncomfortable or violated. The strategy of drinking at increased speeds was a common one that served two purposes. First, it forced clients to quit before driving the bill up too high, and second, sometimes it got the clients so intoxicated that they would pass out and leave the workers alone. Importantly, by slapping the client in an especially tense interaction, Hanh established her power in relation to the men in the room and set boundaries around clients' sexual aggression. In this way, although Hanh and her workers engaged in performances of deference in their everyday interactions, they also drew strict boundaries that men could not cross. . . .

BACKSTAGE BONDS OF FRIENDSHIP

While solidarity on the frontstage makes intuitive sense as a strategy for women to protect one another from clients by spreading individual risk across the group, I anticipated that the women would have fierce rivalries backstage, where they interacted outside of clients' view. However, during my first week at Khong Sao Bar, while I was getting dressed at Hanh's house, she said to me, "When you go in to work, you work for yourself. Do not compete with the other girls or get jealous because they are making more money than you. If I see you competing, I will tell you to leave." At first, I assumed that her words were hollow, but on my first day in the bar all the women gathered around me to help me dress properly and teach me how to get seated at tables. This rite of initiation set the stage for all new workers to build relationships of mutual respect and reciprocity with the other women in the bar.

In all the bars in which I worked, I found myself in a "drama-free" environment, interrupted only rarely by conflicts between women. During the fifteen months that I conducted fieldwork, I witnessed only one fight between the women. This fight was over a client at Khong Sao Bar, and it resulted in the mommy telling both women that she did not want them to return to the bar for at least one week. Instead of rivalry, women's relationships were characterized by mutual support. Workers regularly shared advice on how to dress to accentuate their particular bodies, because they believed that if their coworkers looked attractive, the bar as a whole would regularly attract more clients. . . .

Backstage at each of the bars, I also listened as hostesses helped each other cope with feelings of pain, loss, anguish, and undesirability. They coached each other on how to deal with clients, giving advice that ranged from small things like how to respond to a text message to bigger issues like how to subtly ask for money. When new workers entered into the bar's culture, the older workers usually refrained from providing advice. If a new hostess turned out to be competitive, the older workers would isolate her and make her work life unpleasant. However, if the new worker was humble and noncompetitive, then after a few weeks she became part of a familial environment where women shared stories, clothing, tips, and advice.

The strong bonds that tied workers together allowed the women to create a positive working environment. Many of the hostesses looked forward to coming to work because the workspace provided them with a sense of community in a stigmatized profession. In fact, the women felt so closely tied to their workplaces that they came into work on their days off simply to spend time with the other women backstage. The bars were also a place where hostesses and former hostesses celebrated their birthdays, held bachelorette parties before getting married, and cried through heartbreak and grief. The bonds created at work extended beyond the workplace, since many of the women traveled together to each other's hometowns when a family member passed away or to escape the hectic pace of city life. . . .

BOUNDARIES OF LOVE, SEX, AND ROMANCE

In addition to providing workers with protection and community in the bars, mommies also helped them cultivate the skills necessary to cater to their clients' desires. For these women, escaping the long hours and harsh working conditions they had experienced as factory workers or maids, and gaining autonomy in sex work, hinged on their ability to develop what Parreñas (2011: 103–6) terms "emotional capital," the naturalization of flirtation in their mannerisms and actions. This crucial skill allowed them to maintain the emotional attachments of customers and keep them coming back to the bars. . . . Like the Filipina hostess-workers in Parreñas's study, the sex workers in Vietnam cultivated emotional relationships with various clients to gain greater control over their labor in the bars.

To do this, they relied on the mommies to help them draw boundaries and establish a kind of intimacy predicated on the workers' consent to having sex with their clients.

The mommies in all four niche markets held similar moral philosophies with respect to worker–client relationships. They trained their workers in how to dress, walk, talk, and carry a conversation in order to keep their clients interested. One of the most important skills that the mommies tried to teach their workers was how to maintain boundaries around their emotions and to differentiate between emotional labor as a performance and real feelings of love. While all mommies cautioned their workers not to fall in love with their clients too easily, they differed in their views about the possibility of long-term relations.

The mommies in Khong Sao Bar and Lavender, which catered to local Vietnamese men, other Asian businessmen, and Viet Kieu men, all had strict rules about dating and relationships. Hanh, Tho, and Duyen all believed that it was acceptable to have relationships with men outside the bar, but that a worker should never devote all her time to one man. They also warned workers that falling in love with a client would lead them down a difficult path. . . .

Although some workers in all the bars indeed fell in love with their clients, most found themselves back in the bar within a few months following their heartbreaks. Many of the women who worked in Khong Sao Bar and Lavender often referred to their work as part of a business in which they each served as the mistress of many men. Thi, a twenty-year-old worker at Lavender, said to me, "Sometimes I dream about meeting the right person and falling in love, but right now I care more about money than love. The men I work for will never marry someone like me; they have wives and women who their families know and accept. If I fall in love with one person, I cannot have many men take care of me.". . .

The structure of relationships was different for women who catered to Western men. Lilly, at Secrets, opened what she called a "relationship bar," which was distinct from a "hooker bar" because the workers did not engage in direct sex-for-money exchanges. In opening the bar, Lilly hoped to target Western expatriates living and working in Vietnam on a long-term or recurring basis. On several occasions, I listened as Lilly advised the women working in her bar: "I pay you to work here so you do not have to sleep with men for money. Men out there are all the same. They play and then they get bored. If you are too easy, they will say okay, then play with someone else. You [should] date many men, and then fall in love later." Lilly advised her workers to date many men and then decide later so that they could take their pick among a variety of men. She wanted the workers to engage in long-term relationships with men who were committed to them and who were willing to help them experience upward mobility. . . .

All the women told me they wanted to hold out for the client who could take the best care of them. This meant women had multiple boyfriends while in the process of selecting long-term partners. During my time working in the bar, two of the women who had been employed there for over a year had long-term relationships with multiple men and decided that it was time to quit working in the bars and settle down with only one of them. I went to their bachelorette parties and attended their weddings. The work culture at Secrets created a structure where workers saw men not merely as clients but also as potential boyfriends and even husbands. . . .

Unlike women in popular-media accounts of human trafficking, most of the women I interviewed entered sex work because the labor conditions in the bar were much better than labor conditions in the factories or in homes where they were employed as domestic workers. When we move beyond sensationalized media accounts and take a deeper look inside the bars, it is clear that there was a moral order to the organizational structure inside each bar. The moral codes guided (a) how the mommies managed the workers in the bar, (b) frontstage relationships with clients, (c) backstage relationships among workers, and (d) the emotional boundaries around love. In contrast to findings in previous studies that describe sex work as dangerous labor rife with competition, the vast majority of the workers in my study believed in and succeeded in creating a collaborative work environment. Workers shared clothing, tips on how to engage with clients, and life stories that nurtured strong ties among them. These bonds led workers to come into the bar on their days off to celebrate birthdays and engagements and to mourn the deaths of family members. . . .

REFERENCES

Chin, Christine. 2013. *Cosmopolitan Sex Workers: Women and Migration in a Global City*. New York: Oxford University Press.

Goffman, Erving. 1959. *The Presentation of Self in Everyday Life*. New York: Doubleday.

Kristof, Nicholas, and Sheryl WuDunn. 2010. *Half the Sky: Turning Oppression into Opportunity*. New York: Random House.

Parreñas, Rhacel. 2011. *Illicit Flirtations*. Palo Alto, CA: Stanford University Press.

PERFORMING WITHOUT A NET? SAFER SEX IN PORN

WENDY CHAPKIS

In 1999, in a letter to the editor of *POZ* magazine, prominent sex worker–rights activist Priscilla Alexander argued that strict condom use, not mandatory testing of performers, should be used to control HIV transmission in the production of heterosexual porn.[1] She was outraged that the industry's response to an HIV outbreak the previous year, when one actor transmitted the virus to six women on set, was to agree to more frequent and accurate testing: "Getting tested for HIV and other STDs is not a preventative measure," she scoffed. Furthermore, she argued, adult industry performers are workers "who should be protected by occupational safety and health regulations no less than those in a mine, factory, or any other worksite that has occupational health hazards." Like hard hats for construction workers, "condoms, latex dams, gloves and non-penetrative acts" for performers should be required, Alexander insisted (Alexander, 1999).

In 1999, I agreed with Alexander about the importance of mandatory condom use. Two decades later, I have a very different view. I have now come to accept that testing in porn can be a preventive measure and that mandatory condom laws do not necessarily enhance worker safety. Both of these insights were initially surprising to me.

My early approach to the notion of safer sex in porn was formed, like Alexander's, by my perspective on prostitution. Mandatory testing in prostitution is useless in protecting the health of prostitutes because it focuses exclusively on workers, not their clients (Alexander, 1987; Brandt, 1985; Emilio and Freedman, 1988; Walkowitz, 1980). The lack of interest in the "contamination" of sex workers—rather than by them—has exposed wave after wave of prostitutes to infection (Chapkis, 1997: 165–66; see also Banach, 1999; Loff, Gaze, and Fairley, 2000; Schneider and Stoller, 1995).

I assumed that the same lens could be applied to other sectors of the sex trade, including the adult film industry. Based on the history of prostitution health regulations, I accepted the argument that testing would also fail to protect the health of porn performers. But as I studied the debates around safer sex in the adult film industry, I was reminded that the category "sex worker" is not an undifferentiated one. In fact, conditions within the sex trade are so diverse that strategies that diminish occupational safety in one sector may actually enhance it in another. Mandatory testing, it turns out, is an excellent example of that complexity.

Despite the diverse conditions within the sex trade, my background in prostitution studies did help sensitize me to some critical questions. In particular, I was primed to ask who benefits from sex work–related social policies (workers? the so-called general public? clients/customers? third parties?). I also knew to ask whether sex workers themselves had been at the table when those policies were being crafted.

I knew that, in the adult film industry, condom-free commercial sex is of benefit to consumers who don't want the reality of HIV to intrude on their fantasies or who enjoy watching performers play without a visible net. Producers, of course, always benefit from making whatever the consumer wants. On the other hand, many—most?—performers, I assumed, would be well served by strict condom-use policies on set. Why then, I wondered, weren't adult industry performers at the forefront of efforts to pass mandatory condom laws? An early clue was that mandatory condom policies hadn't been drafted by performers but rather by Michael Weinstein, the CEO of the country's largest AIDS organization, the AIDS Healthcare Foundation (AHF). Workers in straight porn instead supported a system of mandatory testing, reporting, and excluding actors who were HIV positive from performing. In the aftermath of the 1998 HIV outbreak, the one that prompted Alexander's letter, it was a performer, Sharon Mitchell,[2] working with some of the biggest studios, who created and operated a new, more rigorous, and centralized mandatory testing protocol (Kirby, 1999).

In order to keep testing in the hands of performer-advocates rather than producers, Mitchell founded a nonprofit organization called Adult Industry Medical (AIM). Testing results were stored by AIM in a database, AIMCheck, that could be used by workers and producers to ensure that only HIV-negative individuals were allowed to perform in straight porn (Voss, 2015: 199).[3] Testing took place at the AIM clinic, where performers had access to culturally competent health care services offered by the organization. AIM also served an educational and support function for those in the trade, producing a video for workers on how best to navigate the industry ("Porn 101") and hosting 12-step meetings for performers struggling with substance abuse.

Producers were encouraged to allow workers to use condoms for anal and vaginal sex, which they agreed to do "despite grumblings over the presumed financial downside" (Kirby, 1999). According to one prominent adult film star, Nina Hartley, it was now up to women performers to demand condoms be used: "Women have to learn to stand up and say, 'No condom, no scene,'" Hartley proclaimed. Permission by producers, she argued, should be enough: "Just

being told they're allowed to is all they need" (Kirby, 1999).

Mitchell, however, remained skeptical, fearing workers' well-being would lose out to the bottom line. The testing protocol developed by AIM, she observed, was created precisely as a response to that reality: "We formed an agency in an outbreak," she said, "[because] the talent in the industry has always been viewed as expendable" (Kirby, 1999). The use of condoms on set would be great, she argued, but it wasn't up to the performers to make that happen; Mitchell observed, "A little compliance from producers and manufacturers would help" (Kirby, 1999). In fact, as Georgina Voss points out in "Trade Organizations, Industry Legitimacy and Corporate Responsibility in Pornography," "AIM's approach to health care provision was underpinned by the core supposition that the majority of porn studios would not use condoms in production. . . . Any health care strategy that was targeted at the industry would therefore have to work around this fact" (Voss, 2015: 198).

In the absence of a practice of widespread condom use in straight porn, frequent mandatory testing, Mitchell concluded, represented the performers' best available protection against HIV transmission (Kirby, 1999).[4] The mission of AIM, she said, was simply "to give people information to help save their lives" (Kirby, 1999).

THE PROBLEM OF CHOICE

As the low incidence of condom use in straight porn suggests, the "right to use condoms" has never directly translated into the ability to actually demand that they be used. Worker power, not just producer permission, would be necessary for that. In a competitive industry, workers willing to perform without the safety net of condoms have had a distinct market advantage over those who demand condom use. In the heterosexual porn industry, contract workers with no guarantee of continued employment have, therefore, been unlikely to demand condoms even if they were formally allowed to do so.

In a recent study of contrasting approaches to managing occupational risk in the gay porn industry (where condoms have more routinely been used) and straight porn (where mandatory testing has been employed), David Schieber quotes a performer in the straight industry who admits she would prefer to use condoms, but "you will not get hired again if you ask for one" (Schieber, 2017). Another performer explained that "if I were to go on set and be like 'I want to use a condom today,' they would send me home and they would call somebody that wasn't going to use a condom" (ibid.). A producer confirmed workers' concerns: If a performer asked for condoms, he said, "It's, like, mmm bye. We'll replace you today. . . . If you say you are condom-only, you're out of here. You're done" (ibid.). Schieber concludes that, in the straight porn industry, "the actual options are choosing to work without condoms or choosing to no longer work at all" (Schieber, 2017).[5]

Despite this reality, as late as 2016, Dana Van Gorder of the HIV advocacy organization Project Inform argued that "it is important to protect the health of adult performers, and condoms should always be available for them on set. . . . [A]s adults [they should] make a choice about the best option for them" (Rewire Analysis, 2016). But clearly, "choice" is constrained at best.

This problem isn't caused just by greedy and unscrupulous producers. As Mariella Mosthof from *Bustle* magazine observes, "The reality of modern porn-making is that many performers self-distribute via indie operations, camming, and other forms of amateur work" (Mosthof, 2016). Yet, even independent workers may not feel free to incorporate condoms because of "market demands." The suggestion that workers have unlimited choice is as illusory in the adult film industry as it is in other contingent occupations.

Under these conditions, performers in the straight industry determined that mandatory testing provided the best protection. Their decision was supported by the fact that the AIM protocol was surprisingly effective in reducing HIV transmission. From 1999 (when Sharon Mitchell founded Adult Industry Medical) through 2004, AIM administered 80,000 HIV tests with no reported incidents of HIV transmission in the heterosexual porn industry (Tannen, 2004). But in 2004, the limitations of the "test, identify, and exclude" strategy were revealed when three female adult industry performers contracted HIV after having sex with a male performer who had apparently been exposed to the virus a week earlier (too soon for an accurate HIV test) on a porn set outside the country. The industry immediately agreed to a moratorium on filming while AIM completed a process of partner-identification. Their efforts met with praise from the AIDS coordinator for the City of Los Angeles, who announced in August of 2004 that AIM's "testing and partner tracking procedure is better than any public health entity I can imagine. Between that and post-exposure prophylaxis being available, a system with their containment policy is highly effective" (Tannen, 2004).

From 2004 to 2010, there were no further HIV transmissions despite the fact that more than 350,000 sex scenes were filmed without condoms during the period (Egan Morrissey, 2006). AIM's protocol helped to ensure that HIV rates remained lower among performers in the straight porn industry than in the general public (Voss, 2015: 199).

THE OPPOSITE OF WORKER-CONTROLLED POLICY: THE ADVENT OF CONDOM LAWS

But the fact that the mandatory testing protocol was largely effective did not silence those outside the industry who advocated mandatory condom use. Michael Weinstein of the AHF continued to insist that testing was an inadequate response to the risk of HIV; the AIM protocol, he argued, served only to undermine efforts to require condom use in porn. AIM was targeted by the AHF through picketing and multiple complaints to federal and state agencies (Voss, 2015: 199; Kernes, 2010). In 2011, the AIDS Healthcare Foundation—with a budget equal to that of Planned Parenthood (Glazek, 1999)—even brought a lawsuit against AIM, a small, underfunded organization. AHF argued that AIM had violated performers' rights by asking them to sign a voluntary waiver of medical privacy in order to make their test results available to producers. Later the same year, AIM suffered a second body blow when a shadowy anti-porn group, "Porn Wikileaks,"[6] hacked AIM's database and publicly posted performers' personal information online.

The financial and emotional cost of the lawsuit and the hacking incident brought the organization down. AIM filed for bankruptcy in 2011 and closed in May of that year. Adult industry performer and activist (and former AHF model for their safe-sex campaigns) Eric Paul Leue described AHF's lawsuit against AIM as typical for the deep-pocketed organization: "AHF has sued counties, cities, and departments of health, and has bullied smaller organizations into submission with litigation that real nonprofits cannot afford to fight," he said (King, 2015).

Forcing AIM into bankruptcy and closure was considered a victory by the AIDS Healthcare Foundation despite the fact that, as *LA Weekly* reported, "The sudden shutdown [of AIM] leaves the industry without an STD safety net, which could play into the hands of AHF (you could always use condoms, they would argue)" (Romero, 2011). Weinstein himself declared the closure a good thing because performers had been "poorly served by AIM and are poorly served by an industry that places profits above worker safety. . . . Now that AIM has closed and the industry's 'fig leaf' is gone, the responsible thing for the industry to do is to put performers' health first and require condom use on all adult film sets" (ibid.). But, not surprisingly, the heterosexual porn industry did not suddenly change its views on responsible HIV prevention and require condom use on set. Instead, the industry trade organization, the Free Speech Coalition, simply created an industry-run mandatory testing system to replace the work of performer-controlled AIM.

TURNING TO THE STATE: THE PROBLEM OF ENFORCEMENT

In response, Weinstein turned to the state for enforcement: "If the porn industry won't protect its own workers," he argued, "it is time for the Los Angeles County Department of Public Health—the government body charged with safeguarding the health and welfare of its citizens—to enforce condom use on all adult film sets in the County" (Romero, 2011). To this end, in 2012, the AIDS Healthcare Foundation funded a successful countywide initiative, Measure B, mandating condom use in porn in Los Angeles. The ordinance also provided an enforcement mechanism involving warrantless and unannounced inspections of porn sets by county health officials. Passage of Measure B, according to Weinstein, ushered in "a great day for performers and safer sex in our society" (Lin, 2012).

The industry, however, immediately challenged the law in court, blocking implementation for several years. Ultimately, the ordinance was upheld, but key provisions relating to enforcement were struck down, in particular the strategy of unscheduled inspections. According to U.S. District Judge Dean Pregerson, "Given that adult filming could occur almost anywhere, Measure B would seem to authorize a health officer to enter and search any part of a private home in the middle of the night, because he suspects violations are occurring. This is unconstitutional because it is akin to a general warrant" (Abram, 2017).

Despite being held up in the courts for five years, simply the threat of regulation produced immediate and significant effects—though not AHF's intended ones. Adult film permit requests in Los Angeles County plummeted by 95 percent, from over 485 applications (covering approximately 5,000 films) in 2012 to just 40 in 2013; by 2015 only 26 permits were requested (Ng, 2016). As the owner of Penthouse Global Media observed, adult film producers were simply "doing it off the grid . . . [and the law was] driving production to states that are less regulated and therefore less safe" (Ng, 2016). In 2014, Penthouse Entertainment announced that they were shooting in Brazil and Europe because "it's just too complex to shoot here" (Rogers, 2014). The head of the Free Speech Coalition reported that other producers had "moved to Las Vegas, although none want to be mentioned by name for fear of bringing condom activists after them" (Rogers, 2014).

The decline in the number of films produced with permits in Los Angeles, operating under the AIMCheck protocol, soon yielded the predictable result: a case of HIV transmission on an adult film set in Nevada (AP, 2014a). According to the Associated Press, in 2014 "one actor likely infected the other during unprotected sex at a film shoot in Nevada where testing was less stringent than industry standards" (AP, 2014a). The Free Speech Coalition observed: "Non-compliant shoots are one of the chief dangers of pushing the adult industry" out of California (AP, 2014a).

The Los Angeles County law, Measure B, was only one of AHF's attempts to enforce mandatory condom use in pornography. In 2009, the AIDS Healthcare Foundation submitted a formal petition to the California Occupational Safety and Health Administration (Cal/OSHA),

the state's workplace safety enforcement agency, to require more active enforcement of condom regulations. Since the 1990s, the agency had already determined that performers were required to wear condoms in adult films but rarely enforced the provision (Ng, 2016). In 2016, after six years of study, Cal/OSHA voted against amending the regulations to increase enforcement. Instead they announced they would continue to "enforce existing regulations and investigate complaints in the adult film industry" (Abram, 2016). In 2014 and 2015, a total of only four citations were issued despite widespread flouting of condom provisions (Woodyard, 2016). The minimal number of citations reflected the lack of complaints by adult industry performers.

Because performers appeared to be unenthusiastic about bringing complaints against producers, Weinstein and the AHF turned again to the legislative arena. Rather than reaching out to performers for guidance on how to enhance occupational safety in the adult film industry, Weinstein instead attempted to go around them entirely through a statewide citizens' initiative in 2016. Proposition 60 would have required condom use on porn sets throughout the state and expanded the class of people able to file complaints for noncompliance. Under the proposed law, *any California resident* could sue producers if they believed condoms had not been used in a production and Cal/OSHA had failed to investigate. If the lawsuit prevailed, the individual "whistleblower" would receive a 25 percent cut of any financial judgment (McPhate, 2016). The president of the Adult Performer Advocacy Committee expressed alarm at the prospect that the proposed legislation would "incentivize people looking for a reason to harass porn actors" (Pressberg, 2016).

Adding to performers' concerns was the decision by the AHF to resurrect pernicious stereotypes of sex workers as pools of contagion; according to the statewide Proposition 60 campaign, mandatory condom measures were needed because "the diseases contracted in the porn studios don't always stay in the studios or the porn industry" (Woodyard, 2016). Adult industry workers felt both stigmatized and shut out of the process of developing policies that would impact their lives: "This wasn't just about condoms—there was a big part that threatened performer privacy and safety," said Ela Darling, a performer and the president of the Adult Performer Advocacy Committee. "We tried to initiate dialogue with AHF. They stonewalled us. All the while claiming to speak for us, while refusing to speak to us" (Baume, 2017). Performers mobilized effectively against the measure and, despite being outspent 4 to 1 by the AHF, the initiative was defeated in November 2016.

Strict enforcement of mandatory condom use in pornography has now been rejected in the courts, by Cal/OSHA, and by the California voting public (outside of Los Angeles County).[7] But this begs the question: if "workers' choice" remains an illusion and laws to prohibit condom-free pornography are largely unenforceable (and may undermine existing protections), what can be done to enhance adult industry workers' occupational safety?

MEDICAL SCIENCE ADDS TO THE SAFER-SEX TOOLBOX

Fortunately, in the twenty-first century, safety nets can be woven out of more than just latex. While condoms can be very effective in preventing HIV transmission, they are no longer the only means available. Two medical approaches to HIV prevention—daily pre-exposure prophylaxis (PrEP) and treatment-as-prevention—are proving to be as effective as consistent condom use. PrEP involves the use of the drug Truvada by those who are HIV negative as a preventative strategy. Recent studies suggest that, "if taken daily as directed, Truvada reduces risk of transmission of HIV by 99 percent" (Garcia,

2016). (For more discussion of PrEP, see Reading 39 in Chapter 7.)

Given the extraordinary effectiveness of PrEP, it might seem surprising that the AIDS Healthcare Foundation (virtually alone among all major AIDS organizations) rejects PrEP and continues to insist that condoms are not only the best, but the only reasonable response to HIV. According to Weinstein, "If something comes along that's better than condoms, I'm all for it, but Truvada is not that. Let's be honest: It's a party drug" (AP, 2014b).[8] Most physicians (and the American Medical Association itself) take a less ideological and more pragmatic view of PrEP. As the director of the HIV program at New York's Mount Sinai Hospital, Dr. Demetre Daskalakis, argues, "For folks who are having a significant amount of unprotected sex, it's a slam dunk—not only giving them protective medicine, but engaging them in testing, a whole package of regular health care" (AP, 2014b).

PrEP is not the only biomedical prevention method that drastically reduces the risk of HIV transmission in condom-free sex. Most HIV-positive people treated with antiretroviral therapies (ART) can now reduce the amount of HIV in their bodies to undetectable levels.[9] In the fall of 2017, the CDC released a statement announcing that viral suppression prevents HIV transmission: "Across three different studies, including thousands of couples and many thousands of acts of sex without a condom or pre-exposure prophylaxis (PrEP), no HIV transmissions to an HIV-negative person were observed when the HIV-positive person was virally suppressed" (McCray and Mermin, 2017). According to the CDC, "people who take ART daily as prescribed and achieve and maintain an undetectable viral load have effectively no risk of sexually transmitting the virus to an HIV-negative partner."[10]

With these new HIV transmission prevention tools, it may be possible to develop new protocols that, for example, test for viral load rather than HIV status. This would have the additional benefit of eliminating the discriminatory effects of current protocols in the straight industry that rely on testing and excluding workers who are HIV positive.

CONSUMER RESPONSIBILITY AND WORKER ADVOCACY

But Weinstein and the AHF are correct about at least one thing: safer-sex strategies that rely on testing and biomedical interventions continue to place the responsibility for HIV prevention exclusively on workers, leaving producers and consumers off the hook. It is worth repeating that consumers' preference for condom-free porn effectively denies workers access to all the preventive tools they might otherwise have at their disposal.[11]

As porn performer and producer Christopher Daniel Zeischegg (aka Danny Wylde) reminds us, purchasing any commercial product "includes the choice to financially support its mode of production. If consumers buy more of a certain kind of porn, then more of that kind of porn will be produced. . . . It's time for consumers who want more ethical porn to educate themselves about who's producing it, and to use their dollars to support it" (Zeischegg, 2013: 269).[12]

Whether consumers care about ethical production and workers' rights, however, remains an open question. Adult film actress Tasha Reign worked hard to defeat Proposition 60 and expressed relief that voters rejected the criminalization of condom-free productions; but she worried that, for a lot of consumers, the takeaway message was that they were right not to want "condoms in their porn, which is selfish and counteracts my efforts to increase sex worker input" (Mosthof, 2016).

"Sex worker input" has been the key missing component in the development of policies that directly impact their lives. Without having workers at the table, it has been possible to develop policies that would provide warrantless inspections, incentives for those outside the industry to file complaints, and public access to performers' legal names and addresses. The resulting campaigns made use of old stereotypes about the supposed threat diseased sex workers pose to the "general public." It is no surprise, then, that these proposals have been rejected by those they were meant to protect. Insofar as those outside the industry have been successful in passing these laws, like Measure B, the result has been enhanced occupational risk to workers by pushing the industry underground or out of state. As a 2017 editorial in the *Los Angeles Daily News* observes, "Short of repealing the misguided, pointless Measure B [mandatory condom law], the least the county should do is ensure the measure actually accomplishes its ostensible purpose of keeping producers safe. Working with the industry is the best way to do that" (Editorial Board, 2017).

But it's not, in fact, "the producers" that need protection; nor is it only "the industry" that should be the focus of collaborative efforts. Instead, *workers* must be front and center in creating effective policies. As Reign points out, workers resist bad laws like Measure B and Proposition 60 because they do not address their needs: "Performers matter! What we do is important and sex workers have a voice," she insists (Mosthof, 2016).

When it comes to adult industry performers, as with all marginalized populations, policies must be developed in collaboration *with* them, not just *for* them. Whatever strategies are to be pursued, sex workers must be instrumental in crafting and implementing them; nothing about them without them.[13]

ACKNOWLEDGMENTS

Thank you to Elizabeth Lowell for research assistance and to Gabriel Demaine and Erica Rand for careful editing.

NOTES

1. The adult film industry is divided between productions marketed to heterosexual and gay male consumers. The "straight" industry has resisted condom use throughout the AIDS epidemic, relying instead on testing to exclude HIV-positive performers; the gay industry, in contrast, has largely made use of condoms. In a recent article about these contrasting approaches, Schieber argues that the straight industry has employed a "logic of profit maximization" (providing condom-free porn preferred by consumers), while the gay industry has instead used a "logic of civil rights and solidarity" in which condoms are used to prevent the identification and stigmatization of HIV-positive performers through testing (see Schieber, 2017). It is important to note, however, that these different approaches to HIV-transmission prevention reflect not just different logics but also very different conditions confronting heterosexual and gay consumers and performers in the 1980s when the policies were instituted. While HIV was epidemic in gay communities, it was far less prevalent among heterosexuals in the United States. Among gay men, embracing sexuality in the midst of the deadly epidemic made condom use essential; it was the only reliable strategy to prevent transmission in populations heavily affected, with a high incidence of HIV already present within that community. Heterosexuals in the United States were much less affected in the early decades of the epidemic; for this reason, the use of condoms was a harder sell to the (viewing) public. Over the past twenty years, as other tools have become available within the gay community to prevent HIV transmission (including treatment as prevention and PrEP, as discussed elsewhere in this reading), gay barebacking porn (filmed without condoms) has become increasing popular; apparently "the logic of profit maximization" affects the gay industry as well. This reading, however, will focus on the straight porn industry.

2. Mitchell left performing in 1996, when she was followed home by a "fan" who raped her, broke her nose, and crushed her larynx (Anthony, 2004). She was engaged in completing graduate work in human sexuality and training as a phlebotomist when she was hired by the industry to investigate the 1998 HIV outbreak.

3. In "gay porn," condoms have been routinely used until quite recently, with the increasing popularity of so-called barebacking videos. See Schieber (2017) for a useful discussion of the reasons for the choice of condoms over testing in gay porn.

4. Prior to AIM's protocols, the industry had much less rigorous standards involving easily forgeable photocopied documentation that a performer had tested negative sometime in the past 30 to 90 days (depending on the producer) (Kirby, 1999).

5. Because condom use has been routine in gay porn, the dynamic in that sector of the industry is quite different (see Schieber, 2017).

6. The Porn Wikileaks website, which published the legal names, addresses, and other personal information about performers, features "wildly racist and homophobic rants" (Abowitz, 2011).

7. Los Angeles County not only passed Measure B but was one of only four counties in the state that voted in favor of Proposition 60.

8. Weinstein challenges the effectiveness of PrEP by raising questions about compliance: "The bottom line is that people won't adhere and take the pill. That's what studies have shown. If this catches on as a public health strategy, that means there are going to be people who will take Truvada irregularly and some will be infected, and some develop drug resistance" (Curry, 2016). Of course, the same is true of condoms, as the president of the HIV Medicine Association points out: "Obviously, there are lots of gay men who are not using condoms"; insisting on condom use for everyone is, he said, "a moralist view that leads to infections" (Heitz, 2011).

9. The Centers for Disease Control and Prevention defines "viral suppression" as fewer than 200 copies/ml or undetectable levels.

10. See also the Prevention Access Campaign's "Undetectable Equals Untransmittable" (https://preventionaccess.org/faq).

11. Evidence of the important role of the consumer in driving industry practices can be found in the fact that, after the 1998 HIV outbreak, the heterosexual industry experimented with condom use but sales declined by 30 percent. This led to an end to the condom experiment on many sets (Kriegel, 2012).

12. One strategy being pursued is an effort to create a kitemark for consumers that would indicate good practices in pornography, similar to the Fairtrade mark (Minter, 2015).

13. The phrase "nothing about us without us" was adopted in the 1990s by disability rights activists in the United States and has circulated widely in social justice movements of the early twenty-first century.

REFERENCES

Abowitz, R. 2011. "Porn Wikileaks." *Daily Beast*. March 31. www.thedailybeast.com/porn-wikileaks-the-person-behind-the-website-scaring-porn-stars.

Abram, S. 2016. "Porn Industry Wins Battle against California Regulations over Condoms, Eyewear on Film Shoots." *Los Angeles Daily News*. February 18. www.dailynews.com/2016/02/18/porn-industry-wins-battle-against-california-regulators-over-condoms-eyewear-on-film-shoots.

———. 2017. "LA's Condoms in Porn Law Gets a Mixed Legal Ruling." *Los Angeles Daily News*. August 28. www. dailynews.com/2013/08/17/las-condoms-in-porn -law-gets-a-mixed-legal-ruling-2.

Alexander, P. 1987. "Prostitution: a Difficult Issue for Feminists." In F. Delacoste and P. Alexander (Eds.). *Sex Work*. Pittsburgh: Cleis Press. 184–230.

———. 1995. "Sex Workers Fight against AIDS." In B. Schneider and N. Stoller (Eds.). *Women Resisting AIDS*. Philadelphia: Temple University Press. 99–128.

———. 1999. Letter to the Editor. *POZ*. July 1. www.poz.com/article/To-the-Editor-10372-5889.

Anthony, A. 2004. "Risky Business." *The Guardian*. August 1. www.theguardian.com/theobserver/2004 /aug/01/features.magazine37.

AP. 2014a. "HIV Scare in US Porn Industry after Two Actors Test Positive." *The Guardian*. December 31. www .theguardian.com/us-news/2014/dec/31/hiv-scare-porn -actors-positive-nevada.

———. 2014b. "Divide over HIV Prevention Drug Truvada Persists." *USA Today*. April 6. www.usatoday.com/story /news/nation/2014/04/06/gay-men-divided-over-use-of -hiv-prevention-drug/7390879/.

Banach, L. 1999. "Sex Work and the Official Neglect of Occupational Health and Safety." *Social Alternatives*, July, 18(3): 17–22.

Baume, M. 2017. "California's Prop 60 Failed, but Condoms in Porn Is Hardly a Dead Issue." Slate.com. January 5. www.slate.com/blogs/outward/2017/01/05 /california_s_prop_60_condoms_in_porn_bill_failed _but_the_fight_continues.html.

Brandt, A. 1985. *No Magic Bullet*. New York: Oxford University Press.

Chapkis, W. 1997. *Live Sex Acts*. NY: Routledge.

Curry, T. 2016. "Commentary: AHF's Michael Weinstein Gets It Wrong—Again." *The Advocate*. January 21. www .advocate.com/commentary/2016/1/21/ahfs-michael -weinstein-gets-it-wrong-again.

Daily News. 2012. "Nine Porn Actors Test Positive for Syphilis." *Los Angeles Daily News*. August 28. www .dailynews.com/2012/08/28/nine-porn-actors-test-positive -for-syphilis-san-fernando-valley-adult-film-trade-group -reports/.

D'Emilio, J., and E. Freedman. 1998. *Intimate Matters*. New York: Harper and Row.

Editorial Board. 2017. "Porn Producers Should Be Heard." *Los Angeles Daily News*. August 29. www.dailynews .com/2017/08/29/porn-producers-should-be-heard-by -l-a-county-officials/.

Egan Morrissey, T. 2006. "Does the Porn Industry Have the Secret to Successful HIV Prevention?" *Jezebel*. November 16. https://jezebel.com/5958096/does -the-porn-industry-have-the-secret-to-successful -hiv-prevention.

Garcia, M. 2016. "Why Michael Weinstein Gets Blamed for PrEP Myths." *HIV Plus*. February 4. www .hivplusmag.com/prevention/2016/2/04/why-michael -weinstein-gets-blamed-prep-myths.

Glazek, C. 1999. "The CEO of HIV." *New York Times*. April 26. www.nytimes.com/2017/04/26/magazine/the-ceo -of-hiv.html?_r=0.

Heitz, D. 2011. "Michael Weinstein Remembers Popping Penicillin." I'm Still Josh. www.imstilljosh.com/lgbtprep /why-the-leader-of-americas-largest-hiv-care-organization -wants-you-to-wear-a-condom/.

Kernes, M. 2010. "HHS Dismisses AHF Complaint, Closes AIM Investigation." AVN.com. August 2. https://avn.com/business/articles/legal/hhs-dismisses -ahf-complaint-closes-aim-investigation-405797.html.

King, M. "The Angry Fallout from the AIDS Healthcare Foundation Scandal." My Fabulous Disease. April 2015. http://marksking.com/my-fabulous-disease/the-angry -fallout-from-the-aids-healthcare-foundation-scandal/.

Kirby, D. 1999. "LA Confidential: HIV panic seized porn last year," *POZ*. April 1. www.poz.com/article/L-A -Confidential-1488-5968.

Kriegel, D. 2012. "Condom Conundrum." Ventura Blvd. https://venturablvd.goldenstate.is/condom-conundrum/.

Lin, R. 2012. "L.A. City Council OKs Law Requiring Condom Use by Porn Performers." *Los Angeles Times*. January 18. http://articles.latimes.com/2012/jan/18/local /la-me-0118-porn-condoms-20120118.

Loff, B., B. Gaze, and C. Fairley. 2000. "Prostitution, Public Health and Human Rights." *Lancet*. November. 356 (9243): 1764. www.thelancet.com/pdfs/journals /lancet/PIIS0140-6736(00)03219-0.pdf.

McCray, E., and J. Mermin. 2017. "Dear Colleague." Information from CDC's Division of HIV Prevention. September 27. www.cdc.gov/hiv/library/dcl/dcl/092717 .html.

McPhate, M. 2016. "California Today: Requiring the Use of Condoms in Adult Films." *New York Times*. October 4. www.nytimes.com/2016/10/04/us/california-today -condoms-adult-films.html?_r=0.

Minter, H. 2015. "Meet the Woman Who Wants to Disrupt the Porn Industry: Could Introducing a Kitemark Change Working Practices in Porn?" *The Guardian*. November 25. www.theguardian.com/women-in -leadership/2015/nov/25/regulate-the-porn-industry -nichi-hodgson.

Mosthof, M. 2016. "The Porn Industry Scored a Huge Election Victory." *Bustle*. December 16. www.bustle.com /articles/194488-the-porn-industry-scored-a-huge -election-victory-with-prop-60s-defeat-but-theyre-just-too.

Ng, D. 2016. "L.A. County Saw a 95% Drop in Porn Film Permits." *Los Angeles Times*. November 15. www .latimes.com/business/hollywood/la-fi-ct-porn-condom -la-20161111-story.html.

Panzer, Javier. 2016. "Most Californians Support Initiative to Require Adult-Film Actors to Use Condoms." *Los Angeles Times*. September 15. www.latimes.com/politics /la-pol-ca-condom-initiative-prop-60-poll-20160915 -snap-story.html.

Pressberg, M. 2016. "Californians Reject Condoms in Porn Ballot Measure." *The Wrap*. November 9. www.thewrap .com/californians-reject-condoms-porn-ballot-measure -proposition-60/.

Rewire Analysis. 2016. "Proposition 60 Is about More than Just Condoms in Porn." *Rewire*. November 2. https:// rewire.news/article/2016/11/02/californias-proposition -60-just-condoms-porn/.

Rogers, J. 2014. "LA Porn Permits Fall But Films Keep Being Produced." *San Diego Tribune*. August 6. www.sandiegouniontribune.com/sdut-la-porn-permits -fall-but-films-keep-being-produced-2014aug06-story .html.

Romero, D. 2011. "Porn Clinic AIM Closes for Good, Valley-Based Industry Scrambles to Find New STD Testing System." *Los Angeles Weekly*. May 3. www .laweekly.com/content/printView/2398023.

———. 2015. "Nevada Cracks Down on California Porn Producers." *Los Angeles Weekly*. January 7. www.laweekly.com/news/nevada-cracks-down-on -california-porn-producers-5325246.

Schieber, D. 2017. "Money, Morals, and Condom Use: The Politics of Health in Gay and Straight Adult Film Production." *Social Problems*. February 9.

Schneider, B., and N. Stoller (Eds.). 1995. *Women Resisting AIDS*. Philadelphia: Temple University Press.

Tannen, T. 2004. "Sharon Mitchell, Head of the Adult Industry Medical Clinic." *The Lancet*. August 28. 16921–3. www.thelancet.com/journals/lancet/article/PIIS0140 -6736(04)16921-3/fulltext.

Voss, G. 2015. "Trade Organizations, Industry Legitimacy and Corporate Responsibility in Pornography." In L. Comella and S. Tarrant (Eds.). *New Views on Pornography*. Santa Barbara, CA: Praeger. 191–216.

Walkowitz, J. 1980. *Prostitution and Victorian Society*. Cambridge: Cambridge University Press.

Woodyard, C. 2016. "California Voters Reject Condoms for Porn Actors." *USA Today*. November 8. www.usatoday .com/story/money/2016/11/08/californians-vote-condom -use-porn-actors/93464012/.

Zeischegg, C. 2013. "Our Pornography." In T. Taormino et al. (Eds.). *The Feminist Porn Book*. NY: Feminist Press. 265–70.

SEX MATTERS: FUTURE VISIONS FOR A SEX-POSITIVE SOCIETY

ELROI J. WINDSOR, JASMINE SURYAWAN, AND
ELISABETH O. BURGESS

The title of this book, *Sex Matters*, is a double entendre. First, the book presents issues related to the *matters* of sex, for readers to consider. Each chapter addresses numerous contexts for understanding sexuality in contemporary society. We hope that these diverse topics have offered readers a greater appreciation for the study of sexuality. By applying a sociological lens to sex matters, readers can begin to understand the complex ways that social factors shape human sexuality. In addition to relaying these issues about sex, the book's title compels readers to take sex more seriously. We believe that sex *matters*. Sex and sexuality are meaningful subjects that require attention, both scholarly and personal. Our Epilogue explores why sex matters and how we talk about the matters of sex. We aim to identify the potential for productive change by envisioning a more sex-positive society, starting with deconstructing recent representations of sexuality.

SEXUALITY: REPRESENTATIONS AND POLITICS

In the United States, people live in a sex-saturated society. Few would refute this claim. But the visibility of sexual imagery does not speak to the meanings and messages they illustrate. Recent years have brought more diverse sexualities to a range of media outlets. Non-normative sexualities are increasingly visible in both mainstream and alternative television and film. As younger generations become more media literate, especially regarding social media and Internet-based productions, they have the ability to create and engage with sexuality representations in new and interesting ways.

Media representations give us an idea about current understandings of sexualities, but political controversies also shape the public discourse of sex in meaningful ways. The social institutions of government and law have always constructed and controlled our notions of appropriate sexuality. Recently, the United States has seen a shift in sexual politics, especially regarding the topic of nonconsensual sexual acts. By recounting some of these stories below, we illustrate how controversies continue to regulate sexuality.

Media Representations of Nonnormative Sexuality

One of the most influential social institutions is the media. Media have the power to help construct sexuality. For much of the history of modern media, portrayals of normative sexuality have abounded, permeating all genres of film and television. However, more recently representations beyond monogamous, heterosexual couplings have appeared on screens—to varying degrees of ridicule and critique. The last decade has seen an influx of representations of queer and nonmonogamous sexualities. While there is still a dearth of portrayals of nonnormative sexualities in film and on television, members of sexual minority communities more often assess the quality of representations in media.[1] Tales of gay, lesbian, and transgender individuals as ridiculous, dangerous, or tragic—common in the past—are no longer as pervasive. Although these narratives are still present, such as the "Bury Your Gays" trope where disproportionate numbers of LGBTQ television characters die,[2] queer fans tolerate them less, favoring more multifaceted, developed characters. In addition, industry powerhouses occasionally recognize these nonnormative portrayals for their merit. For example, Barry Jenkins's *Moonlight*, a film that traces the life of a gay black man, received three Academy Awards in 2017.[3] What made this moment especially heartening for fans and LGBTQ audience members was that this film beat out the heterosexual romantic musical *La La Land* for the coveted Best Picture award, making it the first LGBTQ film to receive this accolade.[4]

Another first from 2017 was the coming-out story of Todd Chavez, a character on Netflix's anthropomorphic adult animation show *Bojack Horseman*. In the third episode, Todd comes out as asexual, and throughout the season he sporadically attends a support group for asexual people where he learns more about his identity.[5] This representation makes visible a seldom-discussed sexual identity and presents asexuality as one aspect of Todd's character rather than as the only relevant attribute. And, in the last few years, portrayals of polyamory and ethical nonmonogamy have appeared more often in media.[6,7] Season 4 of Amazon's *Transparent* and the first season of *She's Gotta Have It*, Netflix's 2017 adaptation of Spike Lee's 1987 film, both address poly-amory in explicit terms, though some viewers critique how the latter portrays polyamory and black women's sexuality as "selfish" and "uncertain."[8] Importantly, online companies produce these shows. These companies do not build storylines around advertising breaks and have more freedom in showing sexual content than television networks.[9]

Still, network television is pushing the boundaries by including more nonnormative sexual representations in shows for all ages. In the Disney Channel's *Andi Mack*, a show already presenting many "firsts" in terms of racial identity and family dynamics, 13-year-old Cyrus told his friend that he had feelings for Jonah, becoming the network's first character to come out as gay. This scene, from the second season premiere, was prescreened by both PFLAG [Parents, Families and Friends of Lesbians and Gays] and GLAAD, further validating the network's attempt to portray sexuality in a sensitive manner. While there was backlash, the show also received support: its ratings increased by 72 percent after the season 1 premiere.[10] Freeform, a network owned by Disney, broke ground in season 5 of *The Fosters* with one of the first sex scenes on television to include a teen transgender character. The scene involved Callie, a cisgender teen girl, and her transgender boyfriend, Aaron, communicating their desires and boundaries to one another before having sex for the first time.[11] The portrayal of Aaron's character is especially poignant, partly because the actor, Elliot Fletcher, is himself trans. This choice reflects an integral component of representing nonnormative sexuality: the need to consider not only how the stories are told, but who is allowed to tell them.

In addition to film and television, widespread use of technology and the Internet has changed the way that people consume, interact with, and create media. Now more than any time previously, those who embody queer sexualities are the ones telling their own stories. The last decade has seen a rise in LGBTQ web series, or shows created exclusively online through websites like YouTube. Some are produced by companies, such as supernatural lesbian romance *Carmilla*, which was sponsored by Kotex and has gained enough of a following that a full-length film is in the works.[12] Many others are independently produced, such as

Brown Girls and *Couple-ish*,[13] which involve lesbian and queer identities, and *Unicornland*, which involves polyamory.[14] While most corporate and independent visual media still present heteronormative and mononormative sexuality, examples of nonnormative sexual representations contribute to greater variety of sexual identities, behaviors, and practices. These representations challenge audiences to question their assumptions about sexuality. Although variability does not automatically result in changes in attitudes, younger audiences engage with these media and construct sexuality in newer ways than previous generations.

Shifting Sexual Politics

As media representations showcase more diverse and positive images related to sexuality, the political landscape of the United States remains more precarious. After decades of LGBTQ advocacy and political engagement, the U.S. Supreme Court ruled in favor of nationwide same-sex marriage legalization on June 26, 2015.[15] This major victory for the LGBTQ community received backlash from conservatives. In a highly publicized case, Kentucky county clerk Kim Davis refused to issue marriage licenses to same-sex couples. Despite receiving support from some conservatives, in July 2017, Davis lost her battle, resulting in jail time, and the state of Kentucky had to pay legal fees of over $200,000.[16] After this important win for LGBTQ rights, the national debate turned to employment and housing discrimination, adoption rights, disproportionate violence against queer and trans people of color, and transgender rights more broadly.[17] For example, the rise of anti-transgender initiatives, such as so-called bathroom bills, attempt to limit access to sex-segregated public areas based on assigned sex at birth. In addition, fourteen states have proposed legislation that would limit the rights of transgender students

in public schools.[18] Yet, in some regions, these initiatives received national backlash, as organizations and companies boycotted states, resulting in significant loss of revenue.[19]

The election of Donald Trump as president of the United States in 2016 has continued to bolster conservative initiatives, with regressive policy changes and legislation. In July 2017, Trump declared, via Twitter, that transgender individuals would be unable to serve in the military. Although a federal judge blocked this order, the ban could be reinstated at a later date.[20] Trump also signed legislation to cut funding to Planned Parenthood and issued an executive order that prevents U.S. funding from going to abortion counseling in nongovernmental organizations globally.[21] These rapid shifts in policy illustrate how quickly issues can be redefined, reinforcing the ways that sexuality is socially constructed and controlled through court cases and legislative action.

But the social control of sexuality is often met with resistance. Trump's election ignited a swell of activism, epitomized by the 2017 Women's March on Washington, which drew hundreds of thousands of protesters during Trump's inauguration in D.C. and sparked many additional protests around the country and the world.[22] Disgusted by Trump's attitudes toward women, many protesters donned pink "pussyhats" and chanted "Pussy grabs back!" as a way to promote women's empowerment and challenge Trump's claim that being a celebrity gave him the ability to grab women's genitalia at will.[23] Despite attempts by the organizers of the march to center intersectional feminist issues like sexual violence and reproductive justice,[24] some trans women, disabled women, and women of color criticized the march for centering the experiences of white, able-bodied cis women and presenting an essentialist view of womanhood.[25] However, the protests invigorated many, inspiring more feminist activism throughout the year.[26]

The #MeToo movement represents another type of resistance to the status quo by illuminating sexual misconduct in the workplace. Originally created in 2006 by Tarana Burke to center the experiences of black women and girls,[27] the movement gained momentum as thousands of people shared stories of sexual harassment and assault on social media using the #MeToo hashtag.[28] Attention to these issues has exposed the sexual predatory behaviors of celebrities such as Harvey Weinstein, Kevin Spacey, Matt Lauer, and Louis C.K., and the list of predators continues to grow. Of course, evidence of Trump's predatory sexual harassment emerged before the election and played a part in igniting the #MeToo movement. This climate has brought renewed attention to "rape culture," or the ways our society normalizes sexual violence.[29] Despite some concerns about the movement's emphasis on victimhood and the conflation of all sexual blunders as violence,[30] the #MeToo movement has sparked a national conversation about sexual assault and the need for enthusiastic consent in sexual encounters.[31] Finally, the mainstream public is paying attention to what feminists have been writing about for decades.

Why Sex Matters

Changes in media representations and political climates exemplify how U.S. society manages sexuality. As more diverse sexualities gain visibility, these positive images broaden the framework of normative sexuality. Media help construct meanings around sex that render previously "deviant" acts unremarkable and mundane. This discourse paves the way for acceptance for communities previously marginalized, such as people who are LGBTQ, asexual, or interested in polyamorous relationships.

Although media may contribute to sexual diversity, we must remember that many of these representations are fictional and do not necessarily reflect mainstream public opinion. As evidenced in legal and governmental contexts, sex continues to be embroiled in controversy. While one political agency may advance conservative agendas about sex, another may react with fervent resistance. The passion and furor that propel sexual politics demonstrate that sex does indeed matter—to many different people, in many different ways. These contested narratives send mixed messages about sex, and people still struggle with defining *healthy* sexuality.

TOWARD A SEX-POSITIVE SOCIETY

As sexuality scholars, we believe that dominant sexual attitudes of people in the United States suffer from an overly negative outlook. Positive messages about sex are scarce and are typically found within sexual minority communities, like those catering to swinging, BDSM, and polyamory.[32] To conclude this book, we want to present readers with new, sex-positive ways of thinking about sexuality. We want to promote sexuality as important for individuals and our larger society.

Sex positivity asserts, at its core, that people benefit from holding positive attitudes about sexuality. It is not a simple assertion that sex is good,[33] nor does it mean that sex should pervade every part of life. Having a sex-positive outlook on sexuality means valuing the diverse ways people have consensual sex, and affirming those who choose not to engage in sex at all.[34] It involves directing a critical analysis toward the ways socialization affects sexuality and inhibits sexual liberation.[35] Despite the proliferation of sex in media, the United States is not a sex-positive society.[36] An abundance of messages about sex is not the same as being sex-positive. A positive sexuality can help us become more physically, emotionally, and psychologically satisfied. To be sex-positive is to recognize that sex can be enriching. It is to assert that *sex matters*.

Affirming Sexual Diversity

An important tenet of a sex-positive ideology is respect for sexual diversity. Sex positivity rejects the notion that there is such a thing as "normal" sex.[37] People experience pleasure in abundant ways. Bodies provide us with unique sensations worthy of exploration. Sexual enjoyment is different for everyone. Sex positivity recognizes that constraining sexual agendas socially control people's behaviors. Without this restrictive management, people might have fuller sex lives. The ideology of sex positivity recognizes that the public discourse of sex typically does not promote empowerment. Social inequalities based on gender, race, sexual identity, class, size, age, and ability can play out in sexual relationships. As these categories intersect, power dynamics may color sexual encounters.[38,39] Embracing sex positivity would mean practicing freedom and respect, even within relationships that choose to play with erotic power dynamics.

Sex positivity also acknowledges the need to represent sexuality in diverse ways. In media, sex-positive approaches include varied depictions of consensual sexual acts. People should have the right to choose to engage with or abstain from these representations without persecution. Similarly, sex positivity acknowledges that sexually explicit material can be an important part of pleasure for some people.[40] Similarly, commercial sex can be entertaining and empowering for both producers and consumers.[41,42] Sex-work economies could be more sex-positive if they included the fair pay, benefits, security, and safety features characteristic of some conventional forms of employment.

Consenting to Sex

Consent is another core feature of sex positivity. This ideology stresses the importance of sex as consensual and voluntary, not coerced or required.[43] In practicing sex-positive sex, people need to understand and respect each other's boundaries, and recognize that feelings can change in any given situation. In addition to affecting performance and satisfaction, the use of alcohol and drugs can confuse people's limits,[44] so it is important to ensure consent is maintained throughout the encounter.

In promoting consent, it is also important to consider legal "age of consent" issues. A sex-positive approach recognizes the problems in assigning a singular numerical value to the ability to consent to sex. While some youth are sexually and emotionally mature, we must find ways to end sexual violence against children and work to ensure that they are not exploited. Protecting children, however, can also restrict their sexual agency.[45] Respecting young people's developing sexualities means equipping them with knowledge about their bodies, helping them establish personal boundaries, and empowering them to decide when and how to become sexually active.[46]

Issues of consent become more complicated for people with limited cognitive abilities. A sex-positive approach acknowledges the rights of all people to sexual agency[47] and sexual education.[48] It also appreciates that people with cognitive disabilities, particularly young women, face a high risk of victimization. Moreover, for some older adults, the onset or progression of dementia may lead to changes in sexual behavior, including misinterpreting the actions of others.[49,50] Overall, a sex-positive approach values the sexual agency of all individuals, regardless of age or cognitive ability, and strives to create a society where sex is always consensual and voluntary.

The #MeToo movement has not only brought the topic of consent to a larger audience, but has expanded conversations on what consent looks like in practice. The widespread confusion about what constitutes consent is understandable given that its legal definition differs across states.[51] The controversial allegations of sexual misconduct against comedian Aziz Ansari exemplify the need for a discussion of "affirmative consent," which can only occur when all persons involved in a sexual encounter verbally agree to the sexual activity.[52] Taking affirmative consent a step further, practicing "enthusiastic consent" means making sure your partner is actually enjoying what is happening. Given the problem of sexual assault, especially for young adults,[53] ensuring sexual encounters are consensual is an important part of sex-positive behavior.

While consent is a crucial starting point of sex, it should not be the ultimate goal. As Rebecca Traister argues, consensual sex can still be bad sex.[54] A sex-positive approach would account for the "orgasm gap" that exists in heterosexual encounters, or the ways men's pleasure takes the forefront while women's pleasure is treated as optional, if it is even considered at all.[55] In light of research showing this gender inequality in sexual interactions,[56,57] sex-positive approaches resist this trend and work to ensure that everyone experiences pleasure during sex.

Promoting Sexual Health

Practicing sex positivity begins with oneself, and each of us has different expectations about what counts as sexual health. By exploring our own bodies, we can understand our likes and dislikes. Masturbation can be a healthy part of sexuality. It can be an effective way to explore our sexualities so that we can have more satisfying sex with our partners.[58] Through partnering, we can further practice sex positivity by finding people to share in our sexual desires. Partnering can enhance our sexual growth. For some people, sex is best in monogamous relationships. For others, polyamory is ideal. A sex-positive approach to sexual exploration respects the partnering choices people make, including an acceptance of asexuality as a legitimate choice for some people.[59]

Promoting sexual health is crucial in a sex-positive society. Regardless of health status, a sex-positive approach to partnering aims to reduce both risks of transmitting sexually transmitted infections (STIs) and the stigma associated with having them. Campaigns like "#ShoutYourStatus" aid in destigmatization by dispelling misconceptions about living with an STI.[60] Sexual health also seeks effective ways to address people's sexual problems. Treating sexual "dysfunction" should extend beyond prescriptions for assorted pharmaceutical drugs. Sex therapies should move beyond focusing on rote genital performance, understanding that sex is about emotions, attraction, and desire. In managing sexual health, people need access to comprehensive, nonjudgmental health care. Fostering sexual health includes safe, affordable access to contraceptive and procreative choices. Sex positivity maintains that sexuality information and assistance should be made available to people who live in institutions and require care from attendants. If desired, sex can be enjoyed by people with diverse embodiments and abilities.[61]

Educating People

Education is an important means to a sex-positive society. Sex education is appropriate at all stages of life because learning about sex is a lifelong process.[62] Information about sex and sexuality should be accessible, comprehensive, and catered to the audience. Sex-positive sex education does not limit discussion to sexual risk and reproduction. Instead, it emphasizes the benefits of consensual sex, including discussions of pleasure, desire, variety, and communication. To become sex-positive, people need to learn about bodies. Education should include details about sexual anatomy and nongenital erogenous zones and how to explore what feels good both solo and with partners. Sex-positive education should acknowledge that sex can be amazing, but sometimes it is just good and at times it is not great. By emphasizing that good sex is not just about developing appropriate techniques and skills, but also a result of open communication about desires and limits, sex-positive education should continue across the life course in order to accommodate changing bodies, relationships, and social norms.

Educating people about sex is a big responsibility. Social institutions already manage information about sex, and people learn about sex from numerous individuals like peers and family members. A sex-positive approach to education recognizes that multiple agents can effectively deliver healthy information about sex. Some excellent resources already exist online[63] and in innovative text messaging systems designed to educate young people.[64] New approaches, such as the website OMGYes, move beyond the rigid curriculum of middle school health classes or awkward discussions with medical providers and offer research-based advice that caters to women's pleasure.[65] Ultimately, supportive sex education would allow individuals to learn about and explore their sexualities based on their own personal and spiritual values.[66]

In addition, quality research on sexuality is essential to educating people. We believe that before we can accurately teach about sexuality, we must be able to understand and critique sexuality from multiple perspectives. Unfortunately, mainstream science typically marginalizes contemporary sexualities research. It is customary to find studies published in specialty journals by isolated scholars and ignored by mainstream academia and media. A sex-positive model of sexualities research recognizes that sexuality is relevant to many disciplines (including sociology, anthropology, psychology, medicine, art, and history), but also that research on sexualities may be interdisciplinary and not easily regimented into narrow academic boxes. To promote sex positivity, academic departments and funding agents should value and promote sex research of diverse sexualities.[67] In addition, researchers could become more versed in conveying their findings to media, and journalists could move beyond focusing on the sensational aspects of the research.[68] Effective sex research informs effective sex education and enhances broader cultural discussions about sexuality.

In writing this Epilogue, we aspired to provide readers with new ways of thinking about sexuality. As we have shown, the meanings and implications of sex and sexuality are hotly contested in U.S. society. Sex remains a source of controversy. We believe that this discourse has the potential to change by producing more varied perspectives. The #MeToo movement offers an example of expanding conversations around sexuality. Ultimately, we advocate using a sex-positive approach that involves diverse contributions to help foster sexual liberation. Although our discussion of sex positivity is not exhaustive, we hope that this concluding section, like the book as a whole, allows readers to critically consider the sexual status quo. Ultimately, our presumption that *sex matters* begs some kind of action. What about these "sex matters" *matters* to you?

NOTES

1. Allen, Samantha. 2017. "Hey, TV Producers: Let LGBTQ Characters Live and Love Equally." *Daily Beast*, November 11. Retrieved January 17, 2018 from https://www.thedailybeast.com/hey-tv-producers-let-lgbtq-characters-live-and-love-equally.

2. Phillips, Andrew. 2017. "62 Lesbian and Bisexual Female Characters Killed over Past Two Television Seasons." *Out*, July 11. Retrieved January 12, 2018 from https://www.out

.com/news-opinion/2017/7/11/62-lesbian-bisexual-female
-characters-killed-over-past-two-television-seasons.

3. Barton, Amy. 2017. "Moonlight Wins 3 Oscars Including 2017 Best Picture." Oscars, February 27. Retrieved January 12, 2018 from http://oscar.go.com /news/winners/moonlight-wins-3-oscars-including-2017 -best-picture.

4. O'Hara, Mary Emily. 2017. "'Moonlight Makes Oscars History as 1st LGBTQ Best Picture Winner." NBC News, February 27. Retrieved January 12, 2018 from https://www .nbcnews.com/feature/nbc-out/moonlight-makes-oscars -history-1st-lgbtq-best-picture-winner-n726116.

5. Henderson, Taylor. 2017. "Bojack Horseman's Todd Chavez Is Doing Big Things for Asexual Visibility." *Pride*, September 12. Retrieved January 12, 2018 from https:// www.pride.com/tv/2017/9/12/todd-chavez-tvs-first -openly-asexual-character-and-people-are-emotional.

6. National Public Radio. 2017. "It's Polyamorous Polysaturation–Unconventional Relationships Abound on TV." *All Things Considered*, May 24. Retrieved January 23, 2018 from https://www.npr.org/2017/05/24/529862830/its -polyamorous-polysaturation-unconventional-relationships -abound-on-tv.

7. Novick, Ilana. 2017. "TV Is Finally Starting to Get Polyamory Right." *Vice*, April 10. Retrieved January 13, 2018 from https://www.vice.com/en_nz/article/vvk5q9/tv -is-finally-starting-to-get-polyamory-right.

8. Dionne, Evette. 2017. "'She's Gotta Have It' Butchers Polyamory and Queerness." *Bitch Media*, November 29. Retrieved January 13, 2018 from https://www.bitchmedia .org/article/shes-gotta-have-it-review.

9. Plaugic, Lizzie, and Ross Miller. 2015. "How Netflix and Amazon Have Changed the Rules of TV." *The Verge*, December 30. Retrieved January 17, 2018 from https:// www.theverge.com/2015/12/30/10647736/netflix -hulu-amazon-original-shows-streaming-tv-2015.

10. Nilles, Billy. 2017. "Andi Mack's Cast and Creator Reflect on Crafting Disney's First LGBT Storyline: 'I Wanted It to Feel Like Acceptance.'" *E! News*, November 3. Retrieved January 13, 2018 from http://www.eonline.com/news/891452 /andi-mack-s-cast-creator-reflect-on-crafting-disney-s-first -lgbt-storyline-i-wanted-it-to-feel-like-acceptance.

11. Bradley, Laura. 2017. "Inside The Fosters' Groundbreaking Callie-Aaron Sex Scene." *Vanity Fair*, August 23. Retrieved January 13, 2018 from https://www.vanityfair.com /hollywood/2017/08/the-fosters-aaron-callie-sex-scene -relationship-elliot-fletcher-interview.

12. Van Kampen, Stephanie. 2017. "How a Little Canadian Web Series about a Lesbian Vampire Became a Worldwide Hit." *CBC News*, October 24. Retrieved January 13, 2018 from http://www.cbc.ca/news/entertainment/carmilla-web -series-movie-1.4367622.

13. Costa, Daniela. 2017. "Web Series about LGBTQ Women and Femmes of Color to Watch." *Teen Vogue*, March 31. Retrieved January 13, 2018 from https://www.teenvogue .com/story/web-series-about-lgbtq-women-femmes-of-color.

14. Novick, Ilana. 2017. "TV Is Finally Starting to Get Polyamory Right." *Vice*, April 10. Retrieved January 13, 2018 from https://www.vice.com/en_nz/article/vvk5q9/tv -is-finally-starting-to-get-polyamory-right.

15. De Vogue, Ariane, and Jeremy Diamond. 2015. "Supreme Court Rules in Favor of Same-Sex Marriage Nationwide." *CNN*, June 27. Retrieved January 17, 2018 from http://www.cnn.com/2015/06/26/politics/supreme -court-same-sex-marriage-ruling/index.html.

16. Stevens, Matt. 2017. "Kentucky Must Pay $224,000 After Dispute over Same-Sex Marriage Licenses." *New York Times*, July 21. Retrieved January 17, 2018 from https:// www.nytimes.com/2017/07/21/us/kentucky-taxpayers-gay -marriage.html?ribbon-ad-idx=4&rref=world&module=Arro wsNav&contentCollection=U.S.&action=swipe&region=Fi xedRight&pgtype=article.

17. Branson-Potts, Hailey. 2015. "LGBT Activists Say the Fight Doesn't End at Marriage." *Los Angeles Times*, July 12. Retrieved January 17, 2018 from http://beta.latimes.com /local/california/la-me-lgbt-activism-20150712-story.html.

18. Kralik, Joellen. 2017. "'Bathroom Bill' Legislative Tracking." *National Conference of State Legislatures*, July 28. Retrieved January 17, 2018 from http://www.ncsl.org /research/education/-bathroom-bill-legislative-tracking 635951130.aspx.

19. Abadi, Mark. 2016. "North Carolina Has Lost a Staggering Amount of Money over Its Controversial 'Bathroom Law.'" September 21, *Business Insider*. Retrieved January 26, 2018 from http://www.businessinsider.com /north-carolina-hb2-economic-impact-2016-9.

20. Cooper, Helen. 2017. "Transgender People Will Be Allowed to Enlist in the Military as a Court Case Advances." *New York Times*, December 11. Retrieved January 17, 2018 from https://www.nytimes.com/2017/12/11/us/politics /transgender-military-pentagon.html?ribbon-ad-idx=4 &rref=world&module=ArrowsNav&contentCollection=Pol itics&action=swipe&region=FixedRight&pgtype =article.

21. Davis, Julie H. 2017. "Trump Signs Law Taking Aim at Planned Parenthood Funding." *New York Times,* April 13. Retrieved January 17, 2018 from https://www.nytimes .com/2017/04/13/us/politics/planned-parenthood-trump .html.

22. Hartocollis, Anemona, and Yamiche Alcindor. 2017. "Women's March Highlights as Huge Crowds Protest Trump: 'We're Not Going Away.'" *New York Times*, January 21. Retrieved January 18, 2018 from https://www.nytimes .com/2017/01/21/us/womens-march.html.

23. Darrough, Celia. 2017. "What Do the Pink Hats Mean? The Women's March and The Pussyhat Project Have a Purposeful Message." *Bustle*, January 21. Retrieved January 18, 2018 from https://www.bustle.com/p/what -do-the-pink-hats-mean-the-womens-march-the-pussyhat -project-have-a-purposeful-message-32088.

24. Women's March on Washington. 2017. "Unity Principles." Retrieved January 18, 2018 from https://static1 .squarespace.com/static/584086c7be6594762f5ec56e/t/587 ffb20579fb3554668c111/1484782369253/WMW+Guiding +Vision+%26+Definition+of+Principles.pdf.

25. Mosthof, Mariella. 2017. "If You're Not Talking about the Criticism Surrounding the Women's March, Then You're Part of the Problem." *Bustle*, January 30. Retrieved January 19, 2018 from https://www.bustle.com/p/if-youre -not-talking-about-the-criticism-surrounding-the-womens -march-then-youre-part-of-the-problem-33491.

26. Cauterucci, Christina. 2018. "The Women's March Was Just the Beginning." *Slate*, January 17. Retrieved January 18, 2018 from https://slate.com/news-and-politics/2018/01 /the-womens-march-was-just-the-beginning.html.

27. Burke, Tarana. 2017. "#MeToo Was Started for Black and Brown Women and Girls. They're Still Being Ignored." *Washington Post*, November 9. Retrieved January 19, 2018 from https://www.washingtonpost.com/news/post-nation /wp/2017/11/09/the-waitress-who-works-in-the-diner-needs -to-know-that-the-issue-of-sexual-harassment-is-about-her -too/?utm_term=.9834832b93c9.

28. Schmidt, Samantha. 2017. "#MeToo: Harvey Weinstein Case Moves Thousands to Tell Their Own Stories of Abuse, Break Silence." *Washington Post*, October 16. Retrieved January 18, 2018 from https://www.washingtonpost.com /news/morning-mix/wp/2017/10/16/me-too-alyssa-milano -urged-assault-victims-to-tweet-in-solidarity-the-response -was-massive/?utm_term=.3cb41b1df882.

29. Women against Violence against Women. 2014. "What Is Rape Culture?" Retrieved January 18, 2018 from http:// www.wavaw.ca/what-is-rape-culture/.

30. Walters, Suzanna Danuta. 2017. "Between Sexual Assault and Sex Panic." *Ms. Magazine*, November 30. Retrieved January 22, 2018 from http://msmagazine .com/blog/2017/11/30/sexual-assault-sex-panic/?utm _source=facebook&utm_medium=Social&utm_campaign =SocialWarfare.

31. Hudson, Laura. 2018. "Forget the Backlash—We Need #MeToo Now more than Ever." *The Verge*, January 15. Retrieved January 18, 2018 from https://www.theverge .com/2018/1/15/16893734/metoo-movement-backlash.

32. Society for Human Sexuality. 2007. "A New Look at Sex." Retrieved January 16, 2018 from http://citeseerx.ist .psu.edu/viewdoc/download?doi=10.1.1.729.9818&rep=re p1&type=pdf.

33. Glickman, Charlie. 2000. "The Language of Sex Positivity." *Electronic Journal of Human Sexuality* 3, July 6. Retrieved January 16, 2018 from http://www.ejhs.org /volume3/sexpositive.htm.

34. Mogilevsky, Miri. 2016. "10 Things Sex Positivity Is Not." *Everyday Feminism*, August 22. Retrieved January 16, 2018 from https://everydayfeminism.com/2016/08 /10-things-sex-positivity-is-not/.

35. Fabello, Melissa A. 2014. "3 Reasons Why Sex-Positivity without Critical Analysis Is Harmful." *Everyday Feminism*, May 14. Retrieved January 16, 2018 from https:// everydayfeminism.com/2014/05/sex-positivity-critical -analysis/.

36. Moore, Thomas. 1997. "Sex (American Style)." *Mother Jones*, 22(5): 56–64.

37. Ibid., supra 32.

38. Collins, Patricia Hill. 2000. *Black Feminist Thought: Knowledge, Consciousness, and the Politics of Empowerment*. New York and London: Routledge.

39. Lorde, Audre. 1978 (1984). "Uses of the Erotic: The Erotic as Power." In *Sister Outsider: Essays and Speeches by Audre Lorde*. Freedom, CA: The Crossing Press. 53–59.

40. The Center for Sexual Pleasure and Health. 2018. "Sex-Positive and Feminist Friendly Porn." Retrieved January 16, 2018 from http://www.thecsph.org/the -csph-resources/web-resources/sex-positive-basics/pleasure /sex-positive-and-feminist-friendly-porn/.

41. Frank, Katherine. 2002. "Stripping, Starving, and the Politics of Ambiguous Pleasure." In Merri Lisa Johnson (Ed.) *Jane Sexes It Up: True Confessions of Feminist Desire*. New York and London: Four Walls Eight Windows. 171–206.

42. Hartley, Nina. 1987. "Confessions of a Feminist Porno Star." In Frédérique Delacoste and Priscilla Alexander (Eds.) *Sex Work: Writings by Women in the Sex Industry*. Pittsburgh: Cleis Press. 142–44.

43. Ibid., supra 32.

44. Ibid.

45. Egan, R. Danielle, and Gail L. Hawkes. 2008. "Imperiled and Perilous: Exploring the History of Childhood Sexuality." *Journal of Historical Sociology*, 21(4): 355–67.

46. Melby, Todd. 2001. "Childhood Sexuality." *Contemporary Sexuality*, 35(12): 1–5.

47. Wilkerson, Abby L. 2002. "Disability, Sex Radicalism, and Political Agency." *NWSA Journal*, 14(3): 33–57.

48. Rurangirwa, Jacqueline, Kim Van Naarden Braun, Diana Schendel, and Marshalyn Yeargin-Allsopp. 2006. "Healthy Behaviors and Lifestyles in Young Adults with a History of Developmental Disabilities." *Research in*

Developmental Disabilities, 27(4): 381–99. References and further reading may be available for this article. To view references and further reading you must purchase this article.

49. Loboprabhu, Sheila, Victor Molinari, Kimberly Arlinghaus, Ellen Barr, and James Lomax. 2005. "Spouses of Patients with Dementia: How Do They Stay Together 'Till Death Do Us Part'?" *Journal of Gerontological Social Work*, 44(3/4): 161–74.

50. Tabak, Nili, and Ronit Shemesh-Kigli. 2006. "Sexuality and Alzheimer's Disease: Can the Two Go Together?" *Nursing Forum*, 41(4): 158–66.

51. Cooney, Samantha. 2018. "The Aziz Ansari Allegation Has People Talking about 'Affirmative Consent.' What's That?" *Time*, January 17. Retrieved January 19, 2018 from http://time.com/5104010/aziz-ansari-affirmative-consent/.

52. Ibid.

53. Armstrong, Elizabeth, Laura Hamilton, and Brian Sweeney. 2006. "Sexual Assault on Campus: A Multilevel, Integrative Approach to Party Rape." *Social Problems*, 53(4): 483–99.

54. Traister, Rebecca. 2015. "The Game Is Rigged." *The Cut*, October 20. Retrieved January 19, 2018 from https://www.thecut.com/2015/10/why-consensual-sex-can-still-be-bad.html.

55. Ibid.

56. Armstrong, Elizabeth A., Paula England, and Alison C. K. Fogarty. 2012. "Accounting for Women's Orgasm and Sexual Enjoyment in College Hookups and Relationships." *American Sociological Review*, 77(3): 435–62.

57. Cole, Nicki L. 2017. "The Orgasm Gap: What It Is, Why It Exists, and What to Do about It." *ThoughtCo.*, November 27. Retrieved January 17, 2018 from https://www.thoughtco.com/lets-talk-about-the-orgasm-gap-baby-3026207?utm_campaign=wilat&utm_medium=email&utm_source=cn_nl&utm_content=11323591&utm_term=.

58. Ibid., supra 31.

59. Petchesky, Rosalind Pollack. 1999 (2001). "Sexual Rights: Inventing a Concept, Mapping an International Practice." In Mark Blasius (Ed.) *Sexual Identities, Queer Politics*. Princeton, NJ: Princeton University Press. 118–39.

60. Depasse, Emily. 2016. "This Is What It's Like to Actually #ShoutYourStatus Online." *Thought Catalogue*, April 18. Retrieved January 19, 2018 from http://thoughtcatalog.com/emily-depasse/2016/04/this-is-what-its-like-to-actually-shoutyourstatus-online/.

61. Office of the Surgeon General. 2001. *The Surgeon General's Call to Action to Promote Sexual Health and Responsible Sexual Behavior*. Rockville, MD: Office of the Surgeon General. Retrieved January 23, 2018 from https://www.ncbi.nlm.nih.gov/books/NBK44216/.

62. Ibid.

63. For examples of sex-positive websites for youth, see www.sexetc.org, www.amplifyyourvoice.org, www.plannedparenthood.org/learn/teens, and www.goaskalice.columbia.edu. Retrieved January 22, 2018.

64. Hoffman, Jan. 2011. "Sex Education Gets Directly to Youths, Via Text." *New York Times*, December 30. Retrieved January 22, 2018 from http://www.nytimes.com/2011/12/31/us/sex-education-for-teenagers-online-and-in-texts.html.

65. A subscription-based website focusing on sex-positive approaches to understanding women's pleasure, OMGYes uses videos and testimonials to "explore specific ways women increase sexual pleasure" (https://www.omgyes.com).

66. Sexuality Information and Education Council of the United States. "Position Statements: Sexuality Education." Retrieved January 22, 2018 from http://www.siecus.org/index.cfm?fuseaction=page.viewPage&PageID=494&varuniqueuserid=63126375175#sexuality%20education.

67. Ibid., supra 59.

68. McBride, Kimberly R., Stephanie A. Sanders, Erick Janssen, Maria Elizabeth Grabe, Jennifer Bass, Johnny V. Sparks, Trevor R. Brown, and Julia R. Heiman. 2007. "Turning Sexual Science into News: Sex Research and the Media." *Journal of Sex Research*, 44(4): 347–58.

INDEX